LAW

OF

MASS COMMUNICATIONS

FREEDOM AND CONTROL OF PRINT AND BROADCAST MEDIA

By

DWIGHT L. TEETER, JR., Ph.D.

Professor and Dean, College of Communications
University of Tennessee

DON R. LE DUC, J.D., Ph.D.

Professor and Chairman, Department of Mass Communication
University of Wisconsin—Milwaukee

SEVENTH EDITION

Westbury, New York
THE FOUNDATION PRESS, INC.
1992

COPYRIGHT © 1969, 1973, 1978, 1982, 1986, 1989 THE FOUNDATION PRESS, INC.
COPYRIGHT © 1992 By THE FOUNDATION PRESS, INC.

615 Merrick Ave.
Westbury, N.Y. 11590

All rights reserved
Printed in the United States of America

Library of Congress Cataloging-in-Publication Data

Teeter, Dwight L.
    Law of mass communications : freedom and control of print and
broadcast media / by Dwight L. Teeter, Don R. Le Duc — 7th ed.
        p.   cm.
    Rev. ed. of : Law of mass communications / by Harold L. Nelson. 6th
ed. 1989.
    Includes index.
    ISBN 0-88277-981-8
    1. Press law—United States. 2. Telecommunication—Law and
legislation—United States. I. Le Duc, Don R. II. Nelson, Harold L. (Harold
Lewis) Law of mass communications. III. Title.
KF2750.N4 1992
343.73099'8—dc20
[347.303998]

                                                              92–11005

T. & L. Mass Comm. 7th Ed.–FP

FOR TISH AND ALICE

*

PREFACE TO SEVENTH EDITION

It was all much simpler once, just a generation ago. When the first edition of Law of Mass Communications was published in 1969, "electronic media" still referred only to radio and television. The founding author of this book, however, the University of Wisconsin's Professor Harold L. Nelson, saw transformations coming: He referred in 1969 to the "ever-accelerating rate of change in many areas of the law of mass communications." Dr. Nelson had been assigned by The Foundation Press to continue Professor Frank Thayer's *Legal Control of the Press,* which was a standard text through four editions, from 1944 to 1962.

Professor Nelson changed the book's title to its present *Law of Mass Communications,* and added his student, Dwight Teeter, as co-author. Dr. Nelson's work—beyond this book—includes his *Libel in News of Congressional Investigating Committees* and his law journal articles. He is especially well known to historians for his highly respected *Freedom of the Press from Hamilton to the Warren Court* and for his articles exploring the origins of press freedom in colonial America.

With the Sixth Edition in 1989, Professor Nelson left active participation in this book; Teeter was joined by Professor Don R. Le Duc of the University of Wisconsin-Milwaukee, a communications attorney and former broadcaster. Authors Teeter and Le Duc adhere to words written by Professor Nelson in the Preface to the First Edition in 1969:

> We . . . hope that implicit and explicit in this volume is an awareness of the legal process in a democracy. Such an awareness . . . is part of the requisite knowledge of communications law. As social protest of the 1960s [or 1990s!] sweeps American society, it gives life to heirs of an ancient priesthood of intolerance and suppression. The authors believe it imperative that journalists as well as lawyers and historians know about . . . Thomas Jefferson, John Stuart Mill, and Justices Oliver Wendell Holmes, Jr., Louis D. Brandeis, and Benjamin Nathan Cardozo.

For communications law, what is past is precedent, and the present, as historians will tell you, is only the cutting edge of the past. This book is designed to be useful on several levels:

> First, gaining added appreciation for (or dismay over) the workings of the legal process.

> Second, surveying areas of law essential for those mass communications practitioners who hope to "stay out of legal trouble," areas including—to name three examples—libel, invasion of privacy, and copyright.

v

Third, outlining and suggesting ways of coping with explosively growing problems of getting access to governmental records and meetings.

Fourth, acquainting students with new contours of our mediated information environment. To that end, this edition emphasizes the convergence of information delivery systems and looks at eddying patterns in regulation and deregulation.

To reach for such goals is to try to contend with the dazzling variety of changes in mass media law since 1969. Back then, the Supreme Court was about to consider—and to affirm—the authority of the Federal Communications Commission (FCC) to impose the Fairness Doctrine on broadcasters. Although the 1960s had seen greater judicial recognition of First Amendment rights for the press, the broadcast industry then seemed destined to remain forever under strict governmental supervision.

But in 1972, in a communications common carrier ruling that seemed only distantly related to the mass media, the FCC adopted its "Open Skies" satellite policy. Within a few short years, many of the basic concepts of mass communications law became far more complex.

The "Open Skies" policy was designed with communications satellite development in mind, promoting use of satellites through lower rates resulting from marketplace competition. Unforeseen at the time was how that one policy choice would undermine the traditional network-based foundation for American broadcast service and how it would undercut the structure of federal broadcast regulation.

By the mid-1980s, most of the broadcast regulatory structure had collapsed, and the three television networks that in 1969 appeared to be impregnable bastions of corporate power had been rendered so vulnerable that none of them could avoid being taken over by others. During that same era, the "Open Skies" policy also triggered the explosive growth of modern cable TV, encouraging its emergence as a new, uniquely different form of mass communicator. Cable TV delivered a full spectrum of media services not fitting neatly into either of the traditional "press" or "broadcast" models of mass communications law.

In 1969, broadcasting still functioned primarily as an entertainment medium while the press provided the public with its news. Now, however, a quarter of a century later, "all-news" radio stations operate in most major American cities, as a 24-hour-a-day global cable news channel offers up-to-the-minute coverage of events throughout the world. Here again low-cost satellite linkage has been the catalyst for this new broadcast journalism role, a change that has affected the print media as well. In response to this competitive challenge, newspapers and news magazines have reacted with more colorful layouts and lighter stories, attempting to enhance their ability to entertain as some elements of broadcasting and cable TV seek to increase their capacity to inform.

Even our domestic mass media ownership policies have been influenced profoundly by the communication satellite. Now that such satellites have ushered in the era of commercial television throughout Western Europe, an evergrowing demand for the type of mass appeal programs America's media organizations are best able to provide has led a number of foreign conglomerates to acquire American mass entertainment properties. If American media organizations can resist foreign take-overs only through mergers, what then? Does foreign media control pose a greater threat to diversity of media voices in the United States than the degree of domestic media consolidation needed to avoid foreign take-overs?

Because the pace of change accelerates with each passing year, it is now more important than ever for a mass communications law text to consider how governmental and industry policy decisions about the use of fiber optics, digital audio transmission, personal communication, ISDN, portable uplinks, high definition TV, and many other technologies are likely to shape future mass media organizations and services and those laws that govern them.

Any discussion of future trends or policy or law is speculative, of course, but awareness of issues apt to shape the future may help to avoid getting hit from the blind side by change. Charles F. Kettering once said that he was interested in the future because he intended to spend the rest of his life there. We all share that interest, and that is why this text extends a bit beyond current policies to suggest how this field—and laws governing it—are likely to evolve.

Some changes are apparent in this Seventh Edition of Law of Mass Communications. In addition to substantial updating and revision throughout the book, note Professor Le Duc's new emphasis in Chapter 16, "Media Ownership: Consolidation and Globalization," and his all-new Chapter 17, "Distributing Mass Communications." The entire textbook reflects the authors' emphasis on the merging of print and broadcast law.

The authors wish to thank those who have helped us in preparing this Seventh Edition. Beverly Klein, Vice President for Advertising of Milwaukee's Journal/Sentinel Company, again assisted us by granting permission to use her organization's advertising acceptance guidelines. We thank Professor Ruane Hill, the University of Wisconsin-Milwaukee, for his support. Special thanks go to librarians at the University of Wisconsin-Milwaukee; to Professor Steven M. Barkan, Director of the Law Library, Marquette University; to William J. Beintema, Director of the Law Library and to Jean E. Moore, Instructor in the Law Library, both of the University of Tennessee.

PREFACE TO SEVENTH EDITION

We thank them and add our grateful acknowledgment for all the support and help of Letitia Teeter and Alice Le Duc.

DWIGHT L. TEETER, JR.
DON R. LE DUC

March, 1992

SUMMARY OF CONTENTS

	Page
Preface to Seventh Edition	v

PART I. HISTORICAL AND CONSTITUTIONAL FOUNDATIONS OF FREE EXPRESSION

Chapter
1. Freedom and Control ... 1
2. The First Amendment and the Print Media: Historical Background and Today's Law ... 22
3. The First Amendment and Electronic Media ... 79

PART II. MASS COMMUNICATIONS LAW AND THE CITIZEN

4. Defamation: Libel and Slander ... 100
5. The Constitutional Defense Against Libel Suits ... 145
6. Defending Against Libel Suits Under State Law ... 195
7. The Law of Privacy and the Media ... 248
8. Obscenity ... 329

PART III. MASS COMMUNICATIONS AND GOVERNMENT

9. Regulating Broadcasting ... 373
10. Deregulation and the New Media ... 402
11. Regulation of Advertising ... 432
12. Copyright: Protection and Constraint ... 489

PART IV. FACT GATHERING AND CITIZENS' RIGHTS

13. Shielding Information From Disclosure ... 543
14. Legal Problems in Reporting Legislative and Executive Branches of Government ... 591
15. Legal Problems in Reporting Courts ... 635

PART V. CONVERGING MEDIA AND THE LAW

16. Media Ownership: Consolidation and Globalization ... 694
17. Distributing Mass Communications ... 743

SUMMARY OF CONTENTS

APPENDICES

App.   **Page**

A. Abbreviations --- 761

B. Selected Court and Pleading Terms -------------------------- 765

C. Some Notes On the Legal Process---------------------------- 771

D. Bibliography--- 778

E. The Society of Professional Journalists and ASNE Codes
    of Ethics-- 784

F. Communications Act of 1934 (Major Provisions)------------ 789

TABLE OF CASES--- 811

INDEX --- 825

TABLE OF CONTENTS

                                                                    Page
PREFACE TO SEVENTH EDITION v

PART I. HISTORICAL AND CONSTITUTIONAL FOUNDATIONS OF FREE EXPRESSION

Chapter 1. Freedom and Control 1

Sec.
1. The Worth of Freedom 4
2. The Constitutional Guarantees 8
3. "The Intent of the Framers" 19

**Chapter 2. The First Amendment and the Print Media:
Historical Background and Today's Law** 22
4. Seditious Libel: Ancient Enemy of Freedom 22
5. Prior Restraint 37
6. Prior Restraint: Licensing 52
7. Forcing Communication to Occur 58
8. Criminal Libel 61
9. Taxation 69
10. The Contempt Power and Criticizing Courts 76

Chapter 3. The First Amendment and Electronic Media ... 79
11. From Radiotelegraphy to Broadcasting 79
12. Spectrum Space: From Crisis to Control 84
13. Rationalizing Governmental Regulation 88
14. Spectrum Scarcity and Expanding New Media Channels 93
15. The Convergence of "Broadcast" and "Press" Law 96

PART II. MASS COMMUNICATIONS LAW AND THE CITIZEN

Chapter 4. Defamation: Libel and Slander 100
16. Defamation Defined 100
17. The Five Elements of Libel 105
18. Libelous Words Classified 112
19. Opinion and Rhetorical Hyperbole 125
20. Emotional Distress and Mental Anguish 128
21. The Form of the Libel 131
22. Broadcast Defamation 133

Sec.   **Page**

23. Extrinsic Circumstances, Libel Per Se, and Libel Per Quod _____ 139
24. Damages _____ 141

Chapter 5. The Constitutional Defense Against Libel Suits 145
25. The Public Principle _____ 145
26. Defense Against Public Officials' Suits _____ 146
27. Defense Where Public Figures and Public Issues Are Concerned _____ 154
28. Defining "Public Figure" _____ 159
29. Actual Malice _____ 171
30. Special Issues: Juries, Summary Judgment, Neutral Reporting, Discovery _____ 184

Chapter 6. Defending Against Libel Suits Under State Law 195
31. Determining Who Is "Private" _____ 195
32. Ending Strict Liability in Libel _____ 198
33. Qualified Privilege as a Defense _____ 207
34. Truth as a Defense _____ 222
35. Opinion and Fair Comment as Defenses _____ 227
36. Retraction _____ 241

Chapter 7. The Law of Privacy and the Media _____ 248
37. Development of Privacy Law _____ 248
38. "Intrusion" as Invasion of Privacy _____ 255
39. Publication of Private Matters _____ 269
40. False Publications Which Invade Privacy _____ 290
41. Appropriation of Plaintiff's Name or Likeness _____ 298
42. Defenses: Newsworthiness, the Constitution, and Consent _____ 307
43. Defenses: Limitations and Problems _____ 323

Chapter 8. Obscenity _____ 329
44. The Common Law Origins _____ 329
45. The Roth Landmark _____ 333
46. Monitoring Compliance: The Federal Review Era _____ 338
47. Encouraging State Standards: The Miller v. California Era _____ 346
48. Balancing Conflicting Societal Interests _____ 354

PART III. MASS COMMUNICATIONS AND GOVERNMENT

Page

Chapter 9. Regulating Broadcasting _____ 373

Sec.

49. Licensing Broadcasters _____ 373
50. Renewing the Broadcast License _____ 376
51. Broadcast Program Standards _____ 379
52. Political Access Rules _____ 388
53. Fairness Doctrine Obligations _____ 392
54. Personal Attacks and Political Editorials _____ 397
55. Public Broadcasting _____ 399

Chapter 10. Deregulation and the New Media _____ 402

56. Regulating Cable TV _____ 402
57. Modern Federal Cable TV Policy _____ 408
58. New Media Competition _____ 414
59. Deregulation and the Marketplace _____ 423

Chapter 11. Regulation of Advertising _____ 432

60. From *Caveat Emptor* to Consumer Protection _____ 432
61. Federal Administrative Controls: The Federal Trade Commission _____ 434
62. Literal Truth Is Not Enough _____ 445
63. Corrective Advertising Orders of the FTC _____ 449
64. Other Federal Administrative Controls _____ 454
65. The Printers' Ink Statute _____ 458
66. Lotteries _____ 459
67. Self-Regulation _____ 460
68. The Right to Refuse Service _____ 462
69. Broadcast Advertising _____ 469
70. Advertising and the Constitution _____ 473

Chapter 12. Copyright: Protection and Constraint _____ 489

71. Development of Copyright Law _____ 489
72. Securing a Copyright _____ 496
73. Originality _____ 501
74. Infringement and Remedies _____ 503
75. Copyright, Unfair Competition and the News _____ 513
76. The Defense of Fair Use _____ 520
77. Broadcast Music Licensing Rights _____ 538

PART IV. FACT GATHERING AND CITIZENS' RIGHTS

Page

Chapter 13. Shielding Information From Disclosure 543

Sec.

78. The Government Contempt Power 543
79. Refusing to Testify About Sources and Information 550
80. Protecting Newsrooms From Search and Telephone Records From Disclosure 583

Chapter 14. Legal Problems in Reporting Legislative and Executive Branches of Government 591

81. The Problem of Secrecy in Government 591
82. Access and the Constitution 595
83. Records and Meetings of Federal Government 600
84. Access to "Security" Information, Covering Wars 617
85. Records and Meetings in the States 627

Chapter 15. Legal Problems in Reporting Courts 635

86. Access to Judicial Proceedings 635
87. Free Press *Versus* Fair Trial 636
88. Pre-Trial Publicity 640
89. Publicity During Trial: Cameras in the Courtroom 644
90. Notorious Cases: The Shadow of *Sheppard.* 651
91. External Guidelines and Self–Regulatory Efforts 659
92. Restrictive Orders and Reporting the Judicial Process 663
93. Access to Criminal Trials and Civil Matters 674

PART V. CONVERGING MEDIA AND THE LAW

Chapter 16. Media Ownership: Consolidation and Globalization 694

94. International Dimensions of Media Ownership 694
95. The Trend Toward Media Concentration 696
96. Newspaper Antitrust Law 706
97. Electronic Media Ownership Policies 725
98. The Globalization of American Media 739

Chapter 17. Distributing Mass Communications 743

99. Mass Media and the Common Carrier Connection 743
100. The Telephone Network Competitor 745
101. Communication Law and the Challenge of Change 753

TABLE OF CONTENTS

APPENDICES

App.		Page
A.	Abbreviations	761
B.	Selected Court and Pleading Terms	765
C.	Some Notes On the Legal Process	771
D.	Bibliography	778
E.	The Society of Professional Journalists and ASNE Codes of Ethics	784
F.	Communications Act of 1934 (Major Provisions)	789

	Page
TABLE OF CASES	811
INDEX	825

*

LAW

OF

MASS COMMUNICATIONS

FREEDOM AND CONTROL OF PRINT
AND BROADCAST MEDIA

*

Part I

HISTORICAL AND CONSTITUTIONAL FOUNDATIONS OF FREE EXPRESSION

Chapter 1

FREEDOM AND CONTROL

Sec.
1. The Worth of Freedom.
2. The Constitutional Guarantees.
3. "The Intent of the Framers."

A major test of a nation's freedom is the degree of liberty its people have in speaking, writing, and publishing. The hand of authority rests lightly on speech and press at some places and times, heavily at others. But its presence is felt everywhere, including the nations of the Western World which generally consider themselves the most freedom-loving of all.

Some degree of legal control over expression has been in place even in the freest societies through history. Although values of free speech and press may be considered paramount and exalted, there are circumstances where other values may take priority and win in a conflict over rights. The individual's right to a good reputation limits verbal attacks through the law of civil libel. In wartime, assertions of national security may be given precedence over press freedom. Multitudes of laws regulating business, industry and trade apply fully to the commercial press, to advertising, to public relations, and to broadcasting and newer communication technologies.

The goal of this textbook is to serve students in a first or survey course in communication law. A major reason for this book is to help journalists try to "stay out of trouble," to learn something about the pitfalls of libel and slander, invasion of privacy, and copyright infringement. Perhaps the examples and discussion offered here can serve, as legal historian James Willard Hurst has suggested of his field, like training for wrestlers: to help keep their balance, to avoid being upset by sudden and unexpected onslaughts.[1] And on many occasions, of course, atten-

---

[1] James Willard Hurst, Introductory Lecture, course on Legal History, University of Wisconsin–Madison, Spring, 1961.

1

tion to ethical behavior will prevent legal questions from arising at all.

This book will provide students with some "how to" information, especially in chapters dealing with access to information.[2] It also tries to give students some understanding of the legal systems of the United States, especially as they interact with the sweeping field vaguely called "communication law." The law of mass communications can *not* be taught as if it is some compartmentalized area marked off by logical boundaries. Of necessity, this book cuts across most areas covered in a law school curriculum:

Constitutional Law deals with the basic governmental framework, as with a state constitution or the federal Constitution. The federal Constitution—the highest law of the land—divides government powers into the legislative, executive, and judicial branches. Powers of government are apportioned among those branches, and the document also lists, in the First Ten Amendments, powers that the U.S. government may *not* bring to bear on its citizens.

The federal Constitution is one of many constitutions in the United States. There are, after all, fifty-one legal systems—the federal system plus fifty state systems. In addition, there are charters governing the organization and operation of cities and counties. Keep in mind that the federal Constitution is the highest law of the land: state constitutional provisions in conflict with it are not enforceable.

By their nature, as basic or "organic" law, constitutions are not easily changed. As spelled out in the federal Constitution, it takes the vote of three-fourths of the states (via states' legislatures or called constitutional conventions) to amend the Constitution.

The First Amendment guarantee of freedom of speech and press is of central importance to this book. If a law or state or lower federal court decision is declared "unconstitutional" by the Supreme Court of the United States, that law or decision is null and void.

Most of the nation's law is *statutory:* made by legislatures, from Congress to state legislatures to county boards and city councils. If the meaning of a statute is at issue in a legal case or controversy, the meaning of the statute can be interpreted by courts. This search for meaning, called *statutory construction,* tries to define vague terms in the statute, often by digging back into the statute's *legislative history.* What did the legislature intend to do when it passed the measure?

There are abundant examples of statutes directly affecting the communication media. Consider, for example, the basic federal

---

[2] See Chapters 14 and 15.

anti-obscenity law, 18 U.S.C.A. § 1461 [Title or Volume 18, United States Code, at Section 1461.] That statute, passed more than a century ago, forbids sending obscene material through the mails or in interstate commerce. But what is obscene? The statute is unclear. As discussed in Chapter 8, U.S. courts have devoted much energy trying to define "the obscene."

Statutory law was not always the most important branch of law in the United States. Well into the nineteenth century, *common law*—law "found" or "discovered" by judges—was the most important point of growth. Actual judge-made law-making involving an entire area has been rare during the past century. It has been suggested that because of the rarity of common-law creation in this century, there has grown up considerable scholarly fascination with the law of privacy. Privacy law is largely common-law, made by courts instead of legislatures.

Equity is an area which originated in England centuries ago. The Chancellor devised a court—called a Court of Chancery or a Court of Equity (based on what was fair or equitable)—to decide disputes which did not fit into the ordinary framework of the regular or "law" courts. Courts in the United States have combined the functions, and now are said to "sit in both law and equity." Pieces of "equity" remain and are sometimes in the news. For example, in some situations the monetary award remedy available by winning a lawsuit would not be appropriate. Sometimes, what is "equitable" is to have a court order someone to do something (as in a writ of "mandamus," which is Latin for "we demand), or not to do something (as by a court granting an injunction or "cease and desist" order.

One of the most famous First Amendment cases featured in this book—the "Pentagon Papers" to be discussed in Chapter 2—involved the Supreme Court's overturning a lower court's injunction forbidding *The New York Times* from publishing a series of secret documents on the Viet Nam conflict.

Administrative law has grown rapidly in the past century. As the nation grew more complex, Congress found itself overmatched by commercial and industrial growth involved in the industrial revolution and the nation's westward expansion. Beginning in 1890 with the Interstate Commerce Commission (to regulate railroads), Congress delegated some of its power to an agency. Similar agencies followed; two having particular applicability to the mass media are the sometime regulator of advertising, the Federal Trade Commission (FTC), established in 1914, and the Federal Communications Commission (FCC, established in 1934 but actually following a pattern set by the Federal Radio Commission Act of 1927).

Additionally, the federal Executive branch has the power to make a kind of law through *executive orders*. For example, the "Confidential," "Secret" and "Top Secret" document classifications were established in 1951 by a Presidential executive order by Harry S Truman, and remain in effect today.

Another way of classifying legal actions is as *criminal* and *civil* actions. *Black's Law Dictionary* (Rev. Fifth Ed.) defines a crime as an offense against the state. A crime can be accomplished by *omission*, failing to perform a legally commanded duty (e.g. failure to register for the draft) or *commission* (e.g. killing someone on purpose with a blunt instrument). The latter example could lead to a charge of murder, or wrongful taking of another's life. Crimes are variously classified as *misdemeanors* (minor crimes, usually carrying a jail term of less than a year) and *felonies* (major crimes, generally defined as carrying a jail term of more than a year).

Crimes to be taken up in this book include obscenity, seditious libel, and some aspects of copyright infringement.

Civil Law includes personal damage actions ("lawsuits") in which a person asks for "the establishment, recovery, or redress of private and civil rights." If a publication hurts your reputation by printing a false and harmful statement about you, you could bring a legal action ("sue"), asking for "damages" (see "money"). Much of this book is taken up with discussion of damage actions in the areas of libel, invasion of privacy, and copyright infringement.

Another term which is a staple area in law school curricula is *tort*. It is simply a French word meaning "wrong," and the law assumes that if persons have serious wrongs done to them, they ought to be able to sue for compensation. Libel is a tort. Invasion of privacy is a tort.

For a further exposure to legal terminology, please see Appendices B and C of this book.

SEC. 1. THE WORTH OF FREEDOM

Major values underlying free speech and press include society's need for maximum flow of information and opinion, and the individual's right to fulfillment.

Freedom to speak, to write, to travel—and to criticize governments and government officials—now seems as natural as breathing to most residents of the United States. Late in the Twentieth Century, North Americans generally take for granted systems of representative self-government, with legislative and executive officials—and some judges as well—selected at regular intervals via secret ballots.

Taking freedoms for granted can be the world's most dangerous complacency. Particular concern should be directed at official efforts to discourage dissent or to push for some particular orthodoxy. If dissenters' freedoms are not protected, then all freedoms are in danger. Sometimes, individuals will find that they hold views that are widely despised, and will take risks in speaking out, especially in times of great social or political tension. And if there is no dissent, the results may be disastrous. Consider the words of Martin Niemoeller, haunted by the millions of Jews killed in Hitler's Holocaust: [3]

> First they came for the socialists, and I did not speak out—because I was not a socialist. Then they came for the trade unionists, and I did not speak out—because I was not a trade unionist. Then then came for the Jews, and I did not speak out—because I was not a Jew. Then they came for me—and there was no one left to speak for me.

One test of freedom is the ability to go unpunished after venting severe criticism of those holding political power. And, if a government official can check over what you've written and deny you the right to publish it, that's pre-publication censorship. More than three hundred years ago, the now-legendary poet John Milton (*Paradise Lost*) argued against pre-publication censorship by church authorities, who then had power inseparable from government. Writing in 1644, Milton declared that because religious truth was so essential to the fate of mankind the authorities should open up the arena for debate. Truth was the only safe basis for a society's life, he said: [4]

> And though all the winds of doctrine were let loose to play upon the earth, so truth be in the field, we do injuriously, by licensing and prohibiting, to misdoubt her strength. Let her and falsehood grapple; who ever knew Truth put to the worse, in a free and open encounter?

Those words from John Milton—expressing what is often called the "diversity principle"—still resound in 20th Century American law, in key court decisions on the scope of freedom.[5]

---

[3] Martin Niemoeller, Exile in the Fatherland, ed. by H.G. Locke (Grand Rapids, MI: Eerdmans, 1986), p. viii.

[4] John Milton, Areopagitica (Chicago, 1953). See Thomas I. Emerson, The System of Freedom of Expression (New York: Random House, 1970), Chap. 1, for discussion of social and individual values of free expression. See also Vincent Blasi, The Checking Value in First Amendment Theory, 1977 Am.Bar Found.Res.J. 523.

[5] See, e.g., the dissent by Justice O.W. Holmes, Jr., in Abrams v. United States, 250 U.S. 616, 40 S.Ct. 17 (1919) and Justice Hugo L. Black's opinion for the Court in Associated Press v. United States, 326 U.S. 1, 65 S.Ct. 1416 (1945). See also

In 1988, for example, New York Times columnist Anthony
Lewis quoted from a Miltonian-sounding expression of the diversity principle written by Supreme Court Justice Robert H. Jackson
in 1943: After referring to the United States as a country of
" 'individualism and rich cultural diversities,' " Justice Jackson
wrote for the Court in support of a freedom to differ.[6]

> "If there is any fixed star in our constitutional constella-
> tion, it is that no official, high or petty, can prescribe
> what shall be orthodox in politics, nationalism, religion or
> other matters of opinion . . ."

It is not always easy to separate society's need and the
individual's right as the two grounds for freedom of expression. If
the individual's right is thoroughly protected, the social good in
the confrontation of ideas presumably follows. The English writer
John Locke, often called the philosophical father of the American
Revolution, argued persuasively late in the 17th Century in favor
of the individual's rights. In words which later echoed in the
Declaration of Independence, Locke wrote of the "natural right" of
every person to life, liberty, and property. His ideological de-
scendants included speech and press as one of these liberties,
equally applicable to all men in all times and situations.[7]

In the Twentieth Century, social good arguments have been
more compelling than natural rights as a basis for freedom and
control of expression. Society's stake in free speech and press is
plain in the structure and functioning of a self-governing people.
Only through a "clash of ideas in the open marketplace"[8] can
working truths be reached. The social good argument runs that
the widest diversity of opinion and information must flow through
channels of debate and discussion to arrive at worthwhile solutions to problems adding up to sound public policy. Although
Milton's pleas for freer debate were couched in terms of seeking
religious truth, Twentieth Century theorists and judges have
found the confrontation of idea against idea and fact against fact
essential to all kinds of "truth," whether in social relations,
politics, economics or art.

Over the years, the range of rationales for the practice of open
debate in the United States and the Western World has expanded.
Both the individual and society benefit from free interchange of

discussion in Zechariah Chafee, Jr., Free Speech in the United States (Cambridge,
Mass., 1964 [6th printing of 1941 ed.]), pp. 3, 29, 298, 316, 325, 559–561.

[6] West Virginia State Board of Education v. Barnette, 319 U.S. 624, 63 S.Ct. 1178
(1943). Justice Jackson wrote for the Court in a 7–2 decision that children of
Jehovah's Witnesses could not be compelled to salute the flag because this ceremo-
ny conflicted with their religious beliefs.

[7] John Locke, Second Treatise of Government, ed. Thomas P. Peardon (N.Y.,
1952); Leo Strauss, Natural Right and History (Chicago, 1953).

[8] Cf. Holmes, supra note 5.

ideas, and rationales for such benefits include goals of sound public policy, fulfillment of the potential of human beings, and creation of societies where—with openness—individuals need not distrust each other.[9]

Both judges and lawyers have based their arguments for freedom on both the social and the individual good. Barrister Francis L. Holt, whose early Nineteenth Century book on libel was one of the English texts relied on in developing American law, put primary emphasis on freedom of the press. Holt called that freedom one of the "rights of nature * * * that is to say, of the free exercise of our faculties." But press freedom was more than an individual natural right, for it produced a common good. He declared the English system of liberty which overcame feudal anarchy and monarchial despotism as being "the fruit of a free press."[10]

Some important Twentieth Century judges have spoken similarly, linking individual and societal freedom. The late Justice Hugo Black of the United States Supreme Court pointed out in Braden v. United States (1961)[11] that "There are grim reminders all around this world that the distance between individual liberty and firing squads is not always as far as it seems."[12] Twenty years earlier, in Bridges v. California (1941), he wrote of society's stake. He warned that contempt of court citations—judge-imposed fines and jail terms—against newspapers for commenting on trials in progress would "produce their restrictive results at the precise time when public interest in the matters discussed would naturally be at its height."[13]

It should not be suggested that the worth of freedom to the individual and to society goes unchallenged. Freedom is always a risk, and in any society, some hate and fear the expression of ideas contrary to their own. Is it permissible to denigrate races, nationalities or religions? Should pornographers be allowed to "subordinate" women in demeaning or violent depictions? Should a socialist newspaper be allowed to publish in times of threat from "alien ideologies"? Even today, after almost two centuries under the First Amendment to the Constitution proclaiming freedom of

[9] For discussion of the range of values making up the worth of freedom of expression, see Blasi, 544–567.

[10] Francis L. Holt, The Law of Libel . . . in the Law of England, ed. Anthony Bleecker (New York: 1818), quoted in H.L. Nelson, Freedom of the Press from Hamilton to the Warren Court (New York, 1967), pp. 19–20. The individual right claimed emphasis anew in the 1970s. See Thomas I. Emerson, First Amendment Doctrine and the Burger Court, 68 Calif.L.Rev. 422, 424–7; Ronald Dworkin, Is the Press Losing the First Amendment?, New York Review, Dec. 4, 1980, 49–57.

[11] 365 U.S. 431, 445–446, 81 S.Ct. 584, 593 (1961).

[12] See also Branzburg v. Hayes, 408 U.S. 665, 92 S.Ct. 2646, 2668 (1972).

[13] 314 U.S. 252, 268, 62 S.Ct. 190, 196 (1941). See also Robert O'Neill, "Second Thoughts on the First Amendment," 13 N.Mex.L.Rev. 577, Summer 1983.

speech and press, many Americans would answer that *true freedom* protects only virtuous or responsible communication.

But who is to say what is responsible? Suppose that the Constitution of the United States were to be amended to make the press both free and responsible. Perhaps the wording might say something like this: [14]

> In accordance with the interest of the people and in order to strengthen and develop the . . . system . . . citizens . . . are guaranteed freedom of speech, of the press, and of assembly, meetings, and of street processions and demonstrations.

That is a quotation from an actual 1977 constitution of another nation, one which then had little freedom. It is printed with only a few words deleted: the words "socialist," "working people," and "of the U.S.S.R." Even though it proclaimed "freedom," it was apparent that in such a system, speech can be "free" only as rulers interpret speech and press as operating responsibly in support of an existing order, "to strengthen and develop the system." [15]

There is also the related view that true "liberation" of societies is not possible as long as toleration of aggression in national policies is practiced, or if racial, religious, or class hatred may be stirred up. Following this position, some ideas and policies must be forbidden, for to permit them to be expressed is to tolerate conditions that perpetuate servitude and misery.[16]

If a society has free expression, that very freedom may lead to its destruction. The right to challenge the very principle of free expression is, of course, a good indicator of the extent of freedom in a society. " * * * Man can *seem* to be free in any society, no matter how authoritarian, as long as he accepts the postulates of the society, but he can only *be* free in a society that is willing to allow its basic postulates to be questioned." [17]

SEC. 2. THE CONSTITUTIONAL GUARANTEES

Federal and State Constitutions all guarantee freedom of expression but some State Constitutions declare that citizens are responsible for the abuse of that right.

Protection for the dissenters as well as the advocates of the status quo is part of the basic, organic law of the United States.

---

[14] See F.J.M. Feldbrugge, ed., The Constitutions of the USSR . . . (The Netherlands, 1979, see Art. 50, p. 101.

[15] Ibid.

[16] Robert P. Wolff, Barrington Moore, Jr. and Herbert Marcuse, A Critique of Pure Tolerance (Boston, 1965) p. 87ff.

[17] John B. Wolfe, in Wilbur Schramm, Responsibility in Mass Communication (New York, 1957) p. 106.

The Federal and State constitutions unanimously give free expression a position of prime value.

The Americans who wrote and in 1791 adopted the Bill of Rights of the United States Constitution followed a theme in Anglo–American liberty. Those Americans who had seen the breaking of the ties connecting them to Britain in 1776 with the Declaration of Independence drew on a long history of struggle against arbitrary power. With their lively knowledge of their past, they knew of the Englishmen who in 1215 forced King John to sign the Magna Charta—the "large charter" of rights promising lawful rule by duly constituted authority and trial by jury. They knew also of the Englishmen who passed the Habeas Corpus Act in 1679 saying that persons could not be imprisoned except by lawful authority, and of the English Bill of Rights of 1689.[18]

This sense of history doubtless impelled Americans, after the War for Independence, to set down the framework of government—first of the emerging states after the Declaration of Independence, and later the Articles of Confederation and Constitution—*in writing*. Government's powers were to be made explicit.[19]

The Constitution of 1787, adopted after weeks of meetings *in secret* by the Constitutional Convention in Philadelphia, proposed much more centralization of power in the national government than did the nation's first constitution, the Articles of Confederation. Although the Constitution of 1787 is much revered today, and was elevated virtually to the level of Divine inspiration by the 1987 Bicentennial Celebration, it should be kept in mind that the Constitution was—and is—a practical political "frame of government" document.[20]

Although much rhetoric has flowed over the Bill of Rights and the First Amendment, the practical political fact remains that the Bill of Rights—and the First Amendment—were political afterthoughts, compromises. Strong Antifederalist opposition led supporters of the Constitution to conclude that the required nine (of thirteen) states would never ratify the Constitution as written.[21] The Antifederalists pushed a boisterous campaign to prevent adoption of the Constitution, claiming it would create a tyrannous, monolithic national government that would trample liberties then enjoyed by the people under the Articles of Confederation. Supporters of the Constitution defused their opposition enough to

[18] Winston Churchill, The Birth of Britain (New York, 1956, pp. 252–254; Leonard W. Levy, Emergence of a Free Press (Oxford, 1985), Chs. 1 and 2.

[19] Sanford Levinson, Constitutional Faith (Princeton, N.J., 1988) pp. 30–31.

[20] Jackson Turner Main, The Antifederalists: Critics of the Constitution (Chapel Hill, 1961), *passim.*

[21] Ibid., 158–161.

secure ratification in the states by pledging to add a Bill of Rights to place explicit limits on the national government, providing a list of rights that the United States could not infringe.[22]

After initial reluctance to see a Bill of Rights added, James Madison—as a representative to the First Congress from Virginia—served as a major draftsman and the prime mover in getting the Bill of Rights passed for submission to the states. Madison, although staunchly for civil liberties, had questioned whether a national Bill of Rights would be effective. Later, evidently seeing both substance and political usefulness, Madison finally managed—after several months—to get Congress to consider drafting proposed amendments. Such delay suggests that Congress found other matters more pressing than the promised Bill of Rights. (Although some boosterish renditions of journalism history of the after-dinner speech variety claim the First Amendment was listed first because it was considered most important, it seems to have become the first merely because a couple of early draft amendments were edited out.) On the last day of 1791, state ratification of the Bill of Rights gave force to these words making up the First Amendment: [23]

> Congress shall make no law respecting an establishment of religion, or prohibiting the free exercise thereof; or abridging the freedom of speech, or of the press; or the right of the people peaceably to assemble, and to petition the Government for a redress of grievances.

The meaning of the First Amendment was by no means clear. The noted Constitutional historian Leonard Levy once contended that a long and bitter civil war—called by Americans the War for Independence—was hardly a good time for the birth or nurturing of civil liberties. In an inspired phrase, Levy asserted in 1960: "There is even reason to believe that the Bill of Rights was more the chance product of political expediency on all sides than of principled commitment to personal liberties." [24]

In the late Eighteenth Century, and even today, "freedom of speech and press" was an ill-defined and much-debated phrase. But however unsettled the nation's founders were about expanding the reach of free expression beyond that in England, they stated a broad principle in firmly protective terms, and left it to future generations to interpret.[25]

The states adopted their own constitutions, some beginning as early as 1776 and then revising the documents over the years.

---

[22] Ibid.

[23] U.S. Constitution, Amendment 1.

[24] Levy, Legacy of Suppression (Cambridge, Mass., 1960), pp. vii–viii.

[25] Levy, Emergence, pp. 348–349.

Freedoms of speech and press evidently were not seen as "absolutes;" this was recognized, over time, by most states' constitutions. Nearly all agreed that freedom of expression could be "abused," although that "abuse" was not defined. Typically, the sentence in the state constitution that started with the guarantee of free expression ended with a qualification. The Constitution of Pennsylvania of 1790 said: "The free communication of thoughts and opinions is one of the invaluable rights of man, and every citizen may freely speak, write and print on any subject, being responsible for the abuse of that liberty." [26]

As the Federal Constitution's First Amendment left the "freedom of speech and press" to future interpretation, the state constitutions tended to leave "abuse" to later definition. The principle resembled that expressed by Sir William Blackstone, prestigious English legal authority whose famed *Commentaries,* published in 1765–1769, amounted to a kind of legal Bible for the lawyers of the emerging United States. Blackstone's definition of press freedom declared: [27]

> The liberty of the press is indeed essential to the nature of a free state: but this consists in laying no *previous* restraints upon publications, and not in freedom from censure for criminal matter when published. Every freeman has an undoubted right to lay what sentiments he pleases before the public: to forbid this, is to destroy the freedom of the press: but if he publishes what is improper, mischievous, or illegal, he must take the consequences of his own temerity.

Blackstone's formulation had great force as state legal systems emerged. In times before law schools, when would-be lawyers "read law" as assistants to experienced lawyers, a law practice would often be started with two books: the Bible and a copy of Blackstone. Note that Blackstone's definition of freedom guaranteed little beyond no pre-publication censorship. As will be discussed in later sections, criticism of government which Blackstone likely would have considered illegal "abuse" of press freedom now is fully protected as courts interpret the Constitution.

Gitlow v. New York (1925)

Each state's power to define what it considered abuse of free expression long went unchallenged before the Federal courts. But in 1925, the United States Supreme Court in effect *nationalized* the First Amendment.[28]

[26] Constitution of Pennsylvania, Art. 1, § 7.

[27] 4 Blackstone Commentaries 151, 152.

[28] 268 U.S. 652, 666, 45 S.Ct. 625, 630 (1925).

A hapless radical, Benjamin Gitlow, had been charged with violating the criminal anarchy law of the state of New York. That statute defined criminal anarchy as the doctrine " '. . . that organized government should be overthrown by force or violence, or by assassination of the executive head or of any of the officials of government, or by any other means.' " The state's statute also made it a crime to advocate, advise or teach such a doctrine. Gitlow and friends had circulated "The Left Wing Manifesto," which advocated "revolutionary mass action" to establish Communist Socialism.[29]

Ironically, even though the Supreme Court of the United States found that a New York jury was warranted in finding Gitlow guilty of advocating governmental overthrow, it also held that the protections of the First Amendment were applicable to the states through the Fourteenth Amendment, which had been adopted in 1868 to protect the rights of slaves freed by the Civil War. The Fourteenth Amendment declares that *no state* shall "deprive any person of life, liberty or property, without due process of law * * *."[30] In the Gitlow case, the Supreme Court for the first time held the "liberty" mentioned in the Fourteenth Amendment. Until Gitlow v. New York (1925), state courts' rulings on freedom of expression cases were allowed to stand without review by the U.S. Supreme Court. In the Gitlow decision, however, Justice Sanford wrote for the seven-man majority of the Court that: [31]

> * * * we may and do assume that freedom of speech and of the press—which are protected by the First Amendment from abridgment by Congress—are among the fundamental rights and "liberties" protected by the due process clause of the Fourteenth Amendment from impairment by the States.

These words did not help Ben Gitlow; since the Supreme Court had upheld his conviction, he went to jail. Two members of the Supreme Court—Justices Oliver Wendell Holmes and Louis D. Brandeis—dissented, saying that the "Manifesto" posed little threat of doing harm, let alone a "clear and present danger" [32] from the small minority who shared Gitlow's views. In later years, when the Supreme Court of the United States tended to be more tolerant and supportive of expression than many state courts, the 1925 decision in Gitlow v. New York proved to be the case which opened the door to the Supreme Court review of state

[29] Chafee, op. cit., pp. 318–325.

[30] U.S. Constitution, Amendment 14.

[31] 268 U.S. 652, 672, 45 S.Ct. 625, 630 (1925).

[32] 268 U.S. 652, 672, 45 S.Ct. 625, 632 (1925).

courts' actions involving speech and press. After the Gitlow case the Fourteenth Amendment took its place with the First Amendment as a major protection for expression. By "bringing the First Amendment home to the states," the Gitlow decision made possible the landmark case limiting pre-publication censorship, Near v. Minnesota ex rel. Olson (1931),[33] and the famous decision protecting the news media against libel suits by public officials, New York Times Co. v. Sullivan (1964).[34]

The Fifth Amendment

One other amendment to the Federal Constitution also applies to expression. This is the Fifth Amendment, which has language similar to part of the Fourteenth Amendment.[35] The Fifth Amendment says "No person shall be compelled in any criminal case to be a witness against himself, nor be deprived of life, liberty, or property, without due process of law." [36]

When those words are taken together with the First Amendment's command protecting "the freedom of speech, or of the press," the Fifth Amendment may be read as helping guarantee the liberty to speak or write. The Fifth Amendment also provides protection for a witness against self-incrimination. The right against self-incrimination stems from a revolting practice, common in England until the Seventeenth Century, of forcing people—often through torturing them—to testify against themselves. Again, knowledge of history by the men who wrote and adopted the Bill of Rights no doubt come into play. One person who became a symbol to that generation was "Freeborn John" Lilburne, one of the most contentious figures in the history of England's freedoms. Brought before the secret Court of the Star Chamber in 1641 for his alleged importation of anti-government and heretical books, Lilburne was whipped and pilloried because he refused to take an oath to testify against himself. He then petitioned Parliament for compensation for the wrongs he had suffered. Parliament declared Lilburne's sentence "illegal and against the liberty of the subject," and voted him an indemnity of 3,000 pounds. Lilburne had won the day for the "right not to accuse oneself," a right given constitutional status in the U.S. when the Fifth Amendment was ratified 150 years later, in 1791.[37]

Think again about the wording of the First, Fifth and Fourteenth Amendments to the Constitution as discussed in the preced-

---

[33] 283 U.S. 697, 51 S.Ct. 625 (1931).

[34] 376 U.S. 254, 84 S.Ct. 710 (1964).

[35] U.S. Constitution Amendment 14.

[36] Ibid., Amendment 5.

[37] Erwin N. Griswold, The First Amendment Today (Cambridge, 1955) pp. 3, 4.

ing pages. The First Amendment says, with no limiting words that "Congress shall make no law . . . abridging the freedom of speech, or of the press . . ." On the other hand, both the Fifth and the Fourteenth Amendments, say that persons *can* be deprived of life, liberty, or property through due process of law. Further, many State constitutions state that although there is freedom of speech and press, those freedoms can be abused, and the abusers of those freedoms held responsible. Even in a Constitution granting freedoms, certain boundaries for speech and press were suggested.

Boundaries For Freedom

As the final authority on what the Constitution means, it has fallen to the Supreme Court of the United States to say what expression is protected—or "constitutional" and what is not protected. Although the First Amendment says "Congress shall make no law * * * abridging freedom of speech, or of the press * * *," the nation's courts have been unable to draw an exact, ruler-straight line between the permissible and the punishable. American theorists, courts, legislatures, and laymen have stated the boundaries of expression in various ways. If a scale could be made with "freedom" at one end and "restraint" at the other, most Americans would cluster toward "freedom."

Of all American spokesmen, the late Justice Hugo L. Black most flatly stated the position for a right of unlimited expression, interpreting the First Amendment as an "absolute" command forbidding any restraint on speech and press: [38]

> I believe when our Founding Fathers * * * wrote this [First] Amendment they * * * knew what history was behind them and they wanted to ordain in this country that Congress * * * should not tell the people what religion they should have or what they should believe or say or publish, and that is about it. It [the First Amendment] says "no law," and that is what I believe it means.
>
> * * *
>
> I have no doubt myself that the provision, as written and adopted, intended that there should be no libel or defamation law in the United States.

Although such ringing statements made Justice Black a hero to many journalists and civil libertarians, such words might also cause consternation among legal historians. Many legal scholars, writing before and after Justice Black, have contended that such

---

[38] Edmond N. Cahn, "Justice Black and First Amendment 'Absolutes': A Public Interview," 37 N.Y.U.L.Rev. 548 (1962).

historical assertions were flawed by one-sidedness, ignoring abundant contrary evidence of libel actions brought by the generation that adopted the First Amendment.[39]

The late philosopher Alexander Meiklejohn also favored a kind of "absolute" freedom, but only in the realm of expression of political ideas. Speaking in the mid–1950s, when anti-Communism had reached heights known as McCarthyism and efforts to curb Communists' freedom were powerful, Meiklejohn declared: [40]

> The first amendment * * * admits of no exceptions. It tells us that the Congress, and by implication, all other agencies of Government are denied any authority whatever to limit the political freedom of the citizens of the United States.

Such "absolute" positions, however, although theoretically appealing to some, have never found official acceptance or support in the United States. Perhaps the myths of history still cling to ideas of freedom. Even though Twentieth Century courts are still quoting John Milton's plea against censorship from roughly three and one half centuries ago, Milton's expanded concept of freedom did not include those whose religion and morals he could not accept.[41] And only a few years after writing the famed *Areopagitica*, Milton himself had official employment . . . as a censor. Ever since Milton, the case for freedom of expression has been qualified and limited in various ways as efforts are made to define the boundaries of legal control.

Writing about 1765, Sir William Blackstone's vastly influential commentaries expounded the doctrine that government shall lay no restraint on writers *before* publication, but may punish them *after* publication of anything violating the law. (The problem here, of course, is that if it is against the law to criticize government, going to jail or being executed after publication is likely to discourage other dissident speakers or writers.)

Briefly, here are some other concepts to keep in mind as you consider efforts to define freedom of expression:

Liberty v. License: This old distinction line that rolls easily off the tongue but has little operational content is often heard. It is

[39] See, e.g., Paul Murphy, "Time to Reclaim: The Current Challenge of American Constitutional History," 69 Amer.Hist.Rev. 64–654 (1963); Dwight L. Teeter and MaryAnn Yodelis Smith, "Mr. Justice Black's Absolutism: Notes on His Use of History to Support Free Expression," in Everette Dennis, et al., eds., Justice Hugo Black and the First Amendment (Ames, Iowa, 1978).

[40] Alexander Meiklejohn, Testimony of Nov. 14, 1955, U.S. Senate, Committee on Judiciary, Sub–Committee on Constitutional Rights, "Security and Constitutional Rights," pp. 14–15.

[41] See, e.g., Court's opinion by Black, J., in Associated Press v. United States, 326 U.S. 1, 8–10, 65 S.Ct. 1416, 1419 (1945).

said, "Liberty is not the same as licentiousness." (Beyond personal predilections, it is impossible to say where one notion begins and the other leaves off.)

Bad Tendency: "Intent"—or presumed intent—was and is used as a gauge for testing whether someone would have to be legally responsible for a communication. For example, individuals accused of opposing or disrupting the United States war effort during World War I were often convicted and jailed for words which in more recent years would be regarded as innocent expression.

Consider the case of Jacob Abrams. He and some other Russian immigrants were convicted of violating the Espionage Act of 1917, as amended in 1918. The 1918 amendment, since repealed, made punishable (among other things) any false statements harmful to the war effort. The statute went further, forbidding [42]

". . . any disloyal, profane, scurrilous or abusive language about the form of government of the United States, or the Constitution . . . or the military or naval forces of the United States, or the flag . . . or the uniform of the United States . . .

Jacob Abrams and his friends were convicted of violating that statute by throwing leaflets out of a manufacturing building in New York. One leaflet, headlined "THE HYPOCRISY OF THE UNITED STATES AND HER ALLIES" did not criticize the war efforts of the U.S. against Germany. Instead, it protested United States taking part with other nations in sending an expeditionary force into Russia, calling for workers in munitions factories to strike so bullets made by them would not strike down Russians.[43] There was no proof that such pamphleteering had any harmful effect or caused one less bullet to be made in a munitions factory. But World War I was a time of war hysteria and freedoms taken for granted in peacetime were cast aside. The pamphlet's fervent language, denouncing President Woodrow Wilson and "the plutocratic gang in Washington" was then enough to convince a jury to convict Abrams and three others.[44]

The U.S. Supreme Court upheld the conviction, basing its decision not on any demonstrable harm from the pamphlets, but on their "bad tendency." Writing for the Court, Justice Clarke declared that [45]

[42] U.S. Stats. at Large, vol. XL, p. 553ff.

[43] Abrams v. United States, 250 U.S. 616, 40 S.Ct. 17 (1919); see also Zechariah Chafee, Jr., Free Speech in the United States (Cambridge, 1941 ed.) 114ff.

[44] Chafee, p. 109ff.

[45] 250 U.S. 616, 621, 40 S.Ct. 17, 19 (1919).

It will not do to say, as is now argued, that the only intent of these defendants was to prevent injury to the Russian cause. Men must be held to have intended, and to be accountable for, the effects their acts were likely to produce.

Marketplace of Ideas: That prosecutor's delight, the "bad tendency" test, was enough for a majority of the Supreme Court to uphold Abrams' conviction. In dissent, Justice Oliver Wendell Holmes presented a moving expression of the "marketplace of ideas" philosophy. He built on the ideas of John Milton, and those of the Nineteenth Century British philosopher John Stuart Mill. In *On Liberty,* Mill wrote that members of society needed access to many kinds of ideas, false as well as true, to discern the truth. Mill declared that government had no legitimate power to suppress opinions: [46]

If all mankind minus one were of one opinion, and only one person were of the contrary opinion, mankind would be no more justified in silencing that one person, than he, if he had the power, would be justified in silencing mankind.

In the *Abrams* dissent, Justice Holmes wrote: [47]

In this case sentences of twenty years imprisonment have been imposed for the publishing of two leaflets that I believe the defendants had as much right to publish as the Government has to publish the Constitution now vainly invoked by them.

* * *

Persecution for the expression of opinions seems to me perfectly logical. If you have no doubt of your premises or your power and want a certain result with all your heart you naturally express your wishes in law and sweep away all opposition. * * * But when men have realized that time has upset many fighting faiths, they may come to believe even more than they believe the very foundations of their own beliefs that the ultimate good desired is better reached by free trade in ideas—that the best test of truth is the power of the thought to get itself accepted in the competition of the market, and that truth is the only ground upon which their wishes safely can be carried out. That at any rate is the theory of our constitution. It is an experiment, as all life is an experiment. Every year if not every day we have to wager our salvation upon some prophecy based upon imperfect knowledge.

[46] Mill, On Liberty (New York: Appleton-Century, 1947) p. 16.
[47] 250 U.S. 616, 629, 40 S.Ct. 17, 22 (1919).

Expression v. Action—In 1919, shortly before the *Abrams* case, Justice Holmes wrote for the Court's majority in Schenck v. United States. Schenck and his co-defendants had mailed circulars in violation of the Espionage Act of 1917, urging men who had been called to military service to resist the draft. Writing for a unanimous Court, Holmes created some famous, flashing phrases which seemed to offer promise to protect some kinds of anti-government expression, even in wartime. Justice Holmes then stated the famous *clear and present danger test.*[48]

We admit that in may places and in ordinary times the defendants in saying all that was said in the circular would have been within their constitutional rights. But the character of every act depends upon the circumstances in which it is done. The most stringent protection of free speech would not protect a man in falsely shouting fire in a theatre and causing a panic. * * * The question in every case is whether the words used are used in such circumstances and are of such a nature as to create a clear and present danger that they will bring about the substantive evils that Congress has a right to prevent. It is a question of proximity and degree. When a nation is at war many things that might be said in time of peace are such a hindrance to the effort that their utterance will not be endured . . .

The clear and present danger test did not free Schenck, nor was it to be used by Supreme Court majorities in support of free expression for two decades to come.[49] Although this test was a minority view, its development by Justices Holmes and Brandeis in later dissents—as in Abrams v. United States (1919)—served as a rallying point for libertarians for years.[50]

The clear and present danger test asked judges to assess the *likelihood* that dissident speech would be transmitted into illegal action. At what point, however, does "expression" become so dangerous that it creates a "clear and present danger?"

A major formulation by Thomas I. Emerson, one of the nation's foremost First Amendment scholars, was expressed this way in 1970: [51]

The central idea of a system of freedom of expression is that a fundamental distinction must be drawn between conduct which consists of "expression" and conduct which

[48] 249 U.S. 47, 52, 39 S.Ct. 247, 249 (1919).

[49] See Bridges v. California, 314 U.S. 252, 62 S.Ct. 190 (1941), for use of that test in a contempt case.

[50] See Chafee, *passim.*

[51] Emerson, The System of Freedom of Expression, p. 17.

consists of "action." "Expression" must be freely encouraged. "Action" can be controlled.

SEC. 3. "THE INTENT OF THE FRAMERS"

"Law office history"—assertions by judges, lawyers and politicians that they know the "intent of the Framers"—sometimes makes law affecting First Amendment rights.

Statements continue to be heard about the "intent of the Founding Fathers" or the "Framers" on the true meaning of the national constitutional provision on freedom of the press. This is a cautionary note for readers of court decisions or legal arguments which purport to offer *the* meaning of The First Amendment or some other facet of the Constitution of the United States. If you believe such legal arguments, the authors of this book have some real estate and a bridge they'd like to sell you.[52]

First, there's what might be called the journalistic fallacy, talking about the First Amendment as if it contained only guarantees for freedom of speech and press. But read what that Amendment says: it is a group of rights protecting religion, speech, press, assembly, and petition . . . mentioned in that order, for whatever order of mention is worth. The exact words say:

ARTICLE I

Congress shall make no Law respecting an establishment of religion, or prohibiting the free exercise thereof; or abridging the freedom of speech, or of the press; or the right of the people peaceably to assemble, and to petition Government for a redress of grievances.

Obviously, the First Amendment is not just about speech and press. As civil libertarians frequently observe, it is a bundle of rights, and whatever affects one part of that Amendment almost certainly will have repercussions for the other rights it lists.

When you hear a politician assert that "all history proves," brace yourself for a whopper. And be similarly skeptical about lawyers' and judges' use of history-as-argument or history-as-precedent. The legal process in this nation, after all, is an adversary system, and selective perception of evidence—especially historical evidence—is not infrequent in the judicial system.[53]

Many of the following pages will contain assertions made by judges, lawyers, and journalists about the intent underlying the

[52] See, Levy, Original Intent and the Framers' Constitution (New York: 1988) pp. xii–xiii, 377.

[53] Charles Miller, The Supreme Court and the Uses of History (Cambridge, Mass. Belknap Press, 1969).

First Amendment as it applies—to name just a few examples—to criticism of government, or prior restraint, access to information, defamation, or invasion of privacy.

If scholars or judges talk about "the First Amendment intent of the Framers," regard their words skeptically. Face it, the Framers were the men who met in secret, behind closed doors—so much for their intent concerning access to information?—in Philadelphia during the spring and summer of 1787. If someone insisted that their true intent on free speech or press or religion could be found in that document, then what? The body of the Constitution mentioned nothing at all about the rights guaranteed by the First Amendment. Members of the Constitutional Convention signed the document they produced in 1787. Although the Constitution was ratified by the necessary nine states in 1788, and although the new government began in the spring of 1789 the Bill of Rights was not adopted by the states until the end of 1791.

It has been said that the War for Independence and the troubled early years of the struggling new United States of America, instead of securing rights for speech and press, came close to eradicating them.[54] As historian Leonard W. Levy once argued, the First Amendment and the Bill of Rights were "chance products of political expediency," created to overcome the objections of the Antifederalists who were seeking another constitutional convention to undo the document aiming toward a centralized, truly national government. Under that analysis, the Bill of Rights was drafted out of pragmatism, to overcome Antifederalist charges that freedom of speech, press, assembly, and religion would be taken away under a monolithic new government. Other charges included taking away of right to trial by jury and that a heartless national government would torture people until they confessed to crimes they had not committed. Pay specific attention to the language of the First Amendment: it does *not* say that freedoms of speech and press shall not be abridged. It says that Congress (not the states) "shall make no law." True, the Federalists argued that the various states had their own free speech and press guarantees, but the Antifederalists anti-ratification arguments dealt with what the new national government *might* do.

Anthony Lewis has written that a meaningful understanding of "original intent" would have to include posthumous reading of the minds of the different groups of men who drafted the Constitution, and the men who were voting in the ratifying conventions of each state. The intent behind the Bill of Rights is even harder to discern: there is hardly any record of the legislative history of

---

[54] Levy, Legacy of Suppression (Cambridge: Belknap/Harvard, 1960) p. 182; Jackson Turner Main, op. cit., pp. 160–161.

what members of the First Congress meant in offering the Amendments in 1789.[55]

The Constitution and the Bill of Rights have not remained frozen in time. It is likely that this nation was able to celebrate 200 years under its Constitution because it is a brief, broadly stated "frame of government." And it may be asserted with safety that the First Amendment has been changed, over time, as courts—however haltingly or imperfectly—interpreted new meanings into the document. And the Framers' intent? As David A. Anderson has argued, ". . . [M]ost of the Framers perceived, however dimly, naively, or incompletely, that freedom of the press was inextricably related to the new republican form of government and would have to be protected if their vision of government by the people was to succeed." [56]

[55] Anthony Lewis, review of Leonard W. Levy's Original Intent and the Framers' Constitution (New York: Macmillan, 1989), New York Times Book Review, Nov. 6, 1988, p. 11.

[56] David A. Anderson, The Origins of the Press Clause, 30 UCLA L.Rev No. 3 (February, 1983), p. 537.

Chapter 2

THE FIRST AMENDMENT AND THE PRINT MEDIA: HISTORICAL BACKGROUND AND TODAY'S LAW

Sec.
4. Seditious Libel: Ancient Enemy of Freedom.
5. Prior Restraint.
6. Prior Restraint: Licensing.
7. Forcing Communication to Occur.
8. Criminal Libel.
9. Taxation.
10. The Contempt Power and Criticizing Courts.

It has been said that the present is only the cutting edge of the past. This is especially true in law, with courts for the most part looking to earlier decisions, "following precedent." In studying struggles for freedom of expression, it is easy to wonder if there is much that is new. Old patterns of control—ancient enemies of freedom—may be traced to authoritarian philosophies hundreds and hundreds of years old. Major controls over the press well known in Seventeenth and Eighteenth Century England and America set the pattern for battles for freedom of expression which have continued into the last decades of the Twentieth Century.[1] Patterns of control continue, and so do the fights against them.

SEC. 4. SEDITIOUS LIBEL: ANCIENT ENEMY OF FREEDOM

Sedition—defined roughly as expression attacking government's form, laws, institutions, or officers—is a criminal charge many centuries old. In the United States of the Twentieth Century the crime has been restricted by court rulings.

The crime of seditious libel or "sedition" has a long and bloody history. Generally, sedition has been defined as attacking government (its form, laws, institutions) or government officers (including, in Seventeenth Century England, members of the Royal family).

[1] Fredrick S. Siebert, Freedom of the Press in England, 1476–1776 (Urbana: Univ. of Illinois Press, 1952). This is the classic treatment of the instruments of control. See also Norman L. Rosenberg, Protecting the Best Men: An Interpretive History of the Law of Libel (Chapel Hill: Univ. of North Carolina Press, 1986), and Leonard W. Levy, Emergence of a Free Press (New York: Oxford, 1985).

Consider the case of William Prynn, a prude who advocated strict Puritanism. In his book, *Histrio–Mastix,* he denounced such popular pastimes as dancing, hunting, Christmas-keeping, and play-going. How did this attack government? The attack was inferred from Prynn's assertion that lewd women and whores acted in plays: It seems the Queen of England had taken part in a pastoral play at Somerset House. Prynn was fined £10,000 and given life imprisonment. In addition, he was pilloried (made to "stand in the stocks," held in a frame in a public square where passers-by could revile him) and had his ears cropped off.[2] A year later, in 1637, Dr. John Bastwick and Henry Burton were treated similarly by the infamous Court of the Star Chamber for their attacks on the Pope. Mob demonstrations against authority followed Prynn's sentencing. He was released from prisons by the Long Parliament in 1641 after Puritan forces had gained ascendancy in England and after the abolition of the Court of the Star Chamber.[3]

Today, treason is thought of as betraying a nation to an enemy, and conjures up visions of spying or sabotage or of the notorious "Tokyo Rose" who made pro-Japanese broadcasts to American military forces during World War II. Treason is a crime punishable by death. It had been defined very broadly in England since 1352, in the time of Edward III. Treason then meant not only making war against the King or giving aid and comfort to enemies, it also included "compassing the death of the king," or imagining his death. (Put this concept in a Twentieth Century form: How many times have citizens heard and read comments "imagining the death of the President of the United States?" What about comments on candidates for Vice President of whom it is asked, "Do you want this person only a heartbeat away from the Presidency?")

Consider the case of John Twyn, who printed a book called *A Treatise on the Execution of Justice.* Writing was included in "compassing the death of the king," and at a 1663 session of the Old Bailey court in London Twyn was indicted for treason. The book contended that a ruler is accountable to the people, and that the people may take up arms against and even kill a king who refuses accountability. Although Twyn had not written the book, he refused to say who did. And as the printer, he then received the full weight of the law's brutality. The judge pronounced the sentence of guilty: [4]

> . . . "that you be . . . drawn upon a hurdle [sledge] to the place of execution; and there you shall be hanged by

[2] 3 Howell's State Trials 561 (1632–3).

[3] Siebert, pp. 123–125.

[4] Howell's State Trials 513 (1663).

the neck, and being alive, shall be cut down, and your privy-members shall be cut off, your entrails shall be taken out of your body, and you living, the same to be burnt before your eyes; your head to be cut off, your body to be divided into four quarters. . . . And the Lord have mercy upon your soul.

Martyrs to the principle of free expression had their impact as spokesmen for a new philosophy such as John Milton and John Locke had theirs. But the legal principle of seditious libel remained in force: if people criticized government, they did so at their peril. Seditious libel soon was transported to the English colonies in America, although punishments for the crime never descended to the level of cruelty inflicted on the drawn-and-quartered John Twyn.

Sedition in America: The Zenger Trial

At least four colonial Americans faced sedition prosecutions for printed words before the most celebrated criminal trial of the colonial period took place in 1735. The outcome of that famous trial—involving *New York Weekly Journal* printer John Peter Zenger—still symbolizes press struggles for freedom to criticize government, even late in the Twentieth Century.

Zenger became a hero of press freedom by getting into the middle of a bitter factional dispute in New York colony politics. New York Governor William Cosby, a greedy and autocratic man, was opposed by lawyer James Alexander, a leader of the powerful Lewis Morris faction. Alexander wrote anonymous attacks labeling Governor Cosby a tyrant and oppressor of the colony. Those attacks were published in John Peter Zenger's *New York Weekly Journal.*[5]

The colony's attorney general tried, unsuccessfully, to get a grand jury to indict the printer. Thwarted in that direction the attorney general brought charges of sedition on his own, filing an "information" with the New York court. Zenger was jailed, and remained there for eight months awaiting trial for seditious libel. While Zenger sat in jail, Alexander—as the behind-the-scenes political agitator—kept the *Journal* printing and the campaign against Governor Cosby simmering. Wearing his lawyer's hat, Alexander prepared to defend Zenger. He was unable to do so, however, because Chief Justice De Lancey, who had been appointed by Cosby, disbarred Alexander from practicing law. Alex-

[5] Stanley Nider Katz, A Brief Narrative of the Case and Trial of John Peter Zenger (Cambridge: Harvard, 1963); Harold L. Nelson, "Seditious Libel in Colonial America," 3 Am.Jour.Legal History 160 (1959).

ander then turned to Andrew Hamilton of Philadelphia to plead Zenger's case.

The original "Philadelphia lawyer," Hamilton had built a reputation as the ablest attorney in the colonies. The dignity of age, his utter confidence, and his bold advocacy that the court discard old patterns of thinking about sedition came to bear in an irresistible way with jurors already sympathetic to Zenger's cause. The law of sedition had long held that the defendant was not to be permitted to plead that his offending words against government were true; the truth, it was held, only aggravated the offense, for it was more likely than falsehood to cause the target to seek violent revenge and breach the community's peace. Furthermore, the law had given the jury only a minor role in a sedition trial: its job was to decide whether the accused had, indeed, printed the words. It was up to the court to decide whether they were illegal words.

Jockeying with Chief Justice De Lancey, Hamilton urged the jury to recognize truth as a defense for Zenger, and argued that the jury should decide "the law"—the libelousness of the words— as well as the fact of printing. Blocked by the judge from pursuing these points far, he shifted his tactic and went to the importance of permitting men to criticize their governments:[6]

> Men who injure and oppress the people under their administration provoke them to cry out and complain, and then make that very complaint the foundation for new oppressions and prosecutions. I wish I could say there were no instances of this kind. But to conclude, the question before the Court and you, gentlemen of the jury, is not of small or private concern; it is not the cause of a poor printer, nor of New York alone, which you are trying. No! it may, in its consequences, affect every freeman that lives under a British government, on the main of America. It is the best cause; it is the cause of liberty; and I make no doubt but your upright conduct, this day, will not only entitle you to the love and esteem of your fellow citizens, but every man who prefers freedom to a life of slavery, will bless and honor you as men who have baffled the attempts of tyranny; and by an impartial and uncorrupt verdict, have laid a noble foundation for securing to ourselves, our posterity, and our neighbors, that to which nature and the laws of our country have given us a right—the liberty—both of exposing and opposing arbitrary power in these parts of the world at least, by speaking and writing truth.

[6] Stanley Katz (ed.). A Brief Narrative . . . pp. 2–9.

Hamilton ended his plea in an emotion-charged courtroom; De Lancey delivered a confusing charge to the jury, which retired to deliberate. In a short time the jury emerged with a "not guilty" verdict. There were celebrations in the streets that night; there were printings and re-printings of the Hamilton plea for years to come, more even in England than in the colonies. The court trial for seditious libel was finished for the colonial period as an instrument for control of the press. Not for 40 years or more would seditious libel be used again in America.[7]

It was the elected Assembly, or lower house of the colonial legislature, that was the most successful and most active force in official control of Eighteenth Century colonial printers. Jealous of its powers under the view that it was Parliament in miniature, and unwilling to have its acts criticized, this agency of government disciplined printer after printer. Even as it emerged as the main check on the powers of the Crown's governors, even as it showed itself as the seat of government support for the movement for independence, the Assembly demonstrated its aversion to popular criticism. Its instrument for control was the citation for contempt ("breach of privilege"), and it haled a long line of printers before it for their "seditious" attacks on its performance. The legislative contempt citation was a legislative sedition action.

Historian Leonard Levy has demonstrated the relative power and activity of the Assemblies in respect to the press. Up and down the seaboard, printers were brought to the legislative bar and there were forced to kneel and beg the pardon of the stern law-makers, swear that they meant no harm by their writings, and accept rebuke or imprisonment. Printer James Franklin's irony put him in jail in 1722; he had speculated that the Massachusetts government might get around to outfitting a ship to pursue a pirate "sometime this month, wind and weather permitting." New Yorkers James Parker and William Weyman were jailed for an article on the poverty of Orange and Ulster counties; the Assembly construed it as a reflection upon its stewardship. These were only a few actions among many, and they continued to the eve of the Revolutionary War in some colonies.[8]

[7] Harold L. Nelson, Seditious Libel in Colonial America, 3 Am.Journ.Legal History 160 (1959).

[8] Levy, Emergence of a Free Press, 71–84. No other historian has stimulated others to study 18th-Century American press freedom as has Levy, whose thesis that the First Amendment was not intended by the Framers to end the British common law of seditious libel in America has aroused many to dissent. Revising his early, provocative Legacy of Suppression (1960) in Emergence of a Free Press (1985), and conceding some errors and misinterpretations in Legacy, he responds directly to many of the protestors but concedes nothing central to his main thesis. See Emergence of a Free Press, passim, for many of the confrontations.

The great article of faith that heads America's commitment to free expression was adopted in 1791 by men who had not yet thought through all that "free speech and press" implies. The First Amendment to the Constitution states that "Congress shall make no law * * * abridging freedom of speech, or of the press * * *." Although some then argued over precisely what they meant by the words, none spoke doubts about the importance of the principle. They were deeply aware of the lasting symbolic power of the courageous Zenger in accepting prison in the cause of free press. They knew well the spirited, soaring arguments for free press by England's famed "Cato," printed and re-printed in the little colonial newspapers. Behind them lay the great pamphleteering and newspapering that had raised sedition to an art in bringing the colonies to revolt against the Mother country, printed words indispensable in bringing down the most powerful nation on earth.

Yet in the searing newspaper debates of the nation's first years, with Federalists and anti-Federalists indulging in political vitriol seen by many as seditious and thus criminal, the axioms of centuries were with them. It still seemed to many that no government could stand if it could not at some point punish its critics, if their new government was meant to last. Some words surely were illegal. Not, perhaps, in the realm of religion, where James Madison, among others, argued an unlimited freedom to speak and write; but could sedition be given such scope? It was the party of Thomas Jefferson that gave an answer, in the debates and sequel of the Alien and Sedition Acts of 1798–1800.

The Alien and Sedition Acts, 1798–1800

In the complex story about the reluctant retreat of the crime of sedition through more than 150 years of American history, no episode stands out more than the controversy of 1798–1800 over the Alien and Sedition Acts. It was only seven years after the adoption of the Bill of Rights and its First Amendment that the Acts were written, at a time of high public and official alarm. With France and England in conflict through the 1790s, America had been pulled by both toward war. The Republicans—Jefferson's party—had favored France, while the Federalists sided with England. Angered at Jay's Treaty of 1794 with England, which she felt placed America on the side of her enemy, France had undertaken the raiding of American shipping. America's envoys, sent to France to negotiate a settlement, were faced with a demand for an American war loan to France, and a bribe of a quarter-million dollars. This unofficial demand as a price for negotiations was revealed to Americans as the notorious "X, Y, Z Affair." Now most of America was incensed; President John

Adams called for war preparation, which his Federalist Congress set about in 1797.[9]

The Republicans, although they suffered heavy political losses because of the nation's war fever, did not abandon their support of France. Stigmatized in the refusal to do so, associated by the Federalists with the recent French Revolution and its Terror, and beleaguered on all sides for their continued opposition to Britain, the Republicans were in deep trouble. And in this context, the Federalist Congress passed the Alien and Sedition Acts as measures to control opposition to America's war policy and to the Federalist majority party.

It was the Sedition Act that struck most lethally at opposition and at the Republicans. The Act made it a crime to publish or utter false, scandalous, and malicious criticism of the President, Congress, or the government with the intent to defame them or bring them into disrepute.[10]

Fourteen indictments were brought under the Act, all against Republican newspapermen and publicists, and all 14 resulted in convictions.[11] The first action put Rep. Matthew Lyon in jail for four months and cost him a fine of $1,000. He had claimed that under President Adams, the Executive Branch showed "an unbounded thirst for ridiculous pomp, foolish adulation, and selfish avarice," and that the public welfare was "swallowed up in a continual grasp for power." Anthony Haswell, Republican editor of the (Bennington) *Vermont Gazette,* came to Lyon's defense while the latter was in prison. He wrote that Lyon was held by "the oppressive hand of usurped power," and said that the federal marshal who held him had subjected him to indignities that might be expected of a "hard-hearted savage." Haswell's fine was $200 and his term in federal prison two months.[12]

Its back to the wall under the attempt of the Federalists to proscribe it as a party of disloyalty and subversion, the Republican Party put forth spokesmen who declared that the idea of sedition was odious to a self-governing society, and denied that the federal government had any kind of power over the press. The Acts, the Jeffersonian Republicans said, were unconstitutional in making it a crime to criticize the President and government. No matter that the Acts permitted the defenses for which Andrew Hamilton had argued in defending Zenger: truth was of little use in defending opinions (how to prove the truth of an opinion?); and jury

[9] James M. Smith, Freedom's Fetters (Ithaca: Cornell Univ.Press, 1956), Chap. 2. This is the leading work on the Alien and Sedition Acts.

[10] Ibid., Chap. 6.

[11] Ibid., p. 185.

[12] Each trial is treated in Smith, Chaps. 11–17.

power to find the law could be circumvented by judges in various ways. A people, they argued, cannot call itself free unless it is superior to its government, unless it can have unrestricted right of discussion. No natural right of the individual, they contended in Philosopher John Locke's framework, can be more important than free expression. The Jeffersonians rested their case on their belief in reason as the central characteristic of men, and on the people's position of ascendancy over government.[13] The radical Thomas Cooper dissected one by one the arguments for permitting a sedition power in government.[14] Calmly and systematically, lawyer Tunis Wortman worked out philosophical ground for freedom in the fullest statement of the group.[15] James Madison, St. George Tucker, and others drove home the arguments.

The unpopularity of the Alien and Sedition Acts and outrage at the prosecutions of Republican printers helped defeat the Federalist Party and President John Adams in 1800. President Jefferson was committed to letting the Acts lapse, and they died in early 1801. The nation would see no federal peacetime sedition act again for 140 years. Furthermore, the alternative route of using the common law as a basis for federal sedition actions was closed to the government only a few years later. The Supreme Court ruled in cases of 1812 and 1816 that federal courts had been given no authority over common-law crimes by the Constitution, and that whatever question there had been about the matter had been settled by public opposition to such jurisdiction.[16]

The fear and hatred of French revolutionary doctrine had been real factors in the passage of the Alien and Sedition Acts. Different fears, different hatreds led to suppressive laws in the South about a generation later, when states began passing laws to silence Abolitionists. The anti-slavery drive, coupled with incidents such as Nat Turner's slave rebellion, caused paroxysms of fear among Southerners that their "peculiar institution" and the shape of society and government would be subverted and destroyed. Laws were passed—sedition laws, though not labeled as such in statute books—making it a crime to advocate the abolition of slavery or to argue that owners "have no property" in slaves, and denying abolitionist literature access to the mails.[17] The

[13] Levy, Chap. 10. And see Chap. 9 for evidence that several Jeffersonians had no objection to a sedition power in *state* governments.

[14] Political Essays (Phila.: Printed for R. Campbell, 1800), pp. 71–88.

[15] Treatise Concerning Political Enquiry, and the Liberty of the Press (New York: Printed by George Forman, 1800).

[16] United States v. Hudson and Goodwin, 11 U.S. (7 Cranch.) 32 (1812); United States v. Coolidge, 14 U.S. (1 Wheat.) 415 (1816).

[17] Three Virginia laws passed between 1832 and 1848 are in Nelson, Freedom of the Press from Hamilton to the Warren Court, pp. 173–178.

suppression of anti-slavery argument became almost total in most of the South by 1850.

Sedition in World War I

Sedition actions surfaced again in the early Twentieth Century when both state and federal lawmakers acted to check criticism of government in response to alarm at the rise of socio-political protest. Prosecutions to punish verbal attacks on the form of government, on laws, and on government's conduct, found new life at the federal level some 100 years after they had been discredited by the Alien and Sedition Act prosecutions of 1798–1800. The actions focused on a new radicalism, flourishing in the poverty and sweat-shop conditions of industrial cities and in the lumber and mining camps of the West. Whether seeking an improved life for the deprived, driving for power, or fostering revolution, socialists, anarchists, and syndicalists advocated drastic change in the economic and political system. Laws and criminal prosecutions rose to check their words.[18]

In the aftermath of the assassination of President William McKinley in 1901, the states of New York, New Jersey and Wisconsin passed laws against anarchists' advocating the destruction of existing government. Congress passed the Immigration Act of 1903, barring from the country those who believed in or advocated the overthrow of the United States government by violence. Industrial turbulence, the growth of the Industrial Workers of the World, the surge of right- and left-wing socialism, contributed to alarm in the nation. And as the varied voices of drastic reform and radical change rose loud in the land, the coming of World War I increased their stridency: This, they insisted, was a "Capitalists' war," fostered and furthered for industrial profit. By 1918, national alarm was increased by the victory of revolutionary communism in Russia.[19]

World War I brought a wave of legislation across the states to make criminal the advocacy of violent overthrow of government. Yet it was the federal government's Espionage Act of 1917 and its amendment of 1918 to include sedition that put most muscle into prosecution for criminal words. Foremost among forbidden and prosecuted statements were those that were construed to cause insubordination or disloyalty in the armed forces, or to obstruct

[18] William Preston, Jr., Aliens and Dissenters, Federal Suppression of Radicals, 1903–1933 (Cambridge: Harvard Univ.Press, 1963).

[19] Ibid.; Paul L. Murphy, World War I and the Origins of Civil Liberties in the United States (New York, 1979); H.C. Peterson and Gilbert C. Fite, Opponents of War, 1917–1918 (Madison: Univ. of Wis.Press, 1957).

enlistment or recruiting.[20]   Some 1,900 persons were prosecuted for speech, and possibly 100 newspapers and periodicals were barred from the mails.[21]   Polemics in pamphlet form, as well as books, also were the cause of prosecutions.

The best-known of the Socialist newspapers prosecuted under the Espionage Act were the *New York Call,* the *Masses,* also of New York, and the *Milwaukee Leader.*   In the last of these, editor Victor Berger had denounced the war, the United States government, and munitions makers.   Postmaster General Albert Burleson considered this the kind of opposition to the war forbidden by the Espionage Act, and excluded it from the mails as the Act provided.   Further, he said, the repeated attacks on the war effort in the Leader were evidence that it would continue doing the same in the future, and on these grounds, the Leader's second-class mail permit should be revoked.   He was upheld in his revocation of the permit by the United States Supreme Court, and the Leader was thus denied the low-rate mailing privilege from 1917 until after the war.[22]

Pamphleteers of the left were convicted under the Espionage Act and under state anarchy and sedition acts.   The famous case of Schenck v. United States, in which Schenck was prosecuted for polemics that actually went to the matter of resisting the draft, brought Justice Oliver Wendell Holmes' articulation of the clear and present danger test: [23]

> We admit that in many places and in ordinary times the defendants in saying all that was said in the circular would have been within their constitutional rights.   But the character of every act depends upon the circumstances in which it was done * * *.   The question in every case is whether the words used are used in such circumstances and are of such a nature as to create a clear and present danger that they will bring about the substantive evils that Congress has a right to prevent.   It is a question of proximity and degree.   When a nation is at war many things that might be said in time of peace are such a hindrance to its effort that their utterance will not be endured * * *.

As noted earlier, this new test did not free Schenck, and it did not protect radicals seen as illegally opposing the war; they went to

[20] 40 U.S. Statutes 217.   For state laws, see Zechariah Chafee, Jr., Free Speech in the United States (Boston, 1941), pp. 575–597.

[21] Chafee, p. 52.

[22] United States ex rel. Milwaukee Social Democratic Pub. Co. v. Burleson, 255 U.S. 407, 41 S.Ct. 352 (1921).

[23] 249 U.S. 47, 39 S.Ct. 247 (1919).

jail. Its plain implications, however, were that old tests were too restrictive for the demands of freedom under the First Amendment. As elaborated and developed in subsequent opinions by Holmes and Justice Brandeis against restrictive interpretations of free expression,[24] the test helped force the Court to think through the meaning of the First and Fourteenth Amendments, and served as a rallying-point for libertarians for decades to come.

As noted on page 12, above, another milestone in the Supreme Court's consideration of sedition cases was reached in a post-war case, Gitlow v. People of New York.[25] Here the 1902 New York statute on anarchy was invoked against the publication of the "left Wing Manifesto" in a radical paper called *Revolutionary Age.* It advocated and forecast mass struggle, mass strikes, and the overthrow of the bourgeoisie after a long revolutionary period. Convicted, business manager Benjamin Gitlow appealed to the Supreme Court. It upheld his conviction under an old test of criminality in words—whether the words have a tendency to imperil or subvert government.

But even as it upheld conviction, the Court wrote a single short paragraph accepting a principle long sought by libertarians: It said that the Fourteenth Amendment's barrier to states' depriving citizens of life, liberty, or property without due process of law protected liberty of speech and press against invasion by the states. Before *Gitlow,* the Supreme Court had tightly restricted the scope of the "liberty" protected by the Fourteenth Amendment; it had left it up to each state to say what liberty of speech and press was. After *Gitlow,* the Supreme Court would review state laws and decisions on free expression.[26]

The Smith Act of 1940

Immediately after World War I, the thrust of revolutionary communism had spurred the Attorney General of the United States to urge the passage of a federal peacetime sedition act. His call for such a peacetime measure (the Espionage Act of 1917 had applied only to war) brought concerted opposition; the move was stopped although widespread deportation of Russians and other aliens for their ideas and words was accomplished. But 20 years later, similar fears engendered with the coming of World War II and the activity of domestic communists brought success for a similar bill. This was the Alien Registration Act of 1940, known

[24] Notably Abrams v. United States, 250 U.S. 616, 40 S.Ct. 17 (1919); Gilbert v. State of Minn., 254 U.S. 325, 41 S.Ct. 125 (1920); Gitlow v. People of State of New York, 268 U.S. 652, 45 S.Ct. 625 (1925); Whitney v. People of State of California, 274 U.S. 357, 47 S.Ct. 641 (1927).

[25] 268 U.S. 652, 45 S.Ct. 625 (1925).

[26] Ibid., at 666, 45 S.Ct. at 630.

as the Smith Act for Rep. Howard W. Smith of Virginia who introduced it.[27] For the first time since the Alien and Sedition Acts of 1798, America had a federal peacetime sedition law. The heart of its provisions, under Section 2, made it a crime to advocate forcible or violent overthrow of government, or to publish or distribute material advocating violence with the intent to overthrow government.

The Act was to have little or no impact upon the mass media of general circulation. They advocated the *status quo,* not radical change or revolution. But for speakers, teachers, and pamphleteers of the Communist Party, the Smith Act came to mean a great deal. Fewer than 20 persons had been punished under the Alien and Sedition Acts of 1798–1801; it is estimated that approximately 100 persons were fined or imprisoned under the Smith Act between 1940 and 1960.[28] In one sense, however, the Smith Act was less suppressive than its ancestor: The Alien and Sedition Acts had punished criticism of government officials, Congress, and the laws, an everyday exercise of the press, but the Smith Act limited the ban to advocating violent overthrow.

The government made its first move in 1943. Leaders of a revolutionary splinter, the Socialist Workers Party which followed Russia's banished Trotsky, were the target. They were brought to trial in Minneapolis and convicted for the advocacy of violent overthrow in their printed polemics. The Court of Appeals sustained the conviction, and the United States Supreme Court refused to review the case.[29]

But the Communist Party was much more the target of government prosecution than the little group of Trotskyites. In the context of the cold war between the United States and the U.S. S.R. following World War II, almost 10 years of prosecution took place. The first case, Dennis v. United States, brought major figures in the Communist Party to trial and convicted 11 of them.[30] The charges were that they had reconstituted the American Communist Party in 1945, and conspired to advocate violent overthrow of the government.

For almost nine months the trial went on in federal district court under Judge Harold Medina. The nation was fascinated and bored in turn as the defense introduced complex legal challenges to the trial and the prosecution introduced exhibit after exhibit.

[27] 54 U.S. Statutes 670.

[28] Don R. Pember, The Smith Act as a Restraint of the Press, Journalism Monographs # 10, May 1969; Zechariah Chafee, Jr., The Blessings of Liberty (Phila., N.Y.: J.B. Lippincott Co., 1954), p. 22.

[29] Dunne v. United States, 138 F.2d 137 (8th Cir.1943).

[30] 341 U.S. 494, 71 S.Ct. 857 (1951).

Newspapers, pamphlets, and books were employed as evidence of
the defendants' intent, from the *Daily Worker* to *The Communist
Manifesto*. Scores of pages were read into the record, as the
government sought to show conspiracy by publishing and circulating the literature of revolutionary force. Judge Medina followed
the doctrine of the *Gitlow* case in instructing the jury that
advocacy or teaching of violent overthrow of the government was
not illegal if it were only "abstract doctrine." What the law
forbade was teaching or advocating "action" to overthrow the
government.[31] The jury found that the 11 did, indeed, conspire to
advocate forcible overthrow. The Court of Appeals upheld the
conviction and the case was accepted for review by the Supreme
Court of the United States.

The justices wrote five opinions, three opinions concurring in
conviction and two dissenting. Chief Justice Vinson wrote the
opinion that carried the most names (three besides his). He said
that free expression is not an unlimited or unqualified right, and
that "the societal value of speech must, on occasion, be subordinat-
ed to other values and considerations." [32] But a conviction for
violation of a statute limiting speech, he said, must rest on the
showing that the words created a "clear and present danger" that
a crime would be attempted or accomplished. Thus he went to the
famous Holmes rule first expressed in the *Schenck* case in 1919,
and interpreted it as follows: [33]

> In this case we are squarely presented with the
> application of the "clear and present danger" test, and
> must decide what that phrase imports. We first note that
> many of the cases in which this Court has reversed
> convictions by use of this or similar tests have been based
> on the fact that the interest which the State was attempt-
> ing to protect was too insubstantial to warrant restriction
> of speech. * * * Overthrow of the Government by force
> and violence is certainly a substantial enough interest for
> the Government to limit speech. Indeed, this is the
> ultimate value of any society, for if a society cannot
> protect its very structure from armed internal attack, it
> must follow that no subordinate value can be protected.
> * * * Certainly an attempt to overthrow the Govern-
> ment by force, even though doomed from the outset be-
> cause of inadequate numbers or power of the revolution-
> ists, is a sufficient evil for Congress to prevent.

[31] United States v. Foster, 80 F.Supp. 479 (S.D.N.Y.1948). Upon appeal, this case
became United States v. Dennis et al., 183 F.2d 201 (2d Cir.1950).

[32] Dennis v. United States, 341 U.S. 494, 71 S.Ct. 857 (1951).

[33] Ibid., at 508–509, 71 S.Ct. at 866–867.

Having thus rejected the position that likelihood of success in committing the criminal act is the criterion for restricting speech, Chief Justice Vinson adopted the statement of the Court of Appeals in interpreting the clear and present danger test. Chief Judge Hand had written: "In each case [courts] must ask whether the gravity of the 'evil,' discounted by its improbability justifies such invasion of free speech as is necessary to avoid the danger." [34] Vinson was arguing that the danger need not be immediate when the interest (here, self-preservation of government) is important enough.

Deep disagreement in the Court over thus limiting the scope of free expression appeared in the dissents of Justices Black and Douglas. The latter could see no clear and present danger to the government and state in the words and papers of the 11 Communists. Neither as a political force nor as a disciplined corps of poised saboteurs did Justice Douglas see them as a threat: [35]

> Communists in this country have never made a respectable or serious showing in any election * * *. Communism has been so thoroughly exposed in this country that it has been crippled as a political force. Free speech has destroyed it as an effective political party. It is inconceivable that those who went up and down this country preaching the doctrine of revolution which petitioners espouse would have any success.
>
> * * *
>
> * * * Free speech—the glory of our system of government—should not be sacrificed on anything less than plain and objective proof of danger that the evil advocated is imminent.

Through most of the 1950's, cases under the Smith Act continued to move through the courts. But in the wake of the decision in Yates v. United States in 1957, prosecutions dwindled and died out. In this case, the Supreme Court reversed the conviction of 14 Communist Party leaders under the Smith Act. Its decision turned in large part on the difference between teaching the need for violent overthrow as an abstract theory or doctrine, and teaching it as a spur to action.[36] Since the trial court had not required the jury which found the defendant guilty to make the distinction, the conviction was reversed. There was no reference to the famous clear and present danger doctrine.

The Warren Court—so called for chief Justice Earl Warren who had been appointed in 1953—had grown less and less willing

[34] Ibid., at 510, 71 S.Ct. at 867.

[35] Dennis v. United States, 341 U.S. 494, 71 S.Ct. 857 (1951).

[36] Yates v. United States, 354 U.S. 298, 77 S.Ct. 1064 (1957).

to uphold convictions under the Smith Act, and with the *Yates* decision, charges against many other defendants in pending cases were dismissed in lower courts. The Smith Act soon lapsed into disuse, and in the several versions of a bill for the broad reform of the federal Criminal Code that labored toward adoption by Congress beginning in 1977, the Act was omitted and thus scheduled for repeal.[37]

Yates had found that the trial judge's instructions had allowed conviction for mere advocacy without reference to its tendency to bring about forcible action, and overturned the convictions. In 1969, the Supreme Court was presented with the appeal of a Ku Klux Klan leader who had been convicted under the Ohio Criminal Syndicalism statute for advocating the duty or necessity of crime, violence or unlawful methods of terrorism to accomplish political reform. The leader, Brandenburg, had been televised as he made a speech in which he said the Klan was "not a revengent [sic] organization, but if our President, our Congress, our Supreme Court, continues to suppress the white, Caucasian race, it's possible that there might have to be some revengeance taken." He added that "We are marching on Congress * * * four hundred thousand strong."

The Supreme Court reversed the conviction. Citing precedent since *Dennis*, it said: [38]

> These later decisions have fashioned the principle that the constitutional guarantees of free speech and free press do not permit a State to forbid or proscribe advocacy of the use of force or of law violation except where such advocacy is directed to inciting or producing imminent lawless action and is likely to incite or produce such action. * * * A statute which fails to draw this distinction impermissibly intrudes upon the freedoms guaranteed by the First and Fourteenth Amendments.

The "inciting" or producing imminent lawless action clause has been called merely a version of the "clear and present danger" test.[39] It has continued to serve a protective role. Words challenging the authority of the state have brought criminal conviction at trial, but under the test have continued to find protection

[37] For other controls on news media embraced by the Act (S.1437), see Reporters Committee for Freedom of the Press, News Media Alert, Aug. 1977, pp. 4–5.

[38] Brandenburg v. Ohio, 395 U.S. 444, 89 S.Ct. 1827 (1969).

[39] Gerald Gunther, Cases and Materials on Constitutional Law, 9th ed., Mineola, N.Y. 1975, p. 1128; Thomas I. Emerson, "First Amendment Doctrine and the Burger Court," 68 Univ. of Calif.L.Rev. 422, 445–46, feels the "incitement" test is subject to "serious objections," including its permitting government to interfere with expression "at too early a state."

upon appeal to the Supreme Court.[40] Less than an absolute barrier to government's control of expression, the *Brandenburg* test is a strong element in the heavy crippling of the sedition action.[41]

SEC. 5. PRIOR RESTRAINT

Despite authoritative statements that the chief purpose of the First Amendment guarantee is to prevent previous restraints upon publication, prior restraints have continued to be exerted into the late Twentieth Century.

In perhaps the most influential First Amendment decision by the Supreme Court of the United States, Chief Justice Charles Evans Hughes wrote that it is generally considered ". . . that it is the chief purpose of the [First Amendment] guarantee to prevent previous restraint on publication." [42] Journalists and civil libertarians have long counted pre-publication censorship as the most despised of all controls. Prior restraint's origins may be traced back virtually as long as there has been printing. It was tied in Sixteenth and Seventeenth Century England to requiring printers to get permission or license from government to publish. And then censors often pored over every word, to make sure that nothing harmful to those in authority would be printed.

Obviously, if government can stop publication before it occurs, that is the ultimate in repressiveness. Although it is true that a person may be deterred from publishing by the threat of post-publication punishment (as in the case of libel, invasion of privacy, or obscenity), that is not the issue here. As the U.S. Supreme Court has said: "If it can be said that a threat of criminal or civil sanctions after publication 'chills' speech, prior restraint 'freezes' it . . . ." [43]

The power in government to approve who might publish, or to order non-publication—under threat of punishment—has a long and oppressive history. In revolutionary America, the leaders and printers considered that whatever the quicksilver phrase "freedom of the press" meant, it meant an end to prior restraint.[44] If the press were to act as a check on government or to aid society by spreading knowledge and opinion needed for a self-governing socie-

[40] Hess v. Indiana, 414 U.S. 105, 94 S.Ct. 326 (1973); Healy v. James, 408 U.S. 169, 92 S.Ct. 2338 (1972).

[41] See Harry Kalven, "The New York Times Case: a Note on 'The Central Meaning of the First Amendment' ", 1964 Sup.Ct.Rev. 191.

[42] Near v. Minnesota ex rel. Olson, 283 U.S. 697, 713, 51 S.Ct. 625, 630 (1931).

[43] Nebraska Press Ass'n v. Stuart, 427 U.S. 539, 559, 96 S.Ct. 2791, 2803 (1976), 1 Med.L.Rptr. 1064.

[44] Levy, Emergence of a Free Press, Chaps. 6, 8.

ty, prior restraint could not be tolerated. Society's chief weapon against the institution which possessed the power of guns and police was words.

Government attempts to use prior restraint have taken place, with almost predictable regularity, when some form of crisis occurs. During pre-Civil War days when Abolitionists' agitating threatened "the peculiar institution" of slavery, the South often used prior restraint as a weapon. Postmasters regularly refused to deliver mailings from Northern anti-slavery societies. And during the Civil War, Northern generals would occasionally shut down pro-South ("Copperhead") publishers. President Abraham Lincoln himself ordered the closing of newspapers on one occasion.[45] Later in the Nineteenth Century, heavy restrictions on publishing and distributing of materials discussing sex were extensively used, and prior restraint was part of the control. Postal and customs officials' use of prior restraint, in peacetime to control materials labeled "obscene" and in wartime to stop "sedition," was vigorous and frequent through the first third of the Twentieth Century.[46]

The area of prior restraint expanded in the Twentieth Century in matters not related to governmental acts of self-protection. As discussed in Chapter 3—and still ordained by the number of frequencies available—there is the governmental licensing of all broadcasters to prevent overcrowding the airwaves. There are also many areas in which courts can issue injunctions against speaking, publishing, or distributing words or symbols—and those are prior restraints. For example, the Federal Trade Commission can issue "cease and desist" orders against anticompetitive or deceptive ads, and can order advertisers to publish corrective statements.[47] Copyright law provides for court-issued injunctions to restrain illegal use of copyrighted materials.[48]

The U.S. Supreme Court has approved prohibition of newspaper publication of material from pre-trial "discovery" proceedings.[49] During the 1970s, in fact, a striking extension of prior restraint burst out as courts across the nation forbade publishing of accounts of part or all of the records in pre-trial hearings and even in trials. No phase of prior restraint has been more alarming to the media in recent years (see Chapter 11).

[45] Russel Blaine Nye, Fettered Freedom (East Lansing: Michigan State, 1951).

[46] Vincent Blasi, Toward a Theory of Prior Restraint, 66 Minn.L.Rev. 11, 14–15 (Nov.1981).

[47] Anon., The FTC's Injunctive Authority Against False Advertising of Food and Drugs, 75 Mich.L.Rev. 745 (March 1977).

[48] 17 U.S.C.A. §§ 502, 503.

[49] E.g. Seattle Times Co. v. Rhinehart, 467 U.S. 20, 104 S.Ct. 2199 (1984), 10 Med. L.Rptr. 1705.

Later chapters will detail aspects of prior restraint. In this chapter, the special concern goes to government's claims to suppress, on its own behalf, attacks on its personnel and structure, or words constituting danger to national security.

Near v. Minnesota

Mr. Chief Justice Hughes' majority opinion in Near v. Minnesota, a case of 1931, established groundwork that may be seen as a watershed which turned United States Supreme Court majorities in the direction of expanded press freedom.[50]

That decision grew out of scruffy origins. Howard Guilford and J.M. Near were publishing partners in producing *The Saturday Press*, a Minneapolis "smear sheet" which charged that gangsters were in control of Minneapolis gambling, bootlegging and racketeering, and that the city law enforcement and government agencies and officers were derelict in their duties. It vilified Jews and Catholics. And it published the articles that eventually required the Supreme Court of the United States to make one of its most notable descriptions of the extent of freedom of the press in America.

Publication of *The Saturday Press* was halted when a Minnesota statute authorizing prior restraint of "nuisance" or "undesirable" publications was invoked. That statute declared that any person publishing a "malicious, scandalous and defamatory newspaper, magazine or other periodical" could be found guilty of creating a nuisance and could be enjoined from future wrongdoing.[51] Near and Guilford were indeed brought into court after a temporary injunction ordered cessation of all activity by their paper. After the hearing, the injunction was made permanent by a judge, but with the provision that *The Saturday Press* could resume publication if the publishers could persuade the court that they would run a newspaper without objectionable content described in the Minnesota "gag law" statute.[52]

Near and Guilford appealed to the Supreme Court, which found in their favor by the margin of five votes to four. Speaking for the Court, Chief Justice Charles Evans Hughes noted the importance of this case: "This statute, for the suppression as a public nuisance of a newspaper or periodical, is unusual, if not unique, and raises questions of grave importance transcending the

---

[50] Near v. Minnesota ex rel. Olson, 283 U.S. 697, 51 S.Ct. 625 (1931); Paul L. Murphy, Near v. Minnesota in the Context of Historical Developments, 66 Minn.L. Rev. 95 (Nov.1981); Fred W. Friendly, Minnesota Rag (N.Y., 1981).

[51] Chapter 285, Minn.Sess.Laws 1925, in Mason's Minn.Stats., 1927, Secs. 10123–1 to 10123–3.

[52] Near v. Minnesota ex rel. Olson, 283 U.S. 697, 702–707, 51 S.Ct. 625, 628 (1931).

local interest involved in the particular action." Hughes declared of this prior restraint, "This is the essence of censorship." [53]

Hughes then turned to history-as-precedent to answer the question of whether a statute authorizing such proceedings in restraint of publication was consistent with the concept of liberty of the press, declaring here that the chief purpose of the constitutional guaranty is to prevent previous restraints.

He embarked upon a two-fold modification of the old English authority, Blackstone. Blackstone would have had *no prior restraint,* period. The Chief Justice, however, conceded that such a prohibition against all prior restraint might be "stated too broadly," and said that " * * * the protection even as to previous restraint is not absolutely unlimited." In a few exceptional cases, limitation of the principle of "no prior restraint" could be recognized: [54]

> No one would question but that a government might prevent actual obstruction to its recruiting service or the publication of sailing dates of transports or the number and location of troops. On similar grounds, the primary requirements of decency may be enforced against obscene publications. The security of the community life may be protected against incitements to acts of violence and the overthrow by force of orderly government. The constitutional guaranty of free speech does not "protect a man from an injunction against uttering words that may have all the effect of force."

Although Blackstone's "no prior restraint" was thus modified, another aspect of Blackstone was liberalized. Blackstone had approved punishing the publication of criticisms of government or government officials. But Hughes said that the press had a right—and perhaps even a duty—to discuss and debate the character and conduct of public officers. [55]

> . . . [T]he administration of government has become more complex, the opportunities for malfeasance and corruption have multiplied, crime has grown to most serious proportions, and the danger of its protection by unfaithful officials and of the impairment of the fundamental security of life and property by criminal alliances and official neglect, emphasizes the primary need of a vigilant and courageous press, especially in great cities.

[53] Ibid., at 707, 713, 51 S.Ct. at 627, 630.

[54] Ibid., at 716, 51 S.Ct. at 631.

[55] Ibid., at 719–720, 51 S.Ct. at 632–633.

The fact that the liberty of the press may be abused by miscreant purveyors of scandal does not make any the less necessary the immunity of the press from previous restraint in dealing with official misconduct. Subsequent punishment for such abuses as may exist is the appropriate remedy, consistent with constitutional privilege.

Despite the four dissenting votes, Near v. Minnesota has stood since 1931 as one of the most important decisions of the Supreme Court. *Near* was the first case involving newspapers in which the Court applied the provisions of the First Amendment against states through the language of the Fourteenth Amendment.[56] And it was to serve as important precedent for protecting the press against government's demands for suppression.

It was 40 years before the press again collided with government bent on protecting its own interest and functions through prior restraint. On June 30, 1971, the United States Supreme court cleared the confrontation with a decision hailed by many news media with such headlines as "VICTORY FOR THE PRESS" and "The Press Wins and the Presses Roll." [57] These triumphant headlines were tied to the "Pentagon Papers" case. Early in 1971, *New York Times* reporter Neil Sheehan was given photocopies of a 47–volume study of the United States involvement in Vietnam titled *History of the United States Decision–Making Process on Vietnam Policy.* On Sunday, June 13, 1971, the *New York Times* —after a team of reporters had worked with the documents for three months—published a story headlined: "Vietnam Archive: Pentagon Study Traces 3 Decades of Growing U.S. Involvement." Within 48 hours after publication, Attorney General John Mitchell sent a telegram to the Times, urging that no more articles based on the documents be published, charging that the series would bring about "irreparable injury to the defense interests of the United States." [58] The Times chose to ignore Attorney General Mitchell's plea, and columnist James Reston angrily wrote: "For the first time in the history of the Republic, the Attorney General of the United States has tried to suppress documents he hasn't read about a war that hasn't been declared." [59]

After the Times' refusal to stop the series of articles, the Department of Justice asked U.S. District Court Judge Murray I.

[56] William A. Hachten, The Supreme Court on Freedom of the Press: Decisions and Dissents (Ames, Ia.: Iowa State Univ. Press, 1968), p. 43.

[57] Newsweek, Time, July 12, 1971.

[58] Don R. Pember, "The Pentagon Papers Decision: More Questions Than Answers," Journalism Quarterly 48:3 (Autumn, 1971) p. 404; New York Times, June 15, 1971, p. 1.

[59] New York Times, June 16, 1971, p. 1.

Gurfein to halt publication of the stories. Judge Gurfein, who was serving his first day as a federal judge, issued a temporary injunction on June 15, putting a stop to the Times' publication of the articles. But silencing the Times did not halt all publication of the "Pentagon Papers." *The Washington Post*—and a number of other major journals—also weighed in with excerpts from the secret report. The Justice Department likewise applied for—and was granted—a temporary restraining order against *The Washington Post*.[60]

After two weeks of uncertainty, the decision by the Supreme Court of the United States cleared the papers for publication. *New York Times* Managing Editor A.M. Rosenthal was jubilant: "This is a joyous day for the press—and for American society." *Time* added, "Certainly the Justice Department was slapped down in its efforts to ask the courts to enjoin newspapers, and will not likely take that route again."[61] Despite such optimism, some observers within the press were disturbed by the outcome of the *"Pentagon Papers"* case. Not only were there three dissents against lifting the injunction among the nine justices, there was also deep reluctance to do so on the part of two of the majority justices. Furthermore, federal court injunctions had now, for the first time in American history, been employed to impose prior restraint upon newspapers, and the courts had preserved those injunctions intact for two weeks.

The Court's decision was short. It refused to leave in effect the injunctions which the Justice Department had secured against the Times and the Post, and quoted Bantam Books v. Sullivan:[62]

> "Any system of prior restraints of expression comes to this Court bearing a heavy presumption against its constitutional validity." Bantam Books, Inc. v. Sullivan, 372 U.S. 58, 83 S.Ct. 631 * * * (1963); see also Near v. Minnesota ex rel. Olson, 283 U.S. 697, 51 S.Ct. 625 * * * (1931). The Government "thus carries a heavy burden of showing justification for the imposition of such a restraint." Organization for a Better Austin v. Keefe, 402 U.S. 415, 91 S.Ct. 1575, 1578 (1971).

With those words, a six-member majority of the Court ruled that the government had not shown sufficient reason to impose prior restraint. Of the six, four found nothing in the facts of the case to qualify their positions. Justices Hugo L. Black and Wil-

---

[60] For a clear account of the cases' journeys through the courts, see Pember, pp. 404–405.

[61] Time, July 12, 1971, p. 10.

[62] New York Times Co. v. United States, 403 U.S. 713, 714, 91 S.Ct. 2140, 2141 (1971).

liam O. Douglas expressed abhorrence for prior restraint, Douglas saying "uninhibited, robust and wide-open debate" on public questions was essential, and "The stays in these cases that have been in effect for more than a week constitute a flouting of the principles of the First Amendment as interpreted in Near v. Minnesota * * *." [63]

Justice William J. Brennan, Jr., although not subscribing to an absolutist position about prior restraint, nevertheless declared that it was permissible in only a "single, extremely narrow" class of cases, as when the nation was at war or when troop movements might be endangered. For all the government's alarms as to possible dangers of nuclear holocaust if secrecy were breached, it had not presented a case that publication of the Pentagon Papers would cause such an event. Therefore: [64]

> * * * every restraint issued in this case, whatever
> its form, has violated the First Amendment—and none
> the less so because the restraint was justified as necessary
> to examine the claim more thoroughly.

With reluctance, Justices Byron White and Potter Stewart joined the majority. Stewart approved secrecy in some contexts, and said he was convinced that the Executive branch of government was correct in attempting to suppress publication of some of the documents here. But he voted with the majority, he said, because he could not say that disclosure of any of the Pentagon Papers "will surely result in direct, immediate, or irreparable damage to our Nation * * *." [65] White said that if any of the published material proved, after publication, to be punishable under the Espionage Act of 1917, the newspapers now stood warned: "I would have no difficulty in sustaining convictions under [the Espionage Act] on facts that would not justify * * * the imposition of a prior restraint." [66]

Justice Marshall declared that Congress had twice rejected proposed legislation that would have given the President war-time powers to prohibit some kinds of publication. And, he said, it would be inconsistent within the concept of separation of powers for the Court to use its contempt power to prevent behavior that Congress had specifically declined to prohibit.[67]

Dissenting, Justice Harlan wrote that disputes about matters so grave as the alleged contempt and publication of the Pentagon Papers needed more time to resolve, and he voted to support the

[63] Ibid., at 724, 91 S.Ct. at 2146.

[64] Ibid., at 727, 91 S.Ct. at 2148.

[65] Ibid., at 730, 91 S.Ct. at 2149.

[66] Ibid., at 735–738, 91 S.Ct. at 2152–2154.

[67] Ibid., at 746, 91 S.Ct. at 2157.

injunctions.[68] He found that the Court had been almost "irresponsibly feverish in dealing with these cases" of such high national importance in only a few days' time. Justice Blackmun agreed with Harlan, and added in a shrill indictment of the press: [69]

> If, however, damage has been done, and if, with the Court's action today, these newspapers proceed to publish the critical documents and there results therefrom "the death of soldiers, the destruction of alliances, the greatly increased difficulty of negotiation with our enemies, the inability of our diplomats to negotiate," to which list I might add the factors of prolongation of the war and of further delay in the freeing of United States prisoners, then the Nation's people will know where the responsibility for these sad consequences rests.

It should be recognized that no new legal course was charted by the *Pentagon Papers* case. After a delay of two weeks—a prior restraint imposed by lower federal courts at the insistence of the Department of Justice—the Supreme Court allowed the press to resume publication of the documents. By a 6–to–3 margin, the Supreme Court adhered to Near v. Minnesota, that classic case which, by a 5–to–4 margin, forbade prior restraint except in time of war, or when the materials involved were obscene, or when there was incitement to violence or to the overthrow of the Government.

The *Pentagon Papers* case underlines the important truth that no freedom is ever won, once and for all. Consider this statement:

> Some people may think that leaders of the free press would perhaps accomplish more if their claims of constitutional right were less expansive. I do not agree with this. I say it is their duty to fight like tigers right down to the line and not give an inch. This is the way our freedoms have been preserved in the past, and it is the way they will be preserved in the future.

No editor, publisher, or reporter said that. The quotation is from a statement by U.S. Senior Circuit Judge for the Second Circuit Harold R. Medina. Judge Medina's words emphasize an obvious but necessary history lesson. Each freedom has to be rewon by each succeeding generation. And sometimes, as is apparently true during the latter third of the Twentieth Century,

[68] Ibid., at 753, 91 S.Ct. at 2161.

[69] Ibid., at 763, 91 S.Ct. at 2165. Blackmun was quoting the dissent of Judge Wilkey in the Pentagon Papers case involving the Washington Post in the Court of Appeals for the Second Circuit, United States v. Washington Post Co., 446 F.2d 1327 (D.C.Cir.1971).

freedom has to be fought for again and again within one generation.

Doom for national security had been forecast by officials of the State Department as they testified against permitting the Times to continue publishing the Pentagon Papers, one of them declaring that further publication would "irreparably harm the United States." But, as Times columnist Anthony Lewis remarked some five years later, "the Republic still stands," and "Today, hardly anyone can remember a single item of the papers that caused all the fuss." [70]

A multi-volume history of policy-making in the Vietnam War was not the publication at issue, however, when at the end of the decade the federal government learned that *The Progressive,* a magazine of Madison, Wis., was about to print an article titled "The H–Bomb Secret: How We Got It, Why We're Telling It." The manuscript, the U.S. Attorney charged, carried the deepest of technical secrets relating to the security of our weapons. Publication would endanger national security and that of the world, and in the process would violate the U.S. Atomic Energy Act of 1954 by making public "restricted data" about thermonuclear weapons. The government sought and got a temporary injunction against publication of the article by journalist Howard Morland. [71]

Morland swore that everything in the article was in the public domain, that he had in no way been forced to secret sources for the information; the government denied that this was the case. While the trial was in mid-course, it also came to light that similar information had been available to the public by accident, for a time, in a government science laboratory. [72] Federal District Judge Robert Warren was fully aware of the Supreme Court's rule that "any prior restraint on publication comes into court under a heavy presumption against its constitutional validity." Warren found the revelation of secret technical details about the H-bomb quite different, however, from revealing a secret history of war-policy making. He found that publication offered the possibility of "grave, direct, immediate and irreparable harm to the United States," and said: [73]

[70] "Congress Shall Make No Law," New York Times, Sept. 16, 1976, p. 39.

[71] United States v. Progressive, Inc., 467 F.Supp. 990 (W.D.Wis.1979), 4 Med.L. Rptr. 2377. Major prior restraint cases are discussed by U.S. Circuit Judge J.L. Oakes in "The Doctrine of Prior Restraint Since the Pentagon Papers," 15 U.Mich. Journ.L. Reform 497 (Spring, 1982).

[72] United States v. Progressive, Inc., 486 F.Supp. 5 (W.D.Wis.1980), 5 Med.L.Rptr. 2441.

[73] United States v. Progressive, Inc., 467 F.Supp. 990 (W.D.Wis.1979), 4 Med.L. Rptr. 2377, 2380.

* * * because the government has met its heavy burden of showing justification for the imposition of a prior restraint on publication of the objected-to technical portions of the Morland article . . . the Court finds that the objected-to portions of the article fall within the narrow area recognized by the Court in Near v. Minnesota in which a prior restraint on publication is appropriate.

Yet Warren's deep concern at the possible outcome of publication ("I'd want to think a long, hard time before I'd give a hydrogen bomb to Idi Amin.") was questioned in the national debate and discussion which surged over the case. The government, it was asserted, had not shown that publication would result in "direct, immediate, or irreparable damage to the Nation" that the Pentagon Papers decision had insisted was necessary to justify prior restraint. The field of journalism was divided in its support.[74]

The Progressive and Morland, seizing on implications of the Atomic Energy Act that conceivably rendered even innocent conversations about nuclear weapons subject to classification ("classified at birth") insisted that no real secrets had been told. They appealed, and prior restraint held through six months of court process. Suddenly intruding into the matter was the publication on Sept. 16, 1979, of a long letter in the Madison, Wis. *Press Connection,* a daily of 11,000 circulation, from an amateur student of the nuclear bomb. A copy of a letter from computer programmer Charles Hansen to Sen. Charles Percy of Illinois, it included a diagram and list of key components of an H–bomb. Other newspapers which had received copies had not yet published it when, on the following day, the government moved to drop its court action to bar publication of the Morland article. A U.S. Justice Department spokesman said that the Hansen letter had exposed three "crucial concepts" that the government was trying to protect from publication.

Morland's article was published. *The Progressive* set about trying to raise $200,000 from the public, which was the cost, it said, of defending. No prosecution of the *Press Connection* or other newspapers that published the Hansen letter materialized. Judge Warren dismissed the case against *The Progressive* on Sept. 4, 1980.[75]

Not only the security of the United States' war effort and the provisions of the Atomic Energy Act have made a groundwork for

---

[74] Civil Liberties, No. 328, June 1979, p. 1; Ben Bagdikian, "A Most Insidious Case," Quill, 67:6, June 1979, pp. 21, 22; "Editors and Lawyers Share Mixed Views on Story Ban," Editor & Publisher, March 17, 1979, p. 13.

[75] Milwaukee Journal, Sept. 4, 1980, Part 2, pp. 1, 10.

the government's demand for prior restraint. Rules of administrative agencies can furnish the same.[76] The CIA is experienced in the matter. Its employee Victor L. Marchetti resigned from the agency and, with John Marks, wrote *The CIA and the Cult of Intelligence*. This, the CIA charged upon learning of its existence in manuscript form, violated the secrecy contract Marchetti had signed when first employed, promising not to divulge any classified information without specific permission from the CIA.[77] It obtained an injunction in federal district court, the judge ordering Marchetti to submit all writings about the CIA or intelligence work to the Agency for review as to whether it contained classified information that had not been released to the public. As the case proceeded (the Supreme Court of the United States denied certiorari),[78] the CIA's scrutiny of the manuscript resulted in its demand that 339 deletions be performed. "It was the Devil's work we did that day," said Marchetti's attorney, Melvin L. Wulf, after he and the authors spent hours literally cutting out passages of the manuscript—perhaps as much as 20 per cent.[79] Resisting all the way, Marchetti finally won agreement from the court that all but 27 of the 339 deletions would be restored.[80] The book was finally published with blank spaces and the prominent, repeated notation: DELETED.

Frank Snepp, strategy analyst for the CIA in Vietnam, succeeded in getting his case against the CIA to the Supreme Court. He, too, had resigned from the agency and written a book—*Decent Interval*—about his experiences. He, too, had signed an agreement not to publish without first submitting the manuscript to the CIA, and the agency brought legal action. The Supreme Court, by a 6–3 vote, ruled that Snepp had broken his contract, approved an injunction requiring Snepp to submit future writings for publication review, and ruled that he must give all profits from the sale of the book to the CIA through a "constructive trust" imposed on him by the court.[81] He had a fiduciary obligation to the CIA and had breached his trust by publishing.

The government had not alleged that classified or confidential information was revealed by the Snepp book. Rather, it alleged

[76] Ithiel de Sola Pool, "Prior Restraint," New York Times, Dec. 16, 1979, p. E19, portrays unintended prior restraint on research publication through elaborate funding rules of the U.S. Dept. of Health, Education, and Welfare—"a nightmare of bureaucracy run wild, producing results that no one intended."

[77] United States v. Marchetti, 466 F.2d 1309 (4th Cir.1972).

[78] Marchetti v. United States, 409 U.S. 1063, 93 S.Ct. 553 (1972).

[79] Melvin D. Wulf, Introduction to Victor Marchetti and John D. Marks, The CIA and the Cult of Intelligence (New York: Alfred A. Knopf, 1974), p. xxv.

[80] Ibid., p. xxiv.

[81] Snepp v. United States, 444 U.S. 507, 100 S.Ct. 763 (1980), 5 Med.L.Rptr. 2409.

"irreparable harm" in his failure to clear the material with the CIA, and the Supreme Court approved the lower courts' finding that publication of unreviewed material "can be detrimental to vital national interests even if the published information is unclassified." [82]

If the agent published unreviewed material in violation of his fiduciary and contractual obligation, said the court, the constructive trust remedy simply "required him to disgorge the benefits of his faithlessness * * *." Snepp "disgorged" about $138,000, the proceeds from *Decent Interval.*[83]

The Snepp case was more than just a case of prior restraint applied through the administrative machinery, law reporter Anthony Lewis of the *New York Times* found. For the fiduciary, constructive-trust formulation was a far-reaching legal theory: [84]

> * * * one that could apply to hundreds of thousands of federal government employees. For Snepp * * * had no greater access to secrets than do vast numbers of people in the State and Defense Departments * * *. Any one of them, under the theory of the Snepp case, can now be enjoined from talking to a reporter—or have his profits seized if he writes a book.

Non-disclosure agreements similar to that which Snepp and Marchetti had signed so appealed to President Ronald Reagan that in 1983, he issued a directive requiring them of all persons who had access to classified government information, numbering—declared protesting media—more than 100,000 employees. The President withdrew the directive in the face of congressional and media protest.[85]

If the emergence of non-disclosure agreements in the decade beginning with Marchetti appeared as one more example of government creativity in devising prior restraints in the name of national security, predictably enough that newly minted instrument was not the end of invention in prior restraint. In 1982, the Secretary of State's denial of a passport to former CIA agent Philip Agee was upheld by the United States Supreme Court: Agee had asserted his purpose of exposing CIA agents abroad, driving them out of the countries where they operated, and obstructing the operations and recruitment efforts of the CIA, and had taken measures to do so. These statements and actions, the

---

[82] Ibid., 2411.

[83] Herbert Mitgang, "Royalties to the Treasury," New York Times Book Review, Aug. 31, 1980.

[84] New York Times, Feb. 25, 1980.

[85] Directive on Safeguarding National Security Information, 9 Med.L.Rptr. 1759 (1983).

Court said, were no more protected by the First Amendment than those prohibited in Near v. Minnesota half a century earlier.[86] By 1982, Congress and the President had effected a law making it a crime for news media to make public the names of secret U.S. intelligence agents or their sources.[87]

Prior Restraint and the High School Press

As was evident from the discussion of Near v. Minnesota (1931), the key case on prior restraint, not all pre-publication censorship is unconstitutional. Early in 1988, in Hazelwood School District v. Kuhlmeier,[88] the U.S. Supreme Court held that public school officials have the power to impose pre-publication censorship on student newspapers. The newspaper involved in this case, *Spectrum,* was published at Hazelwood High School near St. Louis, Mo.

The newspaper was to be six pages long in its 1983 school-year-end edition as produced by the school's Journalism II class. On May 10, 1983, Principal Robert Reynolds was shown proofs for the edition due to appear on May 13. The proofs were taken to the principal by an interim newspaper adviser; the regular Journalism II instructor had left Hazelwood East for another job just 12 days earlier.

After Principal Reynolds was shown page proofs, he objected to publication of two stories. One described three Hazelwood East students' experiences with pregnancies; the other discussed the effect of divorce on students at the school. Although the pregnancy story used fictitious names to mask identities, the principal decided that the masking was insufficient. Evidently he also thought that the article's references to sex and birth control were not appropriate for some of the younger students in the school. Finally, he was concerned that a student was identified by name in the divorce story, and that the student's parents had not been given the opportunity to respond.

Apparently believing that there was no time for redoing the stories—and that the paper could not appear at all at school year's end if delays occurred—Principal Reynolds deleted two entire pages containing the stories he found offensive. The deleted pages contained other articles—on teen marriages, runaways, juvenile delinquency, and a general article on teenage pregnancy. Principal Reynolds later testified that he had no objection to those

[86] Haig v. Agee, 453 U.S. 280, 101 S.Ct. 2766 (1981), 7 Med.L.Rptr. 1545.

[87] News Media and the Law, Sept./Oct. 1982, 39.

[88] 484 U.S. 260, 108 S.Ct. 562 (1988), 14 Med.L.Rptr. 2081.

articles; they were deleted only because they were on the same pages with the articles that troubled him.[89]

Cathy Kuhlmeier and two other former Hazelwood East students who had been newspaper staffers claimed Reynolds' action violated their First Amendment rights, and sought injunctive relief and monetary damages in a Federal district court.

The trial court upheld the principal's actions. Deletion of the divorce article on invasion-of-privacy grounds was held reasonable, as was the principal's desire to avoid younger students' exposure to "unsuitable material." Further, the district court concluded that the principal was justified in having a " 'serious doubt that the article complied with the rules of fairness which are standard in the field of journalism and which were covered in the textbook used in the Journalism II class.' " [90]

The Eighth Circuit Court of Appeals, however, reversed the district court, holding that the newspaper was both a part of the school's curriculum *and* and public forum, " 'intended to be operated as a conduit for student viewpoints.' " Since the newspaper was a public forum, the appeals court held, school officials could not censor its contents except when necessary " ' ". . . to avoid material and substantial interference with school work or discipline . . . or with the rights of others." ' " [91]

The Court of Appeals thus found no evidence in the trial court's record to indicate that the principal could have predicted reasonably that the articles would be disruptive or cause disorder. Also, the court added that the articles could have caused no tort liability for libel or privacy, and concluded that school officials had violated the students' First Amendment rights.

The U.S. Supreme Court granted certiorari and reversed the Court of Appeals, thus upholding the principal's prior restraint of the newspaper. Justice White wrote for the majority in this 5–3 decision. He outlined circumscribed freedoms available to students in public high schools. Although quoting from the famous language of the Vietnam war armband protest case—Tinker v. Des Moines Independent Community School District [92]—public school students do not " 'shed their constitutional rights at the schoolhouse gate' "—Justice White then took a restrictive tack. He declared that "the First Amendment rights of students in the

[89] 484 U.S. at 264, 108 S.Ct. at 566 n., 14 Med.L.Rptr. at 2082–2083, 2083 n.

[90] Hazelwood School Dist. v. Kuhlmeier, 484 U.S. 260, 264, 108 S.Ct. 562, 566 (1988), 14 Med.L.Rptr. 2081, 2083.

[91] Ibid., at 265, 108 S.Ct. at 567, 14 Med.L.Rptr. at 2083.

[92] See Tinker, 393 U.S. at 511, 89 S.Ct. at 739, quoted in Ibid.

public schools 'are not automatically co-extensive with the rights of adults in other settings.' " [93]

Student rights must be applied " 'in the light of special characteristics of the school environment.' " Quoting Bethel School District No. 403 v. Fraser (1986), he wrote that a school need not tolerate speech that is inconsistent with its educational mission, even though government could not censor such speech outside the school. (The Bethel case involved disciplining a student who had made a campaign speech in behalf of a student politician; the speech was replete with sexual double entendres.) [94]

Justice White's majority opinion declared that the *Spectrum* was not a forum for public expression: It was a part of the school's curriculum, a regular educational activity. He also interpreted the school board's policy statement supporting free expression for school-sponsored publications as suggesting "at most that the administration will not interfere with the students' exercise of those First Amendment rights that attend the publication of a school-sponsored newspaper. It does not reflect an intent to extend those rights by converting a curricular newspaper into a public forum." [95]

The majority opinion also said that a school in its capacity of publisher may " 'dissassociate itself' " from speech which is disruptive, or which sets a bad example in terms of speech that is "ungrammatical, poorly written, inadequately researched, biased or prejudiced, vulgar or profane, or unsuitable for immature audiences."

This meant, the Court said, that educators

. . . do not offend the First Amendment by exercising editorial control over the style and content of student speech in school-sponsored expressive activities so long as their actions are reasonably related to legitimate pedagogical concerns.

In dissent, Justice William J. Brennan, Jr., joined by Justices Marshall and Blackmun, said that when the students enrolled in that Journalism II course, they expected a civics lesson. They argued that only substantially disruptive speech should be censored, conceding that poor grammar, writing or research would disrupt or subvert the school's curricular purpose.[96]

The same cannot be said of official censorship designed to shield the *audience* or dissociate the *sponsor*

[93] Ibid.

[94] 478 U.S. 675, 106 S.Ct. 3159 (1986).

[95] 484 U.S. at 270, 108 S.Ct. at 569, 14 Med.L.Rptr. at 2085, 2086.

[96] 484 U.S. at 290, 108 S.Ct. at 580, 14 Med.L.Rptr. at 2091, 2094.

from the expression. Censorship so motivated . . . in no way furthers the curricular purpose of a student *newspaper,* unless one believes that the purpose of the school newspaper is to teach students that the press ought never to report bad news, express unpopular views, or print a thought that might upset its sponsors.

* * *

The young men and women of Hazelwood East expected a civics lesson, but not the one the Court teaches them today.

At least two kinds of fallout can now be seen from the bombburst unleashed by *Hazelwood.* On the one hand, censorship of high school (and some college) papers increased dramatically after that decision. Director Mark Goodman of the Student Press Law Center (SPLC) reported that as the 1988 *Hazelwood* decision began to be put to use, calls to the SPLC (mostly about threatened or actual censorship) doubled in the first half of 1990.[97] On the other hand, all was not bleak. By the fall of 1991, four states—California, Colorado, Iowa, and Massachusetts—had passed statutes providing student journalists with protection for free expression, and adoption in New Jersey was expected. Efforts to pass similar legislation continues in a number of other states.

State-by-state action now seems the student journalists' best chance to overcome *Hazelwood.* As Justice Brennan and others have suggested, the more expansive among state constitutions may offer help. That is, some state charters may provide leverage to overcome mechanical application of the *Hazelwood* rule that if high school journalism is embedded in a class setting, it is not a First Amendment-protected public forum.[98]

SEC. 6: PRIOR RESTRAINT: LICENSING

When licensing power over expression amounts to prior censorship, it is constitutionally forbidden. Broadcasting, however, has long been a "special case," outside some First Amendment protections of the print media.

Licensing is one aspect of that most hated of all controls over the media: prior censorship. And—as is discussed in Chapter 3, licensing is still alive in the United States. That chapter discusses the Federal Communications Commission's system of allocating broadcast frequencies "in the public interest, convenience, or necessity." [99]

[97] Student Press Law Center Report, Fall, 1990, p. 3.

[98] SPLC Report, Fall, 1991, pp. 3, 11.

[99] See Chapter 3 on the matter of broadcast station licensing.

Past forms of licensing, as in England in the Sixteenth and Seventeenth Centuries, meant that only licensed printers—persons who had the approval of the government—were allowed to print. Late in the Twentieth Century, licensed broadcast stations—or the braver ones among them—seem to find the intestinal fortitude to criticize government from time to time, knowing full well that broadcast re-licensing largely has become a routine matter.

If licensing broadcasting stations seems a comparatively benign form of that ancient control—although it has its vociferous critics—other kinds of licensing raise sharper-edged issues. Consider the American Nazis decision to march, displaying swastikas, through a mostly Jewish neighborhood in Skokie, Illinois, in 1977. Nazi leader Frank Collin asked a number of Chicago suburbs for permits (licenses) for demonstrations in their parks or on their streets. Skokie officials responded that the Nazis would have to post an insurance bond of $350,000 as a hedge against property damage.[1]

The American Civil Liberties Union (ACLU), which lost many Jews from its membership over this issue, was cast in the ironic role of defending the Nazis' right to march and to demonstrate. The Illinois Supreme Court supported the ACLU position and struck down the licensing attempt by the Village of Skokie. The court said:[2]

> The display of the Swastika, as offensive to the principles of a free nation or the memories it recalls may be, is symbolic political speech intended to convey to the public the beliefs of those who display it. It does not, in our opinion, fall within the doctrine of "fighting words," and that doctrine cannot be used here to overcome the heavy presumption against the constitutional validity of prior restraint.

So it may be seen that licensing battles reoccur. England's authoritarian licensing system was allowed to expire in 1695, but no battle for freedom ever seems to be won once and for all.[3] Major weapons against licensing in the Twentieth Century were hammered out by repeated battles by Jehovah's Witnesses. The struggles of the Jehovah's Witnesses were noteworthy: Time and again they fought their cases all the way to the Supreme Court of the United States and ultimately won. This religious group, as

---

[1] See Areyeh Neier, *Defending My Enemy: American Nazis, the Skokie Case, and the Risks of Freedom* (New York: E.P. Dutton, 1979).

[2] *Village of Skokie v. National Socialist Party of America*, 69 Ill.2d 605, 14 Ill. Dec. 890, 373 N.E.2d 21 (1978).

[3] Fredrick S. Siebert, *Freedom of the Press in England, 1476–1776* (Urbana, Ill: University of Illinois Press, 1952), pp. 260–263.

Professor William A. Hachten noted, endured great suffering. The ACLU reported, for example, that in one six-month period of 1940, 1488 men, women and children in the sect were victims of mob violence in 355 communities in 44 states." [4] Professor J. Edward Gerald wrote that the Witnesses made themselves unpopular with their refusal to salute the American flag and with their disdain for most if not all organized religion, including denunciations of the Catholic Church. Likewise, their persistent street sales of literature and doorbell ringings for their causes often irritated non-believers. [5]

The Jehovah's Witness cases are useful reminders that the right of freedom of expression belongs not only to media corporations but to the people. Furthermore, a landmark case won by the Witnesses—Lovell v. City of Griffin, Georgia [6]—is crucially important because it explicitly gives constitutional protection to *distribution* of literature as well as to publication.

Alma Lovell, a Jehovah's Witness, was convicted in a municipal court in Griffin, Ga., and sentenced to 50 days in jail when she refused to pay a $50 fine. Her crime? She had not received advance permission from the City Manager of Griffin to pass out literature, as required by a municipal ordinance.

Alma Lovell simply could not be bothered with such technicalities. She regarded herself as a messenger sent by Jehovah and believed that applying to the City Manager for permission would have "been 'an act of disobedience to His commandments.' " The Supreme Court, however, regarded the city ordinance as far more than a mere technicality. Speaking for a unanimous Court, Chief Justice Charles Evans Hughes denounced the ordinance. [7]

We think that the ordinance is invalid on its face. Whatever the motive which induced its adoption, its character is such that it strikes at the very foundation of the freedom of the press by subjecting it to license and censorship.

The liberty of the press is not confined to newspapers and periodicals. It necessarily embraces pamphlets and leaflets. These indeed have been historic weapons in the defense of liberty, as the pamphlets of Thomas Paine and others in our own history abundantly attest. * * *

[4] William A. Hachten, The Supreme Court on Freedom of The Press (Ames, Iowa: Iowa State University Press, 1968), p. 73.

[5] Hachten, p. 74; Lovell v. City of Griffin, Georgia, 303 U.S. 444, 58 S.Ct. 666 (1938).

[6] 303 U.S. 444, 58 S.Ct. 666 (1938).

[7] Lovell v. City of Griffin, 303 U.S. 444, 451–452, 58 S.Ct. 666, 669 (1938). Mr. Justice Cardozo took no part in this decision.

The ordinance cannot be saved because it relates to distribution and not to publication. "Liberty of circulating is as essential to that freedom as liberty of publishing; indeed, without circulation, the publication would be of little value." Ex parte Jackson, 96 U.S. 727, 733, 24 L.Ed. 877.

Since the ordinance of the City of Griffin was not limited to " 'literature' that is obscene or offensive to public morals or that advocates unlawful conduct," the ordinance could not be upheld. In Schneider v. New Jersey, the Supreme Court reviewed four cities' ordinances. Three of these anti-littering ordinances in effect punished distributors should the recipient of a leaflet throw it to the ground. The Supreme Court held that such ordinances were unconstitutional.[8]

"Time, Place and Manner"

Such cases, of course, do not mean that advocates can distribute anything they want at any time or place. What the courts call "time, place and manner" restrictions may be upheld as lawful if they are administratively even-handed and do not favor some kinds of content over others.

As Justice Owen Roberts wrote for the Court in deciding the Town of Irvington Jehovah's Witness case (above): [9]

> We are not to be taken as holding that commercial soliciting and canvassing may not be subjected to such regulation as the ordinance requires. Nor do we hold that the town may not fix reasonable hours when canvassing may be done . . .

Jehovah's Witnesses were to have many other days in court, defending freedoms of religion, speech and press guaranteed by the First Amendment and protected from state encroachment by the Fourteenth Amendment. The persistence of this religious group, annoying to some, has resulted in some of the Supreme Court's most sweeping language in support of the First Amendment.[10]

In writing the words used to decide that another city license was unconstitutional in Jones v. City of Opelika (1942), Justice Harlan Fiske Stone asserted a favored position for the First

[8] 308 U.S. 147, 60 S.Ct. 146 (1939).

[9] Ibid.

[10] See also other Jehovah's Witness cases: Jones v. Opelika, 316 U.S. 584, 62 S.Ct. 1231 (1942); Martin v. Struthers, 319 U.S. 141, 63 S.Ct. 862 (1943); Douglas v. Jeannette, 319 U.S. 157, 63 S.Ct. 877 (1943); Murdock v. Pennsylvania, 319 U.S. 105, 63 S.Ct. 870 (1943).

Amendment, a "preferred position" view generally out of judicial favor by the 1980s. He wrote: [11]

> The First Amendment is not confined to safeguarding freedom of speech and freedom of religion against discriminatory attempts to wipe them out. On the contrary the Constitution, by virtue of the First and Fourteenth Amendments, has put those freedoms in a preferred position.

Lowe v. SEC (1985)

A licensing effort by the Securities and Exchange Commission (SEC) was slapped down in the spring of 1985 by an 8–0 vote of the Supreme Court of the United States. The SEC, concerned about regulating many things affecting the health of the nation's financial communities, set about licensing financial news media.[12]

Take the case of Christopher Lowe, operator of the "Lowe Investment & Financial Letter." He ran afoul of SEC contentions that it had the power to require permission to publish, plus the power to get injunctions to stop publications if SEC dictates were not obeyed. Lowe had been a licensed investment adviser, operating within the provisions of the Investment Advisers Act of 1940, and founded his newsletter in 1974.[13]

Lowe, however, fell on hard times. He was convicted of stock fraud, of check kiting, and of tampering with evidence.

Until 1981, he had been registered with the S.E.C., but that registration was withdrawn in 1981 after Lowe's convictions in New York for securities law violations, fraud, and bad checks. As News Media & the Law reported, "Lowe stopped giving individual advice on investments after his license was revoked, but continued to publish the newsletters.[14] In 1981, the S.E.C. issued an order, revoking Lowe's registration as an investment adviser, and forbidding him to associate with any investment advisers.[15] As the U.S. Court of Appeals reported as it upheld the S.E.C. action in trying to halt Lowe's newsletters,[16]

> No contention is made that any of the information published in the [Lowe] advisory services has been false or

[11] "SEC Attacks Financial Press," The News Media & The Law, November/December 1984, p. 4.

[12] Ibid.

[13] "Publisher Elated By S.E.C. Victory," The New York Times, June 12, 1985, p. 30.

[14] News Media & the Law, November/December, 1984, p. 4

[15] Ibid.; see also "Newsletter Setback for S.E.C.," The New York Times, June 11, 1985, p. 33.

[16] SEC v. Lowe, 725 F.2d 892 (2d Cir.1984), 10 Med.L.Rptr. 1225, 1226.

materially misleading. Nor is it alleged that Lowe himself * * * has profited through personal or corporate investments from the investment advice offered.

Saying that it believed that the Lowe case added up to permissible regulation of economic activity, the court added: "we believe that the Investment Advisers Act withstands constitutional scrutiny under the First Amendment doctrine relating to commercial speech as well." [17]

The Supreme Court disagreed, finding—without reaching constitutional analysis—that the SEC had overreached its authority. Writing for the Court, Justice John Paul Stevens said that Congressional legislation creating the S.E.C. gave the regulatory body no jurisdiction over investment publications.

The New York Times noted that the Supreme Court did not rule out all S.E.C. control over investment newsletters. If a newsletter's publishers had an interest in some stock they were recommending—or if the publication contained information that was purposely misleading or false—then the S.E.C. could have power over the situation under the Investment Advisers Act of 1940.[18]

Other Forms of Prior Restraint

Government pre-publication censorship continues to be discouraged by courts, but—as discussed earlier—it can occur. In addition, prior restraint may occur in other contexts, cropping up in connection with topics covered in following chapters of this book. Courts are petitioned for prior restraint orders—injunctions against publication—in areas of law including defamation,[19] privacy,[20] copyright,[21] obscenity,[22] access to government information,[23]

[17] Ibid., at p. 1231.

[18] Lowe v. S.E.C., 472 U.S. 181, 105 S.Ct. 2557 (1985); "Newsletter Setback for S.E.C.," The New York Times, June 11, 1985, p. 33.

[19] For an annotated listing of prior restraint cases in general, see Floyd Abrams, "Prior Restraints," in James C. Goodale, chairman, Communications Law 1990 (New York: Practising Law Institute, 1990), pp. 423–618. See Chs. 4 and 5, below, on defamation. Libel decisions refusing to grant injunctions to plaintiffs include Dworkin v. Hustler Magazine, Inc., 634 F.Supp. 727 (D.Wyo.1986), and Lothschuetz v. Carpenter, 898 F.2d 1200 (6th Cir.1990).

[20] Similarly to defamation, courts have been reluctant to issue injunctions to plaintiffs in privacy cases. See Abrams, op. cit., p. 484. See Organization for a Better Austin v. Keefe, 402 U.S. 415, 91 S.Ct. 1575 (1971).

[21] See Ch. 13, above, and Abrams, op cit., pp. 515–531. Injunctions occur more frequently in trademark disputes, although they are occasionally granted—temporarily—in copyright cases. See, e.g., Rosemont Enterprises, Inc. v. Random House, Inc., 256 F.Supp. 55 (S.D.N.Y.1966), reversed at 366 F.2d 303 (2d Cir.1966).

[22] See Ch. 7, above.

[23] See Ch. 9, above.

and advertising/commercial speech.[24] Although courts, in general, grant prior restraint orders grudgingly, the issue lives on. In libel, for example, courts usually will not halt defamatory publications via injunction. In copyright law and other areas dealing with business relationships, pre-publication injunctions may be found frequently enough that they are not aberrations. Prior restraint assumes so many guises that it can not safely be said that battles against pre-publication controls are ever won, once and for all time.

SEC. 7. FORCING COMMUNICATION TO OCCUR

The other side of prior restraint (preventing communication in the first place) is forcing communication to occur. Except for the broadcast media, forcing communication to occur generally is forbidden.

Forcing communication to take place is closely connected with—is often the "flip side" of—a system of prior restraint. As Fredrick Siebert showed in his pathbreaking study of the development of freedom of expression in England from 1476 to 1776, printers who did not publish what they were told to print by government often put themselves in real peril.[25] Similarly, in the early years of Britain's American colonies, printers—who needed government subsidies to survive—had to display "Published by Authority" on their newspapers. Such printers often learned that they dared not deviate from printing only the official accounts— edited for public consumption—of the meetings (held in secret) of colonial legislatures of Governor's councils.[26]

After the War for Independence and the creation of the United States, the development of strongly competing political factions—and later, political parties—helped distribute "official printing" business while criticizing government raucously.[27] Later, in the first four decades of the Nineteenth Century, the rise of mass circulation newspapers supported primarily by advertising helped free the press from government.[28]

[24] See Ch. 11, above. See especially Posadas De Puerto Rico Associates v. Tourism Co., 478 U.S. 328, 106 S.Ct. 2968 (1986).

[25] Siebert, Freedom of the Press in England, 1476–1776; Clyde A. Duniway, The Development of Freedom of the Press in Massachusetts (Cambridge: Harvard Univ. Press, 1906), pp. 104–05.

[26] Jean Folkerts and Dwight L. Teeter, Jr., Voices of a Nation (New York: Macmillan, 1989), pp. 18–23.

[27] See, e.g., Jackson Turner Main, The Antifederalists: Critics of the Constitution (Chapel Hill: Univ. of North Carolina Press, 1961); Teeter, Press Freedom and the Public Printing: Pennsylvania, 1775–1783, Journalism Quarterly XLV (Autumn, 1968), p. 445.

[28] Folkerts & Teeter, op. cit., pp. 129–149.

Over time, the libertarian ideas borrowed from England evolved, with arguments taken from John Milton from the Seventeenth Century and from "Country Whig" philosophers of the Eighteenth Century.[29] Those ideas developed in the crucible of American politics into the ideas that government should keep hands off the press, allowing criticism of government through a "free marketplace of ideas," assuming that truth would win over falsehood in the process of argumentation.

This "marketplace of ideas" philosophy became a kind of received truth, cited with the force of binding precedent by the Supreme Court of the United States in important Twentieth Century decisions.[30] But when major riots occurred after the assassination of Martin Luther King, law professor Jerome Barron articulated a troubling and persistent viewpoint. He argued that lack of access to media of communication by disadvantaged minorities showed that government should intervene .to give the voiceless a voice. Otherwise, people left voiceless were going to "take it to the streets," violently.[31]

In an age of mass communication, Barron asserted, the members of the public must have access to the columns and airwaves of the mass media. Barron elaborated the position that for many decades the high cost of ownership had barred countless voices from a part in the "marketplace of ideas." The media—giant in size and cost, relatively few in number, and owned by largely likeminded entrepreneurs devoted to the economic and political *status quo*—have the power to deny citizens the right to have their message communicated widely.

The media themselves, in Professor Barron's view, are crucial barriers to a diversity of opinion and fact in the marketplace. "At the very minimum," Barron wrote, "the creation of two remedies is essential—(1) a nondiscriminatory right to purchase editorial advertisements in daily newspapers, and (2) a right of reply for public figures and public officials defamed in newspapers." [32]

Professor Barron's "right of access to the press" ideas were tested—and found wanting—in a famed 1974 decision by the U.S. Supreme Court. In Miami Herald v. Tornillo, the Supreme Court took on a case that had arisen in Florida under that state's "right of reply" statute. The Miami Herald had refused to print a reply

[29] See Chapter 1, Sec. 1; see also Norman L. Rosenberg, Protecting the Best Men (Chapel Hill: Univ. of North Carolina Press, 1985).

[30] See, e.g., the classic newspaper antitrust case of Associated Press v. United States, 326 U.S. 1, 28, 65 S.Ct. 1416, 1418 (1945).

[31] Access to the Press—a New First Amendment Right, 80 Harv.L.Rev. 1641 (1967).

[32] Jerome A. Barron, Freedom of the Press for Whom? (Bloomington: Indiana Univ. Press, 1973), p. 6.

by a political candidate, Pat L. Tornillo, Jr., to a Herald editorial criticizing his candidacy for the Florida legislature. When Tornillo asked for his right of reply in the columns of the newspaper, he was refused access, so he sued.

The Florida Supreme Court upheld Tornillo's arguments, and said he should have a right of reply to the print media similar to the right granted under the equal opportunities and fairness doctrines to persons attacked by broadcast media and cable. (See Chapter 9.) At this writing the "equal oppportunities" ["equal time"] law for political candidates is still in force, as is the "personal attack" portion of the Federal Communications Commission's fairness doctrine. Other portions of that doctrine, however were repealed by the FCC in 1987.) The First Amendment, said the Florida Court, "is not for the benefit of the press so much as for the benefit of us all," and added: [33]

> The right of the public to know all sides of a controversy and from such information to be able to make an enlightened choice is being jeopardized by the growing concentration of the ownership of the mass media into fewer and fewer hands, resulting ultimately in a form of private censorship.

The Supreme Court of the United States, however, reversed the Florida court.[34]

In so doing, the nation's highest court conceded the dangers of concentration of media ownership, cross-channel ownership and chains and syndicates all of which focused great power to inform and to influence public opinion in the hands of a few. However valid those arguments, the Court said, government coercion by a remedy such as a right of reply "brings about a confrontation with the express provisions of the First Amendment."

Chief Justice Warren Burger wrote for a unanimous court in rejecting the arguments advanced by Pat Tornillo and Jerome Barron. Reviewing past decisions of the Court, the Chief Justice declared: [35]

> The clear implication has been that any such compulsion to publish that which " 'reason' tells them [editors] should not be published" is unconstitutional. A responsible press is an undoubtedly desirable goal, but press responsibility is not mandated by the Constitution and like many other virtues it cannot be legislated.

[33] Tornillo v. Miami Herald Pub. Co., 287 So.2d 78 (Fla.1973).

[34] Miami Herald Pub. Co. v. Tornillo, 418 U.S. 241, 94 S.Ct. 2831 (1974).

[35] Ibid. Quotes and paraphrases following are from Chief Justice Burger's majority opinion at 2838–2840.

The Florida statute, the Court said, penalized on the basis of the content of a newspaper. The penalty is increased cost of production, and taking up space that could go to other material the paper may have preferred to print. Infinite expansion of its size to accommodate replies that a statute might require is not to be expected of a newspaper.

But cost aside, the Florida statute failed "to clear the barriers of the First Amendment because of its intrusion into the function of editors." The functions of choosing content, determining size of the paper and treatment of public issues, may be fair or unfair, said the Chief Justice. He added that "[i]t has yet to be demonstrated how governmental regulation of this crucial process can be exercised consistent with First Amendment guarantees of a free press . . ."

The Tornillo decision developed no reasoning as to why newspapers were exempt, but broadcasting need not be, from the requirements of furnishing opportunities to reply. Once again, as in other circumstances, the First Amendment's shield proved stronger for printed journalism than for broadcasting.[36]

SEC. 8. CRIMINAL LIBEL

Control of words critical of officials and other citizens was provided by criminal libel law in the states, beginning in the nation's early years, building to strength between 1880 and 1920, and almost disappearing in the years after World War II.

Like the vampire legend, criminal libel never quite seems to die out. Even though it was conventional wisdom to assert during the 1970s and 80s that criminal libel is essentially dead in the United States, don't tell that to South Carolina newsman Jim Fitts. Mr. Fitts spent two days in jail on criminal libel charges in 1988 for his paper's denunciations of two state legislators, and 24 states still had criminal libel statutes on their books in 1988.[37]

In origins, criminal libel overlaps the old crime of sedition: law making verbal attacks on government applied also to words that assailed government officials. That may be seen earlier in this chapter in Section 4's discussion of the Alien and Sedition Acts of 1798. After the death of the Alien and Sedition Acts in 1801, statutes making libel a crime began to proliferate in the states.

[36] See below, Chapter 9.

[37] "Column Puts Publisher in Jail," The News Media & The Law,: Summer, 1988, pp. 3–4.

Keep the phrase *criminal libel* in mind, distinguishing it from *civil libel.* A *criminal* charge or case is brought by an official or agency of government; if a defendant is convicted at trial he or she is subject to imprisonment, payment of a fine, or possibly both. *Civil* libel—dealing with publications (including broadcasts) which are false and which harm a person's *reputation* —do not involve criminal penalties. The person winning a civil libel case can receive "damages"—money—for reputational damage caused by the defendant.

The Jeffersonians who successfully did away with the Federalists' Alien and Sedition Acts had a limited sense of freedom themselves. The Jeffersonians, hating the *national* sedition law when brought to bear on their newspapers and editors, nevertheless accepted the power to punish political speech when it was held by the states.[38] Supposedly, citizens could control their local-state affairs and check tendencies toward oppression close to home more easily than they could check a remote, centralized national government.

Laws of the new states provided that libel could be a crime whether it was aimed at plain citizens or government men. That the laws went under the name "criminal libel" laws instead of under the hated term "seditious libel" made them no less effective as tools for prosecution of those who attacked officials.

The states drew up safeguards against some of the harshest features of the old English law of libel. The principles that Andrew Hamilton pleaded for in defending Zenger emerged as important ones early in the Nineteenth Century as states embarked upon prosecutions. Truth slowly was established as a defense in criminal libel actions, and juries were permitted to find the law under growing numbers of state constitutions and statutes as the century progressed. A celebrated early case in New York encouraged the spread. It stemmed from a paragraph reprinted by Federalist editor Harry Croswell from the *New York Evening Post* attacking President Thomas Jefferson: [39]

> Jefferson paid Callender [a Republican editor] for calling Washington a traitor, a robber, and a perjurer; for calling Adams a hoary-headed old incendiary, and for most grossly slandering the private characters of men who he well knew to be virtuous.

The great Federalist leader, Alexander Hamilton, in 1804 took the case after Croswell had been convicted of criminal libel in a jury trial in which he had not been permitted to show the truth of his charge. Hamilton argued that "the liberty of the press con-

[38] Levy, Emergence of a Free Press, Chaps. 9 and 10; Berns, pp. 89–119.
[39] People v. Croswell, 3 Johnson's Cases at 337 (N.Y.1804).

sists of the right to publish with impunity truth with good motives for justifiable ends though reflecting on government, magistracy, or individuals." This, of course, made the intent of the publisher crucial. He also urged that the jury be allowed to find both the law and the facts of the case. He lost, the appeals court being evenly divided; but the result was so repugnant to people and lawmakers that the New York Legislature in 1805 passed a law embracing the principles that Hamilton urged.[40]

In the states' adoption of Hamilton's formula (a few, indeed, made truth a defense no matter what the motives of the writer) there was an implied rejection of an ancient justification for punishing libel as a crime against the state. The old reasoning was that the truer the disparaging words, the more likely the insulted person to seek violent revenge, breaching the peace. If the words were false, the logic ran, they could be demonstrated as such. Thus the legal aphorism of the Eighteenth Century: "the greater the truth, the greater the libel."

But Nineteenth Century American courts were reluctant to give truth a protected position in the law, even though statutes seemed to endorse the position that the public needs to know the truth. As legislatures adopted truth as a defense in libel statutes through the Nineteenth Century, courts nevertheless clung tenaciously to breach of the peace as an overriding excuse for punishing libel.[41] While few statutes or constitutions retained words' "tendency to breach the peace" as a basis for criminality in libel in the Twentieth Century, judges who wanted to employ it found it readily accessible in common law principles.

Criminal libel actions were few through most of the Nineteenth Century. They surged in number in the 1880s and held at some 100 reported cases per decade for 30 years or more. Not all, by any means, were brought for defamation of public officials in the pattern of seditious libel actions.[42] But criticism of police, governors, mayors, judges, prosecutors, sheriffs, and other government officials was the offense in scores of criminal libel cases.

Of all of them, the most famous was that stemming from the abortive attempt of President Theodore Roosevelt to punish the *New York World* and the *Indianapolis News* for charging deep corruption in the nation's purchase of the title to the Panama

[40] An Act Concerning Libels, Laws of the State of New York, Albany, 1805.

[41] Elizabeth Goepel, "The Breach of the Peace Provision in Nineteenth Century Criminal Libel Law," (Univ. of Wis.1981), unpublished Master's thesis.

[42] John D. Stevens, et al., Criminal Libel as Seditious Libel, 43 Journalism Quar. 110 (1966); Robert A. Leflar, The Social Utility of the Criminal Law of Defamation, 34 Texas L.Rev. 984 (1956). Stevens et al. found that about one-fifth (31) of the 148 criminal libel cases reported in the half-century after World War I grew out of charges made against officials.

Canal from France. Enraged especially by the *World* and its publisher, Joseph Pulitzer, President Roosevelt delivered a special message to Congress. He charged that Pulitzer was responsible for libeling the United States Government, individuals in the government, and the "good name of the American people." He called it "criminal libel," but his angry words carried his accusation deep into various realms of sedition.[43]

There is little indication that the failure of Roosevelt's action deterred lesser officials at lower levels of government from instituting criminal libel actions. Not until more than a decade later, after World War I, did a sharp decline in the number of actions set in, dropping from approximately 100 per decade to far smaller numbers.[44] Courts increasingly came to take the position that civil libel suits to recover damages were much to be preferred to criminal libel prosecutions, which more and more seemed inappropriate to personal squabbles between citizens. Furthermore, violent revenge—breach of the peace—was rarely to be seen in connection with defamation. No longer were the evils of duelling as a way of avenging verbal insults part of life, real though they had been to the Seventeenth and Eighteenth Centuries. Also, the defamed ordinarily had more to gain through a civil judgment for money damages than through a criminal conviction that helps only in the sense that it is a "moral victory."

Yet as the number of cases retreated—to about 15 in the decade of the 1940s—the tendency of harsh words to cause breach of the peace clung to the law's provisions and reasoning in several states. Thus this test was applied to a newspaper article about the police chief of New Britain, Conn., which charged him and his family with bootlegging. "The gist of the crime is, not the injury to the reputation of the person libeled, but that the publication affects injuriously the peace and good order of society," said the Connecticut Supreme Court in upholding the conviction of the newspaper.[45] And as late as 1961 in the same state, it was made plain that the law still held—and that the crime lay in the mere *tendency* of the words to create a breach of the peace, and that "it is immaterial that no one was incited to commit any act by reason of the libel * * *."[46]

Criminal Libel of Groups

Perhaps adding tenacity to the shrinking offense of criminal libel was a highly unusual case of 1952 that claimed the attention

[43] House of Rep.Docs., 60 Cong., 2 Sess., § 1213 (Dec. 15, 1908), pp. 3–5.

[44] Stevens, op. cit.

[45] State v. Gardner, 112 Conn. 121, 124, 151 A. 349, 350 (1930).

[46] State v. Whiteside, 148 Conn. 208, 169 A.2d 260 (1961).

of much of the world of civil liberties. It involved a special and rarely employed version of the ancient criminal libel law—that under some circumstances, *groups* could be libeled and the state could bring criminal action against the libeler. Beauharnais v. Illinois was decided in 1952 with a finding of "guilty." [47] It involved a leaflet attack on the African Americans in Chicago, at a time when the memory of Hitler Germany's mass killing of Jews was fresh in the minds of the nation. Migration of blacks from the south into northern cities was swelling. Beauharnais, president of the White Circle League, had organized his group to distribute the leaflets, and they did so in downtown Chicago. Among other things the leaflet called for city officials to stop "the further encroachment, harassment, and invasion of the white people * * * by the Negro * * *", and predicted that "rapes, robberies, knives, guns, and marijuana of the negro" surely would unite Chicago whites against blacks.

Beauharnais was prosecuted and convicted under an Illinois law making it unlawful to exhibit a publication which "portrays depravity, criminality, unchastity, or lack of virtue of a class of citizens, of any race, color, creed or religion which said publication * * * exposes the citizens of any race, color, creed or religion to contempt, derision, or obloquy or which is productive of breach of the peace or riots." [48]

The charges against Negroes, said the Court, were unquestionably libelous; and the central question became whether the "liberty" of the Fourteenth Amendment prevents a state from punishing such libels when they are directed not at an individual, but at "designated collectivities." The Court said that only if the law were a "wilful and purposeless restriction unrelated to the peace and well-being of the State," could the Court deny a state power to punish utterances directed at a defined group.

Justice Frankfurter found that for more than a century, Illinois had been "the scene of exacerbated tension between races, often flaring into violence and destruction." He cited the murder of abolitionist Elijah Lovejoy in 1837, the "first northern race riot"—in Chicago in 1908—in which six persons were killed, and subsequent violence in the state of Illinois down to the Cicero, Ill. race riot of 1951. He concluded that "In the face of this history and its frequent obligato of extreme racial and religious propagan-

[47] 343 U.S. 250, 72 S.Ct. 725 (1952). See also People v. Spielman, 318 Ill. 482, 149 N.E. 466 (1925). Also "Knights of Columbus" cases: People v. Turner, 28 Cal.App. 766, 154 P. 34 (1914); People v. Gordan, 63 Cal.App. 627, 219 P. 486 (1923); Crane v. State, 14 Okl.Cr. 30, 166 P. 1110 (1917); Alumbaugh v. State, 39 Ga.App. 599, 147 S.E. 714 (1929). And see Joseph Tannehaus, Group Libel, 35 Cornell L.Q. 261 (1950).

[48] Beauharnais v. Illinois, 343 U.S. 250, 251, 72 S.Ct. 725, 728 (1952).

da, we would deny experience to say that the Illinois legislature was without reason in seeking ways to curb false or malicious defamation of racial and religious groups." [49]

Four members of the court delivered strong dissents to the majority opinion that sustained Beauharnais' conviction. Justice Hugo Black stated much of the case against the concept of group libel as an offense acceptable to American freedom. Calling the law a "state censorship" instrument, Black said that permitting states to experiment in curbing freedom of expression "is startling and frightening doctrine in a country dedicated to self-government by its people."[50]

By 1992, hate-crime legislation was adopted in most states: All but four states—Alaska, Nebraska, New Mexico and Wyoming—had hate crime statutes. Thirty-one states' laws closely followed a model of the Anti-Defamation League of B'nai B'rith calling for both criminal sanctions and civil penalties. In 1992, the U.S. Supreme Court was to decide R.A.V. v. St. Paul, a test of a city ordinance's application to a 17-year-old accused of cross-burning in a black family's fenced yard.[51]

Criminal Libel of Officials

In 1966, the Court focused on breach of the peace in common law criminal libel, and found that it did not square with the First Amendment. Merely to say that words which tend to cause breach of the peace are criminal, is too indefinite to be understandable, the court said. The case, Ashton v. Kentucky,[52] involved a pamphlet in which Ashton charged a police chief with law-breaking during a strike of miners, a sheriff with attempts to buy off a prosecution, and a newspaper owner with diverting food and clothing collected for strikers to anti-strike workers. Ashton was convicted under a definition of criminal libel given, in part, by the judge as "any writing calculated to create disturbances of the peace." The Supreme Court said that without specification that was too vague an offense to be constitutional: [53]

In the second case, the Supreme Court's 1964 ruling in the civil libel action New York Times Co. v. Sullivan produced a heavy impact on the decaying bastions of criminal libel as applied to

---

[49] Ibid., at 258–261, 72 S.Ct. at 731–733. Illinois dropped this statute in 1961, but later enacted a hate-crime law.

[50] Ibid., at 270, 272, 273, 72 S.Ct. at 737, 738, 739.

[51] Mary Deibel, "Hate Crimes," Scripps-Howard News Service, Knoxville News-Sentinel, Dec. 1, 1991, p. F–1, and see Hadley Arkes, "Civility and Restriction of Speech: Rediscovering the Defamation of Groups," 1974 Sup.Ct.Rev. 281–335; City of Chicago v. Lambert, 47 Ill.App.2d 151, 197 N.E.2d 448 (1964).

[52] 384 U.S. 195, 86 S.Ct. 1407 (1966).

[53] Ibid., at 198, 86 S.Ct. at 1409–1411.

criticism of public officials. The *Sullivan* decision said that critical words must be used with actual malice if they were to be the object of a *civil* libel action against officials, and now the Supreme Court moved the same rule into the field of *criminal* libel. The case was Garrison v. Louisiana.[54] Here Garrison, a prosecuting attorney for the State of Louisiana, gave out a statement at a press conference attacking several judges of his parish (county) for laziness and inattention to their official duties. He was convicted of criminal libel, and his case ultimately reached the Supreme Court.

The Court cited the Times v. Sullivan rule defining actual malice—that a public official might recover damages as a remedy for civil libel only if it could be shown that there was knowing falsity or reckless disregard for truth.[55]

> The reasons which led us so to hold ∗ ∗ ∗ apply with no less force merely because the remedy is criminal. The constitutional guarantees of freedom of expression compel application of the same standard to the criminal remedy. Truth may not be the subject of either civil or criminal sanctions where discussion of public affairs is concerned. And since "∗ ∗ ∗ erroneous statement is inevitable in free debate ∗ ∗ ∗" only those false statements made with the high degree of awareness of their probable falsity demanded by New York Times may be the subject of either civil or criminal sanctions. For speech concerning public affairs is more than self-expression; it is the essence of self-government.

The Louisiana court's ruling that Garrison's criticism of the judges constituted an attack on the personal integrity of the judges, rather than on their official conduct, was not accepted. The state court had said that Garrison had imputed fraud, deceit, and dishonesty to the judges and malfeasance in office. But, said the United States Supreme Court:[56]

> Of course, any criticism of the manner in which a public official performs his duties will tend to affect his private, as well as his public, reputation. The New York Times rule is not rendered inapplicable merely because an official's private reputation, as well as his public reputation, is harmed. The public official rule protects the paramount public interest in a free flow of informa-

[54] 379 U.S. 64, 85 S.Ct. 209 (1964); Harry Kalven, "The New York Times Case: a Note on the Central Meaning of the First Amendment," 1964 Sup.Ct.Rev. 191.

[55] Ibid., at 74, 85 S.Ct. at 215. Mr. Garrison was famous again in 1992 because of his depiction as a seeker after truth in Oliver Stone's "JFK," a movie about the President's 1963 assassination.

[56] Ibid., at 77, 85 S.Ct. at 217.

tion to the people concerning public officials, their servants. To this end, anything which might touch on an official's fitness for office is relevant. Few personal attributes are more germane to fitness for office than dishonesty, malfeasance, or improper motivation * * *.

As criminal libel cases arose on rare occasions during the decade after *Garrison,* several state statutes were found in violation of the Constitution—Pennsylvania's,[57] Arkansas',[58] and in 1976, California's. In the last of these, an action was brought against the publisher of the *L.A. Star,* a weekly tabloid of southern California, by the Los Angeles city attorney. The Star had published a photo superimposing a picture of a well-known actress' face on an unidentified nude female body in "a sexually explicit pose."[59] At trial and on appeal, the California criminal libel statute was held unconstitutional. For one thing, it provided that truth was a defense to a charge of criminal libel only if it were published with good motives and for justifiable ends, and since the *Sullivan* case, that had been an unconstitutional limitation on the truth defense. Further, the law provided that an injurious publication is presumed to be malicious if no justifiable motive is shown, and malice may not be presumed but must be alleged and proved. Burdened with these rules out of the past which now were rejected under an outlook in the Supreme Court of the United States that over a 50-year period had slowly freed the press from ancient restrictions of English origin and American adoption, the criminal libel statute of California was shredded by the decision. The Supreme Court of the state said that "any attempt at draftmanship on the part of the court to save the remainder of the statute would transgress both the legislative intent and the judicial function and would be a flagrant breach of the doctrine of separation of powers."[60] Broken and impotent, the law was an unlikely candidate for salvage by the state's legislature.

Criminal libel continues to be rare, but the impulse behind such law—to punish dissidents, to silence criticism, by no means is gone. As Norman L. Rosenberg has noted, although the means for suppression or intimidation may vary, the end remains the same.[61]

[57] Commonwealth v. Armao, 446 Pa. 325, 286 A.2d 626 (1972).

[58] Weston v. State, 258 Ark. 707, 528 S.W.2d 412 (1975). See also Williamson v. State of Georgia, 249 Ga. 851, 295 S.E.2d 305 (1982), 9 Med.L.Rptr. 1703, striking down the state's criminal libel statute.

[59] Press Censorship Newsletter No. VI, Dec.-Jan. 1974–75, p. 31.

[60] Eberle v. Municipal Court, Los Angeles Judicial District, 55 Cal.App.3d 423, 127 Cal.Rptr. 594, 600 (1976). For a suggestion that criminal libel may not be dead, see Keeton v. Hustler Magazine, 465 U.S. 770, 104 S.Ct. 1473 (1984), fn. 6, 10 Med.L.Rptr. 1405.

[61] See Norman L. Rosenberg, Protecting the Best Men: An Interpretive History of Libel (Chapel Hill: University of North Carolina Press), p. 6.

Over time in the United States, when those in power could no longer use seditious or criminal libel effectively to muzzle or to punish dissent, they switched to lawsuits for civil libel.[62] The key question, then, revolves around the concept of *political* libel, regardless of the label the particular legal action may carry.[63]

SEC. 9.　TAXATION

The mass media are constitutionally protected from discriminatory or punitive taxation.

Taxation has long been a fighting word to the press. Taxes on the press instituted in England were called "taxes on knowledge" because they raised the purchase price of pamphlets and other printed materials beyond the means of most persons. Taxation also came to be a hated symbol of control and oppression in American history. The British Stamp Act of 1765 imposed great hardships on printers in colonial America, taxing newspapers, advertisements, pamphlets and many legal documents and became a great rallying cry for colonists who resisted British authority.[64] Such a storm of protest arose in the colonies, reflected in angry writings in newspapers and pamphlets and, ultimately, in mobs which forced British stamp agents to resign. Faced with such furious opposition, Parliament repealed the Stamp Taxes as they affected printer-editors.

If American colonists hated the Stamp Act taxes and argued against them in terms of "freedom of the press," American memories also were very short. In 1785, only two years after the War of Independence officially ended, the state of Massachusetts passed a newspaper stamp tax.

Howls of protest echoing the Stamp Act disturbances soon resounded from the Massachusetts newspapers. One writer calling himself "Lucius" declared that the tax on newspapers was a "*stab to the freedom of the people.*" He acknowledged that the tax of a penny on each copy seemed small, but "Lucius" added that "tyranny begins small:" a tax of even a half-penny an issue could be a precedent for a tax of £100 on each issue.[65] Such protests quickly led the to the repeal of the Massachusetts stamp tax on newspapers later in 1785, although the state's legislature soon

---

[62] Ibid., Chapter 4 and 5.

[63] Ibid., p. 7.

[64] Arthur M. Schlesinger, Prelude to Independence: The Newspaper War on Britain, 1763–1776 (New York: Knopf, 1958), p. 68.

[65] Massachusetts Centinel, May 28, 1785.

enacted a tax on newspaper ads.[66] The advertising tax was repealed in 1788.[67]

Newspapers and other units of the mass media of communications are businesses. As such, the media are not immune from taxation just like other business enterprises, as long as the taxes fall with a more or less even hand upon the press as well as other businesses. *Discriminatory* or *punitive* taxation, however, raises quite different issues. The classic case in United States constitutional law occurred during the 1930s and involved the flamboyant Huey "Kingfish" Long, the political boss and governor of Louisiana who entertained dreams of someday becoming President. The Supreme Court decision in Grosjean, Supervisor of Accounts of Louisiana, v. American Press Co., Inc.[68] effectively halted a Huey Long-instigated attempt to use a punitive tax to injure newspapers which opposed Long's political regime.

During the 1930s, Louisiana's larger daily newspapers were increasingly expressing opposition to Long's political machine. Louisiana's larger newspapers' sniping at Governor Long's dictatorial posturings soon brought about retaliation. The Louisiana legislature passed a special two per cent license tax on the gross receipts of all newspapers, magazines, or periodicals having a circulation of more than 20,000 copies per week.[69] Of Louisiana's 163 newspapers, only 13 had circulations of more than 20,000 per week. Of these 13 newspapers to which the tax applied, 12 were opponents of Long's political machine.[70] This transparent attempt to silence newspaper critics was challenged in the courts by nine Louisiana newspaper publishers who produced the 13 newspapers then appearing in the state which had circulations of more than 20,000 copies a week.

In declaring the Louisiana tax unconstitutional, a noted conservative—Justice George Sutherland—spoke for a unanimous Supreme Court. Justice Sutherland, a man not revered for his felicity of expression, may indeed have had some able assistance in writing what has come to be known as "Sutherland's great opinion in *Grosjean.*" It has been asserted that Sutherland's opinion included a proposed concurring opinion which had been drafted by

[66] Ibid., July 6, July 30, 1785.

[67] Clyde Augustus Duniway, Freedom of the Press in Massachusetts (New York, 1906), p. 137.

[68] 297 U.S. 233, 56 S.Ct. 444 (1936).

[69] Grosjean v. American Press Co., 297 U.S. 233, 240, 56 S.Ct. 444, 445 (1936).

[70] J. Edward Gerald, The Press and the Constitution 1931–1947 (Minneapolis, University of Minnesota Press, 1948) p. 100; William A. Hachten, The Supreme Court on Freedom of the Press: Decisions and Dissents (Ames, Iowa: Iowa State University Press 1968) p. 77; Grosjean v. American Press Co., 297 U.S. 233, 56 S.Ct. 444, 445 (1936).

the famed liberal Justice Benjamin Nathan Cardozo, and which the Court wished to add into Justice Sutherland's opinion.[71]

Whether assisted by Cardozo or not, the Sutherland opinion in Grosjean remains noteworthy. Justice Sutherland began with a historical overview of government-imposed dangers to freedom of expression, including reference to John Milton's 1644 "Appeal for the Liberty of Unlicensed Printing" and to the end of the licensing of the press in England in 1695. As Sutherland noted, "mere exemption from previous censorship was soon recognized as too narrow a view of the liberty of the press." Sutherland wrote that taxes in Eighteenth Century England were quite commonly characterized as "taxes on knowledge." [72]

Justice Sutherland asserted that if taxes had been the only issue, many of England's best men would not have risked their careers and their lives to fight against them. The issue in England for many years, however, involved discriminatory taxation designed to control the press and silence criticism of government. The *Grosjean* opinion added: [73]

> The framers of the First Amendment were familiar with the English struggle, which had then continued for nearly eighty years and was destined to go on for another sixty-five years, at the end of which time it culminated in a lasting abandonment of the obnoxious taxes. The framers were likewise familiar with the then recent [1785–1788] Massachusetts [stamp tax] episode . . .

Justice Sutherland rejected the State of Louisiana's argument that the English common law in force when the Constitution was adopted forbade only prior restraints on the press and said nothing about forbidding taxation.[74] In reply, Sutherland quoted from a great 19th century American constitutional scholar, Judge Thomas Cooley, and declared that Cooley had laid down the test to be applied.[75]

> The evils to be prevented were not the censorship of the press merely, but any action of the government by means of which it might prevent such free and general discussion of public matters as seems absolutely essential to prepare the people for an intelligent exercise of their rights as citizens.

[71] Irving Brant, The Bill of Rights: Its Origin and Meaning (New York: Bobbs–Merrill, 1965) pp. 403–404.

[72] Grosjean v. American Press Co., 297 U.S. 233, 249, 56 S.Ct. 444, 449 (1936).

[73] Grosjean v. American Press Co., 297 U.S. 233, 247–248, 56 S.Ct. 444, 448 (1936).

[74] Grosjean v. American Press Co., 297 U.S. 233, 249, 56 S.Ct. 444, 449 (1936).

[75] Grosjean v. American Press Co., 297 U.S. 233, 249, 56 S.Ct. 444, 449 (1936), quoting 2 Cooley's Constitutional Limitations (8th ed.) p. 886.

Application of this test led Justice Sutherland to rule that the Louisiana gross receipts tax on its larger newspapers was an unconstitutional abridgement of the First and Fourth Amendments. Sutherland declared: [76]

> It is not intended by anything we have said to suggest that the owners of newspapers are immune from any of the ordinary forms of taxation for support of the government. But this is not an ordinary form of tax, but one single in kind, with a long history of hostile misuse against the freedom of the press.
>
>   *   *   *
>
> The tax here involved is bad not because it takes money from the pockets of the appellees. If that were all, a wholly different question would be presented. It is bad because, in the light of its history and of its present setting, it is seen to be a deliberate and calculated device in the guise of a tax to limit the circulation of information to which the public is entitled in virtue of the constitutional guaranties. A free press stands as one of the great interpreters between the government and the people. To allow it to be fettered is to fetter ourselves.
>
> The form in which the tax is imposed is in itself suspicious. It is not measured or limited by the volume of advertisements. It is measured alone by the extent of the circulation of the publication in which the advertisements are carried, with the plain purpose of penalizing the publishers and curtailing the circulation of a selected group of newspapers.

Despite these ringing words, it should be noted again that the communications media are not exempt from paying non-discriminatory general business taxes. A case in point involved *The Corona Daily Independent*, a California newspaper which challenged a $32-a-year business license tax imposed by the City of Corona. The newspaper, which had paid the tax in a number of previous years, in 1951 refused to pay the tax. The newspaper went to court, arguing that the tax violated freedom of the press as guaranteed by the First and Fourteenth Amendments. However, the California Appellate Court ruled: [77]

---

[76] Grosjean v. American Press Co., 297 U.S. 233, 250–251, 56 S.Ct. 444, 449 (1936). Accord: See *City of Baltimore v. A.S. Abell Co.*, 218 Md. 273, 145 A.2d 111, 119 (1958). It was held that Baltimore city ordinances imposing taxes on advertising media were unconstitutional in that they discriminatorily taxed newspapers and radio and television stations. About 90 per cent of the impact of the taxes was on those businesses.

[77] City of Corona v. Corona Daily Independent, 115 Cal.App.2d 382, 252 P.2d 56 (1953), certiorari denied 343 U.S. 833, 74 S.Ct. 2 (1953). See also *Giragi v. Moore*, 44 Ariz. 74, 64 P.2d 819 (1937) (general sales tax law placing a one per cent tax

There is ample authority to the effect that newspapers and the business of newspaper publication are not made exempt from the ordinary forms of taxes for the support of local government by the provisions of the First and Fourteenth Amendments.

The general rule is that the media are businesses and are subject to general laws which regulate business. As it was said by the Supreme Court of the United States in 1939 in *Associated Press v. National Labor Relations Board:* [78]

The business of the Associated Press is not immune from regulation because it is an agency of the press. The publisher of a newspaper has no special immunity from the application of general laws. He has no special privileges or immunities to invade the rights and liberties of others. He must answer for libel. He may be punished for contempt of court. He is subject to the anti-trust laws. Like others he must pay equitable and nondiscriminatory taxes on his business.

Grosjean v. American Press Co. remains the leading case for the proposition that the mass media are constitutionally protected from discriminatory or punitive taxation. The *Grosjean* case, as seen on earlier pages, dealt with a garish fact situation, a transparent attempt by Louisiana Governor Huey "Kingfish" Long and his allies to silence newspaper critics.

Unlike the *Grosjean* situation, the State of Minnesota was operating out of more defensible motives during the 1970s when it enacted a "use tax" on paper and ink consumed applicable to newspapers. This apparently was only a revenue measure, not an attempt to control or to punish the press. Even so, the Supreme Court of the United States voided the tax by an 8–1 margin. The tax was held unconstitutional because it singled out the press for special treatment.

upon businesses' sales or gross income not unconstitutional as applied to newspapers); Arizona Publishing Co. v. O'Neil, 22 F.Supp. 117 (D.Ariz.1938), affirmed 304 U.S. 543, 58 S.Ct. 950 (1938).

[78] Associated Press v. National Labor Relations Board, 301 U.S. 103, 132–133, 57 S.Ct. 650, 656 (1937). See Lee Enterprises, Inc. v. Iowa State Tax Commission, 162 N.W.2d 730, 734, 754–755 (Iowa 1969). Ten corporations, including newspapers, radio and television broadcasters, advertising agencies and firms engaged in retail merchandising and in the auto business challenged an Iowa tax law known as Section 25 of Division VII, Iowa House File 702. With that measure, the Iowa General Assembly had amended the state's revenue statutes, including as taxable "the gross receipts of * * * directors, shoppers guides and newspapers whether or not circulated free or without charge to the public, magazine, radio and television advertising * * *." The Iowa Supreme Court held that the tax does not violate freedom of the press as guaranteed in either the United States or Iowa Constitutions because the law was of general application and not discriminatory.

"Use taxes" are imposed by states to discourage their citizens from purchasing items in other states which have lower sales taxes. Minnesota's newspapers were exempted from use taxes until 1971, when the state began taxing the cost of paper and ink used in producing a publication.[79] In 1974, another change in the tax law exempted a publication's first $100,000 of ink and paper consumed from the 4% use tax.[80]

The $100,000 exemption meant that only the largest of Minnesota's publishers were liable to pay the tax. Only 11 publishers, producing 14 of the state's 388 paid-circulation newspapers, had to pay the tax in 1974. The Minneapolis Star and Tribune Company was the major revenue source from the tax. Of $893,355 collected in 1974, $608,634 was paid by the Star and Tribune.[81]

The Star and Tribune Company sued, asking a refund of the use taxes paid from January 1, 1974, to May 31, 1975. The company contended that the use tax violated freedom of the press and equal protection of the laws as guaranteed by the First and Fourteenth Amendments.[82] The Minnesota Supreme Court ruled the use tax constitutional,[83] and the Supreme Court of the United States then noted probable jurisdiction.[84]

Justice Sandra Day O'Connor wrote for an 8–1 Supreme Court in declaring the Minnesota tax unconstitutional on its face because it singled out publications for unique treatment under the state's law.

Justice O'Connor declared that there is evidence that differential taxation of the press would have troubled the Framers of the First Amendment. "A power to tax differentially, as opposed to a power to tax generally, gives government a powerful weapon against the taxpayer selected." [85] Her opinion also suggested the threat of burdensome taxes might operate as a form of censorship, making the press wary of publishing the critical comments which often allow it to serve as an important restraint on government.

Justice William Rehnquist's dissenting opinion declared that the Supreme Court's concern " * * * seems very much akin to protecting something so much that in the end it is smothered."

[79] Minn.Stat.Ann. §§ 297A.14, 287A.25i.

[80] Minn.Stat.Ann. § 297A.14.

[81] Minneapolis Star and Tribune Co. v. Minnesota Commissioner of Revenue, 460 U.S. 575, 103 S.Ct. 1365, 1368 (1983), 9 Med.L.Rptr. 1369.

[82] Ibid.

[83] Minneapolis Star and Tribune Co. v. Commission of Revenue, 314 N.W.2d 201 (Minn.1981).

[84] Minneapolis Star and Tribune Co. v. Minnesota Commissioner of Revenue, 457 U.S. 1130, 102 S.Ct. 2955 (1982).

[85] Ibid., at 586, 103 S.Ct. at 1372.

He expressed doubts that the Framers of the First Amendment would have seen such a use tax as an abridgement of the press. Furthermore: [86]

> The Court recognizes in several parts of its opinion that the State of Minnesota could avoid constitutional problems by imposing on newspapers the 4% sales tax that it imposes on other retailers.

Justice Rehnquist calculated that if a sales tax had been in effect in 1974 and 1975, the Star and Tribune's liability would have been more than $3.6 million, compared to less than $1.3 million paid in use taxes during those years. Such a differential treatment under the use taxes, Rehnquist concluded, actually benefited the press.[87]

Even though the media are protected from discriminatory or punitive taxation by the First Amendment, a 1987 Ad Tax dispute in Florida was a sign of things to come. In 1987, Florida passed a 5% business service sales tax which included taxes on mass media advertising. That tax on services cast a wide net: other services declared taxable included accounting, legal services, and pest control.[88]

Although that clumsily designed tax on services quickly fell under its own weight and a barrage of media complaints, that Florida episode symbolizes federal and state governments' ceaseless hunt for new revenues. Because governments are exhausting traditional sources of money, various aspects of the media industry present inviting possibilities for taxation which could well be held to be constitutional.

Small wonder that Florida's legislature repealed that tax within a matter of months. USA Today gave examples of the unwieldiness of the Florida tax as it would have applied to advertising: [89]

> IBM might pay $200,000 for a 30–second commercial during NBC's St. Elsewhere. If Floridians are 5% of the nationwide TV audience, IBM theoretically would pay $10,000 to reach them. So IBM's tax liability for that commercial would be 5% of $10,000, or $500.

Although that services tax died in Florida in 1987, it was evident in the early 1990s that legislatures all over the nation were in hot pursuit of new sales revenues. The New York Times

---

[86] Ibid., at 597, 103 S.Ct. at 1378.

[87] Ibid., at 604, 103 S.Ct. at 1382.

[88] Marilyn Marks, "Florida Ends Tax on Services . . .", Governing, January, 1988, p. 57; "Governor Acts to End Florida Tax," The New York Times, Sept. 19, 1987, p. 21.

[89] James Cox, "Big advertisers balk at new Florida sales tax," USA Today, Sec. B, p. 1, June 23, 1987.

and Presstime magazine reported in fall, 1992, that a tax on circulation was under consideration in California, and that other states might soon follow that approach. In addition, as of fall, 1992, there were 14 states, including California, taxing newspaper sales, with sales taxes proposed in seven other states.[90]

The basic rule remains: the press may not be singled out for "differential treatment" when being taxed. That does not mean the press will pay less in taxes than other kinds of businesses.

SEC. 10. THE CONTEMPT POWER AND CRITICIZING COURTS

Criticism of judges while cases were pending was long considered an interference with justice, and was punishable as contempt of court.

The offense known as "constructive contempt of court"— notably, contempt shown toward judges in newspaper criticism— had a long and sometimes troublesome life in the United States. This nation had been in existence almost 150 years before the U.S. Supreme Court issued decisions virtually demolishing that word crime.

Judges had—and still have—power to control what goes on in their courtrooms, or to punish persons who are under their jurisdiction and disobey court orders. That is the "direct contempt" power. If a person stands up in a courtroom and screams obscenities at a judge, the judge can use his or her "summary" power— can declare that person in contempt of court, and can sentence that individual *on the spot* to pay a fine, serve a jail term, or both. And journalists, as discussed in Chapter 13, sometimes run afoul of the contempt power when they defy court orders to reveal sources for stories or information gathered in the course of reporting.

The constructive contempt control over the press lay in the power of judges to punish their critics while cases were pending in court. Even though English precedent for such a power was weak, the American judiciary took this power unto itself and extended it.[91]

[90] Alex S. Jones, "Newspapers See a Threat of Spreading Sales Taxes," The New York Times, Sept. 19, 1991, p. C6, using a graphic from Presstime magazine. States shown with sales taxes on newspapers: Alabama, Arizona, California, Delaware, Florida, Hawaii, Georgia, Idaho, Kansas, Kentucky, Missouri, North Carolina, Virginia, and West Virginia. States where taxes were proposed in 1992 included Connecticut, Maine, Maryland, Minnesota, Mississippi, South Carolina, and South Dakota.

[91] Walter Nelles and Carol Weiss King, Contempt by Publication in the U.S., 28 Col.L.Rev. 401–431, 525–562 (1928).

Judges taking such power upon themselves proved upsetting, and Pennsylvania and New York both passed statutes early in the Nineteenth Century to curb judges' power over published criticism. And in 1831, Congress passed a similar law. The reason for the Congressional action came from an attorney, Luke Lawless, who had been found in contempt by Federal Judge James H. Peck. Lawless, who had published newspaper articles critical of the judge's handling of land claims, had sought the impeachment of Judge Peck. Judge Peck retaliated by finding the lawyer in contempt and suspending him from the practice of law for eighteen months.

The House of Representatives ultimately impeached (brought charges) against Judge Peck, but the Senate ultimately found Peck not guilty by the narrowest of margins.[92]

But Congress wanted no more punishment for criticism of judges in the press. Only a month after the impeachment proceedings against Judge Peck, Congress passed an act in 1831 saying that federal judges might punish only misbehavior taking place "in the presence of the courts ∗ ∗ ∗ or so near thereto as to obstruct the administration of justice." [93]

Many states' judges, however, were not ready to permit criticism. The main line of cases from the mid-Nineteenth Century until 1941 found judges asserting their "immemorial power": to cite and punish for newspaper criticism taking place far from their courtrooms.[94]

Two rules emerged: "pendency" and "reasonable tendency." The pendency rule meant that criticism of courts and judges could not be published while a case was still pending. That included attempts to influence judges or participants in cases or publishing false or inaccurate reports of trials. "When a case is finished," said Justice Oliver Wendell Holmes, Jr., in a federal case in 1907, courts are subject to the same criticism as other people . . ." Published criticism could then be labeled as interference with the judicial process and punished as contempt.[95]

The "reasonable tendency" judicial concept meant that there did not have to be any proof of harm to the judicial process from published criticism. A "tendency" to create such harm would be

[92] Arthur J. Stansbury, Report of the Trial of James H. Peck (Boston: Hilliard Gray & Co., 1833).

[93] Nelles and King, op. cit. at p. 430, citing Act of Mar. 2, 1831, c. 98, 4 Stat. 487.

[94] Ronald L. Goldfarb, The Contempt Power (New York, 1963).

[95] Patterson v. Colorado ex rel. Attorney General, 205 U.S. 454, 27 S.Ct. 556 (1907).

enough to cite for contempt, the U.S. Supreme Court said in a 1918 decision.[96]

Note that Justice Holmes, who wrote for the majority in the 1907 Patterson v. Colorado decision involving criticism of pending cases, valued the role of a free press more when he dissented from a 1918 decision involving "reasonable tendency." He declared that the Court's majority erred in upholding a contempt citation against a Toledo newspaper. His dissent invoked the 1831 federal statute, so long forgotten. Holmes wrote, "so near thereto" means so near as actually to obstruct justice, and misbehavior means more than unfavorable comment or disrespect.[97]

Then in a series of decisions in the 1940s, the Supreme Court yielded up its long-standing power, telling the entire judicial branch to do the same. In Bridges v. California,[98] Justice Hugo Black's majority opinion shredded both the pending case rule and the reasonable tendency test. In *Bridges*, trial-court judges had convicted Californians for contempt-by-publication for admonishing courts about pending cases. Black said that such contempt orders silence discussion when public interest would be at its height, and that any moratorium on public discussion—which could last for years during a case's "pendency" was not an insignificant abridgement of freedom of expression. Black also said that neither a reasonable tendency nor an "inherent tendency" of words to interfere with courts was enought to support a contempt order. A "clear and present danger" to the administration of justice had to be shown.[99] The clear and present danger rule was used in other cases to overturn contempt-by-publication convictions. The rare contempt conviction for criticizing courts now is almost certain to be overturned on appeal.[1]

[96] Toledo Newspaper Co. v. United States, 247 U.S. 402, 421, 38 S.Ct. 560, 564 (1918).

[97] Ibid., at 422, 38 S.Ct. at 565.

[98] 314 U.S. 252, 62 S.Ct. 190 (1941).

[99] 314 U.S. at 268–269, 62 S.Ct. at 196–197.

[1] See Pennekamp v. Florida, 328 U.S. 331, 66 S.Ct. 1029 (1946); Craig v. Harney, 331 U.S. 367, 67 S.Ct. 1249 (1947), Wood v. Georgia, 370 U.S. 375, 82 S.Ct. 1364 (1962), and Cooper v. Rockford Nsprs., 34 Ill.App.3d 645, 339 N.E.2d 477 (1975).

Chapter 3

THE FIRST AMENDMENT AND ELECTRONIC MEDIA

Sec.
11. From Radiotelegraphy to Broadcasting.
12. Spectrum Space: From Crisis to Control.
13. Rationalizing Governmental Regulation.
14. Spectrum Scarcity and Expanding New Media Channels.
15. The Convergence of "Broadcast" and "Press" Law.

The constitutional history of American broadcasting is neither as extensive nor as impressive as that of the American press. Yet nothing in the language of the Constitution itself denies to broadcasting any of those free speech rights now being exercised by the press. Why, then, should American broadcasting have its own separate and less extensive body of constitutional law? What prevents a broadcaster from simply claiming that full legacy of First Amendment protections already won for American mass media by the press?

The answers to these questions can be found in the earliest days of radio regulation in the United States, when the federal government began to draw those legal distinctions that would isolate broadcasting from all other forms of American mass communication, restricting it to a much narrower range of constitutionally protected free speech rights.

SEC. 11. FROM RADIOTELEGRAPHY TO BROADCASTING

Broadcasting began in the United States as a service regulated by laws designed for an entirely different form of communication.

It all began with Guglielmo Marconi, who never wanted to be the "father of radio" and in reality—wasn't. Marconi was interested only in discovering some way to transmit telegraphic code through space, so he could offer the owners of the world's great merchant fleets a global communications system capable of delivering messages directly to their ships at sea. In 1901, Marconi demonstrated the effectiveness of his new "radiotelegraphy" device, and immediately began building "wireless" stations to relay telegraphic messages to vessels following every major trade route of the world.

Marconi expected to profit from his invention by selling or leasing the equipment he manufactured to all the large shipping companies of Europe and North America. It soon became apparent, however, that in freeing the telegraph from the constraints of its wire, he had created an open communications network, accessible to everyone possessing a transmitter or receiver obtained from any source. To discourage those in the maritime service from purchasing their wireless devices from a growing number of competitors, Marconi instructed his own operators not to acknowledge or relay radio messages from vessels known to be using non-Marconi radiotelegraphy equipment.[1]

International reaction to Marconi's decision was prompt and vigorous. What might have been viewed as a sensible business policy for a land based communications service seemed brutal and barbaric at sea, where refusal to relay a distress signal could easily imperil the lives of innocent ship passengers and crews.

The first radio law enacted in the United States, "The Wireless Ship Act of 1910"[2], dealt only with this single issue in the field of maritime radiotelegraphy, requiring that large ocean-going vessels leaving American ports carry wireless equipment, and making it unlawful for any ship wireless operator to refuse to exchange telegraphic messages with any other radiotelegraphy operator on sea or shore.

As the number of radio-equipped vessels increased with each passing year, interference caused by the growing volume of ship-to-shore transmissions became a serious problem. International maritime radiotelegraphy conferences were held in Berlin in 1903 and 1906, and in London in 1912 to negotiate treaty arrangements for the supervision of these radio communications that each country would be expected to enforce though its own national laws.[3]

The United States complied with these international obligations by enacting the "Radio Act of 1912"[4], requiring all wireless companies operating within the United States to transmit only on

[1] Because Marconi attempted to design a "closed" communication system, not intended for the general public but only those using his equipment, he could be described more accurately as the father of "narrowcasting", forerunner of modern subscriber-only pay-TV services, rather than broadcasting.

[2] Public Law 262, 61st Congress June 24, 1910. This requirement was imposed only on vessels carrying 50 or more people, and travelling more than 200 miles between ports.

[3] These international negotiations took on a special urgency after the sinking of the Titanic in April 1912. The ship rammed an iceburg in the north Atlantic, and sunk three hours later. Some 700 of her 2,200 passengers and crew were saved, but a nearby ship that might have been able to save many more lives failed to respond to her distress call because no wireless operator was on duty during the early morning hours when the Titanic was sinking.

[4] Public Law 264, 62nd Congress, August 13, 1912.

frequencies approved for their use by the Commerce Department. This law authorized stations engaged in maritime communication to select and use two separate radio frequencies, while all other operators were restricted to a single frequency. In addition, those not engaged in either business or maritime radio communication message delivery service were relegated to a less attractive frequency band, and were restricted to a maximum of one kilowatt of transmission power.

American radio experimenters who tried from time to time to "broadcast" to anyone who might be listening, rather than directing their messages to a specific receiver, were placed in this miscellaneous category of communication service by the Radio Act.

Reginald Fessenden, an early radio experimenter, designed the first wireless equipment capable of transmitting the sound of the human voice in 1906. But Fessenden, as Marconi, had no interest in "broadcasting" to the general public. His "radiotelephone", as the name suggests, was developed only to allow voice as well as telegraph messages to be delivered by wireless transmission anywhere in the world.[5]

In reality, of course, there was no American broadcast audience of any size to serve in 1906, because the complicated and expensive radio receivers of this era were still being designed and produced only for business use, while the inexpensive "crystal" detector receiver that had recently been developed was difficult to tune, needed earphones to pick up its faint sounds, and required some knowledge of electricity to assemble and operate.

From 1906 through 1917, the only broadcast service available anywhere in the United States was being provided by a rather small band of amateur radio operators in various parts of the country who enjoyed spending an evening or two each week transmitting a blend of recorded music and commentary to an equally small group of amateur radio enthusiasts who had constructed the reception equipment necessary to hear their broadcasts.

During this same period, the continuing expansion in the volume of private radio communications began to overcrowd that band of frequencies that had originally been allocated to maritime and business service in 1912. But although the Department of Commerce was urged by several radio industry leaders to reclaim for business radio those spectrum assignments that had been made to amateur broadcast operators, the Department refused to do so,

[5] For a more complete account of this early history of broadcasting, see Christopher H. Sterling and John M. Kittross, Stay Tuned: A Concise History of American Broadcasting (Belmont, CA: Wadsworth Publishing, 1977), pp. 16–46.

declaring that such experimentation would continue to be tolerated as long as it did not interfere in any way with the more important and useful communication functions of private radio.

This era of toleration ended in 1917, when the United States entered World War I, and the only important radio communication function became support of the war effort. In April 1917 all radio transmission equipment not under government control was ordered dismantled, and the United States Navy was granted emergency power to develop the most effective radio equipment possible by ordering all American radio manufacturers to pool their conflicting radio patents and to coordinate their research efforts.

The immediate effect of this wartime control was to transform radio equipment manufacturing in the United States into a growth industry. The U.S. Navy alone had purchased 10 million dollars of radio equipment from these suppliers by the end of 1917, and the government imposed "patent pool" stimulated more technological advances during two years it remained in effect than the industry itself had been able to achieve in almost two decades of fierce competition.

But then, with the American radio equipment manufacturers producing transmitters and receivers at a record pace, the war came to an end in November 1918, ending at the same time the massive military market for radio equipment. Soon afterwards the Navy announced its intention to abandon its program protecting radio manufacturers from patent infringement claims, setting off an incredibly complex series of mergers and cross-licensing agreements to maintain those arrangements that had permitted the industry to develop so rapidly during the war-time era.

By June 1921 these corporate maneuvers created a patent pooling, cross-licensing combination among General Electric, Westinghouse, the newly formed Radio Corporation of America (RCA) and American Telegraph and Telephone (AT&T) that made them the dominant force in the field of American radio equipment manufacturing and marketing.[6] At the same time, these corporate giants entered into a formal agreement granting to General Electric and Westinghouse exclusive rights to manufacture radio receivers that RCA would market as sales agent for the two companies.

RCA, General Electric and Westinghouse each realized that to create public demand for their radio receivers, they would have to provide regular broadcast service themselves. In September 1921

---

[6] For a much more detailed discussion of these corporate negotiations, including a description of AT&T's important role in this trade combination, see Sterling–Kittross, op.cit, pp. 53–58.

this service began, as the Department of Commerce starting issuing the nation's first regular broadcast licenses.

Yet, even before the first of these new stations went on the air, this two-decade history had already begun to determine the future status of broadcasting as a mass medium in the United States. The Radio Act of 1912 had been designed for communication common carriers; services that did not communicate themselves, but merely served as channels to deliver the messages of others.[7] As a very secondary service within this regulatory scheme, broadcasting was tolerated but never recognized as having any unique rights of its own as a communications medium.

The Act made access to the electromagnetic spectrum a privilege, subject to governmental approval. Those private radio services regulated under its provisions had no legal basis for challenging this type of federal control because as common carriers they were already subject to other similar regulatory constraints upon their operations.[8] Since experimental broadcasting was authorized under the same law, it was simply assumed that its privilege of operation was also dependent upon government approval, a position no small and disorganized band of radio amateurs was likely to challenge.

Thus, as the radio era was beginning in the United States, a precedent had already been established for making the broadcaster's right to communicate a conditional one, requiring a government license. At this point, however, the decision of whether or not to issue such a license was still being made solely on the basis of engineering criteria; deciding in each case whether the broadcast license application could be granted without creating an unacceptable level of interference with other existing radio services in the area in which it would be operating. This single

---

[7] This vital distinction between the rights and obligations of communication common carriers, such as telephone and telegraph companies, and broadcasters would not be drawn until 1927, when the Federal Radio Commission was granted authority over broadcasting, and the Department of Commerce retained authority only to regulate common carriers under an entirely different set of standards. Today, the Federal Communications Commission regulates both types of communication services, but under the different types of standards established in 1927.

[8] A "communications common carrier" at law is one who provides message delivery facilities for public use. Because most carriers, such as local telephone companies, exercise at least limited monopoly power over the service they offer, they are subject to regulation to ensure that they furnish this public access in a non-discriminatory manner, provide all necessary services, and establish reasonable rates for those services. In contrast, a broadcaster has no general obligation to provide either free or paid public access to the station's facilities. Instead, the broadcast licensee has complete editorial control over the content of each message transmitted and is legally responsible for the content of every message delivered to the public. These distinctions are reflected in the Communications Act of 1934, at Sections 153(b) and 153(h) that declare "a person engaged in radio communication shall not . . . be deemed to be a common carrier."

criterion for licensing did not pose any threat to the free speech rights of the broadcaster, but the precedent of licensing itself would soon serve as the basis for a much broader range of government controls.

SEC. 12. SPECTRUM SPACE: FROM CRISIS TO CONTROL

Unprepared for rapid growth of broadcasting, Congress was forced to react with regulatory legislation outdated by the time it was enacted.

RCA, Westinghouse and General Electric all applied for broadcast licenses in 1921, as did a number of other smaller radio manufacturers and retailers. By 1923, almost half (46%) of the radio stations on the air were being operated by radio manufacturers, dealers, or department stores selling radio receivers.[9] Except for its promotional value in marketing radio receivers, there was as yet no other financial incentive for providing broadcast service, because at the time it was still not considered to be appropriate to broadcast advertising messages.

As Secretary of Commerce Herbert Hoover told industry representative at the Third National Radio Conference in 1924,

> I believe that the quickest way to kill broadcasting would be to use it for direct advertising. The reader of the newspaper has an option whether he will read an ad or not, but if a speech by the President is to be used as the meat in a sandwich of two patent medicine advertisements, there will be no radio left.[10]

By 1926, however, this opposition had become less intense and stations were permitted to begin broadcasting commercials; although they were still discouraged from accepting advertising that described the qualities of a specific product or mentioned its selling price.

During this same period, another significant change was taking place in American broadcasting. When radio began in 1921, there were an estimated 60,000 radio receivers in the United States, or approximately one radio for every 500 American households. This broadcast audience of 1921 was still primarily one of radio experimenters, testing the sensitivity of their homemade receivers each evening by attempting to "pull in" as many different static-laden signals as possible from stations in distant states. By 1926, the typical household radio came encased in a handsome

[9] Sydney W. Head, Broadcasting in America, 2nd ed. New York, Houghton Mifflin, 1972, p. 137.

[10] Herbert Hoover at the Third National Radio Conference, October 6–10, 1924 as quoted in Sterling–Kittross, op. cit, p. 49.

wooden cabinet for display and use in the family livingroom. The set's storage battery had been replaced by a convenient wall plug, and its speaker allowed the entire family to listen to its favorite radio programs together every evening. By this time there were already 4.5 million radio households and by 1928, eight million, or more than 25% of all homes in the United States.[11]

Unfortunately, as the number of new American broadcast stations increased proportionately during this same era, it soon became impossible to prevent one station's transmissions from interfering with those of other radio stations using the same or even an adjacent frequency channel. When the Secretary of Commerce began issuing the broadcast licenses in 1921, only two different frequency channels were allocated to be used by every broadcast station in the nation.[12] In 1922, the Department of Commerce hurriedly added a third channel for broadcast service, and the following year, developed a far more comprehensive frequency allocation plan that set aside 73 new frequency channels exclusively for broadcast use. Yet, even though this new license assignment plan seemed well designed from an engineering standpoint to protect against future broadcast band interference, the Commerce Department's power to enforce the plan was dependent upon that very narrow base of regulatory authority it had been granted by the Radio Act of 1912.

Although the 30 radio stations using the broadcast spectrum in 1921 had swelled to 530 stations by 1924, Congress continued to disregard annual requests of the Secretary of Commerce to provide him the broader authority he needed to deal with this ever increasing problem of broadcast interference. As one scholar in this field suggests, Congress may have been reluctant to act because

> the nature of broadcasting had not yet been clearly defined, and it was difficult to pass a law to regulate an unknown quantity.[13]

Whatever the reason for this reluctance, the failure of Congress to revise the antiquated radiotelegraphy legislation soon placed the Commerce Department in a difficult position. When the Secretary of Commerce tried to enforce the Department's new broadcast frequency allocation plan by denying a license on the grounds of insufficient spectrum space to accommodate it, a feder-

[11] Sterling and Kittross, op.cit., p. 533.

[12] In September 1921, 833.3 Khz was the frequency to be used for all regular news and entertainment broadcast stations, while 618.6 Khz was set aside for broadcast of special government weather or crop information reports.

[13] Head, op.cit, p. 158.

al court could find nothing in the Radio Act of 1912 that gave him the right to make such a regulatory judgment.[14]

Despite the fact that this decision suggested quite clearly that the Department's license assignment plan was not legally enforceable, most major broadcast organizations continued to comply voluntarily with its provisions, realizing that it was in their best interests to do so. As Commerce Secretary Hoover pointed out to industry leaders at each of National Radio Conferences held between 1921 and 1925, broadcasting could continue to avoid direct governmental control only as long as self-regulation maintained an orderly, interference free broadcast service.

Unfortunately, self-regulation gave the radio industry no legal authority to compel any of its more than 500 licensed broadcasters to comply with Commerce Department directives, as Congress had given the Department no legal power to punish such noncompliance. As a result, the entire broadcast licensing and frequency assignment structure during this period had to rest upon the fragile hope that no broadcaster would ever compel the Commerce Department to rely upon the Radio Act of 1912 again as its only means of enforcing those regulatory policies the Department had adopted to solve the interference problems the industry had been experiencing.

That hope ended in 1926, and the voluntary licensing plan collapsed within a matter of months. Zenith Radio Corporation, a receiver manufacturer, had grown dissatisfied with the two hours a week it was authorized to broadcast on the frequency it was forced to share with several other stations in the Chicago area. Believing that it deserved the same type of broadcast license privileges that Westinghouse, General Electric, RCA and other radio industry competitors had been granted, Zenith reacted when the Commerce Department rejected its application to change frequencies by shifting to the frequency channel the Department had denied it. Although Secretary Hoover was reluctant to have the Commerce Department's licensing authority tested in federal court, there was really no other choice under these circumstances. The frequencies Zenith was using without permission had been reserved for Canadian stations by international agreement, an agreement that legally obligated the Department to protect those interests. In addition, after Zenith had defied the Commerce Department in this way, other stations announced their intention to follow its example.

As expected, when the Commerce Department tried to enforce its frequency assignment decision in federal court, the court found nothing in the Radio Act of 1912 that authorized its enforcement,

---

[14] Hoover v. Intercity Radio Company, 52 App.D.C. 339, 286 Fed. 1003 (1923).

or that permitted the Secretary of Commerce to do anything more than issue broadcast licenses upon request.[15] Required from this point onward simply to approve each broadcast application as submitted, the Department was forced to issue more than 200 new licenses during the remainder of 1926, creating an intolerable level of broadcast interference in urban areas throughout the United States.

Realizing that radio service under these conditions could not survive for long, leaders of broadcast industry themselves began demanding that broadcasting be regulated by the federal government. As the year 1926 was ending, even President Calvin Coolidge, never an ardent supporter of government control, was urging Congress to enact legislation to regulate broadcasting, justifying his position by pointing out that

> . . . many more stations have been operating than can be accommodated within the limited number of wave lengths available; further stations are now in the process of construction; many stations have departed from the scheme of allocation set down by the Commerce Department and the whole service of this most important public function has drifted into such chaos as seems likely, if not remedied, to destroy its great value.[16]

In March of the following year, Congress passed the Radio Act of 1927.[17] A new agency, the Federal Radio Commission, was created to administer the Act. Having failed in the past to provide the Commerce Department with the authority needed to protect the technical quality of broadcast transmissions, Congress now lurched in the opposite regulatory direction, granting the new Commission power not only over the engineering aspects of radio, but over the "public interest" qualities of broadcast programming as well. As the one of the co-authors of the new Radio Act declared at the time:

> We have reached the definite conclusion that the rights of our people to enjoy this means of communication can be preserved only by the repudiation of the idea underlying the 1912 law that anyone who will may transmit and by the assertion in its stead of the doctrine that the right of the public is superior to the right of any individual to use the airwaves.[18]

[15] United States v. Zenith Radio Corporation, 12 F.2d 614 (D.C.Ill.1926).

[16] As quoted in Frank J. Kahn (ed.) Documents of American Broadcasting (3d ed.) Englewood Cliffs, NJ; Prentice Hall, 1978, pp. 15–17.

[17] Public Law 632, 69th Congress.

[18] Senator Wallace H. White, as quoted by Commissioner Robert T. Bartley in FCC mimeo. 1336 (January 29, 1934).

Although the Act expressly prohibited censorship of broad-casting, it did officially empower an agency of the federal govern-ment to grant or revoke the right to communicate by radio on the basis of the quality of that communication.[19] While not as severe a constraint upon freedom of expression as actual censorship, this unique degree of governmental influence authorized over broad-cast free speech during the past six decades has resulted in all electronic mass media being relegated to a less privileged status in terms of constitutional protections, unable to assert that full range of First and Fourteenth Amendment rights recognized by the courts as properly belonging to the American press.

In the last analysis, broadcast self-regulation had failed pri-marily because Congress itself had failed to sense the growing popularity and importance of the broadcast medium before the problem of chaotic interference compelled immediate legislative action. If Congress had simply revised the obsolete Radio Act of 1912 to give the Secretary of Commerce the broadcast licensing the authority he had requested, it seems quite likely that the interference crisis of 1926 could have been averted.

In that sense, then, self-regulation actually may have worked too well, because in cooperating as effectively as it did with the Department of Commerce's licensing plan to reduce the degree of broadcast interference through the years, the radio industry al-lowed Congress to postpone and delay consideration of the federal government's proper role in the field of broadcast communication until it was too late for such a profound and complex question to be raised, much less answered.

SEC. 13. RATIONALIZING GOVERNMENT REGULATION

Although a number of arguments have been advanced to justify federal broadcast regulation, the judiciary has relied upon only one in affirming this right of govern-ment control, the rationale of spectrum scarcity.

The Federal Radio Commission began with the assumption that Congress had provided it with sufficient legal authority to regulate broadcast programming. As the agency declared in one of its first annual reports to Congress,

[19] Section 29 of the Radio Act of 1927 stated in part, "Nothing in this Act shall be understood or construed to give the licensing authority the power of censorship over the radio communication or signals transmitted by any radio station, and no regulation or condition shall be promulgated or fixed by the licensing authority which shall interfere with the right of free speech by means of radio communica-tion." This statutory provision was incorporated as Sec. 326 of the current broadcast law, The Communications Act of 1934.

The radio act specifies that the commission shall exercise no censorship over programs. Nevertheless, the kind of service rendered by a station must be a means of appraising its relative standing and must be considered by the commission in making assignments.[20]

In 1930 the Commission decided for the first time to refuse to renew a broadcast license solely on the basis of what it deemed to be programming not in the public interest. The broadcaster appealed, contending that allowing a federal agency to determine what was proper or permissible broadcast program content constituted a form of censorship clearly prohibited by the Radio Act.

The federal court disagreed, upholding the Commission's action by observing,

> There has been no attempt on the part of the commission to subject any part of appellant's broadcasting matter to scrutiny prior to its release. In considering the question whether the public interest, convenience or necessity will be served by a renewal of the applicant's license, the commission has merely exercised its undoubted right to take note of appellant's past conduct, which is not censorship.[21]

A second FRC denial of license renewal based primarily on inadequate broadcast programming performance was also sustained by a federal court the following year. In appealing the agency's action, the broadcaster invoked First Amendment as well as the non-censorship provision of the Radio Act, arguing that even if a federal licensing decision based upon the quality of broadcast communication was not "censorship" as defined by the Act, it was at least an unconstitutional abridgement of a broadcaster's right of freedom of expression.

Once again the court disagreed, upholding the agency's right to consider a broadcaster's past programming efforts in deciding whether to renew a broadcast license, and declaring that such a review of program content was

> . . . neither censorship nor prior restraint, nor is it a whittling away of the rights guaranteed by the First Amendment, or an impairment of their free exercise.[22]

In each of these cases, the Federal Radio Commission's position may have been strengthened by the fact that the broadcasters

[20] Federal Radio Commission, Third Annual Report (Washington: Government Printing Office, 1929) p. 3.

[21] KFKB Broadcasting Ass'n v. Federal Radio Commission, 47 F.2d 670 (D.C.Cir. 1931).

[22] Trinity Methodist Church, South v. Federal Radio Commission, 62 F.2d 850, 853 (D.C.Cir.1932).

involved were both rather notorious characters with long and well documented histories of using their stations for their own personal benefit. "Doc" Brinkley, owner of KFKB, was a diploma-mill physician who used the airwaves to sell his patent medicines and fabulous "goat gland" operation, guaranteed to rejuvenate the lagging sexual powers of older men, while Reverend Shuler, whose church owned the Trinity Methodist station, seemed to specialize in defaming public officials. Describing Shuler's conduct while on the air, the federal court said:[23]

> On one occasion he announced over the radio that he had certain damaging information against a prominent unnamed man which, unless a contribution (presumably to the church) of a hundred dollars was forthcoming, he would disclose. As a result he received contributions from several persons . . . He alluded slightingly to Jews as a race, and made frequent and bitter attacks on the Roman Catholic religion . . .

The FRC also may have been benefited to some extent in gaining judicial approval of its authority over broadcast program content from its special relationship with the federal court that reviewed its actions. The Court of Appeals for the District of Columbia was designated by statute to be the court to hear all appeals from FRC actions and during this period it seemed particularly willing to apply the doctrine of "judicial forbearance"; that is, not substituting its own judgment for that of the regulatory agency unless that agency decision was found to be clearly in error.[24]

It's important to note, however, that during this entire FRC era, the United States Supreme Court never had considered, much less affirmed, the authority of the government agency to evaluate the quality of broadcast programming in deciding whether an applicant would be granted the right to communicate with a broadcast audience.[25] In 1934, Congress replaced the FRC with the Federal Communications Commission, consolidating regulation of both broadcast and communication common carrier services in the same agency, but controlling each separately under different provisions of the Communications Act of 1934.[26]

In 1937, the FCC launched an investigation of broadcast networks to determine whether the virtual monopoly control they

[23] Ibid, at 852.

[24] See Don Le Duc, Thomas McCain, "The Federal Regulatory Commission in Federal Court: Origins of Broadcast Doctrines", Journal of Broadcasting, Fall 1970, pp. 393–410.

[25] The Trinity Methodist decision had been appealed, but the Supreme Court declined to review the lower court decision. 285 U.S. 599 (1933).

[26] Public Law 416, 73rd Congress, 1934.

exercised over the production and distribution of popular evening radio programming in the United States was in the public interest. In the FCC's view, these networks were using their programming power to force stations seeking to affiliate with them to delegate to the networks too much authority over each station's broadcast scheduling decisions.

In order to prevent these broadcasters from delegating to a network the power to determine a station's programming policies, the FCC adopted rules in 1941 that limited the amount of network broadcast time that any affiliate station could carry, and provided for the revocation of the broadcast license of any station that exceeded this limit.[27]

The networks challenged the Commission's new rule, alleging among other things that by establishing limitations in advance upon the amount of time a broadcast station could devote to any specific type of programming, the federal government was encroaching upon the First Amendment protected free speech rights of the broadcaster. Justice Felix Frankfurter, speaking for a unanimous Supreme Court, provided the first clear expression of the court's willingness to allow the federal government to establish and enforce programming standards in the field of broadcast speech.[28] Frankfurter wrote:[29]

> The question here is simply whether the Commission, by announcing that it will refuse licenses to persons who engage in specified network practices . . . is thereby denying such persons the constitutional right of free speech . . . The licensing system established by Congress in the Communications Act of 1934 was a proper exercise of its power over commerce. The standard it provided for the licensing of stations was the "public interest, convenience or necessity". Denial of a station license on that ground, if valid under the Act, is not a denial of free speech.

The underlying rationale for this position, Frankfurter explained, was that unlike other mass media, being allowed by government to broadcast was a privilege, not a right because,[30]

[27] CFR 47 §§ 3.101–3.108. The FCC was forced to impose these rules upon individual radio stations because the networks used telephone circuits rather than spectrum space to distribute their programming to affiliated stations, and therefore did not require a FCC issued broadcast license to operate.

[28] Although the decision was unanimous, Justices Black and Rutledge took no part in the consideration of this case.

[29] National Broadcasting et al. v. United States et al., 319 U.S. 190, 226–227, 63 S.Ct. 997, 1014 (1943).

[30] Ibid., at 213, 63 S.Ct. at 1008.

. . . its facilities are limited; they are not available to all who may wish to use them; the radio spectrum simply is not large enough to accommodate everybody.

In essence, then, the court held that by accepting the privilege of using the limited and valuable public resource of spectrum space, each broadcast licensee also assumed an obligation to exercise this privilege for the benefit of the public; an obligation the FCC had the authority to enforce on behalf of the public.

The Supreme Court did not return to this specific broadcast free speech question again for more than a quarter of a century, but when it finally did so in 1969, Justice White, speaking once more for a unanimous court, explained its "spectrum scarcity" justification for broadcast content control even more clearly and forcefully than it had been described in the earlier Supreme Court decision.[31]

Although broadcasting is clearly a medium afforded First Amendment interest, differences in the characteristics of new media justify differences in the First Amendment standards applied to them . . . When there are substantially more individuals who want to broadcast than there are frequencies to allocate, it is idle to posit an unabridgeable First Amendment right to broadcast comparable to the right of every individual to speak, write or publish . . . the people as a whole retain their interest in free speech by radio and their collective right to have the medium function consistently with the ends and purposes of the First Amendment. It is the right of the viewers and listeners, not the right of the broadcasters, which is paramount.

Scarcity of broadcast spectrum space remains the only legal justification for federal regulation of broadcast programming in the United States. Following the sensible judicial practice of phrasing exceptions to general legal rules as narrowly as possible, the federal courts have been unwilling to adopt any broader rationalization for this governmental role in media free speech than absolutely necessary, fearing that expanding the basis for media content control might encourage this uniquely threatening power to extend beyond its intended range.[32]

---

[31] Red Lion Broadcasting Co. v. FCC, 395 U.S. 367, 386–390, 89 S.Ct. 1794, 1805–1806 (1969).

[32] A number of other rationales have been suggested through the years for imposing content controls on broadcasting, while protecting other media from similar governmental constraints, including broadcasting's unique prevasiveness and influence upon our society, its unique accessibility to children in the home, and its status as the only medium operating under government license.

So long as broadcasting remained the dominant electronic mass medium in the United States, there was nothing particularly unfair about all regulatory authority being based upon the legal concept of scarcity of spectrum space. Broadcasters might complain about their "second class" mass communications status in comparison to the press, but at least all FCC regulations applied equally to every station competing for the same broadcast audience.

All this changed, however, when cable TV began for the first time to pose a serious competitive challenge to broadcasting in the late 1970s. Unlike broadcasting, cable TV systems did not require broadcast spectrum channels to deliver their programming, and so the FCC had no constitutional basis for imposing the same type of regulatory controls upon a cable system as it was imposing upon its broadcast competitor. Now, the issue was no longer simply whether broadcasters should enjoy the same degree of freedom of expression as the American press, but whether within the field of electronic media itself, radio and television, should be singled out by law as being the only forms of mass communication that remain subject to government content control.

SEC. 14. SPECTRUM SCARCITY AND EXPANDING NEW MEDIA CHANNELS

The federal government has moved toward deregulation largely because it seems inequitable to impose regulation upon certain forms of electronic media that cannot legally be imposed upon others.

Although the FCC never attempted to license cable TV operators, the agency did use its regulatory authority over those microwave systems cable TV required to import their television signals to dictate cable TV programming policies. The Commission's technique was simply to adopt rules prohibiting the use of microwave relay services by cable systems not conforming to the agency's programming standards. Since virtually every cable system needed those additional television channels from distant markets to attract subscribers, this indirect regulatory influence upon cable programming worked quite effectively.

In 1968 the Supreme Court was asked for the first time to consider whether the FCC could exert this type of influence over a communications medium Congress had not granted it legal authority to regulate directly. The court affirmed this authority, but suggested quite clearly that it's scope was limited.[33]

[33] United States v. Southwestern Cable Co., 392 U.S. 157, 88 S.Ct. 1994 (1968).

These is no need here to determine in detail the limits of the Commission's authority to regulate CATV. It is enough to emphasize that the authority we recognize today . . . is restricted to that reasonably ancilliary to the effective performance of the Commission's various responsibilities for the regulation of television broadcasting.

Four years later, in reviewing a FCC rule that required all major cable TV systems to originate one channel of television programming themselves, the Supreme Court, in a 5–4 decision, again affirmed the Commission, but with Chief Justice Burger's warning that such a cable programming requirement,[34]

strains the outer limits of even the open-ended and pervasive jurisdiction that has evolved by decisions of the Commission and the Courts.

That limit of judicial toleration was finally reached in 1979, when the Supreme Court reviewed FCC regulations requiring cable TV systems serving more than 3,500 subscribers to set aside certain system channels for public access programming. The cable operator argued that by denying the system the right to decide who should be allowed access to these channels, or how these channels should be programmed, the FCC had deprived cable TV of constitutionally protected editorial control over the nature of its programming services.

The Court agreed with this argument, but chose to overturn the cable TV access rules without considering their First Amendment implications. Instead, the Court found the rules to be unenforceable because they treated cable TV systems as communication "common carriers," forced to provide access to all, and Congress had not authorized the FCC to impose this type of communication obligation upon either broadcasting or cable.[35]

In 1977, a federal appeals court struck down FCC rules attempting to protect broadcasters from the competitive threat of cable delivered pay–TV services. In Home Box Office, Inc. v. Federal Communications Commission [36], the court found that Commission restrictions imposed upon the type of programming pay–TV could provide were not within the regulatory powers granted the agency by Congress. Although this finding in itself determined the outcome of the case, the court also discussed the

---

[34] United States v. Midwest Video Corp., 406 U.S. 649, 92 S.Ct. 1860 (1972).

[35] Federal Communications Commission v. Midwest Video Corp., 440 U.S. 689, 99 S.Ct. 1435 (1979). A communications "common carrier" is an organization such as a telephone or telegraph company in the business of conveying messages that others pay to have delivered.

[36] 567 F.2d 9 (D.C.Cir.1977).

broader First Amendment implications of such federal cable TV program regulation. In essence, it pointed out that while incidental constraints upon cable TV free speech might be permissable to achieve some broader electronic media policy objective, there was no reasonable justification for believing in this situation that pay–TV would siphon away the most popular programs from traditional broadcast services. As the court observed, "where the First Amendment is concerned, creation of such a rebuttable presumption of siphoning without clear record support is simply impermissible."

As the 1980s began, it was apparent that the federal courts were no longer sympathetic with FCC efforts to impose content controls of any kind upon cable TV systems. While the courts still chose to overturn Commission cable policies on the basis of these regulations exceeding the authority granted the agency by Congress, it was doubtful that any cable programming legislation Congress might adopt could actually withstand First Amendment challenge in the courts.

At this point, then, the FCC began moving in the opposite regulatory direction. Although as an agency of Congress, the Commission was compelled to continue to enforce all requirements imposed upon broadcasters by the Communications Act of 1934, the FCC started rescinding every radio and television rule of its own that no longer seemed justified by the less active regulatory role in broadcasting it intended to play in the future.

At the same time, the Commission began actively to encourage the development of other new electronic media, authorizing direct broadcast satellite (DBS), low power TV (LPTV) and multi-point, multi-channel distribution systems (MMDS) under standards much less stringent than those traditionally imposed upon broadcast license applicants.[37]

The underlying policy objective of both deregulation and new media system authorization has been to create such a vast electronic media marketplace of viewing and listening alternatives for American audiences that there will be no need for any further intervention on the part of the federal government to protect public interests in electronic mass communication. The Supreme Court has already acknowledged the impact such an electronic marketplace of ideas could have upon the traditional spectrum scarcity justification for broadcast regulation observation. Justice Brennan observed, in a footnote comment, that,[38]

[37] These systems and their regulation will be discussed in more detail in Chapter 10.

[38] Note 11, FCC v. League of Women Voters of California, 468 U.S. 364, 104 S.Ct. 3106 (1984).

The prevailing rationale for broadcast regulation based upon spectrum scarcity has come under increasing criticism in recent years. Critics . . . charge that with advent of cable and satellite technology, communities now have access to such a wide variety of stations that the scarcity doctrine is obsolete . . . We are not prepared, however, to reconsider our long standing approach without some signal from Congress or the FCC that technological developments have advanced so far that some revision of the system of broadcast regulation may be required.

Is the time approaching, then, when all legal distinctions between broadcasting and the press will be abolished? Will the rights of the "fourth" and "fifth" estates eventually merge, creating a single body of constitutionally protected mass communication freedom of expression?

SEC. 15. THE CONVERGENCE OF "BROADCAST" AND "PRESS" LAW

Technological advances have begun to blur traditional legal distinctions between "broadcast" and "press" mass communication functions.

When broadcast regulation began in the United States during the 1920s, the only obvious similarity between radio news program and the daily newspapers was the teletype machine they both relied upon for their national and international wire service stories. As far as news production and distribution was concerned, while the radio journalist simply read scripted news items transmitted through the electromagnetic spectrum, the press still relied upon the complex "hot-type" publishing process to produce the daily newspaper.[39]

Today, both broadcast and press journalists write their stories on CRT's (cathode ray tube) word processors linked to a central computer, and a newspaper like the *Wall Street Journal* is distributed nationally by satellite transmission of facsimile pages to local printing plants across the nation, where plates of every page are made and each issue of the *Journal* is then published for delivery to subscribers in that area of the country.

But what if these facsimile pages were relayed instead by satellite directly to every television household equipped to reproduce them, eliminating local publishing and distribution

---

[39] "Hot type" refers to producing images on paper by the complex and expensive process of setting them in molten lead, rather than recreating them photographically on paper. During that era, newspaper copy was typed, set in print by a linotype operator, proofed, made up into pages, mat molded, and then bundled as it rolled off the press to be shipped by truck for local delivery.

costs, and allowing immediate access to each news item in the paper as it was being transmitted? Would such a change in the method of delivering a newspaper also alter its First Amendment status as a communications medium?

Recent federal case law suggests that it could. The Commission has attempted on several occasions to exempt specialized spectrum services similar to this satellite newspaper relay network from its full range of traditional broadcast regulatory requirements, but federal courts have had difficulty finding any legal justification for such exemptions.

The problem for the courts is that Congress, through its Communications Act of 1934, has imposed specific regulatory obligations on each class of broadcast spectrum users that the FCC, as an agency of Congress, has no legal authority to modify or reduce.

In 1981, the Commission sought to encourage the growth of teletext service in the United States.[40] To stimulate its development, the FCC decided to minimize the program content responsibilities of those pioneering this service by exempting teletext from most of the political access requirements imposed on regular broadcasters.[41] In Telecommunications Research and Action Center v. FCC,[42] the court rejected this FCC action, finding no justification in the Communications Act for excusing this particular type of broadcast service from those general requirements Congress had imposed on all broadcasters.[43] Similarly, in National Association of Broadcasters v. FCC,[44] the court denied the Commission the right to exempt direct broadcast satellite opera-

[40] "Teletext" is an information service TV stations can provide to households with specially equipped receivers. The station transmits a continuing sequence of some 500 pages or frames of different news or information items, using a small portion of its television channel not needed for regular TV service, and each household can select from the index of pages provided the specific pages or frames of information they want to retain and read on their screens.

[41] In the Matter of Amendment of Parts 2, 73 and 76 of the Commission's Rules to Authorize the Transmission of Teletext by TV Stations, 53 RR 2d 1309 (1983). The FCC justified its exemptions by described teletext as being not a regular, but only an "ancilliary" broadcast service and therefore not requiring the full range of political content controls applied to broadcasting.

[42] 801 F.2d 501 (D.C.Cir.1986).

[43] The FCC was allowed to exempt teletext from Fairness Doctrine requirements, but that was only because the majority of the court found Fairness not to be a Congressionally imposed obligation.

[44] 740 F.2d 1190 (D.C.Cir.1984). Also see Telecommunications Research and Action Center v. FCC, 836 F.2d 1349 (D.C.Cir.1988) where an attempt by the Commission to exempt Instructional Television Fixed Service (ITFS) licenses from Congressionally mandated broadcast minority preference standards was also struck down by the court.

tors from ownership and political access requirements imposed on all other broadcast licensees.[45]

At the moment, then, it appears that a newspaper might well be transformed by law into a "broadcaster" by the simple act of deciding to distribute its pages directly to the subscriber through the broadcast spectrum, rather than leaving those identical pages imprinted on paper at the front door of the same household.

While this example might seem to illustrate how illogical law can be at times, what it really demonstrates is the difficulties that legal reasoning faces when distinctions that once were useful and sensible no longer are as beneficial or logical. During an era when only broadcasters delivered their messages through the spectrum, there may have been valid legal reasons for defining their communication rights differently from other media that did not use this public resource. But now as that area is coming to an end, we face a future, as one noted writer is this field has said where,[46]

> . . . the industries of print and the industries of telecommunications will no longer be kept apart by a fundamental difference in their technologies. The economic and regulatory problems of the electronic media will thus become the problems of the print media too . . . The issues that concern telecommunications are now becoming issues for all communications as they all become forms of electronic processing and transmission.

But even though media technology may merge in time to blur traditional differences between broadcasting and the press, that time has not yet come. The American legal system continues to recognize these traditional distinctions, and so broadcasting remains a special area in this field, still isolated from the main body of mass communication law.

Communication by broadcasting remains a government granted privilege, thereafter dependent upon continued governmental approval for its exercise. A federal agency retains the authority to impose conditions upon this right, limiting the a broadcaster's

---

[45] Recently, however, in National Ass'n for Better Broadcasters v. FCC, 849 F.2d 665 (D.C.Cir.1988), at least one panel of DC Court of Appeal judges did affirm an FCC regulatory finding that broadcast spectrum transmissions not intended for the general public (such as encoded pay-TV transmissions) could be legally classified as "non-broadcast" services, and thereby exempted from regulations that Congress had designed solely for regular broadcasters. See also, Subscription Video, 62 RR2d 389 (1987), the rule-making proceeding in which the Commission first proposed this legal distinction between broadcast transmissions intended for the general public, and those services intended only for that segment of the public willing to pay for them.

[46] Ithiel de Sola Pool, On Free Speech in An Electronic Age: Technologies of Freedom, (Cambridge: Harvard University Press, 1983) p. 42.

freedom of expression, and the government reserves to itself the power to decide whether quality of that broadcast communication merits a continuation of the privilege to communicate.

For this reason, then, while it is important to be aware of that powerful technologically driven movement toward media convergence that is almost certain to exert an ever increasing influence upon basic principles of broadcast and electronic media law in the future, it is at least equally important to understand the actual regulatory environment in which these media are still operating today.

Part II

MASS COMMUNICATIONS LAW AND THE CITIZEN

Chapter 4

DEFAMATION: LIBEL AND SLANDER

Sec.
16. Defamation Defined.
17. The Five Elements of Libel.
18. Libelous Words Classified.
19. Opinion and Rhetorical Hyperbole.
20. Emotional Distress and Mental Anguish.
21. The Form of the Libel.
22. Broadcast Defamation.
23. Extrinsic Circumstances, Libel Per Se, and Libel Per Quod.
24. Damages.

SEC. 16. DEFAMATION DEFINED

Defamation is communication which exposes persons to hatred, ridicule, or contempt, lowers them in the esteem of others, causes them to be shunned, or injures them in their business or calling. Its categories are libel—broadly, printed, written or broadcast material—and slander—broadly, spoken words of limited reach.

Brace yourselves. The next three chapters are intended to serve as lessons in self-defense for persons working in mass communications fields. These chapters deal with defamation, the term which includes the "twin torts" of libel and slander. Chances are good that if you work in as a journalist that you will be sued for defamation, which the law classifies as a tort, a civil wrong other than breach of contract for which the legal remedy is a court action for monetary damages.[1]

Chances of being sued are substantial, for one thing, because there are so many lawyers in the United States. By 1992, the United States had more than two-thirds of all the lawyers in the world, more than 800,000. And lawyers litigate. Back in 1987, Americans filed lawsuits at the rate of 15 million a year, roughly one for every sixteen of us. Understandably, libel and invasion of

[1] William L. Prosser, The Law of Torts (St. Paul: West Publishing Co., 1964) 3d ed., 2. For another enduring work on defamation, see Robert Sack, Libel, Slander, and Related Problems (New York: Practising Law Institute, 1980).

privacy lawsuits are on the rise. The average cost of defending a libel suit may run as high as $100,000 or even $150,000, and that refers only to legal costs and not to money paid out in a lost lawsuit. And litigation that might sting a large newspaper or radio station or its insurance company could ruin a small media outfit.

Although more attention to fair play and ethical considerations might well stave off many of the libel suits now brought against the media, a free society by its nature is going to allow communication which harms many reputations. Freedom, after all, is a risk. Although society has a strong interest in the free flow of information, there is also a societal stake in allowing protection of one's reputation.

This chapter deals with the basics of libel: It discusses its elements to alert you to situations in which a problem might arise. The next chapter talks about the constitutional defense to libel growing out of 1964's New York Times v. Sullivan landmark and about older, more traditional defenses to libel under state law.

Protecting one's reputation and society's strong interest in providing such protection justify libel suits. As Supreme Court Justice Potter Stewart said, an individual's right to the protection and comfort of his own good name "reflects no more than our basic concept of the essential dignity and worth of every human being—a concept at the root of any decent system of ordered liberty." [2] At the same time, First Amendment values—freedom, an informed citizenry, and media that serve as a check on government—justify strong defenses against the suit. "It is important to safeguard First Amendment rights; it is also important to give protection to a person who is defamed, and to discourage * * * defamation in the future. A balance must be struck." [3]

This "balancing," however, is not an exact process. The late William L. Prosser, long considered America's leading torts scholar, expressed this disenchanted view: [4]

> It must be confessed . . . that there is a great deal of the law of defamation which makes no sense. It contains anomalies and absurdities for which no legal writer ever has had a kind word, and it is a curious compound of a strict liability imposed upon innocent defendants . . . with a blind and almost perverse refusal to compensate the plaintiff for real and very serious harm.

[2] Rosenblatt v. Baer, 383 U.S. 75, 92, 86 S.Ct. 669, 679 (1966).

[3] Maheu v. Hughes Tool Co., 569 F.2d 459, 480 (9th Cir.1977).

[4] Prosser, Law of Torts, 4th ed. (1971), at p. 737.

As a distinguished study asserted in 1987, the law of libel aims at one thing and hits another. This study, entitled Libel Law and the Press: Myth and Reality, noted that the law assumes that by suing, plaintiffs whose reputations have been injured can somehow be made whole by receiving money. That study found, however, that plaintiffs tend to be more interested in correction of falsity and in "setting the record straight." [5]

Damages justly termed "staggering" by the Libel Defense Resource Center, are often returned by juries, whose multi-million-dollar awards to plaintiffs ($40 million in one case) are nearly always drastically reduced by judges, but which, nevertheless, in one case finally totalled $3.05 million. In addition, attorneys' fees may be even greater than such an award. In one extraordinary case of 1985, costs to *Time* magazine were estimated as $3 million for its successful defense; and in another—arguably the most-publicized libel case in the nation's history—one estimate was $8 million in legal costs for both sides, although the plaintiff dropped his suit before it reached the jury. Such prospects may lead media to avoid the huge costs of defending a drawn-out trial by settling out of court—for $800,000 in case of a 1984 agreement by the *Wall Street Journal.*[6]

Today's defamation law carries with it much ancient historical baggage. If it is hard to understand today, chalk that up to its past. Defamation traced a tortuous course through the medieval and early modern courts of England. Feudal and then ecclesiastical (church) courts had jurisdiction over libel as a crime before libel moved haltingly into the common law courts, where people would sue for "damages" (money) for injury to their reputations. Difficulties arose, for example, when printing became more common. Then it seemed important to separate damage done by the spoken word (slander), which was fleeting, from damage done by the printed word, which might be more harmful because it was permanent and more widely diffused than speech. Rules that made sense several centuries ago turned into confusing anachronisms that lived on into the age of television and communication satellites.[7]

In bringing defamation substantially under the U.S. Constitution, the landmark *Sullivan* decision was one factor that tended to wipe out a major complicating element in the law as applied to

[5] Randall P. Bezanson, Gilbert Cranberg, and John Soloski, Libel Law and the Press: Myth and Reality (New York: The Free Press, 1987).

[6] Sharon v. Time, Inc., Time, Feb. 4, 1985, 64; Westmoreland v. CBS, New York Times, Feb. 19, 1985, 1, Feb. 20, 1985, 13; 10 Med.L.Rptr. # 25, 6/19/84, News Notes, citing LDRC Report of July 29, 1984.

[7] Prosser, 2nd ed. 754, 769; John Kelly, "Criminal Libel and Free Speech," 6 Kans.L.Rev. 295 (1958); Anon., "Developments in the Law, Defamation," 69 Harv. L.Rev. 875 (1956).

media: the division of defamation into libel (written defamation) and slander (spoken). Because radio broadcasting was speech, some states considered broadcast defamation to be slander; because it relied on written scripts, other states called it libel; because in combining slander and libel rules for broadcasting, one court was persuaded that a new name was called for, a judicial flyer into creative linguistics produced the name "defamacast." [8] *Sullivan*—the New York Times v. Sullivan case discussed in Section 26—treated the matter as libel, and where *Sullivan* applied, states were to follow suit.

Meanwhile, the prestigious American Law Institute (ALI) resolved the question for its followers by emphasizing the extensive harm that a defamatory broadcast to thousands or millions could do to a reputation. It followed, said ALI, that the more severe penalties of libel should result from broadcast defamation, rather than the lesser ones of slander which had been shaped centuries before to compensate for unenhanced oral denigration to small audiences. Thus the ALI said: "* * * defamation by any form of communication that has the potentially harmful qualities characteristic of written or printed words is to be treated as libel." [9]

The ALI pronouncement that libel should encompass broadcasting was by no means the first time that adjustments in the law had attached "libel" to varied media of communication. Before broadcasting, the Twentieth Century had produced motion pictures, and they had rather early been ruled to be libelous, if defamatory. Long before movies arrived—at least as early as the celebrated case of People v. Croswell in 1804—pictures and signs were included within libel. [10]

The most-used definition of libel is that it is a false statement about an individual which exposes him to "hatred, ridicule, or contempt, or which causes him to be shunned, or avoided, or which has a tendency to injure him in his office, profession or trade." [11] While that definition takes in a wide reach of words, it is nevertheless probably too narrow. Courts recognize mental anguish and personal humiliation as the bases of libel. Prosser pointed

[8] D.H. Remmers, "Recent Legislative Trends in Defamation by Radio," 64 Harv. L.Rev. 727, 1951; Prosser, 2nd ed. 754, 769–81; Grein v. La Poma, 54 Wash.2d 844, 340 P.2d 766 (1959); American Broadcasting-Paramount Theaters, Inc. v. Simpson, 106 Ga.App. 230, 126 S.E.2d 873 (1962).

[9] Restatement, Second, Torts, Vol. 3, 182. Some states have abolished the distinction between libel and slander, e.g. Illinois: Brown & Williamson Tobacco Corp. v. Jacobson, 713 F.2d 262 (7th Cir.1983), 9 Med.L.Rptr. 1936, 1939. But see Nevada Broadcasting Co. v. Allen (Nev.Sup.Ct.1982), 9 Med.L.Rptr. 1770.

[10] Movies: Youssoupoff v. Metro-Goldwyn-Mayer Pictures, 51 L.Q.Rev. 281, 99 A.L.R. 864 (1934); Pictures: People v. Croswell, 3 Johns Cases 337 (N.Y.1804).

[11] Sir Hugh Fraser, Libel and Slander (London: 1936), 7th ed., p. 3; Perry v. Columbia Broadcasting System, Inc., 499 F.2d 797 (7th Cir.1974).

out that words which would cause most people to sympathize with the target have been held defamatory, such as an imputation of poverty, or the statement that a woman has been raped.[12] If a person is lowered in the estimation or respect of the community, he is not necessarily hated, held in contempt, or shunned.

To have definitions such as the above is by no means always to be able to predict what will be held libelous. The legal axiom which says that "every definition in the law is dangerous" most certainly applies to defamation. Whether words are defamatory depends, in part, on the temper of the times and current public opinion; "words harmless in one age, in one community, may be highly damaging to reputation at another time or * * * place."[13] While it was probably not defamation to falsely call one a Communist in the 1930s, several later cases have found the appellation libelous.[14]

It must be understood that in a suit where it is shown that the plaintiff has been libeled—money damages are not necessarily awarded. There are various circumstances in which the law protects media against liability for libeling. Chapter 5 is devoted to the defenses that furnish these protections.

Anyone who is living may be defamed—unless that person is so notorious as a criminal as to be "libel-proof" and courts will not accept that person's libel action—[15] and so may a corporation or partnership where its business standing or practices are impugned. A voluntary association organized for purposes not connected with profit or the self-interest of the organizers also may be defamed.[16] However, it is not possible for one to be defamed through an insult or slur upon someone close to him, such as a member of his family.[17] Nor can a dead person be defamed,[18] nor

[12] Time, Inc. v. Firestone, 424 U.S. 448, 96 S.Ct. 958 (1976); Prosser, 2nd ed. p. 756.

[13] Mencher v. Chesley, 297 N.Y. 94, 75 N.E.2d 257 (1947).

[14] Spanel v. Pegler, 160 F.2d 619 (7th Cir.1947); Levy v. Gelber, 175 Misc. 746, 25 N.Y.S.2d 148 (1941); Gertz v. Robert Welch, Inc., 418 U.S. 323, 94 S.Ct. 2997 (1974).

[15] Cardillo v. Doubleday & Co., Inc., 518 F.2d 638 (2d Cir.1975).

[16] Americans for Democratic Action v. Meade, 72 Pa.D. & C. 306 (1951); New York Society for the Suppression of Vice v. MacFadden Publications, Inc., 129 Misc. 408, 221 N.Y.S. 563 (1927), affirmed 222 App.Div. 739, 226 N.Y.S. 870 (1928); Mullins v. Brando, 13 Cal.App.3d 409, 91 Cal.Rptr. 796 (1970); Friends of Animals, Inc. v. Associated Fur Manufacturers, Inc., 46 N.Y.2d 1065, 416 N.Y.S.2d 790, 390 N.E.2d 298 (1979), 4 Med.L.Rptr. 2503.

[17] Gonzales v. Times Herald Printing Co., 513 S.W.2d 124 (Tex.Civ.App.1974); Wildstein v. New York Post Corp., 40 Misc.2d 586, 243 N.Y.S.2d 386 (1963); Security Sales Agency v. A.S. Abell Co., 205 Fed. 941 (D.Md.1913); but "daughter of a murderer" has been held libelous: Van Wiginton v. Pulitzer Pub. Co., 218 Fed. 795 (8th Cir.1914).

[18] McBeth v. United Press International, Inc., 505 F.2d 959 (5th Cir.1974). But see Canino v. New York News, Inc., 96 N.J. 189, 475 A.2d 528 (1984), 10 Med.L. Rptr. 1852, where a libel action filed before death did not abate at death.

in most circumstances a group. A government entity, such as the city of Philadelphia, cannot bring a civil libel action.[19]

Large groups such as business executives in general, or labor, or a political party, or all the Muslims of the world, or an ethnic group of a large city, cannot sue for libel. When, however, a defamatory statement is leveled against a small group, each member may be considered by the law to be libeled, and the individuals may bring separate suits even though no one has been singled out. It is by no means clear what the upper limit of a "small group" might be.

SEC. 17. THE FIVE ELEMENTS OF LIBEL

The plaintiff in a libel suit must plead that there was Publication, Identification, Defamation, Fault and Injury.

Potential libel suit defendants—and that includes all of us—need to know (as do lawyers filing libel suits) that five conditions must be present before a suit can hope to succeed. (This discussion assumes that the action for defamation will have been filed in a timely fashion to conform to the deadline set by the state where the suit is filed: the *statute of limitations*. In most states, the statute of limitations is one year after publication, and in most others two or three years.)[20]

The five necessary conditions for suit are:

1. Publication
2. Identification
3. Defamation
4. Fault
5. Injury

Publication

Publication means circulation of a statement. It may be in printed, written form, or, in the case of broadcasting and movies, oral. Even signs or statues may qualify as a form of publication.

The first of the five allegations the party filing a libel suit must consider is that the derogatory statement was published.

---

[19] City of Philadelphia v. Washington Post Co., 482 F.Supp. 897 (E.D.Pa.1979), 5 Med.L.Rptr. 2221.

[20] Half of the states—any states not listed here plus the District of Columbia—have a one-year statute of limitations. States with two-year statutes include Alabama, Alaska, Connecticut, Delaware, Hawaii, Idaho, Indiana, Iowa, Maine, Minnesota, Missouri, Montana, Nevada, North Dakota, South Carolina, South Dakota, Washington, and Wisconsin. Arkansas, Massachusetts, New Hampshire, and Vermont's limitations are three years, and the Florida statute of limitations is four years. Oddly, the Tennessee statute of limitations is six months for slander but one year for libel.

Publication can occur only if it is made to the person defamed and one other person. A communication can't harm a reputation unless it is spread to at least one person besides the target. Although the mass media ordinarily publish to huge audiences, it is worth remembering that no more than a "third person" need to be involved for publication to take place. In one case, a man dictated a letter to his secretary accusing the addressee of grand larceny. The secretary typed the letter and it was sent through the mail. The letter's recipient brought a successful libel suit: the court held that publication took place at the time the stenographic notes were read and transcribed.[21]

For the printed media, courts of most states call the entire edition carrying the alleged libel one publication. That is, an over-the-counter sale of back copies of a newspaper weeks or months after they were first printed would not constitute further publication. That is known as the "single publication rule." [22] Where this is not the rule, there is a chance that a plaintiff can stretch the statute of limitations indefinitely, perhaps by claiming a separate publication in a newspaper's selling a February issue the following December. In Tocco v. Time, Inc., it was held that the publication takes place at the time a magazine is mailed to subscribers, or put in the hands of those who will ship the edition to wholesale distributors.[23] That approach, however, is not universally accepted. To the contrary, Osmers v. Parade Publications, Inc., stated that a publication date is when the libel was "substantially and effectively communicated to a meaningful mass of readers—the public for which the publication was intended, not some small segment of it." [24]

Identification

To bring a successful libel action—once publication has been established—a plaintiff must also demonstrate that he or she was *identified* in the alleged libel. Plaintiffs must show that the statement complained about refers to them.

Most of the time, the identification is obvious. A plaintiff's name or picture is used, right along with the statements claimed to be defamatory. But sometimes identification may occur in a less direct way: in one case, a camera shop answered a competitor's ads with these words:

[21] Ostrowe v. Lee, 256 N.Y. 36, 175 N.E. 505 (1931). See also Arvey Corp. v. Peterson, 178 F.Supp. 132 (E.D.Pa.1959).

[22] Sack, op. cit., p. 91.

[23] 195 F.Supp. 410 (E.D.Mich.1961).

[24] 234 F.Supp. 924, 927 (S.D.N.Y.1964).

USE COMMON SENSE * * *
You Get NOTHING for NOTHING!
WE WILL NOT

1. Inflate the prices of your developing to give you a new roll free!

2. Print the blurred negatives to inflate the price of your snapshots!

The Cosgrove Studio sued for libel, claiming that ad implied Cosgrove used dishonest business practices. In upholding a damage award for Cosgrove, a Pennsylvania appeals court made an important point: Identification of the defamed need not be by name. "A party need not be specifically named, if pointed to by description or circumstances tending to identify him," the court held.[25]

Cautious journalists check and double-check identifications and addresses. All too frequently, publication of a typographical error, wrong initials, or an incorrect address may result in a totally unintended identification. Such a slip-up by a careless editor or reporter can falsely link an innocent person with a crime, or immorality, or unethical business conduct that forms the basis for a libel suit.

Some libel cases may instill caution bordering on paranoia. Special care is indicated, for example, in those unusual circumstances where a publication wishes to do a story about a person endeavoring to cope with a socially stigmatized condition such as AIDS or cocaine addiction. It might be the publication decides that the story needs to be told, but that it can be reported only if the source's request not to be identified is honored. If a fictitious name is used to mask identity, ethically that should be made clear in the story. Take care, however, that the "fictitious" identity does not somehow identify some real-life individual.

In a famed English case, E. Hulton & Co. v. Jones,[26] the *Sunday Chronicle* had published a story from a correspondent in France about a supposedly fictitious person named Artemus Jones. He had been seen, the story said, keeping company with a woman who was not his wife. The Chronicle soon learned, through the filing of a libel suit, that there was a *real* Artemus Jones. Jones told the court that some of his friends believed the story was about him. It was found that the identification was sufficient for Jones, a lawyer, to collect damages of £1750.

---

[25] Cosgrove Studio & Camera Shop, Inc. v. Pane, 408 Pa. 314, 182 A.2d 751 (1962). See also Grove v. Dun & Bradstreet, Inc., 438 F.2d 433 (3d Cir.1971), and Dictaphone Corp. v. Sloves (N.Y.Sup.1980), 6 Med.L.Rptr. 1114.

[26] A.C. 20, 1909, 2 K.B. 444 (1910).

In a far more recent case in the United States, Springer sued Viking Press for libel, complaining that she was identifiable to friends as the model for a prostitute in a novel written by Tine, a former friend. The book, Ms. Springer claimed, described the prostitute's physical characteristics as highly similar to her own. Both Ms. Springer and the fictional prostitute lived on the same street in Manhattan, she said, and both received gifts of a diamond and a necklace from a boyfriend, both spoke fluent French and dated Iranian men.

A New York court said that there was similarity between Ms. Springer and the fictional prostitute, and refused to grant Viking Press's motion to dismiss the libel suit.[27]

Identification cannot be established by a person who says that an attack on a large heterogeneous group libels her because she happens to belong to it. To suggest some examples, derogatory statements about a political party, an international labor union, the Presbyterian Church, or the Rotary Club do not identify individuals so as to allow them to bring a libel action.

If, however, the attack is on a small sub-group of an organization, that's quite different. Suppose a defamatory attack is made on the directors of the Smithjones County Democratic Party, on the officers of a labor union (whether it be a national or local unit), or the presiding elders of a church, or on the civic club's officers. Then, each individual member of the attacked sub-group may be able to establish identification—even though his or her name was not used—and bring suit.

A sleazy book—*U.S.A. Confidential*—resulted in the often cited—and often misinterpreted—case known as Neiman–Marcus Co. v. Lait. That case set down these guidelines:

(1) Where the group or class libeled is large, none can sue even though the language used is inclusive.

(2) When the group or class libeled is small, and each and every member of the group or class is referred to, then any individual member can sue.

(3) That while there is a conflict in authorities where the publication complained of libeled some or less than all of a designated small group, the federal court ruling in the Neiman–Marcus case said it would allow such an action.

Those guidelines were drawn from a garish fact situation. Authors Jack Lait and Lee Mortimer claimed in *U.S.A. Confidential* that swingers looking for a "good time" need look no further in Dallas than that city's famed department store, Neiman–Marcus. The book's chapter on Dallas asserted that all of the store's

---

[27] Springer v. Viking Press (N.Y.Sup.1980), 7 Med.L.Rptr. 2040.

models (there were nine) were prostitutes, the highest-paid in town. The book also said that the "nucleus of the Dallas fairy colony" was in the Neiman–Marcus men's store (which had 25 salesmen). Finally, these fearless authors declared that the store's "salesgirls" (there were 382) were prostitutes too, cheaper and more fun than the models.[28]

In applying these rules to the facts, the court dismissed the lawsuits of the saleswomen (382 was simply too large a group to have identification take place), but allowed the suits of the models and the salesman.

But please note what the Neiman–Marcus case did NOT say. It did not say that if a group is larger than 25, you can publish anything you want about that group. In point of cold legal fact, identification has been held to take place when an unnamed person was a member of defamed groups with memberships as high as 53.[29] Despite ill-considered suggestions to the contrary, then, 25 is not a magic number.

Defamation

Is the publication or broadcast defamatory? The third necessary allegation asserts that the statement indeed did defame. That says in effect that the words injured reputation, or, in some circumstances, caused emotional distress. Plaintiffs must assert that defamation occurred, although—as with the elements of publication and identification—they may not be able to prove defamation at trial.

The court decides whether a publication is libelous *per se* (by itself). But when the words complained of can have two meanings—one innocent and the other damaging—it is for the jury to decide in what sense the words were understood by the audience. Both judge and jury, in their interpretation of the statement claimed to be defamatory, should give language its common and ordinary meaning.[30]

[28] 107 F.Supp. 96 (S.D.N.Y.1952); 13 F.R.D. 311 (1952).

[29] See Brady v. Ottaway Newspapers, Inc., 84 A.D.2d 226, 445 N.Y.S.2d 786 (1981), 8 Med.L.Rptr. 1671, where a plaintiff policeman who was a member of a group of 53 unnamed policemen was not barred from bring a libel suit. Courts also have held that members of a jury can be defamed [Byers v. Martin, 2 Colo. 605 (1875)]; all four officers of a labor union [De Witte v. Kearney & Trecker Corp., 265 Wis. 132, 60 N.W.2d 748 (1953)]. Another court, however, has held that a libel action would not work against a magazine which attacked all distributors of the controversial anti-cancer drug laetrile [Schuster v. U.S. News & World Report, Inc., 602 F.2d 850 (8th Cir.1979), 5 Med.L.Rptr. 1773.] Also, a newspaper was ruled not to have identified individuals when 21 individuals of a town police department sued following publication of a printed rumor about one unidentified officer. Arcand v. Evening Call Pub. Co., 567 F.2d 1163 (1st Cir.1977).

[30] Peck v. Coos Bay Times Pub. Co., 122 Or. 408, 259 P.2d 307, 311 (1927); Prosser, 4th ed., p. 746.

Fault

A fourth element of libel that the aggrieved person must allege and persuasively demonstrate is "fault" on the part of the publisher or broadcaster.

"Fault" is part of the complex legal geometry which has developed in the aftermath of New York Times Co. v. Sullivan (1964) [31]. Journalists need to know about courts' renditions of just what "fault" is, but they should also know that this is lawyer's territory. Journalists without law degrees and a real specialty in communication law should not bet their employers' money and their careers on knowing what "fault" means in a given time and place (libel laws do vary from state to state and time to time).

The concept of fault is taken up in depth in Chapter 5. Suffice it to say here that the cases growing out of New York Times v. Sullivan (1964) have added up to some squirmy, stretchy "rules" about determining fault. As will be seen in Chapter 5, "public officials" or "public figures" who claim that they have been injured by a defamatory falsehood have to meet a tough standard of proof called "actual malice."

"Actual malice" as defined in New York Times v. Sullivan meant that public officials (and added later in other cases, public figures) would have to prove that the libel was published ". . . with knowledge that it was false or with reckless disregard of whether it was false or not." [32]

It should be evident that such a standard gives the press a very large benefit of the doubt; it is difficult for a public person to prove that the news organization knew something was false, for example. Private persons—that is, people who are not classed as public officials or public figures by a court—have to meet a lesser, easier standard of proof. They have to prove only that the defamation complained of was negligently published, or published without the "due care" that would be used by an "average person of ordinary sensibilities." [33] But as is discussed in some detail in Chapter 5, courts have not sent clear signals about just who is or is not a "public official" or "public figure."

Because clear guidelines are not available, journalists should not take it upon themselves to decide close calls about who is a "public official" or a "public figure." That suggests that deadline-

[31] 376 U.S. 254, 84 S.Ct. 710 (1964).

[32] 376 U.S. 254, 279–80, 84 S.Ct. 710, 725 (1964).

[33] See Gertz v. Welch, Inc., 418 U.S. 323, 94 S.Ct. 2997 (1974); see also Black's Law Dictionary.

time discussions such as the following hypothetical conversation should not happen.

> Rather Nott, Reporter: "It's a great story, but the competition is on to it too. We've got to get it published. I can't get at any other sources until tomorrow."

> Molly Typo, Editor: "Let's go with it on Page 1. After all, the persons we're writing about are well known here. They're public figures. And two of them used to serve on the school board."

Perhaps the old Associated Press motto should be repeated to Mr. Nott and Ms. Typo: "Get it first, but get it right." Beyond that, the reporter and editor had better get some expert advice—and no doubt the blessing of their bosses—before proceeding to publish. How good are the sources and the evidence assembled so far? And would a court be likely to say that the people to be written about are "public figures?" It takes more than an offhand newsroom guess to make someone into a public figure. A knowledgeable attorney should be able to make a better guess (and it may be just that). In any case, the newsroom folks ought to be aware, for example, that the Texas Supreme Court declared an elected county surveyor to be a private figure.[34] And that a jet-setter with a nationally famous last name was a private figure, said the U.S. Supreme Court, even though she gave news conferences during her divorce trial.[35]

In summary, a public official or public figure must show evidence that the fault of the news medium amounted to *actual malice:* knowledge that the communication was false or reckless disregard as to its truth or falsity. A private individual who sues for libel must bring evidence that the fault amounted at least to *negligence* by the news medium. In the absence of some evidence of the appropriate level of fault, a libel suit will no more "stick" (be accepted for trial) than if there is no publication, identification, or defamation. Many courts have rejected libel suits and discharged them without trial (granted "summary judgment" to the defendant) for this defect. Fault and summary judgment will be treated further in Chapter 5.

"Actual Injury"

Finally, there is the fifth element that needs to be pleaded by a plaintiff in a libel suit: "actual injury." The private-person plaintiff must demonstrate loss or reputational injury of some

---

[34] Foster v. Laredo Newspapers, Inc., 19 TX S.Ct.Jrnl. 390, 541 S.W.2d 809 (1976), cert. denied 429 U.S. 1123, 97 S.Ct. 1160 (1977).

[35] Time, Inc. v. Firestone, 424 U.S. 448, 96 S.Ct. 958 (1976).

kind. Actual injury may include a showing in court of out-of-pocket money loss, of impairment of reputation and standing in the community, of personal humiliation, and of mental anguish and suffering, as the Supreme Court of the United States said in Gertz v. Robert Welch, Inc.[36]

SEC. 18. LIBELOUS WORDS CLASSIFIED

Five categories or kinds of words may be identified in organizing the field of libel. (Libel also may be classified according to libel *per se*, or words defamatory on their face; and libel *per quod*, or words defamatory when facts extrinsic to the story make them damaging. See Sec. 23.)

Danger signals to help journalists avoid libel can be raised by grouping the kinds of statements and the circumstances which have brought suits into classes. A study of reported libel cases found that the large majority of accusations by plaintiffs were that they had been falsely accused of "crime, moral failings, and incompetence in trade or profession." [37] In the following pages, five categories are used to help clarify that which can bring hatred, ridicule, contempt, loss of esteem, humiliation, or damage in one's trade or profession.

1. Damage to the Esteem or Social Standing in Which One Is Held

Of the various ways in which a person may be lowered in the estimation in which he is held, none has brought as many libel suits as a false charge of crime. The news media cover the police and crime beat daily; the persistent possibility of a mistake in names and addresses is never absent. And the courts hold everywhere that it is libel to charge one erroneously with a crime. It is easy to get a libel case based on such a charge into court, even though it has become harder to win it under court doctrine of the 1960s, 1970s, and 1980s.

Thus to print falsely that a person is held in jail on a forgery charge,[38] or to say incorrectly that one has illicitly sold or distributed narcotics,[39] is libelous on its face. To say without legal

---

[36] 418 U.S. 323, 348–350, 94 S.Ct. 2997, 3011–3012.

[37] Marc Franklin, Winners and Losers and Why: a Study of Defamation Litigation, Am. Bar Foundation Research Journ. 1980, Summer, 499.

[38] Oklahoma Pub. Co. v. Givens, 67 F.2d 62 (10th Cir.1933); Barnett v. Schumacher, 453 S.W.2d 934 (Mo.1970).

[39] Snowden v. Pearl River Broadcasting Corp., 251 So.2d 405 (La.App.1971).

excuse that one made "shakedown attempts" on elected officers,[40] or committed bigamy,[41] perjury,[42] or murder [43] is libelous.

There is no substitute as a protection against libel suits for the ancient admonition to the reporter: "Accuracy always." [44] Failure to check one more source of information before writing a story based upon a plausible source has brought many libel suits.

The *Saturday Evening Post* published a story titled "They Call Me Tiger Lil" in its Oct. 26, 1963 issue. The subject was Lillian Reis Corabi, a Philadelphia night club owner and entertainer. The article connected her in various ways with murder and theft, quoting a police captain as saying she and others were responsible for a death by dynamite, and in other ways connecting her with burglary and an apparent drowning. The *Post* argued that the words complained of were not defamatory, but the Pennsylvania Supreme Court upheld the trial judge in his finding some 18 paragraphs of the article "capable of defamatory meaning." It defined defamation as that which "tends so to harm the reputation of another as to lower him in the estimation of the community * * *." [45] The court's decision thus found the elements of libel present in the story, although it agreed with the lower court that because of a grossly excessive award of damages by the jury—$250,000 in compensatory and $500,000 in punitive damages—there should be a new trial.[46]

Nor was the *Post* successful in arguing that libel was not present in a story on Mafia activities on Grand Bahama Island, in which it carried a photo of a group of people including Holmes, a tourist. The photo caption referred to "High-Rollers at the Monte Carlo club," and said that the club's casino grossed $20 million a year with a third "skimmed off for American Mafia 'families'." Holmes, the focal point of the picture and a man in no way connected with Mafia, sued for libel. The *Post*, saying the story was not defamatory, moved for a judgment on the pleadings; but

[40] Bianco v. Palm Beach Newspapers, Inc., 381 So.2d 371 (Fla.App.1980), 6 Med.L. Rptr. 1485.

[41] Taylor v. Tribune Pub. Co., 67 Fla. 361, 65 So. 3 (1914); Pitts v. Spokane Chronicle Co., 63 Wash.2d 763, 388 P.2d 976 (1964).

[42] Milan v. Long, 78 W.Va. 102, 88 S.E. 618 (1916); Riss v. Anderson, 304 F.2d 188 (8th Cir.1962).

[43] Shiell v. Metropolis Co., 102 Fla. 794, 136 So. 537 (1931); Frechette v. Special Magazines, 285 App.Div. 174, 136 N.Y.S.2d 448 (1954).

[44] For a classic mixup in names: Francis v. Lake Charles American Press, 262 La. 875, 265 So.2d 206 (1972).

[45] Corabi v. Curtis Pub. Co., 441 Pa. 432, 273 A.2d 899, 904 (1971).

[46] Corabi v. Curtis Pub. Co., 437 Pa. 143, 262 A.2d 665, 670 (1970). See Sec. 24 of this chapter for a discussion of types of damages awarded in libel cases.

the court held that a jury case was called for and that a jury might find libel.[47]

The failure of a reporter to check the proper source for an address caused an error in identities in a story about a man who pleaded guilty to breaking into business establishments—and the result was a $60,000 libel judgment against a newspaper company. In taking the details of the trial for "breaking" from the court records, the reporter omitted the address of Anthony Liquori of Springfield, the convicted man, and later extracted an address from a telephone book. Unfortunately, the telephone-book address was for a different man of the same name, and, using it, the reporter wrote that Anthony Liquori of 658 Cooper St., Agawam, Mass., had been convicted. The innocent Liquori brought a libel action. The Massachusetts Appeals Court said that there was negligence in not checking the address with court personnel or the attorney for the accused. The court upheld the jury award of damages.[48]

The news story which states incorrectly that a person has been *convicted* of a crime, as in the Liquori case, may be more dangerous than the one which wrongly suggests or states that he is *accused* of crime. But whatever the difference, the latter can cause libel suits, as we have seen above in the suggestion that Corabi was associated with major crimes.

It should be obvious that one should beware of publishing words imputing sexual acts outside prevailing moral codes, or that falsely state that a woman has been raped. Esteem and social standing, it is plain, are at stake. Courts everywhere regard written or printed statements charging without foundation that a woman is immoral as actionable libel. The charge of indiscretion need not be pronounced; any statement fairly imputing immoral conduct is actionable.[49]

Pat Montandon, author of *How To Be a Party Girl*, was to discuss her book on the Pat Michaels "Discussion" show. *TV Guide* received the show producer's advance release, which said that Montandon and a masked, anonymous prostitute would discuss "From Party-Girl to Call-Girl?" and "How far can the 'party-girl' go until she becomes a 'call-girl'." *TV Guide* ineptly edited the release, deleting reference to the prostitute and publishing this: "10:30 Pat Michaels—*Discussion* 'From Party Girl to Call Girl.' Scheduled guest: TV Personality Pat Montandon and au-

---

[47] Holmes v. Curtis Pub. Co., 303 F.Supp. 522 (D.S.C.1969).

[48] Liquori v. Republican Co., 8 Mass.App.Ct. 671, 396 N.E.2d 726 (1979), 5 Med.L. Rptr. 2180.

[49] Baird v. Dun & Bradstreet, 446 Pa. 266, 285 A.2d 166 (1971); Wildstein v. New York Post Corp., 40 Misc.2d 586, 243 N.Y.S.2d 386 (1963); Youssoupoff v. Metro-Goldwyn-Mayer, 50 Times L.R. 581, 99 A.L.R. 964 (1934).

thor of 'How to Be a Party Girl'." Montandon sued for libel and won $150,000 in damages.[50]

On the other hand, a woman who posed in the nude for a film maker but later got his agreement not to show the film, was unsuccessful in a libel action following his breaking of the agreement. She charged that his showing of the film to people who knew her caused her shame, disgrace and embarrassment. But the court said that "a film strip which includes a scene of plaintiff posing in the nude does not necessarily impute unchastity", and that it was not libel *per se.*[51]

Esteem and social standing can be lowered in the eyes of others by statements concerning political belief and race as well as by those grouped under crime and under sexual immorality in the preceding pages. To take political belief first, the salient cases since the late 1940's have largely involved false charges of "Communist" or "Red" or some variant of these words indicating that one subscribes to a generally hated political doctrine. But before these, a line of cases since the 1890's produced libel convictions against those who had labeled others as anarchists, socialists, or fascists.

In the days of Emma Goldman and Big Bill Haywood, it was laid down by the courts that to call one "anarchist" falsely was libelous;[52] when socialism protested capitalism and America's involvement in World War I, "red-tinted agitator" and "Socialist" were words for which a wronged citizen could recover;[53] in the revulsion against Nazi Germany and Japan during World War II, false accusations of "Fascist" and "pro-Jap" brought libel judgments.[54]

Magazines, columnists, newspapers, and corporations have paid for carelessness indulged in by charging others as "Communist" or "representative for the Communist Party." The "basis for reproach is a belief that such political affiliations constitute a threat to our institutions * * *."[55]

[50] Montandon v. Triangle Publications, Inc., 45 Cal.App.3d 938, 120 Cal.Rptr. 186 (1975).

[51] McGraw v. Watkins, 49 A.D.2d 958, 373 N.Y.S.2d 663 (1975). But contra, see Clifford v. Hollander (N.Y.Civ.1980), 6 Med.L.Rptr. 2201, where a photo of a nude woman, identified falsely as that of a woman journalist, was held libelous.

[52] Cerveny v. Chicago Daily News Co., 139 Ill. 345, 28 N.E. 692 (1891); Wilkes v. Shields, 62 Minn. 426, 64 N.W. 921 (1895).

[53] Wells v. Times Printing Co., 77 Wash. 171, 137 P. 457 (1913); Ogren v. Rockford Star Printing Co., 288 Ill. 405, 123 N.E. 587 (1919).

[54] Hartley v. Newark Morning Ledger Co., 134 N.J.L. 217, 46 A.2d 777 (1946); Hryhorijiv v. Winchell, 180 Misc. 574, 45 N.Y.S.2d 31 (1943).

[55] Anon., "Supplement," 171 A.L.R. 709, 712 (1947). Grant v. Reader's Digest Ass'n, Inc., 151 F.2d 733 (2d Cir.1945). And see Wright v. Farm Journal, 158 F.2d

In the famous case of Gertz v. Robert Welch, Inc.,[56] the trial court found that the publication of the John Birch Society had libeled Chicago Attorney Elmer Gertz in charging falsely that he was a "Leninist," a "Communist-fronter," and a member of the "Marxist League for Industrial Democracy." Gertz was awarded $400,000. In another case, where one organization called another "communist dominated" and failed to prove the charge in court, $25,000 was awarded to the plaintiff organization.[57]

Not every insinuation that a person is less than American, however, is libelous. Goodman, a selectman of Ware, Mass., phoned a call-in radio talk-show of the Central Broadcasting Corp. station, WARE, to deliver his opposition to a proposed contract for the local police union, at issue in the town prior to a citizen vote on the matter. During his extended and agitated discussion, he said that " * * * if we do not get together and stop the inroad of communism, something will happen." A libel suit was brought by the police local's parent union against Central Broadcasting, and the Massachusetts Supreme Judicial Court held that this fragment of Goodman's statement was "mere pejorative rhetoric," and an "unamiable but nonlibelous utterance." [58]

The law of libel's past is racist. Where the courts held an incorrect racial identification libelous in the United States, the word at issue was usually "Negro" or some variant thereof and the locale generally below the Mason–Dixon line. Although it is to be hoped that no American court could issue such a judgment today, at least as far back as 1791 and as recently as 1954, cases in the South allowed whites to recover damages for being called Negro or black.[59]

Finally, there are many words among those lowering esteem or social standing that defy classifying. Appellations that may be common enough in the excited conversation of neighborhood gossips can turn to actionable libel when reduced to print or writing. It has been held actionable on its face to print and publish that

976 (2d Cir.1947); Spanel v. Pegler, 160 F.2d 619 (7th Cir.1947); MacLeod v. Tribune Pub. Co., 52 Cal.2d 536, 343 P.2d 36 (1959).

[56] 306 F.Supp. 310 (N.D.Ill.1969); 418 U.S. 323, 94 S.Ct. 2997 (1974).

[57] Utah State Farm Bureau Federation v. National Farmers Union Service Corp., 198 F.2d 20 (10th Cir.1952). See also Cahill v. Hawaiian Paradise Park Corp., 56 Hawaii 522, 543 P.2d 1356 (1975).

[58] National Ass'n of Government Employees, Inc. v. Central Broadcasting Corp., 379 Mass. 220, 396 N.E.2d 996 (1979). Also McAuliffe v. Local Union No. 3, 29 N.Y.S.2d 963 (Sup.1941); McGraw v. Webster, 79 N.M. 104, 440 P.2d 296 (1968); "pro-Castro," Menendez v. Key West Newspaper Corp., 293 So.2d 751 (Fla.App. 1974).

[59] See, e.g., Eden v. Legare, 1 Bay 171 (1791); Strauder v. West Virginia, 100 U.S. (10 Otto) 303 (1879); Jones v. R.L. Polk & Co., 190 Ala. 243, 67 So. 577 (1915); Natchez Times Pub. Co. v. Dunigan, 221 Miss. 320, 72 So.2d 681 (1954).

one is "a liar," [60] "a skunk," [61] or "a scandalmonger"; [62] "a drunk-ard," [63] "a hypocrite," [64] or "a hog"; [65] or to call one heartless and neglectful of his family.[66] Other actionable epithets include link-ing a person to a swastika symbol,[67] or calling one a "despicable human being," [68] or a "bitch" (implying a woman is a prostitute).[69] Name-calling where private citizens are concerned is occasionally the kind of news that makes a lively paragraph, but the alert and responsible reporter recognizes it for what it is and decides wheth-er to use it on better grounds than its titillation value.

2. Damage Through Ridicule

It is pointless to try to draw too narrow a line between words that ridicule and those that lower esteem and social standing. That which ridicules may at times have the effect of damaging social standing. Yet that which attempts to satirize, or which makes an individual appear uncommonly foolish, or makes fun of misfortune has a quality distinct enough to serve as its own warning signal.

Ridicule must be more than a simple joke at another's ex-pense, for life cannot be so grim that the thin-skinned, the solemn, and the self-important may demand to go entirely unharried. But when the good-humored barb penetrates too deeply or carries too sharp a sting, or when a picture can be interpreted in a deeply derogatory manner, ridicule amounting to actionable libel may have occurred.

To sensationalize the poverty of a woman so as to bring her into ridicule and contempt, and to make a joke out of the desertion of a bride on her wedding day [70] have been held libelous. A famed case arose from a photo in an advertisement that accidentally

[60] Melton v. Bow, 241 Ga. 629, 247 S.E.2d 100 (1978); Paxton v. Woodward, 31 Mont. 195, 78 P. 215 (1904); Smith v. Lyons, 142 La. 975, 77 So. 896 (1917); contra, Bennett v. Transamerican Press, 298 F.Supp. 1013 (S.D.Iowa 1969); Calloway v. Central Charge Service, 142 U.S.App.D.C. 259, 440 F.2d 287 (1971).

[61] Massuere v. Dickens, 70 Wis. 83, 35 N.W. 349 (1887).

[62] Patton v. Cruce, 72 Ark. 421, 81 S.W. 380 (1904).

[63] Giles v. State, 6 Ga. 276 (1848); cf. Smith v. Fielden, 205 Tenn. 313, 326 S.W.2d 476 (1959).

[64] Overstreet v. New Nonpareil Co., 184 Iowa 485, 167 N.W. 669 (1918).

[65] Solverson v. Peterson, 64 Wis. 198, 25 N.W. 14 (1885).

[66] Brown v. Du Frey, 1 N.Y.2d 649, 151 N.Y.S.2d 649, 134 N.E.2d 469 (1956).

[67] Mullenmeister v. Snap-On Tools, 587 F.Supp. 868 (S.D.N.Y.1984).

[68] Smith v. McMullen, 589 F.Supp. 642 (S.D.Tex.1984).

[69] Stone v. Brooks, 253 Ga. 565, 322 S.E.2d 728 (1984).

[70] Moffatt v. Cauldwell, 3 Hun. 26, 5 Thomp. & C. 256 (N.Y.1874), but "poverty" and "unemployment" have been held not actionable words: Sousa v. Davenport, 3 Mass.App.Ct. 715, 323 N.E.2d 910 (1975); Kirman v. Sun Printing & Pub. Ass'n, 99 App.Div. 367, 91 N.Y.S. 193 (1904).

gave the illusion of a "fantastic and lewd deformity" of a steeple-chaser holding a riding crop.[71]

Yet there is room for satire and exaggeration. *Boston Magazine* published a page titled "Best and Worst Sports," including the categories "sports announcer," "local ski slopes," and "sexy athlete," some categories plainly waggish, some straightforward and complimentary. Under "sports announcer," the best was named and given kudos; and then appeared: "*Worst:* Jimmy Myers, Channel 4. The only newscaster in town who is enrolled in a course for remedial speaking." Myers sued, lost at trial for failure to establish defamation, and appealed.[72]

The Massachusetts Supreme Judicial Court described the appearance of the magazine's page, with its title, lampooning cartoons, and a mood of rough humor in the words, including "one-liners" and preposterous propositions under such titles as "Sports Groupie." It ruled that the statement about Myers made on such a page would not reasonably be understood by a reader to be an assertion of fact. "Taken in context, it can reasonably be considered to suggest that Myers should have been so enrolled," even though the words read "is enrolled." The words stated "a critical judgment, an opinion." And since Myers was himself available to the critic's audience, being often on view, his performances were in line with the rule that facts underlying opinions could be assumed—the performances "furnished the assumed facts from which the critic fashioned his barb." The court said that words such as these are meant to "sting and be quickly forgotten". Although for the plaintiff who "is the victim of ridicule, the forgetting may not be easy," the law refuses to find a statement of fact where none has been uttered. This was opinion, and if such "is based on assumed, nondefamatory facts, the First Amendment forbids the law of libel from redressing the injury." [73]

The columnist Jimmy Breslin of the former *New York Herald Tribune* has a fine talent for satire, and a libel suit based on his account of barkeep Hyman Cohen's encounter with murder was not successful. Cohen was a witness to the murder of one Munos at the Vivere Lounge in New York City. Fearing for his life if he talked to authorities about the killers, he denied for a time that the murder had happened at the Lounge or that he had witnessed it. He also fled the city. Breslin's column about Cohen was written after he had interviewed police, the district attorney and

[71] Burton v. Crowell Pub. Co., 82 F.2d 154 (2d Cir.1936).

[72] Myers v. Boston Magazine Co., Inc., 380 Mass. 336, 403 N.E.2d 376 (Mass.Sup. Jud.Ct.1980), 6 Med.L.Rptr. 1241.

[73] Ibid., 1243, 1245.

Cohen's employer, and had read about and inspected the scene of the murder. The column began:

> Among New Yorkers out of town for the week end, and out of town for a lot of week ends to come if he has his way, is Mr. Hyman Cohen, of the Bronx. His friends say that he went to the Catskills for the rest of the summer, but there is a feeling that the Catskills are not quite far enough away for Hy at present.
>
>   *   *   *
>
> Hy is a man who once liked this city very much. Particularly, he liked the part of the city they make television shows about. Gunmen, action guys; they were Hy's idea of people.   *   *   *
>
> Hy is a bartender, and it all started a couple of summers ago when he worked at a hotel in the Catskills and found himself pouring drinks for some underworld notables. He never really got over this. When the summer ended, Hy came back to New York and he was no longer Hy Cohen of the Bronx. He was Hy Cohen of the Rackets. He wore a big, snap-brim extortionist's hat, white on white shirts and a white tie. And when he would talk, especially if there were only a few people at the bar and they all could listen, Hy would begin talking about all the tough guys he knew. This was Hy's field.

The court held that though the article was not literally true in every detail, "it presented a fair sketch of a confident talkative bartender who was reduced to speechlessness, self-effacement and flight by gangsters * * *." [74] It explained why it was not libelous: [75]

> With sardonic humor Breslin described Cohen's frantic flight to avoid the murderous gangsters as well as to escape the police who were hot on the killer's trail. The humor was not funny, except on the surface. Murder and terror are * * * the subjects of satire which superficially conceals a tragic or solemn happening. Our courts have held that mere exaggeration, irony or wit does not make a writing libelous unless the article would be libelous without the exaggeration, irony or wit.

While a living man whose obituary has mistakenly been printed may feel annoyed and injured, and may attract unusual attention and perhaps a rough joke or two as he walks into his

[74] Cohen v. New York Herald Tribune, Inc., 63 Misc.2d 87, 310 N.Y.S.2d 709, 725 (1970).

[75] Ibid., 724. See also Sellers v. Time Inc., 299 F.Supp. 582 (E.D.Pa.1969); Fram v. Yellow Cab Co. of Pittsburgh, 380 F.Supp. 1314 (W.D.Pa.1974).

office the next morning, he has not been libeled. As one court said, death "is looked for in the history of every man," and where there is notice of a death that has not occurred, "Prematurity is the sole peculiarity." [76] Yet an erroneous report of death has been held to be the cause of an action for "negligent infliction of emotional distress"—an injury closely related to defamation.[77]

3. Damage Through Words Imputing Disease or Mental Illness

The law has long held that diseases which may be termed "loathsome, infectious, or contagious" may be libelous when falsely attributed to an individual. That which is "loathsome" may change with time and changing mores, of course, but venereal disease, the plague, leprosy, small pox and AIDS to fit this description. Anyone alleged to be at present suffering from any of these diseases is likely to be shunned by his fellows. And if the disease carries the stigma of immorality, such as venereal disease or alcoholism or addiction, it may be libelous to say of a person that he formerly had it, although he has since been cured.

To charge without legal excuse that one has leprosy was held libelous in Lewis v. Hayes; the imputation of venereal disease was held libelous in King v. Pillsbury.[78] An incorrect assignment of mental impairment or of mental illness to a person is libel on its face.[79] The magazine *Fact* published in its September-October issue of 1964, an article billed as "The Unconscious of a Conservative: A Special Issue on the Mind of Barry Goldwater." Goldwater was the Republican Party's candidate for president and a senator from Arizona at the time. He was portrayed in one of two articles as "paranoid," his attacks on other politicians stemming from a conviction that "everybody hates him, and it is better to attack them first." A *Fact* poll of psychiatrists, asked to judge whether Goldwater was psychologically fit to serve as president, also was reported on. A jury found libel and awarded Goldwater $1.00 in compensatory damages and $75,000 in punitive damages.[80]

[76] Cohen v. New York Times Co., 153 App.Div. 242, 138 N.Y.S. 206 (1912); Cardiff v. Brooklyn Eagle, Inc., 190 Misc. 730, 75 N.Y.S.2d 222 (1948).

[77] Rubinstein v. New York Post Corp. (N.Y.Sup.Ct.1983), 9 Med.L.Rptr. 1581. Emotional distress is treated in Sec. 20, below.

[78] 165 Cal. 527, 132 P. 1022 (1913); King v. Pillsbury, 115 Me. 528, 99 A. 513 (1917); Sally v. Brown, 220 Ky. 576, 295 S.W. 890 (1927).

[79] Cowper v. Vannier, 20 Ill.App.2d 499, 156 N.E.2d 761 (1959); Kenney v. Hatfield, 351 Mich. 498, 88 N.W.2d 535 (1958). But not in Virginia: Mills v. Kingsport Times-News, 475 F.Supp. 1005 (W.D.Va.1979), 5 Med.L.Rptr. 2288.

[80] Goldwater v. Ginzburg, 414 F.2d 324 (2d Cir.1969).

4. **Damaging One in His Trade, Occupation, or Profession**

So long as one follows a legal calling, he has a claim not to be defamed unfairly in the performance of it. The possibilities are rich for damaging one through words that impugn honesty, skill, fitness, ethical standards, or financial capacity in his chosen work, whether it be banking or basket-weaving. Observe some of the possibilities: that a University was a "degree mill;"[81] that a contractor engaged in unethical trade;[82] that a clergyman was "an interloper, a meddler, a spreader of distrust;"[83] that a schoolmaster kept girls after school so that he could court them;[84] that a jockey rode horses unfairly and dishonestly;[85] that an attorney was incompetent,[86] and that a corporation director embezzled.[87]

By no means every statement to which a businessman, tradesman or professional takes exception, however, is libelous. Thus Frederick D. Washington, a church bishop, sued the *New York Daily News* and columnist Robert Sylvester for his printed statement that Washington had attended a nightclub performance at which a choir member of his church sang. The bishop argued that his church did not approve of its spiritual leaders' attending nightclubs, and that he had been damaged. The court said the account was not, on its face, an attack on the plaintiff's integrity, and called the item a "warm human interest story" in which there was general interest. This was not libel on its face and the court upheld dismissal of Bishop Washington's complaint.[88]

Nor did David Brown convince the court that there was libel in a pamphlet that opposed his attempt to get a zoning change from the City Council of Knoxville, Tenn. The pamphlet attacked a change that would have permitted Brown to build apartments in a residential district, and asked the question: "Have the 'Skids Been Greased' at City Council?" Brown sued for libel, arguing that the question suggested he had bribed the City Council and that it had accepted the bribe. But the court held that the question did not suggest bribery in its reasonable and obvious meaning; but rather, that pressure in the form of political influence had been brought to bear on certain Council members to

[81] Laurence University v. State, 68 Misc.2d 408, 326 N.Y.S.2d 617 (1971). Reversed on grounds that State official's words were absolutely privileged, 41 A.D.2d 463, 344 N.Y.S.2d 183 (1973).

[82] Greenbelt Co-op. Pub. Ass'n v. Bresler, 253 Md. 324, 252 A.2d 755 (1969), reversed on other grounds 398 U.S. 6, 90 S.Ct. 1537 (1970).

[83] Van Lonkhuyzen v. Daily News Co., 195 Mich. 283, 161 N.W. 979 (1917).

[84] Spears v. McCoy, 155 Ky. 1, 159 S.W. 610 (1913).

[85] Wood v. Earl of Durham, 21 Q.B. 501 (1888).

[86] Hahn v. Andrello, 44 A.D.2d 501, 355 N.Y.S.2d 850 (1974).

[87] Weenig v. Wood, 169 Ind.App. 413, 349 N.E.2d 235 (1976).

[88] Washington v. New York News Inc., 37 A.D.2d 557, 322 N.Y.S.2d 896 (1971).

expedite matters. This was not libel. Had the pamphlet said that "palms are greased at the City Council," that would have been libel on its face and actionable.[89]

A margin of protection also exists in the occasional finding by a court that mistakenly attributing a single instance of clumsiness or error to a professional man is not enough to damage him. Rather, such cases have held, there must be a suggestion of more general incompetency or lack of quality before a libel charge will hold. One court said:[90]

> To charge a professional man with negligence or unskillfulness in the management or treatment of an individual case, is no more than to impute to him the mistakes and errors incident to fallible human nature. The most eminent and skillful physician or surgeon may mistake the symptoms of a particular case without detracting from his general professional skill or learning. To say of him, therefore, that he was mistaken in that case would not be calculated to impair the confidence of the community in his general professional competency.

5. Damage to a Corporation's Integrity, Credit, or Ability to Carry on Business

It is possible to damage the reputation of a corporation or partnership by defamation that reflects on the conduct, management, or financial condition of the corporation.[91] To say falsely that a company is in shaky financial condition, or that it cannot pay its debts, would be libelous, as would the imputation that it has engaged in dishonest practices. While a corporation is an entity quite different from the individuals that head it or staff it, there is no doubt that it has a reputation, an "image" to protect.

Publishing or broadcasting casual statements that a business or corporation is "broke" or "going bankrupt" or "has a rotten credit rating" can be risky business indeed unless you are prepared to prove the truth of such statements in court. When Dun & Bradstreet—which is in the business of giving credit ratings—

[89] Brown v. Newman, 224 Tenn. 297, 454 S.W.2d 120 (1970). An official who resigned from a "financially troubled bank" was not libeled: Bordoni v. New York Times Co., Inc., 400 F.Supp. 1223 (S.D.N.Y.1975).

[90] Blende v. Hearst Publications, 200 Wash. 426, 93 P.2d 733 (1939); November v. Time, Inc., 13 N.Y.2d 175, 244 N.Y.S.2d 309, 194 N.E.2d 126 (1963); Holder Const. Co. v. Ed Smith & Sons, Inc., 124 Ga.App. 89, 182 S.E.2d 919 (1971). But see Cohn v. Am-Law, Inc. (N.Y.Sup.Ct.1980), 5 Med.L.Rptr. 2367, where defamation was found in a magazine story saying an attorney went "unprepared" to a single hearing.

[91] Dupont Engineering Co. v. Nashville Banner Pub. Co., 13 F.2d 186 (D.C.Tenn. 1925); Electric Furnace Corp. v. Deering Milliken Research Corp., 325 F.2d 761 (6th Cir.1963); Golden Palace, Inc. v. National Broadcasting Co., Inc., 386 F.Supp. 107 (D.D.C.1974).

published erroneous information indicating falsely that a Greenmoss Builders had filed for bankruptcy, that was held to be defamatory. Both the Vermont courts and the United States Supreme Court agreed that a $350,000 award should be paid to the building firm.[92]

Charging dishonest or unethical behavior by a firm can also result in a successful defamation suit. Although tobacco companies have received much flak, the Chicago TV station WBBM—owned by the CBS Network—found in 1988 that such a firm could still be libeled. The Supreme Court denied *certiorari,* leaving intact a $3 million damage award in the case of Brown & Williamson Tobacco Corp. v. Jacobson and CBS, Inc.

Back in 1981, Jacobson had delivered a "Perspective" report denouncing the makers of Viceroy cigarettes for hiring advertising "slicksters" to create an advertising strategy to "hook" the young. The strategy used by Brown & Williamson, Jacobson said, was taken from a report recommending that smoking be portrayed to youth as a kind of rite of passage involving wearing a bra or shaving, or drinking wine or beer. The broadcast added up to an accusation of unethical youth-oriented advertising by Brown & Williamson for its Viceroy cigarettes, thus endangering the health of the impressionable young.[93] That huge judgment—one of the largest media libel awards to survive appeals—is only part of the story. The case of Brown & Williamson v. CBS provides multiple lessons about things journalists should not do.

This Walter Jacobson report attacking the cigarette manufacturer was said to be based on a "confidential report in the files of the federal government." Such a report did exist in the files of the Federal Trade Commission (FTC); it had been prepared by a research firm working for Ted Bates & Co., an ad agency once employed by Viceroy Cigarettes' parent company, Brown & Williamson.

At one point, a *confidential* FTC report had assumed, evidently erroneously, that Viceroy had adopted a "hook the young" ad strategy. A researcher for the CBS station—Michael Radutzky—had learned of the FTC report from a newspaper article, and even received copies of some pages of that report. However, Radutzky couldn't persuade FTC staffers to send him copies of the confidential report; the staffers would only "confirm that the report and its findings were accurate."

[92] Dun & Bradstreet, Inc. v. Greenmoss Builders, Inc., 472 U.S. 749, 105 S.Ct. 2939 (1985).

[93] Certiorari denied 485 U.S. 993, 108 S.Ct. 1302 (1988), upholding the judgment of the United States Court of Appeals, Seventh Circuit. See 827 F.2d 1119 (7th Cir. 1987) 14 Med.L.Rptr. 1497.

The FTC's ambiguous response to Radutzky, however, was contradicted directly by a Thomas Humber, a spokesman for Brown & Williamson. Humber told Radutzky that Brown & Williamson had rejected the strategy suggested in documents submitted by the Ted Bates ad agency.[94]

> Humber stated [to Radutzky, according to Humber's notes] that the proposals referred to in the FTC report were similar to a proposed libelous story that a young inexperienced reporter might submit to his editors but that it was corrected by a news organization's editors and attorneys. Humber stated that in such a case no legitimate criticism could be leveled at the news organization.

In response to a request from Jacobson, researcher Radutzky had searched unsuccessfully for "pot, wine, beer and sex" ads for Viceroy cigarettes. Radutzky had made lengthy notes as he conducted interviews and read those pages of the FTC report provided to him by a newspaper reporter. Radutzky also made handwritten entries on the margins of the FTC report pages he had, and also developed an 18–page sample script.

The jury, however, never saw this work by Radutzky. Before the trial, Radutzky "destroyed all of his contemporaneous interview notes, five of the ten pages of the FTC report . . . and fifteen of the original eighteen pages of the sample script." [95]

Radutzky testified that he had destroyed those materials while "housecleaning" after a district court had dismissed an original Brown & Williamson libel complaint. The lawsuit, however, was later reinstated and, as the Court of Appeals noted, the destruction of materials violated CBS policy. The Court of Appeals concluded that Brown & Williamson had proved "by clear and convincing evidence that the defendants either knew the Perspective [Jacobson's commentary] was false or in fact entertained serious doubts as to its truth," thus allowing the district court jury's verdict against the TV station to stand. Furthermore, "[t]he most compelling evidence of actual malice submitted to the jury was the intentional destruction of critical documents by Jacobson's researcher. . . ." [96]

A number of lessons may be taken from this case, including:

(1) Let a story's facts determine its conclusions, not the other way around.

[94] Brown & Williamson Tobacco Corp. v. Jacobson, 827 F.2d 1119, 1123 (7th Cir. 1987).

[95] Ibid.; see Stuart Taylor, Jr., "Justices Uphold $3 million Libel Award on CBS," The New York Times, April 4, 1988.

[96] Ibid.

(2) Try to present "both sides" or "several sides" of a controversy. It is dangerous for a reporter or a commentator to decide that only one side of an issue should be presented.

(3) Publishers and broadcasters need to develop clear policies about preparation of news or commentary reports. In any event, once a legal proceeding has started . . . and until it has concluded, beyond possibility of re-filing or appeal—notes, memos, tapes, or videotapes may not be destroyed safely.

SEC. 19.   OPINION AND RHETORICAL HYPERBOLE

In defining "libel," many abusive words arising in heated controversies are treated as statements of opinion, or rhetorical hyperbole, and as such are not libelous.

Courts have increasingly come to rule that the agitated, heated dialogue of encounters such as political controversy and labor dispute deserve strong protection against libel actions when it is reported in the media.   Rich name-calling that grows out of spirited and hot argument is protected because it is essentially opinion, or it is "rhetorical hyperbole"—extravagant or fanciful exaggeration.

As for opinion, the rule takes force from the Supreme Court's statement in Gertz v. Robert Welch, Inc. in 1974: [97] "Under the First Amendment there is no such thing as a false idea.   However pernicious an opinion may seem, we depend for its correction not on the conscience of judges and juries but on the competition of other ideas."

In the *Old Dominion* case of 1974,[98] shortly after *Gertz* was decided, the Supreme Court found that the word "scabs" applied by publications of union letter-carriers against named, non-union letter-carriers was opinion, and not libel.   The publications were used in on-going efforts to organize remaining non-union people. In a long statement accompanying the names, the publication used many pejorative terms in defining "scab," including "traitor." The named non-union people brought a libel action and were awarded damages which were upheld by the Virginia Supreme Court.   The union appealed, and the United States Supreme Court reversed the verdict, 6–3, Justice Marshall writing the majority opinion.   He reviewed the verbal rough-and-tumble of labor organizing dispute, and cited precedent that had refused to consider

[97] 418 U.S. 323, 339–340, 94 S.Ct. 2997, 3007 (1974).   Opinion is treated in detail in Sec. 35, Chap. 6, below.

[98] Old Dominion Branch No. 496, National Ass'n of Letter Carriers, AFL–CIO v. Austin, 418 U.S. 264, 94 S.Ct. 2770 (1974).

this language libel. Speaking of the union publication's definition
of the word "scab," derived partly from an old description of scabs
by the novelist Jack London, he said: [99]

> The definition's use of words like "traitor" cannot be
> construed as representations of fact. . . . Such words
> were obviously used here in a loose, figurative sense to
> demonstrate the union's strong disagreement with the
> views of those workers who oppose unionization. Expres-
> sion of such an opinion, even in the most pejorative terms
> is protected * * *.

It was opinion that brought a libel suit against reporter Jack
Newfield and his publisher, for charges against New York Judge
Dominic Rinaldi in Newfield's Book, *Cruel and Unusual Justice.*
Newfield called Rinaldi one of New York's 10 worst judges, and in
detailed, illustrative cases about the judge's work, said that large-
scale heroin dealers and people close to organized crime got
lenient treatment from the judge, while blacks and Puerto Ricans
received long sentences. Newfield called for Rinaldi's removal
from the bench. Rinaldi sued. Newfield and his publisher eventually won a summary judgment (i.e., a decision in their favor
without going to trial).[1]

Newfield's attacks on Rinaldi were largely opinion, the New
York Court of Appeals found, and the facts supporting them were
set forth in the book. The court quoted Gertz v. Welch, "there is
no such thing as a false idea"), and added that opinions "false or
not, libelous or not, are constitutionally privileged and may not be
the subject of private damage actions provided that the facts
supporting the opinion are set forth." The free flow of information to the people concerning the performance of their public
officials is essential. "Erroneous opinion must be protected so
that debate on public issues may remain robust and unfettered." [2]

At the same time that Justice Marshall ruled in *Old Dominion* (above, p. 125) that statements of opinion in such agitated
circumstances were not to be held libelous, he also characterized
the words as no more than "rhetorical hyperbole": " * * * Jack
London's 'definition of a scab' is merely rhetorical hyperbole, a
hasty and imaginative expression of the contempt felt by union
members toward those who refuse to join." [3] Hyperbole earlier

[99] Ibid., at 284, 94 S.Ct. at 2781.

[1] Rinaldi v. Holt, Rinehart & Winston, Inc., 42 N.Y.2d 369, 397 N.Y.S.2d 943, 366
N.E.2d 1299 (1977), certiorari denied 434 U.S. 969, 98 S.Ct. 514 (1977), 2 Med.L.
Rptr. 2169.

[2] Ibid., at 380; 366 N.E.2d at 2173; see Gertz v. Welch, 418 U.S. 323, 340, 94 S.Ct.
2997, 3007 (1974).

[3] Old Dominion Branch No. 496, National Ass'n of Letter Carriers, AFL–CIO v.
Austin, 418 U.S. 264, 2782, 94 S.Ct. 2770, 2782 (1974).

had been described as not libelous in the *Greenbelt* case, decided in 1970 by the Supreme Court.[4]   Real estate developer Charles Bresler was petitioning the Greenbelt, Md., City Council for zoning changes that would allow him to build high-density housing on some of his land.   Simultaneously, the city was trying to buy a tract of Bresler's land on which to build a school.

As the Supreme Court said, the situation provided Bresler and the council with much bargaining leverage against each other. Community controversy arose over the matter, and several tumultuous city council meetings were held at which citizens emphatically spoke their minds.   The *Greenbelt News Review* reported the meetings at length, including charges by citizens that Bresler's negotiating position was "blackmail," and a case of "unethical trade."   Bresler sued and a jury awarded him a total of $17,000 in compensatory and punitive damages.   The Maryland Court of Appeals upheld the judgment, and the newspaper took its case to the United States Supreme Court, which reversed the lower courts.   The *News Review*, it said, was performing its function as a community newspaper when it published the reports.   The reports were accurate, full and fair, with Bresler's proposal given proper coverage.   The court said:[5]

> It is simply impossible to believe that a reader who reached the word "blackmail" in either article would not have understood exactly what was meant: it was Bresler's public and wholly legal negotiating proposals that were being criticized.   No reader could have thought that either the speakers at the meeting or the newspaper articles reporting their words were charging Bresler with the commission of a criminal offense.

To find libel for such rhetorical hyperbole, the Court said, would "subvert the most fundamental meaning of a free press, protected by the First and Fourteenth Amendments."

Numerous decisions following *Greenbelt* and *Letter Carriers* have found words in similar settings to be matters of opinion or hyperbole, and sometimes both as Justice Marshall did in the latter.   In the *Myers* decision (above, p. 118), "the only sports announcer enrolled in a course for remedial speaking" was ruled to be opinion and "rhetorical license."   In a Missouri case, the Court of Appeals has ruled that "sleazy sleight-of-hand" written by a newspaper of an attorney was opinion and not libelous.[6]

In other cases, however, defendants have asserted that their words were hyperbole or opinion without success.   The United

[4] Greenbelt Cooperative Pub. Ass'n v. Bresler, 398 U.S. 6, 90 S.Ct. 1537 (1970).

[5] Ibid.

[6] Anton v. St. Louis Suburban Newspapers, Inc., 598 S.W.2d 493 (Mo.App.1980).

States Labor Party published a leaflet opposing a candidate for the Baltimore City Council, charging him with a "SS [Nazi] background" and asserting that he had had associations with the Gestapo—charges which, in a libel suit, won $30,000 for the plaintiff. On appeal, the Labor Party argued that its words were merely "rhetorical hyperbole" and so not libelous. But the Maryland Supreme Court said no: Rhetorical hyperbole exists only when a reader could not possibly understand the statement to be a fact—and the general public which saw the leaflet had nothing to prevent its understanding that the words did not mean what they said.[7] Similarly, a California court refused to agree that it was either opinion or hyperbole where the newsletter of a citizens' group charged a councilman with "outright extortion" and "blackmail."[8]

SEC. 20. EMOTIONAL DISTRESS AND MENTAL ANGUISH

Accompanying libel's damage to reputation is a newer partner whose presence in recent years has become a disagreeable reality for libel defendants, even though it remains an infrequent visitor.[9] Widely termed intentional or negligent "infliction of emotional distress," it refers to the power of words and pictures to carry psychological, rather than reputational harm. A tort separate from defamation in many states, it exists in other states as part of the law of defamation. Thus Justice Powell of the United States Supreme Court said, in discussing harmful components of defamatory falsehood in the 1974 *Gertz* case, that among them are "personal humiliation, and mental anguish and suffering."[10]

Mary Alice Firestone's suit for libel—against *Time* magazine for an erroneous report that her husband had won his divorce action on grounds of adultery—was allowed even though she had withdrawn her claim for harm to reputation before trial. She won a judgment for $100,000, in other words, for emotional anguish.[11] The much-publicized case of Carol Burnett followed, in which she recovered damages in a libel suit against the National Inquirer,

[7] U.S. Labor Party v. Whitman, 442 U.S. 919, 99 S.Ct. 2842, 61 L.Ed.2d 286 (1979).

[8] Good Government Group of Seal Beach v. Superior Court, 22 Cal.3d 672, 150 Cal.Rptr. 258, 586 P.2d 572 (1978); McManus v. Doubleday & Co., Inc., 513 F.Supp. 1383 (S.D.N.Y.1981), 7 Med.L.Rptr. 1475.

[9] Terrance C. Mead, "Suing Media for Emotional Distress," 23 Washburn Law Journ. 24, Fall 1983. Mead found only 18 cases in which emotional distress was part of libel actions, out of 484 against media defendants between 1977 and 1981. See David A. Anderson, Reputation, Compensation, and Proof, 25 William and Mary L.Rev. # 5, 1983–84, 747, 756–64.

[10] Gertz v. Robert Welch, Inc., 418 U.S. 323, 349–350, 94 S.Ct. 2997, 3011–3012 (1974).

[11] Time, Inc. v. Firestone, 424 U.S. 448, 460, 96 S.Ct. 958, 968 (1976).

almost entirely for emotional distress over the magazine's portrayal of her as "drunk, rude, uncaring and abusive" at a restaurant.[12]

In the mid–1980s, the emerging separate tort of infliction of mental injury offered a substantial threat to the press. But in 1988, that threat was lessened by the U.S. Supreme Court's decision in Hustler v. Falwell, which held that the First Amendment protects parodies—even Hustler magazine's mock ad which said Rev. Falwell's first sexual experience had been in an outhouse, with his mother, while she was drunk.

Following what then seemed to be a trend, Rev. Falwell sued Hustler magazine and its publisher, Larry Flynt, for libel *plus* invasion of privacy *plus* intentional infliction of emotional distress.

Not surprisingly, even though the fine print said "ad parody—not to be taken seriously"—a U.S. district court jury was sympathetic to Rev. Falwell. (After all, Flynt had declared, while giving a pre-trial deposition, that his intent in publishing the parody was to "assassinate" the minister's reputation.)[13] Sympathetic or not, the jury found that Falwell had not been libeled: "no reasonable person would believe that the parody was describing actual facts about Falwell." The jury also declined to find that his privacy had been invaded. Jurors, however, seized upon the idea of infliction of mental injury and awarded Falwell $200,000: $100,000 in compensatory damages, plus $50,000 in punitive damages against Flynt and $50,000 against his magazine.

The Court of Appeals, Fourth Circuit—like the trial court—concluded that Rev. Falwell was a public figure.[14] That public figure status meant that defendants Flynt and Hustler Magazine were entitled "to the same level of first amendment protection in an action for intentional infliction of mental distress that they would receive in an action for libel."[15] Even so, the Court of Appeals found the ad parody so offensive that it affirmed the trial court's ruling.[16] The U.S. Supreme Court disagreed.

Chief Justice William Rehnquist defined the issue as whether the First Amendment limits a state's authority to protect its citizens from intentional infliction of mental distress. He wrote, "We must decide whether a public figure may recover damages for

[12] Burnett v. National Inquirer (Cal.Sup.1981), 7 Med.L.Rptr. 1321.

[13] David Margolick, "Some See Threat in Non–Libel Verdict of Falwell," The New York Times, Dec. 10, 1986, p. 6.

[14] Hustler Magazine v. Falwell, 485 U.S. 46, 108 S.Ct. 876 (1988), 14 Med.L.Rptr. 2281, 2282.

[15] Falwell v. Flynt, 797 F.2d 1270, 1274 (4th Cir.1986), 13 Med.L.Rptr. 1145.

[16] 485 U.S. at 50, 108 S.Ct. at 879, 14 Med.L.Rptr. at 2283.

emotional harm caused to him by an ad parody offensive to him, and doubtless gross and repugnant in the eyes of most." [17]

To the surprise of many, Chief Justice Rehnquist then set about a sweeping re-affirmation of First Amendment principles—principles which he has questioned or derided in other cases.[18] He wrote approvingly of the free flow of ideas and opinions on matters of public interest as being at the heart of the First Amendment. " '[T]he freedom to speak one's mind is not only an aspect of individual liberty—and thus a good unto itself—but also is essential to the common quest for truth and the vitality of society as a whole.' " [19]

Chief Justice Rehnquist wrote that under the First Amendment robust political debate will result in speech critical of public officials or public figures who are " 'intimately involved in the resolution of important public questions, or, by reason of their fame, shape events in areas of concern to society at large.' " [20]

The Chief Justice emphasized, however, that freedom of expression is not an absolute. The First Amendment does not mean that ". . . any speech about public figures is immune from sanction in the form of damages." Although false statements—unknowingly false statements—will be protected to insure breathing space needed to ensure open debate, knowingly or recklessly false statements are valueless and will not be protected.[21]

Rehnquist wrote that the law does not regard an intent to inflict emotional harm with much solicitude. He termed it understandable that most jurisdictions have created civil liability when such conduct is sufficiently outrageous. But Reverend Falwell, powerful individual and sometime candidate for President, was a public figure involved ". . . in the world of debate about public affairs, [where] many things done with motives that are less than admirable are protected by the First Amendment." [22]

Chief Justice Rehnquist declared that any system of civil damages that might teach Flynt a lesson would also endanger a long and valued tradition of caustic American political caricatures—verbal and visual—and cartoons. He pointed to the prominent role in political debate played by satire and political

[17] Ibid.

[18] See, e.g., Rehnquist opinion in Wolston v. Reader's Digest Ass'n, Inc., 443 U.S. 157, 99 S.Ct. 2701 (1979). He there rejected the argument that a person who engages in criminal conduct automatically becomes a limited-purpose public figure. See also his opinion in Time, Inc. v. Firestone, 424 U.S. 448, 96 S.Ct. 958 (1976).

[19] 485 U.S. at 50, 108 S.Ct. at 879, 14 Med.L.Rptr. at 2283.

[20] Ibid., quoting Associated Press v. Walker, 388 U.S. 130, 164, 87 S.Ct. 1975, 1996 (1967).

[21] Ibid., 485 U.S. at 52, 108 S.Ct. at 880, 14 Med.L.Rptr. at 2283–2284.

[22] Ibid., 485 U.S. at 52, 108 S.Ct. at 880, 14 L.Rptr. at 2284.

cartoons, and to the impact of images enduring over the years: Lincoln's gangly frame, Teddy Roosevelt's glasses and teeth, Franklin D. Roosevelt's cigarette holder and jutting jaw.

Even though Falwell argued that the Hustler magazine parody was so outrageous that it should be deprived of First Amendment protection, the Court disagreed. True, wrote the Chief Justice, "*Hustler* is at best a distant cousin of . . . political cartoons . . . and a rather poor relation at that." The Chief Justice expressed doubts that a sufficiently precise standard could be found safely to distinguish Flynt's publication from political cartoons in general.[23]

The Falwell case is important. University of Texas law professor David A. Anderson termed it a tremendous victory because it "'. . . cuts off the main avenues of the emotional distress claim" and . . . because it is such a ringing affirmation of the principles of New York Times v. Sullivan.'"[24]

SEC. 21. THE FORM OF THE LIBEL

Damage may be caused by any part of the medium's content, including headlines, pictures and advertisements.

Whatever is printed or broadcast is disseminated at the peril of the publisher. A picture may be as libelous as words; a headline, in some states, may be libelous even though modified or negated by the story that follows. Libelous copy in an advertisement leaves the publisher liable along with the merchant or advertising agency that furnished it.

A 1956 decision explains how headlines and closing "tag-lines" of a news story can be libelous (even though in this case the newspaper defended itself successfully). One story in a series published by the *Las Vegas Sun* brought a libel suit because of its headline and closing tag-line advertising the next article in the series. The headline read "Babies for Sale. Franklin Black Market Trade of Child Told." The tag-line promoting the story to appear the next day read "Tomorrow—Blackmail by Franklin." The body of the story told factually the way in which attorney Franklin had obtained a mother's release of her child for adoption. Franklin sued for libel and won. But the *Sun* appealed, claiming among other things that the trial judge had erred in instructing the jury that the words were libelous. The *Sun* said that the language was ambiguous, and susceptible of more than one interpretation.

---

[23] Ibid., 2285.

[24] Margaret G. Carter, "Press Breathes Sigh of Relief after the Falwell Decision," Presstime, April, 1988, p. 34.

But the Nevada Supreme Court [25] said that the headline and tagline were indeed libelous. Under any reasonable definition, it said, "black market sale" and "blackmail" "would tend to lower the subject in the estimation of the community and to excite derogatory opinions against him and hold him up to contempt." Then it explained the part that the headline had in creating a libel: [26]

> Appellants * * * contend, the headline must be qualified by and read in the light of the article to which it referred and the tag-line must be qualified by and read in the light of the subsequent article to which it referred.

> This is not so. The text of a newspaper article is not ordinarily the context of its headline, since the public frequently reads only the headline * * *. The same is true of a tag-line or leader, since the public frequently reads only the leader without reading the subsequent article to which it refers. The defamation of Franklin contained in the headline was complete upon its face * * *. The same is true of the tag-line.

The dangers of libel in advertisements, of course, have been shown at page 107 in the case of Cosgrove Studio & Camera Shop, Inc. v. Pane.[27] As for pictures, pictures standing alone, without caption or story with them, would rarely pose danger of defamation, but almost invariably in the mass media, illustration is accompanied by words, and it is almost always the combination that carries the damaging impact. In an issue of *Tan*, a story titled "Man Hungry" was accompanied by a picture taken several years earlier in connection with a woman's work as a professional model for a dress designer. With it were the words "She had a good man—but he wasn't enough. So she picked a bad one!" On the cover of the magazine was the title, "Shameless Love."

The woman sued for libel, and the court granted her claim for $3,000. "There is no doubt in this court's mind that the publication libeled plaintiff," the judge wrote. "A publication must be

[25] Las Vegas Sun, Inc. v. Franklin, 74 Nev. 282, 329 P.2d 867 (1958). The *Sun* won the appeal on other grounds.

[26] Ibid., at 869. New York and Louisiana follow the same rule: Schermerhorn v. Rosenberg, 73 A.D.2d 276, 426 N.Y.S.2d 274 (1980), 6 Med.L.Rptr. 1376, Forrest v. Lynch, 347 So.2d 1255 (La.App.1977), 3 Med.L.Rptr. 1187. But in some states, the meaning of headline and story *taken together* govern the finding: Ross v. Columbia Newspapers, Inc., 266 S.C. 75, 221 S.E.2d 770 (1976); Sprouse v. Clay Communication, Inc., 158 W.Va. 427, 211 S.E.2d 674 (1975); Adreani v. Hansen, 80 Ill.App.3d 726, 36 Ill.Dec. 259, 400 N.E.2d 679 (1980), 6 Med.L.Rptr. 1015.

[27] 408 Pa. 314, 182 A.2d 751 (1962).

considered in its entirety, both the picture and the story which it illustrates." [28]

During a program broadcast in Albuquerque, N.M., over station KGGM–TV, the secretary of a Better Business Bureau was speaking about dishonest television repairmen. He held up to the camera a newspaper advertisement of the Day and Night Television Service Company. . . . The speaker said that some television servicemen were cheating the public:

> This is what has been referred to in the trade as the ransom. Ransom, the ransom racket. The technique of taking up the stuff after first assuring the set owner that the charges would only be nominal, and then holding the set for ransom . . . .

The New Mexico Supreme Court pointed up the effect of combining the picture and the words: "Standing alone, neither the advertisement nor the words used . . . could be construed as libel. But the two combined impute fraud and dishonesty to the company and its operators." [29]

The use of the wrong picture in an advertisement may give the foundation for actionable libel, as decided in Peck v. Tribune Co.[30] The use of false or unauthorized testimonials in advertisements also may constitute libel.[31]

SEC. 22. BROADCAST DEFAMATION

Broadcasting's vast audience gives vast potential for harm in defamation, and it is now treated as libel instead of the lesser wrong of slander. Special problems arise in broadcast libel uttered without advance warning by participants in programs.

While defamation suits during the early decades of radio were sometimes brought under the rules of slander—spoken defamation—the offense today is handled as libel. The American Law Institute finds that "defamation by any form of communication that has the potentially harmful qualities characteristic of written or printed words is to be treated as libel." [32] Broadcasting's wide diffusion of its programs to millions, and its prestige and impact

[28] Martin v. Johnson Pub. Co., 157 N.Y.S.2d 409, 411 (1956). See also Farrington v. Star Co., 244 N.Y. 585, 155 N.E. 906 (1927) (wrong picture); Wasserman v. Time, Inc., 138 U.S.App.D.C. 7, 424 F.2d 920 (1970), certiorari denied 398 U.S. 940, 90 S.Ct. 1844 (1970).

[29] Young v. New Mexico Broadcasting Co., 60 N.M. 475, 292 P.2d 776 (1956); Central Arizona Light & Power Co. v. Akers, 45 Ariz. 526, 46 P.2d 126 (1935).

[30] Peck v. Tribune Co., 214 U.S. 185, 29 S.Ct. 554 (1909).

[31] Foster–Milburn Co. v. Chinn, 134 Ky. 424, 120 S.W. 364 (1909).

[32] Restatement Second, Torts, Vol. 3 p. 182.

among audiences, makes it potentially much more damaging than the slanderous speech of one to another in a neighborhood gathering, or of one to an audience in a lecture hall. *Media Law Reporter,* the publication that gathers and reprints court decisions from all jurisdictions in the nation, has no "Slander" subtitle in its classification guide.

If there were a rare case in which broadcasting defamation might still be ruled slander, it would be somewhat harder for the offended person to get his case into court than if his case were libel. Ancient rules persist that protect spoken defamation more than written. Thus slander plaintiffs must show precise, special damages—monetary loss—to get many cases into court. That rule applies in all cases except those arising from offending words that impute crime, loathsome or contagious disease, or unchastity or immorality in a female, or injure one in business or calling. And special damages are hard to establish at trial.

That is not to say that broadcasting presents no special libel circumstances different from those of the printed media. For one thing, a study of a three-and-one-half-year period of all defamation decisions reported among the official published court cases, showed that radio and television were the defendants in 32 cases (26 television, 6 radio), compared to 94 for newspapers, 25 for magazines, and 12 for books. For whatever reasons, thus, the raw numbers of reported cases suggest that broadcasters are less frequently confronted with the libel peril than newspapers.[33]

But even if broadcasters are sued less frequently than print media, that could change. It could mean that the lessened emphasis on broadcast news in recent years—following the Federal Communications Commission's lifting of requirements as it "deregulates"—has cut the amount of news and public affairs content generating lawsuits.[34] Keep in mind, however, that one of the largest libel awards in a mass media setting—$3.05 million—came in Brown & Williamson v. Jacobson and CBS. That case resulted from inaccurate portrayal of the tobacco company's advertising tactics.[35]

Offerings such as CBS's "60 Minutes" and ABC's "20/20" tend to generate libel and privacy actions: they dare to do investigative programs. Also, it is clear that if sued successfully, networks do have the deep pockets to pay large damage awards.

[33] Franklin, 479, 488.

[34] In re Deregulation of Radio, 84 FCC 2d 968, 49 R.R.2d 1 (1981); for TV deregulation of content, see 56 R.R.2d 1005 (1984).

[35] Brown & Williamson Tobacco Corp. v. Jacobson, 827 F.2d 1119 (7th Cir.1987), 14 Med.L.Rptr. 1497.

Beyond news or news-related shows, entertainment programming creates what some lawyers term "exposure to suit." Comedic silliness can generate litigation. David Letterman was sued for defamation in 1987 for making a statement parodying an ad featuring "Martha Raye, actress, denture wearer." Letterman said, " 'I saw the most terrifying commercial on television last night, featuring Martha Raye, actress, condom user.' " Ms. Raye's defamation suit failed on grounds that Letterman's quip could not be taken as a statement of fact. Further, Letterman did make a retraction, stating it was "only a joke." [36]

But suppose a defamatory "ad lib" occurs—a spontaneous statement fired off by a gifted comedian in mid-broadcast? A famous old case—Summit Hotel Co. v. NBC (1939) [37]—provides some background. The famed Jazz Singer, Al Jolson, was appearing on an NBC program sponsored by Shell Petroleum; Jolson actually was being paid by the J. Walter Thompson advertising agency, which had been hired by Shell. A golf champion appearing on the show said that his first job was at the Summit Hotel. Jolson blurted an unscripted ad lib: "That's a rotten hotel." Summit sued NBC.

Was NBC to be held to strict accountability for the words, as a newspaper is held strictly accountable for anything it publishes? Or would the nature of the communication process by radio, incompatible with total advance control by the broadcast company, permit a different treatment? The court took into account the special character of broadcasting, and held that the rule of strict accountability did not apply: [38]

> Publication by radio has physical aspects entirely different from those attending the publication of a libel or a slander as the law understands them.
>
> *   *   *
>
> A rule unalterably imposing liability without fault on the broadcasting company under any circumstances is manifestly unjust, unfair and contrary to every principle of morals *   *   *.
>
> *   *   *
>
> We therefore conclude that a broadcasting company that leases its time and facilities to another, whose agents carry on the program, is not liable for an interjected defamatory remark where it appears that it exercised due care in the selection of the lessee, and, having inspected

[36] Raye v. Letterman (Ca.Sup.Ct., L.A. County, 1987), 14 Med.L.Rptr. 2047.

[37] 336 Pa. 182, 8 A.2d 302 (1939).

[38] Summit Hotel Co. v. National Broadcasting Co., 336 Pa. 182, 199, 204, 8 A.2d 302, 310, 312 (1939).

and edited the script, had no reason to believe an extemporaneous defamatory remark would be made. Where the broadcasting station's employe or agent makes the defamatory remark, it is liable, unless the remarks are privileged. . . .

Radio Talk Shows

The popular radio format of the call-in talk-show presents a similar problem. Louisiana and Wyoming courts have settled actions against telephoned libel in diametrically opposed ways. The announcer for the call-in program of station WBOX of Bogalusa, La., asked call-ins not to use specific names and places unless they were willing to identify themselves, in fairness to all people. A call-in by an unidentified person associated the Pizza Shanty with narcotics, and said that Dr. Newman "is writing those prescriptions," and "Guerry Snowden [manager of a drug store] is filling them and they are selling them down there." The announcer broke in repeatedly, trying to get the name of the caller, but did not succeed. Snowden, Newman and Blackwell of the Pizza Shanty sued, and a jury awarded them $4,000, $5,000, and $2,500 respectively. The station appealed, and in upholding the judgments, the Louisiana Appeals Court explained in detail why the station's behavior was reckless disregard of truth or falsity:[39]

> The procedure employed amounted to an open invitation to make any statement a listener desired, regardless of how untrue or defamatory it might be, about any person or establishment, provided only that the declarer identify himself. * * * Such an eventuality was easily foreseeable and likely to occur, as it in fact did. In our judgment, the First Amendment does not protect a publisher against such utter recklessness.

The vastly different outlook of the Wyoming courts was delivered in the case Adams v. Frontier Broadcasting Co., 1976.[40] Here a caller to a talk-show charged falsely that businessman Adams (a former state official) "had been discharged as Insurance Commissioner for dishonesty," and Adams sued. The trial court ruled that he did not have a suit, because the station did not have "reckless disregard" for truth or falsity in failing to use a delay device to cut dangerous words off the air. Adams appealed, and the Wyoming Supreme Court upheld the trial court. It said that requiring stations to use the delay system would mean that[41]

[39] Snowden v. Pearl River Broadcasting Corp., 251 So.2d 405 (La.App.1971).

[40] 555 P.2d 556 (Wyo.1976), 2 Med.L.Rptr. 1166.

[41] Ibid., 564–567, 2 Med.L.Rptr. at 1173–75.

⁎ ⁎ ⁎ broadcasters, to protect themselves from judgments for damages, would feel compelled to adopt and regularly use one of the tools of censorship, an electronic delay system. While using such a system a broadcaster would be charged with the responsibility of concluding that some comments should be edited or not broadcast at all. Furthermore, we must recognize the possibility that the requirement for the use of such equipment might, on occasion, tempt the broadcaster to screen out the comments of those with whom the broadcaster ⁎ ⁎ ⁎ did not agree and then broadcast only the comments of those with whom the broadcaster did agree.

The court said that uninhibited, robust, wide-open debate "must, in the balance, outweigh the ⁎ ⁎ ⁎ right of an ⁎ ⁎ ⁎ official or public figure to be free from defamatory remarks." Reports such as the call-ins, the court added, are a modern version of the town meeting, and give every citizen a chance to speak his mind on issues.

Electronic News Gathering (ENG)

Reported defamation decisions involving Electronic News Gathering (ENG)—the technology for picturing events live! *live!* LIVE! from the scene to the living room—had not appeared by late 1988. With developing areas of law, courts will look to similar fact situations, reasoning by analogy from the past to see whether principles applied previously can be stretched to create rules of law to govern new cases and controversies.

ENG technology, with small cameras (mini-cams) which journalists use to relay reports instantaneously from a scene—by microwave transmission from a remote truck back to the television studio and onto the air and home TV screens, unedited. So is the television station liable if during an ENG report an interviewee utters—without any warning—a defamatory comment?

If the Wyoming decision just discussed on the preceding page is followed, then broadcasters could relax to some extent about the dangers inherent in using ENG equipment. The Wyoming decision valued free discussion over a system of taped delays that might justify broadcasters in airing only those views agreeable to them.[42]

On the other hand, if the Louisiana court's reasoning is followed—to the effect that using live ENG transmissions with

---

[42] Ibid. See also Teeter and David A. Anderson, "ENG and the Law: An Introduction," chapter in Richard D. Yoakam and Charles F. Cremer, ENG: Television News and the New Technology, 2nd ed. (New York: Random House, 1989) pp. 321–322.

little or no ability to control defamatory blurtings or sign-wavings is negligent or reckless behavior—then use of ENG technology in spot news situations will become chancy indeed.[43] Perhaps the safest course is to pass up some of the freewheeling, competitively advantageous use of live ENG reports. Instead, the live feed from the scene of a news story could be taped and reviewed by a news producer for possible editing of obviously defamatory material— before sending the pictures on to the television station's viewers. But that course, obviously, dispels the advantage of live broadcasting, and mistakes in not removing defamatory material during the "live-delayed" tape editing might also create liability for a television station.

The Candidate for Public Office

A special problem in broadcast defamation grew in the special relationship of the political candidates and the broadcast media. The famous Section 315 of the federal Communications Act of 1934[44] says that if a station decides to carry one political candidate's message on the air, it must carry those of any of his political opponents who may seek air time. The station is specifically barred from censoring the candidate's copy.

For decades, this put the station in a difficult position. If it refused air time to all candidates, it could be criticized for refusing to aid the democratic political process, even though it was within the law in so doing. But suppose that it accepted the responsibility of carrying campaign talks: Then, if it spotted possible defamation in the prepared script of the candidate about to go on the air, it had no way of denying him access to its microphone and no power to censor. The law in effect forced the station to carry material that might very well damage it.

Several cases arose in which campaign talk produced defamation for which stations were held liable.[45] But in 1959, a case from North Dakota reached the Supreme Court of the United States and the problem was settled in favor of the beleaguered broadcasters. A.C. Townley, some 30 years after he had been a major political figure in upper midwest states, returned to the political arena in 1956. He ran for the U.S. Senate in North Dakota. Under the requirements of Section 315, radio station WDAY of Fargo, N.D., permitted Townley to broadcast a speech in reply to two other candidates. In it, Townley accused the Farmers Educational and Cooperative Union of America of conspiring to "estab-

---

[43] Snowden v. Pearl River Broadcasting Corp., 251 So.2d 405 (La.App.1971).

[44] 48 Stat. 1088, as amended, 47 U.S.C.A. § 315(a).

[45] Houston Post Co. v. United States, 79 F.Supp. 199 (S.D.Tex.1948); Sorensen v. Wood, 123 Neb. 348, 243 N.W. 82 (1932); Daniell v. Voice of New Hampshire, Inc., 10 Pike & Fischer Radio Reg. 2045.

lish a Communist Farmers Union Soviet right here in North Dakota." The FECUA sued Townley and WDAY for libel. The North Dakota courts ruled that WDAY was not liable and FECUA appealed.[46]

The Supreme Court held that stations did not have power to censor the speeches of political candidates. For with that power, it said, "Quite possibly if a station were held responsible for the broadcast of libelous material, all remarks evenly [sic] faintly objectionable would be excluded out of an excess of caution," and further, a station could intentionally edit a candidate's "legitimate presentation under the guise of lawful censorship of libelous matter."[47] The Court was confident that Congress had intended no such result when it wrote Section 315.

FECUA also argued that Section 315 gave no immunity to a station from liability for defamation spoken during a political broadcast even though censorship of possibly libelous matter was not permitted. The court said:[48]

> Again, we cannot agree. For under this interpretation, unless a licensee refuses to permit any candidate to talk at all, the section would sanction the unconscionable result of permitting civil and perhaps criminal liability to be imposed for the very conduct the statute demands of the licensee.

In ruling that WDAY was not liable for defamation in campaign broadcasts under Section 315, the Supreme Court gave great weight to the principle of maximum broadcast participation in the political process. And it relieved stations of an onerous burden that they had formerly carried in the furtherance of that participation.

SEC. 23. EXTRINSIC CIRCUMSTANCES, LIBEL PER SE, AND LIBEL PER QUOD

Facts extrinsic to the story itself sometimes are necessary to make out a defamatory meaning; such "libel per quod" is distinguished from "libel per se" which ordinarily means that the words are defamatory on their face.

In most cases of libel, the hard words that cause a suit are plain to see or hear in the written word or broadcast. They carry the derogatory meaning in themselves: "thief" or "swindler" or "whore" or "communist" is defamatory on its face if falsely

[46] Farmers Educational and Cooperative Union of America v. WDAY, Inc., 360 U.S. 525, 79 S.Ct. 1302 (1959).

[47] Ibid., at 530, 79 S.Ct. at 1305.

[48] Ibid., at 531, 79 S.Ct. at 1306.

applied to a person. Words that are libelous on their face are called libel *per se.*[49]

But on some occasions, words that have no apparent derogatory meaning turn out to be libelous because circumstances outside the words of the story itself become involved. In the classic case, there was no apparent derogatory meaning in a brief but erroneous story saying that a married woman had given birth to twins. But many people who read the story knew that the woman had been married only a month.[50] Facts extrinsic to the story itself gave the words of the story a libelous meaning. Where extrinsic facts turn an apparently harmless story into defamation, it is called by many American courts libel *per quod.*[51]

In a records column in the *Spokane Chronicle,* this entry appeared on April 21, 1961: "Divorce Granted Hazel M. Pitts from Philip Pitts." In these words alone there was no defamation. But the divorce had taken place on Feb. 2, 1960, 14 months earlier, and now Pitts had been married to another woman for several months. Some of his acquaintances and neighbors concluded that Pitts had been married to two women at once and was a bigamist. Extrinsic facts made the story libelous, and the Pittses were awarded $2,000.[52]

In some jurisdictions it is held that where extrinsic facts are involved in making out a libel, the plaintiff must plead and prove special damages. These damages are specific amounts of pecuniary loss that one suffers as a result of libel, such as cancelled contracts or lost wages.

The magazine *Life* published a story on May 20, 1966, dealing with electronic eavesdropping. With it was a picture of Mary Alice Firestone, her estranged husband, and Jack Harwood who had a business in electronic "snooping," especially in connection with divorce suits. The story read:[53]

> TWO–WAY SNOOP. In Florida, where electronic eavesdropping is frequently employed in divorce suits, private eyes like Jack Harwood of Palm Beach shown above with some of his gear, do a thriving business. Harwood, who boasts, "I'm a fantastic wire man," was hired by tire heir Russell Firestone to keep tabs on his estranged wife, Mary Alice. * * * She in turn got one

[49] 33 Am.Jur. Libel and Slander § 5; Martin v. Outboard Marine Corp., 15 Wis. 2d 452, 113 N.W.2d 135, 138 (1962); Prosser, p. 782.

[50] Morrison v. Ritchie & Co., 39 Scot.L.R. 432 (1902).

[51] 53 C.J.S. Libel and Slander § 8a; Prosser, p. 781; Electric Furnace Corp. v. Deering Milliken Research Corp., 325 F.2d 761, 764–765 (6th Cir.1963).

[52] Pitts v. Spokane Chronicle Co., 63 Wash.2d 763, 388 P.2d 976 (1964).

[53] Firestone v. Time, Inc., 414 F.2d 790, 791 (5th Cir.1969).

of Harwood's assistants to sell out and work for her and, says Harwood "He plays just as rough with the bugs as I do." * * * A court recently ordered Russell and Mary to stop spying on each other.

Mrs. Firestone brought suit for libel per quod, saying that the story injured her in her pending marital litigation. The trial court dismissed her complaint, but the U.S. Circuit Court of Appeals ruled that she had a case, reversing the trial court. It said:[54]

> We are of the opinion that appellant's allegations of injury to her pending marital litigation constitute allegations of "special damages" for libel per quod which are sufficient to withstand a motion to dismiss. While it may be difficult indeed [for Mrs. Firestone] to prove these damages, we are not convinced that they are so speculative that she could not prove them under any circumstances.

SEC. 24. DAMAGES

Compensatory or general damages are granted for injury to reputation, special damages for specific pecuniary loss, and punitive damages as punishment for malicious or extremely careless libel.

Courts and statutes are not entirely consistent in their labeling of the kinds of damages that may be awarded to a person who is libeled. Generally, however, three bases exist for compensating the injured person.

The first is that injuring reputation or causing humiliation ought to be recognized as real injury, even though it is impossible to make a scale of values and fix exact amounts due the injured for various kinds of slurs. If such injury is proved, "general" or "compensatory" damages are awarded.

There is also harm of a more definable kind—actual pecuniary loss that a person may suffer as a result of a libel. It may be the loss of a contract or of a job, and if it can be shown that the loss is associated with the libel, the defamed may recover "special" damages—the cost to him. It is plain, however, that some states use the term "actual damages" to cover both pecuniary loss and damaged reputations. Thus it was held in Miami Herald Pub. Co. v. Brown:[55]

[54] Ibid.

[55] 66 So.2d 679, 680 (Fla.1953). See, also, Ellis v. Brockton Pub. Co., 198 Mass. 538, 84 N.E. 1018 (1908); Osborn v. Leach, 135 N.C. 628, 47 S.E. 811 (1904).

Actual damages are compensatory damages and include (1) pecuniary loss, direct or indirect, or special damages; (2) damages for physical pain and inconvenience; (3) damages for mental suffering; and (4) damages for injury to reputation.

The third basis for awarding damages is public policy—that persons who maliciously libel others ought to be punished for the harm they cause. Damages above and beyond general and actual damages may be awarded in this case, and are called punitive or exemplary damages. Some states deny punitive damages, having decided long ago that they are not justified. For almost a century, Massachusetts, for example, has rejected punitive damages, under a statement by the famed Oliver Wendell Holmes, Jr., then judge of the Massachusetts high court: "The damages are measured in all cases by the injury caused. Vindictive or punitive damages are never allowed in this State. Therefore, any amount of malevolence on the defendant's part in and of itself would not enhance the amount the plaintiff recovered by a penny * * *." [56]

Huge amounts of damage are often claimed, and sometimes awarded although juries' judgments of such astronomical sums as $5,000,000 or $25,000,000 are invariably cut back by trial judges or by appeals courts. Thus not only "private" persons, but also public officials and public figures, even under the requirements of proving actual malice, have in recent years won major damage awards. Some sizable amounts include as $114,000 compensatory plus $100,000 punitive damages (charge of soliciting bribes);[57] $250,000 plus interest (dishonest practices in real estate);[58] $85,000 (sadistic, paranoid);[59] $450,000 (fixed a football game);[60] $350,000 plus possible $50,000 court costs (connections with underworld);[61] $400,000, of which $300,000 was punitive damages (false charge of "Communist"),[62] and $3,000,000 (tobacco company accused of ad strategies to "hook" young smokers).[63]

A California court jury in 1981 awarded $1.6 million to America's beloved comedienne, Carol Burnett, who was falsely portrayed by the *National Enquirer,* said the judge in the case, as

[56] Burt v. Advertiser Newspaper Co., 154 Mass. 238, 245, 28 N.E. 1, 5 (1891).

[57] Cape Publications, Inc. v. Adams, 336 So.2d 1197 (Fla.App.1976), certiorari denied 348 So.2d 945 (Fla.1977).

[58] Sprouse v. Clay Communication, Inc., 158 W.Va. 427, 211 S.E.2d 674 (1975).

[59] Goldwater v. Ginzburg, 414 F.2d 324 (2d Cir.1969).

[60] Curtis Pub. Co. v. Butts, 388 U.S. 130, 87 S.Ct. 1975 (1967).

[61] Alioto v. Cowles Communications, Inc., 430 F.Supp. 1363 (N.D.Cal.1977). Four trials were conducted over eight years before ex-Mayor Alioto of San Francisco won the judgment.

[62] Gertz v. Robert Welch, Inc., 680 F.2d 527 (7th Cir.1982), 8 Med.L.Rptr. 1769.

[63] Brown & Williamson Tobacco Corp. v. Jacobson, 827 F.2d 1119 (7th Cir.1987).

"drunk, rude, uncaring and abusive" in the Rive Gauche restaurant, Los Angeles.[64] The judge disagreed with the jury only in the amount of damages, which he cut in half to $50,000 compensatory plus $750,000 punitive, and the punitive total was cut to $150,000 by the California Court of Appeal more than two years after the jury trial.[65]

"Miss Wyoming" of 1978, Kimerli Jayne Pring, won a jury award of $25 million in punitive damages plus $1.5 million in compensatory damages from *Penthouse* magazine in 1981. She alleged that a *Penthouse* story falsely implied that she was sexually promiscuous and immoral. The staggering punitive award was quickly halved by Federal District Court Judge Clarence C. Brimmer, who said that the reduced figure must be one that would exceed *Penthouse's* libel insurance protection of $10 million if the magazine were to be punished. *Penthouse*, of course, appealed the enormous remainder, and after another year received the judgment: the article could be reasonably understood by readers as only a "pure fantasy," not as defamation of Pring.[66]

One of the largest libel judgments on record against a newspaper is $9.2 million granted in 1980 by an Illinois circuit court jury to a builder for words that the *Alton Telegraph* never published. The offending words were in a memo from two Telegraph reporters to a Justice Department task force on crime, alleging connections of Alton citizens with organized crime. The paper filed for bankruptcy to delay the force of the judgment until the outcome of its appeal was known, and in May 1982, the U.S. Bankruptcy Court for the Southern District of Illinois approved a settlement reported to be $1.4 million between the Telegraph and the central complainant, realtor James Green.[67] The "chill" induced upon future investigative reporting by a newspaper of modest size by such an award takes meaning from the Telegraph's publisher, who said: "Let someone else stick their neck out next time." [68] Since then, that family-owned newspaper has been sold—to a newspaper group.

Courts—as well as media and their attorneys—find evidence in such astronomical awards of hatred and resentment of media by

[64] Burnett v. National Enquirer, Inc. (Cal.Super.Ct.1981), 7 Med.L.Rptr. 1321, 1323.

[65] Burnett v. National Enquirer Inc., 144 Cal.App.3d 991, 193 Cal.Rptr. 206 (1983), 9 Med.L.Rptr. 1921, appeal dismissed 465 U.S. 1014, 104 S.Ct. 1260 (1984).

[66] Pring v. Penthouse Intern., Ltd., 695 F.2d 438 (10th Cir.1982), 8 Med.L.Rptr. 2409.

[67] News Media & the Law, June/July 1982, p. 20.

[68] Carley, How Libel Suit Sapped the Crusading Spirit of a Small Newspaper, Wall St. Journal, Sept. 29, 1983, p. 1; Marc Franklin, What Does "Negligence" Mean in Defamation Cases? 6 Comm/Ent 259, 277 (Winter 1984).

juries. Widespread anti-media attitudes in the public of recent decades [69] are likely to be represented among the cross-section of people that comprises a jury: attitudes that media are overpowerful, arrogant, unfair, immoral, inaccurate, and invaders of privacy. In Guccione v. Hustler Magazine, Inc.[70] the Ohio Court of Appeals looked at a jury award of some $40 million to Guccione. Even though the trial judge had reduced it to about 1/13 of that amount, the Appeals Court said, the jury award was so influenced by passion and prejudice and was so grossly excessive as to indicate the jury's intent to drive *Hustler* out of business. The Court ordered a new trial on the issue of damages.

[69] Max McCombs, Opinion Surveys Offer Conflicting Views as to How Public Views Press, presstime, Feb. 1983, p. 4; "The Media's Credibility Gap," Washington Post National Weekly, April 29, 1985, 38.

[70] 7 Med.L.Rptr. 2077 (1981).

Chapter 5

THE CONSTITUTIONAL DEFENSE
AGAINST LIBEL SUITS

Sec.
25. The Public Principle.
26. Defense Against Public Officials' Suits.
27. Defense Where Public Figures and Public Issues Are Concerned.
28. Defining "Public Figure".
29. Actual Malice.
30. Special Issues: Juries, Summary Judgment, Neutral Reporting, Discovery.

SEC. 25. THE PUBLIC PRINCIPLE

**News media defend against libel suits on grounds of their
service to the public interest.**

As shown in the previous chapter, libel may be an old area of
law, but its perils and pitfalls are exceedingly real today. This
chapter deals with defenses to libel both new and old. Sweeping
changes in libel law since 1964 have changed not only the law of
defamation but also have altered key interpretations of the Constitution of the United States.

The American Constitution was nearly two hundred years old
before courts, attorneys, and journalists concluded that it ought to
protect speech and press against libel actions. It was in 1964 that
the Supreme Court of the United States ruled in New York Times
Co. v. Sullivan that public officials who sued for libel would have
to clear a First Amendment barrier rather than the long-used
lesser barriers of state laws and precedents. The emergence of
multiple suits claiming formerly unheard-of amounts of damages
threatened losses so high as to turn "watchdog" media into sheep.
The public interest in vigorous, unintimidated reporting of the
news was endangered. The society could not accept self-censorship on the part of media "chilled" by fear of libel awards. The
United States Constitution itself, through the First Amendment,
would provide the shield for discussion of public matters that the
narrow vagaries of many state libel laws denied and that the
public welfare demanded.

Striking as the new application of the Constitution was, it
really amounted to an extension of the "public principle" inherent
in centuries-old defenses against libel suits. Defenses had grown in
the context of the need of an open society for information. Society
needs full discussion in media if its citizens are to participate in

decisions that affect their lives, are to have the opportunity to choose, are to maintain ultimate control over government. Those who claimed harm to their reputations might find their suits unavailing if certain public concerns and values were furthered by the publication: Where the hard words were the truth, or were privileged as in news of court proceedings, or were fair criticism of performances by artists and others, the public had a real stake in receiving those words. Media, which pursued their own self-interest in defending against libel awards, made their claims on the basis of the public interest. State libel laws that honored this principle in the Nineteenth Century remain in effect today.

The First Amendment protection raised by the Supreme Court in the 1964 *Sullivan* case told public officials they would have to accept more fully the verbal rough-and-tumble of political life. Most notably, they would have to show that the news medium published the offending words with *actual malice*—knowledge of falsity, or reckless disregard for falsity.

Libel suits remain at the forefront of media's legal encounters. Suits do not drop in number, jury awards to plaintiffs are often astronomical and are sometimes found by courts to reflect deep jury prejudice against media, defense attorneys' fees may reach six or seven figures, public hostility toward media is widespread and intense. The self-censorship and "chill" that the *Sullivan* decision was intended to avert nevertheless has penetrated some newsrooms, diluting investigative reporting. Journalists, legal scholars, the American Civil Liberties Union, and others have urged strengthening of the *Sullivan* doctrine.[1] They are of course opposed by some who feel that *Sullivan* has been too protective of media.[2]

SEC. 26. DEFENSE AGAINST PUBLIC OFFICIALS' SUITS

Under the doctrine of New York Times Co. v. Sullivan, the First Amendment broadly protects the news media from judgments for defamation of public officials.

The Supreme Court of the United States handed down a decision in 1964 that added a great new dimension of protection to

[1] Anthony Lewis, The Sullivan Case, The New Yorker, Nov. 5, 1984, 52; Marc Franklin, Good Names and Bad Law: a Critique of Libel Law and a Proposal, 18 Univ.S.F.L.Rev. 1, Fall 1983; Symposium, Defamation and the First Amendment: New Perspectives, 25 William & Mary L.Rev. 1983–1984, Special Issue; Michael Massing, The Libel Chill: How Cold Is It Out There?, Columbia Journ. Rev., May/ June, 1985, 31; Gilbert Cranberg, ACLU Moves to Protect All Speech on Public Issues from Libel Suits, Civil Liberties, Feb. 1983, 2.

[2] Jan Greene, Libel Plaintiffs Organize Against Media, 1985 Report of Society of Professional Journalists, Sigma Delta Chi, Freedom of Information '84–'85, 4; Bruce E. Fein, New York Times v. Sullivan: an Obstacle to Enlightened Public Discourse ∗ ∗ ∗, quoted in 11 Med.L.Rptr. # 3, 12/18/84, News Notes.

news media in the field of libel. It said that news media are not liable for defamatory words about the public acts of public officials unless the words are published with "actual malice". This defined the word "malice" with a rigor and preciseness that had been lacking for centuries and in a way that gave broad protection to publication. Public officials, it said, must live with the risks of a political system in which there is "a profound national commitment to the principle that debate on public issues should be uninhibited, robust, and wide-open * * *." Even a factual error, it said, will not make one liable for libel in words about the public acts of public officials unless malice is present.

The case was New York Times Co. v. Sullivan.[3] It stemmed from an "editorial advertisement" in the Times, written and paid for by a group intensely involved in the struggle for equality and civil liberties for the American Negro. Suit was brought by L. B. Sullivan, Commissioner of Public Affairs for the city of Montgomery, Ala., against the Times and four Negro clergymen who were among the 64 persons whose names were attached to the advertisement.

The since-famous advertisement, titled "Heed Their Rising Voices," recounted the efforts of southern Negro students to affirm their rights at Alabama State College in Montgomery and told of a "wave of terror" that met them. It spoke of violence against the Reverend Martin Luther King, Jr. in his leadership of the civil rights movement:[4]

Heed Their Rising Voices

As the whole world knows by now, thousands of Southern Negro students are engaged in wide-spread, nonviolent demonstrations in positive affirmation of the right to live in human dignity as guaranteed by the U.S. Constitution and the Bill of Rights. In their effort to uphold these guarantees, they are being met by an unprecedented wave of terror by those who would deny and negate that document which the whole world looks upon as setting the pattern for modern freedom * * *.

* * *

In Montgomery, Alabama, after students sang "My Country, 'Tis of Thee" on the State Capitol steps, their leaders were expelled from school, and truck-loads of

---

[3] 376 U.S. 254, 84 S.Ct. 710 (1964).

[4] Ibid., facing 292, see also Anthony Lewis, *Make No Law* (New York: Random House, 1991).

police armed with shotguns and tear-gas ringed the Alabama State College Campus. When the entire student body protested to state authorities by refusing to re-register, their dining hall was padlocked in an attempt to starve them into submission.

*　*　*

Again and again the Southern violators have answered Dr. King's protests with intimidation and violence. They have bombed his home almost killing his wife and child. They have assaulted his person. They have arrested him seven times—for "speeding," "loitering" and similar "offenses." And now they have charged him with "perjury"—a *felony* under which they could imprison him for *ten years*. Obviously, their real purpose is to remove him physically as the leader to whom the students and millions of others—look for guidance and support, and thereby to intimidate *all* leaders who may rise in the South *　*　*. The defense of Martin Luther King, spiritual leader of the student sit-in movement, clearly, therefore, is an integral part of the total struggle for freedom in the South.

Sullivan was not named in the advertisement, but claimed that because he was Commissioner who had supervision of the Montgomery police department, people would identify him as the person responsible for police action at the State College campus. He said also that actions against the Rev. King would be attributed to him by association.

It was asserted by Sullivan, and not disputed, that there were errors in the advertisement. Police had not "ringed" the campus although they had been there in large numbers. Students sang the National Anthem, not "My Country, 'Tis of Thee." The expulsion had not been protested by the entire student body, but by a large part of it. They had not refused to register, but had boycotted classes for a day. The campus dining hall was not padlocked. The manager of the Times Advertising Acceptability Department said that he had not checked the copy for accuracy because he had no cause to believe it false, and some of the signers were well-known persons whose reputation he had no reason to question.

The trial jury ruled that Sullivan had been libeled and awarded him $500,000, the full amount of his claim. The Supreme Court of Alabama upheld the finding. But the Supreme Court of the United States reversed the decision, holding that the Alabama rule of law was "constitutionally deficient for failure to provide the safeguards for freedom of speech and of the press that are required by the First and Fourteenth Amendments * * *."

The Court said there was no merit to the claim of Sullivan that a paid, commercial advertisement does not ever deserve constitutional protection. The Court said the advertisement: [5]

> . . . communicated information, expressed opinion, recited grievances, protested claimed abuses, and sought financial support on behalf of a movement whose existence and objectives are matters of the highest public concern * * *. That the Times was paid for publishing the advertisement is as immaterial in this connection as is the fact that newspapers and books are sold * * *. Any other conclusion would discourage newspapers from carrying "editorial advertisements" of this type, and so might shut off an important outlet for the promulgation of information and ideas by persons who do not themselves have access to publishing facilities—who wish to exercise their freedom of speech even though they are not members of the press. The effect would be to shackle the First Amendment * * *.

The Court said that the question about the advertisement was whether it forfeited constitutional protection "by the falsity of some of its factual statements and by its alleged defamation of respondent".

The Court rejected the position that the falsity of some of the factual statements in the advertisement destroyed constitutional protection for the Times and the clergymen. "[E]rroneous statement is inevitable in free debate, and * * * it must be protected if the freedoms of expression are to have the 'breathing space' that they 'need to survive,' * * *" it ruled. Quoting the decision in Sweeney v. Patterson,[6] it added that " 'Cases which impose liability for erroneous reports of the political conduct of officials reflect the obsolete doctrine that the governed must not criticize their governors * * *. Whatever is added to the field of libel is taken from the field of free debate.' "

Elaborating the matter of truth and error, it said that it is not enough for a state to provide in its law that the defendant may plead the truth of his words, although that has long been considered a bulwark for protection of expression:[7]

> A rule compelling the critic of official conduct to guarantee the truth of all his factual assertions—and to

[5] Ibid., at 266, 84 S.Ct. at 718.

[6] 76 U.S.App.D.C. 23, 128 F.2d 457, 458 (1942).

[7] New York Times Co. v. Sullivan, 376 U.S. 254, 279, 84 S.Ct. 710, 725 (1964).

do so on pain of libel judgments virtually unlimited in amount—leads to * * * "self-censorship." Allowance of the defense of truth, with the burden of proving it on the defendant, does not mean that only false speech will be deterred. Even courts accepting this defense as an adequate safeguard have recognized the difficulties of adducing legal proofs that the alleged libel was true in all its factual particulars * * *. Under such a rule, would-be critics of official conduct may be deterred from voicing their criticism, even though it is believed to be true and even though it is in fact true, because of doubt whether it can be proved in court or fear of the expense of having to do so * * *. The rule thus dampens the vigor and limits the variety of public debate.

This was the end for Alabama's rule that "the defendant has no defense as to stated facts unless he can persuade the jury that they were true in all their particulars." But the decision reached much farther than to Alabama: Most states had similar rules under which public officials had successfully brought libel suits for decades. In holding that the Constitution protects even erroneous statements about public officials in their public acts, the Court was providing protection that only a minority of states had provided previously.

Having decided that the constitutional protection was not destroyed by the falsity of factual statements in the advertisement, the Court added that the protection was not lost through defamation of an official. "Criticism of their official conduct," the Court held, "does not lose its constitutional protection merely because it is effective criticism and hence diminishes their official reputations." [8]

Then Mr. Justice Brennan, who wrote the majority decision, stated the circumstances under which a public official could recover damages for false defamation: Only if actual malice were present in the publication: [9]

> The constitutional guarantees require, we think, a federal rule that prohibits a public official from recovering damages for a defamatory falsehood relating to his official conduct unless he proves that the statement was made with "actual malice"—that is, with knowledge that it was false or with reckless disregard of whether it was false or not.

Malice in the new context was no longer the vague, shifting concept of ancient convenience for judges who had been shocked or

[8] Ibid., at 273, 84 S.Ct. at 722.

[9] Ibid., at 279–280, 84 S.Ct. 725–726.

angered by words harshly critical of public officials. It was not the oft-used "evidence of ill-will" on the part of the publisher; it was not "hatred" of the publisher for the defamed; it was not "intent to harm" the defamed. Rather, the actual malice which the plaintiff would have to plead and prove lay in the publisher's knowledge that what he printed was false, or else disregard on the part of the publisher as to whether it was false or not.

The old, tort-based libel requirement that the publisher would have to prove the truth of his words disappeared in Brennan's formulation: No longer would the publisher carry the burden; instead, the plaintiff official would have to prove falsity. Further, it would not be enough for the plaintiff to prove knowing or reckless falsity by "the preponderance of evidence". Instead, he would have to prove it "with convincing clarity." Also, to learn whether the trial court had properly applied the law in this important case over how expression might be regulated, the appellate courts were to independently review the trial record itself to make sure that there had been no forbidden intrusion on free expression.[10]

As court interpretation and litigation proceeded after these drastic revisions of the libel law of centuries, New York Times Co. v. Sullivan came to be recognized as the most important First Amendment case for decades. Famed attorney Floyd Abrams termed the decision "majestic," and "one of the most far reaching, extraordinary, and beautiful decisions in American history." [11]

The United States Constitution's guarantee of freedom of speech and press—which of course rules in all states as well as in federal courts [12]—thus protects all that is said about a public official in his public conduct except the malicious. But did "public official" mean every person who is employed by government at any level? Justice Brennan foresaw that this question would arise, but said in a footnote in the *Sullivan* case: "It is enough for the present case that respondent's position as an elected city commissioner clearly made him a public official * * *." [13]

---

[10] Ibid., at 285, 84 S.Ct. 728. Reaffirmed 20 years later by the Supreme Court in Bose Corp. v. Consumers Union, 466 U.S. 485, 104 S.Ct. 1949 (1984), 10 Med.L.Rptr. 1625, 1636–1639, this rule was held to govern all appellate courts in the determination of actual malice under *Sullivan,* rather than a lesser legal standard which provides that trial-court findings of fact are not to be set aside by appellate courts unless they are "clearly erroneous." Appeals courts have usually practiced independent review: LDRC Bulletin # 13, Spring 1985, 2.

[11] 10 Med.L.Rptr. # 17, 4/24/84, News Notes.

[12] Dodd v. Pearson, 277 F.Supp. 469 (D.D.C.1967); Beckley Newspapers Corp. v. Hanks, 389 U.S. 81, 88 S.Ct. 197 (1967).

[13] New York Times Co. v. Sullivan, 376 U.S. 254, 282 n. 23, 84 S.Ct. 710, 727 n. 23 (1964).

In 1966, Rosenblatt v. Baer helped the definition. Newspaper columnist Alfred D. Rosenblatt wrote in the *Laconia Evening Citizen* that a public ski area which in previous years had been a financially shaky operation, now was doing "hundreds of percent" better. He asked, "What happened to all the money last year? And every other year?" Baer, who had been dismissed from his county post as ski area supervisor the year before, brought a suit charging that the column libeled him. The New Hampshire court upheld his complaint and awarded him $31,500. But when the case reached the United States Supreme Court, it reversed and remanded the case. It said that Baer did indeed come within the "public official" category:[14]

> Criticism of government is at the very center of the constitutionally protected area of free discussion. Criticism of those responsible for government operations must be free, lest criticism of government be penalized. It is clear, therefore, that the "public official" designation applies at the very least to those among the hierarchy of government employees who have, or appear to the public to have, substantial responsibility for or control over the conduct of governmental affairs.

The Court also said that the *Sullivan* rule may apply to a person who has left public office, as Baer had, where public interest in the matter at issue is still substantial.

Meanwhile, cases that did not reach the United States Supreme Court were working their way through state courts. During 1964, the Pennsylvania court applied the rule to a senator who was candidate for re-election.[15] Shortly, state legislators were included,[16] a former mayor,[17] a deputy sheriff,[18] a school board member,[19] an appointed city tax assessor,[20] and a police sergeant.[21] A state legislative clerk was ruled a public official, in his suit against a former state senator who accused the clerk of wiretap-

[14] Rosenblatt v. Baer, 383 U.S. 75, 86 S.Ct. 669 (1966).

[15] Clark v. Allen, 415 Pa. 484, 204 A.2d 42 (1964).

[16] Washington Post Co. v. Keogh, 125 U.S.App.D.C. 32, 365 F.2d 965 (1966); Rose v. Koch and Christian Research, Inc., 278 Minn. 235, 154 N.W.2d 409 (1967).

[17] Lundstrom v. Winnebago Newspapers, Inc., 58 Ill.App.2d 33, 206 N.E.2d 525 (1965).

[18] St. Amant v. Thompson, 390 U.S. 727, 88 S.Ct. 1323 (1968).

[19] Cabin v. Community Newspapers, Inc., 50 Misc.2d 574, 270 N.Y.S.2d 913 (1966).

[20] Eadie v. Pole, 91 N.J.Super. 504, 221 A.2d 547 (1966).

[21] Suchomel v. Suburban Life Newspapers, Inc., 84 Ill.App.2d 239, 228 N.E.2d 172 (1967).

ping when he was actually doing his clerk's duty in trying to identify a telephone caller of obscenities.[22]

In some cases, it has been held that one retains public-official status despite lapse of time: A former federal narcotics agent was designated "public official" in his libel suit for a story about his official misconduct, despite the fact that he had left office six years earlier.[23] And since 1971, the Supreme Court's rule has been that a charge of criminal conduct against a present official, no matter how remote in time or place the conduct was, is always "relevant to his fitness for office," and that he must prove actual malice in a libel suit.[24]

Although "public official" would seem to be readily identifiable, many questions remain. Courts and commentators have long taken the view that holding a government position almost automatically gives one the status of public official. But in a case of 1979, Hutchinson v. Proxmire, the Supreme Court said in a footnote that "public official" is not synonymous with "public employee"; that matter remains unsettled.[25] In a Texas case, a county surveyor who brought a libel suit against a newspaper for its criticism of his work as an engineering consultant to a municipality was ruled not to be a public official but a private person in his consultant's work.[26] And in a federal case of 1980, the Court of Appeals for the Fourth Circuit ruled that the Iroquois Research Institute, employed by the Fairfax County (Va.) Water Authority as a research consultant in a county project, was not a public official. Relying on the Rosenblatt v. Baer decision (above, p. 152), the court said that Iroquois was in the sole role of a scientific factfinder, merely reporting the facts it found to the Water Authority. It had no control over the conduct of government affairs, made no recommendations, was little known to the public, and exercised no discretion.[27] It was private.

Nine major media organizations unsuccessfully urged the United States Supreme Court to review the appeals court decision for Iroquois, asserting that the case "presents perhaps the most

[22] Martonik v. Durkan, 23 Wash.App. 47, 596 P.2d 1054 (1979), 5 Med.L.Rptr. 1266.

[23] Hart v. Playboy Enterprises (D.C.Kan.1979), 5 Med.L.Rptr. 1811.

[24] Monitor Patriot Co. v. Roy, 401 U.S. 265, 91 S.Ct. 621 (1971).

[25] 443 U.S. 111, 119 n. 8, 99 S.Ct. 2675, 2680 n. 8 (1979). See David A. Elder, "The Supreme Court and Defamation: a Relaxation of Constitutional Standards," Kentucky Bench and Bar, Jan. 1980, pp. 38–39.

[26] Foster v. Laredo Newspapers Inc., 541 S.W.2d 809 (Tex.1976), certiorari denied 429 U.S. 1123, 97 S.Ct. 1160 (1977).

[27] Arctic Co., Ltd. v. Loudoun Times Mirror et al., 624 F.2d 518 (4th Cir.1980), 6 Med.L.Rptr. 1433, 1435.

significant unresolved issue in the constitutional law of defamation ∗ ∗ ∗." [28] The Supreme Court denied review and the case
went back to trial court with Iroquois confirmed for trial as a
private agency.

SEC. 27. DEFENSE WHERE PUBLIC FIGURES AND PUBLIC ISSUES ARE CONCERNED

**The doctrine of New York Times Co. v. Sullivan extends the
requirement of proving actual malice to public figures,
such as non-official persons who involve themselves in
the resolution of public questions.**

In the *Rosenblatt* case treated above, Justice William O.
Douglas of the Supreme Court wrote a separate concurring opinion. In it he raised the question of what persons and what issues
might call for an extension of the *Sullivan* doctrine beyond "public officials." He said:[29]

> ∗ ∗ ∗ I see no way to draw lines that exclude the
> night watchman, the file clerk, the typist, or, for that
> matter, anyone on the public payroll. And how about
> those who contract to carry out governmental missions?
> Some of them are as much in the public domain as any so-
> called officeholder. ∗ ∗ ∗. [T]he question is whether a
> public *issue* not a public official, is involved.

Back in 1966, the decision in a suit brought by the noted
scientist and Nobel Prize winner, Dr. Linus Pauling, indeed said
that not only "public officials" would have to prove malice if they
were to succeed with libel suits.

Pauling sued the *St. Louis Globe-Democrat* claiming libel in
an editorial entitled "Glorification of Deceit." It referred to an
appearance by Pauling before a subcommittee of the United States
Senate, in connection with Pauling's attempts to promote a nuclear test ban treaty. It read in part: "Pauling contemptuously
refused to testify and was cited for contempt of Congress. He
appealed to the United States District Court to rid him of the
contempt citation, which that Court refused to do." Pauling said
that he had not been cited for contempt, that he had not appealed
to any court to rid himself of any contempt citation, and that no
appeal was expected.

[28] 6 Med.L.Rptr. # 31 (Dec. 9, 1980), News Notes; John Consoli, "Consultants to
Gov't. Aren't Public Figures," Editor & Publisher, Jan. 17, 1981, 9.

[29] Rosenblatt v. Baer, 383 U.S. 75, 89, 86 S.Ct. 669, 678 (1966).

The federal court conceded that Pauling was not a "public official" such as the plaintiff in New York Times Co. v. Sullivan. But it added: [30]

> We feel, however, that the implications of the Supreme Court's majority opinions are clear. Professor Pauling, by his public statements and actions, was projecting himself into the arena of public controversy and into the very "vortex of the discussion of a question of pressing public concern". He was attempting to influence the resolution of an issue which was important, which was of profound effect, which was public and which was internationally controversial * * *.
>
>   *   *   *

Pauling took his case to the United States Supreme Court, but that court denied certiorari, and the lower court's decision stood. [31]

Walker v. A.P. (1967)

While public figure Linus Pauling was thus being embraced within the *Sullivan* rules, another man who had formerly been a general in the United States Army was undertaking a set of "chain" libel suits. This was retired Maj. Gen. Edwin A. Walker, who after a storm of controversy over his troop-indoctrination program had resigned from the Army in 1961. Opposed to the integration of the University of Mississippi, he had in 1962 appeared on the scene there when rioting took place over the enrollment of an African-American, James H. Meredith. An Associated Press dispatch, circulated to member newspapers around the nation, said that Walker had taken command of a violent crowd and had personally led a charge against federal marshals. Further, it described Walker as encouraging rioters to use violence.

Walker's chain libel suits totalled $23,000,000 against the *Louisville Courier-Journal* and *Louisville Times* and their radio station; against *Atlanta Newspapers Inc.* and publisher Ralph McGill; against the Associated Press, the *Denver Post*, the *Fort Worth Star-Telegram* and its publisher, Amon G. Carter, Jr.; against *Newsweek*, the Pulitzer Publishing Co. (*St. Louis Post-Dispatch*), and against the *Delta* (Miss.) *Democrat-Times* and its editor, Hodding Carter. [32]

Walker's case reached the Supreme Court of the United States through a suit against the Associated Press which he filed in Texas. He had been awarded $500,000 by the trial court. The

[30] Pauling v. Globe-Democrat Pub. Co., 362 F.2d 188, 195–196 (8th Cir.1966).

[31] Pauling v. National Review, Inc., 49 Misc.2d 975, 269 N.Y.S.2d 11 (1966).

[32] Editor & Publisher, Oct. 5, 1963, p. 10.

Texas Court of Civil Appeals upheld the judgment, and stated without elaboration that the Times v. Sullivan rule was not applicable. The Supreme Court of Texas denied a writ of error,[33] and the United States Supreme Court granted certiorari.

The U.S. Supreme Court decided Associated Press v. Walker and Curtis Publishing Co. v. Butts in the same opinion.[34] Wallace Butts was former athletic director of the University of Georgia, and had brought suit against Curtis for a story in the *Saturday Evening Post* that had accused him of conspiring to "fix" a football game between Georgia and the University of Alabama. Neither Walker nor Butts was a "public official" and the late Justice John M. Harlan's opinion said explicitly that the Court took up the two cases to consider the impact of the Times v. Sullivan rule "on libel actions instituted by persons who are not public officials, but who are 'public figures' and involved in issues in which the public has a justified and important interest." [35]

Four opinions were delivered by the Court. All agreed that a publication about a "public figure" deserves First Amendment protection. All agreed that both men were public figures. All agreed that Walker should not recover damages against the AP, and most agreed that Butts should recover.

Walker was a "public figure," said Justice John Harlan in writing for four members of the Court, "by his purposeful activity amounting to a thrusting of his personality into the 'vortex' of an important public controversy." Agreeing, in writing for three members, Chief Justice Earl Warren said that "Under any reasoning, General Walker was a public man" in whose conduct society had a substantial interest. Warren said that giving a public figure, such as Walker, an easier burden to meet than a public official in recovering damages for libel [36]

> * * * has no basis in law, logic or First Amendment Amendment policy. Increasingly in this country, the distinction between governmental and private sectors are blurred * * *.

> Under any reasoning, General Walker was a public man in whose public conduct society and the press had a legitimate and substantial interest.

[33] Associated Press v. Walker, 393 S.W.2d 671 (Tex.Civ.App.1965).

[34] Curtis Pub. Co. v. Butts, 388 U.S. 130, 87 S.Ct. 1975 (1967).

[35] Ibid., at 134, 87 S.Ct. at 1980.

[36] Ibid., at 163–165, 87 S.Ct. at 1995–1997.

Harlan argued that the public figure should not have to meet as difficult a standard of proof as the public official. He articulated a lower barrier for the former: [37]

> We consider and would hold that a "public figure" who is not a public official may * * * recover damages for a defamatory falsehood whose substance makes substantial danger to reputation apparent, on a showing of highly unreasonable conduct constituting an extreme departure from the standards of investigation and reporting ordinarily adhered to by responsible publishers.

Then he examined AP's reporting in the Walker case and found no such departure from responsible reporting standards: The AP story was news which required immediate dissemination, the correspondent was competent and his dispatches were internally consistent with a single exception. [38]

So public figure Walker lost his case because Harlan found no "extreme departure from responsible reporting" by the Post and Warren found no "actual malice." But public figure Butts, according to both opinions, should win his case against the *Saturday Evening Post,* and keep the $460,000 that he had been awarded at trial. The Post had stated that Butts had revealed his school's football secrets to Alabama coach Paul Bryant just before a game between the schools. The article said that one George Burnett had accidentally been connected, in using the telephone, to the conversation between the two in which Butts told Bryant the secrets. According to the article, Burnett made notes of the conversation as he listened, and the Post obtained his story. Justice Harlan's analysis of the Post's methods of investigation— analysis that was noted with approval in the separate opinion of chief Justice Warren—found the Post wanting. He said, in part: [39]

> The evidence showed that the Butts story was in no sense "hot news" and the editors of the magazine recognized the need for a thorough investigation of the serious charges. Elementary precautions were, nevertheless, ignored. The Saturday Evening Post knew that Burnett had been placed on probation in connection with bad check charges, but proceeded to publish the story on the basis of his affidavit without substantial independent support. Burnett's notes were not even viewed by any of the magazine personnel prior to publication. John Carmichael who was supposed to have been with Burnett when the phone call was overheard was not interviewed. No

[37] Ibid., at 155, 87 S.Ct. at 1991.

[38] Ibid., at 158–159, 87 S.Ct. at 1993–1994.

[39] Ibid., at 157, 87 S.Ct. at 1992.

attempt was made to screen the films of the game to see if Burnett's information was accurate, and no attempt was made to find out whether Alabama had adjusted its plans after the alleged divulgence of information.

Again, there was the application of different standards by Harlan and Warren. Harlan found this kind of reporting to be "highly unreasonable conduct constituting an extreme departure from the standards of investigation and reporting ordinarily adhered to by responsible publishers." And in Chief Justice Warren's opinion, it was evidence of "reckless disregard" of whether the statement were false or not.

Justices Black and Douglas joined the three who endorsed Warren's opinion on a single matter—applying the same actual malice requirement to public figures as to public officials. Thus five justices provided a majority for this standard to prevail over Harlan's "extreme departure" standard. Further, Warren had said he could not believe that "a standard which is based on such an unusual and uncertain formulation" as Harlan's could either guide a jury or afford "the protection for speech and debate that is fundamental to our society and guaranteed by the First Amendment." [40] While Justice Harlan's attempt to place an easier burden upon public figures than public officials through his "extreme departure" standard was persuasive for a few lower courts,[41] his formulation came ultimately to be flatly rejected as a rule for public persons' libel suits.[42]

Then in the famous case of Rosenbloom v. Metromedia, Inc.,[43] in 1971, a plurality of three justices of the U.S. Supreme Court approved extending the actual malice requirement in libel whenever the news was a "matter of public interest." It denied recovery for libel to George Rosenbloom, distributor of nudist magazines in Philadelphia, a private citizen involved in a matter of public interest. Metromedia radio station WIP had said Rosenbloom had been arrested on charges of possessing obscene literature, and linked him to the "smut literature rackets." Later acquitted of obscenity charges, Rosenbloom sued for libel in the

[40] Ibid., at 163, 87 S.Ct. at 1995.

[41] Cerrito v. Time, Inc., 302 F.Supp. 1071 (N.D.Cal.1969); Fotochrome Inc. v. New York Herald Tribune, Inc., 61 Misc.2d 226, 305 N.Y.S.2d 168 (1969); Holmes v. Curtis Pub. Co., 303 F.Supp. 522, 525 (D.S.C.1969); Buckley v. Vidal, 50 F.R.D. 271 (S.D.N.Y.1970); Cervantes v. Time, Inc., 330 F.Supp. 936 (E.D.Mo.1971). See esp. Chapadeau v. Utica Observer-Dispatch, Inc., 38 N.Y.2d 196, 379 N.Y.S.2d 61, 341 N.E.2d 569 (1975) for the New York courts' development of a "fault" standard in libel cases brought by private persons under Gertz v. Robert Welch, Inc., 418 U.S. 323, 94 S.Ct. 2997 (1974).

[42] Hunt v. Liberty Lobby, 720 F.2d 631 (11th Cir.1983), 10 Med.L.Rptr. 1097, 1109.

[43] 403 U.S. 29, 91 S.Ct. 1811 (1971).

WIP broadcasts, and won $275,000 in trial court before losing upon the station's appeal. In the U.S. Supreme Court, five justices agreed that Rosenbloom should not recover. Three of them endorsed the "matter of public interest" rationale, laid out in Justice William J. Brennan's plurality (not a majority) opinion: [44]

> If a matter is a subject of public or general interest, it cannot suddenly become less so merely because a private individual is involved, or because in some sense the individual did not "voluntarily" choose to become involved. The public's primary interest is in the event * * *. We honor the commitment to robust debate on public issues, which is embodied in the First Amendment, by extending constitutional protection to all discussion and communication involving matters of public or general concern, without regard to whether the persons involved are famous or anonymous.

Lower courts accepted the plurality opinion as ruling. The sweep of "matter of public or general interest" was so powerful that few libel suits, whether by public or private persons, were won. Commentators on press law forecast the disappearance of libel suits. But in mid-1974, hardly three years after *Rosenbloom,* the support of a three-justice plurality in that decision for the "matter of public interest" interpretation revealed itself as a shaky foundation. A five-man majority of the U.S. Supreme Court rejected it as a rule in Gertz v. Robert Welch, Inc.[45]

SEC. 28. DEFINING "PUBLIC FIGURE"

Distinguishing a public from a private person under *Gertz* rests on either of two bases—fame, notoriety, power or influence that render one a public figure for all purposes, or the status that makes one a public figure only for a limited range of issues. In either case, the person assumes special prominence in the resolution of public controversy.

Elmer Gertz, a Chicago lawyer, was retained by a family to bring a civil action against Policeman Nuccio who had shot and killed their son and had been convicted of second degree murder. *American Opinion,* a monthly publication given to the views of the John Birch Society, carried an article saying that Gertz was an architect of a "frame-up" of Nuccio, that he was part of a communist conspiracy to discredit local police, and that he was a Leninist

[44] Ibid., at 52, 91 S.Ct. at 1824.

[45] 418 U.S. 323, 94 S.Ct. 2997 (1974). For the position that the "public interest" criterion sould be the rule, see Anthony Lewis, New York Times v. Sullivan Reconsidered * * *, 83 Columbia L.Rev. 603 (1983).

and a "Communist-fronter." Gertz, who was none of these things, brought a libel suit and for six years battled the shifting uncertainties of the courts' attitudes toward "public official," "public figure," and "matter of public interest" for the purposes of libel. A jury found libel *per se* and awarded Gertz $50,000 in damages, disallowed by the trial judge and also by the Seventh Circuit Court of Appeals: [46] Because the *American Opinion* story concerned a matter of public interest, Gertz would have to show actual malice on its part, even though he might be a private citizen. Objecting, Gertz appealed to the U.S. Supreme Court.

Private Individuals Exempted From Actual Malice Rule

With four other justices agreeing, Justice Powell wrote for the majority.[47] The plurality opinion in Rosenbloom v. Metromedia, relied on by the Circuit Court, should not stand. Justice Powell had no quarrel with requiring public officials and public figures to prove actual malice in their libel suits. But he reasoned that the legitimate state interest in compensating injury to the reputation of private individuals—of whom, it was found, Gertz was one— requires that such persons be held to less demanding proof of fault by the offending news medium—only "negligence," rather than the stern actual malice standard. They are at a disadvantage, compared with public officials and public figures, where they are defamed: [48]

> Public officials and public figures usually enjoy significantly greater access to the channels of effective communication and hence have a more realistic opportunity to counteract false statements than private individuals normally enjoy. Private individuals are therefore more vulnerable to injury, and the state interest in protecting them is correspondingly greater. * * *
>
> An individual who decides to seek governmental office must accept certain necessary consequences of that involvement in public affairs. He runs the risk of closer public scrutiny than might otherwise be the case.
> * * *
>
> Those classed as public figures stand in a similar position. Hypothetically, it may be possible for someone to become a public figure through no purposeful action of his own, but the instances of truly involuntary public

---

[46] Gertz v. Robert Welch, Inc., 471 F.2d 801 (7th Cir.1972). A dozen years after Gertz brought his first action, a federal jury awarded him $400,000 upon re-trial, and the Seventh Circuit Court of Appeals upheld the award: Gertz v. Welch, Inc., 680 F.2d 527 (7th Cir.1982), 8 Med.L.Rptr. 1769.

[47] Gertz v. Robert Welch, Inc., 418 U.S. 323, 94 S.Ct. 2997 (1974).

[48] Ibid., at 344–346, 94 S.Ct. at 3009–3010.

figures must be exceedingly rare. For the most part those who attain this status have assumed roles of special prominence in the affairs of society.

* * * the communications media are entitled to act on the assumption that public officials and public figures have voluntarily exposed themselves to increased risk of injury from defamatory falsehoods concerning them. No such assumption is justified with respect to a private individual. He has not accepted public office nor assumed an "influential role in ordering society." * * *

Dissenting Justices Douglas and Brennan wanted to affirm the Court of Appeals finding that anyone—including Gertz—would have to prove actual malice in offending words from a story of general or public interest. Brennan felt that the *Gertz* decision damaged the protection which mass media ought to have under the First Amendment. Douglas repeated his view that the First Amendment would bar Congress from passing any libel law; and like Congress, "States are without power 'to use a civil libel law or any other law to impose damages for merely discussing public affairs'." [49]

Brennan, who had written the plurality opinion in *Rosenbloom,* reiterated his point there: "Matters of public or general interest do not 'suddenly become less so merely because a private individual is involved, or because in some sense the individual did not "voluntarily" choose to become involved'." [50] He said it is unproved and highly improbable that the public figure will have better access to the media. The ability of all to get access will depend on the "same complex factor * * *: the unpredictable event of the media's continuing interest in the story." As to the assumption that private people deserve special treatment because they do not assume the risk of defamation by freely entering the public arena, he stated that " * * * voluntarily or not, we are all 'public' men to some degree." [51]

Gertz Is Not a "Public" Person

Returning, now, to Gertz and the finding that he was a private individual rather than a public person: The Supreme Court majority first brushed off the notion that he might be considered a public *official.*

He'd never had a paid government position, and his only "office" had been as a member of mayor's housing committees years before. As for the suggestion that he was a "de facto public

[49] Ibid., at 356, 94 S.Ct. at 3015.
[50] Ibid., at 362, 94 S.Ct. at 3018.
[51] Ibid., at 364, 94 S.Ct. at 3019.

official" because he had appeared at the coroner's inquest into the murder (incidental to his representing the family in civil litigation): If that made him a "public official," the court said, all lawyers would become such in their status as "officers of the court," and that would distort the plain meaning of the "public official" category beyond all recognition.[52]

But the thorny possibility that Gertz was a public *figure* remained. Because lower courts have so frequently drawn on the Supreme Court's treatment of the matter in *Gertz*, detail is called for here.

To start with, the court said, persons in either of two cases "assume special prominence in the resolution of public questions." [53] In either case, "they invite attention and comment."

> [Public figure] designation may rest on either of two alternative bases. In some instances an individual may achieve such pervasive fame or notoriety that he becomes a public figure for all purposes and contexts. More commonly, an individual voluntarily injects himself or is drawn into a particular public controversy and thereby becomes a public figure for a limited range of issues. In either case such persons assume special prominence in the resolution of public questions.

1. The first of the two—deemed a public figure for all purposes and in all contexts: One should not be deemed a public personality for all aspects of his life, "absent clear evidence of general fame or notoriety in the community and pervasive involvement in the affairs of society."

Gertz was not a public figure under this first category. He had, indeed, been active in community and professional affairs, serving as an officer of local civil groups and various legal agencies. He had published several works on law. Thus he was well-known in some circles. But he had "achieved no general fame or notoriety in the community." No member of the jury panel, for example, had ever heard of him.

2. The second of the two—where "an individual voluntarily injects himself * * * into a particular public controversy and thereby becomes a public figure for a limited range of issues." Alternative wording used by the court was that "commonly, those classed as public figures have thrust themselves "into the vortex"

[52] Ibid., at 350, 94 S.Ct. at 3012.

[53] Ibid., at 352, 94 S.Ct. at 3013. Succeeding definitions and procedure in determining "public figure" are taken from *Gertz*, pp. 3009 and 3013.

of particular public controversies in order to influence the resolution of the issues involved." [54]

In determining the status of this person who has no general fame or notoriety in the community, the court said the procedure should be one of "looking to the nature and extent of an individual's participation in the particular controversy giving rise to the defamation." In this statement, the Court was rejecting the trend under *Rosenbloom* to examine the *topic* of the news to determine whether the public principle held, and instead to examine the *individual* and his role in public life. Doing this for Attorney Gertz, the court found again that he was not a public figure: He had played only a minimal role at the coroner's inquest, and only as the representative of a private client; he had had no part in the criminal prosecution of Officer Nuccio; he had never discussed the case with the press; and he "did not thrust himself into the vortex of this public issue * * *" nor "engage the public's attention in an attempt to influence its outcome." Gertz was not, by this second basis, a public figure, and he would not, consequently, have to prove that *American Opinion* libeled him with actual malice. The Supreme Court ordered a new trial.

The modification of *Sullivan* and *Rosenbloom* by *Gertz* was a damaging retreat in protection, in the eyes of media commentators. Now, journalists suspected that although there were gains for the media under *Gertz*—in requiring plaintiffs to show fault and in limiting the reach of punitive damages—it was on the whole a great door-opener for libel suits by private plaintiffs who no longer had to prove actual malice.

David A. Anderson, legal scholar and former journalist, argued that even under the protection of the *Rosenbloom* interpretation, the self-censorship by the press which *Sullivan* had sought to minimize in establishing the malice rule and other safeguards, was real.[55] He wrote that the unconventional, non-established media, sometimes known as the "alternative" press, and the world of magazines, are forced to self-censorship under *Gertz*. The people about whom the alternative press writes are frequently from spheres of life not much handled by the established newspaper media, and thus not established as "public figures." Often financially marginal, the unconventional media face a further problem in the high cost of legal defense. Anderson's worry over

---

[54] As a variant of the "limited range of issues" public figure, the Court identified the person who has not *voluntarily* entered a public controversy, but is *drawn* into it. Subsequent decisions have heavily vitiated this concept. See M.L. Rosen, "Media Lament: the Rise and Fall of Involuntary Public Figures," 54 St. John's L.Rev. 487, Spring 1980.

[55] David A. Anderson, Libel and Press Self-Censorship, 53 Tex.L.Rev. 422 (1975); for an historic pattern supporting Anderson, see Norman L. Rosenberg, *Protecting the Best Men* (Chapel Hill: University of North Carolina Press, 1986).

self-censorship, whether under *Gertz* or under Draconian jury awards even where the greater protection of *Sullivan* applies, runs strongly through the world of the media.[56]

Courts Determine the "Public" and the "Private" under *Gertz*

Whatever the level of press self-censorship under *Gertz* may be, subsequent cases show that media need to be discriminating. Sometimes, distinguishing the "public" from the "private" is not easy, even for the judge, who makes the decision before the case goes to the jury. One judge has said that the two concepts are "nebulous," and "Defining public figures is much like trying to nail a jellyfish to the wall." [57]

The first of the two *Gertz* categories of public figures is those who "occupy positions of such persuasive power and influence they are deemed public figures for all purposes." This was the case with Myron Steere, attorney for Nellie Schoonover in her trial and conviction for first degree murder. Some time after the trial, an Associated Press story said that the Kansas State Board of Law Examiners had recommended to the Kansas Supreme Court that it publicly censure Steere for his conduct of the defense. The examiners found, among other things, that Steere had entered into a "contingency agreement" with Mrs. Schoonover, providing that he would get all but $10,000 of her late husband's estate if she was acquitted. Steere sued broadcasters and newspapers for libel, charging inaccuracies in the stories.[58] The trial court held that he would have to prove actual malice, for he was a public figure for all purposes, and the Kansas Supreme Court agreed, finding that "appellant was a public figure for all purposes by virtue of his general fame and notoriety in the community." Then it described the reach and breadth of Steere's involvement in the life of the community: he had practiced law in the county for 32 years and had been the county attorney for 8 of those years.[59]

> * * * He has achieved a position of some influence in local affairs capped by his representation of Nellie Schoonover in her well publicized, famous murder trial. We find the totality of his experience in Franklin County

[56] 10 Med.L.Rptr. # 13, 3/27/84, News Notes; 10 Med.L.Rptr. # 34, 8/21/84, News Notes.

[57] Rosanova v. Playboy Enterprises, Inc., 411 F.Supp. 440, 443 (S.D.Ga.1976).

[58] Steere v. Cupp, 226 Kan. 566, 602 P.2d 1267 (1979), 5 Med.L.Rptr. 2046. And see Sprouse v. Clay Communication, 158 W.Va. 427, 211 S.E.2d 674 (1975), 1 Med.L. Rptr. 1695, 1704.

[59] Ibid., 573–74, 1273–74, 2050–51. Note, General Public Figures Since Gertz v. Welch, 58 St. John's L.Rev. 355 (Winter 1984).

gave Myron Steere the requisite fame and notoriety in his community to be declared a public figure for all purposes.

Not only a *person* may be a "public figure." In Ithaca College v. Yale Daily News Pub. Co., Inc., the facts started with the publication of "The Insider's Guide to the Colleges 1978–79," 404 pages of material compiled and edited by the *Yale Daily News*. Through stringers, the editors obtained information on many colleges, and published of Ithaca College such statements as "Sex, drugs, and booze are the staples of life." Ithaca College sued for libel, charging falsity and damage to its business and academic reputation. While Ithaca terms itself a "private" college, the New York Supreme Court said it could not be such in a libel suit.[60] The college assumes a role as a qualified educator of many students, serves the public good, is responsible for fair dealing with its students, the court ruled. It is recognized to be of "general fame or notoriety in the community [with] pervasive involvement in the affairs of society." The court decided that the college was a "public figure for all purposes." Similarly, corporations also may be classified as "public figures."[61]

Far more common than the person of general fame or notoriety who is a public figure for all purposes is the individual who is such for a "limited range of issues." Thus Dr. Frederick Exner for two decades and more had been "injecting" and "thrusting" himself into the fluoridation-of-water controversy through speeches, litigation, books, and articles. When he brought a libel suit for a magazine's criticism of his position, he was adjudged a public figure for "the limited issue of fluoridation" by having assumed leadership and by having attempted to influence the outcome of the issue. He had taken the role of "attempting to order society" in its concern with fluoridation.[62]

Harry Buchanan and his firm were retained to perform accounting services for the Finance Committee to Re-elect the President in 1971. Common Cause brought suit in 1972 to force the Committee to report transactions, and Buchanan's deposition was taken in the matter. In reporting the suit, Associated Press compared matters involving Buchanan with the handling of money by convicted Watergate conspirator Bernard L. Barker. Buchanan sued AP for libel, and on the question whether he was a public figure, the court said "yes." There was intense interest in campaign finances at the time Buchanan was working for the Committee. The system he helped set up for the Committee and

---

[60] 105 Misc.2d 793, 433 N.Y.S.2d 530 (1980), 6 Med.L.Rptr. 2180.

[61] See WTSP–TV, Inc. v. Vick (Fla.Cir.Ct.1985), 11 Med.L.Rptr. 1543. But see Blue Ridge Bank v. Veribanc, Inc., 866 F.2d 681 (4th Cir.1989).

[62] Exner v. American Medical Ass'n, 12 Wash.App. 215, 529 P.2d 863 (1974).

the cash transactions in which he took part, were legitimate matters of public scrutiny and concern. Buchanan was a key person for attempts to investigate. He was an agent of the committee who voluntarily accepted his role, and as such a public figure.[63]

A businessman-president of a state bailbond underwriters' association attacked a Pennsylvania state commission's report on bailbond abuses and attempted to have the commission dissolved; he had injected himself into controversy and was a public figure.[64] The United States Labor Party is a public political organization actively engaged in publishing articles, magazines, and books, and is a public figure "at least in regard to those areas of public controversy * * * in which [it has] participated.[65] The Church of Scientology seeks to play an influential role in ordering society, has thrust itself onto the public scene, and is a public figure.[66] So is a Roman Catholic priest who has actively involved himself in the debate over the independence of Northern Ireland, through radio, television, and speeches.[67]

If the above persons and organizations strike one as plainly appropriate public figures, where does the problem arise? What of the above-quoted comment by a judge: "Defining public figures is much like trying to nail a jellyfish to the wall."? The fact is that there have been hard cases—occasionally notorious, and often deeply disturbing to media people who express dismay at courts' finding certain individuals to be private even though in the public eye. Two circumstances illustrate problems:

First: Not rarely, citizens who become involved in any of myriad proceedings of government turn out to be "private" under new rules, whereas journalists' long-standing presumption has been that government proceedings are public and almost inevitably make public figures out of participants.

We may start with the most spectacular, notorious case in the line of separating "private" from "public" persons since *Gertz.* Mary Alice Firestone—wife of a prominent member of the wealthy industrial family and member of the "society" elite of Palm Beach, Fla. (the "sporting set," as U.S. Supreme Court Justice Marshall called it)—went to court to seek separate maintenance from her husband, Russell. He counterclaimed for divorce on grounds of

---

[63] Buchanan v. Associated Press, 398 F.Supp. 1196 (D.D.C.1975).

[64] Childs v. Sharon Herald (Pa.Ct.Com.Pls.1979), 5 Med.L.Rptr. 1597.

[65] United States Labor Party v. Anti-Defamation League (N.Y.Sup.Ct.1980), 6 Med.L.Rptr. 2209.

[66] Church of Scientology of California v. Siegelman, 475 F.Supp. 950 (S.D.N.Y. 1979), 5 Med.L.Rptr. 2021.

[67] McManus v. Doubleday & Co., Inc., 513 F.Supp. 1383 (S.D.N.Y.1981), 7 Med.L. Rptr. 1475.

adultery and extreme cruelty. The trial covered 17 months, both parties charging extramarital escapades ("that would curl Dr. Freud's hair," the trial judge said). Several times during the 17 months, Mrs. Firestone held press conferences. She subscribed to a clipping service. *Time* magazine reported the trial's outcome: Russell Firestone was granted a divorce on grounds of extreme cruelty and adultery, *Time* said. But the trial judge had not, technically, found adultery, and Mrs. Firestone sued *Time* for libel.[68] A jury awarded her $100,000 and *Time* appealed, arguing that Mrs. Firestone was a public figure and as such would have to prove actual malice in *Time's* story.

Justice Rehnquist, writing for the majority of five of the U.S. Supreme Court, said "no" to *Time's* appeal. He quoted various passages from the *Gertz* definition of "public figure" which he said did not fit Mrs. Firestone: "special prominence in the resolution of public questions," "persuasive power and influence," "thrust themselves to the forefront of particular public controversies in order to influence the resolution of the issues involved." The crux of the matter was that, for all the publicity involved: [69]

> Dissolution of marriage through judicial proceedings is not the sort of "public controversy" referred to in *Gertz*, even though the marital difficulties of extremely wealthy individuals may be of interest to some portion of the reading public.

In spite of her position in the "Palm Beach 400," her press conferences, and her clipping service, Mrs. Firestone was a "private" individual, and her "private" marital affairs did not "become public for the purposes of libel law solely because they are aired in a public forum."

Predictably, news media were outraged at the designation of Mrs. Firestone as "private." Accustomed to thinking of official proceedings including divorce trials as public matters which could be reported without fear of injuring the privacy of the participants, journalists had to make a conscious effort to think of Mrs. Firestone as in some sense private. Their effort was made more difficult in that her position in society had for years before the divorce placed her among the "newsworthy" and in the public eye. And with her use of clipping services and press conferences during the drawn-out divorce trial, her "public" character had seemed confirmed. What might the decision mean for future cases?

Three years after *Firestone*, the Supreme Court took up another case whose background was also a public court proceeding. And again, the fact that a libel plaintiff's suit arose from his

[68] Time, Inc. v. Firestone, 424 U.S. 448, 96 S.Ct. 958 (1976).

[69] Ibid., at 454, 96 S.Ct. at 965.

involvement in an official public matter did not destroy private status for his libel suit. Ilya Wolston had been summoned in 1958 to appear before a grand jury that was investigating espionage, but failed to appear. Later, he pleaded guilty to a charge of criminal contempt for failing to respond to the summons and accepted conviction. Sixteen years later, *Reader's Digest* published a book by John Barron on Soviet espionage in the U.S. The book said erroneously that the FBI had identified Wolston as a Soviet intelligence agent. Wolston sued for libel. He asserted that he had been out of the limelight for many years, and that if he had been a public figure during the investigations, he now deserved to be considered private. The lower courts disagreed, saying the long lapse of time was immaterial, that Soviet espionage of 1958 continued to be a subject of importance, and that Wolston thus remained a public figure. He appealed to the Supreme Court, which by a vote of 8–1 reversed the lower courts and determined that Wolston was a private person who would not have to prove actual malice in his libel suit against the *Reader's Digest*. Justice Rehnquist wrote: [70]

> We do not agree with respondents and the lower courts that petitioner can be classed as such a limited-purpose public figure. First, the undisputed facts do not justify the conclusion of the District Court and the Court of Appeals that petitioner "voluntarily thrust" or "injected" himself into the forefront of the public controversy surrounding the investigation of Soviet espionage. * * * It would be more accurate to say that petitioner was dragged unwillingly into the controversy. The government pursued him in its investigation. Petitioner did fail to respond to a grand jury subpoena, and this failure, as well as his subsequent citation for contempt, did attract media attention. But the mere fact that petitioner voluntarily chose not to appear before the grand jury, knowing that his action might be attended by publicity, is not decisive on the question of public figure status.

On the date of the *Wolston* decision, another Supreme Court ruling on the definition of public figure was handed down, and again the decision cast the public figure into a narrower light than a host of journalists felt warranted. This time, the Court said that researcher Ronald Hutchinson, who had received some $500,000 in federal government grants for his experiments, including some on monkeys' response to aggravating stimuli, was a private figure.[71] He would not have to prove actual malice in his libel suit against

[70] Wolston v. Reader's Digest Ass'n, Inc., 443 U.S. 157, 99 S.Ct. 2701 (1979).

[71] Hutchinson v. Proxmire, 443 U.S. 111, 99 S.Ct. 2675 (1979).

Sen. William Proxmire of Wisconsin, who had labeled Hutchinson's work "monkey business" and had given a "Golden Fleece of the Month Award" to government funding agencies which he ridiculed for wasting public money on grants to Hutchinson. A Proxmire press release, a newsletter, and a television appearance were involved, all following Proxmire's announcement of the Award on the senate floor.

Concerned about the narrowing of the definition of "public figure," media attorney James C. Goodale had reasoned in advance of the decision that the lower courts' holding that Hutchinson was, indeed, a public figure deserved to be upheld in the Supreme Court. "Clearly information about how our government grants money and who gets it," he said, "should be the subject of unlimited comment by anyone—especially by a U.S. Senator." [72]

The Supreme Court, however, did not see it that way. It reversed the lower courts, saying that their conclusion that Hutchinson was a public figure was erroneously based upon two factors: one, his success in getting federal grants and newspaper reports about the grants, and two, his access to media as represented by news stories that reported his response to the Golden Fleece Award. But: [73]

> Hutchinson did not thrust himself or his views into public controversy to influence others. Respondents have not identified such a particular controversy; at most, they point to concern about general public expenditures. But that concern is shared by most and relates to most public expenditures; it is not sufficient to make Hutchinson a public figure. If it were, everyone who received or benefited from the myriad public grants for research could be classified as a public figure.

"Subject-matter classifications"—such as general public expenditures—had been rejected in *Gertz* as the touchstone for deciding who would have to prove actual malice, the Court said: instead, the person and his activities must be the basis. And, finally, the Court said it could not agree that Hutchinson had such access to the media that he should be classified as a public figure; his access was limited to responding to the announcement of the Golden Fleece Award.

[72] "Court Again to Consider Who Is A Public Figure," National Law Journal, Feb. 8, 1979, 23.

[73] Hutchinson v. Proxmire, 443 U.S. 111, 134–135; 99 S.Ct. 2675, 2688 (1979). Proxmire was reported to have settled the suit out of court for $10,000, and the Senate was reported to have assumed his trial costs of more than $100,000. D.S. Greenberg, "Press Was a Co-Villain in Proxmire's Golden Gimmick," Chicago Tribune, April 17, 1980.

Second: Other circumstances complicate the defining of public figures. Justice Powell's definition in *Gertz* and various courts' since (as in *Firestone, Wolston,* and *Hutchinson*), make it crucial to decide whether the person has voluntarily injected himself into a matter of public controversy to help resolve that controversy. American courts, unfortunately, have not drawn clear or predictable lines to separate "public figures" from "private persons." Even so, it may be said that there are many public figures besides those who voluntarily "get involved" and try to influence the outcome of public issues. (Please note, as discussed later in Section 35, older tort law, dating back long before New York Times v. Sullivan, has traditionally provided the defense of "fair comment for media that are sued for their critiques of authors' works, restaurants, plays, celebrities and public entertainers.) [74]

Recent decisions have defined the following as "all-purpose" or "pervasive" public figures: Entertainers Carol Burnett [75] and Johnny Carson,[76] a famed evangelist who comments often on politics and who has talked of running for President,[77] or a candidate for elective city office.[78] In seeming contradiction, a famous jet-setter with a household-word name (Firestone) [79] was held to be a private person. Efforts to define public figure become especially troublesome where corporations are concerned.[80] For example, an insurance company—because of its power and influence—was held to be a public figure inviting attention and comment from the media.[81] On the other hand, the Supreme Court of the United States refused to hear an Oregon case in which it was held that corporations—specifically, banks—are *not* automatically public figures.[82] Note that this case was decided in 1986, several years before the savings and loan and banking crisis became big news, complete with allegations of U.S. Senators' involvement in keeping regulators at bay in exchange for campaign donations.

If persons truly were not public figures before getting media coverage, the mere fact of that coverage will not make them public figures. At times however—although rarely—unwilling persons,

---

[74] Prosser, 813–813.

[75] Burnett v. National Enquirer (Cal.1981), 7 Med.L.Rptr. 1321.

[76] Carson v. Allied News Co., 529 F.2d 206 (7th Cir.1976).

[77] Hustler Magazine v. Falwell, 485 U.S. 46, 108 S.Ct. 876 (1988).

[78] Redmond v. Sun Publishing Co., 239 Kan. 30, 716 P.2d 168 (1986).

[79] Time, Inc. v. Firestone, 424 U.S. 448, 96 S.Ct. 958 (1976).

[80] Robert Drechsel and Deborah Moon, "Corporate Libel Plaintiffs and the News Media," 21 Am.Bus.L.Journ. 127 (Summer, 1983).

[81] American Benefit Life Ins. Co. v. McIntyre, 375 So.2d 239 (Ala.1979), 5 Med.L. Rptr. 1124.

[82] Bank of Oregon v. Independent News, Inc., 298 Or. 434, 693 P.2d 35 (1985), cert. denied 474 U.S. 826, 106 S.Ct. 84 (1985).

through no fault of their own, can become "involuntary public figures." [83]   For the most part, however, there are mainly two kinds of "public figures:" The person who, nationally or locally, has pervasive or all-purpose fame, and the "vortex" public figures who thrust themselves into public issues, particularly in an effort to influence the course of events in some significant way.

The safest generalization for journalists is not to generalize: Get legal advice on close calls whether a person is a "public figure" or a "private figure."   At times, courts have ruled that some persons holding elective office—such as an elected but un-salaried county surveyor [84] or a justice of the peace [85]—are private persons.

SEC. 29.   ACTUAL MALICE

Courts examine reporting procedures in testing for actual malice, and find reckless disregard for falsity much more often than knowledge of falsity.

If a libel plaintiff is found by the judge to be a public official or public figure, his next move is to try to show that the offending words were published with actual malice. This term, as we have seen, is defined by the Supreme Court as reckless disregard for falsity in the words, or as knowledge that the publication is false. The burden is on the plaintiff to prove falsity, although the defendant may well undertake to demonstrate truth—a complete defense.

It is worth remembering that, as was said earlier (p. 147), the actual malice of *Sullivan* is quite different from the concept "malice" as it is usually understood. The word ordinarily has to do with hostility, ill will, spite, intent to harm—as, indeed, it was defined in libel law for generations before *Sullivan*, and as it continues to be defined in its tort-related sense in state libel law where the constitutional standard does not apply.

The Supreme Court has said that "actual malice" is a "term of art, created to provide a convenient shorthand expression for the standard of liability that must be established" [86] where public

---

[83] See, e.g., Wolston v. Reader's Digest Ass'n, Inc., 443 U.S. 157, 167, 99 S.Ct. 2701, 2707 (1979), and Waldbaum v. Fairchild Publications, Inc., 627 F.2d 1287, 1295 (D.C.Cir.1980), citing Gertz v. Welch, 418 U.S. 323, 94 S.Ct. 2997 (1974), recognizing that—at least in theory—an involuntary public figure could exist.

[84] Foster v. Laredo Newspapers, Inc., 19 TX S.Ct.Jrnl. 390, 541 S.W.2d 809 (Tex. 1976), cert. denied 429 U.S. 1123, 97 S.Ct. 1160 (1977).

[85] Guinn v. Texas Newspapers, Inc., 738 S.W.2d 303 (Tex.App.1987), 16 Med.L. Rptr. 1024, cert. denied 488 U.S. 1041, 109 S.Ct. 864 (1989). A error-filled article referred to "Guinn," not to Judge Guinn, asserting that Guinn had been convicted of a felony. (In point of fact, Guinn had been the attorney for the convicted thief.)

[86] Cantrell v. Forest City Pub. Co., 419 U.S. 245, 95 S.Ct. 465 (1974).

persons bring libel suits. The court that is trying the libel issue must direct itself to the factual issue as to the defendant's subjective knowledge of actual falsity or his high degree of awareness of probable falsity before publishing.[87]

Very soon after *Sullivan* had established the new definition of actual malice, the Supreme Court began the process of defining "reckless disregard." In Garrison v. Louisiana,[88] a criminal libel action, it said that reckless disregard means a "high degree of awareness of probable falsity" of the publication, and in 1968 in St. Amant v. Thompson, it said that for reckless disregard to be found, "There must be sufficient evidence to permit the conclusion that the defendant in fact entertained serious doubts as to the truth of his publication.[89]

Garrison was convicted of criminal libel, and the Supreme Court of the United States reversed the conviction. It said that the fact that the case was a criminal case made no difference to the principles of the Times v. Sullivan rule, and that malice would have to be shown. And the "reckless disregard" of truth or falsity in malice, it said, lies in a "high degree of awareness of probable falsity" on the part of the publisher. Nothing indicated that Garrison had this awareness of falsity when he castigated the Louisiana judges.[90]

Since the first case providing the constitutional protection in libel, the courts have been at pains to distinguish between "reckless disregard of truth" and "negligence." [91] Negligence is not enough to sustain a finding of actual malice. In the leading case, the Court went to this point. Errors in the famous advertisement, "Heed Their Rising Voices," could have been discovered by the *New York Times* advertising staff had it taken an elevator up a floor to the morgue and checked earlier stories on file. Failure to make this check, the Supreme Court said, did not constitute "reckless disregard"; at the worst it was negligence, and negligence is not enough to indicate malice.[92]

In Washington Post v. Keogh, a Congressman sued the newspaper for a story by columnist Drew Pearson which the Post carried. The story accused the congressman of bribe-splitting. The Post did not check the accuracy of the columnist's charges. The Federal Court of Appeals held that the Post showed no

[87] Orr v. Argus-Press Co., 586 F.2d 1108 (6th Cir.1978).

[88] 379 U.S. 64, 74, 85 S.Ct. 209, 216 (1964).

[89] St. Amant v. Thompson, 390 U.S. 727, 731, 88 S.Ct. 1323, 1325 (1968).

[90] 379 U.S. 64, 85 S.Ct. 209 (1964).

[91] Priestley v. Hastings & Sons Pub. Co. of Lynn, 360 Mass. 118, 271 N.E.2d 628 (1971); A.S. Abell Co. v. Barnes, 258 Md. 56, 265 A.2d 207 (1970).

[92] New York Times Co. v. Sullivan, 376 U.S. 254, 288, 84 S.Ct. 710, 730 (1964).

reckless disregard in not verifying Pearson's charge, regardless of Pearson's shaky reputation for accuracy. The court held that to require such checking by the Post would be to burden it with greater responsibilities of verification than the Supreme Court required of the *New York Times* in the landmark case. It said: [93]

> Verification is * * * a costly process, and the newspaper business is one in which survival has become a major problem. * * * We should be hesitant to impose responsibilities upon newspapers which can be met only through costly procedures or through self-censorship designed to avoid risks of publishing controversial material.

In the foregoing decisions in *Garrison, St. Amant,* and *Keogh,* courts defined reckless disregard by saying what it is *not.*

Later decisions have held that "internal inconsistencies" in a reporter's story do not make reckless disregard; [94] nor does the possibility that the reporter harbored "animosity", or a "grudge" or "ill will" toward the plaintiff; [95] nor does a combination of a reporter's failure to investigate, plus his possession (but omission from the story) of material contradictory to the hard words, plus the fact that the material was not "hot news" and so could have been further checked. [96] And to repeat, reckless disregard is not carelessness or negligence, which are flaws found often enough in news stories but which must be accepted in news of public persons if freedom is to have the "breathing space" it requires to survive. The jury recognized this in the famous case of Ariel Sharon v. Time, Inc.: While it found *Time* magazine's story about public official Sharon to be false defamation, it said specifically that *Time* was negligent and careless, but not possessed of reckless disregard. *Time* had erred but not lied, and was not liable for any of the $50 million that Sharon sought. [97]

The cases of public-person plaintiffs who must accept without compensation the negligent, the careless—indeed the "irresponsible" and the "unreasonable" [98]—sometimes warrant the journalist's reflection: Floyd Rood, a tireless worker and publicist in youth assistance efforts including drug rehabilitation, was said in

[93] Washington Post Co. v. Keogh, 125 U.S.App.D.C. 32, 365 F.2d 965, 972–973 (1966).

[94] Foster v. Upchurch, 624 S.W.2d 564 (Tex.1981), 7 Med.L.Rptr. 2533.

[95] Lancaster v. Daily Banner-News Pub. Co., Inc., 274 Ark. 145, 622 S.W.2d 671 (1981), 8 Med.L.Rptr. 1093; Curtis v. Southwestern Newspapers, 677 F.2d 115 (5th Cir.1982), 8 Med.L.Rptr. 1651.

[96] McNabb v. Oregonian Pub. Co., 69 Or.App. 136, 685 P.2d 458 (1984), 10 Med.L. Rptr. 2181.

[97] Time, Feb. 4, 1985, 64; 599 F.Supp. 538 (S.D.N.Y.1984).

[98] Lawrence v. Bauer Pub. & Printing Ltd., 89 N.J. 451, 446 A.2d 469 (1982), 8 Med.L.Rptr. 1536, 1543.

a news story to have begun a money-raising project "to help solve his drug addiction problem." The word "his" was wrong; it had accidentally been changed from "the" in wire transmission. He lost his suit.[99] Alderwoman Glover, said erroneously by a newspaper to have had abortions, could not recover for libel, for the newspaper had been no more than negligent in its mistake.[1]

Turning now to cases where reckless disregard *was* found in news: The earliest was the 1967 case, Curtis Publishing Co. v. Butts, discussed at pages 156 to 158, in which the former athletic director of the University of Georgia sued for a *Saturday Evening Post* story accusing him of conspiring to "fix" a football game between Georgia and Alabama. The Post had relied on the story of Burnett, a man serving on probation in connection with bad check charges, had not seen Burnett's notes about the alleged telephone conversation he said he had overheard, had not interviewed a man supposedly in the company of Burnett at the time of the phone conversation. Furthermore, the story was not "hot news" that demanded immediate publication. In the words of Chief Justice Earl Warren, this was reckless disregard of whether the statements were true or false.[2]

Investigative Reporting and the Tavoulareas Case (1985)

To journalists, investigative reporting is a high calling, a valued enterprise. They don't mind when they are called "muckrakers" when they try to find and to expose societal ills or corporate or governmental wrongdoing. It came as a shock, therefore when for a time the Washington Post was on the losing end of a $2 million libel award, with its investigative aggressiveness being used against the paper as evidence of its "actual malice."

The feisty and aggressive Mobil Oil Co. president, William Tavoulareas, sued the Post for a story saying he had "set up" his son to head an international tanker fleet carrying petroleum, and implying misuse of his corporate position. Tavoulareas, a public figure, sued the Post for $100 million, claiming actual malice (knowing falsity or reckless disregard for the truth) by the newspaper.[3] The jury agreed and awarded him $250,000 compensatory and $1.8 million punitive damages. But after reviewing the facts at length, the judge threw out the jury award (rendered a "judgment n.o.v."). He said that while the story in question was far short of being a model of fair, unbiased investigative journalism,

---

[99] Rood v. Finney, 418 So.2d 1 (La.App.1982), 8 Med.L.Rptr. 2047.

[1] Glover v. Herald Co., 549 S.W.2d 858 (Mo.1977), 2 Med.L.Rptr. 1846.

[2] Curtis Pub. Co. v. Butts, 388 U.S. 130, 155, 87 S.Ct. 1975 (1967).

[3] Tavoulareas v. Washington Post Co., 567 F.Supp. 651 (D.D.C.1983), 9 Med.L. Rptr. 1553.

there was "no evidence in the record * * * to show that it contained knowing lies or statements made in reckless disregard of the truth," and no evidence to support the jury's verdict.[4]

The U.S. Court of Appeals, District of Columbia Circuit, reversed the trial judge on a 2–1 vote, and reinstated the jury verdict of $2.05 million.[5] The majority found clear and convincing evidence of reckless disregard under the rules of *Butts, St. Amant,* and *Garrison* (see text at p. 172, above)—and added these other indicators of fault in the story: (1) The story carried on its face the warning to the newspaper that it had high potential for harm to Tavoulareas' reputation; (2) the journalists "were motivated by a plan to 'get' the plaintiffs, and deliberately slanted, rejected and ignored evidence contrary to the false premise of the story"; (3) the reporter's interview notes "reflect exactly the opposite of what he was told by the interviewees"; (4) the newspaper refused to retract the story or to print Tavoulareas' letter to the paper.[6]

In elaborating, Judge George MacKinnon (joined by Judge and later Supreme Court Justice Antonin Scalia) raised alarm among journalists. The Post's policy of exposing wrongdoing in public life might be characterized as "hard hitting investigative journalism" or as "sophisticated muckraking," the Court said, and either "certainly is relevant to the inquiry of whether a newspaper employee acted in reckless disregard of whether a statement is false or not." The suggestion that a newspaper's devotion to these two honored traditions in journalism might be evidence of reckless disregard of falsity shocked the field.

Judge J. Skelly Wright, at almost total odds with the court majority, spoke for countless journalists in his long, ranging dissent that rejected MacKinnon's analysis. Holding that a newspaper policy of investigative journalism and muckraking could be evidence of reporters' acting in reckless disregard of falsity endangered the First Amendment, Wright declared:[7]

It is a conclusion fraught with the potential to shrink the First Amendment's "majestic protection" * * *.

[4] Ibid., 1555, 1561.

[5] Tavoulareas v. Washington Post, 759 F.2d 90 (D.C.Cir.1985), 11 Med.L.Rptr. 1777. The same judges denied a petition of the Post to re-hear the case on another 2–1 vote, 763 F.2d 1472 (D.C.Cir. 1985); but the 3-member panel's decision was vacated by the full Circuit Court (10 judges), which voted to hear the case *en banc*: Ibid., 1481.

[6] Ibid., 1809–1810.

[7] Ibid., 1798, 1821–22. For similar reactions from journalists, see Peter Prichard, *Tavoulareas Case Returns—with Bite,* Quill, May 1985, 25; Anthony Lewis, *Getting Even,* New York Times, 4/11/85, A27; Anon., *Press Must Be Tough, but Fair,* Milwaukee Journal, 4/12/85, 14.

Muckraking—a term developed when writers like Lincoln Steffens, Ida Tarbell, and Upton Sinclair relentlessly exposed pervasive corruption—may be seen to serve that high purpose even if it offends and startles * * *.

Wright found in the majority opinion "deep hostility to an aggressive press" that "is directly contrary to the mandates of the Supreme Court and the spirit of a free press," and concluded that "neither a newspaper's muckraking policy nor its hard-hitting investigative journalism should *ever* be considered probative of actual malice."

Ultimately, the Washington Post was rescued by a rehearing of the case by the full panel of the U.S. Court of Appeals for the District of Columbia. That court (with Supreme Court Justice–Designate Antonin Scalia not participating) voted 7–1 to throw out the jury's $2.05 million verdict. The court decided that actual malice had not been proven against the Washington Post. Further, a reputation for "sensational" or investigative reporting was *not* to be taken as evidence of actual malice.[8]

Court-determined indicators of "reckless disregard" (which amount to court-determined standards of news reporting) do not end with those at issue in *Tavoulareas*. They include: where a reporter did not make personal contact with anyone involved in the event before writing;[9] where a publication relied on an obviously biased source, was advised of the falsity of information, and published with no further investigation of the story;[10] where the publication printed although the story was inherently improbable.[11] Ill will of the reporter toward the subject of the story may in some cases contribute to a finding of reckless disregard.[12]

Defining Reckless Disregard: Harte–Hanks v. Connaughton (1989)

The *Connaughton* decision of 1989 marked the first time in two decades that the U.S. Supreme Court held against the media in a public figure libel case.[13] (Keep in mind, however that the media have lost some public figure libel cases over the years. See,

[8] Tavoulareas v. Washington Post Co., 817 F.2d 762 (D.C.Cir.1987), cert. denied by the Supreme Court of the United States, 484 U.S. 870, 108 S.Ct. 200 (1987).

[9] Akins v. Altus Newspapers, Inc., 609 P.2d 1263 (Okl.1977).

[10] Stevens v. Sun Pub. Co., 270 S.C. 65, 240 S.E.2d 812 (1978).

[11] Hunt v. Liberty Lobby, 720 F.2d 631 (11th Cir.1983), 10 Med.L.Rptr. 1097, 1107.

[12] Cochran v. Indianapolis Newspapers, Inc., 175 Ind.App. 548, 372 N.E.2d 1211 (1978), 3 Med.L.Rptr. 2131; Tavoulareas v. Washington Post, 759 F.2d 90, 114 (D.C. Cir.1985), 11 Med.L.Rptr. 1777, 1820, vacated 763 F.2d 1472 (1985), affirmed 817 F. 2d 762 (D.C.Cir.1987).

[13] Harte–Hanks Communications, Inc. v. Connaughton, 491 U.S. 657, 109 S.Ct. 2678 (1989), 16 Med.L.Rptr. 1881; News Media & the Law, Summer, 1989, p. 16.

for example, the $3.05 million libel loss incurred in Brown & Williamson v. Jacobson in 1987.) [14]

Harte–Hanks Communications, Inc. v. Connaughton says that the media may be held responsible for defamation in reporting on a candidate for public office if a jury could reasonably find "actual malice" misconduct by news organizations. The key here seemed to turn on how "reckless disregard for the truth" was defined.

The case arose in 1983 because of judicial election reporting by the Hamilton, Ohio, Journal–News, which was owned by Harte–Hanks until 1986. The newspaper published a story about municipal judge candidate Daniel Connaughton. The newspaper, which had endorsed Connaughton's opponent, published assertions that Connaughton had promised a grand jury witness and her sister jobs and trips if they would provide testimony embarrassing to his opponent for the judgeship.[15] (It did not help appearances that the Journal–News was in a circulation battle with the Cincinnati Enquirer, a newspaper which endorsed Connaughton.)

Connaughton lost the election, and sued the Hamilton Journal–News for defamation. The newspaper tried to defend itself by asserting a "neutral reportage" (see pages 189–192) privilege to present accurate and unbiased accounts of charges against a public figure/political candidate. The newspaper asked unsuccessfully for a summary judgment.[16]

Hindsight suggests that the Journal–News exposed itself to liability by failing to investigate thoroughly. When questioned by a reporter, Connaughton reportedly denied offering grand jury witnesses jobs or trips. Perhaps most damaging to the newspaper; it published its attack on Connaughton without interviewing key sources—who had been identified to the newspaper as such—whose denials should have put an end to the derogatory stories about Connaughton. Also, the newspaper decided not to listen to tape recordings available to it which could have provided additional information. As Justice John Paul Stevens wrote for the Court: [17]

> . . . [D]iscrepancies in the testimony of Journal News witnesses may have given the jury the impression that the failure to conduct a complete investigation involved a deliberate effort to avoid the truth.

[14] Brown & Williamson Tobacco Corp. v. Jacobson, 827 F.2d 1119 (7th Cir.1987), 14 Med.L.Rptr. 1497, cert. denied 485 U.S. 993, 108 S.Ct. 1302 (1988).

[15] 491 U.S. 657, 660, 109 S.Ct. 2678, 2682 (1989), 16 Med.L.Rptr. at 1883.

[16] Ibid.

[17] Harte–Hanks Communications, Inc. v. Connaughton, 491 U.S. 657, 684, 109 S.Ct. 2678, 2694 (1989), 16 Med.L.Rptr. at 1881, 1893.

And that adds up to actual malice. The key lesson for journalists is that they must not cut corners. They should always assume that non-journalists—such as members of a jury—may eventually be looking over their shoulders. The practical reporter's internal voice must keep asking: "If we publish this, will I be able to explain what I did to a jury?"

The jury in the Connaughton case did not believe the newspaper's explanations, and assessed damages totaling $200,000: $5,000 compensatory, and $195,000 punitive.[18] Upholding that outcome, Justice Stevens wrote:[19]

> . . .[I]t it clear that the conclusion concerning the newspaper's departure from accepted standards and the evidence of motive were merely supportive of the court's ultimate conclusion that the record "demonstrated a reckless disregard as to the truth or falsity . . . [of the largely unsupported allegations against Connaughton] . . . and thus provided clear and convincing proof of 'actual malice' as found by the jury." 842 F.2d at 847. Although courts must be careful not to place too much reliance on such factors, a plaintiff is entitled to prove the defendant's state of mind through circumstantial evidence, see Herbert v. Lando, 441 U.S. 153, 150 (1979).

Knowing falsity

The "reckless disregard" aspect of actual malice, is shown rather often in libel suits. But the second aspect—knowing falsehood—is far less frequently found. One case involved a suit by State Sen. Richard Schermerhorn of New York. He was interviewed by reporter Ron Rosenberg of the Middletown *Times Herald Record* about the senator's proposal for the redevelopment plan (the NDDC) in Newburgh. They discussed community controversy about whether minorities' chances for benefiting from NDDC were sufficient. Rosenberg wrote a story which was published under the headline SCHERMERHORN SAYS NDDC CAN DO WITHOUT BLACKS. There was no reference to this in the story. A storm of protest against the senator arose, and Senators Beatty and von Luther proposed a resolution of censure in the Senate against Schermerhorn. In a later story, Beatty was quoted as saying that he had access to tapes in which Schermerhorn made subtle anti-black and anti-Semitic statements.

---

[18] Damages are discussed in Sec. 24.

[19] Harte–Hanks Communications, Inc. v. Connaughton, 491 U.S. 657, 667, 109 S.Ct. 2678, 2686 (1989), 16 Med.L.Rptr. at 1886. Justice Stevens also emphasized judges' constitutional duty to " 'exercise independent judgment and determine whether the record establishes actual malice with convincing clarity,' " quoting Bose v. Consumer's Union, 466 U.S. 485, 514, 104 S.Ct. 1949, 1967 (1984): See 10 Med.L.Rptr. 1625, 1882.

Schermerhorn denied making the headline statement and told his Senate colleagues that if there were tapes showing he had made such statements, he would be unfit to serve in the Senate and would resign. He brought a libel suit, and charged knowing falsehood.[20] At trial, Rosenberg agreed that Schermerhorn had not told him what the headline reported, and that a copy editor—who was never produced at the trial—had written it. But both von Luther and Beatty testified, that, in telephone calls to them, Rosenberg had assured them that Schermerhorn had said that the NDDC could do without blacks, and von Luther added that Rosenberg volunteered that he had a tape in which Schermerhorn made racial and ethnic slurs. The tape was never produced, although both senators testified that they made repeated requests for it.

The jury was unconvinced that a copy editor who never showed up for Rosenberg's trial had written the headline, and in addition, the jury had von Luther's and Beatty's testimony that Rosenberg assured them the headline was accurate. The jury brought in a verdict of $36,000 in damages for Schermerhorn. The New York Supreme Court, Appellate Division, upheld the verdict on three of four counts saying "In our view, then, the evidence was sufficient to sustain the jury's determination that Rosenberg * * * had composed a defamatory headline with actual knowledge that the matter asserted therein was false." [21]

Making Up Quotes: Knowing Falsity or Reckless Disregard? Masson v. New Yorker Magazine (1991)

If a writer alters an interview subject's quotations materially, is that "knowing falsity?" In Masson v. New Yorker Magazine,[22] the U.S. Supreme Court took up issues that are enough to make a journalism ethics teacher downright twitchy. A 1989 U.S. Court of Appeals decision had been portrayed—as a Time magazine headline put it—giving journalists "The Right to Fake Quotes." [23] That and other similar headlines overstated the reach of the 2–1 Ninth Circuit decision.[24] The immediate issue decided by the Supreme Court resulted in a ruling that a famous psychiatrist could overcome a summary judgment ruling and thus force New Yorker magazine to trial on his libel suit.

[20] Schermerhorn v. Rosenberg, 73 A.D.2d 276, 426 N.Y.S.2d 274 (1980), 6 Med.L. Rptr. 1376.

[21] Ibid., 1381. See also Morgan v. Dun & Bradstreet, Inc., 421 F.2d 1241 (5th Cir. 1970); Sprouse v. Clay Communication, Inc., 158 W.Va. 427, 211 S.E.2d 674 (1975).

[22] Masson v. New Yorker Magazine, Inc., 501 U.S. ___, 111 S.Ct. 2419 (1991), 18 Med.L.Rptr. 2241.

[23] Time, Aug. 21, 1989, p. 49; see also Editor & Publisher, Aug. 12, 1989, p. 16.

[24] Masson v. New Yorker Magazine, Inc., 881 F.2d 1452 (9th Cir.1989), 16 Med.L. Rptr. 2089.

Psychiatrist Jeffrey M. Masson sued for defamation based on a 1983 two part article by Janet Malcolm which was published in The New Yorker, and later published in book form by Knopf. The article/book was based on Ms. Malcolm's extensive tape-recorded interviews Dr. Masson and dealt with his dismissal from his post as projects director of the Sigmund Freud Archives.

In his lawsuit, Dr. Masson argued that Ms. Malcolm had ". . . fabricated words attributed to him with quotation marks, and misleadingly edited his statements to make him appear 'unscholarly, irresponsible, vain [and] lacking impersonal [sic] honesty or moral integrity.'" [25] Masson contended that the magazine and Knopf knew of author Malcolm's misconduct before the book and the article were published.

All three defendants were granted summary judgments by a federal district court on the grounds that Dr. Masson had not established actual malice: "'No clear and convincing evidence exists that would justify a holding that . . . [the defendants] entertained serious doubts about the truth of the disputed passages.'" [26]

As a public figure, Dr. Masson was required by the Constitution to prove actual malice, and he had argued that a jury could find that standard of fault based on evidence deliberately fabricated quoted that had been attributed to him. Dr. Masson presented evidence that several quotes ascribed to him did not appear on Ms. Malcolm's tape recordings, and contended that the writer herself had altered other quotes.

For purposes of this appeal, the Court of Appeals assumed that the quotations had been altered knowingly, deliberately. Even so, author Malcolm's more colorful renditions of Dr. Masson's remarks to her in interviews did not seem to the Court of Appeals to be more harmful to the psychiatrist's reputation than the actual words he had used.

For example, Masson contended that Malcolm had made up this quote, which was not in the tape recordings but which was in Malcolm's handwritten interview notes: "I was like an intellectual gigolo—you get your pleasure from him, but you don't take him out in public." [27]

[25] 881 F.2d at 1453, 16 Med.L.Rptr. at 2089–2090.

[26] 881 F.2d at 1454, 16 Med.L.Rptr. at 2090.

[27] 881 F.2d at 1456–1457, 16 Med.L.Rptr. at 2089–2090 (1989); see also Masson v. New Yorker Magazine, Inc., 501 U.S. ___, 111 S.Ct. 2419, 18 Med.L.Rptr. 2241, 2244 (1991).

Or, Ms. Malcolm's interview tapes recorded Dr. Masson describing his plans to occupy Maresfield Gardens after Anna Freud's death: [28]

> "[I]t is an incredible storehouse. I mean, the library, Freud's library alone is priceless in terms of what it contains: all his books with his annotations in them; the Shreber case annotated, that kind of thing. It's fascinating."

Ms. Malcolm's published version of the interview, however, veered away from the words just quoted. She put the following inside direct quotation marks, as if Dr. Masson's exact words were being reproduced: [29]

> " 'It was a beautiful house, but it was dark and sombre and dead. Nothing ever went on there. I was the only person who ever came. I would have renovated it, opened it up, brought it to life. Maresfield Gardens would have been a center of scholarship, but it would also have been a place of sex, women, fun. It would have been like the change in *The Wizard of Oz*, from black-and-white into color.' "

Even though the Supreme Court's 7–2 decision held that New Yorker and Ms. Malcolm could not escape a libel trial via summary judgment,[30] the substance of the majority opinion was a great relief to lawyers for the news media.[31] Writing for the Court, Justice Anthony M. Kennedy held that deliberate misquotation of a public figure can not be libel unless the changed wording substantially changes the meaning of what really was said.[32]

Some excerpts from Justice Kennedy's opinion follow: [33]

> In general, quotation marks around a passage indicate to the reader that the passage reproduces the speaker's words verbatim. They inform the reader that he or she is reading the statement of the speaker, not a paraphrase or other indirect interpretation by an author. By providing this information, quotations add authority to the statement and credibility to the author's work.

[28] Masson v. New Yorker Magazine, Inc., 501 U.S. ___, 111 S.Ct. 2419 (1991), 18 Med.L.Rptr. 2241, 2245.

[29] Ibid.

[30] "Summary judgment" procedures terminate a lawsuit unless the plaintiff can make a good showing of having a strong case.

[31] Linda Greenhouse, "Justices Refuse to Open a Gate for Libel Cases," The New York Times, June 21, 1991, p. A–1.

[32] Masson v. New Yorker Magazine, Inc., 501 U.S. ___, 111 S.Ct. 2419 (1991), 18 Med.L.Rptr. 2241, 2250.

[33] Masson v. New Yorker Magazine, Inc., 501 U.S. ___, 111 S.Ct. 2419 (1991), 18 Med.L.Rptr. 2241, 2248.

* * *

A fabricated quotation may injure reputation in at least two senses, either giving rise to a conceivable claim of defamation. First, the quotation might injure because it attributes an untrue factual assertion to the speaker. An example would be a fabricated quotation of a public official admitting he had been convicted of a serious crime when in fact he had not.

Second, regardless of the truth or falsity of the factual matters asserted within the quoted statement, the attribution may result in injury to reputation because the manner of expression or even the fact that the statement was made indicates a negative personal trait or an attitude the speaker does not hold.

* * *

Justice Kennedy noted that in some circumstances, as in a printed hypothetical conversation or in a work of fiction, a writer's use of quotation marks will not be understood be readers to mean the reproduction of actual conversations.[34]

The work at issue here, however, as with much journalistic writing, provides the reader no clue that the quotations are being used as a rhetorical device or to paraphrase the speaker's actual statements. To the contrary, the work purports to be nonfiction, the result of numerous interviews. At least a trier of fact could so conclude.

* * *

The constitutional question we must consider here is whether, in the framework of a summary judgment motion, the evidence suffices to show that respondents acted with the requisite knowledge of falsity or reckless disregard as to truth or falsity.

* * *

In some sense, any alteration of a verbatim quotation is false. But writers and reporters by necessity alter what people say, at the very least to eliminate grammatical and syntactical infelicities.

Editing to "fix" an interviewee's syntax is by no means an agreed-upon procedure. For one thing, if a print journalist is reporting on words captured "live" in all their ungrammatical splendor, editorial splicing to make a flaming illiterate's words read as if they were spoken by George Will or Sam Donaldson will make the print media appear foolish. Also, what if the grammati-

[34] Masson v. New Yorker Magazine, Inc., 501 U.S. ___, 111 S.Ct. 2419 (1991), 18 Med.L.Rptr. 2241, 2248–2250.

cal atrocities are spoken by, say, a State Higher Education Commissioner or a U.S. Department of Education official? Can they be edited into proper English truly deceiving the public?

Justice Kennedy's decision spoke cautiously to the issues at hand, declaring: [35]

> If every alteration constituted the falsity required to prove actual malice, the practice of journalism, which the First Amendment standard is designed to protect, would require a radical change, one inconsistent with our precedents and First Amendment principles.
>
> * * *
>
> We conclude that a deliberate alteration of the words uttered by a plaintiff does not equate with knowledge of falsity for purposes of *New York Times v. Sullivan . . .* and *Gertz v. Robert Welch . . .* unless the alteration results in a material change in the meaning conveyed by the statement. The use of quotations to attribute words not in fact spoken bears in a most important way on that inquiry, but it is not dispositive in every case.
>
> Deliberate or reckless falsification that comprises actual malice turns upon words and punctuation only because words and punctuation express meaning. Meaning is the life of language. And for the reasons we have given, quotations may be a devastating instrument for conveying false meaning. In the case under consideration, readers of In the Freud Archives may have found Malcolm's portrait of petitioner especially damning because so much of it appeared to be a selfportrait, told by petitioner in his own words. And if the alterations of petitioner's words gave a different meaning to the statements, bearing upon their defamatory character, then the device of quotations might well be critical in finding the words actionable.

The Supreme Court's majority thus overturned the summary judgment, ruling that defendants Janet Malcolm and the New Yorker magazine could be taken to trial on the issue of libel. In a minority opinion, Justices White and Scalia argued that under New York Times v. Sullivan, reporting a known falsehood is sufficient proof of actual malice.[36]

Journalists and legal commentators differed on the impact of the case of Masson v. New Yorker. Jane Kirtley, director of the

[35] Masson v. New Yorker Magazine, Inc., 501 U.S. ___, 111 S.Ct. 2419 (1991), 18 Med.L.Rptr. 2241, 2249–2251.

[36] Masson v. New Yorker Magazine, Inc., 501 U.S. ___, 111 S.Ct. 2419 (1991), 18 Med.L.Rptr. 2241, 2255.

Reporters Committee for Freedom of the Press, said " '[a] lot more reporters are going to start using tape recorders in addition to notebooks—a kind of belt and suspenders protection.' " [37] The New York Times, however, said editorially that the Supreme Court had produced a measured decision meaning that [38]

> . . . fallible journalists won't be held to stenographic exactitude for everything they put between quotation marks. Yet if a deliberately altered quote makes the speaker look like a self-confessed fool or rascal, the journalists had better be prepared to defend themselves in court.

Keep in mind that in applying for a summary judgment, Ms. Malcolm and the New Yorker were forced, in submitting that motion, to admit for purposes of argument that quotes were falsified deliberately. As the case was returned to a Federal District Court for trial, said a spokeswoman for the New Yorker, that meant " '. . . an opportunity for Ms. Malcolm to speak directly' to Masson's charges. . . . 'No quotations were made up by Janet Malcolm.' " [39]

SEC. 30. SPECIAL ISSUES: JURIES, SUMMARY JUDGMENT, NEUTRAL REPORTING, DISCOVERY

Juries

If "actual malice" leaves journalists uncertain about the fine distinctions and contradictions among courts, it presents a broader problem for juries called upon to analyze and employ it in deciding libel suits.[40] Jurors' minds must be cleared of predispositions to consider that the ill will or spite associated in plain English with "malice" is not really at issue, but rather, knowing or reckless falsehood by the publisher. This may involve a difficult "turn-around" in jurors' thought processes, and possibly resentment at the idea that a writer/publisher who harbors spite, hatred, or ill will against the plaintiff nevertheless may be legally immune from a libel judgment. Justice Potter Stewart said, after 15 years' experience with the Times v. Sullivan actual malice, that he "came greatly to regret" the Court's employment of that term: [41]

---

[37] Tony Mauro, "Journalists may need taped evidence of quotes," USA Today, June 21, 1991, p. 8A.

[38] "Misquotations, Measured," The New York Times, June 21, 1991, p. A12.

[39] Mauro, loc. cit.

[40] Marc Franklin, "Good Government and Bad Law ∗ ∗ ∗," 18 Univ.S.F.L.Rev. 1, 8 (1983); 10 Med.L.Rptr. # 12, 3/20/84, News Notes, 8 Ibid. # 39, 11/30/82, News Notes; Randall P. Bezanson, Gilbert Cranberg, and John Soloski, Libel Law and the Press: Myth and Reality (New York: The Free Press, 1987), p. 237 and passim.

[41] Herbert v. Lando, 441 U.S. 153, 199, 99 S.Ct. 1635, 1661 (1979).

For the fact of the matter is that "malice" as used in the New York Times opinion simply does not mean malice as the word is commonly understood. In common understanding, malice means ill will or hostility * * *. As part of the * * * standard enunciated in the New York Times case, however, "actual malice" has nothing to do with hostility or ill will * * *.

And if judge and attorneys in the case succeed in making the legal definition clear to the jury, there remains another problem for jurors enmeshed in libel law: That harsh words are proved false may be almost insurmountable evidence of media liability for some jurors, but that, of course, is not the case, for the falsity must be knowing or reckless. Justice Goldberg of the United States Supreme Court warned of problems for juries in New York Times Co. v. Sullivan: [42] "The requirement of proving actual malice * * * may, in the mind of the jury, add little to the requirement of proving falsity, a requirement which the Court recognizes not to be an adequate standard."

After trial Judge Oliver Gasch in *Tavoulareas* found the jury's verdict of some $2 million unsupportable and disallowed it, Attorney Steven Brill interviewed five of the six jurors.[43] Brill found that they did not understand that falsity must be knowing or reckless to justify an award. They further believed that the *Post* was required to show the truth of its charges, whereas, of course, the rule actually was that Tavoulareas was required to show falsity.[44]

Brill asserted that the *Post* attorneys did not drum these points into the jury's minds, and talked to the jury of ordinary citizens in language appropriate to lawyers not laymen. As for Judge Gasch, his instructions to the jury consisted of almost two hours of review of legal points involved, bound to be difficult for jurors.[45]

A procedure widely praised as a clarification of the task for a jury was initiated in 1985 by Federal Judge Abraham Sofaer. Ariel Sharon, former defense minister of Israel, brought a libel suit for $50 million against *Time* magazine for its report that Sharon had discussed with Christian Phalangists of Lebanon the need for them to take revenge against assassins, just before the massacre of hundreds of Palestinians by Phalangists. In his

[42] 376 U.S. 254, 299, 84 S.Ct. 710, 736 (1964).

[43] Steven Brill, "Inside the Jury Room at the Washington Post Libel Trial," American Lawyer, Nov. 1982, 1, 93, 94.

[44] Ibid., 1, 90.

[45] Ibid., 92. The Libel Defense Resource Center prepared a manual of jury instructions on libel: LDRC Bulletin # 10, Spring 1984, 1–2. Proof of Actual Malice in Defamation Actions: an Unsolved Dilemma, 7 Hofstra L.Rev. 655, 701.

instructions, Judge Sofaer had the jury take up three questions, one at a time, and report its finding on each before proceeding. First, he asked the jury, was the story defamatory? ("Yes," the jury found.) Next, was it false? ("Yes," the jury found.) Finally, was it done with actual malice? ("No," the jury found, and thus, *Time* was not liable for damages.) [46]

In the libel case brought by Gen. William C. Westmoreland against CBS in 1985—perhaps unequalled in the publicity attending it and costliness to the participants— [47] Judge Pierre Laval used another device to aid the jury: He simply barred the use of the confusing term "actual malice" during the trial, substituting the "state of mind" of the journalists as a clearer criterion.[48] Westmoreland, who sued for "CBS Reports'" accusation that he engaged in a "conspiracy" to understate enemy troop strength when he was Commander of United States forces during the Vietnam War, withdrew his suit after 18 weeks of testimony. The jury was never put to the test of grappling with "actual malice" and "state of mind."

The troubling problem of legal technicalities' confronting lay juries by no means ends the question of how media faced with libel suits need to cope with the jury setting.[49] For example, widespread anti-media attitudes of recent decades are likely to be represented among the cross-section of people that often comprises a jury. A juror's support for media's rights to publish may be qualified by resentment and lack of trust in media for what the juror considers arrogance, inaccuracy, and invasion of privacy by media.

The many awards by juries of enormous judgments for libel— particularly punitive damages (see pages 142 to 144)—suggest powerfully that jurors often are disposed to punish media. Jurors often, also, tend to sympathize with the individual whose reputation, feelings, and status among his friends seem tarnished by the rich media corporation, seen by the jury as callous and careless. Where unfairness in media stories is at issue in libel trials, such proclivities may heavily qualify the rights of free expression.

Summary Judgment

If a judge at the threshold of a libel trial finds that a plaintiff is a public figure or public official, the case moves at once to a

[46] Time, Feb. 4, 1985, 64, 66.

[47] The 18-week trial may have cost the parties well over $10 million in expenses, New York Times, Feb. 19, 1985, 10, 26; and see Ibid., from mid-October 8, 1984, to Feb. 19, 1985, for the extent of coverage.

[48] Washington Post National Weekly Edition, March 11, 1985, 28.

[49] See James J. Brosnahan, First Amendment Jury Trials, 6 Litigation 4, 28 (Summer 1980); see Bezanson, et al., op. cit.

second pretrial consideration, of great importance to the defending news medium and the plaintiff. The plaintiff alleges actual malice, and the defendant ordinarily denies it and moves that the judge dismiss the case in a "summary judgment" for the defendant. Winning such a motion avoids a trial. Avoiding libel trials is desirable for a number of reasons. First, to defend the average libel suit through a trial will cost an average of $175,000, according to a 1991 study by John Soloski.[50] Second, the extended distraction and emotional drain of a libel suit add up to a real threat to vigorous reporting.

The importance of summary judgment to the media's defense and to the public need for robust, uninhibited, wide-open reporting was laid out in the decision in Washington Post Co. v. Keogh,[51] an early case that interpreted Times v. Sullivan:

> In the First Amendment area, summary procedures are * * * essential. For the stake here, if harassment succeeds, is free debate. One of the purposes of the *Times* principle, in addition to protecting persons from being cast in damages in libel suits filed by public officials, is to prevent persons from being discouraged in the full and free exercise of their First Amendment rights with respect to the conduct of their government.

In ruling on the motion for summary judgment by the defendant, the judge must make a decision: Is there a "genuine issue of material fact"—a substantial claim by the plaintiff supported by evidence—that there was knowing or reckless falsity in the publication? [52]

Chief Justice Warren Burger of the United States Supreme Court in 1979 wrote a famous footnote—number 9 in Hutchinson v. Proxmire—casting doubt on the appropriateness of summary judgment in libel cases. Lower courts take his admonition into account and sometimes have found it a basis for denial of summary judgment, but summary judgment is granted defendants far more often in libel suits brought by public people than it is denied.[53] Despite the famed footnote, many defamation actions—

---

[50] John Soloski, draft proposal for The Libel Law Reform Movement (with Randall Bezanson), to be published in 1992 by the Guilford Press of New York; "Libel Law and Journalistic Malpractice: A Preliminary Analysis of Fault in Libel Litigation," paper presented to the Law Division at the August, 1991, convention of the Association for Education in Journalism and Mass Communication.

[51] 125 U.S.App.D.C. 32, 365 F.2d 965, 968 (1966).

[52] Restatement, Second, Torts, Vol. 3, p. 220. Cerrito v. Time, Inc., 449 F.2d 306 (9th Cir.1971); Hayes v. Booth Newspapers, Inc., 97 Mich.App. 758, 295 N.W.2d 858 (1980), 6 Med.L.Rptr. 2319.

[53] Hutchinson v. Proxmire, 443 U.S. 111, 99 S.Ct. 2675 (1979). Yiamouyiannis v. Consumers Union of U.S., Inc., 619 F.2d 932 (2d Cir.1980), 6 Med.L.Rptr. 1065. Defendants' motions for summary judgment in the 1980s have been successful

perhaps as many as 75 per cent of those brought by public figures or officials in the last decade—have been ended by grants of summary judgments to media defendants.

In a decision helpful to the media, the Supreme Court ruled in Jack Anderson v. Liberty Lobby, Inc., (1986) that public official or public figure suits must be ended before trial by summary judgment unless libel can be shown with "convincing clarity." Anderson was sued after articles said to portray Willis Carto and Liberty Lobby as Neo Nazi, racist, and fascist.

Plaintiffs Carto and Liberty Lobby argued against the summary judgment, saying that the researcher for the Jack Anderson column's articles had relied on several unreliable sources and because there were inaccuracies in the articles. Writing for the Supreme Court, Justice White wrote that trial judges must decide, based on pre-trial affidavits, whether a public plaintiff can meet the actual malice standard by "clear convincing evidence." If not, summary judgment should be granted.[54]

Police Chief Prease alleged in a suit that stories in the Akron, (O.) *Beacon Journal* libeled him. Assistant Managing Editor Timothy Smith said that all statements in the stories were made in good faith with no serious doubts about their accuracy, and the Chief did not refute Smith. Thus the judge found that there was no issue between them about actual malice—no "genuine issue of material fact" that would have to be argued before a jury for decision. He granted summary judgment for the newspaper.[55]

But the United States Court of Appeals, Fourth District, found such an issue in Fitzgerald v. Penthouse Intern., Ltd.,[56] and reversed a trial court's grant of summary judgment to *Penthouse*. Fitzgerald, a specialist in the use of dolphins as military weapons, sued *Penthouse* for an article about his work that might have been construed as an allegation of espionage—selling dolphins trained as "torpedoes" to other nations, for "fast bucks." The Court found that *Penthouse* relied almost exclusively for its story upon a questionable source, and detailed his "many bold assertions about the United States intelligence community" which in some cases "invite skepticism." It quoted St. Amant v. Thompson: [57] Recklessness may be found "where there are obvious reasons to doubt the veracity of the informant or the accuracy of his reports." Fitzgerald had presented a factual question about whether *Pent-*

about 75% of the time, and Burger's "footnote 9" has been used rarely: Libel Defense Resource Center Bulletin # 13, Spring 1985, 10.

[54] 477 U.S. 242, 106 S.Ct. 2505 (1986), 12 Med.L.Rptr. 2297.

[55] Prease v. Poorman (Ohio Com.Pls.1981), 7 Med.L.Rptr. 2378.

[56] 691 F.2d 666 (4th Cir.1982), 8 Med.L.Rptr. 2340.

[57] 390 U.S. 727, 732, 88 S.Ct. 1323, 1326 (1968).

house had "obvious reasons to doubt" its source; *Penthouse* would have to go to trial on the matter of actual malice.

Neutral Reportage

A sometimes useful—but not-to-be-trusted—defense against libel lawsuits goes under the name of "neutral reportage." The neutral reportage argument is one which lawyers sometimes use on behalf of media clients, but as of 1992, that defense had not attained the status of a reliable constitutional defense.

Back in 1977, Judge Irving Kaufman of the U.S. Court of Appeals, Second Circuit, pioneered the neutral reportage concept in Edwards v. National Audubon Society, Inc.[58] Judge Kaufman wrote for the court that the Constitution protects accurate, unbiased news reporting of accusations made against public figures regardless of the reporter's view of their truth. (This concept is related to the long-standing common-law and statutory doctrine of qualified privilege—immunity from successful libel suit for fair and accurate reports of official proceedings (See Sec. 33, at pages 207–221).

The case arose when The New York Times carried a story reporting accurately a National Audubon Society's written statement that some scientists were paid to lie about the effects of the pesticide DDT upon birds. This outraged scientists who were implicated, and they brought a libel suit against the Society and the Times. Overturning a jury verdict for the scientists, Judge Kaufman wrote for the Court of Appeals that "a libel judgment against the *Times,* in face of this finding of fact, is constitutionally impermissible." He reasoned: [59]

> At stake in this case is a fundamental principle. Succinctly stated, when a responsible, prominent organization like the National Audubon Society makes serious charges against a public figure, the First Amendment protects the accurate and disinterested reporting of those charges, regardless of the reporter's private views of their validity. * * * What is newsworthy about such accusations is that they were made. We do not believe that the press may be required under the First Amendment to suppress newsworthy statements merely because it has serious doubts regarding their truth.

Judge Kaufman applied this doctrine only to situations where the press was not taking sides or was deliberately distorting

[58] 556 F.2d 113 (2d Cir.1977). See Kathryn D. Sowle, "Defamation and the First Amendment: The Case for a Constitutional Privilege of Fair Report," 54 NYU Law Review 469 (June, 1969).

[59] Edwards v. National Audubon Society, Inc., 556 F.2d 113, 120 (2d Cir.1977).

statements in order to launch a personal attack. But in this case, the judge said, reporter John Devlin of The Times wrote an accurate account, did not take the Audubon Society's side in his article. Further, Devlin's article included the scientists' indignant responses to the Audubon Society's charges. Judge Kaufman's opinion termed Devlin's work "an exemplar of fair and dispassionate reporting. . . . Accordingly, we hold that it was privileged under the First Amendment." [60]

Welcome as the "neutral reportage" concept was to the news media, it quickly was met by an opposing view from another U.S. Court of Appeals. Writing in Dickey v. CBS (1978), Judge Hunder ruled for his court that "no constitutional privilege of neutral reportage exists." [61] That case involved a libel action resulting from a television broadcast of a pretaped talk show in which a Pennsylvania Congressman accused a public figure of accepting payoffs. Although CBS won the case, it was not on "neutral reportage" grounds, which Judge Hunder said flew in the face of the much-cited decision in St. Amant v. Thompson (1964) [62] (mentioned earlier at page 172.) Judge Hunder criticized the Audubon decision: [63]

> While the Second Circuit [in Edwards v. Audubon Society] found that there can be no liability despite the publisher's "serious doubts" as to truthfulness, *St. Amant* holds that for libel against a public figure to be proved, "[t]here must be sufficient evidence to permit the conclusion that the defendant in fact entertained *serious doubts* as to the truth of his publication. Publishing with such doubts shows reckless disregard for truth or falsity and demonstrates actual malice."
>
>   *   *   *
>
> We therefore conclude that a constitutional privilege of neutral reportage is not created * * * merely because an individual newspaper or television or radio station decides that a particular statement is newsworthy.

Since the Dickey case of 1978, the concept of neutral reportage has had an uneven and generally unpredictable history of acceptance and rejection, but it may be said that at times it has proven to be a useful defense for the media. A number of states have accepted the neutral reportage doctrine, including Florida

[60] Ibid.

[61] Dickey v. CBS Inc., 583 F.2d 1221 (3d Cir.1978).

[62] 390 U.S. 727, 731, 88 S.Ct. 1323, 1325 (1968).

[63] Dickey v. CBS, Inc., 583 F.2d 1221, 1225–1226 (3d Cir.1978).

and Ohio; [64] others have rejected it. [65] In Illinois in the 1980s, one Appellate Court adopted the neutral report privilege, another rejected it, and the state's Supreme Court refused to consider the issue. [66]

Efforts to use—and get wider recognition for—the defense of neutral reportage continued into the 1990s. When the defense has succeeded, it has been in situations where the plaintiff was a public figure and where the report involved was fair and accurate without the espousal of a point of view by the news medium. [67] For example, the defense failed in Cianci v. New Times Publishing Co. There, *New Times* was found by the Second Circuit (enunciator of the *Edwards* doctrine) to have violated many of the qualifications limiting the privilege. The publication was flatly denied the neutral reportage privilege for its story suggesting falsely that a mayor had been a rapist. [68]

In 1989, in a case setting (at least temporarily) a record for punitive damages against a newspaper in a case surviving the appeals process, the neutral reportage case was reject as inapplicable. The Pittsburgh Post–Gazette paid (including $561,000 in interest) damages totaling $2.8 million. (Of that amount, a total of $2 million was in punitive damages.) In that case, DiSalle v. P–G Publishing Co. [69], a Pennsylvania court held:

". . . [I]f neutral reportage is to be recognized as a constitutional privilege, it can offer protection irrespective of the publisher's belief in the truth or falsity of the charges only when a public official or public figure levels a false charge against a public official or figure.

On the other hand, as attorney Robert McGough said after representing the Pittsburgh–Post Gazette in this case, newspapers commonly report on accusations by private parties against public

---

[64] El Amin v. Miami Herald Pub. Co. (Fla.1983), 9 Med.L.Rptr. 1079; Horvath v. Telegraph (Ohio App.1982), 8 Med.L.Rptr. 1657. See especially John B. McCrory et al., "Constitutional Privilege in Libel Law," in James C. Goodale, Communications Law 1990, Vol. I (New York: Practising Law Institute, 1990), pp. 185–192.

[65] New York: Hogan v. Herald Co., 84 A.D.2d 470, 446 N.Y.S.2d 836 (1982), 8 Med.L.Rptr. 1137, affirmed 58 N.Y.2d 630, 458 N.Y.S.2d 538, 444 N.E.2d 1002 (1982), 8 Med.L.Rptr. 2567; Kentucky: McCall v. Courier–Journal and Louisville Times Co., 623 S.W.2d 882 (Ky.1981), 7 Med.L.Rptr. 2118; Michigan: Postill v. Booth Newspapers, Inc., 118 Mich.App. 608, 325 N.W.2d 511 (1982), 8 Med.L.Rptr. 2222.

[66] Fogus v. Capital Cities Media, Inc. 111 Ill.App.3d 1060, 67 Ill.Dec. 616, 444 N.E.2d 1100 (1982), 9 Med.L.Rptr. 1141, 1143.

[67] Goodale, loc. cit.

[68] Cianci v. New Times Publishing Co., 639 F.2d 54 (2d Cir.1980), 6 Med.L.Rptr. 1625.

[69] Albert Scardino, "Pittsburg Paper Pays $2.8 million Libel Award," The New York Times, July 12, 1989, p. 9; DiSalle v. P.G. Publishing Co., 375 Pa.Super. 510, 544 A.2d 1345, 1363 (1988), 15 Med.L.Rptr. 1874.

officials " 'without knowing or caring whether the accusation is true . . . In Pennsylvania, it is now not enough to report the accusation accurately.' " [70]

Neutral reportage, then, is an unreliable defense. The policy decision to publish or broacast a story involving defamatory charges—even against a person or entity appearing to be a "public official" or a "public figure"—should be checked out not only by journalists but by their legal advisers before publication.

Discovery

The libel plaintiff knows that he will be faced at the outset of his action with a motion for summary judgment by the defendant, and seeks evidence in advance of the trial to counter the motion he knows will come. Often using "discovery proceedings," his attorney confronts the defendant with questions aimed at helping prepare the case. Meanwhile, the defendant news medium is interrogating the plaintiff in similar discovery. Plaintiffs commonly seek evidence, during discovery, of actual malice on the part of the journalist, for their "threshold" showing of this essential ingredient at the outset of the trial. Another element often sought is the identity of confidential sources of the reporter's information—persons quoted in a story, but not named. Refusal by the journalist to testify in discovery proceedings can result in citation for contempt of court.

In one of the most celebrated media cases of the 1970s, Barry Lando and Mike Wallace of CBS' "60 Minutes" refused to answer questions in discovery proceedings that sought to probe their "state of mind" in preparing a segment on one Col. Anthony Herbert. Herbert, a public figure, was suing for words in the broadcast which, he said, portrayed him as a liar in his accusations that his superiors covered up reports of Vietnam War crimes. He was seeking evidence of actual malice on the part of Lando and Wallace. Confronted in discovery proceedings that lasted a year and produced almost 3,000 pages of Lando's testimony alone, Lando refused to respond when it came to inquiries into his state of mind in editing and producing the program, and into the editorial process in general. He said this was a realm of journalistic work that must not be intruded upon for fear of its chilling effect on expression protected by the First Amendment.

While the Court of Appeals, Second District, held on a 2–1 vote that First Amendment interests warranted an absolute evidentiary privilege for Lando, the U.S. Supreme Court reversed, saying that the First Amendment does not prohibit plaintiffs from directly inquiring into the editorial processes of those whom they

---

[70] Scardino, loc. cit.

accuse of defamation.[71] Journalists in libel cases had been testifying as to their motives, discussions, and thoughts relating to their copy, for a century and more before Times v. Sullivan without objecting to the process, said Justice White in writing the majority opinion; and Times v. Sullivan "made it essential to proving liability that plaintiffs focus on the conduct and state of mind of the defendant." He elaborated: [72]

> To be liable, the alleged defamer of public officials or of public figures must know or have reason to suspect that his publication is false. In other cases proof of some kind of fault, negligence perhaps, is essential to recovery. Inevitably, unless liability is to be completely foreclosed, the thoughts and editorial processes of the alleged defamer would be open to examination.

A few newspaper editorials and media voices recognized that the *Herbert* decision had broken no new ground and presented no fresh menace to the First Amendment, but attacking of the Supreme Court was far more common as media took the view that the justices had violated the integrity of the "editorial process" and the First Amendment.[73] Alarmed reactions of shock over presumed new damage by the Court to the First Amendment were often without understanding that what the Court was finding was in line with what lower courts had found for decades or for a century. In general, press reactions spoke eloquently to journalists' superficial education in the history of press freedom, and to their necessary occupational fix upon the world's current "hot scoop," unalloyed by knowledge of the history in which their own First Amendment roots were embedded.

Discovery in libel had arrived to stay, the *Herbert* case confirming its applicability. Said one media attorney: [74] "While there was an outcry from some representatives of the press at the time, it now seems unlikely that the opinion will have any dramatic effect. Before *Herbert* journalists had routinely testified about the editorial process in establishing their freedom from 'actual malice' or 'fault.' As a result of *Herbert,* they will continue to do so."

Because the discovery process can be so intrusive, sensible journalists (or public relations of advertising people who get involved in litigation) should always conduct themselves carefully. Self-protective reporters have long understood that their story

[71] Herbert v. Lando, 441 U.S. 153, 99 S.Ct. 1635 (1979), 4 Med.L.Rptr. 2575.

[72] Ibid., at 160, 99 S.Ct. at 1641, 4 Med.L.Rptr. at 2578.

[73] Editorials on File, April 16–30, 1979, pp. 437–446.

[74] Robert D. Sack, "Special Discovery Problems in Media Cases," Communications Law 1980, I, 235, 242 (Practicing Law Institute 1980).

notes (or tape recordings, or video out-takes) may be subpoenaed as part of the discovery process in litigation. If you and your newspaper are being sued for libel by a mayor, do you want to explain the doodles you've sketched on your note pad to a jury? What if you've drawn a passable likeness of the mayor but added fangs? But—as pointed out in Chapter 4 at page 125—even if you have embarrassing materials in your notes or in a video outtakes, do *not* destroy any materials relating to litigation once "the papers have been filed" to start a legal action. Don't destroy such materials while there is still any possibility of an appeal or further proceedings. If you do, the court may assume that destruction of materials subject to discovery is evidence of actual malice,[75] or of contempt of court.

[75] See Brown & Williamson Tobacco Corp. v. Jacobson, 827 F.2d 1119 (7th Cir. 1987), discussed at pp. 123–125.

Chapter 6

DEFENDING AGAINST LIBEL SUITS
UNDER STATE LAW

Sec.
31. Determining Who Is "Private".
32. Ending Strict Liability in Libel.
33. Qualified Privilege as a Defense.
34. Truth as a Defense.
35. Opinion and Fair Comment as Defenses.
36. Retraction.

SEC. 31. DETERMINING WHO IS "PRIVATE"

Since the 1974 decision in Gertz v. Robert Welch, Inc. provided that private persons' libel suits have a lower barrier to clear than public persons', determining who is "private" has been of first importance in defamation actions.

If a person brings a libel suit against a news medium, one of the defense attorney's fondest hopes is that the judge will rule that the plaintiff is a public person: A "public official" or a "public figure." As discussed in the preceding chapter, the public person has to prove "actual malice" in order to win a libel suit.[1]

This chapter concentrates on what happens when private persons bring libel suits. When that happens, news media generally make use of state statutes and state constitutions as their defenses,[2] thanks to the important decision in Gertz v. Robert Welch.[3] In *Gertz,* the U.S. Supreme Court said that society's stake in getting news about private persons is not as great as where public persons are involved. To put it another way, society places a high value in protecting private persons against libel. Thus, private persons may meet a less stern test—proving negligence—than having to meet the constitutional barrier of proving actual malice.

The reasons for this were detailed in an earlier discussion of *Gertz* (above, Sec. 28). Briefly, the Court said that private people

---

[1] See Sec. 25, above. Public persons have to prove "actual malice"—publication of a defamatory falsehood with knowledge of falsity or reckless disregard for the truth.

[2] See Robert D. Sack and Stuart D. Karle, "Common Law Libel and the Press: A Primer," in James C. Goodale, chairman, Communications Law 1991, Vol. 1 (New York: Practising Law Institute, 1991), pp. 1–88; Comment, "The Impending Federalization of Missouri Defamation Law," 43 Mo.L.Rev. 270 (1978), discussing relationships of traditional and constitutional principles in the law of defamation.

[3] 418 U.S. 323, 94 S.Ct. 2997 (1974).

have not accepted the risk of exposing themselves to the rough-and-tumble give-and-take of public scrutiny and controversy associated with public life. Further, it said, private people do not have the access to media that public people do, to refute false and disparaging news. Another reason that is sometimes given is that private people do not have the immunity from successful libel suits that public officials have in making statements from the platform of libel-proof official proceedings.[4]

To begin, then, who is a private person? A central test, we learned earlier, is that one is private unless he voluntarily thrusts himself into the "vortex" of public controversy in order to influence the outcome of that controversy. It is worth repeating earlier points: One, of course, is that a person's presence in an official proceeding which is open to the public does not automatically destroy his private status (as with Ilya Wolston, Attorney Gertz, Mrs. Firestone, above).

Another is that the media cannot make a private person public merely by bringing the person into the news. That is illustrated by Hutchinson, of course, and also by Mrs. Mary Troman.[5] Mrs. Troman was drawn into a public controversy by a newspaper which, she said, implied that her home was a gang headquarters when it was no such thing. The court ruled that she was private. She had not in any way "injected" herself into a public controversy, nor had she invited public attention or comment.[6]

For example, in Chapter 5 we saw an attorney declared a public figure for all purposes (p. 164): Myron Steere had been county attorney for eight years, with substantial publicity. He also had been special counsel for the board of county commissioners in a controversy over a new courthouse and was an officer and representative for many professional, fraternal and social activities. He had achieved influence in local affairs in his 32-year career in law practice in the county was now capped by representing a woman in her well-publicized, famous murder trial.

Yet attorney Paul Littlefield was not a public figure even though involved in a topic of public interest—his own disciplinary proceedings by the Iowa State Bar Association and the Iowa Supreme Court for practicing law while he was on probation. He brought a libel suit for an erroneous news story about the proceedings, and was declared a public figure by the trial court, which said he was drawn into a public forum and debate as a result of his "purposeful act of practicing law in Iowa in direct contraven-

---

[4] Ibid., at 344–45, 94 S.Ct. at 3009–3010.

[5] Troman v. Wood, 62 Ill.2d 184, 340 N.E.2d 292 (1975).

[6] Ibid.

tion of his probation." But the U.S. Court of Appeals for the 8th district did not agree. It was Littlefield's status as a person, not the high public interest in his story, that was crucial: [7]

> We fail to see anything in Littlefield's status indicating that he has ready access to effective means of self-help or that he has voluntarily assumed the risks of public exposure by thrusting himself into a public controversy with a view toward influencing its resolution.

Shifting from professional people to the realm of business and commerce, corporations and business firms are intensely "public" in their reliance on the public's patronage. That may or may not be enough to make them public figures in libel actions. A San Francisco department store, City of Paris, advertised a close-out sale, and media reported widely its going-out-of-business. The store's agent in the sale, Vegod Corp., was said by KGO–TV to have brought inferior goods in during the sale, the story relying on the Better Business Bureau as its source for charges which included the "deceiving" of the public. Vegod sued, and claimed to be "private." The California Supreme Court agreed in a decision that said of the "public controversy test": [8]

> Criticism of commercial conduct does not deserve the special protection of the actual malice test. Balancing one individual's limited First Amendment interest against another's reputation interest * * *, we conclude that a person in the business world advertising his wares does not necessarily become part of an existing public controversy.

In 1985, the United States Supreme Court ruled in a case where it found a plaintiff to be a private person involved in a matter of *private* concern. Greenmoss Builders sought punitive damages from Dun & Bradstreet's false, confidential report, sent to five subscribers to its credit-reporting service, that Greenmoss had declared bankruptcy. Presumed and punitive damages had been barred to private plaintiffs in Gertz v. Robert Welch unless they could show actual malice. But Justice Lewis Powell wrote in a 5–4 decision that the *Gertz* rule applied only where the subject was a matter of public concern, and that this credit report was "solely in the individual interest of the speaker and its specific

---

[7] Littlefield v. Fort Dodge Messenger, 614 F.2d 581, 584 (8th Cir.1980), 5 Med.L. Rptr. 2325, certiorari denied 445 U.S. 945, 100 S.Ct. 1342. See also Dodrill v. Arkansas Democrat Co., 265 Ark. 628, 590 S.W.2d 840 (1979), certiorari denied 444 U.S. 1076, 100 S.Ct. 1024 (1980), a "private" attorney. Gertz himself, of course, was a "private" attorney.

[8] Vegod Corp. v. ABC, 25 Cal.3d 763, 160 Cal.Rptr. 97, 603 P.2d 14 (1979), 5 Med. L.Rptr. 2043, 2045. And see Robert E. Drechsel and Moon, D., Corporate Libel Plaintiffs and the News Media * * *, 21 Am. Business L.Journ. 127, Summer 1983.

business audience."[9] The special protection given to speech by the *Gertz* rule and by *Sullivan*—to further robust debate on public issues—was not applicable here. The Court upheld a jury award to Greenmoss of $50,000 presumed (compensatory) damages and $300,000 punitive damages.

SEC. 32. ENDING STRICT LIABILITY IN LIBEL

The law may no longer presume injury to persons as a result of false defamation even though it is libelous on its face.

Gertz v. Robert Welch, Inc. told private people they would not have to meet the constitutional demand of proving actual malice against publishers in bringing libel suits. What, then, would be required of them? Justice Powell wrote for the majority that the states might set their own standards of liability for private people to prove, except that the Constitution would not permit states to impose "liability without fault." Powell was saying that state standards could not include an ancient rule in libel *per se*—that for those words which are damaging on their face, the law presumes injury to reputation and liability for libel by the publisher; the only question is the amount of damages that may be recovered.[10] This was the long-standing rule of "strict liability" in libel, and the Court was saying that the media must be shielded from strict liability. The standard of fault for private people to prove, Powell said, need be no more than "negligence," instead of the "actual malice" of *Sullivan*. The Powell opinion significantly returned to the states much of the jurisdiction in libel cases that had been lost to them through the sweep of *Sullivan*, even as it made it plain that there must not be a return to "automatic" liability for defamation.

The *Gertz* majority then turned its attention to damage awards, outlining further restrictions on the states. The states have a "strong and legitimate ＊ ＊ ＊ interest in compensating private individuals for injury to reputation," but compensation may not be limitless. A private plaintiff proving negligence can collect only "compensation for actual injury," otherwise known as "compensatory" or "general" damages.[11] To collect punitive damages, private persons (like public officials or public figures) have to prove "actual malice" rather than mere negligence. It found that awarding presumed damages ("compensatory" or "general" damages) or punitive damages where there is no demonstrated loss,

[9] Dun & Bradstreet, Inc. v. Greenmoss Builders, Inc., 472 U.S. 749, 105 S.Ct. 2939, 2947 (1985).

[10] Gertz v. Robert Welch, Inc., 418 U.S. 323, 346, 94 S.Ct. 2997, 3010 (1974); Prosser, 780–781.

[11] Gertz v. Robert Welch, Inc., 418 U.S. 323, 348, 94 S.Ct. 2997, 3011 (1974).

"unnecessarily compounds the potential of any system of liability for defamatory falsehood to inhibit the vigorous exercise of First Amendment freedoms."[12]

Precisely what the Court meant by the permitted "compensation for actual injury" was not spelled out, but Justice Powell made it plain that he was not speaking strictly of compensation for proved dollar losses flowing from false defamation: [13]

> We need not define "actual injury," as trial courts have wide experience in framing appropriate jury instructions in tort action. Suffice it to say that actual injury is not limited to out-of-pocket loss. Indeed, the more customary types of actual harm inflicted by defamatory falsehood include impairment of reputation and standing in the community, personal humiliation, and mental anguish and suffering. * * * all awards must be supported by competent evidence concerning the injury, although there need be no evidence which assigns an actual dollar value to the injury.

The Negligence "Standard"

The Court's reliance on the ambiguous label of "negligence" has caused substantial problems for media defendants ever since the 1974 decision in Gertz v. Welch. As Justice Brennan predicted in his dissent, the majority opinion in *Gertz* requires media to observe a "reasonable care standard (i.e. the "negligence standard"). Such a fluid concept, he suggested, could give state court juries intent on punishing unpopular views "a formidable weapon for doing so." He argued that the negligence concept in libel cases would lead to self-censorship because publishers would feel compelled to weigh carefully "a myriad of uncertain factors before publication. Even if recovery were limited under rules requiring proof of "actual injury" to reputation, that would not stop self-censorship arising from fear of having to defend a publication or broadcast against libel suit.[14]

Brennan feared that the decision would damage the media's protection, and Chief Justice Burger thought it could inhibit some editors.[15] Justice Byron White, on the other hand, declared the decision endangered the ordinary citizen who might be defamed. White's opinion, the longest in the case, placed his central objec-

---

[12] Gertz v. Robert Welch, Inc., 418 U.S. 323, 348–351, 94 S.Ct. 2997, 3011–3012 (1974).

[13] Ibid.

[14] Ibid., at 366, 94 S.Ct. at 3020.

[15] Ibid., at 354, 94 S.Ct. at 3014.

tions to the majority in its "scuttling the libel laws of the States in
* * * wholesale fashion."[16]

The majority accomplished this, he said: [17]

> • By requiring the plaintiff in defamation actions to
> prove the defendant's culpability beyond the act of pub-
> lishing defamation (i.e., the plaintiff could no longer have
> an actionable case by merely showing "libel *per se;*" he
> would also have to prove "fault" on the part of the
> publisher—variously referred to in the Gertz opinions as
> "negligence" or lack of "reasonable care");

> • By requiring the plaintiff to prove actual damage
> to reputation resulting from the publication (i.e., no long-
> er would harm be presumed and general damages auto-
> matic as under the libel *per se* rule);

In addition, White deplored the fact that it would no longer be
possible to recover punitive damages by showing malice in the
traditional (tort-related) sense of ill will; now the *Sullivan* malice—knowing falsehood or reckless disregard of truth—would be
required. White found that all of this deprived the private citizen
of his "historic recourse" to redress damaging falsehoods under
libel *per se,* as recognized by all 50 states.

Standards of Fault in the States

In *Gertz,* the Supreme Court's majority put the burden of
defining the standard of fault to be used onto the state courts:
"We hold that, so long as they do not impose liability without
fault, the States may define for themselves the appropriate standard of liability for a publisher or broadcaster of defamatory
falsehood injurious to a private individual."[18] The result, unsurprisingly, has been to create an even greater lack of uniformity in
libel law among the states.

It has been said that "the legal concept of fault is grounded
upon breach of a standard of conduct." As John B. McCrory and
his co-authors have noted, the question will arise whether the
standard of conduct is going to be the traditional "reasonable
man" standard of general negligence law, or whether a standard
of conduct set by the media industry will be used as the guide-
post.[19]

16 Ibid., at 370, 94 S.Ct. at 3022.

17 Ibid., at 374–377, 94 S.Ct. at 3024–3025.

18 Ibid., at 346, 94 S.Ct. at 3010.

19 John B. McCrory, Robert C. Bernius, Robb M. Jones, and J. Gregory Bishop,
Constitutional Privilege in Libel Law, in James C. Goodale, Chairman, Communications Law 1987, Vol. II, P. 788.

Both kinds of standards pose problems for media defendants. With the reasonable person standard, the non-journalists sitting on juries (some call them "earth people") seem to have an inborn belief that no reasonable people could *ever* be journalists: journalists are intrusive and tell things that shouldn't be told. And if an industry standard is used—such as "standards of investigation and reporting ordinarily adhered to by responsible publishers" [20]—then expert witnesses for a lawsuit's two sides will no doubt disagree over what those standards properly should be. And once again, non-journalists—jurors and judges—will be sitting in a position to second-guess reporters, editors, and broadcasters.

As John McCrory and co-authors have detailed, most states—a total of 32 late in 1991—have designated their standard as the "negligence" of which Justice Powell wrote in *Gertz*.[21]

But states were not restricted to this standard. Some states have chosen other standards which are more difficult for plaintiffs to prove against media defendants. For example, New York has fashioned a standard known by the shorthand label of "gross irresponsibility by the news medium." [22]

In addition, John McCrory and colleagues have listed four states—Alaska, Colorado, Indiana, and New Jersey—as using an "actual malice" standard, at least as applied to private individuals involved in a matter of public interest.[23] In addition, three states—Connecticut, Louisiana, and Montana—were listed as "undecided" on a standard of fault in defamation cases as of late 1991.[24]

Negligence

In no part of journalism law have the courts more clearly and consistently entered the realm of setting journalistic standards than where they judge the level of "fault"—whether the fault of actual malice or the fault of negligence or gross irresponsibility. Courts examine carefully the reporting and writing process at least as much when a plaintiff is private as when he is public.

In Tennessee, the state Supreme Court decided that it was up to the jury to say whether there had been negligence in a report-

[20] Cf. Curtis Pub. Co. v. Butts, 388 U.S. 130, 87 S.Ct. 1975 (1967).

[21] McCrory, et al., in Goodale, Chairman, Communications Law 1991 (Vol. I), at pp. 249–253.

[22] Chapadeau v. Utica Observer–Dispatch, Inc., 38 N.Y.2d 196, 379 N.Y.S.2d 61, 341 N.E.2d 569 (1975). The similarity to Justice John Marshall Harlan's standard for public figures to meet in Curtis Pub. Co. v. Butts, 388 U.S. 130, 87 S.Ct. 1975 (1967), discussed above at p. ___, is too striking to avoid a connection.

[23] McCrory, et al., op. cit. at 254.

[24] Ibid., at 255.

er's reliance on a single police record to suggest mistakenly that a woman was an adulterer. Using the "arrest report" of the Memphis police, a Press-Scimitar reporter wrote a story saying that Mrs. Nichols had been shot. The suspect, said the story, was a woman who went to the Nichols home and found her own husband there with Mrs. Nichols. The story used "police said" and "police reported" in attribution, the reporter testifying that these were common terms used to indicate that a source was either a written police record or a policeman's spoken words.

Had the reporter gone to the police record called the "offense report," he would have learned that not only was Mrs. Nichols with the suspect's husband (named Newton), but also Mr. Nichols and two neighbors. There would thus have been no suggestion that Mrs. Nichols was having an adulterous affair and had been "caught" by Mrs. Newton. Almost a month later, the newspaper printed a story correcting the implication of the first story. But Mrs. Nichols sued for libel, and testified at trial that the article had torn up her home, children, and reputation, that the family had had to move, that she had had telephone calls asking how much it cost to get the newspaper to run the correcting account. A friend testified that after the initial story, people gossiped about Mrs. Nichols and "said that she was a whore." Before the case went to the jury for decision, the trial court granted the newspaper a directed verdict: While "no fault had been shown" on the part of the reporter, the trial court said, it did note its uncertainty as to what standard of fault was required on the basis of *Gertz*. The Tennessee Court of Appeals, which reversed the trial court decision on several grounds, said that the standard of liability was "ordinary care." The case then went to the Tennessee Supreme Court, which in upholding the Court of Appeals and sending the case back for trial, laid down Tennessee's requirement upon private libel plaintiffs: negligence.[25]

> In determining the issue of liability the conduct of defendant is to be measured against what a reasonably prudent person would, or would not, have done under the same or similar circumstances. This is the ordinary negligence test that we adopt, not a "journalistic malpractice" test whereby liability is based upon a departure from supposed standards of care set by publishers themselves * * *.

In General Products v. Meredith, an article on wood stoves in *Better Homes and Gardens Home Plan Ideas Magazine* warned against fire danger with the use of triple-walled chimneys in

[25] Memphis Pub. Co. v. Nichols, 569 S.W.2d 412, 418 (Tenn.1978), 4 Med.L.Rptr. 1573.

certain stoves. The manufacturer (found to be "private") of one type, not subject to the hazards of creosote buildup, brought suit. The federal District Court denied part of the magazine's motion for summary judgment, saying that there was evidence of possible negligence by the reporter in his fact gathering: [26]

> * * * he relied on an earlier book and article and did not examine them directly, but drew on his general recall of their content. He did not contact the author of either source for an update, was not aware that the information in the magazine article had been repudiated by a subsequent article in another publication, and did not contact anyone in the industry on testing relevant to his subject.

A KARK–TV reporter who happened to be near the scene of police activity in a shopping center store was alerted to the fact, and a camera crew from the station was sent. The crew filmed the scene of police handcuffing two men and placing them in a squad car. Reporter Long questioned the police but got no comment, and interviewed a store clerk from whom she received vague responses. Her story accompanying the broadcast film called the event a "robbery attempt," and said that the two men "allegedly held a store clerk hostage." But the handcuffed men were never arrested, merely detained until police determined that the "tip" on which they acted was false and there had been no robbery attempt. On libel trial, each plaintiff was awarded $12,500.[27]

The Arkansas Supreme Court said there was enough evidence of reporting negligence for the trial court to send that issue to the jury: [28]

> * * *. We cannot say that a news report with its sources consisting of information from a police scanner, uncorroborated by police on the scene, in conjunction with an eye-witness account by a news reporter who did not know the surrounding circumstances of what she observed, will be found to be due care as a matter of law
> * * *.

If reports from a police "scanner" were suspect in that case, a news story about a gunshot death, based on a written report to media from a police "hot line" was not negligent. The hotline

[26] General Products Co., Inc. v. Meredith Corp., 526 F.Supp. 546 (E.D.Va.1981), 7 Med.L.Rptr. 2257, 2261.

[27] KARK–TV v. Simon, 280 Ark. 228, 656 S.W.2d 702 (1983), 10 Med.L.Rptr. 1049. The Arkansas Supreme Court reversed and remanded the case because of the trial court's error in permitting the jury to consider punitive damages, even though it granted none.

[28] Ibid., at 704, 10 Med.L.Rptr. at 1051.

established to lessen the need for interviews with police. The reporter, who had often used the "hot line" and found it reliable, accurately quoted the report's statement that the shooting occurred during a domestic argument. Later, the shooting was ruled accidental. The husband sued the newspaper for implying that he intentionally shot his wife, saying the reporter should have waited for a more "official" report. The Court found no negligence.[29] Nor, in another case, was there negligence in a reporter's failure to interview all eight persons arrested on drug charges, before publishing a story in which a father and son of the same name were confused. The court said that the reporter "undoubtedly could have taken additional steps to insure the accuracy of his facts." But he had talked with several officials, with an attorney, and with neighbors of the raided house, and had listened to a tape of a news conference about the event. His "procedures were well within the bounds of professionalism in the news gathering business." The court found no negligence.[30]

Illinois' Supreme Court adopted negligence as its standard, saying recovery might be had on proof that the defendant knew the statement to be false, or "believing it to be true, lacked reasonable grounds for that belief." It added that a journalist's "failure to make a reasonable investigation into the truth of the statement is obviously a relevant factor." [31] And it quoted the Kansas Supreme Court with approval as further elaboration of what "negligence" means: " * * * the lack of ordinary care either in the doing of an act or in the failure to do something. * * * The norm usually is the conduct of the reasonably careful person under the circumstances." [32]

If it's any help to the reporter, it may be noted that the word "care" is used in various courts' discussions of negligence: simply the "care" of the reasonably prudent person in the Arizona and Tennessee cases above; "ordinary care" in the Illinois/Kansas wording above; "reasonable care" (Washington),[33] "due care" (Ohio).[34]

One analyst has found that a decade's use of the negligence standard has demonstrated high uncertainty and severe contradic-

[29] Phillips v. Washington Post (D.C.Sup.Ct.1982), 8 Med.L.Rptr. 1835.

[30] Horvath v. Ashtabula Telegraph (Ohio App.1982), 8 Med.L.Rptr. 1657, 1662.

[31] Troman v. Wood, 62 Ill.2d 184, 340 N.E.2d 292, 298–299 (1975).

[32] Ibid., 299; Gobin v. Globe Pub. Co., 216 Kan. 223, 531 P.2d 76 (1975).

[33] Taskett v. KING Broadcasting Co., 86 Wash.2d 439, 445, 546 P.2d 81, 85 (1976).

[34] Thomas H. Maloney and Sons, Inc. v. E.W. Scripps Co., 43 Ohio App.2d 105, 334 N.E.2d 494 (1974).

tions in results, plus a likelihood that it produces self-censorship by media. He wrote that the *Gertz* approach has failed.[35]

"Gross Irresponsibility"

In New York, the fault of negligence is not serious enough for a private individual to maintain a libel suit. The New York Court of Appeals has specified that, where the subject matter is of public concern, recovery for the private individual depends on his establishing "that the publisher acted in a grossly irresponsible manner without due consideration for the standards of information gathering and dissemination ordinarily followed by responsible parties." [36] The Utica *Observer-Dispatch* had reported two different episodes involving drug-charge arrests in a single story. At one point, it incorrectly brought together school teacher Chapadeau and two other men at a drug-and-beer party, referring to "the trio." Chapadeau was not there, and he brought a libel action. The Court of Appeals noted the error but also pointed out that the story was written only after two authoritative agencies had been consulted, and that the story was checked by two desk hands at the newspaper. "This is hardly indicative of gross irresponsibility," said the court. "Rather it appears that the publisher exercised reasonable methods to insure accuracy." [37] Summary judgment for the newspaper was upheld. It was denied, however, where a television reporter who had broadcast an account of fraudulent practices concerning burial expenses could recall little or nothing about his sources and how he obtained the information, and made little or no effort to authenticate his report. A jury, said the appeals court, would have to decide whether that was gross irresponsibility.[38]

Actual Malice

Private-person plaintiffs face a tougher test in some states, including Indiana, Colorado, and Wisconsin. Indiana is one of a minority of states continuing to adhere to the *Rosenbloom* plurality view that private persons involved in a matter of public interest

---

[35] Marc Franklin, What Does Negligence Mean in Defamation Cases?, 6 Comm/ Ent 259, 276–281 (Winter, 1984), and see pp. 266–271 for an excellent analysis of journalistic practices as examined by courts under the negligence standard.

[36] Chapadeau v. Utica Observer-Dispatch, Inc., 38 N.Y.2d 196, 379 N.Y.S.2d 61, 64, 341 N.E.2d 569, 571 (1975). The similarity to U.S. Supreme Court Justice Harlan's recommended standard for public figures to meet, in Curtis Pub. Co. v. Butts, 388 U.S. 130, 87 S.Ct. 1975 (1967), above, p. 117, is too striking to avoid a connection.

[37] Ibid., at 65, 341 N.E.2d at 572. See also Goldman v. New York Post Corp., 58 A.D.2d 769, 396 N.Y.S.2d 399 (1977).

[38] Meadows v. Taft Broadcasting Co., Inc., 98 A.D.2d 959, 470 N.Y.S.2d 205 (1983), 10 Med.L.Rptr. 1363.

need to prove actual malice to collect libel damages. Indiana's Court Appeals, ruling in 1974 only six months after Gertz v. Welch was decided by the U.S. Supreme Court, said that Indiana's own constitution called for this rigorous barrier to recovery for libel, rather than for a negligence standard. The court said that differentiating requirements between public and private persons' libel suits "makes no sense in terms of our constitutional guarantees of free speech and press." [39]

In Colorado, similarly, the state supreme court has denied plaintiffs use of the *Gertz* negligence rule. A defamation defendant should be held liable in Colorado "if, and only if, [the publisher] knew the statement to be false and made the statement with reckless disregard for whether it was false or not."

The Colorado Supreme Court evidently believed that freedom of expression would be damaged with a weaker standard of fault than Times v. Sullivan actual malice.[40] And Wisconsin's Supreme Court has intimated several times that private plaintiffs would have to prove actual malice if the stories they sued over involved items of public interest.[41]

It should be obvious from these examples that there is great variation in libel law from state to state, and that the late William L. Prosser was correct when he wrote animatedly about the haphazard, unplanned growth of this area of law.[42]

Proving "Actual Injury"

Having proved fault at some level—actual malice, negligence, gross irresponsibility—the plaintiff next, as we saw in Justice Powell's majority opinion in the landmark *Gertz* case, must go on to prove actual injury. No longer, as under old tort rules, will injury be presumed in libel cases except where the plaintiff shows *Sullivan* malice. Powell said that this could include various injuries—"impairment of reputation and standing in the community, personal humiliation, and mental anguish and suffering," as well as actual out-of-pocket loss.

[39] Aafco Heating and Air Conditioning Co. v. Northwest Publications, 162 Ind. App. 671, 321 N.E.2d 580 (1974); see also Chang v. Michiana Telecasting (N.D.Ind. 1987), 14 Med.L.Rptr. 1889, 1900.

[40] Walker v. Colorado Springs Sun, Inc., 188 Colo. 86, 538 P.2d 450 (1975), cert. denied 423 U.S. 1025, 96 S.Ct. 469 (1975).

[41] Denny v. Mertz, 106 Wis.2d 636, 318 N.W.2d 141 (1982); for state-by-state coverage updated each year, see, e.g. Henry R. Kaufmann, ed., LDRC 50–State Libel Survey 1988 (New York: Libel Defense Resource Center, 1988).

[42] Prosser, Law of Torts, 4th ed. (1976), pp. 737–738.

Attorney Paul Littlefield, in a case treated above,[43] was not successful in showing injury. Littlefield had been prohibited from the practice of law for three years, after he had been convicted of attempting to commit a felony. Further, he was found to have resumed practicing in violation of his probation. He brought a libel suit against the Fort Dodge Messenger for an erroneous report (it said he had pleaded guilty to a felony, a more serious offense than "attempting to commit a felony"). His injury, he testified, was that he was dismissed from his employment with the federal government after his superviser made a trip to Fort Dodge, Ia., where he learned of Littlefield's disbarment. The court denied that there was injury: [44]

> Littlefield failed to prove either (1) that his superviser ever believed him to be a felon, or (2) that such belief, rather than knowledge of his disbarment, was the motivating factor in his termination. Moreover, Littlefield failed to prove any link between the article of which he complains, published in 1974, and his superviser's 1976 discovery of his disbarment. Thus, Littlefield failed to prove any actual damage resulting from the article.

SEC. 33. QUALIFIED PRIVILEGE AS A DEFENSE

News media may publish defamation from legislative, judicial or other public and official proceedings without fear of successful libel or slander action; fair and accurate reports of these statements are privileged.

Since long before the landmark year 1964 and the constitutional defense developed in and after New York Times Co. v. Sullivan, libel suits have been defended under statutory and common law provisions termed *qualified privilege, fair comment and criticism,* and *truth.* As noted earlier, the theory that free expression contributes to the public good in a self-governing society underlies the older defenses as well as the constitutional defense.

In some circumstances it is so important to society that people be allowed to speak without fear of a suit for defamation that their words are given immunity from a finding of libel or slander. The immunity is called privilege. For purposes of the mass media, it is applicable especially in connection with government activity.[45]

---

[43] Littlefield v. Fort Dodge Messenger, 614 F.2d 581 (8th Cir.1980), 5 Med.L.Rptr. 2325, certiorari denied 445 U.S. 945, 100 S.Ct. 1342 (1980).

[44] Ibid., at 584, 5 Med.L.Rptr. at 2327.

[45] For other circumstances where it applies, see Prosser, pp. 804–805; see also Robert Sack, in Goodale, ed., Communications Law 1991 (Vol. I) on "Fair Report," pp. 59–70.

The paramount importance of full freedom for participants in court, legislative or executive proceedings to say whatever bears on the matter, gives all the participants a full immunity from successful libel action. The immunity for the participant in official proceedings is called "absolute" privilege. No words relevant to the business of the proceeding will support a suit for defamation. If a person is defamed in these proceedings, he cannot recover damages.

Public policy also demands, in an open society, that people know to the fullest what goes on in the proceedings; for this reason, anyone who reports proceedings is given an immunity from successful suit for defamation. For the public at large, "anyone" ordinarily means the mass media. The protection is ordinarily more limited for the reporter of a proceeding than for the participant in the proceeding. It is thus called "qualified" (or "conditional") privilege.[46]

It may be argued that the mere fact of a person's participation in an official proceeding makes him a "public figure," and so puts him under the rigorous requirements of proving *Sullivan's* actual malice in a libel suit. The response, of course, is that neither Attorney Gertz nor Mrs. Firestone became a public figure through taking part in official court proceedings that resulted in news stories about them. Both received damages for libel. (Ch. 5).

It has been held that any citizen has *absolute* immunity in any criticism he makes of government. The City of Chicago brought a libel suit against the *Chicago Tribune,* claiming damages of $10,000,000 through the *Tribune's* campaign coverage in 1920. The stories had said that the city was broke, that its credit "is shot to pieces," that it "is hurrying on to bankruptcy and is threatened with a receivership for its revenue."

The court denied the city's claim. It said that in any libelous publication concerning a municipal corporation, the citizen and the newspaper possess absolute privilege.[47]

Every citizen has a right to criticize an inefficient government without fear of civil as well as criminal prosecution. This absolute privilege is founded on the principle that it is advantageous for the public interest

---

[46] A few states give absolute privilege to press reports of official proceedings, e.g. Thompson's Laws of New York, 1939, Civ.P. § 337, Wis.Stats.1931, § 331.05(1). And as we have seen in Ch. 3, Sec. 14, broadcasters are immune from defamation suits brought for the words of politicians in campaign broadcasts: Farmers Educational & Coop. Union of America v. WDAY, Inc., 360 U.S. 525, 79 S.Ct. 1302 (1959).

[47] City of Chicago v. Tribune Co., 307 Ill. 595, 139 N.E. 86, 90 (1923).

that the citizen should not be in any way fettered in his statements . . . .[48]

Qualified privilege in reporting official proceedings is the heart of the concern here. The privilege arose in the law of England, the basic rationale having been developed before the start of the nineteenth century in connection with newspaper reports of court proceedings.[49] While American courts relied on English decisions, America was ahead of England in expanding the protection for press reports. The immunity was broadened to cover the reporting of legislative and other public official proceedings by the New York legislature in 1854, 14 years before privilege for reporting legislative bodies was recognized in England.[50] Other states readily adopted the New York rule.

In America a famous figure in jurisprudence stated the heart of the rationale for qualified privilege in an early case that has been relied upon by American courts countless times since. Judge Oliver Wendell Holmes, Jr., then of the Massachusetts bench and later a justice of the United States Supreme Court, wrote the words in Cowley v. Pulsifer (1884).[51] Publisher Royal Pulsifer's *Boston Herald* had printed the content of a petition seeking Charles Cowley's removal from the bar, and Cowley sued. Judge Holmes wrote that the public must have knowledge of judicial proceedings, not because one citizen's quarrels with another are important to public concern,

> * * * but because it is of the highest moment that those who administer justice should always act under the sense of public responsibility, and that every citizen should be able to satisfy himself with his own eyes as to the mode in which a public duty is performed.

The advantage to the nation in granting privilege to press reports, he stressed, is "the security which publicity gives for the proper administration of justice."[52]

While the privilege is "qualified" in the sense that it will not hold if the report of the proceeding is made with malice, it also requires that the story be a fair and accurate account of the proceeding, and not engage in comment. Most states hold the story must be one of a "public and official proceeding," not a

---

[48] Grafton v. ABC, 70 Ohio App.2d 205, 435 N.E.2d 1131 (1980), 7 Med.L.Rptr. 1134, 1136, quoting Capital District Regional Off-Track Betting Corp. v. Northeastern Harness Horsemen's Ass'n, 92 Misc.2d 232, 399 N.Y.S.2d 597, 598 (1977).

[49] Curry v. Walter, 170 Eng.Rep. 419 (1796); King v. Wright, 101 Eng.Rep. 1396 (1799).

[50] New York Laws, 1854, Chap. 130; Wason v. Walter, L.R. 4 Q.B. 73 (1868).

[51] 137 Mass. 392, 394 (1884).

[52] Ibid.

report of related material that emerges before, after, or in some way outside the proceeding.

Fair and Accurate Reports

Errors can destroy qualified privilege: careless note-taking by a reporter at a court trial, the constant danger of a misspelled name, the arcane and technical jargon and findings of law courts, and all the slip-ups of life with tight deadlines. Further, if the report of an official proceeding is not fair to people involved in it, the reporter can be in trouble. We have seen in the previous chapter how Mrs. Firestone won a libel judgment for $100,000 from Time, Inc., for its error in reporting that her husband's divorce was granted on grounds of adultery.

In the case of Anthony Liquori of Agawam, Mass., a newspaper reporter made an error in an address after extracting other materials from a court record about a "breaking" case in which a man of the same name from Springfield pleaded guilty and was convicted. The reporter took an address from a phone book; the innocent Liquori was wrongly identified and sued the Republican Company, publisher of the Springfield papers which carried separate stories, both erroneous. The Republican defended with a plea of qualified privilege, arguing that the defense should hold "because the newspaper articles were a substantially accurate report of a judicial proceeding." [53] It asserted that since only the address of the accused was inaccurate, it had published an article which was "substantially true and accurate and entirely fair," and that no more was required. But citing several previous cases about fair and accurate press reports of official proceedings, the Massachusetts Appeals Court said: [54] " * * * an article which labels an innocent man as a criminal because it refers erroneously to his street address, which the reporter gained from a source outside the court records, is neither substantially accurate nor fair." It denied qualified privilege for the Republican. A wrong name, taken accurately from official police records, on the other hand, is privileged. [55]

Not every inaccuracy in reporting proceedings is fatal, however. Privilege did not fail in Mitchell v. Peoria Journal-Star, Inc., [56]

---

[53] Liquori v. Republican Co., 8 Mass.App.Ct. 671, 396 N.E.2d 726, 728 (1979), 5 Med.L.Rptr. 2180.

[54] Ibid., at 728–29, 5 Med.L.Rptr. at 2181.

[55] Biermann v. Pulitzer Pub. Co., 627 S.W.2d 87 (Mo.App.1981), 7 Med.L.Rptr. 2601. See also Murray v. Bailey, 613 F.Supp. 1276 (N.D.Cal.1985), 11 Med.L.Rptr. 1369. Report saying plaintiff arrested for drunk driving and assault and battery privileged as fair report when in fact plaintiff had been arrested for public intoxication and resisting arrest. Book author's later erroneous statement "convicted of drunken driving" held not privileged.

[56] 76 Ill.App.2d 154, 221 N.E.2d 516 (1966).

merely because the news story of a court action for liquor ordinance violation got the violators' place of arrest wrong. In Josephs v. News Syndicate Co., Inc.,[57] the newspaper did not lose privilege because somehow the reporter incorrectly slipped into his story of a burglary arrest the statement that the accused had been found under a bed at the scene of the burglary.

Opinion and Extraneous Material

One way to destroy immunity for a news story is to add opinion or material extraneous to the proceeding. It is necessary for reporters to stick to the facts of what comes to light under officials' surveillance. Radio station KYW in Philadelphia broadcast a "documentary" on car-towing rackets, and Austin Purcell sued for defamation. The broadcast had used a judicial proceeding as a basis—a magistrate's hearing at which Purcell was convicted of violating the car-tow ordinance. (Purcell later was exonerated, on appeal.) But the producer of the documentary wove into his script some material he had gathered from other sources—the voices of a man and a woman telling how they had been cheated, a conversation with detectives, and something from the district attorney. Anonymous voices on the tape called Purcell a "thug" and a "racketeer." The producer added comment of his own to the effect that "the sentencing of a few racketeers is not enough." Said the court:

That was defamation, the court said, and it was not protected by qualified privilege. The documentary lost the protection because it contained "exaggerated additions".[58]

"Old–Style Malice"

New York Times Co. v. Sullivan gave the term "malice" a restricted meaning and one increased in rigor and precision, where public officials and figures are concerned. This malice means that the publisher knew his words were false, or had reckless disregard for whether they were false or not. Malice before that decision was defined in many ways—as ill will toward another, hatred, intent to harm, bad motive, lack of good faith, reckless disregard for the rights of others, for example. People who claimed that news stories of government proceedings libeled them, often charged "malice" in the stories, in terms such as these. Such definitions are still alive for libel that does not

[57] 5 Misc.2d 184, 159 N.Y.S.2d 537 (1957).

[58] Purcell v. Westinghouse Broadcasting Co., 411 Pa. 167, 191 A.2d 662, 666 (1963). Ibid., 668. See also Jones v. Pulitzer Pub. Co., 240 Mo. 200, 144 S.W. 441 (1912); Robinson v. Johnson, 152 C.C.A. 505, 239 Fed. 671 (1917); Embers Supper Club, Inc. v. Scripps-Howard Broadcasting Co., 9 Ohio St.3d 22, 457 N.E.2d 1164 (1984), 10 Med.L.Rptr. 1729.

proceed under the constitutional protection. One case shows a court's feeling its way in dealing with the question.

An influential discussion of malice comes from the Restatement (Second) of Torts for 1977, which says that malice requires "wrongful motivation," not mere spite, hatred or ill will. And further, a showing that a defendant simply disliked a plaintiff would not be enough. As attorney and libel expert Robert Sack has written,[59]

> [I]t is not enough in most jurisdictions for a plaintiff to demonstrate that a defendant disliked the plaintiff, or that such animosity was *part* of the motive for the defamatory motive. It must be demonstrated that the improper motive was predominant.

Robert Sack also noted that courts have not done a careful job of distinguishing between (old style) malice—wrongful motivation—and "actual malice" as the term is used in constitutional cases.[60]

Consider a case in which the St. Paul Dispatch was accused of a malicious report based on a complaint filed in district court. The newspaper's story said that William and Frank Hurley had been accused of depleting almost all of the estate of an aged woman before her death. Some $200,000 was involved. The Hurleys sued for libel, saying that the report was malicious and therefore not privileged.

The court did not agree, and in effect said the paper had showed neither "old style malice" (an inaccurate report " 'made solely for the purpose of causing harm to the person defamed' " nor the harder to prove "actual malice" under the New York Times rule. The court ruled the Hurleys could not win their suit because they could produce no evidence of malice at the trial.[61]

Other courts have used old definitions of malice, where qualified privilege is pleaded, alongside knowing or reckless falsehood. Thus one says there is no malice in that which "the publisher reasonably believed to be true"; another speaks of malice as "intent to injure," and another of malice as "ill will." [62]

---

[59] Robert Sack, Libel, Slander and Related Problems (New York: Practising Law Institute, 1980), p. 330, discussing Restatement (Second) of Torts § 603, Comment a (1977).

[60] Ibid., p. 331.

[61] Hurley v. Northwest Publications, Inc., 273 F.Supp. 967, 972, 974 (D.Minn. 1967).

[62] Bannach v. Field Enterprises, Inc., 5 Ill.App.3d 692, 284 N.E.2d 31, 32 (1972); and Brunn v. Weiss, 32 Mich.App. 428, 188 N.W.2d 904, 905 (1971). See, also, Orrison v. Vance, 262 Md. 285, 277 A.2d 573, 578 (1971), 3 Med.L.Rptr. 1170.

Official Proceedings

Reports of official activity outside the proceeding—the trial, the hearing, the legislative debate or committee—may not be protected. Some official activity has the color of official proceeding but not the reality.

To start with the courts: Any trial including that of a lesser court "not of record" such as a police magistrate's furnishes the basis for privilege.[63] The ex parte proceeding in which only one party to a legal controversy is represented affords privilege to reporting.[64] So does the grand jury report published in open court.[65]

In many states, the attorneys' "pleadings" filed with the clerk of court as the basic documents starting a lawsuit are *not* proceedings that furnish protection. In those states the judge must be involved; an early decision stated the rule that for the immunity to attach, the pleadings must have been submitted "to the judicial mind with a view to judicial action," [66] even if only in pretrial hearings on motions.

A 1927 New York decision, as so often in defamation, led the way for several states' rejecting this position and granting protection to reports of pleadings. Newspapers had carried a story based on a complaint filed by Mrs. Elizabeth Nichols against Mrs. Anne Campbell, claiming the latter had defrauded her of $16,000. After the news stories had appeared, Mrs. Nichols withdrew her suit. Mrs. Campbell filed libel suit. Acknowledging that nearly all courts had refused qualified privilege to stories based on pleadings not seen by a judge, the New York Court of Appeals said it would no longer follow this rule. It acknowledged that it is easy for a malicious person to file pleadings in order to air his spleen against another in news stories, and then withdraw the suit. But it said that this can happen also after judges are in the proceeding; suits have been dropped before verdicts have been reached. It added that newspapers had so long and often printed stories about actions started before they reached a judge, that "the public has learned that accusation is not proof and that such actions are at times brought in malice to result in failure." [67] The newspapers won.

[63] McBee v. Fulton, 47 Md. 403 (1878); Flues v. New Nonpareil Co., 155 Iowa 290, 135 N.W. 1083 (1912); See also Sack, *loc. cit.*

[64] Metcalf v. Times Pub. Co., 20 R.I. 674, 40 A. 864 (1898).

[65] Sweet v. Post Pub. Co., 215 Mass. 450, 102 N.E. 660 (1913).

[66] Barber v. St. Louis Post Dispatch Co., 3 Mo.App. 377 (1877); Finnegan v. Eagle Printing Co., 173 Wis. 5, 179 N.W. 788 (1920).

[67] Campbell v. New York Evening Post, 245 N.Y. 320, 327, 157 N.E. 153, 155 (1927).

That set up what is sometimes called the "Campbell Rule," which says that pleadings may be reported on, fairly and accurately, as soon as they are filed with a court and before a judge has acted upon them. Perhaps 20 states follow this rule today. That is, the filing of a pleading is a reportable public and official act appears to be a public and official act in the course of judicial proceedings in the District of Columbia and in the following states: Alabama, California, Georgia, Kentucky, Nevada, New York, Ohio, Pennsylvania, South Carolina, Tennessee, Texas, Washington and Wyoming.

The Campbell Rule, increasingly, seems to be "the modern rule," with more and more courts' language tending toward making the contents of pleadings starting a lawsuit a public record to be reported upon.[68] That is fortunate for reporters, editors and broadcast news directors, many who long have assumed that once a pleading is filed with a court clerk, it is fair game.

But other states have not chosen to follow this rule. Massachusetts specifically rejected it in 1945. *The Boston Herald-Traveler* had published a story based on pleadings filed in an alienation of affections case, had been sued for libel, and had lost. The state Supreme Court said: [69]

> * * * the publication of accusations made by one party against another is neither a legal nor a moral duty of newspapers. Enterprise in that matter ought to be at the risk of paying damages if the accusations prove false. To be safe, a newspaper has only to send its reporters to listen to hearings rather than to search the files of cases not yet brought before the court.

Even in those jurisdictions where "pleadings" are privileged, careful adherence to basic rules of reporting is a must. That is, it should be made clear where the information is from: Attribution to the privileged document is good self-protection. The best rule, of course, is to play fair. Ethical reporters and editors will want to make sure that stories explicitly say that a pleading beginning a lawsuit tells only the plaintiff's side of the story. Reporters may wish to go further, phoning lawsuit defendants or the defendants attorneys to give them an opportunity to comment. (It is likely that defendants may be unwilling to comment in the face of pending litigation, but it never hurts to ask and it will indicate reportorial fairness.)

[68] Henry R. Kaufman, ed., Libel Defense Resource Center (LDRC) 50–State Survey, 1991 (New York: LDRC, 1991).

[69] Sanford v. Boston Herald-Traveler Corp., 318 Mass. 156, 61 N.E.2d 5 (1945): But see Sibley v. Holyoke Transcript-Telegram Pub. Co., Inc., 391 Mass. 468, 461 N.E.2d 823 (1984), 8 Med.L.Rptr. 2497.

Stories based on the following situations were outside "official proceedings" of courts and did not furnish news media the protection of qualified privilege: A newsman's interview of ("conversation with") a United States commissioner, concerning an earlier arraignment before the commissioner;[70] the words of a judge[71] and of an attorney[72] in courtrooms, just before trials were convened formally, and the taking by a judge of a deposition in his courtroom, where he was acting in a "ministerial capacity" only, not as a judge.[73] In Bufalino v. Associated Press,[74] the wire service did not actually demonstrate that it relied on FBI records, nor did it identify "officials" upon whom it relied, and did not, thus, show that it was within the scope of privilege. In a Louisiana case,[75] a reporter was outside the privilege by relying on another newspaper's story even though the latter was based on a sheriff's press release.

Executive Officers and Privilege

Shift now to news stories about the executive and administrative sphere of government. When government officials hold a hearing or issue a report or even a press release, absolute privilege usually protects them. And where absolute privilege leads, qualified privilege for press reports ordinarily follows. Yet while major and minor federal officials enjoy the privilege under federal decisions, state courts have not been unanimous in granting it.[76]

The formalized hearings of many administrative bodies have a quasi-judicial character, in which testimony is taken, interrogation is performed, deliberation is engaged in, and findings are reported in writing. The reporter can have confidence in such proceedings as "safe" to report. The minutes of a meeting and audits of a city water commission were the basis for a successful plea of privilege by a newspaper whose story reflected on an engineer.[77] The Federal Trade Commission investigated a firm and an account based on the investigation said that the firm had engaged in false branding and labeling; the account was privileged.[78] A news story reporting that an attorney had charged another with perjury

[70] Wood v. Constitution Pub. Co., 57 Ga.App. 123, 194 S.E. 760 (1937).

[71] Douglas v. Collins, 243 App.Div. 546, 276 N.Y.S. 87 (1934).

[72] Rogers v. Courier Post Co., 2 N.J. 393, 66 A.2d 869 (1949).

[73] Mannix v. Portland Telegram, 144 Or. 172, 23 P.2d 138 (1933).

[74] 692 F.2d 266 (2d Cir.1982), 8 Med.L.Rptr. 2384.

[75] Melon v. Capital City Press, 407 So.2d 85 (La.App.1981), 8 Med.L.Rptr. 1165.

[76] Barr v. Matteo, 360 U.S. 564, 79 S.Ct. 1335 (1959); Prosser, pp. 802–803; Kaufman, LDRC 50-State Survey.

[77] Holway v. World Pub. Co., 171 Okl. 306, 44 P.2d 881 (1935).

[78] Mack, Miller Candle Co. v. Macmillan Co., 239 App.Div. 738, 269 N.Y.S. 33 (1934).

was taken from a governor's extradition hearing, a quasi-judicial proceeding, and was privileged.[79]

Also, investigations carried out by executive-administrative officers or bodies without the dignity of hearing-chambers and the gavel that calls a hearing to order ordinarily furnish privilege. For example, a state tax commissioner audited a city's books and reported irregularities in the city council's handling of funds. A story based on the report caused a suit for libel, and the court held that the story was protected by privilege.[80]

Yet not every investigation provides a basis for the defense of qualified privilege; reporters and city editors especially need to know what the judicial precedent of their state is. In a Texas case, a district attorney investigated a plot to rob a bank, and obtained confessions. He made them available to the press. A libel suit brought on the basis of the resulting news story was won; the confessions were held insufficient executive proceedings to provide the protection.[81]

"Proceedings" that need especially careful attention by the reporter alert to libel possibilities are the activities of police. Police blotters, the record of arrests and charges made, are the source for many news stories. Their status as a basis for a plea of privilege varies from state to state.[82] The *Washington Star* based a story on an item from a police "hot line," a device for serving news media. The story erroneously reported that a man shot his wife during a quarrel and the man sued for libel. (The jury granted him $1.00 in damages.) So far as qualified privilege for a news story based on the police "hot line" was concerned, the court denied it. A police log of "hot line" reports, the court held, is only an informal arrangement between police and media and is not an official record to which privilege attaches.[83]

Oral reports of preliminary investigations by policemen do not support a plea of privilege in some states. The *Rutland Herald* published a story about two brothers arrested on charges of robbery, and included this paragraph:

> Arthur was arrested on information given to police by the younger brother, it is said. According to authorities, Floyd in his alleged confession stated that Arthur waited

[79] Brown v. Globe Printing Co., 213 Mo. 611, 112 S.W. 462 (1908).

[80] Swearingen v. Parkersburg Sentinel Co., 125 W.Va. 731, 26 S.E.2d 209 (1943).

[81] Caller Times Pub.Co. v. Chandler, 134 Tex. 1, 130 S.W.2d 853 (1939). But see Woolbright v. Sun Communications, Inc., 480 S.W.2d 864 (Mo.1972).

[82] Sherwood v. Evening News Ass'n, 256 Mich. 318, 239 N.W. 305 (1931); M.J. Petrick, "The Press, the Police Blotter and Public Policy," 46 Journalism Quarterly 475, 1969.

[83] Phillips v. Evening Star Newspaper Co., 424 A.2d 78 (D.C.App.1980), 6 Med.L. Rptr. 2191.

outside the window in the rear of the clothing store while Floyd climbed through a broken window the second time to destroy possible clues left behind.

A suit for libel was brought, and the court denied qualified privilege to the story. It reviewed other states' decisions on whether statements attributed to police were a basis for privilege in news, and held that "a preliminary police investigation" is not a proper basis.[84]

The State of New Jersey has provided by statute that "official statements issued by police department heads" protect news stories, and Georgia has a similar law.[85] In other states, courts have provided the protection through decisions in libel suits. In Kilgore v. Koen,[86] privilege was granted to a story in which deputy sheriffs' statements about the evidence and arrest in a case involving a school principal were the newspaper's source.

Legislative Branch Reporting

As for the legislative branch, the third general sphere of government, state statutes have long declared that the immunity holds in stories of the legislative setting. A New York law led the way in this declaration even before the privilege was recognized in England.[87] For debates on the floor of Congress or of a state legislature, there has been no question that protection would apply to news stories. A few early cases indicated that stories of petty legislative bodies such as a town council[88] would not be privileged; but today's reporter need have little fear on this count.

In news stories about a New Jersey municipal council meeting, the city manager was quoted as saying that he was planning to bypass two policemen from promotion because they were insubordinate and "I should have fired them." There was some question as to whether the meeting was the regular one, or a session held in a conference room later. The New Jersey Supreme Court said that that didn't matter. It was not only an official but also a public meeting, at which motions were made by councilmen, sharp discussion was held, and the city manager was queried by councilmen. Privilege held for the newspaper.[89]

---

[84] Lancour v. Herald & Globe Ass'n, 111 Vt. 371, 17 A.2d 253 (1941); Burrows v. Pulitzer Pub. Co., 255 S.W. 925 (1923); Pittsburgh Courier Pub. Co. v. Lubore, 91 U.S.App.D.C. 311, 200 F.2d 355 (1952).

[85] Henry R. Kaufman, LDRC 50–State Survey 1990–91, pp. 249 and 263, citing O.G.C.A. § 51–5–7 and N.J.S.A. 2A:43–1.

[86] 133 Or. 1, 288 P. 192 (1930).

[87] New York Laws, 1854, Chap. 130; Wason v. Walter, L.R. 4 Q.B. 73 (1868).

[88] Buckstaff v. Hicks, 94 Wis. 34, 68 N.W. 403 (1896).

[89] Swede v. Passaic Daily News, 30 N.J. 320, 153 A.2d 36 (1959).

One question about reporting legislatures was settled in a series of "chain" libel suits in the 1920s against several major newspapers. The "qualified privilege" immunity holds for news reports of committees of legislative bodies.[90] (Chain libel suits exist where one plaintiff sues a publisher in several states or jurisdictions on the basis of one allegedly defamatory report.)

Legislative committees have a long history of operating under loose procedural rules.[91] Irregular procedures raise the question whether committee activity always meets the requirements of a "legislative proceeding" which is the basis for immunity in news reports.[92] In reporting committee activity, the reporter may sense danger signals if the committee:

Holds hearings without a quorum;

Publishes material that its clerks have collected, without itself first investigating charges in the material;

Has not authorized the work of its subcommittees;

Has a chairman given to issuing "reports" or holding press conferences on matters that the committee itself has not investigated.

When state and congressional investigating committees relentlessly hunted "subversion" in the 1940s and 1950s, thousands of persons were tainted with the charge of "communist" during the committee proceedings. High procedural irregularity was common. Yet only one libel case growing out of these irregular proceedings reached the highest court of a state, and the newspaper successfully defended with a plea of privilege.[93]

Again, there is much variation concerning privilege from jurisdiction to jurisdiction. It may be generalized that accurate and fair accounts of meetings which are both open to the public and deal with matters of public concern are privileged.[94] Matters get trickier when there is a newsworthy story which becomes available through confidential or secret reports dealing with charges of official misconduct.

[90] Cresson v. Louisville Courier-Journal, 299 Fed. 487 (6th Cir.1924).

[91] Walter Gellhorn (ed.), The States and Subversion (Ithaca: Cornell Univ.Press, 1952); Ernst J. Eberling, Congressional Investigations (New York: Columbia Univ. Press, 1928); more recently, lax legislative evidence rules have resulted in dropping prosecutions against "Iran-contra" scandal defendants. (Because of such loose procedures, it was determined those defendants who testified before Congress on TV later could not get a fair trial.) See, e.g., David Johnston, "Judge in Iran-Contra Trial Drops Case Against North After Prosecutor Gives Up," The New York Times, Sept. 17, 1991, p. A1.

[92] H.L. Nelson, Libel in News of Congressional Investigating Committees (Minneapolis: Univ. of Minn.Press, 1961), Chs. 1, 2.

[93] Coleman v. Newark Morning Ledger Co., 29 N.J. 357, 149 A.2d 193 (1959).

[94] Sack, in Goodale, ed., Communications Law 1991, Vol. I, p. 62.

The American Broadcasting Co. was sued after it telecast correspondent Bettina Gregory's five part series of news reports about scandals in the General Services administration (GSA). From a confidential source, ABC received—and used as source material—some leaked GSA internal reports. Those reports led to broadcasting assertions that Excelon Security Co., which had been under GSA contract to provide security services, had provided guards who did not have security clearances.

The ABC broadcast added that unnamed top federal, county, and city officials said "the President of Excelon is alleged to have connection with organized crime."

Excelon president Salvatore J. Ingenere sued, arguing that the documents were erroneous and were not privileged because the GSA documents were internal memos not intended for publication. Ingenere lost his suit when the U.S. district court ruled that ". . . the Massachusetts common law fair use report privilege extends to the fair and accurate reporting of confidential government reports that reveal possible government misconduct." [95]

Public Proceedings

The Restatement (Second) of Torts, that oft-quoted and influential summary of how law *ought* to be, says: [96]

> The publication of defamatory matter * * * in a report of an official action or proceeding or of a meeting open to the public that deals with a matter of public concern is privileged if the report is accurate and complete and a fair abridgement of the occurrence is reported.

Way back in 1854, the New York legislature enacted a statute saying something quite similar to the passage from the Restatement, dealing with a "fair and true report * * * of any judicial, legislative or public official proceeding." [97] Some 102 years later, in 1956, the New York legislature removed the word "public" from that statute. The change was made after editorial campaigning by New York City newspapers. The deletion of the word "public" made it possible to have immunity in publishing news of an official proceeding even though the proceeding was not public.[98]

[95] Ingenere v. ABC (D.Mass.1984), 11 Med.L.Rptr. 1227.

[96] Restatement (Second) of Torts, S 611 (1977).

[97] New York Laws, 1854, Chap. 130; Danziger v. Hearst Corp., 304 N.Y. 244, 107 N.E.2d 62 (1952).

[98] Editor & Publisher, May 5, 1956, p. 52; See New York State Legislative Annual, 1956, pp. 494–495. Shiles v. News Syndicate Co., 27 N.Y.2d 9, 313 N.Y.S.2d 104, 107, 261 N.E.2d 251 (1970).

McCurdy v. Hughes, 63 N.D. 435, 248 N.W. 512 (1933).

In some cases, efforts to use the fair report privilege as a defense to libel suits growing out of coverage of secret government proceedings do no succeed. Despite the elimination of the word "public" from from the New York statute, the state Court of Appeals ruled in 1970 that news stories of matrimonial proceedings—secret under New York law—are protected by qualified privilege.

That New York situation carries a message to all mass communicators: *Know the law of the state in which you work.* Outside of New York, journalists sometimes have lost immunity when they reported libelous stories after gaining access to secret governmental or quasi-governmental proceedings. In an old case, McCurdy v. Hughes, a newspaper reported on a secret meeting of a disciplinary board of a state bar association in which a complaint against an attorney was considered. The attorney brought a libel suit for derogatory statements in the story and won.[99]

Reporting gets tricky for the news media in those times where a meeting or record is not both *public* and *official*. Obviously, some government records do not have public status. If news media publish such non-public or secret materials containing defamatory information, the public interest in those materials needs to be compelling to afford the media protection from liability.

Take, for example, Time magazine's 1978 publication of an article about suspected criminal activities of a Congressman from Pennsylvania named Daniel J. Flood. The Medico v. Time, Inc. defamation suit resulted, beginning when the magazine—in an article tying the Congressman to the Mafia—published these words: "The suspected link, the Wilkes-Barre firm of Philip Medico and his brothers. The FBI discovered more than a decade ago that [Congressman Daniel] Flood steered Government business to the Medicos and often traveled in their company jet." Time's article was based on secret FBI files.[1]

In addition, the magazine story called Medico a member of an organized crime "family" and referred to him as a Mafia "capo" or chief. Time magazine, however, argued that the gist of its article was that the Federal Bureau of Investigation had recorded "Pennsylvania Rackets Boss" Russell Bufalino's description of Philip Medico.

The trial court refused to find that Time's article could be defended as true, but ultimately held that the article was protect-

---

[99] McCurdy v. Hughes, 63 N.D. 435, 248 N.W. 512 (1933).

[1] Medico v. Time, Inc., 643 F.2d 134, 141 (3d Cir.1981), 6 Med.L.Rptr. 2529, 2535, cert. denied 454 U.S. 836, 102 S.Ct. 139 (1981).

ed under Pennsylvania's common law privilege to report official proceedings. The court recognized that Time had summarized secret FBI reports which had been given the magazine without authorization. But because Time's article was a fair and accurate report of the FBI documents, the trial judge ruled that publication was privileged. Recognizing the great public concern over allegations of wrongdoing by a member of Congress, it was held that secret FBI documents concerning Philip Medico were " 'a report of an official proceeding or meeting.' " [2]

Upholding the trial court, a U.S. Court of Appeals found that important "policies underlie the fair report privilege." First is an "agency theory," where one who reports on a public, official proceeding represents people who could not attend. But, said the appeals court, the agency rationale would not work for proceedings or reports not open to the public.[3] A second policy—and the one the appeals court embraced—is a "theory of public supervision: [4] "

> As public inspection of courtroom proceedings may further the just administration of the laws, public scrutiny of the records of criminal investigatory agencies may often have the equally salutary effect of fostering among those who enforce the laws "the sense of public responsibility." For example, exposing the content of agency records may, in some cases, help ensure impartial enforcement of the laws.

A final note about the word "public" in connection with qualified privilege: The immunity to lawsuit for reporting is clearest when the meeting or record is both *public* and *official*. Perhaps there is an emerging standard suggesting that even if a meeting or record is not both public and official, it is important for the community to know what is happening where matters of public welfare and concern are involved.[5] As for private gatherings of stockholders, directors, or members of an association or organization, they are no basis for privilege in news reports.

[2] Ibid., pp. 137–139.

[3] Ibid., p. 139.

[4] Ibid., p. 140, quoting Judge (later Mr. Justice) Oliver Wendell Holmes from Cowley v. Pulsifer, 137 Mass. 392, 384 (1884) on the desirability for those who administer justice to "always act under the sense of public responsibility;" further, all citizens should be able to see for themselves how public duties are performed.

[5] See Sack and Karle, op. cit., p. 61, citing Kilgore v. Younger, 30 Cal.3d 770, 796, 180 Cal.Rtpr. 657, 673, 640 P.2d 793, 797 (S.Ct.Cal.1982), and Crane v. Arizona Republic, 729 F.Supp. 698 (D.C.Cal.1989); see also Phoenix Newspapers, Inc. v. Choisser, 82 Ariz. 271, 312 P.2d 150 (1957); Pulvermann v. A.S. Abell Co., 228 F.2d 797 (4th Cir.1956).

SEC. 34. TRUTH AS A DEFENSE

Most state laws provide that truth is a complete defense in libel cases, but some require that the publisher show "good motives and justifiable ends." The United States Supreme Court has not ruled on whether truth may ever be subjected to civil or criminal liability.

The defense of truth (often called "justification") in civil libel has ancient roots developed in the common law of England. It was taken up by American courts as they employed the common law in the colonial and early national periods, and was transferred from the common law to many state statutes. Its basis appeals to common sense and ordinary ideas of justice: Why, indeed, should an individual be awarded damages for harm to his reputation when the truth of the matter is that his record does not merit a good reputation? To print or broadcast the truth about persons is no more than they should expect. In addition the social good may be served by bringing to light the truth about people whose work involves them in the public interest.

It is held by some courts that truth alone is a complete defense, regardless of the motives behind its publication, and this squares with the libel statutes in most states. Some state laws continue to qualify, and provide that truth is a defense if it is published "with good motives and justifiable ends." [6] The qualifying term goes back to 1804, when Alexander Hamilton used it in his defense of newspaperman Harry Croswell in a celebrated New York criminal libel case.[7] So far as the comatose *criminal* libel offense is concerned, however, the United States Supreme Court has ruled that the Hamiltonian qualification is unconstitutional, and may not be required of a defendant.[8]

The Supreme Court has shied away from ruling that truth is always a defense in libel. Justice White wrote in Cox Broadcasting Co. v. Cohn that the Court had not decided the question "whether truthful publications may ever be subjected to civil or criminal liability." Earlier cases, he said, had "carefully left open the question" whether the First Amendment requires "that truth be recognized as a defense in a defamation action brought by a private person * * *." [9]

[6] State statutes and constitutional provisions are collected in Angoff, op cit. See also Note, 56 N.W.Univ.L.Rev. 547 (1961); Garrison v. Louisiana, 379 U.S. 64, 85 S.Ct. 209 (1964), footnote 7.

[7] 3 Johns.Cas. 337 (N.Y.1818).

[8] Garrison v. Louisiana, 379 U.S. 64, 85 S.Ct. 209 (1964).

[9] 420 U.S. 469, 490, 95 S.Ct. 1029, 1043–1044 (1975). But see Restatement, Second, Torts, § 581A, p. 235, which says "There can be no recovery in defamation for a statement of fact that is true * * *."

The Burden of Proving Truth

Since the Supreme Court rules of *Sullivan* and *Gertz* have made it plain that some level of fault on the part of the media must be shown—from knowing falsity to negligence—the burden of pleading and showing falsity has largely been on the plaintiff where he is a public person. Yet the *Restatement of Torts (Second)* takes the position that it cannot yet be said that the burden is inescapably on the plaintiff: [10]

> Placing the burden on the party asserting the negative necessarily creates difficulties, and the problem is accentuated when the defamatory charge is not specific in its terms but quite general in nature. Suppose, for example, that a newspaper published a charge that a storekeeper short-changes his customers when he gets a chance. How is he expected to prove that he has not short-changed customers when no specific occasions are pointed to by the defendant?

Some courts have said that the burden of proof rests on the plaintiff to show defamation and to prove damages. It is clear that defendants in libel suits frequently have been at pains to prove that an alleged libel is true.[11] In 1986, however, in Philadelphia Newspapers v. Hepps, the U.S. Supreme Court held 5–4 that it is unconstitutional to put the burden of proving truth on a media defendant where the story involved deals with a matter of public concern.

The *Hepps* case was a close call, a 5–4 decision, but it nevertheless tilted the scales in favor of the media for expression "of a public concern." Justice Sandra Day O'Connor wrote for the majority that the old " * * * common-law presumption that defamatory speech is false cannot stand when a plaintiff seeks damages against a media defendant for speech of public concern." [12]

The news media, in other words, should not be punished for statements that *may* be true. This decision invalidated similar rules in eight other states, including New Jersey. Before the Hepps decision, a dozen or more other states—including New York

[10] Ibid., § 613, p. 310. And see Robert Sack, Libel, Slander, and Related Problems, 135–136.

[11] See Memphis Pub. Co. v. Nichols, 569 S.W.2d 412 (Tenn.1978), 4 Med.L.Rptr. 1573.

[12] Philadelphia Newspapers, Inc. v. Hepps, 475 U.S. 767, 106 S.Ct. 1558, 1561 (1986), 12 Med.L.Rptr. 1977, 1981.

and Connecticut—had already shifted the burden of proof concerning falsity to the plaintiffs.[13]

Not every detail of an allegedly libelous story must be proved accurate in order to rebut a charge of "falsity," but rather, that the story is "substantially" true.[14] But no formula can measure just what inaccuracy will be tolerated by a particular court.

The *New York World-Telegram and Sun* tried to establish truth of the following statement from its pages, but failed:

> John Crane, former president of the UFA now under indictment, isn't waiting for his own legal developments. Meanwhile, his lawyers are launching a $$$$$$ defamation suit.

Focusing on the word "indictment," Crane brought a libel suit against the newspaper and the columnist who wrote the item. He said that the defendant knew or could have learned the falsity of the charge by using reasonable care.

The defendants tried to dodge the libel action, arguing that the facts about John Crane already had been widely punished and commented up by the press of the city. The lame argument that the phrase "under indictment" was used in a figurative, non-legal sense failed, and Crane won his suit against the newspaper. The court held that "under indictment" means a legal action by a grand jury to begin criminal charges, and that the use of the term to mean accusation by private persons is rare.[15] In any case, you cannot prove the truth of one charge against a person by showing he or she was suspected or guilty of another.[16]

The same term—"indictment"—was used by another newspaper in an incorrect way, but was held *not* to be libelous. The word appeared in connection with conflict-of-interest findings discussed in an editorial. A councilman was never truly indicted, but rather was charged by delivery of a summons, and convicted. The court held that "indictment" was substantially accurate, and although technically incorrect, did not constitute defamation.[17]

Thus loose usage of certain technical terms does not always destroy a plea of truth. This is what a court ruled when a

[13] Stuart Taylor, Jr., Supreme Court Adds Protection for News Media in Libel Actions, The New York Times, April 22, 1986.

[14] Hein v. Lacy, 228 Kan. 249, 616 P.2d 277 (1980), 6 Med.L.Rptr. 1662, 1666; Prosser, 825.

[15] Crane v. New York World Telegram Corp., 308 N.Y. 470, 126 N.E.2d 753 (1955); Friday v. Official Detective Stories, Inc., 233 F.Supp. 1021 (E.D.Pa.1964).

[16] Sun Printing and Pub. Ass'n v. Schenck, 40 C.C.A. 163, 98 Fed. 925 (1900); Kilian v. Doubleday & Co., 367 Pa. 117, 79 A.2d 657 (1951); Yarmove v. Retail Credit Co., 18 A.D.2d 790, 236 N.Y.S.2d 836 (1963).

[17] Schaefer v. Hearst Corp. (Md.Super.1979), 5 Med.L.Rptr. 1734.

Massachusetts newspaper said that a man named Joyce had been "committed" to a mental hospital when actually he had been "admitted" to the hospital at the request of a physician as the state law provided. The newspaper's words that caused the man to bring a libel suit were that the man "charges * * * that his constitutional rights were violated when he was committed to the hospital last November." In ruling for the newspaper which pleaded truth, the court said: [18]

> Strictly * * * "commitment" means a placing in the hospital by judicial order * * *. But the words [of the news story] are to be used in their "natural sense with the meaning which they could convey to mankind in general." This meaning of the word "commitment" was placing in the hospital pursuant to proceedings provided by law. In so stating as to the plaintiff * * * the defendant reported correctly.

Of course, the newsman who is highly attuned to nuances in word meanings may save his newspaper the expense and trouble of even a successful libel defense by avoiding gaffes such as confusing "commit" with "admit." While news media continue to be staffed in part by writers insensitive to shades of meaning, however, they may take some comfort in the law's willingness to bend.

Courts frequently hold that truth will not be destroyed by a story's minor inaccuracies. Thus truth succeeded although a newspaper had printed that the plaintiff was in police custody on August 16, whereas he had been released on August 15; [19] and it was not fatal to truth to report in a news story that an arrest, which in fact took place at the Shelly Tap tavern, occurred at the Men's Social Club.[20]

In accord with the maxim that "tale bearers are as bad as tale tellers," it is no defense for a news medium to argue that it reported accurately and truthfully someone else's false and defamatory statements. The broadcaster or newspaper reporter writes at the employer's peril and at his or her own peril, too. The words "it is reported by police" or "according to a reliable source" do not remove from the news medium faced with a libel suit the job of proving that the allegation or rumor itself is true.[21] Liability under the "republication" rule persists.[22]

[18] Joyce v. George W. Prescott Pub. Co., 348 Mass. 790, 205 N.E.2d 207 (1965).

[19] Piracci v. Hearst Corp., 263 F.Supp. 511 (D.Md.1966), affirmed 371 F.2d 1016 (4th Cir.1967).

[20] Mitchell v. Peoria Journal-Star, Inc., 76 Ill.App.2d 154, 221 N.E.2d 516 (1966).

[21] Miller, Smith & Champagne v. Capital City Press, 142 So.2d 462 (La.App.1962); Dun & Bradstreet, Inc. v. Robinson, 233 Ark. 168, 345 S.W.2d 34 (1961).

[22] Cianci v. New Times Pub. Co., 639 F.2d 54 (2d Cir.1980), 6 Med.L.Rptr. 1625, 1629–1630.

Even though every fact in a story is truthful, an error of omission can result in libel. Recall, now, from page 202, the *Memphis Press-Scimitar's* accurate facts about the shooting of Mrs. Nichols. A woman had gone to the home of Mrs. Nichols, and there, the newspaper said on the basis of a police arrest report, found her own husband (Newton) with Mrs. Nichols. The implication of an adulterous affair between the two was plain in the story, all of whose facts were accurate. Mrs. Nichols brought libel suits. The Press-Scimitar had omitted much from the story, as shown by a separate police document (the "offense report"): Not only were Mrs. Nichols and Mr. Newton at the home, but also Mr. Nichols and two other people. Had these facts been in the news story, there would have been no suggestion of an affair. The Press-Scimitar pleaded truth of its words, but the Tennessee Supreme Court said: [23]

> In our opinion, the defendant's reliance on the truth of the facts stated in the article in question is misplaced. The proper question is whether the *meaning* reasonably conveyed by the published words is defamatory * * *. The publication of the complete facts could not conceivably have led the reader to conclude that Mrs. Nichols and Mr. Newton had an adulterous relationship. The published statement, therefore, so distorted the truth as to make the entire article false and defamatory. It is no defense whatever that individual statements within the article were literally true.

Even ill will and an intent to harm will not affect truth where it is said of a public person; knowing or reckless falsehood must be shown.[24] As we have seen, however, against a *private* person's suit, some states provide that truth is a good defense only if made with good motives and for justifiable ends—that ill will (the "malice" of tort law) may defeat the defense.[25] Belief in the truth of the charge may be useful in holding down damages, if it can be established to the satisfaction of the court. Showing honest belief indicates good faith and absence of malice, important to the mitigation of general damages and the denial or lessening of punitive damages to the successful suit-bringer in a libel case.

An article about a public official's criminal conviction failed to state that, upon retrial, the official was acquitted, and the defense of truth was denied the magazine.[26] Also, courts have

---

[23] Memphis Pub. Co. v. Nichols, 569 S.W.2d 412, 420 (Tenn.1978), 4 Med.L.Rptr. 1573, 1579. See also for true facts but false implication, Dunlap v. Philadelphia Newspapers, Inc., 301 Pa.Super. 475, 448 A.2d 6 (1982), 8 Med.L.Rptr. 1974.

[24] Schaefer v. Lynch, 406 So.2d 185 (La.1981), 7 Med.L.Rptr. 2302.

[25] Sack, 130–131.

[26] Torres v. Playboy Enterprises (D.S.Tex.1980), 7 Med.L.Rptr. 1182.

refused to accept the plea of truth where news media would not identify anonymous sources upon whom defamatory stories were based.[27]

SEC. 35. OPINION AND FAIR COMMENT AS DEFENSES

State statutes and the common law provide the doctrine of fair comment and criticism as a defense against libel suits brought by people and institutions who offer their work to the public for its approval or disapproval, or where matters of public interest are concerned. Despite a view that it has become obsolete under recent constitutional protection for opinion, media and courts continue to use it.

Fair Comment Under Common Law and State Statutes

Opinion embraces comment and criticism. The defense of fair comment was shaped to protect the public stake in the scrutinizing of important public matters. Comment and criticism have permeated news and editorial pages and broadcasts, explaining, drawing inferences, reacting, evaluating. The law protects even scathing criticism of the public work of persons and institutions who offer their work for public judgment: public officials and figures; those whose performance affects public taste in such realms as music, art, literature, theater, and sports; and institutions whose activities affect the public interest such as hospitals, schools, processors of food, public utilities, drug manufacturers. Under fair comment legal immunity against a defamation action is given for the honest expression of opinion on public persons and/or matters of public concern.[28]

Even the most public persons have some small sphere of private life. Although one's private character of course can deeply affect one's public acts, there are circumstances in which comment on private acts and personal character is not embraced by the protection of fair comment.[29] The wide sweep of *Sullivan*, it will be remembered, protects only statements about public persons' *public* acts; and courts continue to hold that public persons retain a private sphere.[30]

[27] Dowd v. Calabrese, 577 F.Supp. 238 (D.D.C.1983), 10 Med.L.Rptr. 1208, 1213.

[28] Prosser, 812–816; Harper and James, Law of Torts (Boston, 1956). See also New York Times Co. v. Sullivan, 376 U.S. 254, 271, 84 S.Ct. 710, 721 (1964) quoting Cantwell v. Connecticut, 310 U.S. 296, 310, 60 S.Ct. 900, 906 (1940).

[29] Post Pub. Co. v. Moloney, 50 Ohio St. 71, 89, 33 N.E. 921 (1893); Harper and James, 461.

[30] Zeck v. Spiro, 52 Misc.2d 629, 276 N.Y.S.2d 395 (1966); Stearn v. MacLean-Hunter Ltd., 46 F.R.D. 76 (S.D.N.Y.1969); Standke v. B.E. Darby & Sons, Inc., 291

"*FACTS.*" States have varied in their fair comment rules. Most have said that the protection for comment does not extend to that which is falsely given out as "fact". This presents at the outset the often difficult problem of separating facts—which are susceptible of proof—and opinion—which cannot be proved true or false. Prof. Robert Sack writes that nothing in the law of defamation "is any more elusive than distinguishing between the two." [31] But beyond the problem of making that often cloudy distinction is the diversity of rules from state to state. The majority have insisted on the rule of "no protection for misstatement of fact." Oregon's Supreme Court, for example, held "it is one thing to comment upon or criticize * * * the acknowledged or proved act of a public man, and quite another to assert that he has been guilty of particular acts of misconduct." [32] Under this interpretation, "charges of specific criminal misconduct are not protected as 'opinions'." [33]

But a minority of states provide protection for false statement of fact, the variation being illustrated by Snively v. Record Pub. Co.,[34] a California decision. The Los Angeles police chief brought a libel action against the *Los Angeles Record* for a cartoon which, he said, suggested he was receiving money secretly for illegal purposes. The California Supreme Court held that even if the charge of criminality were false, the cartoon was protected by fair comment:

Political cartoons, indeed, tend to receive additional "running room" from the courts. They may be regarded not as careful statements of fact, but as exaggerated or hyperbolic assertions which by their nature stretch facts to make a point.[35]

Michigan's fair comment statute likewise has been held to protect false statements of fact such as a charge of "fraud" against a real estate developer. The Sixth Circuit Court of Appeals said in Orr v. Argus-Press Co.[36] that the state's statute protected both opinion

Minn. 468, 193 N.E.2d 139, 144 (1971). Note, Fact and Opinion after Gertz v. Robert Welch, Inc., 34 Rutgers L.Rev. 81, 88–89 (Fall 1981).

[31] Sack, 155. See also Gregory v. McDonnell Douglas Corp., 17 Cal.3d 596, 131 Cal.Rptr. 641, 644–645, 552 P.2d 425, 428–429 (1976).

[32] Marr v. Putnam, 196 Or. 1, 246 P.2d 509, 524 (1952); Otero v. Ewing, 162 La. 453, 110 So. 648 (1926).

[33] Cianci v. New Times Pub. Co., 639 F.2d 54, 63 (2d Cir.1980), 6 Med.L.Rptr. 1625, 1635; Restatement (Second) of Torts, # 571.

[34] 185 Cal. 565, 571, 198 P. 1, 3 (1921).

[35] See Keller v. Miami Herald Pub. Co., 778 F.2d 711 (11th Cir.1985), and discussion in Goodale, ed. Communications Law 1991, at p. 120.

[36] 586 F.2d 1108, 1113–1114 (6th Cir.1978), 4 Med.L.Rptr. 1594, 1696–1697; Schultz v. Newsweek, Inc., 668 F.2d 911, 919 (6th Cir.1982), 7 Med.L.Rptr. 2552, 2558. See also Rouch v. Enquirer and News of Battle Creek, 427 Mich. 157, 398 N.W.2d 245 (1986).

and fact about matters of public interest if the statement "be honestly believed to be true, and published in good faith" (i.e., without the "ill-will" malice of the common law).

The protection in states such as the above two—California and Michigan—is broad and deep. It applies to *any story on a matter of public concern or interest.* In such, whether the plaintiff is private or public does not matter. If there is honest belief and no ill-will malice on the part of the news medium, false statements of fact are protected. Could private citizens Hutchinson and Wolston (above, pp. 168–169) have won their suits under such rules? Suing under Gertz v. Robert Welch, Inc.,[37] it will be recalled, both could win by showing "negligence" on the part of the news medium. But negligence does not destroy the protection of fair comment under California and Michigan laws.

In point is the case of private citizen Rollenhagen of Orange, Calif., an auto mechanic about whom CBS aired a television story. After one of his customers had complained to police about his charges for repairs, they arrested him for failure to give a written estimate in advance of auto repairs as required by law, handcuffed him, and led him past a CBS camera crew. CBS interviewed Rollenhagen and police—who said the customer had been victimized—and then ran the story. Rollenhagen sued charging false defamation, and the California Court of Appeal ruled that the story was protected by the state law of fair comment on matters of public interest. It said that while *Gertz* had recently permitted states to let private persons recover where there was negligence in a story of public concern, California had not adopted that rule, but rather had stuck with its half-century-old fair comment law: [38] The subject of auto repair was a matter of general public interest.

A question of "fact" faces the writer under some states' rules of fair comment: the comment must be based on facts—facts stated with the comment, or facts that are known or readily available to the reader. The Fisher Galleries asked art critic Leslie Ahlander of the *Washington Post* to review an exhibition of paintings by artist Irving Amen. Later, Mrs. Ahlander's column carried this comment:

> [The Amen prints and paintings] are so badly hung among many commercial paintings that what quality they might have is completely destroyed. The Fisher Galleries should decide whether they are a fine arts gallery or a

[37] 418 U.S. 323, 94 S.Ct. 2997 (1974).

[38] Rollenhagen v. Orange, 116 Cal.App.3d 414, 172 Cal.Rptr. 49 (1981), 6 Med.L. Rptr. 2561, 2564. See Calif. Civil Code, Sec. 47, sub. 3, granting qualified privilege to all publications concerning a matter of legitimate public interest.

commercial outlet for genuine "hand-painted" pictures. The two do not mix.

Fisher sued for libel, and the *Post* defended on the grounds of fair comment and criticism. Fisher argued that in order for opinion to be protected by the fair comment doctrine, the facts upon which it is based must be stated or referred to so that the reader may draw his own conclusions. The court acknowledged that this is the rule in some jurisdictions.[39] But it instead took that view that the facts do not necessarily have to be stated in the article, but may be facts "known or readily available to the persons to whom the comment or criticism is addressed * * *."[40]

Besides the problem of "fact," the ancient question of what constituted "malice" entered the picture and had much to do with what was "fair." Malice would destroy the protection of fair comment; and malice for centuries before New York Times Co. v. Sullivan had been defined in various ways. Furthermore, various characteristics of "unfair" expression were sometimes treated as suggesting malice. Thus from state to state and jurisdiction to jurisdiction, malice could be pretty much what the court felt it ought to be: ill-will, enmity, spite, hatred, intent to harm; "excessive publication,"[41] vehemence,[42] words that were not the honest opinion of the writer,[43] words which there was no "probable cause to believe true,"[44] words showing reckless disregard for the rights of others, words which a reasonable man would not consider fair.[45] Malice still can be "adduced"[46] from such qualities of expression in some jurisdictions where qualified privilege or fair comment is at issue.

Thus the West Virginia Supreme Court held in denying fair comment's protection against the *Charleston Gazette* which had tongue-lashed several legislators who sued it for saying, among other things, that they had sold their votes:[47]

> While it is very generally held that fair comment as to matter of public affairs is not actionable, * * * it appears to be definitely settled if such comment is unfair

[39] A.S. Abell Co. v. Kirby, 227 Md. 267, 176 A.2d 340 (1961); Cohalan v. New York Tribune, 172 Misc. 20, 15 N.Y.S.2d 58 (1939).

[40] Fisher v. Washington Post Co., 212 A.2d 335, 338 (D.C.App.1965).

[41] Pulliam v. Bond, 406 S.W.2d 635, 643 (Mo.1966).

[42] England v. Daily Gazette Co., 143 W.Va. 700, 104 S.E.2d 306 (1958).

[43] Russell v. Geis, 251 Cal.App.2d 560, 59 Cal.Rptr. 569 (1967).

[44] Taylor v. Lewis, 132 Cal.App. 381, 22 P.2d 569 (1933).

[45] James v. Haymes, 160 Va. 253, 168 S.E. 333 (1933).

[46] Goldwater v. Ginzburg, 414 F.2d 324, 342 (2d Cir.1969).

[47] England v. Daily Gazette Co., 143 W.Va. 700, 104 S.E.2d 306, 316 (1958).

or unreasonably violent or vehement, immunity from liability is denied. "Matters of public interest must be discussed temperately. Wicked and corrupt motive should never be wantonly assigned. And it will be no defense that the writer, at the time he wrote, honestly believed in the truth of the charges he was making, if such charges be made recklessly, unreasonably, and without any foundation in fact * * *. [T]he writer must bring to his task some degree of moderation and judgment." Newell, Slander and Libel * * *.

But in another state—Iowa—there was no suggestion in a Supreme Court decision that "matters of public interest must be discussed temperately." Journalists everywhere know the case of the Cherry sisters, one of the most famous in the annals of libel in America. The *Des Moines Leader* successfully defended itself in their libel suit, using the defense of fair comment. It started when the Leader printed this:

> Billy Hamilton, of the *Odebolt Chronicle* gives the Cherry Sisters the following graphic write-up on their late appearance in his town: "Effie is an old jade of 50 summers, Jessie a frisky-filly of 40, and Addie, the flower of the family, a capering monstrosity of 35. Their long skinny arms, equipped with talons at the extremities, swung mechanically, and anon waved frantically at the suffering audience. The mouths of their rancid features opened like caverns, and sounds like the wailing of damned souls issued therefrom. They pranced around the stage with a motion that suggested a cross between the *danse du ventre* and fox trot,—strange creatures with painted faces and hideous mien. Effie is spavined, Addie is stringhalt, and Jessie, the only one who showed her stockings, has legs and calves as classic in their outlines as the curves of a broom handle."

There was nothing moderate about Billy Hamilton's criticism of these three graces, but the Iowa Supreme Court said that that did not matter. What Hamilton wrote about the three sisters, and the Leader reprinted, was fair comment and criticism: [48]

> One who goes upon the stage to exhibit himself to the public, or who gives any kind of a performance to which the public is invited, may be freely criticized. He may be held up to ridicule, and entire freedom of expression is guaranteed to dramatic critics, provided they are not actuated by malice or evil purpose in what they write. * * * Ridicule is often the strongest weapon in the

[48] Cherry v. Des Moines Leader, 114 Iowa 298, 86 N.W. 323 (1901).

hands of a public writer; and, if fairly used, the presumption of malice which would otherwise arise is rebutted * * *.

Opinion Under the Constitution

Opinion defenses against defamation, although remarkably useful, sometimes promise more than they deliver. True, as noted in Chapter 4 (Sec. 19), the First Amendment has been held to protect exaggerated, extravant give-and-take in labor and political disputes. In such settings, deep feelings give rise to name-calling, to "rhetorical hyperbole" that is not to be construed literally.

Examples of epithets protected in labor or political disputes include:

— "Scabs" and "traitors" as used in a union publication against non-union workers.[49]

— "Blackmail" and "unethical trade" in a land-use dispute.[50]

— "Fellow traveler of the fascists" in a denunciation of a leader of a political fringe group.[51]

Such opinion was protected by courts, defined as immunized by *the context in which it occurred,* in labor or political disputes.[52]

With less than perfect consistency, courts distinguish hyperbole from specific charges of crime and wrongdoing. For example, charging one with a "SS [Nazi] background" and being associated with the Gestapo are not opinion or hyperbole, nor is "outright extortion" spoken of a councilman.[53]

In addition to such protection for rhetorical hyperbole, additional constitutional immunity was deduced by many courts from a dictum—a kind of judicial aside—written by U.S. Supreme Court Justice Lewis Powell in the majority opinion in Gertz v. Robert Welch, Inc.[54]

Under the First Amendment there is no such thing as a false idea. However pernicious an idea may seem, we

[49] Old Dominion Branch No. 496, Nat. Ass'n of Letter Carriers, AFL–CIO v. Austin, 418 U.S. 264, 94 S.Ct. 2770 (1974).

[50] Greenbelt Cooperative Pub. Ass'n v. Bresler, 398 U.S. 6, 90 S.Ct. 1537 (1970).

[51] Cianci v. New Times Pub. Co., 639 F.2d 54, 62 (2d Cir.1980), 6 Med.L.Rptr. 1625, 1631, quoting Buckley v. Littell, 539 F.2d 882 (2d Cir.1976).

[52] Sack, 157–58, 160–61.

[53] Good Government Group of Seal Beach, Inc. v. Superior Court, 22 Cal.2d 672, 150 Cal.Rptr. 258, 586 P.2d 572 (1978).

[54] 418 U.S. 323, 339–340, 94 S.Ct. 2997, 3007 (1974). For cases boldly using *Gertz* to create an "opinion defense," see also Miskovsky v. Oklahoma Publishing Co., 654 P.2d 587 (Okl.1982), cert. denied 459 U.S. 923, 103 S.Ct. 235 (1982), 8 Med.L.Rptr. 2302; see also discussion in Goodale, ed., Communications Law 1991, Vol. I, at pp. 102–103, including In re Yagman, 796 F.2d 1165, 1186 (9th Cir.1986): " ' "an opinion is simply not actionable defamation." ' "

depend for its correction not on the conscience of judges and juries but on the competition of other ideas. But there is no constitutional value in false statements of fact.

Under this statement apparently giving an absolute protection for opinion, the Second Restatement of Torts (1977) said—prematurely, it has turned out—that common-law fair comment had been obliterated. It declared that only where a statement in the form of opinion implies the allegation of undisclosed defamatory facts as the basis is the statement actionable.[55]

Such a statement is "mixed" opinion, and not protected as "pure" opinion is. ("Mixed" opinion refers to an opinion expressed in such a way to appear to be based on facts, and where the opinion is expressed so as to imply there are undisclosed facts justifying the defamatory statement. "Pure" opinion, on the other hand, is based on provable facts which are explicitly stated as support for the opinion. [Restatement (Second) of Torts (1977), S566, Comment b.])

After *Gertz*, many courts enthusiastically supported—and added to—the Supreme Court's statement that "there is no thing as a false idea." Under that slogan, constitutional support flourished, protecting expressions of opinion against defamation lawsuits. For example, the Massachusetts Supreme Judicial Court, using approaches from *Gertz*, from the Restatement of Torts, and from elements of rhetorical hyperbole. In doing so, it illustrated the horrendous difficulty in distinguishing between fact and opinion.

In that case, reporter Cole was fired from WBZ–TV for "reasons of misconduct and insubordination," an official statement from the general manager said. Newspapers reported the firing and the reasons, and added that station spokesman Konowitz elaborated by telephone to them that "unofficially" the firing also was based on "sloppy and irresponsible techniques". Cole sued for libel, seeking damages for those "unofficial words." In upholding the station's position, the court ruled that Konowitz's words could be viewed only as expressions of opinion regarding Cole's reporting abilities. It said: [56]

Whether a reporter is sloppy and irresponsible with bad techniques is a matter of opinion. The meaning of these statements is imprecise and open to speculation. They cannot be characterized as assertions of fact. They cannot be proved false. "An assertion that cannot be proved

[55] Restatement (Second) Torts (1977), S566, Comment b.

[56] Cole v. Westinghouse Broadcasting Co., Inc., 386 Mass. 303, 435 N.E.2d 1021 (1982), 8 Med.L.Rptr. 1828, 1832–1833. See also Marc A. Franklin, "The Plaintiff's Burden in Defamation ＊ ＊ ＊," 25 William and Mary L.Rev. 825, 868 (1983–1984), arguing that "goodness" and "badness" are evaluative statements, "simply not concepts that can be judicially characterized as being either true or false."

false cannot be held libelous." Hotchner v. Castillo-Puche, 55 F.2d 910, 913 * * *.

It may puzzle journalists that one cannot prove such charges false. After all, the United States Supreme Court and other courts often have canvassed reporters' techniques, finding them acceptable at times despite angry charges by plaintiffs, flawed and faulty at other times, and on the basis of the latter sometimes have granted libel judgments.[57]

But the Massachusetts Court found precedent for its judgment: One writer, for example, had called a judge one of the ten worst judges in New York, said he had made a sufficient pattern of incompetent decisions and should be removed from office. The New York court denied recovery for these "opinions," saying that the defendants had simply expressed "their opinion of his judicial performance," and the judge could not recover "no matter how unreasonable, extreme or erroneous these opinions might be." [58] (The statement that the judge was "probably corrupt," on the other hand, was an accusation of crime that could be proved true or false.) In another case, "liar" merely expressed an opinion and could not be libelous however mistaken the opinion might be.[59] In another, "fascist" and fellow traveller of fascism were matters of opinion and protected ideas—but in this case,[60] the claim that the plaintiff had lied about people in his work as a journalist was ruled to be an assertion of fact.

The unsettled nature of the law as to opinion and comment under the Constitution was strikingly illustrated in Evans v. Ollman, a 1984 decision of the Court of Appeals, District of Columbia Circuit. Eleven judges sitting *en banc* delivered seven opinions. The majority found for two defendant newspaper columnists, and the U.S. Supreme Court refused to accept the plaintiff's

[57] Curtis Pub. Co. v. Butts, 388 U.S. 130, 87 S.Ct. 1975 (1967), finding the Associated Press reporter's techniques blameless and the Saturday Evening Post's constituting "reckless disregard." Where reckless disregard is found, it is commonly for bad reporting techniques.

[58] Citing Rinaldi v. Holt, Rinehart & Winston, Inc., 42 N.Y.2d 369, 376, 380–382, 397 N.Y.S.2d 943, 950–951, 366 N.E.2d 1299 (1977).

[59] Citing Edwards v. National Audubon Soc., Inc., 556 F.2d 113, 131 (2d Cir.1977).

[60] Buckley v. Littell, 539 F.2d 882, 884–885 (2d Cir.1976). Decisions that have found indications of "undisclosed defamatory facts" and denied protection include: Braig v. Field Communications, 310 Pa.Super. 569, 456 A.2d 1366 (1983), 9 Med.L. Repr. 1057, allegation that "Judge Braig is no friend of the Police Brutality Unit"; Nevada Independent Broadcasting Corp. v. Allen, 99 Nev. 404, 664 P.2d 337 (1983), 9 Med.L.Rptr. 1770, in a statement questioning whether a political candidate was "honorable"; Grass v. News Group Publications, Inc., 570 F.Supp. 178 (S.D.N.Y. 1983), 9 Med.L.Rptr. 2129, saying that Lew made the business a great success, while "Alex minded the store back home" and "was always in the shade when Lew was around."

appeal, in effect upholding the decision.[61]   Bertell Ollman, a Marxist professor of political science at New York University under appointment procedures to head the department of government at the University of Maryland, sued syndicated newspaper columnists Evans and Novak. Their column stated that Ollman "is widely viewed in his profession as a political activist," whose "candid writings avow his desire to use the classroom as an instrument for preparing what he calls 'the revolution'." It also reported that an unnamed political scientist said that Ollman "has no status within the profession, but is a pure and simple activist."

Writing for himself and three others, Judge Kenneth W. Starr found this to be opinion protected under the First Amendment and the *Gertz* dictum. Judge Robert Bork, joined by three others, considered the statements in the column to be rhetorical hyperbole, and as such a category of words different from either "fact" or "opinion," but protected by the First Amendment. Judge (now Justice) Antonin Scalia, writing as one of five who dissented in part from the judgment, called the statement as to Ollman's status in the profession "a classic and cooly crafted libel," and treated it as an unprotected statement of fact.[62]

Judge Starr noted the difficulty and the "dilemma" that courts often face in distinguishing between fact and opinion. For doing so, he shaped a four-part test which may be expected to find a part in future decisions that grapple with this deeply perplexing realm of libel law: [63]

1. The inquiry must analyze the common usage or meaning of the words. Do they have a precise meaning such as a direct charge of crime, or are they only loosely definable?

2. Is the statement verifiable—"objectively capable of proof or disproof?"

3. What is the "linguistic" context in which the statement occurs? Here the article or column needs to be taken "as a whole": "The language of the entire column may signal that a specific statement which, standing alone, would appear to be factual, is in actuality a statement of opinion."

4. What is the "broader social context into which the statement fits?" Here there are signals to readers or listeners that what is being read or heard is likely to be opinion, not fact. An example would be the labor dispute of *Old Dominion* (above, p. 125), with its exaggerated rhetoric common in such circumstances.

[61] Ollman v. Evans, 750 F.2d 970 (D.C.Cir.1984), 11 Med.L.Rptr. 1433; appeal refused by Supreme Court, L. Greenhouse, "Supreme Court Roundup," New York Times, 5/29/85, 8.

[62] Ibid., at 1038, 11 Med.L.Rptr. at 1491.

[63] Ibid., at 979–983, 11 Med.L.Rptr. at 1440–1444.

Another signal would be whether the article appeared on an editorial page—where opinion is expected—or in a front-page news story.

Despite the assertion in the Restatement (Second) of Torts in 1977, Gertz v. Robert Welch, Inc., did not obliterate the old libel defense of fair comment. Years later, some courts were still using common-law fair comment.[64]

For example, the Illinois Appellate Court, Fifth District, in 1982 held that repeated charges of "liar" against a county official in a newspaper editorial, and warning of two more years of his "lying leadership," were not protected opinion. For while a single charge of "liar" about a single event had been held not actionable in Illinois, the cumulative force of several such charges was "an actionable assault on the plaintiff's character in general, not mere criticism of his conduct in a particular instance."[65] The Court found that these were factual assertions, not expressions of opinion and not rhetorical hyperbole as argued by the defendant. Once more, the charge of "liar" had been found to be unprotected. It is unsafe, like accusations of criminal activity even in the form of "In my *opinion,* he is a rapist."[66]

Milkovich v. Lorain Journal Co. (1990)

As is evident from the preceding pages, Gertz v. Welch, Inc. (1974) generated numerous court decisions referred to under the general label of a "constitutional opinion defense." This defense was warmly welcomed by many commentators, adopted by many appellate courts, and rejected by some others.[67] When this defense was accepted, it meant that statements of opinion—variously defined—were held not to be actionable defamation. That opinion defense seems to have been diluted, in substantial measure, by the

---

[64] Sack, 178–82; Note, Fact and Opinion after Gertz v. Robert Welch, Inc., 34 Rutgers L.Rev. 81, 126 (Fall 1981); Jerry Chaney, Opinion Dicta New Law of Libel? 10 Med.Law Notes # 2, 5 (Feb., 1983); 10 Med.L.Rptr. # 15, 4/10/84, News Notes; Prosser & Keeton, Law of Torts, 5th ed. (1984), 831; Cianci v. New Times, 639 F.2d 54 (2d Cir.1980), 6 Med.L.Rptr. 1625, 1634. Goodrich v. Waterbury Republican-American, Inc., 188 Conn. 107, 448 A.2d 1317 (1982), 8 Med.L.Rptr. 2329; Orr v. Argus-Press Co., 586 F.2d 1108 (6th Cir.1978); Tawfik v. Loyd (N.D.Tex.1979), 5 Med.L.Rptr. 2067.

[65] Costello v. Capital Cities Media, Inc., 111 Ill.App.3d 1009, 67 Ill.Dec. 721, 445 N.E.2d 13 (1982), 9 Med.L.Rptr. 1434.

[66] Cianci v. New Times Pub. Co., 639 F.2d 54, 63 (2d Cir.1980), 6 Med.L.Rptr. 1625, 1631; Ollman v. Evans, 750 F.2d 970 (D.C.Cir.1984), 11 Med.L.Rptr. 1433, 1443.

[67] See discussion in David A. Anderson, "Is Libel Law Worth Reforming?", 140 *Pa.L.Rev.* (Dec.1991) pp. 505–510.

U.S. Supreme Court decision in a 15–year–old libel case, Milkovich v. Lorain Journal (1990).[68]

Michael Milkovich, Jr., a retired high school wrestling coach whose teams won numerous state championships, taught the news media a practical lesson. Packaging attacks on individuals' reputations as "opinion" appears more risky after the Supreme Court's decision.

In 1974, Milkovich was coaching the Maple Heights (Ohio) High School wrestling team against Mentor High School when a fight broke out. Several persons were hurt. Later, Coach Milkovich was among those testifying in an investigation by the Ohio State High School Athletic Association (OSHAA). His Maple Heights team was put on probation and ruled ineligible for the 1975 state tournament, and Coach Milkovich was censured for his role in the fight. After OSHAA was sued by some Maple Heights parents and wrestlers, an Ohio Court of Common Pleas overturned the probation and ineligibility orders.[69]

The following day, a column by sportswriter J. Theodore Diadiun appeared in the News–Herald, a newspaper published by the Lorain Journal Co. The column's headline said: "Maple beat the law with the 'big lie.'" A headline on the jump page read, "＊ ＊ ＊ Diadiun says Maple told a lie." The column said, in part: [70]

"'＊ ＊ ＊ a lesson was learned (or relearned) yesterday by the student body of Maple Heights High School, and by anyone who attended the Maple–Mentor wrestling meet of last Feb. 8.

＊ ＊ ＊

"'It is simply this: If you get in a jam, lie your way out.

＊ ＊ ＊

"'The teachers responsible were mainly Maple wrestling coach, Mike Milkovich, and former superintendent of schools, H. Donald Scott.

＊ ＊ ＊

"'Anyone who attended the meet, whether he be from Maple Heights or Mentor, or impartial observer, knows in his heart that Milkovich and Scott lied at the hearing after each having given his solemn oath to tell the truth.

"'But they got away with it.

---

[68] Milkovich v. Lorain Journal Co., 497 U.S. ___, 110 S.Ct. 2695 (1990), 17 Med.L. Rptr. 2009.

[69] 497 U.S. at ___, 110 S.Ct. at 2698 (1990), 17 Med.L.Rptr. at 2010.

[70] 497 U.S. at ___, 110 S.Ct. at 2698 (1990), 17 Med.L.Rptr. at 2011.

" 'Is this the kind of lesson we want our young people learning from their high school administrators and coaches?

" 'I think not.' "

Milkovich sued for defamation, and 15 years later—in 1990 the U.S. Supreme Court granted certiorari "to consider the important questions raised by the Ohio courts' recognition of a constitutionally required 'opinion' exception to the application of its defamation laws." [71]

Writing for the Court, Chief Justice William H. Rehnquist summarized cases constitutionally limiting the application of state defamation laws, from New York Times v. Sullivan (1964) through *Gertz* and Philadelphia Newspapers v. Hepps. (See discussions of these cases at text pages 159 ff. and 223.) In addition, the Chief Justice cited Harte–Hanks v. Connaughton (1989) (discussed at page 176): " 'The question whether the evidence in the record in a defamation case is sufficient to support a finding of actual malice is a question of law.' " [72]

The Chief Justice then wrote: [73]

> Respondents would have us recognize . . . still another First Amendment-based protection for defamatory statements which are categorized as "opinion" as opposed to "fact." For this proposition they rely on the following dictum from our opinion in *Gertz:*
>
>> "Under the First Amendment there is no such thing as a false idea. However pernicious an opinion may seem, we depend for its correction not on the conscience of judges and juries but on the competition of ideas. But there is no constitutional value in false statements of fact."
>
> Judge Friendly appropriately observed that this passage "has become the opening salvo in all arguments for protection from defamation actions on ground of opinion, even though the case did not remotely concern the question. Cianci v. New Times Publishing Co., 639 F.2d 54, 62 (C.A.2 1980). Read in context, though, the fair meaning of the passage was merely a reiteration of Justice Holmes' classic "marketplace of ideas" concept * * * [See Chapter 1, Sec. 2.]
>
> Thus we do not think this passage from *Gertz* was intended to create a wholesale defamation exemption for

[71] 497 U.S. ___, 110 S.Ct. at 2701 (1990), 17 Med.L.Rptr. at 2013.

[72] 497 U.S. ___, 110 S.Ct. at 2705 (1990), 17 Med.L.Rptr. at 2016.

[73] 497 U.S. ___, 110 S.Ct. at 2705–2706, 17 Med.L.Rptr. at 2017.

anything that might be labeled "opinion." * * * Not only would such an interpretation be contrary to the tenor and context of the passage, but it would also ignore the fact that expressions of "opinion" may often imply an assertion of objective fact.

If a speaker says, "In my opinion John Jones is a liar," he implies a knowledge of facts which led to the conclusion that Jones told an untruth. Even if the speaker states the facts upon which he bases his opinion, if those facts are either incorrect or incomplete, or if his assessment of them is erroneous, the statement may still imply a false assertion of fact. Simply couching such statements in terms of opinion does not dispel these implications; and the statement, "In my opinion Jones is a liar." can cause as much damage to reputation as the statement "Jones is a liar."

Chief Justice Rehnquist wrote: "It is worthy of note that at common law, even the privilege of fair comment did not extend to 'a false statement of fact, whether it was expressly stated or implied from an expression of opinion.' *Restatement (Second) of Torts* * * * Sec. 566 Comment *a.*" [74]

The Chief Justice expressed a desire to avoid drawing lines between opinion and fact. " * * * [W]e think the ' "breathing space" ' which ' "freedoms of expression require" ' to survive *Hepps,* 475 U.S. at 772, 106 S.Ct. at 1561 (quoting *New York Times,* 376 U.S. at 272, 84 S.Ct. at 721), is adequately secured by existing constitutional doctrine without the creation of an artificial dichotomy between "opinion" and "fact." [75]

Thus, unlike the statement, "In my opinion Mayor Jones is a liar," the statement "In my opinion, Mayor Jones shows his abysmal ignorance by accepting the teachings of Marx and Lenin" would not be actionable. *Hepps* ensures that a statement of opinion relating to matters of public concern which does not contain a provably false factual connotation will receive full constitutional protection.

It is to be doubted that the preceding paragraphs are going to settle legal squabbles over what is "fact," "opinion," or, as the Chief Justice stated earlier, an expression of opinion implying an "objective fact." [76]

[74] 497 U.S. at ___, 110 S.Ct. at 2706 (1990), 17 Med.L.Rptr. at 2017.

[75] 497 U.S. at ___, 110 S.Ct. at 2706 (1990), 17 Med.L.Rptr. at 2017.

[76] 497 U.S. at ___, 110 S.Ct. at 2706 (1990), 17 Med.L.Rptr. at 2018.

Chief Justice Rehnquist listed several decisions limiting the severity of libel laws against defendants: [77]

— The *Bresler–Letter Carriers–Falwell* line of cases, protecting name-calling statements that cannot reasonably be interpreted as representing "actual facts" about a person.

— "The *New York Times, Butts,* and *Gertz* culpability requirements further ensure that debate over public issues remains 'uninhibited, robust and wide-open.' New York Times, 376 U.S., at 270 [1964]."

— Finally, the enhanced independent appellate review required by *Bose Corp.* provides assurance that determinations about libel will be made so as not to "constitute a forbidden intrusion into the field of free expression. *Bose,* 466 U.S. at 490 ∗ ∗ ∗ "

Chief Justice Rehnquist concluded that the language the newspaper columnist used against Coach Milkovich was "loose, figurative or hyperbolic," and that the column's connotation that the coach had committed perjury was susceptible of being proved true or false.[78]

Dissenting, Justice Brennan—joined by Justice Marshall— seemingly agreed with the majority's rendition of the facts in the Milkovich case. Unlike the majority, however, Brennan characterized the columnist's words about the coach as "patently conjecture." Therefore, he disagreed with the finding that columnist Diadiun's statements were actionable because they implied an assertion of fact that the coach had perjured himself. Brennan countered: [79]

Diadiun not only reveals the facts upon which he is relying but makes it clear at which point he runs out of facts and is simply guessing. Read in context, such statements simply cannot reasonably be interpreted as implying such an assertion of fact.

Brennan, in line with his years of supporting press freedom, suggested ways in which conjecture and opinion not grounded in verifiable fact could serve a very real public interest. Justice Brennan asked: [80]

Did NASA officials ignore sound warnings that the Challenger Space Shuttle would explode? Did Cuban– American leaders arrange for John Fitzgerald Kennedy's assassination? Was Kurt Waldheim a Nazi officer? Such

[77] 497 U.S. at ___, 110 S.Ct. at 2706 (1990), 17 Med.L.Rptr. at 2018.
[78] Ibid.
[79] 497 U.S. at ___, 110 S.Ct. at 2711 (1990), 17 Med.L.Rptr. at 2019.
[80] 497 U.S. at ___, 110 S.Ct. at 2714 (1990), 17 Med.L.Rptr. at 2021.

questions are matters of public concern long before all the facts are unearthed, if they ever are.

The *Milkovich* decision means that news organizations are well advised to look to their ethics. Reporters and their bosses had best repress the desire to clobber reputations—especially *private* reputations—with opinion statements if the underlying facts are squishy. The noted media attorney Bruce Sanford put it another way: He predicted that " 'our public debate will be more flannel-mouthed and more cautious' " because of self-censorship to avoid possible libel suits.[81] Caution may be indicated. The Lorain Journal Co. reportedly spent more than $500,000 in defending and losing this libel suit.[82] And, the Milkovich decision does have its strange aspects. As Sanford noted, it is ironic that the more far-fetched " * * * or obviously absurd the commentary, the more constitutional protection it will have." Unsurprisingly, Sanford—along with a number of other lawyers who defend media clients—looked at this decision and predicted tough times ahead for the news media where defamation is concerned.[83]

SEC. 36. RETRACTION

A full and prompt apology following the publication of a libel will serve to mitigate damages awarded to the injured.

The news medium that has libeled a person may retract its statement, and in doing so, hope to lessen the chances that large damages will be awarded to the injured. The retraction must be full and without reservation, it should be no attempt to justify the libel, and it must be given the prominence in space or time that the original charge received. But while a full and timely apology may go to mitigate damages, it is in no sense a complete defense. The law reasons that many persons who saw the original story may not see the retraction.

In spite of a fulsome retraction in one case, it was estimated that the broadcaster involved agreed to an out-of-court settlement in the range of one-fourth to one-half of a million dollars.[84] Under state statutes, a full and prompt retraction serves to negate punitive damages, for it is considered evidence that the libel was not published with common-law malice (ill will). Under the constitutional (*Sullivan*) doctrine, however, retraction is in a some-

[81] Bruce Sanford, "Libel Defeat Is Troublesome For Broadcast News," *Radio Week* July 16, 1990, p. 4.

[82] David Margolick, "How a '74 Fracas Led to a High Court Libel Case," The New York Times, April 20, 1990.

[83] Sanford, loc. cit.

[84] Green v. WCAU–TV, 8 Med.L.Rptr. # 35, 11/2/82, News Notes.

what ambiguous condition, jurisdictions varying in whether it negates actual malice (knowing or reckless falsehood) or not.[85]

Many states have had retraction statutes, some providing that punitive damages may not be awarded if retraction is made properly and the publisher shows that he did not publish with malice. Others have gone further, providing that only special damages may be awarded following a retraction and demonstration of good faith on the part of the publisher. California has the statute most favorable to publishers. It provides that a proper retraction limits recovery to special damages, no matter what the motives of the publisher.[86]

Some retraction statutes have been attacked as unconstitutional, one reason being that they sometimes are applicable only to newspapers and as such are discriminatory. Many persons may publish libel in non-newspaper form, but not have the advantage of retraction statutes in these states. In Park v. Detroit Free Press Co., a Michigan retraction statute was held unconstitutional, the Court holding that "It is not competent for the legislature to give one class of citizens legal exemptions from liability for wrongs not granted to others." [87] The Supreme Court of Kansas held that state's retraction provision unconstitutional. The decision went to the law's preventing recovery of general damages, and said: [88]

> The injuries for which this class of damages is allowed are something more than merely speculative * * *. In short, they are such injuries to the reputation as were contemplated in the bill of rights * * *.

Where punitive damages only are barred to the defamed, however, the constitutionality of the statute ordinarily has been upheld.[89]

"SLAPP" Lawsuits

In the late 1980s, the phrase "getting SLAPPED" took on First Amendment meaning. "SLAPP" became well known as the acronym for "Strategic Lawsuits Against Public Participation."

[85] Donna L. Dickerson, Retraction's Role Under the Actual Malice Rule, 6 Communications and the Law # 4, 39 (Aug. 1984).

[86] T.M. Newell and Albert Pickerell, California's Retraction Statute: License to Libel?, 28 Journ.Quar. 474, 1951. For State retraction statutes, see Sack, App. IV, 589.

[87] 72 Mich. 560, 40 N.W. 731 (1888). See also Madison v. Yunker, 180 Mont. 54, 589 P.2d 126 (1978).

[88] Hanson v. Krehbiel, 68 Kan. 670, 75 P. 1041 (1904).

[89] Comer v. Age Herald Pub. Co., 151 Ala. 613, 44 So. 673 (1907); Meyerle v. Pioneer Pub. Co., 45 N.D. 568, 178 N.W. 792 (1920).

For example, suppose a number of citizens of Clearwater City starts a petition to pressure the Blanking Paper Company upstream to stop polluting the Clearwater River. If pollution controls are too expensive for the paper company at the moment, one alternative—which came into increasing use in the late 1980s—is to sue the petitioners for defamation (or some other legal claim). If, as is likely, the citizens' group does not have pockets as deep as Blanking Paper Company, the citizens may be intimidated into shutting up. If they do, they will have been SLAPPED.

The term SLAPP was coined by Professors Penelope Canan and George W. Pring of the University of Denver. They charted the phenomenon of ordinary-looking civil damage suits which in reality were "clearly reactions against past or anticipated opposition on political issues." [90]

In 1988, Canan and Pring surveyed 100 SLAPP suits. The most frequent legal claims used to try to squelch complaining citizens were defamation, business torts and abuse of process, while other filers opted for claims including conspiracy, violation of civil rights, and nuisance lawsuits.[91]

Although courts ultimately dismiss 80 percent of the SLAPP suits, that may still mean that protesting parties have been silenced because of lengthy, costly litigation. Some states, however, have reacted by considering legislation to slow down SLAPP suits. In 1989, for example, Washington passed a statute giving immunity from civil liability for any person who is sued for giving information to a governmental body.[92]

In addition, some people fight back. Early in 1990, reporter Lee McEachern of KQED–TV, San Francisco, told of three Bakersfield, California, farmers who were sued for placing a newspaper ad critical of J.G. Boswell, "the world's largest farming company."

The farmers counter-sued, and a jury held that the SLAPP lawsuit against them had deprived them of their constitutional rights of speech, press, and petition. The three farmers were awarded damages totaling $13.5 million, McEachern told the MacNeil–Lehrer News Hour.[93]

---

[90] Penelope Canan and George W. Pring, "Studying Strategic Lawsuits Against Public Participation ∗ ∗ ∗," 22 Law and Society Review No. 2 (1988), pp. 385–395.

[91] Ibid.

[92] Amy Dockser Marcus, "Law: Intimidation Lawsuits Creep Up on Critics," Wall Street Journal, Feb. 4, 1990, p. 81.

[93] Lee McEachern, "Focus—Getting Slapped," MacNeil–Lehrer News Hour, Feb. 19, 1990.

Other Costs of Defamation

The damages paid out in defamation cases are only part of the cost to the media, only part of the "chilling effect." Court and lawyer costs can be massive: as high as $10 million for CBS to defend the libel suit brought by General William Westmoreland and more than $3 million for Time magazine to defend against a suit brought by General Ariel Sharon.[94] Beyond court-related costs, there are costs of journalists' and editors/news directors' time spent in giving depositions.

Although there is an elegance and a nobility about New York Times v. Sullivan (1964) and many of the cases following it, the romance of the "constitutional defense" to libel has begun to pall on a number of observers. Eugene Roberts, then editor of The Philadelphia Inquirer, reported late in 1987 that his newspaper was being sued by two state supreme court justices after articles investigating the need for court reform in Pennsylvania.

Roberts said: "The Westmoreland and Sharon cases are the best known, but they are the merest tip of the iceberg." He referred to a $250 million libel suit against California's McClatchy Newspapers, withdrawn after three years of attorneys' fees. And in Arizona, the Sheriff Dick Godbehere of Maricopa County had brought a $64 million libel suit against the Arizona Republic and the Phoenix Gazette.

Roberts suggested that the "actual malice loophole," instead of protecting press freedom as the Supreme Court intended had provided tools of harassment for public officials to use with the help of friendly, anti-media juries.[95]

Katherine P. Darrow, General Counsel of The New York Times had a similarly chilling message late in 1987. She said that the average affirmed award for a person who prevails in a libel suit is $145,000. But that amount—obviously substantially large—did not concern her a great deal. After all, she said, only about 10 per cent of all the libel cases started ever get to trial.

What did worry her was the cost of defense. To handle a hypothetical average suit—including pre-trial matters such as discovery, motions, plus the trial itself and an appeal. Figuring the hours billed at typical rates for the U.S. outside of New York City, she estimated a cost through trial of nearly $150,000.

[94] For extended discussions of these cases, see Renata Adler, Reckless Disregard (New York: Knopf, 1986) and Rodney A. Smolla, Suing the Press (New York: Oxford, 1986).

[95] Eugene L. Roberts, "When Freedom of Expression Becomes a Financial Burden," remarks on receiving the John Peter Zenger award, University of Arizona, Tucson, Nov. 13, 1987.

She said this meant that newspapers will be in for a period of high legal defense expenses. Large newspapers may well be able to survive, and even thrive, but small publications could be chilled into silence by the threat of libel, if not actually sued into oblivion.[96]

And if defamation law is seen as a threat and an harassment for the media, it is not working for most plaintiffs, either. As media lawyer Robert Sack has said, "The few plaintiffs who succeed resemble the remnants of an army platoon caught in an enemy crossfire. Their awards stand witness to their good luck, not to their virtue, their skill, or the justice of their cause." [97] The famed "Iowa Study" of libel showed in the 1980s that plaintiffs chances of winning a libel suit are about one in five. Plaintiffs' attorneys tend to be more optimistic than libel suit success rates justify, but most plaintiffs can see that the odds against winning are long.[98]

The Iowa study indicated, quite simply, that the law of defamation does not and can not work because it is built upon an untenable assumption that libel plaintiffs somehow can be mended by monetary damage awards. But plaintiffs themselves, on the other hand, want to set the record straight, to correct falsehoods published about them.[99]

Media attorney Floyd Abrams has declared, " 'Current libel law simply does work. * * * It doesn't really protect individual reputations, and, on the other hand, it does chill freedom of expression.' " [1] Abrams has company in holding that view. The Libel Dispute Resolution Program of the Iowa Libel Research Project and the American Arbitration Association is proposing an alternative. This program proposes to have disputants who might otherwise wind up as plaintiff and defendant in a defamation lawsuit to agree to submit to an arbitration hearing before a neutral arbitrator.

This proceeding will reach a decision on whether reputational harm has been done and whether the challenged statements are true or false. A brochure describing this project says, "Fault-related questions such as malice, negligence, and the reasonableness of editorial procedures, and discovery * * * will be prohibit-

[96] Katherine P. Darrow, "Libel and Newspapers: Is this the Big Chill?", speech at University of Missouri, Oct. 28, 1987.

[97] Robert Sack, Libel, Slander and Related Problems (New York: Practising Law Institute, 1980) p. xxvii.

[98] Randall P. Bezanson, Gilbert Cranberg, and John Soloski, Libel Law and the Press: Myth and Reality (New York: Free Press, 1987) pp. 72–76.

[99] Ibid., p. 4.

[1] Roselle L. Wissler, et al., "Why Current Libel Law Doesn't Work", The Judges' Journal (Spring 1988) p. 29.

ed." Money damages will not be awarded by the arbitrator, and the remedy is likely to be publication or broadcast of the arbitrator's brief statement of the findings.[2]

Late 1988 saw the proposal of a major Libel Reform Project. This effort by the Annenberg Washington Program of Northwestern University was directed by Newton N. Minow, formerly chairman of the Federal Communications Commission. Mr. Minow also was of the opinion that the modern libel law system works well for no one.

The rationale for the libel reform project may be found in a number of inconclusive defamation cases—cases such as those involving General William Westmoreland against CBS and William Tavoulareas against the Washington Post. After millions of dollars had been expended by both sides in the Westmoreland case, the General withdrew from the suit, with both sides claiming vindication. And Tavoulareas had been awarded $2 million in his lawsuit against the Washington Post. That amount, the Libel Reform Project noted, would have paid the lawyers' fees for Tavoulareas, but the award was overturned on appeal.[3]

The Libel Reform Project's proposed model statute would require that every plaintiff *must* seek a retraction or opportunity to reply before filing suit. If the plaintiff's request were to be granted, there could be no suit.

The plaintiff who does not get a retraction or an opportunity to reply would be entitled to file suit. But the Libel Reform Project's proposed law would hold out an attractive option to avoid the lengthy and expensive process of current libel law. How? By agreeing to a declaratory judgment lawsuit. The only issue in such a suit would be truth or falsity of the defamatory statement. The losing party would pay the winner's attorney's fees.

The proposed statute would adopt the idea of neutral reportage: there could be no liability for accurately reporting the words of others. It would also grant no more than "reasonable compensation based upon proof of actual injury," and would abolish presumed and punitive damages.[4]

There appeared to be little in the way of an initial rush to embrace the Libel Reform Project's suggestions. Criticisms of its proposals surfaced quickly. Attorney Jane Kirtley, executive director of the Reporter's Committee for Freedom of the Press,

---

[2] Resolving Libel Disputes, booklet available from Iowa Libel Research Project, College of Law, University of Iowa, Iowa City, Iowa 52242.

[3] Proposal for the Reform of Libel Law, Annenberg Washington Program in Communications Policy Studies, October 17, 1988, pp. 9–10.

[4] Ibid., pp. 15–17, 19–24.

declared: "There is a fundamental reason why news organizations should object. It is called the First Amendment."

She argued that the Libel Reform Project was in effect urging the jettisoning of the principles of New York Times v. Sullivan, abandoning the doctrine that news media cannot be held responsible for "false statements published without fault."

Kirtley conceded that a declaratory judgment lawsuit would be cheaper to litigate. However, she said: "[T]he cost in human terms—the public pillorying of both complainant and publisher—will not be significantly reduced for the simple reason that the ultimate question of truth is just not that easy to answer." [5]

[5] Jane Kirtley, "Proposal to reform libel law has troubling aspects," Editor & Publisher, Nov. 5, 1988, p. 52ff.

Chapter 7

THE LAW OF PRIVACY AND
THE MEDIA

Sec.
37. Development of Privacy Law.
38. "Intrusion" as Invasion of Privacy.
39. Publication of Private Matters.
40. False Publications Which Invade Privacy.
41. Appropriation of Plaintiff's Name or Likeness.
42. Defenses: Newsworthiness, the Constitution, and Consent.
43. Defenses: Limitations and Problems.

SEC. 37. DEVELOPMENT OF PRIVACY LAW

**Privacy—"the right to be let alone"—is protected by an
evolving area of tort law and has been recognized as a
constitutional right by the Supreme Court of the United
States.**

Privacy—roughly defined as "the right to be let alone" [1]—is
one of the nation's hottest issues in the 1990s. It is often said that
the United States has become "The Information Society." Increasingly, it is difficult for individuals to keep information about
themselves from indiscriminate use by government agencies or
business interests. The worry of the 1970s—when privacy was
seen to be in peril by politicians, legal scholars, anthropologists,
and citizen activists—was the nightmare of the 1980s [2] and may be
the reality of the 1990s.

It can't happen here? Don't bet your life on it. Remember
that government's stake in information about individuals has
implications for *control.* Knowledge is power.

Think about cable television. We are moving steadily toward
a nation interconnected, by satellite transmission if not by wire, to
interactive (two-way) in-the-home cable television systems. The

---

[1] Thomas M. Cooley, A Treatise on the Law of Torts, 2d ed. (Chicago: Callaghan
and Co., 1888) p. 29.

[2] See, e.g., Arthur R. Miller, The Assault on Privacy (Ann Arbor: University of
Michigan Press, 1971); Don R. Pember, Privacy and the Press (Seattle: University
of Washington Press, 1972); Alan Westin, Privacy and Freedom (New York:
Atheneum, 1967); Subcommittee on Constitutional Rights of the Committee on the
Judiciary, United States Senate, Ninety Second Congress, First Session ("The Ervin
Subcommittee"), February 23–25, March 2–4, 9–11, 15 and 17, Parts 1 and 2, pp. 1–
2164, *passim;* Final Recommendations of the Privacy Study Commission, and
Warren Freedman, The Right to Privacy in the Computer Age (New York: Quorum
Books, 1987), and George Orwell, 1984.

cornucopia of services offered by cable television is dazzling. The technology is now here for use of cable TV for shopping, mail delivery, consulting with physicians, communicating with one's elected representatives, answering polls, and on and on. Think also about the price in lost privacy which may be paid for such a collection of services.

So it is that the technology which serves us may also ensnare us. Infrared telephoto lenses "see in the dark." Super-sensitive directional microphones can hear across sizable distances. Dossiers are compiled by credit bureaus, and by myriad government agencies. All of these things were continuing phenomena, parts of what Vance Packard called "The Naked Society" back in 1964.[3] Arthur Miller of the Harvard School of Law produced an all-too prophetic study, The Assault on Privacy, investigating credit bureau abuses and use of systems for data collection and information storage and retrieval. Acknowledging the helpful uses of such technology, Professor Miller then warned: "we must be concerned about the axiom . . . that man must shape his tools lest they shape him."[4]

Privacy is worth fighting for, against governmental stupidity or arrogance, or against the prying of businesses or private individuals. Louis D. Brandeis, one of the Supreme Court's greatest justices, once wrote that the makers of the American Constitution "sought to protect Americans in their beliefs, their thoughts, their emotions and their sensations. They [the Constitution's framers] conferred, as against the Government, the right to be let alone— the most comprehensive of rights and the right most valued by civilized man."[5]

Privacy is a problem for each citizen, a desired right to be fought for and zealously guarded. Privacy is also a communications media problem, one to be reported upon. And finally, privacy is a media problem in another sense because missteps by newspapers, magazines and radio and television stations have resulted in hundreds of privacy lawsuits.

Many of the more humorous—or tragicomic—American court decisions have come from settings involving privacy. When a landlord plants a microphone in the bedroom of a newly married couple, is that an invasion of privacy?[6] When a tavern owner takes a picture of a woman customer against her will—and in the

---

[3] Vance Packard, The Naked Society (New York: David McKay and Co., 1964).

[4] Miller, op. cit., pp. 7–8.

[5] Olmstead v. United States, 277 U.S. 438, 48 S.Ct. 564 (1928).

[6] Such "bugging" was held to be an invasion of privacy. See Hamberger v. Eastman, 106 N.H. 107, 206 A.2d 239, 11 A.L.R.3d 1288 (1964).

women's restroom, later displaying the photograph to patrons at the bar—is that an invasion of privacy?[7]

Such cases, in their rather comical aspects, indicate growing pains in an area of law which is remarkably young. Privacy is nowhere mentioned in the Constitution, and its absence is understandable. In America during the Revolutionary generation, most people lived on farms. Urban residents made up not much more than 10 per cent of the new nation's population. When the Constitution was ratified, Philadelphia, then the nation's largest city, had little more than 40,000 residents. When people were out-of-doors, there was little real need for any specific Constitutional statement of a right to privacy. Indoors, privacy was another matter. In 18th Century America, homes often had living, eating and sleeping accommodations for an entire family in the same room. In public inns, travelers often had to share rooms—and sometimes beds—with other wayfarers.[8]

Although privacy was not mentioned in the Constitution by name, its first eight amendments, plus the Fourteenth Amendment, include the right to be secure against unreasonable search and seizure and the principle of due process of law. Taken together with the Declaration of Independence's demands for the right to "life, liberty and the pursuit of happiness," it can be seen that the founders of the nation had a lively concern for something akin to a "right to be let alone."

Since 1960, the Supreme Court of the United States has recognized privacy as a constitutional right, a right which to some extent protects citizens from intrusions by government or police agencies.[9]

Here, a useful distinction may be made between the *right* of privacy and the *law* of privacy. As Professor James Willard Hurst of the University of Wisconsin Law School has written, American legal history is full of concern for a broad *right* to privacy, represented by interests protected in the Constitution's Bill of Rights. (The Constitution, of course, protects citizens only against *government* actions.) Of this broad *right* to privacy, only small slivers have been hammered into the narrower tort *law* of privacy as enunciated by judges and legislatures.[10]

[7] Yoeckel v. Samonig, 272 Wis. 430, 75 N.W.2d 925 (1956) said this was not an invasion of privacy because Wisconsin's Legislature had twice refused to enact a statute creating the tort. In 1977, Wisconsin Statute § 895.50 recognized all four torts.

[8] Pember, Privacy and the Press, p. 5.

[9] See Mapp v. Ohio, 367 U.S. 643, 81 S.Ct. 1684 (1961): Griswold v. Connecticut, 381 U.S. 479, 85 S.Ct. 1678 (1965).

[10] James Willard Hurst, Law and Conditions of Freedom (Madison, Wis.: University of Wisconsin Press, 1956) p. 8.

The tort *law* of privacy is also quite new. It has been traced to an 1890 *Harvard Law Review* article written by two young Boston law partners, Samuel D. Warren and future Supreme Court Justice Louis D. Brandeis. The article, often named as the best example of the influence of law journals on the development of the law, was titled "The Right to Privacy."

If this law journal article was the start of a law of privacy in America, it should also be noted that the newspaper press may have been involved too. Standard accounts of the origins of the Warren-Brandeis article have it that Warren and his wife had been greatly annoyed by newspaper stories about parties which they gave. This irritation, so the story goes, led to the drafting of the article, now thought to have been written primarily by Brandeis. The co-authors asserted that an independent action for privacy could be found within then-established areas of the law such as defamation and trespass to property. Warren and Brandeis wrote: [11]

> The press is overstepping in every direction the obvious bounds of propriety and of decency. Gossip is no longer the resource of the idle and of the vicious, but has become a trade which is pursued with industry as well as effrontery. To satisfy a prurient taste the details of sexual relations are spread broadcast in the columns of the daily papers. To occupy the indolent, column upon column is filled with idle gossip, which can only be procured by intrusion upon the domestic circle. The intensity and complexity of life, attendant upon advancing civilization, have rendered necessary some retreat from the world, and man, under the refining influence of culture, has become more sensitive to publicity, so that solitude and privacy have become more essential to the individual; but modern enterprise and invention have, through invasions upon his privacy, subjected him to mental pain and distress, far greater than could be inflicted by mere bodily injury.

But as a judge in a Missouri appeals court noted in 1911, the concept of a right of privacy was not new at all. Privacy, the judge wrote, "is spoken of as a new right, when in fact it is an old right with a new name. Life, liberty, and the pursuit of happiness are rights of all men." [12]

More than a century before 1890, when Warren and Brandeis added the word "privacy" to the vocabulary of the law, England's

[11] Samuel Warren and Louis D. Brandeis, "The Right to Privacy," 4 Harvard Law Review (1890) p. 196.

[12] Munden v. Harris, 153 Mo.App. 652, 659–660, 134 S.W. 1076, 1078 (1911).

William Pitt gave ringing affirmation to the idea that "a man's home is his castle." Pitt said: "The poorest man may in his cottage bid defiance to all the forces of the Crown. It may be frail; its roof may shake; the winds may blow through it; the storms may enter,—but the King of England cannot enter; all his forces dare not cross the threshold of the ruined tenement!"

From such beginnings an expanding law of privacy has emerged. In 1901, a package of flour led to an early—and famous—privacy case in New York: Roberson v. Rochester Folding Box Co. The judges of two New York courts were evidently readers of the Harvard Law Review, because they would have allowed recovery in a privacy lawsuit brought by Miss Abigail M. Roberson. She had sued for $15,000 because her likeness was used to decorate posters advertising Franklin Mills flour without her consent. But New York's highest court—the Court of Appeals— ruled that she could not collect because there was no precedent which established a "right of privacy." Despite Miss Roberson's unwilling inclusion in an advertising campaign featuring the slogan of "The Flour of the Family," the Court of Appeals held that if her claim were allowed, a flood of litigation would result, and that it was too difficult to distinguish between public and private persons.[13]

The *Roberson* decision, however, hinted broadly that if the New York legislature wished to enact a law of privacy, it could do so. Considerable public outcry and a number of outraged newspaper editorials greeted the outcome of the *Roberson* case. The next year, in 1903, the New York legislature passed a statute which made it both a misdemeanor and a tort to use the name, portrait, or picture of any person for advertising or "trade purposes" without that person's consent. Note that this was narrowly drawn legislation, limited to the kind of fact situation which had arisen in *Roberson*.[14]

In 1905, two years after the New York privacy statute was passed, the Georgia Supreme Court provided the first major judicial recognition of a law of privacy. An unauthorized photograph of Paolo Pavesich and a bogus testimonial attributed to him appeared in a newspaper advertisement for a life insurance company. The Georgia court ruled that there is a law of privacy which prevents unauthorized use of pictures and testimonials for advertising purposes.[15]

[13] 171 N.Y. 538, 64 N.E. 442, 447 (1902).

[14] New York Session Laws 1903, Ch. 132, §§ 1–2, now known as §§ 50–51, New York Civil Rights Law.

[15] Pavesich v. New England Life Ins. Co., 122 Ga. 190, 50 S.E. 68, 79 (1905).

Since the 1905 *Pavesich* decision, the tort of privacy has grown mightily. The late William L. Prosser, for many years America's foremost torts scholar, suggested that there are four kinds of torts included under the broad label of "invasion of privacy." [16]

1. Intrusion on the plaintiff's physical solitude.

2. Publication of private matters violating the ordinary decencies.

3. Putting plaintiff in a false position in the public eye, as by signing that person's name to a letter or petition, attributing views not held by that person.

4. Appropriation of some element of plaintiff's personality—his or her name or likeness—for commercial use.

It should be noted that these are not mutually exclusive categories; more than one of these four kinds of privacy actions may be present in the same case.

Some or all of those privacy areas have been recognized in nearly every state. The law of privacy—or one of its four sub-tort areas as listed above—has now been recognized by federal courts, in the District of Columbia, and at least 49 states.[17] Court ("common law") recognition had come in most states, and statutes recognizing the law of privacy have been passed in seven states: California, Nebraska, New York, Oklahoma, Utah, Virginia, and Wisconsin. Even in those states which were slow to recognize the law of privacy, privacy interests were apt to be protected under other legal actions such as libel or trespass.[18]

[16] Barbieri v. News-Journal Co., 56 Del. 67, 189 A.2d 773, 774 (1963). The Delaware Supreme Court summarized Dean Prosser's analysis of the kinds of actions to be included by the law of privacy. For fuller treatment, see Prosser's much-quoted "Privacy," 48 California Law Review (1960), pp. 383–423, and his Handbook of the Law of Torts, 4th Ed. (St. Paul, Minn., West Publishing Co., 1971, pp. 802–818).

[17] Victor A. Kovner, Harriette K. Dorsen, Suzanne Telsey, "Recent Developments In Intrusion, Private Facts, False Light, and Commercialization Claims," in James C. Goodale, chairman, Communications Law 1991 Vol. II (New York: Practising Law Institute, 1991); see especially his sampling of recent authorities for the four sub-torts which make up the law of privacy, "State Recognition of the Four Torts," pp. 196ff. Minnesota appeared to be the last holdout in 1991, and even there, some recognition has occurred in the area of appropriation-commercialization.

[18] State privacy statutes include California Civil Code, Section 3344, which is similar to the New York privacy statute, New York Civil Rights Law §§ 50–51. Wisconsin Statute § 895.50 recognized all four torts, thus overruling the notorious intrusion case, Yoeckel v. Samonig, 272 Wis. 430, 75 N.W.2d 925 (1956). A woman brought suit, alleging that her picture had been taken in the restroom of Sad Sam's Tavern. The Wisconsin Supreme Court decided that in the absence of statutory enactment, there was no right to privacy in Wisconsin. For a similar statute, see Nebraska Civil Rights Rev.Stat. § 2–201–211. Utah Code Annotated §§ 76–9–401–403, 406 deals with intrusion, and U.C.A. § 76–9–401, 406 covers misappropriation (right of publicity). Virginia Code § 8.01–40 covers right of publicity; Kovner, op. cit.

Professor Prosser noted that an action for invasion of privacy is much like the old concept *"libel per se:"* a plaintiff does not have to plead or prove actual monetary loss ("special damages") in order to have a cause of action. In addition, a court may award punitive damages. But while actions for defamation and for invasion of privacy have points of similarity, there are also major differences. As a Massachusetts court said, "The fundamental difference between a right to privacy and a right to freedom from defamation is that the former directly concerns one's own peace of mind, while the latter concerns primarily one's reputation." [19]

While such a distinction may exist in theory, in practice the distinction between defamation and invasion of privacy is blurred. As noted previously, in 1890 Warren and Brandeis drew upon a number of old defamation cases on the way to extracting what they called a right to privacy. Privacy, it would seem, may often be regarded as a close cousin of defamation. Some publications, indeed, may be both defamatory and an invasion of privacy, and shrewd attorneys often sued for both libel and invasion of privacy on the basis of a single publication.[20]

Privacy actions also resemble defamation lawsuits in that the right to sue belongs only to the affronted individual. As a rule, relatives or friends cannot sue because the privacy of someone close to them was invaded, unless their own privacy was also invaded. In general, as with defamation, the right to sue for invasion of privacy dies with the individual.[21]

When considering privacy law, two things should be kept in mind:

First, the law of privacy is not uniform. In fact, one judge once compared the state of the law to a haystack in a hurricane. There is great conflict of laws from state to state and from jurisdiction to jurisdiction.

[19] Themo v. New England Newspaper Pub. Co., 306 Mass. 54, 27 N.E.2d 753, 755 (1940). Note that Professor Prosser could not have forecast the U.S. Supreme Court decision in the libel case of Gertz v. Welch, Inc., 418 U.S. 323, 94 S.Ct. 2997 (1974), which demolished the old *libel per se* standard in rejecting the concept of liability without fault.

[20] In general, although invasion of privacy and defamation are often included as elements of the same lawsuit, usually courts have not allowed a plaintiff to collect for both actions in one suit. "Duplication of Damages: Invasion of Privacy and Defamation," 41 Washington Law Review (1966), pp. 370–377; see, also, Brink v. Griffith, 65 Wash.2d 253, 396 P.2d 793 (1964), and Donald Elliott Brown, "The Invasion of Defamation by Privacy," Stanford Law Review 23 (Feb., 1971), pp. 547–568.

[21] Bremmer v. Journal-Tribune Pub. Co., 247 Iowa 817, 76 N.W.2d 762 (1956); Wyatt v. Hall's Portrait Studio, 71 Misc. 199, 128 N.Y.S. 247 (1911). In at least one state, heirs can sue for invasion of privacy. For example, see the Utah intrusion statute, U.C.A. §§ 76–9–401–403, 406.

Second, when courts or legislatures become involved with the law of privacy, they are attempting to balance interests. On one side of the scale, you have the public interest in freedom of the press and the right to publish. On the other side, you have the individual's right to privacy.

SEC. 38. "INTRUSION" AS INVASION OF PRIVACY

Invading a person's solitude, including the use of microphones or cameras, has been held to be actionable.

Journalists are often seen as invaders of privacy *par excellence,* but they are rank amateurs compared to governmental units, including police and intelligence-gathering agencies. In times such as these, journalists are in an anomalous position where privacy is concerned. The federal Privacy and Freedom of Information Acts are somewhat at cross purposes.[22] Obviously, journalists using federal and state Freedom of Information legislation to pry information out of government are at times going to dig up facts which persons involved will feel to be an invasion of their privacy.

In the area called "intrusion on the plaintiff's physical solitude," the media must beware of the modern technology which they call upon increasingly to gather and to broadcast news. Microphones—some of which can pick up quiet conversations hundreds of feet away—and telephoto lenses on cameras should be used with care.

More than 200 years ago, Sir William Blackstone's *Commentaries* (1765) considered a form of intrusion, calling eavesdropping one of a list of nuisances which law could punish. Eavesdroppers were termed "people who listen under windows, or the eaves of a house, to conversation, from which they frame slanderous and mischievous tales." [23] Now, the tort subdivision of intrusion includes matters from illegal entry into a house to surreptitious tape recording (in some instances) to window-peeping.

The camera has been something of a troublemaker. Courts have held that it is not an invasion of privacy to take someone's photograph in a public place. Here, photographers are protected on the theory that they "stand in" for the public, taking pictures of what any persons could see if they were there. It follows, of course, that photographers should beware of taking photos in private places. When journalists or photographers invade private territory, they and their employer could be in trouble.

---

[22] See Chap. 14, Sec. 82, at p. 614.

[23] Sir William Blackstone's Commentaries on the Law, ed. by Bernard C. Gavit (Washington, D.C., Washington Book Co., 1892) p. 823.

Barber v. Time provides a classic example. In 1939, Mrs. Dorothy Barber was a patient in a Kansas City hospital, being treated for a disease which caused her to eat constantly but still lose weight. A wire service (International News Service) photographer invaded her hospital room and took her picture despite her protests. This resulted in stories about Mrs. Barber's illness appearing in Kansas City-area newspapers for several days. Time Magazine then purchased the picture from the wire service, and published it along with a 150-word story taken largely from an original wire-service story. The cutline under the picture said "Insatiable-Eater Barber; She Eats for Ten." Mrs. Barber won $3,000 in damages from Time, Inc.[24]

More recently, a television film crew's intrusion onto private property caused a CBS-owned station huge legal costs, although it wound up paying a minor damage award of only $1,200. Minor award or not, the case of LeMistral v. Columbia Broadcasting System underlines the principle that journalists must ask themselves whether they are attempting to report from a private place. In the LeMistral case, WCBS–TV reporter Lucille Rich and a camera crew charged unannounced into the famous and fashionable LeMistral Restaurant in New York City. The reporter-camera team was doing a series on restaurants cited for health-code irregularities. The arrival of the camera crew—with lights on and cameras rolling—caused a scene of confusion which a slapstick comedian would relish. (Persons lunching with persons other than their spouses were reported to have slid hastily under tables to try to avoid the camera.) The restaurant's suit for invasion of privacy and trespass resulted in a jury award against CBS of $1,200 in compensatory damages and $250,000 in punitive damages. On appeal, the case was sent back to the trial judge for reconsideration and, ultimately, cancellation of the punitive damage award.[25]

If you can see something in a public place, you can photograph it. However, photographs can go too far even in public places if their behavior becomes annoyingly intrusive. Ron Galella, a self-styled "paparazzo," was making a career out of taking pictures of Jacqueline Kennedy Onassis and her children. Paparazzi, in the words of U.S. Circuit Judge J. Joseph Smith, "make themselves as visible to the public and obnoxious to their photographic subjects as possible to aid in the advertisement and wide sale of their works."

[24] Barber v. Time, Inc., 348 Mo. 1199, 159 S.W.2d 291, 295 (1948). Time purchased the picture from "International," a syndicate dealing in news pictures, and mainly followed the wording of an account furnished by United Press.

[25] Le Mistral, Inc. v. Columbia Broadcasting System, 61 A.D.2d 491, 402 N.Y.S.2d 815 (1st Dept.1978); TV Guide, May 3, 1980, p. 6.

Galella's posturing and gesturing while taking pictures of Mrs. Onassis and children ultimately led to issuance of an injunction against the photographer. He was forbidden to approach within 25 feet of Mrs. Onassis or within 30 feet of her children.[26] Temptation proved too strong for Galella, however. In 1981, on four different occasions, Galella was again too close and too obnoxious in his photographic shadowing of Mrs. Onassis (attending a mid-day film in New York City, attempting to board a boat at Martha's Vineyard, going to see a dance performance at New York City's Winter Garden) and Caroline Kennedy (bicycling with a friend on Martha's Vineyard). U.S. District Judge Cooper found Galella to be in contempt of the court's 1975 order, subjecting the persistent photographer to liability for a heavy fine and/or imprisonment.[27]

If photographers can see their quarry from a public spot, without going through strange gyrations or trespassing onto private property, no liability should result. The *Crowley* (La.) *Post-Signal* was sued for invasion of privacy by Mr. and Mrs. James Jaubert. The Jauberts returned from a trip to discover that a photograph of their home had been published on the *Post-Signal's* front page, with this caption: "One of Crowley's stately homes, a bit weatherworn and unkempt, stands in the shadow of a spreading oak."

The Jauberts sought $15,000 for invasion of privacy, including mental suffering and humiliation; they were awarded a total of $1,000 by the trial court. The Louisiana Supreme Court ruled that because the photograph was taken from the middle of the street in front of the Jaubert house, and because passers-by were presented with an identical view, there was no invasion of privacy.[28]

Ethical as well as legal considerations get involved in most privacy cases. In the case known as Cape Publications v. Bridges, Hilda Bridges Pate sued for invasion of privacy for a photograph published by the Florida newspaper, Cocoa Today. During the summer of 1977, Hilda Bridges Pate was abducted by her estranged husband. He went to her place of employment and—at gunpoint—forced her to go with him to their former apartment.[29]

[26] Galella v. Onassis, 487 F.2d 986 (2d Cir.1973).

[27] 533 F.Supp. 1076, 1108 (S.D.N.Y.1982), 8 Med.L.Rptr. 1321–1325.

[28] Jaubert v. Crowley Post-Signal, Inc., 375 So.2d 1386 (La.1979), 5 Med.L.Rptr. 2185.

[29] Cape Publications, Inc. v. Bridges, 423 So.2d 426 (Fla.App. 5th Dist.1982), 8 Med.L.Rptr. 2535. See discussion in The News Media & The Law, Jan./Feb. 1984, at p. 41, noting that the Florida Supreme Court and the Supreme Court of the United States refused to review this decision in fall, 1983.

Police were summoned and were surrounding the apartment. The husband forced her to undress in an effort to prevent her from trying to escape. As Judge Dauksch wrote for the Florida Court of Appeal, Fifth District: "This is a typical exciting emotion-packed drama to which newspeople and others are attracted." He said, in short, it was a newsworthy story.[30]

The husband shot himself to death. Police heard the gunshot, stormed the apartment, and rushed the partially clad Ms. Pate to safety across a public parking lot as she clutched a dishtowel to her body, trying to conceal her nudity. At the trial, a Florida jury awarded Ms. Pate $1 million in compensatory damages and $9 million in punitive damages.

In erasing the damage awards, the Florida appeals court said, "The published photograph is more a depiction of grief, fright, emotional tension and flight than it is an appeal to other sensual appetites." Judge Dauksch said, "The photograph revealed little more than could be seen had * * * (Ms. Pate) been wearing a bikini, and somewhat less than some bathing suits seen on the beaches." Judge Dauksch added that courts should be slow to interfere with newspapers' publishing of news in the public interest.[31]

Dietemann v. Time, Inc.

Over the years, there have been relatively few cases of "intrusion" privacy lawsuits against the news media. Life Magazine—a Time, Inc., publication—bit the privacy bullet, however, in the 1971 decision in Dietemann v. Time, Inc. In that case, reporters from Life, cooperating with the Los Angeles, California district attorney and the State Board of Health, did some role-playing to entrap a medical quack. Reporter Jackie Metcalf and photographer William Ray went to the home of journeyman plumber A.A. Dietemann, a man who was suspected of performing medical services without a diploma or state license. Mrs. Metcalf and Mr. Ray gained admittance to Dietemann's house by claiming that they had been sent by (if you'll pardon the expression) the plumber's friends.

Mrs. Metcalf complained that she had a lump in her breast, and while Dietemann conducted his "examination," Ray was

---

[30] Cape Publications v. Bridges, 423 So.2d 426 (Fla.App. 5th Dist.1982), 8 Med.L. Rptr. 2535, 2536. In footnote no. 2, Judge Dauksch quoted the Restatement (Second) of Torts, S652D, Comment G, on the definition of news: " 'Authorized publicity, customarily regarded as 'news,' includes publications concerning crimes, arrests, police raids, suicides, marriages, divorces, accidents, fires, catastrophes of nature, narcotics-related deaths, rare diseases, etc., and many other matters of genuine popular appeal.' "

[31] 423 So.2d 426, 427 (Fla.App. 5th Dist.1982), 8 Med.L.Rptr. 2535, 2536.

secretly taking pictures. Life later published pictures from Dietemann's home, and also reported on his "diagnosis." He said Mrs. Metcalf's difficulty was caused by eating some rancid butter 11 years, 9 months and 7 days prior to her visit to his home.[32]

Mrs. Metcalf, meanwhile, had a transmitter in her purse, and was relaying her conversations with Dietemann to a receiver/tape recorder in an auto parked nearby. That auto contained the following eavesdroppers: another Life reporter, a representative of the DA's office, and an investigator from the California State Department of Public Health. This detective work resulted in a conviction of Dietemann for practicing medicine without a license. The plumber sued for damages totaling $300,000 for invasion of his privacy. A jury, recognizing that Dietemann was not suing from a position of great strength as a convicted medical man-sans-license, nevertheless awarded Dietemann $1,000 for invasion of privacy.

In an opinion by Judge Shirley Hufstedler, a United States Court of Appeals upheld the damage award, disagreeing with Life magazine attorneys' arguments that concealed electronic instruments were "indispensable tools of investigative reporting." Judge Hufstedler wrote:[33]

> Investigative reporting is an ancient art; its successful practice long antecedes the invention of miniature cameras and electronic devices. The First Amendment has never been construed to accord newsmen immunity from torts or crimes committed during the course of newsgathering.

McCall v. Courier-Journal and Louisville Times Co.

This case is discussed under the general heading of "Intrusion," and that certainly is an element here. Like a number of other privacy cases, however, it involves a number of issues. In this case, there was a libel suit, plus privacy law claims which are labeled "false light;" the false light tort area is discussed later in this chapter. McCall v. Courier-Journal and Times arose when Louisville Times reporters outfitted drug suspect Kristie Frazier's purse with a tape recorder. She had told them that attorney Tim McCall had said that if she would pay him $10,000, he could keep her out of jail. Ms. Frazier then returned to McCall's law office with tape recorder running and had another conversation with him. As the fact situation was summarized by The Reporters Committee for Freedom of the Press:[34]

[32] Dietemann v. Time, Inc., 449 F.2d 245, 246 (9th Cir.1971).

[33] Ibid., at p. 249.

[34] News Media & the Law, Oct.-Nov. 1980, p. 31.

The transcript of the conversation revealed that Mc-Call said that the case could not be "fixed" and warned Frazier not to speak in such terms. But he did say that he was going fishing with one of the judges involved, and that once the prosecutor knew McCall had elicited a substantial fee, he would be more sympathetic to her cause.

While Ms. Frazier was in McCall's office taping their conversation, he asked her several times whether she was using a recording device. She denied doing so. Once Ms. Frazier handed the tape over to Louisville Times reporters it was used as the basis for an article. The article said, in part, "The Times requested that Miss Frazier tape-record the conversation because the newspaper was attempting to investigate her allegations that McCall offered to 'fix' her case for $10,000. However, the Times found no indication of any 'fix.' " The Times, even so, repeated Frazier's allegations.[35]

Attorney McCall sued for invasion of privacy and libel. He declared that the secret taping was a wrongful act, and that he had been libeled because the article implied that he had offered to fix the case and was published in reckless disregard of his rights. McCall asked $6 million in damages. The Louisville Times published a story about McCall's lawsuit, summarizing its first article. McCall then amended his complaint, adding the contention that the Times' second article was libelous, too.

Subsequently, the Kentucky Supreme Court ruled that a summary judgment should not have been granted to the newspaper; the matter should be allowed to go to trial on the libel and false light claims. The Kentucky Supreme Court, however, was not impressed with the intrusion aspect of Attorney McCall's suit, instead concentrating on false light privacy and libel.

The Kentucky Supreme Court sent the case back to the trial court for reconsideration.[36] Before that trial could begin again, the newspaper company agreed to pay Attorney McCall $75,000 to settle the $6 million libel and invasion of privacy lawsuit. Paul Janensch, then executive editor of the Louisville newspapers, said the settlement was reached to avoid another costly and time-consuming trial. On the other hand, McCall's attorney told the Associated Press that the newspaper " 'did not want to face a jury in this community which would call it

---

[35] News Media & the Law, Oct.-Nov. 1980, p. 31.

[36] McCall v. Courier–Journal and Louisville Times Co., 623 S.W.2d 882, 887 (Kentucky 1981), 7 Med.L.Rptr. 2118, 2125.

to account for both the wrongful invasion of McCall's privacy and improper reporting.' "[37]

Cassidy v. ABC

Although people generally may dislike hidden tape recorders, they may be even more hostile to hidden television cameras. Sometimes, as Chicago policeman Arlyn Cassidy learned, you can be on TV at an inopportune moment. Cassidy was working as an undercover vice squad agent assigned to investigate a massage parlor.

Policeman Cassidy testified that he had paid a $30 admission fee to see "de-luxe" lingerie modeling. He was then taken to a small cubicle by one of the models, and noticed "camera lights" on each side of the bed. He told the model the lights made the room warm, and then reclined on the bed and watched the model change her lingerie several times. As an Illinois judge described the scene, Cassidy made several suggestive remarks to the model and then arrested her for solicitation after she "established 'sufficient' physical contact." Three other vice squad officers then joined Officer Cassidy, asking if anyone was in the adjoining room.[38]

At that moment, someone rushed out of Room No. 2, yelling "Channel 7 News." That's right, a camera crew from Chicago's American Broadcasting Company television outlet had been in the adjoining room, filming Officer Cassidy and the model through a two-way mirror. The television station personnel testified that they had received complaints from the massage parlor's manager that his establishment was the subject of police harassment.

The whole television situation rubbed Officer Cassidy the wrong way. He complained that the camera crew's activities violated Illinois' anti-eavesdropping statute [39] and that his common law right to privacy was violated.[40] The Illinois Appellate Court had difficulty in terming a television camera "an eavesdropping device," the more so because the noise of the camera's operation drowned out sounds from the other room. Furthermore, Cassidy had noticed the lights and asked the model whether they were "on TV." She replied, "Sure, we're making movies." Under such circumstances, Officer Cassidy was believed by the court not to have much of an expectation of privacy.

[37] The Associated Press, "Louisville Times, attorney settle suit," story published in The Kentucky Kernel, newspaper of the University of Kentucky, Nov. 24, 1982, p. 5.

[38] Cassidy v. ABC, 60 Ill.App.3d 831, 17 Ill.Dec. 936, 377 N.E.2d 126 (1978).

[39] Ibid., at 937, 377 N.E.2d at 127; see § 14–2, Oh. 38, Ill.Rev.Stat. (1975).

[40] Ibid., at 937, 377 N.E.2d at 127.

In addition, Cassidy's effort to assert a cause of action under the "intrusion" theory of privacy failed, on grounds that Cassidy was a public official on duty at the time he heard those stirring words, "Channel 7 News." [41]

Use of Tape Recorders

The Dietemann and Cassidy cases should inspire journalists to think carefully about their use of cameras, tape recorders, and electronic listening and transmitting gear. Professor Kent R. Middleton, in an important article on journalists' use of tape recorders, concluded: "Reporters may record or transmit conversations they overhear, they participate in, or they record with permission of one party." Recording with the permission of one party—that's called "consensual monitoring" in legal jargon—is what is involved here for the press. [42]

Does one-party consent sound confusing, or merely ludicrous? What would one-party consent do to the law of burglary or of rape? What "consensual monitoring" does as a legal concept is forbid an unauthorized third party from intercepting a conversation, as in the case of an illegal (not-authorized-by-a-court) tap on a telephone line, listening in on two other parties.

Please note that this section is discussing what is legal, and not necessarily what is ethical. The authors of this text know that many reporters often record conversations—particularly telephone conversations—without giving notice that a tape recorder is running.

It is legal in most states for a reporter to conceal a tape recorder in pocket or purse while talking to news sources. Note, however, that roughly one-quarter of the states have statutes outlawing such use of recorders. Professor Middleton reported that such participant monitoring was forbidden by statute in 13 states: California, Delaware, Florida, Georgia, Illinois, Maryland, Massachusetts, Michigan, Montana, New Hampshire, Oregon, Pennsylvania, and Washington. [43] Furthermore, in Shevin v. Sunbeam Television Corporation, the Florida Supreme Court ruled that the Florida statute forbidding interception of telephone messages without consent of all parties involved did not violate a reporter's First Amendment rights. [44]

[41] Ibid., at 938, 942, 377 N.E.2d at 128, 132.

[42] Kent R. Middleton, "Journalists and Tape Recorders: Does Participant Monitoring Invade Privacy?", 2 COMM/ENT Law Journal (1980) at pp. 299–300.

[43] Ibid., pp. 304–309.

[44] Shevin v. Sunbeam Television Corp., 351 So.2d 723 (Fla.1977), rehearing denied 435 U.S. 1018, 98 S.Ct. 1892 (1978). See also Victor A. Kovner, "Recent Developments in Intrusion, Private Facts, False Light, and Commercialization Claims," in James C. Goodale, chairman, Communications Law 1991, Vol. II, pp. 15–26.

Many reporters routinely record telephone conversations without telling the party on the other end of the line, or without a warning "beep" signal as required by the Federal Communications Commission.[45] This kind of surreptitious recording may not violate specific state law, but it is forbidden by telephone company tariffs, as Middleton has written. If a person is somehow caught while secretly recording phone conversations, the telephone company could cut off phone service. That, however, seems to be only a remote possibility.[46] Furthermore, as privacy expert Victor A. Kovner has noted, the FCC in 1983 advanced a "Notice of Proposed Rule-Making" to get rid of the "beep-tone" rule but nothing has come of it. The FCC argued that technology of recent years made the rule in effect unenforceable.[47]

Boddie v. ABC (1984)

In addition to state provisions and telephone company "tariffs" [rules] overseen by the Federal Communications Commission (FCC), there is also the Electronic Communications Privacy Act of 1986.[48] Despite its name, it turns out to be less protective of privacy than the statute it amended where the sneaky interception of voices and other messages by electronic means is concerned.[49]

That 1986 statute altered the 1968 "Federal Wiretap Statute," which had made it a crime and a tort to intercept a wire communication or any oral communication "conducted in a situation carrying with it an expectation of privacy.[50]"

While the 1968 statute was still in force, Sandra Boddie sued the American Broadcasting Companies for a report on its "20/20" program. She sought damages for defamation, false light invasion of privacy, and violation of the Federal Wiretap Statute. The ABC report causing Ms. Boddie's suit discussed allegations that Judge James Barbuto of Akron, Ohio, granted leniency to criminal defendants in exchange for sex.

During 20/20's investigations of Judge Barbuto, ABC television personality Geraldo Rivera interviewed Ms. Boddie. She agreed to be interviewed but refused to appear on camera. Un-

---

[45] Middleton, pp. 304–309.

[46] Ibid., pp. 319–320; Kovner, op. cit., pp. 24–25, citing 47 CFR 64.501; Section 73.1206. FCC Rules.

[47] Kovner, ibid., citing FCC Docket No. 20840, 1983.

[48] Electronic Communications Privacy Act of 1986, Pub.L. No. 99–508, 18 U.S. C.A. § 2510.

[49] See 18 U.S.C.A. § 2511, as discussed in Boddie v. ABC, 694 F.Supp. 1304, 1305–1306 (N.D.Ohio 1988), 16 Med.L.Rptr. 1100, 1101, 1103.

[50] See Marc Franklin and David A. Anderson, *Cases and Materials on Mass Media Law,* 4th ed. (Westbury, N.Y.: Foundation Press, 1989), p. 492.

known to Ms. Boddie, Rivera and an ABC producer/reporter, Charles C. Thompson, recorded her interview by using hidden microphones and a hidden videotape camera. A part of the surreptitiously taped interview was televised by ABC in a broadcast report titled "Injustice for All." [51]

Ms. Boddie's lawsuit against ABC went through several incarnations [52] but ultimately was unsuccessful. She had sued—and her right to a cause of action had been upheld—under the 1968 Federal Wiretap Statute, which provided, in wondrous lawyerly prose: [53]

> "It shall not be unlawful under this chapter for a person not acting under color of law to intercept a wire or oral communication where such person is a party to the communication or where one of the parties has given prior consent to such interception unless such communication is intercepted for the purpose of committing any criminal or tortious act in violation of the Constitution or laws of any State or for the purpose of committing any other injurious act."

In 1986, after the U.S. Court of Appeals (6th Cir.) had ruled that Ms. Boddie had a cause of action under the 1968 Federal Wiretap Statute,[54] Congress amended the statute, removing the vague phrase "any other injurious act."

In 1988, however the U.S. District Court (N.D.Ohio) concluded that the Federal Wiretap Statute, as amending the 1986 Privacy Act, had to be applied in Ms. Boddie's lawsuit, saying that the later Act merely clarified Congressional intent in the 1968 Federal Wiretap Statute.[55]

> * * * Congress never intended, at least in cases involving media defendants and giving rise to First Amendment considerations, to provide a cause of action for gathering and disseminating news that does not raise to the level of a crime or a tort * * *.

So Ms. Boddie came up empty in her lawsuit against Geraldo Rivera and ABC. It is apparent that Congress and the courts involved in this case were willing to protect the media even

[51] Boddie v. American Broadcasting Companies, Inc., 731 F.2d 333, 335 (6th Cir. 1984), 15 Med.L.Rptr. 1923, 1924–1925.

[52] Ibid.

[53] Boddie v. American Broadcasting Companies, Inc., 694 F.Supp. 1304 (N.D.Ohio 1988), 16 Med.L.Rptr. 1100, quoting 1968 Federal Wiretap Statute, 18 U.S.C.A. § 2511(2)(d) at p. 1101.

[54] Boddie v. American Broadcasting Companies, Inc., 694 F.Supp. 1304, 1305 (N.D.Ohio 1988), 16 Med.L.Rptr. 1100, 1101.

[55] Ibid., at 1309, 16 Med.L.Rptr. at 1104.

against outrageous behavior: Tricking Ms. Boddie into a video-taped interview after she had refused to appear on camera.

Pearson v. Dodd

In a case which raises the question of the extent of reportorial involvement in removing documents from the office of a public official, Senator Thomas Dodd of Connecticut failed to collect in an intrusion-invasion of privacy lawsuit against sensational columnists Drew Pearson and Jack Anderson. Pearson and Anderson had done great harm to Dodd's reputation and career. They had published papers taken from Dodd's office files which showed an appropriation of campaign funds for personal purposes.

The exposé of Dodd began during the summer of 1965 when two employees and two former employees of Senator Dodd removed documents from his files, photocopied them, and then replaced the originals in their filing cabinets. The copies were turned over to Anderson, who knew how they had been obtained. The Pearson-Anderson "Washington Merry-Go-Round" column then ran six stories about the Senator, dealing—among other matters—with his relationship with lobbyists for foreign interests.

Dodd argued that the manner in which the information for the columns was obtained was an invasion of his privacy. After hearing Pearson and Anderson's appeal from a lower court judgment,[56] Court of Appeals Judge J. Skelly Wright said that Dodd's employees and former employees had committed improper intrusion when they removed confidential files to show them to outsiders. And what of the journalists?[57]

* * *

> If we were to hold appellants [Pearson and Anderson] liable for invasion of privacy on these facts, we would establish the proposition that one who receives information from an intruder, knowing it has been obtained by improper intrusion, is guilty of a tort. In an untried and developing area of tort law, we are not prepared to go so far.

[56] Dodd v. Pearson, 279 F.Supp. 101 (D.D.C.1968).

[57] 133 U.S.App.D.C. 279, 410 F.2d 701, 704–705 (D.C.Cir.1969). See also Bilney v. Evening Star Newspaper Co., 43 Md.App. 560, 406 A.2d 652 (1979), 5 Med.L.Rptr. 1931, in which a newspaper was sued for intrusion because it had published confidential academic records of members of the University of Maryland basketball team. The records involved were held to be newsworthy, and the lawsuit against the paper was dismissed because it was not demonstrated that reporters had solicited or encouraged reading of confidential records. The material involved came unasked for, from an unnamed source.

Florida Publishing Co. v. Fletcher

In 1972, 17-year-old Cindy Fletcher was alone one afternoon at her Jacksonville, Fla., home when a fire of undetermined origin did severe damage to the house. She died in the blaze. When the Fire Marshal and a police sergeant arrived at the house to make their investigation, they invited news media representatives to join them as was their standard practice.

The Fire Marshal desired a clear picture of the "silhouette" left on the floor after the removal of Cindy Fletcher's body to show that the body was already on the floor before the fire's heat damaged the room. The marshal took one Polaroid photograph of the outline, but that picture was unclear and he had no more film. A photographer for the Florida *Times-Union* was then asked to take the silhouette picture, which was made part of the official investigation files of both the fire and police departments.

This picture was not only part of the investigative record, it was also published—along with other pictures from the fire scene—in a Times-Union story on September 16, 1972. Cindy's mother, Mrs. Klenna Ann Fletcher, first learned of the facts surrounding the death of her daughter by reading the newspaper story and by seeing the published photographs.

Mrs. Fletcher sued the newspaper ["Florida Publishing Company"] and alleged three things: "(1) trespass and invasion of privacy, (2) invasion of privacy, and (3) wrongful intentional infliction of emotional distress—seeking punitive damages.[58] The trial court dismissed Count 2 and granted summary judgments in favor of the newspaper on counts 1 and 3. Speaking to the question of trespass, the trial judge said: [59]

> "The question raised is whether the trespass alleged in Count I of the complaint was consented to by the doctrine of common custom and usage.

> "The law is well settled in Florida that there is no unlawful trespass when peaceable entry is made, without objection, under common custom and usage."

Numerous affidavits had been filed by the news media saying that "common custom and usage" permitted the news media to enter the scene of a disaster.[60]

[58] Florida Pub. Co. v. Fletcher, 340 So.2d 914, 915–916 (Fla.1976).

[59] Quoted at Ibid., p. 916.

[60] Ibid. Affidavits came from such sources as the Chicago Tribune; ABC–TV News, New York; the Associated Press; the Miami Herald; United Press International; the Milwaukee Journal, and the Washington Post.

Mrs. Fletcher appealed from the trial court to Florida District Court of Appeal, First District, which held that she should have been able to go to trial on the issue of trespass.[61] The Florida Supreme Court, however, ruled that no actionable trespass or invasion of privacy had occurred. The Florida Supreme Court quoted approvingly from a dissenting opinion by Florida District Court of Appeal Judge McCord: [62]

> *"It is my view that the entry in this case was by implied consent.*
>
> "It is not questioned that this tragic fire and death were being investigated by the fire department and the sheriff's office and that arson was suspected. The fire was a disaster of great public interest and it is clear that the photographer and other members of the news media entered the burned home at the invitation of the investigating officers.
>
> " * * *
>
> "Implied consent would, of course, vanish if one were informed not to enter at that time by the owner or possessor or by their direction. But here there was not only no objection to the entry, but *there was an invitation to enter by the officers investigating the fire."*

Therefore, there was no trespass by the news media in this case.

When a reporter does not have any kind of permission to be on private property, however, the result could be troublesome. That's one message of a 1980 case, Oklahoma v. Bernstein, as decided by an Oklahoma District Court (Rogers County). Benjamin Bernstein and a number of other reporters had been arrested for trespassing onto private property. In hot pursuit of a newsworthy event, they followed protesting demonstrators onto the construction site of a Public Service Company of Oklahoma (PSO) nuclear power plant, Black Fox Station.

Despite showings of extensive governmental support (e.g. use of eminent domain to acquire part of the site for PSO, government-guaranteed loans, and close continuing supervision from the Nuclear Regulatory Commission), the Black Fox site was held to be private property. Although the Oklahoma court held that protests at the construction site were newsworthy, and although

---

[61] Ibid., pp. 917–918.

[62] Ibid., pp. 918–919. See also Higbee v. Times–Advocate, Inc., (S.D.Cal.1980), 5 Med.L.Rptr. 2372, dismissing a federal violation of civil rights claim but ruling that a photo taken inside plaintiffs' home was a matter of state tort law. Escondido, Calif., law enforcement officers had invited the press to be present during the execution of a search warrant. For a contrary view, see Kent R. Middleton, "Journalists, Trespass and Officials: Closing the Door of Florida Publishing Co. v. Fletcher," 16 Pepperdine Law Rev. 259 (1989).

PSO was trying to minimize news coverage of an important public controversy, the reporters were found guilty of trespass.[63]

Similarly, consider the decision in Anderson v. WROC–TV (1981). Two Rochester, New York, television stations accepted the invitation of Humane Society investigator Ronald Storm to accompany him as he served a search warrant. The warrant authorized Storm to enter the house occupied by Barbara P. Anderson and Joy E. Brenon, to seize animals which might be found confined in an overcrowded, unhealthy situation or not properly cared for.

When investigator Storm served the search warrant, television photographers and reporters accompanied him into the home of Ms. Anderson and Ms. Brenon, and filmed the interior. Ms. Brenon asked the television people to stay outside her home, but they entered anyway. Stories about the search were broadcast that evening on news shows of WROC–TV and WOKR–TV.[64]

Citing Dietemann v. Time, Inc.,[65] the New York Supreme Court, Monroe County, held that the First Amendment right to gather news does not allow members of the press to get away with committing crimes or torts in the course of newsgathering. Reporters are not above the law. In this case, a resident of the house told television station employees to stay out of her house, and they did not do so. In addition, the New York Court distinguished this case from Florida Publishing Company v. Fletcher,[66] discussed earlier at footnote 65.[67]

> Even were it necessary to decide this * * * solely upon the factual differences between * * * [this] case and Fletcher the same result would obtain. In Fletcher the Florida court characterized the fire as "a disaster of great public interest." (340 So.2d at 918). The entry here by the Humane Society investigator can hardly be compared to a fire which took the life of a young person.
>
> * * *
>
> As the plaintiffs correctly argue, one may not create an implied consent by asserting that it exists and without evidence to support it. In passing, and as previously noted, it also appears * * * that the entry was made in disregard of plaintiff Joy Brenon's express instructions to stay out.

[63] Oklahoma v. Bernstein (Okl.D.C., Rogers County 1980), 5 Med.L.Rptr. 2313, 2323–2324.

[64] Anderson v. WROC–TV, 109 Misc.2d 904, 441 N.Y.S. 220 (1981), 7 Med.L.Rptr. 1987, 1988.

[65] 109 Misc.2d 904, 441 N.Y.S. 220, 227 (1981), 7 Med.L.Rptr. 1997, 1990, discussing Dietemann v. Time, Inc., 449 F.2d 245 (9th Cir.1971).

[66] 340 So.2d 914 (Fla.1976).

[67] 109 Misc.2d 904, 441 N.Y.S.2d 220, 227 (1981), 7 Med.L.Rptr. 1987, 1992.

SEC. 39.   PUBLICATION OF PRIVATE MATTERS

With the law of privacy, "truth can hurt."   Unlike the law of defamation, truth is not necessarily a defense to a lawsuit for invasion of privacy.

The case of Dorothy Barber discussed in the last section was not only an incident of "intrusion," but also involved a second subarea of privacy law: "publication of private matters violating the ordinary decencies."   In this area of law, missteps by the mass media have led to a substantial number of lawsuits.   In publishing details of private matters, the media may make accurate reports and yet—at least on some occasions—be found liable for damages. A suit for defamation would not stand where the press has accurately reported the truth, but the press could nevertheless lose an action for invasion of privacy based on the same fact situation.   Here, the truth sometimes hurts.

In most cases, the existence of a public record usually has precluded recovery for invasion of privacy.   Even if persons are embarrassed by publication of dates of a marriage or birth,[68] or information which is a matter of public record,[69] publication accurately based on such records have escaped successful lawsuits. Where there is a legitimate public record—and where the media's use of that record is not forbidden by law—the material generally may be used for publication.   In 1960, the Albuquerque (N.M.) *Journal* published a story which said:[70]

> Richard Hubbard, 16, son of Mrs. Ann Hubbard, 532 Ponderosa, NW, was charged with running away from home, also prior to date, several times endangered the physical and moral health of himself and others by sexually assaulting his younger sister.   *   *   *

The younger sister, Delores Hubbard, sued for invasion of privacy, asserting that she had suffered extreme humiliation and distress and that the story "caused her to be regarded as unchaste, and that her prospects of marriage have been adversely affected thereby."   Attorneys for the newspaper, however, brought proof that the *Albuquerque Journal's* story was an exact copy of an official court record.   In upholding a lower court's judgment for the newspaper, the New Mexico Supreme Court ruled that because this was a public record, the newspaper enjoyed privilege.[71]

[68] Meetze v. Associated Press, 230 S.C. 330, 95 S.E.2d 606 (1956).

[69] Stryker v. Republic Pictures Corp., 108 Cal.App.2d 191, 238 P.2d 670 (1951).

[70] Hubbard v. Journal Pub. Co., 69 N.M. 473, 474, 368 P.2d 147, 148 (1962).

[71] 69 N.M. 473, 474–475, 368 P.2d 147, 148–149 (1962).

It should be apparent that much in the law of privacy is unpredictable, and the "private facts" area is no exception. Consider the lawsuits brought by Oliver Sipple, the ex-Marine who saved President Gerald Ford's life in 1975 by deflecting the aim of a would-be assassin, Sarah Jane Moore. Two days after the incident, the San Francisco Chronicle's famed columnist Herb Caen wrote some words strongly implying that Sipple was a homosexual. Caen wrote that San Francisco's gay community was proud of Sipple's action, and that it might dispel stereotypes about homosexuals.[72]

Sipple objected that his sexual preference had nothing to do with saving the President's life, and filed suit against *The* San Francisco Chronicle, Herb Caen, The Los Angeles Times, and several other newspapers, seeking $15 million in damages. Sipple argued that printing facts about his sexual orientation without his consent exposed him to ridicule. The Los Angeles Times countered that Sipple, as a person thrust into the "vortex of publicity" of an event of worldwide importance had become a newsworthy figure. "[M]any aspects of his life became matters of legitimate public interest." Individuals who become public persons give up part of their right of privacy, the *Times* contended. Finally, in April, 1980, a California trial court—without giving any reasons—dismissed the invasion of privacy suit against the San Francisco Chronicle and other newspapers.[73]

Sipple appealed against the dismissal, asking the California Court of Appeal, First District, to reinstate his privacy lawsuit. The appellate court held, however, that Sipple's case was correctly terminated by the lower court. The Court of Appeal said that the facts about Sipple as a member of San Francisco's gay community were already quite widely known: "in the public domain." In addition, the Court of Appeal held that Sipple was indeed newsworthy after saving President Ford's life.

Sipple, of course, was involved in an event of international importance. When the newsworthiness is less, the privacy protection for individuals may be correspondingly greater. Toni Ann Diaz, for example, had achieved a limited newsworthiness as the first woman student body president at a northern California school, the College of Alameda.

In 1978, Oakland Tribune columnist Sidney Jones published truthful—yet highly private—information about Ms. Diaz.[74]

---

[72] The News Media & The Law, Oct./Nov. 1980, p. 27.

[73] Sipple v. Chronicle Publishing Company, 154 Cal.App.3d 1040, 201 Cal.Rptr. 665 (1st Dist.1984), 10 Med.L.Rptr. 1690, 1693–1694.

[74] Diaz v. Oakland Tribune, Inc., 139 Cal.App.3d 118, 188 Cal.Rptr. 762, 766 (1983), 9 Med.L.Rptr. 1121, 1122.

"More Education Stuff: The students at the College of Alameda will be surprised to learn their student body president Toni Diaz is no lady, but is in fact a man whose real name is Antonio.

"Now I realize, that in these times, such a matter is no big deal, but I suspect his female classmates in P.E. 97 may wish to make other showering arrangements."

The trial court jury awarded Ms. Diaz a total of $775,000, finding that the information about the sex change was not newsworthy and would be offensive to ordinary readers.[75]

In January of 1983, although obviously in sympathy with Ms. Diaz, the California Court of Appeal, First District, sent the matter back to the lower court for a new trial. The appellate court held that the trial judge had committed reversible error in not emphasizing to the jury that a newspaper has a right to publish newsworthy information. Also, it was held that jury instructions should have made it clear that plaintiff Diaz had to carry the burden of proof in trying to show that the article she complained of was not newsworthy.[76]

The court held that there was little evidence that the gender-corrective surgery was part of the public record. It did not consider Diaz's Puerto Rican birth certificate to be a public record in this instance. Given Diaz's efforts to conceal the operation, and considering Diaz's needs for privacy and the notoriety received as the first woman student body president at that college, the question of the story's newsworthiness—the judge said—should have been left to a jury.[77] The court added that there was no merit in the Oakland Tribune's claim that the story was made newsworthy by the changing roles of women in society.

The appellate court then sent the case back to the trial level, but a second jury never heard the Diaz case. After the decision by the California Court of Appeal, First District, the case was reportedly settled out of court for between $200,000 and $300,000.

The case of Howard v. Des Moines Register and Tribune Co. also raised both legal and ethical concerns. *Register* reporter Margaret Engel did an investigative story on a county home, and published the name of a young woman who had undergone forced sterilization. The article included this passage: "He [Dr. Roy C. Sloan, the home's psychiatrist] said the decision to sterilize the resident Robin Woody was made by her parents and himself." The article, based on public records, also noted that the woman

---

[75] The News Media and the Law, Oct./Nov. 1980, p. 28.

[76] 139 Cal.App.3d 118, 188 Cal.Rptr. 762 (1983), 9 Med.L.Rptr. 1121.

[77] 139 Cal.App.3d 118, 188 Cal.Rptr. 762, 763 (1983), 9 Med.L.Rptr. 1121, 1127.

was 18 years old in 1970 at the time of her sterilization, and was not mentally retarded or disabled, but an " 'impulsive, hair-triggered, young girl' in the words of Dr. * * * Sloan." [78]

The *Register* defended itself successfully against a private facts lawsuit, with the court concluding that in this context, use of the defendant's name was justified. In granting the *Register* a summary judgment, an Iowa District Court said that the relationship between the disclosure and a story's newsworthiness should be considered. In this case, use of Robin Woody's name was said to lend personal detail, specificity and credibility to a story on a newsworthy topic, care of residents in a county home.[79]

In at least six states, statutes prohibit publishing the *identity* of a rape victim. Those states are Wisconsin, Florida, South Carolina, Georgia, Alaska, and New York.[80] A case based upon the South Carolina statute resulted in a 1963 Federal District Court ruling indicating that such statutes were valid. However, a 1975 Supreme Court of the United States decision held otherwise when publication of a rape victim's name was based on a public record.[81]

Cox Broadcasting Corp. v. Cohn (1975)

Cox Broadcasting v. Cohn grew out of tragic circumstances. In August, 1971, 17-year-old Cynthia Cohn was gang-raped and died, and six youths were soon indicted for the crimes against her. There was considerable coverage of the event, but the identity of the victim was not disclosed until one defendant's trial began. Some eight months later, in April of 1972, five of the six youths entered pleas of guilty to rape or attempted rape, the charge of murder having been dropped. Those guilty pleas were accepted, and the trial of the defendant who pleaded not guilty was set for a later date.[82]

Georgia had a statute forbidding publication of the identity of a rape victim. Despite this, a television reporter employed by WSB–TV—a Cox Broadcasting Corporation station—learned Cynthia Cohn's name from indictments which were open to public inspection. Later that day, the reporter broadcast her identity as

[78] Howard v. Des Moines Register and Tribune Co., 283 N.W.2d 289, 302 (Iowa 1979).

[79] Ibid., p. 303.

[80] Wis.Stat.Ann. 348.412; West's Fla.Stat.Ann. § 794.03; S.C.Ann.Code § 16–81, and Ga.Stat. § 26–9901; See Kovner et al., in Goodale, ed., op. cit. Vol. II (1991) pp. 46–47.

[81] Cox Broadcasting Corp. v. Cohn, 420 U.S. 469, 95 S.Ct. 1029 (1975); Nappier v. Jefferson Standard Life Ins. Co., 213 F.Supp. 174 (D.S.C.1968).

[82] Cox Broadcasting Corp. v. Cohn, 420 U.S. 469, 471, 95 S.Ct. 1029, 1034–1035 (1975).

part of his story on the court proceedings, and the report was repeated the next day.[83]

Martin Cohn sued Cox Broadcasting, claiming that the broadcasts which had identified his daughter invaded his own privacy by reason of the publication of his daughter's name. After hearing the Cohn case twice, the Georgia Supreme Court ruled that the statute forbidding publication of the name of a rape victim was constitutional ＊ ＊ ＊ " 'a legitimate limitation on the right of freedom of expression contained in the First Amendment.' " [84]

The Supreme Court of the United States disagreed by a vote of 8–1. Writing for the Court, Mr. Justice White said:[85]

> The version of the privacy tort now before us—termed in Georgia the "tort of public disclosure" ＊ ＊ ＊ is that in which the plaintiff claims the right to be free from unwanted publicity about his private affairs, which, although wholly true, would be offensive to a person of ordinary sensibilities. Because the gravamen [gist] of the claimed injury is the publication of information, whether true or not, the dissemination of which is embarrassing or otherwise painful to an individual, it is here that claims of privacy most directly confront the constitutional freedoms of speech and press.

Justice White wrote that truth may not always be a defense in either defamation or privacy actions. First, concerning defamation: "The Court has ＊ ＊ ＊ carefully left open the question whether the First and Fourteenth Amendments require that truth be recognized as a defense in a defamation action brought by a private person as distinguished from a public official or a public figure." Writing about privacy, he continued, "In similar fashion, Time v. Hill, supra, [385 U.S. 374 at 383 n. 7, 87 S.Ct. 534 at 539 (1967)] expressly saved [reserved] the question whether truthful publication of very private matters unrelated to public affairs could be constitutionally proscribed." [86] Thus the Supreme Court recognized—but backed away—from a troubling constitutional question: May a state ever define and protect an area of privacy free from unwanted *truthful* publicity in the press?

Having recognized this problem, Justice White then turned his majority opinion to narrower and safer ground. In *Cox Broad-*

[83] 420 U.S. 469, 471, 95 S.Ct. 1029, 1034–1035 (1975).

[84] 420 U.S. 469, 475, 95 S.Ct. 1029, 1036 (1975). Justices Powell and Douglas filed concurring opinions, and Justice Rehnquist dissented, stating that the Supreme Court did not have jurisdiction in this case for want of a final decree or judgment from a lower court.

[85] 420 U.S. 469, 489, 95 S.Ct. 1029, 1043 (1975).

[86] 420 U.S. 469, 490, 95 S.Ct. 1029, 1044 (1975).

casting, the key question was whether Georgia might impose sanctions against the accurate publication of the name of a rape victim, when that name had been obtained from public records. "[M]ore specifically," White wrote, the issue arose when the rape victim's name was obtained "from judicial records which are maintained in connection with a public prosecution and which themselves are open to public inspection. We are convinced that the State may not do so." [87]

He wrote that the news media have a great responsibility to report fully and accurately the proceedings of government, "and official records and documents open to the public are the basic data of governmental operations." The function of the news media reporting of judicial proceedings "serves to guarantee the fairness of trials and to bring to bear the beneficial effects of public scrutiny upon the administration of justice.[88]

In 1979, the Supreme Court of the United States followed its reasoning from *Cox Broadcasting* in deciding Smith v. Daily Mail Publishing Co. *Smith* was a case which cut across areas of constitutional limitations on prior restraint, privacy, and free press-fair trial considerations. It arose in February, 1978, when a 14-year-old junior high school student in St. Albans, W.Va., shot and killed a 15-year-old fellow student. Reporters for nearby Charleston newspapers learned the identity of the youth accused of the shooting by their routine monitoring of the police radio. The Charleston *Daily Gazette* —and later, the *Daily Mail* —used the youth's name in their stories, in violation of a West Virginia statute forbidding newspapers' use of names of juveniles accused of crimes without a written court order.[89]

The state of West Virginia contended that even though this statute amounted to a prior restraint on speech, the state's interest in protecting the identity of juveniles caught up in the legal process overcame the presumption against the constitutional validity of prior restraints. In declaring the West Virginia statute unconstitutional by a vote of 8–0, Chief Justice Burger wrote: "At issue is simply the power of a state to punish the truthful publication of an alleged juvenile delinquent's name lawfully obtained by a newspaper. The asserted state interest cannot justify the statute's imposition of criminal sanctions on this type of publication." [90]

[87] 420 U.S. 469, 491, 95 S.Ct. 1029, 1044 (1975).

[88] 420 U.S. 469, 492, 95 S.Ct. 1029, 1044–1045 (1975), citing Sheppard v. Maxwell, 384 U.S. 333, 350, 86 S.Ct. 1507, 1515 (1966).

[89] West Virginia Statute § 49–7–3; Smith v. Daily Mail Pub. Co., 443 U.S. 97, 99 S.Ct. 2667 (1979).

[90] 443 U.S. 97, 105, 99 S.Ct. 2667, 2672 (1979). See also the key prior restraint cases as discussed in Chapter 1: Near v. Minnesota ex rel. Olson, 283 U.S. 697, 51

The Florida Star v. B.J.F. (1989)

The general rule for journalists is that if material is part of a public record (such as a record of a judicial proceeding) it can be reported truthfully and accurately without legal penalty. In 1989, the U.S. Supreme Court cautiously upheld this generalization in The Florida Star rape reporting case.[91]

This case arose when a Jacksonville weekly newspaper published an item reporting a woman's complaint to the Sheriff's Department that she had been robbed and sexually assaulted. The department prepared a report using B.J.F.'s full name, and put it in the department's press room. Access to the reports in this room was unrestricted.

A reporter-trainee for The Florida Star copied the report verbatim, and a reporter then wrote an accurate one-paragraph "Police Reports" item, which was published. This violated the newspaper's own policy by identifying a rape victim; the newspaper had not done so previously. This mistake by the newspaper came under a Florida statute making it unlawful to " 'print, publish, or broadcast . . . in any instrument of mass communication' the name of a victim of a sexual offense." [92]

"B.J.F." sued for invasion of privacy, claiming that the Jacksonville weekly negligently had violated the Florida statute. She contended that because of the publication of her name, she had suffered emotional distress, and that her mother had received a threatening phone call from a man who said he would rape B.J.F. again. The plaintiff testified that she had been forced to change her phone number and residence and to get mental health counseling.

Despite the newspaper's plea that it had learned the name from the incident report issued by the Sheriff's Department, and that printing the rape victim's name was an inadvertent violation of the newspaper's own policy, the trial court denied the newspaper's motion to dismiss. The court then accepted plaintiff's motion for a directed verdict, awarding $75,000 in compensatory damages and $25,000 in punitive damages.[93] The directed verdict was upheld by Florida's First District Court of Appeal, and the U.S. Supreme Court noted probable jurisdiction.[94]

S.Ct. 625 (1931); Organization for a Better Austin v. Keefe, 402 U.S. 415, 91 S.Ct. 1575 (1971): New York Times Co. v. United States, 403 U.S. 713, 91 S.Ct. 2140 (1971), and Nebraska Press Ass'n v. Stuart, 427 U.S. 539, 96 S.Ct. 2791 (1976).

[91] 491 U.S. 524, 109 S.Ct. 2603 (1989), 16 Med.L.Rptr. 1801.

[92] Florida Stat. § 794.03, quoted in Ibid.

[93] 491 U.S. at 529, 109 S.Ct. at 2607 (1989), 16 Med.L.Rptr. at 1803.

[94] Ibid.

By a 6–3 majority, the Supreme Court held for the newspaper. Justice Thurgood Marshall's opinion cautiously announced the judgment of the Court: It was carefully confined to the specific fact situation. The Court again avoided deciding the important constitutional issue of whether the press can ever have criminal responsibility or civil liability for publishing a truthful but privacy-invading story.[95] Note also that this decision did not declare unconstitutional the Florida statute making it a crime to publish a rape victim's name.[96]

Justice Marshall turned to Smith v. Daily Mail (1979), discussed above, for his rationale in The Florida Star case, invoking the application of "limited principles that sweep no more broadly than the appropriate context of the instant case:" The Smith v. Daily Mail formulation, Justice Marshall wrote, protects only publication of information which a news medium has

> * * * "lawfully obtained," 443 U.S., at 203. . . . To the extent sensitive information rests in private hands, the government may under some circumstances forbid its nonconsensual acquisition . . . [and publication] * * * To the extent sensitive information is in the government's custody, it has even greater power to forestall or mitigate the injury caused by its release. * * * Where information is entrusted to the government, a less drastic means than punishing truthful publication almost always exists for guarding dissemination of private facts. . . .
>
>   * * *
>
> A third and final consideration is the "timidity and self-censorship" which may result from allowing the media to be punished for publishing certain truthful information. * * *
>
> Applied to the instant case, the *Daily Mail* principle clearly commands reversal. The first inquiry is whether the newspaper "lawfully obtained truthful information about a matter of public significance. 443 U.S. at 103. It is indisputed that the news article describing the assault on B.J.F. was accurate. In addition, appellant [the newspaper] lawfully obtained B.J.F.'s name. * * *

Some of Justice Marshall's words suggested that the Court *might* be willing to look favorably upon publication of truthful information if the statute were narrowly drawn. But where

[95] 491 U.S. at 529, 109 S.Ct. at 2607 (1989), 16 Med.L.Rptr. at 1804.

[96] 491 U.S. at 533–536, 109 S.Ct. at 2609–2610 (1989), 16 Med.L.Rptr. at 1805–1806.

government "has failed to police itself in disseminating information," imposition of damages against the media cannot stand.[97]

Justice Marshall was explicit about his cautious approach to this topic: [98]

> Our holding today is limited. We do not hold that truthful publication is automatically constitutionally protected, or that there is no zone of personal privacy within which the State may protect the individual from intrusion by the press, or even that a State may never punish publication of the name of a victim of a sexual offense. We hold only that where a newspaper publishes truthful information which it has lawfully obtained, punishment may be imposed, if at all, only when narrowly tailored to a state interest of the highest order, and that no such interest is satisfactorily served by imposing liability under Florida statute Sec. 794.03 * * * under the facts of this case.

In a concurring opinion, Justice Scalia said the Florida statute to protect rape victims applied only to the press, and not to gossip and non-media dissemination. "This law has every appearance of a prohibition that society is prepared to impose upon the press but not upon itself: [99]

In dissent, Justice White complained bitterly that for B.J.F. " * * * the violation she suffered at a rapist's knife point marked only the beginning of her ordeal." A week later, while her assailant was still at large an account of the assault identifying B.J.F. by name was published by the newspaper. White wrote that he could not accept the conclusion that a jury award to compensate B.J.F. for harm she suffered somehow violated the First Amendment.[1] White declared that there is no public interest in publishing the names, addresses and phone numbers of the victims of crime, and none in immunizing the press from liability where the State fails in its efforts to protect a victim's privacy.[2]

Salacious details in allegations of sexual misconduct and victimization were much in the news in the fall of 1991. One case involved the televised trial of rape charges against William Kennedy Smith, nephew of Massachusetts Senator Edward Kennedy. The 30–year–old woman who brought the rape charges was identified in a grocery-store tabloid paper. Then, in a lowest-common-denominator approach to journalistic value, some establishment

[97] 491 U.S. at 536, 109 S.Ct. at 2611 (1989), 16 Med.L.Rptr. at 1806.

[98] 491 U.S. at 541, 109 S.Ct. at 2613 (1989), 16 Med.L.Reptr. at 1808–1809.

[99] Ibid.

[1] 491 U.S. at 559, 109 S.Ct. at 2614 (1989), 16 Med.L.Rptr. at 1809.

[2] 491 U.S. at 554, 109 S.Ct. at 2619 (1989), 16 Med.L.Rptr. at 183–184.

news media also identified the complainant. Yet at her trial in a Florida court, when she testified, her face was obscured by an electronically generated blue blur. William Kennedy Smith was acquitted quickly by a six-person jury, but the trial generated nation-wide distaste, and raised the question whether women will now be more reluctant to face the legal process to pursue rape charges.[3]

Since the Supreme Court of the United States ultimately makes much of the outlines of civil and criminal law through its interpretive rulings, Oklahoma Law Professor Anita Hill's charges of sexual harassment against Judge Clarence Thomas, a conservative black nominee, discomfited an all-male U.S. Senate committee. The committee was holding hearings on Judge Thomas's fitness to sit on the Supreme Court and ultimately split 7–7 on whether he should be recommended. The full Senate, by a vote of 52 to 48, confirmed President Bush's nomination.[4] As Newsweek magazine said of both the Smith rape trial and the Thomas hearings: "The televised proceedings were a horror show for anyone who set a premium on privacy."[5]

The "Social Value" Test: A California Aberration?

In decisions separated by 40 years, California courts added an element to privacy law: the existence of a public record did not necessarily serve as a defense to a lawsuit for invasion of privacy. One of the most famous—and wrong-headed—cases involving the disclosure of embarrassing private facts came in the 1931 case of Melvin v. Reid, which for many years was regarded as a leading decision in the law of privacy. Gabrielle Darley Melvin sued when a motion picture—"The Red Kimono"—was made about her life as a prostitute and her trial for murder in 1918. But Gabrielle Darley had been acquitted of the murder charge, and thereafter led a changed life: she got married, found many friends who were not aware of her tawdry past, and became an accepted member of society.[6]

Although the court found that a movie could be made about Mrs. Melvin's life without penalty—because the facts were part of a public record—it was found that damages could be recovered for the use of her name, both in the motion picture and in advertisements for it. Strangely, the California Supreme Court said that

[3] See, e.g., "The Trial You Won't See," Newsweek, Dec. 16, 1991, p. 21; David Margolick, "Smith Acquitted of Rape Charge After Brief Deliberation by Jury," The New York Times, Dec. 12, 1991.

[4] See, e.g., "Dividing Lines" and following articles, Newsweek, Oct. 28, 1991, pp. 24–33.

[5] "Sex Crimes: Women On Trial," Newsweek, Dec. 16, 1991, p. 22.

[6] Melvin v. Reid, 112 Cal.App. 285, 297 P. 91 (1931).

privacy as a tort action did not then (in 1931) exist in California. However, Justice Marks found provisions in the California state constitution, such as Section 1, Article I: "men are by nature free * * * and have certain inalienable rights, among which are pursuing and obtaining safety and happiness."[7]

So it was that Mrs. Melvin won her lawsuit, even though Justice Marks denied the existence of the tort of invasion of privacy in California. One especially curious thing about Melvin v. Reid is that the California Supreme Court gave little heed to the qualified privilege attached to reports made from public records. But then, in 1931, a movie such as "The Red Kimono" was not believed to be a defensible part of "the press" which is protected by the First Amendment.[8] The court suggested strongly that if the motion picture company had used only those aspects of Gabrielle Darley's life which were in the trial record or public record of her case, then the film would have been privileged. Even so, Gabrielle Darley's name surely was part of the public record and it would seem that using it should have been "privileged."

In 1968, *Readers Digest* magazine published an article titled "The Big Business of Hijacking," describing various truck thefts and the efforts being made to stop such thefts. Dates ranging from 1965 to the time of publication were mentioned throughout the article, but none of the hijackings mentioned had a date attached to it in the text.[9]

One sentence in the article said: "Typical of many beginners, Marvin Briscoe and [another man] stole a 'valuable-looking' truck in Danville, Ky. and then fought a gun battle with the local police, only to learn that they had hijacked four bowling-pin spotters."

There was nothing in the article to indicate that the hijacking had occurred in 1956, some 11 years before the publication of the *Reader's Digest* article. In the words of the California Supreme Court, "As a result of defendant's [Reader's Digest's] publication, plaintiff's 11-year-old daughter, as well as his friends, for the first time learned of the incident. They thereafter scorned and aban-

---

[7] This was indeed a curious reading of the state's constitution. Usually, constitutions or bills of rights are seen as protecting individuals from the actions and powers of governments, rather than establishing protection against the actions of other individuals. See Pember, Privacy and the Press, p. 98.

[8] For years, courts were reluctant to accord First Amendment protection to motion pictures. See, e.g., Mutual Film Corp. v. Industrial Commission of Ohio, 236 U.S. 230, 35 S.Ct. 387 (1915); Joseph Burstyn, Inc. v. Wilson, 343 U.S. 495, 72 S.Ct. 777 (1952) was the case which first termed movies a significant medium for the expression of ideas.

[9] Briscoe v. Reader's Digest Ass'n, 4 Cal.3d 529, 93 Cal.Rptr. 866, 868, 483 P.2d 34, 36 (1971).

doned him."[10] Briscoe argued that he had since "gone straight"
and that he had become entirely rehabilitated, and led an exemplary and honorable life, making many friends in respectable
society who were not aware of the hijacking incident in his earlier
life.

Briscoe conceded the truth of the facts published in the
Reader's Digest article, but claimed that the public disclosure of
such private facts humiliated him and exposed him to contempt
and ridicule. He conceded that the *subject* of the article might
have been "newsworthy," but contended that the use of his *name*
was not, and that *Reader's Digest* had therefore invaded his
privacy.

Writing for a unanimous California Supreme Court, Justice
Raymond E. Peters agreed with Briscoe's arguments, saying:[11]

> Plaintiff is a man whose last offense took place 11
> years before, who has paid his debt to society, who has
> friends and an 11-year-old daughter who were unaware of
> his early life—a man who has assumed a position in
> "respectable society." Ideally, his neighbors should recog-
> nize his present worth and forget his past life of shame.
> But men are not so divine as to forgive the past trespasses
> of others, and plaintiff therefore endeavored to reveal as
> little as possible of his past life. Yet, as if in some bizarre
> canyon of echoes, petitioner's past life pursues him
> through the pages of Reader's Digest, now published in 13
> languages and distributed in 100 nations, with a circula-
> tion in California alone of almost 2,000,000 copies.

> In a nation built upon the free dissemination of ideas,
> it is always difficult to declare that something may not be
> published. * * * But the rights guaranteed by the
> First Amendment do not require total abrogation of the
> right to privacy. The goals sought by each may be
> achieved with a minimum of intrusion on the other.

Although the California Supreme Court was not in a position
to award damages to Mr. Briscoe, it did send his case back to a
lower court for trial. Justice Peters declared that although there
was good reason to discuss the crime of truck hijacking in the
media, there was no reason to use Briscoe's name. A jury, in the
view of the California Supreme Court, could certainly find that
Mr. Briscoe had once again become an anonymous member of the
community.[12]

[10] Ibid.

[11] 4 Cal.3d 529, 93 Cal.Rptr. 866, 873–75, 483 P.2d 34, 41–42 (1971).

[12] 4 Cal.3d 529, 93 Cal.Rptr. 866, 875, 483 P.2d 34, 43 (1971).

Despite such sweeping language, Briscoe did not win his lawsuit. The case was removed to the U.S. District Court, Central District of California, where Judge Lawrence T. Lydick granted a summary judgment to the *Reader's Digest.* Judge Lydick concluded that the article complained of by Briscoe was newsworthy and published without [actual] malice or recklessness. Further, the judge concluded that the article disclosed no private facts about Marvin Briscoe and that it did not invade his privacy.[13]

The language of the California Supreme Court in Briscoe lingered on. Take the case of Milo Conklin, who brought suit for invasion of privacy because the *Modoc County Record* published this item under the caption, "Twenty Years Ago Today in Modoc County: MILO CONKLIN has been charged with the murder of his brother-in-law, Louis Blodgett, in Cedarville Sunday."

The statement was true. Conklin had been tried for, and convicted of, Blodgett's murder. He served a prison sentence, completed parole, remarried, fathered two children, and rehabilitated himself. Conklin, at all material times, was a resident of Cedarville, California, a hamlet of 800 in the northeast corner of California. It strains credulity to believe that a town of 800 could forget that it had a convicted murderer in its midst, but the California Court of Appeal, Third District, evidently believed that Conklin's misdeed had been, if not forgotten, at least forgiven. In any case, that court accepted Conklin's argument that his friends and acquaintances for the first time learned of his unsavory past and abandoned him.[14]

The defendant newspaper replied that the statement was privileged under a California statute which says that a privileged publication is made by [15]

> * * * a fair and true report in a public journal, of (1) a judicial, (2) legislative, or (3) other public official proceeding, or (4) of anything said in the course thereof. . . .

Although this statutory language evidently conferred a privilege to protect the *Modoc County Record* from successful suit, the

[13] Briscoe v. Reader's Digest Ass'n (C.D.Cal.1972), 1 Med.L.Rptr. 1852, 1854. This decision in favor of the magazine which was not reported in Federal Supplement, was a kind of "best kept secret;" the finding here (evidently unknown other than in the media law reporting service, Media Law Reporter) was either unnoticed or ignored by courts in deciding Forsher v. Bugliosi, 26 Cal.3d 792, 163 Cal.Rptr. 628, 608 P.2d 716 (1980) and Conklin v. Sloss, 86 Cal.App.3d 241, 150 Cal.Rptr. 121 (3d Dist.1978), 4 Med.L.Rptr. 1998.

[14] Conklin v. Sloss, 86 Cal.App.3d 241, 150 Cal.Rptr. 121 (3d Dist.1978), 4 Med.L. Rptr. 1998, 1999.

[15] West's Ann.Cal.Civil Code § 47, subs. 4.

Briscoe case surfaced again to haunt the press. A California Court of Appeal stated: [16]

> We * * * hold that the absolute privilege conferred by the Civil Code section 47, subdivision 4, applies only to publication of items that are "newsworthy" as defined in Briscoe v. Reader's Digest Association * * *.

As a result, the court held that Conklin's case should be taken to trial on the issue of whether or not publication of items of public record from 20 years before were "newsworthy," leaving the potential for a jury to tell a newspaper its business.

Some of the sting of *Briscoe* may have been lessened, however, by the California Supreme Court's 1980 decision in Forsher v. Bugliosi. Bugliosi, at one time a prosecuting attorney in the trial of Charles Manson and his "Family" for the "Tate-Labianca killings." Bugliosi was co-author of Helter-Skelter, a book purporting to be an inside view of the killings, the trial, and the Manson Family. James Forsher, who was mentioned in the book as having been on the periphery of the Manson Family's activities in a minor and non-criminal way, sued for invasion of privacy and libel. In his privacy claim, Forsher contended that there was no informational or social value in using his name in connection with retelling of past events. Justice Manual's opinion in *Forsher* limited the impact of the *Briscoe* decision to cases involving rehabilitated criminals who were harmed by publication of their criminal records.[17]

> California courts have refrained from extending the Briscoe rule to other fact situations. * * * *Briscoe* * * * [held] that "where the plaintiff is a past criminal and his name is used in a publication, the mere lapse of time may provide a basis for an invasion of privacy suit."
>
> * * *

Time Lapse

One of the problems referred to in Briscoe v. Reader's Digest Ass'n involved the so-called time lapse question.[18] How much time must pass before a person recovers from unwanted publicity, loses his or her newsworthiness, and again can be said to have regained anonymity? Take the case of William James Sidis, a person who did not seek publicity but who was found by it. In

[16] 86 Cal.App.3d 241, 150 Cal.Rptr. 121, 125 (3d Dist.1978), 4 Med.L.Rptr. 1998, 2001. See also Restatement of Torts, § 857, comment c, quoted with approval by the court at 150 Cal.Rptr. 125.

[17] Forsher v. Bugliosi, 26 Cal.3d 792, 163 Cal.Rptr. 628, 636–637, 608 P.2d 716, 724, 726 (1980).

[18] See Chief Justice Raymond E. Peters opinion, 4 Cal.3d 529, 93 Cal.Rptr. 866, 873–75, 483 P.2d 34, 41–42 (1971).

1910, Sidis was an 11-year-old mathematical prodigy who lectured to famed mathematicians. He was graduated from Harvard at 16, and received a great deal of publicity. More than 20 years after his graduation, the New Yorker Magazine—in its August 14, 1937 issue—ran a feature story about Sidis plus a cartoon, with the captions "Where Are They Now?" and "April Fool." The article told how Sidis lived in a "hall bedroom of Boston's shabby south end," working at a routine clerical job, collecting streetcar transfers and studying the history of American Indians. Sidis sued for invasion of privacy, but a United States Court of Appeals ultimately held that he could not collect damages.

The court conceded that the New Yorker had perpetrated "a ruthless exposure of a once public character, who has since sought and has now been deprived of the seclusion of private life." Even so, the lawsuit did not succeed.[19]

> * * * [W]e are not yet disposed to afford to all of the intimate details of private life an absolute immunity from the prying of the press. Everyone will agree that at some point the individual interest in obtaining information becomes dominant over the individual's desire for privacy. * * * At least we would permit limited scrutiny of the "private" life of any person who has achieved, or has had thrust upon him, the questionable and indefinable status of a "public figure." * * *
>
> * * *
>
> The article in the *New Yorker* sketched the life of an unusual personality, and it possessed considerable popular news interest.
>
> We express no comment on whether or not the newsworthiness of the matter printed will always constitute a complete defense. Revelations may be so intimate and so unwarranted in view of the victim's position as to outrage the community's notions of decency. But when focused upon public characters, truthful comments upon dress, speech, habits, and the ordinary aspects of personality will usually not transgress this line.

The court implied that the invasion of privacy must be so severe that it would cause more than minor annoyance to an hypothetical "average" or "reasonable" man of "ordinary sensibilities." William James Sidis was an unusually sensitive man, and it has been speculated that the *New Yorker* article was in large measure responsible for his early death.[20]

[19] Sidis v. F–R Pub. Corp., 113 F.2d 806 (2d Cir.1940).

[20] Prosser, "Privacy," California Law Review, Vol. 48 (1960) at p. 397.

The outcome of the Sidis case represents a general pattern. American courts usually have ruled against "time lapse" privacy lawsuits. Two post-1980 cases support that view: Underwood v. First National Bank [21] and Roshto v. Hebert.[22] In the Underwood case, Thomas G. Underwood sued the First National Bank of Blooming Prairie, Minn. In 1980, the bank published a history of its community. That history included a short summary of the first degree murder trial—and conviction—of Underwood for shooting a policeman to death. Underwood claimed that the version in the book was defamatory (that he had killed the policeman in a running gunfight, not—as said in the book— shooting him when he was down on the ground). Additionally, he argued that the "Hot News" that made him a public figure in 1952 was now "Old News," and that appropriating Underwood's name for such an old story invaded his privacy.[23] The Minnesota District Court, assuming for the sake of argument that the law of privacy has been adopted in Minnesota, nevertheless granted the bank's motion for summary judgment, halting Underwood's libel and privacy suit.[24]

In Roshto v. Hebert, the Heberts' newspaper—The Iberville South—found itself sued for invasion of privacy because of its regular "Page from our Past" feature. In 1973, this weekly newspaper reproduced the entire front page from its April 4, 1952, edition, which included an article about the cattle theft trial of three brothers, Carlysle, Alfred, and E.R. Roshto. Four years later, in 1977, the newspaper reproduced the front page of the November 14, 1952, edition, containing another article about the Roshto brothers—this time discussing their sentencing to prison after their sentences were affirmed on appeal.[25]

The Louisiana Supreme Court ruled in favor of the defendant newspapers, although giving some indications of reluctance: [26]

> Defendants were arguably insensitive or careless in reproducing a former front page for publication without checking for information that might be currently offensive to some members of the community. However, more than insensitivity or simple carelessness is required for the imposition of liability for damages when the publication is truthful, accurate and non-malicious.

[21] Underwood v. First National Bank (Minn.Dist.Ct.1982), 8 Med.L.Rptr. 1278.

[22] Roshto v. Hebert, 439 So.2d 428 (La.1983), 9 Med.L.Rptr. 2417.

[23] 8 Med.L.Rptr. 1278, 1279, 1280.

[24] Ibid., 1281. The judge noted that historically, the Minnesota Supreme Court has been reluctant to recognize the tort of invasion of privacy; it is the last holdout among the 50 states.

[25] Roshto v. Hebert, 439 So.2d 428, 429 (La.1983), 9 Med.L.Rptr. 2417, 2418.

[26] 439 So.2d 428, 432 (La.1983), 9 Med.L.Rptr. 2417, 2420.

Finally, consider the 1983 case of Doe v. Sarasota-Bradenton Television. "Jane Doe" was raped, and agreed to testify against her assailant at his upcoming trial. It was important to her that her name and photograph would not be displayed or photographed in connection with this trial.

In March, 1982, "Jane Doe" testified at the rape trial. A news team from the Sarasota-Bradenton Florida Television Company was present in the courtroom. (As noted in Chapter 15, Section 88, below, under Florida law, news cameras are allowed in that state's courtrooms.) That night, the TV station ran a video tape of the trial featuring "Jane Doe's" testimony. As the video tape ran, a newscaster identified "Jane Doe" by name to the viewing audience.[27]

"Jane Doe" sued the TV station, seeking damages under a Florida statute [28] and for common-law invasion of privacy and for intentional infliction of emotional distress. The trial court found in favor of the television station, dismissing the woman's complaint.[29]

A Florida Court of Appeal agreed that the lawsuit must be dismissed, as under Cox Broadcasting Corp. v. Cohn, a case discussed at pages 272–274 of this book.[30] The Florida District Court of Appeal said:[31]

> In Cox Broadcasting, the Supreme Court [of the U.S.] concluded that the State of Georgia could not punish a reporter and his employer for accurately publishing the name of a deceased rape victim where the information had been obtained from otherwise public judicial records. We agree with the trial court here that Cox Broadcasting controls. We conclude that the fact that the plaintiff in Cox Broadcasting was the deceased victim's father and the appellant here ["Jane Doe"] is the victim herself does not distinguish [differentiate between] the cases.

The District Court of Appeal noted that in both the Cox Broadcasting and the "Jane Doe" cases, the broadcasts complained of contained completely accurate but pain-inflicting information. The Florida court had harsh words for the TV station: [32]

---

[27] Doe v. Sarasota-Bradenton Florida Television Co., Inc., 436 So.2d 328 (Fla.App. 2d Dist.1983), 9 Med.L.Rptr. 2074.

[28] Ibid., quoting Florida Statute section 794.03.

[29] Ibid., at 329, 9 Med.L.Rptr. at 2075.

[30] 420 U.S. 469, 95 S.Ct. 1029 (1975).

[31] Doe v. Sarasota-Bradenton Florida Television Company Inc., 436 So.2d 328 (Fla.App. 2d Dist.1983), 9 Med.L.Rptr. 2074.

[32] Ibid., at 329, 9 Med.L.Rptr. at 2075–2076.

We deplore the lack of sensitivity to the rights of others that is sometimes displayed by such an unfettered exercise of first amendment rights.

* * *

The publication added little or nothing to the sordid and unhappy story; yet, that brief little-or-nothing addition may well affect appellant's [Jane Doe's] well-being for years to come.

The court chastised the prosecution—representatives of the State of Florida—"for not having sought a protective order regarding cameras in the courtroom or other proper steps to support its alleged assurance" to Jane Doe that she could testify in the rape trial without her name and picture being used. Further, the court said that it recognized the frequent conflict between freedom of the press and the right of privacy. It then urged "compassionate discretion" by the media in such situations.[33]

Virgil v. Time, Inc. (1975)

Another case encouraging recovery in a privacy lawsuit *even when a truthful report is made by the news media* is Virgil v. Time, Inc. Sports Illustrated, a Time, Inc. publication, published an article on body surfing in February, 1971. The article devoted much attention to Mike Virgil, a surfer who was well known at "The Wedge," a dangerous beach near Newport Beach, California. Sports Illustrated staff writer Curry Kirkpatrick had interviewed Virgil at length—which obviously required a kind of consent from Virgil—and Virgil had also consented to the taking of pictures by a free-lance photographer working with Kirkpatrick.

Before the article was published, another Sports Illustrated employee called Virgil's home and verified some of the information with his wife. At this point, Virgil "revoked all consent" for publication of the article and photographs and indicated that he did not want his name used in the story. Circuit Judge Merrill summarized Virgil's attempt to revoke his consent.[34]

> While not disputing the truth of the article or the accuracy of the statements about him which it contained, and while admitting that he had known that his picture was being taken, the plaintiff indicated that he thought the article was going to be limited to his prominence as a surfer at The Wedge, and that he did not know that it would contain references to some rather bizarre incidents in his life that were not directly related to surfing.

[33] Ibid., at 330, 9 Med.L.Rptr. at 2076, 2077.

[34] Virgil v. Time, Inc., 527 F.2d 1122, 1124 (9th Cir.1975).

It can be objected that Judge Merrill was placing himself in the editor's chair: is it for a *judge* to say whether some of the "bizarre incidents" in Virgil's life are "not directly related to surfing?" If a person persists in body-surfing at a place known as one of earth's most dangerous beaches, might not some of his other actions—such as extinguishing a cigarette in his mouth, or diving down a flight of stairs because "there were all these chicks around"—illustrate an unusually reckless (and therefore news-worthy?) approach to life? [35]

It was argued for the magazine—which had proceeded, on advice of counsel, to publish the article even after Virgil "re-voked" his consent—that Virgil had voluntarily made public the facts he complained about. Judge Merrill disagreed, in words which frightened reporters and editors: [36]

> Talking freely to a member of the press, knowing the listener to be a member of the press, is not then in itself making public. Such communication can be said to antic-ipate that what is said will be made public since making public is the function of the press, and accordingly such communication can be construed as a consent to publicize. Thus if publicity results it can be said to have been consented to. However, if consent is withdrawn prior to the act of publicization, the consequent publicity is with-out consent.

> We conclude that the voluntary disclosure to Kirkpat-rick did not in itself constitute a making public of the facts disclosed.

Judge Merrill paid particular attention to the Restatement, Second, Torts § 652D (Tentative Draft No. 21, 1975), saying that unless a subject is newsworthy, the publicizing of private facts is not protected by the First Amendment. [37] He then quoted a comment from the Restatement of Torts, Second: [38]

> "In determining what is a matter of legitimate public interest, account must be taken of the customs and con-ventions of the community; and in the last analysis what is proper becomes a matter of the community mores. The line is to be drawn when the publicity ceases to be the giving of information to which the public is entitled, and becomes a morbid and sensational prying into public lives for its own sake. . . ."

[35] Ibid., p. 1125n, quoting the Sports Illustrated article.

[36] Ibid., p. 1127.

[37] Ibid., p. 1128.

[38] Restatement quoted in Ibid., pp. 1129, 1129n.

The prestigious Restatement of Torts, Second described the elements of a lawsuit for publication of embarrassing private facts in a way which has encouraged judges to "play editor." [39]

One who gives publicity to a matter concerning the private life of another is subject to liability to the other for invasion of privacy, if the matter publicized is of a kind that

    (a) would be highly offensive to a reasonable person and

    (b) is not of legitimate concern to the public.

In an action which startled constitutional lawyers, the Supreme Court refused to review the Court of Appeals decision in *Virgil*.[40] This meant that the *Virgil* case went back to the District [trial] Court, which decided—fortunately for Sports Illustrated—that the article about Virgil was "newsworthy." [41] But was this a victory for the magazine? Constitutional law specialists Alan U. Schwartz and Floyd Abrams said otherwise. Schwartz complained, "Under this formula truth becomes immaterial. The test is whether community mores (and *what* community? one may ask) have been offended. The peril to the journalist is extreme." [42] Abrams declared, "the test set forth by the Court in the Virgil case contains language so broad ('morbid and sensational prying'), so open-ended ('a reasonable member of the public') and so subjective ('decent standards') that it makes it all but impossible to determine in advance what may be published and what not." [43]

Campbell v. Seabury Press (1980)

Private facts—sometimes termed the "truthful tort" area—were also at issue in Campbell v. Seabury Press. Civil rights leader Will D. Campbell wrote his autobiography, Brother to a Dragonfly, which included an account of his deceased brother, Joe. Campbell wrote about his brother's addiction to drugs and the effects of that addiction on his personality, his family life, and on Will Campbell himself. Carlyne Campbell, Joe's first wife, sued for defamation and invasion of privacy, complaining about the book's portrayal of her marital relationship with Joe Campbell.

[39] Restatement, Second, Torts, § 652D.

[40] Virgil v. Time, Inc., 527 F.2d 1122, 1130–1132 (9th Cir.1975), certiorari denied 425 U.S. 998, 96 S.Ct. 2215 (1976). Justices Brennan and Stewart said they would have granted certiorari.

[41] Floyd Abrams, "The Press, Privacy and the Constitution," New York Times Magazine, August 21, 1977, pp. 11ff, at p. 13; Virgil v. Sports Illustrated, 424 F.Supp. 1286 (S.D.Cal.1976).

[42] Schwartz, op.cit., p. 32.

[43] Abrams, op.cit., pp. 13, 65.

Seabury Press was granted a summary judgment by the U.S. District Court on grounds that a public interest privilege under the first Amendment protected such disclosures.[44]

Carlyne Campbell appealed, arguing that her lawsuit should not be dismissed because there was no logical connection between the matters of legitimate public interest and her home life with Joe Campbell. The Court of Appeals for the Fifth Circuit upheld the dismissal of her case, and articulated a constitutional rationale favorable to the news media. In a per curiam opinion, Circuit Judges Charles Clark, Robert S. Vance, and Sam D. Johnson wrote: [45]

> The first amendment mandates a constitutional privilege applicable to those torts of invasion of privacy that involve publicity. See Cox Broadcasting Corp. v. Cohn, * * * This broad constitutional privilege recognizes two closely related yet analytically distinct privileges. First is the privilege to publish or broadcast facts, events, and information relating to public figures. Second is the privilege to publish or broadcast news or other matters of public interest. See Smith v. Doss, 251 Ala. 250, 253, 37 So.2d 118, 120 (1948). * * * [This news privilege] is not merely limited to the dissemination of news either in the sense of current events or commentary upon public affairs. Rather, the privilege extends to information concerning interesting phases of human activity and embraces all issues about which information is needed or appropriate so that individuals may cope with the exigencies of their period.

As privacy and media law expert Harvey Zuckman has noted, because of the Fifth Circuit's "liberal outlook on the newsworthiness or public interest privilege, counsel for your newspapers may wish to consider attempting removal of private fact and even 'false light' cases from state courts where they are usually filed to the local United States District Court. If that court is located in Florida, Georgia, Alabama, Mississippi, Louisiana or Texas, it will be governed by the law of the *Campbell* case." [46]

[44] Campbell v. Seabury Press, 614 F.2d 395 (5th Cir.1980), 5 Med.L.Rptr. 1829.

[45] 614 F.2d 395, 396 (5th Cir.1980), 5 Med.L.Rptr. 1829, 1803.

[46] Harvey Zuckman, "The Right of Privacy and the Press," talk at Southern Newspaper Publishers Association seminar, The University of Texas–Austin, Oct. 13, 1980.

SEC. 40. FALSE PUBLICATIONS WHICH INVADE PRIVACY

Putting a person in a false position before the public has proven costly for many publications.

A third sub-area of privacy law, "putting plaintiff in a false position in the public eye," is one which holds great dangers of lawsuits for the mass media. The first invasion of privacy case dealing with the mass media to be decided by the Supreme Court of the United States involved a "false position in the public eye." [47]

This branch of privacy law has roots which go back to an outraged English poet, Lord Byron, who successfully sued to prevent the publication of inferior poems under Lord Byron's name.[48] In more recent years, the media—or people who use the media—have misrepresented the views of other people at their peril.

The old saying that "photographs don't lie" is perhaps true most of the time, but photos—and especially their captions—must be carefully watched by editors. Pictures which would give, or are used in such a way that they give, a misleading impression of a person's character are especially dangerous. The *Saturday Evening Post* was stung by a privacy lawsuit in Peay v. Curtis Publishing Co. The magazine published an article about Washington, D.C., taxicab drivers titled "Never Give a Passenger an Even Break." The court noted that this article painted the city's drivers as "ill mannered, brazen, and contemptuous of their patrons * * * dishonest and cheating when opportunity arises." [49] The *Saturday Evening Post's* article was worth money to cabdriver Muriel Peay, whose picture had been used, without her permission, to illustrate the article.

The Curtis Publishing Company lost another invasion of privacy lawsuit only three years later, and the cause was again careless use of a picture. Back in 1947, ten-year-old Eleanor Sue Leverton was knocked down by a careless motorist. A news photographer snapped a picture of a woman helping the little girl to her feet. This photo was published in a Birmingham, Ala.,

---

[47] Time, Inc. v. Hill, 385 U.S. 374, 87 S.Ct. 534 (1967). It should be noted that this third area of privacy overlaps a fourth area discussed later in this chapter, "appropriation of some element of plaintiff's personality for commercial use." This overlapping is especially apparent in cases involving spurious testimonials in advertisements. See, e.g., Flake v. Greensboro News Co., 212 N.C. 780, 195 S.E. 55 (1938) where a woman's picture was placed, by mistake, in an advertisement; Fairfield v. American Photocopy Equipment Co., 138 Cal.App.2d 82, 291 P.2d 194 (1955).

[48] Lord Byron v. Johnston, 2 Mer. 29, 35 Eng.Rep. 851 (Chancery 1816).

[49] Peay v. Curtis Pub. Co., 78 F.Supp. 305 (D.D.C.1948); Fowler v. Curtis Pub. Co., 78 F.Supp. 303, 304 (D.D.C.1948).

newspaper. To this point, there was no action for invasion of privacy possible for young Miss Leverton.

But 20 months after the little girl was hit by the car, the *Saturday Evening Post* used her picture to illustrate an article headlined "They Ask to Be Killed." The little girl's picture was captioned, "Safety education in schools has reduced child accidents measurably, but unpredictable darting through traffic still takes its sobering toll." In a box next to the headline, these words appeared: "Do you invite massacre by your own carelessness? Here's how to keep them alive." A Federal Court of Appeals said.[50]

> The sum total of all this is that this particular plain-tiff, the legitimate subject for publicity for one particular accident, now becomes a pictorial, frightful example of pedestrian carelessness. This, we think, exceeds the bounds of privilege.

The lesson for photo-editors should be plain: if a picture is not taken in a public place or if that picture—or its caption—places someone in a false light, don't use it. The exception, of course, would be when you have received permission, in the form of a signed release, from the persons pictured. Two invasion of privacy lawsuits by Mr. and Mrs. John W. Gill, one successful and one not, illustrate the point rather neatly.

Mr. and Mrs. Gill were seated on stools at a confectionery stand which they operated at the Farmer's Market in Los Angeles. Famed photographer Henri Cartier-Bresson took a picture of the Gills, as Mr. Gill sat with his arm around his wife. The photograph was used in *Harper's Bazaar* to illustrate an article titled "And So the World Goes Around," a brief commentary having to do with the poetic notion that love makes the world go 'round. Although the Gills sued, they failed to collect from the Hearst Corporation, publisher of the magazine. The court held that the Gills had no right to collect since they took that voluntary pose in public and because there was nothing uncomplimentary about the photograph itself.[51]

Although they couldn't collect from the Hearst Corporation for invasion of privacy, Mr. and Mrs. Gill already had won damages from the Curtis Publishing Company. The *Ladies Home Journal,* a Curtis publication, had printed the very same photograph taken at the Farmer's Market but had made that photo an invasion of privacy by using faulty captions. The *Journal* used the Gills' picture to illustrate an article titled "Love." Under-neath the picture was this caption "Publicized as glamourous,

[50] Leverton v. Curtis Pub. Co., 192 F.2d 974 (3d Cir.1951).

[51] Gill v. Hearst Pub. Co., 40 Cal.2d 224, 253 P.2d 441 (1953).

desirable, 'love at first sight' is a bad risk." The story termed such love "100% sex attraction" and the "wrong" kind. The court held that the article implied that this husband and wife were "persons whose only interest in each other is sex, a characterization that may be said to impinge seriously upon their sensibilities." [52]

Context Providing a "False Light"

A 1984 Texas case suggests that the context in which something is published can cause lawsuits for defamation or for invasion of privacy. Jeannie Braun, trainer of "Ralph the Diving Pig" at Aquarena Springs Resort, San Marcos, Texas, took violent exception to having her picture displayed in Chic, a Larry Flynt-published magazine specializing in female nudity and photos and cartoons of an overtly sexual nature.

Part of Mrs. Braun's job at Aquarena Springs was to tread water while holding out a baby bottle of milk. Ralph the pig would then dive into the pool and feed from the bottle. Pictures and postcards were made of Ralph diving toward Mrs. Braun. Mrs. Braun had signed a release saying the picture could be used for advertising and publicity as long as the photo was used in good taste, without embarrassment to her and her family.

Once the picture appeared in Chic—surrounded by pictures and cartoons full of sexual content (captions on other items included "Lust Rock Rules" and "Chinese Organ Grinder")—Mrs. Braun sued for a total of $1.1 million for defamation and invasion of privacy. After ruling that Mrs. Braun was a private individual, the Court of Appeals for the Fifth Circuit took issue with the trial court's damage awards totaling $95,000. That figure represented defamation damages ($5,000 actual and $25,000 punitive) and false light privacy damages ($15,000 actual and $50,000 punitive). The appeals court said that as a matter of public policy, punitive damages should not be awarded in one case for both defamation and false-light privacy invasion. Therefore, the appeals court said that only the damages assessed for invasion of privacy—$65,000—should be awarded. [53]

Duncan v. WJLA–TV

The "false light" area of law is so close to libel that—with evidently increasing frequency—people sue for both invasion of privacy and defamation. Take the case of Duncan v. WJLA–TV (1984), which illustrated, once again, that incautious picture cap-

---

[52] Gill v. Curtis Pub. Co., 38 Cal.2d 273, 239 P.2d 630 (1952).

[53] Braun v. Flynt, 726 F.2d 245, 258 (5th Cir.1984), 10 Med.L.Rptr. 1497, 1498, 1499, 1507–1508.

tioning (or the television equivalent, "voice-overs") has its perils. A young woman named Linda K. Duncan was standing on a street corner in Washington, D.C. Meanwhile, WJLA–TV was shooting a "journalist-in-the-street" format story featuring reporter Betsy Ashton.

WJLA–TV broadcast two versions of a news story based on this videotaping of Ms. Ashton. For the 6 p.m. newscast, the camera was aimed down K street and focused on pedestrians on the corner behind reporter Ashton. The camera zeroed in on Linda Duncan, as she faced toward the camera and could be seen clearly. Then, the camera shifted back to reporter Ashton, who talked about her story, a new treatment for genital herpes.[54]

For the 11 p.m. newscast, a substantial amount of editing was done. Instead of the street scene including reporter Betsy Ashton in the foreground, reliance was placed on a "voice-over" as spoken by news anchor David Schoumacher. For the 11 p.m. version, Ms. Duncan was seen turning into the camera, and then pausing. As she did so, Schoumacher intoned: "For the twenty million Americans who have herpes, it's not a cure." The 11 p.m. version of the story concluded with Ms. Duncan turning away and walking off down the street.[55]

A United States District Court ruled that the 6 p.m. broadcast was neither defamatory nor a false light invasion of privacy—as far as the 6 p.m. broadcast was concerned. The earlier broadcast was said to provide sufficient context for viewers not to associate the subject matter of the news story with Ms. Duncan. The court said, however, that the 11 p.m. newscast presented different questions and should be submitted to a jury for consideration.[56] Ms. Duncan won a small damage award from WJLA–TV.

Fictionalization

The misuse of pictures or photographs is one way to get involved in a privacy lawsuit. So is *fictionalization*. Fictionalization, as used by the courts, involves more than mere incidental falsity. Fictionalization appears to mean the deliberate or reckless addition of untrue material, perhaps for entertainment purposes or to make a good story better. Although the courts' rules for determining fictionalization are by no means clear, journalists should be warned to look to their ethics and accuracy. "Hyping" or "sensationalizing" a story by adding untrue materials so that a false impression is created concerning the subject of the story may be actionable.

[54] Duncan v. WJLA–TV, Inc., 10 Med.L.Rptr. 1395, 1398.

[55] Ibid.

[56] Ibid.

Triangle Publications, which produced magazines such as *Timely Detective Cases* and *Uncensored Detective,* lost a privacy suit because of fictionalization. Robert H. Garner and Grace M. Smith had become legitimate objects of news interest because they were on trial for the murder of her husband. Mr. Garner and Mrs. Smith were convicted of the murder. Meanwhile, magazines published by Triangle carried numerous articles about the crime, adding some untrue elements to their stories. The magazines claimed that Mr. Garner and Mrs. Smith had had "improper relations with each other." However, after the detective magazines had published their stories, the convictions of Mr. Garner and Mrs. Smith were reversed.

A Federal District Court held that there could be no liability for presenting news about a matter of public interest such as a murder trial. However, Triangle Publications could be liable for a privacy lawsuit because when the magazines [57]

> enlarged upon the facts so as to go beyond the bounds of propriety and decency, they should not be cloaked with and shielded by the public interest in dissemination of "information." * * *

It appears, however, that minor errors in fact will not be sufficient to defeat the defense of newsworthiness, which will be discussed later. In the first media-related privacy case to reach the Supreme Court of the United States, it was held that Constitutional protections for speech and press forbid recovery for false reports "in the absence of proof that the defendant published the report with knowledge of its falsity or in reckless disregard of the truth." [58]

Another lawsuit for fictionalization involved the famed Warren Spahn, the left-handed pitcher who won more than 300 games during a long career with the Boston—and later the Milwaukee—Braves. Spahn was a hero to many baseball card collectors in the 1950s and early 1960s, and some people wanted to cash in on "Spahnie's" success. Writer Milton J. Shapiro and publisher Julian Messner, Inc., brought out a book titled *The Warren Spahn Story,* aimed at a juvenile audience. Throughout this book, Spahn's feats were exaggerated. For one thing, Spahn was portrayed as a war hero, which he was not. An elbow injury finally brought an end to Spahn's career; author Shapiro consistently wrote about Spahn's "shoulder injury." Such inaccuracies were

---

[57] Garner v. Triangle Publications, Inc., 97 F.Supp. 546, 550 (S.D.N.Y.1951). For similar holdings, see Hazlitt v. Fawcett Publications, Inc., 116 F.Supp. 538 (D.Conn. 1953); Reed v. Real Detective Pub. Co., 63 Ariz. 294, 162 P.2d 133 (1945).

[58] Time, Inc. v. Hill, 385 U.S. 374, 388, 87 S.Ct. 534, 542 (1967). See also Binns v. Vitagraph Corp. of America, 210 N.Y. 51, 103 N.E. 1108 (1913); Stryker v. Republic Pictures Corp., 108 Cal.App.2d 191, 238 P.2d 670 (1951).

topped off by page after page of fictional dialogue—words attributed to Spahn and his associates but which had been invented by author Shapiro.[59]

Shapiro and Julian Messner, Inc. argued strenuously that Spahn was a public figure who enjoyed no right to privacy.[60] Justice Charles Breitel of the Appellate Division, New York Supreme Court disagreed with contentions that Spahn no longer possessed a right of privacy, and said the fact that the fictionalization was laudatory was immaterial.[61]

If, indeed, writers cannot suppress the impulse to fictionalize, they would be more likely to avoid a lawsuit if they do not use the names of actual people involved in an event upon which they base their fictionalization. Where there is no identification, courts will not be able to find for the plaintiffs.[62] But where there is both identification and fictionalization, the publisher is in danger of losing a suit.[63]

Cantrell v. Forest City Publishing Co. (1974)

Major fact errors—or large swatches of fictionalizing—in something purporting to be a news story—can mean serious difficulty for the news media. Consider the case known as Cantrell v. Forest City Publishing Company. Mrs. Margaret Mae Cantrell and her son sued the company for an article which appeared in the Cleveland Plain Dealer in August of 1968, claiming that the article placed her and her family in a false light.

The facts underlying the lawsuit were these: In December, 1967, Mrs. Cantrell's husband was killed—along with 43 other persons—when the Silver Bridge across the Ohio River at Point Pleasant, W.Va., collapsed. Cleveland *Plain Dealer* reporter Joseph Eszterhas had covered the disaster and he wrote a news feature on Mr. Cantrell's funeral. Five months later, Eszterhas and photographer Richard Conway returned to Point Pleasant and went to the Cantrell residence. Mrs. Cantrell was not there, so Eszterhas talked to the Cantrell children and photographer Con-

---

[59] Spahn v. Julian Messner, Inc., 43 Misc.2d 219, 230–232, 250 N.Y.S.2d 529, 540–542 (1964).

[60] See Time, Inc. v. Hill, 385 U.S. 374, 87 S.Ct. 534 (1967).

[61] 23 A.D.2d 216, 221, 260 N.Y.S.2d 451, 456 (1965).

[62] Bernstein v. NBC, 129 F.Supp. 817 (D.D.C.), affirmed 98 U.S.App.D.C. 112, 232 F.2d 369 (1956); Smith v. NBC, 138 Cal.App.2d 807, 292 P.2d 600 (1956).

[63] Mau v. Rio Grande Oil Co., 28 F.Supp. 845 (N.D.Cal.1939); Garner v. Triangle Publications, Inc., 97 F.Supp. 546 (S.D.N.Y.1951). But see Leopold v. Levin, 45 Ill.2d 434, 259 N.E.2d 250 (1970), where a fictional treatment of Nathan Leopold's participation in the famed 1924 murder of Bobby Franks was declared to be protected by the First Amendment despite the addition of fictional embellishments.

way took 50 pictures. Eszterhas' story appeared as the lead article in the August 4, 1968, edition of the *Plain Dealer's* Sunday magazine.

The article emphasized the children's old, ill-fitting clothes and the poor condition of the Cantrell home. The Cantrell family was used in the story to sum up the impact of the bridge collapse on the lives of people in the Point Pleasant area. Even though Mrs. Cantrell had not been present during Eszterhas' visit to her home, he wrote: [64]

> "Margaret Cantrell will talk neither about what happened nor about how they are doing. She wears the same mask of non-expression she wore at the funeral. She is a proud woman. She says that after it happened, the people in town offered to help them out with money and they refused to take it."

In a ruling that Mrs. Cantrell should be allowed to collect the $60,000 awarded by a U.S. District Court jury, the Supreme Court said: [65]

> * * * the District Judge was clearly correct in believing that the evidence introduced at trial was sufficient to support a jury finding that the respondents Joseph Eszterhas and Forest City Publishing Company had published knowing or reckless falsehoods about the Cantrells. There was no dispute during the trial that Eszterhas, who did not testify, must have known that a number of the statements in the feature story were untrue. In particular, his article plainly implied that Mrs. Cantrell had been present during his visit to her home and that Eszterhas had observed her "wear[ing] the same mask of non-expression she wore [at her husband's] funeral." These were "calculated falsehoods," and the jury was plainly justified in finding that Eszterhas had portrayed the Cantrells in a false light through knowing or reckless untruth.

Bindrim v. Mitchell

The flip side of a journalist lapsing into fiction is a person who purports to write a novel with a story line which parallels too closely to actual persons and events. In point here is the case of Bindrim v. Mitchell. Although it was a libel action, the plaintiff—Paul Bindrim, Ph.D., a licensed clinical psychologist—could just as well have sued for invasion of privacy under the false light theory.

[64] 419 U.S. 245 at 248, 95 S.Ct. 465 at 468 (1974), quoting Eszterhas, "Legacy of the Silver Bridge," The Plain Dealer Sunday Magazine, Aug. 4, 1968, p. 32, col. 1.

[65] 419 U.S. 245, 253, 95 S.Ct. 465, 470–471 (1974).

Dr. Bindrim used the so-called "Nude Marathon" in group therapy in order to help people shed their psychological inhibitions along with the removal of their clothes. And then a novelist showed up and wanted to join his nude encounter group.[66]

Gwen Davis Mitchell had written a best-selling novel in 1969, and then set about writing a novel about women of the leisure class. When she asked to register in Dr. Bindrim's therapy group, he told her she could not come into the group if she planned to write about it in a novel. Bare-facedly, she said she would attend the sessions for therapeutic reasons and had no intention of writing about the group. Dr. Bindrim then brought to her attention a written contract, which included this language: [67]

> "The participant agrees that he will not take photographs, write articles, or in any manner disclose who has attended the workshop or what has transpired. If he fails to do so he releases all parties from this contract, but remains legally liable for damages sustained by the leaders and participants."

Ms. Mitchell reassured Dr. Bindrim that she would not write about the session, paid her money, signed the contract, and attended the nude marathon. Two months later, she entered into a contract with Doubleday publishers and was to receive $150,000 in advance royalties for her novel, which was subsequently published under the name "Touching." It depicted a nude encounter session in Southern California led by "Dr. Simon Herford." The fictional Dr. Herford was described in the novel as a *psychiatrist,* " 'a fat Santa Claus type with long white hair, white sideburns, a cherubic rosy face and rosy forearms.' "

Dr. Bindrim, on the other hand, a psychologist, was clean shaven and had short hair. He alleged that he had been libeled, because dialogue in the novel set in encounter groups included some sexually explicit language which tapes of actual sessions run by Dr. Bindrim did not contain. As a therapist, the psychologist did not use such insulting and vulgar language.[68]

Despite these differences—and perhaps in part because author Mitchell had actually attended Dr. Bindrim's therapy group—it was held that there were sufficient similarities between the fictional Dr. Herford and the real Dr. Bindrim for identification to have taken place. Also, the situation was not improved for the author because she had signed the contract not to write about the sessions. Doubleday and Ms. Mitchell were ordered to pay dam-

---

[66] Bindrim v. Mitchell, 92 Cal.App.3d 61, 69, 155 Cal.Rptr. 29, 33 (1979), 5 Med.L. Rptr. 1113, certiorari denied 444 U.S. 984, 100 S.Ct. 490 (1979).

[67] 92 Cal.App.3d 61, 69, 155 Cal.Rptr. 29, 33 (1979).

[68] 92 Cal.App.3d 61, 70, 75, 155 Cal.Rptr. 29, 34, 37 (1979).

ages totaling $75,000. This case thus hangs out a warning against slipshod disguising of fictional characters who are based on real, live persons.[69]

SEC. 41. APPROPRIATION OF PLAINTIFF'S NAME OR LIKENESS

The appropriation or "taking" of some element of a person's personality for commercial or other advantage has been a source of many privacy lawsuits.

Often, careless use of a person's name or likeness will be the misstep which results in a privacy action. The first widely known privacy cases, Roberson v. Rochester Folding Box Co.[70] and Pavesich v. New England Life Ins. Co.,[71] both discussed earlier in this chapter, turned on taking a person's name or picture for advertising purposes.

The use of a name, by itself, is not enough to bring about a successful lawsuit. For example, a company could publish an advertisement for its breakfast cereal and say that the cereal "gave Fred Brown his tennis-playing energy." There are, of course, many Fred Browns in the nation. However, should the cereal company, without explicit permission, identify a *particular* individual—such as "Olympic High Hurdle Champion Fred Brown"—then Mr. Brown, the hurdler, would have an action for invasion of privacy. Thus a *name* can be used, as long as a person's *identity* is not somehow appropriated.

A good example of this point is a suit which was brought by a Joseph Angelo Maggio, who claimed that the use of a name— "Angelo Maggio"—in James Jones' best-selling novel, *From Here to Eternity,* invaded his privacy. The court ruled, however, that although the name was the same as that of the plaintiff, the plaintiff's *identity* had not been taken. The fictional "Angelo Maggio" was held not to be the same individual as Joseph Angelo Maggio.[72]

Persons who use the media should develop a kind of self-protective pessimism: it should always be assumed that if something could go wrong and result in a lawsuit, it might indeed go wrong. This is, of course, an almost paranoid approach, but it can help to avoid much grief. Take, for example, the case of Kerby v.

---

[69] 92 Cal.App.3d 61, 82–83, 155 Cal.Rptr. 29, 41 (1979).

[70] 171 N.Y. 538, 64 N.E. 442 (1902).

[71] 122 Ga. 190, 50 S.E. 68 (1905).

[72] People on Complaint of Maggio v. Charles Scribner's Sons, 205 Misc. 818, 130 N.Y.S.2d 514 (1954). See also, Uproar Co. v. National Broadcasting Co., 8 F.Supp. 358 (D.C.Mass.1934), affirmed 81 F.2d 373 (1st Cir.1936); Nebb v. Bell Syndicate, 41 F.Supp. 929 (S.D.N.Y.1941).

Hal Roach Studios, Inc., where a simple failure to check as obvious a reference as a telephone directory led to a lost lawsuit. A publicity gimmick boosting one of the *Topper* movies involved the studio's sending out 100 perfumed letters to men in the Los Angeles area. These gushy letters were signed: [73]

> Fondly,
>
> Your ectoplasmic playmate,
>
> Marion Kerby.

Marion Kerby was the name of one of the characters—a female ghost—portrayed in the movie. Unfortunately for the Hal Roach Studios, there was a real-life Marion Kerby in Los Angeles, an actress and public speaker. She was the only one listed in the Los Angeles telephone directory. Miss Kerby, after being annoyed by numerous phone calls and a personal visit, sued for invasion of privacy, and ultimately collected.[74]

Sometimes the out-and-out use of a person's name or likeness *is* permissible in an advertisement—*if* a court decides that the use of the name or likeness is "incidental." Take Academy Award and Emmy Award-winning actress Shirley Booth, who was vacationing in Jamaica some years ago. A *Holiday* magazine photographer asked, and received, permission to take her picture, and that picture was later used in a *Holiday* feature story about Jamaica's Round Hill resort. Several months later, however, the same picture appeared in full-page promotional advertisements for *Holiday* in *Advertising Age* and *New Yorker* magazines. Beneath the picture of the actress were the words "Shirley Booth and Chapeau, from a recent issue of *Holiday*." [75]

Miss Booth sued *Holiday's* publisher, the Curtis Publishing Co., in New York, claiming invasion of privacy on the ground that *Holiday's* advertising use of that picture was impermissible. New York's privacy statute, after all, prohibits use of a person's name or likeness "for purposes of trade" unless the person involved has given consent.[76] Curtis Publishing responded that this sort of promotional advertising was needed to help magazine sales, thus supporting the public's interest in news.[77]

Miss Booth won $17,500 at the trial level, but that finding was reversed on appeal. Finding for the Curtis Publishing Co., Justice, Charles D. Breitel termed *Holiday's* advertising use of the picture

---

[73] Kerby v. Hal Roach Studios, Inc., 53 Cal.App.2d 207, 127 P.2d 577, 578 (1942).

[74] Ibid., at 578. It should be noted that this case is also a good example of the privacy tort category called "false position in the public eye."

[75] Booth v. Curtis Pub. Co., 15 A.D.2d 343, 223 N.Y.S.2d 737 (1962).

[76] Sections 50–51, New York Civil Rights Law, McKinney's Consolidated Laws, Ch. 6. See 15 A.D.2d 343, 223 N.Y.S.2d 737, at 739 (1962).

[77] Booth v. Curtis Pub. Co., 15 A.D.2d 343, 349, 223 N.Y.S.2d 737, 743–744 (1962).

"incidental," and therefore not prohibited by New York's privacy statute.[78]

As Victor A. Kovner has pointed out, there has been a growing number of misappropriation claims founded on unauthorized use of a person's photograph or likeness, in articles and on covers of magazines and books. "[T]he general rule," Kovner said, "is that a picture reasonably related to an article or book on a matter of public interest will not be actionable." [79]

A case in point is Arrington v. New York Times, where the newspaper—without permission—ran a photograph of a young black man on the cover of its Sunday magazine section. The man's likeness was recognizable, but his name was not used. The newspaper argued that it had taken his picture to illustrate an article titled "The Black Middle Class: Making It," using his picture to illustrate upward mobility of blacks.

Use of Arrington's photo in those circumstances was held not to violate New York's Civil Rights Act, §§ 50–51, dealing with appropriation of a person's name or likeness for commercial purposes.[80]

On the other hand, unauthorized use of a black student's photograph on the cover of a book aimed at students hoping to go to college was ruled to be a violation of the New York Civil Rights Statute. Valerie Spellman was initially awarded $120,000 in compensatory damages and $250,000 in punitive damages, but an appellate court threw out all but $1,500 in compensatory damages. Note that she had given verbal consent to having her picture taken, but never gave the written consent required by the statute.[81]

The Arrington and Spellman cases are "mild" fact situations. Sexy photos or pictures which are published without permission are apt to lead to being sued and, perhaps, to being sued successfully.

The gasp-and-giggle genre of magazines continues to make problems for itself. Take, for example, the fact situations in Ali v. Playgirl. A frontally nude black boxer, his hands taped, was pictured—in something "between representational art and a cartoon"—sitting in the corner of a boxing ring. The features on the black male resembled former heavyweight boxing champion

---

[78] 11 N.Y.2d 907, 228 N.Y.S.2d 468, 182 N.E.2d 812 (1962). See also, University of Notre Dame du Lac v. Twentieth Century-Fox Film Corp., 22 A.D.2d 452, 256 N.Y.S.2d 301 (1965).

[79] Victor A. Kovner, "Privacy," in James C. Goodale, chairman, Communications Law 1987 Vol. I, p. 282.

[80] (New York Supreme Court 1980), 5 Med.L.Rptr. 2581, 2584.

[81] (New York County Civil Court 1978), 3 Med.L.Rptr. 2407, 2408.

Muhammad Ali. Ali's name was not used, but the drawing was accompanied by some doggerel referring to the figure as "the Greatest." Ali, of course, made a career out of calling himself "the Greatest" and came to be so identified in the public mind. Ali was granted a preliminary injunction to halt further circulation of the February, 1978 issue of Playgirl which contained the offensive picture.[82]

Author-playwright A.E. Hotchner's attempt to write an intimate biography of American literary giant Ernest Hemingway led to a privacy suit under the New York statute. Hemingway had died in 1961, and his widow, Mary Hemingway, sued to enjoin Random House from publishing Hotchner's manuscript. Hotchner's biography covered the Nobel laureate's life from 1948, when Hemingway and Hotchner first met in a bar in Havana, Cuba, up to the time of Hemingway's death. New York Supreme Court Judge Harry B. Frank wrote of Hotchner's book: [83]

> The format and narrative style of the work make immediately apparent that it is intended as a subjective presentation from the vantage of the friendship, camaraderie, and personal experiences that the younger author shared with the literary giant. Their adventures, their travels, their meetings are all set forth in detail and the portrait of Hemingway that emerges is shaded in terms of the unique self that he manifested and revealed in the course of his particular relationship with Hotchner.

Mary Hemingway's suit for an injunction complained, among other things, that the Hotchner manuscript violated her statutory right of privacy under Section 51 of the New York Civil Rights Law. Mrs. Hemingway was mentioned in various places throughout the book, and she charged that those references to her amounted to an invasion of her privacy. Judge Frank rejected Mrs. Hemingway's privacy contentions and allowed Random House to publish the book, saying that given the public's need to be informed, a biography of this sort outweighed privacy considerations.[84]

In other lawsuits dealing with "appropriation," it has been held that the taking or appropriation need not be for a financial gain in those jurisdictions where the common-law right of privacy is recognized. Just as long as someone's identity or likeness is used for some advantage, an action for invasion of privacy may succeed. An example of this occurred when a political party used a man's

[82] Ali v. Playgirl, Inc., 447 F.Supp. 723 (S.D.N.Y.1978), 3 Med.L.Rptr. 2541, 2546.

[83] Estate of Hemingway v. Random House, Inc., 49 Misc.2d 726, 268 N.Y.S.2d 531, 534 (1966).

[84] 49 Misc.2d 726, 268 N.Y.S.2d 531, 534 (1966).

name as a candidate when he had not given his consent. [85] However, a number of states—including New York, Oklahoma, Virginia, Utah and California—have privacy statutes requiring proof of monetary advantage gained by the publication.[86] It has often been urged that everything published by the mass media is done "for purposes of trade." [87] If such a construction were allowed, the press might be greatly threatened by privacy suits brought by persons who objected to the use of their names, even in news stories. In defense of press freedom, however, courts have repeatedly held that just because a newspaper, magazine, or broadcasting station makes a profit does not mean that everything published is "for purposes of trade." [88]

Actress Ann-Margret brought an invasion of privacy action under Section 51 of the New York Civil Rights Law, asking damages from *High Society* magazine. She contended that including her photograph, nude to the waist, in a publication known as *High Society Celebrity Skin* amounted to use of her likeness, without her consent, for purposes of trade, and also invaded her right of publicity. Although he dismissed her suit, a sympathetic federal judge wrote: [89]

> The defendants * * * publish a magazine * * * which specializes in printing photographs of well-known women caught in the most revealing situations and positions that the defendants are able to obtain. In view of such content, the plaintiff has attempted to characterize Celebrity Skin as hard-core pornography. That description, however, by contemporary standards, appears inappropriate. A more apt description would be simply "tacky."

Judge Goettel's sympathies might have been with Ann-Margret, but he ruled that she could not collect for invasion of privacy. The actress, "who has occupied the fantasies of many moviegoers over the years," chose to perform unclad in one of her films; that is a matter of public interest.

[85] State ex rel. La Follette v. Hinkle, 131 Wash. 86, 229 P. 317 (1924).

[86] McKinney's N.Y. Civil Rights Law §§ 50–51; Virginia Code 1950, § 8–650; 15 Oklahoma Statutes Anno. § 839.1; Utah Code Ann. 1953, 76–4–8, and § 3344, California Civil Code.

[87] See Joseph Burstyn, Inc. v. Wilson, 343 U.S. 495, 501, 72 S.Ct. 777, 780 (1952); New York Times Co. v. Sullivan, 376 U.S. 254 at 266, 84 S.Ct. 710 at 718 (1964).

[88] See, e.g., Time, Inc. v. Hill, 385 U.S. 374, 395, 87 S.Ct. 534, 546 (1967).

[89] Ann-Margret v. High Society Magazine, Inc., 498 F.Supp. 401, 403–404 (S.D. N.Y.1980), 5 Med.L.Rptr. 1774, 1775.

The judge then expressed a non-authoritarian view of what constitutes newsworthiness, a view which seems to have lost favor in some other courts.[90]   Judge Goettel wrote: [91]

> And while such an event may not appear overly impor-
> tant, the scope of what constitutes a newsworthy event
> has been afforded a broad definition and held to include
> even matters of "entertainment and amusement, concern-
> ing interesting phases of human activity in general."
> Paulsen v. Personality Posters, Inc., * * * 113 F.2d 806
> at 809.   As has been noted, it is not for the courts to
> decide what matters are of interest to the general public.
> See Goelet v. Confidential, Inc. * * * 5 A.D.2d 226 at
> 229–30, 171 N.Y.S.2d 223 at 226.

The Right of Publicity

As a general rule, the right of privacy dies with the individual.   As tort scholar William L. Prosser noted, "there is no common
law right of action for a publication concerning one who is already
dead."   However, as with most general rules, there are exceptions.
A workable lawsuit for invasion of privacy may exist after a
person's death, "according to the survival rules of the particular
state." [92]

Similarly, there is a general rule that relatives have no right
of action for an invasion of the privacy of a deceased person.   A
satirical national television show, "That Was the Week that Was,"
included this statement in a broadcast over the National Broadcasting Company network: "Mrs. Katherine Young of Syracuse,
New York, who died at 99 leaving five sons, five daughters, 67
grandchildren, 72 great grandchildren, and 73 great-great
grandchildren—gets our First Annual Booby Prize in the Birth
Control Sweepstakes."   Two of Mrs. Young's sons sued for invasion of privacy, but failed because there is no relative's right to sue
for invasion of the privacy of a deceased person.[93]

But what about famous people?   What about performers, even
those as wildly different as Bela Lugosi or Elvis Presley?   Their
likenesses, their personas, are still valuable commercial properties

[90] See, e.g., Briscoe v. Reader's Digest Ass'n, 4 Cal.3d 529, 93 Cal.Rptr. 866, 483 P.2d 34 (1971); Virgil v. Time, Inc., 527 F.2d 1122 (9th Cir.1975).

[91] Ann-Margret v. High Society, 498 F.Supp. 401, 405 (S.D.N.Y.1980), 6 Med.L. Rptr. 1774, 1776.

[92] William L. Prosser, Handbook of the Law of Torts, 4th ed., St. Paul, Minn.: West Publishing Co., 1971, at p. 815, citing the highly confusing decision in Reed v. Real Detective Pub. Co., 63 Ariz. 294, 162 P.2d 133 (1945).

[93] Young v. That Was the Week that Was, 423 F.2d 265 (6th Cir.1970); accord: see Maritote v. Desilu Productions, Inc., 345 F.2d 418 (7th Cir.1965); Ravellette v. Smith, 300 F.2d 854 (7th Cir.1962).

long after their deaths. For example, the legal ghost of the late horror-film star Bela Lugosi came back in the courtrooms to haunt Universal Pictures Company, although Universal eventually won its case after a series of lengthy court battles. Lugosi, famed for his portrayal of Count Dracula, died in 1956. In 1960, however, Universal began to capitalize on his fame, entering into licensing agreements to allow manufacturing of a number of items, including shirts, cards, games, kites, bar accessories and masks—all with the likeness of Count Dracula as played by Bela Lugosi.[94]

Lugosi's son and widow sued to recover profits made by Universal Pictures in its licensing arrangements, claiming a "right of property or right of contract which, upon Bela Lugosi's death, descended to his heirs." [95] Although the Lugosis won their suit at the trial court level, the California Supreme Court ultimately voted 4–3 that the exclusive right to profit from his name and likeness did not survive the actor's death. The California Supreme Court said, in adopting California Court of Appeal Presiding Justice Roth's opinion as its own:

> "Such '* * * a right of value' to create a business, product or service of value is embraced in the law of privacy and is protectable during one's lifetime but it does not survive the death of Lugosi.

More has been heard, however, in the area of law involving profiting from celebrities' names or likenesses after their deaths. Courts in different regions of the nation give contradictory signals. Cases involving the legendary Elvis Presley are illustrative:

(1) In Factors, Etc. v. Pro Arts, Inc., the Court of Appeals for the Second Circuit held in 1978 that there *was* a property right in Presley's name and likeness which continued on for his heirs after Presley's death.[96]

(2) On the other hand, the Court of Appeals for the Sixth Circuit concluded in Memphis Development Foundation v. Factors, Etc. that Presley's heirs could *not* assign exclusive rights to use Presley's name and likeness. Thus, a Memphis firm which was selling—without authorization—statuettes of Elvis was allowed to go right on doing just that.[97]

[94] Bela George Lugosi v. Universal Pictures, No. 877875, Memorandum Opinion, Superior Court of the State of California for the County of Los Angeles, published in full in Performing Arts Review, Vol. 3, No. 1 (1972), pp. 19–62.

[95] Ibid., pp. 21, 27–28.

[96] Factors Etc., Inc. v. Pro Arts, Inc., 579 F.2d 215 (2d Cir.1978).

[97] Memphis Development Foundation v. Factors Etc., Inc., 616 F.2d 956 (6th Cir. 1980).

As Victor Kovner has written, there is great disagreement among a number of courts [98] on "survivability" of name and likeness. Any persons, however, can assign rights to commercially develop their names or images.

Beyond that, actors imitating the famed late comedians, Stan Laurel and Oliver Hardy lost a suit to heirs of Laurel and Hardy.[99] Similarly, the right of publicity was recognized in a case involving the late mystery author, Agatha Christie. In this case, heirs of Miss Christie failed to collect, however, because the account was so obviously a fiction.[1]

Other cases have held that there is a kind of a property right in a person's picture or likeness. Bubble-gum "trading cards" offer cases in point. Beginning with Judge Jerome D. Frank's 1953 decision in Haelan Laboratories, Inc., v. Topps Chewing Gum, several cases involved players' photographs. Judge Frank wrote of a "right of publicity" apart from a right of privacy which compensates a person for mental suffering because that person has received unwanted publicity. Judge Frank said: "We think that in addition to an independent right of privacy * * * a man has a right in the publicity value of his photograph, i.e., the right to grant the exclusive privilege of publishing his picture * * *. This right might be called a 'right of publicity.' " [2]

Consider "right of publicity" cases involving outfielder Ted Uhlaender and slugging first baseman Orlando Cepeda. Both sued for compensation for the unauthorized use of their names for advertising or promotional purposes. In the *Uhlaender* case, a court decided that a public figure such as a baseball player has a property or proprietary interest in his public personality. This included his identity, as embodied in his name, likeness, or other personal characteristics. This property interest—in effect the "right of publicity" of which Judge Frank wrote in 1953 in the

---

[98] Kovner, 1991 op. cit., Vol. II at p. 185, citing eight states with commercialization statutes providing for a property right to publicity surviving death: California, Florida, Georgia, Nebraska, Oklahoma, Utah, Virginia, and Tennessee. Tennessee adopted the "Personal Rights Protection Act of 1984—protecting a property right in name, etc.—10 years after death, on June 5, 1984.

See also the remarkably useful LDRC [Libel Defense Resource Center] 50-State Survey 1984: Current Developments in Media Libel and Invasion of Privacy Law, ed. by Henry R. Kaufman. See state-by-state listings on court decisions and relevant statutes.

[99] Price v. Worldvision Enterprises, Inc., 455 F.Supp. 252 (S.D.N.Y.1978), affirmed 603 F.2d 214 (2d Cir.1979).

[1] Hicks v. Casablanca Records, 464 F.Supp. 426 (S.D.N.Y.1978).

[2] Haelan Laboratories, Inc. v. Topps Chewing Gum, Inc., 202 F.2d 866 (2d Cir. 1953).

Haelan Laboratories case—was held in *Uhlaender* to be sufficient to support an injunction against unauthorized appropriation.[3]

As if celebrities such as Bela Lugosi, Elvis Presley, and baseball players didn't add enough flair to the law of privacy, what about Hugo "Human Cannonball" Zacchini? Zacchini was doing his thing at the Geauga County Fair in Burton, Ohio—being shot out of a cannon into a net 200 feet away. This high-calibre entertainer, however, took exception to being filmed by a free-lancer working for Scripps-Howard Broadcasting. Zacchini noted the free-lancer and asked him not to film the performance, which took place in a fenced area, surrounded by grandstands.

The television station broadcast the film of the 15-second flight by Zacchini, with the newscaster saying this: [4]

> "This * * * now * * * is the story of a *true spectator* sport * * * the sport of human cannonballing * * * in fact, the great *Zacchini* is about the only human cannonball around these days * * * just happens that, *where* he is, is the Great Geauga County Fair, in Burton * * * and believe me, although it's not a *long* act, it's a thriller * * * and you really need to see it *in person* to appreciate it. * * *"

Zacchini sued for infringement of his "right of publicity," claiming that he was engaged in the entertainment business, following after his father, who had invented this act. He claimed that the television station had "showed and commercialized the film of his act without his consent," and that this was "an unlawful appropriation of plaintiff's professional property."

The Ohio Supreme Court rejected Zacchini's claims, saying that a TV station has a privilege to report in its newscasts "matters of legitimate public interest which would otherwise be protected by an individual's right of publicity." The TV station could be held liable, but only when the actual intent of the station was to appropriate the benefit of the publicity for some non-privileged private use, or unless the actual intent was to injure the individual involved.[5]

The Supreme Court of the United States disagreed, saying that Zacchini was not contending that his act could not be reported as a newsworthy item.[6]

[3] Uhlaender v. Henricksen, 316 F.Supp. 1277 (D.Minn.1970); Cepeda v. Swift & Co., 415 F.2d 1205 (8th Cir.1969).

[4] Zacchini v. Scripps-Howard Broadcasting Co., 433 U.S. 562, 97 S.Ct. 2849 (1977).

[5] Ibid., at 565–566, 97 S.Ct. at 2852.

[6] Ibid., at 574–579, 97 S.Ct. at 2857–2859.

It is evident, and there is no claim here to the contrary, that petitioner's state-law right of publicity would not serve to prevent respondent from reporting the newsworthy facts about petitioner's act. Wherever the line in particular situations is to be drawn between media reports that are protected and those that are not, we are quite sure that the First and Fourteenth Amendments do not immunize the media when they broadcast a performer's entire act without his consent.

* * *

The broadcast of a film of petitioner's entire act poses a substantial threat to the economic value of that performance.

* * *

We conclude that although the State of Ohio may as a matter of its own law privilege the press in the circumstances of this case, the First and Fourteenth Amendments do not require it to do so.

A five-member majority of the Supreme Court then sent the Zacchini case back to the Ohio courts for a decision on whether the Human Cannonball should recover damages. In dissent, Justice Powell—who was joined by Justices Brennan and Marshall— wondered just what constituted "an entire act." [7] As attorney Floyd Abrams has asked—following Justice Powell's question— does the "entire act" include the fanfare and getting into the cannon, possibly lasting for several minutes? [8]

SEC. 42. DEFENSES: NEWSWORTHINESS, THE CONSTITUTION, AND CONSENT

Traditionally, the media's most useful defense against an invasion of privacy lawsuit has been the concept of "newsworthiness," although the "actual malice" rule may supersede it.

Newsworthiness, for many years, was a splendid defense in "private facts" invasion of privacy lawsuits. It is still a major factor, and in some cases may be *the* prime factor in a successful defense against an invasion of privacy lawsuit. However, a number of cases and the oft-quoted discussion of privacy in the Restatement of Torts, Second, suggest that this defense is undergoing erosion. [9]

---

[7] Ibid., at ___, 97 S.Ct. at 2860.

[8] Floyd Abrams, "The Press, Privacy, and the Constitution," New York Times Magazine, August 21, 1977, at pp. 11ff.

[9] Restatement, Second, Torts, § 652D.

Somewhat as Pontius Pilate asked "What is truth?," one may ask, "What is news?" No two journalists ever seem to be able to agree on a clear-cut definition of the term, but presumably, they know it when they see it. Courts, in numerous privacy cases, have tried with indifferent success to define news and newsworthiness. One court has even called news "that indefinable quality of information which arouses public attention."

Editors and reporters assert that "news is what we say it is" or that news is "whatever interests people." For years, many judges confronted with privacy cases tended to accept journalists' definitions.[10] Two cases discussed at some length in Section 39 of this chapter—Virgil v. Time, Inc. (1975)[11] and Campbell v. Seabury Press (1980)[12]—illustrate the tension between two ways of defining news. In *Virgil,* the Circuit Court judge evidently believed that courts (and juries) should set standards of newsworthiness. Using the Restatement's formulation, judges and juries are to work out a kind of "community standard" in a privacy case, determining whether the matter publicized would be "highly offensive to a reasonable person" and whether it is "of legitimate concern to the public."[13]

In *Campbell,* however, the judge viewed newsworthiness in a way far more favorable to the press. The court there said that the First Amendment commands a newsworthiness privilege. As Harvey Zuckman has pointed out, *Campbell* held that the information publicized need not be limited to news dissemination or commentary on public affairs. The privilege "extends to 'information concerning interesting phases of human activity and embraces all issues about which information is needed or appropriate for coping with the exigencies of their period.'"[14] And that can include information about persons who have not sought out—or who have actively tried to avoid—publicity.

Often, of course, people are caught up in the news when they would much rather retain the anonymity of private persons. But when an event is classified as news, the courts have uniformly forbidden recovery for substantially accurate accounts of an event which is of public interest. A rather extreme case in point here

---

[10] Sweenek v. Pathe News Inc., 16 F.Supp. 746, 747 (E.D.N.Y.1936); Sidis v. F–R Pub. Co., 113 F.2d 806, 809 (2d Cir.1940); Associated Press v. International News Service, 245 Fed. 244, 248 (2d Cir.1917), affirmed 248 U.S. 215, 39 S.Ct. 68 (1918); Jenkins v. Dell Pub. Co., 251 F.2d 447, 451 (3d Cir.1958).

[11] Virgil v. Time, Inc., 527 F.2d 1122 (9th Cir.1975).

[12] Campbell v. Seabury Press, 614 F.2d 395 (5th Cir.1980).

[13] Restatement, Second, Torts, § 652D.

[14] Zuckman, "The Right of Privacy and the Press," presentation at Southern Newspaper Publishers Association law symposium, Austin, Texas, October 13, 1980.

involved the unfortunate John Jacova, who had bought a newspaper at a Miami Beach hotel's cigar counter. As Jacova innocently stood at the counter, police rushed into the hotel in a raid and mistook Jacova for a gambler. Jacova was taken into custody, but was released after he showed identification. Mr. Jacova was understandably annoyed later in the day to see himself on television being questioned by policemen. He sued the television stations for invasion of privacy. He was not allowed to collect, however, because the court ruled that Jacova had become an "unwilling actor" in a news event.[15]

Mrs. Lillian Jones—much against her will—originated the "unwilling public figure" rule in a famous privacy case decided in 1929. Her husband was stabbed to death on a Louisville street in her presence. The Louisville *Herald-Post* published a picture of Mrs. Jones, and quoted her as saying of her husband's attackers: "I would have killed them." The court expressed sympathy and acknowledged the existence of a right to privacy, but added:[16]

> There are times, however, when one, whether willing or not, becomes an actor in an occurrence of public or general interest. When this takes place, he emerges from his seclusion and it is not an invasion of his right to privacy to publish his photograph with an account of such occurrence.

Even in the early 1980s there appeared to be an "involuntary public figure" category in privacy law. But that appears to fly in the face of developments in the law of libel. As discussed in Chapter 5, Section 27, the "involuntary public figure" category has been virtually killed off in libel law by the Supreme Court of the United States.[17] Will the Supreme Court shove the libel rule into the law of privacy, further weakening newsworthiness as a defense? Developments in this area need to be watched carefully by journalists and by their attorneys.

What of people who seek fame, public office, or otherwise *willingly* bring themselves to public notice? Public figures have been held to have given up, to some extent their right to be "let alone." Persons who have sought publicity—actors, explorers, or politicians to give a few examples—have made themselves "news" and have parted with some of their privacy. In one case, a suit by a former husband of movie star Janet Leigh was unsuccessful

---

[15] Jacova v. Southern Radio and Television Co., 83 So.2d 34 (Fla.1955); see, also, Hubbard v. Journal Pub. Co., 69 N.M. 473, 368 P.2d 147 (1962); Elmhurst v. Pearson, 80 U.S.App.D.C. 372, 153 F.2d 467 (1946).

[16] Jones v. Herald Post Co., 230 Ky. 227, 18 S.W.2d 972 (1929).

[17] See also Time, Inc. v. Firestone, 424 U.S. 448, 96 S.Ct. 958 (1976), and Wolston v. Reader's Digest Ass'n, Inc., 443 U.S. 157, 99 S.Ct. 2701 (1979).

despite his protestations that he had done everything he could to avoid publicity. Her fame rubbed off on him.[18]

Even so, when the media go "too far," celebrities can bring successful privacy lawsuits. The taking of a name of a public figure, for example, to advertise a commercial product without his consent would be actionable. Also, even newsworthy public figures can collect damages when fictionalized statements are published about them. Some areas of life are sufficiently personal and private that the media may intrude only at their peril. Private sexual relationships, homes, bank accounts, and private letters of an individual would all seem to be in a danger zone for the media.[19]

Unwilling subjects of photographs or motion pictures have caused considerable activity in the law of privacy. Consider the case of Frank Man, a professional musician who made the scene at the Woodstock Festival in Bethel, N.Y., in August of 1969. At someone's request, Man clambered onto the stage and played "Mess Call" on his flugelhorn to an audience of movie cameras and 400,000 people. Subsequently, Warner Bros., Inc. produced and exhibited a movie under the title of "Woodstock." Man claimed that the producers and distributors of the film included his performance without his consent, and brought suit in New York against Warner Bros.

A United States District Court said:[20]

> The film depicts, without the addition of any fictional material, actual events which happened at the festival. Nothing is staged and nothing is false. * * *

> There can be no question that the Woodstock festival was and is a matter of valid public interest.

Man argued that a movie depicting Woodstock could no longer be treated as news because of the lapse of time. The court replied that "the bizarre happenings of the festival were not mere fleeting news but sensational events of deep and lasting public interest." The court concluded that Frank Man, by his own volition had placed himself in the spotlight at a sensational event. He had made himself newsworthy, and thus deprived himself of any right to collect for invasion of privacy.[21]

[18] Carlisle v. Fawcett Publications, Inc., 201 Cal.App.2d 733, 20 Cal.Rptr. 405 (1962).

[19] See Garner v. Triangle Publications, 97 F.Supp. 546 (S.D.N.Y.1951); Bazemore v. Savannah Hospital, 171 Ga. 257, 155 S.E. 194 (1930); Baker v. Libbie, 210 Mass. 599, 97 N.E. 109 (1912).

[20] Man v. Warner Bros. Inc., 317 F.Supp. 50, 53 (S.D.N.Y.1970).

[21] Ibid.

It should not, however, be inferred that all factual reports of current events have been—or will be—held absolutely privileged. Film Producer Wiseman produced a film—"The Titicut Follies"—which showed conditions in a mental hospital, with individuals identifiable. The film showed naked inmates, forced feeding, masturbation and sadism, and the court concluded that Wiseman's film had—by identifying individuals—gone beyond the consent which mental hospital authorities had given him to make the film. The film was taken out of commercial distribution, but was not destroyed. The court ruled that the film was of educational value, and that it could be shown to special audiences such as groups of social workers, or others who might be moved to work toward improving conditions in mental hospitals.[22]

The protection of newsworthiness may vanish suddenly if a careless or misleading caption is placed on a picture. Consider the case of Holmes v. Curtis Publishing Company.

"MAFIA: SHADOW OF EVIL ON AN ISLAND IN THE SUN" screamed the headline on a feature story in the February 25, 1967 issue of the *Saturday Evening Post*. Published along with the article was a picture of James Holmes and four other persons at a gambling table, evidently playing blackjack. This picture was captioned, "High-Rollers at Monte Carlo have dropped as much as $20,000 in a single night. The U.S. Department of Justice estimates that the Casino grosses $20 million a year, and that one-third is skimmed off for American Mafia 'families.' "

Holmes objected to publication of this article, and sued for libel and invasion of privacy, arguing that the picture and caption had placed him in a false light. Holmes was not mentioned by name in the article, but he was, however, the focal point of the photograph. A United States district court in South Carolina noted that the article dealt with subjects of great public interest—organized crime, the growth of tourism in the Bahama Islands, and legalized gambling.

The court refused to grant the Curtis Publishing Company's motions that the libel and privacy lawsuits by Holmes could not stand because of precedents such as New York Times Co. v. Sullivan[23] and Time, Inc. v. Hill.[24] Instead, the court declared that the libel and privacy issues would have to go to trial:[25]

---

[22] Commonwealth v. Wiseman, 356 Mass. 251, 249 N.E.2d 610 (1969). In 1991, more general showings were allowed. See, also Daily Times Democrat v. Graham, 276 Ala. 380, 162 So.2d 474 (1964), where a woman collected for invasion of privacy after a newspaper used her identifiable picture as she emerged from a "fun house" where a jet of air blew her dress above her waist.

[23] 376 U.S. 254, 84 S.Ct. 710 (1964).

[24] 385 U.S. 374, 87 S.Ct. 534 (1967).

[25] Holmes v. Curtis Pub. Co., 303 F.Supp. 522, 527 (D.S.C.1969).

Certainly defendant's caption is reasonably capable of amounting to a defamation, for one identified as a high-stakes gambler of having a connection with the Mafia would certainly be injured in his business, occupation, and/or reputation.

As to plaintiff's action for privacy, there appears no question that if it were not for defendant's caption beneath plaintiff's photograph, this court would be justified in dismissing plaintiff's invasion of privacy cause of action. But such is not the case. Conflicting inferences also arise from the record as it stands today which preclude disposition of this cause of action summarily.

Time, Inc. v. Hill and "Actual Malice"

The law of privacy is much like a jigsaw puzzle with some pieces missing: it is sometimes hard to discern a meaningful pattern. Just as the defense of newsworthiness—discussed in the preceding section—is in flux, the Constitution-based defense growing out of the 1967 Supreme Court decision in Time, Inc. v. Hill also is undergoing change.

When the Supreme Court weighed the right to privacy against the First Amendment freedom to publish, the freedom to publish was given preference. Time, Inc. v. Hill was noteworthy in one respect because the losing attorney was Richard Milhous Nixon, more recently known as sometime President of the United States. This decision is important because it represents the first time that the Supreme Court decided a privacy case dealing with the mass media.

In 1952, the James J. Hill family was minding its own business, living in the suburban Philadelphia town of Whitemarsh. On September 11, 1952, however, the Hills' anonymity was taken away from them by three escaped prisoners. The convicts held Mr. and Mrs. Hill and their five children hostage in their own home for 19 hours. The family was not harmed, but the Hills—much against their wishes—were in the news.[26] Their story became even more sensational when two of the three convicts who had held them hostage were killed in a shoot-out with police.[27]

In 1953, Random House published Joseph Hayes' novel, The Desperate Hours, a story about a family which was taken hostage by escaped convicts. The novel was later made into a successful play and, subsequently, a motion picture.

[26] 385 U.S. 374, 377, 87 S.Ct. 534, 536 (1967).

[27] Pember, Privacy and the Press, p. 210.

The publicity which led the Hills to sue for invasion of their privacy was an article published in 1955 by *Life* magazine. The article, titled "True Crime Inspires Tense Play," described the "true crime" suffered by the James Hill family of Whitemarsh, Pennsylvania.[28]

Life's pages of photographs included actors' depiction of the son being "roughed up" by one of the escaped convicts. This picture was captioned "brutish convict." Also, a picture titled "daring daughter" showed the daughter biting the hand of a convict, trying to make him drop the gun.[29]

The Joseph Hayes novel and play, however, did not altogether match up with *Life's* assertion that Hayes' writings were based on the ordeal of the Hill family. For one thing, Hayes' family was named "Hilliard," not Hill. Also, the Hills had not been harmed by the convicts in any way, while in the Hayes novel and play the father and son were beaten and the daughter was "subjected to a verbal sexual insult."

Hill sued for invasion of privacy under the privacy sections of New York's Civil Rights Law, which provides that a person whose name or picture was so used "for purposes of trade" without his consent could "sue and recover damages for any injuries sustained by reason of such use.[30]

The Hills sought damages on grounds that the *Life* article "was intended to, and did, give the impression that the play mirrored the Hill family's experience, which, to the knowledge of defendant * * * was false and untrue." In its defense, Time, Inc., argued that "the subject of the article was 'a subject of legitimate news interest,' 'a subject of general interest and of value and concern to the public' at the time of publication, and that it was 'published in good faith without any malice whatsoever * * *.' "[31]

The trial court jury awarded the Hills $50,000 compensatory and $25,000 punitive damages. On appeal, the Appellate Division of the Supreme Court of New York ordered a new trial on the question of damages, but upheld the jury's finding that *Life* magazine had invaded the Hill's privacy. The Appellate Division bore down hard on the issue of fictionalization.[32]

[28] Life, Feb. 28, 1955.

[29] 385 U.S. 374, 377, 87 S.Ct. 534, 536–537 (1967).

[30] Sections 50–51, New York Civil Rights Law, McKinney's Consolidated Laws, Ch. 6.

[31] 385 U.S. 374, 378, 87 S.Ct. 534, 537 (1967).

[32] 385 U.S. 374, 379, 87 S.Ct. 534, 537 (1967), quoting Hill v. Hayes, 18 A.D.2d 485, 489, 240 N.Y.S.2d 286, 290 (1963).

At the new trial on the issue of damages, a jury was waived and the court awarded $30,000 compensatory damages with no punitive damages.

When the *Hill* case reached the Supreme Court, issues of freedom of speech and press raised in the appeal by Time, Inc. were considered. Justice Brennan's majority opinion first dealt with the issue of whether truth could be a defense to a charge of invasion of privacy. Quoting a recent New York Court of Appeals decision, Brennan asserted it was "crystal clear" in construing the New York Civil Rights Statute, "that truth is a complete defense in actions under the statute based upon reports of newsworthy people or event."[33] Brennan added, "Constitutional questions which might arise if truth were not a defense are therefore no concern."[34]

Justice Brennan then wrestled with the issue of fictionalization. He noted that James Hill was a newsworthy person " 'substantially without a right to privacy' insofar as his hostage experience was involved." Hill, however, was entitled to sue to the extent that *Life* magazine "fictionalized" and "exploited for the defendant's commercial benefit." Brennan then turned to a libel case, New York Times v. Sullivan, for guidance.[35]

> Material and substantial falsification is the test. However, it is not clear whether proof of knowledge of the falsity or that the article was prepared with reckless disregard for the truth is also required. In New York Times Co. v. Sullivan * * * we held that the Constitution delimits a State's power to award damages for libel in actions brought by public officials against critics of their official conduct. Factual error, content defamatory of official reputation, or both, are insufficient to an award of damages for false statements unless actual malice—knowledge that the statements are false or in reckless disregard of the truth—is alleged and proved. * * *

> * * *

> We hold that the Constitutional protections for speech and press precluded the application of the New York statute to redress false reports of matters of public interest in the absence of proof that the defendant published the report with knowledge of its falsity or in reckless disregard of the truth.

[33] At the outset of his opinion, Justice Brennan relied heavily upon Spahn v. Julian Messner, Inc., 18 N.Y.2d 324, 274 N.Y.S.2d 877, 221 N.E.2d 543 (1966).

[34] 385 U.S. 374, 383–384, 87 S.Ct. 534, 539–540 (1967).

[35] New York Times Co. v. Sullivan, 376 U.S. 254, 84 S.Ct. 710 (1964), used in Time, Inc. v. Hill, 385 U.S. 374, 386–388, 87 S.Ct. 534, 541–542 (1967).

It should be emphasized that Justice Brennan's opinion in Time v. Hill has not made truth an entirely dependable defense against a lawsuit for invasion of privacy. For one thing, the Supreme Court's adoption of the malice rule from New York Times v. Sullivan applies only to those privacy cases involving falsity. Furthermore, the Supreme Court was badly split in Time v. Hill; a five-Justice majority did vote in favor of *Life* magazine, but only two justices—Potter Stewart and Byron White—agreed with Brennan's use of the "Sullivan rule."

Brennan appeared to prize press freedom's benefits to society more than the individual's right to privacy.[36] If incidental, non-malicious error crept into a story, that was part of the risk of freedom, for which a publication should not be held responsible. Justice Brennan wrote:[37]

* * *

Erroneous statement is no less inevitable in * * * [a case such as discussion of a new play] than in the case of comment upon public affairs, and in both, if innocent or merely negligent, * * * it must be protected if the freedoms of expression are to have the "breathing space" that they "need * * * to survive."

The "breathing space" mentioned by Justice Brennan—a phrase borrowed from New York Times v. Sullivan—indicated that the Court was giving the press a healthy "benefit of the doubt." Press freedom, Brennan declared, is essential to "the maintenance of our political system and an open society." Yet this freedom, he argued, could be dangerously invaded by lawsuits for libel or invasion of privacy.[38]

"We have no doubt," Brennan wrote, "that the subject of the *Life* article, the opening of a new play linked to an actual incident, is a matter of public interest. 'The line between the informing and the entertaining is too elusive for the protection of * * * [freedom of the press].'"[39]

Time, Inc. v. Hill thus erected an important constitutional shield in false-light privacy cases. If persons caught up in the news as "involuntary public figures" are to recover damages for falsity, they must prove "actual malice" as borrowed from the lore of libel: publication of knowing falsehoods or with reckless disregard for whether a statement was false or not. As noted earlier,

[36] See the dissent by Mr. Justice Abe Fortas, which was joined by Chief Justice Earl Warren and by Justice Tom C. Clark, 385 U.S. 374, 411, 416, 87 S.Ct. 534, 554, 556 (1967).

[37] 385 U.S. 374, 388–389, 87 S.Ct. 534, 542–543 (1967).

[38] 385 U.S. 374, 389, 87 S.Ct. 534, 543 (1967).

[39] 385 U.S. 374, 388, 87 S.Ct. 534, 542 (1967), quoting Winters v. New York, 333 U.S. 507, 510, 68 S.Ct. 665, 667 (1948).

the developments in the law of libel have virtually annihilated the "involuntary public person" category, and the question remains whether the "public interest" consideration in privacy law will continue to be a worthwhile defense.[40]

Cantrell v. Forest City Pub. Co., discussed in Section 40 of this chapter, allowed the widow of the victim of the famed collapse of the Point Pleasant Bridge to collect $60,000. The jury found fictionalization amounting to "actual malice" in the sense of a knowing falsehood. However, as noted by Sallie Martin Sharp in a 1981 study, the *Cantrell* majority "* * * invited challenges to the [Time v.] *Hill* opinion when it said:"[41]

> "[T]his case presents no occasion to consider whether a State may constitutionally apply a more relaxed standard of liability for a publisher or broadcaster for false statements injurious to a private person under a false-light theory of invasion of privacy or whether the constitutional standard announced in Time, Inc. v. Hill applies to all false-light cases."

Dr. Sharp found that the Constitution-based defenses growing out of Time, Inc. v. Hill have become increasingly important. Since *Hill* was decided in 1967, she wrote, lower federal and state courts began considering private facts in terms of First Amendment limits * * * "even though the *Hill* case involved false light invasion of privacy."[42]

Beyond that, Victor A. Kovner has asked whether the important libel case of Gertz v. Robert Welch, Incorporated [43]—discussed at length in Section 28 of Chapter 5—whether "actual malice's" application in false light privacy cases is limited to public officials and public figures."[44]

In Wood v. Hustler, one of the frequent lawsuits against this magazine, the Fifth Circuit Court of Appeals took what may be the predominating approach to applying a constitutional standard in a false-light privacy suit by a private person. (Wood v. Hustler involved Hustler Magazine's publishing a stolen nude photo of a

---

[40] See also Time, Inc. v. Firestone, 424 U.S. 448, 96 S.Ct. 958 (1976), and Wolston v. Reader's Digest Ass'n, Inc., 443 U.S. 157, 99 S.Ct. 2701 (1979).

[41] Sallie Martin Sharp, "The Evolution of the Invasion of Privacy Tort and Its Newsworthiness Limitations," Ph.D. dissertation, The University of Texas at Austin, 1981. See also Don R. Pember and Dwight L. Teeter, Jr., "Privacy and the Press Since Time, Inc. v. Hill, 50 Washington Law Review (1974) at p. 77.

[42] Sharp, Ibid.

[43] 418 U.S. 323, 94 S.Ct. 2997 (1974).

[44] Kovner, "Recent Developments in Intrusion, Private Facts, False Light, and Commercialization Claims," in Goodale (1991), op. cit., Vol. II, pp. 112–115.

woman after carelessly accepting a faked consent form.) Circuit Judge Jolly wrote for the court:[45]

> On the particular issue of standard of care under false light [privacy law], the Restatement (Second) of Torts § 652E Caveat & Comments d (1976) leaves open the possibility that liability may be based on a showing of negligence as to truth or falsity. "If Time v. Hill is modified along the lines of Gertz v. Robert Welch, then the reckless-disregard rule would apparently apply if the plaintiff is a public official or public figure and the negligence rule will apply to other plaintiffs." Restatement (Second) of Torts § 652E comment d at 399.

Defenses: Consent

In addition to *newsworthiness,* another important defense to a lawsuit for invasion of privacy is *consent.* Logically enough, if a person has consented to have his privacy invaded, he should not be allowed to sue for the invasion. As Warren and Brandeis wrote in their 1890 *Harvard Law Review* article, "The right to privacy ceases upon the publication of the facts by the individual or with his consent." [46]

The defense of consent, however, poses some difficulties. To make this defense stand up, it must be *pleaded* and *proved* by the defendant. An important rule here is that the *consent* must be as broad as the invasion.

A young man had consented to have his picture taken in the doorway of a shop, supposedly discussing the World Series. But the youth was understandably chagrined when *Front Page Detective* used this photograph to illustrate a story titled "Gang Boy." The Supreme Court of New York allowed the young man to recover damages, holding that consent to one thing is not consent to another. In other words, when a photograph is used for a purpose not intended by the person who consented, that person may be able to collect damages for invasion of privacy.[47]

In the case of Russell v. Marboro Books, a professional model was held to have a suit for invasion of privacy despite the fact that she had signed a release. (In the states which have privacy statutes—California, New York, Oklahoma, Utah, Wisconsin and Virginia—prior consent in writing is required before a person's name or picture can be used in advertising or "for purposes of

---

[45] Wood v. Hustler Magazine, Inc., 736 F.2d 1084 at 1091 (5th Cir.1984), 10 Med. L.Rptr. 2113 at 2117–2118. This case is discussed, below, at pp. 314–315.

[46] Warren and Brandeis, op. cit., p. 218.

[47] Metzger v. Dell Pub. Co., 207 Misc. 182, 136 N.Y.S.2d 888 (1955).

trade.") Miss Russell, at a picture-taking session had signed a
printed release form: [48]

Model Release

The undersigned hereby irrevocably consents to the
unrestricted use by * * * [photographer's name], advertisers, customers, successors and assigns of my name,
portrait, or picture, for advertising purposes or purposes
of trade, and I waive the right to inspect or approve such
completed portraits, pictures or advertising matter used
in connection therewith * * *.

Miss Russell maintained that her job as a model involved
portraying an "intelligent, refined, well-bred, pulchritudinous, ideal young wife and mother in artistic settings and socially approved
situations." Her understanding was that the picture was to depict
a wife in bed with her "husband"—also a model—in bed beside
her, reading.   Marboro books did use the pictures in an advertisement, with the caption "For People Who Take Their Reading
Seriously." Thus far, there was no invasion of privacy to which
Miss Russell had not consented.

Marboro Books, however, sold the photograph to Springs
Mills, Inc., a manufacturer of bed sheets which enjoyed a reputation for publishing spicy ads. The photo was retouched so that the
title of the book Miss Russell was reading appeared to be *Clothes
Make the Man,* a book which had been banned as pornographic.
The advertisement suggested that the book should be consulted for
suitable captions, and also suggested captions such as "Lost Weekend" and "Lost Between the Covers." The court held that Miss
Russell had an action for invasion of privacy despite the unlimited
release that she had signed. Such a release, the court reasoned,
would not stand up "if the picture were altered sufficiently in
situation, emphasis, background, or context * * * liability would
accrue where the content of the picture had been so changed that
it is substantially unlike the original."[49]

Even if a signed release is in one's possession, it would be well
to make sure that the release is still valid. In a Louisiana case, a
man had taken a body-building course in a health studio. This
man had agreed to have "before" and "after" photos taken of his
physique, showing the plaintiff's body in trunks. Ten years later,
the health studio used the pictures in an ad. The court held that
privacy had been invaded.[50]

[48] Russell v. Marboro Books, 18 Misc.2d 166, 183 N.Y.S.2d 8 (1959).

[49] Ibid.

[50] McAndrews v. Roy, 131 So.2d 256 (La.App.1961).

If the topic of consent in media law does not make for wary publishers, it should. Hustler magazine was hoaxed by a snapshot and an un-neighborly neighbor, and lost a $150,000 invasion-of-privacy case as a result. Billy and LaJuan Wood, husband and wife, went for a skinny-dip swim at a secluded spot at a wilderness area in a state park. After swimming, they playfully took several photos of each other in the nude. Billy had the film developed by a business using a mechanical developing process, and they treated the snapshots as private, not showing them to others and keeping them out of sight in a drawer in their bedroom.

One Steve Simpson, a neighbor living in the other side of the Woods' duplex, broke into the Woods' home and stole some of the photos. Simpson and Kelly Rhoades, who was then his wife, submitted the nude photo of LaJuan to Hustler magazine for publication in its "Beaver Hunt" section.

Simpson and Rhoades filled out a consent form that requested personal information. They gave some true information about LaJuan Wood (her identity, and her hobby of collecting arrowheads), but also gave some false information such as LaJuan's age and a lurid sex fantasy attributed to her. Kelley Rhoades forged LaJuan's signature and the photograph and consent form were mailed to Hustler in California. The faked consent form did not list a phone number but gave Kelley Rhoades' address as the place where Hustler was to send the $50 it was to pay for each photo used in the "Beaver Hunt" section.[51]

After Hustler selected LaJuan's photo, Kelley Rhoades received and answered a mailgram addressed to LaJuan and phoned Hustler. A Hustler staff member then had about a two-minute conversation with Rhoades; that was the extent of the magazine's checking for consent.[52]

Hustler magazine urged that the action should fail under the one-year statute of limitations applying to defamation in Texas. The Court of Appeals, however, chose to keep the privacy action alive under a two-year statute of limitations.[53] Hustler further argued that it should not be held liable for placing LaJuan Wood in a false light because it did not publish in reckless disregard of the truth, having no serious doubts about the falsity of the consent

[51] Wood v. Hustler Magazine, Inc., 736 F.2d 1084, 1085–1086 (5th Cir.1984), 10 Med.L.Rptr. 2113–2114.

[52] 736 F.2d 1084, 1086 (5th Cir.1984), 10 Med.L.Rptr. 2113, 2114.

[53] 736 F.2d 1084, 1085 (5th Cir.1984), 10 Med.L.Rptr. 2113, 2114. The Woods had sued for both libel and invasion of privacy; the libel action was ruled out because of the one-year statute of limitations on defamation, Tex.Civ.Stat.Ann.Art. 5524; however, the two-year limitations period of Art. 5526 was held to apply to false-light privacy cases. Billy Woods' invasion of privacy action was disallowed because the publication of the photo did not invade his privacy.

form.[54]   However, the U.S. Court of Appeals for the Fifth Circuit held that since LaJuan Wood was a private figure [55] who need prove only negligent behavior in order to collect damages.   In upholding the trial court damage award to her of $150,000, the Court of Appeals said: [56]

> Hustler carelessly administered a slipshod procedure that allowed LaJuan be placed in a false light in the pages of Hustler Magazine.   The nature of material published in the Beaver Hunt section would obviously warn a reasonably prudent editor or publisher of the potential for defamation or privacy invasion if a consent form was forged.   The wanton and debauched sexual fantasies and the intimate photos of nude models were of such a nature that great care was required in verifying the model's consent.

Cher v. Forum International

Consider the famed entertainer "Cher."   Evidently she is determined to control as much of her performer's image as possible.   She willingly consented to and taped an interview with radio talk show host Fred Robbins, a writer who sells celebrity interviews to magazines.   Cher said she had consented to the interview believing she had an agreement that the resulting article was to appear in *US* magazine.   *US* did not run the interview, but instead returned it to Robbins with a "kill" fee.   Robbins then sold the interview to the sensational tabloid *Star* and to a pocket-sized magazine called *Forum*.   That publication was owned by Forum International, of which Penthouse International owned 80% of the stock.[57]

Cher sued, bringing a legal action which had—among other things—aspects of the "false light" branch of privacy law.   She did not claim that the interview was defamatory, nor did she complain that private facts had been published without her consent.   Instead, her complaint charged breach of contract, unfair competition, and *misappropriation* of her name and likeness and of her *right to publicity*.   Beyond the legal labels, Cher was complaining about the appearance she consented to for a much "tamer" kind of

---

[54] 736 F.2d 1084, 1089 (5th Cir.1984), 10 Med.L.Rptr. 2113, 2116.

[55] See discussion of public figures in defamation law, Chapter 5, Sections 27 and 28.

[56] 736 F.2d 1084, 1092 (5th Cir.1984), 10 Med.L.Rptr. 2113, 2119.

[57] Cher v. Forum International, Ltd., et al., 692 F.2d 634, 638 (9th Cir.1982), 8 Med.L.Rptr. 2484, 2485.

magazine, *US*, only to have it appear in the juicy tabloid *Star* and the generally salacious *Forum*, creating misleading impressions.[58]

Cher accused *The Star* of having falsely represented that she had given that publication an exclusive interview, which would be degrading to her as a celebrity, given the nature of that tabloid. The Court of Appeals held, however, that *The Star's* promotional claim of an "Exclusive Interview" did not constitute knowing or reckless falsity under the doctrine of Time, Inc. v. Hill.[59]   Therefore, the judgment against *The Star* was reversed.[60]

Forum magazine, however, after identifying Fred Robbins as the interviewer, made it appear that *Forum* itself was the poser of the questions put to Cher.   Cher complained through her attorneys that this created the false impression that she had given an interview directly to *Forum*.   She argued that this exploited her celebrity value by implying that she endorsed *Forum*.   Her name and likeness were used in promotional subscription "tear out" ads: "There are certain things that Cher won't tell *People* and would never tell *US*.   She tells *Forum*." [61]

The Court of Appeals ruled that publishers can use promotional ads or literature so long as there is no false claim that a celebrity endorsed the publication involved.   Court of Appeals Judge Goodwin wrote, "* * * [T]he advertising staff [of Forum] engaged in the kind of knowing falsity that strips away the protection of the First Amendment."[62]   The Court of Appeals cut the original damage award to Cher from the trial court's figure of more than $600,000 to roughly $200,000.[63]

When a defendant does not have consent and does invade someone's privacy, good intentions are not a defense.   It may be pleaded that the defendant honestly believed that he had consent, but this can do no more than to mitigate punitive damages.   Some of the consequences of a publication's not getting a clear and specific consent from persons whose pictures were used in a magazine article may be seen in the case of Raible v. Newsweek. According to Eugene L. Raible, a Newsweek photographer visited his home in 1969, and asked to take a picture of Mr. Raible and his children in their yard for use in "a patriotic article."   Then, the October 6, 1969, issue of that magazine featured an article

[58] 692 F.2d 634, 638 (9th Cir.1982), 8 Med.L.Rptr. 2484, 2485.

[59] 385 U.S. 374, 87 S.Ct. 534 (1967).

[60] 692 F.2d 634, 638 (9th Cir.1982), 8 Med.L.Rptr. 2484, 2486.

[61] Ibid.   The U.S. Court of Appeals, 9th Circuit, found that Robbins did not participate in the publishing, advertising, or marketing of the articles, and the trial court judgment against him was vacated.   Also, it was stipulated at the trial court level that there was no contract between Cher and Robbins.

[62] 692 F.2d 634, 640 (9th Cir.1982), 8 Med.L.Rptr. 2484, 2487.

[63] Ibid.; see also News Media & The Law, Sept./Oct. 1983, pp. 17–18.

which was headlined on the cover, "The Troubled American—A Special Report on the White Majority." [64] Newsweek did use Mr. Raible's picture (with his children cropped out of it); he was wearing an open sport shirt and standing next to a large American flag mounted on a pole on his lawn. The article ran for many pages thereafter, with such marginal headlines as "You'd better watch out, the common man is standing up," and "Many think the blacks live by their own set of rules." [65] Mr. Raible sued for libel and for invasion of privacy.

Although Raible's name was not used in the story, the court said it was readily understandable that his friends and neighbors in Wilkinsburg, Pa., might consider him to be typical of the "square Americans" discussed in the article. Raible argued that his association with the article meant that he was being portrayed as a "* * * typical 'Troubled American,' a person considered 'angry, uncultured, crude, violence prone, hostile to both rich and poor, and racially prejudiced.' " [66]

District Judge William W. Knox granted *Newsweek* a summary judgment, thus dismissing Mr. Raible's libel claims. Judge Knox declared that since the article indicated that the views expressed are those of the white majority of the United States—of whom Mr. Raible was one—"then we would have to conclude that the article, if libelous, libels more than half of the people in the United States and not plaintiff in particular." [67]

Judge Knox declared, however, that Mr. Raible's invasion of privacy lawsuit appeared to stand on firmer ground. Directing that Raible's privacy lawsuit go to trial, Judge Knox wrote: [68]

> It is true that if plaintiff [Raible] consented to the use of his photograph in connection with *this article,* he would have waived his right of action for invasion of privacy. However, it would appear to the court that the burden of proof is upon the defendant to show just what plaintiff consented to and the varying inferences from this testimony will have to be resolved by the trier of facts.

[64] Raible v. Newsweek, Inc., 341 F.Supp. 804, 806, 809 (W.D.Pa.1972).

[65] Ibid., p. 805.

[66] Ibid., p. 806. See also De Salvo v. Twentieth Century Fox Film Corp., 300 F.Supp. 742 (D.Mass.1969).

[67] Ibid., p. 807.

[68] Ibid., p. 809.

SEC. 43. DEFENSES: LIMITATIONS
AND PROBLEMS

Privacy is a relatively new region of law which has had much unplanned growth. Complexities and confusions affect defenses to privacy lawsuits.

Journalists should not take much comfort in the defenses available for use against suits for invasion of privacy. As noted in this chapter, the concept of "newsworthiness" can prove to be so elastic that it is dangerously subject to the whims of a judge or jury. Also, some courts now seem to be becoming more restrictive in their definitions of "news" and "public interest." Beyond that, being able to defend successfully against a privacy-invasion suit is only part of the equation: even for winners, the costs in dollars and time expended can be enormous.

As may be seen from reading this chapter, the "privacy" concept is many things: a generalized feeling about a "right to be let alone;" it is a constitutional right against some kinds of *governmental* interference in our lives, and it is a growing and increasingly complex body of tort law. As Victor A. Kovner has suggested, perhaps the privacy area must now receive some drastic rethinking and reworking.[69]

> The torts might simply be referred to as intrusion claims, embarrassing facts or "intimacy" claims, false light claims, misappropriation claims, and right of publicity claims. Privacy has little to do with many of these claims. * * * [O]veruse of the term "invasion of privacy" may only contribute to further misunderstanding of the field and further infringement of First Amendment rights.

Privacy is a new area of law, and has not had the centuries of trial-and-error development that attended the law of defamation. This relative newness is a great source of privacy law's danger for the media. Over time, defenses to defamation were built up: for one thing, truth was made a defense. And where slander is concerned, "special damages"—actual monetary loss—must generally be proved before a plaintiff can collect. Where retraction statutes are in force, a plaintiff must prove special damages once a fair and full apology for the defamation has been published.[70] But with the law of privacy, the media do not have such shields. In only one of the privacy tort sub-groups discussed above—"putting

[69] Kovner, in Goodale, Communications Law 1984, Vol. 2, at p. 251.

[70] When the fact situation giving rise to a privacy action also involves defamation, retraction statutes have been held to apply. Werner v. Times-Mirror Co., 193 Cal.App.2d 111, 14 Cal.Rptr. 208 (1961).

plaintiff in a false position in the public eye"—is truth be a defense to a privacy action. Also, a publication need not be defamatory to invade someone's privacy.

Small wonder, then, that some eminent scholars have viewed the law of privacy as a threat to freedom of the press. Professor William L. Prosser has suggested that the law of privacy, in many respects, comes "into head-on collision with the constitutional guaranty of freedom of the press." He said privacy law may be "capable of swallowing up and engulfing the whole law of public dafamation."[71]

If, for example, a newspaper were to be sued for *both* libel and invasion of privacy for the same article, difficulties in making a defense hold up might well arise. If the publication were defamatory, the newspaper might be able to plead and prove truth as a defense. But proving truth would not halt the privacy suit unless the article had to do with "putting plaintiff in a false position in the public eye." It could be possible, if a plaintiff *alleged* that a newspaper printed "embarrassing private facts," that proving the truth of an article might encourage a sympathetic jury to find against the newspaper for invasion of privacy.

This means that an article containing no defamation, based on true facts, and published with the best of intentions or through an innocent mistake could be the basis for a successful invasion of privacy lawsuit. If, indeed, it becomes easier to collect for an invasion of privacy suit than for a defamation action, it has been suggested that privacy suits may supplant libel actions.[72]

The foregoing discussion has concentrated on invasion of privacy as a tort. Privacy, however, is protected not only by tort law—in which individuals may sue for damages if their privacy is invaded. Since 1960, privacy has become a constitutional right, a right which to some extent protects citizens from intrusions by government or police agencies.[73]

Precisely because privacy is a hot political issue, it needs to be watched carefully lest it do great damage to First Amendment concerns. The Freedom of Information Act of the federal government was passed in 1966, and was amended in 1975. And while that was dedicated to disclosure of information, it was accompanied by a measure dedicated to non-disclosure of information (at least where the press is concerned). The Privacy Act of 1974 was passed

[71] Prosser, Handbook of the Law of Torts, 3rd ed., p. 844; 4th ed. (1971), pp. 815–816; "Privacy," 48 California Law Review 383, 401 (1960).

[72] Zuckman, op. cit., citing I Prentice-Hall Government Disclosure Service, p. 30,001 (1980), and Biweekly Comparison of Key Statutes, National Law Journal, February 11, 1980, pp. 12–14.

[73] John W. Wade, "Defamation and the Right of Privacy," 15 Vanderbilt Law Review 1093, 1121 (1962); Prosser, "Privacy" loc. cit.

in an effort to give citizens some control over the government's enormous system of dosiers, and to let individuals see and correct files about themselves. The Privacy Act also limited disclosure of individually identifiable information by federal agencies.

Some observers have contended that the federal Privacy Act is not in conflict with the Freedom of Information Act. Others, including Supreme Court reporter Lyle Denniston, disagree, arguing that the emphasis on privacy is likely to damage newsgathering through the loss of "inside" sources of information often vital to covering sensitive stories about government. His point is that when bureaucrats are torn between disclosure of information and retention of information, the safest course will seem to be against disclosure.

> As Professor Harvey Zuckman has suggested, the impact of the federal Privacy Act (1974) on the states has been substantial. Just six years after the Privacy Act's adoption, one third of the states had passed some sort of privacy act and a like number had legislated to allow expungement [erasure] of non-conviction arrest records.[74]

But why shouldn't arrest records be sealed? After all, not all persons arrested—and thereby shown to be suspected of committing a crime—*have* committed a crime. Even when an innocent person is arrested, a so-called "criminal record" is created. Why shouldn't such records be sealed—hidden away for all time—or expunged, wiped off the record? Alan Westin has written that there are many instances of suicides and nervous breakdowns resulting from exposures by government investigations, press stories about such situations, and even published research. Westin said this should " 'constantly remind a free society that only grave social need can ever justify destruction of the privacy which guards the individual's ultimate autonomy [over dissemination of information about oneself].' "[75]

On the other hand, in Minnesota, a teen-aged girl was placed in a foster home with a convicted sex offender. The Welfare Department that placed her there did not know about the sex offender because the agency was not allowed access to criminal records. Also, it is—or should be—a truism among journalists that the police and the jails and the courts need the closest scrutiny possible if this society is to retain its key freedoms. In order to preserve due process of law, information about police and

---

[74] Zuckman, op. cit.

[75] Alan F. Westin, Privacy and Freedom (New York: Atheneum, 1970), pp. 33–34, quoted in Wright, op. cit.

judicial activities must be kept public and published in the press. As W.H. Hornby, editor of *The Denver Post*, has declared: [76]

> We still need to know who is in jail and what the charges are against him. We still need to know who has been indicted. If we don't insist on this knowledge, we are in the same position as the Germans who, in their privacy, wondered about the sighing cargoes of those long freight trains that passed in the night.

"Incitement" and Soldier of Fortune

A quite new and potentially expansive area of media liability is termed "incitement." Where the media are concerned, that means bringing a lawsuit against the makers of a publication or movie or audio tape or disc, blaming the media product for some harmful outcome.

One of the flashier examples of this emergent area of law could be found in Eimann v. Soldier of Fortune Magazine, Inc., where a 1988 jury award of $9.4 million ($7.2 million in punitive damages) was made against Soldier of Fortune magazine. A jury ordered the civil damage award, evidently believing that Soldier of Fortune had published an ad offering the services of a hired killer. The classified ad by John Wayne Hearn offered his services as a Vietnam veteran, a weapons specialist who knew jungle warfare, to undertake "high risk assignments." Hearn, indeed, was serving several life terms for shooting Sandra Black to death in her home in Bryan, Texas. Her husband, Robert Black, was sentenced to death for hiring her killer for $10,000.[77]

Predictably, the huge jury verdict caused Editor & Publisher, a trade journal for the newspaper industry, to call for a reversal. "The Texas decision," said Editor & Publisher, "would mean that a reader with a grudge against a publication could bring suit claiming damages for ads believed to be untruthful or misleading unless the publisher investigated every advertising claim."[78]

Soldier of Fortune escaped liability in this case, however, because the U.S. Court of Appeals (5th Cir.) held that this advertisement was innocuously worded and that the magazine, therefore, had no duty to refuse to publish such a classified ad.[79]

---

[76] W.H. Hornby, "Secrecy, Privacy and Publicity," Columbia Journalism Review, March-April, 1975, p. 11, quoted in Clancy, op. cit.

[77] Lisa Belkin, "Magazine is Ordered to Pay $9.4 Million for Killer's Ad," The New York Times, March 4, 1988, p. 9.

[78] Editor & Publisher, "Responsibility for ad content," March 12, 1988.

[79] Eimann v. Soldier of Fortune Magazine, Inc., 880 F.2d 830 (5th Cir.1989), 16 Med.L.Rptr. 2148, 2152.

In a 1991 decision, however, an Alabama federal court found Soldier of Fortune liable for incitement to the tune of $375,000 in compensatory damages and $2 million (reduced by the court from the jury's award of $10 million) in punitive damages. In Braun v. Soldier of Fortune, brothers Michael and Ian Braun sued the magazine for wrongful death and personal injury, claiming that their father had been killed by the person who placed the following classified ad: [80]

> GUN FOR HIRE: 37-year-old professional mercenary desires jobs. Vietnam Veteran. Discreet and very private. Body guard, courier, and other special skills. All jobs considered. Phone (615) * * * or write * * * Gatlinburg, TN 37738.

That advertisement had been placed by Richard Savage. A business associate of Mr. Braun saw the ad and negotiated with Savage. Savage employed Sean Trevor Doutre as a contract killer, with these results: On an August day in 1985, as Richard Braun and his 16-year-old son Michael drove out of their suburban Atlanta home, Doutre stepped in front of the car and fired several shots with an MAC–11 automatic pistol. Father and son rolled out of the car on opposite sides; Doutre fired two shots into the father's head. Doutre then pointed the pistol at 16-year-old Michael Braun, but did not fire. "Instead, Doutre put his finger over his lips signaling Michael to be quiet and ran into the woods." [81]

The Braun court distinguished Savage's Soldier of Fortune ad from the classified ad involved in the Eimann case discussed above. The Braun court refused to grant the magazine summary judgment, holding that the ad carrying phrases such as "Gun for Hire" and "Discreet and Very Private" and "All jobs considered" was far more explicit than the "facially innocuous" language in the ad in the Eimann case. The court held that Soldier of Fortune's ad had harmed the Braun family: [82]

> This is no strained construction. A risk becomes unreasonable when its magnitude outweighs the social utility of the act or omission that creates the risk. See Restatement (Second) of Torts Sec. 291. The risk in the Savage ad was the risk of murder or serious, violent crime.

Although an appeal was likely to be pursued by Soldier of Fortune in the Braun case, that jury's intent to punish conduct

---

[80] Braun v. Soldier of Fortune Magazine, Inc., 757 F.Supp. 1325 (M.D.Ala.1991), 18 Med.L.Rptr. 1732, 1733.

[81] Ibid.

[82] Ibid., at 1329.

perceived as outrageous was clear.[83]   But for the most part, outcomes of incitement cases against the media generally have favored defendants.   One case which received substantial publicity was Herceg v. Hustler, in which a teenage boy died experimenting with "autoerotic asphyxiation" after he read about it in Hustler magazine.   The U.S. Court of Appeals, 5th Circuit, in 1987 reversed a damage award of nearly $200,000 against Hustler.[84] More recently, rock stars Ozzy Osbourne and Judas Priest have been sued by surviving family members of adolescent family members who committed suicide.   Osbourne's lyrics in "Suicide Solution" were held to be entertainment, and that Osbourne's music was not proven to have been intended to cause suicide.   In that case, the grieving relatives did not collect damages.[85]

In an even stranger case, a Nevada judge ruled in Vance v. Judas Priest (1989) that subliminal messages do not have First Amendment protection.   This case involved a lawsuit by anguished survivors of Raymond Belknap, 18, who committed suicide with a 12-gauge shotgun aimed under his chin, and James Vance, 20, injured in a suicide attempt with the same shotgun, survived for several years thereafter.   Vance, horribly disfigured, died three years later in the psychiatric unit of a hospital.

The self-inflicted shootings occurred after Belknap and Vance had spent the afternoon drinking beer, smoking marijuana, and listening to Judas Priest albums.   Arguments for the plaintiffs included assertions that subliminal messages urging self-destruction were present in the records along with the overt heavy-metal themes of death, destruction, violent sex and suicide.

Although the Nevada court held that "the use of audio subliminal messages does not advance. . . . [commonly cited] theories of free speech." [86]   Finding that testimony linking the deaths to the music of Judas Priest was not "inherently incredible," the Nevada district court (2nd District) ordered the case to go to trial. At trial, however, it was held that there was insufficient proof that the defendants put subliminal messages in the songs or that the lyrics caused the suicides.[87]

[83] Ibid.

[84] Herceg v. Hustler Magazine, Inc., 814 F.2d 1017 (5th Cir.1987), 13 Med.L.Rptr. 2345.

[85] McCollum v. CBS, Inc., 202 Cal.App.3d 989, 249 Cal.Rptr. 187 (1988), 15 Med.L. Rptr. 2001.

[86] Vance v. Judas Priest, 16 Med.L.Rptr. 2241, 2257 (Nev.1989).

[87] Outcome of case cited in Victor A. Kovner, Harriet K. Dorsen, and Suzanne L. Telsey, "Recent Developments . . .," in James C. Goodale, ed., Communications Law 1991 (Vol. 2), at p. 105, discussing a New York Times story dealing with Priest v. Belknap Records, Aug. 25, 1990, p. 11.

Chapter 8

OBSCENITY

Sec.
44. The Common Law Origins.
45. The Roth Landmark.
46. Monitoring Compliance: The Federal Review Era.
47. Encouraging State Standards: The Miller v. California Era.
48. Balancing Conflicting Societal Interests.

SEC. 44. THE COMMON LAW ORIGINS

British common law, drawn from an era of soapbox orators and humble printers, provided little guidance in establishing what expression was obscene, and therefore not entitled to constitutional protection in the United States.

One of the nation's most literate and articulate judges—United States Court of Appeals Judge Leonard P. Moore—once wrote about obscenity law with sour resignation. "It is unfortunate," said Moore " * * * that these matters have to come before the courts." [1] He was describing the enormous amounts of time and efforts that American courts—especially the Supreme Court of the United States—have spent grappling with what Justice John Marshall Harlan once termed "the intractable obscenity problem." [2] From the mid–1950s through the 1970s, every term brought the Supreme Court dozens of obscenity cases, causing Justice Robert H. Jackson to observe that it seemed to be becoming the High Court of Obscenity.[3]

Jackson was prophetic. For years, aging, dignified members of the Supreme Court have been compelled to spend countless hours weighing the artistic merit of descriptions or depictions of a mind-boggling assortment of natural and perverse sexual activities. The task soon became a formidable and frustrating one, with Justice Potter Stewart wondering at one point whether the Court might be trying to define what in fact was indefinable.[4]

[1] United States v. Various Articles of Obscene Merchandise, 562 F.2d 185 (2d Cir. 1977).

[2] Interstate Circuit, Inc. v. Dallas, 390 U.S. 676, 88 S.Ct. 1298 (1968).

[3] Statement made in 1948 by Justice Jackson, quoted by Anthony Lewis, "Sex and the Supreme Court," Esquire, June 1963, p. 82.

[4] Concurring opinion in Jacobellis v. Ohio, 378 U.S. 184, 197, 84 S.Ct. 1676, 1683 (1964). Stewart noted in the same opinion that he "knew obscenity when he saw it", but this furnished very little definitional guidance to anyone but Justice Stewart himself.

Why, then, did the Court continue to accept obscenity cases appeals among that less than five percent of all lower court cases it agreed to review each year, thereby denying consideration to a wide range of other vital legal questions it did not have the time to answer? Because unique among the legal classifications relating to expression, if something can be classified by law as being "obscene", it has no protection under either the First or Fourteenth amendments from government control.

In common usage, the term "obscene" has generally applied to those representations of sexual behavior that the average person would find to be,

> Foul, disgusting; offensive to common decency or morality; lewd or lascivious sexual conduct.[5]

The Supreme Court actually created this unwieldy obscenity case load burden for itself by deciding in 1957 that any State law defining obscenity had to conform to specific federal standards it established, or be struck down as infringing upon constitutionally protected freedom of expression.[6] Until that time each State had been free to ban, if it choose to do so, any material falling within its own legislative definition of obscenity.

What no one could foresee in 1957, of course, was that those simple traditional moral values of the Eisenhower decade would soon be swept aside by a frenzied "sexual revolution", driven by unrelenting desires that soon catapulted "adult" entertainment into a growth industry with revenues exceeding $4 billion a year. When this wave of demand crested in the late 1960s, the Court appeared for a time like the fabled Sorcerer's Apprentice, totally unable to control that powerful process it had unleashed.

During the first one hundred years of our history as a nation, obscenity was never a burning issue. Congress had passed the Tariff Act of 1842 that forbade the "importation of all indecent and obscene paintings, lithographs, engravings and transparencies",[7] but it was not until the 1870s that the first major anti-obscenity campaign was launched in this country. Anthony Comstock, a persistent and skillful moral crusader, was able in 1873 to muster enough political support to persuade Congress to pass legislation that made distributing obscene material through the mails a criminal offense.

[5] Webster's New Collegiate Dictionary. New York G. & C. Merriam Co. 1956. This mid–1950s definition reflects the pre-Roth view of what the term describes.

[6] Roth v. United States, 354 U.S. 476, 77 S.Ct. 1304 (1957).

[7] U.S. Public Statutes at Large, Vol. 5, Ch. 270. This, however, may have been at least in part an act of protectionism to preserve the market for these goods for American firms.

This federal law became the forerunner of many other obscenity laws and ordinances enacted by State and local governments. Once these laws had been enacted, it was then up to the American courts to decide how they should be applied. Lacking precedents from earlier American case law, these courts were forced to turn to English common law for guidance, discovering and adopting that rule establish in 1868 in the case of Regina v. Hicklin.

The Hicklin Rule

In *Hicklin,* Lord Chief Justice Cockburn ruled that an anti-Catholic pamphlet, The Confessional Unmasked, was obscene. Lord Cockburn set down this test for obscenity: [8]

> Whether the tendency of the matter charged as obscene is to deprave and corrupt those whose minds are open to such immoral influences and into whose hands a publication of this sort might fall.

This "Hicklin rule" was applied by a number of American courts.[9] Under such a test, a book did not have to offend or harm a normal adult. If it could be assumed that a book might have a bad effect on children or abnormal adults—"those whose minds are open to such immoral influences"—such a book could be suppressed.

American law added the so-called "partly obscene" test to the *Hicklin* rule. This was the practice of judging a book by passages taken of context. If a book had an obscenity in it, the entire book was obscene.[10] Perhaps the most troublesome portion of the *Hicklin* rule was the statement that a book was obscene if it suggested "thoughts of a most impure and libidinous character." [11] This judicial preoccupation with *thoughts* induced by the reading of literature—with no requirement that antisocial actions be tied to the reading matter—has continued to this time. In the law of obscenity, no harm or even likelihood of harm to readers need be shown in order to suppress a book as obscene.[12]

In 1913, Judge Learned Hand wrote an often quoted protest against the *Hicklin* rule, which he termed "mid-Victorian precedent." Although Judge Hand felt compelled to uphold the con-

[8] L.R. 3 Q.B. 360, 370 (1868).

[9] See United States v. Bennett, 24 Fed.Cas. 1093, 1103–1104, No. 14,571 (S.D.N.Y. 1879); Commonwealth v. Friede, 271 Mass. 318, 320, 171 N.E. 472, 473 (1930).

[10] Lockhart & McClure, op. cit., p. 343.

[11] Ibid.

[12] See Roth v. United States, 354 U.S. 476, 490, 77 S.Ct. 1304, 1312 (1957); see also dictum by Mr. Justice Frankfurter, Beauharnais v. Illinois, 343 U.S. 250, 266, 72 S.Ct. 725, 735 (1952).

demnation as obscene of Daniel Goodman's novel *Hagar Revelley,* the judge wrote: [13]

> I question whether in the end men will regard that as obscene which is honestly relevant to the adequate expression of innocent ideas, and whether they will not believe that truth and beauty are too precious to be mutilated in the interests of those most likely to pervert them to base uses. * * *

Despite such moving protests, the *Hicklin* rule remained the leading test of obscenity in America until the 1930s.[14]

The Ulysses Decision

About this time, however, other American courts began to relax enforcement of the *Hicklin* rule to some extent. A mother who wrote a book to help her children learn about sex—and who later published the book at the suggestion of friends—successfully defended herself against charges that the book *(Sex Side of Life)* was obscene.[15] And in 1933, James Joyce's famed stream-of-consciousness novel *Ulysses,* now an acknowledged classic, was the target of an obscenity prosecution under the Tariff Act of 1930.[16]

Customs officers had prevented an actress from bringing *Ulysses* into this country. When *Ulysses* reached trial, Judge John Woolsey—a literate man acquainted with far more than law books—did read the entire book. He attacked the *Hicklin* test head-on and ruled that *Ulysses* was art, not obscenity. His decision has become one of the most noted in the law of criminal words, even though it by no means brought the end of the *Hicklin* rule, which continued to appear, in varying degrees, in the decisions of some other courts.[17] Overrated or not, the *Ulysses* decision represents an often-cited step toward nullifying some of the most restrictive aspects of the old *Hicklin* yardstick.

The *Ulysses* decision provided a new definition of obscenity for other courts to consider: that a book is obscene if it [18]

> tends to stir the sex impulses or to lead to sexually impure and lustful thoughts. Whether a particular book would tend to excite such impulses must be the test by the

[13] United States v. Kennerley, 209 Fed. 119 (S.D.N.Y.1913).

[14] See, e.g., Commonwealth v. Friede, 271 Mass. 318, 320, 171 N.E. 472, 473 (1930).

[15] United States v. Dennett, 39 F.2d 564, 76 A.L.R. 1092 (2d Cir.1930).

[16] United States v. One Book Called "Ulysses," 5 F.Supp. 182 (S.D.N.Y.1933); Paul and Schwartz, op. cit., p. 66.

[17] See e.g., United States v. Two Obscene Books, 99 F.Supp. 760 (N.D.Cal.1951), affirmed as Besig v. United States, 208 F.2d 142 (9th Cir.1953).

[18] United States v. One Book Called "Ulysses," 5 F.Supp. 182, 184 (S.D.N.Y.1933).

court's opinion as to its effect (when judged as a whole) on
a person with average sex instincts.

Only one portion of the old *Hicklin* rule appeared in Judge
Woolsey's *Ulysses* opinion: the emphasis on thoughts produced by
a book as an indicator of a book's obscene effect on a reader. This
judicial preoccupation with thoughts—and the tests outlined by
Judge Woolsey in 1933—are markedly similar to rules for judging
obscenity laid down in the Supreme Court's landmark decision in
the 1957 case of Roth v. United States.[19]

SEC. 45. THE ROTH LANDMARK

**In Roth v. United States, the Supreme Court held that ob-
scenity is not constitutionally protected expression and
set down its most influential standard for judging what
is—or is not—obscene.**

Even though efforts to control obscenity have a long history in
this nation, it was not until the reasonably recent date of 1957—in
the case of Roth v. United States—that the Supreme Court directly upheld the constitutionality of obscenity statutes.[20] This decision remains the most influential case in the law of obscenity
because it declared that both state and federal anti-obscenity laws
are valid exercises of government's police power.

Although this decision is called *Roth,* it actually included two
cases. The Court simultaneously decided a case under the federal
obscenity statute [21] (*Roth*) and under a state statute [22] (People v.
Alberts). Taken together, the *Roth* and *Alberts,* cases thus raised
the question of the constitutionality of both federal and state anti-
obscenity laws.

In the federal prosecution, Roth was convicted of violating the
statute by mailing various circulars plus a book, *American Aphro-
dite*. He was sentenced to what was then the maximum sentence:
a $5,000 fine *plus* a five-year penitentiary term. His conviction
was affirmed by the United States Court of Appeals, Second
Circuit, although the great Judge Jerome M. Frank questioned the
constitutionality of obscenity laws in a powerful concurring opinion. In words which have been called the beginning of the modern
law of obscenity, Judge Frank declared that obscenity laws are
unconstitutionally vague. He noted that Benjamin Franklin,
named Postmaster General by the First Continental Congress, had

[19] 354 U.S. 476, 77 S.Ct. 1304 (1957).

[20] Ibid.

[21] United States v. Roth, 237 F.2d 796 (2d Cir.1956).

[22] West's Ann.Cal.Pen.Code § 311; People v. Alberts, 138 Cal.App.2d 909, 292
P.2d 90 (1955).

written books—including The Speech of Polly Baker—which a
20th Century jury might find obscene. Judge Frank added: [23]

* * *

> The troublesome aspect of the federal obscenity stat-
> ute * * * is that (a) no one can now show that with any
> reasonable probability obscene publications tend to have
> any effects on the behavior of normal, average adults, and
> (b) that under the [federal] statute * * * punishment is
> apparently inflicted for provoking, in such adults, unde-
> sirable sexual thoughts, feelings or desire—not overt dan-
> gerous or anti-social conduct, either actual or probable.

Despite Judge Frank's denunciation of the "exquisite vagueness" of obscenity laws, Roth's conviction was upheld, with the
Court of Appeals refusing to consider the contention that obscenity statutes are unconstitutionally vague curbs on speech and
press. The Supreme Court then granted certiorari, taking jurisdiction of the case.[24]

Alberts v. California

The State of California prosecution against David S. Alberts
went after his mail-order business in Los Angeles. In 1955, he
was served with a warrant and his business office, warehouse and
residence were searched. Hundreds—maybe thousands—of books
and pictures were seized.[25] Such books as "Witch on Wheels,"
"She Made It Pay," and "Sword of Desire"—plus some mail
circulars—were found to be obscene. In discussing "Sword of
Desire," the trial judge [26] did not read the book in its entirety,
showing that the *Ulysses* decision's 1933 holding [27] that a book
should be judged as a whole was not always followed.

Alberts' conviction was upheld by an appellate court. That
court concluded that the words "obscene" and "indecent" were not
unconstitutionally vague. The Supreme Court then noted probable jurisdiction.[28]

In jointly considering the *Roth* and *Alberts* cases, the Court
did not rule on whether the books sold by the two men were in
fact obscene. The only issue reviewed in each case was the

---

[23] 237 F.2d 796, 825 826–827 (2d Cir.1956). See Stanley Fleishman, "Witchcraft
and Obscenity: Twin Superstitions," Wilson Library Bulletin, April, 1965, p. 4.

[24] 352 U.S. 964, 77 S.Ct. 361 (1957).

[25] Fleishman, op. cit., p. 10.

[26] Ibid., Alberts was tried by a judge sitting alone since Alberts had waived jury
trial.

[27] United States v. One Book Called "Ulysses," 5 F.Supp. 182 (S.D.N.Y.1933).

[28] Alberts v. California, 352 U.S. 962, 77 S.Ct. 349 (1957).

validity of an obscenity law on its face.[29] Alberts argued that this mail-order business could not be punished under California law because a state cannot regulate an area pre-empted by the federal obscenity laws. The majority opinion replied that the federal statute deals only with actual mailing and does not prevent a state from punishing the advertising or keeping for sale of obscene literature.[30]

Roth contended, on the other hand, that the power to punish speech and press offensive to morality belongs to the states alone under the powers of the First, Ninth, and Tenth Amendments to the Constitution. The majority opinion discarded this argument, saying that obscenity is not speech or expression protected by the First Amendment.[31] Justice Brennan added, in language which was to greatly affect later decisions in the law of obscenity:[32]

> All ideas having even the slightest redeeming social importance—unorthodox ideas, controversial ideas, even ideas hateful to the prevailing climate of opinion—have the full protection of the guaranties [of free speech and press], unless excludable because they encroach upon the limited area of more important interests. But implicit in the area of more important interests. But implicit in the history of the First Amendment is the rejection of obscenity as utterly without redeeming social importance.

This passage had within it elements of freeing literature. Later cases would make much of the phrase "redeeming social importance" to protect sexy materials, because most literature must have something good you can say about it.[33] Justice Brennan's majority opinion set the stage for obscenity law developments in two ways. First, obscenity laws may be used to punish *thoughts;* overt sexual actions are not needed to bring a conviction.[34] Second—and more important—obscenity is expression *not* protected by the First Amendment.[35] Those are the two main strands in the law of obscenity. Other strands woven in by concurring and dissenting Justices in Roth v. United States fore-

[29] 354 U.S. 476, 77 S.Ct. 1304, 1307 (1957).

[30] 354 U.S. 476, 493–494, 77 S.Ct. 1304, 1314 (1957).

[31] 354 U.S. 476, 492, 77 S.Ct. 1304, 1313 (1957).

[32] 354 U.S. 476, 484, 77 S.Ct. 1304, 1309 (1957).

[33] See, e.g., A Book Named "John Cleland's Memoirs of a Woman of Pleasure" v. Attorney General of Massachusetts, 383 U.S. 413, 419–420, 86 S.Ct. 975, 977–978 (1966).

[34] 354 U.S. 476, 486–487, 77 S.Ct. 1304, 1309–1310 (1957).

[35] 354 U.S. 476, 482, 77 S.Ct. 1304, 1307 (1957).

cast other themes which would crescendo and diminish for the next 30 years in the strange symphony of obscenity law.[36]

The Roth Test

Writing for the Court, Justice Brennan set down this try at defining the undefinable: "Obscene material is material which deals with sex in a manner appealing to prurient interest." [37] "Prurient interest," of course, refers to sexually oriented thoughts. Brennan then articulated "the Roth test" for judging whether or not material is obscene: [38]

> * * * whether to the average person, applying contemporary community standards, the dominant theme of the material taken as a whole appeals to prurient interest.

Subsequent decisions have returned for guidance to these words again and again. This "*Roth* test" rejected some features of the American rendition of the *Hicklin* rule. The practice of judging books by the presumed effect of isolated passages upon the most susceptible persons was rejected because it "might well encompass material legitimately dealing with sex." [39]

Mr. Justice Brennan's words were not wholly libertarian. The *Roth* test is a "deprave and corrupt" test. Under *Roth,* a book could be declared obscene if it could be assumed that it might induce obscene thoughts in an hypothetical average person.[40] There is no need for the prosecution to prove that there is a "clear and present danger" [41] or even a "clear and possible danger" [42] that a book will lead to antisocial conduct.

Roth: Concurrences and Dissents

Chief Justice Earl Warren was evidently puzzled by the idea that *books* rather than persons were defendants in obscenity

---

[36] For example, Chief Justice Earl Warren's concurrence in Roth argued that the conduct of a defendant was the key point in an obscenity prosecution. For a case which turned on the defendant's conduct, see Ginzburg v. United States, 383 U.S. 463, 86 S.Ct. 942 (1966).

[37] 354 U.S. 476, 487, 77 S.Ct. 1304, 1310 (1957). The terms used in the three "tests" approved in Roth—"lustful desire," "lustful thoughts," and "appeal to prurient interest"—all imply that if a book can be assumed to cause or induce "improper" sexual thoughts, that book can be "banned." The "appeal to prurient interest" test was drawn from the American Law Institute's Model Penal Code, Tentative Draft No. 6 (Philadelphia, American Law Institute, May 6, 1957).

[38] 354 U.S. 476, 489, 77 S.Ct. 1304, 1311 (1957).

[39] 354 U.S. 476, 489, 77 S.Ct. 1304, 1311 (1957).

[40] 354 U.S. 476, 486, 77 S.Ct. 1304, 1310 (1957).

[41] 354 U.S. 476, 489, 77 S.Ct. 1304, 1310 (1957).

[42] U.S. 476, 489, 77 S.Ct. 1304, 1310 (1957), citing Dennis v. United States, 341 U.S. 494, 71 S.Ct. 857 (1951).

prosecutions. His brief concurring opinion in *Roth* has proved to be remarkably predictive since 1957. Chief Justice Warren stated that in an obscenity trial, the conduct of the defendant rather than the obscenity of a book should be the central issue: [43]

He concluded that both Roth and Alberts had engaged in "the commercial exploitation of the morbid and shameful craving for materials with prurient effect" and said that the state and federal governments could constitutionally punish such conduct.[44] Justice Brennan's majority opinion in *Roth* has influenced the course of the law of obscenity. So, in an increasing degree in recent years, has Chief Justice Warren's concurring opinion, which insisted that the behavior of the defendant, rather than the nature of the book itself, was the "central issue" in an obscenity case.[45]

Justice Harlan also disagreed with the majority opinion's conclusion that obscenity laws are constitutional because an earlier Supreme Court had found that obscenity is "utterly without redeeming social importance": [46]

> On this basis, the *constitutional* question before us becomes, as the Court says, whether "obscenity," as an abstraction, is protected by the First and Fourteenth Amendments, and the question whether a *particular* book may be suppressed becomes a mere matter of classification, of "fact" to be entrusted to a fact-finder and insulated from independent judgment.

Justice Harlan thus told his fellow justices that the vital question was "what is obscenity?", not "is obscenity good or bad?"

While Harlan asked this challenging question of his brethren on the Court, Justice William O. Douglas was joined by Justice Hugo L. Black in a scathing attack on obscenity laws and obscenity prosecutions. This dissent foreshadowed arguments these Justices would advance in obscenity cases which subsequently followed *Roth* to the Supreme Court. Douglas wrote that Roth and Alberts were punished "for thoughts provoked, not for overt acts nor antisocial conduct." He was unimpressed by the possibility that the books involved might produce sexual thoughts: "The arousing of sexual thoughts and desires happens every day in normal life in dozens of ways." [47]

Problems involving freedom of speech and press, it was argued, must not be solved by "weighing against the values of free

[43] 354 U.S. 476, 495, 77 S.Ct. 1304, 1315 (1957).

[44] 354 U.S. 476, 496, 77 S.Ct. 1304, 1315 (1957).

[45] 354 U.S. 476, 495, 77 S.Ct. 1304, 1314–1315 (1957).

[46] 354 U.S. 476, 497, 77 S.Ct. 1304, 1315 (1957).

[47] 354 U.S. 476, 509, 77 S.Ct. 1304, 1322 (1957).

expression, the judgment of a court that a particular form of expression has 'no redeeming social importance.' " Justice Douglas declared: [48]

[T]he test that suppresses a cheap tract today can suppress a literary gem tomorrow. All it need do is incite a lascivious thought or arouse a lustful desire. The list of books that judges or juries can place in that category is endless.

SEC. 46. MONITORING COMPLIANCE: THE FEDERAL REVIEW ERA

Once the federal court system had asserted its right to review the constitutionality of all State obscenity laws, it found itself overwhelmed not only by the case-load it assumed, but also by the difficulty of defining the obscene in any one uniform and universal way.

Although *Roth* remains the leading decision on obscenity and said much, later court decisions showed that it actually settled very little. Five years after *Roth* the Supreme Court attempted to refine its definition of obscenity in Manual Enterprises, Inc. v. Day, Postmaster General of the United States. In writing for the Court, Justice Harlan termed *MANual* [sic], *Trim,* and *Grecian Pictorial* "dismally unpleasant, uncouth and tawdry" magazines which were published "primarily, if not exclusively, for homosexuals." [49]

Despite this, a majority of the Supreme Court held that these magazines which presented pictures of nude males were not obscene and unmailable because they were not "patently offensive." Harlan wrote: [50]

Obscenity under the federal statute * * * requires proof of two distinct elements: (1) patent offensiveness; and (2) "prurient interest" appeal.

In 1966, the Supreme Court again tackled the tough problem of defining obscenity as decisions were announced in three cases, the "Fanny Hill" case,[51] Mishkin v. New York,[52] and Ginzburg v. United States.[53] First announced was the decision in the *Fanny Hill* case. *Fanny Hill,* or as the book is also known, *Memoirs of a Woman of Pleasure,* was written in England about 1749 by John Cleland. The book was well known in the American colonies and

[48] 354 U.S. 476, 514, 77 S.Ct. 1304, 1324 (1957).

[49] 370 U.S. 478, 481, 82 S.Ct. 1432, 1434 (1962).

[50] 370 U.S. 478, 482–486, 82 S.Ct. 1432, 1434–1436 (1962).

[51] 383 U.S. 413, 86 S.Ct. 975 (1966).

[52] 383 U.S. 502, 86 S.Ct. 958 (1966).

[53] 383 U.S. 463, 86 S.Ct. 942 (1966).

was first published in the United States around 1800. *Fanny Hill*, was also one of the first books in America to be the subject of an obscenity trial: in Massachusetts in 1821.[54] More than 140 years later, Fanny Hill was back in the courts of Massachusetts, as well as in New York, New Jersey and Illinois.

In Fanny Hill, there is not one of the "four letter words" which have so often put more modern literature before the courts. But although the language was quite sanitary, author Cleland's descriptions of Fanny's sexual gyrations left little to the imagination. Even so, some experts—including poet and critic Louis Untermeyer—testified that *Fanny Hill* was a work of art and was not pornographic. The experts, however, were asked by a cross-examining prosecuting attorney if they realized that the book contained "20 acts of sexual intercourse, four of them in the presence of others; four acts of lesbianism, two acts of male homosexuality, two acts of flagellation and one of female masturbation." [55]

Fanny Hill, then, is a frankly erotic novel. Justice Brennan summed up the tests for obscenity which the highest court had approved: [56]

> We defined obscenity in *Roth* in the following terms: "[W]hether to the average person, applying contemporary community standards, the dominant theme of the material taken as a whole appeals to prurient interest." 354 U.S. at 489, 77 S.Ct. at 1311. Under this definition, as elaborated in subsequent cases, three elements must coalesce: it must be established that (a) the dominant theme of the materials taken as a whole appeals to a prurient interest in sex; (b) the material is patently offensive because it affronts contemporary community standards relating to the description or representation of sexual matters; and (c) the material is utterly without redeeming social value.

The Supreme Court of the United States held that the Massachusetts courts had erred in finding that a book didn't have to be "unqualifiedly worthless" before it could be deemed obscene. Justice Brennan, writing for the Court, stated that a book "can not be proscribed unless it is found to be *utterly* without redeeming social value." [57]

---

[54] Commonwealth v. Peter Holmes, 17 Mass. 336 (1821).

[55] Cf. the outraged dissent by Justice Tom C. Clark, 383 U.S. 413, 445–446, 86 S.Ct. 975, 990–991 (1966).

[56] 383 U.S. 413, 418, 86 S.Ct. 975, 977 (1966).

[57] 383 U.S. 413, 419, 86 S.Ct. 975, 978 (1966).

Second, Justice Brennan announced the Court's decision in the *Mishkin* case. Edward Mishkin, who operated a bookstore near New York City's Times Square, was appealing a sentence of three years and $12,500 in fines. Mishkin's publishing speciality was sadism and masochism, and he had been found guilty by New York courts of producing and selling more than 50 different paperbacks. Titles involved included *Dance With the Dominant Whip, and Mrs. Tyrant's Finishing School.*[58] Mishkin's defense, was based on the notion that the books he published and sold did not appeal to the prurient interest of an average person. The average person, it was argued, would be disgusted and sickened by such books.[59]

Justice Brennan's majority opinion, however, dismissed Mishkin's argument.[60]

> Where the material is designed primarily for and primarily disseminated to a clearly defined deviant sexual group, rather than the public at large, the prurient-appeal requirement of the *Roth* test is satisfied if the dominant theme of the material taken as a whole appeals to the prurient interest of the members of that group.

After upholding Mishkin's conviction, Mr. Justice Brennan then turned to the *Ginzburg* case. With this opinion, the Supreme Court brought another element to the adjudication of obscenity disputes: the manner in which the matter charged with obscenity was sold.[61]

The *Ginzburg* case involved three publication: "EROS, a hardcover magazine of expensive format; Liaison, a bi-weekly newsletter; and The Housewife's Handbook on Selective Promiscuity, * * * a short book." Justice Brennan took notice of "abundant evidence" from Ralph Ginzburg's federal district court trial "that each of the accused publications was originated or sold as stock in trade of the sordid business of pandering—'the business of purveying textual or graphic matter openly advertised to appeal to the erotic interest of their customers.' "[62]

Included as evidence of this "pandering" were EROS magazine's attempts to get mailing privileges from the whimsically named hamlets of Intercourse and Blue Ball, Pa. Mailing privileges were finally obtained in Middlesex, N.J.[63]

---

[58] 383 U.S. 502, 514–515, 86 S.Ct. 958, 966–968 (1966).

[59] 383 U.S. 502, 508, 86 S.Ct. 958, 963 (1966).

[60] 383 U.S. 502, 508–509, 86 S.Ct. 958, 963–964 (1966).

[61] 383 U.S. 463, 465–466, 86 S.Ct. 942, 944–945 (1966).

[62] 383 U.S. 463, 467, 86 S.Ct. 942, 945 (1966).

[63] 383 U.S. 463, 467, 86 S.Ct. 942, 945 (1966).

Also, Justice Brennan found "'the leer of the sensualist'" permeating the advertising for the three publications. *Liaison*, for example, was extolled as "Cupid's Chronicle," and the advertising circulars asked, "Are you a member of the sexual elite?" [64] It is likely, however, that publisher Ginzburg believed that the *Roth* test had left him on safe ground, for his advertising proclaimed:

"EROS handles the subject of Love and Sex with complete candor. The publication of this magazine—which is frankly and avowedly concerned with erotica—has been enabled by recent court decisions ruling that a literary piece of painting, though explicitly sexual in content, has a right to be published if it is a genuine work of art."

"EROS is genuine work of art."

The Court was severely split of the *Ginzburg* case, however, with Justices Black, Douglas, Harlan and Stewart all registering bitter dissents. Justice Black set the tone for his dissenting brethren, declaring: [65]

* * * Ginzburg, * * * is now finally and authoritatively condemned to serve five years in prison for distributing printed matter about sex which neither Ginzburg nor anyone else could possibly have known to be criminal.

Justice Harlan accused the court's majority of rewriting the federal obscenity statute in order to convict Ginzburg, and called the new "pandering" test unconstitutionally vague. [66] And Justice Stewart asserted in his dissent that Ginzburg "was not charged with 'commercial exploitation'; he was not charged with 'pandering'; he was not charged with 'titillation.'" Convicting Ginzburg on such grounds, Stewart added, was to deny him due process of law. [67]

Justice Douglas added his denunciation of the condemnation of materials as obscene not because of their content, but because of the way they were advertised. [68]

Protecting the Young: The Ginsberg Case and the "Variable Obscenity" Concept

As if to confound careless spellers, it has happened that one of the most important cases after the Ralph *Ginzburg* case involved a

[64] 383 U.S. 463, 469n, 86 S.Ct. 942, 946 (1966).

[65] 383 U.S. 463, 476, 86 S.Ct. 942, 954 (1966).

[66] 383 U.S. 463, 476, 86 S.Ct. 942, 954 (1966).

[67] 383 U.S. 463, 494, 86 S.Ct. 942, 954 (1966).

[68] 383 U.S. 463, 494, 497, 86 S.Ct. 942, 954, 956 (1966).

man named *Ginsberg*: Sam Ginsberg. In the 1968 *Ginsberg* case, the Supreme Court held by a 6–3 vote that a New York statute which defined obscenity on the basis of its appeal to minors under 17 was not unconstitutionally vague.

Sam Ginsberg and his wife operated "Sam's Stationery and Luncheonette" in Bellmore, Long Island. In 1965, a mother sent her 16-year-old son to the luncheonette to by some "girlie" magazines. The boy purchased two magazines—apparently *Sir* and *Gent* or similar publications—and walked out of the luncheonette. On the basis of this sale, Sam Ginsberg was convicted of violation of a New York law making it a misdemeanor "knowingly to sell * * * to a minor" under 17 "any picture * * * which depicts nudity * * * and which is harmful to minors" and "any * * * magazine * * * which contains * * * [such pictures] and which, taken as a whole, is harmful to minors." [69]

It should be noted that magazines such as the 16-year-old boy purchased from Sam Ginsberg's luncheonette in 1967 had been held *not* obscene for adults by the Supreme Court.[70] However the judge at Sam Ginsberg's obscenity trial found pictures in the two magazines which depicted nudity in a manner that was in violation of the New York statute.

The trial judge found that the pictures were "harmful to minors" under the terms of the New York law.

In affirming Ginsberg's conviction, Justice Brennan approved the concept of "variable obscenity." [71] Brennan noted that the magazines involved in the *Ginsberg* case were not obscene for sale to adults. However, the New York statute forbidding their sale to minors "does not bar the appellant from stocking the magazines and selling them to persons 17 years of age or older." Brennan repeated the holding that obscenity is not within the area of protected speech or press.[72] It was permissible for the state of New York to "accord to minors under 17 a more restricted right than that assured to adults to judge and determine for themselves what sex material they may read or see."

In the case which resulted in the fining and jailing of *Eros* publisher Ralph Ginzburg, the Supreme Court served notice that

[69] Ginsberg v. New York, 390 U.S. 629, 634, 88 S.Ct. 1274, 1277 (1968). The statute is Article 484–H of the New York Penal Law, McKinney's Consol Laws c. 40.

[70] Redrup v. New York, 386 U.S. 767, 87 S.Ct. 1414 (1967).

[71] Ginsberg v. New York, 390 U.S. 629, 635 n., 88 S.Ct. 1274, 1278 n. (1968), quoting Lockhart and McClure, "Censorship of Obsenity: The Developing Constitutional Standards," 45 Minnesota Law Review 5, 85 (1960).

[72] Ginsberg v. New York, 390 U.S. 629, 635, 88 S.Ct. 1274, 1277–1278 (1968); see Butler v. Michigan, 352 U.S. 380, 77 S.Ct. 524 (1957); Roth v. United States, 354 U.S. 476, 77 S.Ct. 1304, 1309 (1957).

not only *what* was sold but *how* it was sold would be taken into account.[73] The *how* of selling or distributing literature can include a legitimate public concern over the materials which minor children see. That is the lesson of the case of Ginsberg v. New York, and that lesson is wrapped up in the concept of "variable obscenity." That is, some materials were found not obscene for adults but are obscene when children are involved.[74]

Indecisiveness: *Redrup* and *Stanley*

In the spring of 1967, the Supreme Court of the United States openly admitted its confusion over obscenity law in a case known as Redrup v. New York.[75] This decision did not *look* important: it took up only six pages in United States Reports and only about four pages were devoted to its unsigned *per curiam* ["by the court"] majority opinion. The other two pages were given over to a dissent by Justice John Marshall Harlan, with whom Justice Tom C. Clark joined. *Redrup* was an important case simply because the Court said that a majority of its members could not agree on a standard which could declare so-called "girlie magazines" and similar publications to be obscene.

Redrup seemed for a time to be the most important obscenity case since Roth v. United States because it was used by both state and federal courts for several years to avoid many of the complexities of judging whether works of art or literature are obscene. On June 12, 1967, the date the Court's term ended that year and less than two months after *Redrup* was decided, the Court reversed 11 obscenity convictions by merely referring to Redrup v. New York.[76] Another dozen state or federal obscenity convictions were reversed during the next year, with *Redrup* being listed as an important factor in each reversal.[77]

The majority opinion in *Redrup* placed significant reliance upon the Court's 1966 decision in Ginzburg v. United States. In *Ginzburg,* discussed earlier in this chapter, it will be recalled that the Court took special notice of the *manner* in which magazines or books were sold.[78] *Redrup* echoed this concern, but also took into account the *recipients* of materials charged with obscenity. The Court suggested that convictions for selling or mailing obscenity should be upheld in three kinds of situations:

[73] Ginzburg v. United States, 383 U.S. 463, 86 S.Ct. 942 (1966).

[74] Ginsberg v. New York, 390 U.S. 629, 88 S.Ct. 1274 (1968).

[75] 386 U.S. 767, 87 S.Ct. 1414 (1967).

[76] Dwight L. Teeter, Jr., and Don R. Pember, "The Retreat from Obscenity: Redrup v. New York," Hastings Law Journal Vol. 21 (Nov., 1969) pp. 175–189.

[77] 386 U.S. 767, 771–772, 87 S.Ct. 1414, 1416–1417 (1967).

[78] 383 U.S. 463, 86 S.Ct. 942 (1966).

(1) Where there is evidence of "pandering" sales as in Ginzburg v. United States.

(2) Where there is a statute reflecting "a specific and limited state concern for juveniles." [79]

(3) Where there is "an assault upon individual privacy by publication in a manner so obtrusive as to make it impossible for the unwilling individual to avoid exposure to it." [80]

Beyond these kinds of forbidden conduct *Redrup* gave little guidance. Perhaps, however, it may be guessed that *Redrup* meant this: If the *conduct* of the seller did not fit the three kinds of prohibited actions listed above, and if the *contents* were not so wretched that they would be held to be "hardcore pornography," [81] then the materials involved were constitutionally protected.[82]

Stanley v. Georgia (1969)

In 1969, there was hope that the Supreme Court of the United States—clearly irritated by obscenity cases which amounted to perhaps five per cent of its total workload—would bring order to that troublesome area of law. The Court's resolution of Stanley v. Georgia added to that hope.[83] The *Stanley* case arose when a Georgia state investigator and three federal agents, operating under a federal search warrant, searched the home of Robert E. Stanley, looking for bookmaking records. Evidence of bookmaking was not found, but the searchers found three reels of 8 millimeter film and—handily—a projector. They treated themselves to a showing and decided—as did a couple of courts—that the films were obscene. When Stanley's appeal reached the Supreme Court, Mr. Justice Thurgood Marshall—writing for a

[79] Redrup v. New York, 386 U.S. 767, 769, 87 S.Ct. 1414, 1415 (1967). Note that (2) above, announced in Redrup on May 8, 1967, forecast with considerable precision the Court's decision in Ginsberg v. New York, 390 U.S. 629, 88 S.Ct. 1274 (1968).

[80] Ibid., citing Breard v. Alexandria, La., 341 U.S. 622, 71 S.Ct. 920 (1951), and Public Utilities Commission of Dist. of Columbia v. Pollak, 343 U.S. 451, 72 S.Ct. 813 (1952).

[81] 386 U.S. 767, 771n, 87 S.Ct. 1414, 1416n, referring to Justice Potter Stewart's quotation, in his dissent in Ginzburg v. United States, of this definition of hardcore pornography, including writings and "photographs, both still and motion picture, with no pretense of artistic value, graphically depicting acts of sexual intercourse, including various acts of sodomy and sadism, and sometimes involving several participants in scenes of orgy-like character. * * * verbally describing such activities in a bizarre manner with no attempt whatsoever to afford portrayals of character or situation and with no pretense to literary value." See Ginzburg v. United States, 383 U.S. 463, 499n, 86 S.Ct. 942, 956n (1966).

[82] 386 U.S. 767, 87 S.Ct. 1414, 1416 (1967).

[83] Stanley v. Georgia, 394 U.S. 557, 89 S.Ct. 1243 (1969).

unanimous Court—overturned the conviction, naming two constitutional rights.[84]

(1) A right growing out of the First Amendment, a "right to receive information and ideas, regardless of their social worth." [85]

(2) A constitutional right to privacy tied to the right to receive information and ideas: [86]

* * * [F]undamental is the right to be free, except in very limited circumstances, from unwanted governmental intrusions into one's privacy. * * * These are the rights that appellant [Stanley] is asserting. * * * the right to satisfy his intellectual and emotional needs in the privacy of his own home.

Because Stanley v. Georgia involved no dangers of either injuring minors or invading the privacy of the general public, the Supreme Court concluded: [87]

We hold that the First and Fourteenth Amendments prohibit making mere private possession of obscene material a crime. Roth and the cases following that decision are not impaired by today's holding. As we have said, the States retain broad power to regulate obscenity; that power simply does not extend to mere possession by the individual in the privacy of his own home.

Taken together, *Redrup* and *Stanley* suggested to some judges that the strictures of obscenity law had been loosened by the Supreme Court. *Redrup* said that the Court could not define anything but hard-core porn, the grossest of the gross. And *Stanley* seemed to say that people had a right to possess sexually explicit literature and films at home. This meant, to some judges, that if you got the stuff home, somebody, somewhere, had to have at least a limited right to sell it to you. Right? [88] Or, what if you had an overpowering urge, as Justice Marshall once phrased it, to receive "information and ideas" by viewing "Raunchy Randy and the Virgins of Venus" at your local X-rated movie parlor? Couldn't you be somehow "publicly private"—sitting there in anonymous darkness of that theater? And you, in such a case, would be in effect a consenting adult whose privacy or other

---

[84] Black, J., concurred in the decision.

[85] 394 U.S. 557, 89 S.Ct. 1243 (1969), citing Winters v. New York, 333 U.S. 507, 510, 68 S.Ct. 665 (1948).

[86] 394 U.S. 557, 564–564, 89 S.Ct. 1243, 1247–1248 (1969).

[87] 394 U.S. 557, 568–569, 89 S.Ct. 1243, 1249–1250 (1969).

[88] See, e.g., Dyson v. Stein, 401 U.S. 200, 91 S.Ct. 769 (1971).

sensibilities were not being intruded upon.[89] Couldn't it be claimed that you have a right to satisfy your "intellectual and emotional needs" in this way? [90]

No to all questions. Take, for example, the Supreme Court's 1971 decision in Byrne v. Karalexis,[91] involving state prosecutions for exhibiting the film "I Am Curious (Yellow). A federal court attempted to extend the Stanley v. Georgia language permitting individuals to receive and possess obscene material to seeing such information in a theater or library. That court said "If a rich Stanley can view a film, or read a book, a poorer Stanley should be free to visit a protected theater or library. We see no reason for saying he must go alone." [92]

But in an unsigned *per curiam* decision, the Supreme Court lifted the federal court's order halting Massachusetts prosecutions of the film. The "right to receive information and ideas" announced in Stanley v. Georgia was minimized, clearing the way for further state prosecutions for exhibiting the film.[93]

SEC. 47. ENCOURAGING STATE STANDARDS: THE MILLER v. CALIFORNIA ERA

In 1973, the Supreme Court returned primary responsibility to the States for deciding what was obscene, as long as those "community standards" established were consistent with basic federal principles of free speech.

The Supreme Court decided in 1973 to permit States once again to determine what constituted obscene expression within their own jurisdictions. In Miller v. California,[94] and in four companion cases decided at the same time, the Court delegated this authority to the States. No state was required to ban obscenity unless it chose to do so, but if it did, those standards it adopted to define obscenity had to conform to basic federal guidelines established by the Court in *Miller.*[95]

[89] See, e.g., United States v. Articles of "Obscene" Merchandise, 315 F.Supp. 191 (S.D.N.Y.1970), and Paris Adult Theatre I v. Slaton, 413 U.S. 49, 93 S.Ct. 2628 (1973).

[90] Stanley v. Georgia, 394 U.S. 557, 89 S.Ct. 1243 (1969).

[91] 401 U.S. 216, 91 S.Ct. 777 (1971).

[92] 306 F.Supp. 1363 at 1366–1367 (D.Mass.1969).

[93] 401 U.S. 216, 91 S.Ct. 777 (1971).

[94] Miller v. California, 413 U.S. 15, 93 S.Ct. 2607 (1973).

[95] Paris Adult Theatre I v. Slaton, 413 U.S. 49, 93 S.Ct. 2628 (1973); United States v. Orito, 413 U.S. 139, 93 S.Ct. 2674 (1973); Kaplan v. California, 413 U.S. 115, 93 S.Ct. 2680 (1973), and U.S. v. Twelve 200-ft. Reels of Super 8 mm Film, 413 U.S. 123, 93 S.Ct. 2665 (1973).

Miller v. California

The most important of the five obscenity cases decided by the Supreme Court on June 21, 1973—and indeed the most important such case since Roth v. United States (1957)—was Miller v. California. In that case, as in the four others of that date, the Court split 5–4, revealing a new coalition among the Justices where obscenity and pornography were concerned. This coalition included Justice Byron R. White (appointed by President John F. Kennedy) and four justices appointed by President Richard M. Nixon (Chief Justice Warren Burger, plus justices Harry Blackmun, William Rehnquist, and Lewis Powell). Dissenting in all five of those obscenity cases were Justices Thurgood Marshall, Potter Stewart, William O. Douglas, and the author of the *Roth* test of 1957 and of many of the obscenity decisions thereafter, Justice William J. Brennan, Jr.

Miller v. California arose when Marvin Miller mailed five unsolicited—and graphic—brochures to a restaurant in Newport Beach. The envelope was opened by the restaurant's manager, with his mother looking on, and they complained to police. The brochures advertised four books, Intercourse, Man-Woman, Sex Orgies Illustrated, and An Illustrated History of Pornography, plus a film titled Marital Intercourse. After a jury trial, Miller was convicted of a misdemeanor under the California Penal Code.[96]

Writing for the majority in *Miller,* Chief Justice Burger ruled that California could punish such conduct. He noted that the case involved "a situation in which sexually explicit materials have been thrust by aggressive sales action upon unwilling recipients or juveniles.

Endeavoring to formulate a new standard, Chief Justice Burger first returned to *Roth's* declaration that obscene materials were not protected by the First Amendment.[97] Then, he denounced the test of obscenity outlined in the Fanny Hill (*Memoirs of a Woman of Pleasure*) case in 1960, nine years after *Roth.* In that case, three justices, in a plurality opinion, held that material could not be judged obscene unless it were proven to be "utterly without redeeming social importance." Burger added: [98]

[96] West's Ann. California Pen. Code § 312.2(a) makes it a misdemeanor to knowingly distribute obscene matter. After the jury trial, the Appellate Department, Superior Court of California, Orange County, summarily affirmed the conviction without offering an opinion.

[97] 413 U.S. 15, 20, 93 S.Ct. 2607, 2613 (1973), citing Roth v. United States, 354 U.S. 476, 77 S.Ct. 1304 (1957).

[98] 413 U.S. 15, 22, 93 S.Ct. 2607, 2613–2614 (1973), citing Memoirs of a Woman of Pleasure v. Massachusetts, 383 U.S. 413, 86 S.Ct. 975 (1966). Emphasis the Court's.

While *Roth* presumed "obscenity" to be "utterly without redeeming social value," *Memoirs* required that to prove obscenity it must be affirmatively established that the material is "*utterly* without redeeming social value." Thus, even as they repeated the words of *Roth,* the *Memoirs* plurality produced a drastically altered test that called on the prosecution to prove a negative, i.e., that the material was "*utterly* without redeeming social value"—a burden virtually impossible to discharge under our criminal standards of proof.

The Chief Justice said that since the 1957 decision in *Roth,* the Court had not been able to muster a majority to agree to a standard of what constitutes "obscene, pornographic material subject to regulation under the States' police power." [99] In 1973, however, Burger found himself in substantial agreement with four other Justices. He made the most of it, setting out general rules on what States could regulate ("hard-core pornography") and rewording the *Roth* and *Memoirs* tests into a standard reducing the burden of proof necessary to convict persons for distribution or possession of sexually explicit materials.[1]

* * * [W]e now confine the permissible scope of such regulation to works which depict or describe sexual conduct. That conduct must be specifically defined by the applicable state law, as written or authoritatively construed. A state offense must also be limited to works which, taken as whole, appeal to the prurient interest in sex, which portray sexual conduct in a patently offensive way, and which, taken as a whole, do not have serious literary, artistic, political, or scientific value.

The basic guidelines for the trier of fact must be: (a) whether "the average person, applying contemporary community standards" would find that the work, taken as a whole, appeals to the prurient interest * * * (b) whether the work depicts or describes, in a patently offensive way, sexual conduct specifically defined by the

[99] 413 U.S. 15, 22, 93 S.Ct. 2607, 2614 (1973).

[1] 413 U.S. 15, 23–24, 93 S.Ct. 2607, 2614, 2615 (1973). Emphasis the Court's. Chief Justice Burger wrote that a State could, through statute, forbid:

"(a) Patently offensive representations or descriptions of ultimate sexual acts, normal or perverted, actual or simulated.

"(b) Patently offensive representations or descriptions of masturbation, excretory functions, and lewd exhibition of the genitals.

"Sex and nudity may not be exploited without limit by films or pictures exhibited or sold in places of public accommodation any more than live sex and nudity can be exhibited or sold without limit in such public places. At a minimum, prurient, patently offensive depiction or description of sexual conduct must have serious literary, artistic, political or scientific value to merit First Amendment protection."

applicable state law, and (c) whether the work, taken as a whole, lacks serious literary, artistic, political or scientific value. We do not adopt as a constitutional standard the "*utterly* without redeeming social value" test of Memoirs v. Massachusetts * * *: that concept has never commanded the adherence of more than three Justices at one time.

The majority opinion then declared that there can be no uniform national standard for judging obscenity or what appeals to "prurient interest" or what is "patently offensive." "[O]ur nation is simply too big and diverse for this Court to reasonably expect that such standards could be articulated for all 50 States in a single formulation * * *"[2] The First Amendment, Burger said, did not require the people of Maine or Mississippi to put up with public depiction of conduct tolerated in Las Vegas or New York City.

Deep disagreement with Justice Brennan sounded throughout the Chief Justice's opinion, providing a rather shrill counterpoint to Burger's main arguments. Brennan, the author of the majority opinion in *Roth* and long considered the Court's obscenity specialist, drew fire because Brennan had experienced a profound change of mind.[3]

Brennan's final rejection of the *Roth* test—and its modifications as expressed in *Memoirs*[4] and in Miller v. California[5]—was based in large measure upon his growing belief that obscenity statutes are unconstitutionally vague. That is, there are "*scienter*" problems: obscenity laws are so formless that defendants often do not have fair notice as to whether publications or films they distribute or exhibit are obscene. Without fair notice, there may occur a "chilling effect" upon protected speech.

Brennan wrote:[6]

[2] 413 U.S. 15, 30, 93 S.Ct. 2607, 2618 (1973).

[3] Brennan, in company with Marshall and Stewart, dissented in all five of the obscenity decisions of the Court on June 21, 1973. Douglas dissented separately in all five cases. Brennan's dissent in Miller was brief, and referred to the major statement of his views in his dissent in the accompanying case of Paris Adult Theatre I v. Slaton, 413 U.S. 49, 69–113, 93 S.Ct. 2628, 2642–2663 (1973). Justice Brennan wrote opinions of the Court (or plurality opinions of the Court) in Roth v. United States, 354 U.S. 476, 77 S.Ct. 1304 (1957); Jacobellis v. Ohio, 378 U.S. 184, 84 S.Ct. 1676 (1964); Ginzburg v. United States, 383 U.S. 463, 86 S.Ct. 942 (1966); Mishkin v. New York, 383 U.S. 502, 86 S.Ct. 958 (1966), and A Book Named "John Cleland's Memoirs of a Woman of Pleasure" v. Attorney General of Massachusetts, 383 U.S. 413, 86 S.Ct. 975 (1966).

[4] 386 U.S. 767, 87 S.Ct. 1414 (1967).

[5] A Book Named "John Cleland's Memoirs of a Woman of Pleasure" v. Attorney General of Massachusetts, 383 U.S. 413, 86 S.Ct. 975 (1966).

[6] Brennan dissent in Paris Adult Theatre I v. Slaton, 413 U.S. 49, 90, 93 S.Ct. 2628, 2651 (1973).

I am convinced that the approach initiated 15 years ago in Roth v. United States * * * culminating in the Court's decision today, cannot bring stability to this area of the law without jeopardizing First Amendment values, and I have concluded that the time has come to make a significant departure from that approach.

* * *

Our experience with the *Roth* approach has certainly taught us that the outright suppression of obscenity cannot be reconciled with the fundamental principles of the First and Fourteenth Amendments. For we have failed to formulate a standard that sharply distinguishes protected from unprotected speech, and out of necessity we have resorted to the *Redrup* approach, which resolves cases as between parties, but offers only the most obscure guidance to legislation, adjudication by other courts, and primary conduct.

* * *

I would hold, therefore, that at least in the absence of distribution to juveniles or obtrusive exposure to unconsenting adults, the First and Fourteenth Amendments prohibit the state and federal governments from attempting wholly to suppress sexually oriented materials on the basis of their allegedly "obscene" contents. Nothing in this approach precludes those governments from taking action to serve what may be strong and legitimate interests through regulation of the manner of distribution of sexually oriented material.

From the *Miller* decision of 1973 well into the 1980s, the Court split 5–4 in many of the obscenity cases it has decided. The majority followed *Miller,* and favored stringent regulation of sexually explicit material. Time and time again, including many *per curiam* decisions in which the Court upheld obscenity prosecutions without an explanatory opinion, Brennan dissented, constantly contending that obscenity can not be described with sufficient clarity to give defendants fair notice.[7]

"Refinements" of *Miller*: *Jenkins* and *Hamling*

To many prosecutors the decisions in *Miller* and its companion cases appeared to allow a kind of local-option in setting the limits of candor or disclosure in sexy books, magazines or films.

---

[7] See, e.g., Trinkler v. Alabama, 414 U.S. 955, 94 S.Ct. 265 (1973); Raymond Roth v. New Jersey, 414 U.S. 962, 94 S.Ct. 271 (1973); Sharp v. Texas, 414 U.S. 1118, 94 S.Ct. 854 (1974); J–R Distributors, Inc. v. Washington, 418 U.S. 949, 94 S.Ct. 3217 (1974). See also Hamling v. U.S., 418 U.S. 87, 140–152, 94 S.Ct. 2887, 2919–2924 (1974).

As a result, Mike Nichols' serious film, *Carnal Knowledge,* became the target of an obscenity prosecution in Albany, Georgia in a case known as Jenkins v. Georgia. The prosecution took place even though it contained no frontal nudity or explicit depictions of sexual acts. The manager of a theater, Billy Jenkins, was convicted under a Georgia statute [8] forbidding distribution of obscene material and was fined $750 and sentenced to 12 months in jail. His conviction was affirmed by the Georgia Supreme Court.

Although agreeing with the Georgia Supreme Court that the U.S. Constitution does not require juries in obscenity cases to be instructed according to a hypothetical statewide standard, the Supreme Court of the United States unanimously reversed Jenkins' conviction. Writing for the Court, Justice William H. Rehnquist ruled that *Carnal Knowledge* was not patently offensive. He referred to Miller v. California, which said that a state statute could forbid patently offensive materials, including

> "representations or descriptions of ultimate sexual acts, normal or perverted, actual or simulated," and "representations or descriptions of masturbation, excretory functions, and lewd exhibition of the genitals."

Because *Carnal Knowledge* did not contain such representations as described in *Miller,* the conviction of Jenkins could not stand.[9]

Pope v. Illinois (1987)

In 1987, the United States Supreme Court tried to clarify obscenity law, declaring that an "objective" or "reasonable person" test should be applied to judging the value of work accused of obscenity, *not* a "community standards" test.

It should be recalled that Miller v. California (1973) set out a three-part test: [10]

(1) Does the material, when viewed by an average person applying contemporary community standards, appeal to prurient interest?

(2) If so, then is the appeal "patently offensive"?

(3) Then, even though the material does appeal to prurient interest in a patently offensive manner; does it deserve free speech protection despite such qualities because of having serious literary, artistic, political or scientific value?

[8] Jenkins v. Georgia, 418 U.S. 153, 156, 94 S.Ct. 2750, 2753 (1974) citing Ga.Code §§ 26–2011, 26–2105.

[9] 418 U.S. 153, 160, 94 S.Ct. 2750, 2755 (1974).

[10] 413 U.S. 15, 23–24, 93 S.Ct. 2607, 2614–1615 (1973).

In Pope v. Illinois—dealing with sales of magazines to Rockford, Illinois police officers in an adult bookstore—the constitutionality of jury instructions under the Illinois obscenity statute was challenged.[11]

At their trials, the defendants argued that the literary or artistic value of a work should be judged objectively, rather than viewed in terms of its conforming to "contemporary community standards." [12] But the jury was instructed instead to decide simply whether the material was obscene by "determining how it would be viewed by ordinary adults in the whole state of Illinois."

Writing for the Supreme Court, Justice White asserted:

> There is no suggestion in our cases that the opinion of the value of an allegedly obscene work is to be determined by reference to community standards. Indeed, Smith v. United States, 431 U.S. 291 (1977) held that, in a federal prosecution for mailing obscene materials, the first and second prongs of the *Miller* test—appeal to prurient interest and patent offensiveness—are issues of fact for the jury to determine applying contemporary community standards. The Court then observed that unlike prurient appeal or patent offensiveness, "[L]iterary, artistic, political, or scientific value . . . is not discussed in *Miller* in terms of contemporary community standards."

The Court attempted to move beyond the "common denominator" of juries' views about what "community standards" might be.

> Just as the ideas a work represents need not obtain majority approval to merit protection, neither, insofar as the First Amendment is concerned, does the value of a work vary from community to community based on the degree of local acceptance it has won. The proper inquiry is . . . whether a reasonable person would find such value in the material, taken as a whole.

Based on this analysis, the Court held the Illinois judges' jury instructions based on community standards concerning the value of materials to be unconstitutional.

The Mapplethorpe Exhibit Case

Concern that mid-American juries lacked the sophistication to distinguish between "art" and "smut" lessened to some extent in October 1990 after a Cincinnati, Ohio jury acquitting a local

[11] 481 U.S. 497, 107 S.Ct. 1918 (1987), 14 Med.L.Rptr. 1001.

[12] This has come to be known as the "SLAPS" test; does the material have *Serious Literary, Artistic, Political* or *Scientific* value that protects it from being classified as obscene.

museum director charged with displaying obscene works.[13]   Dennis Barrie, director of Cincinnati's Contemporary Arts Center, had scheduled an exhibition of pictures by Robert Mapplethorpe, a nationally recognized photographer who died of AIDS in 1989.

The exhibition included five photos of nude men in sadomasochistic poses and two of children with their genitals exposed. The exhibit had attracted little attention in its previous showings in Philadelphia and Chicago, but at its opening in Cincinnati, Barrie and the Museum were charged with pandering obscenity, and unlawfully displaying pictures of nude children, both misdemeanor offenses carrying maximum sentences of one year in jail, and a fine of $5,000.

To simplify the issue, the State called just one witness to testify as to the artistic merit of the exhibit, a self-styled communications "specialist" whose only claimed expertise as an art critic involved writing songs for the "Captain Kangaroo" television show.   In contrast, the defense called more than a dozen expert witnesses, including directors from some of the nation's leading art museums who were unanimous in their assessment of Mapplethorpe as a serious and important artist.

If the prosecution believed the photos themselves would be enough to shock the mostly working class, church-going jury of four men and four women into returning a guilty verdict, they clearly underestimated the intelligence of the panel.   After the trial had ended, several jurors admitted being personally offended by these pictures they felt were "lewd", "grotesque" and "disgusting".[14]   But even though they felt that these photos did appeal to prurient interests and were patently offensive, they accepted the judgment of art experts who believed these works also had artistic merit, and therefore could not be classified as being obscene.

2 Live Crew Case

In June 1990, a U.S. District Court in Fort Lauderdale, Florida had entered a decree forbidding the sale or distribution of a music video "Nasty As They Wanna Be" by rap group 2 Live Crew anywhere within the jurisdiction of the Court.   District Judge Jose A. Gonzales conducted extensive hearings before decid-

[13] Contemporary Arts Center v. Ney, 735 F.Supp. 743 (S.D.Ohio 1990).   Also see "Jury Finds Merit in Mapplethorne Exhibit with Verdict of Not Guilty" Milwaukee Journal, October 7, 1990, p. A1.

[14] Isabel Wilkerson, "Obscenity Jurors Were Pulled 2 Ways But Deferred to Art" New York Times October 10, 1990, p. B1.   Five of the eight jurors had never visited an art museum.

ing that the music video was in fact obscene, and therefore could be prevented from being sold.[15]

A local music store owner, Charles Freeman, sold a copy of the music video to an undercover police officer a few days after the decree had been entered and was convicted of violating this ban. Shortly after Freeman's arrest, 2 Live Crew performed selections from the music video during an all-adult concert in Fort Lauderdale. The three members of the group were each charged with one misdemeanor count of disseminating obscene material, and were tried in October 1991, soon after Freeman's conviction.

The defense maintained that white jurors on the 6 member jury panel would be incapable of understanding this unique form of black artistic expression, but the jury voted unanimously for acquittal, finding that the performance was not obscene.[16] Once again, the verdict turned on the "artistic merit" issue, for the jury accepted the judgment of a black English professor that "rapping" represented a serious black cultural art form, whose words were not to be taken at their face value but to be understood in the historical context of black culture.[17]

In each of these cases, then, those who had predicted that a new wave of artistic censorship would sweep across the nation could take some comfort in the verdicts of two predominately white, working-class juries who respected their obligations as jurors to decide these emotion packed obscenity issues impartially and objectively. Perhaps, then, there is reason to believe that the time-honored American trial by jury system deserves more respect than its erudite critics have been willing to accord it.

SEC. 48   BALANCING CONFLICTING SOCIETAL INTERESTS

As private industry content standards continue to become more permissive, pressure is mounting for laws to protect society from mass culture messages that demean certain groups, or erode fundamental tenets of decency.

[15] Skyywalker Records, Inc. v. Navarro, 739 F.Supp. 578 (S.D.Fla.1990) 17 Med.L. Rptr. 2073. According to testimony presented at the hearings, this single music video contained more than a dozen references urging violent sex, some 200 descriptions of women as either "bitches" or "ho" (whores), 115 explicit terms for male or female genitalia, 87 descriptions of oral sex, 9 descriptions of male ejaculation, 4 extensive descriptions of group sex, all within a general theme glorifying the debasement and humiliation of women.

[16] "Rap Band Members Found Not Guilty in Obscenity Trial," New York Times, October 21, 1990, p. 1.

[17] Another factor that may have aided the defense is that the vocals the prosecution recorded at the concert were virtually unintelligible to the jury, providing very little basis for the jury to find the lyrics to be obscene.

Motion Picture Industry Standards

Until the late 1940s, five major film companies dominated the motion picture business in the United States. Paramount, MGM, Warner Brothers, Twentieth Century Fox and RKO owned more than 3000 of the nation's first-run motion picture theaters and controlled film industry production, distribution and exhibition by following a policy of trade-offs and cross-preferences with other studio-owned theaters to deny some 15,000 independently owned theaters access to these feature films until their box office appeal had diminished.

This concentration of control within the film industry also allowed the major studios to cooperate in adopting and enforcing a code of industry standards to ensure that no feature film would contain themes or scenes that might be offensive to certain segments of the film audience.[18] Independent film producers had no choice but to conform to these standards of decency, because without the industry's "Production Code Seal of Authority" they would be denied access to those essential first-run theaters owned by the major studios.[19]

Then, in 1948, the Justice Department was able to force the major film studios to enter into a Consent Decree, agreeing to divest themselves of their film theaters.[20]

Losing control of these major first-run theaters also meant that these studios lost the capacity to impose industry standards on feature film content. As television viewing increased during the 1950s, film attendance plunged downward from 90 million a week in 1948 to less than 40 million a week only a decade later.[21]

[18] The Motion Picture Producers and Distributors of American (MPPDFA) established a film review office in 1922, largely as a public relations gesture to reduce the bad image resulting from a rash of personal scandals in Hollywood. Known as the "Hay's Office", because of its first director, Will Hays, its role in reviewing film content did not become significant until the major studios adopted a much more stringent set of standards, known as the Production Code, in the mid 1930s.

[19] In many ways this private content supervisory system closely resembled that employed by National Association of Broadcasters. In both cases, a small group of studios or networks were able to avoid offending audiences by exerting their control over the main channels of distribution, and this power that gave them to deny distribution to material they believed was in bad taste. In television as in film, the later fragmentation of that power diminished their ability to continue to perform that function.

[20] United States v. Paramount Pictures, 334 U.S. 131, 68 S.Ct. 915 (1948). The studios were actually given the option of divesting themselves of either their role as film distributors or film exhibitors, but sensing the threat that television would soon pose for film theaters, they chose to retain their more profitable distribution role.

[21] Christopher Sterling and Timothy Haight, eds. The Mass Media: Aspen Institute Guide to Communication Industry Trends (New York: Praeger, 1978) pp. 34–35.

To lure audiences back to the film theaters, their new owners needed motion pictures promising special attractions television couldn't provide. One technique was to use technology to expand the screen, surround the viewer with sound, and portray action on a massive scale.

Another was to book sexier or more provocative dramas than television offered the public. Freed of the constraints of the Hollywood Production Code, theater chains began turning to European producers for daring, far more explicit films than American audiences had ever seen in the past.

At this point a number of local film boards originally formed in the early 1900s, but then dormant for decades as Hollywood closely supervised motion picture content, suddenly came to life as these new independent films began appearing in their communities. Now as these boards, under State authority, began trying to fill that void left by the collapse of industry controls, the issue soon arose about their legal right as government agencies to impose conditions on the local exhibition of feature films.

The first of these cases to challenge the authority of a State to control film content was Burstyn v. Wilson, a 1952 Supreme Court decision involving Roberto Rossellini's film, "The Miracle".[22]

This was a story about a simple-minded goatherd who had been raped by a bearded stranger whom she believed to be St. Joseph. The film was accused not of obscenity but of "sacrilege." The New York Education Department had issued a license to allow showing of "The Miracle," but the Education Department's governing body, the New York Regents, ordered the license withdrawn after the regents had received protests that the film was "sacrilegious." Burstyn appealed the license's withdrawal to the New York Courts, claiming that the state's licensing statute was unconstitutional. New York's courts, however, rejected that argument.

The Supreme Court of the United States ultimately ruled unanimously that the New York statute and the term "sacrilegious" were so vague that they abridged freedom of expression. Although the Court said in *dicta* that a clearly drawn obscenity statute to regulate motion pictures might be upheld, the main

---

[22] Joseph Burstyn, Inc. v. Wilson, 343 U.S. 495, 72 S.Ct. 777 (1952). Some film historians claim that Mutual Film Corp. v. Industrial Commission of Ohio, 236 U.S. 230, 35 S.Ct. 387 (1915) was the first test of film's free speech rights, a test in which a federal court held that a State law could restrict film distribution because film was not a form of protected expression, but rather only a business. What these historians overlook is that it was not until 1927 that the Supreme Court finally recognized the power of federal courts to overturn State laws restricting free speech, so that in this case, determining whether or not film was a protected form of free speech was really irrelevant to the actual decision, and therefore not a precedent controlling future federal court decisions in this field.

thrust of the *Burstyn* decision was toward greater freedom. Not only were films given protection under the First and Fourteenth Amendments, movies which offended a particular religious group need not, for that reason alone, be banned. Thus "sacrilege" can no longer be a ground for censoring movies.

Seven years after the *Burstyn* decision, the Supreme Court—in Kingsley International Pictures Corp. v. New York—again upheld the idea that films are within the protection of the First Amendment. The *Kingsley* decision, however, had within it the possibilities for once again expanding controls over films. The Court specifically refused to decide whether "the controls which a State may impose upon this medium of expression are precisely co-extensive with those allowable for newspapers, books, or individual speech." [23]

Despite the veiled warning in the *Kingsley* opinion that the Supreme Court might once again strengthen controls over motion pictures, a bold attempt was made to get a prior restraint ordinance declared unconstitutional. This was the 1961 case of Times Film Corp. v. City of Chicago, which involved a film with a spicy name: "Don Juan." However, this film was merely a motion picture version of Mozart's opera, "Don Giovanni," obviously not obscene.

Times Film Corporation paid the license fee for "Don Juan," but then refused to submit the film to Chicago's Film Review Board for a pre-screening and a license.

Times Film frontally challenged the licensing arrangement as unconstitutional because it was prior restraint. The Supreme Court of the United States reviewed the case, and in 1961 upheld the ordinance as constitutional by a 5–4 vote. It was denied that there was complete freedom to exhibit any motion picture, at least once. "Nor has it been suggested," the Court said, that all prior restraints are invalid." [24]

Four years later, in Freedman v. Maryland (1965), the Supreme Court invalidated a state prior restraint system. This time, unlike the *Times Film* case, *all* prior restraint was not challenged as unconstitutional. Instead, the Maryland Film Review Board was challenged because it could arbitrarily halt showing of a film, unless the exhibitor fought through a time-consuming appeal procedure involving the Maryland courts. The Maryland system was held invalid because of insufficient procedural safeguards for protection of the film exhibitor. But even Justice Brennan—a

[23] 360 U.S. 684, 689–690, 79 S.Ct. 1362, 1366 (1959).

[24] Times Film Corp. v. Chicago, 365 U.S. 43, 47, 81 S.Ct. 391, 393 (1961), citing Near v. State of Minnesota ex rel. Olson, 283 U.S. 697, 51 S.Ct. 625 (1931).

legendary First Amendment supporter—suggested that an orderly, speedy procedure for prescreening films could be constitutional.[25]

Another Maryland-based system upheld by an affirming vote of the U.S. Supreme Court—in Star v. Preller (1974)—showed that orderly film review could be constitutional. That case upheld Maryland's review statute, which [26]

— Gave the Review Board only five days in which to review and license a film.

— If a license was denied, the Review Board had three days to begin review proceedings before the Baltimore City Circuit Court.

— The court must promptly determine obscenity (or lack of it) after an adversary hearing before the Review Board could make final denial of the license.

— The Board had to bear the burden of proof at all stages of the proceeding.

At this time, then, prior restraint of film is still constitutional, but only when strict procedural safeguards are followed. These film industry decisions reflect the difficult role the Supreme Court has had to play when attempting to balance the free speech rights of a film distributor against the inherent right of each State to protect the welfare of its citizens.

In 1968 the major film studios began a new effort to enhance the image of the industry. Unable any longer to enforce standards of good taste, the studios instead established a rating system designed to inform audiences in advance what type of content each film contained. In the original rating system, a "G" designated films suitable for all audiences; "PG" meant parents were cautioned that some material might not be suitable for children; "R" indicated that children under 17 would not be admitted unless accompanied by a parent or guardian; and "X" meant no one under 17 would be admitted.

The rating system had at least two unintended effects. One was to destroy the appeal of the "G" rated film, as children began refusing to attend those films that adults thought were good for them. In 1968, 32 percent of the films released by major studios had a "G" rating, but by 1988, only 4 percent were rated "G".[27] In

---

[25] Freedman v. Maryland, 380 U.S. 51, 85 S.Ct. 734 (1965). For a similar result, see Interstate Circuit, Inc. v. Dallas, 390 U.S. 676, 88 S.Ct. 1298 (1968).

[26] A1 Star v. Preller, 419 U.S. 956, 95 S.Ct. 217 (1974), affirming 375 F.Supp. 1093 (D.Md.1974).

[27] "MPAA Film Ratings 1968–88" Variety November 8, 1988, p. 26. One example of this fear of the dreadful "G" was the John Wayne, Katherine Hepburn film, "Rooster Cogburn" where the producers insisted that one violent scene be inserted to make certain the film received a "PG" rating instead.

contrast, "R" rated films rose from 22 percent of all major releases in 1968 to 48 percent in 1988, as average age of the film audience dropped from 22 to 16, and "R" became virtually synonymous with this age group's favorite film genre; violent, action packed adventures laced with a suitable amount of gore and mayhem.

The other was to make it virtually impossible to successfully market an "X" rated film. Soon after the code was adopted, a number of major newspaper chains established a policy of refusing to accept display ads for "X" rated films, and several television groups began following the same policy a few years later. In addition, several major video rental organizations refused to handle "X" rated films. In view of these severe constraints an "X" rating imposed on the earnings potential of a picture, Hollywood producers generally insisted on contractual agreements that allowed them to re-edit any film rated as "X" to delete that material that prevented it from receiving a "R" rating.[28]

In time, however, because of the bitter controversies these agreements created between producers-investors and directors attempting to make serious but extremely graphic films such as "Henry and June" or "Tie Me Up! Tie Me Down", the film code was revised in 1990 to distinguish between this type of artistic film effort, reclassified as "NC–17" and the typical hard core pornographic film that retained its "X" classification. Unfortunately, a number of States, as well as newspapers, television stations and video rental organizations, were unimpressed by this distinction drawn by the film industry, and so they continue to treat the "NC–17" rating as nothing more than an artsy "X." [29]

Although the film industry's rating system is far from perfect, it has at least been designed to perform a public service by notifying audiences in advance what type of content they can expect from each film the industry releases.

Recent efforts to persuade the music industry to adopt a similar code system have been far less successful to date. After agreeing in principle in 1985 to label all violently pornographic or sexually explicit record and music video releases, several years passed before six major music distributors finally declared their willingness in 1990 to begin on a voluntary basis to establish standards for applying notification stickers on all musical cassettes and albums containing obscene or otherwise patently offensive material.

[28] "Taking the Hex Out of X" Time, October 8, 1990, p. 79. No film distributor can escape an "X" rating by refusing to submit the film to the rating board, because all unreviewed films are automatically given an "X" rating.

[29] "NC–17 X'd Out at Blockbuster; Wildmon, AFA Boycott" Variety January 21, 1991, p. 27.

Unfortunately, as soon as this agreement was reached, several States began consideration of legislation that would prevent anyone under the age of 18 from purchasing any record or cassette bearing such a label. The music industry immediately went on the offensive, declaring that they would abandon this labelling effort if any State passed such a law abridging their right of free speech.[30]

While this concern for freedom of expression is certainly praiseworthy, another factor that might have some effect on the attitude of these music distributors is that purchasers under the age of 18 not only accounted for 32 percent of all revenues earned by the music industry in 1988, but also represented the largest age segment of buyers for "heavy metal" and "black/urban" music, the two types of music most likely to be affected by any labeling law.[31]

Rights of Women and Children

To this point we have been focusing primarily on the legal rights of those who create, finance and distribute sexually oriented magazines, books, films or music. We have seen that the marketing of these items cannot be restricted unless a State succeeds in enacting a statute prohibiting their dissemination, and that statute conforms in all respects to those protections accorded these corporate entities or individuals by the Constitution.[32]

But what about those in our society who are victimized by these materials? Does media free speech carry with it the privilege to ridicule or insult any group with impunity, secure in the knowledge that they have neither the legal right nor the media connections needed to respond to such attacks? In this era of "Political Correctness", there is a heightened awareness of the sensitivity of various racial and ethnic groups to comments or depictions that would have been considered appropriate only a decade ago, but one group in our society still has not benefitted from this change of attitude.

Today, as in the past, "sexually oriented" magazines, films and music continue to stereotype women either as mindless sex objects constantly seeking gratification, or as subhuman victims to be subjugated and used. During the 1980s, women's groups in the

---

[30] Kevin Zimmerman, "Music Biz Rising to Free–Speech Challenge" Variety, July 25, 1990, p. 53.

[31] Charles Fleming, "Stickers for Minors a Major Headache" Variety, July 25, 1990, p. 1.

[32] These protections, as defined in California v. Miller, require that there be reasonable findings, based on acceptable evidence, that the material in question does appeal to prurient interests in a patently offensive way, and does not have any serious literary, artistic, political or scientific value.

United States mounted two different types of legal attacks on pornographic materials that dehumanize women.

One involved sponsoring an ordinance to authorize local government to suppress pornographic material in order to protect the civil rights of women. The other proposed passage of an ordinance to permit a woman to sue pornographic dealers directly for the distribution of materials that violated her civil rights.

The Minneapolis Approach

In Minneapolis, the women's group opposing pornography thought it unwise to involve government in their efforts to prevent the dissemination of this material. As Wendy Kaminer, one of the group's leaders, wrote, "Feminists need not and should not advocate censorship, but we have every right to organize politically and to protest material that is degrading and dangerous to women." [33] Her solution, as that of Andrea Dworkin and Catharine McKinnon—driving forces behind the Minneapolis ordinance—was to sue for violation of rights. Since they believed that pornography was sex-based discrimination— "the sexually explicit subordination of women, graphically depicted"—then persons offended by such materials should have the right to sue for damages.[34] The ordinance, however, was twice vetoed by Minneapolis Mayor Fraser.

Child Pornography

Although American law has been unsympathetic to the pleas of women to stop the flood of pornographic materials in the United States, child pornography has been treated in an entirely different fashion. Strong legislative measures have been taken to halt something far more dangerous than distributing pornography—however defined—to children. Legislation has been created to outlaw using minors to perform or act in the creation of films, books, or magazine articles or other items depicting the sexual exploitation of children.[35] The measure was designed to put a stop to magazines which could be purchased in 1977 such as "Chicken Delight," "Lust for Children," "Lollitots," and "Child Discipline"

[33] Wendy Kaminer, "Pornography and the First Amendment: Prior Restraint and Private Action" in Take Back the Night, p. 241.

[34] See Attorney General's Commission on Pornography Final Report (1986). Although the report has been criticized for overstating the causal connection between depictions of sexual violence and violent treatment of women, virtually all social scientists who testified before the Commission agreed that constant exposure to such content would be likely to stimulate a more aggressive attitude towards women by men already tending towards such behavior.

[35] Senate Bill 1585, 95th Congress, 1st Session, No. 95-438, "Protection of Children Against Sexual Exploitation Act of 1977; Report of the Committee on the Judiciary, United States Senate, on S. 1585.

that were then being sold. Dr. Judianne Densen-Gerber, president of the Odyssey Institute, made this outraged statement to the Subcommittee on Crime of Congress' Committee on the Judiciary: [36]

> There comes a point where we can no longer defend by intellectualization or forensic debate. We must simply say "I know the difference between right and wrong and I am not afraid to say 'no' or demand that limits be imposed".

> Common sense and maternal instinct tell me that this [child pornography which she found in New York, Philadelphia, Boston, Washington, New Orleans, Chicago, San Francisco, and Los Angeles] goes way beyond free speech. Such conduct mutilates children's spirits; they aren't consenting adults, they're victims. The First Amendment isn't absolute.

This legislation was signed into law on Feb. 6, 1978 by President Carter, was formally called the "Protection of Children Against Sexual Exploitation Act of 1977." This legislation, in the words of U.S. Senators John C. Culver of Iowa and Charles McC. Mathias of Maryland, was intended to do the following: [37]

— Make it a Federal crime to use children in the production of pornographic materials.

— Prohibit the interstate transportation of children for the purpose of engaging in prostitution, and

— Increase the penalty provisions of the current Federal obscenity laws if the materials adjudged obscene involve the use of children engaging in sexually explicit conduct.

This measure tried to correct loopholes in federal obscenity statutes. Before this legislation, there was no federal statute prohibiting use of children in production of materials that depict explicit sexual conduct. This statute defined "minor" as any person under the age of 16 years. Penalties for violation of this statutory provision are two–ten years imprisonment and/or a fine of up to $10,000 on first offense, or five–fifteen years imprisonment and/or a fine of up to $15,000 for subsequent offenses.[38]

[36] Prepared Statement of Judianne Densen-Gerber, J.D., M.D., F.C.L.M., President, Odyssey Institute, for submission to The U.S. House of Representatives, Committee on the Judiciary, Subcommittee on Crime, May 23, 1977.

[37] Form letter sent to the author by Senators Culver and Mathias, circa September 1977; letter to the author of October 19, 1977, by Rep. John Conyers, Jr. of Michigan's First District. See Public Law 95–225.

[38] 18 U.S.C.A. § 2251, Chapter 110—Sexual Exploitation of Children. The Mann Act, 18 U.S.C.A. § 2423, prohibits the interstate transportation of minor females for purposes of prostitution and did not include young males until amended in 1977.

Committees of the U.S. Senate and House of Representatives found a close connection between child pornography and the use of young children as prostitutes. For example, a 17-year-old Chicago youth who had sold himself on the streets for two years, could often earn close to $500 a week by selling himself two or three times a night to perform various sex acts with "chicken hawks" or pose for pornographic pictures or both.[39]

Kidporn and New York v. Ferber (1982)

In 1982, the Supreme Court of the United States made one thing clear about the murky law of obscenity: it will uphold state efforts to punish individuals for the production or sale of "kidporn." In New York v. Ferber, the Court declared valid a New York criminal statute prohibiting persons from knowingly authorizing or inducing a child less than 16 years old to engage in a sexual performance.[40] "Sexual performance" is defined by the New York statute as "'any performance or part thereof which includes sexual performance or part thereof which includes sexual conduct by a child less than sixteen years of age.'" The specific statutory provision tested said: [41]

> A person is guilty [of a class D felony, which carries punishment of up to seven years imprisonment for persons and a fine of up to $10,000 for corporations] of promoting a sexual performance by a child when, knowing the character and content thereof, he produces, directs, or promotes any performance which includes sexual conduct by a child less than sixteen years of age.

The case began when Paul Ira Ferber, proprietor of a Manhattan bookstore specializing in sexually oriented materials, sold two films to undercover police officers. The two films dealt almost exclusively with depictions of boys masturbating. A jury trial convicted Ferber of two counts of promoting a sexual performance and Ferber was sentenced to 45 days in prison. Ferber's convictions were upheld on first appeal, but the New York Court of Appeals said that the statute section under which Ferber was

---

[39] Report of the Committee on the Judiciary, United States Senate on S.1585, Protection of Children Against Sexual Exploitation Act of 1977 (Washington, D.C., 1977), p. 7. See also Robin Lloyd, For Money or Love: Boy Prostitution in America (New York: Vanguard Press, 1976).

[40] 458 U.S. 747, 102 S.Ct. 3348 (1982), 8 Med.L.Rptr. 1809.

[41] McKinney's, New York Penal Law, § 263.1. In addition, as noted by the Court, the New York statute defines a performance as "'any play, motion picture, photograph or dance' or 'any other visual presentation exhibited before an audience.'" See McKinney's, N.Y.Penal Law § 263.4. "Sexual conduct" is defined as "'actual or simulated sexual intercourse, deviate; sexual intercourse, sexual bestiality, masturbation, sado-masochistic abuse, or lewd exhibition of the genitals.'" McKinney's, N.Y.Penal Law § 263.3.

convicted was too sweeping. The New York Court of Appeals held that Section 263.15 might be used to punish sale or promotion of material protected by the First Amendment. Protected material which seemed to come under the New York statute, the appeals court said, included " 'medical books and educational sources, which "deal with adolescent sex in a realistic but nonobscene manner." ' " [42]

The Supreme Court of the United States granted certiorari. In deciding the case, the Court said that that it presented just one question:

> To prevent the abuse of children who are made to engage in sexual conduct for commercial purposes, could the New York State Legislature, consistent with the First Amendment, prohibit the dissemination of material which shows children engaged in sexual conduct, regardless of whether such material is obscene?

Writing for the Court, Justice Byron White said:

> Like obscenity statutes, laws directed at the dissemination of child pornography run the risk of suppressing protected expression by allowing the hand of the censor to become unduly heavy. For the following reasons, however, we are persuaded that the States are entitled to greater leeway in the regulation of pornographic depictions of children.
>
> *First.* It is evident beyond the need for elaboration that a state's interest in "safeguarding the physical and psychological well being of a minor" is "compelling." Globe Newspapers v. Superior Court, 457 U.S. 596, 607, 102 S.Ct. 2613, 2620 (1982), 8 Med.L.Rptr. 1689.
>
> * * *
>
> *Second.* The distribution of photographs and films depicting sexual activity by juveniles is intrinsically related to the sexual abuse of children in at least two ways. First, the materials produced are a permanent record of the children's participation and the harm to the child is exacerbated by their circulation. Second, the distribution network for child pornography must be closed if the production of material which requires the sexual exploitation of children is to be effectively controlled.

Justice White noted the economic motive involved in the production of such materials. " 'It rarely has been suggested that the constitutional freedom for speech and press extends immunity to speech or writing used as an integral part of conduct in

[42] 458 U.S. 747, 102 S.Ct. 3348, 3352 (1982).

violation of a valid criminal statute.' " [43]   Further, classifying child pornography as a category outside protection of the First Amendment is compatible with the Supreme Court's earlier rulings.

The Indianapolis Ordinance: Prior Restraint

In the spring of 1984, the Indianapolis-Marion County City-County Council passed and then amended an ordinance to define, prevent, and prohibit "all discriminatory practices of sexual subordination or inequality through pornography."   Mayor Richard Hudnut signed them into law.[44]   The ordinance said, in part: [45]

16. "Pornography" is defined in the Ordinance as follows:

"(q) Pornography shall mean the graphic sex—sexually explicit subordination of women, whether in pictures or in words, that also includes one or more of the following:

"(1) Women who are presented as sexual objects or who enjoy pain or humiliation; or

"(2) Women are presented as sexual objects who experience sexual pleasure in being raped; or

"(3) Women are presented as sexual objects tied up or cut or mutilated or bruised or physically hurt, or as dismembered or truncated or fragmented or severed into body parts; or

"(4) Women are presented being penetrated by objects or animals; or

"(5) Women are presented in scenarios of degradation, injury, abasement, torture, shown as filthy or inferior, bleeding, bruised, or hurt in a context that makes these conditions sexual, and

"(6) Women are presented as sexual objects for domination, conquest, violation, exploitation, possession, or use, or through postures or positions of sevility or submission or display.

"The use of men, children, or transsexuals in the place of women in paragraphs (1) through (6) above shall also constitute pornography under this section."

[43] Quoting Giboney v. Empire Storage & Ice Co., 336 U.S. 490, 69 S.Ct. 684 (1949).

[44] American Booksellers Association, Inc. v. Hudnut, 598 F.Supp. 1316 (S.D.Ind. 1984).

[45] 598 F.Supp. at 1320 (S.D.Ind.1984), 11 Med.L.Rptr. at 1106, quoting Indianapolis ordinance.

Another part of the ordinance said, "Trafficking in pornography: The production, sale, exhibition, or distribution of pornography" was made unlawful. In addition, the ordinance had a provision saying "any woman may file a complaint as a woman acting against the subordination of women."

In response, the American Booksellers Association—plus other groups and individuals including the Association of American Publishers and the Freedom to Read Foundation of the American Library Association—challenged the constitutionality of the ordinance. It was contended that the ordinance "severely restricts the availability, display and distribution of constitutionally protected, non-obscene materials in violation of the First and Fourteenth Amendments." More specifically, plaintiffs complained that the sweep of the ordinance took in more than materials which are constitutionally unprotected speech (such as obscenity).

Further, these plaintiffs said the ordinance was unconstitutionally vague in not giving notice of what might be a crime.

District Judge Barker's lengthy opinion found multiple defects in the Indianapolis ordinance: it sought to control speech without reference to applicable constitutional requirements; and the expression sought to be controlled may not meet the test for obscenity as spelled out in Miller v. California:

> "(a) whether 'the average person, applying contemporary community standards,' would find that the work, taken as a whole, appeals to the prurient interest, * * *; (b) whether the work depicts or describes, in a patently offensive way, sexual conduct specifically defined by the applicable state law; and (c) whether the work, taken as a whole, lacks serious literary, artistic, political, or scientific value."

In addition, the language of the ordinance was, Judge Barker said, "impermissibly vague." In sum, although government has a recognized interest in prohibiting sex discrimination, Judge Barker said "that interest does not outweigh the constitutionally protected interest in free speech."

On appeal, a three-judge panel of the U.S. Court of Appeals, Seventh Circuit, affirmed the district court's judgment that the Indianapolis anti-pornography ordinance was unconstitutional. Circuit Judge Easterbrook said the ordinance did not refer, as in Miller v. California (1973), to prurient interest, offensiveness, or community standards. Further, it concentrated on particular depictions, not judging a work as a whole, and made it irrelevant whether a work had literary, artistic, political, or scientific value.

> The ordinance contains four prohibitions. People may not "traffic" in pornography, "coerce" others into performing in pornographic works, or "force" pornogra-

phy on anyone. Anyone injured by someone who has seen or read pornography has a right of action against the maker or seller.

The appeals court said, "The subordinate status of women leads to affront and lower pay at work, insult and injury at home, battery and rape on the battery." Even so, the ordinance's definition of pornography was ruled unconstitutional.[46]

A law awarding damages for assaults caused by speech * * * has the power to muzzle the press * * *

Much speech is dangerous. * * * Unless the remedy is very closely confined, it could be more dangerous to speech than all the libel judgments in history.

The victimization argument by no means is ended. Note that in early 1992, the Canadian Supreme Court upheld obscenity provisions in that nation's criminal code, declaring that pornography harms women and can be banned.

The Price of "Free" Speech

Today, obscene expression remains the only major form of communication unprotected by law, but the term "obscene" is now narrowly defined by most courts to include only the most revolting forms of sexually explicit depictions or descriptions. If further efforts are made to extend this legal categorization to include hard-core pornography the Supreme Court may eventually decide to move in one of two opposing directions.

On one hand, the Court could ultimately rule that no valid social purpose is served by continuing its tightly constrained "obscenity exception," and abolish this category of unprotected expression. In this way State or local governments would be denied legal authority to restrict local sale or distribution of any form of magazine, film or video content, and the Court could escape further involvement in this difficult and divisive area of law.

On the other, the Court could decide, in response to a growing awareness of how much media actually shape our perceptions of each other and the world around us, to expand the "obscenity exception" in order to grant recognition to the inherent legal interests of those in our society victimized by violent pornography or other forms of hate literature.

Those who fear any greater government control over the sale or distribution of pornographic material argue that social scien-

---

[46] American Booksellers Association, Inc. v. Hudnut, 771 F.2d 323 (7th Cir.1985); see also, Tamar Lewin, "Canada Court Says Pornography Harms Women and Can Be Banned," The New York Times, Feb. 28, 1992, p. 41.

tists have not yet been able to establish a causal connection between the viewing of pornographic material and acts of sexual violence.[47] Unfortunately, this is about as meaningful as saying that the Earth does not revolve around the Sun because medieval astrologers were unable to demonstrate conclusively that it did. The truth is that because of the awesome complexity of the human mind, and numerous legal and ethical constraints imposed upon behavioral research methodologies, social science remains light years away from being capable of predicting even the most elemental forms of stimulus-response relationships of human behavior. Because of this, it would seem wiser not to rely too heavily on social science at this point for answers to serious questions of public policy. Instead it might be far more sensible to follow the tradition of Scottish juries who in addition to being able to find a defendant guilty or not guilty, were allowed to enter a verdict of "not proven" when common sense indicated conclusively that the defendant had committed the crime, but insufficient evidence existed to support a conviction.

Another argument advanced against government restrictions on the free flow of such material is that if certain groups are offended by the content of some particular magazine, film or video, they can simply refuse to buy it. In reality, however, widespread dissemination of these mass media messages of lust, hate or ridicule provides those who are eager to read or view this material reenforcement of those very distorted stereotypes its victims seek to combat. As non-smokers in a smoke-filled room, we cannot escape a polluted culture environment simply by pretending that it does not exist.

To trust in the power of individual consumer choice to alter the nature of this environment seems about as naive as believing all our ecological problems can be solved through boycotting the products of a few polluters. Recognizing the futility of attempting to save our natural resources through the marketplace alone, the federal government ultimately adopted standards to protect the interests of each citizen in a clean and healthful environment.[48]

---

[47] A government commission on violence produced a report in 1986 claiming that a significant body of research evidence documented such a connection. This study, commonly known as the Meese Report because it was headed by Attorney General Edwin Meese, was widely criticized by a number of social scientists who contended that its conclusions were far broader than warranted. U.S. Department of Justice, Govt. Printing Office, July 9, 1986. For a number of critical comments about the report, see Robert Pear, "Panel Calls on Citizens Panel to Wage National Assault on Pornography" New York Times, June 2, 1986, p. 22.

[48] The National Environmental Policy Act of 1970, 42 U.S.C.A. § 4321 and the creation of the Environmental Protection Agency in 1970, marked the first major federal recognition of the need to preserve the physical environment. Prior to that time, courts tended to be unsympathetic with environmental concerns that limited industrial development. Typical is the comment the court in Gardner v. Interna-

Similarly, unless American law at some point either assumes responsibility for protecting the interests of those who are unfairly portrayed by the media, or recognizes their right to protect these interests on their own, that media atmosphere in which they must exist seems unlikely to improve.

Still another argument against recognizing any legal right of those aggrieved by their media treatment is that law is incapable of making informed judgments about the quality of media content, and may turn from suppressing smut today to suppressing Shakespeare tomorrow. What this argument overlooks is that our system of law has progressed significantly since the days of the Star Chamber and trial by ordeal. If a legislature can define and a court or jury can decide at what point similarity in story or melody line constitutes plagiarism; at what moment the aborting of a fetus becomes the murder of a human being; or at what level of mental capacity an individual can be held accountable for the attempted assassination of a president, it would seem that this same legal system has sufficient sophistication to determine when media content is designed to exploit rather than to entertain.

Yet, despite any arguments to the contrary, the traditional mass communication law text would almost certainly praise any Supreme Court decision that abolished the legal category of obscenity, and criticize any effort to extend its scope to include hardcore pornographic or other similar material. This is because the time-honored approach in this field has been to view every law and each judicial decision solely in terms of whether the industry "won" or "lost"; that is, whether its free speech rights were ultimately extended or diminished.

From this perspective, however, it is easy to overlook the fact that in most of these legal battles there are other individuals, groups and societal issues caught in the crossfire. A "victory" for the industry in the field of libel, for example, represents a defeat for all those who have been unfairly maligned by media in the same manner. Similarly, upholding the right of the press to describe details of a criminal investigation may result in prejudicing a jury against the accused, or allow someone who has actually committed a crime to escape justice because of improper pretrial publicity. Releasing broadcasters from their obligations to provide children's programming may enhance their freedom of expression, but at a cost of reducing the number of shows designed to fulfill the educational and entertainment needs of the young.

tional Shoe Co., 319 Ill.App. 416, 49 N.E.2d 328 (1943), that "the restraining of normal business activity is contrary to public policy." Even as late as 1970, in Boomer v. Atlantic Cement Co., 26 N.Y.2d 219, 309 N.Y.S.2d 312, 257 N.E.2d 870 (1970), a court refused to enjoin industrial pollution because damage caused by the pollution was found to be less than the costs of reducing the pollution.

What this suggests is that the study of mass communication law should involve more than simply tallying wins and loses on a scorecard. Any legal victory for the media must be viewed in a broader context; one that looks beyond gauging how much additional freedom media has won to consider at what societal costs this victory has been achieved, and to what benefit for the public.

From this standpoint, then, it may be difficult to rejoice too heartily the victory by the publisher of some violently pornographic magazine over State law, because the extension of the right to disseminate this material certainly exacts its toll from each woman threatened by its message, at no perceptible benefit to our society except for those who avidly study each page.

In the last analysis, though, the only thing that might prove to be more damaging to the interests of the mass communication industry than a series of legal defeats severely curtailing their freedom of expression might be a series of victories granting them virtually absolute freedom from any legal responsibility for their actions. In that case, individuals deprived of any legal means of influencing the conduct of the media are almost certain to resort to vigilante tactics to protect societal interests they believe are too precious to abandon, and to seek through political pressure controls far more repressive than those the media have succeeded in escaping. Ironically, then, what seems most likely to guarantee the broadest possible range of free expression for media in the United States may actually be the continued presence of sufficient legal controls to guarantee that these media will remain responsive to the concerns of each citizen they serve.

Electronic Media Standards

For broadcasters, transmission of obscene programming is a federal criminal offense, and also grounds for FCC revocation of a broadcast license.[49] In addition, however, the Commission has been attempting to establish more rigorous standards for sexually oriented broadcast programs, prohibiting "indecent" content, which the agency has defined in general terms as being patently offensive descriptions of sexual or excretory activities.[50]

The public appears to expect a far higher standard of good taste from broadcasters, and particularly from television networks, than from other media simply because even in an era when these networks attract only 60 percent of the nation's primetime

[49] For radio and television, this prohibition against the transmission of obscene content is contained in the criminal provisions of 18 U.S.C.A. § 1464. A similar prohibition against the carriage of obscene cable TV programming is contained in the Cable Policy Act, 47 U.S.C.A. § 559.

[50] The FCC's indecency activities are discussed in the following chapter.

viewers, they still remain the most powerful and pervasive force in American mass culture. On a typical evening, any modestly popular situation comedy scheduled by one of the major television networks will be viewed by more Americans than will read any best selling novel or attend any single feature film that entire year. In other words, virtually every network television series producer has a greater opportunity to influence public sentiments, beliefs and values than even the most popular of novelists or film makers.

Until the early 1980s, all broadcast programming was regulated by the federal government. Although the amount of supervisory control the FCC actually exerted over television network program policies was minimal, the fact that a federal agency was authorized by law to make television responsive to the concerns of the public was in itself sufficient to satisfy most citizens.

The deregulation of broadcasting closed this one channel of legal influence that had been open to the average citizen, at a time when the industry was dismantling its own private system of program content standards and looking for ways to attract a younger, more affluent and less traditional group of listeners and viewers.[51]

Competition from the Fox Network and a wide array of cable services forced the three major television networks to become slightly more venturesome during the 1980s, as both series and made-for-TV movies began treating topics that would have been summarily rejected only a decade before. Although very little that was broadcast during this era could have been classified as "indecent", much less obscene, American audiences were not accustomed to even mildly risque programs from a medium readily accessible to children in the home.

Yet, because of the tensions resulting from the sense that broadcasting was beyond the public's legal control, one of the major results of broadcast deregulation has been to popularize the forming of countless local and national private pressure groups, ranging from the religious right to the radical left, from the Gay and Lesbian League to the AFL–CIO, to protect their own perceived interests in broadcast programming. Using various economic threats, these groups have already forced a number of stations to modify their programming policies in response to their

---

[51] Although the FCC's current crusade against "indecent" programs as described in Chapter 7 may deserve criticism for attempting to repress constitutionally protected expression, it is at least an effort by the FCC to demonstrate to the more than 6,000 individuals who write to the agency each year to complain about such programs that the federal government is still trying to be responsive to public concerns about the quality of broadcast service. See, for example, "Defining the Line Between Regulation and Censorship" Broadcasting April 15, 1991, p. 74.

demands. In a very real sense, then, it can be argued that one of the disadvantages of media having largely unfettered legal freedom already is clearly reflected in the recent experiences of the broadcasting industry.

Part III

MASS COMMUNICATIONS AND GOVERNMENT

Chapter 9

REGULATING BROADCASTING

Sec.
49. Licensing Broadcasters.
50. Renewing the Broadcast License.
51. Broadcast Program Standards.
52. Political Access Rules.
53. Fairness Doctrine Obligations.
54. Personal Attacks and Political Editorials.
55. Public Broadcasting.

SEC. 49. LICENSING BROADCASTERS

The licensing process has provided both the legal authority and the procedures essential for the regulation of broadcast service in the United States.

The Radio Act of 1927 marked both the beginning of modern broadcast regulation in the United States, and the end of the principle that access to the airwaves was a basic right of every American citizen, limited only by the availability of spectrum space.[1] Section 11 of the Radio Act reduced this right to the status of a privilege, to be granted by the Federal Radio Commission (FRC) only in circumstances where the agency found that issuing or renewing a broadcast license would serve the "public interest".[2] This same regulatory approach was followed by the Communications Act of 1934, creating the Federal Communications Commission (FCC) to replace the FRC.[3]

Because these governmental bodies were viewed as bestowing a privilege upon those they allowed to broadcast, the United

[1] Section 2 of the Radio Act of 1912 required the Secretary of Commerce to issue licenses upon request, allowing conditions to be imposed upon a license only in instances where its operation might interfere with those of other licensed stations.

[2] Section 11, Radio Act of 1927, "If upon examination of any application for a station license or for the renewal or modification of a station license the licensing authority shall determine that public interest, convenience or necessity would be served by the granting thereof, it shall authorize the issuance, renewal or modification thereof in accordance with such finding."

[3] Communications Act of 1934, Public Law 416, 73d Congress, Secs. 307–309.

States Supreme Court upheld their right as regulatory agencies to impose conditions upon the private use of this public resource of broadcast spectrum space, including the requirement that broadcast programming serve the interests of the public.[4] As a later Supreme Court decision would declare in even stronger terms, such government program standards were seen as enhancing, rather than repressing broadcast freedom of expression because,

> When there are substantially more individuals who want to broadcast than there are frequencies to allocate, it is idle to posit an unabridgeable First Amendment right to broadcast comparable to the right of individuals to speak, write or publish . . . the people as a whole retain their interest in free speech and their collective right to have the medium function consistently with the ends and purposes of the First Amendment.[5]

It is this broadcast licensing power, then, that has furnished the federal government with both the legal authority essential to regulate American broadcast service, and the administrative process necessary to enforce its regulatory policies during the past six decades.

The licensing process itself has always been more a matter of form than of substance. Applications for a construction permit, a broadcast license or renewal of a license each require the completion of countless forms, all filed in multiple copies with the Commission in Washington. There a small desk-bound staff of less than two dozen civil servants processes this paperwork to determine whether each application should be approved.[6]

The forms themselves are generally prepared for the broadcaster by one of the major communication law firms in Washington that specialize in dealings with the FCC. These attorneys, often former FCC employees, are in daily contact with the Commission staff to resolve any problems that might arise from their clients' broadcast filings. In the usual situation, the end result of the process is that the application for the permit, license or license renewal is eventually granted.[7]

[4] National Broadcasting Company, et al. v. United States, et al., 319 U.S. 190, 63 S.Ct. 997 (1943). See also, chapter 3, Sec. 14 of this text for a more extensive discussion of this decision.

[5] Red Lion Broadcasting Co. v. FCC, 395 U.S. 367, 89 S.Ct. 1794 (1969).

[6] For an excellent description of this administrative process, see Barry Cole and Mal Oettinger, Reluctant Regulators: The FCC and the Broadcast Audience (Reading, MA: Addison–Wesley, 1978).

[7] In 1976, for example, the FCC processed 2995 applications for renewal of broadcast licenses of which just 23 were designated for hearing, and only 8 ultimately denied. In other words, 99.2% of all renewal applicants were approved without hearing and only $3/10$ of 1% were eventually denied. Cole, Oettinger, op. cit., p. 147.

However, in that very small percentage of cases where a broadcast license application cannot be approved because "a substantial and material question of fact is presented, or the Commission for any reason is unable to make the finding specified," the applicant is notified of the Commission's intention to hold a hearing before deciding what action should be taken.[8] In most instances, a broadcaster unsuccessful at the informal hearing level still has the right to have this administrative finding reviewed both within the FCC itself and then by the Court of Appeals for the District of Columbia before being forced to accept an adverse Commission decision.[9]

The FCC does not monitor broadcast programming and so at time of renewal, it must depend upon the records or "logs" of programming maintained by each station in determining whether the broadcaster has complied with the program proposals filed with the Commission when the license was last renewed.[10] Although these "composite week" logs reveal nothing more than the title of a program, the number of commercial spots it contained and the time it was broadcast, the agency seldom requests any additional evidence relating to each station's programming performance before renewing its license.[11] This lack of FCC concern about station programming practices is reflected in the fact that of the 142 Commission decisions not to renew a broadcast license between 1934 and 1978, only 18 were based to some extent upon a finding of inadequate program service, a programming-related license revocation rate of less than one station every two years.[12]

In reality, broadcasters have generally conformed to Commission programming and other regulatory policies not because the licensing process has been capable of accurately evaluating their performance, but simply because even the slight possibility of losing a station's license by provoking an FCC hearing has been a

---

[8] U.S.C.A. Title 47, § 309(e).

[9] U.S.C.A. Title 47, § 402(b). Although a broadcaster may also seek U.S. Supreme Court review of an adverse Court of Appeals decision, the Supreme Court agrees to review, or accept certiorari only in a very limited number of appeal situations each year.

[10] In reality, to reduce the administrative burden involved in processing more than 3,000 renewal applications each year, a station is asked to file only seven days of program logs, selected at random by the FCC, from the last licensing period to represent its programming efforts for the entire period.

[11] For a more detailed description of this license renewal process and its flaws, see Don R. Le Duc, Beyond Broadcasting: Patterns in Policy and Law (White Plains, NY: Longman, 1987) pp. 43–56.

[12] John Abel, Charles Cliff III and Frederick Weiss, "Station License Revocations and Denial of Renewal 1934–1969," Journal of Broadcasting (Fall 1970) pp. 411–21; Frederick Weiss, David Ostroff and Charles Cliff III, "Station License Revocations and Denial of Renewal 1969–1979," Journal of Broadcasting (Winter 1980) pp. 69–77.

risk worth avoiding at virtually any cost. This type of indirect rule worked rather effectively as long as the Commission was able to decide for itself when its understaffed Broadcast Bureau was capable of using the license renewal process to enforce certain specific FCC regulatory standards.

Until the mid 1960s, only a competing broadcaster could compel the FCC to conduct a comparative hearing before awarding or renewing a broadcast license of another station in that market, and then only if the evidence clearly indicated that the award could cause intolerable transmission interference or severe economic injury to the complaining broadcaster.[13] In all other situations, the Commission had sole authority to decide whether the public interest demanded that it conduct an elaborate and time consuming hearing before renewing a broadcast license. Not surprisingly, it rarely did.

In 1966, however, a federal court found that the FCC had been wrong in assuming that because the Commission was created to protect the interests of the public, members of the public themselves had no right to become involved in a broadcast licensing proceeding.[14] This decision, granting to members of a broadcast audience the power to organize, petition and appeal to the federal courts if the Commission refused to hold formal hearings to review the performance of a broadcast station serving their community, set off such a massive barrage of "citizen group" license challenges that the entire structure of American broadcast regulation seemed imperiled for a time.

SEC. 50.   RENEWING THE BROADCAST LICENSE

Recognizing the right of citizen groups to challenge the renewal of a broadcast license created new constraints upon broadcast freedom of expression.

During the period from 1970 to 1977, the FCC received a total of 447 citizen petitions or objections involving the licenses of 936 broadcast stations; almost 10 percent of all the commercial broadcasters then being licensed by the Commission.[15] Many in the broadcast industry felt that they had been betrayed by the courts, and abandoned by a Commission no longer capable of protecting them from private pressures. After complying with FCC rules for almost a half century with the understanding that the agency

---

[13] Title 47, U.S.C.A. § 316(b).

[14] Office of Communication of the United Church of Christ v. FCC, 359 F.2d 994 (D.C.Cir. 1966).

[15] Comptroller General, Report to the Congress, "Selected FCC Regulatory Policies and Consequences for Commercial Radio and Television," CED 79–62, 4 June 1979, p. 17.

posed the only threat to their licenses, they were now suddenly being forced to defend themselves from citizen challenges as well, attacks upon an unprotected flank that left them vulnerable to interest group demands.

The FCC tried to end this seige of license renewal challenges in 1970 by proposing rules that made it virtually impossible to deny license renewal to an existing broadcast station, but a federal court refused to allow these rules to be adopted.[16] By the end of the 1970s this "citizen group" movement had lost its momentum, frustrated by the Commission's skilled use of constant procedural delay to deny them the hearings they sought. But this chaotic era of widespread license challenge had convinced the broadcast industry that it could no longer rely upon the FCC or the Communications Act of 1934 to protect their broadcast licenses from challenge.

Instead, the primary political objective for broadcasters during the 1980s became convincing Congress to adopt new legislation capable of sheltering existing broadcast station licenses from citizen group attack much more effectively at time of renewal. In 1981, Congress did act to reduce the dimensions of the license renewal problem to some extent by increasing the length of each television station license from three years to five, and lengthening each radio license period from three years to seven.[17] However, Congress has refused thus far to grant the industry the broad license renewal protection it has been seeking, forcing the FCC to try to provide these safeguards under the more restrictive language of the Communications Act of 1934.[18]

The Commission's decision to attempt to protect broadcasters from citizen organized license challenges is based upon the belief that such private pressure can pose a greater, if more subtle threat to broadcast freedom of expression that any federal regulatory policy may have posed in the past. Although the First Amendment shields broadcasting from government censorship, it provides no legal protection against private pressure. In addition, while government regulation is a public process, open for all to observe, interest group negotiations typically are conducted in secret, with concessions being granted without public knowledge or consent.

---

[16] The FCC rules were proposed in "Policy Statement Concerning Comparative Hearings Involving Regular Renewal Applicants," 22 FCC2d 424 (1970). The rules were rescinded when challenged by a public service law firm in Citizens Communication Center v. FCC, 447 F.2d 1201 (D.C.Cir.1971).

[17] Omnibus Reconciliation Act of 1981, 95 Stat. 736–37, as amended by Public Law 97–259.

[18] See, for example, "FCC: Time to Modernize Comparative Renewal," Broadcasting, June 27, 1988, p. 35.

Ironically, then, the same FCC that was once viewed by the industry as the enemy of broadcast free speech is now the industry's only ally in the struggle to safeguard those free speech rights from the influence of self-styled "citizen groups."

But why should broadcast industry be so susceptible to such private pressure, particularly since any "citizen group" license challenge will ultimately be brought to the FCC for resolution? Those who champion the First Amendment rights of broadcasting are often critical of stations or networks willing to negotiate their programming practices with these interest groups, arguing that such broadcast organizations have the financial resources to protect, rather than bargain away their precious freedom of expression. What these critics fail to realize is that while a media organization may have such resources, the decision to fight rather than negotiate a license challenge must be made by some highly paid executive within this organization, generally the station manager, whose dependence upon that generous salary to meet monthly mortgage payments and other financial obligations makes this employee far more vulnerable to such private pressure than any abstract concept of broadcast free speech would suggest.

Continuing controversy over station programming practices tends to disrupt normal business operations, is likely to damage a station's public image in the area it serves, and is almost certain to be viewed with alarm and displeasure at the station's corporate headquarters. In addition, even the successful defense of a station's license may result in uncompensated legal expenses ranging from 100,000 to 500,000 dollars.[19] With these facts in mind, then, it may be easier to understand why a number of broadcast stations have yielded to the programming demands of well organized, politically sophisticated pressure groups, and why both the industry and the FCC view such privately negotiated programming concessions with such concern.

The FCC was finally able to adopt a revised set of license renewal rules in 1989, designed to discourage the challenging of a broadcast license merely to profit from a subsequent payment by the licensee to withdraw the challenge.[20] The new rules require that the Commission approve in advance all negotiated settlements between the license holder and a challenger or competing applicant. No settlement will be approved if payments to the

[19] For example, WBBM–TV Chicago viewed it as a "victory" when they were able to settle a license challenge brought by Center City for *only* $187,000; reimbursement of Center City's legal expenses in filing the challenge. See "Settlement Reached in WBBM–TV Chicago Challenge", Broadcasting, July 18, 1988, p. 33.

[20] *Broadcast Renewal Process*, 66 RR2d 708 (1989); petition for reconsideration denied, 67 RR2d 1515 (1990) also see 67 RR2d 1526 (1990) for the adoption of similar standards for citizen petitions to deny applications for new stations, license modifications and transfer applications.

challenger exceed what the FCC finds to be the "legitimate and prudent" expenses actually incurred by the challenger during the proceeding.

In addition, other forms of indirect compensation are now also presumed to violate the agency's settlement standards, such as an agreement by the station to hire or retain any member of the challenging organization or to accept specific programming produced or provided by that organization.

A survey of renewal proceedings conducted soon after the new rules were adopted disclosed a significant decrease in the number of challenges being filed, suggesting that these new procedural safeguards were achieving their desired policy objectives. Encouraged by these results, the FCC decided in May 1990 to impose similar settlement payment restrictions on all future comparative hearings for new broadcast licenses as well.

After two decades of rulemaking and litigation, the Commission finally appears to have developed renewal standards capable of discouraging the filing of improperly motivated license challenges, while at the same time continuing to permit legitimate challenges to be evaluated fairly and impartially. Although the broadcast industry might have hoped for an even more elaborate set of regulatory safeguards to shelter licensees from the threat of other types of unjustified challenges, this appears to be the most extensive protection of a broadcaster licensee's renewal rights that the FCC, as an agency of Congress, has the legal authority to provide.

SEC. 51. BROADCAST PROGRAM STANDARDS

Broadcast program requirements have always been stated in general terms to avoid encroaching unnecessarily upon the free speech rights of the broadcast licensee.

In 1929, only two years after it began regulating broadcast service in the United States, the FRC issued its first comprehensive description of federal broadcast program policy. Beginning a regulatory tradition that would endure until the 1980s, the agency pointed out in this earliest public programming statement that it would not establish any list of preferred program categories. Instead, the FRC simply directed each station to offer its audience a balanced schedule of different types of programs capable of serving the needs of every segment of the station's audience. The Commission described its program policy objectives in this way:

> The tastes, needs and desires of all substantial groups among the public should be met, in fair proportion, by a well-rounded program schedule, in which entertainment,

religion, education and instruction, important public events, discussions of public questions, weather, market reports, news and matters of interest to all members of the family find a place.[21]

The FRC soon discovered, however, that it was difficult to achieve even these rather basic and generalized programming goals because stations had begun to depend upon national broadcast networks to provide a substantial portion of their daily program schedule. Network broadcasting had existed since 1924, but it was not until 1929 that NBC and the newly formed CBS became the dominant national programming and advertising forces in American radio.[22]

Stations were eager to affiliate with one of the major broadcast networks because they offered the type of popular, professionally produced entertainment shows no local station could hope to duplicate. To become a network affiliate, however, a station had to agree to carry a substantial number of network programs each week, and to reserve other portions of its broadcast schedule to be used for whatever programs the network chose to provide.

Both the FRC and the FCC saw the networks as distorting the balance in American broadcast service these agencies sought; furnishing affiliate stations with a vast array of light entertainment shows while offering virtually no public affairs, educational or childrens' programming. Yet neither agency had authority to regulate the networks directly, because networks did not use the broadcast spectrum to distribute their programs, delivering them instead to their affiliated stations through privately leased telephone lines. Since the networks required no broadcast license to operate these non-spectrum programming services, there was no legal basis for imposing any public interest standards upon the shows they were providing their affiliate stations.[23]

Unable to regulate network program practices directly, the FCC began during the late 1930s to use its licensing authority instead to force network affiliate stations to reclaim from their national network the right to program a larger proportion of their own daily broadcast schedule. In 1940, the Commission adopted rules that established strict limits upon the amount of broadcast time any station could devote to network programming, including

[21] In the matter of the application of Great Lakes Broadcasting, 3 FRC Annual Reports 32 (1929).

[22] NBC actually operated two separate radio networks until 1941, the "Red" network which it retained, and the "Blue" network sold in 1941 and renamed the American Broadcasting Company in 1945.

[23] Each network did own and operate broadcast stations itself, (O & O stations) but the tactic of trying to influence national network program practices through regulations imposed upon these network owned stations never worked successfully.

an enforcement provision that allowed the Commission to revoke the broadcast license of any station exceeding these network time limitations.[24]

In 1970, the Commission tried a somewhat similar tactic in television, restricting network affiliate television stations in major markets to only three hours of network supplied prime-time programming each evening.[25] This "Prime Time Access Rule", modified and amended several times to make it more effective, was designed to stimulate local station production during the most popular viewing period of the day, or at the very least to provide non-network program suppliers with access to major market television audiences.

Neither of these efforts were particularly successful. The Commission's vision of a locally oriented broadcast service, offering a broad and balanced assortment of public affairs, educational and other programs overlooked those powerful economic incentives that propelled the broadcast industry towards nationwide delivery of popular entertainment financed by national advertising.

Through the years, however, the FCC and the broadcast networks managed to develop a rather close working relationship on most regulatory issues. The FCC was useful to the networks, because by regulating broadcasting, it shielded the industry from other, more powerful political pressures, and furnished broadcasting with a stable and predictable legal environment in which the networks could prosper. On the other hand, the FCC had to rely upon the networks to carry out programming reforms the Commission did not have the legal authority to achieve on its own.[26]

Although the Commission was constantly involved in efforts to improve the quality of network broadcast service, it was generally reluctant to interfere in any way with the programming practices of individual broadcast stations. As long as stations were not violating any specific FCC programming rule, the agency was willing to allow broadcasters the widest possible discretion in selecting their own format or schedule.

Thus, in 1970, when a classical music station was being sold to investors who intended to change its musical format, the Commission routinely approved the sale, even though a citizens' group had petitioned the FCC to deny the license transfer. Upon appeal, the

[24] FCC rules CFR § 47. 3.101–3.108. The *NBC v. US* Supreme Court opinion that approved these rules is discussed in chapter 3, Sec. 14.

[25] 23 FCC2d 282 (1970); modified by 44 FCC2d 1081, and further modified by 46 FCC2d 829.

[26] For one example of such close FCC–network cooperation, see the "Family Viewing" opinion in Writers Guild of America West, Inc. v. FCC, 423 F.Supp. 1064 (C.D.Cal.1976).

court reversed the Commission decision, ordering the FCC to conduct a hearing to determine whether the sale would result in depriving the audience in that broadcast market of its only source of this type of programming.[27] In response to the FCC's argument that it was not authorized to act as a "national arbiter of taste," the court declared,

> The Commission is not dictating tastes when it seeks to discover what they presently are, and to consider what assignment of channels is feasible and fair in terms of their gratification.[28]

Four years later the Commission was faced with another sale of a classical music station to a group eager to convert it into a "top 40" outlet, and once again the agency approved the sale without permitting the local citizens' group the hearing they had requested to oppose the license transfer and change of format. The court again reversed the FCC decision, this time with the observation that,

> We think it axiomatic that preservation of a format that would otherwise disappear; although economically and technologically viable and preferred by a significant number of listeners, is generally in the public interest.[29]

At this point the Commission decided to conduct a public policy hearing to determine what its future role in such program format controversies should be. At the conclusion of these deliberations, the FCC adopted the rather daring position that despite any instructions it had received from the federal court of appeals, it would no longer allow itself to be involved in any regulation of broadcast station formats because, as the Commission explained it,

> Our reflection . . . has fortified our conviction that our regulation of entertainment formats as an aspect of the public interest would produce an unnecessary and menacing entanglement in matters that Congress meant to leave to private discretion.[30]

A citizens' group immediately appealed this FCC policy decision, but after it had been reversed at the Court of Appeals level, the Supreme Court decided to consider this format regulation issue itself for the first time. In Federal Communications Commission v. WNCN Listeners Guild [31] the Commission's position was

[27] Citizens Committee to Preserve the Voice of Arts in Atlanta v. FCC, 436 F.2d 263 (D.C.Cir.1970).

[28] Ibid, 272 n. 7.

[29] Citizens Committee to Save WEFM v. FCC, 506 F.2d 246 (D.C.Cir.1973).

[30] "Changes in the Entertainment Formats of Broadcast Stations," 37 RR2d 1679, 1976.

[31] 450 U.S. 582, 101 S.Ct. 1266 (1981).

upheld by the court, on the basis that the FCC's format policy reflected a reasonable balance between, "promoting diversity in programming and . . . avoiding unnecessary restrictions upon licensee discretion".

Yet, even though the Commission has been reluctant to become involved in most phases of local station programming, one specific type of programming has been singled out recently by the FCC for close supervision. Both the Radio Act of 1927 and the Communications Act of 1934 contained regulatory provisions authorizing the imposition of a $10,000 fine and the revocation of the license of any station broadcasting obscene, indecent or profane language.[32]

Punishing "obscene" broadcast language presented no constitutional problem for either federal regulatory agency, because speech or conduct found to be obscene is not recognized by American law as meriting First Amendment protection.[33] "Indecent" or "profane" speech, on the other hand, is constitutionally protected, and so regulatory efforts to discourage such utterances or to penalize stations for scheduling an "indecent" or "profane" program impose greater constraints upon the broadcast medium than upon any other form of American mass communication.

In reality, however, the broadcast networks and their industry association, the National Association of Broadcasters (NAB), were able to shield the FRC and FCC from the problem of tasteless broadcast content until the early 1970s. Each of the networks demanded that their affiliated stations follow NAB program standards far more restrictive in areas of public taste than any regulatory agency could have required, and while independent stations were not bound by these agreements, they hesitated to isolate themselves in this way from the protection of the NAB.

As the 1970s began, however, a number of smaller, typically urban market FM stations saw an opportunity to attract a larger audience with a new format called "topless radio", featuring sexually oriented talk shows to capitalize upon the so-called new morality of that era. By 1973, stations adopting the "topless" format had become top-rated during their sex talk segments in several major markets, as letters of complaint from outraged listeners began flooding the FCC.[34]

[32] In 1948, Congress transferred these statutory provisions to the U.S. Criminal Code, Title 18, U.S.C.A. § 1464, because they also contained criminal penalties (imprisonment of up to 5 years) that could be enforced more effectively by the U.S. Justice Department. However, the FCC was granted continuing authority to penalize broadcasters under the new code section.

[33] See chapter 8.

[34] The FCC received more than 2,000 letters from listeners complaining about these programs in 1972; in 1974, they received more than 20,000 letters of

In that same year, the FCC imposed a $2,000 fine upon a station that had presented a particularly explicit discussion of oral sex techniques, pointing out,

> We are emphatically not saying that sex per se is a forbidden subject on the broadcast medium . . . sex and obscenity are not the same things.[35]

but holding that because the program had been broadcast at a time when a substantial number of children could be presumed to be listening, the station had disregarded its public interest responsibilities towards that special segment of its audience. A citizens' group petitioned for a hearing to challenge the Commission's decision, but a federal appeals court upheld both the FCC action and its right to reject such a petition.[36]

In that same year, another station, in a mid-afternoon program, featured an excerpt from a comedy album of George Carlin, his "Filthy Words" routine, discussing in detail the nuances of several of the seven four-letter words he said couldn't be mentioned on radio or television. The FCC issued a declaratory ruling against the station, this time defining its position on indecency with even greater clarity. According to the Commission, "indecent" programming was that which,

> . . . describes, in terms patently offensive as measured by contemporary community standards for the broadcast medium, sexual or excretory activities and organs, at times of the day where there is reasonable risk that children may be in the audience.[37]

The FCC's newly established indecency standard was overturned almost immediately by a federal appeals court, but at that point the Supreme Court intervened to consider whether more stringent restrictions could legally be imposed upon broadcast free speech than other forms of media expression.

The court affirmed the Commission's position, basing its affirmation of the agency's right to hold broadcasting to a higher standard of care in this area of speech upon two special characteristics of the medium, its prevasiveness and its unique accessibility to children.[38] In addition, the crucial factor in the view of the

complaint. "Programming of Violent, Indecent or Obscene Material", Broadcast Management/Engineering, June 1975, pp. 22–24.

[35] Sonderling Broadcasting, 27 RR2d 285 (1973).

[36] Illinois Citizens Committee for Broadcasting v. FCC, 515 F.2d 397 (D.C.Cir. 1974).

[37] Pacifica Foundation, 56 FCC2d 946 (1975).

[38] FCC v. Pacifica Foundation, 438 U.S. 726, 98 S.Ct. 3026 (1978). It's important to note, however, that the FCC's indecency definition was upheld by a narrow 5–4 vote, suggesting quite clearly that its authority to enforce this type of content control would be narrowly construed.

court was that the FCC was not attempting to ban the broadcasting of indecent programs, but only to require that such programs be scheduled at times when they were not likely to reach a large youthful audience.

Although the Supreme Court had affirmed the right of the Commission to treat indecent programming as a nuisance, "channeling" it away from younger viewers or listeners, the new "marketplace" oriented FCC of the 1980s seemed reluctant to exercise this power. Despite complaints from various citizen groups about the explicit nature of certain new "shock" radio formats, the agency decided initially to restrict its definition of "indecent" only to broadcasts containing one or more of those famous seven words George Carlin had uttered in the monologue that led to the *Pacifica* action.[39]

In 1987, however, the Commission, now headed by a new chairman, began to assert the authority approved by the Supreme Court almost a decade before. It sent public notices to two broadcast stations the agency found to be in violation of the rule, and declared its intention to adopt rules reestablishing the broader definition of indecency it had followed during the 1970s.

Following the "channeling" approach the Supreme Court had approved in *Pacifica,* the FCC declared that indecent programming would be prohibited only if broadcast at a time when there was "reasonable risk that children might be in the audience." [40] Until this time the Commission had taken the position that programs scheduled after 10 p.m. could be aired without concern for their accessibility to children. However, audience research revealed that a substantial number of children were still listening or viewing at 10 p.m. each evening. Therefore, the FCC decided upon the time slot of midnight to 6 a.m. as the appropriate period for such "adult" programming, as long as such programs were prefaced with a warning relating to their content.

This new campaign by the Commission to shield young viewers and listeners from indecent broadcast programming was immediately attacked by a coalition of public interest and trade organizations.[41] Upon review, the D.C. Court of Appeals affirmed the

---

[39] The "shock" radio format goes one step beyond "topless", trying to offend the sensibilities of a larger share of the public by using racial jokes, ethnic slurs and other forms of low humor to attract an audience.

[40] New Indecency Enforcement Standards, 62 RR2d 1218 (1987).

[41] Action for Children's Television v. FCC, 852 F.2d 1332 (D.D.C.1988). It is interesting to note that this legal challenge was spearheaded by the nation's largest and most influential advocacy group for the broadcast programming rights of young viewers and listeners. Through the years ACT has constantly campaigned for more extensive government restrictions on broadcast commercials to protect American youth from the damaging effects of advertising, but its leaders apparently saw no similar need to protect young viewers from the damaging effects

fundamental right of the FCC to restrict indecent programming to those hours of the day when children were least likely to be present in the broadcast audience. In this instance, however, the Court held that the Commission had not adequately documented its claim that the midnight to 6 AM period chosen as a "safe harbor" for such programming was actually the most narrowly drawn one capable of realizing this policy objective.

As the FCC was preparing to justify its six hour indecency "harbor" as being least extensive time period required to achieve its goal, Congress acted to make the agency's already vulnerable legal position virtually indefensible. In October 1988 Congress passed legislation that compelled the Commission to enforce an absolute ban on indecent broadcast programming on a 24 hour a day basis.[42] The FCC had no choice but to comply with this Congressional directive, even though it meant that the agency would now be required to prohibit a constitutionally protected form of expression it had sought only to confine within reasonable time limitations.

When the Commission announced its intention to begin enforcing a total ban on indecent programming in January 1989, the same coalition of media and public interest groups was able to obtain an order from the D.C. Court of Appeals preventing the Commission from implementing this new rule until its validity could be determined by the Court. In doing so, however, the Court granted the FCC permission to continue the enforcement of its indecency standards on a conditional basis in order to gather further documentation relating to the nature of this indecent programming to be used when the case was ultimately heard by the Court.

During this period of conditional enforcement, the Commission decided to confine itself to considering only those indecency complaints involving programs broadcast between 6 AM and 8 PM, so as to restrict its review to that portion of the broadcast day when unsupervised children were most likely to be present in the broadcast audience. After completing this review in July 1990 the Commission voted unanimously to adopt a report supporting a 24 hour a day ban of both indecent radio and television program content, arguing that because at least some portion of the broadcast audience was likely to be composed of children at all times of

of indecent programming, defined by the FCC as "describing or depicting sexual or excretory activities in a patently offensive manner." ACT has explained that it opposes any governmental restrictions on "indecent" broadcasts because indecency is expression protected by the First Amendment. The only problem with that explanation is that commercial speech is also expression protected by the First Amendment.

[42] Public Law 100–459, § 608 (1988). Two months later the FCC adopted an order enforcing this ban. See 67 RR2d 1714.

the day and night, anything less than a total ban of such programming would not achieve the objectives of the regulation.[43]

In April 1991 the U.S. Court of Appeals struck down the 24 hour a day ban of indecent broadcast programming, but directed the FCC to consider once again the possibility of establishing a reasonable defined "safe harbor" for indecent content capable of channeling such programs away from children without unduly restricting adult access to them.[44]

Freed by the Court of its Congressionally imposed burden to ban all indecent broadcasting from the airwaves, the FCC may now seek a new "safe harbor" for such content capable of satisfying the broadcast free speech concerns of the Court. A far better solution, though, has been proposed by the National Association of Broadcasters in its plea to all broadcast owners to monitor their station's programming more carefully in order to prevent the transmission of explicit sexual or scatological references intended primarily to shock or offend.

Unfortunately, this plea is likely to be ignored by that small group of broadcasters who have already demonstrated their willingness to do anything, no matter how degrading or tasteless, to attract an audience. That, in turn, will compel the FCC to intrude once more into this sensitive area of broadcast program content, for as Justice Stewart has pointed out,

> Patently offensive, indecent material presented over the airwaves confronts the citizen not only in public, but also in the privacy of the home, where the individual's right to be left alone clearly outweighs the First Amendment rights of the intruder.[45]

---

[43] 67 RR2d 1714 (1990). To understand more clearly the type of content that triggered the FCC action, and motivated the more than 6,000 indecency complaints the FCC has been receiving annually since the mid 1980s, here are a few excerpts from some of those programs broadcast during a time of day when a substantial number of children could be expected to be in the broadcast audience: WLUP Chicago, " * * * went down on that other woman and oh God, you had your tongue in her vagina. It was fabulous * * * "; KSJO, San Jose, "I'd love to lick the matzo balls right off your butt * * * I'd like to have a smorgasbord in your butt. I'd like to have matzos in there with borscht, everything. I'd just have a buffet * * *," WLLZ Detroit, "He puts Penthouse on his desk/he's got big muscles in his wrist/he holds his organ in his fist/He gives his pink dolphin a mighty twist * * * All the girls in the office they say, 'Hard-on, hard-on, beg my pardon.' Walk with an erection"; WMCA New York, "When you can't call welfare people 'sluts' and 'whores,' 'cocksuckers' or 'freeloaders,' then our English language serves no purpose."

[44] ACT v. FCC, 69 RR2d 179 (D.C.Cir.1991).

[45] FCC v. Pacifica Foundation, 438 U.S. 726, 98 S.Ct. 3026 (1978). The court also pointed out in a footnote (28) that those who seek indecent materials are not limited in access to them by this ruling, since they are so readily available from so many other sources in American society.

SEC. 52. POLITICAL ACCESS RULES

Despite deregulation, Congress still requires the FCC to enforce all equal access broadcast requirements.

The "equal time", or more accurately the "equal opportunities" requirement for political candidates has been an obligation imposed upon broadcasting since the Radio Act of 1927 was adopted. Section 18 of the Radio Act became the well known Section 315 of the Communications Act of 1934, stating,

> If any licensee shall permit any person who is a legally qualified candidate for any political office to use a broadcasting station, he shall afford equal opportunities to all other such candidates for that office in the use of such broadcasting station . . .

This section also denied the broadcaster any power of censorship over candidates exercising their rights of access under the terms of Section 315. In 1959, a political candidate used this access to make defamatory remarks about his opponent. The opponent sued the broadcast station for airing these defamatory statements, but in Farmers Educational & Cooperative Union of America v. WDAY, Inc.,[46] the Supreme Court held that in establishing the terms and conditions for such political broadcast access, Congress had preempted state defamation law and created an absolute privilege that shielded the broadcast station from legal liability for statements made by such candidates.

During this same era, television news coverage of public events began raising an question Congress had no reason to consider when Section 315 was adopted. If a political candidate could be seen by viewers in film clips of a news event broadcast by a television station, was such an appearance a "use" of broadcast facilities requiring the station to offer all opponents of that candidate equal access to television time? In 1959 the Commission decided that such an appearance did constitute a "use" under the Act, even though broadcast journalists had pointed out that if each televised glimpse of a candidate triggered an obligation by a station to make free time available to all opponents, it would be virtually impossible for a television station to provide its viewers with adequate local news coverage during an election campaign.[47]

Congress reacted promptly by amending Section 315 to exempt from its equal opportunities requirement any appearance by a legally qualified candidate on a

---

[46] 360 U.S. 525, 79 S.Ct. 1302 (1959).

[47] Columbia Broadcasting System, 26 FCC2d 715 (1959).

(1) bona fide newscast

(2) bona fide news interview

(3) bona fide documentary (if the appearance of the candidate is incidental to the presentation of the subject or subjects covered by the news documentary), or

(4) on-the-spot coverage of bona fide news events (including but not limited to political conventions and activities incidental thereto) . . .

This amendment provided broadcast journalists the protection from equal access obligations necessary to cover most news events, but in special situations not fitting neatly into one of these four exempted categories of coverage, the FCC tended to be reluctant to extend the scope of such exemptions. In 1960, for example, Congress was forced to suspend the application of Section 315 to presidential candidates to allow the television networks to broadcast the famous Kennedy–Nixon debates without being required to provide an equal amount of free network broadcast time to all minor party presidential candidates.

In 1975, however, the Commission reversed its earlier position that neither broadcast coverage of political candidate debates nor candidate press conferences came within the exemption Congress had granted for on-the-spot coverage of bona fide news events.[48] It now held that debates were exempt from Section 315 requirements if they were controlled by someone other than the candidates or the broadcaster, and that full coverage of a press conference would also be exempted if it was "newsworthy and subject to on-the-spot coverage." [49]

The League of Women Voters acted as the independent host of these presidential debates for the television networks in 1976 and 1980. Since 1984, however, the Commission no longer has required the presence of an outside sponsoring organization in order to exempt political debates from 315 requirements, finding no basis for its previous belief that such an independent group was needed to insure impartial coverage of such debates.[50]

[48] Petition of Aspen Institute and CBS, 35 RR2d 49 (1975). In Petition of Henry Geller, et al., 54 RR2d 1246 (1983) the FCC relaxed its political candidates' debates rules still further, allowing broadcasters themselves to sponsor debates between political candidates without being required by Section 315 to extend this right of debate to all candidates for the office is question.

[49] This change in FCC policy was sustained by the court of appeals in Chisholm v. FCC, 538 F.2d 349 (D.C.Cir.1976), cert. denied 429 U.S. 890, 97 S.Ct. 247 (1976). Senator Kennedy challenged the new press conference exemption, claiming that President Carter had used such a conference to attack Kennedy, then a competing presidential candidate. The FCC's position was upheld in Kennedy for President Committee v. FCC, 636 F.2d 432 (D.C.Cir.1980).

[50] The FCC's position was affirmed in League of Women Voters Educ. Fund v. FCC, 731 F.2d 995 (D.C.Cir.1984).

Through the years the FCC has expanded its category of broadcast programs exempted from political access requirements to include entertainment shows that provide news or current event coverage as regularly scheduled segments of the program. In this way, not only "Today", "Good Morning America" and "This Morning" but even "Donahue", "Entertainment Tonight" and "Entertainment This Week" have been able to invite political candidates to discuss public issues without exposing the network or station carrying them to "equal time" demands by rival candidates.[51]

On the other hand, the Commission has held rigidly to its position that any use of station time by a political candidate not expressly exempted by Section 315 creates an obligation for equal access. For example, the FCC has held a station broadcasting a Ronald Reagan film during any campaign period in which he was a political candidate would obligate that station to offer all his legally qualified opponents the same degree of access to its audience.[52]

More significantly, such a policy effectively denies any broadcast performer the right to run for political office. The FCC has defined "use" of broadcast facilities to include virtually any type of on-air performance, including working under an assumed name as the radio host of a weekly dance show.[53] Under this strict interpretation of the rules, as soon as a broadcast performer becomes a political candidate, each subsequent on-air performance obligates the station to provide a similar amount of free air time to each of the employee's political opponents.

In one recent case, station management estimated that it would be required to provide more than 33 hours of free broadcast response time if a television reporter went ahead with his plans to become a candidate for a town council position.[54] Not surprising-

[51] Although the Donahue exemption was originally denied by the FCC, it was subsequently granted in 1984 despite the show's rather sporadic commitment to coverage of significant politcal events or issues. See Multimedia Entertainment 56 RR2d 143 (1984). In justifying its exemption for show business promotional programs such as "Entertainment Tonight," the FCC observed that the news exemption to Section 315 is not based on "the subject matter reported" but only on whether a program "reports news of some area of current events", and for the Commission to make its own independent evaluation of the importance or significance of the information provided would require it to become more deeply involved in an assessment of the quality of a particular program's content than would be constitutionally justified. Request for Declaratory Ruling by Paramount Pictures Corp. (1988).

[52] In re Adrian Weiss, 36 RR2d 292 (1976). See also In re Pat Paulsen, 23 RR2d 861 (1972), affirmed 491 F.2d 887 (9th Cir.1974).

[53] See Letter to WUGN, 40 FCC 2d 293 (1958).

[54] Branch v. FCC, 824 F.2d 37 (D.C.Cir.1987), 14 Med.L.Rptr. 1465.

ly, the reporter was ordered by the station to make an immediate choice between a career in politics and one in broadcasting.

Yet, it would be unfair to blame the FCC too severely for this unfortunate result, because Congress has allowed the Commission virtually no discretion in the enforcement of this broadcast "use" standard. Despite the fact that both the NAB and the Radio Television News Directors Association (RTNDA) have on several occasions urged that Congress amend Section 315 to allow broadcast employees to exercise this basic right of citizenship, Congressional leaders have seemed content to continue treating broadcasting as a less legally privileged medium.

Nowhere is that attitude of Congress more clearly reflected than in legislation it enacted in 1971 to take advantage of broadcasting's status as a federally regulated medium. In that year the Communications Act was amended by Congress to compel each broadcast station to provide candidates for federal office a reasonable amount of broadcast time, and to furnish time for purchase by federal candidates at the lowest rate charged regular advertisers for that same time period.[55] In essence, members of Congress had decided to combat the rising costs of federal election campaigns by imposing upon broadcasting, the only medium controlled by government, requirements designed to reduce their own campaign costs at the broadcast industry's expense. The first major test of this new legislation occured in 1980, when the Carter–Mondale Committee sought to purchase a half hour of prime time from each network to present a documentary portraying President Carter's first term accomplishments just after Carter's formal announcement of his intention to seek a second term. When none of the networks were willing to provide the full 30 minutes of time the Committee demanded, the group filed a complaint with the FCC.[56]

The Commission found the networks in violation of the "reasonable access" rule, and on appeal, the Supreme Court, in a five to four decision, narrowly affirmed this finding.[57]

Whatever the deregulatory trend may be in Washington, members of Congress are not likely to ever voluntarily release broadcasting from the constraints of federal programming regula-

[55] The "reasonable access" amendment created section 312(a)(7) of the Communications Act, and the "lowest rate" provision became section 315(b).

[56] Networks were reluctant to sell a large block of prime time for a political program during a non-election year, aware that inserting such a political documentary into a regular evening lineup of shows would substantially reduce the audience for all programs following the political program the evening it was scheduled. CBS offered a 5 minute prime time segment, and ABC a full 30 minute prime time slot during a non-rating period in January, but the Committee refused these offers.

[57] CBS, Inc. v. FCC, 453 U.S. 367, 101 S.Ct. 2813 (1981).

tion so long as they can continue to gain such political advantages from the "equal opportunities", "lowest advertising rate" and "reasonable access" provisions of the Communications Act of 1934.[58]

SEC. 53.   FAIRNESS DOCTRINE OBLIGATIONS

Although the FCC has repealed the Fairness Doctrine, it has never been declared unconstitutional by the courts, and easily could be reinstituted at any time by Congress or the Commission.

In contrast, the "fairness doctrine", the other major public issue oriented principle of broadcast regulation, has never been as directly related to Congressional self-interest. In fact, Congress never bothered to formally codify the doctrine, simply declaring when amending the "equal opportunities" provision of Section 315 in 1959 that it had no intention of relieving broadcasters,

> . . . from the obligations imposed upon them under this Act to operate in the public interest and to afford reasonable opportunity for the discussion of conflicting views on issues of public importance.[59]

The concept of broadcast "fairness" emerged instead from years of specific decisions made by the FRC and FCC in determining the exact extent of a licensee's obligation to provide the public with balanced coverage of controversial matters of public importance. In 1949, the FCC issued the first formal description of this doctrine, declaring,

> One of the most vital questions of mass communications in a democracy is the development of an informed public opinion through the public dissemination of news and ideas concerning the vital public issues of the day.[60]

Elaborating on this concept, the Commission established a twofold obligation for every broadcaster; to devote a reasonable amount of time to the coverage of important public issues, and to provide this coverage in a fair and balanced manner. In 1969, the Supreme Court had its first opportunity to consider the First Amendment issues raised by the fairness doctrine. Although only one narrow portion of the doctrine, its personal attack rule, was

[58] Congress has always favored the "equal opportunities" provision of Section 315, because while virtually every incumbent can gain constant broadcast access to constituents between elections through news items most local stations are eager to carry, any challenger is restricted by § 315 during the campaign period to access under the same terms and conditions as the incumbent, thus protecting the incumbent's pre-election advantage.

[59] Public Law No. 274, 86th Congress 1959.

[60] Editorializing by Broadcast Licensees, 13 FCC 1246 (1949).

truly at issue, the consolidation of this case with an action brought by a group of broadcast news directors allowed the court to consider the broader constitutional implications of this Commission policy. Justice White, speaking for a unanimous court, declared in affirming the doctrine that the federal government did have the constitutional authority to require broadcasters to furnish their audiences with balanced coverage of controversial issues of public importance because,

> It is the purpose of the First Amendment to preserve an uninhibited marketplace of ideas in which truth will ultimately prevail, rather than to countenance monopolization of that market, whether it be by the Government itself or a private licensee. . . . It is the right of the viewers and listeners, not the right of the broadcasters, which is paramount.[61]

In 1967 the Commission had taken the position that in accepting cigarette advertising, a station obligated itself under the fairness doctrine to present programming or public service announcements balancing the advocacy of smoking with information describing the threat that cigarette smoking posed to health.[62] By establishing this precedent, the FCC soon found itself under pressure from a wide range of interest groups demanding that this "counteradvertising" broadcast obligation be extended to require informational messages criticizing virtually every product advertised on television or radio.

Clearly, expanding the scope of the fairness doctrine in this way would have made it extremely difficult for broadcasters to continue to compete with newspapers or magazines for advertising revenues, since few advertisers would be likely to use a medium that was obligated by law to provide free air time to those who wished to criticize the products they had paid to promote. As a result, when the Federal Trade Commission (FTC) filed a brief with the FCC in 1972 that urged the Commission adopt broadcast counteradvertising rules as a "suitable approach to some of the present failings of advertising which are beyond the FTC's capacity," the FCC realized that it was being maneuvered into a regulatory position that would undercut the financial base of the entire broadcast industry.[63]

In 1974 the Commission rejected this FTC proposal and issued a policy statement effectively removing all product advertising from the requirements of the fairness doctrine, except in situations where the advertising itself expressly raised a controversial

[61] Red Lion Broadcasting Co. v. FCC, 395 U.S. 367, 89 S.Ct. 1794 (1969).

[62] Banzhaf v. FCC, 405 F.2d 1082 (D.C.Cir.1968).

[63] FTC Docket 19.260.

issue of public importance.[64]   In this same policy statement the FCC also tried to clarify basic broadcast obligations under the doctrine, concluding that broadcasters needed only to devote a reasonable amount of time to the coverage of public issues, and through this coverage, to provide opportunities for the presentation of contrasting points of view relating to these issues.

Citizen groups viewed this effort at clarification as an attempt to retreat from regulatory guidelines that in the past had been construed by the agency itself as requiring broadcasters actively to seek out controversial issues of public importance and to assume primary responsibility for providing balanced coverage of these issues.   Eventually, however, the FCC's new, more limited definition of broadcast fairness doctrine obligations was sustained by the courts.[65]

Shortly thereafter, even this more narrowly defined set of fairness obligations began to seem too intrusive upon broadcast freedom of expression for an FCC now committed to a policy of deregulation.   In 1981, the Commission asked Congress to repeal the fairness doctrine, pointing to what it felt was an ever increasing inequity between the programming requirements broadcasters had to accept, and the much less extensive programming obligations the agency could legally impose upon all other forms of competing electronic media service.[66]

When Congress failed to respond to the FCC's request, the agency began an extensive investigation of the doctrine on its own. In 1985, the Commission released a study based upon this investigation that concluded that the fairness doctrine no longer served the public interest.[67]   This was true, according to the report, because a rapid expansion in the number of information services available to American audiences made them far less dependent upon broadcasting to be informed than they had been when the doctrine was adopted.   In the absence of such continuing dependence, further intrusion by government in this area of broadcast free speech was not only unwarranted, in the view of the Commission, but also dangerous, because it offered ample opportunity for political pressure to affect broadcast coverage of public issues.

Congress responded to this FCC report by ordering the agency not to alter any of its existing fairness doctrine enforcement policies for a two year period ending in August 1987.   Instead, the

[64] In the Matter of Handling of Public Issues under the Fairness Doctrine, 48 FCC 2d 1 (1974).

[65] National Citizens Committee for Broadcasting v. FCC, 567 F.2d 1095 (D.C.Cir. 1977), cert. denied 436 U.S. 926, 98 S.Ct. 2820 (1978).

[66] FCC Report No. 5068, Setting Forth Proposals for Amending the Communications Act (Sept. 17, 1981).

[67] Fairness Report, 102 FCC 2d 143 (1985).

Commission was directed to complete, during this two year period, a detailed assessment of various alternative methods the agency might recommend for continuing to protect the public's interest in balanced treatment of controversial issues without infringing to the same extent upon broadcaster editorial discretion.

In the midst of preparing this report criticizing the fairness doctrine, the FCC actually enforced its provisions for the first time in almost a decade. In 1984 the Commission found that Meredith Broadcasting, owner of a television station in Syracuse, New York had violated the doctrine's provisions by refusing to balance editorial advertisements supporting the building of a nuclear power plant with anti-nuclear energy public service announcements pointing out the drawbacks of this source of energy.[68] Perhaps it was purely coincidental that the Commission had decided to begin enforcing the doctrine again at this particular time, but there was certainly a tactical advantage in doing so. As long as Congress remained unwilling to relieve the FCC of its statutory obligation to enforce the fairness doctrine, the agency's only means of escaping this responsibility was through an appeal of a Commission fairness violation decision to the federal courts, where the fairness doctrine could be found unconstitutional, and therefore unenforcible; exactly the issue that this case happened to present.

Although this may have been the strategy the FCC and the industry were following at the time, an unexpected decision by the Court of Appeals for the District of Columbia soon made such elaborate planning unnecessary. It had generally been assumed that the Commission lacked the authority to repeal the fairness doctrine on its own because in amending the Communications Act in 1959, Congress had inserted a statutory provision that appeared to make the doctrine a part of the Act. However, in a decision involving the application of broadcast rules to teletext service, the court found that the language of this provision had not been clear or specific enough to actually codify the fairness doctrine as a part of the Communications Act of 1934.[69]

Soon afterwards this same Court of Appeals reversed and returned the fairness doctrine case involving Meredith Broadcasting to the FCC, avoiding the need to consider any of First Amendment issues it raised by simply instructing the Commission, now free of the obligation to enforce the doctrine, to decide on its own whether this doctrine still served the public interest.[70]

[68] In re Syracuse Peace Council, 57 RR2d 519 (1984).

[69] Telecommunications Research and Action Center (TRAC) v. FCC, 801 F.2d 501 (D.C.Cir.1986).

[70] Meredith Corp. v. FCC, 809 F.2d 863 (D.C.Cir.1987). Because the Supreme Court had found that the fairness doctrine did not infringe upon broadcaster First

As the year 1987 began, members of Congress who wanted to preserve the doctrine realized that they would soon have to add a new, clearly stated "fairness" clause to the Communications Act to prevent the FCC from following the court's advice to exercise its own judgment in deciding whether the doctrine still served the public interest. In May 1987, "fairness" legislation had been passed by both houses of Congress, and a bill codifying the doctrine was sent to the president in mid-June.[71]

During this period of feverish legislative activity, the NAB decided not to oppose this attempt to codify the fairness doctrine, fearing that such opposition might antagonize members of Congress whose support was needed for more important comparative renewal legislation.[72] Even though the broadcast industry had been unwilling to campaign publicly to extend its right of freedom of expression under these circumstances, President Reagan decided on his own to veto the bill, a veto Congress lacked the votes to override.

After this veto, the FCC stood alone in the political spotlight. The Court of Appeals had found no language in the Communications Act compelling the Commission to continue to enforce the doctrine, and Congress had failed in its efforts to incorporate the fairness doctrine in the Act.

The agency was still acting under instructions from Congress not to abandon its enforcement of the doctrine prior to August 1987, when it was to provide Congress with a list of alternative methods for achieving the same objectives of balance in the broadcast coverage of controversial issues. On August 4, 1987, it issued this study Congress had requested.[73] At the same time, however, the agency released its decision in the *Meredith* case, rescinding all broadcast fairness doctrine requirements, except those rules relating to "personal attack" and "political editorializing".[74]

Supporters of the doctrine in Congress reacted angrily to the Commission's action, drafting new fairness legislation while seeking some approach that could shelter it from presidential veto.

Amendment rights in the *Red Lion* case, the lower court obviously preferred to avoid basing its decision on constitutional grounds.

[71] S. 742 was passed by the Senate on April 21 and H.R. 1934 was passed by the House in May. The reconciled bill was vetoed by President Reagan on June 19, 1987, and unable to override the veto, the legislation was returned to committee without action.

[72] "CBS's Bob McConnell and the Story Behind the Veto", Broadcasting, July 6, 1987, p. 33.

[73] Fairness Alternatives, 63 RR2d 488 (1987).

[74] In re Complaint of Syracuse Peace Council Against WVTH, Memorandum Opinion and Order, 63 RR2d 542 (1987). See also "The Decline and Fall of the Fairness Doctrine: Fairness Held Unfair," Broadcasting, Aug. 19, 1987, p. 27.

But despite their best efforts, this second attempt to make the fairness doctrine part of the Communications Act also failed to survive President Reagan's veto in December 1987.

On review, the FCC's decision to rescind the Fairness Doctrine was upheld by a divided three-judge panel.[75] The Court found that the Commission had not acted in an arbitrary or capricious manner in abolishing both of the Doctrine's requirements; to seek out controversial issues of public importance and to cover them in a balanced, impartial fashion. In essence, the majority decision accepted the FCC's conclusions that the Fairness Doctrine did tend to discourage broadcast coverage of controversial public issues and also tended to encourage too great a degree of governmental interference in areas of broadcast freedom of expression.

Each judge wrote a separate opinion. Judge Starr, while concurring in the result, argued that the constitutionality of the Doctrine itself was so closely interwoven into the Commission's action that its validity under the First Amendment needed to be considered independently by the court before reaching its decision. Judge Wald, on the other hand, felt that although no independent consideration of First Amendment issues was necessary, the FCC had not adequately demonstrated the need to repeal the "first prong" of the Doctrine, the requirement "to seek out controversial issues" when finding that the second or "balance" prong no longer serves the public interest.

At the moment, then, the Commission's decision to repeal the basic requirements of the Fairness Doctrine has been sustained by the D.C. Court of Appeals, but because of the Court's refusal to make its decision on constitutional grounds, Congress has still not been precluded from adopting legislation in the future that would once again require the FCC to enforce its requirements.

SEC. 54. PERSONAL ATTACKS AND POLITICAL EDITORIALS

When a broadcast attacks the integrity or character of a person or group, or an editorial supports or opposes a political candidate, the station must promptly notify the person attacked or opposed, furnishing that person with the content of the attack, and offering air time to respond.

An attack upon the character, honesty, or integrity of a person or group during a broadcast of a controversial issue of public importance is one situation still governed by the rules of

---

[75] Syracuse Peace Council v. FCC, 867 F.2d 654 (D.C.Cir.1989). See also the FCC reconsideration of its Meredith Broadcasting decision that formed the basis for this appeal in *Syracuse Peace Council*, 64 RR2d 1073 (1988).

the fairness doctrine. The other occurs when a station broadcasts its editorial support for or opposition to a political candidate.

The reason the Commission decided not to rescind either of these rather specialized fairness rules until giving them further consideration is that neither seemed to infringe directly upon the editorial judgment of the broadcasters.[76]

These Commission rules require that the broadcaster must notify the target of the attack promptly, and furnish this person with a transcript, tape or summary of the attack. Also, an offer of time to reply must be given. Where the licensee has broadcast an editorial endorsing or opposing a political candidate, the opposing candidates are to be notified within 24 hours after the endorsement or attack, and furnished with the transcript and an offer of time.[77]

Personal attacks occurring during bona fide newscasts, news interviews and commentaries are exempted from these fairness requirements.[78] This leaves editorials and documentaries among the types of programs that do impose these special responsibilities upon broadcasters.

Although the FCC contends that notification requirements such as those imposed by personal attack and political editorial rules do not appear to exert the same degree of "chilling effect" upon broadcast freedom of expression as regulation directly affecting program content, there are those who disagree with this assessment. It has been argued, for example, that personal attack rules do not serve the claimed FCC objective of airing the issues in the crucial task of informing the public. Instead, the reasoning goes, it is precisely when issues retreat and name-calling comes to the fore that the personal attack rules require reply opportunity. "To a large extent, the personal attack rules generate name calling exercises, allowing those parties whose personalities are criticized to rebut the charges without requiring rebuttal opportunities on the more substantive issues." [79]

There is no way of being able to determine at this point whether the personal attack and political editorializing rules have been preserved to achieve some long term policy objective of the Commission, or have only been spared until the agency can find a valid justification for their recission. In either case, they now

[76] Another reason for being somewhat reluctant to repeal the "personal attack" rule might be that it was precisely this rule that the Supreme Court found to be constitutional in the *Red Lion* decision. See Syracuse Peace Council, 64 RR 2d 1873 (1988).

[77] 32 Fed.Reg. 10303–ff (1967).

[78] 32 Fed.Reg. 11531 (1967).

[79] Steven J. Simmons, "The FCC Personal Attack and Political Editorializing Rules Reconsidered," Pennsylvania Law Review (Fall 1977) p. 990.

represent the only regulatory vestiges remaining of that once broad and powerful doctrine that shaped the programming policies of broadcast networks and stations throughout the United States.

SEC. 55. PUBLIC BROADCASTING

Created to offer an alternative to commercial radio and television, public broadcasting has been sheltered from direct FCC control by a separate set of regulations.

Unlike most other Western industrial nations, no special provisions were made for non-commercial broadcasting when broadcast regulation began in the United States. Those college and university radio stations that had already received a broadcast license from the Commerce Department during the early 1920s were permitted to remain on the air, but no spectrum space was specifically set aside by either the Radio Act of 1927 or the Communications Act of 1934 to encourage the development of a nationwide educational or cultural broadcasting service.[80]

In 1945, as part of its revised approach to broadcast frequency assignments, the FCC allotted some 10 percent of the new FM service spectrum space to non-commercial applicants and in 1952, following the same approach, it allotted a similar percentage of the television spectrum for non-commercial stations.[81] However, this belated recognition of non-commercial broadcast service did little to stimulate the growth of educational broadcasting in the United States. By 1960, for example, there were only 162 educational FM stations in operation throughout the nation, and only 44 educational television stations.

What these educational television stations lacked in particular was any major source of funding capable of underwriting the

[80] Many of these early college stations were simply experimental projects of a physics or engineering department, and in the absence of any nationwide educational policy mission, the more that 200 noncommercial stations operating in 1927 had dwindled to less than 30 a decade later as their commercial increased and private concerns eagerly sought their frequency assignments. Section 307(c) of the Act of 1934 did require the FCC to report to Congress on the advisability of allocated fixed percentages of radio broadcasting facilities to various types of non-commercial broadcasters but the Commission reported back to Congress in 1935 that existing commercial stations were providing sufficient cultural and education programming to make such special non-commercial allocations unnecessary.

[81] The first FCC attempt to reserve space for non-commercial FM broadcasting actually occurred in 1940, but World War II suspended efforts to implement this allocation plan and it was substantially modified when reintroduced in 1945. Radio broadcast licenses have always been issued nationwide on a first-come, first-serve basis, only conditioned on an applicant being able to establish that transmission on the frequencies assigned will not interfere with other existing radio broadcast signals. In contrast, the FCC's FM and TV license allocation programs have assigned each specific authorized FM or TV channel to a particular locality in the United States, and designed a specified segment of the FM band and a specific proportion of all TV channels for non-commercial use.

massive production costs demanded by even a relatively modest television program schedule. In 1962 the federal government passed the first significant piece of legislation offering financial support for educational television, the Educational Television Facilities Act. Five years later an extremely influential report issued by the Carnegie Commission on Educational Television resulted in Congress enacting the Public Broadcasting Act of 1967. This Act created the Corporation for Public Broadcasting (CPB), a non-profit, non-governmental organization charged with funding all forms of educational broadcasting in the United States.[82]

To protect this new non-commercial service from being dominated by a centralized bureaucracy in Washington, CPB was denied the right to provide any type of broadcast service of its own to the general public. Instead, it was directed to work with existing public broadcast stations to develop new forms of culturally or educationally oriented radio and television programming.

In 1970 CPB and a coalition of public broadcast stations formed the Public Broadcast Service (PBS) and National Public Radio (NPR), organizations established to distribute public radio and television programs to member stations. Four years later CPB and its member television stations created the Station Program Cooperative (SPC) plan, further decentralizing public television operation by making local stations primarily responsible for deciding which specific proposed television series productions will be funded.

When Congress established the Corporation for Public Broadcasting in 1967, it inserted new regulatory language in the Communications Act of 1934 specially designed to govern its functions.[83] The question soon arose whether by creating a separate set of regulatory requirements for public broadcasting, Congress had thereby exempted these stations from all other obligations imposed on broadcasters by the Communications Act.

In Accuracy in Media, Inc. v. FCC a federal court found that specific language in Act of 1967 mandating balanced and objective public broadcast programming meant that Congress rather than the FCC should be primarily responsible for supervising compliance with its directive.[84]

---

[82] The Carnegie Commission had recommended the term "public" rather than "educational" to describe the new non-commercial broadcast services it proposed, contended that to label them as "educational" would unduly restrict their role as alternatives to commercial broadcasting.

[83] Statutory provisions of the Communications Act of 1934 that relate to CPB and public broadcasting are found in Section 390–399 of the Act of 1934.

[84] 521 F.2d 288 (D.C.Cir.1975), cert. denied 425 U.S. 934, 96 S.Ct. 1664 (1976). The court was particularly impressed by the argument that Congress had sought to shelter public broadcasting as much as possible from federal interference, and FCC regulation in the area of program content would operate to undercut that objective.

This special regulatory language that governed non-commercial broadcasting also denied those stations receiving funds from CPB the right to editorialize. In a 5–4 decision, the U.S. Supreme Court struck down this ban as an unconstitutional abridgement of broadcast free speech.[85]

In Muir v. Alabama Educational Television Commission, a majority of the huge en banc panel of 22 federal judges held that public broadcast stations had the same degree of editorial freedom in selecting and scheduling their programming as all other broadcasters.[86] Viewers challenging the refusal of two public broadcast stations to carry a controversial PBS documentary had argued that their tax supported status transformed them into "public forums" with less discretion to ignore the demands of the citizens who provided their funding, but the majority opinion rejected this distinction between commercial and non-commercial public interest standards.

Although most non-commercial licenses in the United States are held by public broadcast stations operated by state or local governments, universities, or school districts, other non-profit organizations are also licensed to broadcast by the FCC. Religious groups or institutions do not qualify for a reserved educational broadcast channel unless the primary emphasis of their programming is on education, but they as well as other community supported broadcasters such as "Pacifica" are authorized to receive a non-commercial broadcast license.

Periodic campaigns have been waged to deny religious broadcasters spectrum space because their opponents contend they are too narrowly oriented to serve the interests of the general public.[87] The FCC has never accepted this argument, however, maintaining that religious and other non-commercial broadcasters perform a useful service by enhancing that degree of diversity available to American broadcast audiences.

[85] FCC v. League of Women Voters of California, 468 U.S. 364, 104 S.Ct. 3106 (1984). In this instance, the station editorializing was not a public broadcaster but rather a non-commercial station that had accepted funding from CPB and therefore came under the federal statute.

[86] 688 F.2d 1033 (5th Cir.1982). The large panel of judges resulted from the consolidation of appeals from two conflicting lower court actions resulting from the refusal of two public broadcast stations to carry the controversial documentary "Death of a Princess" that portrayed Saudi Arabian society as being primitive and barbaric.

[87] See Multiple and Religious Ownership of Educational Stations, 34 RR2d 1217 (1975). The Commission rejected this argument, but does employ the "fair break" principle first described in Noe v. FCC, 260 F.2d 739 (D.C.Cir.1958) requiring a broadcast licensee to give all listeners reasonable access to views opposing those held by the broadcaster.

Chapter 10

DEREGULATION AND THE NEW MEDIA

Sec.
56. Regulating Cable TV.
57. Modern Federal Cable TV Policy.
58. New Media Competition.
59. Deregulation and the Marketplace.

Since 1927, the entire regulatory structure of American broadcasting has rested upon a single base of authority, the privilege of spectrum access, furnishing both the legal justification and the administrative process required for federal control of broadcast service in the United States. Through licensing standards derived from this power, the FRC and FCC labored diligently to create and maintain a nationwide system of locally oriented radio and television stations, with each licensee offered an exclusive territorial right to disseminate programming on one specially reserved set of spectrum frequencies.

Cable television posed the first serious challenge to this traditional regulatory structure, its coaxial cable systems operating without need of spectrum space, and furnishing the capacity to flood previously sheltered broadcast markets with new channels of programming. That flood fragmented television audiences and diminished station advertising revenues.

Cable TV emerged as unexpectedly as radio broadcasting had developed during the 1920s. Once again, the federal government would be forced to react to a crisis it had not foreseen, and to adopt laws to resolve the immediate problem without time to consider the long range policy implications of those laws.

SEC. 56. REGULATING CABLE TV

Cable TV has been regulated by the FCC as a by-product of broadcast service, its presence tolerated only to the extent that it did not impair the quality of that service.

No one actually "invented" cable television. During the 1930s, Bell Labs had perfected coaxial cable, a specially constructed high-capacity conduit capable of delivering a vast number of different communication services within a single wire. Even in the late 1940s, however, when AT & T began using this cable to distribute network programs to affiliated television stations, there was no thought of connecting individual households to such a coaxial delivery system.

402

In truth, the emergence of cable TV was simply an historical accident, caused by a noble but flawed policy effort of the FCC to design a system of "community oriented" local television in the United States. The FCC television allocation plan of 1952 provided for more than 2000 television stations to serve some 1300 different communities throughout the nation.[1] The engineering staff of the Commission had based its television service projections on just such a fully operational system. Unfortunately, only 530 of these 2000 stations were actually in operation at the end of that decade, even though nearly 85 percent of all American homes already were television households.[2]

What the FCC planners had failed to foresee was that no one would apply for a television license in any of those communities that a television network would refuse to serve because they were too small to earn sufficient advertising revenues to justify affiliation. As a result, instead of establishing a nationwide system of local television stations, the Commission succeeded only in creating conditions that would allow a new, more effective system of television program distribution to emerge.

Originally "community antennas", as cable systems were then called, were exactly that—shared master antenna hookups that allowed a cluster of homes located just beyond the coverage area of the nearest television station to receive a marginally acceptable picture.[3] During the early 1950s these crude antennas were viewed as being nothing more than a temporary solution to an immediate problem, destined to disappear in time as newly licensed stations began filling in each of the many gaps remaining in national network television coverage.

Within a few years, however, it became clear the Commission would not abandon its original television station allocation policy, despite the plan's obvious limitations. As late as 1958, some 34 percent of America's television households still could receive only one television channel.[4] Located in less populous markets without an audience base large enough to support additional affiliate television stations, these viewers had access to only one of those

[1] 6th Report and Order, 17 Reg. 3905–4100 (May 2, 1952) allocated 2,053 television stations to 1,291 different communities in the United States, many with populations of less than 50,000.

[2] U.S. Congress, Senate, Committee on Interstate and Foreign Commerce, Television Inquiry: Television Allocations 86th Cong. 2nd sess. 1960, p. 4587.

[3] As in the early days of radio, many of these first community antenna operators were actually appliance stores, trying to stimulate demand for the TV receivers they wanted to sell by providing television reception to households that otherwise would have been unable to receive a broadcast television signal.

[4] U.S. Congress, Senate, Committee on Interstate and Foreign Commerce, "VHF Boosters and Community Antenna Legislation"; Hearings on S. 1739 . . . 86th Congress, 1st sess. 1959, p. 455.

three sources of network fare they were eager to watch each evening.   During this era one enterprising cable TV operator requested permission from the FCC's Common Carrier Bureau to lease a microwave system to import the two missing network program channels from affiliate stations nearest to his system subscribers.[5] Because communication common carrier regulation at that time involved nothing more than a review of the reasonableness of the charges for service, this request was routinely granted.[6]

Microwave relays opened an entirely new domain for CATV operators, allowing them for the first time to enter larger communities where some television service was already available. Until this time, a cable system could enhance only the quality of existing over-the-air television service. Now, however, cable TV could attract subscribers by offering a second or third channel of network programs imported by microwave from affiliate stations in other nearby cities.

Although affiliate stations whose network programs were being exported by CATV systems without payment or permission were the first to complain about this usage, they really sustained no economic injury through this unauthorized carriage of their signals.[7] Few of the programs being exported by CATV were actually owned by these stations, and the wider circulation each station's advertising messages provided through cable dissemination increased, rather than diminished, their potential to earn revenues.

Instead, the damage was being inflicted upon small market television stations located in those communities where the CATV systems were operating. Until this era, station managers had generally been pleased with the community antenna systems that sprang up along the edges of their coverage contours, for they extended a station's effective transmission range at no cost to the broadcaster.

Now, however, these CATV systems were providing competing television channels to subscribers in the broadcaster's own mar-

[5] FCC 54-58; In the Matter of J.E. Belnap. For a discussion of the impact this decision had upon cable TV development and regulation in the 1950s and 1960s, see Don R. Le Duc, Cable Television and the FCC (Philadelphia; Temple University Press, 1973) pp. 74-77.

[6] In a 1961 case, Federal Power Com'n v. Transcontinental Gas P.L. Corp., 365 U.S. 1, 81 S.Ct. 435, the Supreme Court approved the common carrier regulatory approach of looking beyond simple authorization of a service to determine whether the ultimate result of its use would be in the public interest. It was this decision that gave the FCC authority to begin denying cable TV its microwave relay requests in Carter Mountain Transmission Corp. v. FCC, 321 F.2d 359 (D.C.Cir. 1963).

[7] Intermountain Broadcasting & Television Corp. v. Idaho Microwave, Inc., 196 F.Supp. 315 (D.Idaho 1961).

ket, substantially reducing the number of viewers watching the local station's programs. What had been a symbiotic relationship between the station and community antenna had been transformed into a parasitic one, for CATV preyed upon small one station markets in the weakest financial condition. Yet, ironically, it was the marginal nature of these markets that sheltered CATV from immediate federal regulatory reaction. Because the networks and the major stations instrumental in shaping industry policies saw little need to protect the economic welfare of stations in markets that cumulatively represented less than one percent of the total television audience, no effort was made to convince the FCC to intervene to stop this damaging competition.[8]

In 1960, at the urging of several members of Congress whose small market television broadcasters faced such CATV competition, a Congressional committee considered legislation that would place the cable industry under FCC's regulatory jurisdiction. The Commission vigorously opposed the legislation, declaring that it did not believe the cable threat to be severe enough to justify the heavy administrative burden its supervision would impose upon the agency.[9] Ultimately the bill died in committee and because Congress would not adopt any cable TV legislation during the next 20 years, the FCC was forced to operate continually at the very edge of its legal authority when dealing with cable, uncertain when the federal courts might find the agency had exceeded the boundaries of its Congressionally delegated power over cable TV.

Because the federal government had not claimed exclusive control over cable TV, local governments began to exert their own legal authority to impose program service obligations upon cable operators who wanted to construct cable systems in their communities. They were able to do this without unconstitutionally abridging the free speech rights of the cable operator because of one special characteristic of the cable "franchise" agreement.

It was virtually impossible to construct a cable system without obtaining a public "easement" from local government, a legal privilege granting the cable operator the right to cross city streets and other rights-of-way with cable trunk line. Granting this public easement privilege as a part of the cable franchise agreement empowered the municipality in return to impose communication service conditions upon the cable system for the benefit of

---

[8] For a more complete discussion of this era of cable TV growth, see Le Duc, Op. Cit. pp. 82–113.

[9] "In the Matter of Inquiring into the Impact of CATV . . . upon the Orderly Development of Television Broadcasting." Docket 12443, 18 RR2d 1573 (1959). The FCC realized that without constitutional authority to license each cable system, the agency would have no power to prevent the damaging impact CATV competition had upon broadcast stations, and yet would be held responsible for such damage because of being given this responsibility for cable supervision.

the citizens of that community who were the rightful owners of this municipal property.

As large corporations began buying groups of small CATV systems in the early 1960s, they started to exert strong influence upon the industry's trade group, the National Cable Television Association (NCTA), to support, rather than oppose federal regulation of cable TV. These new corporate cable owners found it extremely inconvenient to manage cable systems operating under vastly different local franchise agreements, and so favored the broadest possible federal preemption of cable control to reduce the degree of diversity among these local cable laws.

The NAB and NCTA tried to draft a jointly sponsored cable TV bill to submit to Congress that would grant the FCC at least some type of regulatory authority over cable TV. However, by 1964, bitter factional clashes between the new pro-regulatory and the old anti-regulatory groups within NCTA had become too intense to allow for any hope of future agreement on the "industry concensus" legislation Congress had requested.

As these industry negotiations were ending in failure, several of the larger, corporate owned CATV systems were preparing to enter a number of the "top 100," or largest 100 American broadcast markets, where 90 percent of the nation's television homes were located. Suddenly cable's competitive threat was no longer viewed as a minor one by broadcast industry leaders, and the FCC now shared this viewpoint.

Although the agency had no direct legal authority to regulate cable, it did have such direct authority over the microwave relay services essential for cable TV to attract subscribers in major markets.[10] In 1963, the Commission had actually begun, on a case-by-case basis, to decide whether approving an application for a particular cable microwave relay would lessen the financial capacity of local television stations to provide effective broadcast service. When the FCC began to deny microwave applications on this basis, a federal court upheld the agency's right to use this power to protect the public's interest in maintaining the quality of broadcast television.[11]

[10] To attract paying subscribers in major markets, cable TV had to offer viewers more service than those three network channels virtually all households in urban area could already receive with a simple antenna. This meant that programming from non-network stations in distant markets had to be imported as well, offering different film packages, syndicated programs and sports than local stations provided. Until 1975, when the first communication satellites began operation, there was no other means for delivering television signals from one market to another except by microwave network.

[11] Carter Mountain Transmission Corp. v. FCC, 321 F.2d 359 (D.C.Cir.1963), cert. denied 375 U.S. 951, 84 S.Ct. 442 (1963).

In 1965 the FCC declared that it would no longer authorize any applications to microwave television programs into a "top 100" broadcast market until the agency was able to adopt permanent cable microwave rules.[12] In the end, this "temporary" freeze on microwave applications would actually remain in force for more than seven years, effectively denying the cable TV industry any growth opportunities in the nation's most profitable broadcast markets from 1965 to 1972.

Although the Commission has been widely criticized for suppressing cable industry expansion during this extended period of time, it is only fair to point out that Congress was at least equally to blame for the agency's conduct. The FCC was convinced that it would not be in the public interest to allow the cable industry to undermine the economic stability of television stations, while at the same time offering the public virtually no programming of its own and contributing nothing to the production costs of those television programs it carried.

Cable TV was free to take and distribute whatever broadcast programming it wanted without permission or payment simply because the only legally recognized property rights in these programs were defined by the Copyright Act of 1909, a law adopted long before the birth of radio broadcasting. Because it was written in the era of vaudeville and the musical hall, the Act of 1909 protected copyrighted material from infringement only if it was being "performed" without permission. In 1968, the Supreme Court affirmed earlier decisions by several lower federal courts that mere delivery of a television program by a cable TV system was not a "performance" of that program, and therefore that television programming was not protected by the Copyright Act of 1909 from unauthorized cable TV usage.[13]

Congress had begun efforts to revise the copyright law to include cable TV carriage of broadcast programming in 1965, but it took more than a decade to accomplish this task and cable TV would not actually come under the provisions of the new Copyright Act of 1976 until January 1, 1978.[14] During this entire era, the FCC stood as the broadcast industry's only legal defense again cable TV's unauthorized use of television programming.

[12] "Proposed Rulemaking in Docket 15971", 1 FCC2d 463 (1965). By making this an interim or temporary rule, the FCC protected it from being challenged in federal court, because the court, except in an exceptional case, will not hear an appeal from an order until the action is final.

[13] Fortnightly Corp. v. United Artists Television, Inc., 392 U.S. 390, 88 S.Ct. 2084 (1968).

[14] Title 17, United States Code, "Copyright Act of 1909" was rescinded and replaced by the new Title 17, as enacted by Public Law No. 94-553, 94th Stat. 2541 (1976).

In 1968 the Supreme Court affirmed for the first time the Commission's use of its microwave relay authority to discourage cable TV from entering major broadcast markets.[15] At that point the FCC announced its intention to launch a series of full scale hearings to develop rules and long range policy for the development of cable TV service in the United States. Four years later the agency completed these deliberations, and in March 1972, it issued these new rules, declaring that the era of modern cable TV service in the United States had finally begun.[16]

In reality, the FCC continued to prevent cable TV systems from importing television signals into the 50 largest broadcast markets, where 75 percent of the television audience was located, until the Copyright Act of 1976 came into force, but at least for the first time in its history, the cable TV would be regulated by rules designed for its systems, rather than solely for the protection of its broadcast industry competitor.

Cable TV had sprung up like a weed in a carefully cultivated garden. In attempting to create favorable conditions for the growth of locally oriented television service, the FCC had succeeded only in providing fertile opportunities for a rival distribution system to take root.

In this environment cable TV was the intruder, the electronic medium to be restrained in order to encourage more useful growth. Seen from this perspective, it is easier to understand why the FCC simply suppressed cable TV, rather than trying to incorporate its systems within plans to provide more effective distribution of the nation's television services. Unfortunately, the damage caused by this repression would become all too apparent in the near future, when the cable industry did not have the financial capacity necessary to fulfill the promises it made to citizens in a number of American cities.

SEC. 57. MODERN FEDERAL CABLE TV POLICY

Cable TV was the first of the "new media," its multi-channel distribution system providing an entirely different form of communication service than the single channel broadcast station.

The 1972 FCC cable rules required every new system being constructed in one of the largest 100 broadcast markets to provide a minimum of 20 channels and to set aside specific channels for

---

[15] United States v. Southwestern Cable Co., 392 U.S. 157, 88 S.Ct. 1994 (1968), in which the high court affirmed the FCC's authority to regulate cable TV's use of television signals as being a reasonable ancillary of its power to regulate broadcasting in the public interest.

[16] "Third Report and Order on Docket 18397", 24 RR2d 1501 (1972).

educational, governmental, leased and public access programming. While the FCC denied local governments any regulatory authority over cable TV's television signal carriage or program origination practices, it allowed municipal or state cable regulators to continue to establish franchise boundaries, select cable operators, determine terms of service and decide upon the amount to be collected as a franchise fee, although each of these powers had to be exercised within standards set by the federal government.

It was difficult for the Commission to regulate cable TV effectively, because the agency had no constitutional authority to deny these non-spectrum communication systems permission to operate. Instead, the agency was limited to denying those cable systems in violation of its rules the right to carry broadcast signals, and if necessary, to enforce this denial through a federal court order. However, since the effect of this order would be to prevent the system's subscribers from receiving those services for which they had paid, it was an action the Commission was obviously reluctant to take.

Initially, the FCC imposed an extremely elaborate system of restrictions upon the importation of television signals to major market cable systems, but after the Copyright Act of 1976 established a system compensating broadcasters and program suppliers for cable TV carriage, the Commission rescinded most of these restraints. By 1983, the only major FCC rule remaining in this field was "must carry", requiring cable TV systems to provide channel space for all local television stations their subscribers could receive over-the-air.

Even though the new copyright law did require cable TV systems to begin paying for the television programming they were importing, the terms and conditions of payment reflected a clear legislative victory for the cable industry. Cable was granted a "compulsory license" by the Copyright Act, compelling television stations and program suppliers to allow cable TV to carry their programs in return for a program use fee to be determined by a government body, the Copyright Royalty Tribunal. The Tribunal was empowered by the Act to collect from each cable system a percentage of that system's gross subscriber revenues to be used to compensate these television program suppliers.[17]

In gaining the "compulsory license", the cable industry was able to avoid having to pay the marketplace value for the programs it used. When the first distribution was made from this cable copyright pool, program suppliers complained bitterly that payments they received from the Tribunal were not only far less

---

[17] This "secondary transmission" cable copyright payment procedure is described in Title 17, U.S.C.A. §§ 801–810.

than the actual value of these programs, but even less than the financial damage they sustained because of this cable TV usage.[18]

In 1982 the Tribunal instituted new proceedings to adjust the amount of subscriber revenues each system would be required to pay into the copyright revenue pool. Until that time, cable systems paid only 0.625 percent of its annual revenues to import one distant television signal, and another 0.425 percent for each additional distant signal imported. Program suppliers urged the Tribunal to increase this fee substantially, because by bringing major feature films packages and popular series programming into areas where they had not yet been sold to local stations, cable TV was significantly diminishing the value, and thus the price of the these features as "first run" attractions for television stations in that market where the cable system was located.[19]

After lengthy deliberations the Tribunal finally decided upon new rates for cable systems to pay for each distant television signal imported, almost 10 times higher than the base percentages established only four years before.[20] Although the cable industry complained bitterly about this massive increase in its copyright fee payments, the actual economic impact of these higher copyright rates upon cable systems was not particularly severe, simply because cable operators were by this time far less dependent upon broadcast stations for cable system programming.[21]

Between 1975 and 1980, satellite delivered pay-TV services, superstations, and advertising supported cable networks not only reduced cable TV's dependence on the broadcast industry for programming, but also furnished cable systems with new sources of revenue. Home Box Office (HBO) launched the first cable pay-TV service in 1975, offering system owners the opportunity to earn profits from a vacant channel by devoting it to the delivery of the HBO service.

[18] The Tribunal collected $15 million from cable systems during 1978, the first year this system was in operation. The distribution formula granted 75% of this money to program and movie syndicators, 12% to sports organizations and only 3.5% to television stations. This allocation was approved by the courts in National Ass'n of Broadcasters v. Copyright Royalty Tribunal, 675 F.2d 367 (D.C.Cir.1982).

[19] This problem became more severe in 1980 when the FCC rescinded its "syndicated exclusivity" rules, that until this time had forced cable TV to "black out" programs on those channels it imported that local stations held exclusive rights to broadcast in that market.

[20] CRT 1982 "Distribution Proceeding and Partial Distribution of Fees" 48 Fed. Reg. 46412 (Oct. 12, 1983). This determination was sustained by the courts in National Cable Television Ass'n v. Copyright Royalty Tribunal, 689 F.2d 1077 (D.C. Cir.1982).

[21] Until 1988, only subscriber revenues earned from imported broadcast signals were subject to the copyright fee. In Cablevision Systems v. MPAA, 836 F.2d 599 (1988), cable systems were required to pay copyright fees on all revenues earned by a tier of service if even one broadcast channel was included in the tier.

In 1977, USA, the first advertising supported cable TV network, began operation. It sought, at least initially, to cover its costs and generate profits solely on the basis of the commercials it could place in its programming. Although cable operators receive no payment from these advertising supported channels, and in most cases are now charged a monthly per subscriber fee for the privilege of carriage, systems can earn money from placing local advertising in network time slots provided, and are likely to attract a greater number of subscribers because of offering these additional channels of programming.

So-called "superstation" cable service began in 1976, when Ted Turner, owner of a small UHF station in Atlanta, started delivering his station's programming by satellite to cable systems throughout the nation. Turner, whose ownership of the Atlanta Braves and part-ownership of the Atlanta Hawks allowed him to offer professional sports as well as the usual assortment of older syndicated series programs, generated his revenues through the higher advertising rates he could charge sponsors for his vastly expanded national cable viewing audience. By the mid–1980s, his service was reaching more than 12.5 million American homes, or roughly one-sixth of all television households in the United States.

By 1980, cable TV system operators could choose among five competing pay-TV services, six "superstations" and more than 40 advertising supported cable networks, such as Entertainment and Sports Network (ESPN), Cable Satellite Public Affairs Network (C–SPAN), Cable News Network (CNN) and a host of other general and specialized program services to fill their systems' channels.

Ironically, this explosive growth in new satellite delivered services that transformed cable TV from a passive relay system for broadcast services into a truly unique and independent electronic medium was also the unanticipated by-product of an FCC major policy decision involving a different form of communication.

When the FCC authorized domestic communication satellite service in 1972, no one could foresee how its competitive "open skies" satellite policy would affect future cable TV service in the United States.[22] Until this time AT&T had held a virtual monopoly over the national distribution of television programming. Broadcast networks were charged a relatively low rate to deliver their programs to affiliate stations, because they were willing to pay for 24 hour a day usage of special AT&T television circuits set aside specifically for this purpose. When other television distributors tried to lease similar circuits from AT&T on an occasional use

---

[22] "Domestic Communication Satellite Facilities," 35 FCC2d 844 (1972).

basis, however, the charge for this service was prohibitively high, because AT&T was forced to reroute thousands of telephone circuits to find the space necessary to deliver a full-sized television channel.

The Commission's policy decision to encourage competition by opening the communication satellite field to any organization meeting basic qualifications standards was not designed with the intention of ending this AT&T monopoly over national television delivery, but rather in the hope of reducing AT&T's domination over nationwide distribution of telephonic, telegraphic and other personal and business messages.[23] However, when Western Union's Westar I and RCA's Americom were finally launched in the mid–1970s, these new satellite system owners were eager to lease their unused delivery channels to video program organizations at rates far lower than AT&T had been charging.

The other factor that had inhibited the growth of new nationwide television services had been the absence of local outlets to distribute these programs. Most broadcast markets had only three television stations, each already affiliated with a major network. As cable TV began to expand during the mid–1970s, however, with the 20 channel system capacity required by the FCC rules, virtually all operators had vacant channels available to serve as those local outlets that national satellite delivered program services required.

Thus, through another fortunate historical accident, the emergence of privately owned, competitively priced national domestic satellite system service happened to coincide with the growing demand of urban multi-channeled cable systems for additional programming to result in the establishment of a much more independent and prosperous cable industry.

Unfortunately, though, extensive campaigns launched by each of the major cable ownership groups to capture as many urban cable franchises as possible once the FCC signal importation restrictions had been lifted, left most of these multiple system owners (MSOs) in a very precarious financial position as the 1980s began. In their eagerness to win franchise agreements from major city governments, each applicant tried to outbid all other competitors by offering an impressive range of communication services without carefully considering the operational costs involved. Adding to their difficulties was the fact that as many of these urban systems were being built in 1978 and 1979, interest

---

[23] The FCC Common Carrier Bureau had begun this policy effort to reduce the AT&T–Bell domination of American personal and business communication services in 1959 by allowing carriers other than AT&T to operate microwave relay networks.

rates on the substantial investment needed for cable construction soared to more than 20 percent.[24]

If the cable industry had been allowed by the FCC to expand gradually in urban markets through the years, it seems reasonable to assume that this period of frantic franchise speculation would have been avoided. Instead, the net result of all this destructive bidding was simply a trail of broken cable franchise promises, denying subscribers those benefits that had earned the MSO its franchise.

During the late 1970s, cable growth came to a virtual halt as financially overextended MSOs sought the additional funding essential to complete those systems they were already committed to build. The timing couldn't have been more unfortunate for the cable industry, because, ironically, that very satellite delivered programming that could have made cable TV sucessful in major television markets was now seen by direct broadcast satellite (DBS), multi-channel, multi-point, distribution system (MMDS) and low power television (LPTV) promoters as being the program services that would allow them to invade these markets and claim that urban audience cable TV was still struggling to reach.[25]

Cable TV had been the first of the "new media". What made cable TV different from broadcasting was its program delivery function. Each radio or television station must depend upon a single channel of communication to entertain and inform its audience and earn its advertising revenues. In contrast, a cable system serves as a broadcast spectrum for its subscribers, allowing them to select from among those various channels of programming it provides.

This difference gave cable TV a tremendous competitive advantage over the individual television station. The cable system did not have to displace a popular, profitable program in order to provide more specialized features for particular segments of the audience. Instead, popular and specialized programs could be distributed simultaneously, attracting as paying subscribers not only those seeking mass appeal features, but also viewers especially interested in sports, politics, religion, culture, news or any of the many other cable delivered services. In fact, cable systems soon began packaging groups of these program channels in various priced "tiers" of subscriber fees, allowing operators to profit to an

[24] For a detailed summary of many of these urban market problems, see "Cable Franchising Update," Broadcasting July 12, 1982, p. 37.

[25] As late as 1981, more than 60% of all American cable TV systems still had no more than a 12 channel delivery capacity, a capacity reduced even further by franchise and FCC signal carriage rules. Sydney Head and Christopher Sterling, Broadcasting in America 4th ed. (Boston: Houghton Mifflin, 1982) p. 296.

even greater extent from the diversity of services the system offered.

Yet, although cable TV was able to exploit this multi-channel distribution system advantage when competing with broadcasting, its massively expensive coaxial distribution system made it vulnerable to challenge from newer multi-channeled systems far less expensive to build, and capable of beginning service much more rapidly than cable.

Until this point, the cable industry had been totally committed to the principle of free competition in a marketplace environment to determine which form of electronic media service should prevail. During the 1980s, that commitment became somewhat less than total.

SEC. 58. NEW MEDIA COMPETITION

The authorization of each new electronic medium made it increasingly more difficult for the FCC to maintain the "level regulatory playing field" it had pledged to provide each competitor.

In 1972, the Commission formulated its "open skies" satellite policy without intending to attempt to stimulate the growth of electronic media services in the United States. During the 1980s, the Commission formulated its "new media technology" policies with exactly this purpose in mind. Only time will tell whether or not the FCC's carefully planned regulatory strategy will be as successful as those results it has achieved largely by chance.

The FCC announced its intention, in October 1980, to establish regulatory policies for the development of direct broadcast satellite (DBS) service in the United States. This action was motivated at least in part by the concern that American lagged behind Canada, Western Europe and Japan in the development of DBS technology. "Direct broadcast" satellites are specially designed to transmit a focused, far more powerful signal covering a more limited amount of territory than the ordinary communication satellite. Because of this greater power, DBS signals can be received on a much smaller "dish" or antenna than the regular satellite, reducing the size and cost to a point where individual households could easily afford to purchase this reception equipment.[26]

Satellite Television Corporation, a subsidiary of Comsat, had submitted a proposal to the FCC in 1979 to develop a six channel

---

[26] The large backyard dish necessary to receive regular satellite transmissions today still costs about $2,000. The tiny DBS dish, only 3 feet in diameter, costs between $400–500, and when mass marketing allows them to be made in quantity, it is estimated that they may retail for only $200–$250.

DBS delivered pay-TV service, to be delivered through a system of several satellites deployed in orbital slots capable of providing nationwide coverage. In October 1981 the Commission accepted this application, and at the same time approved applications from several other organizations interested in providing various forms of DBS service, including CBS, RCA, American Communications, and Western Union Telegraph.[27]

The following year the FCC adopted a simplified set of regulations especially designed for DBS service, exempting these systems from traditional broadcast ownership and political access requirements.[28] The Commission hoped through what it called this "flexible" new approach to avoid imposing unnecessary regulatory burdens upon new media in the earliest stages of their development, before it was clear precisely what type of federal supervision they might require.

The National Association of Broadcasters challenged what it saw as unfair regulatory advantages given an electronic media competitor, and this challenge was sustained on appeal.[29] The court found that the Commission had no right to exempt DBS systems who came within the statutory definition of "broadcasting" from requirements Congress had imposed upon all those providing broadcast service in the United States.

In the end, however, it was not the regulatory but the financial demands of launching and operation that discouraged those who had filed DBS applications with the Commission from actually beginning to provide this service. Subscription Television, the pioneer in this field, abandoned its DBS plans in 1984, and CBS, RCA and others soon followed its example. United States Communications tried a lower powered communication satellite to provide direct-to-home broadcast service to those households with larger dish antennas, but this venture ended in receivership less than two years after it was launched.

From the beginning, DBS promoters realized that it would cost an estimated $150 million to begin even a modest one satellite, three channel service. In the early 1980s, however, it was still assumed that the novel appeal of first run feature films, unedited and uninterrupted by commercials would attract enough DBS subscriber households to recoup these costs in a reasonable period of time. By 1985, as the VCR and the VCR rental stores were becoming national institutions, the appeal of the first run

[27] "Notice of Proposed Policy Statement and Rulemaking in General Docket 80–603," adopted Oct. 22, 1981, 88 FCC2d 100 (1981).

[28] "In the Matter of Inquiry into the Development of Regulatory Policy in Regard to Direct Broadcasting Satellites . . .," 51 RR2d 1341 (1981).

[29] National Association of Broadcasters v. FCC, 740 F.2d 1190 (D.C.Cir.1984).

feature film no longer seemed unique enough to justify such a substantial satellite system investment.

In addition, no DBS system wanted to be the first in space, because until actual demand was created for DBS reception equipment, the price of these units would remain high. In essence, then, the first system would be operating at a loss to stimulate the demand that would lower the unit cost of the antenna, build an audience and then face competition from those who entered the field to serve that audience without having incurred any of these start up expenses.

At this point most experts agree that a DBS service could operate at a profit if it were able to attract at least three million subscribers, or approximately 20 percent of those 15 million American TV households currently beyond the reach of cable TV. Most DBS proposals now envision a service of 80 to 120 digitally compressed video channels offering both basic program services and a selection of pay-per-view movie options.

For a time it seemed that "Sky Cable," a true high power DBS proposal uniting NBC, Rupert Murdoch's News Corporation, Cablevision and Hughes would emerge by the mid–1990s as a dominant DBS force in the United States. This one billion dollar venture envisioned 108 channels of video services, capable of being received anywhere in the continental United States on an 18 inch dish antenna and reception equipment costing less than the 300 dollars.

But as the year 1990 ended, this consortium collapsed, leaving the satellite supplier Hughes as the only partner still eager to continue the project. The failure of Congress to amend the Cable Policy Act so as to prevent major cable MSOs from denying DBS operators access to cable network programs obviously discouraged the three media investors. Yet it seems that an even more compelling reason for the pullout by Murdoch and NBC was the need to reduce parent company debt loads during a period of recession.

Hubbard Broadcasting (USSB) joined Hughes in an effort to revive this DBS project in June 1991, but the $50 million USSB tendered to build the first of its two satellites represents only a small percentage of the funds that must be raised before the system can become operational. Hughes succeeded in obtaining the most favorably situated satellite orbit position assignment from the FCC but even though it has the competitive advantage of being able to serve the entire continental United States from its orbital location, it must still find the additional capital and video programming sources necessary to launch its system.

TCI, the largest and most influential cable MSO, has also applied through its subsidiary, Tempo, for a DBS orbital slot. Because its prospects of obtaining even the limited number of channel allocations it is eligible to receive are not encouraging, there is some possibility that TCI might eventually join the Hughes–Hubbard DBS venture and provide both the funding and the cable program services it now lacks.[30]

Two other satellite ventures are planning to use medium power satellites requiring larger and more expensive household dish and reception equipment. "Primestar," (formerly "K Prime") a group of cable MSOs and GE American Communication, has already launched a trial run service, offering 10 channels of basic cable networks and superstations to rural homes in some 38 communities. Only a small number of households subscribed during the first six months of operation, unwilling to invest the 600 dollars necessary for the reception of this temporary service, or the 30 dollars a month subscriber fee required to view such a limited number of channels. Some in the satellite industry see "Primestar" as nothing but an attempt by its cable TV owners to erode public confidence in DBS by launching an inferior service that will fail and thereby discourage future DBS marketing efforts. "Primestar" obviously denies this charge, but whether by chance or design, it has certainly done nothing thus far to enhance the image of DBS.

The other major medium power satellite contender is "Sky Pix," a venture headed by Northwest Starscan. Sky Pix had hoped to include among its 80 channels of programming at least 40 channels of pay-per-view films but when Comsat Video, its feature film supplier, backed out of the deal, Sky Pix was forced to begin searching again both for new sources of capital and new program services.

The cable industry claims that the new channel compression technology it is developing will by the end of this decade allow it to increase by a factor of 10 the number of channels its systems have the capacity to deliver. This they believe will provide them with a significant competitive advantage over even the most advanced DBS system, restricted by available spectrum space to no more than 120 digitally compressed channels of service.

In reality, however, digital compression could have exactly the opposite effect. Without even considering how the cable industry

---

[30] When TCI's subsidiary company applied for a DBS orbital slot assignment in 1989, its application was challenged on character grounds because one of the parent company, TCI's cable TV system operators had been convicted of violating the anti-trust laws in 1986. This challenge was eventually withdrawn but the delay it caused could result in TCI failing to receive even that limited group of DBS channels it had sought.

will find the funds to obtain or produce sufficient programming and services to fill 100, let alone 500 video channels, the fact is that cable TV channel expansion must take place gradually through the years, on a system-by-system basis and is unlikely to extend into those rural cable markets targeted by DBS systems within the foreseeable future. On the other hand, the moment a DBS satellite is launched its entire nationwide system of channels are digitally compressed and capable immediately of offering its entire audience that abundance of services made possible by this new technology.

Perhaps the most important benefit that digital band compression can offer both cable TV and DBS is in furnishing them with the additional frequency space required to deliver future high definition television (HDTV) services. If the FCC does adopt a uniform standard for HDTV transmissions as scheduled in 1993, this in itself might provide the impetus necessary for DBS service to begin developing in the United States.

In contrast to DBS, satellite master antenna television (SMARTV) systems are not really "new technology" at all, but simply a modern version of the old fashioned community antenna. SMARTV operators erect large satellite receiving dishes on top of high-rise apartment buildings in major cities, and then distribute the satellite delivered programming received through cable to each apartment in the complex.

SMARTV systems charge apartment subscribers for their wired service, just as cable systems do. However, unlike cable TV, these self-contained systems do not cross city property to deliver their service, and so do not require an easement or franchise grant from the municipality in order to operate.[31]

Although these systems serve only those tenants within a single building, and so are not in competition with cable TV on a city-wide basis, they still can have a damaging impact upon cable revenues by depriving a cable system its most profitable potential subscriber revenues. The per subscriber cost of cabling a densely populated high-rise building has been estimated to be five to ten times lower than serving individual households, so each new SMARTV system doesn't simply deprive cable an additional group of subscribers, but also denies it the most valuable type of service opportunity.

[31] SMARTV systems are also unlike the 2.5 million "home dish" installations, where individual households receive their programming direct from satellite. SMARTV operators are licensed by satellite programmers to distribute their channels for profit, sharing these profits with the programmers. Home dish owners are not licensed in this manner, but most satellite services now scramble their transmissions so that these individuals must pay to unscramble and view these transmissions.

Municipal governments have tended to be very sympathetic to cable TV in this situation, because local cable systems typically pay the city from three to five percent of their annual subscriber revenues as a franchise fee. In 1983, a SMARTV operator in New Jersey was prevented from installing a satellite reception system because of failing to comply with the regulatory requirements of the New Jersey Cable Television Act. The operator requested the FCC to intervene and deny state or local governments the right to regulate SMARTV construction or operation.

State officials argued that since the FCC had chosen not to regulate SMARTV systems, state and local authorities retained the right to impose rules upon these systems so as to balance their competitive relationship with locally regulated cable TV. The FCC rejected this argument, denying state or local governments any regulatory authority over SMARTV, despite the competitive threat these unregulated services might pose for cable TV. Another state cable regulatory body immediately challenged the FCC's decision to preemptive SMARTV jurisdiction, but the Commission was affirmed on appeal.[32]

In 1982, the court had also affirmed the FCC's authority to assert preemptive federal control over all microwave relay services.[33] Microwave is a very high frequency radio relay, developed by AT&T in the 1940s to substitute whenever possible for more expensive telephone wire or cable trunk lines. A microwave relay, unlike a regular radio transmission, must be focused like a beam of light, and travels in a narrow path as aimed for some 25 to 30 miles unless obstructed, as light would be obstructed, by a hill or tall building.

Until the late 1970s, microwave networks were used almost exclusively to send information or messages from one place to another. At that point, some multi-point system (MDS) operators in urban areas began to develop new microwave markets by relaying pay-TV programs to hotels and high-rise apartments. The design of a MDS system differs in one significant respect from that of the traditional point to point microwave relay. While the relay service consists of a single beam traveling in a straight line, MDS systems transmit several beams of microwave signals simultaneously that fan out from their transmission hub in different directions like spokes on a wheel. This design not only made it possible for a MDS system to deliver its pay-TV channel to virtually any hotel or apartment building within range of one of

[32] New York State Commission on Cable Television v. FCC, 749 F.2d 804 (D.C.Cir. 1984).

[33] Orth–O–Vision, 44 RR2d 329 (1978), reconsidered 48 RR2d 503 (1980); affirmed in New York State Commission on Cable Television v. FCC, 669 F.2d 58 (2d Cir. 1982).

its transmissions, but also to deliver the same pay-TV service directly to every individual household in the path of one of these beams as well.

It was at this point that the FCC moved in to prevent the New York cable commission from establishing regulatory standards to control the competitive impact of MDS upon cable TV. MDS itself posed nothing more than a minor competitive threat to cable TV, because each MDS system had been assigned only one television channel of microwave frequencies.

In 1983, however, the FCC revised its rules to create a more powerful new major market competitor for cable, the "multi-channel, multi-point distribution service" (MMDS). The Commission reallocated frequencies from another microwave service to provide each of those new MMDS systems it would license sufficient microwave bandwidth to deliver four separate channels of television service, with the right to lease additional microwave frequency bands for television delivery from other operators in that market.[34]

After receiving more than 16,500 applications for MMDS licenses during the brief period the agency had set aside to accept such filings, the FCC decided to select successful applicants by means of a lottery, rather than trying to evaluate each license application individually.[35] The Commission held the first of these lotteries in September 1985, but the growth of MMDS, also known as "multi-channel television" (MCTV) and "wireless cable" has been far less spectacular thus far than originally expected.

The most successful of the systems are those that serve major urban markets without any significant cable TV system competition. MMDS systems have already started operation in Philadelphia, San Francisco, Washington D.C., Cleveland and several smaller markets. The Cleveland operation is undoubtedly the most impressive at the moment, offering 12 channels of service, including "Showtime" pay TV.[36]

MMDS operators are claiming that the cable TV industry is conspiring with cable program suppliers to deny "wireless cable" the type of premium pay-TV and satellite network services these systems need to attract subscribers.[37] However, the fact that MMDS has been unable to compete in markets where cable TV is already in operation may simply suggest that no electronic medi-

[34] ITFS Service, 54 RR2d 107 (1983).

[35] Further Notice of Proposed Rulemaking in General Docket 80–122, adopted Oct. 12, 1983, 48 Fed.Reg. 49309. Congress had granted the FCC the authority to use a lottery to select licensees in the Omnibus Spending Bill of 1981.

[36] "Wireless Cable Ready to Grow," Broadcasting Oct. 5, 1987, p. 46.

[37] "Microband Fights for 'Wireless Cable'", Variety August 3, 1988, p. 80.

um restricted by spectrum space limitations to less than a dozen channels can ever hope to attract subscribers away from a wired system offering three to four times that number of program channels.

The final "new medium" of this era was actually an old fashioned single channel distribution system, which is probably the reason it has failed thus far to have any significant impact upon American electronic media service. The concept of low power television (LPTV) was drastically revised by the Commission in March 1982, to transform it from a one-per-applicant, noncommercial broadcast public access service to a facility that could be group owned, operated as part of a nationwide network and used to distribute scrambled pay-TV services.[38] Changing the orientation of these stations attracted a substantial amount of interest, and within a matter of weeks, the FCC was buried under a backlog of 32,000 applications for the 4,000 LPTV licenses available to be issued.

The FCC began processing these applications in September 1983, issuing licenses, using a lottery process, at a rate of about 100 a month. In 1988, however, less than 10 percent of those original licenses were actually in use, with some 380 LPTV stations on the air and another 150 in the construction permit stage.[39] Perhaps after the initial enthusiasm had worn off, those who had so eagerly sought the opportunity to operate a LPTV station realized more clearly than the Commission what the future prospects actually were for a small single channel medium in a world of multi-channel media competitors.

Although it may be too soon to evaluate the successes and failures of the Commission's "new media" competition policies of the early 1980s, certain characteristics of this competition now seem clearer than they did only a few years ago.

The one unexpected factor that made competitive conditions for new media far more difficult than anticipated was the impressive resurgence of the cable industry from 1981 through 1985, as national economic conditions improved, and interest rates dropped substantially. The number of cable subscribers more than doubled during these four years, increasing from 7.8 to 20.4 million, as the number of homes offered cable TV service rose from 43 to 72 percent of all American television households.[40] The FCC began these "new media" proceedings in 1980 with the assumption that cable TV growth in major markets had been

[38] "Report and Order on Docket 78–253", adopted Mar. 4, 1982, 17 Fed.Reg. 21468.

[39] "By the Numbers", Broadcasting April 4, 1988, p. 14.

[40] Arthur D. Little, "Prospects for Cable TV; Outlook 1985–1990" May 1985.

stunted, leaving gaping holes in national satellite service coverage that could be filled by DBS, MMDS and LPTV. By the time the Commission was able to begin licensing this "new media" applicants in 1984 and 1985, those holes were being filled instead by revitalized urban cable TV systems, making it difficult for these "new media" with their unproven service record and far more limited channel capacity to attract an audience.

The greatest problem for these "new media" is that they have lacked any unique communication services of their own to attract viewers away from established media. DBS operators had seen themselves as "first run pay-TV feature film distributors" until the VCR made this appeal far less powerful. MMDS, SMARTV and LPTV offered no program channels that cable TV couldn't furnish, and had less capacity to provide alternative viewing choices than their cable competitor. As a result, it seems unlikely that any of these "new media" in their present form can survive direct cable TV competition unless they are able to develop unique entertainment or informational features not available from cable, or can provide service at a cost so much lower than cable TV that they will be able to attract viewers on that basis alone.[41]

While the first years of this "new media" era may not have revealed any challenger as yet capable of displacing cable TV in urban markets, it did reveal for the first time the incredibly difficult task the FCC would have in trying to maintain a "level regulatory playing field" among competing forms of electronic mass media.[42] The Commission has pledged its commitment to the principal of fair and equitable regulatory treatment of all electronic media, but as the agency discovered during this era, its authority to achieve this objective is restricted in several ways.

For one thing, as the FCC learned in the DBS case, it has only limited discretion in designing its rules to reflect the special characteristics of the medium being regulated.[43] Although the

[41] It's been estimated to cost approximately $2,000 per subscriber to provide service to a cable TV customer, but only $400 to provide a MMDS subscriber with the necessary dish antenna and conversion equipment. At this point, however, perhaps because of lower sales volume, MMDS subscriptions are still priced somewhat higher than comparable cable rates; e.g. $18.95 in Cleveland for 12 basic MMDS delivered program channels and one premium service, "Showtime".

[42] The powerful cable TV challenger looming in the distance is the local telephone company, already wired to each subscriber home, and moving towards a optic fiber network system that would have the capacity to deliver far more video channels than cable. At this point, telephone companies are denied by federal law the right to deliver video service, but if this policy should be modified in the future, cable would face the most powerful competitive threat it has ever experienced.

[43] In June 1988, the D.C. Court of Appeals affirmed an FCC ruling that neither subscription TV nor direct broadcast satellites are "broadcast" technologies, allowing the agency to exempt these distribution systems from certain regulatory requirements imposed by Congress on broadcasters. National Ass'n for Better Broadcasting v. FCC, 849 F.2d 665 (D.C.Cir.1988). The FCC had argued that

agency might believe certain basic broadcast standards to be irrelevant to satellite communication, hindering rather than encouraging its development, it is required by law to enforce all requirements established by Congress for that class of communication service without concern for their effect upon that particular medium.

For another, as the Commission discovered in the SMARTV and MMDS preemption controversies, since it could not free cable TV from lawful local regulation, its only alternatives were to allow similar local restraints to be imposed upon these media, or to grant them a freedom cable TV did not enjoy.   It chose regulatory freedom over a "level playing field" for SMARTV and MMDS, as the court forced it to choose the "level playing field" over regulatory freedom in the DBS case, but in neither instance did the Commission achieve the true equality in regulatory treatment it was seeking.

Unfortunately, this principle is becoming more difficult for the FCC to observe with each passing year, because as each new medium attempts to expand its own special rights and interests, it is virtually impossible for the Commission to maintain that balance among media regulatory constraints it has promised to preserve.

SEC. 59. DEREGULATION AND
THE MARKETPLACE

As the level of electronic media competition increases, each medium appears to be less concerned with freeing itself from government control than with finding a regulatory solution to its own competitive problems.

The greatest obstacle in the path of FCC efforts to establish a equitable regulatory environment in which all electronic media can compete under the same general legal obligations is the Communications Act of 1934. As long as Congress is recognized by the courts as having the constitutional authority to impose

"broadcasting", as defined by the Communications Act of 1934, applies only to spectrum transmissions intended for the general public. Because neither STV nor DBS transmissions were intended for general public, but only for those members of the audience willing to pay for the decoding of these transmissions, the Court agreed that the agency need not apply to these services Congressional regulations intended only for traditional broadcasters. During the same year, however, a different 3-judge D.C. Court of Appeals panel denied the FCC authority to award Instructional Television Fixed Service (ITFS) licenses by lottery without complying with Congressional minority preference requirements relating to such lottery awards. Telecommunications Research and Action Center v. FCC, 836 F.2d 1349 (D.C.Cir.1988). These conflicting decisions make it difficult to determine exactly how much discretion the FCC actually has in attempting to modify statutory requirements to encourage new media development.

conditions upon the exercise of broadcast free speech, the Commission has no choice but to enforce those conditions.

Because of this obligation, it is difficult for the FCC to provide broadcasting with a truly level regulatory playing field, for while the agency must require broadcasters to conform to various programming standards, the agency's constitutional authority to impose similar content standards upon competing electronic media is far less extensive.[44] More significantly, perhaps, because the FCC is powerless to reduce the regulatory burden of the broadcast industry, the only alternative it has for restoring balance to the "playing field" is to increase those legal obligations it imposes upon all other electronic media.

As these circumstances might suggest, the FCC is constantly being pressured by the broadcast industry to extend and expand its regulatory controls over cable TV and other media competitors. It was the National Association of Broadcasters that challenged the Commission's attempt to limit the regulatory obligations of DBS systems, and that ultimately prevented the FCC from carrying out its proposed policy of "flexible" supervision of new media. Similarly, the broadcast industry opposed the creation of low power television stations because the FCC had established no "local service" requirements for these facilities.[45] Through the years, however, broadcast pressure for more extensive regulation has been most consistently applied to the field of cable television.

Every Commission effort to reduce the federal constraints on cable TV system operation has been attacked by a broadcast organization, and on several occasions the NAB has threatened to turn to Congress for relief when the FCC, in its deregulatory fervor, seemed too eager to release cable TV systems from various regulatory requirements of the past.[46] This industry pressure became even more intense in 1985, when a federal court found that the Commission's cable TV "must carry" rules were far too broad in their scope to be legally enforcible.[47]

The FCC had adopted rules in the mid 1960s that made it mandatory for cable systems to carry all locally viewed television stations. The agency's basis for enacting this regulation at that time was that in the absence of such a requirement, a cable operator might be tempted to injure a local station economically

[44] Congress itself imposed the equal access for political candidates obligations of Sec. 315 upon cable TV program origination channels when it enacted the Federal Elections Campaign Act of 1971; Pub.L. No. 92–225, 86 Stat. 3 (1972).

[45] "Notice of Proposed Rulemaking in BC Docket 78–258, 82 FCC2d 47 (1980).

[46] See, for example, Malrite T.V. of New York v. FCC, 652 F.2d 1140 (2d Cir 1981) cert. denied 454 U.S. 1143, 102 S.Ct. 1002 (1982) opposing FCC recission of the cable distant signal and syndicated exclusivity rules.

[47] Quincy Cable TV, Inc. v. FCC, 768 F.2d 1434 (D.C.Cir.1985).

by refusing to deliver its signal to cable subscribers, and substitute for it a distant station affiliated with the same network. The court did not declare the concept of "must carry" to be unconstitutional on its face, but simply held that the magnitude of this potential problem was not great enough to justify the degree of interference the rule imposed upon the free speech rights of the cable system to select the programming it would deliver to its subscribers. Initially, the FCC decided not to appeal this decision or attempt to re-draft the "must carry" rules in narrower terms that might satisfy the court, but under extreme pressure from the NAB and several members of Congress, the Commission was forced, within a few weeks, to reverse its position.[48]

In March 1986 the NAB was successful in wresting significant cable signal carriage concessions from the NCTA. By August of the same year, the FCC had adopted new "must carry" rules closely following the terms of this consensus agreement.[49] However, the court had not been a party to this carefully coordinated consensus, and in December 1987 it struck down this second effort to impose signal carriage requirements upon cable TV as still being unreasonably intrusive upon cable's First Amendment rights.[50]

Prevented by the court from regulating cable TV in this way, the FCC decided to pursue another tactic to limit cable TV's programming choices. When the Commission reopened its "must carry" proceedings in 1985, it had indicated that if mandatory carriage should prove to be unenforcible, it might decide instead to reimpose its syndicated exclusivity rule upon cable systems. At the time, this was seen as nothing more than subtle pressure to encourage the NCTA to come to terms on a "must carry" consensus agreement.

When "must carry" requirements were overturned by the court, however, the FCC, at the urging of the broadcast industry, actually carried out its threat, proceeding not only to draft new syndicated exclusivity rules, but also to make a formal recommendation to Congress that cable TV's compulsory copyright license be revoked as well.[51]

[48] Compare "FCC Decides Against Must–Carry Appeal," Broadcasting August 15, 1985, p. 28 with "Must Carry: Coming to a Boil at FCC," Broadcasting Sept. 23, 1985, p. 23.

[49] "Must Carry Rules", 61 RR2d 792 (1986).

[50] Century Communications Corp. v. FCC, 835 F.2d 292 (D.C.Cir.1987).

[51] "Amendment to Parts 73 and 76 of the Commission's Rules Relating to Program Exclusivity in the Cable and Broadcast Industries", 2 FCC Rcd. 2393 (1987); "Compulsory Copyright License for Cable Retransmission", 2 FCC Rcd. 2387 (1987).

These syndicated exclusivity rules, repealed by the FCC in 1980, required cable systems to delete from their channels any programming imported from distant stations that local stations held exclusive right to broadcast in the market served by the system.[52] The Commission had concluded when repealing these rules that forcing a cable system to "black out" various program channels on a regular basis imposed a costly administrative burden on the cable operator, frustrated and inconvenienced the system's viewers, and was no longer necessary to protect the economic interests of local stations. But only eight years later, the agency seemed convinced that these same rules were both reasonable and necessary.

Lacking any logical explanation for this change in regulatory attitude, it can only be assumed that "syndicated exclusivity" illustrates how the FCC's "level playing field" principle can result in increasing the regulatory burdens of broadcast industry media competitors. When judicial recognition of cable TV's freedom of expression denied the Commission the authority needed to maintain the regulatory balance it sought between broadcast and cable program carriage rights, the agency simply imposed other signal carriage restraints upon cable to restore that balance.

Challenging the basic fairness of cable's compulsory copyright license places the cable industry in a rather uncomfortable position, because no trade group has been more vocal than the NCTA in championing a "marketplace" solution for all media regulatory questions. Perhaps it is only fair to make cable TV rely upon that marketplace it admires so much to establish the price its systems must pay for the programming they use. Yet, the FCC's decision to raise this issue of cable's compulsory license only as part of its broader mandatory carriage inquiry suggests that the agency's main concern is not to provide equitable relief for program suppliers, but simply to demonstrate to the cable TV industry what unpleasant consequences might result if cable systems should actually dare to assert their rights to deny carriage to local television stations.[53]

Although the FCC has not been sympathetic to cable industry's pleas to allow local authorities to impose upon MMDS and SMARTV operations the same type of franchise obligations required of cable systems in order to equalize their regulatory burden, it did attempt to balance their local media regulatory

[52] These requirements were repealed by "In the Matter of Community Antenna Television Syndicated Program Exclusivity Rules", 48 RR2d 171 (1980).

[53] The FCC has in fact informally supported legislation introduced in Congress to condition a cable system right to compulsory license upon whether or not the system is voluntarily carrying all local broadcast signals. "Compulsory License" Broadcasting, August 22, 1988, p. 11.

requirements in another way. Rather than increasing the regulatory burden of these new media competitors, the agency has worked instead to reduce the degree of authority local franchise regulators can exercise over cable TV. To achieve this objective, the FCC began a campaign to claim exclusive federal control over a number of cable TV regulatory powers previously exercised by local cable franchising bodies, pressuring the National League of Cities (NLC), the lobbying group for city governments, to seek a consensus agreement with the NCTA on federal legislation to regulate cable before the Commission's preemptive actions diminished local cable TV authority to a point where NLC would have no bargaining power left in these negotiations.[54]

The Cable Policy Act of 1984 that resulted from this consensus did much to free cable TV from local regulation.[55] Although the cable franchising process remains under the jurisdiction of state or local cable agencies, these agencies are now subject to a wide range of federal constraints.

Franchise authorities are prohibited from specifying particular programming or information services that applicants for a franchise are required to provide, are denied the right to impose any content standards whatsoever on constitutionally protected cable programming, and can not prevent an operator from deleting any program service that the operator believes is "commercially impracticable" for the system to carry.[56]

Renewal of a cable franchise is virtually guaranteed, furnishing a cable operator the type of shelter from regulatory pressure any broadcaster would envy.[57] The Act also denies the franchising authority the right to regulate cable TV as a common carrier meaning, among other things, that the cable operator has the right to refuse to provide any type of access to system channels

[54] During this era, the FCC denied municipalities the right to regulate the rates of any cable service other than the "basic," lowest-price tier of service in Community Cable TV 54, RR2d 1351 (1983) and opened dockets to consider establishing stricter franchise fee limitations and access requirements. Pressure was increased still further by the Supreme Court decision in Capital Cities Cable, Inc. v. Crisp, 467 U.S. 691, 104 S.Ct. 2694 (1984) that held that states could impose no content restrictions on broadcast signals imported to local cable systems because the FCC had preempted this area of cable regulation.

[55] 47 U.S.C.A. §§ 521–559.

[56] 47 U.S.C.A. §§ 544–545.

[57] A cable franchise can not be denied renewal unless the cable regulator can establish that the operator has substantially violated the terms of the existing franchise agreement, has provided unreasonably inadequate service, lacks the necessary financial, technical or legal ability to fulfill the promises made in the proposal or has filed a renewal proposal that does not adequately meet the future needs of the community. The decision to deny may be appealed, and in federal court, and the franchise authority has the burden of establishing the reasonableness of its action. 47 U.S.C.A. § 546.

other than that offered by its public, educational and government access channels.

Franchise fees are fixed at a maximum of 5 percent of system gross revenues, and the cable franchise authority no longer has any control over the rates charged system subscribers.[58] Considering the fact that a city does grant a cable system a valuable and essential public property right of easement, and therefore has both the right and the obligation to obtain in return certain benefits for the use of this public property, the Cable Act appears to have extended federal preemptive power over local cable regulation about as far as federal law could logically reach.

Yet, this new recognition of cable TV's First Amendment rights carries with it certain risks many in the cable industry seem unwilling to face.[59] For one thing, judicial recognition of cable's First Amendment right to be free of "must carry" requirements was not something the NCTA had sought.[60] The mandatory carriage rules had been challenged by one maverick cable operator, not the industry itself, because the NCTA understood this obligation to be only a minor part of a larger reciprocal agreement in effect with the NAB, whereby cable would carry local television signals in return for the broadcast industry's continuing support for compulsory licensing and cable deregulation policies.[61]

Even more significantly, complete First Amendment recognition of cable TV's rights as a communications medium could imperil the most precious right each system possesses, it's exclusive franchise agreement. Recently, unsuccessful cable franchise applicants in several cities have attempted to force local regulatory bodies to allow them to build competing cable systems without a franchise in the local cable system's service area, arguing that

[58] Maximum franchise fees are established by 47 U.S.C.A. § 542. Section 543 still allows regulation of basic rates, but only in localities unable to receive three television stations off air. The FCC was granted authority by Congress to determine when "effective TV service" was lacking so as to require continued rate regulation. This standard, challenged in American Civil Liberties Union v. FCC, 823 F.2d 1554 (D.C.Cir.1987) was sustained by the court. The FCC amended these rules to include more specific technical standards in 64 RR2d 1276 (1988).

[59] For a useful discussion of cable TV's First Amendment concerns, see "Cable's Catch–22: Whether to Be or Not to Be a Full First Amendment Player," Broadcasting, Dec. 21, 1987, p. 28.

[60] "FCC Must–Carry Rules Overturned by a Washington Appeals Court," Variety Dec. 16, 1987, p. 34.

[61] It's important to realize, when considering the close working relationship between the NAB and NCTA in many policy areas, that the two industries are not really that distinct, since over ⅓ of all cable systems are owned by broadcast interests.

preventing them from doing so unconstitutionally abridges their right to communicate with the public.[62]

Considering the severe threat that such a First Amendment position would pose for all major cable companies now operating under an exclusive franchise agreement, it is not surprising that the NCTA has steadfastly opposed what the cable industry sees as being this "unrealistically absolutist" view of freedom of expression.[63]

On the other hand, several cable TV operators safe from competitive challenge have been vigorously asserting their own First Amendment status, not to protect their freedom of expression, but simply to avoid paying franchise fees they claim impose a discriminatory burden upon their activities as a communications medium.[64]

Nothing in this recent history of electronic media deregulation seems to reveal strong support from any segment of the media industry for either a more competitive media marketplace or a broader recognition of electronic media free speech rights.[65] In fact, *Broadcasting,* the "fifth estate's" own trade journal, has begun for the first time in the magazine's history to publish editorials critical of both broadcast and cable TV industry leaders for being so eager to trade away their free speech rights simply to

[62] The most famous of these cases is City of Los Angeles v. Preferred Communications, Inc., 476 U.S. 488, 106 S.Ct. 2034 (1986). The Supreme Court remanded this case to a California District Court for a determination of whether the exclusive cable TV franchise might be justified in this case because of other, more compelling societal needs the agreement served. The trial court judge held that several of the city's major cable franchise requirements to be more restrictive than necessary to achieve the municipality's proper regulatory objective of providing for safe and efficient use of utility poles and conduits. It upheld provisions favoring local franchise applicants, but struck down those limiting the length of the franchise agreement, requiring state-of-the-art equipment, and compelling the operator to provide six free public access and two leased channels, finding in each case that these constraints on the free speech rights of the cable applicant were greater than necessary to realize any valid public policy objective of the city. Preferred Communications Inc. v. City of Los Angeles, 68 RR2d 121 (C.D.Cal.1990). See also Century Federal, Inc. v. City of Palo Alto, Cal., 648 F.Supp. 1465 (N.D.Cal.1986) where a decision by several California cities to grant an exclusive cable franchise was declared by the court to be a clearly unconstitutional abridgment of free speech.

[63] Op. cit., footnote 61.

[64] Central Telecommunications, Inc. v. TCI Cablevision, Inc., 800 F.2d 711 (8th Cir.1986); Erie Telecommunications, Inc. v. City of Erie, 659 F.Supp. 580 (W.D.Pa. 1987).

[65] In fact, in July 1988 the NAB commissioned and published a study opposing a "marketplace" approach to broadcast service in the United States. Titled "Is More Necessarily Better?" the report criticizes FCC efforts to license additional broadcast facilities that the agency's engineering bureau indicates can operate without creating interference for existing stations. In this report, this marketplace concept is described as being both ineffective and destructively competitive. "NAB Shies Away from Crowded Marketplace", Broadcasting, July 4, 1988, p. 47.

safeguard their immediate economic interests.[66] Responding to a
strongly worded letter from a broadcast lobbying group pointing
out that *Broadcasting*'s magazine had no right to speak for the
industry, it commented editorially,

> . . . "Committed to the First Amendment and the Fifth
> Estate" has been represented on this page for almost 57
> years without facing challenge from a significant portion
> of the industry we cover . . . We have never said we
> were speaking for the industry; on the other hand, until
> these recent divisions, it appeared that the magazine and
> the industry leadership were in essential agreement. Our
> policy hasn't change; one wonders what has.

* * *

> If broadcasters are content to operate more as crown
> carriers than as First Amendment speakers, then little
> may be lost by submitting to the fairness doctrine as well.
> And if the theory is that broadcasters will enjoy more
> economic benefit from a public interest standard than
> they will pay to the government in tribute, then you pays
> your money and you takes your chance. Our own view is
> that broadcasters stand to lose their freedom and keep
> their insecurity—the worst of both worlds.[67]

Why should the broadcast industry, finally free of what industry leaders have always described as the "chilling" free speech
effects of Fairness Doctrine, now be negotiating with Congress for
its return? Or, why should an industry so bitterly opposed to its
second class status as a regulated medium be willing at this point
to accept continuing government supervision of program content if
an opportunity exists at last to escape these constraints upon
broadcast free speech? The answer is simply that for the typical
broadcaster, a guaranteed right of license renewal is far more
precious than any abstract concern about freedom of expression.
If the price for such renewal legislation is acceptance of the
Fairness Doctrine, the industry seems willing to pay it. By the
same token, if total programming freedom would come only at the
cost of a spectrum use fee or public auction of spectrum space,

[66] See, for example, "On the Sidelines", Broadcasting, April 27, 1987, p. 122,
criticizing the broadcast industry's willingness to deal away the "Fairness Doctrine" in return for comparative license renewal relief; "Cutting and Running",
Broadcasting June 27, 1988, p. 90, opposing industry acceptance of permanent
federal free speech restrictions to obtain guarantees of continued spectrum usage
without charge, and "Fish or Fowl?" Broadcasting, December 21, 1987, p. 112,
urging the cable TV industry not to sell out its free speech rights simply to shield
its franchises from competition.

[67] "Hanging in There for the First Amendment", Broadcasting July 25, 1988, p.
114.

broadcast free speech does not appear at the moment to be worth that price.[68]

Similarly, while the cable TV industry seeks First Amendment recognition as a medium, it does not desire complete freedom of expression if the price for free speech includes the loss of its exclusive franchise privilege. Nor does the cable industry see anything contradictory in supporting a marketplace approach for establishing the price of its cable subscriber fees, and yet opposing such an approach for establishing the price it must pay for cable programming.

In this way, the media industries are no different from other political and economic groups in our society, in that they can distinguish between a general principle and its specific application in deciding when a theoretical commitment must be abandoned to achieve a particular goal. Thus, to media leaders, "free speech," "deregulation" and "marketplace" are not sacred ends in themselves, but simply concepts invoked to realize certain industry objectives; and therefore useful only to the extent that they aid in attaining those objectives.

In that sense, then, while "freedom of expression" remains a noble aspiration for all electronic media, it is often the first casualty in policy skirmishes among media competitors. Deregulation has not as yet resulted in freeing electronic media from government content control, in large part because winning such "free speech" rights has not been a primary policy objective of electronic media during this era. Perhaps at some future date, when the competitive boundaries of each of these media empires have been more clearly established, that time may finally arrive.

---

[68] During the past decade, Congress has considered a number of bills that would have transformed broadcasting's "public interest" programming responsibilities into a simple financial obligation for use of a public resource. By paying the reasonable value for the license privilege, a broadcaster would thereby be freed of any responsibilities to the public in terms of program service. Because of this, all federal broadcast content regulation would end when this legislation took effect. The broadcast industry has not supported any of these "reasonable value" bills. One reason for the industry's lack of enthusiasm for this approach might be reflected in the fact that the value of one Chicago network television license was recently estimated to be in excess of $600 million.

Chapter 11

REGULATION OF ADVERTISING

Sec.
60. From *Caveat Emptor* to Consumer Protection.
61. Federal Administrative Controls: The Federal Trade Commission.
62. Literal Truth Is Not Enough.
63. Corrective Advertising Orders of the FTC.
64. Other Federal Administrative Controls.
65. The Printers' Ink Statute.
66. Lotteries.
67. Self-Regulation.
68. The Right to Refuse Service.
69. Broadcast Advertising.
70. Advertising and the Constitution.

SEC. 60. FROM *CAVEAT EMPTOR* TO CONSUMER PROTECTION

The history of advertising in the United States has seen a gradual change away from the motto of *caveat emptor* ("let the buyer beware").

It is hardly news that advertising is both a necessity and a nuisance in American society. It encourages and advances the nation's economy by providing information to the public about goods and services. Although its economic role in supporting the news media has been criticized, advertising has paid the bills for most of the news and vicarious entertainment which we receive. Historically, we owe advertising another debt. The rise of advertising in the 19th Century did much to free the press from excessive reliance on political parties or government printing contracts which tended to color news columns with their bias.

Despite advertising's undeniably worthwhile contributions, this chapter unavoidably must emphasize the seamy side of American salesmanship. We will concentrate to a great extent upon issues raised by cheats and rascals. There can be little question that all too much advertising has been—and is—inexact, if not spurious and deceitful. Better units of the communications media now operate their advertising as a business with a definite obligation to the public. The realization evidently has dawned that unless advertising is both truthful and useful, the public may react unfavorably.

Advertising in the United States has a colorful if sometimes sordid past. From the first days of the nation throughout the

Nineteenth Century, the philosophy motivating advertising was largely *laissez faire*. Too much advertising, in spirit if not to the letter, resembled this 1777 plug for "Dr. RYAN's *incomparable* WORM *destroying* SUGAR PLUMBS, *Necessary to be kept in all* FAMILIES:" [1]

> The plumb is a great diurectic, cleaning the veins of slime; it expels wind, and is a sovereign medicine in the cholic and griping of the guts. It allays and carries off vapours which occasion many disorders of the head. It opens all obstructions in the stomach, lungs, liver, veins, and bladder; causes a good appetite, and helps digestion.

Such exploitation of the *laissez faire* philosophy went unpunished for more than a century of this nation's existence. There was little or no regulation; what would be termed unreliable or even fraudulent advertising was published by some of the most respectable newspapers and periodicals. The general principle seemed to be that advertising columns were an open business forum with space for sale to all who applied.

Before 1900, advertising had little established ethical basis. The liar and the cheat capitalized on glorious claims for dishonest, shoddy merchandise. The faker lured the ill and suffering to build hopes on pills and tonics of questionable composition. Cures were promised by the bottle. Fortunes were painted for those who invested in mining companies of dubious reliability. Foods were frequently adulterated.

Exposés of frauds and fraud promoters who were using advertising to ensnare new prospects were important early in the Twentieth Century. Mark Sullivan exposed medical fakes and frauds in the *Ladies Home Journal* in 1904. Upton Sinclair's novel, *The Jungle,* revolted readers with its description of filthy conditions in meat-packing plants. Spurred by such exposés, Congress passed the Pure Food and Drug Act in 1906. Despite being a truth-in-labeling measure the 1906 statute did nothing to insure truth in advertising.[2]

Campaigning against advertising chicanery, many magazines and newspapers exposed fraudulent practices.[3] Some newspapers of this period, including the Cleveland Press and other Scripps-McRae League papers, monitored advertisements, refusing those which appeared to be fraudulent or misleading. A Scripps-McRae official asserted that the newspaper group turned away approxi-

[1] Pennsylvania Gazette, March 12, 1777.

[2] Ibid.

[3] H.J. Kenner, The Fight for Truth in Advertising (1936) pp. 13–14; Alfred McClung Lee, The Daily Newspaper in America (1937), p. 328.

mately $500,000 in advertising revenue in one year by rejecting advertisements.

Such self-regulation has grown considerably over the years, and legal restraints have grown, too. People working in advertising come under all the laws which affect other branches of mass communications, including libel, invasion of privacy, copyright infringement, and obscenity. In addition, there are batteries of statutes and regulatory powers aimed at advertising *in addition to* the laws which affect, for example, the editorial side of a newspaper. There's the Food and Drug Administration (FDA), the Securities Exchange Commission (SEC), the Federal Communications Commission (FCC), and quite an alphabet soup of other federal agencies which gets into the advertising regulation act. Beyond that, there is increasing activity at the state level to attempt to control false or deceptive advertising. This chapter, then, can be only a sparse survey of advertising regulatory structures.

SEC. 61. FEDERAL ADMINISTRATIVE CONTROLS: THE FEDERAL TRADE COMMISSION

The most important federal government controls over advertising have been exercised by the Federal Trade Commission, which has experienced considerable controversy in recent years.

The Federal Trade Commission

Over the last 90 years, the Federal Trade Commission became more important than other official controls over advertising. The FTC Act was passed in 1914 to supplement sanctions against unfair competition which had been provided by the Sherman Anti-Trust Act of 1890 and by the Clayton Act of 1914.[4] Gradually, the FTC grew in power and assumed an increasingly important place in regulating advertising.

By the 1960s, as will be discussed later in this section, there was increasing criticism that the FTC was a do-nothing agency, and efforts were made to reorganize[5] and to strengthen[6] the

[4] Sherman Act, 26 Stat. 209 (1890), 15 U.S.C.A. § 1; Clayton Act, 38 Stat. 730 (1914), 15 U.S.C.A. § 12.

[5] See Report of "Nader's Raiders," The Consumer and the Federal Trade Commission—A Critique of the Consumer Protection Record of the FTC, published in 115 Congressional Record 1539 (1969); William F. Lemke, Jr., "Souped Up Affirmative Disclosure Orders of the Federal Trade Commission," 4 University of Michigan Journal of Law Reform (Winter, 1970), p. 193. See also Charles McCarry, Citizen Nader (New York: Saturday Review Press, 1972); American Bar Association, Report of the ABA Commission to Study the Federal Trade Commission, reprinted as Appendix II, pp. 123–244, "Federal Trade Commission Procedures," Hearings Before the Subcommittee on Administrative Practice and Procedures of the Committee on the Judiciary, United States Senate, First Session, Ninety-First Congress, Part I (Washington, D.C.: Government Printing Office, 1970).

[6] See note 6 on page 435.

commission. Ironically, when the FTC became really assertive during the late 1970s, that set about a backlash that actually weakened its efforts to regulate advertising.

The question may be raised whether American society—as represented by Congress—*really* wishes to regulate advertising. After all, only a small segment of the FTC's budget (74 million in 1990–91)—less than 3 million was used to regulate (or *try* to regulate) deceptive advertising. And advertising is more than a $100 billion dollar industry in the United States today. When some advertisers—e.g. Bayer Aspirin, Anacin, and Bufferin—spend more on television advertising each year than the FTC has in its annual budget to attend to the regulation of all products which are advertised in interstate commerce, one senses something of a mismatch. While the FTC Act was conceived to prevent monopoly and restraint of trade, checking dishonest advertising long has been regarded as a principal activity of the Commission.[7]

This change of emphasis, created partly by criticisms of advertising, has not been without major opposition on the part of American business. There was—and is—fear that the government would so shackle advertising and sales efforts that business enterprise and even freedom of the press would be hampered.

The Federal Trade Commission is an example of administrative rule and law-making authority delegated by Congress. Five Federal Trade Commissioners are appointed by the President and confirmed by the Senate for five-year terms. No more than three of the five commissioners may be from the same political party. In any case, the FTC has long been criticized as insufficiently active in protecting consumers.

In 1969, an American Bar Association study concluded that FTC activity had been declining while FTC staff and budget increased. The report contended that the FTC had mismanaged its resources, and that it had failed to set goals and provide necessary guidance for its staff.[8]

Extensive reorganizations of the FTC were carried out after the ABA study. A Bureau of Consumer Protection was created to handle consumer protection activities. The Bureau's responsibility extends not only to the enforcement of consumer protection statutes but also to the development of Trade Regulation Rules

[6] See, e.g., Consumer Product Warranties and Federal Trade Commission Improvements Act ("Moss-Magnuson Act"), Pub.L. 93–637, 88 Stat. 2183 (1975).

[7] During fiscal year 1990, e.g., the FTC reported it had compelled firms involved in a wide range of fraudulent trade practices to pay American consumers more than $50 million in compensation while forcing those involved in deceptive trade marketing schemes to refund $30 million to customers misled by such actions: "FTC Asks for 11% Increase for FY 1992," Broadcasting, March 25, 1991, p. 82.

[8] See footnote 5, above.

(with the force of law), of industry guidelines, and of consumer protection programs.[9]

The Bureau of Consumer Protection is responsible for enforcing the FTC Act where deceptive or unfair marketing practices of national or interstate scope are concerned. A sub-unit of the Bureau, the Division of Advertising Practices, is said by the FTC to have as its goal "* * * the promotion of the free flow of truthful information in the marketplace. Its law enforcement activities focus on:" [10]

- Advertising claims, particularly those relating to safety or effectiveness, for food and drugs sold over the counter.

- Performance and energy-savings claims for solar products, furnaces, storm windows, residential siding, wood-burning products, gas-saving products, motor oils, and other products that are marketed by emphasizing their energy conservation features.

- Advertising directed at children.

- Cigarette advertising, which includes monitoring for deceptive claims; operating a tobacco-testing laboratory to measure tar, nicotine, and carbon monoxide content of cigarettes; and reporting to Congress annually on cigarette labeling, advertising, and promotion.

The FTC, long expected to help enforce a crazy quilt of statutes, gets involved with the Truth-in-Lending Act, the Fair Credit Reporting Act, the Wool Products Labeling Act, the Textile Fiber Products Identification Act, and the Fur Products Labeling Act, plus other statutes for which the FTC has enforcement responsibilities.

The FTC machinery tries to enforce Section 5 of the Federal Trade Commission Act, which says: "Unfair methods of competition in commerce, and unfair or deceptive practices in commerce, are declared unlawful." [11]

Early FTC cases which came before the courts cast doubt on the Commission's powers over advertising.[12] However, in 1921, something as mundane as partly wool underwear masquerading as real woolies gave the FTC the case it needed to establish its authority. For many years the Winsted Hosiery Company had

[9] George Eric Rosden and Peter Eric Rosden, The Law of Advertising (New York Matthew Bender, 1973, 1985 and updated 2 vols.) Vol. 2, § 32.05; see also Gerry Thain, "Advertising Regulation," 1 Fordham Urban Law Journal (1973), pp. 367–381.

[10] "A Guide to the Federal Trade Commission," FTC pamphlet, 1984, pp. 7–8.

[11] 15 U.S.C.A. § 45(a)(1).

[12] Federal Trade Commission v. Gratz, 253 U.S. 421, 40 S.Ct. 572 (1920); L.B. Silver Co. v. Federal Trade Commission of America, 289 Fed. 985 (6th Cir.1923).

been selling its underwear in cartons branded with labels such as "Natural Merino," "Natural Wool," or "Australian Wool." In fact, none of this company's underwear was all wool, and, some of its products had as little as 10 per cent wool.

The FTC complaint against Winsted Hosiery asked the company to show cause why the use of its brands and labels which seemed deceptive should not be discontinued. After hearings, the FTC issued a cease and desist order against the company. On appeal, the FTC lost, with a United States Circuit Court saying: the agency was powerless to prevent use of misleading labels.[13]

In 1922, however, the Supreme Court of the United States upheld the FTC in language broad enough to support the Commission's power to control false labeling and advertising as unfair methods of competition. Speaking for the Court, Justice Brandeis declared that the Commission was justified in its conclusions that the hosiery company's practices were unfair methods of competition. He authorized the Commission to halt such practices. Brandeis said, "when misbranded goods attract customers by means of the fraud which they perpetrate, trade is diverted from the producer of truthfully marked goods."[14]

Despite the efforts of the Federal Trade Commission, the idea of consumer protection had little support from the Courts during the early 1930s. In 1931, the *Raladam* case, for example, cut sharply into the FTC's attempts to defeat the ancient, amoral doctrine of caveat emptor, "let the buyer beware." The Raladam Company manufactured an "obesity cure" containing "dessicated thyroid." This preparation, sold under the name of "Marmola," was advertised in newspapers and on printed labels as being the result of scientific research. It was claimed that "Marmola" was "safe and effective and may be used without discomfort, inconvenience, or danger of harmful results to health."

The FTC complaint focused upon the likelihood of actual physical harm to consumers who used Marmola believing it safe as claimed. The Supreme Court, however, disallowed the FTC's order that the Raladam Corporation cease such advertising. Speaking for the Court, Justice George Sutherland ruled that Section 5 of the FTC Act did not forbid the deception of consumers unless the advertising injured competing business in some way. Accordingly, the FTC was not allowed to work directly for consumer protection.[15]

[13] Winsted Hosiery Co. v. Federal Trade Commission, 272 Fed. 957, 961 (2d Cir. 1921).

[14] Federal Trade Commission v. Winsted Hosiery Co., 258 U.S. 483, 493–494, 42 S.Ct. 384, 385–386 (1922).

[15] Federal Trade Commission v. Raladam Co., 283 U.S. 643, 644, 51 S.Ct. 587, 589 (1931).

The FTC's authority over advertising grew slowly. As late as 1936—when the FTC had been in operation for some 22 years—the famed Judge Learned Hand of a U.S. Circuit Court decided a case against the FTC and in favor of an advertising scheme for encyclopedias which involved false representation. The publisher of the encyclopedias tried to lure customers into believing that the company gave them a set of encyclopedias "free," and that the customer's payment of $69.50 was only for a loose leaf supplement to the encyclopedia. The $69.50 was actually the combined regular price for both books and supplements. Despite this, Judge Hand could declare:[16] "Such trivial niceties are too impalpable for practical affairs, they are will-o'-the-wisps, which divert attention from substantial evils."

When this case reached the Supreme Court, Justice Hugo L. Black reacted indignantly, saying the sales method used to peddle the encyclopedia "successfully deceived and deluded its victims."[17] In overturning Judge Hand's "let the buyer beware" ruling in the lower court, Justice Black added:[18]

> The fact that a false statement may be obviously false to those who are trained and experienced does not change its character, nor take away its power to deceive others less experienced. There is no duty resting upon a citizen to suspect the honesty of those with whom he transacts business. Laws are made to protect the trusting as well as the suspicious. The best element of business has long since decided that honesty should govern competitive enterprises, and that the rule of caveat emptor [let the buyer beware] should not be relied upon to reward fraud and deception.

In 1938, the year after the Supreme Court endorsed the concept of consumer protection from advertising excesses, Congress acted to give the FTC greater authority over deceptive advertising. The 1938 Wheeler-Lea Amendment changed Section 5 of the Federal Trade Commission Act to read: "Unfair methods of competition *in commerce,* and unfair or deceptive acts or practices in commerce, are hereby declared unlawful.[19] Note the italicized phrase. These words were added by the Wheeler-Lea Amendment, and this seemingly minor change in phrasing proved to be of great importance. The italicized words removed the limits on FTC authority imposed by the *Raladam* decision. No longer

[16] Federal Trade Commission v. Standard Educ. Society, 302 U.S. 112, 116, 58 S.Ct. 113, 115 (1937), quoting Judge Hand's opinion in the same case in the Circuit Court, 86 F.2d 692, 695 (2d Cir.1936).

[17] 302 U.S. 112, 117, 58 S.Ct. 113, 115 (1937).

[18] 302 U.S. 112, 116, 58 S.Ct. 113, 115 (1937).

[19] 52 Stat. 111 (1938); 15 U.S.C.A. § 45. Italics added.

would the FTC have to prove that a misleading advertisement harmed a competing business. Now, if an advertisement deceived consumers, the FTC's enforcement powers could be put into effect.[20]

Aiming at false advertising, the Wheeler-Lea Amendment also inserted Sections 12 and 15(a) into the Federal Trade Commission Act. Section 12 provides:[21]

> It shall be unlawful for any person, partnership, or corporation to disseminate, or cause to be disseminated, any false advertisement—(1) by United States mails, or in [interstate] commerce by any means, for the purpose of inducing, or which is likely to induce, directly or indirectly, the purchase in commerce of food, drugs, devices or cosmetics.

Section 15(a) of the FTC Act says:

> The term 'false advertising' means an advertisement, other than labeling, which is misleading in a material respect; and in determining whether any advertisement is misleading, there shall be taken into account (among other things) not only representations made or suggested by statement, word, design, device, sound, or any combination thereof, but also the extent to which the advertisement fails to reveal facts material in the light of such representations or material with respect to consequences which may result from the use of the commodity * * *.

Such statutory changes gave the FTC some of the power it sought to protect consumers. As FTC Commissioners Everett MacIntyre and Paul Rand Dixon wrote in the 1960s, the Wheeler-Lea "amendment put the consumer on a par with the businessman from the standpoint of deceptive practices."[22]

Even so, this commission was often called "toothless" and other less flattering things. The delays which have attended FTC enforcement procedures—especially those involved in lengthy court battles—became legendary. An often cited example was the famed "Carter's Little Liver Pills" case. In 1943, the FTC decided that the word "liver" was misleading, and a classic and lengthy battle was on. Carter's Little Liver Pills had been a well known laxative product for 75 years. It took the FTC a total of 16

---

[20] Ibid.; Earl W. Kinter, "Federal Trade Commission Regulation of Advertising," Michigan Law Review Vol. 64:7 (May, 1966) pp. 1269–1284, at pp. 1275–1276, 1276n.

[21] Section 12, 52 Stat. 114 (1938), 15 U.S.C.A. § 52; Section 15(a), 52 Stat. 114 (1938), 15 U.S.C.A. § 55(a).

[22] Everette MacIntyre and Paul Rand Dixon, "The Federal Trade Commission After 50 Years," Federal Bar Journal Vol.24:4 (Fall,1964) pp. 377–424, at p. 416.

years—from 1943 to 1959—to win its point before the courts and get "liver" deleted.[23]

In addition, the FTC could not hope to regulate all advertising in interstate commerce—it could merely regulate by example, by pursuing a relatively small number of advertisers who appeared to operate in a deceptive fashion, in hopes that this would encourage others to tone down their advertising claims. It has been objected that during most of the FTC's history, it had tended to go after "little guys" or unimportant issues, too often ignoring misdeeds by big and powerful corporations which tied into important issues.

Beyond that, the FTC's enforcement machinery, for the most part, was creaky and slow. If an advertising campaign on television is deemed "deceptive" or "false and misleading" by the FTC, the ad campaign might have run its course (generally three months, six months, or nine months) before the FTC could have any impact. In lawyer's jargon, such cases had become moot, or meaningless by the time they were finally resolved.

The FTC has several weapons to use against misleading advertising:

(1) *Assurance of Voluntary Compliance (Non-Adjudicative)—* If the FTC believes the public interest is served, it may halt an investigation by accepting a promise that a questioned practice will be stopped. The Commission accepts such a promise only in rare cases, and then after considering the seriousness of the advertising practice complained of and the prior record and good faith of the party involved.

(2) *Consent Orders*—Instead of litigating an FTC complaint, a respondent may enter into an agreement amounting to a cease and desist order for consideration by the Commission. If this agreement is approved by the FTC, the order is placed in the public record for 60 days. During that period, interested persons may file comments concerning the order. If a consent order is approved by the FTC, it will have the force of adjudicative orders (discussed below). Respondents in consent order proceedings do not admit violations of the law.[24]

(3) *Adjudicative Orders*—These are based on evidence from a record developed during a proceeding that starts when the FTC issues a complaint. The proceeding is conducted before an Administrative Law Judge who serves as the

[23] Carter Products, Inc. v. Federal Trade Commission, 268 F.2d 461 (9th Cir.1959), certiorari denied 361 U.S. 884, 80 S.Ct. 155 (1959).

[24] Federal Trade Commission, Your FTC: What It Is and What It Does (U.S. Government Printing Office, 1977), p. 26.

initial trier of facts. After hearings, the judge will issue a decision within 90 days. That decision may be reviewed by the FTC, and if not appealed or if upheld, a cease and desist order will issue. Appeals from a final FTC decision may be made to a U.S. Court of Appeals, and ultimately, to the Supreme Court of the United States. Unless a cease and desist order is appealed within 60 days, it becomes self-executing. Violation of such an order is punishable by a civil penalty of $10,000 a day for each offense.[25]

(4) *Publicity*—The FTC publicizes complaints and cease-and-desist orders which it promulgates. News releases on such subjects are regularly issued to the media, and publicity has proven to be a strong weapon at the Commission's disposal.[26]

It can be seen from the foregoing list of FTC activities that the Commission is not dependent solely on harsh actions such as cease and desist orders or court procedures. The Commission also takes positive steps to attempt to clarify its view of fair advertising practices. The Commission has three major programs which attempt to secure voluntary compliance. These are:

1. INDUSTRY GUIDES. This program involved issuing interpretations of the rules of the Commission to its staff. These guides are made available to the public, and are aimed at certain significant practices of a particular industry, especially those involved in advertising and labeling. The guides can be issued by the Commission as its interpretation of the law without a conference or hearings, and, therefore, in a minimum of time.

2. ADVISORY OPINIONS. In 1962, the FTC began giving advisory opinions in response to industry questions about the legality of a proposed industry action. Advisory opinions generally predict the FTC's response, although the Commission reserves the right to reconsider its advice if the public interest so requires.[27]

3. TRADE REGULATION RULES. The FTC publishes a notice before issuing a Trade Regulation Rule on a specific practice. Industry representatives may then comment on the proposed Trade Regulation before the rule is adopted and put into effect.[28]

[25] Ibid.; Rosden & Rosden, op. cit., Vol. II, § 25.06.

[26] Federal Trade Commission, Your FTC: What It Is and What It Does, p. 19.

[27] Rosden and Rosden, Vol. II, § 32.04.

[28] Ibid.

Voluntary compliance with laws and FTC rules is not always forthcoming. The FTC sometimes is compelled to begin a case against an advertiser. Cases sometimes open after a complaint from an aggrieved citizen or a competitor who has suffered a loss because of what he believes to be illegal activity. The FTC also screens advertisements, looking for false or misleading statements. When a suspicious advertisement is found, a questionnaire is sent to the advertiser. The FTC may also request samples of the product advertised, if practicable. If the product is a compound, its formula may be requested. Copies of all advertisements published or broadcast during a specified period are requested, together with copies of supplementary information such as booklets, folders, or form letters.

Product samples may be inspected by the FTC or referred to another appropriate government agency for scientific analysis. If false or misleading advertising claims are indicated by such an examination, the advertiser is advised of the scientific opinions of the Commission's experts. The advertiser is allowed to submit evidence in support of his advertisement.

Recently the FTC has become much more active in challenging nutritional claims made for various food products in our health-obsessed society. The agency is currently developing standards to be used to determine when a processed food can be called "lite" or "light", and is challenging the right of those marketing productions with a substantial amount of saturated fat from claiming they are "cholesterol free".

Strengthening the FTC—The 1970s

Strengthening of the FTC's regulatory powers came in 1973 in a stealthy fashion. While an energy crisis absorbed attention of Congress and of the public in 1973, a rider to the Trans-Alaska Pipeline Authorization Act gave the FTC powers which it had sought for years.[29] Thanks to that rider, the FTC was given the power to go to a federal court and ask for an injunction against an advertisement which is—in the eyes of the Commission—clearly in violation of federal law prohibiting false or misleading advertising. This injunctive sanction is not likely to be much used because it is so drastic. However, an injunction could—in critical instances— put a stop to ads which might otherwise continue to run through their campaign cycle, be it three months or six months or nine months, before the FTC could act.

[29] 15 U.S.C.A. § 53. See Note, " 'Corrective Advertising' Orders of the Federal Trade Commission," 85 Harvard Law Review (Dec.1971), pp. 485–486. The FTC already has injunctive powers to deal with advertising for products which could pose an immediate health threat to consumers: medical devices, foods, drugs, and cosmetics.

More help was on the way for the FTC. In January, 1975, the "Consumer Product Warranties and Federal Trade Commission Improvements Act"—hereafter referred to as the Moss-Magnuson Act—was signed into law by President Gerald R. Ford.[30] One part of this measure was designed to provide minimum disclosure standards for written consumer product warranties.

Before the Moss-Magnuson Act, jurisdiction of the FTC was limited to advertising *in* interstate commerce. In 1941, the Supreme Court held that an Illinois company which limited its sales to wholesalers located only in Illinois was not "in [interstate] commerce,"[31] and was thus beyond the reach of FTC control. Now, under the new statute, the FTC can regulate advertising *affecting* commerce. A small change, on the surface, but not in actuality. This wording change gave the FTC the power, in effect, to say that *all* commerce affects interstate commerce, and therefore is under FTC jurisdiction.[32]

Also, the Moss-Magnuson Act gave the power to the Commission to get beyond of "regulation by example"—that is, to do more than let a shave cream manufacturer know with a cease-and-desist order that an advertising campaign was considered misleading by the FTC. The FTC was enabled to issue Trade Regulation Rules which can apply to an entire product type or industry. Trade Regulation Rules—when formally issued by the FTC—have the force of law. Fines for violation of a Trade Regulation Rule through misleading advertising can draw fines of up to $10,000 a day, so the FTC was given the clout to get advertisers to pay attention.[33]

Weakening the FTC—The 1980s

Although the Magnuson-Moss Act strengthened FTC powers, the activist stance of the FTC during the late 1970s brought a counter-attack from the business community plus 1980 legislation to weaken the FTC. Although the Great Sugar Imbroglio was by no means the only source of the FTC's troubles, it may be used as an example of Commission behavior that horrified business and industry. In 1977 and 1978,[34]

> [t]he FTC staff proposed rules that would have resulted in a ban of most children's television advertising. The FTC primarily premised its far-reaching rulemaking proceeding on "unfairness," a standard with few legal precedents,

[30] Pub. L. 93–637, 88 Stat. 2183 (1975).

[31] Federal Trade Commission v. Bunte Bros., 312 U.S. 349, 61 S.Ct. 580 (1941).

[32] Moss-Magnuson Act, Pub.L. 93–637, 88 Stat. 2183 (1975).

[33] Ibid.

[34] Foote and Mnookin, op. cit., p. 90.

rather than on "deception," a well-established standard with more confining limits.

Issues involved in the regulation of children's advertising—including FTC hearing on whether some sugary foods should be banned—provided a sticky situation for the commission. In 1977 and 1978, FTC Chairman Michael Pertschuk made a variety of statements critical of techniques used in children's advertising.

The FTC soon began a major trade regulation rulemaking procedure on "Children's Advertising," under Section 18 of the Magnuson-Moss Act.[35] The Association of National Advertisers and the Kellogg Company, after asking without success that Pertschuk disqualify himself from hearings on the subject, then went to court for an order to restrain Pertschuk from further involvement. It was contended that the chairman had prejudged fact issues and would not be able to participate fairly in the rulemaking procedure.[36] Pertschuk, in fact, had said: " 'Advertisers seize on the child's trust and exploit it as a weakness for their gain. * * *' " and " 'Cumulatively, commercials directed at children tend to distort the role of food. * * * Rarely is their emphasis on good nutrition.' "[37]

A U.S. district court disqualified Pertschuk from the proceeding, saying that administrative hearings must both be fair and look fair, and that Pertschuk did not meet that standard. Late in 1979, however, the U.S. Court of Appeals, District of Columbia Circuit, ruled that Pertschuk's dual role of advocate and administrator was permissible; the Association of National Advertisers had not shown that the Chairman's mind was unalterably closed concerning the proceeding on children's advertising.[38]

The FTC Improvements Act of 1980

Although that Court of Appeals supported the FTC's activism, Congress in 1980 passed the whimsically named Federal Trade Commission Improvements Act of 1980.[39] A few more such "improvements" and the FTC can pack it in. This legislation removed "unfairness"[40] as a basis for regulation of commercial

[35] 15 U.S.C.A. § 57a.

[36] Med.L.Rptr. 1716 (1979).

[37] The News Media & The Law, Vol. 3: No. 2 (May/June 1979), p. 18.

[38] 5 Med.L.Rptr. 2233, 2236, 2245–2247. Despite this ruling, Pertschuk withdrew from the administrative rulemaking procedure. See P. Cameron DeVore and Robert D. Sack, Advertising and Commercial Speech, in James C. Goodale, chairman, Communications Law 1980, Vol. II (New York: Practicing Law Institute, 1980) p. 487.

[39] Pub.L.No. 96–252, 94 Stat. 374 (1980).

[40] Foote and Mnookin, op. cit., pp. 90–91; see also discussion in text in preceding footnote number 36.

advertising. Instead of being able to forbid "unfair" ads the FTC will have to show out-and-out *deception,* which is harder to prove. Also, the 1980 act removed FTC powers to make rules on children's advertising and the funeral industry. In addition, the FTC now has Congress breathing down its neck. Under the 1980 "Improvements Act," there is established a 90-day review period for any FTC Trade Regulation Rules. If both Houses of Congress pass a resolution objecting to the rule, the rule is overturned. This procedure has been called the "two-House legislative veto." [41]

As advertising law experts Earl W. Kintner, Christopher Smith, and David B. Goldston have said: [42]

> Although the Federal Trade Commission Improvements Act of 1980 restrains some of the Commission's more controversial initiatives, the legislation does not alter the Commission's basic enforcement authority. Congressional criticism of the Commission, however, already has and will likely continue to cause the Commission to enter new frontiers of trade regulation law much more cautiously.

SEC. 62. LITERAL TRUTH IS NOT ENOUGH

Even literally true statements may cause an advertiser difficulty if those statements are part of a misleading advertisement.

Sometimes even the *literal truth* can be misleading. When truth misleads in an advertisement, the FTC is able to issue a "cease and desist" order and make it stick. A photo album sales scheme offers a case in point. Door-to-door salesmen told customers that for $39.95, they could take advantage of a "once in a lifetime combination offer" and receive a "free" album by purchasing 10 photographic portraits at the "regular price" of the photographs alone.

The FTC ordered the company selling the photo albums to stop suggesting that its albums were given away free, when in fact the albums were part of a $39.95 package deal. The company was also ordered to stop claiming that it sold only to "selected persons" and that a special price was involved. The photo album company retorted that its sales pitch was the literal truth, and that the

[41] Pub.L.No. 96–252, 94 Stat. 374 (1980), § 21, discussed in Earl W. Kintner, Christopher Smith, and David B. Goldston, "The Effect of the Federal Trade Commission Improvements Act of 1980 on the FTC's Rulemaking and Enforcement Authority," 58 Washington University Law Quarterly No. 4 (Winter, 1980) pp. 847–859, at 853. This legislative veto provision stays in effect until September 30, 1982, and contains a provision for expedited judicial review should this provision's constitutionality be attacked through a lawsuit.

[42] Kintner, Smith and Goldston, op. cit., pp. 858–859.

FTC's cease and desist order should, therefore, be set aside by the courts.[43] The company argued that its customers actually were "selected;" that the word "few" is a relative term which is very elastic, and that the $39.95 price was in fact "promotional" because it tended to support the sale of the albums.

A U.S. Court of Appeals upheld the FTC's cease and desist order. The Circuit Court announced that there should be a presumption of validity when courts reviewed FTC orders involving advertising. Tendencies of advertisements to mislead or deceive were held to be factual questions which would be determined by the FTC. Finally, the Circuit Court vigorously upheld the idea that even literal truthfulness of statement cannot protect an advertisement if it is misleading. A statement may be deceptive even if the constituent words may be literally or technically construed so as not to constitute a misrepresentation.[44]

In a 1981 deceptive advertising case, the Federal Trade Commission pursued Reader's Digest Association, claiming that a sweepstakes mail solicitation campaign was unfair and deceptive. The solicitation involved a direct mass mailing, "promising money or merchandize to a small percentage of those who returned the sweepstakes entry forms." The United States Court of Appeals, Third Circuit, ruled that Reader's Digest had violated an earlier consent order promising to cease distributing confusing simulated checks. The court assessed Reader's Digest a whopping $1.75 million penalty for violation of the consent order.[45]

Television Ad Mock–Ups

To what extent can "reality" be suspended during the filming of a television commercial without producing an ad that improperly misleads the public? Products such as butter and ice cream that would melt under hot studio lights must be adulterated in some fashion in order to be filmed; new cars are parked under powerful floodlights to accentuate the sheen of their finishes, and the complexions of many of those breathtakingly beautiful models shown in cosmetic ads have been artfully retouched in the photo lab. Do such common practices actually deceive consumers and cause them to buy goods they would otherwise refuse to purchase?

The FTC attempted to establish a standard of non-deception in this field of television advertising during the early 1960s that is not likely to be recorded in the annals of history as one of

[43] Kalwajtys v. Federal Trade Commission, 237 F.2d 654, 655–656 (7th Cir.1956).

[44] 237 F.2d 654, 656 (7th Cir.1956).

[45] United States v. Reader's Digest Association, Inc., 662 F.2d 955 (3d Cir.1981), 7 Med.L.Rptr. 1921, 1924.

bureaucracy's finest hours. The FTC's great "sandpaper caper" dragged on for five years at substantial expense to the American taxpayer and only minimal benefit to the American consumer.[46]

An aerosol shaving cream client, Rapid Shave, had commissioned the Ted Bates advertising agency to produce a series of television commercials dramatizing the superior qualities of their product. Realizing that all shaving creams were pretty much alike, some creative genius at the agency came up with the idea of demonstrating on camera that Rapid Shave could not only soften tough beards but even soften the roughest type of sandpaper. Everyone bought the concept but when the agency tried to film the commercial, the shaving cream dampened the sandpaper, causing it to rip as it was being shaved. Rather than abandon such a brilliant idea, the agency decided instead to coat a piece of plastic with sand to make it look like sandpaper, and use this plastic replica in these ads.

As the "sandpaper" was shown being shaved in the commercial, an announcer intoned, "To prove RAPID SHAVE'S super-moisturizing power, we put it right from the can onto this tough dry sandpaper. It was applied ＊ ＊ ＊ soak ＊ ＊ ＊ and off in a stroke." [47]

Believing that few consumers would rush out to buy Rapid Shave simply to shave their sandpaper, Colgate–Palmolive, the manufacturer of Rapid Shave, was shocked when the FTC issued a complaint contending that this ad constituted a deceptive advertising practice. However, when the FTC's hearing examiner discovered that sandpaper actually could be shaved with Rapid Shave after it had soaked to the paper for an hour or so, he dismissed the complaint.[48]

Unwilling to allow the public to be led astray by this unscrupulous sandpaper hoax, the FTC reversed its examiner's finding and issued a cease-and-desist order declaring that all depictions in advertisements that were not "accurate representations were illegal."

But when a Court of Appeals considered the FTC order, it expressed concern that the flexible Article 5 of the FTC Act was being used in a new area. Article 5 provides:

[46] Federal Trade Commission v. Colgate-Palmolive Co., 380 U.S. 374, 85 S.Ct. 1035 (1965). For an amusing account of this case, see Daniel Seligman, "The Great Sandpaper Shave: A Real-Life Story of Truth in Advertising," Fortune (Dec.1964) pp. 131–133ff.

[47] 380 U.S. 374, 376, 85 S.Ct. 1035, 1038 (1965).

[48] 380 U.S. 374, 376–377, 85 S.Ct. 1035, 1038 (1965).

Unfair methods of competition in commerce, and unfair or deceptive acts or practices in commerce, are declared unlawful.[49]

The Circuit Court of Appeals concluded that the FTC was going too far in declaring all mock-ups illegal. The court declared, "where the only untruth is that the substance [the viewer] sees on the screen is artificial, and the visual appearance is otherwise a correct and accurate representation of the product itself, he is not injured.[50]

In May, 1963, the Commission issued its final order that Colgate and Bates cease and desist from: [51]

Unfairly or deceptively advertising any * * * product by presenting a test, experiment or demonstration that (1) is represented to the public as actual proof of a claim made for the product which is material to inducing a sale, and (2) is not in fact a genuine test, experiment or demonstration being conducted as represented and does not in fact constitute actual proof of the claim * * *.

Although Colgate and Bates also challenged the 1963 FTC order, the Supreme Court of the United States made the order stick. Note that the use of *all* mock-ups in televised commercials was not forbidden as deceptive. The Court found that "the undisclosed use of plexiglas" in the Rapid Shave commercials was "a material deceptive practice." But there is a fine line between the forbidden kind of "demonstration" in the Rapid Shave commercial and an acceptable "commercial which extolled the goodness of ice cream while giving viewers a picture of a scoop of mashed potatoes appearing to be ice cream." The Court tried to draw such a distinction, stating: [52]

In the ice cream case the mashed potato prop is not being used for additional proof of the product claim, while the purpose of the Rapid Shave commercial is to give the viewer objective proof of the claims made. If in the ice cream hypothetical the focus of the commercial becomes the undisclosed potato prop and the viewer is invited,

[49] 380 U.S. 374, 376n, 85 S.Ct. 1035, 1038n, quoting 38 Stat. 719, as amended, 52 Stat. 111, 15 U.S.C.A. § 45(a)(1).

[50] 380 U.S. 374, 381, 85 S.Ct. 1035, 1040 (1968), quoting 310 F.2d 89, 94 (1st Cir. 1962).

[51] 380 U.S. 374, 382, 85 S.Ct. 1035, 1041 (1965), quoting Colgate Palmolive Co., No. 7736, FTC May 7, 1963. This clause was added by the FTC for the benefit of Ted Bates & Co., because advertising agencies do not always have all the information about a product that a manufacturer has. The clause said, " 'provided, however, that respondent [Bates] neither knew nor had reason to know that the product, article or substance used in the test, experiment, or demonstration was a mock-up or a prop.' "

[52] 380 U.S. 374, 390, 85 S.Ct. 1035, 1045, 1047 (1965).

explicitly or by implication, to see for himself the truth of the claims about the ice cream's rich texture and full color, and perhaps compare it to a "rival product," then the commercial has become similar * * * [to the Rapid Shave commercial.] Clearly, however, a commercial which depicts happy actors delightedly eating ice cream that is in fact mashed potatoes or drinking a product appearing to be coffee but which is in fact some other substance is not covered by the present order.

Marbles In The Soup

The Campbell Soup Company, however, slipped over the fine line between "demonstration" and "deception," at least in the eyes of the Federal Trade Commission. Campbell Soup consented to stop the practice of putting marbles in bowls of soup to force solid chunks of meat and vegetables to the surface, making them visible to viewers of television ads.[53]

SEC. 63. CORRECTIVE ADVERTISING ORDERS OF THE FTC

The Federal Trade Commission has attempted to enforce truth in advertising by requiring some advertisers to correct past misstatements.

After being roughly handled by critics ranging from Ralph Nader to the American Bar Association during the late 1960s, the Federal Trade Commission of the 1970s became much more active than in previous years. Symptomatic of this increased activity was an FTC complaint against Standard Oil Company of California. The company's advertising had been claiming that its Chevron gasoline, thanks to an additive called F–310, could significantly decrease harmful substances in auto exhaust emissions, thus helping to reduce air pollution. This sort of "we're good for the environment" advertising has been termed "Eco-Porn" (ecological pornography) by cynical critics of advertising.

The FTC issued a cease and desist order to halt allegedly misleading F–310 advertising claims, but the matter did not end there. The FTC also demanded that the Standard Oil Company run "corrective" ads for a year, disclosing that its earlier advertising campaign had included false and deceptive statements. The Commission said that 25 per cent of the advertising for Chevron—either published space or broadcast time—should be devoted to

---

[53] Campbell Soup Co., 3 Trade Reg.Rep. Para. 19,261 (FTC, 1970); the Campbell Soup Co. consented to stop the practice of putting marbles in soup bowls to force solid chunks of meat and vegetables to the surface of the soup so as to be visible to viewers of television ads.

making "affirmative disclosures" about the earlier advertising.[54] An FTC administrative judge dismissed charges against the F–310 ads, but he was then overruled by the Commission. The FTC then re-instituted its cease-and-desist order. The U.S. Court of Appeals for the Ninth Circuit held that the FTC was correct in concluding that the F–310 commercials had a tendency to mislead consumers. However, the FTC was held to have erred in having issued an order against Standard Oil Company asking the company to refrain from making certain representations about F–310 "or any other product in commerce" unless every statement is true and completely substantiated. The court said that order was too broad, and had to be narrowed to deal only with gasoline additive F–310.[55]

Other corporate defendants in cases where the FTC has sought to obtain corrective advertising include Coca Cola, for claims made about nutrient and vitamin content of its Hi-C fruit drinks,[56] and ITT Continental Baking Company, for ads implying that eating Profile Bread could help people to lose weight. The FTC charged that Profile was different from other bread only in being more thinly sliced, meaning that there were seven fewer calories per slice. ITT Continental Baking Company consented to a cease and desist order which does two things: first, it prohibits all further claims of weight-reducing attributes for Profile Bread, and second, the company has to devote 25 per cent of its Profile advertising for one year to disclosing that the bread is not effective for weight reduction.[57]

Such orders, however, were mere palliatives, and did nothing to solve the FTC's great problems with delays. Delays of from three to five years between issuance of an FTC complaint and final issuance of a cease and desist order were commonplace. Meanwhile, the advertiser was free to continue his advertising campaign: "By the time the order has become final, the particular campaign has probably been squeezed dry, if not already discarded in favor of a fresh one." [58]

---

[54] 3 Trade Reg.Rep.Para. 19,420 (FTC Complaint issued, Dec. 29, 1970). See also William F. Lemke, Jr., "Souped Up Affirmative Disclosure Orders of the Federal Trade Commission," 4 University of Michigan Journal of Law Reform (Winter, 1970) pp. 180–181; Note, " 'Corrective Advertising' Orders of the Federal Trade Commission," 85 Harvard Law Review (December, 1971) pp. 477–478.

[55] Standard Oil Co. of California v. FTC, 577 F.2d 653, 658 (9th Cir.1978).

[56] 3 Trade Reg.Rep. Para. 19,351 (FTC, 1970).

[57] 3 Trade Reg.Rep. Para. 19,780 (FTC, Aug. 17, 1971); Note, " 'Corrective Advertising' Orders of the Federal Trade Commission," 85 Harvard Law Review (December, 1971), p. 478.

[58] Note, "Corrective Advertising' Orders of the Federal Trade Commission," 85 Harvard Law Review (December, 1971), pp. 482–483.

The FTC—as if to confound some of its earlier critics—showed increasing willingness to move against advertising campaigns by big-name firms or products. "Listerine Antiseptic Mouthwash," a product of the Warner-Lambert Company had advertised its product for years as preventing or alleviating the common cold. The FTC ordered in 1972 that Warner-Lambert disclose in future advertisements that: "Contrary to prior advertising, Listerine will not help prevent colds or sore throats or lessen their severity." Hearing the case on appeal, the Court of Appeals for the Fifth Circuit affirmed the order, but dropped the phrase "Contrary to Prior Advertising." [59] Writing for the court in 1977, Circuit Judge J. Skelly Wright found persuasive scientific testimony that gargling Listerine could not help a sore throat because its active ingredients could not penetrate tissue cells to reach viruses.[60] "[T]he Commission found that the ability of Listerine to kill germs by millions on contact is of no medical significance in the treatment of colds or sore throats. Expert testimony showed the bacteria in the oral cavity, the 'germs' which Listerine purports to kill, do not cause colds and play no role in cold symptoms." In this case the Warner-Lambert Company was not playing for small monetary stakes. The FTC required the corrective advertising statement to appear in Listerine advertising until about $10 million had been spent on touting the mouthwash.

The Warner-Lambert Company also played for high legal stakes challenging the very authority of the FTC to issue "corrective advertising" orders. The Commission contended, on the other hand, that the affirmative disclosure that Listerine will not prevent colds or lessen their severity is needed to give effect to a cease and desist order which would remove the misleading claim from the mouthwash's ads.[61]

The Court of Appeals upheld the FTC's order against Listerine, approving the Commission's standard for imposing corrective advertising. The FTC standard said if a deceptive advertisement played a substantial role in creating or reinforcing "in the public's mind a false and material belief which lives on after the false advertising ceases," then there is clear harm to competitors and to the consuming public. Since merely ceasing the ad cannot avert injury to the public, the FTC said it could require corrective ads: "affirmative action designed to terminate the otherwise continuing ill effects of the advertisement." [62]

[59] Warner-Lambert Co. v. FTC, 562 F.2d 749, 762 (D.C.Cir.1977).

[60] Ibid., p. 754.

[61] Ibid., p. 756.

[62] Ibid., p. 762.

Comparative Advertising

People reading or viewing advertising sometimes see claims made that Product A is "better," "more effective," etc. than Product B. This is what is known as "comparative advertising" and has been encouraged by the Federal Trade Commission in the belief that this will assist consumers in getting more needed information about products. This comparative advertising, however, must be susceptible of substantiation; false and misleading comparative statements will draw legal consequences.

For example, consider American Home Products [makers of Anacin] v. Johnson and Johnson [makers of Tylenol]. Anacin ads based on the theme "Your Body Knows" contended that Anacin was superior to Tylenol, that it was more effective in reducing inflammation, and that it worked faster than Tylenol. Johnson and Johnson [Tylenol] complained to the three television networks that the Anacin advertising was deceptive and misleading. American Home Products [Anacin] countered by suing Johnson and Johnson, claiming that the makers of Tylenol violated the Lanham Trademark Act by disparaging a competitor's product,[63] and seeking an injunction against the Tylenol folks.[64]

This lawsuit backfired, however, because a federal district court dismissed the American Home Products [Anacin] suit and instead slapped a permanent injunction on American Home Products forbidding publishing of a misleading advertisement.[65]

In a comparative advertising case that involved both advertising regulation and copyright law, Triangle Publications—publishers of *TV Guide* magazine—sued Knight-Ridder Newspapers, publishers of *The Miami Herald*. *The Herald* developed a new supplement for its Sunday edition; a guide to television programs. *The Herald* began a campaign of newspaper and television ads late in 1977, promoting its own new TV listing supplement. For example, one such ad used a "Goldilocks and the Three Bears" theme, emphasizing that *The Herald*'s supplement was bigger than *TV Guide* and smaller than another magazine * * * and therefore presumably "just right."

The *TV Guide* complaint stemmed from *The Miami Herald*'s use of a photograph of a copyrighted *TV Guide* cover in a *Herald* promotional ad. Even though it was held that the defendant *Miami Herald* had exceeded "fair use"—see Section 82 of Chapter

---

[63] Lanham Trademark Act, 44 Fed.Reg. 4738 § 43(a), cited in DeVore and Sack, op. cit., p. 475.

[64] American Home Products Corp. v. Johnson and Johnson, 436 F.Supp. 785 (S.D. N.Y.1977), affirmed 577 F.2d 160 (2d Cir.1978).

[65] Ibid.

14, discussing fair use in copyright law. Ultimately, it was held that *The Herald*'s use of the *TV Guide* cover in the context of a truthful comparative advertisement was indeed a fair use.[66]

Advertising Substantiation

Since the early 1970s, the FTC has set down requirements that advertisers keep available proof—"substantiation," in FTC terminology—to back up their claims. At the start of its substantiation efforts, the Commission demanded of entire industries—e.g. soap and detergents, air conditioners, deodorant manufacturers—that they come forward to back up their claims. An early case in the substantiation area was the FTC proceeding, In re Pfizer, Inc., decided in 1972. Pfizer, a chemical/drug manufacturing concern, had advertised its "Un-Burn" product with claims that its application would stop the discomfort of sunburn by tuning out nerve endings. The FTC told Pfizer that unless it could prove such a claim, that would be considered an unfair (and therefore illegal) trade practice. That meant an advertiser should have "a reasonable basis [for its claims] before disseminating an ad."[67] As Associate Director for Advertising Practices Wallace S. Snyder wrote in 1984, " * * * ads for objective claims imply that the advertiser has a prior reasonable basis for making the claim. In light of the implied representation of substantiation, therefore, a performance claim that lacks a reasonable basis is deceptive."[68]

Growth in State Regulation of Advertising

In the 1980s, a time in which "deregulation" was a major theme of the Reagan Administration, one effect was a continued scaling back of the aggressiveness of the nation's prime governmental regulator of advertising, the Federal Trade Commission. But from the mid–1980s on, occasional comments were heard from leaders in the advertising business to the effect that deregulation had its problems, too. Although "getting government off the back of business and the public" was good for political mileage, when FTC regulation diminished, state regulatory efforts to some extent moved into the void. Perhaps it might be said that regulators, like nature, abhor a vacuum.

[66] Triangle Publications, Inc. v. Knight-Ridder Newspapers, Inc., 626 F.2d 1171 (5th Cir.1980), affirming 445 F.Supp. 875 (S.D.Fla.1978), 3 Med.L.Rptr. 2086; see also DeVore and Sack, op. cit., p. 476.

[67] Wallace S. Snyder, "Advertising Substantiation Program," in Christopher Smith and Christian S. White, chairmen, The FTC 1984 (New York: Practising Law Institute, 1984), p. 121; In re Pfizer, Inc., 81 FTC 23 (1981).

[68] Snyder, loc. cit., citing General Dynamics Corp., 82 FTC 488 (1973), and also Firestone Tire & Rubber Co., 81 FTC 398 (1972), affirmed 481 F.2d 246 (6th Cir. 1972), certiorari denied 414 U.S. 1112, 94 S.Ct. 841 (1973).

Advertising executives have reason to worry as state ad regulation becomes more insistent. Whatever their feelings about the FTC, state-to-state regulatory differences threaten to assemble a crazy-quilt pattern of regulations.

Part of the rise of more aggressive state regulation of advertising may be found in the National Association of Attorneys' General. In February, 1988, Daniel Oliver, then chairman of the Federal Trade Commission, expressed some doubts about the states' consumer-protection, saying the state attorneys general were exceeding their authority. Oliver added, "Obviously, deregulation gives the opportunity for the most restrictive of attorneys general to bring cases that will have national effect, and that's not what the American consumer needs." [69]

The New York Times reported that attorneys general of New York, Texas, California, Missouri, Kansas, Illinois, Minnesota and Wisconsin created a study group to look into consumer complaints about airline fares. "The group reported last fall that airline advertising was deceptive and that it amounted to a 'bait-and-switch' practice," and later distributed enforcement guidelines on false advertising. [70]

One consumer advocate even told The Times that many activists now work with state attorneys general, getting action to resolve complaints also filed—evidently with little result—with Federal agencies. [71]

SEC. 64. OTHER FEDERAL ADMINISTRATIVE CONTROLS

In addition to the Federal Trade Commission, many other federal agencies—including the Food and Drug Administration, the Federal Communications Commission, and the United States Postal Service—exert controls over advertising in interstate commerce.

Although of paramount importance as a control over advertising, the FTC does not stand alone among federal agencies in its fight against suspect advertising. Federal agencies which have powers over advertising include:

(1) The Food and Drug Administration

(2) The United States Postal Service

(3) The Securities and Exchange Commission

[69] M.D. Hinds, "States Are Taking Lead on Consumer Protection," The New York Times, Feb. 8, 1988, p. 12.

[70] Ibid.

[71] Ibid.

(4) The Alcohol and Tobacco Tax Division of the Internal Revenue Service

Such a list by no means exhausts the number of federal agencies which, tangentially at least, can exert some form of control over advertising. Bodies such as the Civil Aeronautics Board and perhaps the Interstate Commerce Commission and the Federal Power Commission have power to curtail advertising abuses connected with matters under each agency's jurisdiction.[72]

1. Food and Drug Administration

The Food and Drug Administration's (FDA) activities in controlling labelling and misbranding overlap the powers of the FTC to a considerable degree. The Pure Food and Drug Act gives the FDA jurisdiction over misbranding and mislabeling of foods, drugs, and cosmetics.[73] The FTC, however, was likewise given jurisdiction over foods, drugs, and cosmetics by the Wheeler-Act Amendment.[74] The FTC and the FDA have agreed upon a division of labor whereby FTC concentrates on false advertising and the FDA focuses attention on false labelling.[75] However, this division of labor is quite inexact. Pamphlets or literature distributed with a product have been held to be "labels" for purposes of FDA enforcement.[76]

2. The U.S. Postal Service

Postal controls over advertising can be severe. Congress was provided with lawmaking power to operate the postal system under Article I, Section 8 of the Constitution. This power was long delegated by Congress to a Postmaster General and his Post Office Department. It has long been established that the mails could not be used to carry things which, in the judgment of Congress, were socially harmful.[77] The Postmaster General had the power to exclude articles or substances which Congress has proscribed as non-mailable. With the passage of the Postal Reor-

---

[72] See Note, "The Regulation of Advertising," Columbia Law Review Vol. 56:7 (Nov. 1956) pp. 1019–1111, at p. 1054, citing 24 Stat. 378 (1887), 49 U.S.C.A. § 1 (ICC); 41 Stat. 1063 (1920), 16 U.S.C.A. § 791(a) (FTC); 52 Stat. 1003 (1938), as amended, 49 U.S.C.A. § 491.

[73] 52 Stat. 1040 (1938), 21 U.S.C.A. § 301.

[74] See "The Wheeler Lea Amendment" to the Federal Trade Commission Act, 52 Stat. 111 (1938), as amended, 15 U.S.C.A. § 45(a)(1).

[75] See, for example, 2 CCH Trade Reg.Rep. (10th ed.), Paragraph 8540, p. 17,081 (1954).

[76] See United States v. Kordel, 164 F.2d 913 (7th Cir.1947); United States v. Article of Device Labeled in Part "110 V Vapozone," 194 F.Supp. 332 (N.D.Cal. 1961).

[77] See, for example, early federal tax laws on obscenity discussed in Chapter 11, or see Public Clearing House v. Coyne, 194 U.S. 497, 24 S.Ct. 789 (1904).

ganization Act of 1970, the Post Office Department was abolished as a Cabinet-level agency, and was replaced by the United States Postal Service, a subdivision of the Executive branch.[78]

Perhaps the Postal Service's greatest deterrent to false advertising is contained in the power to halt delivery of materials suspected of being designed to defraud mail recipients.[79] The Postal Service can order nondelivery of mail, and can impound suspected mail matter.[80]

The administrative fraud order is not the only kind of mail fraud action available to the Postal Service. Instead of administrative procedure through the Service, a *criminal* mail fraud case may be started. Criminal cases are prosecuted by a U.S. attorney in a United States District Court. Conviction under the federal mail fraud statute can result in a fine of up to $1,000, imprisonment for up to 5 years, or both.[81] Criminal fraud orders are used when the U.S. Postal Service wishes to operate in a punitive fashion. The administrative fraud orders, on the other hand, are more preventive in nature.

3. The Securities and Exchange Commission

Securities markets are attractive to fast-buck artists, so the sale and publicizing of securities are kept under a watchful governmental eye. Most states have "Blue Sky" laws which enable a state agency to halt the circulation of false or misleading information about the sale of stocks, bonds or the like.[82] The work of the Securities and Exchange Commission, however, is far more important in protecting the public.

After the stock market debacle of 1929, strong regulations were instituted at the federal level to prevent deceptive statements about securities. Taken together, the Securities Act of 1933 [83] and the Securities Exchange Act of 1934 [84] gave the S.E.C. great power over the sale and issuance of securities.

Sale of securities to investors cannot proceed until complete and accurate information has been given, registering the certificates with the S.E.C.[85] A briefer version of the registration statement is used in the "prospectus" circulated among prospec-

[78] 39 U.S.C.A. § 3003.

[79] Ibid.

[80] Ibid.

[81] 18 U.S.C.A. § 1341; Ague, ibid., p. 61.

[82] See Note, "The Regulation of Advertising," Columbia Law Review op. cit. p. 1065.

[83] 48 Stat. 74 (1933), 15 U.S.C.A. § 77.

[84] 48 Stat. 881 (1934), as amended, 15 U.S.C.A. §§ 78(a)–78(jj).

[85] 48 Stat. 77 (1933), as amended, 15 U.S.C.A. § 77(f).

tive investors before the stock or bond can be offered for sale.[86]   If misleading statements have been made about a security "in any material respect" in either registration documents or in the prospectus, the Commission may issue a "stop order" which removes the right to sell the security.[87]   Furthermore, unless a security is properly registered and its prospectus accurate, it is a criminal offense to use the mails to sell it or to advertise it for sale.[88]

An unscrupulous seller of securities has more to fear than just the S.E.C.   Under a provision of the United States Code, a person who has lost money because he was tricked by a misleading prospectus may sue a number of individuals, including persons who signed the S.E.C. registration statement and every director, officer, or partner in the firm issuing the security.[89]

4. The Alcohol and Tobacco Tax Division, Internal Revenue Service

Ever since this nation's unsuccessful experiment with prohibition, the federal government has kept a close eye on liquor advertising.   The responsible agency is the Alcohol and Tobacco Tax Division of the Internal Revenue Service.[90]   Liquor advertising may not include false or misleading statements, and may not disparage competing products.   False statements may include misrepresenting the age of a liquor, or claiming that its alcoholic content is higher than it is in reality.[91]

The Alcohol and Tobacco Tax Division has harsh sanctions at its disposal.   If an advertiser violates a regulation of the Division, he is subject to a fine, and could even be put out of business if his federal liquor license is revoked.[92]

The FTC and other federal agencies by no means provide the whole picture of controls over advertising.   There are many state regulations affecting political advertising and legal advertising by government bodies, but they cannot be treated here.   States also regulate the size and location of billboards, but space does not permit discussion of these statutes.   We now turn to consideration of some of the ways in which states have regulated commercial advertising in the mass media.

[86] 48 Stat. 78 (1933), 15 U.S.C.A. § 77(j).

[87] 48 Stat. 79 (1933), as amended, 15 U.S.C.A. § 77(h)(b) and (d).

[88] 48 Stat. 84 (1933), as amended, 15 U.S.C.A. § 77(e).

[89] 48 Stat. 82 (1933), 15 U.S.C.A. § 77(k).

[90] 49 Stat. 481 (1936), as amended, 27 U.S.C.A. § 205.

[91] Ibid.

[92] Ibid.

SEC. 65.   THE PRINTERS' INK STATUTE

Most states have adopted some version of the model statute which makes fraudulent and misleading advertising a misdemeanor.

One of the best known restraints upon advertising exists at the state level in the various forms of the Printers' Ink statute adopted in 48 states.   *Printer's Ink* magazine, in 1911, advocated that states adopt a model statute which would make false advertising a misdemeanor.   Leaders in the advertising and publishing world realized the difficulty in securing prosecutions for false advertising under the usual state fraud statutes.   Considerable initiative in gaining state enactment of Printers' Ink statutes was generated through the Better Business Bureau and through various advertising clubs and associations.

All but two states—Delaware and New Mexico—have some version of the Printers' Ink statute on their books.[93]   Although the Printers' Ink statute is famous, its fame is greater than its present-day usefulness as a control over advertising.   Relatively few relevant cases exist which indicate that the statute has seen little use in bringing cheating advertisers to court.   The Printers' Ink statute may still be useful as a guideline, or in providing a sanction which local Better Business Bureaus may threaten to invoke even if they seldom do so.[94]

The Printers' Ink statute is aimed and enforced primarily against advertisers rather than against units of the mass media which may have no knowledge that an ad is false or misleading.[95]   This statute was widely adopted, apparently because the common law simply did not provide adequate remedies against false advertising, especially in an economy which has grown so explosively.

The model statute is more flexible than common law prosecutions or fraud statutes.   It does not make *scienter,* guilty knowledge or intent to publish false advertisements an element of the offense.   A number of states, however, have variants of the Printers' Ink statute which are not as comprehensive as the model law in that some element of *scienter* must be shown for conviction.[96]

[93] "Basis for State Laws on Truth in Publishing—The Printers' Ink Model Statute," Reprint, Printers' Ink Publishing Corp., 1959.   Note, "Developments in the Law—Deceptive Advertising," Harvard Law Review, op. cit., p. 1122.

[94] Note, "The Regulation of Advertising," op. cit. p. 1057.

[95] Ibid., pp. 1059–1060;   State v. Beacon Publ. Co., 141 Kan. 734, 42 P.2d 960 (1935).

[96] Note, "Developments in the Law of Deceptive Advertising," Harvard Law Review loc. cit.

A major and obvious difficulty with the Printers' Ink statute—and with all attempts to control advertising—is that concepts of "truth" and "falsity" tend to elude definition. What is misleading, deceptive, or untrue is not defined in the model statute. The problem of making such a determination is left up to the jury.

SEC. 66.   LOTTERIES

Federal and state prohibitions on advertising or publicizing of lotteries are changing as many states have started lotteries as revenue measures.

The theory of laws forbidding advertising or publicizing lotteries is that the public needs to protected from gambling. And in practice, most journalists paid scant attention to the federal and state lottery ad statutes. As a practical matter, church bingo socials or merchants' promotional lottery schemes are rarely prosecuted.

What then, is a lottery? There are three elements:

(1) *Consideration*—This usually means money paid to purchase a lottery ticket or a chance on an auto or some other item which a service organization is offering to raise money. But in some states, consideration need not be money paid. Just the effort required to enter a contest, as going to a store to get an entry blank orhaving to mail a product label, at times has been termed "considertion." [97]

(2) *Prize*—A prize in a lottery is something of value, and generally of greater worth than the consideration invested.

(3) *Chance*—The element of chance—the gambling element—is what led Victorian–era Congressmen to pass the first federal statutes against lotteries in 1890. There can, however, be an element of certainty accompanying the buying of chances in a lottery. For example, if a woman buys a newspaper subscription she is certain to receive the newspaper which includes a chance in a prize contest, but—many years ago—one court termed that promotion a lottery.[98]

In May 1990, a new federal law, the "Charity Games Act", went into effect, permitting print or broadcast promotion and advertising of lotteries conducted by non-profit organizations and of all official state lotteries in any state conducting such lotter-

---

[97] Brooklyn Daily Eagle v. Voorhies, 181 Fed. 579 (C.C.N.Y.1910).

[98] Stevens v. Cincinnati Times–Star Co., 72 Ohio St. 112, 73 N.E. 1058 (1905).

ies.[99] The new law also allows commercial corporations to advertise occasional lotteries as long as such a promotional activity is not related to the corporation's usual course of business.

However, the new federal law still recognizes the right of a state to ban such mail and broadcast advertising for lotteries or other games of chance not legal in that state.

Lotteries are forbidden in the electronic media and in the print media.[1] Section 1307 of the U.S. Code, however, allows a station to broadcast information about lotteries in their service areas—into an adjoining state, for example—as long as the station's own state has a legalized lottery scheme.[2]

Under the First Amendment, meanwhile, it seems that bona fide news about lotteries should not be able to be forbidden, although trying to draw lines separating "news" from "promotion" from "advertising" could get sticky.[3] Into the 1990s, more change is apt to occur in laws regulating lotteries and other gambling, at both state and federal levels. The scramble for added revenue has put many states into authorized lottery schemes, and society seems increasingly tolerant of gambling.

SEC. 67. SELF–REGULATION

Leading communications companies have developed standards to govern their acceptance or rejection of advertising.

Publishers and broadcasters must know the legal status of advertising. If it can be proved that they knew that an advertisement is fraudulent, they may be held responsible for that ad along with the person or company who placed it in the publication. Advertising departments on many newspapers, moreover, often serve as a kind of advertising agency. In this capacity, the advertising staff must be able to give knowledgeable counsel and technical advice to advertisers.

In general, publishers are not liable to the individual consumer for advertising which causes financial loss or other damage unless the publisher or his employees knew that such advertising was fraudulent or misleading. The absence of liability for damage, however, does not mean that there is an absence of responsibility to the public generally and to individual readers of a publication.

[99] Public Law 100–667, 132, amending Sec. 43(a) Title 15 USC 1125(a).

[1] 18 U.S.C.A. §§ 1301–1305.

[2] 18 U.S.C.A. § 1307.

[3] See U.S.C.A. § 1302, n. 15, 1988 pocket part.

The newspaper or broadcast station which permits dishonest or fraudulent advertising hurts its standing with both its readers and its advertisers. Publishers and broadcasters, who perceive psychological and economic advantages in refusing dishonest advertising, also appear to be becoming more cognizant that they have a moral duty to protect the public.

Responsible media units go to great lengths to ensure that advertising which they publish or broadcast is honest. Some newspapers' advertising acceptance statements, such as the one used by the Dallas Morning News, are very specific, spelling out advertisements which will not be accepted for publication. For example, the Dallas Morning News says it will not accept "bait and switch" ads: "Advertisements describing goods not available and not intended to be sold on request, but used as 'bait' to lure customers." Other newspapers provide long lists of ads that are not acceptable; some include fortune tellers, palm readers, and faith healers, along with forbidding publication of ads for illegal or harmful activities or substances.[4]

The Milwaukee Journal and The Milwaukee Sentinel, like The Dallas Morning News, have long been recognized as reputable newspapers with high standards of conduct. Their advertising acceptance guidelines are presented below, with the permission of Journal/Sentinel, Inc., because they are both brief and inclusive.[5]

ADVERTISING GUIDELINES

JOURNAL/SENTINEL INC.

The confidence our readers have in *The Milwaukee Journal* and the *Milwaukee Sentinel* extends to the advertising columns as well as news and editorial. Reader confidence is obviously vital to the success of Journal/Sentinel, Inc. and of economic value to our many advertisers.

Our advertising guidelines, over many years, have helped insure the credibility of our columns, and although specific guidelines are reviewed as new products and services enter the marketplace, the basic concepts remain.

Our policy is to refrain from publishing advertising that is untrue, deceptive or misleading; that makes unfair competitive statements; that violates law or standards of decency; or that is fraudulent.

[4] Advertising Standards of Acceptability in the Dallas Morning News, pamphlet dated August, 1983.

[5] Used by permission. The help of Beverly Klein, Vice President for Advertising, is gratefully acknowledged.

Our paramount concern is reader confidence. We do, based on a combination of past experience, judgement and general community standards, refuse to accept certain types of advertising. We are always willing to review.

As a newspaper, it is our belief that we have a duty to our readers to accept responsible opinion-type advertisements without regard to the editorial positions of either paper. Fear of an idea or thought is inherently inconsistent with the First Amendment. However, we shall not knowingly publish a libelous or defamatory statement or purported fact that cannot be reasonably verified.

Reproduced with the permission of
Journal/Sentinel Inc.

SEC. 68. THE RIGHT TO REFUSE SERVICE

A newspaper or magazine is not a public utility and therefore may choose those with whom it cares to do business.

A newspaper or magazine is a private enterprise and as such may carry on business transactions with whom it pleases. If its managers so desire they may refuse to sell newspapers to individuals or news agents, or to publish news stories about any particular event or on any opinion. By weight of legal authority, a newspaper is not a public utility.

There is pressure to create a "right of access" to advertising if not to the news space of the media. Arguments heard with increasing frequency run something like this:[6]

> The free marketplace of ideas is not working at all well during the latter third of the 20th Century. Competition among newspapers, magazines, and the electronic media is so diminished that only ideas acceptable to the nation's establishment can gain a hearing. Laissez faire in the media has come to mean, as John P. Roche once said in another context, "Every man for himself—as the elephant said, dancing among the chickens." Government has an affirmative obligation to stop the discriminatory refusal of advertisements and notices in publications.

Such arguments, at this writing, have not succeeded. If a change does come which affects the right to refuse advertising, it

---

[6] See, e.g., Jerome A. Barron, "Access to the Press—A New First Amendment Right," Harvard Law Review Vol. 80 (1967), p. 1641; Willard H. Pedrick, "Freedom of the Press and the Law of Libel," Cornell Law Quarterly Vol. 49 (1964) p. 581; Report of the 1968 Biennial Conference of the American Civil Liberties Union, New York, Sept., 1968; Gilbert Cranberg, "New Look at the First Amendment," Saturday Review, Sept. 14, 1968, pp. 136–137; Simon Lazarus, "The Right of Reply," New Republic, Oct. 5, 1968.

would seem that advertising with a political or otherwise socially significant message might first be forced upon publishers before the right to refuse ordinary commercial advertising would be affected. An old but important case decided in 1931 declared:[7]

> The newspaper business is an ordinary business. It is a business essentially private in nature—as private as that of the baker, grocer, or milkman, all of whom perform a service on which, to a greater or less extent, the communities depend, but which bears no such relation to the public as to warrant its inclusion in the category of businesses charged with the public use. If a newspaper were required to accept an advertisement, it could be compelled to publish a news item. If some good lady gave a tea, and submitted to the newspaper a proper account of the tea, and the editor of the newspaper, believing that it had no news value, refused to publish it, she, it seems to us, would have as much right to compel the newspaper to publish the account as would a person engaged in business to compel a newspaper to publish an advertisement of the business that the person is conducting.

> Thus, as a newspaper is strictly a private enterprise, the publishers thereof have a right to publish whatever advertisements they desire and to refuse to publish whatever advertisements they do not desire to publish.

Non-private entities, however—such as transit authorities or state-owned publications—can not refuse advertising with impunity. A California case involved a group called Women for Peace. In 1964, Women for Peace sought to place advertising placards in buses owned by the Alameda-Contra Costa Transit District. The placards said:

> "Mankind must put an end to war or war will put an end to mankind." President John F. Kennedy.

> Write to President Johnson: Negotiate Vietnam. Women for Peace, P.O. Box 944, Berkeley.[8]

The private advertising agency which managed advertising for the transit district rejected the placards. It was declared that "political advertising and advertising on controversial subjects are not acceptable unless approved by the [transit] district, and that

---

[7] Shuck v. Carroll Daily Herald, 215 Iowa 1276, 1281, 247 N.W. 813, 815, 87 A.L.R. 975 (1933). See also Friedenberg v. Times Publishing Co., 170 La. 3, 127 So. 345 (1930); In re Louis Wohl, Inc., 50 F.2d 254 (D.Mich.1931). See also Miami Herald Pub. Co. v. Tornillo, 418 U.S. 241, 94 S.Ct. 2831 (1974).

[8] Wirta v. Alameda-Contra Costa Transit District, 68 Cal.2d 51, 64 Cal.Rptr. 430, 432, 434 P.2d 982, 984 (1967).

advertising objectionable to the district shall be removed
* * *." [9]

After a trial and two appeals, the Women for Peace finally
won their case in 1967 before the California Supreme Court. The
court said that the ad was protected by the First Amendment and
that once a public facility is opened for use of the general public,
arbitrary conditions cannot be imposed upon the use of that
facility.[10]

The California Supreme Court declared.[11]

> We conclude that defendants, having opened a forum
> for the expression of ideas by providing facilities for
> advertisements on its buses, cannot for reasons of admin-
> istrative convenience decline to accept advertising expres-
> sing opinions and beliefs within the ambit of First
> Amendment protection.

In 1969, a college newspaper was told it could not refuse
political advertising. A number of non-students wished to place
political ads in the *Royal Purple,* the offical campus newspaper at
Wisconsin State University-Whitewater. Their requests for advertising space were denied on the ground that the newspaper had a
policy against accepting "editorial advertisements"—those advertisements expressing political views. Refusal of the advertisements led to suits charging that the plaintiffs' First and Fourteenth Amendment rights had been violated by Wisconsin, acting
through the regents of the state colleges, and by the university
itself. This refusal, it was claimed, amounted to "state action"
because the board of regents—a state agency—had delegated poli-
cy-setting powers to the president of the university and to the
student publications board.[12]

U.S. District Judge James Doyle ruled that the *Royal Purple*
should have accepted the advertisements: [13]

> Defendant's acceptance of commercial advertisements
> and of those public service advertisements that do not
> "attack an institution, group, person or product" and
> their rejection of editorial advertisements constitutes an
> impermissible form of censorship.

[9] Ibid.

[10] 68 Cal.2d 51, 64 Cal.Rptr. 430, 433, 434 P.2d 982, 985 (1967), citing Danskin v.
San Diego Unified School District, 28 Cal.2d 536, 171 P.2d 885 (1946).

[11] 68 Cal.2d 51, 64 Cal.Rptr. 430, 432, 434 P.2d 982, 984 (1967).

[12] Lee v. Board of Regents of State Colleges, 306 F.Supp. 1097 (W.D.Wis.1969).

[13] Ibid., 1101, affirmed 441 F.2d 1257 (7th Cir.1971).

There can be no doubt that defendants' restrictive advertising policy—a policy enforced under color of state law—is a denial of free speech and expression.

En route to that holding Judge Doyle found that the *Royal Purple* was indeed a newspaper, and that letters to the editor—even if accepted for publication—would not be a proper substitute for a paid advertisement. Advertisements offered certain advantages in presentation, including options for large type, photographic display, and repeated publication as "some of the modes of expression available in an editorial advertisement that might not be available in a letter to the editor." [14]

Note that the theme of state action runs through all of the above cases in which courts have listened with sympathy to demands that advertisements be accepted. That is, the agency refusing to accept an advertisement was either a transit authority funded by public money [15] or an official campus newspaper on a tax-supported campus which had advertising acceptance rules set up under delegated state authority.[16] In the absence of a strong showing of state action, however, the general rule is that advertisements may be refused by the print media.

One possible exception to that rule—and a rare and hard to prove exception at that—might be if a newspaper, for example, refused ads in some sort of an anticompetitive scheme to injure another business. One example is offered by Home Placement Service v. Providence Journal Company, in 1982. The U.S. Court of Appeal for the First Circuit ruled that a newspaper's refusal to accept classified ads from a rental referral business was held to violate antitrust provisions of the Sherman Act.

This was a special case, however. On the one hand, it is understandable why the Providence Journal didn't want to carry Homefinders' ads. Homefinders would advertise a property with an untraceable location, and then—once someone called the phone number listed in the ad—the person was told that the listed property was " 'no longer available, but if the prospective tenant would merely come to Homefinders' office and pay the fee of $20, other listings would be made available.' " On the other hand, the newspaper's refusal of the ads appeared a bit strange because The Providence Journal, the only metro daily in the area, itself served as a rental referral agency through its advertising columns. The Court of Appeal said that the evidence in the case " * * *

---

[14] Ibid., p. 1101.

[15] Cf. Kissinger v. New York City Transit Authority, 274 F.Supp. 438, 441 (S.D. N.Y.1967); Wirta v. Alameda-Contra Costa Transit District, 68 Cal.2d 51, 64 Cal. Rptr. 430, 432, 434 P.2d 982, 984 (1967).

[16] Lee v. Board of Regents of State Colleges, 441 F.2d 1257 (7th Cir.1971), affirming 306 F.Supp. 1097 (W.D.Wis.1969).

indicates the simplest form of attempted strangulation of a competitor by refusal to deal." The Court said this conduct violated both Sections 1 and 2 of the Sherman Act.[17]

One other situation where an ad refusal might bring legal trouble involves contract law. If a newspaper has entered into a contract to carry advertising, and then refuses to do so, that could be a problem. That's the message from a 1982 Indiana case, Herald-Telephone v. Fatouros, a case involving a political ad which was accepted—as was payment for the ad—and then the message was refused because it might be "inflammatory." The Indiana Court of Appeals, Fourth District, said: [18]

> * * * we agree * * * that a newspaper has a right to publish or reject advertising as its judgment dictates. However, once a newspaper forms a contract to publish an advertisement, it has given up the right to publish or not publish the ad unless that right is specifically reserved or an equitable defense to [refusing] publication exists.

In more usual cases, however, the media are free to refuse ads, as in Person v. New York Post Corp., 1977. The plaintiff asked a court order to prevent the newspaper from refusing to run a "tombstone" ad on a financial matter. Instead, the federal district court declared that it is a newspaper's prerogative to accept or reject ads as it sees fit.[19]

The *Resident Participation* Case

One of the most eloquent pleas for forced access to advertising space can be found in an air pollution dispute in Denver, Colorado. The setting in Denver should be idyllic—a city ringed by the magnificent Rocky Mountains, close to some of the American continent's most spectacular scenery. But not all was well in Denver during the late 1960's: on some days, Denver residents suffered from an eyeburning smog which would seem more at home in Los Angeles, California, roughly 950 miles away.

When word got out that Pepcol, Inc.—a subsidiary of the giant conglomerate Beatrice Foods, Inc.—was going to build a rendering plant within the city limits of Denver, a protest resulted. A citizens group calling itself Resident Participation of Denver,

[17] Home Placement Service, Inc. v. Providence Journal Co., 682 F.2d 274, 276, 279 (1st Cir.1982), 8 Med.L.Rptr. 1881, 1884, reversed in part at 739 F.2d 671 (1st Cir.1984). Although lawyers' fees ran to over $35,000, the *treble damage* award was a mere $3.

[18] Herald Telephone v. Fatouros, 431 N.E.2d 171 (Ind.App. 4th Dist.1982), 8 Med. L.Rptr. 1230m, 1231.

[19] Person v. New York Post Corporation, 427 F.Supp. 1297 (E.D.N.Y.1977), affirmed 573 F.2d 1294 (2d Cir.1977).

spurred by visions of a malodorous plant processing "dead animals, guts, and blood" and producing "disgusting" garbage,[20] attempted to place advertisements in Denver's two competing daily newspapers, the *Denver Post* and the *Rocky Mountain News*. The newspapers rejected the ads on the ground that the proposed wording called for a boycott of Beatrice Foods products, and boycott advertising is forbidden by Colorado statute.[21]

Undaunted, the Resident Participation group re-worded its advertising copy to avoid any reference to boycott, but listed each Beatrice Foods products as Meadow Gold milk, cheese, and ice cream, and Zooper Dooper fruit drinks and ice cream. The advertisement, as rewritten, included suggested letters: readers were to be asked to clip out, sign, and mail the letters, thereby protesting the rendering plant project to city and state officials. Both newspapers again refused to print the advertisements.[22]

Resident Participation then sought a court order under the First Amendment to force the newspapers to punish the advertisements. The newspapers countered with arguments that the First Amendment forbids only official abridgments of free speech and press, not merely private ones, and this was an argument the ecology group was unable to overcome. Nevertheless, Resident Participation argued strenuously to have the court consider the newspapers refusals to publish the advertisements as a kind of official or state action. The citizens' group argued:[23]

> * * * state action is present in this case because defendant newspapers enjoy a special relationship with the State of Colorado and City of Denver which involves those governments in the newspaper business and because the papers "enjoy monopoly control in an area of vital public concern."

Resident Participation also contended that the state and city are involved in the newspaper business because of sections of the Colorado Revised Statutes which require that legal notices be published in newspapers of general circulation.[24] Other provisions which were said to make newspapers a public business included a statute which exempts editors and reporters from jury service,[25]

---

[20] Plaintiffs Exhibit "A," Resident Participation, Inc. Newsletter quoted in brief in Resident Participation of Denver, Inc. v. Love, 322 F.Supp. 1100 (D.Colo.1971). The authors wish to thank Thomas A Stacey, graduate student in journalism at the University of Wisconsin-Madison, for his assistance.

[21] Colo.Rev.Stat.Ann. § 80–11–12.

[22] Resident Participation of Denver, Inc. v. Love, 322 F.Supp. 1100, 1101 (D.Colo. 1971).

[23] Ibid., 1102.

[24] Colorado Rev.Stat.Ann. §§ 49–10–3, 49–8–1, 49–22–5, 49–22–11 (1963).

[25] Colo.Rev.Stat.Ann. § 7801–3 (1963).

and a Denver ordinance which allows newspaper vending machines on public property, including sidewalks.[26]

A three-judge federal district court rejected these arguments with dispatch, saying it could find nothing "remotely suggesting that these measures are sufficient to justify labeling the newspapers conduct state action."[27]   Chief Circuit Judge Alfred A. Arraj said that where private conduct is concerned, there has to be great justification for concluding that the private party serves as an alter ego for government, either because officialdom has in some important way become involved with the private party, or because the private party performs a function of a governmental nature.

As the Resident Participation case showed, general circulation newspapers cannot be compelled to accept and publish controversial advertisements.   Some newspapers, however, publish controversial political advertisements as a matter of responsibility to the public.   In the spring of 1972, for example, The New York Times published two advertisements which drew considerable protest from readers.   The first advertisement, signed by a group of citizens calling themselves "The National Committee for Impeachment," demanded the removal from office of President Richard M. Nixon, alleging violations of law and the Constitution in his prosecution of the Vietnam war.   A second advertisement, an open letter to President Nixon signed by Norman F. Dacey, inveighed against the President for a Middle East policy termed "blind support" for Israel.[28]

Readers responded to these advertisements with hundreds of letters, and many of those letters criticized *The Times* for publishing such emotionally loaded and politically heated ads, opinions with which neither *The Times*—nor a large part of its readership agreed.   That criticism of *The Times* was expressed so frequently and with such obvious sincerity that *The Times* published an editorial, "Freedom to Advertise," stating the principles which guide The Times in accepting controversial advertising on topics of political or social importance.   The editorial declared:[29]

* * *

As we see it, the issue goes to the very heart of the freedom and responsibility of the press. *The Times* believes it has an obligation to afford maximum reasonable opportunity to the public to express its views, however much opposed to our own, through various outlets in this newspaper including the advertising columns.

[26] Denver Municipal Code, §§ 339G, 334.1–2.

[27] 322 F.Supp. 1100, 1103 (D.C.Colo.1971).

[28] See New York Times, May 31 and June 6, 1972.

[29] New York Times, June 16, 1972.   © 1972 by The New York Times Company.

It has long been held by American courts that a newspaper or magazine is a private enterprise, and that it may choose to omit certain news items or to refuse certain advertising. In recent years, and in part because of the thrust given to a "new right of access" by Professor Jerome Barron, the old "right to refuse ads" has undergone considerable challenge. Nevertheless, this generalization may still be made: unless the publication or agency which is to carry an advertisement is clearly some sort of a public entity because of some kind of "state action," an advertisement lawfully may be refused.

Take the case of a film exhibitor who was angered because the *Los Angeles Times* altered advertising copy for a movie, The Killing of Sister George, slightly changing a drawing of a female figure and omitting a reference to "deviate sexual conduct". *The Times,* by virtue of its enormous advertising revenues, was said by the film distributor to have attained a "substantial monopoly in Southern California." It was further argued that the *Times's* "semi-monopoly and quasi-public position" amounted to state action. The United States Court of Appeals for the 9th Circuit rejected the film distributors arguments, saying: "Unlike broadcasting, the publication of a newspaper is not a government conferred privilege. As we have said, the press and the government have had a history of disassociation." [30]

The right to refuse ads seems to be holding solidly into the 1990s.

SEC. 69. BROADCAST ADVERTISING

Broadcasters also have the right to refuse to accept advertising messages, except for federal political candidate ads during an election period.

In Columbia Broadcasting System Inc v. Democratic National Committee, the Supreme Court held that radio and television stations are not legally required to broadcast any advertisements they do not want to accept.[31] By a 7–2 vote, the Court recognized a right for broadcasting similar to the print media's "right to refuse service".

This case dealt with the efforts of a political party and an anti-war group to get airtime for their respective viewpoints. Business Executives' Move for a Vietnam Peace (BEM) was the anti-war group that filed a complaint with the FCC alleging that a

[30] Associates & Aldrich Co. v. Times Mirror Co., 440 F.2d 133, 136 (9th Cir.1971); see also Adult Film Ass'n of America v. Times Mirror Co., 3 Med.L.Rptr. 2292, Civil Action No. C217216 (L.A.Cty.Sup.Ct.1978), upholding a newspaper's right to refuse ads.

[31] CBS, Inc. v. Democratic Nat. Committee, 412 U.S. 94, 93 S.Ct. 2080 (1973).

radio station in Washington D.C., WTOP had violated the fairness doctrine by refusing to sell the group time to broadcast a series of one-minute spot announcements against the Vietnam conflict. WYOP refused, saying it already had presented full and fair coverage of all important viewpoints concerning U.S. policy in Southeast Asia.

A few months later, the Democratic National Committee (DNC) sought a declaratory ruling from the FCC on this statement:

> That under the First Amendment . . . and the Communications Act, a broadcaster may not, as a general policy, refuse to sell time to responsible entities . . . for comment on public issues.

The Commission rejected the demands of both DNC and BEM, but the Court of Appeals reversed the FCC, declaring that a flat ban on paid public-issue announcements was "in violation of the First Amendment, at least when other types of paid announcements are accepted." [32]

The Supreme Court, however, upheld the FCC's decision by a margin of 7 to 2. Chief Justice Burger's plurality opinion—he was joined by Justices Rehnquist and Stewart—concluded that broadcast licensees were not common carriers.

He compared a newspaper's right of editorial judgment with that of a broadcast licensee, finding that the broadcaster's degree of freedom was somewhat less extensive than that of the newspaper publisher. Broadcasters are supervised—and periodically licensed—by the FCC which must "oversee without censoring." [33] Even so, the opinion declared, government control over broadcast licensees is not broad enough to transform their stations into "common carriers" or "public utilities", compelled to accept and deliver whatever message any individual might be willing to pay to have transmitted.

Burger wrote,

> For better or worse, editing is what editors are for, and editing is selection and choice of material. That editors—newspaper or broadcast—can and do abuse this power is beyond doubt, but that is not reason to deny the discretion Congress provided. Calculated risks of abuse are taken in order to preserve higher values.

The concurring and dissenting opinions galloped off in several directions. Justice Douglas's concurrence declared that TV and

[32] Business Executives' Move for Vietnam Peace v. FCC; Democratic National Committee v. FCC, 450 F.2d 642 (D.C.Cir.1971) overturning Business Executives, 24 FCC2d 242 (1970) and Democratic National Committee, 25 FCC2d 216 (1970).

[33] 412 U.S. 94, 93 S.Ct. 2080 (1973).

radio stand in the same protected position under the First Amendment as newspapers and magazines. And Douglas, along with Justice Stewart, was highly critical of any claimed "right of access", arguing that if government can *require* publication, then freedom of the press would be lost. Justices Brennan and Marshall dissented from the majority view, contending that if time could not be purchased for the airing of controversial political and social viewpoints, then broadcasting would continue to be filled with nothing but bland, noncontroversial programming.

Based upon this decision, then, a broadcaster has the judicially recognized right to refuse to sell commercial time to anyone except those within that one specific category guaranteed advertising access by Congress; legally qualified candidates for federal elective offices.[34]

Action for Children's Television (ACT), a citizens' group, has been pressuring the FCC since the early 1970s to reduce the amount of commercialism in television programs produced for children. In 1986, the Commission eliminated the commercial guidelines it had established for television broadcast licensees, including limitations on the number of commercial minutes per hour of programs designed for children.[35] ACT challenged this FCC action, and the Court of Appeals sustained the challenge, declaring that the Commission had not presented adequate justification for its assumption that the marketplace would operate to prevent over-commercialization of children's programs.[36]

In October 1988, a consensus children's television advertising bill, reflecting the compromise agreement the NAB had negotiated with various interest groups, was enacted by Congress but vetoed by President Reagan.[37]

[34] Title 47 Section 312(a)(7) provides that station licenses may be revoked for refusing to allow reasonable access or to allow the purchase of reasonable amounts of time by legally qualified candidates for federal elective offices. For a more detailed discussion of this requirement, see chapter 12.

[35] Programming Commercialization Policies, 60 RR2d 526 (1986).

[36] Action for Children's Television v. FCC, 821 F.2d 741 (D.C.Cir.1987). For more than a half century, the National Association of Broadcasters had been actively involved in limiting the amount of commercialization in programs designed for children, working with the networks to voluntarily limit the number of commercial minutes per hour. In 1982, however, the Justice Department decided to bring an antitrust action against the NAB, charging that its commercial codes were in constraint of trade. At that point, the NAB was forced to enter into a consent agreement to abandon all efforts to negotiate for further limitations upon broadcast advertising. See United States v. National Association of Broadcasters, 536 F.Supp. 149 (D.D.C.1982). As a result, the FCC's recission of its commercial time limitations in 1986 left broadcasters free of any regulatory or self regulatory constraints upon commercialization.

[37] "Congress, in Overtime, Passes TVRO, Children's Ad bills," Broadcasting, October 24, 1988, p. 27.

Two years later Congress passed new legislation with many of the same provisions contained in the earlier compromise agreement. This time, however, President Bush's failure to veto the "Children's Television Act" allowed it to become law in October 1990.[38] The Act limits advertising contained in weekday television or cable TV programs intended for children to 10½ minutes per hour, while allowing 12 minutes per hour on the weekend.

In addition, the law also requires broadcasters to meet the educational needs of children or face possible license revocation by the FCC, and establishes a federal endowment to fund the production of educational programs for children. The endowment, to be administered by the National Telecommunications and Information Administration, is scheduled to receive $2 million in 1991 and $4 million in 1992.

At the insistence of Action for Children's Television, the bill also directs the FCC to determine whether certain "super-hero" cartoon strips based on toy characters merchandised by the advertiser constitute "program-length" commercials, and therefore automatically violate the law by exceeding maximum advertising time standards for such programs.

Although the National Association of Broadcasters supported the legislation, its constitutionality has been challenged by the Radio–Television News Directors Association. The RTNDA claims the bill violated the First Amendment rights of broadcasters by requiring them, "to provide programming and supporting advertising material as the federal government demands." [39]

Yet even if the Act does prove to be constitutional, its value in protecting children from the hazards of over-commercialization may turn out to be less significant than hoped. Recent studies of children's viewing behavior have revealed a continuing downward trend in the amount of time spent watching broadcast television each day.[40] These studies do not suggest that children are actually viewing less video entertainment each year, but rather that they are spending more of their time watching rented cassettes on the family VCRs where they can expose themselves to program-length commercials like "The Care Bears Battle the Freeze Machine", "Transformers: The Ultimate Doom" or "Mutant Ninja

[38] *Children's TV Act of 1990*, PL 101–437, 47 U.S.C.A. §§ 303a, 303b, 394. Implimented by the FCC, *In the Matter of Policies and Rules Concerning Children's Television Programming*, 68 RR2d 1615 (1991). See also, "President's Pocket Unveto Allows Children's Bill to Become Law," *Broadcasting*, October 22, 1990, p. 35.

[39] "Media Groups Challenge Kidvid Bill Constitutionality," *Variety* January 28, 1991, p. 44.

[40] See, for example, Nielsen 1990, Report on Television.

Turtles" to their hearts' content without interference from any well-intentioned adult interest group.

SEC. 70.   ADVERTISING AND THE CONSTITUTION

Beginning in 1975, some commercial advertising began to receive protection under the First Amendment.

Commercial speech often is referred to as a stepchild of the First Amendment.   Over the years, commercial speech—or advertising, to use an everyday term—was denied freedoms of speech and press granted to unconventional religious minorities,[41] to persons accused of blasphemy,[42] to free-love advocates,[43] and to persons sued for defaming public officials or public figures.[44] During the 1970s and 1980s, the Supreme Court—however grudgingly and qualifiedly—held that just because a message is disseminated as paid-for advertising does not wipe out all First Amendment protection for that message.[45]   By the early 1990s, however, Supreme Court backing for constitutional support for advertising evidently was backsliding.[46]

Back in 1942, evidently with little reflection or receiving of evidence, the Supreme Court of the United States denied advertising First Amendment protection in Valentine v. Chrestensen.[47]   In 1940, F.J. Chrestensen owned a World War I submarine moored at an East River pier in New York City.   As World War II threatened to engulf the U.S., Chrestensen was trying to make money by charging for tours of a "U–Boat."   New York City officials, however, ordered him not to distribute handbills advertising the submarine.   Chrestensen's handbill listed an admission fee.   New York City Police Commissioner Lewis J. Valentine said that the city's Sanitary Code forbade distributing commercial advertising matter in the streets.[48]

---

[41] Minersville School Dist. v. Gobitis, 310 U.S. 586, 60 S.Ct. 1010 (1940).

[42] Joseph Burstyn, Inc. v. Wilson, 343 U.S. 495, 72 S.Ct. 777 (1952).

[43] Kingsley Intern. Pictures Corp. v. Regents of N.Y.U., 360 U.S. 684, 688–689, 79 S.Ct. 1362, 1365 (1959).

[44] See New York Times Co. v. Sullivan, 376 U.S. 254, 84 S.Ct. 710 (1964) and later cases, including Rosenblatt v. Baer, 383 U.S. 75, 86 S.Ct. 669 (1966); Curtis Pub. Co. v. Butts, Associated Press v. Walker, 388 U.S. 130, 87 S.Ct. 1975 (1967), and St. Amant v. Thompson, 390 U.S. 727, 88 S.Ct. 1323 (1968).

[45] Bigelow v. Virginia, 421 U.S. 809, 95 S.Ct. 2222 (1975); Virginia State Board of Pharmacy v. Virginia Citizens Consumer Council, 425 U.S. 748, 96 S.Ct. 1817 (1976).

[46] See Posadas De Puerto Rico v. Tourism Co., 478 U.S. 328, 106 S.Ct. 2968 (1986); Board of Trustees of the State University of New York v. Fox, 492 U.S. 469, 109 S.Ct. 3028 (1989), and Austin v. Michigan Chamber of Commerce, 494 U.S. 652, 110 S.Ct. 1391 (1990).

[47] 316 U.S. 52, 62 S.Ct. 920 (1942).

[48] Valentine v. Chrestensen, 316 U.S. 52, 54, 62 S.Ct. 920, 921 (1942).

Chrestensen changed his handbill. One side then consisted of a notice about the submarine, but reference to the admission fee was deleted. The other side of the redone handbill was used to protest against city policies he disliked. Police officials then told Chrestensen he could distribute a handbill criticizing the city, but that invitation to visit the submarine was a commercial ad and was not permitted. In 1942, the Supreme Court held unanimously that although streets may be used to communicate information and disseminate opinion, the Constitution does not restrain government from controlling "purely commercial advertising." [49]

The Court's decision in Valentine v. Chrestensen was brief, only five pages in the official *United States Reports.* Mr. Justice Owen J. Roberts' opinion for the Court—which slipped in the virtually unsupported statement that commercial advertising is not entitled to First Amendment protections—ignored a number of relevant cases he might well have cited.[50]

But that's where matters stood; 1942's Valentine v. Chrestensen decision stated the law for some years to come. In 1959, in a now-famous concurring opinion in Cammarano v. United States, Justice William O. Douglas complained that the Chrestensen decision was "casual, almost offhand. And it has not survived reflection." Cammarano, a beer distributor, had tried to deduct, as a business expense, a contribution to a fund used to buy political ads to oppose a ballot measure which would have turned all wine and beer sales over to a state agency. Although he concurred in the decision denying Cammarano the IRS deduction, Justice Douglas wrote: " * * * I find it impossible to say that the owners of the * * * business who were fighting for their lives in opposing these initiative [ballot] measures were not exercising First Amendment rights." [51]

N.Y. Times v. Sullivan (1964) and Advertising

Oddly enough, a "breakthrough" case toward protecting advertising under the Constitution is little thought of as a "commercial speech case." In part, however, that's exactly what the landmark 1964 libel decision of New York Times v. Sullivan was. In that case, the Supreme Court granted First Amendment protection for advertisements which deal with important political or

---

[49] Ibid.

[50] See Mr. Justice William O. Douglas's concurring opinion in Cammarano v. United States, 358 U.S. 498, 513–515, 79 S.Ct. 524, 533–535 (1959), listing two cases prior to the Chrestensen case which approved broad control over commercial advertising: Fifth Avenue Coach Co. v. New York, 221 U.S. 467, 31 S.Ct. 709 (1911), and Packer Corp. v. Utah, 285 U.S. 105, 52 S.Ct. 273 (1932). Justice Douglas noted that in the latter case, no First Amendment issue was raised.

[51] 358 U.S. 498, 79 S.Ct. 524 (1959).

social matters. The *Sullivan* case, discussed fully in libel chapters earlier in this book, carefully distinguished the advertising involved in Valentine v. Chrestensen from the advertising at issue in New York Times v. Sullivan. Libel plaintiff Sullivan's attorneys argued that libelous statements had been published in an advertisement by The New York Times. Therefore, the plaintiff's contention was that "the constitutional guarantees of freedom of speech and of the press are inapplicable * * * at least so far as the Times is concerned, because the allegedly libelous statements were published as part of a paid, 'commercial' advertisement." [52]

The Supreme Court held that such a reliance on the rule Valentine v. Chrestensen was "wholly misplaced." Writing for the *Sullivan* majority, Justice William J. Brennan, Jr. declared: [53]

> The publication here [in Times v. Sullivan] was not a "commercial" advertisement in the sense in which the word was used in *Chrestensen*. It communicated information, expressed opinion, recited grievances, protested claimed abuses, and sought financial support on behalf of a [civil rights] movement whose existence and objectives are matters of the highest public concern. * * * That the Times was paid for publishing the advertisement is as immaterial in this connection as is the fact that newspapers and books are sold. * * * Any other conclusion would discourage newspapers from carrying "editorial advertisements" of this type, and so might shut off an important outlet for the promulgation of information and ideas by persons who do not themselves have access to publishing facilities . . .

What advertising, then, was protected by the First Amendment after New York Times v. Sullivan (1964)? Not all advertising—and especially, not advertising for an illegal activity—the Supreme Court said in Pittsburgh Press Co. v. Pittsburgh Commission on Human Relations (1973). A Pittsburgh ordinance empowered the city's human relations commission to issue cease and desist orders against discriminatory hiring practices. The Pittsburgh Press ran "Help Wanted" ads in columns labeled "Jobs—Male Interest," and "Jobs—Female Interest." The city commission sought a cease and desist order.[54]

Arguing for the Pittsburgh Press, attorneys contended that the order violated the First Amendment because it tampered with the newspaper's editorial judgment in accepting and placing ads.

[52] New York Times Co. v. Sullivan, 376 U.S. 254, 265–266, 84 S.Ct. 710, 718 (1964).

[53] Ibid.

[54] 413 U.S. 376, 377, 93 S.Ct. 2553, 2555 (1973).

Writing for the Court's five-member majority, Justice Lewis Powell disagreed: Discrimination in employment is illegal commercial activity under the city's ordinance. "We have no doubt that a newspaper constitutionally could be forbidden to publish a want ad proposing a sale of narcotics or soliciting prostitutes.[55]

Dissenting in *Pittsburgh Press,* Chief Justice Warren Burger declared that the cease and desist order against the newspaper was in fact a prior restraint on publication.[56]

Bigelow v. Virginia (1975)

It should be emphasized that the Court, in New York Times v. Sullivan, drew a distinction between "commercial advertising" which attempted to sell products or services and other kinds of expression. This distinction, however, was too oversimplified. Some products or services—by their very nature—are matters of public debate or controversy, and advertisements for those products or services may have the characteristics and importance of political speech. A 1975 Virginia case involving advertising about the availability and legality of abortions in New York—the case called Bigelow v. Virginia—showed that "commercial speech" can have some degree of constitutional protection.

Early in 1971, an advertisement was published in The Virginia Weekly, a newspaper focusing its coverage on the University of Virginia. Jeffrey C. Bigelow was managing editor and a director of the newspaper when it published this ad: [57]

"UNWANTED PREGNANCY
LET US HELP YOU
Abortions are now legal in New York
There are no residency requirements.
FOR IMMEDIATE PLACEMENT IN
ACCREDITED HOSPITALS AND
CLINICS AT LOW COST
Contact
WOMAN'S PAVILION
515 Madison Avenue
New York, N.Y. 10022
or call any time
(212) 371–6670 or (212) 371–6550
AVAILABLE 7 DAYS A WEEK
STRICTLY CONFIDENTIAL. We will
make all arrangements for you and help
you with information and counseling."

[55] Pittsburgh Press Co. v. Pittsburgh Commission on Human Relations, 413 U.S. 376, 387, 93 S.Ct. 2553, 2560 (1973).

[56] Pittsburgh Press Co. v. Pittsburgh Commission on Human Relations, 413 U.S. 376, 394, 93 S.Ct. 2553, 2563 (1973).

[57] Bigelow v. Virginia, 421 U.S. 809, 810, 95 S.Ct. 2222, 2227 (1975).

A Virginia court convicted Bigelow of violating a section of the Virginia Code: "If any person, by publication, lecture, advertisement, or by the sale or circulation of any publication, or in any other manner, shall encourage or prompt the procuring of an abortion or miscarriage, he shall be guilty of a misdemeanor." [58] The Virginia Supreme Court affirmed Bigelow's conviction, declaring that because the ad involved was a "commercial advertisement," Bigelow's First Amendment claim was not valid. Such an advertisement, said the Virginia Supreme Court, " 'may be constitutionally prohibited by the state, particularly where, as here, the advertising relates to the medical-health field.' " [59]

The Supreme Court overruled the Virginia Supreme Court. Writing for a 7–2 majority, Justice Harry Blackmun concluded that Virginia courts erred in assuming that advertising is not entitled to First Amendment protection. Justice Blackmun distinguished the Virginia case from *Chrestensen.* He wrote that the handbill ad involved in *Chrestensen* did no more than propose a purely commercial transaction, while The Virginia Weekly's ad about abortions "contained factual material of clear 'public interest.' " [60]

The existence of the Women's Pavilion in New York City was "not unnewsworthy" and also pertained to constitutional privacy interests.[61] A State, Justice Blackmun wrote, "may not * * * bar a citizen of another State from disseminating information about an activity that is legal in another State." Although advertising "may be subject to reasonable regulation that serves a legitimate public interest," some commercial speech is still worthy of constitutional protection. "The relationship of speech to the marketplace of products or services does not make it valueless in the marketplace of ideas," Justice Blackmun declared.[62]

What Justice Blackmun's majority opinion called for, of course, is a balancing of interests. The courts, and most especially the Supreme Court, have final say in deciding what is "merely" commercial speech as compared to ads which are "newsworthy" or politically or socially important enough to be anointed with "the public interest." Such vagueness, of course, lends little predictability to this area of law.

[58] Bigelow v. Virginia, 421 U.S. 809, 814, 95 S.Ct. 2222, 2228 (1975).

[59] Bigelow v. Virginia, 421 U.S. 809, 814, 95 S.Ct. 2222, 2229 (1975), quoting Bigelow v. Commonwealth, 213 Va. 191, 193–195, 191 S.E.2d 173, 174–176 (1972).

[60] Bigelow v. Virginia, 421 U.S. 809, 822, 95 S.Ct. 2222, 2233 (1975).

[61] Ibid., citing Roe v. Wade, 410 U.S. 113, 93 S.Ct. 705 (1973), and Doe v. Bolton, 410 U.S. 179, 93 S.Ct. 739 (1973).

[62] Bigelow v. Virginia, 421 U.S. 809, 826, 95 S.Ct. 2222, 2235 (1975).

Virginia State Board of Pharmacy v. Virginia Citizens Consumer Council, Inc. (1976)

What the Supreme Court started in 1975 with the *Bigelow* case continued the next year with the decision in the Virginia State Board of Pharmacy (VSBP) case. In fact, an excellent study of advertising law emphasized—as of 1991—that VSBP represented the decision in which the Supreme Court gave broadest First Amendment protection for commercial advertising.[63]

The Virginia State Board of Pharmacy case was not directly about a political or social issue. Instead, it dealt with a matter of price advertising. It arose because a Virginia statute forbade "the advertising of the price for any prescription drug." This statute was challenged in a lawsuit by two consumer organizations and by a Virginia citizen who had to take prescription drugs on a daily basis. The plaintiffs claimed that the First Amendment entitled users of prescription drugs to receive information from pharmacists—through advertisements or other promotional means—about the price of those drugs.[64]

By a 7–1 vote expressed via Justice Blackmun's majority opinion in *Virginia State Board of Pharmacy*, the Court overturned the state's ban on advertising of prescription drug prices.[65]

> . . . [T]he question whether there is a First Amendment exception for "commercial speech" is squarely before us. Our pharmacist does not wish to editorialize on any subject, cultural, philosophical, or political. He does not wish to report any particularly newsworthy fact, or to make generalized observations even about commercial matters. The "idea" he wishes to communicate is simply this: "I will sell you the X prescription drug at Y price."

The Supreme Court declared that the consumer had a great interest in the free flow of commercial information—perhaps a greater interest than in the day's most important political debate. The individuals hardest hit by the suppression of prescription price information, wrote Justice Blackmun, were the poor, the sick and the old. Therefore, despite the State of Virginia's interest in protecting professionalism among pharmacists, the societal interest in making prescription price information available through

---

[63] For an excellent discussion of the Virginia Board of Pharmacy case and, indeed, of the key cases involving advertising and the First Amendment, see Richard T. Kaplar, Advertising Rights, The Neglected Freedom: Toward a New Doctrine of Commercial Speech (Washington, D.C.: The Media Institute, 1991).

[64] Virginia State Board of Pharmacy v. Virginia Citizens Consumer Council, Inc., 425 U.S. 748, 96 S.Ct. 1817 (1976).

[65] Virginia State Board of Pharmacy v. Virginia Citizens Consumer Council, Inc., 425 U.S. 748, 759–761, 96 S.Ct. 1817, 1824–1825 (1976).

advertising was protected under the First Amendment. Thus, the Supreme Court declared the Virginia statute invalid.[66]

Subsequent cases indicated that commercial speech could receive constitutional protection in a variety of areas. Later in 1976, for example, the Horner–Rausch Optical Co. case, decided by a Tennessee court, declared an administrative regulation against price ads for eyeglasses to be unconstitutional.[67] And in 1977, the U.S. Supreme Court decided the now famous "lawyer ad case," Bates v. State Bar of Arizona.[68] By a 5–4 margin, the Court held that lawyers have a constitutional right to advertise their prices for their various services.

Justice Blackmun's majority opinion in *Bates* said, "[I]t is entirely possible that advertising will serve to reduce, not to advance, the cost of legal services to the consumer." In this case, the consumer's need for information about the cost of legal services was held to outweigh the legal profession's interest in having a regulated self-restraint against virtually all kinds of advertising by attorneys. The majority opinion added that the time, place and manner of advertising may be regulated, and that false or misleading advertising by lawyers may be forbidden.[69]

In holding that advertising by attorneys may not be subjected to blanket suppression, and that the advertisement in question is protected, we, of course, do not hold that advertising by attorneys may not be regulated in any way. * * * Advertising that is false, deceptive or misleading of course is subject to restraint.

* * *

The constitutional issue in this case is only whether the State may prevent the publication in a newspaper of appellants' truthful advertisement concerning the availability and terms of routine legal services. We rule simply that the flow of such information may not be restrained, and we therefore hold the present application of the disciplinary rule against appellants to be violative of the First Amendment.

[66] Virginia State Board of Pharmacy v. Virginia Citizens Consumer Council, Inc., 425 U.S. 748, 763, 96 S.Ct. 1817, 1826 (1976).

[67] Horner–Rausch Optical Co. v. Ashley, 547 S.W.2d 577 (Tenn.App.1976).

[68] Bates v. State Bar of Arizona, 433 U.S. 350, 97 S.Ct. 2691 (1977).

[69] Bates v. State Bar of Arizona, 433 U.S. 350, 383, 384, 97 S.Ct. 2691, 2706, 2708, 2709 (1977). Advertising by attorneys can go too far, however, when it includes a lawyer's visiting the family of a person injured in an auto accident, and even visiting with the driver herself in her hospital room. Personal solicitation of that nature (bedpan chasing?) is unreasonable. See Ohralik v. Ohio State Bar Ass'n, 436 U.S. 447, 98 S.Ct. 1912 (1978). If lawyer advertising is fundamentally misleading, it will not be tolerated: See Peel v. Attorney Registration and Disciplinary Com'n of Illinois, 496 U.S. 91, 110 S.Ct. 2281 (1990).

The Bellotti Case (1978): Protecting Corporate Speech

If abortion clinics, pharmacists, and lawyers have some First Amendment protection for their ads, what about corporations right to exercise political speech? In First National Bank of Boston v. Bellotti (1978),[70] the U.S. Supreme Court invalidated a Massachusetts statute forbidding business corporations from making contributions or expenditures " 'for the purpose of * * * influencing or affecting the vote on any question submitted to the voters, other than one materially affecting the property, business, or assets of the corporation.' " That statute provided that a corporation violating its provisions could be fined $50,000 and that its officers could be fined up to $10,000, imprisoned for up to one year, or both.

The bank wanted to spend money to publicize its views on a Massachusetts constitutional amendment being submitted to voters as a ballot question. The amendment would have allowed the legislature to place a graduated tax on individual incomes. Massachusetts Attorney General Francis X. Bellotti told the First National Bank of Boston that he would enforce the statute. The bank responded with an action asking that the statute be declared unconstitutional. The Supreme Judicial Court of Massachusetts upheld the statute as valid.[71]

The U.S. Supreme Court, however, found the Massachusetts statute unconstitutional. Writing for the Court, Justice Lewis Powell declared that the political argument the bank wished to make "is at the heart of the First Amendment's protection." He added, "[t]he question in this case, simply put, is whether the corporate identity of the speaker deprives the proposed speech of what otherwise would be its clear entitlement to protection." [72]

Justice Powell cited the Court's 1970s commercial speech cases—including *Virginia State Board of Pharmacy*—as illustrating "that the First Amendment goes beyond protection of the press and the self-expression of individuals to prohibit government from limiting the stock of information from which members of the public may draw." Thus corporations' political speech was entitled to First Amendment protection.[73]

[70] First National Bank of Boston v. Bellotti, 435 U.S. 765, 98 S.Ct. 1407 (1978).

[71] First National Bank of Boston v. Attorney General, 371 Mass. 773, 359 N.E.2d 1262 at 1268 (1977).

[72] First National Bank of Boston v. Bellotti, 435 U.S. 765, 778, 98 S.Ct. 1407, 1416 (1978).

[73] First National Bank of Boston v. Bellotti, 435 U.S. 765, 783, 98 S.Ct. 1407, 1409 (1978).

Justice Byron White dissented, and was joined by Justices Brennan and Marshall. He argued that the Massachusetts statute did not infringe on First Amendment interests, but instead protected them. Corporations that had amassed great wealth should thus be prevented from having "an unfair advantage in the political process. White wrote: [74]

> Indeed, what some have considered to be the principal function of the First Amendment, the use of communication as a means of self-expression, self-realization, and self-fulfillment, is not at all furthered by corporate speech.

Freedom of expression for *self-fulfillment* is an important First Amendment value to many theorists. Other scholars hold that the First Amendment's true role is mainly *utilitarian,* to provide sufficient freedom of expression to enable citizens to participate fully and effectively in self-government. However, neither the proponents of self-fulfillment nor the adherents of a utilitarian theory of the First Amendment tend to look kindly on expanding freedom in the area of commercial speech.[75]

In sum, as Justice White suggested in his dissent, the decision in *Virginia State Board of Pharmacy* sent mixed messages. The Court, without firmly grounding its majority opinion in a defensible theory of the First Amendment, wobbled understandably when trying to define commercial messages which have public interest and those which do not. The Court said, rather lamely, that it could detect "commonsense differences" between commercial speech and, say, political speech.[76] If, indeed, Virginia State Board of Pharmacy is to be the all-time highwater mark for commercial speech, then advertising will continue to be the unwelcome passenger in the First Amendment's lifeboat.

Central Hudson (1980) and the Four–Part Test

In 1980, the Supreme Court of the United States created an important test to try to outline just when advertising might be deemed worthy of constitutional protection. This case, Central Hudson Gas & Electric Corp. v. Public Service Commission of New York, involved a commission order that the utility stop promoting consumption of electricity. This order was promulgated during an energy shortage, under the assumption that cutting Central Hud-

---

[74] First National Bank of Boston v. Bellotti, 435 U.S. 765, 809, 98 S.Ct. 1407, 1433 (1978).

[75] For discussion of such First Amendment values, see Kaplar, op. cit., pp. 38–40, and Steven Shiffrin, "The First Amendment and Economic Regulation: Away from a General Theory of the First Amendment," 78 Northwestern U.L.Rev. 1212 (1983, at pp. 1223–1251).

[76] Footnote 24 in Virginia Pharmacy case, discussed in Kaplar, op. cit., at p. 52.

son's "buy appliances" advertising might assist in energy conservation. The U.S. Supreme Court, however, invalidated New York's ban on promotional advertising by electric utilities. Justice Powell, writing for an 8–1 Court, laid out a four-part test: [77]

> In commercial speech cases, then, a four-part analysis has developed. At the outset, we must determine [1] whether the expression is protected by the First Amendment. For commercial speech to come within that provision, it at least must concern lawful activity and not be misleading. [2] Next, we ask whether the asserted governmental interest is substantial. If both inquiries yield positive answers, we must determine [3] whether the regulation directly advances the governmental interest asserted, and [4] whether it is not more extensive than necessary to serve that interest.

Because advertising promoting use of electricity was seen as protected by the First Amendment, and because the ad was neither misleading nor "unlawful," the New York regulation was overturned as unconstitutional. Although the state had a substantial interest in energy conservation, the state's regulation was more extensive than necessary. No demonstration was made that the state's interest in energy conservation could not have been served adequately by a more limited restriction on the content of promotional advertisements. [78]

Narrowing Constitutional Protection: Posadas de Puerto Rico v. Tourism Company (1986)

For eleven years deciding the abortion advertising case of Bigelow v. Virginia (1975), [79] the U.S. Supreme Court held that if a product or service was legal and was the subject of public or corporate interest, truthful ads for that product or service had First Amendment protection. [80] As noted earlier in this Section, this protection covered ads for abortion referral services, prices of

---

[77] Central Hudson Gas & Electric Corp. v. Public Service Com'n of New York, 447 U.S. 557, 100 S.Ct. 2343 (1980).

[78] Central Hudson Gas & Elec. Corp. v. Public Service Com'n, 447 U.S. 557, 100 S.Ct. 2343 (1980). See also a related case, Consolidated Edison Co. of New York, Inc. v. Public Service Commission of New York, 447 U.S. 530, 100 S.Ct. 2326 (1980), 6 Med.L.Rptr. 1518. There, the Court struck down an order forbidding the utility's including in mailings statements of "Con Ed's" views on public policy controversies. Powell, quoting First National Bank of Boston v. Bellotti, 435 U.S. 765, 98 S.Ct. 1407 (1978), wrote for the Court that the Commission's censorship attempt "strikes at the heart of the freedom to speak."

[79] 421 U.S. 809, 95 S.Ct. 2222 (1975).

[80] See also New York Times Co. v. Sullivan, 376 U.S. 254, 84 S.Ct. 710 (1964), the pivotal libel case extending First Amendment protection to ads dealing with major social or political concerns.

prescription drugs, eyeglasses, lawyers, banks' political stances, promotions by a public utility, even during an energy shortage.

This expansiveness ground to a halt in July, 1986, when the Supreme Court ruled that government may forbid truthful ads for some products or services, even though they are legal for sale. Not surprisingly, this 1986 case—involving Puerto Rico's regulations against local ads promoting gambling in Puerto Rico's legal casinos—alarmed the tobacco and liquor industries in the United States.[81]

The Puerto Rico Legislature, when it legalized regulated casino gambling in 1948, also provided that " '[n]o gambling room shall be permitted to advertise . . . to the public of Puerto Rico.' " [82] The Tourism Company of Puerto Rico, a governmental agency, created regulations to implement the no-advertising-in-Puerto Rico ban called for by the statute.

When a hotel-casino challenged the advertising regulations as unconstitutional, it did seem to have plenty to complain about. The regulations were sweepingly broad. For example, consider this Tourism Company memo: [83]

"This prohibition includes the use of the word 'casino' in matchbooks, lighters, envelopes, inter-office and/or external correspondence, invoices, napkins, brochures, menus, elevators, glasses, plates, lobbies, banners, flyers, paper holders, pencils, telephone books, directories, bulletin boards or in any hotel dependency or object which may be accessible to the public in Puerto Rico."

When the case reached the U.S. Supreme Court, Justice (subsequently Chief Justice) William H. Rehnquist wrote for the Court's five member majority. He said the issue was whether the Puerto Rico statute and regulations "impermissibly suppressed commercial speech in violation of the First Amendment and the equal protection and due process guarantees of the United States Constitution." [84]

Justice Rehnquist said that this case involved " * * * the restriction of pure commercial speech which does 'no more than propose a commercial transaction.' " [85] That meant, he wrote, that First Amendment discussion of this case was controlled by the four-part analysis set forth in the Central Hudson Gas &

[81] Stuart Taylor, Jr., "High Court, 5–4, Sharply Limits Constitutional Protection for Ads," The New York Times, July 2, 1986, p. 2 (National Edition).

[82] Posadas De Puerto Rico Associates v. Tourism Co. of Puerto Rico, 478 U.S. 328, 332, 106 S.Ct. 2968, 2972 (1986), 13 Med.L.Rptr. 1003, 1035.

[83] 478 U.S. at 333, 106 S.Ct. at 2873, 13 Med.L.Rptr. at 1035.

[84] 478 U.S. at 328, 106 S.Ct. at 2971, 13 Med.L.Rptr. at 1034.

[85] 478 U.S. at 340, 106 S.Ct. at 2976, 13 Med.L.Rptr. at 1038–1039.

Electric Corp. case discussed earlier in this Section. Recall that the *Central Hudson* test of whether commercial speech qualified for First Amendment protection involved four questions:

(1) Does ad concern a lawful activity?, and is *not* fraudulent or misleading?

(2) Does government have a substantial interest in restricting this commercial speech?

(3) Does the regulation directly advance that governmental interest?

(4) Is the regulation more extensive than necessary to serve that governmental interest?

The Court's majority opinion concluded that advertising of casino gambling in Puerto Rico "concerns a lawful activity and is not misleading or fraudulent, at least in the abstract." [86]   Even so, Justice Rehnquist's majority opinion deferred to Puerto Rico's legislative judgment: It was not an unreasonable policy choice to believe that excessive casino gambling by Puerto Rico's residents would produce great harm to citizens welfare. The Court's majority concluded that the hotel/casino's First Amendment claims had been rejected properly.

He wrote acidly that even though products or activities including cigarettes, alcoholic beverages, and prostitution had been legalized for sale in some jurisdictions did not mean that their advertising could not be limited.[87]

In dissent, Justice Brennan (joined by Justices Blackmun and Marshall) depicted the Court's majority as encroaching substantially on free expression. He conceded that government may regulate the content of commercial speech to stop dissemination of false, deceptive, or misleading information. Brennan noted that for a decade before *Posadas* was decided, the U.S. Supreme Court consistently invalidated restrictions which would deprive consumers of accurate information about products and services legally offered for sale. Justice John Paul Stevens also dissented, calling the Puerto Rico ad prohibitions a regime of prior restraint articulating a hopelessly vague and unpredictable standard.[88]

The extent of the fall-out from *Posadas* in shriveling gains toward admittedly limited First Amendment protection for advertising remains to be seen. It might be argued that the Court bowed too low in the direction of federalism, of letting various states or jurisdictions create their own rules legislatively without federal judicial interference. What, however, was the net effect in

[86] 478 U.S. at 340–341, 106 S.Ct. at 2975, 13 Med.L.Rptr. at 1039.

[87] 478 U.S. at 346, 106 S.Ct. at 2977.

[88] 478 U.S. at 361, 106 S.Ct. at 2988.

Puerto Rico? Citizens of that Commonwealth surely know the casinos are there in various hotels. After all, they work in the casinos, and may gamble there if they choose, whether or not those gaming establishments are advertised locally in addition to in northern American cities to attract *turista* dollars.

More significantly, the Posadas decision makes it far more difficult to overturn State laws that constrain commercial free speech. The Central Hudson test Justice Rehnquist claimed to be applying in the Posadas case had permitted States to use only the "least restrictive means" available in regulating advertising messages. In fact, however, Posadas simply requires a State to demonstrate that any advertising laws it adopts are "reasonable" ones.[89]

Banning All Tobacco Ads?

In any event, the interplay of the *Posadas* decision with efforts to get rid of tobacco advertising truly had the attention of cigarette manufacturers in the late 1980s and early 1990s. Back in 1972, of course, the U.S. Supreme Court affirmed—with no explanation—an Act of Congress barring cigarette ads from radio and television. And, in the 1980s, the American Medical Association, among others, urged a ban on all cigarette advertising, including newspapers, magazines, and billboards. Complaints rose from the tobacco and liquor interests that such a ban on print advertising would be unconstitutional. Voices raised in such protests included the American Tobacco Institute and the American Civil Liberties Union.[90]

The growing chorus of concern about interrelationships between tobacco and health may indeed mean that the banning of cigarette ads from radio and television may be only the first wave of control. Starting in 1986, Rep. Michael Synar (D–Okla.) repeatedly introduced legislation calling for banning "consumer sales promotion" of all tobacco products. That means all forms of tobacco intended for human consumption: cigarettes, little cigars, pipe or loose rolling tobacco, chewing tobacco, snuff, and so on.

Tobacco use has been targeted by virtually all doctors as the largest preventable cause of death in the United States, and is assailed as associated with the unnecessary deaths of more than 300,000 Americans annually.

[89] See Denise M. Trauth and John L. Huffman, "The Commercial Speech Doctrine: Posadas Revisionism," Communication and the Law (Feb. 1988), pp. 43–56.

[90] See "Smoking, Smoke and Free Speech," New York Times editorial, Aug. 15, 1986, p. 22; "Free speech under assault," Mobil Oil Corp. ad, The New York Times, Dec. 18, 1986.

Unsurprisingly, this has led to multiple efforts to pass legislation to silence the messenger, to put a stop to advertising of tobacco products. For example, consider Rep. Synar's 1986 bill to outlaw "commercial sales promotion of tobacco products. "Commercial sales promotion" included not only radio and TV commercials but also newspaper and magazine ads. That Synar bill also proposed forbidding of premiums and samples, and of sponsorship of athletic, artistic, or other events under the registered brand name of tobacco products.[91]

Regulatory proposals have not been received tamely by the tobacco industry. In the late 1980s, the tobacco industry wrapped itself in the American flag and the Bill of Rights, barraging mailboxes with freedom-invoking arguments seeking citizen support against added taxes on tobacco products and against efforts to ban tobacco ads.

Strengthening Government Ad Regulation: State University of New York v. Fox (1990)

Greater willingness by the Supreme Court to allow state regulation of commercial messages showed in 1990 in a decision seemingly based on a trivial fact situation. The U.S. Supreme Court treated the facts of the case as if "Tupperware Parties" had been held in a State University of New York (SUNY) dormitory. This sales technique—a presentation made by students in this instance representing American Future Systems (AFS)—violated a regulation forbidding private commercial enterprises from operating on New York State university campuses.

Salesperson Todd Fox was arrested by SUNY–Cortland campus police while conducting a demonstration in a dorm. Ultimately, after a trial, a federal district court held that SUNY dormitories were not a public forum and that the regulation was reasonable in view of a dormitory's purpose.[92] The student salespersons' claim that their First Amendment rights were abridged by the university, however, was upheld by the U.S. Court of Appeals for the Second Circuit.[93] The Second Circuit court turned to Part Four of the *Central Hudson* test, holding that the regulation applied by SUNY–Cortland was defective in that it did not

---

[91] H.R. 1272, 100th Congress, 1st Sess. (Feb. 25, 1987). See also "Advertising of Tobacco Products," Hearings before the Subcommittee on Health and the Environment, House of Representatives, 99th Congress, 2nd Sess., July 18 and Aug. 1, 1986. For a discussion of 1989 and 1990 bills to curtail tobacco and alcohol ads, see Kaplar, op. cit., pp. 6–8.

[92] Board of Trustees of the State University of New York v. Fox, 492 U.S. 469, 109 S.Ct. 3028 (1989).

[93] Ibid., at 471, 109 S.Ct. at 3030.

apply the least restrictive means of regulating commercial speech.[94]

The U.S. Supreme Court, however, overturned the Court of Appeals, thus upholding the university regulation about commercial activity in dormitories. Writing for a Court divided 6–3, Justice Antonin Scalia again diluted Central Hudson's fourth part (commercial speech regulations should be accomplished by the "least restrictive means").[95] With Justice Scalia's wording, the regulation of commercial speech should represent "not necessarily the least restrictive means but * * * a means narrowly tailored to achieve the desired objective." [96]

Scalia argued it was essential for the Court to maintain clear distinctions between commercial and non-commercial expression in order to protect traditional free speech rights from being eroded by those restraints States might lawfully impose on advertising messages. Yet, as Justice Blackmun, joined by Justices Marshall and Brennan, pointed out, to achieve this objective Scalia appeared to be indulging in the same type of judicial activism that conservative jurists had criticized so vehemently in the past.[97]

Austin v. Michigan Chamber of Commerce (1990)

Although the Supreme Court found constitutional support for corporate political advertising in First National Bank of Boston v. Bellotti (1978), a 1990 decision marked a retreat in that area. In Austin v. Michigan Chamber of Commerce, the Supreme Court voted 6–3 to uphold a Michigan statute forbidding corporations from using their general treasury funds for "independent expenditures" to support or oppose political candidates seeking state offices.[98] In other words, corporate political ad expenditures concerning candidates had to be made from separate funds used only for political purposes.

In essence, this decision simply permitted a State to prevent wealthy private organizations from financing a political campaign directly from their own general resources. Even so, it can be seen as diminishing to some extent those broad guarantees of corporate free speech granted by the Court in the Central Hudson case.[99]

Despite this post-Posadas tendency of the Court to recognize a more extensive role for State law in the field of commercial speech

[94] Ibid., at 473, 109 S.Ct. at 3022–3033.

[95] Ibid., at 475, 109 S.Ct. at 3035.

[96] Ibid., at 475, 109 S.Ct. at 3035.

[97] Ibid., at 479, 109 S.Ct. at 3038.

[98] Austin v. Michigan Chamber of Commerce, 494 U.S. 652, 110 S.Ct. 1391 (1990).

[99] Central Hudson Gas & Elec. Corp. v. Public Service Com'n of New York, 447 U.S. 557, 100 S.Ct. 2343 (1980).

regulation, it seems unlikely that those Constitutional protections given this type of expression during the 1970s will be greatly lessened.[1] Instead, it is more likely that the Court simply will permit States to begin exercising broader regulatory control over the advertising of certain specific products such as tobacco or liquor, where the public policy interests of the State are most clearly evident, and where social values of those products being marketed are most difficult to defend.

[1] For a review of recent federal judicial decisions applying the Posadas test, see Roxanne Hovland and Ronald E. Taylor, "Advertising and Commercial Speech Since the 1986 Posadas Case," Journalism Quarterly (Winter, 1990), pp. 1083–1089.

Chapter 12

COPYRIGHT: PROTECTION AND CONSTRAINT

Sec.
71. Development of Copyright Law.
72. Securing a Copyright.
73. Originality.
74. Infringement and Remedies.
75. Copyright, Unfair Competition and the News.
76. The Defense of Fair Use.
77. Broadcast Music Licensing Rights.

SEC. 71. DEVELOPMENT OF COPYRIGHT LAW

Copyright is the right to control or profit from a literary, artistic or intellectual production.

A furious Mark Twain once declared that every time copyright law was to be made, then all the idiots assembled. That was back around the turn of the century, and his anger was fueled by his helplessness to prevent unscrupulous individuals from making unauthorized use of his writings. In fact, Twain lobbied for passage of the Copyright Act of 1909, which was to remain the basic law for almost 70 years.

By the mid-1970s, that horse-and-buggy-era statute was pathetically out-of-date. Over the years, amendments to the 1909 statute were not sweeping, and were analogous to re-arranging the deck chairs on the Titanic. Copyright law was a prime example of an area where technology ran off and left efforts to regulate it. Think about 1909. The photocopying machine was unknown, and so were computers and communications satellites. Radio ("wireless") was a scientific curiosity and movies were little beyond the "magic lantern" stage.

The first major change in copyright statutes since 1909 was signed into law October 19, 1976, by President Gerald R. Ford, and went into effect January 1, 1978.[1] Passage of that law was a remarkable event. Copyright revision had been underway in Congress since 1961, with massive snags lurking all about. Where onrushing technology did not cause problems, vigorously competing special interest groups did. Take photocopying. Teachers and

---

[1] One of the more useful sources in studying these changes in House of Representatives Report No. 94–1476, "Copyright Law Revision." Title 17, United States Code, "Copyrights," was amended in its entirety by Public Law 94–553, 94th Congress, 94 Stat. 2541 (1976). Also essential for study of this field is Melville B. Nimmer, Nimmer on Copyright, 4 vols. (New York: Matthew Bender, 1963–1988).

librarians wanted few if any restraints on photocopying, while authors and publishers wanted to halt any copying which could cut into the sale of so much as one book or magazine.[2]

Copyright Defined

Black's Law Dictionary defines copyright as: [3]

The right of literary property as recognized and sanctioned by positive law. An intangible, incorporeal right granted by statute to the author or originator of certain literary or artistic productions, whereby he is invested, for a limited period, with the sole and exclusive privilege of multiplying copies of the same and publishing and selling them.

Such definitions aside, journalists must have a basic understanding of this complicated, frustrating area of law. Perhaps this area of law is so complex because it draws authority from a number of bases: Anglo-American literary history and common law, state and federal laws, court decisions, plus Article I, Section 8 of the Constitution of the United States: [4]

The Congress shall have power * * * to promote the Progress of Science and useful Arts by securing for limited Times to Authors and Inventors the exclusive Right to their respective Writings and Discoveries.

Passage of the first federal copyright statute as early as 1790 indicates that America's Revolutionary generation had a lively concern about the need for copyright protection. Additional copyright statutes were enacted during the 19th century.[5]

History of Copyright

Underlying the words of Article I, Section 8 of the Constitution was the principle of copyright, which had been known since ancient times. It is known that the Republic of Venice in 1469 granted John of Speyer the exclusive right to print the letters of Pliny and Cicero for a period of five years.[6]

The development of printing increased the need for some form of copyright. Although printing from movable type began in 1451

---

[2] For a view of efforts to resolve such disputes, see H.R. Report No. 94–1476, "Copyright Law Revision," pp. 66–70. The guidelines there were later approved by the Senate-House conference committee which hammered out the final bill.

[3] Black's Law Dictionary, 5th ed. (St. Paul, Minn., West Publishing Co.) p. 304.

[4] Benjamin Kaplan and Ralph S. Brown, Jr., Cases on Copyright (Brooklyn, Foundation Press, 1960) pp. 22–52.

[5] Thorvald Solberg, Copyright Enactments of the United States, 1783–1906. Washington, 1906.

[6] R.C. DeWolf, Outline of Copyright Law (Boston: John W. Luce, 1925) p. 2.

and although Caxton introduced printing into England in about 1476, the first copyright law was not passed in England until 1790 in the "Statute of 8 Anne." Before this time, the printing business was influenced in two distinct ways. First, printing gave royalty and government in England the opportunity to reward favored individuals with exclusive printing monopolies. Second, those in power recognized that printing, unless strictly controlled, tended to endanger their rule.

Hoping to control the output of the printing presses, Queen Mary I granted a charter to the Stationers Company in 1556. The Stationers Company, a guild of printers, thus was given a monopoly on book printing. Simultaneously these printers were given the authority to burn prohibited books and to jail the persons who published them.[7] The Stationers Company acted zealously against printers of unauthorized works, making use of terrifying powers of search and seizure. Tactics paralleling those of the Inquisition were used defending the doctrines of the Catholic Church against the burgeoning Reformation movement.[8]

The Stationers Company remained powerful into the seventeenth century, with its authority augmented by licensing statutes. The Act of 1662, for example, confined printing to 59 master printer members of the Stationers Company then practicing in London, and to the printers at Oxford and Cambridge Universities. The privileged position of the Stationers Company in England during the sixteenth and seventeenth centuries underlies the development of the law of copyright of more recent times. Printers who were officially sanctioned to print by virtue of membership in the Stationers Company complained when their works were issued in pirated editions by unauthorized printers.[9]

In time, the guild printers who belonged to the Stationers Company began to recognize a principle now known as "common law copyright." They began to assume that there was a common law right, *in perpetuity,* to literary property. That is, if a man printed a book, duly approved by government authority, the right to profit from its distribution remained with that man, or his heirs, forever.[10]

Authors, like England's printers, came to believe that they also had some rights to profit from their works. Authors joined printers in the latter half of the seventeenth century in seeking

[7] Philip Wittenberg, The Law of Literary Property (New York: World Publishing Co., 1957), pp. 25–26; Fredrick S. Siebert, Freedom of the Press in England, 1476–1776 (Urbana: University of Illinois Press, 1952) pp. 22, 65, 249.

[8] Siebert, op. cit., pp. 82–86; Mrs. Edward S. Lazowska, "Photocopying, Copyright, and the Librarian," American Documentation (April, 1968) pp. 123–130.

[9] Siebert, pp. 74–77, 239.

[10] Wittenberg, op. cit., pp. 45–46.

Parliamentary legislation to establish the existence of copyright. In 1709, Parliament passed the Statute of 8 Anne, believed to have been drafted, in part, by two famed authors, Joseph Addison and Jonathan Swift. This statute recognized the authors' rights, giving them—or their heirs or persons to whom they might sell their rights—exclusive powers to publish the book for 14 years after its first printing. If the author were still alive after those 14 years, that person could renew copyright for an additional 14 years.[11]

This limitation of copyright to a total of 28 years displeased both authors and printers. They complained for many years that they should have copyright in perpetuity, forever, under the common law. In 1774, the House of Lords, acting in its capacity of a court of the highest appeal, decided the case of Donaldson v. Beckett.

This 1774 decision was of enormous importance to the history of American law, because it outlined the two categories of copyrights, *statutory copyright* and *common law copyright*. The House of Lords ruled that the Statute of 8 Anne, providing a limited 28 year term of copyright protection, had superseded the common law protection for *published* works. Only *unpublished* works, therefore, could receive common law copyright protection in perpetuity. An author was to have automatic, limitless common law copyright protection for his creations only as long as they remained unpublished. But once publication occurred, the author or publisher could have exclusive right to publish and profit from his works for only a limited period of time as decreed by legislative authority. The Statute 8 Anne, as upheld by the House of Lords in Donaldson v. Beckett, is the ancestor of modern copyright legislation in the United States.[12]

When the first federal copyright statute was adopted in the United States in 1790, implementing Article I, Section 8 of the Constitution, it gave the federal government *statutory* authority to administer copyrights. Since there was no common law authority for federal courts, questions involving *common law* copyright remained to be adjudicated in state courts.[13] In the 1834 case of Wheaton v. Peters, the Supreme Court of the United States enunciated the doctrine of common law copyright in America: [14]

[11] Siebert, op. cit., p. 249; Wittenberg, Ibid., pp. 47–48.

[12] Burr. 2408 (1774); Lazowska, op. cit., p. 124.

[13] Wheaton v. Peters, 33 U.S. (8 Pet.) 591 (1834); W.W. Willoughby, Constitutional Law of the United States, p. 446.

[14] 33 U.S. (8 Pet.) 591 (1834); Hirsch v. Twentieth Century-Fox Film Corp., 207 Misc. 750, 144 N.Y.S.2d 38, 105 U.S.P.Q. 253 (1955).

That an author at common law has a property right in his manuscript, and may obtain redress against any one who endeavors to realize a profit by its publication, cannot be doubted; but this is a very different right from that which asserts a perpetual and exclusive property in the future publication of the work, after the author shall have published it to the world.

Congress tried to do away with state authority over common law copyrights, phasing them out of existence with Sec. 301 of the Copyright Act of 1976. Of course, there would have to be a transitional period: Sec. 301 specifically preserved common law copyrights which were in effect before January 1, 1978—the effective date of the 1976 Copyright Act.

In point of fact, state laws affecting copyrights continue to have real effects. For example, Bette Midler, "The Divine Miss M," won $400,000 from the Ford Motor Company for using a singer imitating her voice in a series of TV commercials.

The Young and Rubicam advertising agency, tried to attract young urban professionals with songs evoking memories of when the Yuppies were in college. The ad agency tried to get the original performers who had made songs famous. Failing in that attempt, the agency then had ten songs recorded by "sound alikes"—including an imitation of Ms. Midler's rendition of the 1973 song hit, "Do You Want to Dance?".

Ms. Midler sued Ford Motor Company and Young and Rubicam for wrongful use of her singing voice without her consent. The U.S. Court of Appeals, 9th Circuit, held that although "a voice is not copyrightable," when a famous professional singer's distinctive voice is deliberately imitated in order to sell a product, that may be held to be a tort under California law.[15]

Common law copyright had both advantages and disadvantages. Its advantages were that it was automatic and perpetual so long as a manuscript or creation was not published. An author could circulate a manuscript among friends, could use it in class for experimental teaching materials, or, perhaps, could send it to several publishing houses without publication in the technical, legal sense. In general, as long as the manuscript was not offered to the general public, common law copyright protection remained intact.

[15] Midler v. Ford Motor Co., 849 F.2d 460, 462 (9th Cir.1988), 15 Med.L.Rptr. 1623–1625, citing 17 U.S.C.A. § 102(a) for the principle that a voice is not copyrightable because sounds are not "fixed." See "Supreme Court Roundup," The New York Times (Nat'l. Ed.), March 3, 1992, p. A10.

Published works, however, had to have a copyright notice—for example, © John Steinbeck, 1941—in a specified place on a book or manuscript or other copyrightable item or the work would fall into the public domain. That meant that once "in the public domain" the work lacked copyright protection, and that anyone who wished to do so could republish the work for his or her own profit.[16]

The Copyright Act of 1976 was intended to allow the federal government to supersede entirely the states' authority to deal with copyright. The federal statute's language certainly sounds preemptive: " * * * no person is entitled to any such [copy] right or equivalent right in any such work under the common law or statutes of any State." [17] Confusingly and annoyingly for persons looking for uniformity in copyright law, state power impinging on copyright has not gone away.

As Howard B. Abrams has pointed out, the vaguely defined tort of "misappropriation" as dealt with in state courts has led to a chaotic situation in conflict with Sec. 301 of the 1976 Copyright Act. So, is copying to continue to be both a misappropriation ("wrongful taking") under the laws of various states or is it to be equivalent to an action for copyright infringement under the federal Copyright Act of 1976? Howard B. Abrams has written: [18]

> If anything, § 301 [of the 1976 Copyright Act] has frustrated congressional intent to create "a single Federal system" and proliferated the "vague borderline areas between State and Federal protection" which Congress so sincerely yet so artlessly sought to avoid.

The Nature of Copyright

Copyright is an exclusive, legally recognizable claim to literary or pictorial property. It is a right, extended by federal statute, to entitle originators to ownership of the literary or artistic products of their minds. Before launching into more detailed discussion of provisions of the copyright statute now in force, consider the following three principles:

(1) *Facts or ideas cannot be copyrighted.* Copyright applies only to the literary style of an article, news story, book, or other intellectual creation. It does *not* apply to the

[16] 17 U.S.C.A. § 102.

[17] H.R. Report No. 94–1476, pp. 146–149.

[18] Howard B. Abrams, "Copyright, Misappropriation, and Preemption: Constitutional and Statutory Limits of State Law Protection," pp. 75–147 in David Goldberg, Chairman, Current Developments in Copyright Law, 1985 (New York: Practising Law Institute), at p. 147, quoting H.R. Report No. 94–1476 (1976), at p. 130. See also Abrams' pp. 83ff, for discussion of state cases endeavoring to deal with copying of sound recordings.

themes, ideas, or facts contained in the copyrighted material. Anyone may write about any subject. Copyright's protection extends only to the particular manner or style of expression. What is "copyrightable" in the print media, for example, is the order and selection of words, phrases, clauses, sentences, and the arrangement of paragraphs.[19]

(2) *Copyright is both a protection for and a restriction of the communications media.* Copyright protects the media by preventing the wholesale taking of the form of materials, without permission, from one person or unit of the media for publication by another person or unit of the media. Despite the guaranty of freedom of the press, newspapers and other communications media must acquire permission to publish material that is protected by copyright.[20]

(3) *As a form of literary property, copyright belongs to that class of personal property including patents, trade-marks, trade names, trade secrets, good will, unpublished lectures, musical compositions, and letters.*

　　(a) Copyright, it must be emphasized, is quite different from a patent. Copyright covers purely composition, style of expression or rhetoric, while a patent is the right given to protect a novel idea which may be expressed physically in a machine, a design, or a process.

　　(b) Copyright may be distinguished from a trademark in that copyright protects a particular literary style while a trade-mark protects the sign or brand under which a particular product is made or distributed.

　　(c) When someone sends you a letter, you do not have the right to publish that letter. You may keep the letter, or throw it away; indeed, you can do anything you wish with the letter but publish it. Although the recipient of a letter gets physical possession of it—of the paper it is written upon—the copyright ownership remains with the sender.[21]

---

[19] Kaeser & Blair, Inc. v. Merchants Ass'n, Inc., 64 F.2d 575, 577 (6th Cir.1933); Eisenschiml v. Fawcett Publications, Inc., 246 F.2d 598 (7th Cir.1957).

[20] Cf. Chicago Record-Herald Co. v. Tribute Ass'n, 275 Fed. 797 (7th Cir.1921).

[21] Baker v. Libbie, 97 N.E. 109, 210 Mass. 599 (1912); Ipswich Mills v. Dillon, 260 Mass. 453, 157 N.E. 604 (1927). See also Alan Lee Zegas, "Personal Letters: A Dilemma for Copyright and Privacy Law," 33 Rutgers Law Review (1980) pp. 134–164. Writers who seek relief for unauthorized publication may sue for recovery under both copyright and privacy theories, although the author suggests that those areas of law offer writers inadequate protection.

SEC. 72. SECURING A COPYRIGHT

Essentials in acquiring a copyright include notice of copyright, application, deposit of copies in the Library of Congress, and payment of the required fee.

What May Be Copyrighted

Reflecting awareness that new technologies will emerge and that human ingenuity will devise new forms of expression, the language of the new copyright statute is sweeping in defining what may be copyrighted. Section 102 says: [22]

(a) Copyright protection subsists * * * in original works of authorship fixed in any tangible medium of expression, now known or later developed, from which they can be perceived, reproduced, or otherwise communicated, either directly or with the aid of a machine or device. Works of authorship include the following categories:

(1) literary works;

(2) musical works, including any accompanying words;

(3) dramatic works, including any accompanying music;

(4) pantomimes and choreographic works;

(5) pictorial, graphic, and sculptural works;

(6) motion pictures and other audiovisual works; and

(7) sound recordings.

(b) In no case does copyright protection for an original work of authorship extend to any idea, procedure, process, system, method of operation, concept, principle, or discovery, regardless of the form in which it is described, explained, illustrated, or embodied in such work.

The Copyright Notice

Under the 1976 statute, once something has been published the omission of a copyright notice or an error in that notice does not destroy the author or creator's protection.[23] Section 405 gives a copyright owner up to five years to register a work with the Register of Copyrights, Library of Congress, Washington, D.C., even if that work has been published without notice. (Formerly, under the 1909 statute, publication without notice could mean that the authors lost any copyrights in their works if a defective

[22] 17 U.S.C.A. § 102.

[23] 17 U.S.C.A. §§ 405, 406.

notice—or no notice at all—was used.)[24] The copyright owner, however, must make a reasonable effort to add a copyright notice to all copies or phonorecords distributed in the United States after the omission has been discovered.[25]

Section 401 makes the following general requirement about placing copyright notices on "visually perceptible copies."[26]

> Whenever a work protected under this title [Title 17, United States Code, the copyright statute] is published in the United States or elsewhere by authority of the copyright owner, a notice of copyright in this section shall be placed on all publicly distributed copies from which the work can be visually perceived, either directly or with the aid of a machine or device.

The copyright notice shall consist of these three elements: [27]

(1) the symbol © (the letter C in a circle), or the word "Copyright" or the abbreviation "Copr."; and

(2) the year of first publication of the work; in the case of compilations or derivative works incorporating previously published material, the year date of the first publication of the compilation or derivative work is sufficient. The year date may be omitted where a pictorial, graphic, or sculptural work, with accompanying text matter, if any, is reproduced in or on greeting cards, postcards, stationery, jewelry, dolls, toys, or any useful articles; and

(3) the name of the owner of copyright abbreviation by which the name can be recognized or a generally known alternative designation of the owner.

If a sound recording is being copyrighted, the notice takes a different form. The notice shall consist of the following three elements: [28]

(1) The symbol ℗ (the letter P in a circle); and

(2) the year of first publication of the sound recording; and

(3) the name of the owner of copyright in the sound recording, or an abbreviation by which the name can be recognized, or a generally known alternative designation of the owner; if the producer of the sound recording is named on the phonorecord labels or containers, and if no other

---

[24] Leon H. Amdur, Copyright Law and Practice (New York: Clark Boardman Co., 1936), pp. 64–65; Holmes v. Hurst, 174 U.S. 82, 19 S.Ct. 606 (1899).

[25] 17 U.S.C.A. § 405.

[26] 17 U.S.C.A. § 401(a).

[27] 17 U.S.C.A. § 401(b).

[28] 17 U.S.C.A. § 402(b), (c).

name appears in conjunction with the notice, the producer's name shall be considered a part of the notice.

The copyright statute adopts one of the former law's basic principles: in the case of works made for hire, the employer is considered the author of the work (and therefore the initial copyright owner) unless there has been an agreement to the contrary. The statute requires that any agreement under which the employee will own rights be in writing and signed by both the employee and the employer.[29]

The copyright notice shall be placed on the copies "in such manner and location as to give reasonable notice of the claim of copyright." Special methods of this "affixation" of the copyright notice and positions for notices on various kinds of works will be prescribed by regulations to be issued by the Register of Copyrights.[30]

Duration of Copyright

A most welcome change under the Act of 1976 set copyright duration at the life of the owner plus 50 years. This replaced the fouled-up and complicated system of the 1909 statute of an initial period of 28 years plus a renewal period of another 28 years. Renewals had to be applied for, and if unwary copyright owners waited a full 28 years to apply for their second term, they had waited too long and their works became part of the public domain—everybody's property. Also, the U.S. system was badly out of step with a great majority of the world's nations which had adopted a copyright term of the author's life plus 50 years. As noted in the legislative commentary accompanying the 1976 statute,[31]

> * * * American authors are frequently protected longer in foreign countries than in the United States . . . [This] disparity in the duration of copyright has provoked * * * some proposals of retaliatory legislation. * * * The need to conform the duration of U.S. copyright to that prevalent throughout the rest of the world is increasingly pressing in order to provide certainty and simplicity in international business dealings. Even more important, a change in the basis of our copyright term would place the United States in the forefront of the international copyright community. Without this change, the possibility of future United States adherence to the Berne Copyright Union would evaporate, but with

[29] 17 U.S.C.A. § 201(b); see discussion of this section in House of Representatives Report No. 94–1476, "Copyright Law Revision."

[30] 17 U.S.C.A. § 401(c).

[31] H.R. Report No. 94–1476, p. 135, discussing 17 U.S.C.A. § 302.

it would come a great and immediate improvement in our copyright relations.

Existing works already under statutory copyright protection at the time of passage of the new copyright statute have had their copyright duration increased to 75 years. Works now in their first 28-year copyright under the old system must be renewed if they are in their 28th year, but the second term will be expanded to 47 years to provide a total of 75 years' protection. For copyrighted works in their renewal term, 19 years will be added so that copyright on such works will exist for a total of 75 years.[32] Congress repeatedly extended the terms of expiring copyrights from 1964 to 1975, in anticipation of the enactment of copyright revision.[33]

In October, 1988, the Senate finally ratified an agreement bringing the United States within the Berne Copyright Union.[34] At the same time Congress approved legislation revising the Copyright Act of 1976 to conform to the terms of Berne Convention. Film and video distributors, music and publishing industry leaders all favored ratification, believing that participation in this international agreement would secure a much higher measure of protection for the creative efforts of American producers and authors.

One legal effect of the United States having joined the Berne Copyright Union is that since March 1, 1989, when this international agreement became a part of American copyright law, all American and other creators of intellectual property who are citizens of member nations enjoy full copyright protection whether or not their works display an official notice of copyright. This means that from that time onward, any work published without a copyright notice will no longer pass into public domain simply because of the absence of such a notice.

Despite this new copyright protection, including the legal notice on copyrighted materials is still a far wiser course of action to follow, because a notice of copyright discourages use of copyrighted materials without permission. A copyright notice prevents anyone using such materials from later claiming "innocent" infringement of the copyrighted work.

Copyright Registration and Deposit

As in the past, copyright registration will be accomplished by filling out a form obtainable from:

[32] 17 U.S.C.A. § 304.

[33] See H.R. Report No. 94–1476, p. 140.

[34] Paul Harris, "Senate Ratifies States Entry Into Berne Treaty," Variety, October 26, 1988, p. 1.

Register of Copyrights
Library of Congress
Washington, D.C. 20559

(In addition, corresponding with the Publications Division of the Copyright Office (address above) can yield much helpful information. Information Package 109 contains sample forms, and be sure to ask for Copyright Office R–1, Copyright Basics. The Copyright Office information service—as of 1992—was available by calling (202) 479–0700 weekdays between 8:30 a.m. and 5 p.m. A copyright hotline is provided for ordering specific forms: (202) 707–9100.)

The Register of Copyrights will require (with some exceptions specified by the Copyright Office), that material deposited for registration shall include two complete copies of the best edition.[35] (The deposit of two copies of each work being copyrighted has built the collections of the Library of Congress.) These copies are to be deposited within three months after publication, along with a completed form as prescribed by the Register of Copyrights.[36] A fee of $10 must be paid for most items being copyrighted.[37] It should be noted that registration is required before any action for copyright infringement can be started.[38]

If an individual carries out a "bluff copyright"—that is, places a copyright notice on a work at the time of publication without bothering to register it and deposit copies as outlined above, that person could have some difficulties with the Register of Copyrights. The Register of Copyrights may demand deposit of such unregistered works. Unless deposit is made within three months, an individual may be liable to pay a fine of up to $250. If a person "willfully or repeatedly" refuses to comply with such demand, a fine of $2,500 may be imposed.[39]

Authors and the Copyright Act of 1976

The sweeping copyright revision which went into effect in 1978—compared to its 1909 predecessor—is truly the author's friend. As Professor Kent R. Middleton has pointed out, authors' ownership of rights under the old statute was precarious indeed. "One change," Middleton wrote, "which makes copyright divisible,

---

[35] 17 U.S.C.A. § 407. Other useful circulars available in 1989 from the Publications Division of the Copyright include Circular Ric, Copyright Registration Procedures; Circular R22, How to Investigate the Copyright Status of a Work, and Circular R21, Reproduction of Copyrighted Works by Educators and Librarians.

[36] 17 U.S.C.A. § 407.

[37] Payment of fees is specified by 17 U.S.C.A. § 708.

[38] 17 U.S.C.A. § 411; see also 17 U.S.C.A. § 205.

[39] 17 U.S.C.A. § 407(d).

gives the author greater flexibility in selling his work to different media. The other, vesting initial ownership with the creator of a work, makes the author's title more secure."[40]

Under the 1909 statute, a single legal title was held by a "proprietor" to any writing or artistic creation. Typically if an author sold the right to publish a work, he sold *all* rights to his creation.[41] Under the revised statute, authors can sell *some* rights or *all* rights as they wish. In that way, a writer may sell "one-time rights"—for use of his work only once—and then will keep other rights to re-sell the same work. For example, a magazine article—such as "The Urban Cowboy," published in *Esquire Magazine* —became the basis for a smash motion picture of the same name. Under § 201 of the revised copyright act, an author retains ownership in anything he does unless he or she *expressly* signs away all rights to a publisher.[42]

Free-lance journalists should beware of the phrase "work made for hire." Under both the old and new laws, a work produced while working for an employer constituted a "work made for hire," and all rights in that work belong to the employer. As Professor Middleton has warned, "a free-lancer's commissioned work may also be considered a work made for hire if a publisher can get a free lancer to agree."[43]

Journalists should also pay attention to what kinds of rights they are selling. If you sell "all rights," your financial stake in a piece of work is at an end. Perhaps it would be better for you to sell "first serial rights"—which will allow, for example, a magazine to publish your writing one time anywhere in the world. Then, the rights to that work revert to you, the author. Or, you might sell first North American rights, which would allow publication of your work one time in this part of the world, but not anywhere else.[44]

SEC. 73. ORIGINALITY

The concept of originality means that authors or artists have done their own work, and that their work is not copied from or grossly imitative of others' literary or artistic property.

[40] Kent R. Middleton, "Copyright and the Journalist: New Powers for the Free-Lancer," Journalism Quarterly 56:1 (Spring, 1979), p. 39.

[41] Harry G. Henn, "Ownership of Copyright, Transfer of Ownership," in James C. Goodale, chairman, Communications Law 1979 (New York: Practising Law Institute, 1979) pp. 709–711.

[42] 17 U.S.C.A. § 201.

[43] Middleton, op. cit., p. 40.

[44] The Writer's Market.

Originality is a fundamental principle of copyright; originality implies that the author or artist created the work through his own skill, labor, and judgment.[45] The concept of originality means that the particular work must be firsthand, pristine, not copied or imitated. Originality, however, does not mean that the work must be necessarily novel or clever, or that it have any value as literature or art. What constitutes originality was explained in an old but frequently quoted case, Emerson v. Davies. The famed Justice Joseph Story of Massachusetts wrote in 1845: [46]

> In truth, in literature, in science and in art, there are, and can be, few, if any, things, which, in an abstract sense, are strictly new and original throughout. Every book in literature, science, and art, borrows, and must necessarily borrow, and use much which was well known and used before.

The question of originality seems clear in concept but this quality of composition is not always easy to separate and identify in particular cases. This is true especially when different authors have conceived like expressions or based their compositions upon commonly accepted ideas, terms, or descriptions in sequence. It must be borne in mind that an idea as such cannot be the subject of copyright; to be eligible for copyright, ideas must have particular physical expressions, as signs, symbols, or words. As was stated in Kaeser & Blair, Inc. v. Merchants' Association, Inc., "copyright law does not afford protection against the use of an idea, but only as to the means by which the idea is expressed." [47]

Similarly, a recent Supreme decision has held that no amount of "sweat of the brow" labor ever merits copyright protection in itself unless accompanied by some degree of originality.[48] Rural Telephone, a small Kansas phone company, had invested a substantial amount of time compiling a directory that listed the names and addresses of its subscribers in several different communities.

When Feist Publications sought to publish a regional phone directory, Rural refused to give Feist permission to include Rural's copyrighted white pages in this directory. Feist proceeded to incorporate the Rural listings in its regional telephone directory without permission, altering some of the information to conform to

[45] American Code Co. v. Bensinger, et al., 282 Fed. 829 (2d Cir.1922).

[46] 8 Fed.Cas. 615, No. 4,436 (C.C.Mass.1845).

[47] 64 F.2d 575, 577 (6th Cir.1933). See also, Holmes v. Hurst, 174 U.S. 82, 19 S.Ct. 606 (1899); Eisenschiml v. Fawcett Publications, Inc., 246 F.2d 598, 114 U.S. P.Q. 199 (7th Cir.1957).

[48] Feist Publications, Inc. v. Rural Telephone Service Co., Inc., 499 U.S. 504, 111 S.Ct. 1282 (1991).

its own directory format, but publishing many of the listings exactly as they appeared in the Rural telephone directory.

Justice O'Connor, speaking for the Court, explained that although both the Copyright Act of 1909 and 1976 recognized the right of a compiler to claim copyright protection for a collection of facts, a subsequent compiler was free to use those same facts in preparing a competing work so long as the new work did not follow exactly the same selection and arrangement of those facts.

Here the Court found that although Rural had devoted sufficient effort to make its white pages useful, it had not done so in a sufficiently creative way to make the work original.[49] As the Court itself had explained this crucial distinction between effort and originality almost a century ago,

> The right secured by copyright is not the right to forbid the use of certain words or facts or ideas by others; it is a right to that arrangement of words which the author has selected to express his ideas which the law protects.[50]

SEC. 74. INFRINGEMENT AND REMEDIES

Violation of copyright includes such use or copying of an author's work that his possibility of profit is lessened.

Anyone who violates any of the exclusive rights spelled out by Sections 106 through 108 of the copyright statute is an infringer. Section 106 provides that copyright owners have the exclusive rights to do and to authorize any of the following: [51]

(1) to reproduce the copyrighted work in copies or phono records;

(2) to prepare derivative works based upon the copyrighted work;

(3) to distribute copies or phonorecords of the copyrighted work to the public by sale or other transfer of ownership, or by rental, lease or lending;

---

[49] Ibid., at ___, 111 S.Ct. at 1290.

[50] Holmes v. Hurst, 174 U.S. 82, 19 S.Ct. 606 (1899); Van Rensselaer v. General Motors Corp., 324 F.2d 354 (6th Cir.1963).

[51] 17 U.S.C.A. § 106. Note, however, that these "exclusive rights" are subject to limitations as spelled out in §§ 107 ("Fair Use"), 108 ("Reproduction by Libraries and Archives,"), 109 ("Effect of transfer of a particular copy or phonorecord"), and 110 ("Exemption of certain performances and displays," as by instructors or pupils in teaching activities in non-profit educational institutions.) See, also, §§ 111–118, dealing with secondary transmissions by cable TV systems, ephemeral recordings, pictorial, sculptural and graphic works, sound recordings, plays, juke boxes, computers and information systems, and certain works' use in non-commercial broadcasting.

(4) in the case of literary, musical, dramatic, and choreographic works, to perform the copyrighted work publicly, and

(5) in the case of literary, musical, dramatic and choreographic works, pantomimes, and motion pictures and other audiovisual works, including the individual images of a motion picture or other audiovisual work, to display the copyrighted work publicly.

The next section of the statute—Section 107—inserted sizable limitations on the above-enumerated "exclusive rights" by sketching—in broad terms—the judicially created doctrine of fair use. Fair use is discussed in some detail in Section 76 later in this chapter.

It should be kept in mind that copyright law is now analogous to old wine in a new bottle. The "bottle" which holds this area of law together, so to speak, is the new statute. But its provisions, by and large, will be interpreted to a considerable extent in terms of copyright cases—some decided many years ago.

In order to win a lawsuit for copyright infringement, a plaintiff must establish two separate facts, as the late Circuit Judge Jerome N. Frank wrote some years ago: "(a) that the alleged infringer copied from plaintiff's work, and (b) that, if copying is proved, it was so 'material' or substantial as to constitute unlawful appropriation." [52] Even so, the material copied need not be extensive or "lengthy" in order to be infringement. "In an appropriate case," Judge Frank noted, "copyright infringement might be demonstrated, with no proof or weak proof of access, by showing that a simple brief phrase, contained in both pieces, was so idiosyncratic in its treatment as to preclude coincidence.[53] Judge Frank also noted that even a great, famous author or artist might be found guilty of copyright infringement. He wrote, "we do not accept the aphorism, when a great composer steals, he is 'influenced'; when an unknown steals, he is 'infringing.' "[54]

Copyright protection continues even though a usurper gives away the copyrighted material or obtains his profit on some associated activity. The old case of Herbert v. Shanley Co. (1917) is relevant here. Shanley's restaurant employed musicians to play at mealtimes. Victor Herbert's song "Sweethearts," was performed, but no arrangement had been made with Herbert or his representatives to use the song. Defendant Shanley argued that he had not infringed upon Herbert's copyright because no profit came from music which was played merely to lend atmos-

[52] Heim v. Universal Pictures Co., 154 F.2d 480, 487 (2d Cir.1946).
[53] Ibid., p. 488.
[54] Ibid.

phere to his restaurant. The Supreme Court of the United States, however, held that Shanley had benefited from the playing of the music.[55]

As under the former statute, a court may, in its discretion, award full court costs plus a "reasonable attorney's fee" to the winning party in a copyright lawsuit.[56] A plaintiff in an infringement suit also may opt to ask for "statutory damages" rather than actual damage and profits: [57]

(1) * * * the copyright owner may elect, at any time before final judgment is rendered, to recover, instead of actual damages and profits, an award of statutory damages for all infringements involved in the action, with respect to any one work, for which any one infringer is liable individually, or for which any two or more infringers are liable jointly and severally, in a sum of not less than $250 or more than $10,000 as the court considers just. * * *

(2) In a case where the copyright owner sustains the burden of proving, and the court finds, that infringement was committed willfully, the court in its discretion may increase the award of statutory damages to a sum of not more than $50,000. In a case where the infringer sustains the burden of proving, and the court finds, that such infringer was not aware and had no reason to believe that his or her acts constituted an infringement of copyright, the court in its discretion may reduce the award of statutory damages to a sum of not less than $100.

If you own a copyright and it is infringed upon, you have an impressive arsenal of remedies or weapons under the 1976 copyright statute.

For openers, if you know that someone is infringing on your copyright or you can prove is about to do so, a federal court has the power to issue temporary and final injunctions "on such terms as it may deem reasonable to prevent or restrain injunctions." [58] Furthermore, this injunction may be served on the suspected copyright infringer anywhere in the United States.[59] That's a form, in other words, of prior restraint at the disposal of an affronted copyright owner.

[55] 242 U.S. 591, 37 S.Ct. 232 (1917).

[56] 17 U.S.C.A. § 505.

[57] 17 U.S.C.A. § 504(c)(1), (2).

[58] 17 U.S.C.A. § 502(a). For an example of an unsuccessful attempt to get an injunction, see Belushi v. Woodward, 598 F.Supp. 36 (D.D.C.1984), 10 Med.L.Rptr. 1870. The case involved widow of actor John Belushi asking that author Bob Woodward and publisher Simon & Schuster be enjoined from publishing book because of allegedly unauthorized use of her copyrighted photo.

[59] 17 U.S.C.A. § 502(b).

A copyright owner may also apply to a federal court to get an order to impound "on such terms as it may deem reasonable, * * * all copies or phonorecords claimed to have been made or used in violation of the copyright owner's exclusive rights."[60] And, if a court orders it as part of a final judgment or decree, the articles made in violation of the copyright owner's exclusive rights may be destroyed or otherwise disposed of.[61]

A copyright infringer, generally speaking, is liable for either of two things: (1) the copyright owner's actual damages and any additional profits of the infringer * * * or (2) statutory damages.[62]

Actual Damages and Profits

Consider the statute's language on "actual damages and profits": [63]

The copyright owner is entitled to recover the actual damages suffered by him or her as a result of the infringement, and any profits of the infringer that are attributable to the infringement and are not taken into account in computing actual damages. In establishing the infringer's profits, the copyright owner is required to present proof only of the infringer's gross revenue, and the infringer is required to prove his or her deductible expenses and the elements of profit attributable to factors other than the copyrighted work.

"Damages are awarded to compensate the copyright owner for losses from the infringement, and profits are awarded to prevent the infringer from unfairly benefiting from a wrongful act."[64]

In seeking to recover profits from a copyright infringer, the burden of proof falls upon the plaintiff to show the gross sales or profits arising from the infringement. The copyright infringer is permitted to deduct any legitimate costs or expenses which he can prove were incurred during publication of the stolen work. The winner of a suit to recover profits under copyright law can receive only the *net profits* resulting from an infringement. As the Supreme Court of the United States has declared, " 'The infringer is liable for actual, not for possible, gains.' "[65]

[60] 17 U.S.C.A. § 503(a).

[61] 17 U.S.C.A. § 503(b).

[62] 17 U.S.C.A. § 504(a).

[63] 17 U.S.C.A. § 504(b).

[64] H.R.Rep. No. 94–1476 (Sept. 3, 1976), "Copyright Law Revision," p. 161.

[65] Sheldon v. Metro-Goldwyn Pictures Corp., 309 U.S. 390, 400–401, 60 S.Ct. 681, 683 (1940); Golding v. R.K.O. Pictures, Inc., 35 Cal.2d 690, 221 P.2d 95 (1950).

Net profits can run to a great deal of money, especially when the work is a commercial success as a book or motion picture. Edward Sheldon sued Metro-Goldwyn Pictures Corp. and others for infringing on his play, "Dishonored Lady" through the production of the Metro-Goldwyn film, "Letty Lynton." A federal district court, after an accounting had been ordered, found that Metro-Goldwyn had received net profits of $585,604.37 from their exhibitions of the motion picture.[66]

Mr. Sheldon did not get *all* of Metro-Goldwyn's net profits from the movie, however. On appeal, it was held that Sheldon should not benefit from the profits that motion picture stars had made for the picture by their talent and box-office appeal. Sheldon, after his case had been heard by both a United States Court of Appeals and the Supreme Court of the United States, came out with "only" 20 per cent of the net profits, or roughly $118,000. It still would have been much cheaper for Metro-Goldwyn simply to have bought Sheldon's script. Negotiations with Sheldon for his play had been started by Metro-Goldwyn, but were never completed. The asking price for movie rights to the Sheldon play was evidently to be about $30,000, or slightly more than one-fourth of the amount the courts awarded to the playwright.[67]

Copyright cases involving music have proved to be difficult. The evidence in such cases is largely circumstantial, resting upon similarities between songs. The issue in such a case, as one court expressed it, is whether "so much of what is pleasing to the ears of lay listeners, who comprise the audience for whom such popular music is composed, that defendant wrongfully appropriated something which belongs to the plaintiff."[68]

More than "lay listeners" often get involved in such cases, however. Expert witnesses sometimes testify in copyright infringement cases involving music. But it can happen that the plaintiff who feels that his musical composition has been stolen, and the defendant as well, will *both* bring their own expert witnesses into court, where these witnesses expertly disagree with each other.[69]

In proving a case of copyright infringement—and not just for those cases dealing with music—it is often useful if plaintiffs can show that the alleged infringement had "access" to the original work from which the copy was supposed to have been made. Such

[66] Sheldon v. Metro-Goldwyn Pictures Corp., 26 F.Supp. 134, 136 (S.D.N.Y.1938), 81 F.2d 49 (2d Cir.1936), 106 F.2d 45 (2d Cir.1939).

[67] 309 U.S. 390, 398, 407, 60 S.Ct. 681, 683, 687 (1940); see Nimmer, op. cit., § 14.03 fn. 30 (1988).

[68] Arnstein v. Porter, 154 F.2d 464, 473 (2d Cir.1946).

[69] Ibid.

"access" needs to be proved by the plaintiff, if only by the circumstantial evidence of similarity between two works.

During the 1940s, songwriter Ira B. Arnstein tried to show that the noted composer, Cole Porter, not only had access to his work, but that Porter had taken freely from Arnstein. The courts declared that Porter had not infringed upon any common law or statutory copyrights held by Arnstein. Porter's victory in the courts was hard-won, however.

Arnstein began a copyright infringement lawsuit against Cole Porter in a federal district court. Arnstein charged that Porter's "Begin the Beguine" was a plagiarism from Arnstein's "the Lord is My Shepherd" and "A Mother's Prayer." He also claimed that Porter's "My Heart Belongs to Daddy" had been lifted from Arnstein's "A Mother's Prayer."

On the question of access, plaintiff Arnstein testified that his apartment had been burglarized and accused Porter of receiving the stolen manuscripts from the burglars. Arnstein declared that Porter's "Night and Day" had been stolen from Arnstein's "I Love You Madly," which had never been published but which had been performed once over the radio. Technically, this meant that Arnstein's "I Love You Madly" had never been published.

In reply, Porter swore that he had never seen or heard any of Arnstein's compositions, and that he did not know the persons said to have stolen them. Even so, Arnstein's lawsuit asked for a judgment against Porter of "at least one million dollars out of the millions this defendant has earned and is earning out of all the plagiarism."[70]

At the original trial, the district court directed the jury to bring in a summary verdict in favor of Porter. Arnstein then appealed to a U.S. Circuit Court of Appeals, where Judge Jerome Frank explained what the appellate court had done. The Circuit Court of Appeals had listened to phonograph records of Cole Porter's songs and compared them to records of Arnstein's songs. As he sent the case back to a district court, jury, Judge Frank wrote:

> * * * we find similarities, but we hold that unquestionably, standing alone, they do not compel the conclusion, or permit the inference, that defendant copied. The similarities, however, are sufficient so that, if there is enough evidence of access to permit the case to go to the jury, the jury may properly infer that the similarities did not result from coincidence.

[70] Ibid., 474.

The jury then found that Cole Porter's "Begin the Beguine" had indeed been written by Cole Porter.

Similarly, the U.S. Court of Appeals, Second Circuit ruled that A.A. Hoehling could not collect damages from Universal City Studios in a dispute involving the motion picture, *The Hindenburg*. Back in 1962, Hoehling—after substantial research—published a copyrighted book, *Who Destroyed the Hindenburg?* That book advanced the theory that a disgruntled crew member of The Graf Zeppelin had planted a crude bomb in one of its gas cells.

Ten years later, after consulting Hoehling's book plus many other sources, Michael MacDonald Mooney published his own book, *The Hindenburg*. Mooney's book put forward a similar cause for the airship's destruction, but there was also evidence that authors pre-dating Hoehling had suggested the same cause for the explosion. Circuit Judge Kaufman said for the court: [71]

> All of Hoehling's allegations of copying, therefore, encompass material that is non-copyrightable as a matter of law * * *.
>
> * * *
>
> * * * in granting * * * summary judgment for defendants, courts should assure themselves that the works before them are not virtually identical. In this case, it is clear that all three authors relate the story of the Hindenburg differently.
>
> In works devoted to historical subjects, it is our view that a second author may make significant use of prior work, so long as he does not bodily appropriate the expression of another. *Rosemont Enterprises, Inc.*, 366 F.2d at 310. This principle is justified by the fundamental policy undergirding the copyright laws—the encouragement of contributions to recorded knowledge * * * Knowledge is expanded as well, by granting new authors of historical works a relatively free hand to build upon the work of their predecessors.

In Litchfield v. Spielberg, the U.S. Court of Appeals for the Ninth Circuit decided in 1984 that a copyright infringement/unfair competition lawsuit involving the movie *E.T.—The Extraterrestrial* was—if not out of this world—at least legally insupportable. Lisa Litchfield claimed that her copyrighted one-act musical play, Lokey from Maldemar, had been infringed upon by *E.T.*, the box-office smash hit. As the appeals court put it, the issue, in

[71] Hoehling v. Universal City Studios, Inc., 618 F.2d 972, 979–980 (2d Cir.1980), 6 Med.L.Rptr. 1053, 1057–1058.

addition to that of infringement, was whether the lower court had acted properly in granting defendants a summary judgment.[72]

After independently reviewing the facts, the Court of Appeals held: [73]

> There is no substantial similarity * * * between the sequences of events, mood, dialogue and characters of the two works. Any similarities in plot exist only at the general level for which plaintiff cannot claim copyright protection. * * *
>
>   * * *
>
> As is too often the case, Litchfield's action was premised "partly upon a wholly erroneous understanding of the extent of copyright protection; and partly upon that obsessive conviction, so common among authors and composers, that all similarities between their works and any others to appear later must be ascribed to plagiarism." *Dellar v. Samuel Goldwyn, Inc.,* 150 F.2d 612 (2d Cir. 1945).

As noted earlier in this chapter, facts or ideas are not copyrightable, only the style in which they are expressed. An additional gloss was put on this by a 1978 case, Miller v. Universal City Studios, which raised the question whether the research effort put into gathering facts is copyrightable.

Pulitzer Prize-winning reporter Gene Miller of The Miami Herald collaborated on writing a book with Barbara Mackle about her ordeal in a famous kidnapping incident. Ms. Mackle was held for ransom while literally buried alive in a box with seven days' life-sustaining capacity. She was rescued from the box on the fifth day. Miller worked an estimated 2500 hours in researching and writing this book.

A Universal Studios executive, William Frye, then offered Miller $15,000 for rights to use the Miller-Mackle account in a television "docudrama." Miller refused, asking for $200,000. At this point, negotiations between Miller and the studio collapsed, but the studio proceeded to produce and air a docudrama titled "The Longest Night." This production had obvious similarities to the Miller-Mackle book, and Miller sued for copyright infringement.[74]

The script writer had proceeded to write "The Longest Night" on the assumption that his studios had closed a deal with Miller

---

[72] Litchfield v. Spielberg; MCA, Inc.; Universal City Studios, Inc.; Extraterrestrial Productions; Kennedy; Tanen, and Mathison, 736 F.2d 1352 (9th Cir.1984) 10 Med.L.Rptr. 2101, 2102–2103.

[73] 736 F.2d 1352, 1355 (9th Cir.1984), 10 Med.L.Rptr. 2102, at 2105–2106.

[74] Miller v. Universal City Studios, Inc., 460 F.Supp. 984, 985–986 (S.D.Fla.1978).

for rights to the book and that he could proceed to write the script on that basis. Even so, Universal City Studios argued that no matter how hard Miller had worked to research the facts in the Mackle kidnapping case, he "may not monopolize those facts because they are historical facts and everyone has the right to write about them and communicate them to the public." The court disagreed with Universal City Studios' argument, saying: [75]

> To this court it doesn't square with reason or common sense to believe that Gene Miller would have undertaken the research involved in writing of *83 Hours Till Dawn* (or to cite a more famous example, that Truman Capote would have undertaken the research required to write *In Cold Blood*) if the author thought that upon completion of the book a movie producer or television network could simply come along and take the profits of the books and his research from him.

On appeal, however, Universal City Studios won a reversal of the judgment. The U.S. Court of Appeals, Fifth Circuit, ruled that Universal should have a new trial "＊ ＊ ＊ because the case was presented and argued to the jury on a false premise: that the labor of research by an author is protected by copyright." The Court of Appeals added that its decision was difficult to reach because there was "＊ ＊ ＊ sufficient evidence to support a finding of infringement ＊ ＊ ＊ under correct theories of copyright law." In sum, the Court of Appeals did not believe that *research* is copyrightable, only the manner in which it is *presented*. "It is well settled that copyright protection extends only to an author's expression of facts and not to the facts themselves." [76]

Sometimes, in dealing with a major Hollywood film studio, establishing infringement is actually less difficult than forcing the studio to make an honest disclosure of a film's earnings. Humorist Art Buchwald sold a screen treatment (a story outline) to Paramount in 1983 for a movie featuring Eddie Murphy. Paramount subsequently made the movie, "Coming To America" that followed the general plot line of Buchwald's treatment, but refused to honor its contract to pay Buchwald the $250,000 and 19% of the film's net profits specified by the agreement.

Although Paramount contended that the Buchwald screen treatment was only one of several the studio had used in preparing a shooting script, and that three other writers were claiming similar rights in the picture, the Court found that a substantial number of obvious parallels between Buchwald's treatment and

---

[75] Ibid., p. 987 n. 988.

[76] Miller v. Universal City Studios, Inc., 650 F.2d 1365, 1368 (5th Cir.1981).

the actual screen play justified a holding that the movie was based primarily upon his work.[77]

However, when Buchwald sought to claim his share of the film's profits, Paramount's accountants maintained that even though the film had grossed more than $125 million in all media sales worldwide, there were no profits to share with him because the studio's account books still showed a net loss for the film of $18 million.[78] The judge was not impressed by studio bookkeeping that appeared to be far more creative than the film itself, and insisted on an independent analysis of the accounting procedures employed by Paramount before making his final award to Buchwald. Efforts to trace these elusive profits are still continuing as this book goes to press.

Alex Haley, author of the best-seller *Roots*, was sued for both copyright infringement and unfair competition by Margaret Walker Alexander. Ms. Alexander claimed that Haley's book, published in 1976, was drawn substantially from her novel, *Jubilee*, published in 1966, and a pamphlet, *How I Wrote Jubilee*, published in 1972. A federal district court granted Haley a summary judgment, finding that no copyright infringement had occurred. The court said: [79]

> Many of the claimed similarities are based on matters of historical or contemporary fact. No claim of copyright protection can arise from the fact that plaintiff has written about such historical and factual items, even if we were to assume that Haley was alerted to the facts in question by reading *Jubilee*. * * *

> Another major category of items consists of material traceable to common sources, the public domain, or folk custom. Thus, a number of claimed infringements are embodiments of the cultural history of black Americans, or of both black and white Americans planning out the cruel tragedy of white-imposed slavery. Where common sources exist for the alleged similarities, or the material that is similar is otherwise not original with the plaintiff, there is no infringement. * * * This group of asserted infringements can no more be the subject of copyright protection than the cause of a date or the name of a president or a more conventional piece of historical information.

[77] Buchwald v. Paramount Pictures Corp. (Cal.1990), 17 Med.L.Rptr. 1257.

[78] "Par to Buchwald; We're $18–Mil in Hole," *Variety* February 28, 1990, p. 5.

[79] Alexander v. Haley, 460 F.Supp. 40, 44–45 (S.D.N.Y.1978).

Criminal Penalties

There can be *criminal* penalties for copyright infringement. The new statute ups the ante where phonorecord or movie pirates are concerned. Section 506 provides: [80]

> (a) CRIMINAL INFRINGEMENT.—Any person who infringes a copyright willfully and for purposes of commercial advantage or private financial gain shall be fined not more than $10,000 or imprisoned for not more than one year, or both: *Provided, however,* That any person who infringes willfully and for purposes of commercial advantage or private financial gain the copyright in a sound recording shall be fined not more than $25,000 or imprisoned for not more than one year, or both, for the first such offense and shall be fined not more than $50,000 or imprisoned for not more than two years, or both, for any subsequent offense.

Criminal penalties—fines of up to $2,500—await any person who, "with fraudulent intent," places on any article a notice of copyright that is known to be false. Similar fines may be levied against individuals who fraudulently remove a copyright notice, or who knowingly make misstatements in copyright applications or related written statements.[81]

SEC. 75. COPYRIGHT, UNFAIR COMPETITION, AND THE NEWS

The news element of a story is not subject to copyright, although the style in which an individual story is written may be protected from infringement. Reporters, in short, should do their own reporting.

Any unauthorized and unfair use of a copyrighted news story constitutes an infringement which will support either lawsuits for damages or an action in equity to get an injunction against further publication. Although a news story—or even an entire issue of a newspaper—may be copyrighted, the *news element* in a newspaper story is not subject to copyright. News is *publici juris*—the history of the day—as was well said by Justice Mahlon Pitney in the important 1918 case of International News Service v. Associated Press. Justice Pitney wrote: [82]

---

[80] 17 U.S.C.A. § 506. See also § 507, which orders a three-year statute of limitations for both criminal prosecutions and civil proceedings under the Copyright Statute.

[81] 17 U.S.C.A. § 506(c), (d) and (e).

[82] 248 U.S. 215, 39 S.Ct. 68, 71 (1918).

A News article, as a literary production, is the subject of copyright. But the news element—the information respecting current events in the literary production, is not the creation of the writer, but is a report of matters that ordinarily are publici juris; it is the history of the day. It is not to be supposed that the framers of the Constitution, when they empowered Congress to promote the progress of science and useful arts, by securing for limited times to authors and inventors the exclusive rights to their respective writings and discoveries (Const. Art. 1, § 8, par. 8), intended to confer upon one who might happen to be first to report an historic event the exclusive right for any period to spread the knowledge of it.

The Associated Press had complained of news pirating by a rival news-gathering agency, International News Service. The Supreme Court granted the Associated Press an injunction against the appropriation, by INS, of non-copyrighted AP stories while the news was still fresh enough to be salable. This was true even though in that era, and until the Copyright Act of 1976, material was not copyrighted unless it carried the © symbol and notice at the time of publication. "The peculiar value of news," Justice Pitney declared, "is in the spreading of it while it is fresh; and it is evident that a valuable property interest in the news, as news, cannot be maintained by keeping it secret."

Justice Pitney also denounced the taking, by INS, of AP stories, either by quoting or paraphrasing. Justice Pitney wrote that INS, "in appropriating * * * news and selling it as its own is endeavoring to reap where it has not sown, and by disposing of it to newspapers that are competitors * * * of AP members is appropriating to itself the harvest of those who have sown."[83]

What, then, can a newspaper or other communications medium do when it has been "beaten" to a story by its competition? It must be emphasized that the historic case of International News Service v. Associated Press did *not* say that the "beaten" news medium must sit idly by. "Pirating" news, of course, is to be avoided: pirating has been defined as "the bodily appropriation of a statement of fact or a news article, with or without rewriting, but without independent investigation or expense."[84] However, first-published news items may be used as "tips." When one newspaper discovers an event, such as the arrest of a kidnaper, its particular news presentation of the facts may be protected by copyright. Even so, such a first story may serve as a tip for other newspapers or press associations. After the first edition by the

[83] 248 U.S. 215, 239–240, 39 S.Ct. 68, 71–72 (1918).

[84] 248 U.S. 215, 243, 39 S.Ct. 68, 74 (1918).

copyrighting news organization, other organizations may independently investigate and present their own stories about the arrest of the kidnaper. In such a case, the time element between the appearance of the first edition of the copyrighting newspaper and the appearance of a second or third edition by a competing newspaper might be negligible as far as the general public is concerned; only a few hours. If other newspapers or press associations make their own investigations and obtain their own stories, they do not violate copyright.

However, to copy a copyrighted news story—or to copy or paraphrase substantially from the original story—may lead to court action, as shown in the 1921 case of Chicago Record-Herald Co. v. Tribune Association. This case arose when the *New York Tribune* copyrighted a special news story on Germany's reliance upon submarines. This story, printed in the *New York Tribune* on Feb. 3, 1917, was offered for sale for exclusive publication in the *Chicago Herald.* The *Herald* declined this opportunity, and the *Chicago Daily News* then purchased the Chicago rights to the story.

With full knowledge that the *Tribune's* story on the German submarine campaign was fully copyrighted, the *Herald* nevertheless ran a version of the same story featuring identical paragraph after identical paragraph on the morning of Feb. 3.

The *Chicago Daily News* then refused to publish the story or to pay the *New York Tribune* for it. The *Daily News,* having agreed to purchase an exclusive story, had the right to refuse a story already published in its market. The publishers of the *New York Tribune* successfully sued the *Chicago Herald* for infringement.

The judge declared that the *New York Tribune's* original story "involves authorship and literary quality and style, apart from the bare recital of the facts or statement of news." So, although facts are not copyrightable, the style in which they are expressed is protected by law.

As noted in International News Service v. Associated Press (1918), the AP won its case despite the fact that the news stories it telegraphed to its members were not copyrighted. There, the Supreme Court of the United States held that the AP had a "quasi property" right in the news stories it produced, even after their publication. Once the Supreme Court found that such a "quasi property" right existed, it then declared that appropriation of such stories by INS amounted to unfair competition and could be stopped by a court-issued injunction against INS.[85]

[85] See reference to this case at footnote 82, above. The case of International News Service v. Associated Press was cited as important by the more recent case of

Far more recently, a newspaper—the Pottstown, Pa., *Mercury*—won an unfair competition suit against a Pottstown radio station, WPAZ, getting an injunction which prevented WPAZ "'from any further appropriation of the newspaper's local news without its permission or authorization.'" [86] The court noted that businesses, radio, television, and newspapers were "competing with each other for advertising which has become a giant in our economy." This court viewed the Pottstown *Mercury's* news as "a commercial package of news items to service its advertising business." In the rather jaundiced view of the Pennsylvania Supreme Court, advertising has become virtually all-important, with "the presentation of news and entertainment almost a subsidiary function of newspapers, radio and television stations." Although copyright infringement was not the precise issue here, the Pennsylvania Supreme Court found itself able to punish the radio station for appropriating news stories under the area of law dealing with unfair competition. The court said:[87]

> * * * for the purpose of an action of unfair competition the specialized treatment of news items as a service the newspaper provides for advertisers gives the News Company [publishers of the Pottstown *Mercury*] a limited property right which the law will guard and protect against wrongful invasion by a competitor whereas, for the purpose of an action for the infringement of copyright, the specialized treatment of news is protected because the law seeks to encourage creative minds."

The limited property right in news is to some extent waived by member organizations of the Associated Press. All A.P. members are entitled to all *spontaneous* news from areas served by other A.P. member newspapers or broadcasting stations. Membership in the Associated Press includes agreement to follow this condition as stated in Article VII of the A.P. bylaws:

> Sec. 3. Each member shall promptly furnish to the [A.P.] Corporation all the news of such member's district, the area of which shall be determined by the Board of Directors. No news furnished to the Corporation by a member shall be furnished by the Corporation to any other member within such member's district.

> Sec. 4. The news which a member shall furnish to the Corporation shall be all news that is spontaneous in origin, but shall not include news that is not spontaneous

Pottstown Daily News Pub. Co. v. Pottstown Broadcasting Co., 411 Pa. 383, 192 A.2d 657, 662 (1963).

[86] Ibid.

[87] 411 Pa. 383, 192 A.2d 657, 663–664 (1963).

in its origin, or which has originated through deliberate and individual enterprise on the part of such member.

A.P. member newspapers or broadcasting stations are expected to furnish spontaneous or "spot" news stories to the Associated Press for dissemination to other members throughout the nation. However, Section 3 of the A.P. By-Laws (above) will protect the news medium originating such a story within its district. If a newspaper copyrights a spot news story about the shooting of a deputy sheriff by a gambler, other A.P. members could use the story despite the copyright. By signing the A.P. By-Laws, the originating newspaper has given its consent in advance for all A.P. members to use news stories of *spontaneous* origin. On the other hand, if a newspaper copyrights an exposé of gambling in a city based on that newspaper's individual enterprise and initiative, the other A.P. members could not use the story without permission from the copyrighting newspaper.

Roy Export Company v. CBS

Eagerness to present the news as effectively as possible in pressure situations may sometimes lead to disregard of ownership rights. Evident lack of concern about such rights cost the Columbia Broadcasting System $717,000 [88] in copyright and unfair competition damages for missteps making a documentary on the occasion of the death of film legend Charlie Chaplin. In 1977, CBS broadcast a film biography of Chaplin, including film clips from six Chaplin-motion pictures. Exclusive rights in those films were held by several parties, including the first-named plaintiff in this case, Roy Export Company Establishment of Vaduz, Liechtenstein.[89]

The events leading to this lawsuit are traceable to 1972, when the Academy of Motion Picture Arts and Sciences (AMPAS) arranged to have a film tribute made from highlights of Chaplin's films. This tribute was broadcast by NBC-TV in connection with an appearance by Chaplin at the 1972 Academy Awards ceremo-

[88] Roy Export Co. Establishment of Vaduz, Liechtenstein v. CBS, 672 F.2d 1095, 1097 (2d Cir.1982), 8 Med.L.Rptr. 1637, 1639. See footnote 6: "Of the compensatory total, $7,280 was for statutory copyright infringement, $1 was for common-law copyright infringement, and $300,000 was for unfair competition. The punitive damages were divided between the common-law claims: $300,000 for common-law copyright infringement and $110,000 for unfair competition."

[89] 672 F.2d 1095 (2d Cir.1982), 8 Med.L.Rptr. 1637, cert. denied 459 U.S. 826, 103 S.Ct. 60 (1982). This case was complicated, Circuit Judge Newman said, by troublesome questions coming from pre-1978 common law protection for intellectual property, plus challenges to statutory copyrights, "on the ground that the work lost its common copyright prior to January 1, 1978, entered the public domain, and therefore was not eligible for statutory copyright." Judge Newman cited M. Nimmer, Nimmer on Copyright, Sec. 4.01 [B].

nies. It was understood that excerpts compiled in that tribute were to be used only on that one occasion.[90]

In 1973, CBS started work on a retrospective of Chaplin's life, to be used as a broadcast obituary when Chaplin died. CBS made repeated requests for permission to use excerpts from Chaplin's films, but was rebuffed. CBS was told that the copyright owners were involved in producing their own film biography of Chaplin titled "The Gentleman Tramp." That production used some of the same footage used in the Academy Awards show compilation, but did not use that compilation itself. CBS, meanwhile, made a "rough cut" of a Chaplin obituary/biography. The network was offered a chance to purchase rights to show "The Gentleman Tramp" in 1976 and 1977, but did not do so.

Chaplin died on Christmas day, 1977. CBS had its "rough cut" biography ready to use, but instead used a copy of the 1972 Academy Award show compilation which CBS had obtained from NBC. CBS put together a new biography, depending heavily "on what CBS knew to be copyrighted material." This hastily assembled new biography was broadcast on December 26, 1977.[91]

Roy Export Company and other copyright owners of Chaplin films then sued CBS for copyright infringement and for unfair competition. The latter claim said the CBS broadcast competed unfairly with the copyright owners' own Chaplin retrospective, "The Gentleman Tramp." A jury trial in a U.S. district court found CBS liable to the plaintiffs for $307,281 compensatory and $410,000 punitive damages.

In its appeal, CBS asserted that the First Amendment provides a general privilege to report newsworthy events such as Chaplin's death, and that this privilege shielded the network from liability. CBS claimed that the main reason for Chaplin's fame was his films, and that it would be meaningless to try to provide a full account of his life without making use of his films. Circuit Judge Newman summed up the network's First Amendment argument:[92]

> In CBS's view, the 1972 Academy Awards ceremony, at which the Compilation received its single public showing, was an "irreducible single news event" to which the showing of the Compilation was integral. The significance of the ceremony, CBS contends, was not simply that Chaplin appeared after a twenty-year exile provoked by Senator [Joseph] McCarthy's investigations, but that a collection of his work was shown, thereby bringing home

[90] 672 F.2d at 1098 (2d Cir.1982), 10 Med.L.Rptr. at 1639.

[91] Ibid.

[92] 672 F.2d 1095, 1099 (2d Cir.1982), 10 Med.L.Rptr. 1637, 1640.

to the American people both what they had been deprived of by McCarthyism and how ludicrous had been the attempt to find subversion and political innuendo in Chaplin's films. CBS concludes that the plaintiff's claims for infringement of the copyright in the films and the compilation must give way to an asserted First Amendment news-reporting privilege.

The Court of Appeals found CBS's First Amendment arguments "unpersuasive," resting on a theory that someday, some way, there might be an inseparability of news value and copyrighted work to the extent that copyright would have to yield. Judge Newman wrote, however: "No Circuit that has considered the question * * * has ever held that the First Amendment provides a privilege in the copyright field distinct from the accommodation embodied in the 'fair use' doctrine." And in a footnote he added,[93]

> Fair use balances the public interest in the free flow of ideas and information with the copyright holder's interest in exclusive proprietary control of his work. It permits use of the copyrighted matter " 'in a reasonable manner without [the copyright owner's] consent, notwithstanding the monopoly granted to the owner.' " Rosemont Enterprises, Inc., v. Random House, Inc., 366 F.2d 303 (2d Cir.1966), cert. denied 385 U.S. 1009, 87 S.Ct. 714 * * * (1967) * * *.

The Roy Export case and Unfair Competition

CBS also argued that the plaintiffs could not maintain a claim that the network's December 26, 1977, broadcast unfairly competed with the plaintiffs' rights in "The Gentleman Tramp." CBS asserted the unfair competition claim rested on "misappropriation" of films under New York state law, " * * * and that a state law claim based on misappropriation of federally copyrighted materials is pre-empted * * * "[94] The Court of Appeals replied:

> An unfair competition claim involving misappropriation usually concerns the taking and use of the plaintiff's property to compete against the plaintiff's use of the same property, e.g. International News Service v. Associated Press * * * [248 U.S. 215, 39 S.Ct. 68 (1918)] By contrast, in this case the Compilation was taken and used to compete unfairly with a different property, "The Gentleman Tramp." Despite the unusual facts, we are satisfied that the plaintiffs have established an unfair competition tort under New York law.

[93] 672 F.2d 1095, 1099 (2d Cir.1982), 10 Med.L.Rptr. 1637, 1640.

[94] 697 F.2d at 1104–1105 (2d Cir.1982), 10 Med.L.Rptr. at 1644–1645.

* * *

CBS unquestionably appropriated the "skill, expenditures and labor" of the plaintiffs to its own commercial advantage. Its actions, in apparent violation of its own and the industry's guidelines, were arguably a form of "commercial immorality." We are confident that the New York courts would call that conduct unfair competition.

The Court of Appeals ruled that the damages of more than $700,000 against CBS should stand, including the punitive damage awards totaling $410,000. Judge Newman wrote, "The deterrent potential of an award of $410,000 must be measured by its likely effect on a national television network with 1977 earnings of some $217,000,000 * * *."[95]

We now turn to a discussion of a major defense against claims of copyright infringement: the doctrine of "fair use."

SEC. 76. THE DEFENSE OF FAIR USE

The fair use doctrine—invented by courts to allow some use of others' works—was made explicit by the Copyright Act of 1976. Major cases—such as *Sony* and *The Nation* magazine—continue to add to the definition of fair use in a piecemeal fashion.

The copyright law phrase "fair use" made a good deal of news during the mid-1980s. Its growth in importance is quite remarkable, stemming as it does from judicial wriggling many years ago. Its growth may be understood as being fueled, in a major way, by onrushing technological changes. Recent examples of important fair use cases decided by the Supreme Court—and which are taken up later in this Section—are Sony Corporation of America v. Universal City Studios, Inc.,[96] and Harper & Row Publishers, Inc. v. Nation Enterprises.[97]

The old 1909 copyright statute gave each copyright holder an exclusive right to "print, reprint, publish, copy and vend the copyrighted * * *." As stated in that Act, it was an *absolute* right; the wording was put in terms so absolute that even pencil-and-paper copying was a violation of the U.S. Copyright Act.[98] Because the 1909 statute's terms were so stringent, if enforced to the letter, it could have prevented anyone except the copyright holder from making any copy of any copyrighted work. Such a

---

[95] 697 F.2d at 1107 (2d Cir.1982), 10 Med.L.Rptr. at 1646.

[96] 464 U.S. 417, 104 S.Ct. 774 (1984).

[97] 471 U.S. 539, 105 S.Ct. 2218 (1985).

[98] See 17 U.S.C.A. § 10 of the statute which preceded the Copyright Statute of 1976: Verner W. Clapp, "Library Photocopying and Copyright: Recent Developments," Law Library Journal 55:1 (Feb., 1962) p. 12.

statute was clearly against public policy favoring dissemination of information and knowledge and was plainly unenforceable. As a result, courts responded by developing the doctrine called "fair use."

American courts assumed—in creating a judge-made exception to the absolute language of the 1909 copyright statute—that "the law implies the consent of the copyright owner to a fair use of his publication for the advancement of science or art." [99] The fair use doctrine, although a rather elastic yardstick, was a needed improvement. The 1976 copyright statute has distilled the old common law copyright doctrine into some statutory guidelines. Factors to be considered by courts in determining whether the use made of a work in any particular case is a fair use include: [1]

(1) the purpose and character of the use, including whether such use is of a commercial nature or is for nonprofit educational purposes;

(2) the nature of the copyrighted work;

(3) the amount and substantiality of the portion used in relation to the copyrighted work as a whole; and

(4) the effect of the use upon the potential market for or value of the copyrighted work.

What, then, is fair use? In 1964, one expert asserted that fair use of someone's copyrightable materials exists "somewhere in the hinterlands between the broad avenue of independent creation and the jungle of unmitigated plagiarism." [2] No easy or automatic formula can be presented which will draw a safe line between fair use and infringement. Fifty words taken from a magazine article might be held to be fair use, while taking one line from a short poem might be labeled infringement by a court. The House of Representatives Committee on the Judiciary said this in its report on the 1976 copyright statute: [3]

General intention behind the provision

The statement of the fair use doctrine in section 107 offers some guidance to users in determining when the principles of the doctrine apply. However, the endless variety of situations and combinations of circumstances that can rise in particular cases precludes the formulation of exact rules in the statute. The bill endorses the

[99] Wittenberg, op. cit., p. 148, offers a good non-technical description of fair use before it was expanded in 1967. See section 44 in this chapter.

[1] 17 U.S.C.A. § 107.

[2] Arthur N. Bishop, "Fair Use of Copyrighted Books," Houston Law Review, 2:2 (Fall, 1964) at p. 207.

[3] H.R. Report No. 94–1476, discussing the fair use provisions of 17 U.S.C.A. § 107.

purpose and general scope of the judicial doctrine of fair use, but there is no disposition to freeze the doctrine in the statute, especially during a period of rapid technological change. Beyond a very broad statutory explanation of what fair use is and some of the criteria applicable to it, the courts must be free to adapt the doctrine to particular situations on a case-by-case basis. Section 107 is intended to restate the present judicial doctrine of fair use, not to change, narrow, or enlarge it in any way.

Generally speaking, courts have been quite lenient with quotations used in scholarly works or critical reviews. However, courts have been less friendly toward use of copyrighted materials for commercial or non-scholarly purposes, or in works which are competitive with the original copyrighted piece.[4] The problems surrounding the phrase "fair use" have often arisen in connection with scientific, legal, or scholarly materials. With such works, it is to be expected that there will be similar treatment given to similar subject matters.[5] A crucial question, obviously, is whether the writer makes use of an earlier writer's work without doing substantial independent work. Wholesale copying is *not* fair use.[6] Even if a writer had no intention of making unfair use of someone else's work, that writer still could be found liable for copyright infringement.[7] The idea of independent investigation is of great importance here. Copyrighted materials may be used as a *guide* for the purpose of gathering information, provided that the researcher or writer then performs an original investigation and expresses the results of such work in his or her own language.[8]

Fair Use and Public Interest

Although many earlier cases expressed a narrow, restrictive view of the doctrine of fair use, some important decisions since the mid-1960s have emphasized the idea of *public* interest. This changed approach is of great importance to journalists and scholars, for where there are matters which are newsworthy or otherwise of interest to the public, courts will consider such factors in determining whether a fair use was made of copyrighted materi-

---

[4] Eisenschiml v. Fawcett Publications, Inc., 246 F.2d 598 (7th Cir.1957); Benny v. Loew's Inc., 239 F.2d 532 (9th Cir.1956), affirmed 356 U.S. 43, 78 S.Ct. 667 (1958), rehearing denied 356 U.S. 934, 78 S.Ct. 770 (1958); Pilpel and Zavin, op. cit., pp. 160–161.

[5] Eisenschiml v. Fawcett Publications, Inc., 246 F.2d 598 (7th Cir.1957), certiorari denied 355 U.S. 907, 78 S.Ct. 334 (1957).

[6] Benny v. Loew's Inc., 239 F.2d 532 (9th Cir.1956), affirmed 356 U.S. 43, 78 S.Ct. 667 (1958), rehearing denied 356 U.S. 934, 78 S.Ct. 770 (1958).

[7] Wihtol v. Crow, 309 F.2d 777 (8th Cir.1962).

[8] Jeweler's Circular Pub. Co. v. Keystone Pub. Co., 281 Fed. 83 (2d Cir.1922), certiorari denied 259 U.S. 581, 42 S.Ct. 464 (1922).

als. A key case here is the 1967 decision known as Rosemont Enterprises, Inc. v. Random House, Inc. and John Keats. This case arose because Howard Hughes, a giant in America's aviation, oil and motion picture industries had a passionate desire to remain anonymously out of the public eye. A brief chronology will illustrate how this copyright infringement action came about:

• January and February, 1954: *Look* magazine, owned by Cowles Communications, Inc., published a series of three articles by Stanley White, titled "The Howard Hughes Story."

• In 1962, Random House, Inc., hired Thomas Thompson, a journalist employed by *Life* magazine, to prepare a book-length biography of Hughes. Later, either Hughes or his attorneys learned of the forthcoming Random House book. An attorney employed by Hughes warned Random House that Hughes did not want this biography and "would make trouble if the book was published." Thompson resigned from the project, and Random House then hired John Keats to complete the biography.

• Rosemont Enterprises, Inc., was organized in September, 1965 by Hughes' attorney and by two officers of his wholly-owned Hughes Tool Company.

• On May 20, 1966, Rosemont Enterprises purchased copyrights to the *Look* articles, advised Random House of this, and five days later brought a copyright infringement suit in New York. Attorneys for Rosemont somehow had gained possession of Random House galley proofs of the Random House biography of Hughes then being published: "Howard Hughes: a Biography by John Keats." [9]

Rosemont Enterprises sought an injunction to restrain Random House from selling, publishing, or distributing copies of its biography of Hughes because the book amounted to a prima facie case of copyright infringement. With his five-day-old ownership of the copyrights for the 1954 Look magazine articles, Hughes was indeed in a position to "cause trouble" for Random House.

The trial court agreed with the Rosemont Enterprises argument that infringement had occurred, and granted the injunction against Random House, holding up distribution of the book. The trial court rejected Random House's claims of fair use of the Look articles, saying that the privilege of fair use was confined to "materials used for purposes of criticism or comment or in scholarly works of scientific or educational value." This district court took the view that if something was published "for commercial purposes"—that is, if it was designed for the popular market—the doctrine of fair use could not be employed to lessen the severity of

[9] Rosemont Enterprises, Inc. v. Random House, Inc. and John Keats, 366 F.2d 303, 304–305 (2d Cir.1966).

the copyright law.[10] The district court found that the Hughes biography by Keats was for the popular market and therefore the fair use privilege could not be invoked by Random House.[11]

Circuit Judge Leonard P. Moore, speaking for the Circuit Court of Appeals, took another view. First of all, he noted that the three *Look* articles, taken together, totalled only 13,500 words, or between 35 and 39 pages if published in book form. Keats' 1966 biography on the other hand, had 166,000 words, or 304 pages in book form. Furthermore, Judge Moore stated that the *Look* articles did not purport to be a biography, but were merely accounts of a number of interesting incidents in Hughes' life. Judge Moore declared: [12]

> * * * there can be little doubt that portions of the *Look* article were copied. Two direct quotations and one eight-line paraphrase were attributed to Stephen White, the author of the articles. A mere reading of the *Look* articles, however, indicates that there is considerable doubt as to whether the copied and paraphrased matter constitutes a material and substantial portion of those articles.

> Furthermore, while the mode of expression employed by White is entitled to copyright protection, he could not acquire by copyright a monopoly in the narration of historical events.

In any case, the Keats book should fall within the doctrine of fair use. Quoting a treatise on copyright, Judge Moore stated: "Fair use is a privilege in others than the owner of a copyright to use the copyrighted material in a reasonable manner without his consent, notwithstanding the monopoly granted to the owner * * *." [13]

Judge Moore demanded that public interest considerations— the public's interest in knowing about prominent and powerful men—be taken into account. He wrote that "public interest should prevail over possible damage to the copyright owner." He complained that the district court's preliminary injunction against Random House deprived the public of the opportunity to become acquainted with the life of a man of extraordinary talents in a number of fields: "A narration of Hughes' initiative, ingenuity, determination and tireless work to achieve his concept of perfec-

[10] Ibid., p. 304, citing the trial court, 256 F.Supp. 55 (S.D.N.Y.1966).

[11] Ibid.

[12] Ibid., pp. 306–307, certiorari denied 385 U.S. 1009, 87 S.Ct. 714 (1967).

[13] Ibid., p. 306, quoting Ball, Copyright and Literary Property, p. 260 (1944).

tion in whatever he did ought to be available to a reading public." [14]

The Zapruder Case

A stunning event—the assassination of President John F.
Kennedy—gave rise to a copyright case which added luster to the
defense of fair use in infringement actions. On November 22,
1963, dress manufacturer Abraham Zapruder of Dallas stationed
himself along the route of the President's motorcade, planning to
take home movie pictures with his 8 millimeter camera. As the
procession came into sight, Zapruder started his camera. Seconds
later, the assassin's shots fatally wounded the President and
Zapruder's color film caught the reactions of those in the President's car.

On that same day, Zapruder had his film developed and three
color copies were made from the original film. He turned over
two copies to the Secret Service, stipulating that these were
strictly for governmental use and not to be shown to newspapers
or magazines because Zapruder expected to sell the film. Three
days later, Zapruder negotiated a written agreement with *Life*
magazine, which bought the original and all three copies of the
film (including the two in possession of the Secret Service). Under
that agreement, Zapruder was to be paid $150,000, in yearly
installments of $25,000. *Life,* in its November 29, 1963, issue then
featured thirty of Zapruder's frames. *Life* subsequently ran more
of the Zapruder pictures. *Life* gave the Commission appointed by
President Lyndon B. Johnson to investigate the killing of President Kennedy permission to use the Zapruder film and to
reproduce it in the report.[15]

In May of 1967, *Life* registered the entire Zapruder film in the
Copyright office as an unpublished "motion picture other than a
photoplay." Three issues of *Life* magazine in which the Zapruder
frames had been published had earlier been registered in the
Copyright office as periodicals.[16] This meant that *Life* had a valid
copyright in the Zapruder pictures when Bernard Geis Associates
sought permission from *Life* magazine to publish the pictures in
Josiah Thompson's book, Six Seconds in Dallas, a serious, thoughtful study of the assassination. The firm of Bernard Geis Associ-

[14] Ibid., p. 309. And, at p. 311, Judge Moore discussed Rosemont's claim that it
was planning to publish a book: "One can only speculate when, if ever, Rosemont
will produce Hughes' authorized biography."

[15] Time Inc. v. Bernard Geis Associates, 293 F.Supp. 130, 131–134 (S.D.N.Y.1968).
Although the Commission received permission from Time, Inc. to reproduce the
photos, the Commission was told that it was expected to give the usual copyright
notice. That proviso evidently was disregarded by the Commission.

[16] Ibid., p. 137.

ates offered to pay *Life* a royalty equal to the profits from publication of the book in return for permission to use specified Zapruder frames in the book. *Life* refused this offer.

Having failed to secure permission from *Life* to use the Zapruder pictures, author Josiah Thompson and his publisher decided to copy certain frames anyway. They did not reproduce the Zapruder frames photographically, but instead paid an artist $1,550 to make charcoal sketch copies. Thompson's book was then published, relying heavily on the sketches, in mid-November of 1967. Significant parts of 22 copyrighted frames were reproduced in the book.[17]

The court ruled that *Life* had a valid copyright in the Zapruder film, and added that "the so-called 'sketches' in the book are in fact copies of the copyrighted film. That they were done by an 'artist' is of no moment." The Court then quoted copyright expert Melville B. Nimmer:[18]

> "It is of course, fundamental, that copyright in a work protects against unauthorized copying not only in the original medium in which the work was produced, but also in any other medium as well. Thus copyright in a photograph will preclude unauthorized copying by drawing or in any other form, as well as by photographic reproduction."

The court then ruled that the use of the photos in Thompson's book was a copyright infringement, "unless the use of the copyrighted material in the Book is a 'fair use' outside the limits of copyright protection."[19] This led the court to a consideration of fair use, the issue which is " 'the most troublesome in the whole law of copyright.' "[20] The court then found in favor of Bernard Geis Associates and author Thompson, holding that the utilization of the Zapruder pictures was a "fair use."[21] The court said:

> There is an initial reluctance to find any fair use by defendants because of the conduct of Thompson in making his copies and because of the deliberate appropriation in the Book, in defiance of the copyright owner. Fair use presupposes "good faith and fair dealing." * * * On the other hand, it was not the nighttime activities of Thompson which enabled defendants to reproduce copies of Zapruder frames in the Book. They could have secured such frames from the National Archives, or they could

[17] Ibid., pp. 138–139.

[18] Ibid., p. 144, citing Nimmer on Copyright, p. 98.

[19] Ibid., p. 144.

[20] Ibid., quoting from Dellar v. Samuel Goldwyn, Inc., 104 F.2d 661 (2d Cir.1939).

[21] Ibid., p. 146.

have used the reproductions in the Warren Report [on the assassination of President Kennedy] or in the issues of *Life* itself. Moreover, while hope by a defendant for commercial gain is not a significant factor in this Circuit, there is a strong point for defendants in their offer to surrender to *Life* all profits of Associates from the Book as royalty payment for a license to use the copyrighted Zapruder frames. It is also a fair inference from the facts that defendants acted with the advice of counsel.

In determining the issue of fair use, the balance seems to be in favor of defendants.

There is a public interest in having the fullest information available on the murder of President Kennedy. Thompson did serious work on the subject and has a theory entitled to public consideration. While doubtless the theory could be explained with sketches * * * [not copied from copyrighted pictures] * * * the explanation actually made in the Book with copies [of the Zapruder pictures] is easier to understand. The Book is not bought because it contained the Zapruder pictures; the Book is bought because of the theory of Thompson and its explanation, supported by the Zapruder pictures.

There seems little, if any, injury to plaintiff, the copyright owner. There is no competition between plaintiff and defendants. Plaintiff does not sell the Zapruder pictures as such and no market for the copyrighted work appears to be affected. Defendants do not publish a magazine. There are projects for use by plaintiff of the film in the future as a motion picture or in books, but the effect of the use of certain frames in the Book on such projects is speculative. It seems more reasonable to speculate that the Book would, if anything, enhance the value of the copyrighted work; it is difficult to see any decrease in its value.

Copyright and a Comparative Ad

The publishers of TV Guide magazine were piqued by The Miami Herald's using pictures of TV Guide covers in an advertising campaign. The Miami Herald was indulging in "comparative advertising," whimsically suggesting that the newspaper's Sunday television listing supplement was a better product. In one television ad for the Miami Herald supplement, a Goldilocks and the Three Bears skit suggested that the newspaper's TV guide was "just right" for humans.[22]

[22] Triangle Publications, Inc. v. Knight-Ridder Newspapers, Inc., 445 F.Supp. 875, 876 (S.D.Fla.1978).

TV Guide complained about the use of its name and cover picture in the *Herald's* advertisements, charging copyright violation and asking an injunction against the paper. However, a U.S. Court of Appeals upheld dismissal of the copyright lawsuit, on fair use grounds: [23]

> We are simply unable to find any effect—other than possibly *de minimis*—on the commercial value of the copyright. To be sure, the Herald's advertisements may have had the effect of drawing customers away from TV Guide. But this results from the nature of advertising itself and in no way stems from the fact that TV Guide covers were used.

Harper & Row v. Nation Enterprises (1985)

The defense of fair use, often helpful in fending off lawsuits for copyright infringement, can be pushed too far. The Supreme Court of the United States served notice in 1985 that the fair use doctrine at times may not prevent liability for unauthorized publishing, even the material involved is highly newsworthy. Nation Magazine—reputedly America's longest continuously published weekly magazine—in 1979 received an unauthorized copy of former President Gerald R. Ford's memoirs. Nation Editor Victor Navasky received the draft from an undisclosed source; this writing was the result of a collaboration between Ford and Trevor Armbrister, a senior editor of Reader's Digest.[24]

Nation Magazine carried an article developed by Navasky from the unauthorized copy, published in its issue of April 3, 1979, and was just over 2,000 words long. Harper & Row and The Reader's Digest Association, Inc., sued for copyright infringement. At the trial court level, U.S. District Judge Owen found that Navasky knew that the memoirs were soon to be published in book form by Harper & Row and Reader's Digest, with some advance publication rights assigned to Time Magazine. Judge Owen wrote: [25]

> However, believing that the draft contained "a real hot news story" concerning Ford's pardon of President Nixon * * * Navasky spent overnight or perhaps the next twenty-four hour period quoting and paraphrasing from a number of sections of the memoirs. Navasky added no comment of his own. He did not check the material. As

[23] 626 F.2d 1171 (5th Cir.1980).

[24] Harper & Row Publishers, Inc. and Reader's Digest Ass'n, Inc. v. Nation Enterprises and Nation Associates, 557 F.Supp. 1067, 1069 (S.D.N.Y.1983), 9 Med.L. Rptr. 1229.

[25] Ibid.

he later testified, "I wasn't reporting on the truth or falsity of the account; I was reporting the fact that Ford reported this * * *" Part of Navasky's rush apparently was caused by the fact that he had to get the draft back to his "source" with some speed.

The Nation's article was about 2,250 words long, of which 300 to 400 words were taken from the Ford memoirs manuscript. Nation's publication may be said to have skimmed some of the more newsworthy aspects from the manuscript, which Harper & Row and Reader's Digest Association, as copyright holders, were preparing to market. For one thing, the copyright owners had negotiated a pre-publication agreement in which Time Magazine agreed to pay $25,000 ($12,500 in advance and the balance at the time of publication) for rights to excerpt 7,500 words from Mr. Ford's story of his pardon of President Nixon.

The Supreme Court of the United States said that The Nation had timed its publication to "scoop" Time Magazine's planned article. As a result of Nation's publication, Time cancelled its article and refused to pay the remaining $12,500 to Harper & Row and to Reader's Digest Association.[26] Writing for the Court, Justice Sandra Day O'Connor found that Nation's publication was not covered by the fair use defense: [27]

> * * * The Nation has admitted to lifting verbatim quotes of the author's original language totalling between 300 and 400 words and constituting some 13% of The Nation article. In using generous verbatim excerpts of Mr. Ford's unpublished manuscript to lend authenticity to its account of the forthcoming memoirs, The Nation effectively arrogated to itself the right of first publication, an important marketable subsidiary right. * * * [W]e find that use of the copyrighted manuscript, even stripped to the verbatim quotes conceded by The Nation to be copyrightable expression, was not a fair use within the meaning of the Copyright Act.

Justice O'Connor examined the tension between racing to publish news first and copyright: [28]

> In our haste to disseminate news, it should not be forgotten that the Framers intended copyright itself to be the engine of free expression. By establishing a marketable right to the use of one's expression, copyright supplies the economic incentive to create and disseminate ideas.

[26] Harper & Row Publishers, Inc. v. Nation Enterprises, 471 U.S. 539, 105 S.Ct. 2218 (1985), 11 Med.L.Rptr. 1969, 1971.

[27] 471 U.S. 539, 105 S.Ct. 2218, 2225 (1985), 11 Med.L.Rptr. 1969, 1973.

[28] 471 U.S. 539, 105 S.Ct. 2218, 2230 (1985), 11 Med.L.Rptr. 1969, 1978.

Further, she held that a writer's public figure status did not create a waiver of the copyright laws: [29]

> In view of the First Amendment protections already embodied in the Copyright Act's distinction between copyrightable expression and uncopyrightable facts and ideas, and the latitude for scholarship and comment traditionally afforded by fair use, we see no warrant for expanding the doctrine of fair use to create what amounts to a public figure exception to copyright. Whether verbatim copying from a public figure's manuscript in a given case is or is not fair must be judged according to the traditional equities of fair use.

The Court's majority opinion marched through the Copyright Statute's list of four factors to be considered in determining whether a use is "fair:"

(1) *The Nature and Purpose of the Use*—Justice O'Connor said the general purpose of The Nation's use was "general reporting." Part of this, however, was The Nation's stated purpose of scooping the forthcoming hardcover books and the excerpts to be published in Time Magazine. This, Justice O'Connor said, had " * * * the intended purpose of supplanting the copyright holder's commercially valuable right of first publication." [30]

(2) *Nature of the Copyrighted Work*—Justice O'Connor wrote that President Ford's narrative, "A Time to Heal" was "an unpublished historical narrative or autobiography." She said the unpublished nature of the work was critical to considering whether use of it by The Nation was fair. Although substantial quotes might qualify as fair use in a review or discussion of a published work, "the author's right to control the first public appearance of his expression weighs against such use of the work before its release." [31]

(3) *Amount and Substantiality of the Copying*—"Stripped of the verbatim quotes, the direct takings from the unpublished manuscript constitute at least 13% of the infringing article. * * * The Nation article is structured around the quoted excerpts which serve as its dramatic focal points."

(4) *Effect on the Market*—Noting that Time Magazine had cancelled its projected serialization of the Ford memoirs

29 471 U.S. 539, 105 S.Ct. 2218, 2230–2231 (1985), 11 Med.L.Rptr. 1969, 1978.

30 471 U.S. 539, 105 S.Ct. 2218, 2232 (1985), 11 Med.L.Rptr. 1969, 1978.

31 471 U.S. 539, 105 S.Ct. 2218, 2232 (1985), 11 Med.L.Rptr. 1969, 1980.

and had refused to pay $12,500, Justice O'Connor said those occurrences were direct results from the infringement. "Rarely will a case of copyright infringement present such clear cut evidence of damage." [32]

Thus a six-member majority concluded that The Nation's use of the Ford memoirs was not a fair use. This meant that a Court of Appeals finding that The Nation's publication was overturned, and that The Nation was liable to pay the $12,500 in damages, matching the amount which Time Magazine had refused to pay the copyright holders after the unauthorized publication.

Justice William J. Brennan, Jr.—who was joined by Justices Byron White and Thurgood Marshall—dissented. "The Court holds that The Nation's quotation of 300 words from the unpublished 200,000-word manuscript of President Gerald R. Ford infringed the copyright," wrote Brennan. He said the Court's majority reached this finding even though the quotations related to a historical event of undoubted significance—the resignation and pardon of President Richard M. Nixon. Brennan added that "this zealous defense of the copyright owner's prerogative will, I fear, stifle the broad dissemination of ideas and information copyright is intended to nurture." [33]

Brennan concluded,[34]

> The Court's exceedingly narrow approach to fair use permits Harper & Row to monopolize information. This holding "effect[s] an important extension of property rights and a corresponding curtailment in the free use of knowledge and of ideas." International News Service v. Associated Press, 248 U.S. at 263 (Brandeis, J., dissenting). The Court has perhaps advanced the ability of the historian—or at least the public official who has recently left office—to capture the full economic value of information in his or her possession. But the Court does so only by risking the robust debate of public issues. * * *"

Using J.D. Salinger's Letters Held Not a "Fair Use"

J.D. Salinger is a highly regarded novelist and short story writer, best known for his novel, "The Catcher in the Rye". His last work was published in 1965, and since that time he has been trying to avoid any publicity about himself, refusing to grant interviews or to respond to any inquiries about his private life.

[32] 471 U.S. 539, 105 S.Ct. 2218, 2233 (1985), 11 Med.L.Rptr. 1969, 1981.

[33] 471 U.S. 539, 105 S.Ct. 2218, 2240 (1985), 11 Med.L.Rptr. 1969, 1983.

[34] 471 U.S. 539, 105 S.Ct. 2218, 2254 (1985), 11 Med.L.Rptr. 1969, 1994–1995.

Ian Hamilton, a respected literary critic for *The London Sunday Times,* contacted the reclusive author in 1983 to tell him that he intended to write a biography about Salinger to be published by Random House. Although Salinger responded that he did not want to have his biography written during his lifetime, Hamilton spent the next three years completing the work, titled "J.D. Salinger: A Writing Life".

Lacking any cooperation from Salinger himself, Hamilton relied heavily upon information contained in letters Salinger had written to various friends during his early years as a writer. These letters had been donated by their recipients to several university libraries, but Salinger was apparently unaware that they would be available to Hamilton.

When Salinger read the galley proofs of the book Random House planned to publish, he notified the publisher that he would attempt to block its publication unless all direct quotations from these private letters he had written his friends were deleted.

Responding to these objections, Hamilton revised his work, omitting most of the direct quotations from Salinger's letters, but still paraphrasing very closely some 59 passages from this correspondence. As Random House was about to publish this revised version of the biography, Salinger sued to prevent publication, claiming among other things that such extensive reliance upon passages from his unpublished letters exceeded the reasonable bounds of fair use.

After originally granting Salinger's request for a preliminary injunction, a lower federal court had decided to lift the injunction and allow publication when a U.S. Court of Appeals intervened, ordering that this ban on publication be made permanent.[35] In its attempt to follow the Supreme Court's concept of fair use as defined in the Harper & Row case, this Court of Appeals decision placed special emphasis upon the fact these letters of Salinger's were unpublished.

That Supreme Court opinion had declared that "the scope of fair use is narrower with respect to unpublished works." Following this argument, the court found that because an author's privilege to incorporate unpublished material of another in his own work was a relatively limited one, and because Hamilton had

---

[35] 13 Med.L.Rptr. 1954 (1987). The Supreme Court has declined to review this decision, so the ban on the publication of the book remains permanent. "Supreme Court Refuses to Review Salinger Ruling," New York Times, October 6, 1987, p. 11. On the other hand, in Maheu v. CBS, 201 Cal.App.3d 662, 247 Cal.Rptr. 304 (1988), 15 Med.L.Rptr. 1548, a California court refused to allow an action for copyright infringement by an assistant of Howard Hughes for the unauthorized use of correspondence he received from Hughes because of his failure to obtain copyright protection for this unpublished correspondence that was copyrightable.

relied so heavily upon the unpublished letters of Salinger in his biography, he had clearly exceeded the reasonable boundaries of permissible fair use.

In essence, then, the "nature of the copyrighted work" and "the amount and substantiality of the portion used" were the two elements of the Harper & Row decision that this court emphasized in finding that Hamilton's biography of Salinger had abused this legal privilege.

In Craft v. Kobler, the material to be used was from several copyrighted works but the result was exactly the same.[36] In this case an author completing a biography of Igor Stravinsky sought to include in his manuscript passages from the copyrighted works of the composer's personal assistant. Here again the problem was one of excessive usage of the work of others, because the passages to be taken from these copyrighted works of the plaintiff represented nearly three percent of the total biography, and included many richly descriptive paragraphs about Stravinsky based upon the assistant's special knowledge of him.

Technology and Fair Use: The Sony "Betamax" Decision (1984)

The Supreme Court of the United States seemed to squirm on the issue of whether or not home taping of television programs was legal. The Court even postponed its decision, evidently in hopes that Congress would act, taking the Court off the hook.[37] Finally, in January, 1984, the Court said by 5–4 vote that video recorders are legal for sale and home use under the Copyright Statute and the doctrine of fair use.[38]

The case of Sony Corporation v. Universal City Studios is an excellent symbol of a basic and continuing problem in the history of copyright law. Technological advances outrun legislative and judicial efforts to contain them. As Professor David Lange of Duke Law School said after the Betamax decision that the new technologies have caused copyright problems because it " 'is possible for people to duplicate copyrighted works in their private homes more frequently than ever before.' " And Professor Arthur R. Miller of Harvard Law School said the Copyright Act of 1976— which became operational on January 1, 1978—" 'was obsolete

---

[36] Craft v. Kobler, 667 F.Supp. 120 (S.D.N.Y.1987), 14 Med.L.Rptr. 1617.

[37] Stephen Wermeil "Taping of TV Programs at Home Is Approved 5–4 by Supreme Court," Wall Street Journal, Jan. 18, 1984, p. 3.

[38] Sony Corporation of America v. Universal City Studios, Inc., 464 U.S. 417, 104 S.Ct. 774 (1984).

from the day it went into effect, at least in terms of technology.' " [39]

With its decision in the "Betamax Case," the Supreme Court produced great economic news for the Sony Corporation and others who make and sell video tape recorders (VTRs). This case arose when Universal City Studios and Walt Disney productions sued, claiming that use of Sony Betamax VTRs in homes by private individuals constituted copyright infringement.

In 1979, a federal district court held off-the-air copying for private, non-commercial use to be a "fair use." Plaintiffs had not proved to the court's satisfaction that harm to copyrighted properties was being done by such taping.[40] But in 1981, the United States Court of Appeals for the Ninth Circuit overturned that ruling, holding that makers and distributors of home video recorders were liable for damages if the machines were used to tape programs broadcast over-the-air.[41]

The Supreme Court, after granting certiorari, agreed in mid-1982 to hear Sony's appeal from the Court of Appeals holding. The Court, however, held the case over into a second term, and had it argued a second time in October, 1983.[42]

Writing for a five-Justice majority, Justice John Paul Stevens said that an average member of the public uses a VTR principally to record a program he or she cannot see as it is being telecast, and then use the home recording to watch the program at another time. This "time-shifting" practice, Justice Stevens said, enlarges the viewing audience: [43]

> * * * [A] significant amount of television programming may be used in this manner without objection from the owners of the copyrights on the programs. For the same reason, even the two respondents in this case, who do assert objections to time-shifting * * * were unable to prove that the practice has impaired the commercial value of their copyrights * * *

Justice Stevens noted that Universal and Disney studios were not seeking damages from individual Betamax users whom they claimed infringed their copyrights. Instead, they charge Sony with "contributory infringement. To prevail, they have the burden of proving that users of Betamax have infringed their copy-

---

[39] Stuart Taylor, Jr., "Decision a Basis for Further Action," The New York Times, Jan. 18, 1984, p. 43.

[40] 480 F.Supp. 429, 452–453 (D.Cal.1979).

[41] 659 F.2d 963 (9th Cir.1981).

[42] 464 U.S. 417, 104 S.Ct. 774, 777 (1984); Wermeil, loc. cit.

[43] 464 U.S. 417, 104 S.Ct. 774, 778 (1984).

rights and that Sony should be held responsible for that infringement." [44]   Justice Stevens added, [45]

> If vicarious liability is to be imposed on * * *
> [Sony] * * *, it must rest on the fact that they have sold
> equipment with constructive knowledge of the fact that
> their consumers may use that equipment to make unauthorized copies of copyrighted material.   There is no
> precedent in the law of copyright for the imposition of
> vicarious liability on such a theory.

The Betamax decision was limited to noncommercial home uses.   "If the Betamax were used to make copies for a commercial or profit-making purpose, such use would be presumptively unfair," Justice Stevens said. [46]   Thus the Sony case is clearly distinguishable from a situation where off-the-air taping is being done for commercial reasons. [47]

Importantly, Justice Stevens concluded that the home use of VTRs for noncommercial purposes was a fair use. [48]

> * * * [To] the extent that time-shifting expands
> public access to freely broadcast television programs, it
> yields societal benefits.   Earlier this year, in Community
> Television of Southern California v. Gottfried, __ U.S.
> __, __, n. 12, 103 S.Ct. 885, 891–892, 74 L.Ed.2d 705
> (1983), we acknowledged the public interest in making
> television broadcasting more available.   Concededly, that
> interest is not unlimited.   But it supports an interpretation of the concept of "fair use" that requires the copyright holder to demonstrate some likelihood of harm
> before he may condemn a private act of time-shifting as a
> violation of federal law.

Justice Stevens concluded the opinion of the Court with a summary of findings and with an invitation to Congress to provide legislative guidance in this case: [49]

> In summary, the record and findings of the District
> Court lead us to two conclusions.   First, Sony demonstrated a significant likelihood that substantial numbers of

[44] 464 U.S. 417, 104 S.Ct. 774, at 785 (1984).

[45] 464 U.S. 417, 104 S.Ct. 774, at 787 (1984).

[46] 464 U.S. 417, 104 S.Ct. 774, 792 (1984).

[47] Melville B. Nimmer, Nimmer on Copyright, Vol. 3, § 13.5[F] (New York: Matthew Bender, 1963, 1980), citing Elektra Records Co. v. Gem Electronic Distributors, Inc., 360 F.Supp. 821 (E.D.N.Y.1973) (taping of copyrighted records for commercial redistribution ruled infringing) and Walt Disney Productions v. Alaska Television Network, Inc., 310 F.Supp. 1073 (W.D.Wash.1969) (videotaping for commercial use).

[48] 464 U.S. 417, 104 S.Ct. 774, 795 (1984).

[49] 464 U.S. 417, 104 S.Ct. 774, 796 (1984).

copyright holders who license their works for broadcast on free television would not object to having their broadcasts time-shifted by private viewers. And second, respondents failed to demonstrate that time-shifting would cause any likelihood of nominal harm to the potential market for, or the value of, their copyrighted works. The Betamax is, therefore, capable of substantial noninfringing uses. Sony's sale of such equipment to the general public does not constitute contributory infringement of respondent's copyrights.

* * *

One may search the copyright act in vain for any sign that the elected representatives of the millions of people who watch television every day have made it unlawful to copy a program for later viewing at home, or have enacted a flat prohibition against the sale of machines that make such copying possible.

It may well be that Congress will take a fresh look at this new technology, just as it so often has examined other innovations in the past. But it is not our job to apply laws that have not yet been written. Applying the copyright statute, as it now reads, to the facts as they have been developed in this case, the judgment of the Court of Appeals must be reversed.

Justice Blackmun, joined by Justices Marshall, Powell, and Rehnquist, dissented.[50]

It is apparent from the record and from the findings of the District Court that time-shifting does have a substantial adverse effect upon the "potential market for" the Studios' copyrighted works. Accordingly, even under the formulation of the fair use doctrine advanced by Sony, time-shifting cannot be deemed a fair use.

Justice Blackmun added that the case should have been sent back to District Court for additional findings of fact on the matter of infringement and contributory infringement.[51]

Parody and Fair Use

Can a parody be fair use? The "Saturday Night Live" television program did a skit poking fun at New York City's public relations campaign and its theme song. In this four-minute skit, the town fathers of Sodom discussed a plan to improve their city's image. This satire ended with the singing of "I Love Sodom" to

[50] 464 U.S. 417, 104 S.Ct. 774, 811 (1984).

[51] 464 U.S. 417, 104 S.Ct. 774, 815 (1984).

the tune of "I Love New York." In a per curiam opinion, the U.S. Court of Appeals, Second Circuit rejected the complaint of Elsmere Record Co., owner of copyright to "I Love New York." "Believing that, in today's world of often unrelieved solemnity, copyright law should be hospitable to the humor of parody," the Court of Appeals approved District Judge Goettel's decision granting the defendant National Broadcasting Company a summary judgment on ground that the parody was a fair use.[52]

Judge Goettel's opinion said, in words useful for understanding both the concept of fair use and its application to parodies charged with copyright infringement: [53]

> In its entirety, the original song "I Love New York" is composed of a 45 word lyric and 100 measures. Of this only four notes, D C D E (in that sequence), and the words "I Love" were taken in the Saturday Night Live sketch (although they were repeated 3 or 4 times). As a result, the defendant now argues that the use it made was insufficient to constitute copyright infringement.

> This court does not agree. Although it is clear that, on its face, the taking involved in this action is relatively slight, on closer examination it becomes apparent that this portion of the piece, the musical phrase that the lyrics "I Love New York" accompanies, is the heart of the composition. * * * Accordingly, such taking is capable of rising to the level of a copyright infringement.

> Having so determined, the Court must next address the question of whether the defendant's copying of the plaintiff's jingle constituted a fair use which would exempt it from liability under the Copyright Act. Fair use has been defined as a "privilege in others than the owner of the copyright to use the copyrighted material in a reasonable manner without his consent, notwithstanding the monopoly granted to the owner of the copyright.

Judge Goettel then reviewed the four criteria set out by the 1976 copyright revision, 17 U.S.C.A. § 107 [quoted at the beginning of this Section], and compared those criteria to relevant cases on the fair use doctrine. He quoted copyright specialist Melville B. Nimmer, who has said, " 'short of * * * [a] complete identity of content, the disparity of functions between a serious work and a

---

[52] Elsmere Music, Inc. v. NBC, 623 F.2d 252 (2d Cir.1980), 6 Med.L.Rptr. 1457.

[53] Elsmere Music, Inc. v. NBC, 482 F.Supp. 741, 742 (S.D.N.Y.1980), 5 Med.L. Rptr. 2455, 2456.

satire based upon it, may justify the defense of fair use even where substantial similarity exists.' " [54]

Plaintiff Elsmere Records argued that "I Love Sodom" was not a valid parody of "I Love New York." Elsmere pointed to two raunchy cases in which copyright infringement was found because use of copyrighted material was not parodying the material itself, but was instead using someone's intellectual property, without permission, to make statements essentially irrelevant to the original work.[55] Elsmere Records cited MCA, Inc. v. Wilson, in which the song "Cunnilingus Champion of Company C" was held to infringe the copyright of "Boogie Woogie Bugle Boy of Company B." [56] And in Walt Disney Productions v. Mature Pictures Corporation, the court held that using the copyrighted "Mickey Mouse March" as background for a teen-age group sex scene in a "Happy Hooker" movie was not fair use.[57]

However, Judge Goettel found that the Saturday Night Live sketch validly parodied the plaintiff's jingle and the "I Love New York" ad campaign. Also, he ruled that the parody did not interfere with the marketability of a copyrighted work. Therefore, he held that the sketch was a fair use, and that no copyright violation had occurred.

SEC. 77. BROADCAST MUSIC LICENSING RIGHTS

Electronic media must obtain copyright clearance for the music they use through private agreements with organizations that represent the composers and publishers of this music.

In 1923 the National Association of Broadcasters (NAB) was founded primarily to negotiate an agreement with the American Society of Composers and Publishers (ASCAP) to allow radio stations to broadcast the copyrighted music of the society's composers and music publishers.

ASCAP had been formed in 1914 as a performing rights, copyright licensing agency for a group of music publishers and their composers whose works were being performed in music halls

---

[54] Nimmer on Copyright, § 13.05[C], at 13–60–61 (1979), quoted by Judge Goettel at 482 F.Supp. 741 at 745 (S.D.N.Y.1980), 5 Med.L.Rptr. 2455, 2457.

[55] 482 F.Supp. 741, 745 (S.D.N.Y.1980), 5 Med.L.Rptr. 2455, 2457.

[56] MCA, Inc. v. Wilson, 425 F.Supp. 443 (S.D.N.Y.1976).

[57] 389 F.Supp. 1397 (S.D.N.Y.1975). Similarly, in Fisher v. Dees, 794 F.2d 432 (9th Cir.1986), 13 Med.L.Rptr. 1167, a U.S. Court of Appeals Court found that a parody of the plaintiff composers' song "When Sunny Gets Blue," performed as "When Sunny Sniffs Glue," took no more from the copyrighted song than was necessary to reasonably accomplish its purpose. It was neither obscene nor immoral in nature, and was parody entitled to fair use protection.

and in Vaudeville theaters without permission or payment.[58] When radio stations began broadcasting recorded music of AS-CAP's composers and publishers during the early 1920s, the organization demanded copyright royalties for this program use.

During this pioneering era of broadcasting, stations were not yet permitted to sell commercial time and so until the early 1930s these radio station music licensing payments were little more than token contributions. By 1932, however, as radio was emerging as one of the few profitable industries during the Great Depression, ASCAP suddenly demanded a 300 percent increase in its broadcast music licensing fees.

For a time the NAB was able to convince its member stations to fill their schedules with the few public domain compositions they had on record, but when ASCAP offered a lower rate to newspaper owned stations, opposition collapsed and broadcasters agreed to this massive rate hike.

In 1937 the broadcast industry attempted to dilute ASCAP's absolute power over broadcast music rights by encouraging the formation of a rival group, Broadcast Music Incorporated (BMI), hoping that competition for broadcast business would force AS-CAP to reduce its fees. The tactic worked for a short time, but soon BMI began bargaining as aggressively as ASCAP during each renegotiation of its licensing agreements.

When television began to emerge during the 1950s as the dominant electronic medium in the United States, the "blanket license" approach that both ASCAP and BMI used to grant broadcast use of their music was challenged by the television industry. Most radio stations had been willing to accept this type of license that granted them full broadcast use of music from ASCAP and BMI composers in return for a payment of less than one percent of their annual advertising revenues. For television stations, however, with their far larger advertising revenues, and their far less extensive use of music, neither the blanket license nor the per-use alternative offered by ASCAP or BMI seemed reasonably related to the actual value a station owner received from such music usage.

Beginning in 1950, the All–Industry Television Station Music License Committee, negotiating on behalf of its member stations, sought some other type of arrangement with the music licensing groups that would reflect more accurately the minimal benefits the blanket license offered television stations. Although each new

---

[58] During this era, sheet music was still the primary source of income for the music industry. Publishing companies would either hire composers and lyricists to write the songs that would be published and sold to the public or purchase songs from established composers. Today a music publisher simply promotes and produces musical recordings.

round of negotiations resulted in a further reduction of the percentage of advertising revenues to be charged during the subsequent license period, neither ASCAP nor BMI was willing to abandon a licensing structure that by 1970 was providing an estimated 20–25 percent of their annual music rights revenue.[59]

After failing to reach agreement with the music licensing organizations on a satisfactory alternative to the blanket license, CBS, acting on behalf of the television networks, began an antitrust action against ASCAP and BMI in 1969. CBS alleged that these organizations had acted in concert to prevent the composers and publishers they represented from dealing directly with the television networks or its producers who sought to purchase broadcast music rights from the parties who held title to them, in restraint of trade and in direct violation of section 1 of the Sherman Antitrust Laws.[60]

In 1981, the U.S. Supreme Court held that the blanket license was not a per se violation of the Act, and on remand the Court of Appeals then dismissed the action.[61] In 1978 a group of local television stations began their own antitrust action against ASCAP and BMI, alleging the same type of anticompetitive practices. Unlike CBS, however, these local stations were successful in convincing a lower court that the blanket music licensing agreements did constitute an illegal restraint of trade.[62] According to the opinion, what made the conduct of ASCAP and BMI anticompetitive was their concerted effort to discourage program producers from obtaining directly from composers complete copyright clearance for broadcast usage of the programs they produced. The court found that, unlike the television networks, individual stations did not have sufficient bargaining power to force music licensing organizations to alter their practices, and therefore they required the protection the law provided in order to be capable of bargaining with ASCAP and BMI on equal footing.

ASCAP and BMI challenged this federal trial court decision, and a federal appeals court reversed the lower court holding, finding that the difference in the degree of bargaining power exercised by the stations and the networks was not substantial enough to require a finding that the music licensing organizations were acting in restraint of trade.[63]

[59] "Broadcasters Press On Against ASCAP, BMI," *Variety* January 8, 1986, p. 209.

[60] CBS v. ASCAP, 620 F.2d 930 (2d Cir.1980).

[61] BMI v. CBS, 441 U.S. 1, 99 S.Ct. 1551 (1979).

[62] Buffalo Broadcasting Co. v. ASCAP, 546 F.Supp. 274 (S.D.N.Y.1982).

[63] Buffalo Broadcasting Co. v. ASCAP, 744 F.2d 917 (2d Cir.1984).

When the U.S. Supreme Court refused to review this appellate court decision, broadcasting turned immediately to Congress to obtain through legislation what it had been unable to gain through litigation. During recent years the NAB has been attempting during each session of Congress to obtain passage of a law that would legally obligate every television producer to acquire full musical broadcast performance rights to all programs to be distributed for television broadcast. Although none of these "source licensing" bills have been adopted by Congress, the NAB continues in its lobbying efforts because it believes that such "source licensing" would clear at least 90 percent of the musical content now broadcast by television stations throughout the United States, making it possible for networks and most television stations to avoid the need of a "blanket" music license from ASCAP or BMI.

Because payment arrangements for electronic media usage of copyrighted music are not established by the statutory provisions of the Copyright Act, all terms and conditions of usage must be negotiated between the music licensing organizations and representatives of electronic media. Considering the amount of money involved, it is not surprising that so many of these efforts have ended up in litigation, requiring the courts to define for the parties the reasonable value of the music rights involved.

Recently, pay-TV organizations have begun to have their day in court. Early in 1991, HBO negotiated an interim settlement with BMI, agreeing to pay the broadcast music performing rights organization a monthly fee for use of BMI music until a federal court determines whether BMI can rightfully demand music rights payments both from a pay-TV service that is providing programming and each cable system that is distributing it.[64] One week later ASCAP, the other major broadcast music licensing organization, negotiated a similar interim settlement with Showtime.[65]

This entire electronic media music performing rights controversy is yet another illustration of technology complicating the process of effectively compensating the creative artist for the use of that individual's intellectual property. Paying some arbitrarily determined amount of money to a licensing organization to be divided in almost as arbitrarily a fashion among that group of artists it represents is certainly far less efficient or cost effective than direct negotiations between the purchaser and the artist.[66]

[64] "BMI Makes Deal with HBO; Lawsuit Dropped," *Variety* January 14, 1991, p. 121.

[65] "ASCAP, Showtime Settle on Fees," *Variety* January 21, 1991, p. 90.

[66] Cable TV's compulsory license to allow it to pay a percentage of its subscriber revenues into a pool to compensate those who own the TV programs the system has imported from a distant broadcast market operates in basically the same fashion as

Unfortunately, though, what was possible in the days when a Vaudeville or music hall producer could purchase from a publisher the performing rights to a single musical score for a show that would run for six months is now virtually impossible for the typical radio station listing twenty different musical compositions on each hour's playlist.

the broadcast music licensing agreement, but in cable TV's situation the pooling arrangement is created by the Copyright Act and administered by a government agency, the Copyright Royalty Tribunal.

Part IV

FACT GATHERING AND CITIZENS' RIGHTS

Chapter 13

SHIELDING INFORMATION FROM DISCLOSURE

Sec.
78. The Government Contempt Power.
79. Refusing to Testify About Sources and Information.
80. Protecting Newsrooms From Search and Telephone Records From Disclosure.

SEC. 78. THE GOVERNMENT CONTEMPT POWER

Persons who disobey the orders of courts may be cited, tried and convicted for contempt of court, the coercive power that underlies the courts' authority. The legislative branch has similar power. Journalists most often have come in conflict with the contempt power when they have refused court orders to disclose confidential information.

The common law has long provided that relationships between certain people are so personal and intimate that their confidences deserve protection against legally compelled disclosure. The clergyman and penitent, the physician and patient, the attorney and client, the husband and wife all share information that in some circumstances warrants unbroken confidentiality. The law has resisted expanding the protection to other interpersonal relationships, and even in the few listed above it has carefully avoided establishing any never-failing or absolute protection against the general rule: When government requires a citizen's testimony in furthering its legitimate ends such as ensuring fair judicial process or making laws, it is the citizen's duty to appear and testify.[1]

Printers of the American colonial period universally provided many contributors with anonymity, and occasionally resisted demands of the legislative branch to reveal their names. Early in nationhood, journalists continued to refuse demands of Congress and legislatures to break confidences, and as the Nineteenth Century progressed, sought expansion of the common law's protec-

---

[1] 8 J. Wigmore, Evidence, 2286, 2290, 2394 (J. McNaughton Rev.Ed.1961).

tion to their own setting. They argued that journalistic ethics and their own professional livelihood required that they keep confidences. Especially in reporting corruption in government, they added, the public interest required that the news be told and that sometimes the news could be told only if they promised their source confidentiality. Their success was modest indeed, but by the end of the century, a start was made toward legal protection when the State of Maryland passed the nation's first "shield law" for journalists—a law that recognized a journalist's privilege to not reveal confidential sources. Within the next three or four decades, a few more states joined Maryland in establishing journalists' privilege by statute.[2] Broad protection, however, was to await the decade of the 1970s, when the First Amendment, increased numbers of state statutes, and the federal common law were brought to bear.

The authority of government to compel testimony and to respond to journalists' refusal to break confidences is its contempt power—to declare that refusals to testify are contempt of authority, and to punish the person in contempt with imprisonment. The clash between the demand and refusal comes to resolution in the exercise of this power.

Annette Buchanan wrote a story for her college newspaper, the University of Oregon *Daily Emerald,* about the use of marijuana among students at the University. She said that seven students, whom she did not name, gave her information. And when the district attorney asked her to name the sources of information to a grand jury that was investigating drug use, and subsequently a judge directed her to do so, she refused. A reporter should be privileged not to reveal her sources, she said, and not to break confidences. To betray a pledge of secrecy to a source, Buchanan added, would be a signal to many sources to "dry up." The judge, and upon appeal the Oregon Supreme Court, found her in contempt of court for refusing to obey the judge's order, and she was sentenced to a brief jail term.[3]

Buchanan's was a case of "direct" contempt: it took place in the presence of the judge. Goss, a television personality, was not within shouting distance of the court when on his program he attacked witnesses in a divorce case in which he was accused of adultery with the wife. For his attempt to prevent witnesses from

[2] The history of journalists' privilege not to reveal information is best told by A. David Gordon, "Protection of News Sources: the History and Legal Status of the Newsman's Privilege," Ph.D. dissertation, unpublished (Univ. of Wis., 1970). See also Thomas H. Kaminski, "Congress, Correspondents and Confidentiality in the 19th Century: a Preliminary Study," Journalism History, 4:3, Autumn 1977, pp. 83–87. For a recent overview, see The News Media & The Law, Fall, 1989.

[3] State v. Buchanan, 250 Or. 244, 436 P.2d 729 (1968), certiorari denied 392 U.S. 905, 88 S.Ct. 2055 (1968).

giving testimony unfavorable to him by vilifying them, he was convicted of contempt which takes place away from the court, by publication, called indirect or "constructive" contempt.[4] On appeal, his conviction was overruled, the court holding that his broadcasts were no real danger to justice because while the targets might have been angered by his words, they had no reason to feel threatened in their testimony by them.[5]

In the *Goss* case of contempt by publication as in the *Buchanan* case of direct contempt, a judge ruled initially that the reporter's acts interfered with the administration of justice—that the acts were contemptuous of court. In each case, the judge convicted the reporter under his inherent power to punish for the interference, punishment for contempt being the basis of all legal procedure and the means of courts' enforcing their judgments and orders.[6]

The cases diverged in their outcomes, Buchanan failing in her appeal, Goss succeeding in his. Indeed, the outcomes illustrate the fortunes of reporters in recent years in similar circumstances. Direct contempt is a current, serious problem for the press; constructive "indirect" contempt has almost vanished, as we saw in Chapter 2, Sec. 10, and needs no further treatment in this chapter.

Summary procedure is the ordinary procedure in contempt. In it, the judge accuses, tries, and sentences in his own case without resort to trial by jury. It is often justified by reference to the British legal writer of the 18th Century, Sir William Blackstone, who wrote:[7]

> Some * * * contempts may arise in the face of the court; as by rude and contumelious behavior; by obstinacy, perverseness, or prevarication; by breach of the peace; or any wilful disturbance whatever; others, in the absence of the party; as by disobeying or treating with disrespect the king's writ, or the rules of process of the court; by perverting such writ or process to the purposes of private malice, extortion, or injustice * * true ones, without proper permission) of causes then depending in judgment * * *.
>
> The process of attachment for these and the like contempts must necessarily be as ancient as the laws themselves * * *. A power therefore in the supreme courts of justice to suppress such contempts by an imme-

[4] People v. Goss, 10 Ill.2d 533, 141 N.E.2d 385, 390 (1957).

[5] Goss v. State of Illinois, 204 F.Supp. 268 (N.D.Ill.1962), reversed on other grounds, 312 F.2d 257 (7th Cir.1963).

[6] Sir John C. Fox, History of Contempt of Court (Oxford, 1927), p. 1.

[7] Blackstone, pp. 284, 285.

diate attachment of the offender results from the first principles of judicial establishments and must be an inseparable attendant upon every superior tribunal.

For the United States, an act declaratory of the law of contempt in the federal courts, passed in 1831, is the basis of contempt proceedings before federal judges. State courts likewise possess the power to punish for contempt, under authority of inherent power or statute, or both.[8] State courts have ignored or denied acts by state legislatures to limit this power.[9] For example, in State v. Morrill (1855) an Arkansas court was faced with a state statute limiting contempt proceedings to specified acts not including out-of-court publications. The court ruled that the statute was not binding upon the judiciary, for it must have power to enforce its own process, and the contempt power which provides this springs into existence upon the creation of the courts.[10] Without this authority, courts would be powerless to enforce their orders.

Attempts by Congress and state legislatures to limit contempt to certain specific classifications have not been universally successful. The legislative and judicial branches of government are coordinate under the "separation of powers" doctrine that gives each branch of government autonomy in its own sphere. While the legislative branch of any governmental unit has the power to make the law, the judicial branch has inherent rights to enforce its orders, rules, writs, or decrees. Even in states where there is a strict definition of what constitutes contempt, under special circumstances there is precedent for the courts' considering their inherent power above the legislative enactment.[11]

Some headway has been made by those who pose a more general challenge to the contempt power of courts, and who assert that jury trials should be substituted for a judge's summary proceeding. It is sometimes objected by these that American traditions are violated where a judge may sit as accuser, prosecutor, and judge in his own or a fellow judge's case: "It is abhorrent to Anglo-Saxon justice as applied in this country that one man, however lofty his station or venerated his vestments, should have the power of taking another man's liberty from him."[12] There are flaws in the Blackstonian position that summary procedure is an

---

[8] Act of Mar. 2, 1831, c. 99, 4 Stat. 487.

[9] State v. Morrill, 16 Ark. 384 (1855) is an influential case mimicked by courts elsewhere to protect their "inherent" contempt powers from legislative limitations.

[10] Ibid., 384, 407.

[11] Farr v. Superior Court of Los Angeles County, 22 Cal.App.3d 60, 99 Cal.Rptr. 342, 348 (1971).

[12] Ballantyne v. United States, 237 F.2d 657, 667 (5th Cir.1956); J. Edward Gerald, The Press and the Constitution, pp. 30–31.

"immemorial power" of judges in all contempt cases;[13] and the United States Supreme Court in 1968 addressed itself to the problem and said that the old rule did not justify denying a jury trial in serious contempt cases. It ruled in Bloom v. Illinois [14] that "If the right to jury trial is a fundamental matter in other criminal cases, * * * it must also be extended to criminal contempt cases." The length of the sentence imposed was used by the Court as the test of "seriousness," which it found in a two-year jail term given Bloom.

Legislative Contempt and the Press

In addition to courts, legislative bodies are jealous of their power to cite for contempt. Congressional and state legislative investigating committees sometimes seek the testimony of reporters who have special knowledge about subjects under the committees' official inquiry. Citations for contempt have occurred when reporters have refused to answer lawmakers' questions, and occasionally, over the last two centuries, convictions have been had.

The legislative power to cite for contempt derives its force from the power possessed by the English Parliament, on which both the legislatures and the Congress were modeled.[15] No limitations are imposed upon Congress in its punishment for either disorderly conduct or contempt, but in Marshall v. Gordon,[16] it was held that the punishment imposed could not be extended beyond the session in which the contempt occurs.

The Supreme Court has conceded to Congress the power to punish nonmembers for contempt when there occurs "either physical obstruction of the legislative body in the discharge of its duties, or physical assault upon its members, for action taken or words spoken in the body, or obstruction of its officers in the performance of their official duties, or the prevention of members from attending so that their duties might be performed, or finally, for refusing with contumacy to obey orders, to produce documents or to give testimony which there was a right to compel." [17]

Seldom has a reporter gone to jail for refusing to reveal to Congress a source of information. One of the cases involved Z.L. White and Hiram J. Ramsdell, Washington correspondents of the *New York Tribune*. They published what they claimed was the "Treaty of Washington," a document being studied by the Senate

[13] W. Nelles and C.W. King, "Contempt by Publication in the United States," 28 Col.L.Rev. 408 (1928).

[14] 391 U.S. 194, 88 S.Ct. 1477, 1485 (1968).

[15] Max Radin, Anglo American Legal History, pp. 63, 64.

[16] 243 U.S. 521, 37 S.Ct. 448, L.R.A.1917F, 279, Ann.Cas.1918B, 371 (1917).

[17] Ibid.

in a closed session. They refused to say from whom they got the copy, were tried and convicted of contempt by the Senate, and were committed to the custody of the Sergeant at Arms until the end of the Session.[18]

Congress has not in many decades chosen to try and convict for contempt. Instead, it has cited for contempt and certified the persons cited to the district attorney of the District of Columbia for prosecution under a law that gives the courts power to try such cases.[19]

It is uncertain how far the principles of freedom of the press protect a reporter from contempt charges if he refuses to answer the questions of a Congressional Committee. Journalists have argued that the First Amendment sharply limits Congress in questioning and investigating the press: Congress may investigate only the matters on which it may legislate, they point out, and the First Amendment says that "Congress shall make no law ＊ ＊ ＊ abridging freedom of ＊ ＊ ＊ the press."

"The Selling of the Pentagon"

In 1971, a prize-winning television documentary by CBS, "The Selling of the Pentagon," raised a storm of protest against alleged bias in the film's portrayal of the American military's public information programs. Selective editing for the documentary, the military charged, distorted the intent, management and messages of the military. The House of Representatives Commerce Committee, under its chairman Rep. Harley O. Staggers, undertook an investigation of the matter, and CBS president Frank Stanton refused to furnish the committee parts of film edited out of the final version. In response to the subpoena ordering him to appear with the materials, he appeared but declared that furnishing materials would amount to a violation of freedom of the press. The Committee voted 25 to 13 to recommend to Congress a contempt citation. The House, however, turned down the recommendation, Rep. Emanuel Celler declaring that "The First Amendment towers over these proceedings like a colossus. No tenderness of one member for another should cause us to topple over this monument to our liberties." [20]

---

[18] U.S. Senate, Subcommittee on Administrative Practice and Procedure of Committee on the Judiciary, The Newsman's Privilege, 89 Cong., 2 Sess., Oct. 1966, pp. 57–61. Nineteenth century investigations of news media and reporters were not rare according to Kaminski, op.cit., p. 85.

[19] 2 U.S.C.A. §§ 192, 194.

[20] Congressional Record, 117:107, July 13, 1971, p. 6643.

Daniel Schorr and Congress

In the 1970s, newsman Daniel Schorr, then of CBS, came under protracted investigation by Congress, and heavy fire from a segment of the media, for his refusal to testify. Schorr had obtained a copy of the Pike Committee (House Intelligence Committee) report on operations of the Central Intelligence Agency, which the House of Representatives had voted should be kept secret after heavy pressure not to disclose it from the federal administration. National security, the administration said, was at stake. Schorr broadcast some of the contents; passed the report to the *Village Voice* which published much of it; was investigated for several months during which he was suspended by CBS; and finally came before the House Ethics Committee.[21] Under a congressman's solemn admonition against publishers' taking it "upon themselves to publish secret and classified information against the will of Congress and the people," [22] Schorr illuminated the rationale for a journalist's refusing to reveal sources, saying in part: [23]

> For a journalist, the most crucial kind of confidence is the identity of a source of information. To betray a confidential source would mean to dry up many future sources for many future reporters. The reporter and the news organization would be the immediate losers. The ultimate losers would be the American people and their free institutions.
>
> But, beyond all that, to betray a source would be to betray myself, my career, and my life. It is not as simple as saying that I refuse to do it. I cannot do it.

Unlike the committee that recommended on Stanton, the Ethics Committee did not recommend to the full House that Schorr be cited for contempt. He was released from subpoena without revealing his source.

The courts have not decided contempt of Congress cases on First Amendment grounds, one of them saying, "We shrink from this awesome task" of drawing lines between the investigative power of Congress and the First Amendment rights of a member of the press. Instead, the courts have found other reasons for reversing convictions of newsmen—such as faulty indictments—

[21] See Daniel Schorr, Clearing the Air (New York: Houghton Mifflin, 1977), passim; "The Daniel Schorr Investigation," Freedom of Information Center Report, # 361, Oct. 1976.

[22] Anthony Lewis, "Congress Shall Make No Law * * *," New York Times, Sept. 16, 1976, p. 39.

[23] I. William Hill, "Schorr Sticks to His Refusal to Name Source," Editor & Publisher, Sept. 25, 1976, p. 14.

who were found in contempt of Congress for refusing to answer questions.[24]

Deja vu set in early in 1992, when reporters Nina Totenberg (National Public Radio) and Timothy Phelps (Newsday) balked at answering Senate questions. They faced subpoenas to reveal the sources of their reports of Professor Anita Hill's charges of sexual harassment against Supreme Court nominee—and ultimately Supreme Court Justice—Clarence Thomas.[25] The Senate soon dropped the inquiry.

SEC. 79. REFUSING TO TESTIFY ABOUT SOURCES AND INFORMATION

Journalists' clashes with courts for refusing to testify as to sources and information were infrequent until the 1970s when the incidence multiplied manyfold. Protection has developed under the First Amendment, the common law, and state statutes.

The refusal to testify before grand juries and courts about confidential sources has become a familiar phenomenon of the 1970s and 1980s. Subpoenas to appear and testify were for decades only an occasional problem for journalists whose stories suggested to officialdom that the reporters had information of use to government; there are probably fewer than 40 reported contempt cases before 1965 for refusal to testify when subpoenaed. But in 1969 and 1970 the sometime problem of subpoenas changed to a burst, and across the nation reporters faced demands that they appear and testify. No one was able to track down every subpoena issued during these years and in 1971 and 1972. In a two-and-one-half-year segment of this period, 121 subpoenas for news material were said to have gone to CBS and NBC alone, and in three years, more than 30 to Field Enterprises newspapers.[26] A high level persisted, the U.S. attorney general approving 42 subpoena requests of reporters betwen May 1975 and November 1976.[27]

In particular demand were reporters who had been reporting widespread social and political turmoil. Grand juries wanted these journalists to reveal their confidential sources as well as to surrender their unpublished notes and records, unused photo-

[24] Shelton v. United States, 117 U.S.App.D.C. 155, 327 F.2d 601 (1963); 89 Editor & Publisher 12, July 7, 1956. Russell v. United States, 369 U.S. 749, 767, 82 S.Ct. 1038, 1049 (1962).

[25] Neil A. Lewis, "Constitutional Test Is Seen in Inquiry in Leak to Press," The New York Times, Feb. 3, 1992, p. A9.

[26] House of Rep. Committee on the Judiciary, Subcommittee No. 3, 92 Cong., 2d sess., "Newsmen's Privilege," Hearings, Oct. 4, 1972, p. 204; Sept. 27, 1972, p. 134.

[27] "Justice Department Subpoenas Fewer Reporters," News Media and the Law 1:1 (Oct.1977), p. 30.

graphs, tape recordings and television film "outtakes." To much
of this, reporters responded "no" with intensity and solidarity.[28]
Their unwritten code of ethics stood in the way of breaking
confidences, they said; but more important, if they broke confidences they would become known as untrustworthy and their
sources would dry up, thereby harming or destroying their usefulness as news gatherers for the public, and their own status as
professionals would be damaged. Moreover, some argued, compelling them to disclose their news sources was tantamount to making them agents of government investigation.

As for turning over unused film, files, photos and notes, some
media adopted the policy of early destruction of unpublished
materials after *Time, Life, Newsweek,* the *Chicago Sun-Times,*
CBS, NBC and others were called by subpoena, or in the name of
cooperation with government, to deliver large quantities of news
materials.[29] According to Attorney General John Mitchell, who
served under President Nixon, journalists' willingness to accept
contempt convictions and jail terms rather than reveal confidences, along with their unyielding protests to government, made
the controversy "one of the most difficult issues I have faced
* * *."[30] The storm of objection to subpoenas issuing from the
Department of Justice led attorneys general to issue "Guidelines
for Subpoenas to the News Media"—a set of instructions to Justice
Department attorneys over the nation—that sought to resolve
testimonial questions with reporters through negotiating rather
than through subpoenas except in the last resort.[31]

The Constitutional Protection

Journalists who assumed or asserted that the First Amendment guarantee of freedom of the press has protected the craft
historically against compelling testimony had not reckoned with
the course of court decisions. Privilege cases were adjudicated for
most of a century under the common law or state statutes without
the Constitution's even entering the picture. Not until 1958, in

[28] S.Res. 3552, 91 Cong., 2d Sess., 116 Cong.Rec. 4123–31, 1970; Noyes & Newbold, "The Subpoena Problem Today," Am.Soc. Newspaper Editors Bull., Sept.
1970, pp. 7–8; Editor & Publisher, Feb. 7, 1970, p. 12. For several journalists'
positions, see U.S. Congress, Senate, Committee on the Judiciary, Newsmen's
Privilege Hearings Before the Subcommittee on Constitutional Rights, 93rd Cong.,
1st Sess., 1973, passim.

[29] Columbia Journalism Rev., Spring 1970, pp. 2–3.

[30] Editor & Publisher, Aug. 15, 1970, pp. 9–10.

[31] Department of Justice, Memo No. 692, Sept. 2, 1970. The guidelines were
adjusted and developed by subsequent attorneys general. See "Guidelines on News
Media Subpoenas," 6 Med.L.Rptr. 2153 (11/5/80) for more recent guidelines.

Garland v. Torre,[32] was the first claim to First Amendment protection an issue in the reported cases.

Here, Marie Torre, columnist for the *New York Herald Tribune*, attributed to an unnamed executive of a broadcasting company, certain statements which actress Judy Garland said libeled her.   In the libel suit, Torre refused to name the executive, asserting privilege under the First Amendment.   She was cited for contempt and convicted, and the appeals court upheld the conviction.   "The concept that it is the duty of a witness to testify in a court of law," the Second Circuit Court of Appeals said, "has roots fully as deep in our history as does the guarantee of a free press." It added that if freedom of the press was involved here, "we do not hesitate to conclude that it too must give place under the Constitution to a paramount public interest in the fair administration of justice."[33]   Subsequent claims to constitutional protection were likewise denied in other cases.[34]

The Branzburg Case (1972)

The United States Supreme Court in 1972 ruled for the first time on whether the First Amendment protects journalists from testifying about their confidential sources and information.   The cases of three newsmen who had refused to testify before grand juries during 1970 and 1971 were decided together in Branzburg v. Hayes.[35]   Paul Branzburg, a reporter for the *Louisville Courier-Journal,* had observed two people synthesizing hashish from marijuana and written about that and drug use, and had refused to answer the grand jury's questions about the matters.   Paul Pappas, a television reporter of New Bedford, Mass., had visited Black Panther headquarters during civil turmoil in July 1970, and refused to tell a grand jury what he had seen there.   Earl Caldwell, a black reporter for the *New York Times* in San Francisco, who had covered Black Panther activities regularly for some years, was called by a federal grand jury and had refused to appear or testify.

Only Caldwell received protection from the lower courts.   The federal district court of California and the Ninth Circuit Court of Appeals ruled that the First Amendment provided a qualified privilege to newsmen and that it applied to Caldwell.[36]   The

---

[32] 259 F.2d 545 (2d Cir.1958), certiorari denied 358 U.S. 910, 79 S.Ct. 237 (1958).

[33] Ibid., at 548–549.

[34] In re Goodfader's Appeal, 45 Hawaii 317, 367 P.2d 472 (1961); In re Taylor, 412 Pa. 32, 193 A.2d 181 (1963); State v. Buchanan, 250 Or. 244, 436 P.2d 729 (1968), certiorari denied 392 U.S. 905, 88 S.Ct. 2055 (1968).

[35] Branzburg v. Hayes, 408 U.S. 665, 92 S.Ct. 2646 (1972).

[36] Application of Caldwell, 311 F.Supp. 358 (N.D.Cal.1970); Caldwell v. United States, 434 F.2d 1081 (9th Cir.1970).

Kentucky Court of Appeals refused Branzburg protection under either the Kentucky privilege statute, or the First Amendment interpretation of the Caldwell case.[37] And the Supreme Judicial Court of Massachusetts, where no privilege statute existed, rejected the idea of a First Amendment privilege.[38]

The Supreme Court of the United States found that none of the three men warranted First Amendment protection. It reversed the Caldwell decision of the lower federal court and upheld the Kentucky and Massachusetts decisions, in a 5–4 decision.[39] It said that the First Amendment would protect a reporter if grand jury investigations were not conducted in good faith, or if there were harassment of the press by officials who sought to disrupt a reporter's relationship with his news sources.[40] But it found neither of these conditions present here. The journalist's obligation is to respond to grand jury subpoenas as other citizens do and to answer questions relevant to commission of crime, it said.

The Caldwell decisions in lower courts had focused on the need of recognition for First Amendment protection for the news gathering process; the Supreme Court said "It has generally been held that the first Amendment does not guarantee the press a constitutional right of special access to information not available to the public generally * * *," and "Despite the fact that news gathering may be hampered, the press is regularly excluded from grand jury proceedings, our own conferences, the meetings of other official bodies gathered in executive session * * *."[41]

The reporters had asserted that the First Amendment should take precedence over the grand jury's power of inquiry. The Supreme Court said that at common law, courts consistently refused to recognize a privilege in journalists to refuse to reveal confidential information, and that the First Amendment claim to privilege had been turned down uniformly in earlier cases, the courts having concluded "that the First Amendment interest asserted by the newsman was outweighed by the general obligation of a citizen to appear before a grand jury or at trial, pursuant to a subpoena, and give what information he possesses."[42] It said that the only constitutional privilege for unofficial witnesses before grand juries is the Fifth Amendment privilege against compelled self-incrimination, and the Court declined to create another.

[37] Branzburg v. Pound, 461 S.W.2d 345 (Ky.1970); Branzburg v. Hayes, 408 U.S. 665, 92 S.Ct. 2646 (1972).

[38] In re Pappas, 358 Mass. 604, 266 N.E.2d 297 (1971).

[39] Branzburg v. Hayes, 408 U.S. 665, 92 S.Ct. 2646 (1972).

[40] Ibid., at 706–709, 92 S.Ct. at 2669–2670.

[41] Ibid., at 682, 684, 92 S.Ct. at 2657, 2658.

[42] Ibid., at 684, 686, 92 S.Ct. at 2658, 2659.

The reporters argued that the flow of news would be diminished by compelling testimony from them. The Supreme Court said it was unconvinced, and "the evidence fails to demonstrate that there would be a significant constriction of the flow of news to the public if the Court reaffirms the prior common law and constitutional rule regarding the testimonial obligations of newsmen."[43]

The reporters said the freedom of the press would be undermined. The Court said this is not the lesson that history teaches, for the press had operated and thrived without common law or constitutional privilege since the beginning of the nation.[44]

The Supreme Court said that while the Constitution did not provide the privilege sought, Congress and the state legislatures were free to fashion standards and rules protecting journalists from testifying by passing legislation.

Concurring, Justice Lewis F. Powell, Jr., expanded, in general terms, the possibilities for first Amendment protection for journalists subpoenaed to testify. "The Court," he said, "does not hold that newsmen * * * are without constitutional rights with respect to the gathering of news or in safe-guarding their sources. * * * the courts will be available to newsmen under circumstances where legitimate First Amendment interests require protection." And where they claim protection, Powell said, "The asserted claim to privilege should be judged on its facts by the striking of a proper balance between freedom of the press and the obligation of all citizens to give relevant testimony * * *."[45] His opinion was to become central to many subsequent cases.

The dissenting justices wrote two opinions. One was that of Justice William O. Douglas, who said that a reporter's immunity from testifying is "quite complete" under the First Amendment and a journalist "has an absolute right not to appear before a grand jury * * *."[46]

Concurring for himself and two others, Justice Potter Stewart argued for a qualified privilege. He called the majority's opinion a "crabbed view of the First Amendment" that reflected a disturbing insensitivity to the critical role of an independent press. And he said that in denying the protection, "The Court * * * invites state and federal authorities to undermine the historic independence of the press by attempting to annex the journalistic profession as an investigative arm of government." Justice Stewart said the protection was essential, not "for the purely private

[43] Ibid., at 692, 92 S.Ct. at 2662.

[44] Ibid., at 698, 92 S.Ct. at 2665.

[45] Ibid., at 708, 710, 92 S.Ct. at 2670, 2671.

[46] United States v. Caldwell, 408 U.S. 665, 719, 92 S.Ct. 2686, 2691 (1972).

interests of the newsman or his informant, nor even, at bottom, for the First Amendment interests of either partner in the news-gathering relationship."[47]

> Rather it functions to insure nothing less than democratic decisionmaking through the free flow of information to the public, and it serves, thereby, to honor the "profound national commitment to the principle that debate on public issues should be uninhibited, robust, and wide-open."

Stewart indicated what he felt the government should be required to do in overriding a constitutional privilege for the reporter:[48]

> * * * it is an essential prerequisite to the validity of an investigation which intrudes into the area of constitutionally protected rights of speech, press, association and petition that the State *show a substantial relation between the information sought and a subject of overriding and compelling state interest.*
>
> * * *
>
> Government officials must, therefore, demonstrate that the information sought is *clearly* relevant to a *precisely* defined subject of governmental inquiry. * * * They must demonstrate that it is reasonable to think the witness in question has that information. * * * And they must show that there is not any means of obtaining the information less destructive of First Amendment liberties.

These were essentially the requirements placed upon government by the lower courts in holding that Caldwell had been protected by the First Amendment, and Stewart endorsed that decision. He would have upheld the protection for Caldwell, and vacated and remanded the Branzburg and Pappas judgments.

Largely innocent of the history of the shield, reporters and editors expressed shock and dismay that the First Amendment did not protect the reporters in the Supreme Court's *Branzburg* decision.[49] A few years later, William H. Hornby wrote that the decision had "beclouded what American newsmen had come to assume was a traditional privilege—to refuse to testify either as to

[47] Branzburg v. Hayes, 408 U.S. 665, 737, 92 S.Ct. 2646, 2678 (1972).

[48] Ibid., at 739–742, 92 S.Ct. at 2679–2680.

[49] See generally Columbia Journalism Review, 10:3, Sept.–Oct. 1972, for articles by Norman E. Isaacs, Benno C. Schmidt, Jr., and Fred W. Friendly. The only extensive history of journalists' privilege is Gordon, op.cit.

the source or the content of information received under confidential circumstances."[50]

After the *Branzburg* decision, many journalists predicted doom for press freedom. Those predictions were premature: buried within *Branzburg* were statements which said the First Amendment was still around and could be used in confidentiality cases. There was Justice White's plurality opinion, which said that journalists would be protected against the harassment of bad-faith investigations. Justice Powell's concurrence said that courts would protect journalists "where legitimate First Amendment interests require protection." And Justice Stewart's dissent, as matters turned out, contained concepts that courts quickly came to use in subsequent cases to protect journalists. (See discussion following page 560.)

Then only months after *Branzburg* was decided, the U.S. Court of Appeals, Second Circuit, gave the doom-predictors a most welcome surprise. That court said that journalist Alfred Balk was *protected* by the First Amendment in his refusal to name a source. Balk had once written an article on discriminatory real estate practices—"block busting" for the Saturday Evening Post. Civil rights advocates, in a court action, sought to have Balk reveal the identity of one of his confidential sources ("Vitcheck," a pseudonym). Balk refused, on grounds tht Vitcheck gave him the information in confidence. The trial court ruled in Balk's favor, and the appeals court affirmed. The decision stood because the Supreme Court of the United States—for whatever reason—refused to grant certiorari.[51]

The court found that the identity of Vitchek did not go to the heart of the appellants' case, and that, anyway, there were other available sources that the appellants could have tried to reach and that might have disclosed Vitchek's identity (*vide* Stewart, dissent in *Branzburg*). It said that the majority in *Branzburg* had applied traditional First Amendment doctrine, which teaches that First Amendment rights cannot be infringed absent a "compelling" or "paramount" state interest (once more, Stewart).[52]

Even though the *Branzburg* majority emphasized public interest in grand jury investigation of crimes, this case found that "there are circumstances, at the very least in civil cases, in which the public interest in non-disclosure of a journalist's confidential sources outweighs

[50] William H. Hornby, "Journalists Split in Shield Law Imbroglio," IPI Report, 25:3, March 1976, p. 8.

[51] Baker v. F & F Investment Co., 470 F.2d 778 (2d Cir.1972), certiorari denied 411 U.S. 966, 93 S.Ct. 2147 (1973).

[52] Ibid., 783–785. See also United States v. Orsini, 424 F.Supp. 229 (E.D.N.Y. 1976).

the public and private interest in compelled testimony. The case before us is one where the First Amendment protection does not yield."

Here was a line of reasoning (one which took its departure from the widely damned *Branzburg* decision) that was to prove a protection for the journalist in the court-room faceup in which his testimony was being demanded with increasing and truly disturbing frequency. In civil cases, the public's interest was likely to weigh with the journalist's refusal to name his sources, and thus the journalist's position would outweigh the private litigant's demand for disclosure. It was the start of courts' using *Branzburg* in both civil and criminal to establish a qualified privilege under the First Amendment for journalists who claimed protection not to reveal sources.

Quickly other courts brought the privilege into play.[53] In a case decided in 1973, the District Court for the District of Columbia ruled on a demand of the Committee for the Re-Election of the President (Nixon) for news materials.[54] The Committee was party to civil actions arising out of the break-in at the Watergate offices of the Democratic National Committee. It had obtained subpoenas for reporters or management of the *New York Times,* the *Washington Post,* the *Washington Star-News,* and *Time* magazine to appear and bring all papers and documents they had relating to the break-in. The media ("movants") asked the court to quash the subpoenas.

Judge Richey defined the issue: Were the subpoenas valid under the First Amendment? He distinguished this case from Branzburg, noting that the re-election committee was not involved in criminal cases, but civil. He felt, furthermore, that the cases were of staggering moment: " * * * unprecedented in the annals of legal history." "What is ultimately involved in these cases * * * is the very integrity of the judicial and executive branches of our Government and our political processes in this country."[55]

Not only did the civil nature of the cases involving the re-election committee weigh for the media in Richey's opinion. He saw a chilling effect in the enforcement of the subpoenas upon the flow of information about Watergate to the press and thus to the public:[56]

> This court stands convinced that if it allows the discouragement of investigative reporting into the highest

---

[53] See Press Censorship Newsletter, IX, April–May 1976, pp. 46, 48–9; Loadholtz v. Fields, 389 F.Supp. 1299 (D.Fla.1975).

[54] Democratic National Committee v. McCord, 356 F.Supp. 1394 (D.D.C.1973).

[55] Ibid., 1395–1397.

[56] Ibid., 1397.

levels of Government no amount of legal theorizing could allay the public suspicions engendered by its actions and by the matters alleged in these lawsuits.

Then Richey balanced; as Justice Powell had instructed in *Branzburg,* a reporter's claim to privilege should be judged " * * * 'on its facts by the striking of a proper balance between freedom of the press and the obligation of all citizens to give relevant testimony'."   Richey said that here, "The scales are heavily weighted in the Movants' [media's] favor."   For the Committee for the Re-Election of the President had made no showing that "alternative sources of information have been exhausted or even approached. Nor has there been any positive showing of the materiality of the documents and other materials sought by the subpoenas [i.e., that the materials sought "go to the heart of the claim"]." [57]

Even the legal proceeding which the lead opinion in *Branzburg* was so concerned to elevate above reporter's privilege— namely, the grand jury investigation—could in some circumstances give way to the journalist's claim.

This happened in the case of Lucy Ware Morgan, who for three years fought a 90-day contempt sentence for refusing to disclose her source, and finally won.[58]   Her story in the St. Petersburg, Fla., *Times* brought two actions against her to compel her to say who told her of a grand jury's secret criticism of Police Chief Nixon.   The Florida Supreme Court found the story innocuous.   It overruled the lower court which had found that the mere preservation of secrecy in grand jury proceedings outweighed any First Amendment considerations.   The high state court said "A nonspecific interest, even in keeping the inner workings of the Pentagon secret, has been held insufficient to override certain First Amendment values."[59]   It found further that the proceedings against Morgan had an improper purpose—namely, "to force a newspaper reporter to disclose the source of published information, so that the authorities could silence the source."   Then it called on the leading case in precedent:[60]

> The present case falls squarely within this language in the *Branzburg* plurality opinion: "Official harassment of the press undertaken not for purposes of law enforce-

[57] Ibid., 1398. On exhausting the sources of information, see also Connecticut State Board of Labor Relations v. Fagin, 33 Conn.Sup. 204, 370 A.2d 1095 (1976), 2 Med.L.Rptr. 1765, 1766; Altemose Const. Co. v. Building Trades Council of Philadelphia and Vicinity, 443 F.Supp. 492 (E.D.Pa.1977), 2 Med.L.Rptr. 1878.

[58] Morgan v. State, 337 So.2d 951 (Fla.1976).

[59] Ibid., 955.

[60] Ibid., 956.

ment but to disrupt a reporter's relationship with his news sources would have no justification."

Thus with *Branzburg* supporting, First Amendment protection for the reporter's shield was being discovered.[61] No court conceded that the privilege under the First Amendment was an "absolute" protective shield for the journalist in all conceivable circumstances. In applying the First Amendment, courts widely started with Justice Powell's instruction in *Branzburg* ("striking a proper balance between freedom of the press and the obligation of all citizens to give relevant testimony"), and then used criteria such as those advocated by Justice Stewart in his *Branzburg* dissent (whether the testimony sought from reporters was clearly relevant, whether the subject was one of overriding state interest, whether all other means of obtaining the sought-after information had first been exhausted). In most cases in which the First Amendment was employed, the procedure worked out to provide protection.[62]

But the First Amendment shield sometimes dropped. For one thing, in balancing the journalist's right to a shield against the need of the state or a plaintiff, as Powell instructed, courts sometimes found that the hurdles such as Stewart's criteria were surmounted by those seeking testimony, and the balance tipped against the journalist. This could happen at trial, or in pre-trial discovery procedure (see Chap. 5, Sec. 30) in which plaintiffs were attempting to obtain from journalists certain facts that would help them establish their cases. Also, some courts interpreted *Branzburg* to deny a First Amendment shield of any kind.

To go first to the hurdles which the state in criminal cases, or the plaintiff in civil cases, would have to clear before overcoming the journalist's First Amendment qualified privilege, these have been expressed in several ways. The most-used rules[63] are that the party seeking the information from the journalist must show:

[61] Gora, p. 28. Gora's handbook, prepared for the American Civil Liberties Union, despite being dated, should be available to every reporter and editor. It covers true-to-life, practical problems in several fields of law that involve journalists, using a "Q" and "A" approach.

[62] United States v. Hubbard, 493 F.Supp. 202, 206, 209 (D.D.C.1979), 5 Med.L. Rptr. 1719; Montezuma Realty Corp. v. Occidental Petroleum Corp., 494 F.Supp. 780 (S.D.N.Y.1980), 6 Med.L.Rptr. 1571; Application of Consumers Union of United States, Inc., 495 F.Supp. 582 (S.D.N.Y.1980), 6 Med.L.Rptr. 1681; Hart v. Playboy Enterprises (D.Kan.1978), 4 Med.L.Rptr. 1616; United States v. DePalma, 466 F.Supp. 917 (S.D.N.Y.1979), 4 Med.L.Rptr. 2499; Zelenka v. State, 83 Wis.2d 601, 266 N.W.2d 279 (1978).

[63] Others have included: Plaintiff must show that the information "is necessary to prevent a miscarriage of justice" Florida v. Taylor (Fla.Cir.Ct.1982), 9 Med.L. Rptr. 1551; there is "reasonable possibility that information sought would affect the verdict" State v. Rinaldo, 36 Wash.App. 86, 673 P.2d 614 (1983), 9 Med.L.Rptr. 1419; the action is not "facially frivolous or patently without merit" Winegard v. Oxberger, 258 N.W.2d 847, 852 (Iowa 1977).

• That the information sought can be obtained from no other source or by means less destructive of First Amendment interests:

• That the information is centrally relevant to the party's case ("goes to the heart of the claim," or is information for which the party has a "compelling need").

• That the subject is one of "overriding and compelling state interest."

As we saw on the preceding pages, the journalist won because the plaintiffs failed to show that the materials sought "went to the heart of their claim," or that the information might not be available from an alternative source, other parties seeking information have been more successful in piercing the shield of the First Amendment. That was the case in Winegard v. Oxberger,[64] decided by the Iowa Supreme Court in 1977.

Winegard v. Oxberger (1977)

Diane Graham, a reporter for the *Des Moines Register,* wrote articles about legal proceedings brought by Sally Ann Winegard to dissolve her claimed common-law marriage to John Winegard. The articles quoted Sally's attorney extensively. John, who denied that there had been a marriage, brought a libel suit and invasion of privacy action against the attorney, who had told John that he had spoken with reporter Graham, but who denied saying the alleged libel. Then John sought, through discovery proceedings before the trial, to obtain from Graham or the Register any information they had in connection with the preparation of the articles.

Graham was subpoenaed, and refused to answer questions about conversations with her sources or their identity, and about preparation and editing of the articles. She said that the First Amendment and the Iowa Constitution protected her. She and the Register applied to the court for an order quashing the subpoena; John Winegard moved to compel discovery; and Judge Oxberger ruled for Graham and the Register, saying that a qualified privilege under the First Amendment protected Graham.

Winegard appealed to the Iowa Supreme Court, which reversed the trial court and said that Judge Oxberger had erred in denying John's motion to compel discovery by reporter Graham. The Supreme Court said that a First Amendment qualified privi-

---

[64] 258 N.W.2d 847 (Iowa 1977), certiorari denied 436 U.S. 905, 98 S.Ct. 2234 (1978), 3 Med.L.Rptr. 1326. See also Goldfeld v. Post Pub. Co. (Conn.Sup.1978) 4 Med.L.Rptr. 1167; In re Powers (Vt.Dist.1978), 4 Med.L.Rptr. 1600.

lege existed, but was lost to Graham upon the application of the Court's "three-pronged standard." [65]

First, it said that John's basic discovery objective "is necessary and critical to his cause of action" against the attorney; John "needs to know what was said to Graham and by whom." Second, the Court said, John's questioning of Sally's attorney resulted in the attorney's denying "having made statements attributed to him by Graham's articles. Under these circumstances we find Winegard did reasonably exercise and exhaust other plausible avenues of information," and that "Graham is apparently the only remaining person who could conceivably provide the information essential to Winegard's invasion of privacy and defamation action." And as for the last of the "three-prong standard," the Court said there was nothing in the record to suggest that John's action against the attorney "is facially frivolous or patently without merit." For good measure, the unanimous opinion said that the Court found no cause to hold that John was abusing judicial process to force a "wholesale disclosure of a newspaper's confidential sources of news," nor that John was embarked upon a course "designed to annoy, embarrass or oppress Graham.[66] John won the case for compelled disclosure.

Some courts have denied or doubted that any First Amendment protection exists. The Massachusetts Supreme Judicial Court did so in the case of Paul Pappas,[67] and reaffirmed that position in 1982.[68] A Connecticut Superior Court has said that the First Amendment gives no greater protection to the electronic media "than the same action by any other citizen," nor "any privilege to refuse to reveal information solely because the writers deem it confidential." [69] Idaho's Supreme Court once read Branzburg v. Hayes, the leading case,[70] to mean that "no newsman's privilege against disclosure of confidential sources exists

[65] Winegard v. Oxberger, 258 N.W.2d 847, 852 (Iowa 1977).

[66] The Iowa Court relied directly on the first of the shield cases in which a reporter claimed a First Amendment protection—Garland v. Torre, 259 F.2d 545 (2d Cir.1958), which continues to carry weight with courts in frequent citations. An example is Silkwood v. Kerr-McGee Corp., 563 F.2d 433 (10th Cir.1977), 3 Med. L.Rptr. 1087, 1091.

[67] In the Matter of Paul Pappas, 358 Mass. 604, 266 N.E.2d 297 (1971).

[68] Corsetti v. Massachusetts, 458 U.S. 1306, 103 S.Ct. 3 (1982), 8 Med.L.Rptr. 2113 and reporter's jail term for contempt commuted in 1982, 8 Med.L.Rptr. # 28, 9/14/82, News Notes. In 1984, the Massachusetts Supreme Judicial Court was asked by a governor's task force to promulgate rules about journalists' privilege, and recommended details for protection of journalists asserting such, the Court having denied until then any recognition of privilege: 10 Med.L.Rptr. # 41, 10/16/84, News Notes.

[69] Rubera v. Post-Newsweek (1982), 8 Med.L.Rptr. 2293, 2295.

[70] 408 U.S. 665, 92 S.Ct. 2646 (1972), 1 Med.L.Rptr. 2617.

* * *." [71]   In 1985, however, the Idaho Supreme Court recognized a reporter's right to protect source confidentiality in both criminal and civil cases.[72]

For journalists, the best defense against subpoenas probably is a "good offense."   That is, if a news organization is known to judges and prosecuting attorneys as one willing to fight against subpoenas—even to the point of having reporters and editors go to jail to resist yielding up confidential sources or information—chances of subpoenas being served doubtless are lessened.

In re Farber (1978)

A shield case which arose in New Jersey cost its media principals more than any other in the 1970s.   It was the famous In re Farber.[73]   Before it had run its course, in fines alone it had cost the *New York Times* approximately $265,000, at the rate of $5,000 per day and including a flat $101,000 and had sent reporter Myron Farber to jail for 40 days.   Farber had written lengthy articles about deaths at a New Jersey hospital, and their possible connection with drugs.   A grand jury probe of the matter resulted in the indictment of Dr. Mario Jascalevich for murder, and after he went to trial, Farber and the Times were subpoenaed to bring thousands of documents to the court for *in camera* inspection.   The Times and Farber demanded a hearing before turning over materials.   But the trial judge refused a hearing, saying he would have to examine the documents before deciding whether the shield law would protect them against disclosure to Jascalevich.   Facing contempt citations, the Times and Farber appealed unsuccessfully; the contempt findings went into effect, with jail for Farber and the $5,000-a-day fine against the Times pending its bringing forth the materials.

Appealing once more, the newspaper and reporter reached the New Jersey Supreme Court.   That court denied that the First Amendment provided any privilege to remain silent, interpreting Branzburg v. Hayes to be a flat rejection of that notion.   In response to the journalists' claim to privilege, the New Jersey court said that U.S. Supreme Court Justice White, had "stated the

[71] Caldero v. Tribune Pub. Co., 98 Idaho 288, 562 P.2d 791 (1977), 2 Med.L.Rptr. 1490, 1495.

[72] In re Contempt of Wright, 108 Idaho 418, 700 P.2d 40 (1985).

[73] In re Farber, 78 N.J. 259, 394 A.2d 330 (1978), 4 Med.L.Rptr. 1360, 1362; see also Anon., "Lets Stand Contempts Against New York Times," News Media & the Law, Jan. 1979, 4–5. For a step-by-step account of the complex process applied to the Times and Farber, see Anon., "Reporter Jailed; N.Y.Times Fined," Ibid., Oct. 1978, 2–4. Farber and the Times were ultimately pardoned of the contempt conviction by the Governor of New Jersey, and the $101,000 criminal contempt fine was returned: 7 Med.L.Rptr. # 42, 2/2/82, News Notes.

issue and gave the Court's answer in the first paragraph of his opinion":[74]

> "The issue in these cases is whether requiring newsmen to appear and testify before state or federal grand juries abridges the freedom of speech and press guaranteed by the First Amendment. We hold that it does not."

> * * *

> Our conclusion that appellants cannot derive the protection they seek from the First Amendment rests upon the fact that the ruling in *Branzburg* is binding upon us and we interpret it as applicable to, and clearly including, the particular issue framed here. It follows that the obligation to appear at a criminal trial on behalf of a defendant who is enforcing his Sixth Amendment rights is at least as compelling as the duty to appear before a grand jury.

Having settled the First Amendment issue for New Jersey, the court went on to say that the Times and Farber of course deserved a hearing such as they sought, but that they had aborted it by refusing to submit the material subpoenaed for the court to examine in private—and that such an examination is no invasion of the New Jersey shield statute. "Rather, it is a preliminary step to determine whether, and if so to what extent, the statutory privilege must yield to the defendant's constitutional rights."

It added, however, that in future similar cases there should be a preliminary determination before being compelled to submit materials to a trial judge—in which the party seeking the materials would show the relevancy of them to his defense, and that the information could not be obtained from any less intrusive source. This, it said, did not stem from any First Amendment right, but rather, it would seem necessary from the legislature's "very positively expressed" intent, in passing the shield law, to protect confidentiality of media sources.

Farber was released from jail in October 1978, following the acquittal of Jascalevich by a jury at the end of an eight-month trial. The judge suspended penalties against him and the Times. The New Jersey legislature began work on a bill to prevent a recurrence of the Farber incident, and on Feb. 28, 1981, Governor Byrne signed a law saying that a criminal defendant would have to prove at a subpoenaed journalist's hearing that the material sought was relevant and unavailable elsewhere, and that the hearing would be held before the start of the criminal trial.[75]

[74] In re Farber, 78 N.J. 259, 394 A.2d 330 (1978), 4 Med.L.Rptr. 1360, 1362.

[75] New York Times, Feb. 28, 1981, p. 25. Maressa v. New Jersey Monthly, 89 N.J. 176, 445 A.2d 376 (1982), 8 Med.L.Rptr. 1473, 1475–1476.

It should be clear that despite the language of shield laws or of court precedent erecting some sort of a "shield" for journalists, such shields often turn out to be of little help at crunch time. First Amendment attorney James C. Goodale, for example, looked at the Farber case and exclaimed about the persistent ineffectiveness of New Jersey's shield statute. He complained that Farber had been shipped off to jail without a hearing, even though there was a statute stating that Farber was totally protected against requests for confidential sources and even though there are scores of decisions upholding claims of privilege even in states where there is no shield statute.

Journalists need to keep up with the kaleidoscopically shifting patterns of shield protection. One way of managing this is to subscribe to The News Media & the Law, published four times a year by the Reporters Committee for Freedom of the Press, and which puts out periodic guides on the status of shield laws from jurisdiction to jurisdiction.[76]

Confidentiality Under the Federal Common Law

Even as journalists' successes in asserting a First Amendment privilege not to testify were proving about as frequent as were their failures, in 1979 the United States Third Circuit Court of Appeals discovered and applied an added basis of privilege for journalists to rely on in refusing to divulge sources: the federal common law. In 1979, Judge Sloviter wrote that the Court of Appeals, Third Circuit, had concluded "that journalists have a federal common law privilege, albeit qualified, to refuse to divulge their sources."

Riley v. Chester (1979)

That case began when Policeman Riley of Chester, Pa., a candidate for mayor, alleged that Mayor Battle and Police Chief Owens had violated his constitutional right to freedom to conduct his campaign, by surveillance of his activity, by conducting investigations of his performance as a policeman, and by public announcements of the investigations. He sought a preliminary injunction from federal court to restrain them from continued activities of this kind. Reporter Geraldine Oliver was called as a witness concerning her news story which reported that Riley had been suspended as a policeman, docked, and officially reprimanded, and that he had been investigated on several occasions during

---

[76] "Reporters Have Rights, Too," The Nation, Nov. 3, 1979, pp. 435–436; The Reporters Committee for Freedom of the Press, Suite 504, 1735 Eye Street, N.W., Washington, D.C. 20006. The Reporters Committee has an all-day, every-day libel and freedom of information hotline, including emergency legal aid on subpoena questions: Toll free 800–F–FOI–AID. In Washington, D.C., area, (202) 466–6313.

his 13 years as a policeman. She refused to give the source of her information and under an order by the trial judge was cited for civil contempt. She appealed, and the Third Circuit Court reversed the contempt citation.[77]

The Court found that Riley had not first exhausted other sources of information that might have "leaked," including other reporters, Battle, and Owens. Nor had Riley shown that the information sought to be disclosed was more than marginally relevant to his case—a matter "of most significance." Criteria such as these were applicable to the case of anyone seeking disclosure, the Court said, under any standard. And with that, it applied the standard of the federal common law, emerging from Rule 501 of the Federal Rules of Evidence and the legislative history of the Rule. The importance of the decision for journalists' privilege emerges not so much in the finding for Oliver as for the general matter of journalists' privilege.[78]

The Court then added:

> The strong public policy which supports the unfettered communication to the public of information, comment and opinion and the Constitutional dimension of that policy, expressly recognized in Branzburg v. Hayes, lead us to conclude that journalists have a federal common law privilege, albeit qualified, to refuse to divulge their sources.

In two later federal common law cases in the Third Circuit, the reporter's shield was denied. One, concerning a newspaper reporter's refusal to say whether she had conversations with a U.S. attorney in the "Abscam" prosecutions, ruled that the information was crucial to the defendant's case and that it could be obtained only from the reporter. The court followed standard judicial procedure in choosing to decide the case on common law instead of a First Amendment standard: "'. . . [W]e ought not to pass on questions of constitutionality ∗ ∗ ∗ unless such adjudication is unavoidable ∗ ∗ ∗.'"[79]

In the other case, a television network was ordered by a court to submit to a pre-trial, *in camera* [in private, in the judge's chambers] proceeding. In that proceeding film, audio tapes, and written transcripts were to be revealed concerning persons whom the government intended to call as witnesses in a trial. The TV network refused and appealed the order. But the order was

---

[77] Riley v. Chester, 612 F.2d 708 (3d Cir.1979). For a state decision bottomed explicitly on common law as providing privilege, see Senear v. Daily Journal-American, 97 Wash.2d 148, 641 P.2d 1180 (1982), 8 Med.L.Rptr. 1151, 1152.

[78] Ibid., 713, 714.

[79] United States v. Criden, 633 F.2d 346, 349 (3d Cir.1980).

upheld so far as it applied to the named persons whom the government intended to call, but was overturned as to other people, whose testimony was not relevant.[80]

Confidentiality Under State Statutes and in State Courts

The mixed results for confidentiality under the First Amendment and the federal common law, meanwhile, were characteristic of developments under state shield statutes and state court decisions. Media Attorney Robert Sack has said that shield laws are like insurance policies, in that "they cover absolutely everything except what happens to you."[81] If, as attorney Joel Gora had said in the journalistic climate of discouragement under *Branzburg,* "the situation is far from bleak," there were nonetheless more than enough jailings to warrant confusion and anger among journalists. Probably more reporters were going to jail in the 1970s for refusal to reveal sources, than for any offense since 1798–1800 and the Alien and Sedition Acts.[82] The interpretations of the legitimacy of journalists' privilege under state laws and rulings contributed heavily to this unlovely fact. Yet it was plain by the 1980s that the large majority of state (and federal) jurisdictions had recognized qualified shield protection. Further, the number of actions by mid-decade was declining; media Attorney James C. Goodale found state shield laws increasingly effective.[83]

State Shield Laws

The Supreme Court in *Branzburg* made it plain that either Congress or the states or both might pass laws providing a shield. Attempts in state legislatures to adopt shield laws (15 antedated *Branzburg*) were sometimes successful in following years, the total of old and new having reached 28 in number by 1990. In addition, 16 other states' courts had adopted a qualified privilege in case decisions by that year, while a few rejected the privilege.[84] Some statutes provided a privilege that appeared "absolute," while others qualified the protection in various ways. Alabama's, passed in 1935 and amended in 1949, was one of those that, on the

---

[80] United States v. Cuthbertson, 630 F.2d 139 (3d Cir.1980), 6 Med.L.Rptr. 1545.

[81] 9 Med.L.Rptr. # 7, 3/15/83, News Notes.

[82] Quill, 61:1, Jan. 1973, p. 28.

[83] Note, "Developments in the News Media Privilege: the Qualified Constitutional Approach Becoming Common Law," 33 Maine L.Rev. 372, 441 (1981); 10 Med.L. Rptr. # 47, 11/27/84, News Notes.

[84] The News Media & the Law, Fall 1987, special section on source confidentiality; see also Henry R. Kaufman, ed., LDRC (Libel Defense Resource Center), 50–State Survey 1988 (New York: LDRC, 1988), *passim*; See also "Confidential Sources and Information," 1990 guide for reporters, The Reporters Committee for Freedom of the Press.

surface, seemed absolute—as long as a person could claim to be with a journalistic organization:[85]

> No person engaged in, connected with, or employed on any newspaper, or radio broadcasting station or television station, while engaged in a news gathering capacity shall be compelled to disclose in any legal proceeding or trial, before any court or before a grand jury of any court, before the presiding officer of any tribunal or his agent or agents or before any committee of the legislature or elsewhere the sources of any information procured or obtained by him and published in the newspaper, broadcast by any broadcasting station or televised by any television station on which he is engaged, connected with or employed.

Among states that hedged the privilege, Illinois, for example, said that a person seeking the reporter's information could apply for an order divesting the reporter of the privilege. The application would have to state the specific information sought, its relevancy to the proceedings, and a specific public interest which would be adversely affected if the information sought were not disclosed. And the court would have to find, before taking away the privilege, that all other available sources of information had been exhausted and that disclosure of the information was essential to the protection of the public interest involved.[86]

But absolute or qualified, state laws might contain loopholes through which under certain conditions, journalists could lose the privilege. Branzburg, before seeking constitutional protection, had failed to receive protection under Kentucky's statute. The statute gave him a firm shield, as a newspaper employee, against disclosing before a court or grand jury, the source of information procured by him and published in a newspaper. But the Kentucky court held that he himself was the source of information for a story reporting his observation of the manufacture of hashish by others. He would have to give the identity of the manufacturer— to identify those whom he saw breaking the law. It was contempt for him to refuse to do so.[87]

New York's shield law is termed "absolute" in its protection, and even protects a journalist against testifying before a grand

---

[85] Ala.Code § 12–21–142 (Cum.Supp.1988). See Jacqueline L. Jackson, "Shield Laws Vary Widely," Presstime, May 1981, p. 14; See also New Jersey's, Maressa v. New Jersey Monthly, 89 N.J. 176, 445 A.2d 376 (1982), 8 Med.L.Rptr. 1473.

[86] Ill.Legis.H.Bill 1756, 1971, Gen. Assembly.

[87] Branzburg v. Pound, 461 S.W.2d 345 (Ky.1970). For a similar position under New York's statute, see People v. Dupree, 88 Misc.2d 791, 388 N.Y.S.2d 1000 (1976); for Texas, Ex parte Grothe, 687 S.W.2d 736 (Tex.Cr.App.1984); 10 Med.L.Rptr. 2009.

jury.[88]   But it applies only to information obtained under the "cloak of confidentiality," and did not protect CBS against producing, under subpoena, video and audio takes and outtakes not made under promises of confidentiality.[89]   California's constitution immunizes against contempt convictions for refusing to testify, but not against various other sanctions [90] nor does it protect certain free-lance authors.   California's shield statute projects unpublished or "out-take" materials.[91]   Ohio's shield law protects against disclosure only of the source of the information, not against disclosure of information in notes, tapes, and records from the source.[92]

The William Farr Case

A case whose permutations enmeshed a reporter for eight years was that of William Farr, reporter for the *Los Angeles Herald Examiner* and later the *Los Angeles Times*.   Reporting the murder trial of Charles Manson, Farr learned that a Mrs. Virginia Graham had given a statement to a district attorney in the case, claiming that a Manson "family" member, Susan Atkins, had confessed taking part in the multiple crimes and told of the group's plans for other murders.   The judge in the case had ordered attorneys, witnesses and court employees not to release for public dissemination, any content or nature of testimony that might be given at the trial; but Farr obtained copies of the Graham statement, according to him from two attorneys in the case.   The court learned that he had the statement.   Farr refused to tell the court the names of the sources, and published a story carrying sensational details.   Later, he identified a group of six attorneys as including the two.   The judge queried them, and all denied being the source.   Once more the court asked Farr for his sources, and he continued to refuse under the California reporters' privilege law.[93]   The court denied him protection under the statute and he appealed.

[88] Beach v. Shanley, 62 N.Y.2d 241, 476 N.Y.S.2d 765, 465 N.E.2d 304 (1984), 10 Med.L.Rptr. 1753.

[89] People v. Korkala, 99 A.D.2d 161, 472 N.Y.S.2d 310 (1984), 10 Med.L.Rptr. 1355; see also Knight-Ridder Broadcasting, Inc. v. Greenberg, 70 N.Y.2d 151, 518 N.Y.S.2d 595, 511 N.E.2d 1116 (1987), 14 Med.L.Rptr. 1299.

[90] KSDO v. Superior Court Riverside County, 136 Cal.App.3d 375, 186 Cal.Rptr. 211 (1982), 8 Med.L.Rptr. 2360.   Also New York: Oak Beach Inn Corp. v. Babylon Beacon, 62 N.Y.2d 158, 476 N.Y.S.2d 269, 464 N.E.2d 967 (1984), 10 Med.L.Rptr. 1761; see Calif. Constitution Art. I, § 2, subd. (b).

[91] In re Van Ness (Cal.3d 1982), 8 Med.L.Rptr. 2563; Evidence Code of Calif. (§ 1070).

[92] Ohio v. Geis, 2 Ohio App.3d 258, 441 N.E.2d 803 (1981), 7 Med.L.Rptr. 1675.

[93] West's Ann.Cal.Evidence Code § 1070 (1966).

The appeals court upheld the conviction for contempt, essentially under the doctrine of the "inherent power" of courts to regulate judicial proceedings without interference from other government branches—a principle, as we have seen, reaching far back in the history of contempt. It said that courts' power of contempt is inherent in their constitutional status, and no legislative act could declare that certain acts do not constitute a contempt. If Farr were immunized from liability, it would violate the principle of separation of powers among the three branches of government; it would mean that the legislative branch could interfere with the judicial branch's power to control its own officers:[94]

> Without the ability to compel petitioner to reveal which of the six attorney officers of the court leaked the Graham statement to him, the court is without power to discipline the two attorneys who did so, both for their violations of the court order [concerning no publicity] and for their misstatement to the court that they were not the source of the leak.

Farr served 46 days in jail before he was released pending a further appeal, and in his uncertain freedom lived with the possibility of indeterminate, unlimited imprisonment if his appeal failed and he persisted in refusing to reveal his sources. That "coercive" sentence was later ruled by the courts to have no further purpose, as there was no likelihood that continuing it would induce Farr to testify. It was still possible, however, that he might have to serve a further "punitive" sentence for his contempt. Five years after the opening of the case against Farr— on Dec. 6, 1976—he was finally freed from the latter possibility by ruling of the California Court of Appeal, Second District.[95] He had served the longest jail term on record in the United States for refusing to reveal news sources, and his case had lasted longer than any other.

But his ordeal was not over. Two of the six attorneys whom he had identified brought a libel suit for $24 million against him. The trial court and the California Appellate Court ruled that the shield law did not protect him from answering questions in the case.[96] The long contest ended in April 1979. The libel plaintiffs had missed the five-year statute of limitations for bringing an action, and Farr's attorney convinced the trial court that their

[94] Farr v. Superior Court of Los Angeles County, 22 Cal.App.3d 60, 99 Cal.Rptr. 342, 348 (1971). New Mexico's Supreme Court ruled similarly that that state's shield law was without effect where testimony before courts was concerned: Ammerman v. Hubbard Broadcasting, Inc., 89 N.M. 307, 551 P.2d 1354 (1976).

[95] In re Farr, 64 Cal.App.3d 605, 134 Cal.Rptr. 595 (1976); Milwaukee Journal, Dec. 7, 1976.

[96] 64 Cal.App.3d 605, 134 Cal.Rptr. 595 (1976). See also Quill, Nov. 1977, p. 14.

failure was a result of insufficient effort to bring the case to trial. The judge dismissed the suit.[97]   The adhesive web of process had finally dissolved.

Sixteen months later, Californians voted to elevate the state's shield for journalists to a better-fortified position than that of a statute; they passed Proposition 5, which placed the shield directly into the State Constitution.[98]

In 1982, one test demonstrating the limitation of the new California shield came when Riverside (Calif.) policemen brought a libel suit against KSDO radio and its reporter, Hal Brown, for a story that implicated police in drug traffic.   They demanded Brown's notes and memoranda.[99]   And while the journalists won in their refusal to yield the material, they did so under *First Amendment* protection, said the court of appeal: the police had failed to show that the information was not available from any other source, or that the desired material went to the heart of their case.[1]

But so far as California's constitutional shield was concerned, said the court, decades of assumptions about its protective reach were mistaken: All it does is protect a journalist from contempt conviction.   It does not stop courts from taking other actions in a libel case, as here, where journalists themselves are defendants: Their refusal to testify about information needed by the plaintiff could result in the court's striking their defense, or even awarding the plaintiff a default judgment.   The court said that the shield law[2]

> * * * does not create a privilege for newspeople, rather, it provides an immunity from being adjudged in contempt.   This rather basic distinction has been misstated and apparently misunderstood by members of the news media and our courts as well.

Though vulnerable under any law journalists occasionally got more protection from their states' courts than the statutes suggested might be available.   One loophole in several "absolute" statutes was the lack of provision protecting the reporter from revealing *information* that he had gathered, even though it protected him from revealing the *source* of that information.   Robert L. Taylor,

[97] Anon., "William Farr's Seven [sic] Year Fight to Protect Sources Is Victorious," News Media & the Law, Aug./Sept. 1979, 22.

[98] Anon., "Californians Vote to Include a Newsmen's Shield in the State Constitution," Quill, July/August 1980, 9; Calif.Const. § 2, subd. (b).

[99] KSDO v. Superior Court of Riverside County, 136 Cal.App.3d 375, 186 Cal. Rptr. 211 (1982), 8 Med.L.Rptr. 2360.

[1] Ibid., at 216, 8 Med.L.Rptr. at 2366.

[2] Ibid., at 213, 8 Med.L.Rptr. at 2362.

president and general manager, and Earl Selby, city editor of the *Philadelphia Bulletin,* were convicted of contempt of court for refusing to produce documents in a grand jury investigation of possible corruption in city government. Both were fined $1,000 and given five-day prison terms. They appealed, relying on the Pennsylvania statute stating that no newsman could be "required to disclose the source of any information" that he had obtained. "Source" they said, means "documents" as well as "personal informants." The Pennsylvania Supreme Court, reversing the conviction, agreed. The court said that the legislature, in passing the act, declared the gathering of news and protection of the source of news as of greater importance to the public interest than the disclosure of the alleged crime or criminal.[3]

Shield Laws and Libel

Finally, there is the frequent case of whether a shield against testifying is justified where a newspaper and reporter are sued for libel. If a reporter refuses to reveal an unnamed source who had allegedly libeled the plaintiff, may the plaintiff be foreclosed from discovering and confronting his accuser? Who, besides the reporter, can identify the accuser? Conversely, if the sources must be revealed, then is it not possible "for someone to file a libel suit as a pretext to discover the reporters' sources and subject them to harassment"?[4] This line of actions, of course, produced the suit which, perhaps more than any other, alerted the news world to the possibilities of danger in required testimony—Garland v. Torre, of 1958. As Marie Torre in that case, most other reporters since then who have been sued for libel have argued fruitlessly that they should not be required to name the source.

Shield statutes of Oregon, Rhode Island, and Tennessee provide expressly that the privilege is not available to persons sued for libel.[5] Supreme Courts of Massachusetts[6] and Idaho, which have no shield statutes, reject reporters' claims that there is an alternative First Amendment protection against the requiring of testimony—including testimony about sources of alleged libel. An Idaho decision, in which certiorari was denied by the United States Supreme Court, confirmed a 30-day jail sentence for report-

[3] In re Taylor, 412 Pa. 32, 193 A.2d 181, 185 (1963). The Reporters Committee 1990 Guide, "Confidential Sources of Information," lists "absolute" and "qualified privilege" states as to both confidential sources *and* information.

[4] Gora, p. 40.

[5] Gora, p. 247. See Kaufman, op. cit., at footnote 84, above, *passim*, for comments on state shield statutes.

[6] Dow Jones & Co., Inc. v. Superior Court, 364 Mass. 317, 303 N.E.2d 847 (1973).

er-editor Jay Shelledy.[7] He had quoted a "police expert" as criticizing state narcotics agent Michael Caldero who had been involved in a shooting incident. He was sued for libel by the agent, and, refusing to reveal the name of the expert, was held in contempt. The trial judge decided not to press the contempt citation, however, finding that another course of action would be more helpful to Caldero: The court would treat Shelledy's failure to identify the police expert "as an admission by the defendant Shelledy that no such 'police expert' exists, and the jury shall be so instructed."[8] The trial proceeded; the jury was instructed, and in place of the shield that his now-spent effort had hoped to raise, the jury served as armor: It brought in the verdict that Shelledy's article was not libelous.

The Caldero trial judge's ruling that Shelledy "had no source" was unusual but not unique. Only months before, one case in precedent had used the move—a decision by the New Hampshire Supreme Court. A former police chief sued for libel after a newspaper cast doubt on his truthfulness, alleging that he had failed polygraph tests. Its staff refused to reveal the sources of the accusation. The court, after determining that the sought-after testimony was "essential to the material issue in dispute," and "not available from any source other than the press," granted the chief's motion to compel disclosure. The newspaper appealed, and the New Hampshire Supreme Court felt that there was a better way to enforce the trial court's order than by holding the newspaper in contempt.[9]

> We are aware * * * that most media personnel have refused to obey court orders to disclose, electing to go to jail instead. Confining newsmen to jail in no way aids the plaintiff in proving his case. Although we do not say that contempt power should not be exercised, we do say that something more is required to protect the rights of a libel plaintiff. Therefore, we hold that when a defendant in a libel action, brought by a plaintiff who is required to prove actual malice under *New York Times*, refuses to disclose his sources of information upon a valid order of

[7] Caldero v. Tribune Pub. Co., 98 Idaho 288, 562 P.2d 791 (1977), certiorari denied 434 U.S. 930, 98 S.Ct. 418 (1977).

[8] Anon., "Lewiston reporter Wins Jury Verdict in Libel Case," News Media & the Law, Oct./Nov.1980, 10–11, Downing v. Monitor Pub. Co. Inc., 120 N.H. 383, 415 A.2d 683 (1980), 6 Med.L.Rptr. 1193.

[9] Downing v. Monitor Pub. Co. Inc., 120 N.H. 383, 415 A.2d 683, 686 (1980), 6 Med.L.Rptr. 1193, 1195; see also Sprague v. Walter, 518 Pa. 425, 543 A.2d 1078, 1086 (1988), in which the Pennsylvania Supreme Court held that a reporter-defendant in a libel case could invoke the state's shield law to protect the identity of sources. And the jury was to draw *"no inference either favorable or adverse"* from the invoking of the shield law as to the reliability of an unidentified source.

the court, there shall arise a presumption that the defendant had no source. The presumption may be removed by a disclosure of the sources a reasonable time before trial.

Successful Shield Claims

Nonetheless, the frequent success of the claim to the shield (usually where plaintiffs fail to show necessity, relevancy, and unavailability of the information) occasionally can extend to the libel situation, where the reporter is so likely to be vulnerable because he is the only source of the information sought. Before Marie Torre ever pleaded for protection in a libel case, a decision under the shield law of Alabama had furnished it to a reporter who refused to reveal sources of a story on prison conditions.[10] New York, New Jersey, and Pennsylvania protect, in varying degree, confidentiality in libel cases.[11]

Even in Idaho (which has no shield law and whose Supreme Court has interpreted *Branzburg* to provide no First Amendment protection), the appeal process has brought relief to journalists who fruitlessly sought a shield in discovery proceedings in a libel case. Sierra Life Insurance Co. demanded the names of confidential sources for a series of stories about the firm's financial difficulties, written by reporters for the *Twin Falls Times-News*.[12] Through complex legal processes, the reporters and the newspaper alleged that their stories were true and refused to name sources. In response, the trial judge ruled that Idaho provided no protection for them, struck all their defenses, and entered a "default" judgment against them for $1.9 million.

But the Idaho Supreme Court reversed the trial court. It did not feel that the refusal to testify should stand in the way of the newspaper's employing defenses—truth and lack of a connection between the stories and the damages suffered. Striking defenses in this case, it agreed, amounted to unwarranted punishment of the newspaper. And it said that Sierra had failed to show that its inability to discover the sources damaged its ability to prove the

[10] Ex parte Sparrow, 14 F.R.D. 351 (N.D.Ala.1953). Federal courts have provided protection in some libel cases also: Mize v. McGraw-Hill, Inc., 82 F.R.D. 475, 86 F.R.D. 1 (S.D.S.Tex.1979), 5 Med.L.Rptr. 1156; Bruno & Stillman, Inc. v. Globe Newspaper Co., 633 F.2d 583 (1st Cir.1980), 6 Med.L.Rptr. 2057.

[11] Respectively, Oak Beach Inn Corp. v. Babylon Beacon, Inc., 62 N.Y.2d 158, 476 N.Y.S.2d 269, 464 N.E.2d 967 (1984), 10 Med.L.Rptr. 1761; Maressa v. New Jersey Monthly, 89 N.J. 176, 445 A.2d 376 (1982), 8 Med.L.Rptr. 1473; D'Alfonso v. A.S. Abell Co., 765 F.2d 138 (4th Cir.1985), 9 Med.L.Rptr. 1015; and Hatchard v. Westinghouse Broadcasting Co., 516 Pa. 184, 532 A.2d 346 (1987): Reporters have to yield up evidence in a libel suit when it does not reveal identify of sources of confidential information.

[12] Sierra Life Insurance Co. v. Magic Valley Newspapers, Inc., 101 Idaho 795, 623 P.2d 103, (1980), 6 Med.L.Rptr. 1769.

news stories false, which would be necessary to its case. It remanded the case, with "guidance" to the trial judge which included the Supreme Court's suggestion that the confidential sources' identity might not be relevant.[13]

Summarizing Issues in Confidentiality

The Branzburg decision having hedged the constitutional protection that the news world sought, the media turned to lobbying for statutes at the state and federal levels, and to strengthening existing state statutes. The number of states with statutes reached 28 by 1991,[14] about half of them passed during the 1960s and 1970s.

At the federal level, the major news organizations tried periodically for passage of a federal shield law, with—as of early 1989—no success. They found strong support and strong opposition among congressmen. It was estimated back in early 1973 that more than 50 bills offering a shield had been introduced,[15] and more appeared in subsequent years. Whatever the level of government, the issues were similar.

(1) What are the competing social values in granting or denying journalists an immunity from testifying? The reporter's ethic of not betraying sources, and his property right in not losing his effectiveness and value as a reporter through losing his sources, had long been asserted unsuccessfully in cases under the common law. Now he was grounding his claim in society's loss of his service if he lost his sources through betraying them.

Earl Caldwell was one of a tiny number of reporters who had gained the confidence of the Black Panthers at a time when society had a real need to know about this alienated group. The Ninth Circuit Court of Appeals accepted Caldwell's argument that he would lose the Panthers' confidence if he even entered the secret grand jury chambers, for this extremely sensitive group would not know what he might say under the compulsion of the legal agency.[16] And if Caldwell could not report the Panthers, society was the real loser. This situation illustrated the difference between the values served in the case of privilege for the journalist and that for the doctor, lawyer, or clergyman:[17]

[13] Ibid., at 109, 6 Med.L.Rptr. at 1773.

[14] Reporters Committee 1990 guide, "Confidential Sources of Information."

[15] Thomas Collins, "Congress Grapples with Press Bill," Milwaukee Journal, March 25, 1973, p. 16.

[16] Caldwell v. United States, 434 F.2d 1081, 1088 (9th Cir.1970).

[17] House of Rep. Committee on the Judiciary, Subcommittee No. 3, 92 Cong., 2d Sess., "Newsmen's Privilege," Hearings, Testimony of Victor Navasky, Oct. 5, 1972, p. 236.

" * * * the doctor-patient privilege is there to make it possible for patients to get better medical care. A journalist's privilege should be there not only to make it possible for a journalist to get better stories, but to contribute to the public's right to know. So in that sense it is a more critical privilege than some of these other privileges, which are based primarily on the relationship between two people."

Asserting an equal service in the cause of the "public's right to know" was the position that in many circumstances, government-as-the-public sought information from reporters vital to the public welfare. In State v. Knops,[18] an "underground" newspaper editor refused to tell a grand jury the names of people to whom he had talked about the bombing of a university building that killed a researcher, and about alleged arson of another university building. "[T]he appellant's information could lead to the apprehension and conviction of the person or persons who committed a major criminal offense resulting in the death of an innocent person," said the Wisconsin Supreme Court in denying privilege to editor Mark Knops.[19] Here government was saying that the journalist was practicing secrecy similar to that which he so often criticized in government, and that government was trying to serve the public's right to know about a major crime.

The Janet Cooke Debacle

A few reporters, meanwhile, rejected the notion that the privilege was either needed by or appropriate to the journalist. They said that most journalists of the nation had done their work for decades without a shield. And they worried about unethical reporters using a shield law to hide behind in dishonest reporting.

In point was the episode—dismaying to journalists everywhere—of the fabricated story of rookie reporter Janet Cooke of the *Washington Post* in 1981. Her account of an unnamed eight-year-old heroin addict, whose identity she refused to disclose to her editors out of alleged fear of death from the child's "supplier," was awarded a Pulitzer Prize. But the award was scarcely announced when a standing challenge to the story's accuracy by city officials (resisted by Post editors who had insisted on shielding their reporter from disclosure of her sources), took strength from the revelation that Cooke had falsified her biographical resumé in applying for a position at the Post. Faced with the dual challenge, she confessed that she had made up the story and resigned. The Post returned the Pulitzer Award with agonized apologies to

---

[18] State v. Knops, 49 Wis.2d 647, 183 N.W.2d 93 (1971).

[19] Ibid., at 99.

readers, the city, and the field of journalism. No law court, no threat of contempt was involved, but the parallels were too close for comfort. The integrity of a shield claimed by a reporter and afforded by editors had been shattered; and so, too, in some measure, had that of a great newspaper, and the fact-gathering principle of special treatment—privilege—for the journalist.[20]

(2) Can the news gathering function be protected by a qualified immunity, or must it be absolute? Hard positions for absolute shields were taken by many journalists and their organizations including the directors of the American Newspaper Publishers Association and those of the American Society of Newspaper Editors.[21]

Yet "absolute" protection was an illusion, as we have seen in the previous section.[22] And a federal statute of any kind became a more and more remote possibility as years of drafting, committee work, and lobbying failed.[23]

(3) Also at issue was the question: Who deserves the shield? and following that: Would not defining "reporter" in effect be to license journalists and thus bring them under state control? The United States Supreme Court in denying Paul Branzburg protection summarized the question and found that deciding it would bring practical and conceptual difficulties of a high order:[24]

> Sooner or later, it would be necessary to define those categories of newsmen who qualified for the privilege, a questionable procedure in light of the traditional doctrine that liberty of the press is the right of the lonely pamphleteer who uses carbon paper or a mimeograph just as much as of the large metropolitan publisher who utilizes the latest photo-composition methods. . . . Freedom of the press is a "fundamental personal right" which "is not confined to newpapers and periodicals. It necessarily embraces pamphlets and leaflets. . . . Almost any author may quite accurately assert that he is contributing to the flow of information to the public, that he relies on confidential sources of information, and that these sources will be silenced if he is forced to make disclosures before a grand jury.

[20] Jerry Chaney, "Level With Us, Just How Sacred Is Your Source?", Quill, March 1979, 28; Quill, 61:4, April 1973, 38. Paul Magnusson, "Reporter's Lies Undermine Paper, Profession," Wisconsin State Journal, April 19, 1981, Sec. 4, p. 6; Robert H. Spiegel, "Notes from Pulitzer Juror," Wisconsin State Journal, April 21, 1981, Sec. 1, p. 6.

[21] Quill, 61:1, Jan. 1973, 29.

[22] AP Log, Sept. 3–9, 1973, pp. 1, 4.

[23] Press Censorship Newsletter No. IX, April–May 1976, p. 53.

[24] Branzburg v. Hayes, 408 U.S. 665, 702, 92 S.Ct. 2646, 2668 (1972).

Troubling as the question was, it did not deter states as they adopted statutes from 1970 onward. New York's 1970 law defined "professional journalist" and "newscaster" in its law that protected only those agencies normally considered "mass media"—newspaper, magazine, news agency, press association, wire service, radio or television transmission station or network.[25] Illinois, in its 1971 statute, defined "reporter" as one who worked for similar media.[26] Neither included books among the media immunized; neither included scholars and researchers among the persons immunized. In two cases, courts have ruled that state statutes which gave protection specifically to newspapers did not protect magazines.[27] But in late 1977, the U.S. Court of Appeals, Tenth Circuit, ruled that Arthur Buzz Hirsch, a film maker engaged in preparing a documentary on Karen Silkwood who had died mysteriously in a puzzling auto accident in Oklahoma, was indeed protected by the First Amendment in refusing to disclose confidential information concerning his investigation. This was the case despite the fact that the Oklahoma shield law gave protection only to those "regularly engaged in obtaining, writing, reviewing, editing or otherwise preparing news."[28]

These issues and questions run deep. They are not likely to be resolved for all sides soon. For the young journalist who will live with them and who may find them coming to bear personally in his professional work, the veteran investigative reporter Clark R. Mollenhoff has some rules of thumb for guidance. Winner of a Pulitzer Prize, Sigma Delta Chi Distinguished Service Awards, and various professional citations, Mollenhoff writes that "You'd better know what you're getting into".[29]

Is a Reporter's Confidentiality Pledge a Contract? Cohen v. Cowles Media (1991)

Ethically, if a reporter promises to protect the identity of a source, that sounds relatively simple. Unless the journalist is released from that pledge by the source, then the journalist—if ordered to testify before a grand jury or in court—must choose between ethically keeping the confidence or refusing to testify and

---

[25] McKinney's N.Y.Civ.Rights Law § 79–h (Supp.1971). In People v. LeGrand, 67 A.D.2d 446, 415 N.Y.S.2d 252 (1979), 4 Med.L.Rptr. 2524, the law was held not to apply to a book author, because the law specifies that only professional journalists and newscasters are shielded.

[26] Ill.Legis.H.Bill 1756, 1971 Gen.Assembly.

[27] Cepeda v. Cohane, 233 F.Supp. 465 (S.D.N.Y.1964); Deltec, Inc. v. Dun & Bradstreet, Inc., 187 F.Supp. 788 (N.D.Ohio 1960).

[28] Silkwood v. Kerr-McGee, see "Court Protects Film Maker's Sources," News Media & the Law, 1:1 (Oct.1977), p. 26.

[29] Quill, March 1979, p. 27, for Mollenhoff's rules.

being fined or jailed for contempt. That is a hard choice, to be sure, but the rules seem understandable.

But matters are not that simple. Refer back to unfortunate Janet Cooke, discussed earlier in this chapter at page 578? She turned in a brilliant story to the Washington Post about an 8–year-old heroin addict, and said that her source was confidential. The Washington Post backed her, and—perhaps due to its own success with "confidentially sourced" stories by Bob Woodward and Carl Bernstein [30]—did not learn who her source was.

Ever since 1981, when it was seen that Ms. Cooke had made up the entire story and had caused the mortified Washington Post to hand back a Pulitzer Prize, most editors have insisted upon knowing the source's identity. This makes sense because if a paper (or broacaster) is going to stake its reputation on a story, it is essential to have a good idea of the source's veracity and reliability. With some editors, also, it is an additional protection for a reporter. As John Seigenthaler of the Nashville Tennessean instructed his staff before his retirement in 1991, he insisted on knowing the identity of a confidential source so he could evaluate both source and information. (Then, if a judge wants to put a reporter in jail for not testifying, the judge may also have to jail the editor).[31]

The case of Cohen v. Cowles Media illustrates a situation in which editors decided—over the reporters' objections—that a confidential source's identity should be edited into a story. Its lesson—as handed down by the Supreme Court of the United States in June of 1991—is that a reporter's oral promise of source confidentiality amounts to a contract. Breaking such a contract may expose the reporter's employing organization to financial liability.

Dan Cohen, a former Minneapolis alderman, had been working as a political consultant to a Republican candidate for governor. Cohen found his candidate trailing badly in the polls late in October of 1982, only weeks before the election. Cohen arranged meetings with reporters from Twin Cities news organizations, including the Minneapolis Star and Tribune, the St. Paul Pioneer Press, and WCCO–TV.

Cohen offered to provide information that a candidate for state-wide election had been convicted of a misdemeanor. (The candidate involved was Marlene Johnson, the Democratic–Farmer–Labor [DFL] candidate for lieutenant governor; the DFL was then far ahead of Republicans in the governor's race. The misde-

---

[30] Cf. Woodward and Bernstein's All the President's Men (New York: Simon & Schuster, 1974).

[31] Seigenthaler comments on July 26, 1988, edition of McNeil–Lehrer News-hour.

meanor was for shop-lifting merchandise worth $6 a dozen years earlier.) [32]

Reporters for both the Star Tribune and the Pioneer Press promised to keep Cohen's identity anonymous, and Cohen then gave the reporters two court documents showing that Marlene Johnson had been "charged in 1969 with three counts of unlawful assembly, and the second that she had been convicted in 1970 of petty theft." (The unlawful assembly charges stemmed from Ms. Johnson engaging in a protest against claimed failure to hire minority workers in city construction, and those charges were dismissed. The shoplifting conviction involved leaving a store without paying for $6 worth of sewing materials. That incident apparently happened, the Supreme Court noted, at a time when Ms. Johnson was emotionally distraught, "and the conviction was later vacated.")

Evidently not liking being caught by Dan Cohen's political dirty trick, reporters for the newspapers interviewed Marlene Johnson to get her comments. Both the Minneapolis and the St. Paul newspapers decided independently to use Dan Cohen's name as the source of their last-minute before the election stories about Johnson. [33]

> In their stories, both papers identified Cohen as the source of the court records, indicated his connection with the Whitney [Republican candidate for governor] campaign, and included denials by Whitney campaign officials of any role in the matter. The same day the stories appeared, Cohen was fired by his employer.

(At least one newsman, David Nimmer of WCCO–TV, listened to Cohen's proposition and refused to use the information. It was "no story," Nimmer said: "A conviction when she was 18 years old for shoplifting needles and thread.") [34]

> Tim McGuire, managing editor of the Star Tribune, said that " * * * disclosure of an 11th–hour dirty trick [in the political campaign] was at least as important as the 12–year–old shoplifting record which Cohen was revealing." [35]

The trial court rejected the newspapers' contentions that the First Amendment erected a barrier to Dan Cohen's lawsuit alleg-

---

[32] Cohen v. Cowles Media Co. (1987), 14 Med.L.Rptr. 1460; News Media & the Law, Summer, 1988, p. 349; Andrew Radolf, "Anonymous Sources," Editor & Publisher, Aug. 27, 1988.

[33] Cohen v. Cowles Media Co., ___ U.S. ___, ___, 111 S.Ct. 2513, 2516 (1991), 18 Med.L.Rptr. 2273, 2274.

[34] MacNeil–Lehrer News Hour, July 26, 1988.

[35] "Verdict on news sources distresses journalists," Associated Press report in Milwaukee Journal, July 23, 1988.

ing fraudulent misrepresentation and breach of contract. By a 5–1 margin, a jury awarded Cohen $200,000 in compensatory damages and $500,000 in punitive damages.[36] In a split decision, however, the Minnesota Court of Appeals overturned the punitive damages award after concluding that Cohen had not established a fraud claim which would support a punitive damage award. That court, however, left standing the $200,000 compensatory damages award.[37]

The Supreme Court of the United States held that the First Amendment does not prohibit a plaintiff from collecting damages for a newspaper's breaking of a promise of confidentiality in exchange for information. Liability could be assessed under Minnesota's "doctrine of promissory estoppel." [38] Justice Byron White wrote for the Court's 5–member majority:

> * * * "[G]enerally applicable laws do not offend the First Amendment simply because their enforcement against the press has incidental effects on its ability to gather and report the news. * * * [T]ruthful information sought to be published must have been lawfully acquired. The press may not with impunity break and enter an office or dwelling to gather news.

The U.S. Supreme Court declared that the Minnesota Supreme Court's "incorrect conclusion that the First Amendment barred Cohen's claim may well have truncated its consideration of whether a promissory estoppel claim had otherwise been established under Minnesota law and whether Cohen's claim could be upheld on a promissory estoppel basis." [39] Or, Justice White wrote, perhaps the Minnesota Constitution might be construed to protect the press from such a promissory estoppel action.

In dissent, Justice Blackmun (joined by Justices Marshall and Souter) argued that a damage claim for promissory estoppel should not be used to punish reporting of truthful information about a political campaign.[40] Justice Souter's dissenting opinion (joined by Marshall, Blackmun, and O'Connor) took the tack that the higher value to be served is an informed public, not a promise kept by a newspaper: [41]

[36] News Media & the Law, Summer, 1988, p. 49.

[37] Ibid., at 50, 18 Med.L.Rptr. at 2276.

[38] Ibid. Black's Law Dictionary says: "*Estoppel.* A man's own act or acceptance stops or closes his mouth to allege or plead the truth." With *promissory estoppel,* " * * * such promise is binding if injustice can be avoided only by enforcement of [the] promise."

[39] Ibid., at ___, 111 S.Ct. at 2519–2520, 18 Med.L.Rptr. at 2277.

[40] Ibid., at ___, 111 S.Ct. at 2520, 18 Med.L.Rptr. at 2279.

[41] Ibid., at ___, 111 S.Ct. at 2523, 18 Med.L.Rptr. at 2280.

The importance of this public interest [the information provided by the press necessary to self-government] is integral to the balance that should be struck in this case. There can be no doubt that the fact of Cohen's identity expanded the universe of information relevant to the choice faced by Minnesota voters in that State's 1982 gubernatorial election, the publication of which was thus of the sort quintessentially subject to strict First Amendment protection.

Justice Souter summarized his dissent, arguing that "the State's interest in enforcing a newspaper's promise of confidentiality [is] insufficient to outweigh the interest in unfettered publication of the information revealed in this case * * *."

Whatever else Cohen v. Cowles Media means, the way it was argued by the newspapers ought to be a tremendous embarrassment to the journalistic world. Journalists have long argued that because they serve the public, they are somehow special and do not have to testify—like ordinary mortals—about the sources of their information. "We gave our word to protect our confidential sources, and courts should respect that." But in the Cohen case, the newspapers wanted it both ways; they wound up appearing to want to be free to give promises to get information, and also to have the luxury of reneging on promises when convenient.

But what of Dan Cohen? This political operative wanted to be a paid political consultant—anonymously—while lobbing bricks over a wall at an opposition candidate. But was he harmed $200,000 worth (the amount of compensatory damages left standing by the Minnesota Supreme Court)? Cohen, who lost a $35,000–a–year job in public relations in 1982 the day the story was published, by 1987 had his own PR firm and earned $97,000.[42]

Ironically, the Minneapolis Star Tribune was twice burned in 1988 on the issue of confidential sources. A second controversy over naming a source resulted in the newspaper halting circulation of its Sunday magazine for July 24, 1988. The New York Times reported that the Star Tribune could not ascertain whether a story to appear in its magazine had breached a secrecy agreement between a source (who is a lawyer) and the author, a freelance journalist.[43] That magazine issue was withheld.

These problems surfaced in a time when journalists were worrying about their ethical standards. Charles J. Lewis, Wash-

[42] "2 Newspapers Lose Suit for Disclosing a Source," Associated Press story in New York Times, July 23, 1988. Early in 1992, the State's Supreme Court upheld the $200,000 jury award. The News Media & The Law, Winter, 1992, p. 2.

[43] Charles J. Lewis, Trading News for Anonymity, The Bulletin of the American Society of Newspaper Editors, April 1988, p. 3.

ington Bureau Chief of the Associated Press, expressed concern about misuse of confidential sources eroding media credibility.

How can readers evaluate stories when sources are not known? For example, news from the State Department tends to follow certain rules: "on the record" means use names and information, but much news called "background" means that information can be used, but only vaguely attributed, as to "U.S. Officials" or "State Department sources." "Deep Background" means no specific attribution, and "off the record" means reporters can't use what they're told except for background.

Bureau Chief Lewis noted that the Associated Press has developed a three-part test which has helped to cut down the number of unattributed stories sent by the wire service.[44]

(1) The information should be newsworthy.

(2) We couldn't get the information elsewhere with attribution.

(3) The information is arguably factual rather than opinion or judgmental.

Beyond that, some sources discover that they have been quoted after they thought they had an agreement that their names would not be used.[45] Sometimes, releasing a source's name is necessary, as when the source has lied. For example, Lt. Colonel Oliver North complained about "leaks" which had led to a story in Newsweek about interception of an Egyptian plane carrying hijackers. Understandably, Newsweek published the rejoinder that the Colonel had failed to mention that he was the source of the leaks.

The Wall Street Journal distinguishes "anonymous sources" from "confidential sources." A memo circulated by managing editor Norman Pearlstine says that anonymous sources are those whose names the Journal has agreed to leave out of the paper but whose identity may later be disclosed, as in defending against a libel suit. A confidential source, on the other hand, is one whose identity the paper has promised to keep secret, even it means losing a lawsuit or going to jail.[46]

Source confidentiality, then, is serious business. Secrecy agreements with sources are not to be entered lightly. Especially worrisome are situations in which reporters' pledges are broken, either by reporters themselves or by their editors.

The basic question is whether the press is to be trusted and credible. Editors wishing to avoid difficulties would do well to

[44] Ibid., p. 5.

[45] Monica Langley and Lee Levine, Broken Promises, Columbia Journalism Review July/August 1986, p. 21.

[46] Ibid., p. 23.

emulate Editor John Seigenthaler of the Nashville Tennessean:
He says the only conceivable time to name a source pledged
confidentiality would be if it turns out that the source has provided false information.[47]

SEC. 80. PROTECTING NEWSROOMS FROM SEARCH AND TELEPHONE RECORDS FROM DISCLOSURE

Courts have not granted First Amendment protection against officials' searches of newsrooms, but Congress and several states have passed laws providing protection. Confidentiality of journalists' telephone-call records that are on file at telephone companies has not been recognized.

When the United States Supreme Court rejects a claim to
First Amendment protection, Congress and state legislatures may
be able to furnish protection by passing laws. The news world's
drive for a statutory privilege against revealing sources—after the
Supreme Court in Branzburg v. Hayes seemed to journalists to
restrict protection under the First Amendment to a shadow—
succeeded in a few states by dint of long, hard work, and failed in
others. The effort to get a law through Congress ground to a
frustrated halt in 1976 and 1977 as we saw above.

But another aspect of confidentiality denied First Amendment
protection by the Supreme Court—shielding news rooms and offices against official searches and seizures of news material—got
an early remedy in the form of state legislation and a national
law—the Privacy Protection Act of 1980.[48] It was passed less than
three years after a Supreme Court decision of May 1978 sent the
news media into a reaction of alarm and denunciation; the very
security of their news rooms and files was at stake. Journalists'
outrage over the decision was widespread at what they saw as the
Court's approval of a "right to rummage" in their offices, a breach
of custom and understanding.

By a 5–3 margin, the Court said in 1978's Zurcher v. Stanford
Daily that newspapers (and all citizens, for that matter) may be
the subjects of unannounced searches as long as those searches are
approved beforehand by a court's issuance of a search warrant.[49]
They need not be suspected of any crime themselves; but as "third
parties" who may hold information helpful to law enforcement,
their property may be searched. A particular issue in this case

---

[47] McNeil–Lehrer News Hour, July 26, 1988.

[48] Pub.Law # 96–440, 94 Stat. 1879, approved Oct. 13, 1980, 6 Med.L.Rptr. 2255.
For summary and discussion of the law and the state actions, see Anon., "Newsroom Searches," News Media & the Law, Oct./Nov. 1980, 3–5.

[49] 436 U.S. 547, 98 S.Ct. 1970 (1978).

was a question of how to interpret the words of the Fourth
Amendment to the Constitution. That amendment says:

> The right of the people to be secure in their persons,
> houses, papers, and effects, against unreasonable searches
> and seizures, shall not be violated, and no Warrants shall
> issue, but upon probable cause, supported by Oath or
> affirmation, and particularly describing the place to be
> searched, and the persons or things to be seized.

The Zurcher case arose during violent demonstrations at
Stanford University on April 9, 1971. Two days later, the *Stanford Daily* carried articles and photographs about the clash between demonstrators and police. It appeared to authorities from
that coverage that a Daily photographer had been in a position to
photograph fighting between students and police. As a result, a
search warrant was secured from a municipal court. The warrant
was issued [50]

> on a finding of "just, probable and reasonable cause for
> believing that: Negatives and photographs and films,
> evidence material and relevant to the identification of the
> perpetrators of felonies, to wit, Battery on a Peace Officer,
> and Assault with a Deadly Weapon, will be located [on the
> premises of the Daily]."

Later that day, the newspaper office was searched by four
police officers, with some newspaper staffers present. The search
turned up only the photographs already published in the Daily, so
no materials were removed from the newspaper's office. In May
of 1971, the Daily and some of its staffers sued James Zurcher, the
Palo Alto chief of police, the officers who conducted the search,
and the county's district attorney.

A federal district court held that the search was illegal. It
declared that the Fourth and Fourteenth Amendments forbade
the issuance of a warrant to search for materials in possession of a
person not suspected of a crime unless there was probable cause to
believe, based on a sworn affidavit, that a subpoena *duces tecum*
would be impractical.

Some translation is needed here. As *New York Times* reporter Warren Weaver, Jr. noted, a subpoena *duces tecum* (that's Latin
for "bring it with you") "can be enforced by a judge only after a
hearing in which the holder of the evidence has the opportunity to
present arguments why the material should not be given to the
government." That process means, of course, that the holder of
the documents sought would have some warning and perhaps even
a chance to "clean up" files. (But if one does tamper with

---

[50] Ibid., at 551, 98 S.Ct. at 1974.

evidence under subpoena—and if that tampering is revealed, it is surely punishable as contempt.) If investigators have a search warrant, on the other hand, the holder of the documents "has no more warning than a knock on the door." [51] In finding in favor of the Stanford Daily, District Judge Robert F. Peckham wrote:[52]

> It should be apparent that means less drastic than a search warrant do exist for obtaining materials from a third party. A subpoena duces tecum, obviously, is much less intrusive than a search warrant: the police do not go rummaging through one's house, office, or desk armed only with a subpoena. And, perhaps equally important, there is no opportunity to challenge the search warrant prior to the intrusion, whereas one can always move to quash the subpoena before producing the sought-after materials. * * * In view of the difference in degree of intrusion and the opportunity to challenge possible mistakes, the subpoena should always be preferred to the search warrant, for non-suspects.

The Daily's lawsuit thus was upheld by a U.S. district court and, five years later, by a U.S. Court of Appeals.[53] The Supreme Court of the United States, however, in a decision announced by Justice White, declared that newspapers are subject to such unannounced "third party" searches as the one involving the *Stanford Daily*. Justice White's majority opinion said:[54]

> It is an understatement to say that there is no direct authority in this or any other federal court for the District Court's sweeping revision of the Fourth Amendment. Under existing law, valid warrants may be issued to search *any* property, whether or not occupied by a third party, at which there is probable reason to believe that fruits, instrumentalities, or evidence of a crime will be found.
>
> * * *
>
> The critical element in a reasonable search is not that the owner of the property is suspected of a crime but that there is reasonable cause to believe that the specific "things" to be searched for and seized are located on the property to which entry is sought.

[51] Warren Weaver, Jr., "High Court Bars Newspaper Plea Against Search," New York Times, June 1, 1978, pp. Al ff, at p. B6.

[52] Stanford Daily v. Zurcher, 353 F.Supp. 124, 130 (N.D.Cal.1972).

[53] 550 F.2d 464 (9th Cir.1977).

[54] Zurcher v. Stanford Daily, 436 U.S. 547, 554–556, 98 S.Ct. 1970, 1975–1977 (1978).

The Court enumerated—and rejected—the following arguments that additional First Amendment factors would forbid use of search warrants and permit only the subpoena *duces tecum*— arguments which held that searches of newspaper offices for evidence of crime would threaten the ability of the press to do its job.[55]

> This is said to be true for several reasons: first, searches will be physically disruptive to such an extent that timely publication will be impeded. Second, confidential sources of information will dry up, and the press will also lose opportunities to cover various events because of fears of the participants that press files will be readily available to the authorities. Third, reporters will be deterred from recording and preserving their recollections for future use if such information is subject to seizure. Fourth, the processing of news and its dissemination will be chilled by the prospects that searches will disclose internal editorial deliberations. Fifth, the press will resort to self-censorship to conceal its possession of information of potential interest to the police.

Justice White's majority opinion brushed aside such arguments and expressed confidence that judges could guard against searches which would be so intrusive as to interfere with publishing newspapers.

Justice Potter Stewart, joined by Justice Thurgood Marshall, dissented, arguing that in place of the unannounced "knock-on-the-door" intrusion, "a subpoena would afford the newspaper itself an opportunity to locate whatever material might be requested and produce it." Then, as did his dissent in Branzburg v. Hayes, his argument hammered at society's need for confidentiality of the journalist's information, and for its constitutional protection.[56]

> Perhaps as a matter of abstract policy a newspaper office should receive no more protection from unannounced police searches than, say, the office of a doctor or the office of a bank. But we are here to uphold a Constitution. And our Constitution does not explicitly protect the practice of medicine or the business of banking from all abridgment by government. It does explicitly protect the freedom of the press.

Justice John Paul Stevens' dissent focused not on First Amendment matters, but on the justification needed to issue a search warrant without running afoul of the Fourth Amendment.

[55] Ibid., at 561–566, 98 S.Ct. at 1977–1982.

[56] Ibid., at 572, 576, 98 S.Ct. at 1985, 1987.

Stevens wrote that every private citizen—not only the media—should be protected.[57]

Students of the problem questioned Justice White's reliance on "neutral magistrates" to protect media from harassment, and to issue warrants only upon reasonable requests whose propriety they could gauge on the basis of probable cause to believe that evidence would be found on the premises to be searched. For one thing, between the 1971 raid on the *Stanford Daily* offices and the Supreme Court decision in 1978, there were at least 14 other searches of media properties. And in addition:[58]

> Journalists should perhaps be forgiven if they regard the protection of "neutral magistrates" as illusory. First, most, if not all, journalists tend to believe the folklore item about police walking around with fill-in-the-blank search warrants already signed by a complacent magistrate. Even if that is rankest slander of the judiciary, statistics on the issuance of search warrants compel the belief that the preconditions for warrant issuance are often improperly administered. "From 1969 through 1976, police sought 5,563 applications for search warrants under the 1968 Omnibus Crime Control Act. Only 15 of these applications were denied." Bluntly, the general rule seems to be that a search warrant sought equals a search warrant granted.

The legislation that Congress passed in 1980 in reaction to the *Zurcher* decision took effect in 1981. It provides a subpoena procedure, and a hearing for those subpoenaed. It prohibits "knock-on-the-door," search-warrant raids of news media offices and those of authors and researchers, by federal, state, and local law enforcement agencies, except in three unusual circumstances. These are: where there is cause to believe that the reporter himself is involved in a crime, where the information sought relates to the national defense or classified information, or where there is reason to believe that immediate action through search warrant is needed to prevent bodily harm or death to a human being.[59] *News Media & the Law* found that at least nine states had adopted their own laws along the same lines, some extending the protection to all private citizens, not only those in the field of writing. While the federal law avoids that reach, it requires the Justice Department to work out guidelines for federal searches

[57] Ibid., at 582–583, 98 S.Ct. at 1990.

[58] Dwight L. Teeter and Singer, S.G., Search Warrants in Newsrooms, 67 Ky.L. Journ. 847, 858 (1978–79).

[59] Pub.Law 96–440, 94 Stat. 1879; 6 Med.L.Rptr. 2255, 2256 (1981). And see "Carter Signs Newsroom Raid Ban," News Media & the Law, Oct./Nov. 1980, 3–5.

that will take into account personal privacy interests of the person to be searched.[60]

Journalists' Telephone Records

Searches of newsrooms slowed after adoption of the Privacy Protection Act of 1980, but—as discussed at the end of this chapter—occasional police or FBI searches (of dubious legality) may occur.[61] And there are other intrusions. In 1976, the Reporters Committee for Freedom of the Press and other journalists lost a case in federal district court to compel AT & T to inform media when government subpoenas were issued for media phone records. The court of appeals also turned down the media, saying that no right of privacy under the First Amendment existed because the records belonged to the telephone company and not the media.[62] In an unsuccessful appeal to the United States Supreme Court to review the decision, the journalists stated the heart of their case for protection of their telephone records:[63]

> The impact of the ruling below cannot be minimized * * *. When government investigators obtain a reporter's toll records * * * they learn the identity of (his) sources. And they also learn * * * much about the pattern of his investigative activities—whom he called, when and in what order he makes calls to develop his leads, what subjects he is looking into and how actively he is exploring these subjects.

In the fall of 1980, it was reported that phone records of the Atlanta bureau of the *New York Times,* as well as those of its bureau chief, Howell Raines, had been subpoenaed in June by the Justice Department. The telephone company had waited 90 days, at the request of the Justice Department, before telling the Times. Shortly thereafter, attorney General Benjamin Civiletti announced new rules for issuing subpoenas for phone records— essentially, that no subpoena is to be issued to media people for their toll phone records without "express authorization" of the Attorney General.[64] This was the extent of protection that the media found.

---

[60] Attorney General's Guidelines for Litigation to Enforce Obligations to Submit Materials for Predissemination Review, 6 Med.L.Rptr. 2261 (1981), dated 12/9/80, and published 1/2/81.

[61] "Police Raid Newspaper Printing Office," News Media & the Law, Aug./Sept. 1980, 25.

[62] Reporters Committee for Freedom of Press v. American Tel. & Tel. Co., 593 F.2d 1030 (D.C.Cir.1978), certiorari denied 440 U.S. 949, 99 S.Ct. 1431 (1979), 4 Med. L.Rptr. 1177.

[63] News Media & the Law, Oct./Nov. 1980, 6.

[64] New York Times, Nov. 13, 1980, A30.

Thus in one more setting, journalists were asserting that secrecy—anathema when employed by the government—was essential to the highest performance of their own craft. And once again, it was clear that deep values in the journalist's work—the "watchdogging" of government and other powerful institutions, and informing the members of an open society about their world— would be overshadowed in some contests where other cherished values sometimes would take precedence.

Newsroom Confidentiality: A Continuing Struggle

Despite passage of the federal Privacy Act of 1980, aimed at protecting newsrooms from searches under most circumstances,[65] the late 1980s saw a number of efforts to search newsrooms. The searches showed that law is not self-executing, and that reporters need a working understanding of the law—with preparation from knowledgable attorneys—when a search is attempted. Searches became sufficiently bothersome in 1988 that the National Association of Broadcasters (NAB) issued a memo urging broadcast stations to review procedures with their attorneys for fending off a search.[66]

When a police department or sheriff asks a judge for a search warrant, there is some likelihood that the judge won't know that the Privacy Protection Act of 1980 forbids searches of newsrooms except in limited situations as noted above, at footnote 59. Despite this statute and despite similar legislation in at least nine states, occasional searches have continued. The News Media & The Law reported in the fall of 1988 that four newsroom searches had taken place between December, 1986, and mid-August of 1988, in Minneapolis and Golden Valley, Minnesota, and in Palm Springs and Los Angeles, California.

The News Media & The Law emphasized that the Privacy Protection Act of 1980 made it illegal for the seizure of either the "work product" or "documentary materials" from persons who are creating newspapers, books or broadcasts.[67] That magazine recommends:

[65] See discussion at footnote 59, above. Those limited occasions in which a federal or state judge may issue a warrant for a newsroom search include a reasonable showing that newsroom personnel are involved in commission of a crime, in possession of contraband or classified or national defense information, or where there is reason to believe that information in a newsroom is needed by authorities to protect human life.

[66] Jane E. Kirtley, Counsel Memo: "Dealing With Newsroom Searches," N.A.B. Info-Pak, October/November, 1988.

[67] News Media & The Law, Fall, 1988, pp. 4–5.

First, journalists in the newsroom should object to the search and, if possible, should stall long enough for the company's lawyer and upper-level management to arrive.

Second, journalists should not interfere with the search, but they do not have to assist in it. The search should be limited by the terms of the warrant to certain areas and to specific materials.

Third, News Media & The Law recommends that a videotape or photographic record be made if the search proceeds.

Finally, once a search has taken place, a lawyer should be consulted about the possibility of suing the governmental agency carrying out the search. If the search is deemed found illegal under the terms of the Privacy Protection Act of 1980, the journalist whose office was searched can collect $1,000 in damages (plus reimbursement for any actual harm done in the search) plus lawyer's fees.[68] It should be apparent that most search warrants issued against newsrooms are illegal and invalid, and journalists should be prepared to fight back. Lawsuits are not the only weapons, however. Publicity about governmental units acting illegally may be the media's strongest weapon in protecting newsrooms from searches.

Obviously, journalists must remain vigilant, ready to contend—by all lawful means—against newsroom subpoenas or searches. While the threat of searches may have abated considerably, newsroom subpoenas seem to be alive and well. In 1991, for example, the Reporters Committee on Freedom of the Press released a study of 4,400 subpoenas asking for notes, tapes, or testimony served on 1,042 news operations during 1989. Significant details included: [69]

— Television stations are far more likely than newspapers to be subpoenaed, and are more likely to comply with subpoenas.

— Responding news organizations (about half of the 2,127 surveyed) indicated that only about 8 percent of the subpoenas were challenged in court. But nearly half of the subpoenas sought material that had actually been published or broadcast.

— News organizations' courtroom challenges to subpoenas were successful more than 75 percent of the time.

[68] Ibid., p. 6; See also Kirtley, op. cit.

[69] Anna America, "News Media Under Legal Siege," Presstime, March, 1991, page 34.

Chapter 14

LEGAL PROBLEMS IN REPORTING LEGISLATIVE AND EXECUTIVE BRANCHES OF GOVERNMENT

Sec.
81. The Problem of Secrecy in Government.
82. Access and the Constitution.
83. Records and Meetings of Federal Government.
84. Access to "Security" Information, Covering Wars.
85. Records and Meetings in the States.

SEC. 81. THE PROBLEM OF SECRECY IN GOVERNMENT

Following World War II, obtaining access to information at various levels of government became an acute problem in American journalism.

Government accountability requires an informed public. Self-government depends on citizens' knowledge of what public officials are doing in the name of the public and with the public's money. Some thoughtful historians of the mass media, however, suggest that more and more power to control information has been amassed by governments and by private centers of wealth and power closely linked to government. For example, Norman L. Rosenberg contended that "the central free-speech issues of the post-World War II era involved the expansion of a vast surveillance apparatus, the growing power of an increasingly monopolistic communications industry, and the problems of its ties to other private and public centers of power." [1]

If such a sorry state of affairs exists, what have journalists been doing about it? Not much and not enough, if one believes Robert M. Entman's contentions: [2]

> Restricted by the limited tastes of the audience and reliant upon political elites for most information, journalists participate in an interdependent news system, not a free market of ideas. In practice . . . the news media fall far

---

[1] Norman L. Rosenberg, Protecting the Best Men (Chapel Hill: Univ. of North Carolina Press, 1986), p. 265; for a discussion of problems of access to information about great concentrations of wealth and power involving stock market scandals, see James B. Stewart, Den of Thieves (New York: Simon and Schuster, 1991).

[2] Robert M. Entman, Democracy Without Citizens: Media and the Decay of American Politics (New York: Oxford University Press, 1989) p. 8.

short of the ideal version of a free press as civic educator and guardian of democracy.

The news media can do only so much in reporting on private power. Much news—especially news which is not favorable to corporate America—comes to reporters via reports from federal, state and local regulatory agencies. Since 1980, especially, the federal government has pruned regulatory activities over business, so that less is learned about private concentrations of power until too late for the news media to serve as an effective sentinel. Then, when a scandal such as the estimated $500 billion savings and loan debacle occurs, disaster strikes, showing government regulators and the news media too often impotent and irrelevant. With newspapers, broadcasting stations and cable TV companies generally owned by large corporations, it is not only the conspiracy buff who wonders if news media have sufficient independence.

Cataclysmic changes now taking place in communications industries, however, may make media concentration only a short-run problem. "Demassification" is occurring and accelerating, which may mean that individuals interconnected via communications networks may begin to overshadow mass media units—including newspapers, broadcast stations, and cable television—in societal importance. The late Ithiel de Sola Pool, a most important communication theorist, expressed the hope that as new communications networks emerge, they will do so under "guidelines that recognize the preferred position of freedom of discourse." [3] Pool also saw that the First Amendment must apply "to the function of communication, not just to the media that existed in the eighteenth century." [4]

Meaningful discourse and meaningful communication on the brink of the 21st Century require that the First Amendment now be given expanded meaning where access to government information is concerned. Growth of governmental power has coincided with expanding government secrecy at all levels and with the rapid changeover to computerized records rather than the more easily accessible paper files. The need for computer-literate reporters and citizens is now the more important as records once freely available in file drawers now require the intervention of a government gatekeeper. Computer searches for information—and finding patterns in that information—can be far more informative to society than yesterday's paper-chases, but only if citizen access is protected under the Constitution and under supporting stat-

[3] Ithiel de Sola Pool, Technologies of Freedom (Cambridge, MA: Belknap Press of Harvard University, 1983) p. 244.

[4] Ibid., p. 246.

utes.[5] As is discussed in Section 82 of this chapter, the Supreme Court of the United States has viewed the Constitution and the First Amendment as something apart from the concept of "a public's right to know" or a "citizen's right to gather information." To that extent, as government grows ever more powerful and the news media increasingly embrace corporate values, it might be argued that the First Amendment has been allowed to become obsolete.

No segment of the American public has been more concerned about tendencies to secrecy in government than journalists. Some feel that it is the central threat to freedom of expression in Twentieth Century America. Accepting, during World War II, the need for extensive secrecy for an enormous war machine in a government bureaucracy grown gigantic, journalists after the war soon detected a broad pattern of continued secrecy in government operations. Access to meetings was denied; reports, papers, documents at all levels of government seemed less available than before officialdom's habits of secrecy developed in the passion for security during World War II. An intense, insistent campaign for access to government information was launched in the 1950's by editors, publishers, reporters, and news organizations. It went under a banner labeled "Freedom of Information," and under the claim that the press was fighting for the "people's right to know."[6]

To combat what they viewed as a severe increase in denial of access to the public's business, journalists took organized action. "Freedom of Information" committees were established by the American Society of Newspaper Editors (ASNE) and by the Society of Professional Journalists—Sigma Delta Chi. The ASNE commissioned newspaper attorney Harold L. Cross to perform a major study on the law of access to government activity. His book, *The People's Right to Know,* was published in 1953 and served as a central source of information. State and local chapters of professional groups worked for the adoption of state access laws. In 1958, a Freedom of Information Center was opened at the University of Missouri School of Journalism, as a clearing house and research facility for those concerned with the subject. Meanwhile, an early and vigorous ally was found in the House Subcommittee on Government Information under Rep. John E. Moss of California, created to investigate charges of excessive secrecy in the Executive branch of government.[7]

[5] See generally, Sissela Bok, Secrets: On the Ethics of Concealment and Revelation (New York: Pantheon, 1983); for a discussion of computerized aids to reporting, see Elliot G. Jaspin, "Just do it!," ASNE Bulletin, Dec. 1991, p. 4ff.

[6] See Annual Reports, Sigma Delta Chi Advancement of Freedom of Information Committee (Chicago, Sigma Delta Chi).

[7] Rep. John E. Moss, Preface to Replies from Federal Agencies to Questionnaire Submitted by the Special Subcommittee on Government Information of the Committee on Government Operations, 84 Cong. 1 Sess. (Nov. 1, 1955), p. iii.

Journalism had powerful allies also in the scientific community. It found that the advance of knowledge in vast areas of government-sponsored science was being slowed, sometimes crippled for years, in the blockage of the flow of research information between and even within agencies of the federal government. Fear of "leakage" of secrets important to defense in the Cold War with the Soviet Union brought administrative orders that were contrary to the tenets of scientists and researchers. A snarl of regulations, rules, and red tape, prevented scientists from sharing their findings with others. Their concern about the damage to the advance of knowledge in science paralleled the news fraternity's alarm about damage to the democratic assumption that free institutions rest on an informed public.[8]

Public understanding of the dangers of official secrecy broadened in the exposé of the Executive's abuse of power in the Watergate episode of the mid-1970's. Earl Warren, retired Chief Justice of the United States, crediting the news media with a share in exposing the fraud and deceit, said if we are to learn from "the debacle we are in, we should first strike at secrecy in government wherever it exists, because it is the incubator for corruption." [9] New recruits entered the battle against official secrecy—Common Cause, the Center for National Security Studies, and Ralph Nader among them.

Although citizens of the United States congratulate themselves upon having an open society, that openness seemed to be in increasing peril in the 1990s. It is one thing to have Freedom of Information legislation at the federal and state levels; it is quite another to find that access is truly open.

In his April, 1987 presidential address to the American Society of Newspaper Editors, Michael Gartner laid out a dirty laundry list of information that is not freely obtainable. Just a few of the many items Gartner listed as being unavailable:

— Information that the government keeps secret for purposes of national defense or foreign policy.

— Information on sources or methods of the Central Intelligence Agency.

— Information concerning virtually anything about the National Security Agency.

— Much of the information at the Consumer Product Safety Commission.

[8] Science, Education and Communications, 12 Bulletin of Atomic Scientists, 333 (Nov.1956); Walter Gellhorn, Security, Loyalty, and Science (Ithaca: Cornell Univ. Press, 1950).

[9] Governmental Secrecy: Corruption's Ally, 60 ABA Journal 550 (May, 1974).

— Information on pre-sentencing investigations and parole reports.

The key to reporting of the legislative and executive branches is persistence: stubbornness in asking questions and virtually endless patience that is often needed in filing and re-filing FOIA (Freedom of Information Act) requests. It took a dozen years of struggle, including three lawsuits, to open the first 1.5 million pages of documents from the Administration of President Nixon, and those pages were mostly trivia and represented less than 4 per cent of the total body of papers.

SEC. 82.   ACCESS AND THE CONSTITUTION

Courts have given little support to the position that the First Amendment includes a right of access to government information.

In many journalists' view, freedom of speech and press and the First Amendment encompass a right to gather government information as much as they encompass the right to publish and distribute it. Constitutional protection against denial of access seems to them only reasonable. The legal scholar Harold Cross argued that "Freedom of information is the very foundation for all those freedoms that the First Amendment of our Constitution was intended to guarantee." [10]

Famed First Amendment legal scholar Thomas I. Emerson held that "we ought to consider the right to know as an integral part of the system of freedom of expression, embodied in the first amendment and entitled to support by legislation or other affirmative government action." He found the argument for "starting from this point * * * overwhelming," and further, that the Supreme Court has in some respects recognized a constitutional right to know.[11]

But the courts have provided scant acknowledgement of a "right of access" under the First Amendment, except for access to public, criminal court trials, declared open as a First Amendment right in a major case of 1980, Richmond Newspapers v. Virginia (detailed in Chap. 15, below). As noted in Chapter 15, some of the *Richmond Newspapers* case's language is so sweeping that it may be the forerunner of a First Amendment *right* to gather information. Our concern here, however, is news-gathering problems in the legislative and executive/administrative branches.

[10] Harold L. Cross, The People's Right to Know (Morningside Heights: Columbia Univ. Press, 1953), pp. xiii–xiv.

[11] Legal Foundations of the Right To Know, 1976 Wash.U.L.Quar. 1–3. See also Jacob Scher, "Access to Information: Recent Legal Problems," Journalism Quarterly, 37:1 (1960), p. 41.

A Right to Travel?

Reporter William Worthy of the *Baltimore Afro-American* in 1956 ignored an order of Secretary of State John Foster Dulles which barred American newsmen from going to Red China to report. When Worthy returned to the United States, the State Department revoked his passport and refused to give him another. Worthy went to court to attempt to regain his passport. The trial court held, without elaborating, that Dulles' refusal to issue the passport did not violate Worthy's rights to travel under the First Amendment. Worthy appealed, but his argument for First Amendment protection failed, the Court of Appeals holding:[12]

> The right to travel is a part of the right to liberty, and a newspaperman's right to travel is a part of freedom of the press. But these valid generalizations do not support unrestrained conclusions. * * *

> Freedom of the press bears restrictions * * *. Merely because a newsman has a right to travel does not mean he can go anywhere he wishes. He cannot attend conferences of the Supreme Court, or meetings of the President's Cabinet or executive sessions of the Committees of Congress.

In another case, Zemel argued that a State Department travel ban was a direct interference with the First Amendment rights of citizens to inform themselves at first hand of events abroad. The United States Supreme Court agreed that the Secretary's denial rendered "less than wholly free the flow of information concerning that country," but denied that a First Amendment right was involved. "The right to speak and publish does not carry with it the unrestrained right to gather information,"[13] the Court said.

On occasion, the U.S. State Department may deny a passport to a person whose foreign travel is thought to create "substantial likelihood of 'serious damage' to national security or foreign policy." The Supreme Court upheld such a passport revocation involving Philip Agee, a dissident former Central Intelligence agent accused of working to expose the cover and sources of CIA employees.[14]

[12] Worthy v. Herter, 270 F.2d 905 (D.C.Cir.1959), certiorari denied 361 U.S. 918, 80 S.Ct. 255 (1959).

[13] Zemel v. Rusk, 381 U.S. 1, 17–18, 85 S.Ct. 1271, 1281 (1965). See also Trimble v. Johnston, 173 F.Supp. 651 (D.D.C.1959); In re Mack, 386 Pa. 251, 126 A.2d 679 (1956).

[14] Haig v. Agee, 453 U.S. 280, 287, 288, 101 S.Ct. 2766, 2771, 2772 (1981).

A Right of Access?

While an occasional lower court or a dissenting judge has found reason for the First Amendment to protect a right of access to government information,[15] the United States Supreme Court has done so only in the setting of public, criminal trials. Justice Potter Stewart delivered a rationale for the denial of a constitutional right of access to government, in a 1975 speech:[16]

> So far as the Constitution goes, the autonomous press may publish what it knows, and may seek to learn what it can.
>
> But this autonomy cuts both ways. The press is free to do battle against secrecy and deception in government. But the press cannot expect from the Constitution any guarantee that it will succeed. There is no constitutional right to have access to particular government information, or to require openness from the bureaucracy. The public's interest in knowing about its government is protected by the guarantee of a Free Press, but the protection is indirect. The Constitution itself is neither a Freedom of Information Act nor an Official Secrets Act.
>
> The Constitution, in other words, establishes the contest, not its resolution. Congress may provide a resolution, at least in some instances, through carefully drawn legislation. For the rest, we must rely, as so often in our system we must, on the tug and pull of the political forces in American society.

Pell v. Procunier (1974)

Saxbe v. Washington Post Co. (1974)

Stewart's speech spelled out in fresh formulation views which he had expressed in writing the majority opinion in Pell v. Procunier.[17] Here, journalists Eve Pell, Betty Segal, and Paul Jacobs challenged a California prison regulation which barred press and other media interviews with specific, individual inmates. Denied their requests to interview prison inmates Apsin, Bly and Guild, they asserted that the rule limited their news-gathering activity and thus infringed freedom of the press under the First

---

[15] Providence Journal Co. et al. v. McCoy et al., 94 F.Supp. 186 (D.R.I.1950); In re Mack, 386 Pa. 251, 126 A.2d 679, 689 (1956); Lyles v. Oklahoma, 330 P.2d 734 (Okl. Crim.1958).

[16] Potter Stewart, Or of the Press, 26 Hastings L.Journ. 631 (1975).

[17] 417 U.S. 817, 94 S.Ct. 2800 (1974). At least 11 states have statutes permitting reporters to interview inmates in confidential settings: Press Censorship Newsletter VII, April–May 1975, p. 61.

and Fourteenth Amendments. They lost in District Court and appealed to the U.S. Supreme Court. Stewart wrote for the majority that the press and public are afforded full opportunities to observe minimum security sections of prisons, to speak about any subject to any inmates they might encounter, to interview inmates selected at random by the corrections officials, to sit in on group meetings of inmates. "The sole limitation on news-gathering in California prisons is the prohibition in [regulation] # 415.071 of interviews with individual inmates specifically designated by representatives of the press." [18]

Before the regulation was adopted, Stewart continued, unrestrained press access to individual prisoners resulted in concentration of press attention on a few inmates, who became virtual "public figures" in prison society and gained great influence. One inmate who advocated non-cooperation with prison regulations had extensive press attention, encouraged other inmates in his purpose, and eroded the institution's ability to deal effectively with inmates in general. San Quentin prison authorities concluded that an escape attempt there, resulting in deaths of three staff members and two inmates, flowed in part from an unrestricted press access policy, and regulation # 415.071 was adopted as a result. Stewart wrote: "The Constitution does not * * * require government to accord the press special access to information not shared by members of the public generally." [19]

Dissenting in this case and in a companion case, Saxbe v. Washington Post Co.[20] which involved an unsuccessful challenge to a Federal Bureau of Prisons rule similar to California's, was Justice Powell. He said that "sweeping prohibition of prisoner-press interviews substantially impairs a core value of the First Amendment." In these cases, he argued, society's interest "in preserving free public discussion of governmental affairs" was great and was the value at stake. Since the public is unable to know most news at first hand, "In seeking out the news the press * * * acts as an agent of the public at large. * * * By enabling the public to assert meaningful control over the political process, the press performs a critical function in effecting the societal purpose of the First Amendment."

Houchins v. KQED Inc. (1978)

Much more restrictive access to a jail was at issue when Sheriff Houchins of Alameda Co., Calif., was ordered by injunction

[18] Pell v. Procunier, 417 U.S. 817, 94 S.Ct. 2800, 2808 (1974).

[19] Ibid., at 834, 94 S.Ct. at 2810.

[20] 417 U.S. 843, 94 S.Ct. 2811 (1974). Powell's statements are at 860–874, 94 S.Ct. at 2820–2826.

to open up his facility to reporters and their cameras and record-ers. His rules had limited journalists to regular, once-a-month tours open to the public in general. No cameras or recorders were allowed, nor was access to a part of the jail where violence had reportedly broken out earlier. KQED, which made a practice of covering prisons in the area and wanted access to shoot film and interview prisoners, took Houchins to court, saying its journalistic usefulness was reduced by his tour rules. The sheriff objected that the access sought would infringe the privacy of inmates, create jail "celebrities" and cause attendant difficulties, and dis-rupt jail operations. He told of other forms of access by which information about the jail could reach the public. The district court agreed with KQED's contentions, and enjoined the sheriff from further blocking of media access "at reasonable times," cameras and recorders included.[21] The California Court of Ap-peals upheld the injunction, saying that the U.S. Supreme Court's *Pell* and *Saxbe* decisions were not controlling.

Houchins appealed to the Supreme Court, and it reversed the lower courts, Chief Justice Warren Burger writing that neither of the earlier cases, nor indeed Branzburg v. Hayes (Chapter 13, above), provided a constitutional right to gather news, or a consti-tutional right of access to government.[22] He agreed that news of prisons is important for the public to have, and that media serve as "eyes and ears" for the public. He said, however, that the Supreme Court had never held that the First Amendment compels anyone, private or public, to supply information. He discussed various ways in which information about prisons reaches the public, and said the legislative branch was free to pass laws opening penal institutions if it wished. But the press, Burger said, enjoys no special privilege of access beyond that which officials grant to the public in general. *Pell* and *Saxbe* would hold, and Houchins' access rules also. Separately, Justice Stewart joined in the decision, differing only to the extent of saying that reporters on tour with the public should be allowed to carry and use their tools of the trade, including cameras and recorders.

Justice Powell, who as we have seen had dissented in *Pell* and *Saxbe,* joined two others in dissenting again, on similar grounds. He and the other dissenters in *Pell* had totaled four, the greatest support that the Supreme Court has furnished for "access to government" as a constitutionally protected principle outside the judicial branch.[23]

---

[21] Houchins v. KQED, Inc., 438 U.S. 1, 98 S.Ct. 2588 (1978), 3 Med.L.Rptr. 2521.

[22] Ibid., at 584–585, 98 S.Ct. at 2523–2524.

[23] Richmond Newspapers v. Virginia, 448 U.S. 555, 100 S.Ct. 2814 (1980), 6 Med. L.Rptr. 1833. For a view that sees the approach of a broad constitutional right of

SEC. 83. RECORDS AND MEETINGS
OF FEDERAL GOVERNMENT

Access to records and meetings of federal executive and administrative agencies is provided under the "Freedom of Information" and the "Sunshine in Government" Acts; the Privacy Act provides for secrecy of records.

The Freedom of Information Act

On July 4, 1966, Pres. Lyndon B. Johnson signed the Federal Public Records Law, shortly to be known as the federal Freedom of Information (FOI) Act.[24] Providing for the public availability of records of executive and administrative agencies of the government, it sprang, President Johnson said, "from one of our most essential principles: a democracy works best when the people have all the information that the security of the Nation permits." He expressed a "deep sense of pride that the United States is an open society in which the people's right to know is cherished and guarded." [25]

The FOI Act replaced section 3 of the Administrative Procedure Act of 1946, which had permitted secrecy if it was required in the public interest or for "good cause." [26] The new law expressed neither this limitation nor another which had said disclosure was necessary only to "persons properly and directly concerned" with the subject at hand. In the words of Attorney General Ramsey Clark, the FOI Act.[27]

> imposes on the executive branch an affirmative obligation
> to adopt new standards and practices for publication and
> availability of information. It leaves no doubt that disclo-
> sure is a transcendent goal, yielding only to such compel-
> ling considerations as those provided for in the exemp-
> tions of the act.

Every federal executive branch agency is required under the FOI Act to publish in the Federal Register its organization plan, and the agency personnel and methods through which the public can get information. Every agency's procedural rules and general

access to government, see Roy V. Leeper, Richmond Newspapers, Inc. v. Virginia and the Emerging Right of Access, 61 Journ.Quar. 615 (Autumn 1984).

[24] 5 U.S.C.A. § 552, amended by Pub.Law 93–502, 88 Stat. 1561–1564. For history, text, and extensive judicial interpretation of this act, and information on the federal Privacy Act, see Allan Adler and Halperin, M.H., Litigation under the Federal Freedom of Information Act and Privacy Act, 1984 (Washington, 1983).

[25] Public Papers of the Presidents, Lyndon B. Johnson, 1966 II, p. 699.

[26] 5 U.S.C.A. § 1002 (1946).

[27] Foreword, Attorney General's Memorandum on the Public Information Section of the Administrative Procedure Act (1967).

policies are to be published. Every agency's manuals and instructions are to be made available for public inspection and copying, as are final opinions in adjudicated cases. Current indexes are to be made available to the public. If records are improperly withheld, the U.S. district court can enjoin the agency from the withholding and order disclosure. And if agency officials fail to comply with the court order, they may be punished for contempt.

Exceptions to that which must be made public are called "exemptions." There are nine of them, some of them revised and tightened against abuse by agencies after a three-year congressional study which brought about amendments effective Feb. 19, 1975:

1. Records "specifically authorized under criteria established by an Executive order to be kept secret in the interest of national defense or foreign policy" and which are properly classified.

2. Matters related only to "internal personnel rules and practices" of an agency.

3. Matters exempt from disclosure by statute.

4. Trade secrets and commercial or financial information obtained from a person and that are privileged or confidential.

5. Inter-agency or intra-agency communications, such as memoranda showing how policy-makers within an agency feel about various policy options.

6. Personnel and medical files which could not be disclosed without a "clearly unwarranted invasion" of someone's privacy.

7. Investigatory files compiled for law enforcement purposes, if the production of such records would interfere with law enforcement, deprive one of a fair trial, constitute an unwarranted invasion of personal privacy, disclose the identity of a confidential source, disclose investigative techniques, or endanger the life or safety of law enforcement personnel.

8. Reports prepared by or for an agency responsible for the regulation or supervision of financial institutions.

9. Geological and geophysical information and data, including maps, concerning wells—particularly explorations by gas and oil companies.

Long delays, high costs for searching and copying documents, and widespread agency reluctance to comply with the original act's provisions characterized its early history.[28] Not only were several exemptions tightened by the amendments; also, rules were passed requiring agencies to inform persons making requests for information within ten days whether or not access would be granted, and to decide upon requests for appeals within 20 days. Uniform schedules of fees—limited to reasonable standard charges for document search and copying—were also mandated in the amendments.[29]

The amendments brought a flood of requests for information, primarily from persons who asked the FBI, the CIA, and the IRS, whether files were kept on them, and, if so, what the files contained. The Justice Department was receiving 2,000 requests per month by August 1975.[30] Media requests mounted under the amendments. One study found more than 400 between 1972 and 1984, but said that was far fewer than the actual total. Another study found that almost 50% of its list came from "public interest" groups, and about one-fourth from media.[31]

Court cases decided under the Act as of mid-1976 totaled 295, half of them less than two years old.[32] The increase suggested the impact of the 1975 amendments. Actions concerning investigatory files (exemption 7) outstripped the pre-amendments leaders, agency memoranda and trade secrets (exemptions 5 and 4). One important change provided for *in camera* review by judges of documents which the Executive Branch might refuse to open on grounds of national defense or foreign policy (exemption 1). Under the original FOI Act, Congress had not provided this, but rather, said Justice Stewart in an acid concurring opinion, had simply chosen "to decree blind acceptance of Executive fiat" that secrecy was called for.[33]

[28] Wallis McClain, "Implementing the Amended FOI Act," Freedom of Information Center Report No. 343, Sept. 1975, p. 1; U.S. Congress, Freedom of Information Act and Amendments of 1974 (P.L. 93–502) Source Book: Legislative History, Texts, and Other Documents. Joint Committee Print (94th Cong., 1 Sess.), Washington: U.S. Government Printing Office, March 1975.

[29] Anon., "FOI Act Amendments Summarized," FOI Digest, 17:1, Jan.-Feb. 1975, p. 5.

[30] Anon., "FOI Act: Access Increases, Some Nagging Problems Remain," FOI Digest, 17:4, July-Aug. 1975, p. 5, citing Wall Street Journal, June 27, 1975; John A. Jenkins, "Ask, and You Shall Receive," Quill, July-Aug. 1975, pp. 22, 24.

[31] Ibid., quoting Attorney Ronald Plesser, 22; Anon., Media Use of FOIA Documented in New Study, 10 Med.L.Rptr. # 34, 8/21/84, News Notes, quoting a study done for the House Subcommittee on Government Information, Justice, and Agriculture; Sam Archibald, Use of the FOIA, Freedom of Information Report # 457, May 1982, 3 (Univ. of Mo.).

[32] Anon., "Justice Dept. Indexes Decided FOIA Cases," FOI Digest, 18:5, Sept.-Oct. 1976, p. 5, citing Congressional Record, Senate, Aug. 2, 1976, p. S13028. Reprinted in Marwick, App. p. 72.

[33] Environmental Protection Agency v. Mink, 410 U.S. 73, 136, 93 S.Ct. 827, 718 (1973).

From government's side of the desk, the FOI Act takes too much time and money.

A Congressional study in 1985 showed that in a year's time, the Federal FOI Act drew 248,000 total requests. Although some agencies approved over 90 percent of the FOI requests, the study did not control for delays in providing information or in fee waivers granted. The Department of State granted less than 30 per cent of its more than 3,000 requests for information, according to the House Subcommittee on Government Information.

With the deluge of requests for information came growing complaints from government agencies that it was too costly and too time-consuming to process FOI Act requests. Costs to the Treasury Department in 1978 alone totalled more than $6 million,[34] and CIA Director William Casey said that FOIA and Privacy Act (below) requests of the agency required 257,420 man-hours of service at a cost of about $2 million. Agencies complained that the act was used by law firms and commercial competitors to learn trade secrets and government enforcement policies, by foreign agents to gain national security information, and by organized crime to discover and thwart criminal investigations.[35]

Congressional efforts to restrict access to various agencies by amending the FOI Act never stop. The 1980s saw several. With President Ronald Reagan's support, the Central Intelligence Agency was authorized by law in 1984 to exempt its operational files on sources and methods from disclosure. In 1983, the 97th Congress passed six measures authorizing withholding by agencies that deal with trade, consumer product safety, income tax, energy, and health.[36]

Exemption 1, the national security exemption, was clarified in an executive order by President Jimmy Carter, effective in 1978, which imposed stricter minimum standards on classification of material. If the disclosure "reasonably could be expected to cause *identifiable* damage to national security," the information was confidential. However, any reasonable doubt should be resolved in favor of declassification, if the public interest in disclosure

[34] "Diverse Legislative Efforts To Amend the FOIA Increase," FOI Digest, Jan.-Feb. 1980, 22:1, p. 5. Rod Perlmutter, Proposed FOIA Amendments—2, Freedom of Information Report # 451, Jan. 1982 (Univ. of Mo.).

[35] "Congress, Courts Mutilate FOI Act," News Media & The Law, Aug.-Sept. 1980, 4:3, p. 16.

[36] Anon., CIA Exemption Bill Passed, News Media & the Law, Nov./Dec. 1984; 8 Med.L.Rptr. # 46, 1/25/83, News Notes; Anon., Note, Developments under the Freedom of Information Act 1983, 1984 Duke Law J. 377, 382; News Media & the Law, Sept./Oct. 1983, 24.

outweighed the damage to national security that "might be reasonably expected from disclosure." [37]

Exemption 1 was also the target of suits involving the definition of "possession" of records. In Forsham v. Harris, a 1980 Supreme Court decision, Justice Rehnquist stated that written data held by a private research firm receiving federal grant money from HEW were not "agency records" if the agency providing the funds had not yet obtained possession of the data. The FOI Act provided no direct access to such data; therefore, HEW had not improperly "withheld" the data. The Act applied not to records that could exist, but only to records that did exist.[38]

In Kissinger v. Reporters Committee for Freedom of the Press, the Supreme Court held that the State Department had not "withheld" records of former Secretary of State Henry Kissinger's phone calls by failing to file a lawsuit to recover documents which Kissinger had improperly donated to the Library of Congress, and which would be unavailable to the public for 25 years.[39] A Justice Department suit was considered, and Kissinger later agreed to a new review of documents to determine whether they are needed for departmental files.[40]

In other developments related to national security, a federal district court judge ruled in Hayden v. National Security Agency/Central Security Service that disclosure of the existence of particular records, obtained through NSA monitoring of foreign electromagnetic signals, could be withheld, since the existence of such records might be more sensitive than their substance.[41]

Openness Is Not Self-Executing

No open records or open meetings victory is ever likely to be won, once and for all. It is simply a fact of life that government officials, especially when under pressure or embarrassed because of mistakes within their agencies, tend to "stonewall" when citizens—including members of the news media—come around asking questions.

Although the Freedom of Information Act, as amended, has been useful in opening government files, any skimming of the

[37] Alan S. Madens, "Developments Under the Freedom of Information Act—1979," 1980 Duke L.J. 139, 146–147.

[38] "The Supreme Court 1979 Term," 94 Harv.L.Rev. 1, 232–237 (1980); Forsham v. Harris, 445 U.S. 169, 100 S.Ct. 977 (1980).

[39] "The Supreme Court 1979 Term," Harv.L.Rev. 1, 232–235; Kissinger v. Reporters Committee for Freedom of the Press, 445 U.S. 136, 100 S.Ct. 960 (1980), 6 Med. L.Rptr. 1001.

[40] "Nixon Tapes Available to Public: Archives Requests More Materials," FOI Digest, May-June 1980, 22:3, p. 1.

[41] Madens, op. cit., 148.

American Civil Liberties Union's annual compendium, Litigation Under the Freedom of Information Act and Privacy Act, will indicate that the federal commitment to open records is flawed. To a mind-boggling degree, federal courts have supported federal bureaucracies in keeping secret materials which the public ought to have available.[42] Consider the following "parade of issues," looking at some litigation situations which arose under a number of the Exemptions to the federal FOIA. Federal agencies tried to withhold information under the exemptions for a variety of reasons (some far-fetched), and were quite often supported in such withholding decisions by federal courts.

Exemption 1—National Security Information. As outlined by the ACLU's guidebook, Litigation Under the Freedom of Information and Privacy Act, it may be seen that "national security" is an almost magical incantation. For example, the Central Intelligence Agency (CIA) is allowed, under a 1984 amendment to the National Security Act of 1947, to exempt "operational" files from the search and review requirements of the FOIA.[43] When will the records be available? (When the operation is "over.") When will the operation be declared "over?" (That's a matter for CIA discretion.) The CIA hangs onto secrets: In some cases, the CIA may turn aside a request for information with the response that for national security reasons, it can neither confirm nor deny the existence of the requested records.[44] For an example of the U.S. Supreme Court's deference to the CIA even in the face of egregious wrongdoing by that agency, see the discussion of CIA v. Sims (1985) at pages 620–622.[45]

Exemption 2—Internal Agency Rules. For example, the Internal Revenue Service (IRS) attempted to withhold its auditing manual, on grounds that this was merely of internal concern. A federal court, however, held—sensibly enough—that the auditing rules used by the IRS should be available to public inspection.[46]

Exemption 3—Information Exempted by Other Statutes. Airworthiness and crash-worthiness of commercial airliners seems to be, simply and obviously, of public interest. Parties interested in comparative air safety records sued the Federal Aeronautics Authority in the 1970s to get access to "Systems Worthiness Analysis Reports." The FAA refused to release the reports, evidently on grounds that disclosing information would be bad for some air

[42] Allan Robert Adler, ed., Litigation Under the Federal Freedom of Information and Privacy Act, 1990 edition (Washington, D.C.: ACLU Foundation, 1990).

[43] Ibid., p. 42.

[44] Ibid., p. 39, citing Phillippi v. CIA, 546 F.2d 1009, 1012–1013 (D.C.Cir.1976).

[45] CIA v. Sims, 471 U.S. 159, 105 S.Ct. 1881 (1985).

[46] Hawkes v. Internal Revenue Service, 467 F.2d 787 at 789 (6th Cir.1972).

carriers' reputations and thus would not be in the public interest. The U.S. Supreme Court upheld this exercise of FAA "discretion," [47] although Congress later amended Exemption 3 to restrict administrators' loopholes and to allow a bit more information in the public interest.[48]

Using the FOIA

The FOI Service Center, a project of the Reporters Committee on Freedom of the Press, periodically issues updated booklets titled "How to Use the FOI Act." This useful guide summarizes the uses of the FOIA as a news-gathering tool, and also provides thumbnail sketches of the Act's disclosure exemptions. This is truly a "do-it-yourself" guide, and even includes sample FOI Act request letters—and, if needed—sample appeal letters. This material is available from The Reporters Committee on Freedom of the Press, 1735 Eye Street, N.W., Washington, D.C. 20006.

The Case of Samuel L. Morison

National security concerns present real dilemmas for the United States. Government secrets and secrecy—in large part a legacy of Cold War tensions between the United States and Communist-bloc countries in the 1950s through the 1980s—now take on a somewhat different glow in the aftermath of the 1991 collapse of the Soviet Union.

Journalists have long complained about excessive secrecy in the United States' defense and intelligence establishments. One way in which journalists were able to combat secrecy, at least to some extent, was by the "leak," where reporters get tipped off to "inside" or confidential information. In 1988, however, the espionage conviction of Samuel Loring Morison worried some journalists lest that conviction might make it more difficult to get news of wrongdoing out of the Pentagon and the defense industry.

Morison was a civilian employee of the U.S. Navy, and also did some "moonlighting" as a freelance correspondent for a weapon's-industry journal published in Britain, Jane's Fighting Ships. Morison saw some photos stamped "Secret" on a co-worker's desk, photos taken from a U.S. KH–11 spy satellite. The photos showed construction work on a Russian nuclear aircraft carrier.

Morison, violating a Navy security pledge he had signed, sent the photos to another publication, Jane's Defence Weekly, which published them. The photos were republished in the U.S. in some newspapers. Morison, arguing unconvincingly that he had leaked

[47] Administrator, Federal Aeronautics Authority v. Robertson, 422 U.S. 255, 95 S.Ct. 2140 (1975).

[48] Adler, op. cit., p. 59.

the pictures to alert the world to a growing Soviet threat,[49] was prosecuted and convicted under an Espionage Statute.[50]   Early in 1988, a three-judge panel of the Court of Appeals, Fourth Circuit, upheld Morison's conviction.[51]   Thirty-one media organizations joined in a friend-of-the-court brief, arguing that if Morison's conviction stood, the flow of needed information to the public would be impeded.   The media groups' amicus brief said: " '[F]or the first time, the court has applied the espionage statute to the dissemination of information to press and public.' " [52]

Court of Appeals Judge Donald Stuart Russell took a hard line in announcing the judgment against Morison.   This intelligence department employee had taken secret intelligence from government files and had "wilfully transmitted or given it to one 'not entitled to receive it.' "   As such, Morison was "not entitled to invoke the First Amendment as a shield to immunize his act of thievery." [53]

The Court of Appeals ruling was allowed to stand by the U.S. Supreme Court, and Morison began serving a jail term in the fall of 1988.[54]   This outcome confirmed fears of some media advocates who argued that the Morison case will discourage government employees from providing information—even evidence of wrongdoing—if that information might be construed as falling under the espionage laws.   Further, reporters may face subpoenas to reveal sources if their stories show that they have turned up information (from whatever sources) that the government believes to be classified.

Investigating the Death of Karen Silkwood

Attempts by media to open records through court cases commonly run afoul of Exemptions 7 and 5—investigatory files and agency memoranda—source materials which are often expected by media to be relevant to criminal activity.   National Public Radio, for example, sought disclosure of records compiled by the Justice Department and the FBI about the perplexing death of Karen Silkwood.   An employee of a manufacturer of plutonium and uranium fuels for nuclear reactors, Silkwood was reportedly driv-

[49] Stuart Taylor, Jr., "Court Ruling on Leaks Could Make it a Crime to Talk to the Press," The New York Times, Sec. 4, P. 7, April 10, 1987.   On leaks, generally, see Stephen Hess, The Government/Press Connection: Press Officers and Their Offices (Washington, D.C.: Brookings Institution, 1984, pp. 75–79, 92–94).

[50] 18 U.S.C.A. §§ 641, 793(d) and (e).

[51] United States v. Morison, 844 F.2d 1057 (4th Cir.1988).

[52] News Notes, in flyleaves of 14 Med.L.Rptr. No. 22 (Nov. 3, 1987).

[53] United States v. Morison, 844 F.2d 1057, 1069 (4th Cir.1988), 15 Med.L.Rptr. 1369, 1378.

[54] Taylor, loc. cit.

ing to attend a meeting with a union official and a newspaper reporter when she was killed in an auto crash. Uncertain evidence suggested that her car might have been driven off the road by another car, and that a file of documents she was supposedly carrying was not recovered. NPR also sought the record of the agency's investigation of the contamination of Silkwood by plutonium.

The Justice Department furnished NPR with some of the requested materials, but refused others. The parts of the death investigation file withheld were the "closing memoranda"—agency materials prepared during its final deliberations—and about 15 pages of notes and working papers of Justice Department attorneys. The Justice Department said that exemption 5 of the FOI Act—intra-agency memoranda or letters—protected these materials from disclosure. The Federal district court agreed,[55] saying the agency memoranda are protected as "papers which reflect the agency's group thinking in the process of working out its policy and determining what its law shall be."[56] The court rejected NPR's argument that the memoranda were "final" opinions, which under the Supreme Court's interpretation of the FOI Act would have been subject to disclosure.[57]

As for Exemption 7 of the FOI Act, protecting from disclosure matters which are "investigatory records compiled for law enforcement purposes" whose release would "interfere with enforcement proceedings * * *.": This applied to the Justice Department investigation of Silkwood's contamination by plutonium, and the court said that the records of the case suggested law-violation in materials-handling by personnel. It said that Congress' intent in writing Exemption 7 was plainly to prevent harm to a "concrete prospective law enforcement proceeding" that might result from disclosure of information. And though the department's leads in the investigation had currently run out, and want of finances for the moment precluded assignment of an investigator to the case, the case was "active." Disclosure would present "the very real possibility of a criminal learning in alarming detail of the government's investigation of his crime before the government has had the opportunity to bring him to justice," said the court in rejecting NPR's request.[58]

[55] National Public Radio et al. v. Bell, 431 F.Supp. 509 (D.D.C.1977), 2 Med.L. Rptr. 1808.

[56] Ibid.

[57] N.L.R.B. v. Sears, Roebuck & Co., 421 U.S. 132, 95 S.Ct. 1504 (1975).

[58] National Public Radio et al. v. Bell, 431 F.Supp. 509 (D.D.C.1977). The investigatory exemption was tightened in lower court cases. Records must be both investigatory *and* compiled for law enforcement purposes: Pope v. United States, 599 F.2d 1383 (5th Cir.1979). The information must be originally gathered for law enforcement purposes: Gregory v. Federal Deposit Insurance Corp., 470 F.Supp.

Exemption 5—agency memoranda—was expanded in Federal Open Market Committee v. Merrill, in which the Supreme Court upheld an agency's refusal to release monthly policy directives while they were in effect, if they contained sensitive information not otherwise available, and if release of the directive would significantly harm the government's monetary functions or commercial interests.[59]

A power of withholding has always been asserted by the President and his Executive Department heads. This is the power exercised under the doctrine of "executive privilege." President George Washington was asked by Congress to make available documents relating to General St. Clair's defeat by Indians. He responded that "the Executive ought to communicate such papers as the public good would permit, and ought to refuse those, the disclosure of which would injure the public * * *."[60] In this case the records were made available to Congress, but many Presidents since have refused to yield records, as have the heads of executive departments. Their power to do so was upheld early in the nation's history by the United States Supreme Court. The famous decision written by Chief Justice John Marshall was delivered in 1803 in Marbury v. Madison, where Marshall said that the Attorney General (a presidential appointee) did not have to reveal matters which had been communicated to him in confidence.[61]

> By the Constitution of the United States, the president is invested with certain important political powers, in the exercise of which he is to use his own discretion, and is accountable only to the country in his political character and to his own conscience.

Justice Marshall elaborated the principle in the trial of Aaron Burr, accused of treason, saying that "The propriety of withholding * * * must be decided by [the President] himself, not by another for him. Of the weight of the reasons for and against producing it he himself is the judge."[62]

Executive privilege came to be asserted and used increasingly during the government's efforts to maintain security in the cold war with the U.S.S.R. following World War II. Presidents Tru-

---

1329 (D.D.C.1979), reversed in part 631 F.2d 896 (D.C.Cir. 1980). Courts have given mixed reactions to records for "improper" investigations. See Lamont v. Department of Justice, 475 F.Supp. 761 (S.D.N.Y.1979), and Irons v. Bell, 596 F.2d 468 (1st Cir.1979). See also Madens, op. cit., at 162–163.

[59] Madens, op. cit., 155.

[60] Francis E. Rourke, Secrecy and Publicity (Baltimore: Johns Hopkins Press, 1961), p. 65. And see Ibid., pp. 64–69, for general discussion of executive privilege.

[61] 5 U.S. (1 Cranch.) 137 (1803).

[62] 1 Burr's Trial 182.

man and Eisenhower used the power to issue orders detailing what might and might not be released from the executive departments; both came under heavy attack from Congress and the news media.[63] President Nixon's Executive Order No. 11–652 of March 8, 1972, replaced and modified rules set by President Eisenhower.

One of the most far-reaching directives of this period was issued by President Eisenhower in 1954. A senate subcommittee was investigating a controversy between the Army and Senator Joseph McCarthy of Wisconsin. President Eisenhower sent to Secretary of the Army Robert Stevens a message telling him that his departmental employees were to say nothing about internal communications of the Department.[64]

> Because it is essential to efficient and effective administration that employees of the executive branch be in a position to be completely candid in advising with each other on official matters, and because it is not in the public interest that any of their conversations or communications, or any documents or reproductions, concerning such advice be disclosed, you will instruct employees of your Department that in all of their appearances before the subcommittee of the Senate Committee on Government Operations regarding the inquiry now before it they are not to testify to any such conversations or communications or to produce any such documents or reproductions.

While the directive was aimed at a single situation and a single Executive Department, it soon became used by many other executive and administrative agencies as justification for their own withholding of records concerning internal affairs.[65] While journalists protested the spread of the practice, and while Congressional allies joined them, there was not much legal recourse then apparent.

The President's powers to restrict access are substantial, used extensively by some and little by others. Journalists have widely asserted that President Ronald Reagan employed these powers more vigorously than his predecessors of many terms. In fact, one of President Reagan's directives placed a "lifelong" nondisclosure restriction on many government employees, although it was partially withdrawn. In his 1982 Executive Order 12,356, he tight-

[63] Rourke, pp. 75–83.

[64] House Report, No. 2947, 84 Cong., 2 Sess., July 27, 1956. Availability of Information from Federal Departments and Agencies. Dwight D. Eisenhower to Sec. of Defense, May 17, 1954, pp. 64–65.

[65] Rourke, p. 74.

ened declassification rules set by President Jimmy Carter, permitting permanent exemption from disclosure of documents in the realm of national security and foreign policy. In 1981, he submitted proposals to the Senate to give the Attorney General power to exempt some kinds of intelligence files from disclosure. In 1983, the Justice Department, with his support, notably tightened the rules for waiving fees charged to those who seek information from government agencies. Under him as Commander in Chief, journalists were kept uninformed and were excluded from the armed forces' invasion of the Caribbean island of Grenada. Journalists found him and his administration much less accessible than his predecessor, and expert at frustrating reporters, one analyst declaring that "bureaucrats have largely succeeded in undermining the FOI Act at will." [66]

A head-on confrontation emerged in the Watergate investigations, as President Richard M. Nixon refused to turn over to a grand jury, tape recordings of conversations with his White House aides. Federal Judge John J. Sirica ruled that the tapes must be submitted to him for *in camera* scrutiny and possible forwarding to the grand jury. The President refused, asserting executive privilege, and said he was protecting "the right of himself and his successors to preserve the confidentiality of discussions in which they participate in the course of their constitutional duties." Special prosecutor Archibald Cox argued it was intolerable that "the President would invoke executive privilege to keep the tape recordings from the grand jury but permit his aides to testify fully as to their recollections of the same conversations." The President fired Cox, and the Attorney General resigned and his deputy was fired before the President yielded the tapes (which of course were to prove central to the discrediting of him and his aides) amid a public cry for his impeachment.[67]

The Supreme Court ruled that executive privilege is not absolute, but qualified. The *in camera* court inspection of the tapes that Sirica ordered, it said, would be a minimal intrusion on the President's confidential communications. The President's claim was not based on grounds of national security—that military or diplomatic secrets were threatened—but only on the ground

[66] Floyd Abrams, The New Effort to Control Information, New York Times Magazine, Sept. 25, 1983, 23; Government Shuts Up, Columbia Journalism Rev., July/Aug. 1982, 31; Executive Order No. 12356 on National Security Information, April 2, 1982, 8 Med.L.Rptr. 1306; 1984 Duke L.Journ. 377, 387, op. cit.; Anon., Reagan Signs New Secrecy Order to Seal More Public Documents, News Media & the Law, June/July 1982, 22; 8 Med.L.Rptr. # 46, 1/25/83, News Notes; Anon., Coverage Efforts Thwarted, News Media & the Law, Jan.-Feb. 1984, 6; Carl Stepp, Grenada Skirmish over Access Goes On, SPJ/SDX, Freedom of Information 84–'85, Report, 5; Steve Weinberg, Trashing the FOIA, Columbia Journalism Rev., Jan./Feb. 1985, 21, 22; Donna A. Demac, Keeping America Uninformed (N.Y., 1984).

[67] New York Times, Sept. 11, 1973, p. 36; Oct. 24, 1973, p. 1.

of his "generalized interest in confidentiality." That could not prevail over "the fundamental demands of due process of law in the fair administration of justice." It would have to yield to the "demonstrated, specific need for evidence in a pending criminal trial." [68]

Subsequent assertions of executive privilege by Nixon involved his post-resignation claim to custody of presidential papers from his term in office—millions of pages of documents and almost 900 tapes—and also his denial of the rights of record companies and networks to copy, sell, and broadcast tapes that had been played at one of the trials arising from Watergate. The Supreme Court ruled in one case that the government should have custody of all but Nixon's private and personal papers,[69] and in the other it granted Nixon's plea to deny networks and record companies the right to copy, sell, or broadcast the tapes.[70]

On July 24, 1979, a U.S. District Court ruled that Nixon's dictabelt "diaries" were not personal and would not be screened for use by archivists. Also, the court ruled that the public should have access to the actual tapes, instead of synopses or transcripts.[71] As of June 1980, National Archives had released 31, or about 12½ hours of conversation, of the 950 tapes, and Nixon was fighting release of another 6,000 hours.[72] Usage of the tapes is restricted: no more than 24 persons may listen at a time, for 45 to 90 minutes depending on the length of the tape played; and listeners are forbidden to make their own recordings of the tapes.[73]

Access to federal officials' papers and claims of executive privilege were active issues during the latter half of the seventies. The Nixon papers cases and the Kissinger "phone calls" case both involved dispute about ownership of executive papers. President Carter signed the Presidential Records Act of 1978, effective January 1981, which clarified ownership of executive branch papers. The National Archives assumes control of presidential papers at the end of a president's last term. Records related to defense and foreign policy, plus presidential appointment records involving trade secrets, may be restricted for 12 years. Papers not

---

[68] United States v. Nixon, 418 U.S. 683, 684–685, 713, 94 S.Ct. 3090, 3095–3096, 3110 (1974).

[69] Nixon v. General Services Administrator, 433 U.S. 425, 97 S.Ct. 2777 (1977).

[70] Nixon v. Warner Communications, Inc., News Media and the Law, 1:1 (Oct. 1977), p. 14. Anon., "High Court Bars Networks' Right To Nixon Tapes," New York Times, April 19, 1978, p. 1.

[71] "Nixon Documents Litigation Reaches Court Settlement," News Media & The Law, March-April 1980, 4:2, p. 50.

[72] "Nixon Tapes Available to Public; Archives Requests More Materials," op. cit. See also, "Anyone Can Hear Nixon Tapes," Wisconsin State Journal, May 29, 1980, p. 12, sec. 1.

[73] Ibid.

restricted become available to the public under the FOI Act as soon as the Archives processes them.[74]

The recorded word, in literally billions of pages of government documents, is the focus of the FOI Act, dedicated to dissemination of this record. But developments during 1979 and 1980 included two Supreme Court decisions involving "reverse-FOI Act" suits, in which persons or organizations submitting information to a federal agency sought to prevent disclosure in response to FOI Act requests. In Chrysler Corp. v. Brown, the Court banned such suits under the FOI Act, stating that while exempt records could be withheld, the Act did not *require* nondisclosure.[75] However, in GTE Sylvania, Inc. v. Consumers Union, the Consumer Product Safety Act was used successfully to exempt information from release unless its accuracy is verified first.[76]

The FOI Reform Act of 1986

Efforts to "improve" or "reform" the Freedom of Information Act mean different things to different people. The "Freedom of Information Reform Act of 1986" had some good news and some bad news for reporters. Apparently to the good, the Act required the Office of Management and Budget (OMB) to allow up to 100 pages of document copying free to journalists, and to make charges only for duplication on lengthier requests. Also helpful is allowing FOI requests of demonstrable importance to the public— e.g. reporters investigating an environmental hazard—to get speeded-up treatment for such requests.

On the other hand, journalists or citizens seeking information about businesses could face tougher slogging. Under the Reform Act, in order to protect proprietary information for businesses, the businesses named in information requests are to be notified. Then, they have 35 days to oppose disclosure. At the same time, Sen. Orrin Hatch (R–Utah) successfully sponsored an amendment to a drug control bill which provided broader FOI exemptions for investigatory records of law enforcement agencies.[77]

[74] Robert Schwaller, "Access to Federal Officials' Papers," FOI Center Report No. 411, October 1979, pp. 7, 8.

[75] Madens, op. cit., pp. 141–142. See also Chrysler Corp. v. Brown, 441 U.S. 281, 99 S.Ct. 1705 (1979).

[76] "Safety Data Release Depends On Who Reaches Courtroom First," News Media & The Law," Feb.-March 1981, 5:1, p. 49; GTE Sylvania, Inc. v. Consumers Union, 445 U.S. 375, 100 S.Ct. 1194 (1980); Consumer Product Safety Commission v. GTE Sylvania, Inc., 447 U.S. 102, 100 S.Ct. 2051 (1980).

[77] Public L. No. 99–570; see also News Media & the Law, Fall, 1986, pp. 28–29, and Spring, 1987, 31–32; see Allan Adler, ed., Litigation Under the Federal Freedom of Information Act, 13th ed. (Washington: ACLU Foundation, p. 6 and Insert, plus pp. 251–264.

Privacy Act of 1974

"After long years of debate, a comprehensive federal privacy law passed the Congress ∗ ∗ ∗ as a solid legislative decision in favor of individual privacy and the 'right to be let alone'," writes attorney James T. O'Reilly.[78] It is a statute shaped to deal with the federal government's gargantuan systems of secret dossiers on citizens, to give citizens access to the content of files that may be kept on them, and to provide citizens with a means for correcting inaccurate content of these files. If agencies are not responsive in making changes, civil suits may be brought against them. A crucial element in the law is that no file may be transferred from one agency to another without the individual's consent, except where the purpose squares with the purpose for which the information was collected.

Under the law, a supposedly exhaustive index to all federal government "data banks" or personal information systems on individuals has been published. Also published in the Federal Register are the categories of individuals on whom records are maintained, and where one can learn whether a particular government agency has information about him.[79] No citizen who inquires about himself need give any reason for a request to examine the record, and may obtain a copy. Some exceptions to citizen access are provided, mostly dealing with law enforcement agencies' records, and including, notably, the CIA and the Secret Service.[80] However, foreign nationals working for the government have no access rights to personnel records about themselves under either the FOI Act or the Privacy Act, according to a U.S. Court of Appeals.[81]

Privacy issues intensified during the 1970s and 1980s, as individuals made greater use of the Privacy Act to see records maintained about them and to amend those records or correct inaccuracies.[82] States also were active in protecting privacy of financial, medical, and criminal records.[83]

[78] "The Privacy Act of 1974," Freedom of Information Report No. 342, Sept. 1975, p. 1.

[79] Anon., "Citizens' Guide to Privacy Act Available," FOI Digest, 18:2 (March-April 1976), p. 2. For an editor's struggle of more than a year to get a file kept on him by the FBI, see John Seigenthaler, "Publisher Finally Gets His FBI Files, or Some of Them," (Memphis) Tennessean, July 10, 1977. False accusations, the FBI said after finally releasing contents of the file, would be purged.

[80] Anon., "Government Information and the Rights of Citizens," 73 Mich.L.Rev. 971, 1317. This study of more than 370 pages describes, analyzes, and criticizes the FOI Act, state open records and meetings laws, and the Privacy Act of 1974.

[81] Raven v. Panama Canal Co., 583 F.2d 169 (5th Cir.1978), certiorari denied 440 U.S. 980, 99 S.Ct. 1787 (1979). See also, "Allows Personnel Files to be Kept From Alien," News Media & The Law, March-April 1980, 4:2, p. 31.

[82] In 1977, of 1,417,214 requests, 1,355,515 were granted either entirely or in part: "Privacy Roundup: Report Shows Increasing Use of Privacy Act by Individuals," FOI Digest, July-Aug. 1978, 20:4, p. 2.

[83] "Poll Shows Privacy Concerns Rising," FOI Digest, May-June 1979, 21:3, p. 2.

Recall that privacy issues also are part of the FOIA; as noted at Page 601, Exemptions 6 (personnel or medical files) and 7 (law enforcement investigatory files) both list privacy. In Department of Justice v. Reporters Committee for Freedom of the Press, the U.S. Supreme Court held—in part for privacy reasons—that FBI "rap sheets"—records of a person's arrests, charges, and jailings. Release of such criminal identification records was held to be a "clearly unwarranted invasion of privacy" under the terms of the FOIA.[84] Most states—all but Wisconsin, Florida, and Oklahoma— follow the federal lead in withholding rap sheets from public inspection.[85]

The additional emphasis on secrecy brought about by the Privacy Act concerns some journalists about loss of inside sources of information in the federal government, and the possibility of tracing "leaks" through the agencies' records of who got access to various files.[86]

Government in the Sunshine Act

As the FOI Act is to federal government records, so the "Sunshine Act"[87] is to federal government meetings. The Act mandates open meetings for regular sessions and quorum gatherings of approximately 50 agencies—all those headed by boards of two or more persons named by the President and confirmed by the Senate. Included are the major regulatory agencies such as the Securities Exchange Commission and the Interstate Commerce Commission—whose meetings always had been secret—and such little-known entities as the National Council on Educational Research and the National Homeownership Foundation board of directors.[88]

All meetings of the named agencies are to be open—with at least one week's public notice—unless agendas take up matters in 10 categories which permit closed sessions. Either a verbatim transcript or detailed minutes of all matters covered in closed sessions is to be kept. And as for the record of open meetings, it is to be kept as minutes and made available to the public at minimal copying cost.

[84] Department of Justice v. Reporter's Committee on Freedom of the Press, 489 U.S. 749, 109 S.Ct. 1468, 16 Med.L.Rptr. 1545 (1989).

[85] Ibid., 489 U.S. at 750, 109 S.Ct. at 1470, 16 Med.L.Rptr. at 1547.

[86] Lyle Denniston, "A Citizen's Right to Privacy," Quill, 63:4, April 1975, p. 16. See also Editor & Publisher, Jan. 31, 1976, p. 9.

[87] 5 U.S.C.A. § 552b. The FOI Act and the Privacy Act of 1974 are in the federal statutes under the same number, as 5 U.S.C.A. § 552a and 5 U.S.C.A. § 552c respectively.

[88] Editor & Publisher, Feb. 26, 1977, p. 32. This account's details of the Sunshine Act are taken largely from James T. O'Reilly, "Government in the Sunshine," Freedom of Information Center Report 366, Jan. 1977; O'Reilly, p. 2.

Closed-to-the-public meetings will hardly be rare, whatever strength the Sunshine Act may prove to generate. The ten categories of subject-matter whose discussion warrants closed doors for meetings of the boards and commissions are much like the exemptions to disclosure under the FOI Act. Abbreviated, the ten are:

1. National defense or foreign policy matters which are properly classified;

2. Internal agency personnel matters;

3. Matters expressly required by law to be held confidential;

4. Confidential commercial or financial information, and trade secrets;

5. Accusations of criminal activity, or of censure, against a person;

6. Matters which if disclosed would be clearly unwarranted invasions of a person's privacy;

7. Law enforcement and criminal investigatory records, subject to the same categories as FOI Act exemption (b)(7);

8. Bank examiners' records;

9. Matters which if disclosed would generate financial speculation (included to protect the Federal Reserve Board Open Market Committee) or which would frustrate agency action which has not been announced;

10. Matters which involve the agency's issuance of a subpoena or participation in hearings or other adjudication-related proceedings.

It may prove significant that the ten exemptions of the Sunshine Act apply to the some 1,300 Advisory Committees spread throughout the Executive Branch of government. These committees of private citizens contribute expertise, advice, and recommendations to government policy making. The members tend to be prominent persons from industries which deal with the agencies they advise.

Ways exist for attacking illegal secrecy under the Sunshine Act. One may seek an injunction in advance to force a pending meeting to be open, and having found one illegal closing of an agency, a court may enjoin the agency from further illegal closings. One may sue, within 60 days after the secret meeting, to require that a transcript be furnished. No financial penalty for illegal meetings may be levied against members themselves, but courts may assign costs or fees against the United States—or against a plaintiff whose suit is found to be "dilatory or frivolous." The range of possibilities for future secrecy or openness is large, and the crystal balls of various observers offer varied forecasts of cheer and gloom.

Attorneys General

Attorneys general have been called on to interpret meetings and records laws in many states. As for meetings, it is occasionally feasible for a reporter to seek "instant action" in the form of an attorney general's opinion, perhaps by placing a phone call even while an illegal secret meeting is in session. Through such maneuvers, enterprising reporters have, on occasion, forced meetings open.

More likely, however, before an opinion can be had, the meeting will have adjourned. Nevertheless, either a formal opinion delivered at the request of a state government agency, or an informal one delivered at the request of a non-official person or entity—such as a reporter or a newspaper—can have a future impact on the behavior of the secretive group or agency. Reporters, of course, should read up on the open-records, open-meetings opinions of attorneys general. The attorney general interprets the law of a state; an "AG's opinion" does not have the force of a court opinion, but it is authoritative until a court has passed on a particular question.[89]

SEC. 84. ACCESS TO "SECURITY" INFORMATION, COVERING WARS

As discussed elsewhere in this text, traditions of openness run afoul of restrictive executive orders, statutes and court decisions in areas where claims of "national security" are raised.

Access in the "Surveillance State"

It is likely that the crucial battle to preserve what journalists have come to see as the central meaning of the First Amendment will be fought in the arena of access to government information. What is talked about here goes beyond the traditional tugging and hauling between reporters and government. Resistance to access by government officials is to be expected: human nature, of course, dictates an unwillingness to look foolish, and government officials—like all of us—dislike revealing mistakes.

Extrapolating from the words of First Amendment historian Norman L. Rosenberg suggests a scary phrase, the "surveillance state." He wrote, "The central free-speech issue of the post-World

---

[89] William Thompson, "FOI and State Attorneys General," Freedom of Information Center Report No. 307, July, 1973, University of Missouri.

War II era involved the expansion of a vast surveillance apparatus, the growing power of an increasingly monopolistic communications industry, and the problems of its ties to other private and public centers of power." [90]

Journalists—and all citizens and public officials—would do well to keep the phrase "surveillance state" in mind, for it conjures up a vision of a society where government watches the people but the people see only what government wants them to see. A surveillance state, in sum, is an old map of hell.

Anyone paying even scant attention to news reports during the late 1980s saw the phrase "national security" often used as a reason why documents could not be released—or used in a federal court—to try Lt. Col. Oliver North on criminal conspiracy charges coming out of the Iran–Contra affair. (North, along with retired Admiral John M. Poindexter, the former National Security Adviser to President Reagan, was the subject of criminal charges relating to illegal sale of arms to Iran and diversion of the proceeds to fund the Nicaraguan Contras.) With those classified documents unavailable, the main charges against North were dropped early in 1989. The Central Intelligence Agency, itself so clandestine that its budget is secret, opposed release of security-classified documents needed to bring North to trial. [91]

The task for reporters or other citizens who try to keep tabs on what government has done or is doing is monumental. In 1988, fourteen years after President Richard M. Nixon resigned in the wake of the Watergate scandal, historian Dan T. Carter complained about difficulties in access to the Nixon Papers as he worked on a biography of former Alabama Governor George Wallace, pursuing tantalizing bits of evidence that Nixon's Republican White House had involved itself strangely in Wallace's Democratic and Third Party political campaigns in the early 1970s.

After Nixon left the White House, he claimed, through his lawyers, that the President had a right to bottle up or even get rid of materials relating to the Presidency. Congress then passed the 1974 Presidential Records Act, declaring Presidential records to be government property and ordering the National Archives to catalog the records, to cull them for national security and privacy-sensitive areas, and to release those records as soon as practicable.

[90] Norman L. Rosenberg, Protecting the Best Men: An Interpretive History of Libel (Chapel Hill: University of North Carolina Press, 1986) p. 266.

[91] Marianne Means, "Dr. Strangelove's super-CIA scheme," column in Austin American–Statesman, July 18, 1987, p. A14; Stephen Engelberg, "Data Disclosure in Contra Case Fought by U.S.," The New York Times, June 4, 1988 (Nat'l. Ed.), p. 9; "House Sets Secret Sum for Intelligence Groups," A.P. story in The New York Times, June 10, 1987, p. 13.

The historian Carter wrote to The New York Times: [92]

> Mr. Nixon's lawyers . . . sent several representatives-untrained in historical study—or archival management—to conduct their own examination of the 1.5 million documents. In April 1987, less than a month before the scheduled opening of the first batch of papers, Mr. Nixon's lawyers demanded that an additional 150,000 documents be withheld.

It should be obvious that the existence of federal and state freedom of information acts does not mean that information is freely available. Ask any knowledgeable investigative reporter, and you will get a litany of complaints about problems in getting access. For example, James Derk of the Evansville (Ind.) Courier used the federal Freedom of Information Act (FOIA) to report on a regional airline.

Although, as described earlier in this chapter at pages 601–602, there are—on paper—just nine broad exemptions to the Federal FOIA, Derk wrote: "I usually run into the unofficial 10th Exemption, known as the 'forget it' exemption." He noted that he received letters saying his requests had been denied for various reasons, or, at times, never got answers at all. "I've been waiting," Derk wrote late in 1988, "for more than two years for a response from the Department of Justice." He added: [93]

> When I get answers, often they are not the answers I sought.

* * *

> In September, I received 1,150 pages of documents from the U.S. Environmental Protection Agency that I had requested in July. The documents were riddled with deletions and I ended up paying 15 cents a page for 118 blank pages, the contents of which were deemed too sensitive for public eyes.

Road-blocks to information often do seem excessive. John Weiner, a history professor reporting the life of former Beatle John Lennon, reported in 1988 that 14–year–old CIA and FBI files about the singer's anti-Vietnam War activities and his work against President Nixon's reelection were withheld. Professor Weiner asked, " 'How can 14–year–old documents on the peaceful activity of a dead rock singer jeopardize national security?' " [94]

[92] Dan T. Carter, "The Nixon Cover–Up Goes On," letter to The New York Times, July 25, 1988, p. 23.

[93] James Derk, "It takes a lot of persistence to make the Freedom of Information Act pay off, ASNE Bulletin, November, 1988, pp. 10–11.

[94] "Educators Assailing Curbs on Data," The New York Times (Nat'l. Ed.), Sept. 14, 1988, p. 26.

Freedom of information requests, however frustrating they may be, can turn up useful results if persistence is maintained. Late in 1988, for example, it was reported by the Durham (N.C.) Morning Herald—which had received more than 2,000 pages in an FOIA request—that the Federal Bureau of Investigation had kept a confidential file on the Supreme Court of the United States from 1932 until at least 1985. That file included evidence that the FBI had wiretapped (evidently without warrants!) or monitored conversations involving four men on the Court, Chief Justice Earl Warren and Justices Abe Fortas, Potter Stewart, and William O. Douglas.[95]

CIA v. SIMS (1985)

A case which provides a disturbing symbol of the power of claimed national security exemptions to shield federal agencies from scrutiny is CIA v. Sims (1985). This Orwellian nightmare of a case concerned a Freedom of Information Act lawsuit to get records on the Central Intelligence Agency's research project code-named MKULTRA. This project, started in 1953 when Richard Helms was CIA deputy director for planning, was to counter Chinese and Soviet advances in brainwashing and interrogation. From 1953 to 1965, the CIA contracted with numerous universities to test the efficacy of certain biological and chemical materials in altering human behavior.[96]

Sims and others sued in 1977 to discover which universities and individuals had taken part in this secret research, but were unsuccessful. The Supreme Court of the United States upheld lower court rulings saying that Exemption 3 of the FOIA Act, in concert with the National Security Act of 1947, allowed the Director of the CIA to decide what should or should not be released—in the national interest—to protect intelligence sources and methods from unauthorized disclosure.[97]

Hidden in that judicial/bureaucratic verbiage is a dangerous dilemma for a society which would be self-governing. If CIA v. Sims is put in human terms, it boils down to this: can a society which would be self-governing adopt the methods of totalitarianism (surreptitious administration of drugs such as LSD to unwitting "subjects?") And, when some aspects of those CIA research projects went terribly wrong—including death of at least two

[95] "FBI Kept Secret File on the Supreme Court," The New York Times, August 21, 1988, p. 13.

[96] CIA v. Sims, 471 U.S. 159, 161, 105 S.Ct. 1881, 1884 (1985), 11 Med.L.Rptr. 2017.

[97] 471 U.S. at 159, 164, 105 S.Ct. 1882, 1885 (1985).

persons and the likelihood of impaired health for other "subjects"—the CIA attempted to cover its tracks.[98]

Because CIA budgetary records are secret, there is no way of tracking down the financial costs. But the MKULTRA project was massive: it consisted of some 149 subprojects which the CIA contracted out to various universities and research foundations. At least 80 institutions—including, apparently, major universities in the U.S. and even in Canada—and 185 private researchers took part in MKULTRA.[99]

But try to keep this in human terms: shouldn't the universities participating—and the researchers who took part in these bizarre and dangerous experiments—be identified? Or if you had a relative who had committed suicide after being dosed with LSD without his permission, in an MKULTRA "research project" might not you want to find out more, to confront those responsible?

According to the Supreme Court decision in CIA v. Sims, you'll get that information only if the Director of the CIA decides that its release would not be harmful to national security interests. And because the CIA had promised the researchers and their institutions—including universities—anonymity, the Director of the CIA could "properly" conclude that such information could not be released, in order to protect "intelligence sources."

The Supreme Court, in upholding the CIA Director's authority to withhold information, said:[1]

> We hold that the Director of the Central Intelligence properly invoked § 102(d)(3) of the National Security Act of 1947 to withhold disclosure of the identities of the individual MKULTRA researchers as protected 'intelligence sources.' We also hold that the FOIA does not require the Director to disclose the institutional affiliations of the exempt researchers in light of the record which supports the Agency's determination of that such disclosure would lead to an unacceptable risk of disclosing the source's identities.

The lesson of CIA v. Sims, is that the Supreme Court gives an enormous benefit of the doubt to government agencies which can claim some kind of "national security" exemption. The MKULTRA project, which brings to mind certain "research" which led to War Crimes trials in the aftermath of World War II, should never

---

[98] 471 U.S. 159, 162n, 105 S.Ct. 1881, 1884n (1985).

[99] 471 U.S. at 162, 105 S.Ct. at 1884 (1985).

[1] Ibid., 471 U.S. at 181, 105 S.Ct. at 1894 (1985).

be repeated. After it came to light, a Presidential Executive Order forbade that kind of research.[2]

But it should be kept in mind that MKULTRA—hardly the CIA's finest hour—became known despite a determined effort to erase all evidence that it had ever existed. When Richard Helms—who had himself suggested the project as a CIA functionary in 1953—became President Nixon's CIA director in the 1970s, he ordered all evidence of the project wiped out. But some of the financial records of the project "inadvertently survived" and came to the attention of Admiral Stansfield Turner, CIA Director under President Carter. Turner turned the information over to the Senate Select Committee on Intelligence, resulting in a major Congressional investigation. But even there, the CIA request to treat the names of the MKULTRA researchers as confidential was honored.[3]

By the late 1980s, other freedom of information problems involving access to computerized records were becoming increasingly important. When is electronically stored information "a record?" How can computerized information be identified with sufficient specificity? As Joe Grimm of the Detroit Free Press has said, both state and federal FOI acts can be used to get computer records that some agencies generally have not deemed to be public. Reporters will need to argue that it is the information, not the way of storing it, that is the record, and news organizations will have to fight this out in the courts, in all likelihood.[4]

One answer where electronic records are concerned is that citizens' groups or newsgathering organizations will have to be willing to be assertive. If what used to be an open public record in a file becomes unavailable or discouragingly expensive when stored electronically, it may be time to go to court. In some states, it may be necessary to lobby legislators to get antiquated statutes updated.

The Reporters Committee on Freedom of the Press makes available "Access to Electronic Records: A Guide to Reporting on State & Local Government in the Computer Age." The Reporters Committee says that in general, electronic records—or at least the pieces of information stored electronically—are subject to federal and state open records laws.[5]

[2] Exec.Order No. 12333, § 2.103 CFR 213 (1982).

[3] Ibid., 471 U.S. at 160, 105 S.Ct. at 1883. See also Stansfield Turner, Secrecy and Democracy: The CIA in Transition (Boston: Houghton Mifflin, (1985).

[4] ASNE Bulletin, November 1988, p. 9.

[5] Reporters Committee on Freedom of the Press, Access to Electronic Records: A Guide to Reporting on State & Local Government in the Computer Age, Rev. 1991, p. 3.

One nasty problem gets the copyright interests of records-management firms tangled up in questions of access to information. For example, access to the computer software may be needed in order to make sense of records, especially for a complicated reporting or research project. State agencies, especially those which have purchased or leased software from private suppliers, may try to deny access to software as a kind of "trade secret." [6]

Access to News of Military Operations

One of the true tests of how free a nation is comes when that nation's government is at war. Some of the givens of wartime include:

— There can be prior restraint when safety of military forces or civilians is at stake.

— Prior restraint can be imposed over dispatches sent or broadcast from a battle zone.

— Correspondents in a war zone may have both their mobility and their access to channels of communication curtailed.

"The Uncensored War" is the title Daniel C. Hallin chose for his study of the media and the war in Vietnam. A myth has grown up, Hallin contends, that because the media were allowed, quite freely, to send home images of war in 'Nam, that the U.S. media somehow "lost the war."

Former President Richard M. Nixon has blamed television for demoralization at home during the latter stages of the Vietnam conflict. Such views of media—particularly, TV—coverage have affected policy. As Hallin noted,[7]

[I]t was the example of Vietnam, for instance, that motivated the British government to impose tight controls on news coverage of the Falklands crisis [of 1982]. Back at home, the Reagan administration, with Vietnam in mind, excluded the media from the opening phase of the invasion of Grenada.

The excessive secrecy of the 1983 Grenada invasion led to earnest press protests, and to some rueful admissions from military officials that they may have gone too far with their controls.

As a result, "press pools" were organized. A small number of journalists representing largely establishment publications and

---

[6] Ibid., p. 6.

[7] Daniel C. Hallin, "The Uncensored War:" The Media and Vietnam (Berkeley: University of California Press, 1986, p. 4; Tom Wicker, "Ghosts of Vietnam," in The New York Times, Jan. 26, 1991, p. 19.

broadcast operations were selected to keep their bags packed, to be "at the ready" should the United States embark on another military action. This arrangement meant that the small number of journalists selected for the pool would share their stories with the far larger number of correspondents and media outlets not selected. When the United States invaded Panama on December 20, 1989, pool correspondents belatedly were put into place to cover actions involving 25,000 highly trained U.S. troops, plus a large assortment of military hardware—tanks, jet fighters, helicopter gunships and Stealth bombers, all to try to capture and arrest General Manuel Noriega. It turned out that the Panama pool was not the solution; it was part of the problem.

From the standpoint of the news media, there was only one thing wrong with the Panama pool arrangement: It didn't work. As Editor & Publisher reported, Secretary of Defense Dick Cheney and his press assistant, Pete Williams, were blamed for the inability of the "National Press Pool" to cover the invasion of Panama effectively.[8]

Fred Hoffman, a former Associated Press reporter who also had served as a Pentagon spokesperson, evaluated the Panama pool experience harshly. It should be noted that Hoffman's evaluative report had been requested by Pete Williams himself.

The Hoffman report complained that Cheney was excessively concerned with secrecy, and concluded that was the reason the pool did not get to the scene until the fighting was nearly over. The press pool—16 reporters—Editor & Publisher quoted from the Hoffman report, which said that in practice sessions during the National Press Pool's five-year history and in covering sea and air battles in the Persian Gulf in 1986–87,[9]

> " * * * reporters demonstrated they could be trusted to respect essential ground rules, including operational security * * *
>
> "Unless the Defense Department's leaders are prepared to extend that trust in hot-war situations, the pool probably will be of little value."

Long after the Panama invasion, many questions remained. How many civilians were killed? On December 20, 1990—exactly a year after the U.S. invasion—U.S. Representative Charles Rangel (D–NY) published his views in The New York Times. He wrote: [10]

[8] George Garneau, "Panning the Pentagon," Editor & Publisher, March 31, 1990, p. 11.

[9] Quoted in Ibid.

[10] Charles B. Rangel, "The Pentagon Pictures," The New York Times (Nat'l.Ed.), Dec. 20, 1990, p. A19.

* * * General Manuel Antonio Noriega sits idly in a Miami jail cell, his trial on charges of drug trafficking delayed by the Government's tape recording of his telephone conversations. But few people know that for the past year Government has been withholding another set of tapes—Government-recorded videotapes of the Panama invasion.

The videotapes of the invasion were taken by highly sophisticated gun cameras aboard Apache attack helicopters. What might those tapes show? They could well suggest that far more civilians died than the U.S. count of 202. (Human rights leaders and some Panamanians have charged that thousands died.) Also, Rangel wrote, as many as 60 percent of the 347 American casualties may have been caused by "friendly fire." [11]

Covering the Persian Gulf War

When President George Bush said that the Persian Gulf war was not to be "another Vietnam," he seemed to refer to his determination to bring enough military resources into play to assure a swift victory. The desire to avoid the "Vietnam syndrome" obviously had fallout for press coverage of the war in the Persian Gulf. Although camera operators on rooftops got spectacular footage of Nintendo-like displays of rockets and tracer bullets, the result of warfare—corpses—was little seen.

In the main, the American press acquiesced in the pooling arrangements. Daniel Hallin's comments on American news media in Vietnam are worth pondering in light of media's coverage of Persian Gulf warfare. Just how independent are the media? Hallin wrote: [12]

> Structurally the American news media are both highly autonomous from direct political control and, through the routines of the news-gathering process, deeply intertwined in the actual operation of government.

Hallin argued that news people combine suspicion of power with a respect for established order, institutions, and authority. Given this anomalous status, small wonder the press—watched most carefully by suspicious military officials—had severe problems in the Persian Gulf. The distinguished military correspondent Malcolm W. Browne, long known for his steadiness and balanced coverage, wrote in January, 1991, that many [13]

[11] Ibid.

[12] Hallin, p. 8.

[13] Malcolm W. Browne, "Conflicting Censorship Upsets Many Journalists," The New York Times, Jan. 21, 1991, p. A8.

* * * news correspondents covering the war with Iraq are bridling under a system of conflicting rules and confusing censorship.

For the first time since World War II, correspondents must submit to near-total military supervision of their work.

Military escorts tagged along with reporters, making it highly unlikely that servicemen and women who were interviewed would speak frankly. At times, escorts interrupted interviews, objecting to questions. When an enlisted man told a reporter how he continued to practice his Christian faith in a country where anything but Muslin rites are not legal, a military "information officer" cut off the interview. The reason? "Military ground rules forbid questions about 'things that we don't know about necessarily.' " [14]

Carol Rosenberg of the Miami Herald and Susan Sachs of Newsday were excluded from covering the First Marine Division in the Persian Gulf because they were thought to have asked "rude questions" of Marine officers. [15]

Uneven application of rules seemed particularly frustrating. Officers in the field would clear a dispatch, only to have it held up somewhere up the line. On the other hand, reporters could understand why a battlefield commander would request that the location of an action not be given, only to have the information withheld in the war zone made public by the Pentagon.

Top brass showed fondness for the spotlight. Malcolm Browne observed that "[t]he Pentagon is clearly eager to be the first to report the most newsworthy information. [16] Later in the war, the Pentagon itself was upstaged by briefings given from Saudi Arabia by General "Stormin Norman" Schwarzkopf.

Despite the grumbling by the press, it surrendered quite meekly to what amounted to military rule, with Cable News Network's Peter Arnett's reports from Baghdad being the most obvious nose-thumbing at pooled journalism. The establishmentarian nature of most American news operations may be seen, perhaps, in the scant coverage given to a lawsuit by Pulitzer Prize-winner Sydney Schanberg, a lawsuit challenging the ground rules for covering Operation Desert Shield (which became "Desert Storm" once the fighting started).

[14] Clarence Page, "Gulf between military, media is so wide that truth has been put in choke hold," Milwaukee Sentinel, Jan. 22, 1991, p. 8, Part 1.

[15] Ibid.

[16] Browne, op. cit.

In that lawsuit, nine publications and four journalists sued Secretary of Defense Cheney and Assistant Secretary of Defense for Public Affairs Pete Williams (among others), seeking an injunction against what were characterized as unfair policies. One press rule, issued January 9, 1991, decreed that media reports from combat pools had to be reviewed by an on-site military public affairs officer before transmission, an obvious cause of delay (or worse).[17]

Despite the pro-Administration-cheerleading-for-the-Persian Gulf war attitudes permeating most of America's news media, the military evidently viewed reporters with less than enthusiasm, if not suspicion or outright hostility. The military controlled its own image during the Persian Gulf war.

SEC. 85. RECORDS AND MEETINGS IN THE STATES

The extent of access in the states varies under statutes providing what shall be open and what closed in the meetings and records of executive, administrative, and legislative agencies.

All states have laws declaring that public policy demands substantial if not maximum disclosure of official business, both meetings and records. Rarely, however, is it conceded that every act or document of officialdom must be open to public scrutiny. Every branch of government in the United States conducts some of its work or maintains some of its records in secret. There are situations in the states as in the federal government's domain which favor secrecy as protection for the individual's private rights and for government's carrying out its work. But the principle of disclosure and openness is as important to the democratic spirit at the state and local levels as it is at the federal level. Thanks to open government efforts pushed by the press and by public spirited citizens in the 1960s and 1970s, by mid–1974 48 states had open-meetings laws.[18]

[17] The journalists bringing the suit were Schanberg (Newsday), novelists E.L. Doctorow and William Styron, and Michael Klare (Nation magazine). The New York Times, the Washington Post, and the Associated Press were not involved in the suit, nor were any of the four big broadcast networks. Plaintiff publications included Harper's, The Nation, Mother Jones, Progressive Magazine, In These Times, and The Village Voice.

[18] All except Miss. and W.Va. by 1974. See John B. Adams, "State Open Meetings Laws: An Overview," Freedom of Information Foundation Series No. 3, July 1974. For another historical treatment, see William R. Henrick, "Public Inspection of State and Municipal Executive Documents," 45 Fordham L.Rev. 1105 (1977). See also "Gaining Access '84," section of the 1985 Freedom of Information Report, Society of Professional Journalists, Sigma Delta Chi.

The great diversity among state open meetings and open records statutes defies easy generalization or detailed discussion here.[19] Citizens who need to know how to get information out of particular governmental units—including reporters—need to brief themselves on the special provisions of each state's access laws. Ignorance of such provisions leaves the citizen or reporter at the mercy of officials who choose not to live up to open records or open meetings statutes.

Efforts are made periodically to generalize across state openness statutes, and even to "rank" state statutes in terms of "more open" or "less open." If one learns one is in a state with a highly rated statute, however, do not relax. Openness statutes—or court decisions, for that matter—tend to be rather like airline tickets— good for this time and purpose only. Keeping records and meetings open takes real diligence on the part of the news media and concerned citizens' groups.

To begin with records kept by government offices, just because many records are generically termed "public" does not necessarily mean "open to inspection by the public or press." The old common law (judge-made) definition of public record is something like this: A written memorial by an authorized public officer in discharge of a legal duty to make a record of something written, said, or done.[20]

So, the word "public" does not imply a general right of inspection. In the statutes, furthermore, various qualifications in the public's right to inspect "public records" exist: [21]

> Some documents which constitute public records under * * * an open records statute have been exempted from disclosure. There may be available to specified individuals [e.g. licensing examination data available only to the individual examined, or reports of mental examinations of school children available only to their parents.] * * * Not all state-affiliated organizations will meet the definition of "agency" within an open records act [e.g., consulting firms and quasi-public corporations are frequently outside the terms of an open records act.]

All the states have certain statutes specifically providing for secrecy. One example is a provision in income tax laws mandating that individual income tax returns be protected from disclo-

---

[19] Of special usefulness is the series Tapping Officials' Secrets: A State Open Government Compendium, a state-by-state project of the Reporters Committee for Freedom of the Press.

[20] Amos v. Gunn, 84 Fla. 285, 94 So. 615, 616 (1922).

[21] Henrick, p. 1112. A qualified right of inspection does exist under common law. Harold L. Cross, The Public's Right to Know (New York: Columbia University Press, 1953), pp. xiii–xiv.

sure. Frequent exemptions appearing in state open records laws have much the same character as the exemptions in the Federal Freedom of Information Act (discussed earlier at page 601), including personnel or medical information, intra- or inter-agency memoranda, preliminary draft documents, and trade secrets. Most if not all states also exempt from disclosure a variety of health department records, juvenile and adoption records, licensing examination data, and public assistance or welfare records.

Modern statute-based open records law contains a major improvement over the old common-law right of inspection. At common law, the right to inspect public records ordinarily depended upon a citizen's having a proper purpose in seeing or copying the record. Relatively few statutes include such a provision. Some states—e.g. Louisiana, Tennessee, Texas—have statutes providing that record custodians may not inquire into a record applicant's motives.[22]

Opening the Records

Most state open records laws provide legal instruments for the record-seeker to use in trying to overcome denial of access. Usually, the record-seeker may apply to a court for an order to disclose (which may take several forms, such as an injunction against secrecy or a writ of mandamus ordering disclosure). In a number of states, denial of access to a record may be appealed to a state's attorney general, and, in Connecticut and New York, to a special, statutorily established, freedom of information review group. Penalties for illegal denial of access are provided in many statutes, ranging from the rare removal from office or impeachment to the more common fine and/or imprisonment.[23]

Personnel information is often difficult to obtain, and that difficulty is often linked to claims of "privacy." Even when such claims to privacy are not well-founded, smoking out newsworthy records may take major effort and expenditure. For example, a New York court at first upheld Monroe County in denying a Gannett Company newspaper's request for personnel information. Gannett had asked for the names, titles and salaries of 276 Monroe County employees laid off because of budget cuts. The county's regulations provided that each of its agencies should make such information on every officer or employee available to the news media.

In upholding denial of the request, a court held that the 276 fired individuals were no longer public employees but had become

[22] Ibid., p. 1131, 1163–1196. See also Anon., "Government Information and the Rights of Citizens," 73 Mich.L.Rev. 971, at 1179 (1975).

[23] Ibid., pp. 1135–36.

private citizens, and that disclosure of information about them would invade their privacy in a damaging way. A New York appellate court, however, approved Gannett's request for information, saying that the information about the laid off employees was not of a personal nature and that any hardship from disclosure had not been documented.[24]

Police Records

Police records are among the most important in all of government, yet rules of states and municipalities about disclosing such records vary tremendously. If citizens and reporters cannot get access to the "blotter" (the police calls log) and the arrest ("booking") log and the jail log on a constant and continuous basis, the possibility of abuse of citizens' rights may tend to become a probability. According to yet another useful survey by the Reporters Committee on Freedom of the Press, most states have laws allowing sealing of investigatory files.[25] And in some states—as in Alabama, Georgia, Mississippi, Montana and New Mexico (among others)—state statutes are silent about access to law enforcement records.[26]

Just because a state does not spell out access to law enforcement records in statutory form, that does not mean that reporters or citizens are without remedy. Sometimes getting access to law enforcement records will take a willingness to sue under an open records statute—or, on a common law basis if no such statute applies—to try to get the records. Practical reporters will tell you, however, that developing a good working relationship with police probably is as valuable an avenue to access to their records as is reliance on statutes or courts to enforce access.

Access to Campus Police Records

Many colleges and universities in the United States, said to be educating the young for democracy, have unfortunate histories where openness of campus police records is concerned. Part of the problem, in recent years, has been the United States Department of Education, which was threatening universities with loss of federal funding if they violated student privacy by releasing "educational records." Strangely, the Department of Education functionaries argued that campus police incident reports were "educa-

[24] Gannett Co. v. Monroe County, 59 A.D.2d 309, 399 N.Y.S.2d 534, at 536 (1977), overruling 90 Misc.2d 76, 393 N.Y.S.2d 676 (1977).

[25] A Guide to Police Records, News Media & the Law, following page 20, Summer, 1987.

[26] Ibid. See also Justin D. Franklin and Robert E. Bouchard, Guide to the Freedom of Information and Privacy Acts, 2nd ed. (New York: Clark Boardman, updated 1990). Contains texts of state open records laws.

tional records" under the Family Educational Rights and Privacy Act ("FERPA").

The issue gained national notoriety in 1989 when Traci Bauer, a campus newspaper editor at Southwest Missouri State University (SMSU) claimed that she was entitled to SMSU Security Office incident reports.

Ultimately, Ms. Bauer sued Paul Kincaid, SMSU's director of university relations, seeking release of SMSU security office records. Triggering the controversy was Ms. Bauer's request to see an incident report about a rape involving a student athlete.[27]

In July, 1989, Kincaid had distributed a policy statement ordering the withholding of SMSU Security Office records, including the verbatim "incident" reports. The SMSU campus is located within the jurisdiction of the Springfield, Mo., police force.

Ms. Bauer's suit claimed that she was entitled to the SMSU incident reports, and that those reports—which were to be filed with the Springfield police by the campus Security Office—were sometimes delayed. She charged that this meant that the Springfield police thus were unable, at times, to investigate on-campus crime promptly. She sought access to the SMSU records under the Missouri Open Records or "Sunshine" Act.

SMSU Officials, whether using the Department of Education edict as an excuse or a reason, expressed fear of losing federal funding if the "incident reports" were released to the public and press contrary to the U.S. Department of Education's (DOE) understanding of FERPA. The DOE had urged campus officials to keep confidential police incident reports as "educational records," all in the name of privacy.[28]

U.S. District Judge Russell G. Clark, however, found that there was credible testimony that " * * * in the past SMSU has concealed or destroyed evidence of contraband and failed or refused to release selected criminal investigation and incident reports concerning sex offenses, student athletes, and university personnel.[29] In addition, Judge Clark noted credible testimony from Mark Goodman, President of the Student Press Law Center, that no federal funds actually had been withheld as the result of disclosure of police information or incident reports.

The judge noted, however, that the U.S. Department of Education had issued warnings to some schools, and that all schools that had been issued warnings voluntarily fell into compliance with the DOE's interpretation of FERPA.

[27] Bauer v. Kincaid, 759 F.Supp. 575 (W.D.Mo.1991).

[28] Ibid., p. 5; Sec. 610.25 of the Missouri Revised Statutes.

[29] Ibid., p. 11.

In sum, Judge Clark ruled that campus crime records were not "educational records," and thus could not be withheld under FERPA.[30]

> [T]his Court concludes that defendants' actions in withholding the criminal investigation and incident reports which contain names and other personally identifiable information, is unconstitutional under the equal protection.

Judge Clark concluded that the criminal investigation and incident reports of SMSU are not exempt from disclosure under Missouri's Sunshine Law.

Evidently intent on making FERPA into a campus secrets act, the U.S. Department of Education was slow to comply with Judge Clark's ruling. As a result, the SPLC and student editors from the University of Tennessee and the University of Colorado sought—and were granted—an injunction to prevent the Department of Education from interfering with the release of campus crime reports.[31]

But obviously, it is the most troublesome or "sensitive" incidents (e.g. rape allegations against a star athlete, sexual harassment by professors, or some breach of law by an administrator) that tend to stir the human impulse to conceal damaging information. The trouble with "just a little secrecy"—whether on campus or elsewhere—is that what is hidden is likely to be precisely what society needs most to know.

Access to Disaster Scenes

When disasters happen—when airplanes fall from the sky or when industrial plants explode—that may be bad news but it is *news*. Reporters and photographers need to get to the news scene to report, yet police officials and rescue workers argue that they don't need members of the media getting in the way or exposing themselves to danger.

A Milwaukee plane crash provided a case in point. At 3:30 p.m. on September 6, 1985, Midwest Airlines Flight 105 crashed in the City of Oak Creek just after takeoff from Milwaukee's General Mitchell Field.

Just after the crash, a Milwaukee County sheriff's department lieutenant in charge of airport security ordered the crash scene secured. Only emergency personnel and equipment were allowed near the crash site. Roadblocks were set up.

---

[30] Ibid., pp. 47–48.

[31] "Judge Orders Release of Campus Crime Reports," The New York Times, March 15, 1991, p. B9, on decision in Student Press Law Center, Lyn D. Schrotgerber (CO), Sam G. Cristy and James C. Brewer, Jr. (TN) v. Lamar Alexander, U.S. Sec. of Education.

An unmarked sedan carrying four employees of Milwaukee station WTMJ–TV rolled through the roadblock, following an emergency vehicle down the only road providing access to the crash site. A detective left his post at the roadblock and pursued the sedan. When he caught up to the vehicle, the WTMJ–TV employees, including Peter Ah King, were getting cameras out of the trunk. The detective told the four news people they were in a restricted area and would have to leave. One individual then asked if three of the TV news people—excluding the driver—could walk back along the road to the non-restricted area and began to do so.[32]

Cameraman Peter Ah King then left the others, jumped a fence bearing "No Trespassing" signs, and ran to a low hill where he took pictures of the crash site. The detective then ordered Ah King to leave; Ah King replied that he would not leave unless he was arrested. Ah King was then arrested on suspicion of disorderly conduct. He was charged under a disorderly conduct statute which says: [33]

> *Disorderly conduct.* Whoever, in a public or private place, engages in violent, abusive, profane, boisterous, unreasonably loud or otherwise disorderly conduct under circumstances in which the conduct tends to cause or provoke a disturbance in guilty of a Class B misdemeanor.

Because Ah King's conduct was not of the kind listed by the statute, one question in appellate review of the case was whether the statute's catch-all phrase ("or otherwise disorderly conduct") would sustain the conviction of the cameraman.

Writing for the Wisconsin Supreme Court, Justice Louis J. Ceci cited the 1972 U.S. Supreme Court decision in Branzburg v. Hayes: [34]

> "Newsmen have no constitutional right of access to the scenes of crime or disaster when the general public is excluded * * *" "Despite the fact that news gathering may be hampered, the press is regularly excluded from grand jury proceedings, our own [the U.S. Supreme Court's] conferences, the meetings of other official bodies gathered in executive session, and the meetings of private organizations."

In addition, Justice Ceci denied that Richmond Newspapers v. Virginia (1980), a case speaking of the right of the public to attend

[32] City of Oak Creek v. Peter Ah King, 148 Wis.2d 532, 436 N.W.2d 285, 286–287 (1989).

[33] Ibid., pp. 1274–1275.

[34] Ibid., pp. 292–293, quoting *Branzburg v. Hayes*, 408 U.S. 665, 684–685, 92 S.Ct. 2646, 2658–2659 (1972).

courtroom proceedings, was inapplicable to the air crash situation under consideration.[35]   Further,

> [o]ur interpretation of * * * [relevant] Supreme Court cases leads us to the conclusion that under the first amendment, the appellant has an undoubted right to gather news from any source by means within the law. However, the appellant does not have a first amendment right of access solely because he is a news gatherer, to the scene of this airplane crash when the public reasonably has been excluded.

Justice Ceci said that while Ah King was disobeying the detective's order and entering a restricted area, other news gatherers were meeting in the airport director's office in line with the rules set out in the General Mitchell Field Media Guide. (That guide states that " 'no representative of the media will be permitted to enter non-public/restricted areas of the airport without an authorized escort.' ")

The crash occurred at 3:30 p.m., and at 4:30 p.m. the airport director held a 15–minute briefing, then taking media representatives to the crash site to photograph or film the scene.

Justice Ceci concluded with some caustic remarks to underscore his holding that the disorderly conduct ordinance was not unconstitutionally vague as applied to cameraman Peter Ah King. Further, he declared that Ah King as a news gatherer had no special First Amendment rights of access to the scene of the airplane crash beyond the general public's right of access. Justice Ceci declared that [36]

> * * * the needs and rights of the injured and dying should be recognized by this court as having preference over newly created "rights" that the dissenting justices would give to a "news gatherer" who is simply trying to beat out his competition and make his employer's deadline.

In dissent, Wisconsin Supreme Court Justice Shirley Abrahamson, joined by Justices Nathan A. Heffernan and William A. Bablitch, wrote that Peter Ah King did not interfere with or obstruct emergency personnel. That said, she concluded: [T]he court can and should take into consideration the media's role as the "eyes and ears" of the public at large.[37]

[35] Ibid., p. 293.
[36] Ibid., pp. 293–294.
[37] Ibid., p. 297.

Chapter 15

LEGAL PROBLEMS IN REPORTING COURTS

Sec.
86. Access to Judicial Proceedings.
87. Free Press *Versus* Fair Trial.
88. Pre-trial Publicity.
89. Publicity During Trial: Cameras in the Courtroom.
90. Notorious Cases: The Shadow of *Sheppard.*
91. External Guidelines and Self–Regulatory Efforts.
92. Restrictive Orders and Reporting the Judicial Process.
93. Access to Criminal Trials and Civil Matters.

SEC. 86. ACCESS TO JUDICIAL PROCEEDINGS

In a free society, judicial processes remain open to public view.

In the fall of 1991, Americans watching cable television were both repelled and fascinated by the televised rape trial—and subsequent acquittal—of William Kennedy Smith. This medical-school graduate, nephew of the late President John F. Kennedy and of Massachusetts Senator Edward Kennedy, was accused of rape by a young woman who—for purposes of television—had an electronically generated blue blob, not a face, as she brought her accusations against young Mr. Smith.

This trial-as-entertainment—in a sense a throwback to the entertainment trials and public hangings provided in small-town America before instantaneous communication—shows just how much, and how little, coverage of the judicial process has changed.[1]

Given the bloody English heritage of secret Star Chamber trials, secret court proceedings are very much against the American grain. Even so, as recently as 1979, the Supreme Court of the United States—with an eye to protecting the rights of defendants in criminal trials—touched off a firestorm of protests from journalists and civil libertarians by suggesting that in some instances, pre-trial hearings (and even trials themselves) could be shut away from public view. That this case was largely shot down by the Supreme Court a year later is of some consolation, true.[2] Even so,

---

[1] Anna Quindlen, "The Glass Eye," The New York Times, Dec. 18, 1991, p. A19.

[2] Gannett Co., Inc. v. De Pasquale, 443 U.S. 368, 99 S.Ct. 2898 (1979), generally overturned by Richmond Newspapers, Inc. v. Virginia, 448 U.S. 555, 100 S.Ct. 2814 (1980).

it is astonishing that the nation's highest court—in 1979—could in effect call into question the basic right to see and report on the criminal justice process.

SEC. 87.   FREE PRESS *VERSUS* FAIR TRIAL

Attorneys, judges and members of the press continue to try to settle long-standing issues in the "free press—fair trial" dispute.

Back in the 1960s, "trial by newspaper" or "trial by mass media" were phrases which were often heard as the bar-press controversy steamed up.   Some attorneys blamed the mass media for many of the shortcomings of the American court system.[3]   In reply, many journalists went to great lengths in trying to justify questionable actions of the news media in covering criminal trials.[4]

Many of the lawyers' arguments contained the assertion that the media were destroying the rights of defendants by publicizing cases before they got to court.[5]   Such publicity, it was said, prejudiced potential jurors to such an extent that a fair trial was not possible.   Editors and publishers—and some attorneys, too— retorted that the media were not harmful, and contended with passion if not historical accuracy that the First Amendment's free press guarantees took precedence over other Constitutional provisions, including the Sixth Amendment.[6]

What about prejudicing jurors by media accounts?   More than 100 years ago, Mark Twain questioned whether an impartial—in the sense of know-nothing—jury was not a perversion of justice. He wrote that the first 26 graves in Virginia City, Nevada, were occupied by murdered men, and their murderers were never punished.

Twain asserted that when Alfred the Great invented trial by jury, news could not travel fast.   Therefore, he could easily find a jury of honest, intelligent men who had not heard of the case they were to try.   Mark Twain swore that with newspapers and the telegraph, the jury system "compels us to swear in juries com-

---

[3] See, e.g., Advisory Committee on Fair Trial and Free Press, Standards Relating to Fair Trial and Free Press (New York, 1966); see also draft approved Feb. 19, 1968, by delegates to the American Bar Association convention as published in March, 1968.

[4] See, e.g., American Newspaper Publishers Association, Free Press and Fair Trial (New York): American Newspaper Publishers Association, 1967, p. 1 and passim.

[5] See footnote 3, above.

[6] American Newspaper Publishers Association, op. cit., p. 1.

posed of fools and rascals, because the system rigidly excludes honest men and men of brains." [7]

Actually, Mark Twain had the history of the jury system wrong. The jury began in 11th Century England, utilizing a defendant's neighbors who were called to serve both as witnesses and as arbiters of fact. It was not until several centuries later that juries stopped serving as witnesses and served only as triers of fact. In addition, Twain's 19th Century exaggeration does not apply to jury selection procedures in the last quarter of the 20th Century. Jurors need not be absolutely ignorant of—or completely unbiased about—a case which is to go to trial. If jurors can set aside their prejudices and biases, and keep an open mind, that is sufficient. [8]

During the past four decades, the free press-fair trial controversy took place against a backdrop of several sensational, nationally publicized trials and the assassinations of President John F. Kennedy in 1963 and Senator Robert Kennedy and Martin Luther King in 1968. Resultant disputes arrayed the media's right to report against defendants' rights to a fair trial, generated new law in the form of several important Supreme Court decisions, and brought forth efforts to make rules to regularize dealings between the media and law enforcement officials. [9]

The assassination of President Kennedy brought problems of "trial by mass media" dramatically to public consciousness. That fact was underscored by the report of a Presidential Commission headed by Chief Justice Earl Warren. The Warren Commission was intensely critical of both the Dallas police and the news media for the reports of the news of that event. The accused assassin, Lee Harvey Oswald, never lived to stand trial, because he himself was assassinated by Jack Ruby in a hallway of Dallas police headquarters. The hallway was a scene of confusion, clogged with reporters, cameramen, and the curious. [10]

The month after Kennedy's slaying, the American Bar Association charged that "widespread publicizing of Lee Harvey Oswald's alleged guilt, involving statements by officials and public disclosures of the details of 'evidence' would have made it extremely difficult to impanel an unprejudiced jury and afford the accused

[7] Mark Twain, Roughing It (New York: New American Library, Signet Paperback, 1962) pp. 256–257.

[8] Rita J. Simon, The Jury: Its Role in American Society (Lexington, Mass. D.C. Health and Company, 1980), p. 5; Murphy v. Florida, 421 U.S. 794, 95 S.Ct. 2031 (1975).

[9] See Advisory Committee on Fair Trial and Free Press, op. cit., passim; see also Irvin v. Dowd, 366 U.S. 717, 81 S.Ct. 1639 (1961); Rideau v. Louisiana, 373 U.S. 723, 83 S.Ct. 1417 (1963); Sheppard v. Maxwell, 384 U.S. 333, 86 S.Ct. 1507 (1966).

[10] Report of the President's Commission on the Assassination of President John F. Kennedy (Washington: Government Printing Office, 1964), p. 241.

a fair trial." [11]   Indeed, had Oswald survived to stand trial, he might not have been convicted.   This was so even though the Warren Commission—after the fact—declared that Oswald was in all likelihood Kennedy's killer.   Under American judicial procedures, it seems possible that Oswald could not have received a fair and unprejudiced trial, and that any conviction of him might have been upset on appeal.[12]

The Warren Commission placed first blame on police and prosecutors, but additionally criticized the media for their part in the events following the President's death.   The Commission said that "part of the responsibility for the unfortunate circumstances following the President's death must be borne by the news media * * *."   Journalists were excoriated by Commission members for showing a lack of self-discipline, and a code of professional conduct was called for as evidence that the press was willing to support the Sixth Amendment right to a fair and impartial trial as well as the right of the public to be informed.[13]

If the reporters behaved badly in Dallas, so did the Dallas law enforcement officials, who displayed "evidence" in crowded corridors and released statements about other evidence.   Conduct of police and other law enforcement officials, however, has by no means been the only source of prejudicial materials which later appeared in the press to the detriment of defendants' rights.   All too often, both defense and prosecution attorneys have released statements to reporters which were clearly at odds with the American Bar Association's Canons of Professional Ethics.   Canon 20, adopted more than 50 years earlier, advised lawyers to avoid statements to the press which might prejudice the administration of justice or interfere with a fair trial.   In any case, lawyers were not to go beyond quotation from the records and papers on file in courts in making statements about litigation.[14]

Canon 20, in theory, could be used as a weapon to punish lawyers who released statements to the press which harmed a defendant's chances for a fair trial.   Although this Canon was adopted by the bar associations of most states, there was rarely a case brought to disbar or discipline an attorney or judge who made prejudicial remarks to the press.[15]

[11] William A. Hachten, The Supreme Court on Freedom of the Press: Decisions and Dissents (Ames, Iowa: Iowa State University Press, 1968), p. 106.

[12] Ibid.

[13] Report of the President's Commission on the Assassination of President John F. Kennedy, p. 241.

[14] Canons of Professional and Judicial Ethics of the American Bar Association, Canon 20.

[15] Donald M. Gillmor, Free Press and Fair Trial (Washington, D.C., Public Affairs Press, 1966) p. 110.

The ABA's Code of Professional Responsibility—which superseded the old ABA Canons—outlined standards of trial conduct for attorneys. Disciplinary Rule DR 7–107 dealt with "Trial Publicity." It says that lawyers who are involved in a criminal matter shall not make "extra-judicial statements" to the news media which go beyond unadorned factual statements.

In 1991, however, the ABA adopted new Standards for Criminal Justice dealing with out-of-court statements by attorneys. If a state or a court jurisdiction accepts these new standards, they will become mandatory in that region.

Lawyers, again, are allowed to make general statements outside of court about "the general nature of the charges against the accused." This approach is new, according to The News Media & The Law, in that it makes it possible for defense lawyers to try to counterbalance harmful pre-trial publicity against their clients. Lawyers, however, must refrain from making statements which are substantially likely to prejudice a criminal proceeding.

Other language of the ABA's 1991 Fair Trial–Free Press standards appeared to whittle away at rules for closing pre-trial criminal proceedings, changing the standard for closure to "substantial likelihood of harm" from the more restrictive "clear and present danger." Also, the ABA weakened its previous strictures against using the contempt power to punish lawyers who violate a judge's restrictive order by talking to the press.[16]

Reporters are not the only offenders in disrupting trials. A quick skimming of the General Index of a legal encyclopedia, *American Jurisprudence,* adds support for such a generalization. The General Index of "Amjur" contains nearly 1,000 categories under the topic, "New Trial." New trials may be granted because something went awry in the original trial, somehow depriving a defendant of the right to a fair trial under the Sixth Amendment. These categories include such things as persons fainting in the courtroom, hissing, technical mistakes by attorneys, prejudice of judges, and misconduct by jurors: Jurors who read newspapers.[17]

Findings of social scientists lend modest support to assumptions about jurors being prejudiced by the mass media.[18] Much more research, however, remains to be done before assertions can

[16] American Bar Association, Code of Professional Responsibility and Code of Judicial Conduct (Chicago, ABA, 1976) p. 37C, ABA 1991 Fair Trial-Free Press Rules; see News Media & The Law, Spring, 1991, p. 22.

[17] 3 Am.Jur., Gen.Index, New Trial.

[18] See, e.g., Mary Dee Tans and Steven H. Chaffee, "Pretrial Publicity and Juror Prejudice," Journalism Quarterly Vol. 43:4 (Winter, 1966) pp. 647–654, and a list of juror prejudice studies on p. 647, notes 4, 5 and 6. But see Don R. Pember, "Does Pretrial Publicity Really Hurt?" Columbia Journalism Review, Sept./Oct. 1984, p. 16.

be made confidently that what a juror reads or learns from the mass media will affect the juror's subsequent behavior. On the other hand, it has been argued that lawyers, before casting aspersions at the press, might consider the question of whether their own legal house is in order. Consider what psychologists can tell lawyers about a fair trial. Consider the rules of procedure in a criminal trial in many states as attorneys make their final arguments to a jury. First, the prosecution sums up its case. Then the defense attorney makes the final argument. And last, the prosecuting attorney makes the final statement to the jury. For years, psychologists have been arguing about order of presentation in persuasion. Some evidence has been found that having the first say is most persuasive; there is other evidence that having the last word might be best.[19] But in many jurisdictions, who gets neither the first say nor the last word during the final arguments before a jury? The defendant.[20]

SEC. 88.   PRE–TRIAL PUBLICITY

Pre-trial publicity which makes it difficult—if not impossible—for a defendant to receive a fair trial was summed up in the Supreme Court cases of Irvin v. Dowd (1961) and Rideau v. Louisiana (1963).

"Pre-trial publicity" is a phrase which is a kind of shorthand expression meaning strain between the press and the courts. The kind of publicity which "tries" a defendant in print or over the air before the real courthouse trial starts—that's the issue here. This section discusses two classic instances of pre-trial publicity, instances in which the news media did not cover themselves with glory: Irvin v. Dowd and Rideau v. Louisiana.

Irvin v. Dowd (1961)

The Irvin case represents the first time that the Supreme Court overturned a state criminal conviction because publicity before the trial had prevented a fair trial before an impartial jury.[21]

The defendant in this murder case, Leslie Irvin, was subjected to a barrage of prejudicial news items in the hysterical wake of six murders which had been committed in the vicinity of Evansville, Indiana. Two of the murders were committed in December, 1954,

[19] See, e.g., Carl I. Hovland, et al., The Order of Presentation in Persuasion, (New Haven: Yale, 1957) passim.

[20] The authors are grateful to Professors Jack M. McLeod and Steven H. Chaffee, of the University of Wisconsin Mass Communications Research Center and Stanford University, respectively for this insight.

[21] Gillmor, op. cit., pp. 116–117.

and four in March, 1955. These crimes were covered extensively by news media in the locality, and created great agitation in Vanderburgh County, where Evansville is located, and in adjoining Gibson County.[22]

Leslie Irvin, a parolee, was arrested in April, 1955, on suspicion of burglary and writing bad checks. Within a few days, the Evansville police and the Vanderburgh County prosecutor issued press releases asserting that "Mad Dog Irvin" had confessed to all six murders, including three members of one family. The news media had what can conservatively be described as a field day with the Irvin case, and were aided in this by law enforcement officials. Many of the accounts published or broadcast before Irvin's trial referred to him as the "confessed slayer of six." Irvin's court-appointed attorney was quoted as saying he had received much criticism for representing Irvin. The media, by way of excusing the attorney, noted that he faced disbarment if he refused to represent the suspect.[23]

Irvin was soon indicted by the Vanderburgh County Grand Jury for one of the six murders. Irvin's court-appointed counsel sought—and was granted—a change of venue. However, the venue change, under Indiana law, was made only from Vanderburgh County to adjoining Gibson County, which had received similar prejudicial accounts about "Mad Dog Irvin" from the news media in the Evansville vicinity.[24]

The trial began in November of 1955. Of 430 prospective jurors examined by the prosecution and defense attorneys, 370— nearly 90 per cent—had formed some opinion about Irvin's guilt. These opinions ranged from mere suspicion to absolute certainty.[25] Irvin's attorney had used up all of his 20 peremptory challenges. When 12 jurors were finally seated by the court, the attorney then unsuccessfully challenged all jurors on grounds that they were biased. He complained bitterly that four of the seated jurors had stated that Irvin was guilty.[26] Even so, the trial was held, Irvin was found guilty, and the jury sentenced him to death. Irvin's conviction was upheld by the Indiana Supreme Court, which denied his motions for a new trial.[27] Protracted appeals brought Irvin's case to the Supreme Court of the United States twice,[28] but

[22] Irvin v. Dowd, 366 U.S. 717, 719, 81 S.Ct. 1639, 1641 (1961).

[23] 366 U.S. 717, 725–726, 81 S.Ct. 1639, 1641, 1645 (1961); Gillmor, op. cit., p. 11.

[24] 366 U.S. 717, 720, 81 S.Ct. 1639, 1641 (1961).

[25] 366 U.S. 717, 727, 81 S.Ct. 1639, 1945 (1961).

[26] 359 U.S. 394, 398, 79 S.Ct. 825, 828 (1959).

[27] Irvin v. State, 236 Ind. 384, 139 N.E.2d 898 (1957).

[28] Irvin's appeal for a writ of *habeas corpus* to a Federal District Court was denied on the basis that he had not exhausted his opportunities to appeal through the Indiana courts. 153 F.Supp. 531 (N.D.Ind.1957). A United States Court of

his case was not decided on its merits by the nation's highest court until 1961.

Then, in 1961, all nine members of the Supreme Court agreed that Irvin had not received a fair trial. The upshot of this was that Irvin received a new trial, although he was ultimately convicted. This time, however, his sentence was set at life imprisonment.[29]

In his majority opinion, Justice Tom C. Clark—a former attorney general of the United States—concentrated on the effect of prejudicial publicity on a defendant's rights. Clark noted that courts do not require that jurors be totally ignorant of the facts and issues involved in a criminal trial. It is sufficient if a juror can render a verdict based on the evidence presented in court.[30]

Justice Clark then considered the publicity Irvin had received, and concluded: "Here the build-up of prejudice is clear and convincing." He noted that arguments for Irvin presented evidence that "a barrage of newspaper headlines, articles, cartoons and pictures was unleashed against him during the six or seven months before his trial" in Gibson County, Indiana. Furthermore, "Evansville radio and TV stations, which likewise blanketed the county, also carried extensive newscasts covering the same incidents." [31]

In a concurring opinion, Justice Frankfurter unleashed a bitter denunciation of "trial by newspapers instead of trial in court before a jury." He stated that the Irvin case was not an isolated incident or an atypical miscarriage of justice. Frankfurter wrote: [32]

> Not a term passes without this Court being importuned to review convictions, had in States throughout the country, in which substantial claims are made that a jury trial has been distorted because of inflammatory newspaper accounts—too often, as in this case, with the prosecutor's collaboration—exerting pressures upon potential jurors before trial and even during the course of trial
> * * *.

Appeals affirmed the dismissal of the writ, 251 F.2d 548 (7th Cir.1958). In a 5–4 decision in 1959, the Supreme Court of the United States sent Irvin's case back to the Federal Court of Appeals for reconsideration. 359 U.S. 394, 79 S.Ct. 825 (1959). The Court of Appeals again refused to grant a writ of *habeas corpus* to Irvin, 271 F.2d 552 (7th Cir.1959). Irvin's case was then appealed to the Supreme Court for the second time.

[29] Gillmor, op. cit., pp. 11–12.

[30] Irvin v. Dowd, 366 U.S. 717, 723, 81 S.Ct. 1639, 1642–1643 (1961).

[31] 366 U.S. 717, 728, 81 S.Ct. 1939, 1645 (1961).

[32] 366 U.S. 717, 730, 81 S.Ct. 1639, 1646–1647 (1961).

Trial by Television: Rideau v. Louisiana (1963)

If Leslie Irvin was mistreated primarily by newspapers during the period before his trial, Wilbert Rideau found that television was the major offender in interfering with his right to a fair trial. Early in 1961, a Lake Charles, La., bank was robbed. The robber kidnaped three of the bank's employees and killed one of them. Several hours later, Wilbert Rideau was arrested by police and held in the Calcasieu Parish jail in Lake Charles. The next morning, a moving picture—complete with a sound track—was made of a 20-minute "interview" between Rideau and the Sheriff of Calcasieu Parish. The Sheriff interrogated the prisoner and elicited admissions that Rideau had committed the bank robbery, the kidnaping, and the murder. Later in the day, this filmed interview was broadcast over television station KLPC in Lake Charles. Over three days' time, the film was televised on three occasions to an estimated total audience of 97,000 persons, as compared to the approximately 150,000 persons then living in Calcasieu Parish.[33]

Rideau's attorneys subsequently sought a change of venue away from Calcasieu Parish. It was argued that it would take away Rideau's right to a fair trial if he were tried there after the three television broadcasts of Rideau's "interview" with the sheriff. The motion for change of venue was denied, and Rideau was convicted and sentenced to death on the murder charge in the Calcasieu Parish trial court. The conviction was affirmed by the Louisiana Supreme Court,[34] but the Supreme Court of the United States granted *certiorari*.[35]

Justice Potter Stewart's majority opinion noted that three of the 12 jurors had stated during *voir dire* examination before the trial that they had seen and heard Rideau's "interview" with the Sheriff. Also, two members of the jury were Calcasieu Parish deputy sheriffs. Although Rideau's attorney challenged the deputies, asking that they be removed "for cause," the trial judge denied this request. Since Rideau's lawyers had exhausted his "peremptory challenges"—those for which no reason need be given—the deputies remained on the jury.[36]

Justice Stewart noted that the *Rideau* case did not involve physical brutality. However, he declared that the "kangaroo

[33] Rideau v. Louisiana, 373 U.S. 723, 724, 83 S.Ct. 1417, 1419 (1963).

[34] 242 La. 431, 137 So.2d 283 (1962).

[35] 371 U.S. 919, 83 S.Ct. 294 (1962).

[36] 373 U.S. 723, 725, 83 S.Ct. 1417, 1418 (1963).

court proceedings in this case involved a more subtle but no less real deprivation of due process of law." Justice Stewart added: [37]

> . . . In this case the people of Calcasieu Parish saw and heard, not once but three times, a "trial" of Rideau in a jail, presided over by a sheriff, where there was no lawyer to advise Rideau of his right to stand mute.

Rideau's conviction was reversed, and a new trial was ordered by the Supreme Court.

SEC. 89. PUBLICITY DURING TRIAL: CAMERAS IN THE COURTROOM

The notorious Lindbergh kidnaping trial of the 1930s and the Estes case of 1965 severely limited still and television cameras in the courtroom. Cameras are returning now in many states, under the Supreme Court's 1981 decision in Chandler v. Florida.

"The Lindbergh Case" and "the trial of Bruno Hauptmann" are phrases heard whenever the free press—fair trial debate heats up. These phrases, of course, refer to the kidnaping in 1932 of the 19-month-old son of the aviator famed for the first solo crossing of the Atlantic. The child's kidnaping was front-page news for weeks, long after the child's body was found in a shallow grave not far from the Lindbergh home in New Jersey.

More than two years later, in September, 1934, Bruno Richard Hauptmann was arrested. His trial for the kidnap-murder of the Lindbergh child did not begin until January, 1935. The courtroom where Hauptmann was tried had a press section jammed with 150 reporters. During the Hauptmann trial, which lasted more than a month, there were sometimes more than 700 newsmen in Flemington, N.J., the site of the trial.[38]

Much of the publicity of the Hauptmann trial was prejudicial, and lawyers and newsmen authored statements which were clearly inflammatory. Hauptmann was described in the press, for example, as a "thing lacking in human characteristics." [39] After the trial—and after Hauptmann's execution—a Special Committee on Cooperation Between the Press, Radio, and Bar was established to search for "standards of publicity in judicial proceedings and methods of obtaining an observance of them." In a grim report issued in 1937, the 18-man committee—including lawyers, editors, and publishers—termed Hauptmann's trial "the most spectacular and depressing example of improper publicity and professional

---

[37] 373 U.S. 723, 727, 83 S.Ct. 1417, 1419 (1963).

[38] John Lofton, Justice and the Press (Boston: Beacon Press, 1966), pp. 103–104.

[39] Lofton, op. cit., p. 124.

misconduct ever presented to the people of the United States in a criminal trial." [40]

One result of the committee's investigation of the Hauptmann trial was the American Bar Association's adoption in 1937 of Canon 35 of its Canons of Professional Ethics. Canon 35 forbade taking photographs in the courtroom, including both actual court sessions and recesses. As updated, Canon 35 declared that broadcasting or televising court proceedings "detract from the essential dignity of the proceedings, distract the participants and witnesses in giving testimony, and create misconceptions * * * and should not be permitted." This was replaced by ABA Canon of Judicial Conduct 3(7): [41]

A judge should prohibit broadcasting, televising, recording, or taking photographs in the courtroom and areas immediately thereto during sessions of court or recesses between sessions * * * The only exceptions involved situations when the judge had given permission, or the filming was to be used only for ceremonial or instructional purposes.

Estes v. Texas

Excesses in televising a trial in Texas during the 1960s meant the end of televising virtually all criminal trials for a period of more than a decade. As is discussed later in this section, however, developments in the late 1970s—capped by the January, 1981 decision of the Supreme Court of the United States in Chandler v. Florida [42]—have seen a substantial movement toward getting both television and still cameras back into state courtrooms. At this writing, however, federal courtrooms are still off limits.

The crucial case of the 1960s involved the swindling trial of flamboyant Texas financier Billie Sol Estes. Estes was ultimately convicted, but not until he had received a new trial as a result of the manner in which a judge allowed his original trial to be photographed and televised. Fallout from the U.S. Supreme Court decision which granted Estes a new trial seemed to rule out cameras in the courtroom. [43]

[40] American Bar Association, "Report of Special Committee on Cooperation between Press, Radio and Bar," Annual Report, Volume 62, pp. 851–866 (1937), at p. 861. See, also, New Jersey v. Hauptmann, 115 N.J.L. 412, 180 A. 809 (Err. & App.1935), certiorari denied 296 U.S. 649, 56 S.Ct. 310 (1935).

[41] American Bar Association, Code of Professional Responsibility and Code of Judicial Conduct, p. 59C. For Canon 35, see ABA, Annual Report, Vol. 62, at p. 1134; see it as updated by Justice John Marshall Harlan in his concurring opinion in Estes v. Texas, 381 U.S. 532, 601n., 85 S.Ct. 1628, 1669n. (1965).

[42] Chandler v. Florida, 449 U.S. 560, 101 S.Ct. 802 (1981).

[43] Estes v. Texas, 381 U.S. 532, 85 S.Ct. 1628 (1965).

Estes came before a judicial hearing in Smith County, Texas, in 1962, after a change of venue from Reeves County, some 500 miles west. The courtroom was packed and about 30 persons stood in the aisles. A New York Times story described the setting for the pre-trial hearing in this way: [44]

> A television motor van, big as an intercontinental bus, was parked outside the courthouse and the second-floor courtroom was a forest of equipment. Two television cameras have been set up inside the bar and four more marked cameras were aligned just outside the gates.
>
> *   *   *
>
> Cables and wires snaked over the floor.

With photographers roaming unchecked about the courtroom, Estes' attorney moved that all cameras be excluded from the courtroom. As the attorney spoke, a cameraman walked behind the judge's bench and took a picture.[45]

After the two-day hearing was completed on September 25, 1962, the judge granted a continuance (delay) to the defense, with the trial to begin on October 22. Meanwhile, the judge established ground rules for television and still photographers. Televising of the trial was allowed, with the exception of live coverage of the interrogation of prospective jurors or the testimony of witnesses. The major television networks, CBS, NBC, and ABC, plus local television station KLTV were each allowed to install one television camera (without sound recording equipment) and film was made available to other television stations on a pooled basis. In addition, through another pool arrangement, only still photographers for the Associated Press, United Press, and from the local newspaper would be permitted in the courtroom.

At its own expense, and with the permission of the court, KLTV built a booth at the back of the courtroom, painted the same color as the courtroom. An opening in the booth permitted all four television cameras to view the proceedings. However, in this small courtroom, the cameras were visible to all.[46]

Despite these limitations the judge placed on television and still photographers, a majority of the Supreme Court held that Estes had been deprived of a fair trial in violation of the due process clause of the Fourteenth Amendment. Chief Justice Warren and Justices Douglas, Goldberg, and Clark asserted that a fair

---

[44] Estes v. Texas, 381 U.S. 532, 553, 85 S.Ct. 1628, 1638 (1965), from Chief Justice Warren's concurring opinion, with which Justices Douglas and Goldberg concurred.

[45] 381 U.S. 532, 553, 85 S.Ct. 1628, 1638 (1965). From concurring opinion by Chief Justice Warren.

[46] 381 U.S. 532, 554–555, 85 S.Ct. 1628, 1638–1639 (1965), from Chief Justice Warren's concurring opinion.

trial could not be had when television is allowed in any criminal trial. Justice Harlan, the fifth member of the majority in this 5–4 decision, voted to overturn Estes' conviction because the case was one of "great notoriety." Even so, it should be noted that Harlan reserved judgment on the televising of more routine cases.

In delivering the opinion of the Court, Mr. Justice Clark wrote: [47]

> We start with the proposition that it is a "public trial" that the Sixth Amendment guarantees to the "accused." The purpose of the requirement of a public trial was to guarantee that the accused would be fairly dealt with and not unjustly condemned. * * *.

Justice Clark then took aim on an assertion that if courts exclude television cameras or microphones, they are discriminating in favor of the print media. Clark retorted, "[t]he news reporter is not permitted to bring his typewriter or printing press." Clark did concede that technical advances might someday make television equipment and cameras quieter and less obtrusive.[48]

In a strongly worded dissent, Justices Stewart, Black, Brennan and White raised constitutional arguments in objecting to the ban on television from courtrooms, at least at that stage of television's development. Justice Stewart expressed doubt that Estes had been deprived of a fair trial by the limited televising of it.[49]

Brennan argued that the *Estes* decision was "*not* a blanket constitutional prohibition against the televising of state criminal trials." [50] Television, said Brennan, was barred by the majority side of *Estes* only from "notorious trials." Nevertheless, from 1965 to 1975, cameras—including television cameras—were kept out of virtually *all* courtrooms.

Cameras in the Courtroom

After 1975, cautious efforts to get cameras back in the courtroom became evident in a number of states. In 1977, the Associated Press Managing Editors Association published a report titled "Cameras in the Courtroom: How to Get 'Em There." The report noted that if "you're going to get your Nikon into that courtroom you've got to have more tools than just a camera. For one thing, you've got to have the clout of your State Supreme Court."

[47] 381 U.S. 532, 538–539, 85 S.Ct. 1628, 1631 (1965).

[48] 381 U.S. 532, 540, 85 S.Ct. 1628, 1631 (1965).

[49] 381 U.S. 532, 601–602, 85 S.Ct. 1628, 1669 (1965).

[50] 381 U.S. 532, 615–616, 85 S.Ct. 1628, 1676–1677 (1965).

The report described a process, beginning with work with a bench-bar-press committee, through demonstrations and carefully regulated experimental photo and TV coverage of either mock or actual trials. Then, a demonstration videotape should be made for use before a hearing to be conducted by the state's supreme court. The final step is writing guidelines for court coverage for adoption by the state supreme court.[51]

Tentatively, a number of states began to allow television, radio and photographic coverage of judicial proceedings. Modern cameras, available-light photography, smaller and quieter television and camera gear: technological advances have helped get cameras back into many courtrooms. More important, however, has been intelligent negotiation by thoughtful members of bench, bar and press who realize that photography in the courtroom, properly used, can be a valuable tool for educating and informing the public.

By 1979, six states allowed some form of television, radio or photographic coverage on a permanent basis.[52] Twelve other states permitted some coverage on an experimental basis, and several others were considering allowing coverage. By mid–1991, there were some 45 states permitting at least some camera access to state judicial proceedings.

Chandler v. Florida: The Lower Courts

A key case testing admission of cameras to courtrooms is Chandler v. Florida.[53] It raised the issue of whether admitting television cameras to a courtroom, over the objection of a participant in a criminal case, made a fair trial impossible.[54]

The *Chandler* case stated the issue in rather extreme form, because in jurisdictions where coverage is permitted, consent of parties is required in most instances.[55] The Supreme Court of the United States held early in 1981 that television coverage had not denied Chandler a fair trial.[56]

Chandler v. Florida also is important because of its interrelationship with another Florida matter, In re Petition of Post-

---

[51] Freedom of Information Committee, APME, "Cameras in the Courtroom: How to Get 'Em There," 1977 Freedom of Information Report, p. 2.

[52] Petition of Post-Newsweek Stations, Florida, Inc., 370 So.2d 764 (Fla.1979), Appendix 2.

[53] Chandler v. State, 366 So.2d 64 (Fla.App.1978), certiorari denied 376 So.2d 1157 (1979), probable juris. noted 446 U.S. 907, 100 S.Ct. 1832 (1980).

[54] 366 So.2d 64, 69 (Fla.App.1978).

[55] See Appendix 2, "Television in the Courtroom—Recent Developments," National Center for State Courts, quoted in entirety in Petition of Post-Newsweek Stations, Florida, Inc., 370 So.2d 764 (Fla.1979).

[56] 449 U.S. 560, 101 S.Ct. 802 (1981).

Newsweek Stations, Florida, Inc., for Change in Code of Judicial Conduct.[57] In that proceeding, the Supreme Court of Florida ruled that electronic media coverage of courtroom proceedings is not in itself a denial of due process of law. However, the court also held that the First and Sixth Amendments do not mandate the electronic media be allowed to cover courtroom proceedings. The Florida Supreme Court then issued a rule to amend 3 A(7) of Florida's Code of Judicial Conduct to allow still photography and electronic media coverage of public judicial proceedings in the appellate and trial courts, subject at all time to the authority of the presiding judge.[58]

The *Post-Newsweek Stations* ruling, with its lengthy appendices spelling out the deployment of equipment and personnel, the kind of equipment to be used, and pooling arrangements for coverage to cut down on in court distractions, has been used elsewhere as a primer for drafting petitions to seek changes in state judicial rules.

Chandler v. Florida: The Trial

Chandler v. Florida involved the burglary trial of two Miami Beach policemen, Noel Chandler and Robert Granger. During their trial, the defendants raised various objections to Florida's [then] Experimental Canon 3 A(7). Under that canon, despite requests from the defendants that live television coverage be excluded, cameras were allowed to televise parts of the trial.[59]

The Supreme Court of Florida denied a petition for a writ of certiorari, asserting a lack of jurisdiction. That court said, "No conflict has been demonstrated, and the question of great public interest has been rendered moot by the decisions in Petition of Post-Newsweek Stations, Florida, Inc., 370 So.2d 764 (Fla.1979)."

The Supreme Court of the United States, however, noted probable jurisdiction in Chandler v. Florida in 1980.[60]

Chandler v. Florida: The Supreme Court

In 1981, the Supreme Court of the United States decided *Chandler* by an 8–0 vote, thus upholding the conviction of two Miami Beach police officers for burglarizing Piccolo's Restaurant. This case—regardless of its outcome—would have been memorable for its fact situation. Officers Noel Chandler and Robert Grander had been chatting with each other via walkie-talkies as they broke

[57] 370 So.2d 764 (Fla.1979).

[58] Ibid., 781.

[59] Chandler v. State, 366 So.2d 64, 69 (Fla.App.1978).

[60] 466 U.S. 907, 100 S.Ct. 1832 (1980).

into the restaurant; they were overheard by an insomniac ham radio operator who recorded their conversations.[61]

Writing for that unanimous Court, Chief Justice Burger based his decision on the principle of federalism. States may work out their own approaches to allowing photographic and broadcast coverage of trials, as long as the Constitution of the United States is not violated.

Chandler and Granger had argued that the very presence of television cameras violated their rights to a fair trial because cameras were psychologically disruptive.[62] Chief Justice Burger wrote for the Court. Burger said: [63]

> An absolute Constitutional ban on broadcast coverage of trials cannot be justified simply because there is a danger in some cases that prejudicial broadcast accounts of pretrial and trial proceedings may impair the ability of jurors to decide the issue of guilt or innocence. * * * [T]he risk of juror prejudice does not warrant an absolute Constitutional ban on all broadcast coverage. * * *
>
> *   *   *
>
> The [appellants] have offered nothing to demonstrate that their trial was subtly tainted by broadcast coverage—let alone that all broadcast trials would be so tainted.

Note that states do not have to admit cameras or broadcast equipment: they *may* do so according to rules which the states develop themselves. Although Florida, unlike most other states which allow cameras in the courtrooms, does not require the permission of the participants in a trial, there are still careful regulations imposed. As noted earlier in this Section,[64] only one television camera and only one still photographer are allowed in the courtroom at one time. Equipment must be put in one place; photographers/camerapersons cannot come and go in the middle of a proceeding, and no artificial light is allowed. Further, if the judge finds cameras disruptive, he can exclude them.[65]

As the Court said in *Chandler,* [66]

> Dangers lurk in this, as in most, experiments, but unless we are to conclude that television coverage under

[61] Chandler v. Florida, 449 U.S. 560, 101 S.Ct. 802 (1981).

[62] The News Media & The Law, 5:1 (Feb./Mar.1981) p. 5.

[63] Chandler v. Florida, 449 U.S. 560, 575, 101 S.Ct. 802, 810 (1981).

[64] Footnote 57, above.

[65] For a good contemporaneous discussion of *Chandler,* see James D. Spaniolo and Talbot D'Alemberte, "Despite 'cameras' ruling, some questions persist," Press-time, March, 1981, p. 16.

[66] 449 U.S. 560, 581, 101 S.Ct. 802, 813 (1981).

all conditions is prohibited by the Constitution, the states must be free to experiment. * * * The risk of prejudice to particular defendants is ever present and must be examined carefully as cases arise.

The Federal Cameras in Courts' Experiment

Even though remarkable gains have been made in getting television and still cameras into state courtrooms, the federal court picture remained unchanged for many years: No cameras in federal courts. With the camera-despising Chief Justice Warren Burger's retirement—replaced by William Rehnquist—a modest experiment in coverage of federal courts began in July, 1991.

Even so, Rule 53 of the Federal Rules of Criminal Procedure (1953) continued in force, and it forbids photographing or making radio broadcasts during a criminal trial. As the Radio–Television News Directors Association (RTNDA) has pointed out, Rule 53 did not explicitly prohibit TV broadcasts, but it might as well, because that's the way courts have interpreted it.

With mounting pressure from the news media, the U.S. Judicial Conference approved a three-year experiment with microphones and cameras in federal courtrooms, to run from July 1, 1991 to June 30, 1994. The experiment deals with substantial media coverage of civil trials and appeals in selected courts, with coverage of criminal trials and appeals forbidden in this experiment.[67]

SEC. 90. NOTORIOUS CASES: THE SHADOW OF *SHEPPARD*

The long ordeal of Dr. Samuel Sheppard ended with the reversal of his murder conviction on grounds that pretrial and during-trial publicity had impaired his ability to get a fair trial.

The Trial of Dr. Sam Sheppard

When the free press—fair trial controversy is raised, the case most likely to be mentioned is that *cause celebre* of American jurisprudence, Sheppard v. Maxwell.[68] This case was one of the most notorious—and most sensationally reported—trials in American history. With perhaps the exception of the Lindbergh kidnap-

---

[67] RTNDA, News Media Coverage of Judicial Proceedings With Cameras and Microphones: A Survey . . . (Washington, D.C., RTNDA, 1991), pp. 9–10. This experimental civil coverage was to occur in six federal district courts and in the U.S. Courts of Appeal for the Second and Ninth Circuits.

[68] 384 S.Ct. 333, 86 S.Ct. 1507 (1966).

ing case of the 1930s, the ordeal of Dr. Sam Sheppard may well have been the most notorious case of the Twentieth Century.

This case began in the early morning hours of July 4, 1954, when Dr. Sheppard's pregnant wife, Marilyn, was found dead in the upstairs bedroom of their home. She had been beaten to death. Dr. Sheppard, who told authorities he had found his wife dead, called a neighbor, Bay Village Mayor Spence Houk. Dr. Sheppard appeared to have been injured, suffering from severe neck pains, a swollen eye, and shock.

Dr. Sheppard, a Bay Village, Ohio, osteopath, told a rambling and unconvincing story to officials: that he had dozed off on a downstairs couch after his wife had gone upstairs to bed. He said that he heard his wife cry out and ran upstairs. In the dim light from the hall, he saw a "form" which he later described as a bushy haired man standing next to his wife's bed. Sheppard said he grappled with the man and was knocked unconscious by a blow to the back of his neck.

He said he then went to his young son's room, and found him unharmed. Hearing a noise, Sheppard then ran downstairs. He saw a "form" leaving the house and chased it to the lake shore. Dr. Sheppard declared that he had grappled with the intruder on the beach, and had been again knocked unconscious.[69]

From the outset, Dr. Sheppard was treated as the prime suspect in the case. The coroner was reported to have told his men, "Well, it is evident the doctor did this, so let's go get the confession out of him.'" Sheppard, meanwhile, had been removed to a nearby clinic operated by his family. While under sedation, Sheppard was interrogated in his hospital room by the coroner. Later, on the afternoon of July 4, he was also questioned by Bay Village police, with one policeman telling Sheppard that lie detector tests were "infallible." This same policeman told Dr. Sheppard, " 'I think you killed your wife.' " Later that same afternoon, a physician sent by the coroner was permitted to make a careful examination of Sheppard.[70]

As early as July 7—the date of Marilyn Sheppard's funeral—a newspaper story appeared quoting a prosecuting attorney's criticism of the Sheppard family for refusing to permit his immediate questioning. On July 9, Sheppard re-enacted his recollection of the crime at his home at the request of the coroner. This re-enactment was covered by a group of newsmen which had apparently been invited by the coroner. Sheppard's performance was reported at length by the news media, including photographs.

[69] 384 U.S. 333, 335–336, 86 S.Ct. 1507, 1508–1509 (1966).

[70] 384 U.S. 333, 337–338, 86 S.Ct. 1507, 1509–1510 (1966).

Front-page headlines also emphasized Sheppard's refusal to take a lie-detector test.[71]

On July 20, 1954, newspapers began a campaign of front-page editorials. One such editorial charged that someone was "getting away with murder." The next day, another front-page editorial asked, "Why No Inquest?" A coroner's inquest was indeed held on that day in a school gymnasium. The inquest was attended by many newsmen and photographers, and was broadcast with live microphones stationed at the coroner's chair and at the witness stand. Sheppard had attorneys present during the three-day inquest, but they were not permitted to participate.[72]

The news media also quoted authorities' versions of the evidence before trial. Some of this "evidence"—such as a detective's assertion that " 'the killer washed off a trail of blood from the murder bedroom to the downstairs section' "—was never produced at the trial. Such a story, of course, contradicted Sheppard's version of what had happened in the early morning hours of July 4, 1954.[73]

The news media's activities also included playing up stories about Sheppard's extramarital love life, suggesting that these affairs were a motive for the murder of his wife. Although the news media repeatedly mentioned his relationship with a number of women, testimony taken at Sheppard's trial never showed that Sheppard had any affairs except the one with Susan Hayes.[74]

The Supreme Court of the United States, in Justice Tom C. Clark's majority opinion in the Sheppard case in 1966, summed up the news accounts in this way: [75]

> The publicity then grew in intensity until his indictment on August 17. Typical of the coverage during this period is a front-page interview entitled: "Dr. Sam: 'I Wish There Was Something I Could Get Off My Chest—but There Isn't.' " Unfavorable publicity included items such as a cartoon of the body of a sphinx with Sheppard's head and the legend below: " 'I Will Do Everything In My Power to Help Solve This Terrible Murder.'—Dr. Sam Sheppard." Headlines announced, *inter alia* [among other things], that: "Doctor Evidence is Ready for Jury," "Corrigan Tactics Stall Quizzing," "Sheppard 'Gay Set' Is Revealed by [Bay Village Mayor Spence] Houk," "Blood Is Found in Garage," "New Murder Evidence Is Found,

[71] 384 U.S. 333, 338, 86 S.Ct. 1507, 1510 (1966).
[72] 384 U.S. 333, 339, 86 S.Ct. 1507, 1510 (1966).
[73] 384 U.S. 333, 340, 86 S.Ct. 1507, 1511 (1966).
[74] 384 U.S. 333, 340–341, 86 S.Ct. 1507, 1511 (1966).
[75] 384 U.S. 333, 341–342, 86 S.Ct. 1507, 1511–1512 (1966).

Police Claim," "Dr. Sam Faces Quiz At Jail on Marilyn's Fear Of Him."

Although the record of Sheppard's trial included no excerpts from radio and television broadcasts, the Court assumed that coverage by the electronic media was equally extensive since space was reserved in the courtroom for representatives of those media.

Justice Clark also noted that the chief prosecutor of Sheppard was a candidate for common pleas judge and that the trial judge, Herbert Blythin, was a candidate for re-election. Furthermore, when 75 persons were called as prospective jurors, all three Cleveland newspapers published their names and addresses. All of the prospective jurors received anonymous letters and telephone calls, plus calls from friends, about the impending Sheppard trial.[76]

During the trial, pictures of the jury appeared more than 40 times in the Cleveland newspapers. And the day before the jury rendered its verdict of guilty against Dr. Sam Sheppard, while the jurors were at lunch in the company of two bailiffs, the jury was separated into two groups to pose for pictures which were published in the newspapers. The jurors, unlike those in the Estes case, were not sequestered ["locked up" under the close supervision of bailiffs]. Instead, the jurors were allowed to do what they pleased outside the courtroom while not taking part in the proceedings.[77]

The intense publicity given the Sheppard case in the news media continued unabated while the trial was actually in progress. Sheppard's attorneys took a "random poll" of persons of the streets asking their opinion about the osteopath's guilt or innocence in an effort to gain evidence for a change of venue. This poll was denounced in one newspaper editorial as smacking of "mass jury tampering" and stated that the bar association should do something about it.

A debate among newspaper reporters broadcast over radio station WHK in Cleveland contained assertions that Sheppard had admitted his guilt by hiring a prominent criminal lawyer. In another broadcast heard over WHK, columnist and radio-TV personality Robert Considine likened Sheppard to a perjuror. When Sheppard's attorneys asked Judge Blythin to question the jurors as to how many had heard the broadcast, Judge Blythin refused to do this. And when the trial was in its seventh week, a Walter Winchell broadcast available in Cleveland over both radio and television asserted that a woman under arrest in New York City for robbery had stated that she had been Sam Sheppard's mistress

---

[76] 384 U.S. 333, 342, 86 S.Ct. 1507, 1512 (1966).

[77] 384 U.S. 333, 345, 353, 86 S.Ct. 1507, 1513, 1517 (1966).

and had borne him a child. Two jurors admitted in open court that they had heard the broadcast. However, Judge Blythin merely accepted the jurors' statements that the broadcast would have no effect on their judgment and the judge accepted the replies as sufficient.[78]

When the case was submitted to the jury, the jurors were sequestered for their deliberations, which took five days and four nights. But this "sequestration" was not complete. The jurors had been allowed to call their homes every day while they stayed at a hotel during their deliberations. Telephones had been removed from the jurors' hotel rooms, but they were allowed to use phones in the bailiffs' rooms. The calls were placed by the jurors themselves, and no record was kept of the jurors who made calls or of the telephone numbers or of the persons called. The bailiffs could hear only the jurors' end of the telephone conversations.[79]

When Sheppard's case was decided by the Supreme Court of the United States in 1966, Justice Tom C. Clark's majority opinion included this ringing statement of the importance of the news media to the administration of justice.[80]

> The principle that justice cannot survive behind walls of silence has long been reflected in the "Anglo-American distrust for secret trials." A responsible press has always been regarded as the handmaiden of effective judicial administration, especially in the criminal field. Its function in this regard is documented by an impressive record of service over several centuries. The press does not simply publish information about trials but guards against the miscarriage of justice by subjecting the police, prosecutors, and judicial processes to extensive public scrutiny and criticism.

Implicit in some of Justice Clark's other statements in his opinion was deep disapproval of the news media's conduct before and during the Sheppard trial. But the news media were by no means the only culprits who made it impossible for Sheppard to get a fair trial. There was more than enough blame to go around, and Justice Clark distributed that blame among the deserving: news media, police, the coroner, and the trial court. The trial judge, Herbert Blythin, had died in 1960, but Justice Clark nevertheless spelled out what Judge Blythin should have done to protect the defendant.

At the outset of Sheppard's trial, Judge Blythin stated that he did not have the power to control publicity about the trial.

[78] 384 U.S. 333, 346, 348, 86 S.Ct. 1507, 1514–1515 (1966).

[79] 384 U.S. 333, 349, 86 S.Ct. 1507, 1515 (1966).

[80] 384 U.S. 333, 349–350, 86 S.Ct. 1507, 1515–1516 (1966).

Justice Clark declared that Judge Blythin's arrangements with the news media "caused Sheppard to be deprived of that 'judicial serenity and calm to which [he] was entitled.'" Justice Clark added that "bedlam reigned at the courthouse during the trial and newsmen took over practically the entire courtroom hounding most of the participants in the trial, especially Sheppard."[81] Justice Clark asserted: [82]

> The carnival atmosphere at trial could easily have been avoided since the courtroom and courthouse premises are subject to the control of the court. As we stressed in *Estes,* the presence of the press at judicial proceedings must be limited when it is apparent that the accused might otherwise be prejudiced or disadvantaged. Bearing in mind the massive pre-trial publicity, the judge should have adopted stricter rules governing the use of the courtroom by newsmen, as Sheppard's counsel requested. The number of reporters in the courtroom itself could have been limited at the first sign that their presence would disrupt the trial. They certainly should have not been placed inside the bar. Furthermore, the judge should have more closely regulated the conduct of newsmen in the courtroom. For instance, the judge belatedly asked them not to handle and photograph trial exhibits lying on the counsel table during recesses.

In addition, the trial judge should have insulated the jurors and witnesses from the news media, and "should have made some effort to control the release of leads, information, and gossip to the press by police officers, witnesses, and the counsel for both sides." [83]

The Judge's Role

The decision in the Sheppard case left its mark in the recommendations of the American Bar Association's "Reardon Report" discussed later in this chapter. The cases discussed in this chapter—*Irvin, Rideau, Estes,* and *Sheppard*—generated new law and suggested strongly that American courts may insist more and more on tighter controls over the information released to the news media in criminal trials by police, prosecution and defense attorneys, and by other employees under the control of the courts. The primary responsibility, however, for seeing to it that a defendant receives a fair trial, rests with the courts. Judges are expected to remain in control of trials in their courts.

[81] 384 U.S. 333, 355, 86 S.Ct. 1507, 1518 (1966).

[82] 384 U.S. 333, 358, 86 S.Ct. 1507, 1520 (1966).

[83] 384 U.S. 333, 359, 361, 86 S.Ct. 1507, 1521–1522 (1966).

A judge with great respect for the press, Frank W. Wilson of a U.S. District Court in Nashville, Tenn., wrote: "Certain it is that the press coverage of crimes and criminal proceedings make more difficult the job that a judge has of assuring a fair trial. But no one has yet shown that it renders the job impossible. In fact, no one has yet shown, to the satisfaction of any court, an identifiable instance of miscarriage of justice due to press coverage of a trial where the error was not remedied." [84]   Note that Judge Wilson said that it is the *judge's* job to assure a fair trial. Judge Wilson declared, "show me an unfair trial that goes uncorrected and I will show you a judge who has failed in his duty." [85]

Judge Wilson thus placed great—some would argue *too* great— [86] reliance upon the remedies which a judge can use to attempt to set things right for the defendant once he has received what the judge considers to be an undue amount of prejudicial publicity. Some of the most important of these trial-level "remedies" are outlined below:

(1) *Change of venue,* moving the trial to another area in hopes that jurors not prejudiced by mass media publicity or outraged community sentiment can be found. This "remedy," however, requires that a defendant give up his Sixth Amendment right to a trial in the "State and *district* wherein the crime shall have been committed * * *." [87]

(2) *Continuance or postponement.* This is simply a matter of postponing a trial until the publicity or public clamor abates. A problem with this "remedy" is that there is no guarantee that the publicity will not begin anew. It might be well to remember the axiom, "justice delayed is justice denied." A continuance in a case involving a major crime might mean that a defendant—even an innocent defendant—might thus be imprisoned for a lengthy time before his trial. A continuance means that a defendant gives up his Sixth amendment right to a *speedy* trial.

(3) *Voir dire* examination of potential jurors. This refers to the procedure by which each potential juror is questioned

[84] Frank A. Wilson, "A Fair Trial and a Free Press," presented at 33rd Annual convention of the Ohio Newspaper Association, Columbus, Ohio, Feb. 11, 1966.

[85] Ibid.

[86] Don R. Pember, Pretrial Newspaper Publicity in Criminal Proceedings: A Case Study (unpublished M.A. thesis, Michigan State University, East Lansing, Mich.) pp. 12–16.

[87] Constitution, Sixth Amendment, emphasis added; Lawrence E. Edenhofer, "The Impartial Jury—Twentieth Century Dilemma: Some Solutions to the Conflict Between Free Press and Fair Trial," Cornell Law Quarterly Vol. 51 (Winter, 1966) pp. 306, 314.

by opposing attorneys and may be dismissed "for cause" if the juror is shown to be prejudiced. (In addition, attorneys have a limited number of "peremptory challenges" which they can use to remove jurors who may appear troublesome to one side or the other. Professor Don R. Pember of the University of Washington says that the voir dire examination is an effective tool and one of the best available trial-level remedies.

(4) *Sequestration,* or "locking up" the jury. Judges have the power to isolate a jury, to make sure that community prejudices—either published or broadcast in the mass media or of the person-to-person variety—do not infect a jury with information during trial which might harm a defendant's chances for a fair trial by an impartial jury. As Professor Pember has said, judges are reluctant to do this today because of the complexities in the life of the average person.[88]

(5) *Contempt of Court.* This punitive "remedy" is discussed at length in Chapter 9. Courts have the power to cite for contempt those actions—either in court or out of court—which interfere with the orderly administration of justice. American courts—until the "gag order" controversies of recent years—have been reluctant to use the contempt remedy to punish pre-trial or during-trial publications. (See Section 92 of this chapter, on "restrictive" or "gag" orders.) Some critics of the American mass media would go even further: they would like to see the British system imported. That would mean using contempt of court citations as a weapon to halt media coverage of ongoing or pending criminal cases.

The British system of contempt citations to regulate media activities has worked well, according to some observers. The British press—knowing that the threat of a contempt citation hangs over it for a misstep—cannot quote from a confession (or even reveal its existence); nor can the British publish material—including previous criminal records—which would not be admissible evidence. One of the things about the British system which is most offensive to American journalists is the prohibition of a newspaper's making its own investigation and printing the results

---

[88] Another trial-level remedy which is more infrequently used is the blue-ribbon jury. When a case has received massive prejudicial publicity, a court may empower either the prosecution or the defense to impanel a special, so-called "blue ribbon" jury. Intelligent jurors are selected through the use of questionnaires and interviews, under the assumption that a more intelligent jury will be more likely to withstand pressures and remain impartial.

of it.   After the trial is concluded, *then* British newspapers can cover the trial.[89]

The *New York Times'* Anthony Lewis has suggested that the British system of using contempt citations to preclude virtually all comment on criminal cases simply could not work in the United States.   While some criminal trials in the United States drag on for years, even trials involving major crimes—including appeals— are usually completed in Britain in less than two months' time.[90] Anthony Lewis has also argued that Britain is a small, homogeneous nation where police or judicial corruption is virtually unknown.   America has not been so fortunate: occasionally corrupt policemen or judges are discovered, and perhaps the media's watchdog function is more needed in reporting on police and courts in this nation than it is in Britain.[91]

SEC. 91.   EXTERNAL GUIDELINES AND SELF–REGULATORY EFFORTS

An external regulatory threat—the fair trial reporting guidelines of the "Reardon Committee"—led to press-bar-bench efforts to agree to rules for covering the criminal justice process.

During the middle 1960s, the American Bar Association again got into the act in attempting to regulate prejudicial publicity.[92] As should be evident from preceding sections, there was plenty of pressure on the ABA to do something.   First, as noted earlier in Section 87, the Warren Commission investigating the assassination of President Kennedy had some harsh things to say about media coverage of the arrest of suspect Lee Harvey Oswald.[93] Then, there had been a chain of cases involving prejudicial publicity—Irvin v. Dowd (1961), [94] Rideau v. Louisiana (1963), [95] Estes v. Texas (1965) [96] and Sheppard v. Maxwell (1966).[97]   Although the

[89] Harold W. Sullivan, Trial by Newspaper (Hyannis, Mass., Patriot Press, 1961).

[90] New York Times, June 20, 1965.

[91] Ibid.

[92] Advisory Commitee on Fair Trial and Free Press, Standards Relating to Fair Trial and Free Press (New York, 1966); see also draft approved Feb. 19, 1968, by delegates to the ABA Convention as published in March, 1968.   For earlier ABA involvement in trying to come to terms with prejudicial publicity see ABA, "Report of Special Committee on Cooperation Between [sic] Press, Radio and Bar," Annual Report, Volume 62, pp. 851–866 (1937).

[93] Report of the President's Commission on the Association of President John F. Kennedy (Washington: Government Printing Office, 1964) p. 241.

[94] 366 U.S. 717, 81 S.Ct. 1639 (1961).

[95] 373 U.S. 723, 83 S.Ct. 1417 (1963).

[96] 381 U.S. 532, 85 S.Ct. 1628 (1965).

[97] 384 U.S. 333, 86 S.Ct. 1507 (1966).

[Attorney General Nicholas DeB.] Katzenbach Guidelines for federal courts and law enforcement officers had met with considerable approval, the ABA's concern continued. Early in 1968, the ABA Convention meeting in Chicago approved the "Standards Relating to Fair Trial and Free Press" recommended by the Advisory Committee headed by Massachusetts Supreme Court Justice Paul C. Reardon.[98] The "Reardon Report," as the document came to be known, was greeted with outraged concern by a large segment of the American media.[99] This report dealt primarily with things that attorneys and judges were *not* to say lest the rights of defendants be prejudiced. For example, if a defendant in a murder case had confessed before trial, that confession should not be revealed until duly submitted as evidence during an actual trial. Most frightening to the media, however, were suggestions that contempt powers be used against the media if they were to publish statements which could affect the outcome of a trial.

The Reardon Report touched off many press-bar meetings, seeking to reach voluntary guidelines on coverage of the criminal arrest, arraignment, hearing and trial process.[1] More than two dozen states adopted voluntary agreements based on conferences among judges, lawyers, and members of the media. States with such guidelines include Colorado, Kentucky, Massachusetts, Minnesota, New York, Oregon, Texas, Washington, and Wisconsin.

In such a setting—in the aftermath of the Warren Commission Report on the Kennedy assassination (which called for curtailment of pretrial news)—the *Sheppard* case came along to illustrate once again just how wretchedly prejudicial news coverage of a criminal trial could become. In that setting, the ABA Advisory Committee on Fair Trial—Free Press (Reardon Committee) was formed.[2]

In many places, a press-bar agreement occurred, leading to construction, by joint press-bar committees in roughly half of the states, of guidelines for the coverage of criminal trials.

[98] Advisory Committee on Fair Trial and Free Press (of the ABA), Approved Draft, op. cit.

[99] See, e.g., American Newspaper Publishers Association, Free Press and Fair Trial (New York: ANPA, 1967) p. 1 and passim.

[1] Advisory Committee on Fair Trial and Free Press, op. cit., 1966 and 1968; "Bar Votes to Strengthen Code on Crime Publicity," Editor & Publisher, Vol. 101 (Feb. 24, 1968) p. 9.

[2] J. Edward Gerald, "Press-Bar Relationships: Progress Since *Sheppard* and Reardon," Journalism Quarterly 47: 2 (Summer, 1970), p. 223. See, also, the Report of the President's Commission on the Association of President John F. Kennedy (1964), and Judicial Conference of the United States Committee on the Jury System, Report of the Committee on the Operation of the Jury Systems on the Free Press—Fair Trial Issue 1–3 (1968).

Wisconsin Fair Trial and Free Press
Principles and Guidelines

In Wisconsin, for example, informal rules titled "Wisconsin Fair Trial and Free Press Principles and Guidelines were drafted by a committee of lawyers and journalists in 1969. These guidelines were reworked and reissued in 1979 and in 1987 in response to changes brought about my cases such as Nebraska Press Association Stuart (1976) and pre–1987 free press-fair trial cases discussed earlier in this chapter.

These are *recommended* principles, for voluntary compliance, and the 1987 version emphasized that they are not binding on anyone. Further, and doubtless in some response to a Washington case which would have made voluntary guidelines mandatory as a condition for covering a trial, Wisconsin's 1987 guidelines specify that they are "not to be applied or used against anyone." [3]

The Wisconsin Guidelines, similarly to those of other states, ask for protection of criminal defendants' presumption of innocence as a shared responsibility among the judiciary, attorneys, news media, and law enforcement agencies. Both access to news of court proceedings and defendants' rights to a fair, unprejudiced trial are recognized as vital rights to be protected. The news media, which have a constitutional and statutory right to report on courts (subject to rare exceptions), and should strive for accuracy, balance, fairness and objectivity.

As to release of information in criminal trials, the guidelines say there should be no restraint on making available to the public, in criminal investigations, the following:

— Information in a public record.

— Information indicating that an investigation is in progress.

— Information on the general scope of an investigation, including a description of the offense.

Non-prejudicial information—such as the defendant's name, age, residence, and place of employment—may also be given, and the circumstances of the arrest may be described.

However, prejudicial information such as the existence of a purported confession, or a defendant's performance on tests related to a crime should not be reported.

[3] See Wisconsin News Reporter's Legal Handbook, 2nd ed. (1987), prepared by the Media–Law Relations Committee, State Bar of Wisconsin, in cooperation with the Wisconsin Broadcasters Assn. and the Wisconsin Newspaper Assn. The Washington case is Federated Publications v. Swedburg. See below at footnote 15.

Federated Publications v. Swedberg (1981)

Voluntary guidelines may become a two-edged sword. In fact, some states reworked their guidelines after the harsh lesson of Federated Publications v. Swedberg as decided by the Supreme Court of the State of Washington. Reworkings of the state guidelines were to re-emphasize their VOLUNTARY nature.

Judge Byron L. Swedberg presided over a trial involving charges of attempted murder. The case, in Whatcom County, north of Seattle, had great notoriety. It involved Veronica Lynn Compton, a woman reputedly the girlfriend of Kenneth Bianchi. Bianchi was known regionally and even nationally as the "Hillside Strangler."

Judge Swedberg refused to grant a defense motion in the case of State v. Compton which would have closed a pretrial hearing to the public. However, the judge conditioned media attendance at the trial upon reporters' signing an agreement to abide by the Washington Bench-Bar-Press Guidelines. Federated Publications, publishers of the Bellingham Herald, challenged Judge Swedberg's order.

The Washington guidelines were created as a voluntary document and had no legal force until Judge Swedberg incorporated them in his order. In that situation, the guidelines—if enforced—would, for example, have stopped the media from reporting on the defendant's previous criminal record or on the existence of a pretrial confession. In most cases, journalists will agree that pre-trial confessions should not be reported until officially accepted as evidence in court. However, situations could conceivably arise where the best judgment of journalists would be to include information about the existence of such a confession in pre-trial stories. As journalist Tony Mauro said in a Society of Professional Journalists Freedom of Information report in 1982,

> * * * [I]n a single stroke, Swedberg made suspect all the guidelines, developed in many instances only after years of delicate negotiations. Editors who were wary in the first place of sitting down with judges and lawyers were given new reasons to be suspicious—if we agree to talk about guidelines, the thinking went, someday they'll be used against us, as with Swedberg.

In upholding Judge Swedberg's ruling that members of the press must agree to abide by the Washington guidelines if so ordered by a judge, Justice Rosellini of the State of Washington's Supreme Court concluded that Swedberg's limitation was "reasonable." He compared the Swedberg situation to the Washington Supreme Court's holding in Federated Publications v. Kurtz. In the Kurtz case, the court held that the public has a right under the state and federal constitutions to have access to judicial proceedings, including pretrial hearings.

Justice Rosellini listed alternatives to closing a courtroom (see discussion of a similar list at page 660 of this Chapter: Continuance (delay), change of venue, change of venire, voir dire, and so forth). Those alternatives, Justice Rosellini wrote, "all involved some compromise of a right or interest of the accused or the State. None of the suggested alternatives involved the exercise of some restraint on the part of the media." He concluded that since his court had the power to exclude all of the public, including the media, he also had the power to impose reasonable conditions upon the media's attendance at a trial.[4]

SEC. 92.   RESTRICTIVE ORDERS AND REPORTING THE JUDICIAL PROCESS

After "gag orders" became a nationwide problem, Nebraska Press Association v. Stuart (1976) halted such prior restraints on the news media.

Bar-press guidelines such as those disclosed in the preceding sections tried to honor both the public's right to know about the judicial process and a defendant's right to a fair trial. Not all was well, however, despite the various meeting-of-minds between press and bar. Another disturbing counter-current was perceived during the late 1960s, starting mainly in California and involving judges issuing "restrictive" or "gag" orders in some cases.[5] In a Los Angeles County Superior Court in 1966, for example, a judge ordered the attorneys in a case, the defendants, the sheriff, chief of police, and members of the Board of Police Commissioners not to talk to the news media about the case in question. The order forbade "[r]eleasing or authorizing the release of any extrajudicial statements for dissemination by any means of public communication relating to the alleged charge or the Accused."

All that could be reported under such an order were the facts and circumstances of the arrest, the substance of the charge against the defendant, and the defendant's name, age, residence, occupation, and family status. If such an arrangement were to be worked out on a voluntary basis between press and bar, that

---

[4] Federated Publications, Inc. v. Swedberg, 96 Wash.2d 13, 633 P.2d 74, 75 (1981), 7 Med.L.Rptr. 1865, 1871, citing Federated Publications, Inc. v. Kurtz, 94 Wash.2d 51, 615 P.2d 440 (1980), 6 Med.L.Rptr. 1577. See also Tony Mauro, "Bench-media misunderstanding threatens press access to courts," FOI '82: A Report from the Society of Professional Journalists, p. 3.

[5] Robert S. Warren and Jeffrey M. Abell, "Free Press—Fair Trial: The 'Gag Order,' A California Aberration," Southern California Law Review 45:1 (Winter, 1972) pp. 51–99, at pp. 52–53.

might be one thing. However, the fact of a judge's *order*—a "gag rule"—worried some legal scholars, and with good reason.

In a New York case during 1971, Manhattan Supreme Court Justice George Postel, concerned about possibly prejudicial news accounts, called reporters into his chambers and laid down what he called "Postel's Law." The trial involved Carmine J. Persico, who had been charged with extortion, coercion, criminal usury ("loan sharking") and conspiracy. Justice Postel admonished the reporters not to use Persico's nickname ("The Snake") in their accounts and not to mention Persico's supposed connections with Joseph A. Columbo, Sr., a person said to be a leader of organized crime. The reporters, irked by Postel's declarations, reported what the judge had told them, including references to "The Snake" and to Columbo.

Persico's defense attorney then asked that the trial be closed to the press and to the public, and Judge Postel so ordered. However, the prosecutor—Assistant District Attorney Samuel Yasgur—complained that the order would set an unfortunate and dangerous precedent. For one thing, Yasgur declared, the absence of press coverage might mean that possible witnesses who could become aware of the trial through the media would remain ignorant of the trial and thus could not come forward to testify. Prosecutor Yasgur added:[6]

> But most importantly, Your Honor, as the Court has noted, the purpose of having press and the public allowed and present during the trial of a criminal case is to insure that defendants do receive an honest and a fair trial.

Newsmen appealed Judge Postel's order closing the trial to New York's highest court, the Court of Appeals. Chief Judge Stanley H. Fuld then ruled that the trial should not have been closed.[7]

> "Because of the vital function served by the news media in guarding against the miscarriage of justice by subjecting the police, prosecutors, and the judicial processes to extensive public scrutiny and criticism," the Supreme Court has emphasized that it has been "unwilling to place any direct limitations on the freedom traditionally exercised by the news media for '[w]hat transpires in the court room is public property.' "

Chief Judge Fuld added that courts should meet problems of prejudicial publicity not by declaring mistrials, but by taking

[6] *New York Times*, "Trial of Persico Closed to Public," pp. 1, 40, November 16, 1971.

[7] Oliver v. Postel, 30 N.Y.2d 171, 331 N.Y.S.2d 407, 414, 282 N.E.2d 306, 311 (1972).

careful preventive steps to protect their courts from outside inter-
ferences. In most cases, Judge Fuld suggested, a judge's caution-
ing jurors to avoid exposure to prejudicial publicity, or to disregard prejudicial material they had already seen or heard, would be
effective. In extreme situations, he said, a court might find it
necessary to sequester ("lock up") a jury for the duration of a
trial.[8]

Although reporters were ultimately vindicated in the *Postel*
case, a Louisiana case went against the press. This case, United
States v. Dickinson, arose when reporters Larry Dickinson and
Gibbs Adams of the Baton Rouge *Star Times* and the *Morning
Advocate* tried to report on a U.S. District Court hearing involving
a VISTA worker who had been indicted by a Louisiana state grand
jury on suspicion of conspiring to murder a state official. The
District Court hearing was to ascertain whether the state's prose-
cution was legitimate. In the course of this hearing, District
Court Judge E. Gordon West issued this order:

> "And, at this time, I do want to enter an order in the
> case, and that is in accordance with this Court's rule in
> connection with Fair Trial—Free Press provisions, the
> Rules of this Court.

> "It is ordered that no * * * report of the testimony
> taken in this case today shall be made in any newspaper
> or by radio or television, or by any other news media."

Reporters Dickinson and Adams ignored that order, and wrote
articles for their newspapers summarizing the day's testimony in
detail. After a hearing, Dickinson and Adams were found guilty
of criminal contempt and were sentenced to pay fines of $300 each.
Appealing to the Court of Appeals for the Fifth Circuit, the
reporters were told that the District Court judge's gag order was
unconstitutional.[9] They were not in the clear, however. The
Court of Appeals sent their case back to the District Court so that
the judge could reconsider the $300 fines. The judge again fined
the reporters $300 apiece, and they again appealed to the Court of
Appeals. This time, the contempt fines were upheld. The Fifth
Circuit Court declared that the reporters could have asked for a
rehearing or appealed against the judge's order not to publish.
Once the appeal was decided in their favor, the court evidently
reasoned, *then* they could publish.[10]

[8] Ibid. See, also, People of the State of New York v. Holder, 70 Misc.2d 31, 332
N.Y.S.2d 933 (1972), and Phoenix Newspapers Inc. v. Jennings, Justice of the
Peace, 107 Ariz. 557, 490 P.2d 563, 566–567 (1971).

[9] United States v. Dickinson, 465 F.2d 496, 514 (5th Cir.1972).

[10] 476 F.2d 373, 374 (5th Cir.1973); 349 F.Supp. 227 (M.D.La.1972). See also
James C. Goodale's "The Press 'Gag' Order Epidemic," Columbia Journalism
Review, Sept./Oct. 1973, pp. 49–50.

Attorney James C. Goodale—then vice president of the *New York Times*—was indignant.

It doesn't take much analysis to see that what the Court has sanctioned is the right of prior restraint subject to later appeal. * * * What this case means, in effect, is that when a judge is disposed to order a newspaper not to report matters that are transpiring in public he may do so, and a newsman's only remedy is to appeal or decide to pay the contempt penalty, be it a fine or imprisonment.

In the fall of 1973, the Supreme Court—evidently not seeing a major issue requiring its attention—refused to grant certiorari, thereby allowing the lower court decision to stand.[11] By 1976, however, the gag issue was an obvious problem. Attorney Jack C. Landau, Supreme Court reporter for the Newhouse News Service and a trustee of the Reporters Committee for Freedom of the Press, came up with some agonizing statistics. From 1966 to 1976, hundreds of restrictive orders were issued by courts against the news media.[12]

Nebraska Press Ass'n v. Stuart (1976)

Although the Supreme Court refused to hear the reporters' appeal in the Dickinson case [13]—thus allowing contempt fines against two reporters to stand—a virtual nationwide epidemic of restrictive orders quickly showed that the Baton Rouge case was no rarity.[14] A ghastly 1976 multiple-murder case in the hamlet of Sutherland, Neb. (population 840) was reported avidly by the mass media. This provided the Supreme Court with the factual setting which led to the Court's clamping down on the indiscriminate issuance of gag orders. The issue was stated succinctly by E. Barrett Prettyman, the attorney who represented the news media in Nebraska Press Association v. Stuart.[15]

The basic question before the Court is whether it is permissible under the First Amendment for a court to issue direct prior restraint against the press, prohibiting in advance of publication the reporting of information revealed in public court proceedings, in public court

[11] 414 U.S. 979, 94 S.Ct. 270 (1973), refusing certiorari in 465 F.2d 496 (5th Cir. 1972).

[12] Jack C. Landau, "The Challenge of the Communications Media," 62 American Bar Association Journal 55 (January, 1976).

[13] 414 U.S. 979, 94 S.Ct. 270 (1973).

[14] Landau, p. 57.

[15] "Excerpts from the Gag Order Arguments," Editor & Publisher, May 1, 1976, p. 46A.

records, and from other sources about pending judicial proceedings.

The nightmarish Nebraska case involved the murder of six members of one family, and necrophilia was involved. Police released the description of a suspect, 29-year-old Erwin Charles Simants, an unemployed handyman, to reporters who arrived at the scene of the crime. After a night of hiding, Simants walked into the house where he lived—next door to the residence where six had been slain—and was arrested.

Three days after the crime, the prosecuting attorney and Simants' attorney jointly asked the Lincoln County Court to enter a restrictive order. On October 22, 1975, the County Court granted a sweeping order prohibiting the release or publication of any "testimony given or evidence adduced * * * ".[16] On October 23, Simants' preliminary hearing was open to the public, but the press was subject to the restrictive order. On that same day, the Nebraska Press Association intervened in the District Court of Lincoln County and asked Judge Hugh Stuart to set aside the County Court's restrictive order. Judge Stuart conducted a hearing and on October 27 issued his own restrictive order, prohibiting the Nebraska Press Association and other organizations and reporters from reporting on five subjects: [17]

> (1) the existence or contents of a confession Simants had made to law enforcement officers, which has been introduced in open court at arraignment; (2) the fact or nature of statements Simants had made to other persons; (3) the contents of a note he had written the night of the crime; (4) certain aspects of the medical testimony at the preliminary hearing; (5) the identity of the victims of the alleged sexual assault and the nature of the assault.

This order also prohibited reporting the exact nature of the restrictive order itself, and—like the County Court's order—incorporated the Nebraska Bar-Press Guidelines.[18]

The Nebraska Press Association and its co-petitioners on October 31 asked the District Court to suspend its restrictive order and also asked that the Nebraska Supreme Court stop the gag order. Early in December, the state's Supreme Court issued a modification of the restrictive order "to accommodate the defendant's right to a fair trial and the petitioners' [i.e., the Nebraska Press Association, other press associations, and individual journal-

16 427 U.S. 539, 542, 96 S.Ct. 2791, 2795 (1976).

17 427 U.S. 539, 543–544, 96 S.Ct. 2791, 2795 (1976).

18 427 U.S. 539, 545, 96 S.Ct. 2791, 2796 (1976).

ists'] interest in reporting pretrial events." This modified order prohibited reporting of three matters: [19]

> (a) the existence and nature of any confessions or admissions made by the defendant to law enforcement officers; (b) any confessions or admissions made to any third parties, except members of the press, and (c) other facts "strongly implicative" of the accused.

The Nebraska Supreme Court did not reply on the Nebraska Bar-Press Guidelines. After interpreting state law to permit closing of court proceedings to reporters in certain circumstances, the Nebraska Supreme Court sent the case back to District Judge Hugh Stuart for reconsideration of whether pretrial hearings in the Simants case should be closed to the press and public. The Supreme Court of the United States granted certiorari.[20]

Writing for a unanimous Supreme Court, Chief Justice Burger reviewed free press-fair trial cases and prior restraint cases. He wrote: "None of our decided cases on prior restraint involved restrictive orders entered to protect a defendant's right to a fair and impartial jury, but the opinions on prior restraint have a common thread relevant to this case." The Chief Justice then quoted from Organization for a Better Austin v. Keefe: [21]

> "Any prior restraint on expression comes to this Court with a 'heavy presumption' against its constitutional validity. * * * Respondent [Keefe] thus carries a heavy burden of showing justification for the imposition of such a restraint. He has not met that burden. * * *"

Chief Justice Burger noted that the restrictive order at issue in the Simants case did not prohibit publication but only postponed it. Some news, he said, can be delayed and often is when responsible editors call for more fact-checking. "But such delays," he added, "are normally slight and they are self-imposed. Delays imposed by governmental authority are a different matter." [22]

The Court then turned to an examination of whether the threat to a fair trial for Simants was so severe as to overcome the presumption of unconstitutionality which prior restraints carry with them. The Chief Justice borrowed Judge Learned Hand's language (oft criticized by libertarians) from a case involving the trial of Communists in 1950: whether the "gravity of the evil," discounted by its improbability, justifies such invasion of free

[19] 427 U.S. 539, 545, 96 S.Ct. 2791, 2796 (1976).

[20] 423 U.S. 1027, 96 S.Ct. 557 (1975).

[21] 402 U.S. 415, 91 S.Ct. 1575 (1971).

[22] 427 U.S. 539, 560, 96 S.Ct. 2791, 2803 (1976).

speech as is necessary to avoid the danger.[23] The Court's review of the pretrial record in the Simants case indicated that Judge Stuart was justified in concluding that there would be intense and pervasive pretrial publicity. The judge could have concluded reasonably that the publicity might endanger Simants' right to a fair trial.

Even so, the restrictive order by the trial court judge was not justified in the view of the Supreme Court of the United States. Alternatives to prior restraint were not tried by the Nebraska trial court. Those alternatives included a change of venue; postponement of the trial to allow public furore to subside, and searching questioning of prospective jurors to screen out those who had already made up their minds about Simants' guilt or innocence. Sequestration ("locking up") of jurors would insulate jurors from prejudicial publicity only after they were sworn, but that measure "enhances the likelihood of dissipating the impact of pretrial publicity and emphasizes the elements of the jurors' oaths." The Chief Justice wrote: [24]

> * * * [P]retrial publicity, even if pervasive and concentrated, cannot be regarded as leading automatically and in every kind of criminal case to an unfair trial.
>
> * * *
>
> We reaffirm that the guarantees of freedom of expression are not an absolute prohibition under all circumstances, but the barriers to prior restraint remain high and the presumption against its use continues intact. We hold that, with respect to the order entered in this case prohibiting reporting or commentary on judicial proceedings held in public, the barriers have not been overcome; to the extent that this order restrained publication of such material, it is clearly invalid. To the extent that it prohibited publication based on information gained from other sources, we conclude that the heavy burden imposed as a condition to securing prior restraint was not met and the judgment of the Nebraska Supreme Court is therefore *reversed.*

Nebraska Press Association v. Stuart was hailed as a sizable victory for the news media. Nevertheless, some scholars were fretful about that decision's ultimate impact. Benno C. Schmidt, then a Columbia University law professor, found some "disturbing undertones." He expressed the fear that the [25]

---

[23] 427 U.S. 539, 562, 96 S.Ct. 2791, 2804 (1976).

[24] 427 U.S. 539, 565, 570, 96 S.Ct. 2791, 2804, 2806 (1976).

[25] Schmidt, "The Nebraska Decision," Columbia Journalism Review, November/December, 1976, p. 51.

* * * Court may have invited severe controls on the press's access to information about criminal proceedings from principals, witnesses, lawyers, the police, and others; it is even possible that some legal proceedings may be closed completely to the press and public as an indirect result of *Nebraska.*

He also worried that the Supreme Court's decision might encourage trial judges to place increasing reliance on stipulations that parties in a trial—lawyers, witnesses, police, etc.—not provide information in the press.

Schmidt was correct in his gloomy assessment of the Simants case; the so-called victory of the press in Nebraska Press Association was hollow. As former Washington Star editor Newbold Noyes has observed:[26]

It was Star Chamber, not publicity, that the founding fathers worried about. Defendants were guaranteed a public trial, not a cleared courtroom. The whole thrust of these amendments was—and must remain—that what happens in the courts happens out in the open, in full view of the citizenry, and that therein lies the individual's protection against the possible tyranny of government. There is no possible conflict between this idea and the idea of a free press.

Gagging Everybody But the Press?

Back in 1978, a trend then was discernible: gag news sources related to a judicial proceeding while leaving the press alone. The net result, of course, was much the same: a diminished flow of information about the judicial process. As trial courts close various courtroom proceedings, seal certain records, and decree that witnesses, attorneys and participants in trials do not speak to reporters, all that can be done is for the news media to fight back by going to court themselves. Noted First Amendment attorneys Dan Paul, Richard Ovelmen, James Spaniolo and Steven Kamp wrote late in 1984: "The most troubling trend in the cases decided during the last twelve months has been the use of gag orders on litigants and trial participants in order to block at the source public access to information concerning judicial proceedings." [27] The leading case? Seattle Times v. Rhinehart.[28]

[26] Speech at the University of Oregon, Ruhl Symposium Lectures, November 21, 1975, reprinted in "The Responsibilities of Power," School of Journalism, University of Oregon, June, 1976, pp. 16–17.

[27] Dan Paul, et al., op. cit., pp. 57–58.

[28] Seattle Times Co. v. Rhinehart, 467 U.S. 20, 104 S.Ct. 2199 (1984), 10 Med.L. Rptr. 1705.

Seattle Times v. Rhinehart (1984)

Keith Milton Rhinehart was the leader of a religious group, the Aquarian Foundation. The Seattle Times had published a number of stories about Rhinehart and the Foundation, a group with fewer than 1,000 members, believers in life after death and the ability to communicate with the dead. Rhinehart was the group's chief spiritual medium.[29] As Justice Powell described articles about Rhinehart in the Seattle Times and the Walla Walla Union-Bulletin: [30]

> One article referred to Rhinehart's conviction, later vacated, for sodomy. The four articles that appeared in 1978 concentrated on an "extravaganza" sponsored by Rhinehart at the Walla Walla State Penitentiary. The articles stated that he had treated 1,100 inmates to a 6-hour-long show, during which he gave away between $35,000 and $50,000 in cash and prizes. One article described a "chorus line of girls [who] shed their gowns and bikinis and sang * * *" The two articles that appeared in 1959 referred to a purported connection between Rhinehart and Lou Ferrigno, star of the popular television program, "The Incredible Hulk."

Rhinehart and five of the female members of the Aquarian Society who had taken part in the presentation at the penitentiary sued for libel and invasion of privacy, claiming that the stories were " 'fictional and untrue.' " They asked damages totalling $14.1 million.

As part of the pre-trial discovery proceedings, the defendant newspapers asked for information about the financial affairs of The Aquarian Foundation, including information on donors. The trial court judge issued a protective order [called a "gag order" by journalists] forbidding the Seattle Times from publishing pre-trial discovery information about the Aquarian Foundation's donors, members, and finances.[31]

A unanimous Supreme Court of the United States upheld the gag order preventing release and publication of deposition material. Writing for the Court, Justice Powell said: [32]

> * * * [I]t is necessary to consider whether the "practice in question [furthers] an important or substantial governmental interest unrelated to the suppression of

---

[29] 467 U.S. 20, 104 S.Ct. 2199, 2202 (1984), 10 Med.L.Rptr. 1705, 1706.

[30] Ibid.

[31] 467 U.S. 20, 104 S.Ct. 2199, 2204 (1984), 10 Med.L.Rptr. at 1707.

[32] 467 U.S. 20, 104 S.Ct. 2199, 2207 (1984), 10 Med.L.Rptr. at 1711.

expression" and whether "the limitation of First Amendment freedoms [is] no greater than necessary or essential to the protection of the particular governmental interest involved." Procunier v. Martinez, 415 U.S. 396, 413, 94 S.Ct. 1800, 1811 (1974) * * *.

* * *

A litigant has no First Amendment right of access to information made available only for purposes of trying his suit. * * * Moreover, pretrial depositions and interrogatories are not public components of a civil trial.

Attorney Dan Paul and co-authors were unconvinced by that reasoning. They wrote: [33]

> None of these reasons is persuasive. First Amendment cases have uniformly recognized that once the press has information in hand, by whatever lawful means, any prohibition on publication is a prior restraint.

Prior Restraint Revisited:
CNN and the Noriega Tapes

The prosecution of Panamanian dictator Manuel Antonio Noriega during 1991 showed that judicial prior restraint still could occur. Although Nebraska Press Association v. Stuart (see text, above) still is regarded as a major bulwark against prior censorship by judges, the bizarre Noriega Tapes case showed that courts, on occasion, still can crack the prior restraint whip.

General Noriega, of course, was a most unusual suspect. Taken into custody after a massive U.S. deployment of armed forces, Noriega took sanctuary in a Vatican consulate. After several days of listening to American rock music played by troops surrounding the Vatican property, General Noriega surrendered. He was then spirited away to a well-appointed jail cell in Florida (outfitted with TV, telephone, and even a paper shredder). (Concerns about a fair trial for a foreign head of state who surrendered after a potent military attack seemed strained: Could a U.S. court *really* find a jury of his peers?)

Suspicion grew that the last thing the U.S. government wanted after Noriega survived the attack on Panama was to get the ex-dictator on the stand where he could sing about his former chums at the Central Intelligence Agency (CIA). In any event, someone got hold of tape recordings of Noriega's Florida jail-cell calls to the office of his attorney, Frank Rubino. The tapes, which Rubino claimed were evidence of a government plot to spy on Noriega's

---

[33] Dan Paul et al., op. cit., p. 59.

legal defense plans, were given to the Cable News Network (CNN).[34]

After CNN announced that it had the tapes, U.S. District Judge William Hoeveler, on November 8, 1990, granted defense attorneys' request for an injunction to prevent CNN's broadcast of the tapes. Although CNN broadcast no taped excerpts of conversations between the general and his attorneys, excerpts of Noriega's calls to others were broadcast.

Judge Hoeveler evidently saw CNN's eagerness to use the tapes as raising two Sixth Amendment questions: Violation of the attorney-client privilege and the possibility of revealing information harmful to Noriega's defense. Even though Judge Hoeveler noted that prior restraints are "presumptively unconstitutional," he held that the barrier laid down by a three-part test in Nebraska Press Association v. Stuart was not insurmountable. The *Nebraska Press* test for justifing prior restraint to prevent prejudicial publicity requires that: [35]

1. Publicity must impair the right to a fair trial.

2. No less restrictive alternative to prior restraint is available or practicable to mitigate effects of the publicity, and

3. A prior restraint would effectively prevent the harm to defendant's rights.

Judge Hoeveler found that in this instance, prior restraint was justifiable, and ordered a temporary injunction against CNN's broadcast of the tapes until the court could review the tapes in CNN's possession. The following day—Nov. 9, 1990—after an emergency appeal by CNN to the Eleventh Circuit Court of Appeals, Judge Hoeveler limited the temporary injunction to ten days. He complained about CNN's refusal to turn over the tapes to him, putting him in the position of having to make rulings without having heard them.

The next day—Nov. 10, 1990—the Court of Appeals ruled that the temporary restraining order should remain in effect. The appellate court upheld Judge Hoeveler's injunction against CNN and his demand for production of the tapes.[36] Meanwhile, CNN indeed had been defiant, for it had broadcast—on Nov. 9—a taped conversation said to be an interchange between Noriega and a legal secretary working for his attorneys. Noriega's attorneys

[34] "Tales of the Tape," Newsweek, Dec. 17, 1990, p. 29; "Eavesdropping on Noriega," Newsweek, Nov. 19, 1990.

[35] U.S. v. Noriega, 18 Med.L.Rptr. 1348, 1349 (D.C., S.D.Fla., Nov. 8 & 9, 1990).

[36] In re Cable News Network, Inc., 18 Med.L.Rptr. 1352, 1358 (11th Cir., 1990.)

asked for dismissal of the charges against their client and that CNN be fined $300,000 each time it played one of the tapes.[37]

CNN then withdrew a bit, agreeing on Nov. 12 to halt playing the tapes until the U.S. Supreme Court could rule. Noriega contended that he was being railroaded and was powerless before an unjust legal system.[38]

On Nov. 18, 1990, moving swiftly only eight days after the Court of Appeals ruling against CNN, the U.S. Supreme Court upheld the injunction, denying CNN's petition for a writ of certiorari.[39]

After this defeat, CNN handed over the Noriega tapes to a federal magistrate who reported his evaluation of the tapes to U.S. District Judge Hoeveler. Anticlimactically, Judge Hoeveler ruled that CNN could broadcast the taped conversations. CNN, however, decided not to put the tapes on the air . . . at least, not immediately.[40] The New York Times confessed to being puzzled by CNN's behavior: Challenging a U.S. district judge, ultimately getting his permission to run the tapes, and then not doing so. A *Times* editorial said:[41]

> The network's actions and news judgments obscure the important feature of its own story. The existence, not the airing, of some tapes requires explanation from the [U.S.] Justice Department. What safeguards [for defendant Noriega] were in place at Miami's Metropolitan Correction Center and how were they violated?

SEC. 93. ACCESS TO CRIMINAL TRIALS AND CIVIL MATTERS

Gannett v. DePasquale (1979) declared that *pre-trial* matters could be closed to press and public; Richmond Newspapers v. Virginia (1980) held that there is a First Amendment right to attend *trials*.

The Supreme Court had some good news for the press in 1978, and it came in the decision in Landmark Communications, Inc. v. Virginia. The Virginian Pilot, a daily newspaper owned by Landmark, late in 1975 published an accurate article reporting on

[37] "CNN to Delay Playing of Noriega Tapes," The New York Times, Nov. 13, 1990, p. A12.

[38] Ibid.; see also David Johnston, "Noriega Tells Judge He's at Mercy of an Unfair and Unjust System," The New York Times, Nov. 17, 1990, p. 1.

[39] Cable News Network, Inc. v. Noriega, ___ U.S. ___, 111 S.Ct. 451, 18 Med.L. Rptr. 1358, 1359 (1990).

[40] David Johnston, "Judge Lifts Ban on Noriega Tapes; No Broadcast is Planned," The New York Times, Nov. 29, 1990, p. A14.

[41] "Odd Behavior in the Noriega Case," The New York Times, Dec. 1, 1990, p. 14.

a pending investigation by the Virginia Judicial Inquiry and Review Commission. The article named a state judge whose conduct was being investigated. Because such proceedings were required to be confidential by the Constitution of Virginia and by related enabling statutes, a grand jury indicted Landmark for violating Virginia law.

The newspaper's managing editor, Joseph W. Dunn, Jr., testified that he had chosen to publish material about the Judicial Inquiry and Review Commission because he believed the subject was a matter of public importance. Dunn stated that although he knew it was a misdemeanor for participants in such an action to divulge information from that Commission's proceedings, he did not think that the statute applied to newspaper reports.[42]

Chief Justice Burger, writing for a unanimous Court, said the issue was whether the First Amendment allows criminal punishment of third persons—including news media representatives—who publish truthful information about proceedings of the Judicial Inquiry and Review Commission. The Court concluded that "the publication Virginia seeks to punish under its statute lies near the core of the First Amendment, and the Commonwealth's interests advanced by the imposition of criminal sanctions are insufficient to justify the actual and potential encroachments on freedom of speech and of the press."

Although the Commission was entitled to meet in secret, and could preserve confidentiality of its proceedings and working papers, the press could not be punished for publication of such information once it has obtained it.[43]

Obtaining information about judicial proceedings, of course, implies access by public and press to those proceedings. And then, after the "good news" of *Landmark Communications* (1978), along came one of the Supreme Court's unpleasant surprises for the press: Gannett v. DePasquale.

Gannett v. DePasquale (1979)

Journalists are taught that government should never be given the power of secret arrest, secret confinement, or secret trial. With its decision in Gannett v. DePasquale, the Supreme Court of the United States said, in effect, that two out of three aren't bad. In a badly fragmented 5–4 vote, with a total of five opinions written, the Court held that the public—including the press—has no right to attend pretrial hearings. The issue in *DePasquale* was narrow: the Gannett Company was seeking to overturn a ruling

---

[42] Landmark Communications, Inc. v. Virginia, 435 U.S. 829, 98 S.Ct. 1535 (1978).

[43] 435 U.S. 829, 838, 98 S.Ct. 1535, 1541 (1978).

barring its reporter from a pretrial hearing and forbidding the immediate release of a transcript of a secret hearing.

The Court's majority, however, did not restrict itself to pretrial hearings. Justice Potter Stewart's majority opinion also declared that the rights guaranteed by the Sixth Amendment did not extend to the public or to the press. Instead, those rights "are personal to the accused. * * * We hold that members of the public [and thus the press] have no constitutional right to attend criminal trials." Joining Justice Stewart in that view were Justices William Rehnquist and John Paul Stevens.

Chief Justice Warren E. Burger joined the opinion of the Court, but argued that by definition, a " * * *; hearing on a motion before trial is not a *trial:* it is a *pre* trial hearing." Mr. Justice Lewis Powell, like the Chief Justice, concurred separately. Justice Powell expressed the belief that the reporter had an interest protected by the First Amendment to attend the pretrial hearing. However, he added that this right of access to courtroom proceedings is not absolute and must be balanced against a defendant's Sixth Amendment fair trial rights. In his concurring opinion, Justice William Rehnquist said that so far as the Constitution is concerned, it is up to the lower courts, "by accommodating competing interests in a judicious manner," to decide whether to open or close a court proceeding.

In a 44-page dissent joined by Justices William Brennan, Byron White, and Thurgood Marshall, Justice Harry Blackmun contended that the Sixth Amendment guarantees the public's right to attend hearings and trials. Justice Blackmun wrote that the Court's majority overreacted to "placid, routine, and innocuous" coverage of a criminal prosecution.

Gannett v. DePasquale arose when 42-year-old former policeman Wayne Clapp did not return from a July, 1976, fishing trip on upstate New York's Lake Seneca. He had been fishing with two men, aged 16 and 21, and those men returned in the boat without Clapp and drove away in Clapp's pickup truck. They were later arrested in Michigan after Clapp's disappearance had been reported and after bullet holes were found in Clapp's boat.

Gannett newspapers, the morning *Democrat & Chronicle* and the evening *Times-Union,* published stories about Clapp's disappearance and reported on police speculations that Clapp had been shot on his own boat and his body dumped overboard. In one story, the *Democrat & Chronicle* reported that the 16-year-old suspect, Kyle Greathouse, had led Michigan police to a place where he had buried Clapp's .357 magnum revolver. Defense attorneys then began taking steps to try to suppress statements made to police, claiming that those statements had been given involuntarily. The defense also tried to suppress evidence turned up in relation to the allegedly involuntary confessions, including the pistol.

During a pretrial hearing, when defense attorneys requested that press and public be excluded, Justice Daniel DePasquale granted the motion, evidently fearing that reporting on the hearing might prejudice defendants' rights in a later trial. Neither the prosecution nor reporter Carol Ritter of the *Democrat & Chronicle* objected to the clearing of the courtroom. On the next day, however, Ritter wrote Judge DePasquale, asserting a right to cover the hearing and asking to be given access to the transcript. The judge, refused to rescind his exclusion order or to grant the press or public immediate access to a transcript of the pre-trial hearing. Judge DePasquale's orders were overturned by an intermediate-level New York appeals court, but were upheld by the state's highest court, the Court of Appeals.[44] The Supreme Court of the United States subsequently granted certiorari.[45]

Although the issue of covering a pretrial hearing on suppression of evidence is technically narrow, it is important. As James C. Goodale, former vice president of *The New York Times,* has written: [46]

> Only a fraction of the criminal cases brought ever go to trial. The real courtroom for most criminal trials in the United States is the pre-trial hearing, where proceedings of a vital public concern often take place. * * * [A] successful suppression motion will probably mean that an account of the improper methods the police have used to extract a certain confession will be brought out only at the pretrial hearing, and nowhere else. * * * [T]his is information which the public needs to have if its public officers are to be held accountable. Without multiplying examples, we need only remember the shocking trials of Ginzburg and Scharansky behind closed doors in Russia in the summer of 1978 to realize that criminal trials in this country must remain open.

Other constitutional scholars and a variety of publications expressed both shock and outrage at the Supreme Court's decision in *DePasquale.* Fear of secret trials is in the American grain. Even though England's despised secret Court of the Star Chamber was abolished in 1641, it has been remembered as a symbol of

[44] Gannett Co., Inc. v. De Pasquale, 43 N.Y.2d 370, 401 N.Y.S.2d 756, 372 N.E.2d 544 (1977), reversing the Supreme Court of the State of New York, Appellate Division, Fourth Department's decision in 55 A.D.2d 107, 389 N.Y.S.2d 719 (1976).

[45] 443 U.S. 368, 99 S.Ct. 2898 (1979).

[46] James C. Goodale, "Open Justice: The Threat of *Gannett,*" Communications and the Law, Vol. 1, No. 1 (Winter, 1979) pp. 12–13.

persecution ever since. The assumption by both public and press has long been that open trials are needed to make sure that justice is done. Harvard Law Professor Lawrence Tribe, a leading scholar, said after *DePasquale* was decided that there " ' * * * will be no need to gag the press if stories can be choked off at the source.' " Allen Neuharth, chairman of The Gannett Co., Inc., declared that " ' * * * those judges who share the philosophy of secret trials can now run Star Chamber justice.' " [47] In any event, the *DePasquale* holding was far removed from Justice William O. Douglas's words in a 1947 contempt of court case, Craig v. Harney: "[w]hat transpires in the court room is public property." [48]

Justice Potter Stewart wrote for the Court: [49]

* * *

Publicity concerning pretrial suppression hearings such as the one involved in the present case poses special risks of unfairness. The whole purpose of such hearings is to screen out unreliable or illegally obtained evidence and insure that this evidence does not become known to the jury. Cf. Jackson v. Denno, 378 U.S. 368, 84 S.Ct. 1774 (1964). Publicity concerning the proceedings at a pretrial hearing, however, could influence public opinion against a defendant and inform potential jurors of inculpatory information wholly inadmissible at the actual trial.

* * *

The Sixth Amendment, applicable to the States through the Fourteenth, surrounds a criminal trial with guarantees such as the rights to notice, confrontation, and compulsory process that have as their overriding purpose the protection of the accused from prosecutorial and judicial abuses. Among the guarantees that the Amendment provides to a person charged with the commission of a criminal offense, and to him alone, is the "right to a speedy and public trial, by an impartial jury." The Constitution nowhere mentioned any right of access to a criminal trial on the part of the public; its guarantee, like the others enumerated, is personal to the accused. See Faretta v. California, 422 U.S. 806, 846, 95 S.Ct. 2525, 2546 (1975) ("[T]he specific guarantees of the Sixth Amendment are personal to the accused.") (Blackmun, J., dissenting).

[47] "Slamming the Courtroom Doors," Time, July 16, 1979, p. 66.

[48] Craig v. Harney, 331 U.S. 367, 374, 67 S.Ct. 1249, 1254 (1947).

[49] Gannett Co., Inc. v. DePasquale, 443 U.S. 368, 378–381, 99 S.Ct. 2898, 2905–2906 (1979).

Our cases have uniformly recognized the public trial guarantee as one created for the benefit of the defendant.

Chief Justice Burger's concurring opinion simply maintained that by definition, a hearing on a motion before trial to suppress evidence is not a *trial*, it is a *pre-trial* hearing. Trials should be open, but pre-trial proceedings are "private to the litigants" and could be closed.

Justice Powell's concurrence argued that the reporter had an interest protected by the First and Fourteenth Amendments in being present at the pretrial suppression hearing. He added: [50]

As I have argued in Saxbe v. Washington Post Co., 417 U.S. 843, 850, 94 S.Ct. 2811, 2815 (1974) (Powell, J., dissenting), this constitutional protection derives, not from any special status of members of the press as such, but rather because "[i]n seeking out the news the press * * * acts as an agent of the public at large," each individual member of which cannot obtain for himself "the information needed for the intelligent discharge of his political responsibilities." Id., at 863, 94 S.Ct., at 2821.

Justice Powell then swung into his balancing act, stating that the right of access to courtroom proceedings is not absolute. It is limited by both the right of defendants to a fair trial and by needs of governments to obtain convictions and to maintain the confidentiality of sensitive information and of the identity of informants. In his view, representatives of the public and the press must be given an opportunity to protest closure motions. Then it would be the defendant's burden to offer evidence that the fairness of his trial would be jeopardized by public and press access to the proceedings. On the other hand, the press and public should have to show that alternative procedures are available which would take away dangers to the defendant's chances of receiving a fair trial.[51]

Justice Rehnquist's concurring opinion scoffed that Justice Powell was advancing the idea " * * * that the First Amendment is some sort of constitutional 'sunshine law' that requires notice, an opportunity to be heard and substantial reasons before a governmental proceeding may be closed to public and press." [52]

Justice Blackmun's lengthy dissent was joined by Justices Brennan, White, and Marshall. Blackmun termed the news coverage of this case "placid, routine, and innocuous" and, indeed,

[50] 443 U.S. 368, 397–398, 99 S.Ct. 2898, 2914 (1979).

[51] 443 U.S. 368, 398–399, 99 S.Ct. 2898, 2915 (1979).

[52] 443 U.S. 368, 405, 99 S.Ct. 2898, 2918 (1979).

relatively infrequent. After a long review of Anglo-American historical and constitutional underpinnings for public trials, he pointed to dangers he saw in closing court proceedings.[53]

> I, for one, am unwilling to allow trials and suppression hearings to be closed with no way to ensure that the public interest is protected. Unlike the other provisions of the Sixth Amendment, the public trial interest cannot adequately be protected by the prosecutor and judge in conjunction, or connivance, with the defendant. The specter of a trial or suppression hearing where a defendant of the same political party as the prosecutor and the judge—both of whom are elected officials perhaps beholden to the very defendant they are to try—obtains closure of the proceeding without any consideration for the substantial public interest at stake is sufficiently real to cause me to reject the Court's suggestion that the parties be given complete discretion to dispose of the public's interest as they see fit. The decision of the parties to close a proceeding in such a circumstance, followed by suppression of vital evidence or acquittal by the bench, destroys the appearance of justice and undermines confidence in the judicial system in a way no subsequent provision of a transcript might remedy. ＊ ＊ ＊

III

＊ ＊ ＊

> On this record, I cannot conclude, as a matter of law, that there was sufficient showing to establish the strict and inescapable necessity that supports an exclusion order. The circumstances also would not have justified a holding by the trial court that there was a substantial probability that alternatives to closure would not have sufficed to protect the rights of the accused.

> It has been said that publicity "is the soul of justice." J. Bentham, A Treatise on Judicial Evidence, 67 (1825). And in many ways it is: open judicial processes, especially in the criminal field, protect against judicial, prosecutorial, and police abuse; provide a means for citizens to obtain information about the criminal justice system and the performance of public officials; and safeguard the integrity of the courts. Publicity is essential to the preservation of public confidence in the rule of law and in the operation of courts.

[53] 443 U.S. 368, 438–439, 448, 99 S.Ct. 2898, 2935–2936, 2940 (1979).

Richmond Newspapers v. Virginia (1980)

On July 2, 1980—exactly one year after the Supreme Court of the United States ruled in Gannett Co., Inc. v. DePasquale [54] that pretrial hearings could be closed—the Court held 7-1 that the public and the press have a First Amendment right to attend criminal trials. The 1980 case, Richmond Newspapers, Inc. v. Virginia, brought joyous responses from the press.

Anthony Lewis of *The New York Times* wrote, "For once a Supreme Court decision deserves that overworked adjective, historic." [55] His newspaper editorialized: "Now the Supreme Court has reasserted the obvious, at least as it pertains to trials. 'A presumption of openness inheres in the very nature of a criminal trial under our system of justice.' " [56] Even though *Richmond Newspapers* did not overrule *Gannett* where pretrial matters are concerned, the Court's 1980 reliance on the First Amendment— and not on the Sixth Amendment as in *Gannett*—gave hope to journalists.

In fact, if Justice John Paul Stevens was correct in his concurring opinion in *Richmond Newspapers*, "This is a watershed case." He continued, [57]

> Until today the Court has accorded virtually absolute protection to the dissemination of information or ideas, but never before has it squarely held that the acquisition of newsworthy matter is entitled to any constitutional protection whatsoever.

Lewis said " * * * the Court today established for the first time that the Constitution gives the public a right to learn how public institutions function: a crucial right in a democracy." [58] Attorney James Goodale said the Richmond case will help reporters to see " 'prisons, small-town meetings, the police blotter' " and other places and documents often closed to the news media in the past.

Years ago, Judge Learned Hand described his career on the bench as "shoveling smoke." In 1979, the Supreme Court unlimbered its smoke generator in the infamous *Gannett* case, ruling by a 5-4 margin that the public and the press did not have a right to attend pre-trial proceedings in criminal cases. Some of the

[54] 443 U.S. 368, 99 S.Ct. 2898 (1979).

[55] Anthony Lewis, "A Right To Be Informed," The New York Times, July 3, 1980, p. A–19.

[56] Editorial, "Wiping the Graffiti Off the Courtroom," The New York Times, July 3, 1980, p. A–18.

[57] Opinion of Mr. Justice Stevens, 448 U.S. 555, 581, 100 S.Ct. 2814, 2830 (1980).

[58] Lewis, loc. cit.

Justices' language billowed beyond pre-trial matters. As noted, Justice Potter Stewart's plurality opinion announcing the Court's judgment in *Gannett* declared that rights guaranteed by the Sixth Amendment did not reach to the public or to the press. Those rights, said Stewart, " * * * are personal to the accused. * * * We hold that members of the public [and thus the press] have no constitutional right to attend criminal trials." [59]

Four members of the Court later made public statements professing shock about the way *Gannett* had been "misinterpreted," and that wholesale closings had not been endorsed by a majority of the Court. Howls of protest arose from the media. Goodale, then executive vice president of *The New York Times*, wrote in 1979 that only a small fraction—perhaps 10 per cent—of all criminal cases reach the trial stage. The real courtroom for most criminal proceedings is the pre-trial hearing. [60]

In the wake of *Gannett*, many pretrial *and* trial proceedings were closed. As a study by The Reporters Committee for Freedom of the Press showed, in the 10 months between the *Gannett* decision of July 2, 1979 and April 30, 1980, there were at least 220 attempts to close criminal justice proceedings. More than half were successful. Jack C. Landau, director of The Reporters Committee, wrote that "[j]udges are closing pre-indictment, trial, and post-trial proceedings, in addition to pre-trial proceedings." [61] *Newsweek* reported that in the year after *Gannett*, 155 proceedings were closed, including 30 actual trials. Four hundred attempts were made to close courtrooms between July, 1979, and May, 1981. [62]

The Richmond case arose when Baltimore resident John Paul Stevenson was convicted of second-degree murder in the slaying of a Hanover County, Virginia, motel manager. In late 1977, however, the Virginia Supreme Court reversed Stevenson's conviction, concluding that a bloodstained shirt belonging to Stevenson had been admitted improperly as evidence. [63] Subsequently, two additional jury trials of Stevenson ended in mistrials, one when a juror had to be excused and the other because a prospective juror may have read about the defendant's previous trials and may have told other jurors about the case before the retrial began.

On September 11, 1978, the same court—for the fourth time—attempted to try Stevenson. Reporters Tim Wheeler of the *Rich-*

[59] Gannett Co., Inc. v. DePasquale, 443 U.S. 368, 99 S.Ct. 2898 (1979).

[60] Goodale, loc. cit.

[61] The Reporters Committee for Freedom of the Press, Court Watch Summary, May, 1980; Southern Newspaper Publishers Association Bulletin, Aug. 10, 1981.

[62] Newsweek, July 14, 1980, p. 24.

[63] Stevenson v. Commonwealth, 218 Va. 462, 237 S.E.2d 779 (1977).

mond Times-Dispatch and Kevin McCarthy of the *Richmond News-Leader,* along with all other members of the public, were barred from the courtroom by Hanover County Circuit Court Judge Richard H.C. Taylor, after defense counsel said: [64]

> "[T]here was this woman that was with the family of the deceased when we were here before. She had sat in the Courtroom. I would like to ask that everybody be excluded from the Courtroom because I don't want any information being shuffled back and forth when we have a recess as to what—who testified to what."

Trial Judge Taylor had presided after two of the previous three trials of Stevenson. After hearing that the prosecution had no objection to the closure, excluded all parties from the trial except witnesses when they testified.[65] Since no one—including reporters Wheeler and McCarthy—had objected to closure, the order was made. Later that same day, however, the Richmond newspapers and their reporters asked for a hearing on a motion to vacate the closure order. Reporters were not allowed to attend the hearing on that order, however, since Judge Taylor ruled that it was a part of the trial. The closure order remained in force.

On the trial's second day, Judge Taylor—after excusing the jury—declared that Stevenson was not guilty of murder, and the defendant was allowed to leave. The Richmond Newspapers then appealed the court closing, unsuccessfully petitioning the Virginia Supreme Court for writs of mandamus and prohibition. The Supreme Court of the United States granted certiorari.

Chief Justice Burger's Opinion

Chief Justice Warren Burger reiterated his view, as stated in Gannett v. DePasquale, that while pre-trial hearings need not be open, trials should be open. In this case, he did not take the Sixth Amendment (right to fair trial) route of the majority in *DePasquale.* [66] Instead, he emphasized that the question in *Richmond Newspapers* [67] was whether the First and Fourteenth Amendments guarantee a right of the public (including the press) to attend trials.

[64] Opinion of Chief Justice Burger, Richmond Newspapers, Inc. v. Virginia, 448 U.S. 555, 559, 100 S.Ct. 2814, 2818 (1980).

[65] Virginia Code § 19.2–2.66, which provided that courts may, in their discretion, exclude any persons from the trial whose presence would impair the trial's conduct, provided that the right of an accused to a fair trial shall not be violated.

[66] Gannett Co., Inc. v. DePasquale, 443 U.S. 368, 99 S.Ct. 2898 (1979).

[67] Richmond Newspapers, Inc. v. Virginia, 448 U.S. 555, 564, 100 S.Ct. 2814, 2821 (1980).

He said that in prior cases, the Court has dealt with questions involving conflicts between publicity and defendants' rights to a fair trial, including Nebraska Press Association v. Stuart,[68] Sheppard v. Maxwell,[69] and Estes v. Texas.[70] But this case, in his view, was a "first:" the Court was asked to decide whether a criminal trial itself may be closed to the public on the defendant's request alone, with no showing that closure is required to protect the right to a fair trial.

After having thus stated the issue, the Chief Justice traced Anglo-American judicial history back to the days before the Norman Conquest and forward through the American colonial experience.[71] In addition to this historical ammunition, Burger quoted Dean Wigmore, who wrote long ago that " '[t]he publicity of a judicial proceeding is a requirement of much broader bearing than its mere effect on the quality of testimony.' " The Chief Justice also found a "significant community therapeutic value" in public trials. He then became expansive about the role of the press as a stand-in for the public, a role often claimed by the press but one which had received little judicial support.[72]

> Looking back, we see that when the ancient "town meeting" form of trial became too cumbersome, twelve members of the community were delegated to act as surrogates, but the community did not surrender its right to observe the conduct of trials. The people retained a "right of visitation" which enabled them to satisfy themselves that justice was in fact being done.

> People in an open society do not demand infallibility from their institutions, but it is difficult for them to accept what they are prohibited from observing.

> * * *

> In earlier times, both in England and America, attendance at court was a common mode of "passing the time." * * * With the press, cinema and electronic media now supplying the representations of reality of the real life drama once available only in the courtroom, attendance at court is no longer a widespread pastime. * * * Instead of acquiring information about trials by firsthand observation or by word of mouth from those

[68] 427 U.S. 539, 96 S.Ct. 2791 (1976).

[69] 384 U.S. 333, 86 S.Ct. 1507 (1966).

[70] 381 U.S. 532, 85 S.Ct. 1628 (1965). The Chief Justice also cited Murphy v. Florida, 421 U.S. 794, 95 S.Ct. 2031 (1975), in which Jack (Murph the Surf) Murphy, unsuccessfully pleaded that prejudicial pre-trial publicity had deprived him of a fair day in court.

[71] Richmond Newspapers, Inc. v. Virginia, 448 U.S. 555, 100 S.Ct. 2814 (1980).

[72] 448 U.S. 555, 572–573, 100 S.Ct. 2814, 2354–2355 (1980).

who attended, people now acquire it chiefly through the print and electronic media. In a sense, this validates the media claim of functioning as surrogates for the public. While media representatives enjoy the same right of access as the public, they often are provided special seating and priority of entry so that they may report what people in attendance have seen and heard. This "contribute[s] to public understanding of the rule of law and to comprehension of the functioning of the entire criminal justice system. ∗ ∗ ∗" Nebraska Press Ass'n v. Stuart, 427 U.S. 539, 587, 96 S.Ct. 2791, 2816 (1976) (Brennan, J., concurring).

Burger than disposed of the State of Virginia's arguments that neither the constitution nor the Bill of Rights contains guarantees of a public right to attend trials. He responded that the Court has recognized that "certain unarticulated rights" are implicit in the Bill of Rights, including the rights of association, privacy, and the right to attend criminal trials. He then inserted footnote 17, which may become important in the future: "Whether the public has a right to attend trials of civil cases is a question not by this case, but we note that historically *both civil and criminal trials* have been presumptively open." [73]

Despite the sweep of Burger's words, he was not saying that all criminal trials must be open to the press and public. Instead, he criticized the conduct of the court in the murder trial of John Paul Stevenson. There, despite its being the fourth trial of the defendant, the judge " ∗ ∗ ∗ made no findings to support closure; no inquiry was made as to whether alternative solutions [such as sequestration of the jury] would have met the need to insure fairness; there was no recognition of any right under the Constitution for the public or press to attend the trial." He concluded: "Absent an overriding interest articulated in findings, the trial of a criminal case must be open to the public. Accordingly, the judgment under review is reversed." [74]

Note that Justice Powell took no part in the consideration or decision of this case. And remember that Powell declared, concurring in Gannett v. DePasquale, that reporters had a *limited* First Amendment right to attend pre-trial hearings. And Justices Blackmun, Brennan, White, and Marshall all agreed that public and press had a right, either under the First or the Sixth Amendment, to attend both pre-trial hearings and trials. Thus, although the First Amendment is not an absolute, it appears that the breadth of the language in *Richmond Newspapers* about *trials* has

[73] 448 U.S. 555, 581, 100 S.Ct. 2814, 2829 (1980), at footnote 17. Emphasis added.

[74] 448 U.S. 555, 581, 100 S.Ct. 2814, 2830 (1980).

once again made attendance at *pre-trial* proceedings an open question.

In his concurring opinion, Justice Stevens said: [75]

> * * * I agree that the First Amendment protects the public and the press from abridgment of their rights of access to information about the operation of their government, including the judicial branch; given the total absence of any record justification for the closure order entered in this case, that order violated the First Amendment.

Justice Brennan, joined by Justice Marshall, presented a marvelously complex concurrence, speaking of the structural value of public access in various circumstances. "But the First Amendment embodies more than a commitment to free expression and communicative interchange for their own sakes; it has a *structural* role to play in securing and fostering our republican form of self-government." He added: [76]

> Open trials assure the public that procedural rights are respected, and that justice is afforded equally. Closed trials breed suspicion of prejudice and arbitrariness, which in turn spawns disrespect for the law. Public access is essential, therefore, if trial adjudication is to achieve the objective of maintaining public confidence in the administration of justice.

Note also that Justice Rehnquist, seeming unconcerned by possible threats of secret judicial proceedings to society, was the only member of the court in both the *Gannett* and *Richmond* cases who could find no support for a right of public and press to attend judicial proceedings under either a Sixth Amendment or First Amendment rationale.[77]

Access Rights Need Defense

Although *Richmond Newspapers* has a much nicer ring than Gannett v. DePasquale, it did leave unanswered questions about the right to cover pre-trial matters, the matters which make up the bulk of our criminal justice process. During the dark days of 1979 and '80, after Gannett v. DePasquale was decided, reporters covering the judicial process began carrying their "Gannett cards." Various organizations made up statements for reporters to read in court when they were about to be ousted from pre-trial

[75] 448 U.S. 555, 584, 100 S.Ct. 2814, 2830 (1980).

[76] 448 U.S. 555, 595, 100 S.Ct. 2814, 2833, 2837 (1980).

[77] 448 U.S. 555, 605, 100 S.Ct. 2814, 2843 (1980).

or trial proceedings. In fact, a Gannett card—literally from the Gannett organization—said: [78]

> "Your honor, I am _____, a reporter for _____, and I would like to object on behalf of my employer and the public to this proposed closing. Our attorney is prepared to make a number of arguments against closings such as this one, and we respectfully ask the Court for a hearing on those issues. I believe our attorney can be here relatively quickly for the Court's convenience and he will be able to demonstrate that closure in this case will violate the First Amendment, and possibly state statutory and constitutional provisions as well. I cannot make the arguments myself, but our attorney can point out several issues for your consideration. If it pleases the Court, we request the opportunity to be heard through counsel."

Reporters, then, should hang on to their "Gannett Cards" and be ready to read them should a judge decide—on application from counsel—to give them the heave-ho from a judicial (including pretrial) proceedings. After all, as attorney James C. Goodale has written, even the *Gannett* case required three conditions before closure of a pre-trial hearing: [79]

(1)   there would be irreparable damage to the defendant's fair trial rights,

(2)   there were no alternative means to deal with the publicity and

(3)   the closure would be effective, i.e. no leaks.

If judicial proceedings are to remain open, reporters will have to stand ready to speak up, to protest closures. And their employers, obviously, will have to stand ready to go to court—to expend the money and energy to try to keep court proceedings open. Without protests and court tests, closures will simply occur. And when contested, closures can often be reversed. Reporters in courts—whether they like it or not—must sometimes be a first line of defense against secret court proceedings.[80]

[78] Other news organizations, such as Knight-Ridder, had similar cards made for their reporters.

[79] James C. Goodale, "The Three-Part Open Door Test in Richmond Newspapers Case," The National Law Journal, Sept. 22, 1980, p. 26.

[80] See James D. Spaniolo, Dan Paul, Parker D. Thomson and Richard Ovemlen, "Access After *Richmond Newspapers*," in James C. Goodale, chairman, Communications Law 1980 (New York: Practising Law Institute, 1980), pp. 385–648, for an intensive discussion of and listing of recent cases involving access to judicial proceedings. See especially pp. 452–456, dealing with access to judicial records.

Access to Courts after *Richmond Newspapers*

During the first few years after Richmond Newspapers v. Virginia (1980), the Supreme Court of the United States filled in some of that decision's promising outlines where coverage of the judicial process is concerned. Four key cases are: [81]

1. Globe Newspaper Co. v. Superior Court (1982).

2. Press-Enterprise Co. v. Superior Court (1984). ("Press Enterprise I")

3. Waller v. Georgia (1984).

4. "Press-Enterprise II (1986).

Globe Newspaper Co. v. Superior Court (1982)

The Boston Globe challenged the constitutionality of a Massachusetts statute providing for the exclusion of the public from trials of certain sex offenses involving victims under the age of 18. Globe reporters had tried unsuccessfully to get access to a rape trial in the Superior Court for the County of Norfolk, Massachusetts. Charges against the defendant in the trial involved forcible rape and forced unnatural rape of three girls who were minors at the time of the trial—two were 16 and one was 17. Writing for the Court, Justice Brennan held that the Massachusetts statute providing for mandatory closure of such cases violated the First Amendment of access to criminal trials. He said: [82]

> The Court's recent decision in Richmond Newspapers firmly established for the first time that the press and the general public have a constitutional right of access to criminal trials. Although there was no opinion of the Court in that case, seven Justices recognized that this right of access is embodied in the First Amendment, and applied to the States through the Fourteenth Amendment.
>
> * * *
>
> * * * [T]he right of access to criminal trials plays a particularly significant role in the functioning of the judicial process and the government as a whole. Public scrutiny of a criminal trial enhances the quality and safeguards the integrity of the factfinding process, with benefits to both the defendant and to society as a whole.

[81] Globe Newspapers v. Superior Court for Norfolk County, 457 U.S. 596, 102 S.Ct. 2613 (1982), 8 Med.L.Rptr. 1689; Press-Enterprise Co. v. Superior Court of California, 464 U.S. 501, 104 S.Ct. 819 (1984), 10 Med.L.Rptr. 1161; Waller v. Georgia, 467 U.S. 39, 104 S.Ct. 2210 (1984), 10 Med.L.Rptr. 1714.

[82] Globe Newspaper Co. v. Superior Court for Norfolk County, 457 U.S. 596, 102 S.Ct. 2613, 2618–2620 (1982), 8 Med.L.Rptr. 1689, 1692–1694.

* * *

We agree * * * that the first interest—safeguarding the physical and psychological wellbeing of a minor is a compelling one. But as compelling as that is, it does not justify a mandatory closure rule, for it is clear that the circumstances of the particular case may affect the significance of the interest. A trial court can determine on a case-by-case basis whether closure is necessary to protect the welfare of a minor victim.

Chief Justice Burger and Justice Rehnquist dissented, complaining that Justice Brennan had ignored " * * * a long history of exclusion of the public from trials involving sexual assaults, particularly those against minors." [83]

Press-Enterprise v. Superior Court (1984)

The Riverside (California) Press-Enterprise was trying to cover a rape trial, and wanted its reporters present during the *voir dire* proceedings, the in-depth questioning of prospective jurors. The newspaper moved that the *voir dire* be open to public and press. The State of California opposed the motion, arguing that with the public and press present, jurors' responses would not be candid, and that this would endanger the entire trial.

Writing for a unanimous Supreme Court, Chief Justice Burger wrote that the roots of open trials reach back to the days before the Norman Conquest in England, and related to that was a "presumptive openness" in the jury selection process.[84] He added:

No right ranks higher than the right of the accused to a fair trial. But the primacy of the accused's right is difficult to separate; from the right of everyone in the community to attend the *voir dire* which promotes fairness.

This fact situation was made harsher by the trial judge's keeping six weeks of the *voir dire* proceedings closed (although three days were open). Media requests for transcripts of the *voir dire* were refused; the California court argued that Sixth Amendment (defendant's right to a fair trial) and juror privacy rights coalesced to support closure of the proceeding. The Supreme Court disagreed. Chief Justice Burger wrote: [85]

The judge at this trial closed an incredible six weeks of *voir dire* without considering alternatives to closure.

[83] 457 U.S. 596, 102 S.Ct. 2613, 2624 (1984), 8 Med.L.Rptr. at 1697.

[84] Press-Enterprise Co. v. Superior Court of California, 464 U.S. 501, 104 S.Ct. 819, 823 (1984), 10 Med.L.Rptr. 1161, 1164.

[85] 464 U.S. 501, 104 S.Ct. 819, 826 (1984), 10 Med.L.Rptr. 1161, 1166.

Later the court declined to release a transcript of the voir dire even while stating that most of the material in the transcript was "dull and boring." * * * Those parts of the transcript reasonably entitled to privacy could have been sealed without such a sweeping order; a trial judge should explain why the material is entitled to privacy.

Waller v. Georgia (1984)

Waller was a defendant charged with violation of Georgia's Racketeer Influenced and Corrupt Organizations (RICO) Act. A pre-trial suppression hearing was held, in which Waller and other defendants asked that wiretap evidence and evidence seized during searches be suppressed—that is, disallowed or declared inadmissible.

The prosecuting attorney asked that the suppression hearing be closed, contending that if the evidence were presented in open court and published, it might become "tainted" and therefore unusable, especially in future prosecutions. The court ordered the suppression hearing closed to all persons except witnesses, the defendants, and lawyers and court personnel. Defendant Waller, however, wanted the hearings to be open.

Writing for the Court, Justice Lewis Powell cited Press Enterprise I approvingly, noting that even though the suppression hearing had been closed for its entire seven days, there was less than two and one-half hours worth of wiretap evidence tapes played in the court.[86]

"Press–Enterprise II"
[Press–Enterprise v. Riverside County Superior Court (1986)]

In 1986, the Supreme Court of the United States continued to back away from its much-criticized decision in Gannett v. DePasquale (1979), which held that pre-trial hearings could be closed to press and public. *De Pasquale*, decided under the Sixth (fair trial) amendment, now seems to have been overruled by "Press Enterprise II, decided under the First Amendment."

In that case, Robert Diaz—a nurse suspected of murdering a dozen hospital patients by lethal injections of huge amounts of the heart drug lidocaine—was to have a hearing to see whether there was probable cause to hold him for trial. The magistrate excluded the press from the hearing, which dragged on for 41 days. The magistrate ordered a trial for Diaz.[87]

[86] Waller v. Georgia, 467 U.S. 39, 42, 104 S.Ct. 2210, 2213 (1984).

[87] 478 U.S. 1, 106 S.Ct. 2735 (1986).

The California Supreme Court upheld the exclusion order, on the ground that there is no general First Amendment right of access to preliminary hearings, not if a judge found there was "a reasonable likelihood of substantial prejudice." [88]

The U.S. Supreme Court overturned that view, stating that the California rule called for a lesser burden of proof than is required under the First Amendment: there should be a "substantial probability" of prejudice before closure could be allowed.[89]

Chief Justice Burger, writing for a total of seven Justices (Stevens and Rehnquist dissented), declared that the interest of free press and of fair trial are not necessarily inconsistent. He added, "[O]ne of the important means of assuring a fair trial is that the process is open to neutral observers." Finally: [90]

> The considerations that led the Court to apply the First Amendment right of access to criminal trials in *Richmond Newspapers* and the selection of jurors in *Press Enterprise I* lead us to conclude that the right of access applies to preliminary hearings as conducted in California.

Access to Civil Matters

Although civil trial coverage may not appear as important or sexy as criminal trials to journalists and civil libertarians, all of the judicial process—criminal or civil, or in law or equity—needs to be open to the public. Public funds pay for the courts and judges, whether the cases involved be criminal or civil. Furthermore, when the judicial process is closed or otherwise hidden from public view, the likelihood is great that private rather than public welfare is being served.

As Professor Bill Loving of the University of Oklahoma has noted, ask Americans about major American auto makers associated with gas-tank fires and the answer will come back: Ford Motor Company and its Pinto. But as Loving pointed out,[91]

> * * * General Motors built cars with designs similar to Ford's and GM cars were involved in numerous accidents in which persons were severely injured or killed because of gas-tank fires and explosions.

[88] Press-Enterprise Company v. Superior Court, 478 U.S. 1, 5, 106 S.Ct. 2735, 2739 (1986).

[89] 478 U.S. 1, 13, 106 S.Ct. 2735, 2743.

[90] 478 U.S. 1, 10, 106 S.Ct. 2735, 2741.

[91] Bill Loving, "Media Access to Civil Court Records," paper presented to the Law Division, Association for Education in Journalism and Mass Communication, Boston, MA, Aug. 1991, p. 1.

The difference between the publicity the two received lay in General Motors' savvy use of the court system to throw up a shield of secrecy over its legal problems

* * *

The problem for the public has assumed these outlines. Suppose that a firm—we'll call it Feckless Industries for purposes of this discussion—is responsible for manufacturing a dangerous product or causing environmental damage through a spill of toxic chemicals. When injured parties become plaintiffs and sue Feckless Industries for damages, then—as long was customary—defendant Feckless could ask the court to issue a secrecy order. Those orders typically take one of these forms: [92]

Protective Orders: This in effect gags persons who receive information from the defendant, thus keeping information damaging to the defendant away from the public, the press, or other litigants.

Confidentiality Agreements: Defendants and plaintiffs often agree to keep details of the lawsuit, including causes of injuries or amounts of settlements, secret.

Sealed Files: When a lawsuit is settled out of court, sealing the files will keep everyone else—the public, environmental health officials, the news media—from knowing just what kind of deal has been cut.

Paul McMasters, Freedom of Information chair for the Society of Professional Journalists in 1990, put the issue of civil litigation secrecy in sharp focus: [93]

"We're not talking about irrelevant facts left in the files of the litigants. We're talking about documents and decisions involving unsafe products, dangerous drugs, toxic wastes, all with potentially devastating effects on people unaware of that danger."

Such records secrecy in civil litigation has long been routine in most jurisdictions. In Texas, however, Justice Lloyd Doggett of the Texas Supreme Court led the fight which resulted in a new standard in that state for sealing court records, saying explicitly that records may not be removed from (civil) court files except as allowed by statute or court rule. Such records are presumed open, and may be closed only upon a showing of a substantial interest outweighing the presumption of openness and any probable adverse effect that sealing records might have on public health or safety. This presumption of openness in Texas does include settle-

[92] Society of Professional Journalists and Association of Trial Lawyers of America, Keeping Secrets: Justice on Trial: Report of the Conference on Courtroom Secrecy, April 25, 1990, p. 5.

[93] Quoted at Ibid.

ment agreements "that seek to restrict disclosure of information concerning matters that have a probable adverse effect upon general public health or safety ＊ ＊ ＊ " [94]

Similarly in 1990, Florida passed its Sunshine in Litigation statute which demands that courts not enter secrecy orders or seal records which would prevent the public from being informed about hazardous products or public hazards in general.[95] And in May, 1990, the Subcommittee on Courts and Administrative Practices of the U.S. Senate Judiciary Committee, chaired by Senator Herbert Kohl of Wisconsin, held hearings on court secrecy with an eye to public policy needs in protecting victims' rights.[96]

[94] Texas Rules of Civil Procedure, Rule 76(a), effective Sept. 1, 1990.

[95] Sunshine in Litigation Act, Sec. 69.081, Florida Statutes, discussed in Keeping Secrets: Justice on Trial, p. 4, and reprinted at pp. 63–64.

[96] Hearings, Subcommittee on Courts and Administrative Procedures, U.S. Senate Committee on the Judiciary, May, 1990.

Part V

CONVERGING MEDIA AND THE LAW

Chapter 16

MEDIA OWNERSHIP: CONSOLIDATION AND GLOBALIZATION

Sec.
94. International Dimensions of Media Ownership.
95. The Trend Toward Media Concentration.
96. Newspaper Antitrust Law.
97. Electronic Media Ownership Policies.
98. The Globalization of American Media.

SEC. 94. INTERNATIONAL DIMENSIONS OF MEDIA OWNERSHIP

Foreign commerce considerations have begun shaping American media ownership policies.

Just a few years ago, when the United States still loomed as an invincible power in the arena of world trade, federal policy generally opposed mergers among major media organizations. Diversity of opinion was the key objective that prompted this policy stance—a position established to prevent a small group of giant corporations from dominating the U.S. marketplace of ideas.

Times have changed, however, and with this nation's ever increasing foreign trade deficit, federal media ownership policy has been altered as well. During the past decade the mass media industries have become one of a very few areas of international commerce still providing the United States with a favorable foreign trade balance.[1]

This fact has not gone unnoticed by other powerful industrial nations. Since the mid–1980s, foreign interests acquired three of America's six major film studios, and two of the nation's three largest music organizations.[2] Only two of the world's ten largest

---

[1] During the 1980s the annual U.S. foreign trade deficit increased from $20 billion in 1980 to $115 billion in 1989. During that same time, our trade *surplus* from foreign sales of U.S. films, films, television programs, music and video cassettes increased from less than $2 billion in 1980 to more than $6 billion in 1988.

[2] During the past decade Rupert Murdoch's News Corporation has acquired the film studio 20th Century Fox and Metromedia Broadcasting; Sony has purchased

694

mass media conglomerates are now American owned, and several of the European and Japanese media groups have been expanding at a more rapid pace than their American competitors.[3]

Because of growing concern that many other American mass media corporations might be tempting foreign takeover targets, mergers to strengthen financial position of domestic mass media properties and enhance their capacity to compete in a global media marketplace have been looked upon with much greater favor in Washington during the past decade.

Yet all this attention being given to foreign trade implications of media ownership in the United States should not obscure the fact that permitting domestic mass media organizations to merge reduces the number of mass cultural options available to the American public, diminishing that level of competition essential for a marketplace of ideas to flourish. So, while it is important to understand why our federal government appears at this point to be allowing and even encouraging national media mergers and consolidations, it is at least equally important to understand what adverse effects this policy may have upon the nature of future media service in the United States.

Clear patterns in national media conglomeration are already beginning to emerge in this nation. At this point then, there are two significant questions to raise and consider. First, why has the federal government been so firmly opposed to such consolidation

Columbia Pictures and Matsushita has taken over MCA, owner of Universal Studios. Technically, Murdoch's acquisition is no longer "foreign," since he is now an American citizen but the organization he controls is still a global conglomerate. In the field of music, Bertelsmann, a German media conglomerate, has bought RCA Music and Sony had acquired CBS Records. Paramount, Disney and the newly conglomerated Time–Warner are the only remaining American owned film studios, and Warner is also the only remaining major music distributor in the United States. Although foreign corporations have been somewhat less interested in acquiring American publishing interests, five of the largest book publishers in the United States are now foreign owned, as well as over 100 magazines, including "TV Guide", "Variety" and "Broadcasting."

[3] Since the recent merger, Time–Warner is now the largest media conglomerate in the world, generating annual revenues of $9 billion. Bertelsmann, the German media conglomerate that also owns RCA Music, Doubleday Publishing, Bantom Books and Dell is in second place, and closing rapidly on Time–Warner. In third place is Berlusconi's Italian media organization Fininvest, and in fourth place is the other American entity, Capital Cities/ABC. Thomson, the Canadian publisher, is the world's sixth largest media corporation and Rupert Murdoch's News Corporation, owner of the Fox Network, TV Guide and Harper & Row, among other American magazines and book publishers, is only slightly smaller than Thompson. The French media conglomerate Hachette is next in size, now the publisher of "Variety" followed by Maxwell, the late British media baron whose estate owns the financially ailing "New York Daily News."

Media observers have become increasingly concerned during the past twenty years about the tendency of corporate media owners to combine and consolidate their control both over local and national sources of public information.

in the past, and secondly, are those fears that prompted that opposition still justified today?

SEC. 95. THE TREND TOWARD MEDIA CONCENTRATION

The natural tendency of media organizations has been to combine and thereby reduce competition, a trend that has become more pronounced during the past two decades.

The disappearance of many daily newspapers—particularly independent, locally owned newspapers—is part of the story. Phrases frequently heard include "concentration of newspaper ownership," "problems of bigness and fewness," and "fewer voices in the marketplace of ideas."[4]

Newspaper ownership patterns are by no means the only points of concern. Professor Ben H. Bagdikian of the University of California-Berkeley—one of the best-known media critics—is an important voice pointing out that media power is political, and that only a small group of corporations have real opportunities to control most of "what America sees, hears, and reads." Bagdikian wrote that finance capitalism and new technologies have forged[5]

> * * * a new kind of central authority over information—the national and multinational corporation. By the 1980s, the majority of all major American media—newspapers, magazines, radio, television, books, and movies—were controlled by fifty giant corporations. These corporations were interlocked in common financial interest with other massive industries and with a few dominant banks.

By 1987, the 50 giant corporations Bagdikian had described in 1982 had merged into just 26 much larger and more powerful media conglomerates.[6]

Until deregulation became the policy of choice in Washington during the late 1970s, this clear pattern of media consolidation would almost certainly have triggered federal antitrust investigations by the Justice Department. At the moment, however, federal media antitrust actions—the focus of this chapter—are not

---

[4] Toby J. McIntosh, "Why the Government Can't Stop Press Mergers," Columbia Journalism Review, December, 1980, pp. 48–50; "America's Press: Too Much Power for Too Few?," U.S. News & World Report, Aug. 15, 1977, pp. 27ff; Kevin Phillips, "Busting the Media Trusts," Harper's Magazine, July 1977, pp. 23ff, and Neil Hickey, "Can the Networks Survive," TV Guide, March 21, 1981, p. 7ff.

[5] Ben H. Bagdikian, The Media Monopoly (Boston: Beacon Press, 1983), book jacket copy, plus quote from p. xv.

[6] Ben Bagdikian, "The 26 Corporations That Own Our Media," Extra, June 1987, p. 1.

politically in vogue. Yet, since fads and fashions change in politics as they do in the real world, it's important to be aware of basic concepts in an area of law that may soon become fashionable once more if the trend towards media consolidation should continue at its present pace.

So what is "antitrust?" Black's Law Dictionary says:[7]

> Antitrust acts. Federal and state statutes to protect trade and commerce from unlawful restraints, price discriminations, price fixing, and monopolies. Most states have mini-antitrust acts patterned on the federal acts. The principal federal antitrust acts are: Sherman Act (1890); Clayton Act (1914); Federal Trade Commission Act (1914); Robinson-Patman Act (1936). See Boycott; Combination in restraint of trade; Price fixing; Restraint of trade; * * *

The nation's premier scholar of the law of mass communications—the late Professor Zechariah Chafee of Harvard University—knew back in 1947 that the problem of concentration of media ownership was of pivotal importance to American society. Chafee asked to what extent antitrust laws should be used to prevent concentration of media units from hindering the free interchange of ideas. Chafee also declared in 1947 that antitrust law problems were the most important facing the press and also the most difficult.[8]

Antitrust law is an area which from time to time causes considerable fright among publishers and broadcasters. For example, the Federal Communications Commission (FCC) proposed in 1970 that broadcast station owners should cut their mass media operations in any community to either broadcast properties or to newspaper ownership. That FCC "proposed rulemaking" was enough to cause a substantial number of cross-ownerships to be split up by their owners. The FCC backed down from its proposal in 1975, issuing a ruling which "grandfathered"—left in effect—most existing local cross-ownerships of broadcast and newspaper properties. A group calling itself The National Citizens Commission for Broadcasting sued the FCC, asking that such cross-ownerships be broken up unless positive showings could be made that such patterns served the public interest.[9] In 1978, the Supreme Court of the United States held that it was within the FCC's authority to decide that existing cross-media ownerships were in

[7] Black's Law Dictionary, Fifth Edition (St. Paul, West Pub. Co., Minn., 1979) p. 86.

[8] Zechariah Chafee, Jr., Government and Mass Communications, 2 vols. (Chicago: University of Chicago Press, 1947) I, p. 537.

[9] National Citizens Committee for Broadcasting v. FCC, 555 F.2d 938 (D.C.Cir. 1977).

the public interest. That upheld the FCC's grandfathering of existing ownership patterns.[10] The FCC, however, made clear it would approve no new local cross-media ownerships.

In certain circumstances, the power of antitrust law over the media can be awesome. The shock wave generated by the *RKO General* case provides one example. The Federal Communications Commission (FCC), claiming (among other things) antitrust law violations by RKO General and its parent company—General Tire and Rubber Company—refused to renew broadcast licenses for three television stations owned by RKO General. With that stroke, the FCC tried to lift the license of WNAC–TV, Boston; WOR–TV, New York City, and KHJ–TV, Los Angeles. RKO General appealed the FCC's decision, setting off lengthy court battles. The antitrust/trade practices complaints were only part of the FCC's proceedings against RKO General. Even though an FCC administrative law judge had found in 1987 that RKO was unfit to hold a broadcast license, the Commission decided against immediate revocation, giving RKO the opportunity to sell its broadcast properties and transfer the station licenses to purchasers the agency had approved.[11]

Also, it should be kept in mind that antitrust law is not exclusively a federal matter. Although this chapter concentrates on federal antitrust activity, state antitrust laws are a formidable thicket. Antitrust experts Conrad M. Shumadine and Michael S. Ives noted in 1980 that although state antitrust prosecutions have been relatively rare, state laws contain some scary provisions. Under the laws of many states, convictions for antitrust violations may result in forfeiture of a corporation's charter. That could add up to dissolving of a corporation based in an individual state or the ouster of a corporation from one state when it is chartered in another state.[12]

This chapter will not consider in any detail the entire range of antitrust activity affecting the media. It is aimed, instead, at the increasingly interrelated question of newspaper and broadcast/ cable ownership situations. It does not take up such matters as exclusive syndication or newspaper distribution problems, nor does it treat important related questions of ownership of magazines, community newspapers and billboards.[13]

[10] FCC v. National Citizens Committee for Broadcasting, 436 U.S. 775, 98 S.Ct. 2096 (1978).

[11] RKO General, 63 RR 2d 866 (1987). See also, "FCC Gives RKO Green Light to Sell Stations," Broadcasting July 25, 1988, p. 33.

[12] Conrad M. Shumadine and Michael S. Ives, "Selected Antitrust Issues of Interest to the Media," in James C. Goodale, editor, Communications Law 1980, Vol. 2 (New York: Practising Law Institute, 1980) pp. 296–298.

[13] Exclusive syndication problems involve features such as columns or comic strips. Such features are offered to major newspapers under an agreement that no

Because of the structure of the newspaper business, the Antitrust Division of the Department of Justice has been unable to make much of an impact on newspaper chains acquiring newspapers like charms for a charm bracelet. The federal government can do little, for example, to prevent a newspaper group from New York from acquiring newspapers far away—as in Texas or California.

The communications media are businesses, and as such, are ringed about by federal and state laws which regulate businesses. Congress has enacted several statutes—most commonly called antitrust laws—which attempt to preserve competition. The most important statements of national antitrust policy are found in the Sherman[14] and Clayton[15] Acts.

The Sherman Act of 1890 begins: "Every contract, combination in the form of a trust or otherwise, or conspiracy, in restraint of trade or commerce among the several states, or with foreign nations, is hereby declared to be illegal."[16] Every person who acts to restrain trade, as mentioned generally above, is guilty of a crime.[17] The Sherman Act prohibits "contracts, combinations * * * or conspiracies in restraint of trade or commerce" and makes it illegal to "monopolize, or attempt to monopolize, or combine or conspire * * * to monopolize * * * trade or commerce."[18]

Criminal prosecution—with penalties of fines, imprisonment, or both—is provided for in the Sherman Act. Fines may reach a maximum amount of $100,000 per individual, and imprisonment for up to three years may also be imposed. A corporation may be fined up to $1 million for violating the Sherman Act. The Act also enables the government to bring suits in equity to get injunctions against violations of the statute. As Chafee observed in 1947, suits in equity are "preferred because it is not always easy for businessmen to know in advance whether their transactions are illegal or not."[19] Also, a person (or business) who has suffered damages because a competitor has violated the Sherman Act may sue the competitor for *treble damages.*

other newspapers within a certain region can publish those particular features. For a discussion of territorial exclusivity problems and distribution problems involving newspapers, see Marc A. Franklin, et al., The First Amendment and the Fourth Estate (Mineola, N.Y.; Foundation Press, 1977 and later editions).

[14] 26 Stat. 209, 15 U.S.C.A. §§ 1–7; P.L. No. 190, 51st Congress (1890).

[15] 38 Stat. 730, 15 U.S.C.A. § 12ff; P.L. No. 201, 63rd Congress (1914).

[16] 15 U.S.C.A. § 1.

[17] 15 U.S.C.A. § 20.

[18] 15 U.S.C.A. §§ 1, 4.

[19] Chafee, op. cit., p. 538.

Treble damages lawsuits work in this way: suppose that the Fluke Manufacturing Company has violated the Sherman Act. The United States Department of Justice takes Fluke Manufacturing to court and gets an order to make it stop monopolistic or trade-restraining practices. An interested spectator, meanwhile, is Fluke's competitor, whom we shall call the Flimsy Manufacturing Company. Flimsy Manufacturing then begins a treble damage antitrust suit, and is able to prove in court that Fluke Manufacturing's illegal business practices cost Flimsy $100,000 in business. However, since this would be a *treble damage* lawsuit, Flimsy Manufacturing would actually collect $300,000 from the competing Fluke company.

The Clayton Act of 1914 added to the government's antitrust enforcement powers, enumerating many acts as illegal when "they tend to lessen competition or to create a monopoly in any line of commerce."[20] Section 7 of the Clayton Act—more commonly called the Celler-Kefauver Act of 1950—is the most important section of the Clayton Act where the media are concerned.[21] The "Celler-Kefauver Act" forbids corporations to acquire stock or assets of a competing corporation "where * * * the effect * * * may be substantially to lessen competition, or tend to create a monopoly."

Upon such vaguely worded provisions of the Sherman and Clayton Acts is built federal antitrust policy. The vagueness of the statutory provisions make antitrust one of the most perplexing branches of public law, especially where newspapers and other units of the communications media are involved.

Increasingly and perhaps inevitably, the business of media is more prominent—and often seems more highly valued—than the social roles of the media. Unfortunately, media theorists who talk about a free press or competition in the marketplace of ideas seem more and more out-of-date. Whatever else they are, the First Amendment rights of speech and press and religion and assembly are supposed to be citizens' rights:

> Congress shall make no law respecting an establishment of religion, or prohibiting the free exercise thereof; or abridging the freedom of speech, or of the press; or the right of the people peaceably to assemble, and to petition the Government for a redress of grievances.

Although it may well be, as historian Leonard W. Levy has argued, that the First Amendment was merely a kind of fortunate political accident, freedom of speech and press are very much in the American grain. It is commonly accepted—or at least given

[20] 15 U.S.C.A. § 18.

[21] 64 Stat. 1125, 15 U.S.C.A. § 18; P.L. 899, 81st Congress (1950).

lip service—that the news media provide incalculably valuable services to society.[22] The media, so the belief goes, create an informed public necessary for meaningful self-government. This is one key reason why the press is shielded by the First Amendment, so that citizens might be informed about government and speak out as necessary. Those are the kinds of assumptions ringed about the First Amendment.

Now, however, there is room for skepticism about the First Amendment as a citizens' right. Increasingly, it demands enormously large amounts of capital to own a newspaper or broadcast station, on the one hand, or to defend oneself against a libel or privacy lawsuit, on the other.

In April 1985, the FCC relaxed its broadcast station ownership restrictions, increasing the number of radio, FM and television properties a licensee could own from 7 to 12 of each type of station.[23] This action set off a massive surge of broadcast industry acquisitions and mergers, resulting in a record-breaking total of $30 billion in broadcast and allied media industry sales transactions occuring before the year ended.[24] Among the more that 100 separate media purchases that each exceeded $10 million, the acquisition of RCA–NBC by General Electric for $6.3 billion, the purchase of ABC by Capital Cities Broadcasting for $3.5 billion and Australian media baron Rupert Murdoch's takeover of Metromedia for $2 billion captured the greatest amount of public attention.

Through acquiring the Metromedia stations, Murdoch's new Fox Network obtained virtually the same amount of network-owned television station audience coverage as his three major network competitors.[25]

Although the pace of this trading in broadcast properties has slowed to some extent since 1985, more than 1,300 broadcast stations were sold in the year 1987 alone, at a value of $7.5 billion.[26] In addition, during this era—

[22] Leonard W. Levy, Emergence of a Free Press (New York: Oxford University Press, 1985), passim.

[23] The following FCC rules were amended for the three broadcast services 47 CFR 73.35(a); 47 CFR 43.240(a) 1; 47 CFR 73.636(a) 1–2; and 47 CFR 76.501. Bowing to Congressional pressure, the FCC did limit to 25% the maximum size of the national television audience that any 12 group owned stations could serve.

[24] "Fifth Estate's $30 Billion-plus Year," Broadcasting December 30, 1985, p. 35.

[25] ABC's owned and operated TV stations reach 24.5% of all American TV households; NBC's O & O stations reach 22.4%; CBS reaches 19.46% and Fox, through its Metromedia holdings, now serves 19.39% of the total TV population. "Television's Top 20," Broadcasting August 31, 1987, p. 33.

[26] "Broadcasting–$7.5 Billion, Cable–$6 Billion," Broadcasting February 6, 1988, p. 61.

— Washington Post Co., bought 17 percent of Cowles Media. (The flagship enterprise of Cowles Media is the Minneapolis Star and Tribune.)

— Advance Publications (S.I. Newhouse, chairman) bought New Yorker Magazine for $142 million.

— U.S. News & World Report sold to Mortimer Zuckerman for $164 million.

Earlier in 84–85, Gannett Company purchased The Des Moines Register and Tribune, plus some smaller papers, for $200 million, and Time, Inc., the huge magazine and cable TV power, bought Southern Progress Corporation, publisher of Southern Living and other profitable magazines, for $480 million.[27] Westinghouse Electric Corporation bought cable television properties from Teleprompter Corporation for $647 million, and the A.H. Belo Corporation—publishers of the Dallas Morning News—acquired Corinthian Broadcasting Corporation's six television stations from Dun & Bradstreet for $606 million.[28] Small wonder that Newsweek Magazine termed this wave of acquisitiveness a "feeding frenzy." Newsweek added: [29]

> For the American news media, accustomed to thinking of themselves as a Fourth Estate, it has been something of a shock to be treated as Wall Street darlings instead. The pell-mell quest for media properties has bid up their sale prices to heady levels.

And *Variety* commented,

> So small businesses were gobbled up by larger companies and corporations were devoured by still larger corporations. And to all this Washington—the FCC and Justice Dept.—said fine. The era of regulation was at an end.[30]

Many journalists (except for business writers, Wall Street Journal types, and the like) have long had the reputation for being financial illiterates. But when the media became such attractive properties in the 1980s, self-interest began to impel journalists to learn some new terms, such as:

"Leveraged Buyout"—This is a deal in which money is borrowed to buy a corporation. Then, the cash flow

[27] Newsweek, "Big Media, Big Money," April 1, 1985, p. 52.

[28] Ibid.

[29] Ibid.

[30] "The Year in Review", Variety, January 8, 1986, p. 159.

from the purchased company is put to work to pay off the interest and principal of the loan.

The purchase of the ABC Network by Capital Cities is a startling example of a leveraged buyout. A Nebraska financier—Warren Buffett—bought Capital Cities stock to provide $517.5 million of the $3.5 billion "Cap Cities" spent to get control of ABC. Note that Cap Cities was much smaller than ABC—its 1984 revenues amounted to $950 million, compared to $3.7 billion for ABC. "It's a little like the canary eating the cat," said Roone Arledge, president of ABC News and Sports.[31]

But then, with media companies, cash flow can be great that enormous loans can be paid off. Alex S. Jones reported in The New York Times that "well-run television stations in major markets can generate pre-tax operating income of over 50 percent * * * cash flow can be 60 percent or more of revenues." Further, cash flow for the more profitable newspapers can range as high as 40 percent or more.[32]

"Friendly Takeover"—As the term implies, it is an amicable merger between two corporations. The Capital Cities Communications-ABC merger again provides a good example. ABC's architect and Chairman, 79-year-old Leonard Goldenson, had for some years been the subject of speculation: who would replace him at the 214-station network? Cap Cities Chairman Thomas Murphy talked with the ABC Executive Vice President, and they agreed that if the FCC ever liberalized its "7-7-7 rule" [see above], the two companies would be a "natural fit." After the FCC changed to its "12-12-12" rule on April 1, 1985, the merger took place.[33]

Similarly, General Electric's purchase of NBC in December of 1985 for $6.3 billion was also a friendly merger. The management of NBC's parent company RCA, had taken defensive measures against a hostile take-over, but was still concerned about its long term vulnerability. The merger, creating the second largest industrial corporation in the nation (excluding the auto industry) provided NBC with a massive infusion of capital, while GE gained re-entry into a field with the strong profit base the

[31] Peter W. Kaplan, "Takeover's Impact Is Uncertain," The New York Times, March 19, 1985, p. 54.

[32] See Geraldine Fabrikant, "3 TV Stations High Margins," The New York Times, July 1, 1985, p. 25.

[33] Newsweek, April 1, 1985, p. 54.

company saw as being essential to support its worldwide manufacturing and marketing activities.[34]

"Hostile Takeover"—There had been rumors that ABC was being stalked for a hostile takeover—a situation in which entrepreneurs buy up a controlling interest in a company's stock, thus gaining effective ownership. The rumors mentioned potential takeover bidders as the Bass brothers of Fort Worth, Texas, and Ted Turner, the feisty and aggressive owner of Atlanta "super-station" WTBS, Cable News Network, the Atlanta Braves baseball team, and so on. But ABC Board Chairman Goldenson said that the network had found no evidence of investors buying up huge blocs of ABC stock, and added that the sale to Capital Cities was not put together to prevent someone less desirable from gaining control of the network.[35]

"Junk Bonds"—A failed hostile takeover, especially one financed with "junk bonds", can sometimes be as damaging for media organizations as a successful takeover. In 1985, Ted Turner, the cable TV magnate, decided he wanted to own CBS. Turner tried, unsuccessfully, to purchase the 67 percent of CBS's common stock required under New York to gain control of the corporation. Since he lacked the $5.4 billion needed to acquire the stock, he attempted to float more than $5 billion of the purchase price in "junk bonds", trying to persuade stockholders to support him by promising them an annual dividend some seven times their current dividend rate.[36]

Although Turner failed in his campaign to take over CBS, the massive expenses the network incurred in fighting off his attack weakened its financial structure, making it much more vulnerable to the next takeover effort by another corporate giant. For a time it seemed that giant might be Coca–Cola, but while CBS executives were

[34] "RCA + GE: Marriage Made in Takeover Heaven," Broadcasting December 16, 1985 p. 43. At the time of the merger, GE did own one television property, KCNC–TV Denver that NBC had previously tried to acquire. With the purchase, it became the 6th NBC owned and operated TV station.

[35] Ibid., p. 53; "Network Blockbuster," Time, April 1, 1985, p. 60.

[36] The term "junk bond" is slang for a bond issued by a company that is too poor a credit risk to borrow money in a conventional manner. These bonds can often be purchased for far less than their stated value (eg. $10,000 face value worth of bonds for $100) because the chance that the company issuing them will ever being able to pay them off is so slight. What usually happens after "junk bonds" have financed the purchase of corporate stock is that the new owner then plunders the assets of the corporate acquired to pay the high rates of return demanded by the bonds tendered to purchase it.

guarding their corporate flanks from attack, the actual takeover of CBS was occuring right behind their backs.

"Inside Takeover"—When Lawrence Tisch used the 24.9% of CBS stock he had recently acquired through his Loews Corporation to become acting chief executive officer (CEO) of CBS in September 1986, the FCC accepted the network's argument that Tisch's stock purchase and CEO appointment did not require Commission review because there had been no actual change in the ownership or control of CBS.[37] Before the year 1986 had ended, however, the 500 network employees he had already fired were among those who had reason to question the FCC's determination that Tisch was not in charge of CBS.

For a few brief weeks, Tisch was viewed as a hero at the network, because he had saved CBS from the rumored take-over move by Coca–Cola. But, as *Time* magazine described it, as Tisch continued to direct a "rapid and ruthless austerity program",

> The September mood of euphoria at CBS suffered accordingly. Says one mid-level executive: "Half the people here curse Tisch." A television producer . . . describes employee morale as "pulverized with fear." Staffers soon coined a bitter name for the layoffs; to be fired was to be "tisched".[38]

In January 1987, Tisch assumed complete control of the network, restructuring its organization and selecting his own managerial staff. Thus, while CBS was not taken over by an outside corporation, it was effectively taken over from within.

When all this merger activity is considered—and there is far more of it than short summary can include—it's clear that the pace of media consolidation in the United States accelerated significantly during the 1980s and shows no sign of slowing down in the foreseeable future. The 50 major media organizations of 1982 that had become only 26 media giants of 1988 are almost certain to continue merging and combining until perhaps only a dozen of them will be dominating every form of American mass culture by the end of this decade.

While reduced competition may mean greater prosperity for the American media conglomerates themselves, it will certainly

[37] "FCC on CBS: No Change in Control," Broadcasting, October 20, 1986, p. 28. The FCC's concern was not about ownership of the network per se, but about control of those licensed broadcast stations owned by CBS, because the Commission is required by Sec. 310(d) of the Communications Act to determine whether the transfer of control over a broadcast license is in the public interest before authorizing any change in ownership or control.

[38] "A Cut Above the Ordinary," Time, December 22, 1986, p. 53.

continue to diminish the vigor of public discourse and discussion totally dependent upon competition for its vitality.

SEC. 96. NEWSPAPER ANTITRUST LAW

Antitrust statutes, as applied to the press, are not in violation of the First Amendment guarantee of freedom of the press.

Until the late 1970s, national rather than international mass media competition was the primary concern of the federal government. During this era the Justice Department was deeply committed to preventing anti-competitive trade practices in the newspaper industry.

Although decided just after the end of World War II, the decision of the Supreme Court of the United States in Associated Press v. United States[39] still ranks as a leading case in antitrust law affecting the media. The Justice Department had brought suit under the Sherman Act[40] to get an injunction preventing the AP from continuing to operate under a restrictive clause in its by-laws. The Associated Press is a cooperative news-gathering organization. Its by-laws forbade AP member newspapers or broadcast stations from selling news to non-members. Other by-law provisions also gave a newspaper which had an AP membership virtual veto power over competing newspapers' attempts to gain AP membership.[41]

Associated Press v. United States (1945)

One of several cases combined under the case name of Associated Press v. United States involved Chicago publisher Marshall Field's efforts to get an AP membership for his Chicago Sun, a new newspaper trying to compete with crusty Col. Robert R. McCormick's Chicago Tribune. The Chicago Tribune protested against the upstart Chicago Sun's AP membership application, trying to prevent the competition from gaining the benefit of the premier news wire service. Once such a protest was made, the AP by-laws then required a majority vote of ALL members of the Associated Press before the new applicant could be admitted to the club.[42] That majority vote—from publisher members of AP, many of whom enjoyed exclusive use of that wire service in their own

[39] 326 U.S. 1, 65 S.Ct. 1416 (1945).

[40] See discussion of the Sherman Act, Section 93, supra, at footnote 15.

[41] Chafee, op. cit., pp. 542–543; Associated Press v. United States, 326 U.S. 1, 9–10, 65 S.Ct. 1416, 1419 (1945).

[42] Chafee, p. 543; Associated Press v. United States, loc. cit. Another newspaper which like the Chicago Sun had applied for AP membership and had been turned down by a 2–1 vote margin of AP members, was the Washington Times-Herald.

publication areas—was most unlikely to occur. Thus Marshall Field's Chicago Sun could not join the AP without Col. McCormick's consent, unless the federal government intervened—in the public interest, of course—to use antitrust laws to force a change in the AP bylaws.

In 1943, the Justice Department charged that the conduct of the AP and the Chicago Tribune constituted "(1) a combination and conspiracy of restraint of trade and commerce in news among the states, and (2) an attempt to monopolize part of that trade." [43] The Associated Press and the Chicago Tribune fought against the Justice Department charges, arguing that the application of the Sherman Act in this case would violate freedom of the press guaranteed by the First Amendment. A majority of the Supreme Court was not impressed by this argument. Writing for the Court, Justice Hugo L. Black said: [44]

> * * *. All are alike covered by the Sherman Act. The fact that the publisher handles news while others handle goods does not, as we shall later point out, afford the publisher a peculiar constitutional sanctuary in which he can with impunity violate laws regulating his business practices.

Finally, Justice Black answered the assertion that the Sherman Act's application to the Associated Press abridged the AP's First Amendment freedom. He declared that it would be strange if the concern for press freedom underlying the First Amendment should be read "as a command that the government was without power to protect that freedom." Black continued, [45]

> Freedom to publish means freedom for all and not for some. Freedom to publish is guaranteed by the Commission, but freedom to combine to keep others from publishing is not. Freedom of the press from governmental interference under the First Amendment does not sanction repression of that freedom by private interests. The First Amendment affords not the slightest support for the contention that a combination to restrain trade in news and views has any constitutional immunity.

Justice Frankfurter added other arguments in favor of government action under the Sherman Act to attempt to control media activities which tended to restrain trade. To Frankfurter, the press was a business, but it was also much more: "in addition to being a commercial enterprise, it [the press] has a relation to the public interest unlike that of any other enterprise pursued for

[43] 326 U.S. 1, 7, 65 S.Ct. 1416, 1418 (1945).

[44] 326 U.S. 1, 8–10, 65 S.Ct. 1416, 1419 (1945).

[45] 326 U.S. 1, 20, 65 S.Ct. 1416, 1424–1425 (1945).

profit." Following this premise, Justice Frankfurter then quoted words written by America's most famous United States District Court judge. The oft-quoted words below came from Judge Learned Hand's lower-court opinion in this same case of Associated Press v. United States,[46]

> * * * that [the newspaper] industry serves one of the most vital of all general interests: the dissemination of news from as many different sources, and with as many different facets and colors as is possible. That interest is closely akin to, if indeed it is not the same as, the interest protected by the First Amendment; it presupposes that right conclusions are more likely to be gathered out of a multitude of tongues than through any kind of authoritative selection. To many this is, and always will be, folly; but we have staked upon it our all.

To Frankfurter, the By-Laws of the Associated Press were a clear restriction of commerce. Such a restriction was unreasonable because it subverted the function of a constitutionally guaranteed free press.

Dissents from Justices Owen J. Roberts and Frank Murphy took a traditional libertarian view: In general, government should leave the press alone. Justice Murphy wrote: [47]

> Today is * * * the first time that the Sherman Act has been used as a vehicle for affirmative intervention by the Government in the realm of dissemination of information. As the Government states, this is an attempt to remove "barriers erected by private combination against access to reports of world news." * * *. [The press associations] are engaged in collecting and distributing news and information rather than in manufacturing automobiles, aluminum or gasoline. We cannot avoid that fact. Nor can we escape the fact that governmental action directly aimed at the methods or conditions of such collection or distribution is an interference with the press, however differing in degree it may be from governmental restraints on written or spoken utterances themselves * * *. We should therefore be particularly vigilant in reviewing a case of this nature, a vigilance that apparently is not shared by the Court today.

[46] 326 U.S. 1, 28, 65 S.Ct. 1416, 1428 (1945), quoting Judge Hand, United States v. Associated Press, 52 F.Supp. 362, 372 (S.D.N.Y.1943).

[47] 326 U.S. 1, 51–52, 65 S.Ct. 1416, 1439 (1945).

Lorain Journal Company v. United States (1951)

Media can violate antitrust laws in one of two general ways. The first is by attempting through acquisition, merger or some other type of corporate restructuring to reduce the level of media competition in an unlawful manner. The second, and far more common type of media antitrust violation is to engage is some form of anti-competitive media business practice. The Lorain Journal case presents a clear illustration of the type of anti-competitive practices antitrust law has been designed to prevent.[48]

The paper had tried and failed to obtain a broadcast license to operate a radio station in the city in which it was located, Lorain, Ohio.[49] Soon afterward, the FCC issued a radio license to an applicant whose station was located in Elyria, Ohio, just eight miles from Lorain.

In an effort to force this competitor out of business, the paper adopted a strict policy of refusing to accept advertising from any local merchants who also purchased any advertising time from the radio station. Because the Lorain Journal reached 99 percent of the area's households, local advertisers had little choice but to avoid buying commercial time from the radio station.

The Justice Department brought a civil antitrust suit against the Journal, charging the paper with attempting to monopolize commerce under the Sherman Act. The newspaper responded by claiming that this government action infringed not only on its constitutionally protected right of free speech, but also its right to accept or refuse advertisements from whomever it pleased.

A federal district court found that Lorain Journal had indeed been attempting to illegally monopolize commerce, and issued an injunction to prevent the paper from continuing its anticompetitive trade practices. The Journal appealed to the Supreme Court but to no avail. In a 7–0 decision, the Court upheld the lower court decision and the injunction that issued from it.

The Court, through Mr. Justice Harold Burton, rejected the argument that the newspaper's "bold, relentless and predatory commercial behavior" was in any way sheltered by the First Amendment and also rejected its asserted right to accept or reject advertisements, saying: [50]

[48] Lorain Journal Co. v. United States, 342 U.S. 143, 72 S.Ct. 181 (1951).

[49] See 92 F.Supp. 794 (N.D.Ohio 1950). See also Mansfield Journal Co. v. FCC, 180 F.2d 28 (D.C.Cir.1950). This refusal of the FCC to grant the license application was based in part on allegations of similar past anti-competitive behavior of the Mansfield Journal, jointly owned with the Lorain Journal, in its advertising practices and its refusal to print the schedules of competing radio stations in its area.

[50] Lorain Journal Co. v. United States, 342 U.S. 143, 155, 72 S.Ct. 181, 187 (1951).

The right claimed by the publisher is neither absolute nor exempt from regulation. [The refusal to accept advertising] * * * as a purposeful means of monopolizing interstate commerce is prohibited by the Sherman Act. The operator of the radio station, equal with the publisher of newspaper, is entitled to the protection of the Act.

Because the findings of fact in a civil or criminal antitrust action brought by the government may be used in a lawsuit for **treble damages** by the injured party, the radio station was later able to sue the Journal and recover three times the damages it actually sustained for advertising revenues lost because of the newspaper's anticompetitive behavior.[51]

Times–Picayune Pub. Co. v. United States (1953)

In this case, the publisher of a morning (Times-Picayune) and an afternoon newspaper (States) in New Orleans would not accept advertising unless a merchant purchased advertising space in both of its newspapers, but did not refuse ads from those who also advertised in a competing afternoon paper (The Item). The Justice Department challenged this advertising practice, claiming that it constituted an anticompetitive "tying agreement"—that is, forcing a customer to buy an unwanted product in order to obtain the one desired. The government contended that most advertisers desired to place their ads in the morning Times–Picayune, with a circulation of 188,000, but were forced by its unit-buying rule to purchase space in its sister afternoon paper, the States, with a circulation of only 105,000.[52] This, of course, would operate to divert potential advertising revenues away from the independent New Orlean's afternoon paper, the Item.

In a 5–4 decision, the Supreme Court disagreed with the Justice Department, finding that there had been no unlawful "tying" because the government had not established that the publisher's morning paper was in fact the desired or "dominant" product or that its afternoon paper the unwanted or "inferior" product for newspaper advertisers. Instead, Justice Tom C. Clark's majority opinion held that the two newspapers—owned by one publisher—were selling identical products: advertising space in a newspaper. But did competition survive? The name of the afternoon paper—after a 1958 merger—is the States-Item.

[51] Elyria–Lorain Broadcasting Co. v. Lorain Journal Co., 298 F.2d 356 (6th Cir. 1961).

[52] 345 U.S. 594, 73 S.Ct. 872 (1953).

United States v. Kansas City Star (1957)

In Kansas City, the morning Times and afternoon and Sunday Star were owned by the same publisher, who also owned a local radio and television station. The Kansas City Post, the Star's only former competitor had gone bankrupt and ceased publication.

Readers were forced to subscribe to all three papers, the Times, and both the afternoon and Sunday Star in order to receive service. Advertisers were also forced to place their ads in all three papers, and there was evidence that merchants who did not advertise in the newspaper were not permitted to buy radio or television commercial time from the newspaper's stations.

In prosecuting its case, the government was able to show that the Star's dominant media position in the Kansas City area gave it the power to exclude competition. The government also assembled evidence to demonstrate that this power had been exercised in a ruthless fashion to coerce both readers and advertisers in a manner that would not have been possible in a truly competitive environment.

The Star was found guilty of criminal violations of antitrust law, as the jury rejected the publisher's argument that the morning and afternoon papers were separate entities in competition with one another. Eventually, after a federal appeals court affirmed the conviction, the Star agreed to a consent decree ending a companion civil suit brought by the government.

This decree, like other consent decrees between an antitrust defendant and the government, was a negotiated settlement. By it terms, the Star agreed, in return for the government ending its civil action, to sell its radio and television stations and never again attempt to purchase any broadcast properties without the prior consent of the government. The decree also prohibited the newspapers from forcing advertisers to buy advertising space in both the Star and the Times in order to have their ads accepted.

Even the consent decree did not end the Star's legal problems. The criminal antitrust conviction was used repeatedly as evidence by would-be competitors who brought treble-damage antitrust suits against the paper. Defending against such lawsuits was an expensive proposition, and a number of such actions were settled out of court.[53]

[53] See e.g. Goodfriend and Levinson v. Kansas City Star Co., 158 F.Supp. 531 (W.D.Mo.1958); Duff v. Kansas City Star Co., 299 F.2d 320 (8th Cir.1962) and Siegfried v. Kansas City Star Co., 193 F.Supp. 427 (W.D.Mo.1961).

United States v. Times–Mirror (1967)

Unlike the Lorain Journal, Times–Picayune or Kansas City Star antitrust actions, the Times–Mirror case did not involve anticompetitive conduct, but rather an attempt through merger to reduce competition.[54] The Times–Mirror Corporation had purchased the San Bernardino (California) Sun, a profitable daily newspaper located about 40 miles from Los Angeles for $15 million. The Pulitzer Corporation of St. Louis had offered to pay the same amount for the Sun, but the Sun's owner decided to accept the Times–Mirror offer instead.

Acquisition of the Sun by the Times–Mirror Corporation was challenged by the Antitrust Division of the Justice Department. The government complained that the merger meant that the publisher of California's largest daily newspaper, the Times, had now gained control of the largest independent daily newspaper in Southern California.

The federal trial judge found that the three San Bernardino County newspapers published by the Sun Corporation constituted the only major advertising competition faced by the Times–Mirror in the area and its primary competitor for subscribers in that region of the state.

Based on these findings, the Court ruled that the purchase of the Sun Company by Times–Mirror violated the antimerger provisions of Section 7 of the Clayton Act. As a result, the Times–Mirror was forced to divest itself of Sun Company stock and present a plan for divestiture that provided for the continuation of the Sun Company as a strong and viable organization.

The Antitrust Division of the Department of Justice held that its victory in the Times-Mirror case was a significant one. In 1968, the leading antitrust lawyer Charles D. Mahaffie, Jr. wrote that the Antitrust Division was "and will continue to be particularly concerned with mergers which may eliminate the actual and potential competition afforded by the suburban, small-city and community papers."[55]

Underlying such a statement was a basic philosophy of communication and freedom of expression filtered through antitrust law. The idea is that many voices in the marketplace of information and opinion—"diversified, quarrelsome, and competitive"—

---

[54] United States v. Times Mirror Co., 274 F.Supp. 606 (W.D.Cal.1967), affirmed by the U.S. Supreme Court without opinion 390 U.S. 712, 88 S.Ct. 1411 (1968).

[55] Charles D. Mahaffie, Jr., "Mergers and Diversification in the Newspaper, Broadcasting and Information Industries," The Antitrust Bulletin Vol. 13 (Fall 1968) pp. 927–935, at p. 928.

are; in the public interest.[56] After the Times-Mirror's acquisition of the San Bernardino Sun was voided, the Sun newspapers were acquired by the nation's largest newspaper group, The Gannett Company, headquartered in Rochester, New York.

United States v. Citizen Publishing Co. (1968) and the "Newspaper Preservation Act" of 1970

In 1969, the Supreme Court of the United States decided a case of great importance to the daily newspaper industry: United States v. Citizen Publishing Company, often called "The Tucson Case." That decision declared "joint operating agreements to be illegal. Such agreements were and are important to the profit margins if not to the very survival of competing newspapers in about two-dozen cities.[57]

The Supreme Court's judgment that joint operating agreements were illegal didn't last long. The ruling brought a wave of protests from publishers whose newspapers are involved in joint operating agreements. On March 12, 1969, just two days after the Court's Tucson decision, a number of bills were offered in both the U.S. House of Representatives and the Senate to legalize joint operating agreements between two newspapers. Those bills tied in with lengthy hearings held by the preceding Congress on the so-called "Failing Newspaper Act."[58]

After the Supreme Court's decision in the Tucson Case, the "Failing Newspaper Act" was given the euphemistic label "Newspaper Preservation Act" and was passed by both houses of Congress.[59] President Nixon signed the bill into law on July 24, 1970. The text of the Newspaper Preservation Act is quoted at length in Appendix—at the end of this book.

Joint operating agreements work in this fashion. Two competing newspapers in one town combine their printing, advertising, circulation and business operations. The news and editorial operations of the two newspapers, however, retain their separate identities. Then, the two newspapers—one published in the morning and the other in the afternoon—can use the same publishing, business and distribution facilities, resulting in substantial economies in operation.

[56] See the classic statement by Judge Learned Hand in United States v. Associated Press, 52 F.Supp. 362, 372 (S.D.N.Y.1943), quoted at 326 U.S. 1, 28, 65 S.Ct. 1416, 1428 (1945), and printed in the text to footnote 52 earlier in this chapter.

[57] Editor & Publisher, Jan. 18, 1969, p. 9. Such cities include Tucson; San Francisco; Madison, Wisconsin, El Paso, Texas, and Honolulu.

[58] See Subcommittee on Antitrust and Monopoly of the Committee on the Judiciary, United States Senate, 90th Congress, First Session, on S. 1312, The Failing Newspaper Act, Part 1, July 12–14, 18–19, 25–26, 1967, at p. 2.

[59] 15 U.S.C.A. §§ 1801–1804.

To say that the Tucson Case obviously worried a number of publishers would be one hellacious understatement. Arguments filed before the Supreme Court in the Tucson Case early in 1969 included an amicus curiae brief filed on behalf of newspaper publishers in 16 cities. In that brief, attorney Robert L. Stern asserted that "a joint operating plant is the only feasible way to preserve competition in cities which cannot support two completely separate newspapers." [60]

The Antitrust Division of the Department of Justice, however, disagreed with the line of thinking argued by attorney Stern. So did a Federal district court, in deciding that the Tucson joint operating agreement was illegal.[61] That joint operating agreement had been in existence since 1940. Then, Citizen Publishing Company (publishers of The Tucson Daily Citizen, an evening paper) and The Star Publishing Company (publishers of The Arizona Daily Star, a morning and Sunday paper) joined forces to form a third corporation: Tucson Newspapers, Inc. Tucson Newspapers, Inc. took over all departments of the two newspapers except news/editorial.

This joint operating agreement was started because—the publishers of the two newspapers later said—they beleived there could not be successful operation of two competing dailies in a city with a population of less than 100,000.

In the district court decision, Chief Justice James A. Walsh found that the joint operating agreement amounted to illegal "price fixing, profit pooling, and market allocations by the parties to the agreement," a violation of the Sherman Act.

In arguments to the Supreme Court of the United States, the Tucson newspapers contended that joint operating agreements were necessary in a number of cities to allow newspapers to survive while maintaining competing news and editorial voices. There were 22 cities with a total of 44 newspapers involved in joint operating agreements similar to the Tucson situation in the mid-1960s. Thus, it was feared that the Justice Department, should it succeed in the Tucson case, would begin antitrust actions against other newspapers' joint operating agreements. That would mean, to use the example of Arizona, that Tucson Newspapers, Inc., could no longer operate single advertising and circulation departments serving both newspapers.[62]

In March of 1969, the Supreme Court of the United States indeed did find the Tucson joint operating agreement illegal.

[60] Editor & Publisher, Dec. 21, 1968, p. 9.

[61] United States v. Citizen Pub. Co., Tucson Newspapers, Inc., Arden Pub. Co. and William A. Small, Jr., 280 F.Supp. 978 (D.Ariz.1968).

[62] Ibid. See also Editor & Publisher, Jan. 18, 1969, p. 9.

Writing for the Court, Mr. Justice Douglas ruled that the agreement was for the purpose of ending competition between the two newspapers.

The Supreme Court thus affirmed the orders issued by the U.S. District Court in the Tucson case. This meant that the Tucson newspapers must "submit a plan for divestiture and reestablishment of the Star as an independent competitor and for modification of the joint operating agreement so as to eliminate the price-fixing, market control, and profit pooling provisions."

It should be noted that Douglas emphasized the "failing company doctrine" as he wrote the majority opinion in the Tucson case. Douglas declared the "only real defense of appellants [the Citizen Publishing Company and its co-defendants] was the failing company defense—a judicially created doctrine." The failing company doctrine means that acquisition of a company by a competitor does not illegally lessen competition if the firm which has been purchased is in grave danger of business failure. Justice Douglas, however, found that the Citizen had not been a failing newspaper in 1940 when it entered the joint operating agreement with the Star, despite the fact that the Citizen was then losing money.[63] The Supreme Court, as Justice Douglas put it, found that "beyond peradventure of doubt" the joint operating agreement between Tucson's two daily newspapers violated antitrust laws.

The Newspaper Preservation Act

As noted earlier, the Supreme Court's decision in the Citizen Publishing Company case was promptly legislated out of existence by the Newspaper Preservation Act.[64] This act's purpose was stated to be maintaining—in the public interest—"a newspaper press editorially and reportorially competitive in all parts of the United States" by legalizing such joint operating agreements. In one sense, this legislation might be viewed as "too little, too late" because by 1969 there were not many cities left with competing, independently owned daily newspapers. In another sense, there is also room for doubt about how truly "independent" newspapers bound together by common financial and business operations will be when a choice has to be made between serving the public

---

[63] 394 U.S. 131, 89 S.Ct. 927 (1969); United States Law Week, Vol. 37, pp. 4208–4212 (March 11, 1969); Barry Schweid, "Newspapers Want Congress to Legalize Joint Operation," Associated Press dispatch in Madison, Wis., Capital Times, March 11, 1969; "Publishers seek relief in Congress," Editor & Publisher, March 15, 1969, p. 9ff. See also International Shoe Co. v. Federal Trade Commission, 280 U.S. 291, 302, 50 S.Ct. 89, 93 (1930).

[64] 15 U.S.C.A. §§ 1801–1804.

interest and serving economic self-interest.[65]   As a result, the Newspaper Preservation Act of 1970 approved all 22 joint operating agreements then in existence, involving 44 daily papers.[66]

The Newspaper Preservation Act was passed despite strenuous objections from the Antitrust Division of the Department of Justice. The government's attorneys expressed fear that if profit pooling or price fixing laws were relaxed to aid newspapers, "many publishers will opt for that way [joint operating agreements] even though they might be capable of remaining fully independent, or of finding other solutions to the difficulties which preserve competition."[67]   Weekly newspapers, small dailies, and the American Newspaper Guild strongly and repeatedly urged against passage of a failing newspaper act, often complaining that joint advertising rates provide newspapers in a joint operation situation with an advantage which competitors simply cannot overcome.[68]

John H. Carlson, writing in the Indiana Law Journal, expressed dismay about the antitrust exemption for so-called failing newspapers.[69]   Carlson declared that the Newspaper Preservation Act, which legalized the *Tucson* arrangement as well as similar operations elsewhere, allowed newspapers which were nowhere close to failing financially to dodge antitrust laws.

Just as Carlson's critique of the Newspaper Preservation Act first appeared in print in the spring of 1971, publisher Bruce Brugman of the *San Francisco Bay Guardian* offered his own critique in the form of a challenge to the Act's constitutionality. *The Bay Guardian,* a monthly with a circulation of 17,000, saw itself in a tough competitive situation. *San Francisco's Chronicle and Examiner* had tied themselves into a joint newspaper operat-

---

[65] See Ben H. Bagdikian, The Media Monopoly (Boston: Beacon Press, 1983, pp. 98–103.

[66] Cities with daily newspapers in JOA in 1970 included: Albuquerque, N.M.; Bristol, Tenn.; Charleston, W.Va.; Columbus, Ohio; El Paso, Texas; Evansville, Ind.; Fort Wayne, Ind; Franklin-Oil City, Pa.; Honolulu; Knoxville, Tenn.; Lincoln, Neb.; Madison, Wis.; Miami, Fla.; Nashville, Tenn.; Pittsburgh, Pa.; Saint Louis, Mo.; Salt Lake City; San Francisco; Shreveport, La.; Tucson, and Tulsa. Since then, Birmingham, Ala., Cincinnati, Ohio, Chattanooga, Tenn., and Seattle, Wn. have gone into JOAs. Dailies in Anchorage, Alaska, dissolved a JOA after a brief period, and The Derrick, Oil City, Pa., ended its JOA in 1985 by buying its partner, the Franklin News-Herald. The Knoxville, TN, News-Sentinel and the Journal ended their JOA at the end of 1991.

[67] Statement of Donald F. Turner, assistant attorney general, Antitrust Division, Department of Justice, before the Senate Judiciary Committee, Subcommittee on Antitrust and Monopoly, on S. 1312, April 1968, p. 18.

[68] See, e.g., The Guild Reporter, Sept. 8, 1967, p. 8; "Failing Newspaper Bill Assailed," Associated Press dispatch in Wisconsin State Journal, Madison, Sec. 1, p. 8, April 17, 1968.

[69] John H. Carlson, "Newspaper Preservation Act: A Critique," Indiana Law Journal 46:392 (Spring, 1971).

ing agreement some years before, in September of 1965. Under that agreement, one newspaper—*The News-Call-Bulletin*—was put to death, and the two remaining dailies carved up the morning (*Chronicle*) and evening (*Examiner*) markets. Printing for the *Chronicle* and the *Examiner* is done by a jointly owned subsidiary, the San Francisco Newspaper Printing Company. The two remaining daily papers' editorial staffs are kept independent, although the two newspapers jointly published a unified Sunday edition. Profits from all operations are shared half-and-half. As a result, the *Chronicle* and *Examiner* have achieved a highly profitable position in San Francisco's daily newspaper market.[70]

Publisher Brugman and the *Bay Guardian* contended that the Newspaper Preservation Act is unconstitutional because it unfairly encourages such a journalistic monopoly. The effect of the Act, they contended, causes it to violate the press freedom guarantee of the First Amendment.

Chief Judge Oliver J. Carter summed up the *Bay Guardian's* arguments:[71]

> The plaintiffs . . . contend that the profit sharing, joint ad rates, and other cooperative aspects of the joint operating agreement enable the defendants to establish and perpetuate a stranglehold on the San Francisco newspaper market. The plaintiffs contend that the Act is unconstitutional because it unfairly encourages this journalistic monopoly.

Judge Carter, however, was not persuaded by such arguments. He ruled that the simple answer to the plaintiffs' contention is that the Act does not authorize any conduct. He added that the Newspaper Preservation Act is a narrow exception to the antitrust laws for newspapers in danger of failing, and that the Act is "in many respects merely a codification of the judicially created 'failing company' doctrine." Although he upheld the Act's constitutionality, Judge Carter's words were not kind to the legislation: [72]

> * * * [T]he Act was designed to preserve independent editorial voices. Regardless of the economic or social

---

[70] Bay Guardian Co. v. Chronicle Pub. Co., 344 F.Supp. 1155, 1157 (N.D.Cal.1972). This court confrontation did not represent a full-dress trial. The plaintiffs originally sought a declaratory judgment that the Act was unconstitutional, but "such an action could not be maintained for technical jurisdictional reasons." See 340 F.Supp. 76 (N.D.Cal.1972). Then, the defendants—including the *Examiner* and the *Chronicle*—"answered the antitrust portions of the complaint by asserting the Act in two affirmative defenses to those claims." Plaintiff *Bay Guardian Co.* then moved to strike those defenses on grounds that the Newspaper Preservation Act is unconstitutional on its face.

[71] 344 F.Supp. 1155, 1157 (N.D.Cal.1972).

[72] Ibid., p. 1158.

wisdom of such a course, it does not violate the freedom of the press. Rather it is merely a selective repeal of the antitrust laws. It merely looses the same shady market forces which existed before the passage of the Sherman, Clayton and other antitrust laws.

The Bay Guardian Company lawsuit, however, contained another wrinkle. It was contended that the *Chronicle* and the *Examiner* were not truly "failing newspapers" and that the *News-Call-Bulletin* should not have been shut down as part of the merger. A $1,350,000 out-of-court settlement was awarded to a number of parties, including the Bay Guardian Company.

Such considerations aside, the importance of the Newspaper Preservation Act should not be overestimated. As Professor Paul Jess of the University of Kansas has noted, the Act did little more than legalize the 22 joint operating agreements already in existence at the time the Act was passed. There has been no great scramble to add to the number of joint operating agreements as such agreements are outlined by the act. The test of the Newspaper Preservation Act provides that to enter a joint operating agreement requires that at least one of the two newspapers must be "failing", or "in probable danger of financial failure." Any new joint operating agreement, furthermore, must be undertaken only after receiving written consent from the Attorney General of the United States. The Attorney General must determine that at least one of the newspapers applying for joint operation is "failing" or "in probable danger of financial failure."

At the 15th anniversary of the Newspaper Preservation Act in 1985, there were still 22 joint operating agreements in the nation, although the cast of newspapers had changed somewhat. As Margaret Genovese noted, further change was occurring. One paper in a "JOA"—The Derrick of Franklin-Oil City, Pennsylvania—had ended the partnership by buying out The News Herald of Franklin. In addition, the Columbus (Ohio) Dispatch was planning to end its JOA with a Scripps-Howard paper, the Columbus Citizen-Journal.[73]

One of the recent JOA partnerships—in Seattle, between the Post-Intelligencer (P–I) and the Times—is speaking of a " 'substantially improved' " financial picture. The P–I had reported losses of averaging $1 a year from 1969 until 1983, but made a profit in 1984, the second year of the JOA—a JOA created despite employees of the P–I hiring an attorney to prevent its creation. Although opponents continue to be heard, the publishers of the Times and the P–I say that their editorial product has improved and that the two papers' news sides are competing briskly.

[73] Margaret Genovese, "JOA," Presstime, August, 1985, pp. 16–17.

In August 1988, in one of his last official acts in office, Attorney General Edwin Meese overruled his own Department of Justice antitrust lawyers and a Department administrative law judge to approve a JOA between Knight-Ridder's Detroit Free Press and Gannett's Detroit News. During the time that Attorney General was considering the proposed agreement, the Free Press, normally the liberal Detroit newspaper, remained discreetly silent about Meese's mounting difficulties with Congress, even admitting in one editorial that "commenting on Mr. Meese's conduct makes us uncomfortable because the Free Press petition for a joint operating agreement with the Detroit News awaits his decision." [74]

After the Attorney General approved the JOA between the Detroit Free Press and the Detroit News, various citizen groups joined together to form a coalition, Michigan Citizens for a Free Press to overturn the Attorney General's decision in federal court. They argued that both newspapers had intentionally adopted short-term practices designed to reduce their revenues, creating artificial losses to justify their application for the JOA. A divided federal court of appeals upheld the JOA but admitted:

> We can envision a perfectly rational different policy, one that would require a showing that the weaker paper was more bloodied before approving a JOA and therefore *might* discourage the sort of competition we saw in Detroit. Congress, however, delegated to the Attorney General and not to us the delicate and troubling responsibility of putting content into the ambiguous phrase 'probable danger of financial failure'. [75]

Rehearing en banc was denied 5–4. The Supreme Court affirmed without opinion, 4–4, Justice White not participating.

The Detroit JOA was the first authorized since 1983, when two Seattle dailies began joint operation after more than two years of Justice Department scrutiny and litigation. At present, there are 19 JOAs in existence in the United States, three less than when Congress grandfathered the 22 joint operations existing when the law was passed in 1970.

Most experts agree that this figure is likely to remain relatively constant in the future, because the number of cities where all the factors exist that are necessary to qualify for the formation of a JOA is quite limited. In addition to those 19 areas where JOAs presently exist, only 23 other cities still have two competing

---

[74] As quoted in Mark Fitzgerald, "Treading Softly," Editor & Publisher, July 30, 1988, p. 12. See also George Garneau, "Detroit JOA Approved," Editor & Publisher, August 13, 1988, p. 14.

[75] Michigan Citizens for an Independent Press v. Thornburgh, 868 F.2d 1285 (D.C. Cir.1989).

daily newspapers, and few of these would qualify for joint operating agreements, either because one of the papers is too weak financially to make a JOA attractive to the other, or because the rivalry between them is too intense to provide a basis for such an agreement.

One expert believes that the number of new JOAs that will be formed in the future can be counted on one hand. The reason is that:

> there's a window of opportunity for a JOA. It's at the time when the second paper still has a large enough portion of the market to make it financially attractive for the larger paper to enter a JOA.[76]

That "window" has already closed in most cities with two competing dailies. In reality, then, it would seem that the Detroit News/Free Press JOA doesn't mark the beginning of a new trend towards operating agreements among rival daily newspapers, but rather one of the last applications of a law designed for competitive situations that are becoming less and less common in major American cities.

Total Market Coverage ("TMC") and The Newspaper Preservation Act

A case involving the Tucson joint operating agreement papers—the Arizona Daily Star and the Tucson Citizen—illustrates an increasingly troublesome wrinkle in antitrust law for newspapers. Obviously trying to offer a more attractive package to advertisers, the Tucson papers—joined together in their business, production, and distribution sides to form the joint operator, Tucson Newspapers, Inc.—tried "Total Market Coverage." A TMC a product designed to keep advertisers from defecting to the local "shoppers," controlled or free-circulation publications. TMCs have often been added—as they were in Tucson—to newspapers, going to every house in an area, often in "zoned" editions tailored to particular locales.[77]

As lawyer George Freeman has written, "The shopper finds competition tougher than it used to be. It is about this time that the shopper realizes that its biggest asset may be an antitrust lawsuit against the [urban daily] newspaper publisher [who has started a TMC]."[78]

---

[76] M. Anderson, "JOA Law at the Turning Point," Presstime 10/89, 6.

[77] Wick v. Tucson Newspaper, Inc., 598 F.Supp. 1155 (D.Ariz.1984), reversed and vacated at 831 F.2d 1066 (9th Cir. 1984).

[78] George Freeman, "Antitrust Actions: At least 25 lawsuits in the last few years have focused on newspapers' total market coverage products," Presstime, January, 1985, p. 8.

In the Tucson-area TMC case, Walter and Robert Wick—publishers of a biweekly newspaper, the Green Valley News & Sun—brought an antitrust action against the Tucson dailies. Green Valley is located about 25 miles from Tucson. The Wicks objected to the TMCs offered by the Tucson papers. The Arizona Star published a " * * * four-page newsprint jacket [which] appears in the Arizona Daily Star on a weekly basis. It is named THE ROUNDUP." It contains as filler advertising inserts called inserts or preprints, and was distributed once a week as a part of the Arizona Daily Star.

As George Freeman explains the operation of a TMC product, the cost of its production is low. Therefore, "the publisher charges little for space (or inserts), offering bargain rates to clients already advertising in the daily."[79]

The Tucson Citizen, the other half of the JOA, was publishing its own TMC—the BULLETIN BOARD—in an identical way. In addition, in order to blanket the area with the TMC product, the Tucson daily newspapers mailed THE ROUNDUP and BULLETIN BOARD to all persons in the area—whether there were subscribing to the Tucson dailies or not.[80]

The court noted that the Tucson papers' joint operating agreement had been declared in violation of the antitrust laws, and that the Newspaper Preservation Act had exempted certain newspapers from the operation of antitrust statutes. The court initially concluded that the biweekly TMC products, THE ROUNDUP and BULLETIN BOARD were not parts of the Tucson Newspapers; they were not sections of daily newspapers. The content of THE ROUNDUP and BULLETIN BOARD was seen as primarily distributing advertising rather than editorial material. Why did this matter? The court said:[81]

> The Court * * * finds that these publications [THE ROUNDUP and BULLETIN BOARD] constitute "shopping newspapers" which were not intended to be included among those activities of a joint operating agreement exempt from the operation of anti-trust laws. The only thing exempted by the Newspaper Preservation Act from the operation of those laws is a newspaper publication * * *. That is a limited exemption and unless it is found to be applicable, the joint operation of these two daily newspapers constitutes a violation of the Sherman Act * * *.

[79] Freeman, loc. cit.

[80] 598 F.Supp. 1155, 1157 (D.Ariz.1984).

[81] Wick v. Tucson Newspaper, Inc., 598 F.Supp. 1155, 1160 (D.Ariz.1984).

The court then issued an injunction to prevent the Arizona Daily Star and the Tucson Citizen from distributing those portions of their papers referred to as ROUNDUP and BULLETIN BOARD to non-subscribers to the dailies. This distribution was forbidden whether by mail or otherwise, and included the "slick" advertising material that ROUNDUP and BULLETIN BOARD provided as "jackets" (covers) for, to any non-subscribers in the Green Valley zip code area.

On reargument several months later, however, the court changed its ruling in part:

> The Court is now advised by counsel that, contrary to the above [the earlier preliminary injunction order and accompanying language], the publication of ROUNDUP and BULLETIN BOARD is being distributed in Green Valley, almost uniformly, without any slick paper inserts.

> Therefore, the prior finding of the Court that there was a contemporary violation of the antitrust laws . . . which was likely to recur is inaccurate as there has been no violation to date. Further, the Court now finds, for reasons and on the authority set forth in the September 5, 1984 Order, that ROUNDUP and BULLETIN BOARD, as distributed in Green Valley, are not "shopping newspapers."

*   *   *

> The Court finds that the portion of ROUNDUP and BULLETIN BOARD printed on newsprint and referred to in both this and the Court's prior opinion as a "jacket" is a "newspaper publication" within the meaning of 15 U.S.C. Sec. 1802(4), and is not a "shopping newspaper" in its present form. It is thus exempt from the antitrust laws.

Other TMC Activity

The TMC antitrust challenge to the Tucson joint operating agreement by no means shows the whole picture of TMC antitrust action. The joint operating agreement was merely a complicating factor. Most dailies, of course, are not parts of joint operating agreements.

Attorney George Freeman has noted that at least 15 lawsuits in the mid 1980s zeroed in on daily newspapers efforts to provide total-market-coverage publications. And that's where the going gets sticky: if an antitrust suit is brought involving a TMC product, then it will be up to a court to discover what may be nearly indiscoverable: Is the intent behind the TMC to compete better for ad revenues or is it to put competing publications out of business? One is good competition; the other is violative of antitrust laws.

Consent Decrees

Court decisions, however, are only a part of the antitrust story affecting the communications media. Also available in antitrust law is a court-adjudicated legal instrument known as a consent decree. Consent decrees—also sometimes called consent judgments—are negotiated final legal settlements between the government and a business. Consent decrees have the force of law once they have been approved by a judge. Such consent decree settlements can take place in civil, but not criminal, antitrust cases.[82]

Where a newspaper or broadcasting station is concerned, antitrust consent decrees have been used in the following fashion. First, civil antitrust suit is filed by the Antitrust Division of the Justice Department against the owners of a newspaper or broadcasting station. In the opinion of the Justice Department, the communications medium involved may have been engaging in anti-competitive business practices.

Second, the owners may decide that it will do them no good to fight the antitrust suit. The owners' attorneys may see that a court battle is almost certain to result in defeat. So, in order to avoid lengthy and expensive trial, attorneys for the owner will sit down with attorneys from the Antitrust Division of the Justice Department. Once a consent agreement is worked out, it means that the owners have promised to stop certain business practices or to divest themselves of certain media units. After the agreement is reached, it is made final by being formalized before a federal district judge.

Consent decrees have the advantage of allowing a defendant to settle a suit without admitting a violation of law. An example of this was the sale, late in 1968, of WREX–TV in Rockford, Ill., by the Gannett Company of Rochester, New York. In that year, the Antitrust Division of the Department of Justice has filed a civil antitrust suit against the Gannett Company, which owned, in addition to WREX–TV, also owned the Rockford Newspaper, the Morning Star and the Register-Republic. Gannett had acquired the two newspapers in 1967, and had purchased WREX–TV in 1962 for $3,500,000. Under the consent decree, the Gannett Company agreed to divest itself of the television station to James

---

[82] As Dr. Lorry Rytting, formerly of the University of Utah noted, the Justice Department is sensitive to charges that criminal antitrust suits might be filed, in effect, to force the signing of civil consent decrees. Department of Justice policy discourages the use of concurrent criminal and civil antitrust complaints. Rytting, "Antitrust Consent Decrees: A Threat to Freedom of the Press?," unpublished paper, School of Journalism, University of Wisconsin, 1967.

S. Gilmore, Jr., president of Gilmore Broadcasting Co., for $6,850,000.[83]

Earl A. Jinkinson, formerly chief of the Midwest Office of Chicago of the Department of Justice's Antitrust Division, has summarized some of the differing ways consent decrees are viewed.[84]

> To the Government attorneys the consent decree is an act of grace granted in order to give the attorneys and the entire staff more time to attend to other ever-pressing and sometimes more important matters. On the other hand, many defense counsel at least profess to believe, erroneously I might add, that the consent decree is a governmental device for winning cases, thrust upon an unwilling defendant which, to adopt the words of Seth Dabney, is like "Byron's maiden who strove and repented, but ultimately consented." To attorneys for private parties injured because of the violation [of antitrust statutes], the consent decree is an abrogation of the duty of the Department of Justice to protect their client's rights.

In 1947, Zechariah Chafee warned that consent decrees could increase the danger to press freedom through heavy use of the antitrust laws. Consent decrees are reached without trials, after secret proceedings. Evidence presented in reaching these decrees is not made public. Furthermore, such decrees are as legally binding as the decision of a federal court, and may be enforced with contempt-of-court sanctions if they are not obeyed.[85]

It has been suggested that the government, when it begins—or which has indicated that it soon may begin—an antitrust action is very much in the driver's seat against the defendant, which may feel compelled to "settle" by way of a consent decree. True, if an owner decides that the terms insisted on by the Antitrust Division violate his rights, he may halt the negotiations for a consent decree and demand a full trial. Trials, however, are expensive, lengthy, and may carry with them publicity which the media owners find damaging.[86]

Whether consent decrees are a threat to press freedom or a boon to media owners which allows them to avoid full-dress antitrust trials, the fact remains that such decrees affecting the mass media are a weapon in government's antitrust arsenal.

[83] The Gannetteer, magazine of the Gannett Co., January 1969, p. 3.

[84] Earl A. Jinkinson, "Negotiation of Consent Decrees," Antitrust Bulletin, Vol. 9: Nos. 5–9 (Sept.-Dec., 1964), pp. 673–690, at pp. 676–677.

[85] Chafee, op. cit. Vol. 2, p. 670.

[86] Rytting, op. cit.

That kind of agreement is by no means a thing of the past. For example, in February of 1984, the Tribune Company—owners of the Orlando (Florida) Sentinel—agreed to a settlement with the Department of Justice to end an antitrust action. Back in 1980, the Sentinel had purchased five publications—two shoppers and three weeklies—for $4.1 million. The Justice Department brought suit, contending that those five acquired publications added up to 20 percent of the advertising in Osceola County, and that the Sentinel already had another 40 percent.

The Chicago-based Tribune Company settled with the Department of Justice, agreeing to sell off the five publications within a year. Also, the agreement forbids the Orlando Sentinel from buying any other publications in its main circulation area for 10 years.[87]

SEC. 97. ELECTRONIC MEDIA OWNERSHIP POLICIES

Traditional electronic media ownership policies have been altered substantially by greater government reliance on deregulation as the policy of choice.

The FCC's primary broadcast ownership policy, as that of the FRC that preceded it, has often been described as favoring the licensing of locally owned stations to provide broadcast audiences with locally produced, community oriented programming. Yet as most government "policies," local ownership was not a specific objective that either regulatory agency worked systematically to attain, but rather only a vague statement of intention appearing periodically in various regulatory pronouncements.[88]

The FCC's efforts to prevent broadcast networks from exerting too much influence upon local station program decisions has been discussed elsewhere in this text.[89] In addition, the Commission adopted rules that prevented any licensee from owning more than one station in a single broadcast market.[90] Later, when television and FM services emerged, the FCC prohibited joint ownership of

[87] SNPA [Southern Newspaper Publishers Assocation] Bulletin, Feb. 10, 1984.

[88] As the President's Task Force on Telecommunications: Final Report (Govt. Printing Office, Wash. D.C.1969) pointed out, the concept of a nationwide system of local stations, "produced a relatively large number of individual stations, but relatively few accessible broadcast signals for the individual listener." Chapter 7, p. 12–13. The industry itself evolved towards national network services popular with broadcast audiences, and federal policy was powerless to impose upon this national system the local orientation Congress had once envisioned.

[89] See Chapter 9, Sec. 49.

[90] 47 CFR § 73.35. It was this rule that lead to the famous NBC case, 319 U.S. 190, 63 S.Ct. 997 (1943) discussed in Chapter 7 of this text.

television and either an AM or FM facility in a single market, but "grandfathered" those already owning such broadcast facilities.[91]

The FCC also has imposed a cap on the number of broadcast stations a single entity can own, a figure recently increased from 21 to 36.[92] In contested license proceedings, the Commission has attempted to broaden the base of broadcast ownership by favoring the candidate without other media holdings. Then in 1975, the agency finally formalized what had been its unofficial policy for the past two decades, adopting rules that prohibited newspaper ownership of any broadcast station within the paper's main service area.[93] In enacting this rule, the FCC "grandfathered" all but those 16 newspaper owners who also owned the only radio or television station in their market.[94]

From 1978 onward the Commission began to retreat from vigorous enforcement of its broadcast ownership policies, relying more heavily on a deregulated marketplace to decide how broadcast licenses should be acquired or transferred.[95] During the same period though, the FCC also began developing new licensing policies to encourage more widespread minority ownership of broadcast stations.

In 1978 the Commission adopted a policy statement offering tax certificates to those selling their broadcast stations to minority owners. These certificates allowed sellers to defer the capital gains tax that otherwise would be imposed on any profits made from the sale. At the same time the agency also authorized anyone whose license renewal had been designated for hearing to avoid possible loss of license by disposing of the broadcast property to a minority owner for a price not in excess of 75% of its fair market value.[96]

---

[91] CFR § 73.240 and CFR § 73.636. To "grandfather" is to enforce a rule only prospectively, allowing those currently in violation of its terms to continue their existing practices without penalty. From an equitable standpoint, grandfathering avoids punishing those who were acting in good faith at a time when their actions were not in violation of law. The greatest drawback of grandfathering, however, is that it creates a privileged class of individuals who are thereafter able to do what all others are prohibited from doing. From a practical point, agencies like the FCC prefer to "grandfather" whenever possible, because in this way they can avoid legal challenges from those who otherwise would be adversely affected by their new rules.

[92] 47 CFR §§ 73.35(a); 43.240(a)1; 1:73.636(a)1–2; 76.501.

[93] 50 FCC 2d 1046, amended on rehearing by 53 FCC 2d 589 (1975).

[94] This decision to grandfather all other newspaper owners of broadcast stations was sustained by the U.S. Supreme Court in FCC v. National Citizens Committee for Broadcasting, 436 U.S. 775, 98 S.Ct. 2096 (1978).

[95] At the FCC's urging, Congress has even authorized the agency to award licenses by chance through use of a lottery, rather than by hearing, Omnibus Reconciliation Act of 1981, 95 Stat. 736–37, but the Commission has used a lottery only to award LPTV, MMDS and other specialized spectrum services to this point.

[96] Minority Ownership of Broadcast Facilities, 44 RR 2d 1051 (1978).

In addition, after having been instructed by the D.C. Court of Appeals in the TV 9, Inc. v. FCC case [97] that, "when the minority ownership is likely to increase diversity of content, especially on opinion and viewpoint, merit should be awarded," the agency began granting "enhancement" points to minority applicants in comparative license hearing cases, thus improving their prospects of being awarded the license.

The FCC's efforts to extend the same rights to women as a minority group was struck down by the Court in Steele v. FCC,[98] because Congress had not authorized women to be classified as a minority in awarding these license preferences. When the *Steele* case was remanded to the Commission for further consideration, the agency indicated that it was no longer certain that granting any minority preferences served the public interest.[99] Alarmed by this apparent change in regulatory attitude, Congress included in its Omnibus Spending Bill of 1987 a provision preventing the agency from repealing or even continuing to reconsider its minority preference policies.[1]

In 1983, Alan Shurberg had filed a license application for television channel 18 in Hartford, Connecticut. Shurberg's application was rejected by the Commission because the current licensee of channel 18, Faith Center, was facing a license revocation hearing. Before the hearing was completed, Faith Center took advantage of the FCC's "distress sale" policy to sell the station to Astroline Communications, an Hispanic partnership qualifying as a minority-owned organization under FCC rules.

Shurberg, a white applicant, challenged this minority preference policy, and in a 2–1 decision, one panel of D.C. Court of Appeals judges upheld the challenge, deciding that this FCC minority ownership program was "not narrowly tailored to reme-

---

[97] 495 F.2d 929 (D.C.Cir.1973), cert. denied 419 U.S. 986, 95 S.Ct. 245 (1974).

[98] 770 F.2d 1192 (D.C.Cir.1985).

[99] The FCC had originally launched its regulatory programs to expand minority ownership of broadcast properties because studies indicated that less than 2 percent of all broadcast stations were owned by minorities in the mid 1970s. When the Supreme Court in Wygant v. Jackson Board of Education, 476 U.S. 267, 106 S.Ct. 1842 (1986) held that mere numerical evidence of minimal minority presence in a particular activity is not sufficient in itself to justify government intervention to rectify racial imbalance in the absence of actual evidence of prior discrimination, this holding undercut the entire basis for the Commission's position, because there was no documentation of any discrimination in the issuance or sale of broadcast licenses.

[1] Pub.L. 100–202 (1987). However, in January 1991, while still serving on the D.C. Court of Appeals, now Supreme Court Justice Clarence Thomas wrote the majority opinion for a divided three-judge panel in Lamprecht v. FCC that overturned the FCC female ownership preference policy on the grounds that Congress had not demonstrated previous discrimination against women who sought to acquire broadcast properties. Harry A. Jessell, "Court Overturns FCC Gender Preference," Broadcasting, February 24, 1992, p. 16.

dy past discriminations or to promote program diversity. Specifically, the program unduly burdens Shurberg, an innocent non-minority, and is not reasonably related to the interest it seeks to vindicate."[2]

Three weeks later a different three judge D.C. Court of Appeals panel in another 2–1 decision upheld the Commission's policy of awarding minority enhancements in comparative hearing situations.[3] In this case Winter Park Communications with 20 percent black ownership and non-minority owned Metro Broadcasting both challenged the FCC's awarding of a new television license in Orlando, Florida to Hispanic-owned Rainbow Broadcasting. In affirming the Commission's decision to grant the license to the Hispanic group the court declared, "the Commission's award of minority enhancements is not a grant of any number of permits to minorities or a denial to qualified non-minorities of the ability freely to compete for permits."

Efforts to resolve these conflicting decisions made by different panels of judges from the same court when neither case was able to obtain sufficient votes to be scheduled for rehearing by a full panel of judges. Because of the importance of this issue, the Supreme Court agreed to hear both cases, and in June 1990 it rendered its decision.

The Court affirmed, by a 5–4 vote, the constitutionality of both the FCC distress sale and its minority preference policies. The decision to uphold these two Commission affirmative action programs surprised many communication lawyers who had expected only Justices Brennan, Marshall and Blackmun to support these measures.[4] This belief become even more widespread after oral arguments before the Court in which all parties seemed to agree that changing the racial characteristics of broadcast ownership would be unlikely to have any significant effect on the nature of broadcast programming, since programming decisions tended to be determined primarily by marketplace considerations.

In the end, however, Justices White and Stevens joined the three strongest proponents of minority preference, influenced perhaps by the special circumstances of this particular type of affirmative action. Justice Brennan, writing for the majority, placed great emphasis on broadcasting's status as a unique institution, legitimately subject to a far wider range of Congressional controls than any other medium simply because a scarcity of spectrum space has required the federal government to regulate the privilege of spectrum access.

[2] Shurberg Broadcasting of Hartford, Inc. v. FCC, 876 F.2d 902 (D.C.Cir.1989).

[3] Winter Park Communications, Inc. v. FCC, 873 F.2d 347 (D.C.Cir.1989).

[4] 58 U.S.L.W. 5054.

Under such circumstances, according to Brennan, Congressional intent must be given special recognition, and as he observed, these particular FCC policies, "have been specifically approved—indeed, mandated—by Congress," through riders attached to FCC appropriation bills in 1988, 1989 and 1990, preventing the FCC from spending any portion of its funding to reconsider the validity of its minority preference policies.

Quoting Justice White's *Red Lion* opinion with approval, Brennan pointed out that since no one has a First Amendment right to broadcast, no applicant has the right to expect that a broadcast license will be granted without consideration of such significant public interest factors such as minority ownership.

In essence, then, the majority opinion affirmed those specific FCC ownership preference programs under review because in this particular instance there was clear evidence of Congressional support for such programs to serve the public interest through encouraging broader minority participation in a field where federal authority is paramount. (The issue of broadcast ownership preferences for women was not considered by the court because it was not involved in FCC actions being appealed.)

Justice O'Connor wrote a scathing 30 page dissent, in which Justices Rehnquist, Scalia and Kennedy joined. She charged the FCC with using "race as a proxy for whatever views it believes to be underrepresented in the broadcast spectrum," adding, "The reflexive or unthinking use of a suspect classification is the hallmark of an unconstitutional policy."

Justice Kennedy also wrote a separate dissent, in which Justice Scalia joined. Kennedy said that he could not accept the argument of the majority that, "the Constitution permits the government to discriminate among its citizens on the basis of race in order to serve interests so trivial as 'broadcast diversity.' "

If this case had been before the Court only a few months later, after Justice Brennan had retired those minority broadcast ownership policies it affirmed might well have been rejected, quite possibly by the 6–3 margin the experts had been predicting before Brennan began working both on his opinion and his colleagues. But even though the FCC's minority ownership policies have now finally been affirmed by the Court, the most crucial test of their value still lies ahead. Will more extensive minority ownership of broadcast properties actually lead to a wider range of broadcast programming designed to meet the special needs of minority viewers and listeners? Perhaps just having a larger number of minority owners deeply involved in the day-to-day programming decisions of a station will achieve this objective, but if its realization is dependent to any extent upon enlightened guidance and direction from the FCC, then the outlook for improved minority broadcast service in the United States because of these policies is not very promising.

Antitrust and Electronic Media Program Ownership Practices

In National Broadcasting Company v. United States[5], the Supreme Court had affirmed the power of the FCC to consider federal antitrust implications of broadcast practices in determining whether broadcast licensees were operating in the public interest. In his opinion, Justice Frankfurter quoted with approval the justification the Commission had advanced for adopting regulations designed to prevent this type of abuse of the broadcast license privilege:

> While many of the network practices raise serious questions under the antitrust law, our jurisdiction does not depend on a showing that they do in fact constitute a violation of the antitrust laws. It is not our function to apply the antitrust laws as such. It is our duty, however, to refuse licenses or renewals to any person who engages or proposes to engage in practices which will prevent either himself or other licensees or both from making the fullest use of radio facilities. This is the standard of public interest . . . which we must apply to all applications for licenses and renewals.[6]

One casualty of the FCC's decade-long policy of deregulation seems to have been this traditional concern for anti-trust implications of broadcast ownership. During the 1980s, the FCC increased the number of TV, AM and FM stations each licensee could own from 7–7–7 to 12–12–12. In 1992, the FCC allowed each licensee to own as many as 30 AM and 30 FM stations as the commission continued to rescind virtually all other regulatory restraints imposed to prevent undue concentration of control.[7]

It is the Justice Department, rather than the FCC, that has primary responsibility for enforcing federal antitrust laws in the field of broadcasting, as in every other area of American com-

[5] National Broadcasting Co. v. United States, 319 U.S. 190, 222–223, 63 S.Ct. 997 (1943).

[6] Ibid., at 219–223, 63 S.Ct. at 1011–1012.

[7] See, for example, "Changing Point of View at the FCC," Broadcasting June 17, 1985, p. 38 that discusses the repeal of the "anti-trafficking" requirement that prevented a station from being sold until it had been owned for at least 3 years; the rule that a single entity could own only one VHF station in a top 50 market, and rules that required FCC approval of all hostile takeovers. See also Edmund L. Andrews, "A New Tune for Radio: Hard Times," The New York Times, March 15, 1992, Sec. 4, p. 3.

merce.[8] However, the courts have given the FCC far greater latitude than the Justice Department to prevent media practices that while not truly "anti-competitive" in terms of the federal law, might operate to constrain "the development of diverse and antagonistic sources of program service." [9]

During the 1980s, the Commission had been contending that there is no longer any need to impose strict regulatory constraints upon broadcast ownership, because electronic media audiences have such a wide range of viewing and listening alternatives today that no combination of conglomerates could possibly deny them their free choice of programming.

Unfortunately, this view of electronic mass communication operation completely overlooks the anti-competitive influences that media conglomerates are capable of exerting upon efforts by entertainment and information services to reach electronic media audiences. From the beginning, broadcasting has acted primarily as a distribution system for the programming of others, and today, all electronic media remain dependent upon the film and music industries for their most popular features.

Radio began this pattern of dependency, as local stations delegated popular "prime time" programming responsibility to a network that in turn relied upon advertising agencies to produce its shows.[10] When television program production became too expensive to be underwritten by advertising agency sponsors in the mid 1950s, the network turned to Hollywood film studios to produce their series programs. With film audiences dwindling because of television competition, these Hollywood producers were only too eager to accept this new type of financial support.

The problem these film producers faced in dealing with the networks, however, was that they were sellers in a market with only three potential buyers who often seemed less interested in obtaining the best program quality than in obtaining the most favorable ownership terms for the programs they agreed to schedule. When Justice Department began an anti-trust action against the three networks in 1972, alleging that they used their dominant position in the field of television program distribution to obtain financial advantages from program producers, the FCC enacted

---

[8] United States v. RCA, 358 U.S. 334, 79 S.Ct. 457 (1959).

[9] Mount Mansfield Television, Inc. v. FCC, 442 F.2d 470, 480 (2d Cir.1971).

[10] American newspapers tried to prevent radio stations from using press wire services for their newscasts, but after a short period of constraint, broadcasting became as dependent upon the newsgathering capacity of the American press during the 1930s as it was dependent upon the music and entertainment industries for its popular programming. The short-term agreement between the press and broadcasting specifying how wire service stories could be handled on radio is published as "The Biltmore Agreement" in Frank J. Kahn, Documents of American Broadcasting 4th ed. (Englewood Cliffs NY: Prentice Hall 1984) p. 101.

"financial interest" rules denying the networks the right to benefit financially from the distribution of any programs they had not
produced themselves.[11]   Not satisfied either by the scope of these
rules or the Commission's commitment to enforce them, the Justice Department continued its anti-trust action until each of the
three networks eventually entered into consent agreements to
alter their program procurement practices.[12]

In enacting its financial interest rules, the FCC explained
quite clearly why it believed these network practices were not
simply damaging to independent producers, but the interests of
the public as well.   As the Commission pointed out, selecting
network programs on the basis of price rather than quality artifi-
cally deprived television audiences of their best possible viewing
opportunities while encouraging those who produced these shows
to be more concerned with production costs than production values.

In 1982 the FCC attempted to rescind these "financial interest" rules, but pulled back when program producers rallied
enough support in Congress to discourage this effort.[13]   During
this same period, the Justice Department had indicated its willingness to release the networks from the terms of their consent
agreements if the Commission repealed these rules.[14]

In 1988, the networks began a new campaign to be released
from these program ownership restrictions.[15]   As might be expected, they based their plea for release upon the FCC's own
argument that there is now such a competitive electronic media
environment that marketplace alone should determine how programs are to be financed and distributed.

In January 1990, Fox Broadcasting petitioned the FCC to be
exempted from the financial interest rules for an 18 month period
to allow it to exceed that 15 hour a week maximum limitation
imposed by the rules on a network's carriage of its own program-

[11] 47 CFR 73.658(j). The Justice Department action was United States v. CBS,
Civ.Action # 74–5399 (C.D.Cal.1974).

[12] For details of these settlements, see "NBC Breaks Ranks: Settles with Justice," Broadcasting November 22, 1976, p. 21; "CBS Settles with Justice," Broadcasting May 12, 1980, p. 29; "It's Settled; ABC, Justice Come to Terms," Broadcasting August 25, 1980.

[13] 54 RR2d 457 (1983). The Hollywood producers were even successful in
enlisting the help of former Actors Guild President Reagan to stop this recission
effort. For a more detailed account of this entire financial interest issue, see Don
R. Le Duc, Beyond Broadcasting: Patterns in Policy and Law (White Plains NY:
Longman, 1987) chapter 5.

[14] "Consent Decree Held Hostage: Justice Department Backs FCC," Variety,
February 2, 1983, p. 84.

[15] "Fin–Syn Phoenix Out of the Ashes," Broadcasting July 4, 1988, p. 30.

ming.[16] Fox contended this 18 month waiver would allow it to take advantage of its ownership of 20th Century Fox film studios to produce programming during this period that would increase its audience and enable it to compete more effectively with the three major television networks.

Instead of responding directly to the Fox petition, the FCC tried to avoid getting caught in the middle of this controversy by directing the television networks and Hollywood film producers to work out some compromise agreement the Commission could then adopt as its new rules. By June 1990, however, it was clear that no compromise agreement could be reached and the FCC was forced to begin its own deliberations to determine whether the rules should be retained, modified or rescinded.

Hollywood producers claimed that the networks had not been bargaining in good faith, because they were confident that the administration would not be sympathetic to a continuation of restrictions on the marketplace behavior of the television networks. That suspicion seemed to be confirmed when the U.S. Justice Department, the Federal Trade Commission and the President's Chief of Staff all urged the Commission to repeal the rules.[17]

The networks argued that to continue to deny them the right to share in the off-network domestic and international sales revenues of those programs they scheduled unfairly eroded their capacity to survive in the much more competitive electronic media environment of the 1990s.

On the other hand, producers claimed that because the networks pay only 75–80 percent of the production costs of those programs they schedule, they have no right to demand a share of those domestic and international syndication revenues producers need to recoup their costs and profit from their own productions. In addition, these producers pointed out that without the protection of the rules, networks would be able to coerce them into granting the networks ownership or monetary concessions because only a very limited number of programs are able to obtain network exposure, and each network can exert a significant influence on a show's popularity by determining where it will be positioned in its schedule, and how heavily it will be promoted.[18]

[16] "Fox Waiver Petition May Be Open Sesame for Fin–Syn Revision." Broadcasting Jan. 29, 1990, p. 19.

[17] "Justice Dept. Urges Fin–Syn Repeal in FCC Filing Flood," Variety June 20, 1990, pg. 47; "White House Sends Loud and Clear Fin–Syn Signal," Broadcasting Feb. 18, 1991, pg. 27.

[18] The ratings success of a program is vitally important to the TV producer, because the amount of money a producer will earn from the $5.7 billion domestic syndication market and $2.3 billion foreign syndication market is largely dependent on the program's popularity during its network run.

Obviously, there is no simple, sensible solution to this extremely complex problem and so in April 1991, by a 3–2 vote, a sharply divided Commission adopted new financial syndication rules that as everyone had expected, pleased none of the parties. The new rules are to remain in effect for four years, subject to repeal at that time if the Commission should find that marketplace conditions no longer require them. During this period the networks may now fill up to 40 percent of the primetime schedule with their own productions, may engage in foreign syndication of television programs and may acquire syndication rights in programs produced by others, but in that case must wait at least 30 days after obtaining these rights before beginning syndication.[19]

The one major benefit the networks did receive from the revised rules was the ability to engage in foreign sales of television programming. Restricted by the old rules to foreign syndication only of those programs the networks themselves produced, network foreign sales have never exceeded $175 million, less than 8 percent of the $2.3 billion earned annually from foreign sales of American television programs.[20]

Ironically, even though this opportunity to share in the vast revenues of international program sales should strengthen the financial position of the networks, it is also likely to make them much more tempting targets for take-over by media giants such as Paramount and Disney, who have not in the past been interested in acquiring a broadcast network because of the FCC's financial interest rules. Now that either Paramount or Disney would be free to produce up to 40 percent of the primetime programs of the network it purchased and engage with only minimal restrictions in both domestic and foreign syndication, this revision of the FCC rules could ultimately result in our broadcast networks becoming a part of the American film industry.[21]

---

[19] 69 RR 2d 341 (1991). This 30 day waiting period has been provided in the rules to give a TV producer who has been coerced by the network into granting it syndication rights adequate opportunity to revoke this permission before the network exercises its right.

[20] "MIP Hip to Net's New Game", Variety, April 22, 1991, p. 1.

[21] "Going Dark At 10," Broadcasting, May 6, 1991, p. 20. This article reports a rumor circulating in the industry that NBC will soon reduce its primetime programming to less than 15 hours a week to no longer qualify as a "network" under the Financial Interest rules and then will be purchased by Paramount Pictures. As this text goes to press, the networks are still unable to exercise these new program syndication rights granted them by the FCC because they remain bound by the terms of the Consent Decree that ended the Justice Department antitrust action two decades ago. The Justice Department is seeking to release the networks from provisions of the Decree that prevent them from engaging in those program syndication practices now permitted by the FCC, but it is up to U.S. District Court Judge Robert Kelleher to decide whether this relief will actually be granted. See "Networks Take Fin–Syn Case to Justice." Broadcasting, July 29, 1991, p. 8.

In an allied development, First Media Corporation, owner of a CBS affiliate station in Orlando, Florida, petitioned the FCC in 1990 to rescind the agency's "Prime Time Access Rule." The current version of the rule, adopted in 1975, requires network affiliate television stations in the nation's largest 50 broadcast markets to set aside one hour of their primetime schedules each evening for non-network programming.[22] First Media argued that such sweeping interference in the programming choices of urban television stations no longer was justified by electronic media marketplace conditions, and therefore improperly infringed upon the First Amendment rights of those broadcasters.

The Commission initially appeared ready to ignore the First Media petition, with FCC Chairman Sikes declaring that a review of PTAR was, "certainly not on the front burner." As *Broadcasting* magazine noted editorially,[23]

> If anything remains sacrosanct in this day and age, it is that no one in his right mind will suggest laying a glove on PTAR. It is that most peculiar of regulations: one that apparently benefits everyone. Creation of PTAR cut back the network inventories and made ABC a competitive third network. It almost singlehandedly created a viable syndication industry * * * and it improved the position of the top 50 independents remarkably.

However, after Disney, Bonneville International and a large coalition of ABC and CBS affiliates joined First Media in asking that the rule be re-examined, the FCC came under increasing pressure to hold hearings to evaluate the continuing validity of this 15 year old policy.[24] Those opposing the rule point out that television producers of those "first-run" game and tabloid news programs that now dominate the first hour of affiliate station primetime schedules no longer need to be guaranteed major market exposure to survive economically, because the vast number of new cable TV networks that have emerged since 1975 now furnish such non-network producers a broad range of purchasers for their shows.

In addition, these PTAR opponents argue that the rule unfairly discriminates against producers of network programs, because it denies them the opportunity to recoup their production expenses through subsequent syndication of these shows in major markets during one of the most lucrative periods of the broadcast day.

[22] 47 CFR § 73.658(k), 1.

[23] "No Larger Than A Man's Hand," Broadcasting, Dec. 10, 1990, p. 138.

[24] "Bonneville Calls for PTAR Relaxation," Broadcasting, Jan. 21, 1991, p. 44.

It seems likely that the FCC will eventually decide to reconsider these rules fashioned for another era and either substantially revise or rescind them.

Although program producers constantly claimed during the 1980s that television networks were engaging in anticompetitive practice, the only broadcast-related antitrust action launched by the Justice Department during the decade was against the National Association of Broadcasters' Radio and Television Codes. These Codes the NAB had developed to prevent over-commercialization and encourage good taste in broadcast programs were challenged by Justice in 1981 as being anticompetitive in nature.[25]

Smaller corporations claimed they could not purchase network television advertising time because the NAB Code specified that each commercial should be no less than 30 seconds in length to avoid cluttering each two minute commercial break with too many different messages. The Codes had no legal effect, but the three networks complied with them voluntarily to enhance the image and reputation of the industry. Because of this compliance, these advertisers contended that the networks refused to sell them the less expensive 10–15 seconds segments of network commercial time they could afford.

Charging that the networks and their affiliate stations were acting in concert to prevent these advertisers from being able to place their ads on television, the Justice Department forced the NAB to agree to a consent decree, pledging to abandon all efforts to negotiate further restrictions on broadcast advertising.

This "victory" of the Justice Department over those who dared to try to limit the number of commercials on American television also had another unintended consequence. When the NAB was forced by the government to end its "program practices" activities in 1981, it provided the industry with a perfect excuse for avoiding any further responsibility for the quality of television programming.

From that time onward, industry representatives could simply explain even though they were eager to cooperate with one another in efforts to improve the overall quality of the programs they broadcast, the Justice Department could once again find such a cooperative industry effort to be anticompetitive in nature.

In November 1990, Congress gave the broadcast and the cable industry the protection they had claimed to be so eager to receive, granting both industries a three year exemption from antitrust laws in order to develop program standards capable of reducing the amount of violence and improper sexual behavior portrayed in

---

[25] United States v. NAB, 536 F.Supp. 149 (D.D.C.1982).

the shows they distributed.[26] Only a month later Congressional leaders began to press for action, suggesting that both industries begin work on such program standards immediately to demonstrate their good faith in striving to improve the quality of their programming.[27]

Although it has been the programming practices of the broadcast networks that have attracted most regulatory attention in the past, some of the competitive tactics of the nation's major cable TV MSOs would seem to deserve similar attention.

In 1980, for example, ATC Home Box Office was the only pay TV service offered by 87 percent of all ATC-owned cable-TV systems. Warner's "The Movie Channel" was the sole pay-TV service available to 80 percent of Warner's cable system subscribers and Teleprompter's jointly owned "Showtime" was the only pay service provided by 78 percent of Teleprompter's cable systems.[28]

Although market demand forced most systems to add other pay-TV services during the 1980s, the recent example of Manhattan Cable TV suggests quite clearly that the tendency to base program carriage decisions upon participation in the service's profits still exists today, always ready to dictate program choices under the right conditions.[29]

Recently, a disturbing new trend has begun to surface in the cable TV programming field. From 1986 onward, MSO ownership and profit participation in new satellite delivered programming services has become the quid pro quo for choosing one service instead of others in competitive contests to fill the last remaining cable channels in many group owned systems.[30] Here, as in the pay TV field of a decade ago, cable conglomerates are using their dominant power over electronic media distribution to obtain economic advantages from those program channels they agree to

[26] Pub.L. 101–650 (1990). Also see "TV Violence Bill Passed by Congress in 11th Hour," Broadcasting, November 5, 1990, p. 90.

[27] "Simon Presses for Revived Programming Code," Broadcasting, December 17, 1990, p. 79.

[28] Paul Kagan Associates, The Pay TV Census, December 31, 1980. The same survey revealed that only 4% of all ATC systems, and 5% of all Teleprompter and Warner systems offered any competing non-owned pay TV services at the time, and no system offered only the pay TV service of a competing MSO.

[29] In December 1987, Manhattten Cable, owned by ATC, entered into a settlement with a local citizens group, agreeing to add to its ATC owned HBO and Cinemax pay TV services a group of non-owned pay TV channels. See "MCTV Forced to Offer Channels Not Affiliated with HBO or Time," Variety December 9, 1987, p. 34.

[30] For a description of this trend, see "Vertical Integration: The Business Behind the Boom in Cable Programming," Broadcasting November 23, 1987, p. 40. Increasing cable system capacity by compressing the size of each channel may lessen the impact of this vertical integration, but it is more likely that this additional channel space will be used for data and pay-per-view services.

deliver, and allowing those financial considerations to dictate which particular communication options they will offer the subscribers they serve. In addition, they are likely to prevent DBS systems from gaining access to any of the cable network programming they own or distribute as they have prevented LPTV and MMDS systems from gaining access to such programming in the past.

And yet, while such influence over entertainment programming is unfortunate, an even greater threat to the interests of the public may be posed by the cable industry's control over those information services cable systems are likely to be distributing in the near future. As a recent Congressional report points out, although cable in the United States is still primarily involved in the dissemination of entertainment services, the 1990s are likely to see a significant expansion in cable's role as a distributor of a wide range of information services as well.[31] Its broadband capacity, providing the ability to handle high volumes of electronic traffic, makes cable the ideal network for computer data, electronic mail, videotex, security monitoring, home banking and other interactive services.

Although such "blue sky" claims have been made for cable during the past two decades, a number of recent studies predict that both a saturation point in terms of increased demand for cable delivered entertainment and the competitive challenge posed by telephone companies will motivate major MSOs to become more deeply involved in developing their own cable-distributed information services during the next few years.[32]

Based upon their past performance, there is every reason to believe that during such a "new information age", cable MSOs will continue to follow their old strategy of denying carriage to any videotex, home banking or other interactive service in which they have no ownership interest. Once again, then, the public as well as the supplier of each communication service will be at the mercy of a media distributor who has the power to demand tribute for the privilege of delivery, and who is free to offer the public only those services for which this tribute has been paid.

It's difficult to believe that this is that "media marketplace" to which the FCC has delegated responsibility for all public entertainment or information programming decisions, or that this is

---

[31] U.S. Congress, Office of Technology Assessment, "Science, Technology and the First Amendment," Special Report. (Washington D.C., GPO 1988) See particularly chapter 3.

[32] See, for example, Yankee Group, "Cable and the Telcos: From Confrontation to Detente," (Cambridge MA: Yankee Group, 1983) or Walter S. Baer, "Telephone and Cable Companies: Rivals or Partners," in Eli Noam (ed.) Video Media Competition (New York: Columbia University Press 1985) p. 187.

the competitive environment the Justice Department will continue to rely upon to protect the interests of the public in these vital areas of mass communication.

And yet, as media mergers continue to consolidate control in the hands of an ever smaller group of media conglomerates, their power to determine what communication services the public will receive solely on the basis of their own financial interest in these services will increase with each passing year.

SEC. 98.　THE GLOBALIZATION OF AMERICAN MEDIA

An expanding international market for film and television productions and mergers to prevent foreign acquisitions of American media could both have a significant impact on future media service in the United States.

Foreign corporations currently are not interested in trying to acquire an American television network because the Communications Act prohibits granting a broadcast license to an alien or any corporation organized under the laws of a foreign government.[33] Because the most valuable assets of each of the three major networks are those television stations they own and operate in the nation's largest television markets, a foreign purchaser would be prevented by law from realizing the greatest benefits of such an acquisition.

Recently, however, because tighter credit controls and declining advertising revenues have resulted in a sluggish market for broadcast station sales, lobbying efforts have begun to convince Congress to rescind this section of the Act so that foreign investors will be able to acquire broadcast properties in the United States.[34] If Congress yields to this pressure, particularly now that the networks have been released from most program syndication restrictions of the old "Financial Interest" rules, it is quite likely that several of the world's largest media conglomerates would be in the market for an American television network.

An even more likely scenario is that one or more of these networks will eventually be purchased by a Hollywood studio.

[33] Title 47, U.S.C.A. § 310(b)1–2. Virtually every nation in the world has a similar citizenship requirement. Rupert Murdoch was not allowed to receive the licenses to those Metromedia television group stations that form the backbone of his Fox television network until he applied for and received American citizenship.

[34] See, for example, the arguments advanced in "Monday Memo," Broadcasting, April 22, 1991, p. 16.

NBC's General Electric is known to be dissatisfied with its broadcast earnings, and CBS continues to struggle financially.[35]

Soon after the FCC amended its financial interest rules in April 1991, rumors began to circulate on Wall Street that GE was preparing to offer Paramount a 50 percent interest in NBC, a rumor that seemed to gain creditability when Brandon Tartikoff, chairman of NBC's Entertainment Group left the network to join Paramount in May 1991.[36]

But even if these rumors turn out to have been premature, it is reasonable to expect that General Electric eventually will sell its marginally profitable television network to an entertainment conglomerate better equipped to produce and promote its programming, while CBS may have no choice but to turn its operations over to a media giant with financial assets necessary to allow it to stay competitive in a global market beset by constantly escalating production costs.

One question that should concern the American public if one or more of the major networks are taken over either by a foreign or domestic mass entertainment conglomerate is how supportive the new owners will be of that vital national and international broadcast journalism service provided by that network they acquire. Although it is true that the present network owners have pared their news department budgets down substantially during the past few years, it is difficult to believe that entertainment giants such as Paramount, Disney or Berlusconi will be even as committed as the current owners are to a service that informs rather than entertains, and does so without increasing a conglomerate's bottom line.

But broadcast journalism isn't the only type of American television programming that may be affected by changing patterns in mass media commerce. As broadcast and satellite services continue to expand in Europe, American television producers have become increasingly unwilling to produce programs for the networks that are too "American" in orientation to attract foreign audiences as well. Because these producers depend on sales to foreign broadcast organizations to recoup a significant portion of production costs not covered by network license payments, they

[35] "Down Year in Profits for the Big Three," Broadcasting, May 6, 1991, p. 19. And also see, "Would NBC Pare to Pact with Paramount?," Variety, April 29, 1991, p. 1.

[36] "Tartikoff Moves From Peacock to Paramount," Broadcasting, May 6, 1991, p. 22. There is also speculation that NBC may reduce its primetime schedule to less than 15 hours a week to make the network even more attractive to a prospective purchaser. The financial interest rules define a "network" as any organization distributing more than 15 hours of primetime programming each week, so by reducing its weekly schedule below that minimum number of hours, a television network would cease to be one in terms of financial interest constraints.

have become more reluctant with each passing year to produce dramas or situation comedies reflecting values that are alien to other cultures.[37]

Foreign television audiences find it much easier to understand and enjoy basic action-adventure series such as "Miami Vice", "Magnum P.I." or "Kojak" than dialogue-driven, American context shows such as "Cheers" or "Thirtysomething". Similarly, Hollywood studios have begun to analyze foreign audience preferences as carefully as domestic audience interests when deciding which major feature films to produce. For example, Warner studio made the third, fourth and fifth sequels to "Police Academy" even though box office revenues in the United States didn't justify their production, simply because of their continued popularity in foreign nations. On the other hand, several major studios rejected the opportunity to produce the 1989 Oscar winning film, "Driving Miss Daisy" because they doubted that foreign film audiences would be attracted to a story about an elderly Jewish Southern woman and her black driver.

In addition, the growing involvement of American television networks in hundreds of European and Japanese co-productions projects also tends to result in the creation of generalized, somewhat simplistic action-oriented television films and series, rather than drama reflecting any particular American issues or values.[38]

This increasing desire of the American mass entertainment industry to produce feature films and television series capable of satisfying the tastes of global television and film audiences will not result in these producers totally ignoring the interests of the largest and most prosperous domestic audience in the world. It will, however, cause them to be more cautious in the future about producing films or television series reflecting uniquely American social issues or concerns. In this way then, that global dominance of our mass entertainment industry that some feared would result in shaping foreign mass cultures in America's image may in the

[37] With the explosive growth of newly authorized private commercial broadcast networks and satellite services, the number of Western European television channels is likely to increase from 74 in 1989 to 97 in 1995, with the 484,000 hours of broadcast time increasing to 602,285 by the end of that period. This should result in Europe alone providing a $2 billion market for US programs, constituting 25% of their total broadcast schedules. See, "Euro TV Boom Seems a Steady Thing," Variety, April 15, 1991, M–2 and "U.S. TV Exports to Rise, Study Says", Variety, February 4, 1991, p. 70. At the same time, 43 percent of the $3.13 billion American film rentals came from foreign countries in 1990, up from only 33 percent in 1985.

[38] For example, CBS now is co-producing films and television series with Antenna 2 (France), ORF (Austria), RAI (Italy) ZDF (Germany), as well as film and broadcast organizations in Switzerland, Spain and the United Kingdom. None of its current co-production projects in production—"Eurocops," "Eureka" and "S.O.S. Disparus" are set in the United States.

end have shaped American mass culture far more significantly than their own.

At the moment federal policy is so preoccupied with reducing the foreign trade deficit and encouraging economic growth that those mass cultural issues raised by media mergers or international film and television trade practices have been virtually ignored. Yet, are American mass media just another domestic industry, whose value to this society is determined solely by the revenues it generates for the United States in international trade? Arguably, a vigorous marketplace of ideas is more vital to the welfare of any nation than a prosperous marketplace for consumer goods.

Reducing media competition through mergers and conglomerations may offer tangible domestic and international trade benefits, but at what cost in diminishing those reading, listening, and viewing options that provide the American public with access to diverse thoughts and ideas? [39]

There are no longer any simple answers to these complex media ownership issues in an era when the globalization of media operations extends the scope of policy considerations beyond national borders. Yet it is important to keep in mind that many of those concerns of the past about media conglomeration and its tendency to concentrate too much influence over our society in the hands of too few still seem to be equally valid today.

[39] Media industry representatives are quick to claim that with technology providing a continuous expansion in the number of electronic channels available for distributing entertainment and information services, there is no need for concern about reduced media competition through mergers. This is about as reassuring as a government promising to increase commerce simply by expanding its network of roads. The critical mass of funds available to produce mass entertainment and news is relatively fixed, and increasing the number of channels through which it can be distributed does not operate to increase the amount of content produced. See Le Duc, Beyond Broadcasting: Patterns in Policy and Law, chapter 7.

Chapter 17

DISTRIBUTING MASS COMMUNICATIONS

Sec.
99. Mass Media and the Common Carrier Connection.
100. The Telephone Network Competitor.
101. Communication Law and the Challenge of Change.

SEC. 99. MASS MEDIA AND THE COMMON CARRIER CONNECTION

Common carriers have played a crucial role in the development of mass communications in the United States.

It was the telegraph that transformed the provincial gazette of the early 1800s into the modern newspaper capable of providing comprehensive coverage of national and world events. The steam-driven rotary press may have launched the era of mass news in the 1830s, but not until telegraph lines of the newly formed Western Union spanned the continent from coast to coast in 1861 did reports of major events occurring in San Francisco, New Orleans or Atlanta begin reaching newsrooms in the Northeast in a matter of minutes rather than days or weeks.

The first Associated Press was formed in 1848, and by the end of the Civil War this cooperative newspooling venture of the nation's largest newspapers provided its member publishers with immediate coverage of events as they happened anywhere in the United States through telegraphed news dispatches from AP reporters at the scene.[1]

Less than a decade later, as the first trans-Atlantic submarine cable began operation, this channel of telegraphed dispatches linked American publishers not only with Europe, but through the British news agency Reuters and the French news agency Havas, with colonial offices of these agencies located throughout the Middle East, Africa and Asia.

[1] During the 1850s, several of the privately owned telegraph companies tried to form their own news organizations in competition with AP. When many of these companies merged to form Western Union in 1861, AP offered to give the new nationwide telegraph company the exclusive right to carry its news dispatches, in return for priority handling of these dispatches. Western Union agreed, and by 1880, these AP transmissions constituted 11 percent of Western Union's total message traffic. By 1880, the volume in telegraphed news traffic was so heavy that Western Union began dedicating private leased lines solely to AP news dispatches. See Robert Thompson, Wiring A Continent (Princeton: Princeton University Press, 1947). The AP organized in 1848 was later supplanted by the Western AP, which survived when the earlier AP went out of business in 1892.

Thus, in less than a half century, the telegraph and those wire services formed to take advantage of this new technology allowed local newspapers in the United States to begin covering the world for their readers. The daily newspaper was no longer isolated from distant events by days or weeks of mail delivery, but connected directly by reports travelling at the speed of light through the wires of the Western Union.

During the late 1920s, it was AT&T, another communications common carrier, whose long distance lines transformed a weak, locally oriented collection of radio stations into a national broadcast medium. In its original license allocation plan, the Federal Radio Commission had established an elaborate system of local and regional broadcast services, but had made no provision for simultaneous nationwide distribution of broadcast programming.

A small group of radio stations had begun using AT&T lines as early as 1923 to pool programs, but it was not until the late 1920s that NBC's two national networks (its second network would later become ABC) and the newly formed CBS leased AT&T's recently completed nationwide broadcast lines to become the dominant forces in American broadcasting. Using these private lines to blanket the nation with broadcast coverage disseminated by affiliated local stations, these networks were able to avoid the constraints the federal government's licensing plan to offer advertisers a massive consumer base no other medium could rival.

Then, when the FCC attempted to establish a system of community oriented television stations in the early 1950s, it was AT&T's long line systems, now augmented by microwave relays, that once again allowed the networks to by-pass the agency's regulations to establish national programming channels where only local services had been envisioned by government planners.

In a very real sense, then, it is entirely possible that if AT&T and its Bell Systems had not established their nationwide system of telephone networks before broadcasting emerged as a mass medium in the United States during the 1920s, our radio and television services of today might be as provincial in nature as our local newspapers were before the advent of the telegraph.

Then, during the mid–1950s, when "community antenna systems" were simply enhancing the quality of the television picture from one or two nearby television stations, it was AT&T's microwave relay systems that allowed cable TV operators to begin importing from distant markets the programs of television networks with no local affiliates. In time, the FCC began restricting this microwave signal importation to preserve its broadcast market system, but not before the cable TV industry was firmly established in the United States.[2] Without this AT&T microwave network, it is quite possible that "community antenna", dependent solely on local television signals, would have withered away as predicted when more television stations began broadcast service during the late 1950s. In that event, of course, there would have been no cable TV industry to emerge during the 1980s with dozens of new program channels, and viewers in the United States today would still have to be content with only four or five viewing alternatives.

In 1972, when the FCC announced its "Open Skies" communication satellite policy, no government planner could foresee how encouraging new operators to provide nationwide satellite common carrier services in competition with AT&T would alter the competitive relationship between broadcasting and cable TV in the United States, or erode the strength of the American television networks. As discussed in Chapter 1, it was this decision by the Commission that eventually allowed cable TV to become a medium in its own right, able through more competitive nationwide video distribution costs to launch its own unique cable networks. In addition, these lower video distribution costs also enabled television stations affiliated with a network to become more independent of the network in making their own programming decisions, because they now had the option of using satellites to obtain their programs directly from feature film, sports or series program syndicators.

In each of these past situations, the communications common carrier has played only a supporting role to the mass medium it has served, providing the distribution function essential for its growth and expansion. But what if a carrier should attempt to take over the medium and become the mass communicator itself?

Until 1982 this would have been an idle question, because federal law prohibited a communications common carrier from offering any service other than its traditional distribution of communication messages. In that year, however, a consent decree negotiated without any serious consideration of its possible implications for mass media, offered AT&T and its former Bell Systems the promise of eventual freedom to expand into other fields including mass communications.

SEC. 100. THE TELEPHONE NETWORK COMPETITOR

When local and national telephone networks are released from legal constraints, they could transform radically the

[2] For a more detailed account of this era, see Don R. Le Duc, Cable TV v. the FCC: A Crisis in Media Control (Temple University Press: Philadelphia, 1973).

current structure of mass media service in the United States.

In 1974 the Justice Department launched a massive antitrust action against AT&T, its wholly owned manufacturing subsidiary, Western Electric and Bell Laboratory, the research and development facility it owned jointly with its Bell Systems. The suit charged AT&T and its subsidiaries with using their dominant position in the telecommunications market to inhibit competition.

The government wanted AT&T to divest itself of one or more of its subsidiaries to avoid the possibility of the company using revenues from its regulated monopoly telephone networks to subsidize its development and promotion of advanced services in competitive areas of the telecommunications marketplace. In addition, the Justice Department believed that breaking up the AT&T–Bell System would deny the company the opportunity to use its monopoly control over its telephone networks in the United States either to block the use of non-AT&T equipment on its lines, or prevent the carriage of rival telecommunication services.

In January 1982 AT&T agreed to the terms of the Justice Department settlement requiring it to divest itself of its 22 Bell Systems, Bell Laboratory and Western Electric in return for the right to enter markets previously denied it because of its regulated common carrier monopoly status. In August of that same year, Federal District Judge Harold Greene indicated he would approve the agreement if certain additional conditions were added. He insisted that the agreement allow the new and independent Regional Bell Operating Companies (BOCs) formed from the old Bell Systems to produce, publish and distribute telephone directory "yellow pages", and prohibited AT&T from offering "electronic publishing"[3] over its own transmission facilities for a minimum period of seven years.

On August 24, 1982, Judge Greene gave final approval to the AT&T divestiture plan.[4] During the next year AT&T spun off its 22 Bell Systems that then merged into seven separate regional telephone and telecommunication systems.[5]

[3] Judge Greene defined "electronic publishing" in legal context as including "the provision of any information which AT&T or its affiliates has, or has caused to be originated, authored, compiled, collected or edited, or in which it has a direct or indirect financial or proprietary interest and which is disseminated to an unaffiliated person through some electronic means."

[4] United States v. AT&T, 552 F.Supp. 131 (D.D.C.1982), affirmed sub nom. Maryland v. U.S., 460 U.S. 1001, 103 S.Ct. 1240 (1983). Thirteen state regulatory commissions contested the consent agreement on various grounds but since only three Supreme Court Justices voted to accept an appeal from the consent agreement (4 are needed to grant review), no further legal challenge was possible.

[5] These new BOCs, still sometimes called Regional Bell Operating Companies (RBOCs) but now more commonly described by the shorter abbreviation, were

In 1984 Greene approved a proposed order filed by the Justice Department to permit the newly formed BOCs to engage in non-telephonic businesses as long as the estimated net revenues of these activities would not exceed 10 percent of the company's telephone service net revenues. Under this standard, the Justice Department allowed several BOCs to enter a wide variety of businesses from equipment leasing and real estate management to retail sales and international consulting.[6]

Judge Greene retained authority to approve or disapprove each new non-telephone venture, and to review the agreement every three years to determine whether conditions had changed sufficiently to authorize BOCs to engage in an even broader range of these activities. However, under the terms of the modified final judgment (MFJ) entered in 1987, the BOCs continued to be prohibited from providing "information services"—a broad category of activities the court defined as including everything from videotex to the operation of a cable TV system.

The non-telephone business revenues of the BOCs increased from a 1986 total of $4.3 billion to $7 billion in 1987, nearly doubling within a single year as its telephone earnings remained relatively stable at $70 billion.[7] To put these industry revenues in perspective, as the seven BOCs were earning this $77 billion in 1987, the entire newspaper industry, including some 1,640 papers, generated combined earnings of $40 billion; some 15,000 broadcast stations earned a total of $24.4 billion, and the nation's 8,800 cable TV systems shared revenues of $14 billion.[8]

And none of these BOC revenues could be earned from those non-telephonic activities that the companies could perform the most effectively; distributing public information, electronic publishing, and video services through its telecommunication networks. At the time of the consent agreement in 1982, the American Newspapers Publishing Association proposed what it called a "diversity principle" to guide future judicial supervision of the BOCs under the terms of the agreement. To ensure the greatest degree of diversity, the press association urged that telephone companies controlling transmission facilities should be barred

Ameritech, Atlantic, Nynex, Bell South, Pacific Telesis, Southwestern Bell and US West. Although they are called "Baby Bells," each of them is large enough to be listed among the Fortune magazine's largest 500 American corporations.

[6] "Broadening Business Horizons for BOCs," Telecommunications, December 1984, p. 42.

[7] "Putting Out Lines in All Directions," Time, May 5, 1986, p. 49. "Baby Bells Prospering", Telecommunications, March 1988, p. 12.

[8] "Broadcasting versus the Telco Monster," Broadcasting, May 8, 1989, p. 44. In 1987, the combined revenues of just two BOCs, Nytex and Bell South in itself exceeded the combined revenues of the entire cable TV industry.

from acquiring any interest in or control over the information content flowing through their facilities.

Although Judge Greene did allow the BOCs to begin offering their customers access to information services in 1987, he did so in a manner consistent with this principle, limiting the companies to the role of a conduit simply distributing to subscribers data bases supplied by others. In 1991, however, Greene was forced to reconsider his position when the D.C. Court of Appeals directed him to either lift the ban or make a finding of fact that allowing the BOCs to enter this information market would operate to lessen competition in this field.[9]

Lacking the evidence required for such a finding, Judge Greene instead agreed to lift the ban at some future date, but only after those opposing its recission had the opportunity to challenge this action on his part. At this point, then, the Bell Companies are still prevented from providing information or electronic publishing services by the terms of the Consent Agreement, and prohibited from offering cable TV services both by Congressional laws and FCC rules.[10] In part, this opposition reflects a concern that competing for information and video service subscribers will tempt the BOCs to neglect their special and primary responsibility to the public to provide efficient, economical and technologically advanced telephone service. Certainly the temptation is there, because providing local telephone service in a monopoly environment furnishes no incentives to improve service, while there is every incentive to divert those profit-regulated payments received from telephone subscribers into competitive investments in videotex and cable TV services without any controls on profits.[11]

But it seems to be "self interest" far more than "public interest" that motivates that political pressure now being applied by the print, broadcast and cable TV industries to preserve the ban on BOC electronic publishing, information or video distribu-

[9] For Judge Greene's initial review holding see, United States v. Western Electric Co., 673 F.Supp. 525 (D.D.C.1987) and 714 F.Supp. 1 (D.D.C.1988). Reversal by the U.S. Court of Appeals, directing Greene to apply a broader range of criteria than those used in his original decision can be found at United States v. Western Electric Co., 900 F.2d 283 (D.C.Cir.1990). Unable to do so, Greene decided instead to vacate his original decision but allow those affected by this reversal to appeal. See, "Ruling Opens Door for Phone Companies," Milwaukee Journal, July 26, 1991, p. C–6.

[10] The FCC prohibited telephone carrier ownership of cable TV systems in 1970. In 1984, Congress established its own ban on this type of cross-ownership in section 533(b)(1) of the Cable Policy segment of the Communications Act of 1934.

[11] A 1989 study commissioned by the National Cable Television Association claimed that despite the constraints of the consent agreement, cross-subsidies between revenues earned from rate-regulated telephone services and non-regulated telecommunication activities were still rampant. "NCTA Attacks Telco Business Practices," Broadcasting, March 20, 1989, p. 72.

tion operations in the United States.[12] For one thing, they simply fear direct competition from seven corporate giants boasting combined capital assets in excess of $225 billion.[13] But far more significantly, they fear the complex and sophisticated electronic distribution systems these capital assets reflect, and that technological potential they may soon be capable of realizing.

Today's telephone network, unlike the modern cable TV system, is all-switched, virtually all-digital and has rapidly become all fiber optic. A "switched" system is one that is totally interactive, allowing each subscriber access to any signal or channel available from switching center, selecting and being charged for that choice at the same instant the specific channel ordered is being sent directly to that subscriber. Thus, unlike even the most advanced cable TV system, the telephone switching center is already capable of responding directly and individually to each subscriber request for any type of communication service from pay-per-view (PPV) feature films to international banking transactions, billing the customer automatically as the service is being provided.[14]

All electronic media are attempting to convert from analog to digital transmission as rapidly as possible, because delivering audio or visual information by binary code rather than in a continuous wave of signals reduces distortion significantly while at the same time allowing the transmission to be compressed into a much narrower channel of frequencies. What may eventually provide the telephone industry with a distinct advantage in this area of new technology is its continuing commitment to developing "Integrated Service Digital Networks" (ISDN), special broadband communications channels capable of distributing a broad array of different types of communication services simultaneously within a single network channel.[15]

[12] In 1990 the British government decided to allow telephone carriers in the United Kingdom to provide cable TV service. Fears arose that this British action might prompt Congress to consider Telco ownership of American cable TV systems more seriously. See, for example, "USTA Girds Its Loins for Fight with Cable Over Telco Entry", Broadcasting, Dec. 11, 1989, p. 35.

[13] "Valuing the Big Three: Telcos Get Bigger," Broadcasting, August 19, 1991, p. 19. All local exchange carrier assets are valued at $300 billion; BOCs account for 3/4 of these total assets. In comparison, cable TV assets are currently valued at only $58 billion and broadcast assets at $29 billion. Broadcast industry revenues in 1990 were estimated to be $23 billion; cable TV, $19 billion and Telco revenues $90 billion.

[14] One example of the impressive service capacity of an all-switched network is provided by the "Video-on-Demand" channels developed for the telephone carrier operated test project in Cerritos, California. "Video-on-Demand" not only allows a subscriber to select any movie offered by the system at any time, but also to control the delivery of the movie by being able to "fast forward," "reverse" or stop the movie to view a still frame whenever desired. This is only possible because of the completely interactive qualities of the telephone "switched network."

[15] The primary barrier in the path of ISDN development has been international politics, with various regions of the world clashing over the one universal set of

But the most impressive advantage the telephone carriers appear to have over the cable TV industry is that 1.5 million miles of fiber optic trunk lines are already in service delivering telephone company voice and data transmissions.[16] A fiber optic circuit is a hair-thin, flexible glass filament that guides pulses of message-delivering light along the length of the narrow fiber. Typical fiber systems carry data at rate of more than a billion digital bits of information per second, and can transport this data for 20 miles without need of amplification.[17] In contrast, the coaxial cable used by cable TV systems can deliver data at a rate of only 1.5 million bits per second and requires amplification at least once every mile.[18]

Studies indicate that fiber optic circuits have the potential to be at least 30 times more cost effective than coaxial circuits, when operating at full capacity and delivering digital signals. At the moment, though, this potential can't be realized because "full capacity" would require a payload of 500 separate video-sized communication channels during an era when those 50 to 60 video channels available contain analog produced programs.[19]

In other words, today's fiber optic networks are still much faster, larger and more efficient than necessary to carry those video services available for them to deliver. At this point, then, using an optic network to deliver cable TV service would be much like buying a Concorde jet to get to work each morning. And, engineers must still solve the "last mile" problem of fiber optic networks, finding some way of reducing the cost of connecting individual homes to the network. Adding subscribers to a coaxial cable system can be accomplished for less than $150 per house-

standards that should be adopted for ISDN operation, so that worldwide ISDN service will be possible.

[16] In contrast, at the end of 1990, cable TV systems had installed only 1,000 miles of fiber optic trunk lines. "Fiber Optics and the Future of Television", NVR Reports, Winter 1991, p. 4.

[17] In addition, fiber optic performance continues improving. In 1990, for example, each fiber optic filament was capable of delivering 100 times the amount of data it could carry in 1980, as the price of the fiber dropped from $3 dollars to 15 cents a yard. Karen Wright, "The Road to the Global Village," Scientific American, March 1990, p. 92.

[18] Because each time a signal is amplified, distortion is introduced by the amplifier, the fact that fiber optic delivered signal can travel 20 times as far as coaxial cable delivered signal without need of amplification not only significantly reduces equipment, installation and maintenance costs, but also substantially diminishes signal distortion.

[19] Technology already being developed for HDTV and cable TV channel compression will be capable of converting video productions for digital transmission easily and inexpensively, but with the huge channel capacity already available to it, this is unlikely to increase fiber optic cost effectiveness in the foreseeable future. The greater problem for the BOCs is that most of these channels are owned by cable MSOs unlikely to permit fiber optic carriage of their programming.

hold, but because there has been no economic inducement as yet to provide fiber optic service to the home, the cost for each hookup is still estimated to be in the range of $1,500–$2,000.[20]

Although these technological and economic problems must be solved before telephone carriers can even consider competing with existing mass media services, the greatest barrier they must surmount is actually a regulatory one. As long as they are restricted by law to the function of telephone service, these companies have great difficulty trying to justify to state and federal regulatory agencies any technological development costs that are not directly related to this phone service. For example, "last mile" fiber optic connection costs remain extremely high largely because telephone regulatory agencies don't believe that telephone companies need to refine this technology simply to provide basic phone service.

This is the reason that telephone carriers have been seeking special "pilot project" exemptions from general federal and state regulations in order to develop these technologies, and why the cable TV industry has so bitterly opposed these exemptions. In 1988, the FCC authorized GTE, a telephone company serving Cerritos, California to construct a state-of-the-art fibre optic cable system within its own service area.[21] Although a federal appeals court eventually found that the Commission had not adequately justified its decision to waive the statutory ban against telco-cable TV cross-ownership, the cable system was almost operational by the time the court made its determination, and no attempt was made to prevent GTE from completing the project.

In July 1990, the Bush administration advocated legislation repealing the section of the Communications Act that currently prohibits telephone company ownership of cable TV systems in areas where the telco furnishes telephone service.[22] The Commission supported the measure and when it eventually died in a Congressional committee, the agency declared its intention to

[20] "Sikes Says Telcos Are Revaluating Fiber to Home," Broadcasting, February 12, 1990, p. 15.

[21] In the Application of General Telephone Company of California, 64 RR2d 1156 (1988). In this case, the FCC chose a non-Bell telephone carrier to avoid interfering with the consent decree that affected only those companies. However, the waiver was still in conflict with section 533(b) of the Communications Act that prohibits a telephone carrier from operating a cable TV in its own service area. In this Cerritos pilot project, GTE will be comparing the effectiveness of three distinctly different types of communication networks: Its traditional "twisted pair" phone lines, a coaxial cable network offering integrated telephone and television service and a fiber optic network offering switched video services.

[22] S 2800 (1990). In 1991, the Bush administration again endorsed legislation to allow telephone companies to enter the cable TV business in a letter Commerce Secretary Robert Mossbacher sent key Congressional leaders on behalf of the President.

provide Congress with a full scale review of all major policy issues raised both by telcos seeking to offer their customers cable TV service and cable TV systems planning to provide telephonic personal communication services (PCS).[23] As Commission Chairman Alfred Sikes explained when announcing the FCC action, "What we are faced with is multi-use technologies and if companies want to use them for more than their traditional businesses, how much sense does it make to preclude them from doing that?"[24]

The Commission is now firmly committed to a policy of encouraging rival communication delivery systems to compete or combine in whatever form they believe they can function most efficiently. This policy is guided by the principle that government should play as limited a role as possible in directing how various video, audio or information services are delivered to the home. As Sikes explains it, whether by telephone fiber optic, coaxial cable, satellite or some hybrid combination of the three, the actual distribution system should be transparent to the message being delivered, a "seamless" universe of communication channels in which the specific method of dissemination is irrelevant as long as the entire system functions in the most effective manner possible.[25]

It is far easier, of course, to proclaim such an foresighted policy than it is to achieve it. Whatever long range benefits might be gained from a merging of separate and overlapping broadcast, satellite, cable TV and telephone distribution services, it is the short term effects of this policy that will decide how each rival medium will respond to it; an impact almost certain to threaten many of each media industry's most fundamental and cherished economic interests.

Yet, even if this particular FCC policy initiative should fail, the trend towards an ever greater degree of consolidation among

[23] Soon afterward the FCC decided to approve the request of three cable industry MSOs, Cox, Cablevision and Continental, to launch experimental personal communication networks to compete with phone companies in their service areas. The operators plan to use their cable systems to link a number of low-powered radio towers together to relay messages to the wireless telephones of those subscribing to their service. The Commission seems likely to also approve the request of "TV Answer", an equipment manufacturer and marketer, for a temporary allocation of spectrum space to allow television stations interested in their device to provide their own interactive video data service. Gen.Docket 91–2, FCC 91–16 (1991). TV Answer is seeking 500 kHz of spectrum space for this service, that would allow the television viewer to select a program, purchase items, respond to opinion polls or exercise other options by delivering a response directly to the television station transmitting the image seen on the television screen.

[24] "Sikes Vows to Act on Telco Entry Question in 1991," Broadcasting, Nov. 26, 1990, p. 58.

[25] "Subject to Change," Broadcasting, Jan. 28, 1991, p. 82.

previously independent video, audio, informational and personal distribution systems seems destined to continue, simply because every media industry will be able to realize substantial savings from combining with others to allow its content to be delivered through a single network rather than continuing to maintain and operate its own distribution facilities.

As all previous "revolutions" in the history of American mass communications, this trend towards consolidation among media delivery systems is likely to occur so gradually and sporadically during this decade and the next that it will again be difficult in the future to point to any specific date when the final form of the new multi-media delivery network was actually determined. But even at this point it is possible to begin considering what effects this tendency is likely to have upon future broadcast, cable TV and newspaper service in the United States and those First Amendment rights now accorded each of these media by American law.

SEC. 101. COMMUNICATION LAW AND THE CHALLENGE OF CHANGE

Changing the way mass media are distributed in the United States could have a profound effect on those legal rights each medium can now assert.

The nation's telephone carriers appear to be in the best position to emerge as the dominant partners in future media merger ventures. In addition to their greater economic power and more advanced distribution systems, the phone companies also have a significant advantage in being able to underwrite the costs of network operation through being able to offer and charge their customers for a far broader range of telecommunications related services than any of their media competitors.[26]

And, in the near future, the 500 video channel capacity of their fiber optic networks that now seems so totally unnecessary could actually be their most significant competitive advantage of all.[27] This vast channel space will not only permit each fiber optic network to carry a large number of "high definition television" (HDTV) channels without reducing its other services, but will also

---

[26] In 1990, for example, telephone carrier local exchange billings in themselves were reported to be in excess of $20 billion, thereby generating 50% of the revenues of the entire newspaper industry, and virtually equalling the earnings of the entire broadcasting industry.

[27] The cable industry is planning to increase dramatically the number of video channels their systems can carry through digital compression of each video signal. In reality, however, this will not increase the coaxial cable actual frequency capacity, but only allow more signals to be delivered within the same space constraints.

make it an ideal distribution system for "pay-per-view" feature films and other special events.[28]

This extensive network channel capacity could also be used to deliver the daily newspaper by facsimile to each subscriber home. With newsprint, ink and distribution now representing at least 35 percent of the operating expenses of the typical newspaper, the substantially reduced costs offered through electronic transmission could prove very attractive to a number of publishers in the future.[29]

On the other hand, electronic publishing could pose a significant competitive threat to the local newspaper if the network were to decide instead to allow the system's customers to select directly from wire services and other news sources those specific news topics of greatest interest to each subscriber.[30] In this way, a subscriber could create a daily "newspaper" that could much more clearly reflect that reader's own particular interests in business, sports, international or entertainment news by drawing upon the resource of that 90–95 percent of those relevant wire stories in each topic area not selected to be published by the local newspaper.[31] Clearly, a vast majority of a newspaper's subscribers would probably prefer to continue to receive their pre-packaged news and advertising directly from the local publisher, but if the competing electronic service would cause only a 5 to 10 percent reduction in

[28] Major film studios have shown great interest in a marketing plan that devotes one network channel to each of a dozen or more of their most popular recent releases that system subscribers could pay to see at any time. In this way they could by-pass pay-TV distribution, where they are generally paid only one license fee by the service for a package of their films, and the video cassette rental market, where because of the "first sale" doctrine, they earn money only from the original sale of a film cassette to the rental store, with all rental proceeds being kept by the store. Because of its "all-switched" configuration, a telco network would allow a viewer to start the film selected at any time, while a cable system could only provide access at certain specific times each day when the film is scheduled to begin.

[29] The 35% figure is derived from Christopher H. Sterling and Timothy Haight, The Mass Media: Aspen Institute Guide to Communication Trends (Praeger, New York, 1976), Table 321–B, p. 166. Industry sources indicate that because of substantial increases in newsprint costs during the 1980s, the actual publishing and distribution costs of the typical daily newspaper may now exceed 40 percent of total operating expenses. In fact, the main reason that no newspaper publisher has attempted electronic distribution is simply that so few American homes are yet equipped to receive facsimile transmissions, and so few cable TV systems serve more than 60 percent of the homes in their market area.

[30] This type of service is already being provided on an experimental basis in New York City, where subscribers may use their phone network to select and print news items arranged by topic from a number of different news sources including USA Today, New York Newsday and some 50 other non-newspaper information providers.

[31] AP, as a press owned cooperative, would obviously oppose having its news items distributed in this manner, but in the end it would probably be forced to provide this new competitor with its service, as it did radio during the mid–1930s.

newspaper subscribership, the impact of even this relatively minor drop in circulation on potential advertising revenues could undercut the financial foundation of a significant number of America's daily newspapers.

The competitive threat that this type of media distribution system poses for poses for television broadcasters is even more severe. Because the typical television station operates primarily only as a distributor of programs produced by others, it is extremely vulnerable to challenge from other delivery systems that are capable of disseminating these same television programs more efficiently and economically.[32] In reality, there is no logical reason why television stations should continue to incur operating expenses in excess of a million dollars a year simply to encumber the valuable public resource of spectrum space with retransmissions of programs it receives by microwave or satellite; programs that actually could be viewed with far greater clarity and less distortion delivered directly to the home through a fiber optic channel. The one unique mass communication role now played by most television stations, the production of local news and other public affairs programs, could continue to be performed, and at a far lower cost by simply delivering these programs through the channels of a wired distribution network.

Cable TV might appear at first glance to be the industry most seriously threatened by a rival media delivery system, but because most major corporate cable TV owners are now almost as deeply involved in the production of entertainment programming as the four television networks, they seem likely to remain as potential partners in future fiber optic network ventures.[33] In addition, cable TV operators have the advantage of already providing video distribution service in most of the major markets telephone carriers are interested in entering, making it much more sensible for the carriers to attempt to merge with, rather than seek to displace the existing system.

Similarly, it is unlikely that telephone carriers will ever try to undercut local network-affiliate television stations by dealing directly with their networks for local program distribution rights,

[32] FCC Commissioner Mimi Dawson was aware of this vulnerability of the television station when she predicted in 1987 that within 15 years all communications would be delivered through fiber optic networks, freeing the valuable public resource of spectrum space for other more beneficial uses. Broadcasting, November 30, 1987. This susceptibility to competitive challenge from new media delivery systems was clearly illustrated during the cable TV era of the 1960s, when without FCC repression of cable system growth, a substantial number of television stations seemed unable to survive.

[33] For some examples of recent major cable MSO production efforts, see John Dempsey, "Star-studded Cable Stable," Variety, June 10, 1991, 1: "Costs May Make Strange Bedfellows of Broadcasting Cable," Broadcasting, April 29, 1991, 27: "ABC Gets Cable Friendlier," Broadcasting, June 17, 1991, 45.

simply because this tactic would anger a large number of Congressional leaders very sympathetic to the concerns of the broadcast industry. Instead, these carriers will probably begin simply by offering each local television station the opportunity to lease a channel to program with 24 hour-a-day news, sports or other features capable of generating additional advertising revenue for the station.[34] The intention, of course, would be to demonstrate to station management the substantial savings that can be realized by abandoning over-the-air transmissions, but should that tactic fail, the carriers would then at least be in a stronger position to launch a public relations campaign creating support for ending the practice of allowing broadcasters to squandering the precious public resource of spectrum space on services that could just as effectively be delivered through a fiber optic network.

As all of this may suggest, the evolution of fiber optic delivery systems in the United States is almost certain to occur in a cautious, tentative manner. Since this is a game without any known rules, different approaches will be taken to achieve the goal of consolidating all major communication services within a single conduit until one of them seems to work more effectively than any of the others. For example, one approach would be for a telephone carrier simply to construct a fiber optic network for a cable TV system, and then lease from that cable operator those channels necessary for the telecommunication services the carrier intends to provide. Another approach would be for a carrier to build and operate the fiber optic network in partnership with some film studio, television network or cable conglomerate, with each partner then managing its own set of communication services. Still another approach would be for the carrier to build and operate the network itself, choosing and furnishing all the system's telecommunications, entertainment and news services.[35]

Each of these divergent approaches will obviously raise a different set of legal issues. And yet, because the pace of this trend towards media consolidation will be gradual and tentative, the federal government is almost certain to ignore these develop-

[34] A number of cable TV systems across the country are already carrying such broadcast originated programs. See, for example, "Cable News Covers Chicago" Variety, April 22, 1991, 22; "Allbritton to Launch All News Cable Channel in D.C." Broadcasting, November 19, 1990, 21; "Cox Proposes California News Channel," Broadcasting, May 6, 1991, 23.

[35] All of these approaches presuppose, of course, that the telephone carrier will be able to act without violating those bans on video distribution now imposed by the consent degree, the FCC and Congress. In reality, though, none of these legal barriers are really as formidable as they may seem. First, non-Bell carriers, such as GTE, are not bound by the consent decree; second, the FCC has already demonstrated in the Cerritos case its eagerness to waive a ban it is trying to rescind, and thirdly, if the carrier gains the cooperation of the local cable carrier, it is unlikely that anyone will assert the Congressional ban in court.

ments until, once again, it is unprepared when the time has come to answer those crucial mass communications policies it has been unable to anticipate.

As we have seen, American law has always defined the rights of each medium on the basis of how it has been delivered to the public—through the spectrum, through wire, through cable, through the printed page—but now, as mergers blur these legal distinctions based on mode of distribution, what new principles of law should be established, and what objectives should they be designed to realize?

If telephone companies, for example, are permitted to provide a full range of mass communication and other informational services to the public, should they be restricted to functioning solely as traditional common carriers, prohibited by law from doing anything but distributing the services of others who have leased their channels? Some assert that to restrict telcos only to this "video dial tone" role would be to improperly abridge their constitutionally protected right to communicate.

Others argue, however, that to permit a telephone carrier to exercise total control over what is likely in time to become the only conduit of communication linking each home with the world would be to vest in one corporate entity far too much power over each individual's access to information and entertainment.

And what should be the legal consequences of distributing television programming through privately owned channels rather than through the public resource of spectrum? If scarcity of spectrum space furnishes the only constitutionally acceptable justification for imposing special content constraints on broadcast programming, then distribution by fiber optic network should finally allow broadcasters to be as free of government control as the press. But once this federal regulation has ended, will the public really be content to permit a force as powerful and pervasive as television, the only visual medium readily accessible to children in the home, to operate free from any degree of societal control whatsoever? [36]

And what threat, if any, to freedom of the press may emerge from electronic publishing of newspapers and magazines? Will the use of a fiber optic network result, as some fear, in bringing

[36] In a perfectly rational realm of law, operating above and beyond political reality, it might be argued because "spectrum scarcity" has been the only justification accepted by the Supreme Court for broadcast regulation, ending the use of spectrum also ends any justification for that regulation. This, however, overlooks the fact that because "spectrum scarcity" has always been conveniently available, the court has never been forced to look beyond it to decide whether other characteristics of broadcasting, and more particularly of television, might continue to justify some degree of federal supervision on other grounds.

newspapers within the supervisory authority of the FCC's Common Carrier Bureau or a State Public Utility Commission? Is it even possible that federal regulations imposing content controls on video channels could also be found by the courts to be equally applicable to print channels using the same electronic distribution system.[37]

These are just a few illustrations of the many equally important and difficult free speech legal issues that remain to be resolved before additional mergers among various forms of communication and mass media distribution systems have further weakened the conceptual framework of First Amendment rights and obligations that has always in the past been founded upon differences in the ways that media messages are delivered.[38]

Because this chapter has ventured out beyond the safe harbor of established law and into the reef-filled waters of speculation, it is quite possible that some of its assertions about future media developments will prove to be incorrect. However, the one assumption about future media service that has constantly proven to be accurate in the past is that whenever the channel capacity of any communications delivery system expands, ingenious entrepreneurs will eventually develop more services than that system is capable of delivering.[39]

If this continues to hold true in the future, then whether fiber optic, coaxial cable or other communication network developments occur exactly as described in this text or not is not as important in

[37] These fears seem less justified than those that relate to the economic threat that fiber optic networks may pose for the daily newspaper, but because the Common Law tradition does not permit a judge or Supreme Court Justice to predict in advance how some hypothetical regulatory or constitutional issue will be decided, it is impossible to be certain at this point how broadly governmental regulatory authority could be exercised over electronic publishing without infringing on the constitutionally protected rights of the publisher.

[38] Another kind of major social policy issue will certainly be raised if broadcast television services now freely available to all citizens are restricted in the future only to those able to subscribe to a fiber optic network. However, since the shift from broadcast to fiber optic delivery of electronic media is apt to be quite gradual, there should be ample time for some political solution to this problem.

[39] Examples include the 10,500 commercial broadcast stations in service in the United States today when experts claimed in the mid–1940s that the economy could support no more than those 1,000 commercial stations then in operation; Intelsat's present generation of satellites providing 600 times the international communication traffic capacity that national telecommunication agencies of the world believed was possible in the mid–1960s, and still not having enough channels to satisfy all demands; America's domestic satellites launched in the mid–1970s at a time when many felt there would never be enough users to make them profitable continue to be launched on a regular basis with long lists of users waiting to lease their transponders; and the cable TV industry, that when required by the FCC to provide 20 channels of service for urban markets in 1972 argued that most of those channels would never be used—that same industry that is now planning band compression for its 50 channel systems to provide as many as 500 channels of service.

the long run as being aware of the fundamental changes in media service and media law these developments are certain to cause. As technology continues to increase the capacity of mass communication distribution systems in the future, that expansion will stimulate the launching of new forms and combinations of media services. That in turn will require a drastic reformulation of mass communication principles derived from our Constitution, but defined by the Congress and the courts during an era when legal distinctions that once were apparent gradually will have disappeared.

The last two decades have brought us, among other changes, a substantial reduction in federal regulatory control over broadcasting in the United States; the creation of modern cable TV as a distinct communications medium with its own specialized sports, music and public affairs channels; the establishment of a totally new national newspaper, USA Today, with a distinctive approach and style that has significantly influenced formats and coverages of daily newspapers across the country; the beginnings of 24 hour-a-day national and global television news channels; ENG and remote television news coverage; the emergence of pay-TV and the VCR; the development of a fourth national television network; the eroding of the network television programming power, and the growth of a new international orientation for the entire American mass entertainment industry.

As significant as these changes have been, it is quite likely that the changes occurring during the next two decades will be even more dramatic.

*

Appendix A

ABBREVIATIONS

A.	Atlantic Reporter.
A.2d	Atlantic Reporter, Second Series.
A.C.	Appeal Cases.
A.L.R.	American Law Reports.
Aff.	Affirmed; affirming.
Ala.	Alabama;—Alabama Supreme Court Reports.
Am.Dec.	American Decisions.
Am.Jur.	American Jurisprudence, a legal encyclopedia.
Am.Rep.	American Reports.
Am.St.Rep.	American State Reports.
Ann.Cas.	American Annotated Cases.
App.D.C.	Court of Appeals, District of Columbia.
App.Div.	New York Supreme Court, Appellate Divisions, Reports.
Ariz.	Arizona; Arizona Supreme Court Reports.
Ark.	Arkansas; Arkansas Supreme Court Reports.
Bing.	Bingham, New Cases, Common Pleas (England).
C.D.	Copyright Decision.
C.J.	Corpus Juris, a legal encyclopedia.
C.J.S.	Corpus Juris Secundum, a legal encyclopedia.
Cal.	California; California Supreme Court Reports.
Can.Sup.Ct.	Canada Supreme Court Reports.
Cert.	Certiorari, a legal writ by which a cause is removed from an inferior to a superior court.
C.F.R.	Code of Federal Regulations.
Colo.	Colorado; Colorado Supreme Court Reports.
Conn.	Connecticut; Connecticut Supreme Court of Errors Reports.
Cranch	Cranch, United States Supreme Court Reports; United States Circuit Court Reports.
Cush.	Cushing (Massachusetts).
D.C.App.	District of Columbia Court of Appeals Reports.
Dall, Dal.	Dallas, United States Supreme Court Reports; Pennsylvania Reports.
Del.	Delaware; Delaware Supreme Court Reports.
Edw.	Edward; refers to a particular king of England; which king of that name is indicated by the date; used to identify an act of Parliament.
Eng.Rep.	English Reports (reprint).
F.	Federal Reporter.

F.2d	Federal Reporter, Second Series.
F.C.C.	Federal Communications Commission Reports.
F.R.D.	Federal Rules Decisions.
F.Supp.	Federal Supplement.
Fed.Cas. or F.Cas.	Reports of United States Circuit and District Courts, 1789–1879.
Fla.	Florida; Florida Supreme Court Reports.
Ga.	Georgia; Georgia Supreme Court Reports.
Ga.App.	Georgia Appeals Reports.
How.St.Tr.	Howell's State Trials.
Hun	Hun, New York Supreme Court Reports.
Ibid.	Ibidem, the same, in the same volume, or on the same page.
Ill.	Illinois; Illinois Supreme Court Reports.
Ill.App.	Illinois Appellate Court Reports.
Ind.	Indiana; Indiana Supreme Court Reports.
Ind.App.	Indiana Appellate Court Reports.
Johns.Cas.	Johnson's Cases (New York).
K.B.	King's Bench Reports (England).
Kan.	Kansas; Kansas Supreme Court Reports.
Ky.	Kentucky; Kentucky Court of Appeals Reports.
L.J.	Law Journal (England).
L.R.Q.B.	Law Reports, Queen's Bench (England).
L.R.A.	Lawyers Reports Annotated.
L.R.A.,N.S.,	Lawyers Reports Annotated, New Series.
L.R.Ex.	Law Reports, Exchequer (England).
L.T.	The Law Times (England).
La.	Louisiana; Louisiana Supreme Court Reports.
La.Ann.	Louisiana Annual Reports.
Mass.	Massachusetts; Massachusetts Supreme Judicial Court Reports.
Md.	Maryland; Maryland Court of Appeals Reports.
Me.	Maine; Maine Supreme Judicial Court Reports.
Mich.	Michigan; Michigan Supreme Court Reports.
Minn.	Minnesota; Minnesota Supreme Court Reports.
Miss.	Mississippi; Mississippi Supreme Court Reports.
Mo.	Missouri; Missouri Supreme Court Reports.
Mo.App.	Missouri Appeals Reports.
Mont.	Montana; Montana Supreme Court Reports.
N.C.	North Carolina; North Carolina Supreme Court Reports.
N.D.	North Dakota; North Dakota Supreme Court Reports.
N.E.	Northeastern Reporter.
N.E.2d	Northeastern Reporter, Second Series.

N.H.	New Hampshire; New Hampshire Supreme Court Reports.
N.J.	New Jersey; New Jersey Court of Errors and Appeals Reports.
N.J.L.	New Jersey Law Reports.
N.M.	New Mexico; New Mexico Supreme Court Reports.
N.W.	Northwestern Reporter.
N.W.2d	Northwestern Reporter, Second Series.
N.Y.	New York; New York Court of Appeals Reports.
N.Y.S.	New York Supplement Reports.
Neb.	Nebraska; Nebraska Supreme Court Reports.
Nev.	Nevada; Nevada Supreme Court Reports.
Ohio App.	Ohio Appeals Reports.
Ohio St.	Ohio State Reports.
Okl.	Oklahoma; Oklahoma Supreme Court Reports.
Ops.	Opinions, as of Attorney General of the United States, or a state.
Or., Ore., Oreg.	Oregon; Oregon Supreme Court Reports.
P.	Pacific Reporter.
P.2d	Pacific Reporter, Second Series.
P.L. & R.	Postal Laws and Regulations (1948 ed.).
Pa.	Pennsylvania District and County Court Reports.
Pa.D. & C.	Pennsylvania District and County Court Reports.
Pa.Super.	Pennsylvania Superior Court Reports.
Paige	Paige, New York Chancery Reports.
per se	In itself or by itself; used in connection with words actionable *per se,* libelous *per se,* or slanderous, *per se.*
Phila. (Pa).	Philadelphia Reports.
Pick.	Pickering, Massachusetts Reports.
Q.B.	Queen's Bench.
R.	Rex king; regina, queen.
R.C.L.	Ruling Case Law.
R.C.P.	Rules of Civil Procedure.
R.I.	Rhode Island; Rhode Island Supreme Court Reports.
R.R.	Pike & Fisher Radio Regulations.
S.C.	South Carolina; South Carolina Supreme Court Reports.
S.D.	South Dakota; South Dakota Supreme Court Reports.
S.E.	Southeastern Reporter.
S.E.2d	Southeastern Reporter, Second Series.

S.W................Southwestern Reporter.

S.W.2d ....Southwestern Reporter, Second Series.

Sandf.................Sandford, New York Superior Court Reports.

Sec. ....Section.

So.................Southern Reporter.

So.2d ....Southern Reporter, Second Series.

Stark. ....Starkie, English Reports.

S.Ct. ....Supreme Court Reporter.

T.L.R. ....Times Law Reports (England).

Tenn.................Tennessee; Tennessee Supreme Court Reports.

Tex.................Texas; Texas Supreme Court (and the Commission of Appeals) Reports.

Tex.Civ.App.........Texas Civil Appeals Reports.

Tex.Cr.R.............Texas Court of Criminal Appeals Reports.

U.S.C. ....United States Code.

U.S.C.A. ....United States Code Annotated.

U.S.P.Q. ....United States Patents Quarterly.

V.................Volume.

Va.................Virginia; Virginia Supreme Court of Appeals Reports.

Vt.................Vermont; Vermont Supreme Court Reports.

W.Va. ....West Virginia; West Virginia Supreme Court of Appeals Reports.

Wash. ....Washington; Washington Supreme Court Reports.

Wash.L.Rep. ....Washington Law Reporter, Washington, D.C.

Whart.................Wharton (Pa.).

Wheat.................Wheaton (U.S.).

Wis.................Wisconsin; Wisconsin Supreme Court Reports.

Wyo.................Wyoming; Wyoming Supreme Court Reports.

Appendix B

SELECTED COURT AND
PLEADING TERMS

Action

A formal legal demand of one's rights made in a court of law.

Actionable per quod

Words not actionable in themselves may be defamatory when special damages are proved.

Actionable per se

Words that need no explanation in order to determine their defamatory effect.

Amicus curiae

A friend of the court or one who interposes and volunteers information upon some matter of law.

Answer

The pleading of a defendant against whom a complaint has been filed.

Appeal

An application by an appellant to a higher court to change the order or judgment of the court below.

Appellant

The person or party appealing a decision or judgment to a higher court.

Appellee

The party against whom an appeal is taken.

Bind over

To hold on bail for trial.

Brief

A written or printed document prepared by counsel to file in court, normally providing both facts and law in support of the case.

Cause of action

The particular facts on which an action is based.

Certiorari

A writ commanding judges of a lower court to transfer to a higher court records of a case so that judicial review may take place.

Change of venue

Removing a civil suit or criminal action from one county or district to another county or district for trial.

Civil action (suit, trial)

Court action brought to enforce, redress, or protect private rights, as distinguished from a Criminal action (q.v.).

Code

A compilation or system of laws, arranged into chapters, and promulgated by legislative authority.

Common law

The law of the decided cases, derived from the judgments and decrees of courts. Also called "case law." Originally, meant law which derived its authority from the ancient usages or customs of England.

Complaint

The initial proceeding by a complainant, or plaintiff, in a civil action.

Contempt of court

Any act calculated to embarrass, hinder, or obstruct a court in the administration of justice, or calculated to lessen its dignity or authority.

Courts of record

Those whose proceedings are permanently recorded, and which have the power to fine or imprison for contempt. Courts not of record are those of lesser authority whose proceedings are not permanently recorded.

Criminal action (trial)

An action undertaken to punish a violation of criminal laws, as distinguished from a Civil action (q.v.).

Damages

Monetary compensation which may be recovered in court by a person who has suffered loss, detriment, or injury to his person, property, rights, or business, through the unlawful or negligent act of another person or party.

De novo

Anew, afresh.   A trial de novo is a retrial of a case.

Dictum (pl. Dicta; also, Obiter Dictum)

An observation made by a judge, in an opinion on a case, that does not go to the main issue—a saying "by the way".

Discovery

A party's pre-trial devices used, in preparation for trial, to obtain facts from the other party.

Due process

Law in its regular course of administration through the courts of justice.   The guarantee of due process requires that every person have the protection of a fair trial.

En banc

A session where the entire membership of a court, instead of one or a few, participates in the decision of an important case.   ("Banc" means the judge's "bench" or place to sit.)

Equity

That system of jurisprudence which gives relief when there is no full, complete and adequate remedy at law; based originally upon the custom of appealing to the King or chancellor when the formality of the common law did not give means for relief.

Estoppel

An admission which prevents a person from using evidence which proves or tends to prove the contrary.

Executive session

A meeting of a board or governmental body that is closed to the public.

Ex parte

> By or concerning only one party. This implies an examination in the presence of one party in a proceeding and the absence of the opposing party.

Ex post facto

> After the fact.

Habeas corpus

> Latin for "you have the body." A writ issued to an officer holding a person in detention or under arrest to bring that person before a court to determine the legality of the detention.

In camera

> In the judge's private chambers or in a courtroom from which all spectators have been excluded.

Indictment

> A written accusation of a crime prepared by a prosecuting attorney and presented for the consideration of a grand jury.

Information

> A formal, written accusation of a crime prepared by a competent law officer of the government, such as a district or prosecuting attorney.

Injunction

> A judicial order in equity directed against a person or organization directing that an act be performed or that the person or organization refrain from doing a particular act.

Judgment

> The decision of a court of law.

Jury

> A group of a certain number of persons, selected according to law and sworn to inquire into certain matters of fact, and to declare the truth from evidence brought before them. A *grand jury* hears complaints and accusations in criminal cases, and issues bills of indictment in cases where the jurors believe that there is enough evidence to bring a

case to trial. A *petit jury* consists of 12 (or fewer) persons who hear the trial of a civil or criminal case.

Mandamus

An extraordinary legal writ issued from a court to a corporation or its officers, to a public official, or to an inferior court commanding the doing of an act which the person, corporation, or lower court is under a duty to perform.

Motion to dismiss

A formal application by a litigant or his counsel addressed to the court for an order to dismiss the case.

Nol pros, nolle prosequi

A formal notification of unwillingness to prosecute which is entered upon the court record.

N.O.V. ("non obstante veredicto")

A judgment by the court in favor of one party notwithstanding a verdict that has been given to the other party.

Plaintiff

The person (including an organization or business) who initiates a legal action.

Pleading

The process in which parties to a lawsuit or legal action alternately file with a court written statements of their contentions. By this process of statement and counter-statement, legal issues are framed and narrowed. These statements are often termed "pleadings."

Preliminary hearing, preliminary examination

A person charged with a crime is given a preliminary examination or hearing before a magistrate or judge to determine whether there is sufficient evidence to hold that person for trial.

Prima facie (pron.: prī ma fā shē)

"At first sight" or "on the face of it." So far as can be judged from the first disclosure.

Reply

The pleading of plaintiff in response to the "answer" of the defendant.

Res adjudicata or res judicata

    A thing decided.

Respondent

    A party who gives an answer to a bill in equity; also, one who opposes a party who has taken a case to a higher court.

Stare decisis

    To stand by the decisions, or to maintain precedent. This legal doctrine holds that settled points of law will not be disturbed.

Subpoena

    A command to appear at a place and time and to give testimony. "Subpoena-duces tecum" is a command to produce some document or paper at a trial.

Summary

    Connoting "without a full trial." A summary judgment is a judge's rule that one party in a lawsuit wins before the conclusion of a full trial.

Venue

    The particular county, city, or geographical area in which a court with jurisdiction may hear and decide a case.

Verdict

    The decision of a jury as reported to the court.

Voir dire

    Denotes the preliminary examination which the court may make of one presented as a witness or juror, where his competency or interest is objected to.

Writ

    A legal instrument in the judicial process to enforce compliance with orders and sentences of a court.

Appendix C

SOME NOTES ON THE LEGAL PROCESS

During the first chapter of this book you were introduced rather rapidly to a wide assortment of legal terms. At that point, you probably did nothing more than to try to memorize as many of these terms as possible, expecting to find one or more of them lurking somewhere on your mid-term exam.

In reality, though, the most effective way of understanding what each of these legal terms actually means is to see how it operates in an actual case situation. Here, for example, are how the terms "criminal", "civil" "common" and "constitutional" law apply to various elements of a case you may have already read about in this book.

A. *Criminal, Civil and Common and Constitutional Law*

In the case of Cox Broadcasting v. Cohn, discussed in earlier in your text, a reporter disclosed the name of a rape victim during a television broadcast. The State of Georgia, where the broadcast originated, had enacted a provision in its criminal code that made it a crime for,

> any news media or other person to print, publish, broadcast, televise or disseminate through any other medium
> * * * the name or identity of any female who may have been raped.

If that official responsible for prosecuting those in that locality violating Georgia's "criminal law", (generally called the "District Attorney") believed that a reporter had violated this statute and thus committed a crime as defined by the criminal code of Georgia, the District Attorney would file a complaint describing the nature of the crime and charging the reporter with having committed it.[1] If the reporter entered a plea of "guilty" to this charge, the criminal court judge would then have the authority to impose any penalties provided by the law for this offense. However, if the reporter should enter a plea of "not guilty", the state would be required to prove "beyond a reasonable doubt" that *each* element of the crime had occurred—in this case that (1) that the defendant reporter had knowingly disclosed the name of a woman

---

[1] Criminal law in most states classifies each crime as being either a "misdemeanor" or a "felony". A misdemeanor is a less serious crime, generally providing for a maximum jail term of less than one year, while a felony is a more serious crime, carrying a prison sentence in excess of one year. In this instance, disclosing the name of a rape victim was classified as being a misdemeanor crime.

(2) who may in fact have been a rape victim (3) and that the reporter's disclosure was disseminated by broadcasting or some other communications medium to the general public. Unless the state can establish beyond a reasonable doubt that each element of the criminal charge has taken place, the defendant reporter must be found "not guilty".

Here, for instance, if the District Attorney could not prove that this disclosure had actually been broadcast or disseminated to the public through some other medium, the charge against the defendant would have had to be dismissed "with prejudice", meaning that the State could not try this reporter again for this same offense.

But even if the reporter had been tried and found not guilty of any criminal offense, he could still be required by "civil law" to compensate anyone damaged because of the disclosure. In other words, even though not guilty of violating a criminal law designed to protect society in general, a reporter could still be required by civil law to pay money damages to any specific individual actually injured by this same act.

Civil law actions can be based either upon statutory rights granted individuals by State legislation or upon traditional rights granted by Anglo Saxon "common law". In the *Cox* case the father of the deceased rape victim argued a "common law" of "privacy" as the basis for a legal action claiming damages from the reporter and his television station employer.[2] Although the state of Georgia had not enacted a law granting an individual the right to sue for invasion of privacy, the Georgia courts did recognize a historic right of privacy developed by past judicial decisions that allowed those damaged by public disclosure of private information to be compensated for their embarrassment or humiliation.[3]

As this civil action to recover damages for invasion of privacy was about to begin, however, an issue of "constitutional law" was raised, delaying the trial until this question could be resolved.

The defendant broadcast station claimed that the rape victim's name had already been revealed to the public before it was disclosed during the television news program, because she had

---

[2] Even though the reporter may have been the one primarily responsible for any damage the father of the deceased rape victim sustained, law suits of this type always attempt to include the media organization as a co-defendant, because juries tend to be far more generous in awarding damages when they are taking them from a giant corporation, rather than an individual. One peculiar issue in this case was that in most jurisdictions, only living persons—and not survivors of the deceased—can sue for invasion of privacy.

[3] At common law, this type of injury is called a "tort", meaning that the law allows a party injured by the act of another to recover damages caused by that act.

been identified by name in the criminal proceedings used to charge her assailants. Under these circumstances, the defendant argued that to compel a broadcast station to pay damages for disclosing a fact that any member of the public could have discovered in the files of the local courthouse improperly penalized a communications medium for exercising its free speech right to disseminate public information.

In essence then, the defendant broadcast station was claiming that no matter how much anguish or embarrassment it might have caused, there should be no civil trial to determine what monetary compensation it should pay for these damages. Instead, the defendant demanded that the case be dismissed immediately without awarding any damages, because to punish a station for reporting information already a matter of public record would improperly inhibit its right of freedom of expression protected by the First and Fourteenth Amendments.

B. *The Judicial Process*

The Supreme Court of Georgia rejected this constitutional argument, finding nothing in either the Georgia state constitution or the federal constitution that guaranteed a broadcaster an absolute right to reveal the identity of an individual whose privacy was expressly protected by Georgia law. This decision meant that the civil action to decide whether the defendants were actually liable for damages caused by their news report could now begin.

Here, however, the Supreme Court of the United States intervened to grant *certiorari*, meaning that it would review the Georgia court's decision to determine if the State court had correctly interpreted the constitutionally protected free speech rights of the broadcast medium under these circumstances. Once again, then, the trial had to be postponed until the Supreme Court was able to decide whether the defendant broadcast station could be held liable for invasion of privacy damages without illegally infringing upon its right of freedom of expression. It takes votes from at least four Justices to grant a *writ of certiorari*.

Eventually, as you may recall, a majority of the Supreme Court Justices joined in a decision that shielded the broadcast defendant from civil liability for any damages caused by the disclosure of information already a matter of public record, finding that to allow a communications medium to be penalized for disseminating facts available to every citizen would "invite timidity and self-censorship and very likely lead to the suppression of many items . . . that should be made available to the public".[4]

---

[4] Cox Broadcasting Corp. v. Cohn, 420 U.S. 469, 95 S.Ct. 1029 (1975).

Thus in *Cox,* as in many of the other cases discussed in this book, there was never any exciting conflict in open court; no trial with its fascinating array of witnesses, caustic cross examinations, angry objections or eloquent closing statements. Instead, clashes between attorneys representing the embittered family of the rape victim and those protecting the free speech rights of the broadcasters occurred in the hushed atmosphere of an appeals court, defined by carefully researched legal arguments in written documents called "briefs", and explained by these attorneys in polite, precisely reasoned statements to the court.

After considering these briefs and arguments, an appeals court determines how to resolve the issue or issues of law raised by the appeal, writing an opinion to explain the legal basis for this decision, and to point out to those lower trial courts under its authority how they should resolve the same legal issue if it should arise again during any legal proceeding in the future.

But what if the trial in the *Cox* case had already taken place before the defense attorneys raised any questions about its constitutionality, and the jury had found that this news broadcast did invade the privacy of the plaintiff, entering a verdict granting the injured party a massive award of monetary damages? In that case, the attorneys for the defendants would have the right to appeal this verdict, asking the court with review authority over the trial judge to consider any material legal issues the appealing attorney claims were not considered, or were decided erroneously during the trial, resulting in the appealing party losing the case.

In our *Cox* case example, the reviewing court judge would then accept briefs and hear arguments on only that single issue raised on appeal, determining whether the free speech safeguards of the First and Fourteenth amendment protect a broadcast station from being held liable for monetary damages caused by disclosure of information already a matter of public record.

This appeals court generally has three options available to it after considering the legal issues it has reviewed. The first option is to *affirm* the lower court decision, indicating that the lower court was correct in its interpretation of the legal issue raised on appeal. The second option is to *reverse and remand* with instructions, finding the lower court to be in error and sending the case back for a new trial or "retrial" in which the judge will follow the guidance of the review court to avoid those errors that caused the first trial to be invalid. In this situation, the third option would be to *vacate* the judgment, declaring that law suit should not have been tried in the first place because the plaintiff had no legal right to bring the action.

Unfortunately, this is seldom the end of the litigation process. The party losing at this appeal court level generally has the right to seek a review of the appeal court decision by a higher level appellate court or the state Supreme Court, and if as in the *Cox* case, an important federal issue has been raised by the litigation, the entire matter can be removed to federal court, where the proceedings begin anew.

A process this slow, expensive and risky is one that provides every incentive for out-of-court settlements and explains why one legal scholar described litigation as being the "pathology" of the law. In reality, then, those appeal court opinions published and discussed in this book can be understood most accurately not as typical cases in communication law, but rather the unusual ones that were considered so important by the parties involved that they were willing to accept the delays, costs and risks of litigation in order to establish that point of law described in the opinion.

C. *Administrative Law and the Courts*

The FCC is an administrative agency, created by Congress to enforce the provisions of the Communications Act of 1934. As a regulatory body, the Commission has been granted authority by Congress to adopt "administrative law" rules to define more clearly those generalized broadcast public interest standards contained in the Communications Act. In addition, the FCC has been empowered by Congress to hold hearings to determine whether a broadcast licensee may have violated Commission rules, or the provisions of the Communications Act, and to impose penalties upon those licensees not conforming to these regulatory standards.

At the same time, Congress has established the Court of Appeals for the District of Columbia as the federal court responsible for reviewing FCC decisions. In a case such as *CBS v. FCC*, described in chapter eight of your text, an administrative law judge held a hearing to determine whether the refusal of CBS to provide air time for the broadcast of a political documentary represented a violation of the reasonable access requirements of section 312(a) of the Communications Act.

As administrative law has been structured by Congress, this hearing is considered to be a "trial court" proceeding, establishing a legal record for the decision that can later be reviewed on appeal by the Court of Appeals for the District of Columbia, and ultimately by the United States Supreme Court if it should decide to accept certiorari.

The finding of the administrative law judge that CBS had violated the access requirements of section 312(a) was reviewed initially within the FCC by review board created expressly for this purpose. When this decision was affirmed by the board, and finally approved by a 4–3 vote of the FCC Commissioners, the network petitioned the D.C. Court of Appeals to review those errors in law alleged to have caused the Commission to improperly interpret the legal requirements of this section of the Act.

As in the *Cox* case, the Court of Appeals had the option of affirming the Commission decision, remanding it for a new hearing on issues it overlooked or improperly decided at the original hearing, or vacating the decision if the appeals court could find no legal basis for the FCC's determination.

In this example, after the appeals court affirmed the FCC decision, the Supreme Court agreed to review the case and eventually also affirmed the Commission's decision by a 6–3 margin, with Justice Berger writing the majority opinion explaining that such a reasonable political access requirement did not improperly infringe upon the free speech rights of the broadcaster because there was "nothing in the First Amendment which prevents Government from requiring a licensee to share his frequency with others * * *"[5]

Understanding these basic legal terms in the context of that system of law in which they operate should help you to become more fully aware of the actual legal effects of those communication law decisions contained in this book. But if you'd be interested in finding and actually reading these or other important communication law opinions on your own, no area of study is organized more logically or indexed more effectively than the field of American law.

D. *Finding Judicial Source Material*

All decisions of the United States Supreme Court are published officially in a series called *US Reports,* and by two commercial publishers in series called *Supreme Court Reporter* (West Publishing) and another called *U.S. Supreme Court Reports, Lawyers' Edition* (Lawyers' Cooperative Publishing Company). Each of these series contains every opinion of the Supreme Court, but West and Lawyers' Cooperative provide additional reference and indexing material as part of their total system of legal publications for lawyers.

Decisions of the federal Courts of Appeal are published in the *Federal Reporter,* and most federal District Court decisions are found in the *Federal Supplement,* both West Publishing series. All reported decisions of state courts are contained in West Publishing's National Reporter System, divided geographically into seven different regional series; the *Atlantic, Pacific, Southern, Southwestern, Southeastern, Northwestern* and *Northeastern.*

---

[5] CBS, Inc. v. FCC, 453 U.S. 367, 101 S.Ct. 2813 (1981).

To locate a particular judicial opinion, all you need to do is to follow the instructions provided by its citation. For example, to find the famous *United Church of Christ v. FCC* case, cited as 359 F2d 994, recognizing that citizen groups had the legal right to challenge the renewal of a broadcast license, you would open the 359th volume of the *Federal Reporter,* 2nd series, and turn to page 994 where the opinion begins.

If your university library doesn't have these legal publications among its holdings, they can all be found in the library of your nearest county courthouse. In addition, you should find a service called *Shepard's Citators* there that allow you, by using various judicial indexing books, to discover whether any later decisions have had any effect upon those legal principles defined by that judicial opinion you've just been reading.

This brief survey of communication law research literature is not intended to do anything more than illustrate how simple the process of legal research can really be. There is no reason to provide a elaborate description of a wide variety of communication law research techniques here, because there are so many excellent books and studies already covering every aspect of this topic in great detail. For further guidance, any of the following books and articles are highly recommended:

1. Cohen, M.L. *How to Find the Law* St. Paul, Minn. West Publishing. (often updated with new editions)

2. Cohen, M.L. *Legal Research in a Nutshell* St. Paul, Minn West Publishing (frequently updated)

3. Foley, J.M. "Broadcast Regulation Research: A Primer for Non–Lawyers," *Journal of Broadcasting* 17/2 (Summer 1973) pp. 147–159.

4. Goehlert, R *Congress and Law Making: Researching the Legislative Process* Santa Barbara, CA Clio Books, 1979.

5. Honigsburg, P.J. *Cluing Into Legal Research* Berkeley, CA Golden Rain Press, 1979.

6. Jacobstein J.M. and R.M. Mersky, *Fundamentals of Legal Research* Mineola, NY Foundation Press, 1977.

7. Le Duc, D.R. "Broadcast Legal Documentation: A Four-Dimensional Guide," *Journal of Broadcasting* 17/2 (Summer 1973) pp. 131–146.

8. Pauwels, C.K., in J.R. Bittner, *Broadcast Law and Regulation* Englewood Cliffs NJ Prentice Hall 1982 pp. 397–411.

9. Price, M.O. and H. Bittner, *Effective Legal Research* Boston Little Brown (1979).

Appendix D

BIBLIOGRAPHY

American Law Institute, Restatement of the Law: Torts. 2d ed. St. Paul, 1977.

Adler, Allan, and M.H. Halperin, Litigation Under the Federal Freedom of Information Act and Privacy Act, Washington, D.C., 1990.

Adler, Renata, Reckless Disregard, New York, 1986.

Angoff, Charles, Handbook of Libel. New York, 1946.

Bagdikian, Ben, The Media Monopoly. Boston, 1983.

Barnouw, Erk, A History of Broadcasting in the United States, 3 vols. (N.Y., 1966–1972).

Barron, Jerome, Freedom of the Press for Whom? Bloomington, Ind., 1973.

Beck, Carl, Contempt of Congress. New Orleans, 1959.

Berns, Walter, The First Amendment and the Future of American Democracy. New York, 1976.

Bezanson, Randall P., Gilbert Cranberg, and John Soloski, Libel Law and The Press: Myth and Reality, New York, 1987.

Blackstone, William, Commentaries on the Law of England, IV, adapted by Robert Malcom Kerr, Boston, 1952.

Blasi, Vincent, The Checking Value in First Amendment Theory, Am. Bar Foundation Research Journal, 1977, # 3.

Bok, Sissela, Secrets. New York, 1983.

Brenner, Daniel L. and William L. Rivers, Free But Regulated: Conflicting Traditions in Media Law. Ames, Iowa, 1982.

Canavan, Francis, Freedom of Expression: Purpose as Limit. Durham, N.C., 1984.

Center for National Security Studies, FOIA Handbook. Washington, D.C., 1979.

Chafee, Zechariah, Jr., Free Speech in the United States. Boston, 1941.

————, Government and Mass Communications, 2 vols. Chicago, 1947.

Chamberlin, Bill F., and Charlene Brown, The First Amendment Reconsidered. Chapel Hill, 1981.

Cline, Victor (ed.), Where Do You Draw the Line? Provo, UT, 1974.

Cooley, Thomas M., Constitutional Limitations. (8th ed.). Boston, 1927.

Cooper, Thomas, The Law of Libel and the Liberty of the Press. New York, 1830.

Denniston, Lyle, The Reporter and the Law. New York, 1980.

Devol, Kenneth S., Mass Media and the Supreme Court, 2d ed. New York, 1976.

Duniway, Clyde A., The Development of Freedom of the Press in Massachusetts. Cambridge, 1906.

Emerson, Thomas I., The System of Freedom of Expression. New York, 1970.

Emery, Walter B., Broadcasting and Government: Responsibilities and Regulations. East Lansing, Mich., 1961.

Folkerts, Jean and Dwight L. Teeter, Voices of a Nation: A History of the Media in the United States. New York, 1989.

Fox, Sir John C., The History of Contempt of Court. Oxford, 1927.

Franklin, Marc A., Mass Media Law Cases and Materials, Westbury, 3rd ed., 1987.

Friendly, Fred, Minnesota Rag. New York, 1981.

Gerald, J. Edward, The Press and the Constitution, 1931–1947. Minneapolis, 1948.

Gillmor, Donald M., Free Press and Fair Trial. Washington, D.C., 1966.

Goldfarb, Ronald L., The Contempt Power. New York, 1963.

Goodale, James, C., Communications Law 1984. New York, 1984.

Gora, Joel M., The Rights of Reporters. New York, 1974.

Hachten, William A., The Supreme Court on Freedom of the Press: Decisions and Dissents. Ames, Iowa, 1968.

Haight, Anne Lyon, Banned Books (rev. 2d ed.). New York, 1955.

Havick, John J., Communications Policy and the Political Process. Westport, Conn., 1983.

Head, Sydney W. and Christopher Sterling, Broadcasting in America. (5th ed.). Boston, 1987.

Hentoff, Nat, History of Freedom of the Press in America. New York, 1980.

Hocking, William E., Freedom of the Press. Chicago, 1947.

Holmes, Oliver Wendell Jr., The Common Law. Boston, 1881.

Hopkins, W. Wat, Mr. Justice Brennan and Freedom of Expression. New York, 1991.

Jolliffe, John, The Constitutional History of Medieval England (2d ed.). London, 1947.

Jones, William, Cases and Materials on Electronic Mass Media. Mineola, N.Y., 1977.

Kahn, F.J., ed., Documents of American Broadcasting, 4th ed. New York, 1984.

Kaufman, Henry R., ed., LDRC 50–State Survey 1984, III. New York, 1984.

Kinsley, Philip, Liberty and the Press. Chicago, 1944.

Konvitz, Milton R., First Amendment Freedoms. Ithaca, 1963.

Le Duc, Don R., Beyond Broadcasting: Patterns in Policy and Law. (New York, 1987).

Levin, Harvey J., Fact and Fancy in Television Regulation. New York, 1980.

Levy, Leonard W., Emergence of a Free Press. New York, 1985.

————, ed., Freedom of the Press from Zenger to Jefferson. Indianapolis, 1966.

————, Legacy of Suppression: Freedom of Speech and Press in Early American History. Cambridge, 1960.

Lewis, Anthony, Make No Law: The Sullivan Case and the First Amendment. New York, 1991.

Lockhart, William B., and Robert C. McClure, Censorship of Obscenity: the Developing Constitutional Standards, 45 Minnesota Law Review 5 (Nov. 1960).

————, Literature, the Law of Obscenity, and the Constitution, 38 Minnesota Law Review (March 1954).

Lofton, John, The Press as a Defender of the First Amendment. Columbia, S.C., 1980.

McCormick, Robert R., The Freedom of the Press. New York, 1936.

Meiklejohn, Alexander, Free Speech and Its Relation to Self Government. New York, 1948.

Miller, Arthur, The Assault on Privacy. Ann Arbor, 1971.

Murphy, Paul, World War I and the Origins of Civil Liberties in the United States. New York, 1979.

Nelson, Harold L., ed., Freedom of the Press from Hamilton to the Warren Court. Indianapolis, 1967.

Nimmer, Melville B., Nimmer on Copyright, 4 vols. New York, 1963–1988.

Odgers, W. Blake, A Digest of the Law of Libel and Slander (6th ed.). London, 1929.

Owen, Bruce M., Economics and Freedom of Expression. Cambridge, 1975.

Parsons, Patrick, Cable Television and the First Amendment. Lexington, MA, 1987.

Paterson, James, Liberty of Press, Speech and Public Worship. London, 1880.

Patterson, Giles J., Free Speech and a Free Press. Boston, 1939.

Paul, James C.N., and Murray L. Schwartz, Federal Censorship: Obscenity in the Mail. New York, 1961.

Pember, Don R., Privacy and the Press. Seattle, 1972.

Peterson, H.C., and Gilbert C. Fite, Opponents of War, 1917–1918. Madison, 1957.

Pilpel, Harriet, and Theodora Zavin, Rights and Writers. New York, 1960.

Powe, Lucas A., Jr., American Broadcasting and the First Amendment, Berkeley, 1987.

———, The Fourth Estate and the Constitution. Berkeley, 1991.

Preston, Ivan, The Great American Blowup. Madison, 1975.

Preston, William, Jr., Aliens and Dissenters. Cambridge, 1963.

Prosser, William L., The Law of Torts. 4th ed. St. Paul, 1971.

Rohrer, Daniel M., Mass Media, Freedom of Speech, and Advertising. Dubuque, Ia., 1979.

Rosden, George Eric and Peter Eric, The Law of Advertising, 2 vols. (New York, 1963, 1976, 1988).

Rosenberg, Norman L., Protecting the Best Men: An Interpretive History of Libel, Chapel Hill, 1986.

Rourke, Francis E., Secrecy and Publicity. Baltimore, 1961.

Sack, Robert D., Libel, Slander, and Related Problems. New York, 1980.

Sanford, Bruce, The Law of Libel and the Right of Privacy. New York, 1984.

Schmidt, Benno C., Jr., Freedom of the Press vs. Public Access. New York, 1976.

Seldes, George, Freedom of the Press. Cleveland, 1935.

Shapiro, Martin, Freedom of Speech: The Supreme Court and Judicial Review. Englewood Cliffs, N.J., 1966.

Siebert, Fredrick S., Freedom of the Press in England, 1476–1776. Urbana, 1952.

Simmons, Steven J., The Fairness Doctrine and the Media. Berkeley, 1978.

Simon, Morton J., Public Relations Law. New York, 1969.

Smith, James Morton, Freedom's Fetters: the Alien and Sedition Laws and American Civil Liberties. Ithaca, 1956.

Smolla, Rodney, Jerry Falwell v. Larry Flynt. Urbana, 1988.

————, Suing the Press. New York, 1986.

Stansbury, Arthur J., Report of the Trial of James H. Peck. Boston, 1833.

Starkie, Thomas, The Law of Slander, Libel, Scandalum Magnatum and False Rumors, with the Practise and Pleadings. London, 1813; 4th ed. by Henry C. Folkard, with notes and references to American Cases by Horace G. Wood. New York, 1877.

Sterling, Christopher, and John Michael Kittross, Stay Tuned: An Informal History of American Broadcasting. Belmont, CA, 1978.

Sullivan, Harold W., Contempts by Publication. New Haven, 1940.

Warren, Samuel D., and Louis D. Brandeis, The Right to Privacy, 4 Harvard Law Review 193 (1890).

Westin, Alan, Privacy and Freedom. New York, 1967.

Winfield, Richard N., New York Times v. Sullivan, the Next Twenty Years (New York, Practising Law Institute, 1984).

Wolff, Robert Paul, Barrington Moore and Herbert Marcuse, A Critique of Pure Tolerance. Boston, 1965.

Wortman, Tunis, Treatise Concerning Political Enquiry, and the Liberty of the Press. New York, 1800.

Yudof, Mark G., When Government Speaks. Berkeley, 1983.

Additional Resources

American Digest System, Decennial Digests, valuable for lists of cases and points adjudicated.

American Jurisprudence, a legal encyclopedia.

Annotated Report System, selected reports and annotations, with summaries of arguments of counsel.

Compilations of Laws Affecting Publications, particularly those put out by various states. Consult managers of various state press associations.

Corpus Juris Secundum, a legal encyclopedia.

Freedom of Information Center, University of Missouri, issues frequent Reports, the FOI Digest (bi-monthly newsletter), and occasional studies covering a wide variety of media-and-law-subjects. Invaluable for state laws on meetings and records.

Law Dictionaries, including Black's, Ballentine's, and Bouvier's.

Law Reviews. Among the outstanding law reviews published under the direction of law schools are Columbia Law Review, Cornell Law Quarterly, Harvard Law Review, Illinois Law Review, Michigan Law Review, Texas Law Review, Wisconsin Law Review, and Yale Law Journal.

Libel Defense Resource Center Bulletin. Reports studies and analyses by the Center, many of them wide-sweeping surveys of aspects of libel nationally.

Media Law Reporter. Bureau of National Affairs, Inc., Washington, D.C. This looseleaf service provides up-to-date coverage of court decisions (full texts) and news notes in communication law, beginning in 1976.

National Reporter System, giving texts of appellate court decisions in various jurisdictions of the nation.

News Media and the Law, publication of the Reporters Committee for Freedom of the Press (formerly Press Censorship Newsletter). Washington, D.C.

Words and Phrases, a legal encyclopedia based on definitions of terms as used in statutes and by the courts.

Appendix E

THE SOCIETY OF PROFESSIONAL JOURNALISTS AND ASNE CODES OF ETHICS

THE SOCIETY OF PROFESSIONAL JOURNALISTS CODE OF ETHICS

The Society of Professional Journalists believes the duty of journalists is to serve the truth.

We believe the agencies of mass communication are carriers of public discussion and information, acting on their Constitutional mandate and freedom to learn and report the facts.

We believe in public enlightenment as the forerunner of justice, and in our Constitutional role to seek the truth as part of the public's right to know the truth.

We believe those responsibilities carry obligations that require journalists to perform with intelligence, objectivity, accuracy and fairness.

To these ends, we declare acceptance of the standards of practice here set forth:

I. Responsibility: The public's right to know of events of public importance and interest is the overriding mission of the mass media. The purpose of distributing news and enlightened opinion is to serve the general welfare. Journalists who use their professional status as representatives of the public for selfish or other unworthy motives violate a high trust.

II. Freedom of the Press: Freedom of the press is to be guarded as an inalienable right of people in a free society. It carries with it the freedom and the responsibility to discuss, question and challenge actions and utterances of our government and of our public and private institutions. Journalists uphold the right to speak unpopular opinions and the privilege to agree with the majority.

III. Ethics: Journalists must be free of obligation to any interest other than the public's right to know the truth.

1. Gifts, favors, free travel, special treatment or privileges can compromise the integrity of journalists and their employers. Nothing of value should be accepted.

2. Secondary employment, political involvement, holding public office and service in community organizations should be

avoided if it compromises the integrity of journalists and their employers. Journalists and their employers should conduct their personal lives in a manner which protects them from conflict of interest, real or apparent. Their responsibilities to the public are paramount. That is the nature of their profession.

3. So-called news communications from private sources should not be published or broadcast without substantiation of their claims to news value.

4. Journalists will seek news that serves the public interest, despite the obstacles. They will make constant efforts to assure that the public's business is conducted in public and that public records are open to public inspection.

5. Journalists acknowledge the newsman's ethic of protecting confidential sources of information.

IV. Accuracy and Objectivity: Good faith with the public is the foundation of all worthy journalism.

1. Truth is our ultimate goal.

2. Objectivity in reporting the news is another goal, which serves as the mark of an experienced professional. It is a standard of performance toward which we strive. We honor those who achieve it.

3. There is no excuse for inaccuracies or lack of thoroughness.

4. Newspaper headlines should be fully warranted by the contents of the articles they accompany. Photographs and telecasts should give an accurate picture of an event and not highlight an incident out of context.

5. Sound practice makes clear distinction between news reports and expressions of opinion. News reports should be free of opinion or bias and represent all sides of an issue.

6. Partisanship in editorial comment which knowingly departs from the truth violates the spirit of American journalism.

7. Journalists recognize their responsibility for offering informed analysis, comment and editorial opinion on public events and issues. They accept the obligation to present such material by individuals whose competence, experience, and judgment qualify them for it.

8. Special articles or presentations devoted to advocacy or the writer's own conclusions and interpretations should be labeled as such.

V. Fair Play: Journalists at all times will show respect for the dignity, privacy, rights, and well-being of people encountered in the course of gathering and presenting the news.

1. The news media should not communicate unofficial charges affecting reputation or moral character without giving the accused a chance to reply.

2. The news media must guard against invading a person's right to privacy.

3. The media should not pander to morbid curiosity about details of vice and crime.

4. It is the duty of news media to make prompt and complete correction of their errors.

5. Journalists should be accountable to the public for their reports and the public should be encouraged to voice its grievances against the media. Open dialogue with our readers, viewers, and listeners should be fostered.

VI. Pledge. Adherence to this code is intended to preserve and strengthen the bond of mutual trust and respect between American Journalists and the American People.

The Society shall—by programs of education and other means—encourage individual journalists to adhere to these tenets, and shall encourage journalistic publications and broadcasters to recognize their responsibility to frame codes of ethics in concert with their employers to serve as guidelines in furthering these goals.

Adopted by the 1973 national convention; revised 1984, 1987.

ASNE STATEMENT OF PRINCIPLES

PREAMBLE

The First Amendment, protecting freedom of expression from abridgment by any law, guarantees to the people through their press a constitutional right, and thereby places on newspaper people a particular responsibility.

Thus journalism demands of its practitioners not only industry and knowledge but also the pursuit of a standard of integrity proportionate to the journalist's singular obligation.

To this end the American Society of Newspaper Editors sets forth this Statement of Principles as a standard encouraging the highest ethical and professional performance.

ARTICLE I: RESPONSIBILITY

The primary purpose of gathering and distributing news and opinion is to serve the general welfare by informing the people and enabling them to make judgments on the issues of the time. Newspapermen and women who abuse the power of their professional role for selfish motives or unworthy purposes are faithless to that public trust.

The American press was made free not just to inform or just to serve as a forum for debate but also to bring an independent scrutiny to bear on the forces of power in the society, including the conduct of official power at all levels of government.

ARTICLE II: FREEDOM OF THE PRESS

Freedom of the press belongs to the people. It must be defended against encroachment or assault from any quarter, public or private.

Journalists must be constantly alert to see that the public's business is conducted in public. They must be vigilant against all who would exploit the press for selfish purposes.

ARTICLE III: INDEPENDENCE

Journalists must avoid impropriety and the appearance of impropriety as well as any conflict of interest or the appearance of conflict. They should neither accept anything nor pursue any activity that might compromise or seem to compromise their integrity.

ARTICLE IV: TRUTH AND ACCURACY

Good faith with the reader is the foundation of good journalism. Every effort must be made to assure that the news content is accurate, free from bias and in context, and that all sides are presented fairly. Editorials, analytical articles and commentary should be held to the same standards of accuracy with respect to facts as news reports.

Significant errors of fact, as well as errors of omission, should be corrected promptly and prominently.

ARTICLE V: IMPARTIALITY

To be impartial does not require the press to be unquestioning or to refrain from editorial expression. Sound practice, however, demands a clear distinction for the reader between news reports and opinion. Articles that contain opinion or personal interpretation should be clearly identified.

ARTICLE VI: FAIR PLAY

Journalists should respect the rights of people involved in the news, observe the common standards of decency and stand accountable to the public for the fairness and accuracy of their news reports.

Persons publicly accused should be given the earliest opportunity to respond.

Pledges of confidentiality to news sources must be honored at all costs, and therefore should not be given lightly. Unless there is clear and pressing need to maintain confidences, sources of information should be identified.

These principles are intended to preserve, protect and strengthen the bond of trust and respect between American journalists and the American people, a bond that is essential to sustain the grant of freedom entrusted to both by the nation's founders.

This Statement of Principles was adopted by the ASNE Board of Directors, Oct. 23, 1975; it supplants the 1922 Code of Ethics ("Canons of Journalism").

Appendix F

COMMUNICATIONS ACT OF 1934
(MAJOR PROVISIONS)

COMMUNICATIONS ACT OF 1934

48 Stat. 1064 (1934), as amended, 47 U.S.C.A. § 151 et seq.

TITLE I—GENERAL PROVISIONS

PURPOSES OF ACT; CREATION OF FEDERAL COMMUNICATIONS COMMISSION

Sec. 151

For the purpose of regulating interstate and foreign commerce in communication by wire and radio so as to make available, so far as possible, to all the people of the United States a rapid, efficient, Nationwide, and world-wide wire and radio communication service with adequate facilities at reasonable charges, for the purpose of the national defense, for the purpose of promoting safety of life and property through the use of wire and radio communication, and for the purpose of securing a more effective execution of this policy by centralizing authority heretofore granted by law to several agencies and by granting additional authority with respect to interstate and foreign commerce in wire and radio communication, there is hereby created a commission to be known as the "Federal Communications Commission," which shall be constituted as hereinafter provided, and which shall execute and enforce the provisions of this Act.

* * *

APPLICATION OF ACT

Sec. 152

(a) The provisions of this Act shall apply to all interstate and foreign communication by wire or radio and all interstate and foreign transmission of energy by radio, which originates and/or is received within the United States, and to all persons engaged within the United States in such communication or such transmission of energy by radio, and to the licensing and regulating of all radio stations as hereinafter provided. . . . The provisions of this Act shall apply with respect to cable service to all persons engaged within the United States in providing such service, and to

789

the facilities of cable operators which relate to such service as provided in title VI.

* * *

TITLE II—COMMON CARRIERS

(omitted)

TITLE III—PROVISIONS RELATING TO RADIO

LICENSE FOR RADIO COMMUNICATION OR TRANSMISSION OF ENERGY

Sec. 301

It is the purpose of this Act, among other things, to maintain the control of the United States over all the channels of interstate and foreign radio transmission; and to provide for the use of such channels, but not the ownership thereof, by persons for limited periods of time, under licenses granted by Federal authority, and no such license shall be construed to create any right, beyond the terms, conditions, and periods of the license. No person shall use or operate any apparatus for the transmission of energy or communications or signals by radio (a) from one place in any Territory or possession of the United States or in the District of Columbia to another place in the same Territory, possession, or district; or (b) from any State, Territory, or possession of the United States, or from the District of Columbia to any other State, Territory, or possession of the United States; or (c) from any place in any State, Territory, or possession of the United States, or in the District of Columbia, to any place in any foreign country or to any vessel; or (d) within any State when the effects of such use extend beyond the borders of said State, or when interference is caused by such use or operation with the transmission of such energy, communications, or signals from within said State to any place beyond its borders, or from any place beyond its borders to any place within said State, or with the transmission or reception of such energy, communications, or signals from and/or to places beyond the borders of said State; or (e) upon any vessel or aircraft of the United States; or (f) upon any other mobile stations within the jurisdiction of the United States, except under and in accordance with this Act and with a license in that behalf granted under the provisions of this Act.

* * *

GENERAL POWERS OF THE COMMISSION

Sec. 303

Except as otherwise provided in this Act, the Commission from time to time, as public convenience, interest, or necessity requires shall:

(a) Classify radio stations;

(b) Prescribe the nature of the service to be rendered by each class of licensed stations and each station within any class;

(c) Assign bands of frequencies to the various classes of stations, and assign frequencies for each individual station and determine the power which each station shall use and the time during which it may operate;

(d) Determine the location of classes of stations or individual stations;

(e) Regulate the kind of apparatus to be used with respect to its external effects and the purity and sharpness of the emissions from each station and from the apparatus therein;

(f) Make such regulations not inconsistent with law as it may deem necessary to prevent interference between stations and to carry out the provisions of this Act: Provided, however, That changes in the frequencies, authorized power, or in the times of operation of any station, shall not be made without the consent of the station licensee unless, after a public hearing, the Commission shall determine that such changes will promote public convenience or interest or will serve public necessity, or the provisions of this Act will be more fully complied with;

(g) Study new uses for radio, provide for experimental uses of frequencies, and generally encourage the larger and more effective use of radio in the public interest;

(h) Have authority to establish areas or zones to be served by any station;

(i) Have authority to make special regulations applicable to radio stations engaged in chain broadcasting;

(j) Have authority to make general rules and regulations requiring stations to keep such records of programs, transmissions of energy, communications, or signals as it may deem desirable;

* * *

(m)(1) Have authority to suspend the license of any operator upon proof sufficient to satisfy the Commission that the licensee—

(A) has violated any provision of any Act, treaty, or convention binding on the United States, which the Commission is authorized to administer, or any regulation made by the Commission under any such Act, treaty, or convention; or

* * *

(D) has transmitted superfluous radio communications or signals or communications containing profane or obscene words, language, or meaning. . . .

* * *

(r) Make such rules and regulations and prescribe such restrictions and conditions, not inconsistent with law, as may be necessary to carry out the provisions of this Act, or any international radio or wire communications treaty or convention, or regulations annexed thereto, including any treaty or convention insofar as it relates to the use of radio, to which the United States is or may hereafter become a party.

(s) Have authority to require that apparatus designed to receive television pictures broadcast simultaneously with sound be capable of adequately receiving all frequencies allocated by the Commission to television broadcasting when such apparatus is shipped in interstate commerce, or is imported from any foreign country into the United States, for sale or resale to the public.

* * *

ALLOCATION OF FACILITIES; TERM OF LICENSES

Sec. 307

(a) The Commission, if public convenience, interest, or necessity will be served thereby, subject to the limitations of this Act, shall grant to any applicant therefor a station license provided for by this Act.

(b) In considering applications for licenses, and modifications and renewals thereof, when and insofar as there is demand for the same, the Commission shall make such distribution of licenses, frequencies, hours of operation, and of power among the several States and communities as to provide a fair, efficient, and equitable distribution of radio service to each of the same.

* * *

(d) No license granted for the operation of a television broadcasting station shall be for a term longer than five years . . . and any license granted may be revoked as hereinafter provided.

Each license granted for the operation of a radio broadcasting station shall be for a term of not to exceed seven years. Upon the expiration of any license, upon application therefor, a renewal of such license may be granted from time to time for a term of not to exceed five years in the case of television broadcasting licenses, for a term of not to exceed seven years in the case of radio broadcasting station licenses, and for a term of not to exceed five years in the case of other licenses, if the Commission finds that public interest, convenience, and necessity would be served thereby. . . .

(e) No renewal of an existing station license in the broadcast or the common carrier services shall be granted more than thirty days prior to the expiration of the original license.

APPLICATIONS FOR LICENSES . . .

Sec. 308

* * *

(b) All applications for station licenses, or modifications or renewals thereof, shall set forth such facts as the Commission by regulation may prescribe as to the citizenship, character, and financial, technical, and other qualifications of the applicant to operate the station; the ownership and location of the proposed station and of the stations, if any, with which it is proposed to communicate; the frequencies and the power desired to be used; the hours of the day or other periods of time during which it is proposed to operate the station; the purposes for which the station is to be used; and such other information as it may require. . . .

ACTION UPON APPLICATIONS; FORM OF AND CONDITIONS ATTACHED TO LICENSES

Sec. 309

(a) Subject to the provisions of this section, the Commission shall determine, in the case of each application filed with it to which section 308 applies, whether the public interest, convenience, and necessity will be served by the granting of such application, and, if the Commission, upon examination of such application and upon consideration of such other matters as the Commission may officially notice, shall find that public interest, convenience, and necessity would be served by the granting thereof, it shall grant such application.

* * *

(d)(1) Any party in interest may file with the Commission a petition to deny any application. . . .

(2) If the Commission finds on the basis of the application, the pleadings filed, or other matters which it may officially notice that there are no substantial and material questions of fact and that a grant of the application would be consistent with subsection (a), it shall make the grant, deny the petition, and issue a concise statement of the reasons for denying the petition, which statement shall dispose of all substantial issues raised by the petition. If a substantial and material question of fact is presented or if the Commission for any reason is unable to find that grant of the application would be consistent with subsection (a), it shall proceed as provided in subsection (e).

(e) If, in the case of any application to which subsection (a) of this section applies, a substantial and material question of fact is presented or the Commission for any reason is unable to make the finding specified in such subsection, it shall formally designate the application for hearing on the ground or reasons then obtaining and shall forthwith notify the applicant and all other known parties in interest of such action and the grounds and reasons therefor, specifying with particularity the matters and things in issue but not including issues or requirements phrased generally. . . .

* * *

(h) Such station licenses as the Commission may grant shall be in such general form as it may prescribe, but each license shall contain, in addition to other provisions, a statement of the following conditions to which such license shall be subject: (1) The station license shall not vest in the licensee any right to operate the station nor any right in the use of the frequencies designated in the license beyond the term thereof nor in any other manner than authorized therein; (2) neither the license nor the right granted thereunder shall be assigned or otherwise transferred in violation of this Act; (3) every license issued under this Act shall be subject in terms to the right of use or control conferred by section 606 of this Act.*

* * *

LIMITATION ON HOLDING AND TRANSFER OF LICENSES

Sec. 310

(a) The station license required hereby shall not be granted to or held by any foreign government or representative thereof.

---

* [Section 606 grants broad powers to the President to utilize communications facilities during wartime or a national emergency.]

(b) No broadcast or common carrier . . . license shall be granted to or held by—

(1) Any alien or the representative of any alien;

(2) Any corporation organized under the laws of any foreign government;

* * *

(d) No construction permit or station license, or any rights thereunder, shall be transferred, assigned, or disposed of in any manner, voluntarily or involuntarily, directly or indirectly, or by transfer of control of any corporation holding such permit or license, to any person except upon application to the Commission and upon finding by the Commission that the public interest, convenience, and necessity will be served thereby. Any such application shall be disposed of as if the proposed transferee or assignee were making application under section 308 for the permit or license in question; but in acting thereon the Commission may not consider whether the public interest, convenience, and necessity might be served by the transfer, assignment, or disposal of the permit or license to a person other than the proposed transferee or assignee.

SPECIAL REQUIREMENTS WITH RESPECT TO CERTAIN APPLICATIONS IN THE BROADCASTING SERVICE

Sec. 311

* * *

(c)(1) If there are pending before the Commission two or more applications for a permit for construction of a broadcasting station, only one of which can be granted, it shall be unlawful, without approval of the Commission, for the applicants or any of them to effectuate an agreement whereby one or more of such applicants withdraws his or their application or applications.

(2) The request for Commission approval in any such case shall be made in writing jointly by all the parties to the agreement. Such request shall contain or be accompanied by full information with respect to the agreement, set forth in such detail, form, and manner as the Commission shall by rule require.

(3) The Commission shall approve the agreement only if it determines (A) that the agreement is consistent with the public interest, convenience, or necessity; and (B) no party to the agreement filed its application for the purpose of reaching or carrying out such agreement. If the agreement does not contemplate a merger, but contemplates the making of any direct or indirect payment to any party thereto in considera-

tion of his withdrawal of his application, the Commission may determine the agreement to be consistent with the public interest, convenience, or necessity only if the amount or value of such payment, as determined by the Commission, is not in excess of the aggregate amount determined by the Commission to have been legitimately and prudently expended and to be expended by such applicant in connection with preparing, filing, and advocating the granting of his application.

* * *

ADMINISTRATIVE SANCTIONS

Sec. 312

(a) The Commission may revoke any station license or construction permit—

(1) for false statements knowingly made either in the application or in any statement of fact which may be required pursuant to section 308;

(2) because of conditions coming to the attention of the Commission which would warrant it in refusing to grant a license or permit on an original application;

(3) for willful or repeated failure to operate substantially as set forth in the license;

(4) for willful or repeated violation of, or willful or repeated failure to observe any provision of this Act or any rule or regulation of the Commission authorized by this Act or by a treaty ratified by the United States;

(5) for violation of or failure to observe any final cease and desist order issued by the Commission under this section;

(6) for violation of section 1304, 1343, or 1464 of title 18 of the United States Code; * or

* [Relevant provisions read as follows:

§ 1304. Broadcasting lottery information

Whoever broadcasts by means of any radio station for which a license is required by any law of the United States, or whoever, operating any such station, knowingly permits the broadcasting of, any advertisement of or information concerning any lottery, gift enterprise, or similar scheme, offering prizes dependent in whole or in part upon lot or chance, or any list of the prizes drawn or awarded by means of any such lottery, gift enterprise, or scheme, whether said list contains any part or all of such prizes, shall be fined not more than $1,000 or imprisoned not more than one year, or both.

§ 1343. Fraud by wire, radio, or television

Whoever, having devised or intending to devise any scheme or artifice to defraud, or for obtaining money or property by means of false or fraudulent pretenses, representations, or promises, transmits or causes to be transmitted by means of wire, radio, or television communication in interstate or foreign commerce, any writings, signs, signals, pictures, or sounds for the purpose of executing such

(7) for willful or repeated failure to allow reasonable access to or to permit purchase of reasonable amounts of time for the use of a broadcasting station by a legally qualified candidate for Federal elective office on behalf of his candidacy.

(b) Where any person (1) has failed to operate substantially as set forth in a license, (2) has violated or failed to observe any of the provisions of this Act, or section 1304, 1343, or 1464 of title 18 of the United States Code, or (3) has violated or failed to observe any rule or regulation of the Commission authorized by this Act or by a treaty ratified by the United States, the Commission may order such person to cease and desist from such action.

(c) Before revoking a license or permit pursuant to subsection (a), or issuing a cease and desist order pursuant to subsection (b), the Commission shall serve upon the licensee, permittee, or person involved an order to show cause [at a hearing] why an order of revocation or a cease and desist order should not be issued. . . .

(d) In any case where a hearing is conducted pursuant to the provisions of this section, both the burden of proceeding with the introduction of evidence and the burden of proof shall be upon the Commission.

* * *

APPLICATION OF ANTITRUST LAWS; REFUSAL OF LICENSES AND PERMITS IN CERTAIN CASES

Sec. 313

(a) All laws of the United States relating to unlawful restraints and monopolies and to combinations, contracts, or agreements in restraint of trade are hereby declared to be applicable to the manufacture and sale of and to trade in radio apparatus and devices entering into or affecting interstate or foreign commerce and to interstate or foreign radio communications. Whenever in any suit, action, or proceeding, civil or criminal, brought under the

scheme or artifice, shall be fined not more than $1,000 or imprisoned not more than five years, or both.

§ 1464. Broadcasting obscene language

Whoever utters any obscene, indecent, or profane language by means of radio communications shall be fined not more than $10,000 or imprisoned not more than two years, or both.

§ 1307. State-conducted lotteries

(a) The provisions of sections 1301, 1302, 1303, and 1304 shall not apply to an advertisement, list of prizes, or information concerning a lottery conducted by a State acting under the authority of State law—

(1) contained in a newspaper published in that State, or

(2) broadcast by a radio or television station licensed to a location in that State or an adjacent State which conducts such a lottery. . . .]

provisions of any of said laws or in any proceedings brought to enforce or to review findings and orders of the Federal Trade Commission or other governmental agency in respect of any matters as to which said Commission or other governmental agency is by law authorized to act, any licensee shall be found guilty of the violation of the provisions of such laws or any of them, the court, in addition to the penalties imposed by said laws, may adjudge, order, and/or decree that the license of such licensee shall, as of the date the decree or judgment becomes finally effective or as of such other date as the said decree shall fix, be revoked and that all rights under such license shall thereupon cease: *Provided, however,* That such licensee shall have the same right of appeal or review, as is provided by law in respect of other decrees and judgments of said court.

(b) The Commission is hereby directed to refuse a station license and/or the permit hereinafter required for the construction of a station to any person (or to any person directly or indirectly controlled by such person) whose license has been revoked by a court under this section.

* * *

FACILITIES FOR CANDIDATES FOR PUBLIC OFFICE

Sec. 315

(a) If any licensee shall permit any person who is a legally qualified candidate for any public office to use a broadcasting station, he shall afford equal opportunities to all other such candidates for that office in the use of such broadcasting station: *Provided,* That such licensee shall have no power of censorship over the material broadcast under the provisions of this section. No obligation is imposed under this subsection upon any licensee to allow the use of its station by any such candidate. Appearance by a legally qualified candidate on any—

(1) Bona fide newscast,

(2) Bona fide news interview,

(3) Bona fide news documentary (if the appearance of the candidate is incidental to the presentation of the subject or subjects covered by the news documentary), or

(4) On-the-spot coverage of bona fide news events (included but not limited to political conventions and activities incidental thereto), shall not be deemed to be use of a broadcasting station within the meaning of this subsection. Nothing in the foregoing sentence shall be construed as relieving broadcasters, in connection with the presentation of newscasts, news interviews, news documentaries, and on-the-spot

coverage of news events, from the obligation imposed upon them under this Act to operate in the public interest and to afford reasonable opportunity for the discussion of conflicting views on issues of public importance.

(b) The charges made for the use of any broadcast station by any person who is a legally qualified candidate for any public office in connection with his campaign for nomination for election, or election, to such office shall not exceed—

(1) During the 45 days preceding the date of a primary or primary runoff election and during the 60 days preceding the date of a general or special election in which such person is a candidate, the lowest unit charge of the station for the same class and amount of time for the same period; and

(2) At any other time, the charges made for comparable use of such station by other users thereof.

(c) For the purposes of this section:

(1) The term "broadcasting station" includes a community antenna television system.

(2) The terms "licensee" and "station licensee" when used with respect to a community antenna television system, mean the operator of such system.

(d) The Commission shall prescribe appropriate rules and regulations to carry out the provisions of this section.

MODIFICATION BY COMMISSION OF CONSTRUCTION PERMITS OR LICENSES

Sec. 316

(a) Any station license or construction permit may be modified by the Commission either for a limited time or for the duration of the term thereof, if in the judgment of the Commission such action will promote the public interest, convenience, and necessity, or the provisions of this Act or of any treaty ratified by the United States will be more fully complied with. No such order of modification shall become final until the holder of the license or permit shall have been notified in writing of the proposed action and the grounds and reasons therefor, and shall have been given reasonable opportunity, in no event less than thirty days, to show cause by public hearing, if requested, why such order of modification should not issue. . . .

(b) In any case where a hearing is conducted pursuant to the provisions of this section, both the burden of proceeding with the introduction of evidence and the burden of proof shall be upon the Commission.

ANNOUNCEMENT WITH RESPECT TO CERTAIN MATTER BROADCAST

Sec. 317

(a)(1) All matter broadcast by any radio station for which any money, service or other valuable consideration is directly or indirectly paid, or promised to or charged or accepted by, the station so broadcasting, from any person, shall, at the time the same is so broadcast, be announced as paid for or furnished, as the case may be, by such person: *Provided,* That "service or other valuable consideration" shall not include any service or property furnished without charge or at a nominal charge for use on, or in connection with, a broadcast unless it is so furnished in consideration for an identification in a broadcast of any person, product, service, trademark, or brand name beyond an identification which is reasonably related to the use of such service or property on the broadcast.

* * *

CENSORSHIP . . .

Sec. 326

Nothing in this Act shall be understood or construed to give the Commission the power of censorship over the radio communications or signals transmitted by any radio station, and no regulation or condition shall be promulgated or fixed by the Commission which shall interfere with the right of free speech by means of radio communication.

JURISDICTION TO ENFORCE ACT AND ORDERS OF COMMISSION

Sec. 401

(a) The district courts of the United States shall have jurisdiction, upon application of the Attorney General of the United States at the request of the Commission, alleging a failure to comply with or a violation of any of the provisions of this Act by any person, to issue a writ or writs of mandamus commanding such person to comply with the provisions of this Act.

(b) If any person fails or neglects to obey any order of the Commission other than for the payment of money, while the same is in effect, the Commission or any party injured thereby, or the United States, by its Attorney General, may apply to the appropriate district court of the United States for the enforcement of such order. . . .

Sec. 402

(a) [Provides that any proceeding to review an order of the Commission not appealable under Sec. 402(b) is within the exclusive jurisdiction of the courts of appeal, venue to lie in the circuit in which the filing party resides or has his principal office, or in the D.C. Circuit.]

(b) [Provides that appeals from licensing decisions and cease and desist orders may be taken to the D.C. Circuit Court of Appeals.]

FORFEITURES

Sec. 503

* * *

(b)(1) Any person who is determined by the Commission, in accordance with paragraph (3) or (4) of this subsection, to have—

(A) willfully or repeatedly failed to comply substantially with the terms and conditions of any license, permit, certificate, or other instrument or authorization issued by the Commission;

(B) willfully or repeatedly failed to comply with any of the provisions of this Act or of any rule, regulation, or order issued by the Commission under this Act or under any treaty convention, or other agreement to which the United States is a party and which is binding upon the United States;

(C) violated any provision of section 317(c) or 509(a) of this Act; or

(D) violated any provision of sections 1304, 1343, or 1464 of Title 18, United States Code;

shall be liable to the United States for a forfeiture penalty. A forfeiture penalty under this subsection shall be in addition to any other penalty provided for by this Act; except that this subsection shall not apply to any conduct which is subject to forfeiture under . . . section 507 of this Act.

(2) The amount of any forfeiture penalty determined under this subsection shall not exceed $2,000 for each violation. Each day of a continuing violation shall constitute a separate offense, but the total forfeiture penalty which may be imposed under this subsection, for acts or omissions described in paragraph (1) of this subsection and set forth in the notice or the notice of apparent liability issued under this subsection, shall not exceed:

(A) $20,000, if the violator is (i) a common carrier subject to the provisions of this Act, (ii) a broadcast station licensee or permittee, or (iii) a cable television operator; or

(B) $5,000, in any case not covered by subparagraph (A).

The amount of such forfeiture penalty shall be assessed by the Commission, or its designee, by written notice. In determining the amount of such a forfeiture penalty, the Commission or its designee shall take into account the nature, circumstances, extent, and gravity of the prohibited acts committed and, with respect to the violator, the degree of culpability, any history of prior offenses, ability to pay, and such other matters as justice may require.

* * *

TITLE VI—CABLE COMMUNICATIONS

PURPOSES

Sec. 521

The purposes of this title are to

(1) establish a national policy concerning cable communications;

(2) establish franchise procedures and standards which encourage the growth and development of cable systems and which assure that cable systems are responsive to the needs and interests of the local community;

(3) establish guidelines for the exercise of Federal, State, and local authority with respect to the regulation of cable systems;

(4) assure and encourage that cable communications provide and are encouraged to provide the widest possible diversity of information sources and services to the public.

(5) establish an orderly process for franchise renewal which protects cable operators against unfair denials of renewal where the operator's past performance and proposal for future performance meet the standards established by this title; and

(6) promote competition in cable communications and minimize unnecessary regulation that would impose an undue economic burden on cable systems.

* * *

CABLE CHANNELS FOR PUBLIC, EDUCATIONAL OR GOVERNMENTAL USE

Sec. 531

(a) A franchising authority may establish requirements in a franchise with respect to the designation or use of channel capacity for public, educational, or governmental use only to the extent provided in this section.

(b) A franchising authority may in its request for proposals require as part of a franchise, and may require as part of a cable operator's proposal for a franchise renewal, subject to section 626, that channel capacity be designated for public, educational, or governmental use, . . .

(c) A franchising authority may enforce any requirement in any franchise regarding the providing or use of such channel capacity. Such enforcement authority includes the authority to enforce any provisions of the franchise for services, facilities, or equipment proposed by the cable operator, which relate to public, educational, or governmental use of channel capacity, whether or not required by the franchising authority pursuant to subsection (b).

* * *

(e) Subject to section 624(d), a cable operator shall not exercise any editorial control over any public, educational, or governmental use of channel capacity provided pursuant to this section.

* * *

GENERAL FRANCHISE REQUIREMENTS

Sec. 541

(a)(1) A franchising authority may award, in accordance with the provisions of this title, one or more franchises within its jurisdiction.

* * *

(3) In awarding a franchise or franchises, a franchising authority shall assure that access to cable service is not denied to any group of potential residential cable subscribers because of the income of the residents of the local area in which such group resides.

* * *

(c) Any cable system shall not be subject to regulation as a common carrier or utility by reason of providing any cable service.

* * *

FRANCHISE FEES

Sec. 542

(a) Subject to the limitation of subsection (b), any cable operator may be required under the terms of any franchise to pay a franchise fee.

(b) For any 12–month period, the franchise fees paid by a cable operator with respect to any cable system shall not exceed 5 percent of such cable operator's gross revenues derived in such period from the operation of the cable system.

* * *

REGULATION OF RATES

Sec. 543

(a) Any Federal agency or State may not regulate the rates for the provision of cable service except to cable subscribers only to the extent provided under this section. Any franchising authority may regulate the rates for the provision of cable service or any other communications service provided over a cable system to cable subscribers, but only to the extent provided under this section.

(b)(1) Within 180 days after the date of the enactment of this title, the Commission shall prescribe and make effective regulations which authorize a franchising authority to regulate rates for the provision of basic cable service in circumstances in which a cable system is not subject to effective competition. Such regulations may apply to any franchise granted after the effective date of such regulations. Such regulations shall not apply to any rate while such rate is subject to the provisions of subsection (c).

(2) For purposes of rate regulation under this subsection, such regulations shall—

(A) define the circumstances in which a cable system is not subject to effective competition; and

(B) establish standards for such rate regulation.

* * *

(c) In the case of any cable system for which a franchise has been granted on or before the effective date of this title, until the end of the 2–year period beginning on such effective date, the franchising authority may, to the extent provided in a franchise—

(1) regulate the rates for the provision of basic cable service, including multiple tiers of basic cable service;

(2) require the provision of any service tier provided without charge (disregarding any installation or rental charge for equipment necessary for receipt of such tier); or

(3) regulate rates for the initial installation or the rental of one set of the minimum equipment which is necessary for the subscriber's receipt of basic cable service.

* * *

RENEWAL

Sec. 546

(a) During the 6–month period which begins with the 36th month before the franchise expiration, the franchising authority may on its own initiative, and shall at the request of the cable operator, commence proceedings which afford the public in the franchise area appropriate notice and participation for the purpose of—

(1) identifying the future cable-related community needs and interests; and

(2) reviewing the performance of the cable operator under the franchise during the then current franchise term.

(b)(1) Upon completion of a proceeding under subsection (a), a cable operator seeking renewal of a franchise may, on its own initiative or at the request of a franchising authority, submit a proposal for renewal.

(2) Subject to section 624, any such proposal shall contain such material as the franchising authority may require, including proposals for an upgrade of the cable system.

(3) The franchising authority may establish a date by which such proposals shall be submitted.

(c)(1) Upon submittal by a cable operator of a proposal to the franchising authority for the renewal of a franchise, the franchising authority shall provide prompt public notice of such proposal and, during the 4–month period which begins on the completion of any proceedings under subsection (a), renew the franchise or, issue a preliminary assessment that the franchise should not be renewed and, at the request of the operator or on its own initiative, commence an administrative proceeding after providing prompt public notice of such proceeding in accordance with paragraph (2) to consider whether—

(A) the cable operator has substantially complied with the material terms of the existing franchise and with applicable law;

(B) the quality of the operator's service including signal quality, response to consumer complaints, and billing practices, but without regard to the mix, quality, or level of cable services or other services provided over the system, has been reasonable in light of community needs;

(C) the operator has the financial, legal, and technical ability to provide the services, facilities, and equipment as set forth in the operator's proposal; and

(D) the operator's proposal is reasonable to meet the future cable-related community needs and interests, taking into account the cost of meeting such needs and interests.

* * *

(3) At the completion of a proceeding under this subsection, the franchising authority shall issue a written decision granting or denying the proposal for renewal based upon the record of such proceeding, and transmit a copy of such decision to the cable operator. Such decision shall state the reasons therefor.

(d) Any denial of a proposal for renewal shall be based on one or more adverse findings made with respect to the factors described in subparagraphs (A) through (D) of subsection (c) (1). . . .

* * *

OBSCENE PROGRAMMING

Sec. 559

Whoever transmits over any cable system any matter which is obscene or otherwise unprotected by the Constitution of the United States shall be fined not more than $10,000 or imprisoned not more than two years, or both.

UNAUTHORIZED PUBLICATION OR USE OF COMMUNICATIONS

Sec. 705

(a) Except as authorized by Chapter 119, Title 18, no person receiving, assisting in receiving, transmitting, or assisting in transmitting, any interstate or foreign communication by wire or radio shall divulge or publish the existence, contents, substance, purport, effect, or meaning thereof, except through authorized channels of transmission or reception, (1) to any person other than the addressee, his agent, or attorney, (2) to a person employed or authorized to forward such communication to its destination, (3) to proper accounting or distributing officers of the various communicating centers over which the communication may be passed, (4) to the master of a ship under whom he is serving, (5) in response to a subpoena issued by a court of competent jurisdiction, or (6) on demand of other lawful authority. No person not being authorized by the sender shall intercept any radio communication and divulge or publish the existence, contents, substance, purport, effect, or meaning of such intercepted communication to any person. No person not being entitled thereto shall receive or assist in receiving any interstate or foreign communication by radio and use such communication (or any information therein contained) for his own benefit or for the benefit of another not entitled thereto. No person having received any intercepted radio communication or having become acquainted with the contents, substance, purport, effect, or meaning of such communication (or any part thereof) knowing that such communication was intercepted, shall divulge or publish the existence, contents, substance, purport, effect, or meaning of such communication (or any part thereof) or use such communication (or any information therein contained) for his own benefit or for the benefit of another not entitled thereto. This section shall not apply to the receiving, divulging, publishing, or utilizing the contents of any radio communication which is transmitted by any station for the use of the general public, which relates to ships, aircraft, vehicles or persons in distress, or which is transmitted by an amateur radio station operator or by a citizens band radio operator.

(b) The provisions of subsection (a) shall not apply to the interception or receipt by any individual, or the assisting (including the manufacture or sale) of such interception or receipt, of any satellite cable programming for private viewing if—

(1) the programming involved is not encrypted; and

(2)(A) a marketing system is not established under which—

(i) an agent or agents have been lawfully designated for the purpose of authorizing private viewing by individuals, and

(ii) such authorization is available to the individual involved from the appropriate agent or agents; or

(B) a marketing system described in subparagraph (A) is established and the individuals receiving such programming have obtained authorization for private viewing under that system.

(c) For purposes of this section—

(1) the term "satellite cable programming" means video programming which is transmitted via satellite and which is primarily intended for the direct receipt by cable operators for their retransmission to cable subscribers;

(2) the term "agent," with respect to any person, includes an employee of such person;

(3) the term "encrypt," when used with respect to satellite cable programming, means to transmit such programming in a form whereby the aural and visual characteristics (or both) are modified or altered for the purpose of preventing the unauthorized receipt of such programming by persons without

authorized equipment which is designed to eliminate the effects of such modification or alteration;

(4) the term "private viewing" means the viewing for private use in an individual's dwelling unit by means of equipment, owned or operated by such individual, capable of receiving satellite cable programming directly from a satellite; and

(5) the term "private financial gain" shall not include the gain resulting to any individual for the private use in such individual's dwelling unit of any programming for which the individual has not obtained authorization for that use.

(d)(1) Any person who willfully violates subsection (a) shall be fined not more than $1,000 or imprisoned for not more than 6 months or both.

(2) Any person who violates subsection (a) willfully and for purposes of direct or indirect commercial advantage or private financial gain shall be fined not more than $25,000 or imprisoned for not more than 1 year, or both, for the first such conviction and shall be fined not more than $50,000 or imprisoned for not more than 2 years, or both, for any subsequent conviction.

(3)(A) Any person aggrieved by any violation of subsection (a) may bring a civil action in a United States district court or in any other court of competent jurisdiction.

(B) The court may—

(i) grant temporary and final injunctions on such terms as it may deem reasonable to prevent or restrain violations of subsection (a);

(ii) award damages as described in subparagraph (C); and

(iii) direct the recovery of full costs, including awarding reasonable attorneys' fees to an aggrieved party who prevails.

(C)(i) Damages awarded by any court under this section shall be computed, at the election of the aggrieved party, in accordance with either of the following subclauses;

(I) the party aggrieved may recover the actual damages suffered by him as a result of the violation and any profits of the violator that are attributable to the violation which are not taken into account in computing the actual damages; in determining the violator's profits, the party aggrieved shall be required to prove only the violator's gross revenue, and the violator shall be required to prove his deductible expenses and the elements of profit attributable to factors other than the violation; or

(II) the party aggrieved may recover an award of statutory damages for each violation involved in the action in a sum of not less than $250 or more than $10,000, as the court considers just.

(ii) In any case in which the court finds that the violation was committed willfully and for purposes of direct or indirect commercial advantage or private financial gain, the court in its discretion may increase the award of damages, whether actual or statutory, by an amount of not more than $50,000.

(iii) In any case where the court finds that the violator was not aware and had no reason to believe that his acts constituted a violation of this section, the court in its discretion may reduce the award of damages to a sum of not less than $100.

(4) The importation, manufacture, sale, or distribution of equipment by any person with the intent of its use to assist in any activity prohibited by subsection (a) shall be subject to penalties and remedies under this subsection to the same extent and in the same manner as a person who has engaged in such prohibited activity.

(5) The penalties under this subsection shall be in addition to those prescribed under any other provision of this title.

*

TABLE OF CASES

Principal cases are in italic type. Non-principal cases are in roman type. References are to Pages.

Aafco Heating & Air Conditioning Co. v. Northwest Publications, Inc., 206

A Book Named 'John Cleland's Memoirs of a Woman of Pleasure' v. Attorney General of Com. of Mass., (Fanny Hill Case), 335, 338, 339, 347, 348, 349

Abrams v. United States, 5, 16, 17, 18, 32

Accuracy in Media, Inc. v. F. C. C., 400

ACT v. FCC, 387

Action for Children's Television v. F.C.C., 852 F.2d 1332, p. 385

Action for Children's Television v. F.C.C., 821 F.2d 741, p. 471

Adams v. Frontier Broadcasting Co., 136

Administrator, F.A.A. v. Robertson, 606

Adreani v. Hansen, 132

Adrian Weiss, In re, 390

Adult Film Ass'n of America v. Times Mirror Co., 469

Akins v. Altus Newspapers, Inc., 176

Alberts, People v., 333, 334

Alberts v. State of California, 334

Alexander v. Haley, 512

Ali v. Playgirl, Inc., 301

Alioto v. Cowles Communications, Inc., 142

Al Star v. Preller, 358

Altemose Const. Co. v. Building and Const. Trades Council of Philadelphia and Vicinity, 558

Alumbaugh v. State, 65

Amendment of Parts 2, 73 and 76 of the Commission's Rules to Authorize the Transmission of Teletext by TV Stations, Matter of, 97

Amendment to Parts 73 and 76 of the Commission's Rules Relating to Program Exclusivity in the Cable and Broadcast Industries, 425

American Ben. Life Ins. Co. v. McIntyre, 170

American Booksellers Ass'n, Inc. v. Hudnut, 771 F.2d 323, p. 367

American Booksellers Ass'n, Inc. v. Hudnut, 598 F.Supp. 1316, p. 365

American Broadcasting–Paramount Theatres, Inc. v. Simpson, 103

American Civil Liberties Union v. F.C.C., 428

American Code Co. v. Bensinger, 502

American Home Products Corp. v. Johnson and Johnson, 452

Americans for Democratic Action v. Meade, 104

Ammerman v. Hubbard Broadcasting, Inc., 569

Amos v. Gunn, 628

Anderson v. WROC–TV, 268

Ann–Margret v. High Soc. Magazine, Inc., 302, 303

Anton v. St. Louis Suburban Newspapers, Inc., 127

Appeal of (see name of party)

Application of (see name of party)

Arcand v. Evening Call Pub. Co., 109

Arctic Co., Ltd. v. Loudoun Times Mirror, 153

Ariel Sharon v. Time, Inc., 173

Arizona Pub. Co. v. O'Neil, 73

Armao, Commonwealth v., 68

Arnstein v. Porter, 507

Article of Device Labeled in Part 110 V Vapozone, United States v., 455

Articles of "Obscene" Merchandise, United States v., 346

Arvey Corp. v. Peterson, 106

A. S. Abell Co. v. Barnes, 172

A. S. Abell Co. v. Kirby, 230

Ashton v. Kentucky, 66

Aspen Institute and CBS, Petition of, 389

Associated Press v. International News Service, 308

Associated Press v. N.L.R.B., 73

Associated Press v. United States, 5, 15, 59, 706, 707, 708

Associated Press, United States v., 708, 713

Associated Press v. Walker, 156

Associates & Aldrich Co. v. Times Mirror Co., 469

AT&T, United States v., 746

Austin v. Michigan Chamber of Commerce, 473, 487

811

Baird v. Dun and Bradstreet, 114
Baker v. F. & F. Inv., 556
Baker v. Libbie, 310, 495
Ballantyne v. United States, 546
Baltimore, City of v. A. S. Abell Co., 72
Bank of Oregon v. Independent News, Inc., 170
Bannach v. Field Enterprises, Inc., 212
Bantam Books, Inc. v. Sullivan, 42
Banzhaf v. F. C. C., 393
Barber v. St. Louis Post Dispatch Co., 213
Barber v. Time, Inc., 256
Barbieri v. News–Journal Co., 253
Barnett v. Schumacher, 112
Barr v. Matteo, 215
Bates v. State Bar of Arizona, 479
Bauer v. Kincaid, 631
Bay Guardian Co. v. Chronicle Pub. Co., 344 F.Supp. 1155, p. 717
Bay Guardian Co. v. Chronicle Pub. Co., 340 F.Supp. 76, p. 717
Bazemore v. Savannah Hospital, 310
Beach v. Shanley, 568
Beacon Pub. Co., State v., 458
Beauharnais v. People of State of Ill., 65, 331
Beckley Newspapers Corp. v. Hanks, 151
Bela George Lugosi v. Universal Pictures, 304
Belushi v. Woodward, 505
Bennett v. Transamerican Press, 117
Bennett, United States v., 331
Benny v. Loew's Incorporated, 522
Bernstein v. National Broadcasting Co., 295
Bethel School Dist. No. 403 v. Fraser, 51
Bianco v. Palm Beach Newspapers, Inc., 113
Biermann v. Pulitzer Pub. Co., 210
Bigelow v. Commonwealth, 477
Bigelow v. Virginia, 473, 476, 477, 478, 482
Bilney v. Evening Star Newspaper Co., 265
Bindrim v. Mitchell, 296, 297, 298
Binns v. Vitagraph Co. of America, 294
Blende v. Hearst Publications, 122
Bloom v. Illinois, 547
Blue Ridge Bank v. Veribanc, Inc., 165
Board of Trustees of State University of New York v. Fox, 473, 486
Boddie v. American Broadcasting Companies, Inc., 731 F.2d 333, p. 264
Boddie v. American Broadcasting Companies, Inc., 694 F.Supp. 1304, pp. 263, 264
Boomer v. Atlantic Cement Co., 369
Booth v. Curtis Pub. Co., 228 N.Y.S.2d 468, p. 300

Booth v. Curtis Pub. Co., 223 N.Y.S.2d 737, p. 299
Bordoni v. New York Times Co., Inc., 122
Bose Corp. v. Consumers Union of United States, Inc., 151, 178
Braden v. United States, 7
Brady v. Ottaway Newspapers, Inc., 109
Braig v. Field Communications, 234
Branch v. F.C.C., 390
Brandenburg v. Ohio, 36, 37
Branzburg v. Hayes, 7, 405, 552, 553, 555, 556, 557, 558, 559, 561, 562, 566, 572, 576, 583, 586, 599, 633
Branzburg v. Pound, 553, 567
Braun v. Flynt, 292
Braun v. Soldier of Fortune Magazine, Inc., 327
Breard v. City of Alexandria, La., 344
Bremmer v. Journal–Tribune Pub. Co., 254
Bridges v. State of Cal., 7, 18, 78
Brink v. Griffith, 254
Briscoe v. Reader's Digest Ass'n, 93 Cal.Rptr. 866, pp. 279, 280, 281, 282, 303
Broadcast Music, Inc. v. Columbia Broadcasting System, Inc., 540
Broadcast Renewal Process, 378
Brooklyn Daily Eagle v. Voorhies, 459
Brown v. Du Frey, 117
Brown v. Globe Printing Co., 216
Brown v. Newman, 122
Brown & Williamson Tobacco Corp. v. Jacobson, 827 F.2d 1119, pp. 123, 124, 134, 142, 177, 194
Brown & Williamson Tobacco Corp. v. Jacobson, 713 F.2d 262, p. 103
Brunn v. Weiss, 212
Bruno & Stillman, Inc. v. Globe Newspaper Co., 573
Buchanan v. Associated Press, 166
Buchanan, State v., 544, 545, 552
Buchwald v. Paramount Pictures Corp., 512
Buckley v. Littell, 232, 234
Buckley v. Vidal, 158
Buckstaff v. Hicks, 217
Bufalino v. Associated Press, 215
Buffalo Broadcasting Co., Inc. v. American Soc. of Composers, Authors and Publishers, 744 F.2d 917, p. 540
Buffalo Broadcasting Co., Inc. v. American Soc. of Composers, Authors and Publishers, 546 F.Supp. 274, p. 540
Burleson, United States ex rel. Milwaukee Social Democratic Pub. Co. v., 31
Burnett v. National Enquirer, 7 Med.Rptr. 1321, pp. 129, 170
Burnett v. National Enquirer, Inc., 193 Cal.Rptr. 206, p. 143
Burrows v. Pulitzer Pub. Co., 217

Burt v. Advertiser Newspaper Co., 142
Burton v. Crowell Pub. Co., 118
Business Executives' Move for Vietnam Peace v. F. C. C., 470
Butler v. State of Michigan, 342
Byers v. Martin, 109
Byrne v. Karalexis, 346

Cabin v. Community Newspapers, Inc., 152
Cable News Network, Inc. v. Noriega, 674
Cablevision Systems Development Co. v. Motion Picture Ass'n of America, Inc., 410
Cahill v. Hawaiian Paradise Park Corp., 116
Caldero v. Tribune Pub. Co., 562, 572
Caldwell, Application of, 552
Caldwell, United States v., 554
Caldwell v. United States, 552, 574
Caller Times Pub. Co. v. Chandler, 216
Calloway v. Central Charge Service, 117
Cammarano v. United States, 474
Campbell v. New York Evening Post, 213
Campbell v. Seabury Press, 288, 289, 308
Campbell Soup Co., 449
Canino v. New York News, Inc., 104
Cantrell v. Forest City Pub. Co., 171, 295, 296, 316
Cantwell v. Connecticut, 227
Cape Publications, Inc. v. Adams, 142
Cape Publications, Inc. v. Bridges, 257, 258
Capital Cities Cable, Inc. v. Crisp, 427
Capital Dist. Regional Off-Track Betting Corp. v. Northeastern Harness Horsemen's Ass'n, 209
Cardillo v. Doubleday & Co., Inc., 104
Carlisle v. Fawcett Publications, Inc., 310
Carson v. Allied News Co., 170
Carter Mountain Transmission Corp. v. F. C. C., 404, 406
Carter Products, Inc. v. Federal Trade Com'n, 440
Cassidy v. American Broadcasting Companies, Inc., 261
CBS, Inc. v. F. C. C., 391
Central Arizona Light & Power Co. v. Akers, 133
Central Hudson Gas & Elec. Corp. v. Public Service Com'n of New York, 481, 482, 484, 486, 487
Central Telecommunications, Inc. v. TCI Cablevision, Inc., 429
Century Communications Corp. v. F.C.C., 425
Century Federal, Inc. v. City of Palo Alto, Cal., 429

Cepeda v. Cohane, 577
Cepeda v. Swift & Co., 306
Cerrito v. Time, Inc., 449 F.2d 306, p. 187
Cerrito v. Time, Inc., 302 F.Supp. 1071, p. 158
Cervantes v. Time, Inc., 158
Cerveny v. Chicago Daily News Co., 115
Chandler v. Florida, 644, 645, 648, 649, 650
Chandler v. State, 648, 649
Chang v. Michiana Telecasting Corp., 206
Changes in the Entertainment Formats of Broadcast Stations, 382
Chapadeau v. Utica Observer-Dispatch, Inc., 158, 201, 205
Cher v. Forum Intern., Ltd., 320, 321
Cherry v. Des Moines Leader, 231
Chicago, City of v. Lambert, 66
Chicago, City of v. Tribune Co., 208
Chicago Record-Herald Co v. Tribune Ass'n, 495
Childs v. Sharon Herald Co., Div. of Ottaway Newspapers, Inc., 166
Chisholm v. F. C. C., 389
Chrysler Corp. v. Brown, 613
Church of Scientology of California v. Siegelman, 166
C.I.A. v. Sims, 605, 620, 621
Cianci v. New Times Pub. Co., 191, 225, 228, 232, 236
Citizen Pub. Co. v. United States, 715
Citizen Pub. Co., United States v., 713, 714
Citizens Committee to Preserve the Voice of Arts in Atlanta v. F. C. C., 382
Citizens Committee to Save WEFM v. F. C. C., 382
Citizens Communication Center v. F. C. C., 377
City of (see name of city)
Clark v. Allen, 152
Clifford v. Hollander, 115
Cochran v. Indianapolis Newspapers, Inc., 176
Cohalan v. New York Tribune, 230
Cohen v. Cowles Media Co., 111 S.Ct. 2513, pp. 579, 581
Cohen v. Cowles Media Co. (Minn.Dist. Ct.1987), 578, 579
Cohen v. New York Herald Tribune, Inc., 119
Cohn v. Am-Law, Inc., 122
Cole v. Westinghouse Broadcasting Co., Inc., 233
Coleman v. Newark Morning Ledger Co., 218
Columbia Broadcasting System, 388

Columbia Broadcasting System, Inc. v. American Soc. of Composers, Authors and Publishers, 540

Columbia Broadcasting System, Inc. v. Democratic Nat. Committee, 469, 470

Comer v. Age–Herald Pub. Co., 242

Commonwealth v. ____ (see opposing party)

Community Antenna Television Syndicated Program Exclusivity Rules, Matter of, 426

Community Cable TV, 427

Complaint of Syracuse Peace Council Against WVTH, Memorandum Opinion and Order, In re, 396

Compton, State v., 662

Compulsory Copyright License for Cable Retransmission, 425

Conklin v. Sloss, 281, 282

Connecticut State Bd. of Labor Relations v. Fagin, 558

Consolidated Edison Co. of New York, Inc. v. Public Service Com'n of New York, 482

Consumer Product Safety Com'n v. GTE Sylvania, Inc., 613

Consumers Union of United States, Inc., Application of, 559

Contemporary Arts Center v. Ney, 353

Contempt of Wright, Matter of, 562

Coolidge, United States v., 29

Cooper v. Rockford Newspapers, Inc., 78

Corabi v. Curtis Pub. Co., 273 A.2d 899, p. 113

Corabi v. Curtis Pub. Co., 262 A.2d 665, p. 113

Corona, City of v. Corona Daily Independent, 72

Corsetti v. Massachusetts, 561

Cosgrove Studio & Camera Shop, Inc. v. Pane, 107, 132

Costello v. Capital Cities Media, Inc., 236

Cowley v. Pulsifer, 209, 221

Cowper v. Vannier, 120

Cox Broadcasting Corp. v. Cohn, 222, 272, 272, 273, 274, 285

Craft v. Kobler, 533

Craig v. Harney, 78, 678

Crane v. Arizona Republic, 221

Crane v. New York World Telegram Corporation, 224

Cresson v. Louisville Courier–Journal, 218

Criden, United States v., 565

Croswell, People v., 62, 103

Curry v. Walter, 209

Curtis v. Southwestern Newspapers, 173

Curtis Pub. Co. v. Butts, 130, 142, 156, 174, 175, 201, 205, 234, 473

Cuthbertson, United States v., 566

Daily Times Democrat v. Graham, 311

D'Alfonso v. A.S. Abell Co., 573

Daniell v. Voice of New Hampshire, Inc., 138

Danskin v. San Diego Unified School Dist., 464

Danziger v. Hearst Corporation, 219

Dellar v. Samuel Goldwyn, Inc., 526

Deltec, Inc. v. Dun & Bradstreet, Inc., 577

Democratic Nat. Committee v. McCord, 557

Dennett, United States v., 332

Dennis v. United States, 33, 34, 35, 36, 336

Dennis, United States v., 34

Denny v. Mertz, 206

DePalma, United States v., 559

Deregulation of Radio, In re, 134

DeSalvo v. Twentieth Century–Fox Film Corp., 322

De Witte v. Kearney & Trecker Corporation, 109

Diaz v. Oakland Tribune, Inc., 270, 271

Dickey v. CBS Inc., 190

Dickinson v. United States, 666

Dickinson, United States v., 476 F.2d 373, p. 665

Dickinson, United States v., 465 F.2d 496, pp. 665, 666

Dickinson, United States v., 349 F.Supp. 227, p. 665

Dictaphone Corp. v. Sloves, 107

Dietemann v. Time, Inc., 258, 259, 268

DiSalle v. P.G. Pub. Co., 191

Dodd v. Pearson, 279 F.Supp. 101, p. 265

Dodd v. Pearson, 277 F.Supp. 469, p. 151

Dodrill v. Arkansas Democrat Co., 197

Doe v. Bolton, 477

Doe v. Sarasota–Bradenton Florida Television Co., Inc., 285

Domestic Communication Satellite Facilities, 411

Douglas v. City of Jeannette, 55

Douglas v. Collins, 215

Dowd v. Calabrese, 227

Dow Jones & Co., Inc. v. Superior Court, 571

Downing v. Monitor Pub. Co. Inc., 572

Duff v. Kansas City Star Co., 711

Dun & Bradstreet, Inc. v. Greenmoss Builders, Inc., 123, 198

Dun & Bradstreet, Inc. v. Robinson, 225

Duncan v. WJLA–TV, Inc., 293

Dunlap v. Philadelphia Newspapers, Inc., 226

Dunne v. United States, 33

Dupont Engineering Co. v. Nashville Banner Pub. Co., 122

Dupree, People v., 567

Dworkin v. Hustler Magazine, Inc., 57
Dyson v. Stein, 345

Eadie v. Pole, 152
Eberle v. Municipal Court, Los Angeles
    Judicial Dist., 68
Eden v. Legare, 116
Editorializing by Broadcast Licensees,
    392
Edwards v. National Audubon Soc.,
    Inc., 189, 191, 234
E. Hulton & Co. v. Jones, 107
Eimann v. Soldier of Fortune Magazine,
    Inc., 326
Eisenschiml v. Fawcett Publications,
    Inc., 495, 502, 522
El Amin v. Miami Herald Pub. Co., 191
Electric Furnace Corp. v. Deering Milli-
    ken Research Corp., 122, 140
Elektra Records Co. v. Gem Electronic
    Distributors, Inc., 535
Ellis v. Brockton Pub. Co., 141
Elmhurst v. Pearson, 309
Elsmere Music, Inc. v. National Broad-
    casting Co., 623 F.2d 252, p. 537
Elsmere Music, Inc. v. National Broad-
    casting Co., Inc., 482 F.Supp. 741, pp.
    537, 538
Elyria–Lorain Broadcasting Co. v. Lo-
    rain Journal Co., 710
Embers Supper Club, Inc. v. Scripps–
    Howard Broadcasting Co., 211
Emerson v. Davies, 502
England v. Daily Gazette Co., 230
E.P.A. v. Mink, 602
Erie Telecommunications, Inc. v. City of
    Erie, 429
Estes v. State of Tex., 645, 646, 647, 656,
    659, 684
Exner v. American Medical Association,
    165
Ex parte (see name of party)

Factors Etc., Inc. v. Pro Arts, Inc., 304
Fairfield v. American Photocopy Equip-
    ment Co., 290
Fairness Alternatives, 396
Fairness Report, 394
Falwell v. Flynt, 129
Farber, Matter of, 562, 563
Farmers Educational & Coop. Union of
    America, North Dakota Div. v.
    WDAY, Inc., 139, 208, 388
Farr, In re, 569
Farr v. Superior Court of Los Angeles
    County, 546, 569
Farrington v. Star Co., 133
F.C.C. v. League of Women Voters of
    California, 95, 401
F. C. C. v. Midwest Video Corp., 94
F. C. C. v. National Citizens Committee
    for Broadcasting, 698, 726

F. C. C. v. Pacifica Foundation, 384, 385,
    387
F. C. C. v. WNCN Listeners Guild, 382
Federal Open Market Committee of
    Federal Reserve System v. Merrill,
    609
Federal P. Com'n v. Transcontinental
    Gas P.L. Corp., 404
Federal Trade Commission v. Bunte
    Bros., 443
F. T. C. v. Colgate–Palmolive Co., 447,
    448
Federal Trade Commission v. Gratz, 436
Federal Trade Commission v. Raladam
    Co., 437, 438
Federal Trade Commission v. Standard
    Education Soc., 438
Federal Trade Commission v. Winsted
    Hosiery Co., 437
Federated Publications, Inc. v. Kurtz,
    662, 663
Federated Publications, Inc. v.
    Swedberg, 661, 662, 663
Feist Publications, Inc. v. Rural Tele-
    phone Service Co., Inc., 502
Fifth Ave. Coach Co. v. City of New
    York, 474
Finnegan v. Eagle Printing Co., 213
Firestone v. Time, Inc., 140
Firestone Tire & Rubber Co., 453
First Nat. Bank of Boston v. Attorney
    General, 480
First Nat. Bank of Boston v. Bellotti,
    480, 481, 482, 487
Fisher v. Dees, 538
Fisher v. Washington Post Co., 230
Fitzgerald v. Penthouse Intern., Ltd.,
    188
Flake v. Greensboro News Co., 290
Florida v. Taylor, 559
Florida Pub. Co. v. Fletcher, 266, 268
Florida Star v. B.J.F., 275
Flues v. New Nonpareil Co., 213
Fogus v. Capital Cities Media, Inc., 191
Forrest v. Lynch, 132
Forsham v. Harris, 604
Forsher v. Bugliosi, 281, 282
Fortnightly Corp. v. United Artists Tel-
    evision, Inc., 407
Foster v. Laredo Newspapers, Inc., 111,
    153, 171
Foster, United States v., 34
Foster v. Upchurch, 173
Foster–Milburn Co. v. Chinn, 133
Fotochrome, Inc. v. New York Herald
    Tribune, Inc., 158
Fowler v. Curtis Pub. Co., 290
Fram v. Yellow Cab Co. of Pittsburgh,
    119
Francis v. Lake Charles American
    Press, 113
Frechette v. Special Magazines, 113

Freedman v. State of Md., 357, 358
Friday v. Official Detective Stories, Inc., 224
Friede, Commonwealth v., 331, 332
Friedenberg v. Times Pub. Co., 463
Friends of Animals, Inc. v. Associated Fur Mfrs., Inc., 104

Galella v. Onassis, 487 F.2d 986, p. 257
Galella v. Onassis, 533 F.Supp. 1076, p. 257
Gannett Co., Inc. v. DePasquale, 99 S.Ct. 2898, pp. 635, 675, 678, 679, 680, 681, 682, 683, 685, 686, 687
Gannett Co., Inc. v. DePasquale, 372 N.E.2d 544, pp. 675, 677, 678, 690
Gannett Co., Inc. v. Monroe County, 630
Gardner v. International Shoe Co., 369
Gardner, State v., 64
Garland v. Torre, 552, 561
Garner v. Triangle Publications, 294, 295, 310
Garrison v. State of La., 67, 68, 172, 173, 175, 222
General Dynamics Corp., 453
General Products Co., Inc. v. Meredith Corp., 202, 203
General Telephone Company of California, Application of, 751
Gertz v. Robert Welch, Inc., 94 S.Ct. 2997, pp. 104, 110, 112, 116, 125, 126, 128, 158, 159, 160, 161, 162, 163, 164, 167, 169, 170, 171, 195, 197, 198, 199, 200, 201, 205, 206, 223, 229, 232, 233, 235, 236, 238, 254, 316
Gertz v. Robert Welch, Inc., 680 F.2d 527, pp. 142, 160
Gertz v. Robert Welch, Inc., 471 F.2d 801, p. 160
Gertz v. Robert Welch, Inc., 306 F.Supp. 310, p. 116
Giboney v. Empire Storage & Ice Co., 365
Gilbert v. Minnesota, 32
Giles v. State, 117
Gill v. Curtis Pub. Co., 292
Gill v. Hearst Pub. Co., 291
Ginsberg v. State of N. Y., 342, 343, 344
Ginzburg v. United States, 154, 336, 338, 340, 341, 343, 344, 349
Giragi v. Moore, 72
Gitlow v. People of State of New York, 11, 12, 32, 34
Globe Newspaper Co. v. Superior Court for Norfolk County, 688, 689
Glover v. Herald Co., 174
Gobin v. Globe Pub. Co., 204
Golden Palace, Inc. v. National Broadcasting Co., Inc., 122
Goldfeld v. Post Pub. Co., 560
Golding v. R. K. O. Pictures, 506
Goldman v. New York Post Corp., 205

Goldwater v. Ginzburg, 120, 142, 230
Gonzales v. Times Herald Printing Company, 104
Goodfader, Appeal of, 552
Goodfriend and Levinson v. Kansas City Star Co., 711
Good Government Group of Seal Beach, Inc. v. Superior Court of Los Angeles County, 128, 232
Goodrich v. Waterbury Republican-American, Inc., 236
Gordan, People v., 65
Goss, People v., 545
Goss v. State of Ill., 545
Grafton, Village of v. American Broadcasting Co., 209
Grant v. Reader's Digest Ass'n, Inc., 115
Grass v. News Group Publications, Inc., 234
Great Lakes Broadcasting, 380
Green v. WCAU–TV, 241
Greenbelt Co-op. Pub. Ass'n v. Bresler, 90 S.Ct. 1537, pp. 127, 232, 240
Greenbelt Co-op. Pub. Ass'n v. Bresler, 252 A.2d 755, p. 121
Gregory v. Federal Deposit Ins. Corp., 608
Gregory v. McDonnell Douglas Corp., 228
Grein v. La Poma, 103
Griswold v. State of Conn., 250
Grosjean v. American Press Co., 70, 71, 72, 73, 75
Grothe, Ex parte, 567
Grove v. Dun & Bradstreet, Inc., 107
GTE Sylvania, Inc. v. Consumers Union of United States, 613
Guccione v. Hustler Magazine, Inc, 144
Guinn v. Texas Newspapers, Inc., 171

Haelan Laboratories, Inc. v. Topps Chewing Gum, Inc., 305, 306
Hahn v. Andrello, 121
Haig v. Agee, 49, 596
Hamberger v. Eastman, 249
Hamling v. United States, 350
Handling of Public Issues under the Fairness Doctrine, Matter of, 394
Hanson v. Krehbiel, 242
Harper & Row Publishers, Inc. v. Nation Enterprises, 557 F.Supp. 1067, p. 528
Harper & Row Publishers, Inc. v. Nation Enterprises, 105 S.Ct. 2218, pp. 520, 529, 530, 531
Hart v. Playboy Enterprises, Inc., 5 Med.Rptr. 1811, p. 153
Hart v. Playboy Enterprises, Inc., 4 Med.Rptr. 1616, p. 559
Harte–Hanks Communications, Inc. v. Connaughton, 176, 177, 178, 238

Hartley v. Newark Morning Ledger Co., 115

Hatchard v. Westinghouse Broadcasting Co., 573

Hawkes v. I.R.S., 605

Hayden v. National Sec. Agency/Central Sec. Service, 604

Hayes v. Booth Newspapers, Inc., 187

Hazelwood School Dist. v. Kuhlmeier, 49, 50, 52

Hazlitt v. Fawcett Publications, Inc, 294

Healy v. James, 37

Heim v. Universal Pictures Co., 504

Hein v. Lacy, 224

Hemingway's Estate v. Random House, Inc., 301

Henry Geller, Petition of, 389

Herald Telephone v. Fatouros, 466

Herbert v. Lando, 184, 193

Herbert v. Shanley Co., 504

Herceg v. Hustler Magazine, Inc., 328

Hess v. Indiana, 37

Hicklin, Regina v., 331, 332, 333, 336

Hicks v. Casablanca Records, 305

Higbee v. Times–Advocate, Inc., 267

Hill v. Hayes, 313

Hinkle, State ex rel. LaFollette v., 302

Hirsch v. Twentieth Century–Fox Film Corporation, 492

Hoehling v. Universal City Studios, Inc., 509

Hogan v. Herald Co., 191

Holder, People v., 665

Holder Const. Co. v. Ed Smith & Sons, Inc., 122

Holmes v. Curtis Pub. Co., 114, 158, 311

Holmes v. Hurst, 497, 502, 503

Holway v. World Pub. Co., 215

Home Box Office, Inc. v. F.C.C., 94

Home Placement Service, Inc. v. Providence Journal Co., 466

Hoover v. Intercity Radio Co., 86

Horner–Rausch Optical Co. v. Ashley, 479

Horvath v. Ashtabula Telegraph, 204

Horvath v. Telegraph, 191

Houchins v. KQED, Inc., 598, 599

Houston Post Co. v. United States, 138

Howard v. Des Moines Register and Tribune Co., 271, 272

Hryhorijiv v. Winchell, 115

Hubbard v. Journal Pub. Co., 269, 309

Hubbard, United States v., 559

Hudson, United States v., 29

Hunt v. Liberty Lobby, 158, 176

Hurley v. Northwest Publications, Inc., 212

Hustler Magazine v. Falwell, 129, 170, 240

Hutchinson v. Proxmire, 153, 168, 169, 170, 187

Illinois Citizens Committee for Broadcasting v. F. C. C., 384

Ingenere v. American Broadcasting Co., Inc., 219

Inquiring into the Impact of CATV . . . upon the Orderly Development of Television Broadcasting, Matter of, 405

Inquiry into the Development of Regulatory Policy in Regard to Direct Broadcasting Satellites . . ., Matter of, 415

In re (see name of party)

Intermountain Broadcasting & Television Corp. v. Idaho Microwave, Inc., 404

International News Service v. Associated Press, 513, 514, 515

International Shoe Co. v. Federal Trade Commission, 715

Interstate Circuit, Inc. v. City of Dallas, 329, 358

Ipswich Mills v. Dillon, 495

Irons v. Bell, 609

Irvin v. Dowd, 81 S.Ct. 1639, pp. 637, 640, 641, 642, 656, 659

Irvin v. Dowd, 79 S.Ct. 825, pp. 641, 642

Irvin v. Dowd, 271 F.2d 552, p. 642

Irvin v. Dowd, 153 F.Supp. 531, p. 641

Irvin v. State, 641

ITFS Service, 420

Ithaca College v. Yale Daily News Pub. Co., Inc., 165

Jack Anderson v. Liberty Lobby, Inc., 188

Jacobellis v. State of Ohio, 329, 349

Jacova v. Southern Radio and Television Company, 309

James v. Haymes, 230

Jaubert v. Crowley Post–Signal, Inc., 257

J.E. Belnap, Matter of, 404

Jenkins v. Dell Publishing Company, 308

Jenkins v. Georgia, 351

Jeweler's Circular Pub. Co. v. Keystone Pub. Co., 522

Jones v. City of Opelika, 55

Jones v. Herald Post Co., 309

Jones v. Pulitzer Pub. Co., 211

Jones v. R. L. Polk & Co., 116

Joseph Burstyn, Inc. v. Wilson, 279, 302, 356, 357, 473

Josephs v. News Syndicate Co., 211

Joyce v. George W. Prescott Pub. Co., 225

J–R Distributors, Inc. v. Washington, 350

Kaeser & Blair v. Merchants' Ass'n, 495, 502

Kalwajtys v. Federal Trade Commission, 446

Kaplan v. California, 346

KARK–TV v. Simon, 203

Keeton v. Hustler Magazine, Inc., 68

Keller v. Miami Herald Pub. Co., 228

Kennedy for President Committee v. F. C. C., 389

Kennerley, United States v., 332

Kenney v. Hatfield, 120

Kerby v. Hal Roach Studios, 299

KFKB Broadcasting Ass'n v. Federal Radio Commission, 89

Kilgore v. Koen, 217

Kilgore v. Younger, 221

Kilian v. Doubleday & Co., 224

King v. _____ (see opposing party)

King v. Pillsbury, 120

Kingsley Intern. Pictures Corp. v. N.Y.U., 357, 473

Kirman v. Sun Printing & Pub. Co., 117

Kissinger v. New York City Transit Authority, 465

Kissinger v. Reporters Committee for Freedom of Press, 604

Knight–Ridder Broadcasting, Inc. v. Greenberg, 568

Knops, State v., 575

Kordel, United States v., 455

Korkala, People v., 568

KSDO v. Superior Court of Riverside County, 568, 570

LaFollette, State ex rel. v. Hinkle, 302

Lamont v. Department of Justice, 609

Lamprecht v. Federal Communications Commission, 727

Lancaster v. Daily Banner–News Pub. Co., Inc., 173

Lancour v. Herald and Globe Ass'n, 217

Landmark Communications, Inc. v. Virginia, 675

Las Vegas Sun, Inc. v. Franklin, 132

Laurence University v. State, 121

Lawrence v. Bauer Pub. & Printing Ltd., 173

L B Silver Co v. Federal Trade Commission of America, 436

League of Women Voters Educ. Fund v. F.C.C., 389

Lee v. Board of Regents of State Colleges, 441 F.2d 1257, p. 465

Lee v. Board of Regents of State Colleges, 306 F.Supp. 1097, p. 464

Lee Enterprises, Inc. v. Iowa State Tax Commission, 73

LeGrand, People v., 577

Le Mistral, Inc. v. Columbia Broadcasting System, 256

Leopold v. Levin, 295

Letter to WUGN, 390

Leverton v. Curtis Pub. Co., 291

Levy v. Gelber, 104

Lewis v. Hayes, 120

Liquori v. Republican Co., 114, 210

Litchfield v. Spielberg, 509, 510

Littlefield v. Fort Dodge Messenger, 197, 207

Loadholtz v. Fields, 557

Lorain Journal Co. v. United States, 709

Lorain Journal Co., United States v., 709

Lord Byron v. Johnston, 290

Los Angeles, City of v. Preferred Communications, Inc., 429

Lothschuetz v. Carpenter, 57

Louis Wohl, Inc, In re, 463

Lovell v. City of Griffin, Ga., 54

Lowe v. S.E.C., 56, 57

Lundstrom v. Winnebago Newspapers, Inc., 152

Lyles v. Oklahoma, 597

Mack, In re, 597

Mack, Miller Candle Co. v. Macmillan Co., 215

MacLeod v. Tribune Publishing Co., 116

Madison v. Yunker, 242

Maheu v. CBS, Inc., 532

Maheu v. Hughes Tool Co., 101

Malrite T.V. of New York v. F. C. C., 424

Man v. Warner Bros. Inc., 310

Mannix v. Portland Telegram, 215

Mansfield Journal Co. v. Federal Communications Com'n, 709

Manual Enterprises, Inc. v. Day, 338

Mapp v. Ohio, 250

Marbury v. Madison, 609

Marchetti v. United States, 47

Marchetti, United States v., 47

Maressa v. New Jersey Monthly, 563, 567, 573

Maritote v. Desilu Productions, Inc., 303

Marr v. Putnam, 228

Marshall v. Gordon, 547

Martin v. City of Struthers, 55

Martin v. Johnson Pub. Co., 133

Martin v. Outboard Marine Corp., 140

Martonik v. Durkan, 153

Masson v. New Yorker Magazine, Inc., 111 S.Ct. 2419, pp. 179, 180, 181, 182, 183

Masson v. New Yorker Magazine, Inc., 881 F.2d 1452, p. 179

Massuere v. Dickens, 117

Matter of (see name of party)

Mau v. Rio Grande Oil, 295

MCA, Inc. v. Wilson, 538

McAndrews v. Roy, 318

McAuliffe v. Local Union No 3, International Brotherhood of Electrical Workers, 116

McBee v. Fulton, 213

McBeth v. United Press Intern., Inc., 104

McCall v. Courier–Journal and Louisville Times Co., 191, 259, 260

McCollum v. CBS, Inc., 328

McCurdy v. Hughes, 219, 220

McGaw v. Webster, 116

McGraw v. Watkins, 115

McManus v. Doubleday & Co., Inc., 128, 166

McNabb v. Oregonian Pub. Co., 173

Meadows v. Taft Broadcasting Co., Inc., 205

Medico v. Time, Inc., 220

Meetze v. Associated Press, 269

Melon v. Capital City Press, 215

Melton v. Bow, 117

Melvin v. Reid, 278, 279

Memphis Development Foundation v. Factors Etc., Inc., 304

Memphis Pub. Co. v. Nichols, 202, 223, 226

Mencher v. Chesley, 104

Menendez v. Key West Newspaper Corp., 116

Meredith Corp. v. F.C.C., 395, 396

Metcalf v. Times Pub. Co., 213

Metzger v. Dell Pub. Co., 317

Meyerle v. Pioneer Pub. Co., 242

Miami Herald Pub. Co. v. Brown, 141

Miami Herald Pub. Co. v. Tornillo, 60, 463

Michigan Citizens for an Independent Press v. Thornburgh, 719

Midler v. Ford Motor Co., 493

Midwest Video Corp., United States v., 94

Milan v. Long, 113

Milkovich v. Lorain Journal Co., 237, 241

Miller v. California, 346, 347, 348, 349, 350, 351, 366

Miller v. Universal City Studios, Inc., 650 F.2d 1365, p. 511

Miller v. Universal City Studios, Inc., 460 F.Supp. 984, p. 510

Miller, Smith and Champagne v. Capital City Press, 225

Mills v. Kingsport Times–News, 120

Milwaukee Social Democratic Pub. Co., United States ex rel. v. Burleson, 31

Minersville School Dist. v. Gobitis, 473

Minneapolis Star and Tribune Co. v. Minnesota Com'r of Revenue, 103 S.Ct. 1365, p. 74

Minneapolis Star and Tribune Co. v. Commissioner of Revenue, 102 S.Ct. 2955, p. 74

Minneapolis Star & Tribune Co. v. Minnesota Commissioner of Revenue, 74

Minority Ownership of Broadcast Facilities, 726

Mishkin v. State of New York, 338, 340, 349

Miskovsky v. Oklahoma Pub. Co., 232

Mitchell v. Peoria Journal–Star, Inc., 210, 225

Mize v. McGraw–Hill, Inc., 573

Moffatt v. Cauldwell, 117

Monitor Patriot Co. v. Roy, 153

Montandon v. Triangle Publications, Inc., 115

Montezuma Realty Corp. v. Occidental Petroleum Corp., 559

Morgan v. Dun & Bradstreet, Inc., 179

Morgan v. State, 558

Morison, United States v., 607

Morrill, State v., 546

Morrison v. Ritchie & Co., 140

Mt. Mansfield Television, Inc. v. F. C. C., 731

Muir v. Alabama Educational Television Com'n, 401

Mullenmeister v. Snap–On Tools Corp., 117

Mullins v. Brando, 104

Multimedia Entertainment, 390

Multiple and Religious Ownership of Educational Stations, 401

Munden v. Harris, 251

Murdock v. Commonwealth of Pennsylvania, 55

Murphy v. Florida, 637, 684

Murray v. Bailey, 210

Must Carry Rules, 425

Mutual Film Corp. v. Industrial Commission of Ohio, 279, 356

Myers v. Boston Magazine Co., Inc., 118, 127

Nappier v. Jefferson Standard Life Ins. Co., 272

Natchez Times Pub. Co. v. Dunigan, 116

National Ass'n for Better Broadcasting v. F.C.C., 98, 422

National Ass'n of Broadcasters v. Copyright Royalty Tribunal, 410

National Ass'n of Broadcasters v. F.C.C., 97, 415

National Ass'n of Broadcasters, United States v., 471, 736

National Ass'n of Government Emp., Inc. v. Central Broadcasting Corp., 116

National Broadcasting Co. v. United States, 91, 374, 381, 723, 730

National Cable Television Ass'n v. Copyright Royalty Tribunal, 410

National Citizens Committee for Broadcasting v. F.C.C., 567 F.2d 1095, p. 394

National Citizens Committee for Broadcasting v. F.C.C., 555 F.2d 938, p. 697

National Public Radio v. Bell, 608
Near v. State of Minn. ex rel. Olson, 13, 37, 39, 41, 49, 274, 357
Nebb v. Bell Syndicate, 298
Nebraska Press Ass'n v. Stuart, 96 S.Ct. 2791, pp. 37, 275, 663, 666, 667, 668, 669, 672, 673, 684
Nebraska Press Association v. Stuart, 96 S.Ct. 557, p. 668
Neiman–Marcus Co. v. Lait, 107 F.Supp. 96, p. 109
Neiman–Marcus v. Lait, 13 F.R.D. 311, p. 109
Nevada Broadcasting Co. v. Allen, 103
Nevada Independent Broadcasting Corp. v. Allen, 234
New Indecency Enforcement Standards, 385
New Jersey v. Hauptmann, 645
New York v. Ferber, 363, 364
New York Society for the Suppression of Vice v. MacFadden Publications, Inc., 104
New York State Com'n on Cable Television v. F.C.C., 419
New York Times Co. v. Sullivan, 13, 66, 67, 102, 103, 110, 145, 146, 147, 149, 151, 152, 154, 155, 156, 163, 164, 170, 171, 172, 173, 183, 185, 187, 191, 193, 195, 198, 200, 207, 208, 211, 223, 227, 230, 238, 241, 244, 247, 302, 311, 314, 473, 475, 476, 482
New York Times Co. v. United States, 42, 275
Nixon v. General Services Administrator, 612
Nixon, United States v., 612
N.L.R.B. v. Sears, Roebuck & Co., 608
Noe v. F.C.C., 401
Noriega, United States v., 917 F.2d 1543, p. 673
Noriega, United States v., 752 F.Supp. 1032, p. 673
Notice of Proposed Policy Statement and Rulemaking in General Docket 80–603, p. 415
Notice of Proposed Rulemaking in BC Docket 78–258, p. 424
November v. Time Inc., 122

Oak Beach Inn Corp. v. Babylon Beacon, Inc., 568, 573
Oak Creek, City of v. Peter Ah King, 633
Office of Communication of United Church of Christ v. F. C. C., 376
Ogren v. Rockford Star Printing Co., 115
Ohio v. Geis, 568
Ohralik v. Ohio State Bar Ass'n, 479
Oklahoma v. Bernstein, 267, 268
Oklahoma Pub. Co. v. Givens, 112

Old Dominion Branch No. 496, Nat. Ass'n of Letter Carriers, AFL–CIO v. Austin, 125, 126, 127, 232, 235, 240
Oliver v. Postel, 664, 665
Ollman v. Evans, 235, 236
Olmstead v. United States, 249
One Book Called 'Ulysses', United States v., 332, 334
Organization for a Better Austin v. Keefe, 57, 275, 668
Orito, United States v., 346
Orr v. Argus–Press Co., 172, 228, 236
Orrison v. Vance, 212
Orsini, United States v., 556
Orth-O-Vision, 419
Osborn v. Leach, 141
Osmers v. Parade Publications, Inc., 106
Ostrowe v. Lee, 106
Otero v. Ewing, 228
Overstreet v. New Nonpareil Co., 117

Pacifica Foundation, 384
Packer Corporation v. State of Utah, 474
Paramount Pictures, United States v., 355
Paris Adult Theatre I v. Slaton, 346, 349
Park v. The Detroit Free Press Co., 242
Pat Paulsen, In re, 390
Patterson v. Colorado ex rel. Attorney General of State of Colorado, 77, 78
Patton v. Cruce, 117
Pauling v. Globe–Democrat Pub. Co., 155
Pauling v. National Review, Inc., 155
Paul Pappas, In re, 553, 561
Pavesich v. New England Life Ins., 252, 298
Paxton v. Woodward, 117
Pearson v. Dodd, 265
Peay v. Curtis Pub. Co., 290
Peck v. Coos Bay Times Pub. Co., 109
Peck v. Tribune Co., 133
Peel v. Attorney Registration and Disciplinary Com'n of Illinois, 479
Pell v. Procunier, 597, 598, 599
Pennekamp v. State of Fla., 79
People v. ____ (see opposing party)
People on Complaint of Maggio v. Charles Scribner's Sons, 298
Perry v. Columbia Broadcasting System, Inc., 103
Person v. New York Post Corp., 466
Peter Holmes, Commonwealth v., 339
Petition of (see name of party)
Pfizer, Inc., In re, 453
Philadelphia, City of v. Washington Post Co., 105
Philadelphia Newspapers, Inc. v. Hepps, 223
Phillippi v. C.I.A., 605

Phillips v. Evening Star Newspaper Co., 216

Phillips v. Washington Post Co., 204

Phoenix Newspapers v. Choisser, 221

Phoenix Newspapers Inc. v. Jennings, 665

Piracci v. Hearst Corp., 225

Pitts v. Spokane Chronicle Co., 113, 140

Pittsburgh Courier Pub. Co. v. Lubore, 217

Pittsburgh Press Co. v. Pittsburgh Com'n on Human Relations, 475, 476

Policies and Rules Concerning Childrens Television Programming, Matter of, 472

Policy Statement Concerning Comparative Hearings Involving Regular Renewal Applicants, 377

Pope v. Illinois, 351, 352

Pope v. United States, 608

Posadas De Puerto Rico Associates v. Tourism Co. of Puerto Rico, 58, 473, 483, 484, 485

Postill v. Booth Newspapers, Inc., 191

Post–Newsweek Stations, Florida, Inc., Petition of, 648, 649

Post Pub. Co. v. Moloney, 227

Pottstown Daily News Pub. Co. v. Pottstown Broadcasting Co., 516

Powers, In re, 560

Prease v. Poorman, 188

Preferred Communications Inc. v. City of Los Angeles, 429

Press–Enterprise Co. v. Superior Court of California for Riverside County, 106 S.Ct. 2735, pp. 688, 690, 691

Press–Enterprise Co. v. Superior Court of California, Riverside County, 104 S.Ct. 819, pp. 688, 689

Price v. Worldvision Enterprises, Inc., 305

Priest v. Belknap Records, 328

Priestley v. Hastings & Sons Pub. Co. of Lynn, 172

Pring v. Penthouse Intern., Ltd., 143

Progressive, Inc., United States v., 486 F.Supp. 5, p. 45

Progressive, Inc., United States v., 467 F.Supp. 990, p. 45

Programming Commercialization Policies, 471

Proposed Rulemaking in Docket 15971, p. 407

Providence Journal Co. v. McCoy, 597

Public Clearing House v. Coyne, 455

Public Utilities Commission of District of Columbia v. Pollak, 344

Pulliam v. Bond, 230

Pulvermann v. A. S. Abell Co., 221

Purcell v. Westinghouse Broadcasting Co., 211

Quincy Cable TV, Inc. v. F.C.C., 424

Raible v. Newsweek, Inc., 321, 322

Ravellette v. Smith, 303

Raven v. Panama Canal Co., 614

Raye v. Letterman, 135

Raymond Roth v. New Jersey, 350

RCA, United States v., 731

Reader's Digest Ass'n, Inc., United States v., 446

Red Lion Broadcasting Co. v. F. C. C., 92, 374, 393, 396, 729

Redmond v. Sun Pub. Co., Inc., 170

Redrup v. State of New York, 342, 343, 344, 345, 349

Reed v. Real Detective Pub. Co., 294, 303

Regina v. _____ (see opposing party)

Reporters Committee for Freedom of Press v. American Tel. & Tel. Co., 588

Resident Participation of Denver, Inc. v. Love, 467, 468

Richmond Newspapers, Inc. v. Virginia, 595, 599, 635, 681, 683, 684, 685, 686

Rideau v. Louisiana, 637, 640, 643, 644, 656, 659

Riley v. City of Chester, 565

Rinaldi v. Holt, Rinehart & Winston, Inc., 126, 234

Rinaldo, State v., 559

Riss v. Anderson, 113

RKO General, 698

Roberson v. Rochester Folding Box Co., 252, 298

Robinson v. Johnson, 211

Roe v. Wade, 477

Rogers v. Courier Post Co., 215

Rollenhagen v. City of Orange, 229

Rood v. Finney, 174

Rosanova v. Playboy Enterprises, Inc., 164

Rose v. Koch & Christian Research, Inc., 152

Rosemont Enterprises, Inc. v. Random House, Inc., 366 F.2d 303, p. 523

Rosemont Enterprises, Inc. v. Random House, Inc., 256 F.Supp. 55, p. 57

Rosenblatt v. Baer, 101, 152, 153, 154, 473

Rosenbloom v. Metromedia, Inc., 158, 161, 163, 205

Roshto v. Hebert, 284

Ross v. Columbia Newspapers, Inc., 132

Roth v. United States, 77 S.Ct. 1304, pp. 330, 331, 333, 334, 335, 336, 337, 338, 341, 342, 343, 347, 348, 349

Roth v. United States, 77 S.Ct. 361, p. 334

Roth, United States v., 333, 334

Rouch v. Enquirer & News of Battle Creek, 228

Roy Export Co. Establishment of Vaduz, Liechtenstein v. Columbia Broadcasting System, Inc., 517, 518, 519
Rubera v. Post–Newsweek Stations of Connecticut, 561
Russell v. Geis, 230
Russell v. Marboro Books, 317, 318
Russell v. United States, 550

Sally v. Brown, 120
Sanford v. Boston Herald–Traveler Corporation, 214
Saxbe v. Washington Post Co., 597, 598, 599
Schaefer v. Hearst Corp., 224
Schaefer v. Lynch, 226
Schenck v. United States, 18, 31, 34
Schermerhorn v. Rosenberg, 132, 179
Schneider v. New Jersey, 55
Schultz v. Newsweek, Inc., 228
Schuster v. U.S. News & World Report, Inc., 109
Seattle Times Co. v. Rhinehart, 38, 670, 671
S.E.C. v. Lowe, 56
Security Sales Agency v. A. S. Abell Co., 104
Sellers v. Time Inc., 119
Senear v. Daily Journal–American, Div. of Longview Pub. Co., 565
Sharon v. Time, Inc., 102
Sharp v. Texas, 350
Sheldon v. Metro–Goldwyn Pictures Corp., 26 F.Supp. 134, p. 507
Sheldon v. Metro–Goldwyn Pictures Corporation, 60 S.Ct. 681, pp. 506, 507
Sheldon v. Metro–Goldwyn Pictures Corporation, 506, 507
Shelton v. United States, 550
Sheppard v. Maxwell, 637, 651, 652, 653, 654, 655, 656, 659, 660, 684
Sherwood v. Evening News Ass'n, 216
Shevin v. Sunbeam Television Corp., 262
Shiell v. Metropolis Co., 113
Shiles v. News Syndicate Co., 219
Shuck v. Carroll Daily Herald, 463
Shurberg Broadcasting of Hartford, Inc. v. F.C.C., 728
Sibley v. Holyoke Transcript–Telegram Pub. Co., Inc., 214
Sidis v. F–R Pub. Corp., 283, 308
Siegfried v. Kansas City Star Co., 711
Sierra Life Ins. Co. v. Magic Valley Newspapers, Inc., 573
Silkwood v. Kerr–McGee Corp., 561, 577
Sipple v. Chronicle Pub. Co., 270
Skokie, Village of v. National Socialist Party of America, 53
Skyywalker Records, Inc. v. Navarro, 354
Smith v. Daily Mail Pub. Co., 274, 276

Smith v. Fielden, 117
Smith v. Lyons, 117
Smith v. McMullen, 117
Smith v. National Broadcasting Co., 295
Snepp v. United States, 47
Snively v. Record Pub. Co., 228
Snowden v. Pearl River Broadcasting Corp., 112, 136, 138
Solverson v. Peterson, 117
Sonderling Broadcasting, 384
Sony Corp. of America v. Universal City Studios, Inc., 520, 533, 534, 535, 536
Sorensen v. Wood, 138
Sousa v. Davenport, 117
Southwestern Cable Co., United States v., 93, 408
Spahn v. Julian Messner, Inc., 221 N.E.2d 543, p. 314
Spahn v. Julian Messner, Inc., 260 N.Y.S.2d 451, p. 295
Spahn v. Julian Messner, Inc., 250 N.Y.S.2d 529, p. 295
Spanel v. Pegler, 104, 116
Sparrow, Ex parte, 573
Spears v. McCoy, 121
Spielman, People v., 65
Sprague v. Walter, 572
Springer v. Viking Press, 108
Sprouse v. Clay Communication, Inc., 132, 142, 164, 179
St. Amant v. Thompson, 152, 172, 173, 175, 190, 473
Standard Oil Co. of California v. F. T. C., 450
Standke v. B. E. Darby & Sons, Inc., 227
Stanford Daily v. Zurcher, 550 F.2d 464, p. 585
Stanford Daily v. Zurcher, 353 F.Supp. 124, p. 585
Stanley v. Georgia, 344, 345, 346
State v. ____ (see opposing party)
State ex rel. v. ____ (see opposing party and relator)
Stearn v. MacLean–Hunter Limited, 227
Steele v. F.C.C., 727
Steere v. Cupp, 164
Stevens v. Cincinnati Times–Star Co., 459
Stevens v. Sun Pub. Co., 176
Stevenson v. Commonwealth, 682
Stone v. Brooks, 117
Strauder v. State of West Virginia, 116
Stryker v. Republic Pictures Corp., 269, 294
Subscription Video, 98
Suchomel v. Suburban Life Newspapers, Inc., 152
Summit Hotel Co. v. National Broadcasting Co., 135
Sun Printing & Publishing Ass'n v. Schenck, 224

Swearingen v. Parkersburg Sentinel Co., 216

Swede v. Passaic Daily News, 217

Sweenek v. Pathe News, 308

Sweeney v. Patterson, 149

Sweet v. Post Pub. Co., 213

Syracuse Peace Council, 64 RR2d 1073, pp. 397, 398

Syracuse Peace Council, In re, 57 RR2d 519, p. 395

Syracuse Peace Council v. F.C.C., 397

Taskett v. KING Broadcasting Co., 204

Tavoulareas v. Washington Post, 817 F.2d 762, pp. 176, 185

Tavoulareas v. Washington Post, 759 F.2d 90, p. 175

Tavoulareas v. Washington Post Co., 174

Tawfik v. Loyd, 236

Taylor, In re, 552, 571

Taylor v. Lewis, 230

Taylor v. Tribune Pub. Co., 113

Telecommunications Research and Action Center v. F.C.C., 836 F.2d 1349, pp. 97, 423

Telecommunications Research and Action Center v. F.C.C., 801 F.2d 501, pp. 97, 395

Themo v. New England Newspaper Pub. Co., 254

Third Report and Order on Docket 18397, p. 408

Thomas H. Maloney & Sons, Inc. v. E. W. Scripps Co., 204

Time Inc. v. Bernard Geis Associates, 525

Time, Inc. v. Firestone, 104, 111, 128, 130, 167, 170, 309, 316

Time, Inc. v. Hill, 290, 294, 295, 302, 311, 312, 313, 314, 315, 316, 321

Times Film Corporation v. City of Chicago, 357

Times Mirror Co., United States v., 712

Times–Picayune Pub. Co. v. United States, 710

Tinker v. Des Moines Independent Community School Dist., 50

Tocco v. Time, Inc., 106

Toledo Newspaper Co. v. United States, 78

Tornillo v. Miami Herald Pub. Co., 60

Torres v. Playboy Enterprises, Inc., 226

Triangle Publications, Inc. v. Knight–Ridder Newspapers, Inc., 626 F.2d 1171, p. 453

Triangle Publications, Inc. v. Knight–Ridder, Newspapers, Inc., 445 F.Supp. 875, p. 527

Trimble v. Johnston, 596

Trinity Methodist Church, South v. Federal Radio Commission, 89

Trinkler v. Alabama, 350

Troman v. Wood, 196, 204

Turner, People v., 65

TV 9, Inc. v. F. C. C., 727

12 200–Foot Reels of Super 8mm. Film, United States v., 346

Two Obscene Books, United States v., 332

Uhlaender v. Henricksen, 306

Underwood v. First Nat. Bank of Blooming Prairie, 284

United States v. ____ (see opposing party)

United States Dept. of Justice v. Reporters Committee For Freedom of Press, 615, 617

United States ex rel. v. ____ (see opposing party and relator)

United States Labor Party v. Anti–Defamation League of B'nai B'rith, 166

United States Labor Party v. Whitman, 128

Universal City Studios, Inc. v. Sony Corp. of America, 659 F.2d 963, p. 534

Universal City Studios, Inc. v. Sony Corp. of America, 480 F.Supp. 429, p. 534

University of Notre Dame du Lac v. Twentieth Century–Fox Film Corp., 300

Uproar Co. v. National Broadcasting Co., 298

Utah State Farm Bureau Federation v. National Farmers Union Service Corp., 116

Valentine v. Chrestensen, 473, 474, 475

Vance v. Judas Priest, 328

Van Lonkhuyzen v. Daily News Co., 121

Van Ness, Matter of, 568

Van Rensselaer v. General Motors Corp., 503

Van Wiginton v. Pulitzer Pub. Co., 104

Various Articles of Obscene Merchandise, Schedule No. 1303, United States v., 329

Vegod Corp. v. American Broadcasting Companies, Inc., 197

Village of (see name of village)

Virgil v. Sports Illustrated, 288

Virgil v. Time, Inc., 286, 288, 303, 308

Virginia State Bd. of Pharmacy v. Virginia Citizens Consumer Council, Inc., 473, 478, 479, 480, 481

Waldbaum v. Fairchild Publications, Inc., 171

Walker v. Colorado Springs Sun, Inc., 206

Waller v. Georgia, 688, 690

Walt Disney Productions v. Alaska Television Network, Inc., 535
Walt Disney Productions v. Mature Pictures Corp., 538
Warner–Lambert Co. v. F. T. C., 451
Washington v. New York News Inc., 121
Washington Post Co. v. Keogh, 152, 172, 173, 187
Washington Post Co., United States v., 44
Wason v. Walter, 209, 217
Wasserman v. Time, Inc., 133
Weenig v. Wood, 121
Wells v. Times Printing Co., 115
Werner v. Times–Mirror Co., 323
Western Elec. Co., Inc., United States v., 748
Westmoreland v. CBS, 102
Weston v. State, 68
West Virginia State Board of Education v. Barnette, 6
Wheaton v. Peters, 492
Whiteside, State v., 64
Whitney v. People of State of California, 32
Wick v. Tucson Newspaper, Inc., 720, 721
Wihtol v. Crow, 522
Wildstein v. New York Post Corp., 104, 114
Wilkes v. Shields, 115
Williamson v. State, 68
Winegard v. Oxberger, 559, 560, 561
Winsted Hosiery Co. v. Federal Trade Commission, 437
Winter Park Communications, Inc. v. F.C.C., 728
Winters v. People of State of New York, 315, 345
Wirta v. Alameda–Contra Costa Transit Dist., 463, 464, 465

Wiseman, Commonwealth v., 311
Wolston v. Reader's Digest Ass'n, Inc., 130, 168, 170, 171, 309, 316
Wood v. Constitution Pub. Co., 215
Wood v. Earl of Durham, 121
Wood v. Georgia, 78
Wood v. Hustler Magazine, Inc., 316, 317, 319, 320
Woolbright v. Sun Communications, Inc., 216
Worthy v. Herter, 596
Wright v. Farm Journal, 115
Wright, King v., 209
Writers Guild of America, West, Inc. v. F.C.C., 381
WTSP–TV, Inc. v. Vick, 165
Wyatt v. Hall's Portrait Studio, 254
Wygant v. Jackson Bd. of Educ., 727

Yagman, Matter of, 232
Yarmove v. Retail Credit Co., 224
Yates v. United States, 35, 36
Yiamouyiannis v. Consumers Union of United States, Inc., 187
Yoeckel v. Samonig, 250, 253
Young v. New Mexico Broadcasting Co., 133
Young v. That Was the Week That Was, 303
Youssoupoff v. Metro-Goldwyn-Mayer Pictures, 103, 114

Zacchini v. Scripps–Howard Broadcasting Company, 306
Zeck v. Spiro, 227
Zelenka v. State, 559
Zemel v. Rusk, 596
Zenith Radio Corp., United States v., 87
Zurcher v. Stanford Daily, 583, 585, 587

INDEX

ABRAMS, FLOYD
Comments about Times v. Sullivan, 151

ACCESS TO GOVERNMENT INFORMA-TION
Campus police records, 630–632
Constitutional right of, 592
Defining "public record", 600–601
Disaster scene access, 632–634
Exceptions to FOIA, 601
Executive privilege, 594, 596, 600
Federal public records law, 600
Federal Sunshine Act, 615
Freedom of Information Act (FOIA), 600
Gulf War coverage, 625–626
Military operations coverage, 623–627
Openness not self-executing, 604–605
People's right to know, 592
Police records, 630
Presidential power over access, 603, 609
Prison access, 597
Privacy Act of 1974, p. 614
Right to travel, 596
Role of state attorneys general, 617
Silkwood case, 607
State meetings, 627
State records, 629
Surveillance records, 617
Watergate cases, 611

ACTUAL MALICE
See, also, Libel
Applied to criminal libel, 64–69
Defined in New York Times v. Sullivan, 151
Forms of, discussed, 171–184
Privacy law, 314

ADAMS, JOHN
Alien and Sedition Acts, 28–29

ADMINISTRATIVE LAW
Defined, 3–4

ADVERTISING
Action for Children's Television (ACT) citizen group, 471–472
Banning tobacco advertising, 485–486

ADVERTISING—Cont'd
Broadcast advertising for children, 471–473
Caveat emptor, 432
Childrens' TV Advertising Act, 471
Comparative advertising, 452–453
Constitutional protections, 473–488
Corporate free speech, 480–481
Corrective advertising orders, 449–451
Early American advertising practices, 432–434
Fairness broadcast requirements, 393–394
Federal Trade Commission,
  Authority, 434–445
  Structure, 434–436
  Federal Trade Commission Improvement Act of 1975 (Moss-Magnuson Act), 443
Federal Trade Commission Improvement Act of 1980 (weakens FTC), 443–444
Food and Drug Administration, 455
Literal truth not enough, 445–449
Lottery advertisements, 459–460
Printers' Ink Statute, 458–459
Right to refuse service
  Broadcast, 469–471
  Press, 462–466
Sandpaper shave case, 467–468
Securities and Exchange Commission, 456
Self-regulation, 460–462
State regulation of, 453–454
Tobacco advertising, banning of, 485–486
U.S. Postal Service controls, 455
Wheeler–Lea amendment, 438–439

ALIEN AND SEDITION ACTS
Passage and prosecutions, 27–30

ALIEN REGISTRATION ACT OF 1940
Bans violent overthrow, 33
Revives peacetime sedition actions, 33

AMERICAN BAR ASSOCIATION
Canon 35 of Professional Ethics, 645

AMERICAN BAR ASSOCIATION—
Cont'd
Canon of Judicial Conduct 3(7) (Florida) on photographing/televising of trials, 649
Disciplinary Rule DR 7–107, p. 639
Fair trial for Lee Harvey Oswald, 638
Reardon Committee report, 659

AMERICAN TELEPHONE AND TELEGRAPH (AT & T)
See, also, Bell Operating Companies
Consent agreement, 746–748
Divestiture of, 746–747
Early radio broadcasting, 82–83
Satellite efforts, 412

ANDERSON, DAVID A.
On Framers' intent, 21

ANTITRUST
Associated Press v. U.S., 706–708
AT & T divestiture, 746–747
Broadcasting and, 730–739
Clayton Act, 700
Consent decrees, 723–725
Criminal activities, 699
Defined, 697
FCC and, 730–731
Financial interest rules, 731–733
Global media ownership trends, 694–696
Kansas City Star case, 711
Lorain Journal case, 709–710
Mergers and takeovers, 696–698
Newspaper Preservation Act, 715–720
Sherman Act, 699
Times–Mirror case, 712–713
Times–Picayune case, 710
Total market coverage, 720–723
Treble damage actions, 700
Trends in anti-trust enforcement, 696, 742

APPROPRIATION
Invasion of privacy, 298–307

AREOPAGITICA
Milton's plea for unlicensed printing, 5

BAD TENDENCY
Test discussed, 16–17

BARRON, JEROME
Right of public access to media, 59

BELL OPERATING COMPANIES
Advantages over cable TV, 749–751, 753
Created by AT & T divestiture, 746
Electronic publishing activities, 748
Digital operation, 750

BELL OPERATING COMPANIES—
Cont'd
Diversity prinicples and, 747
Fiber optic system advantages, 749, 750, 753
Regulatory constraints, 751–752
Threat to newspapers, 754–755

BLACK, HUGO L.
"Absolutes" of First Amendment, 14
Individual, social values of freedom, 7

BLACKMUN, HARRY A.
Dissent in Gannett v. DePasquale, 680
Dissent in Pentagon Papers case, 44

BLACKSTONE, SIR WILLIAM
Criticism of government punishable, 40–41
Free press means no prior restraint, 11, 15

BRANDEIS, LOUIS D.
Co-author, seminal privacy article, 251–252
On worth of privacy, 249

BREACH OF PEACE
Basis for criminal libel, 63

BRENNAN, WILLIAM J., JR.
Broadcasting, minority ownership, 728–729
Obscenity definitions amount to dangerous censorship, 356
Pentagon Papers opinion, 43

BROADCAST DEFAMATION
Discussed, 133–137

BROADCASTING
Airwaves as public resource, 88–93, 373–375
Childrens' advertising, 471–473
Deregulation, 93–96, 382–383, 423–424
Equal opportunities requirement, 388
Extension of the licensing period, 377
Fairness Doctrine advertising, 393–394
Licensing process, 373–376
Minority ownership policies, 726–730
Network influence on programming, 380–381
Non-commercial, 399–401
Ownership restrictions, 730
Spectrum scarcity rationale, 88–93, 373–374
Susceptibility to license challenge, 376–378
"Topless" radio, 383
Willingness to accept regulation, 429–431

BUGGING
Invasion of privacy, 260, 262–263
Telephone wiretapping, 263–265

BURGER, WARREN A.
Right to attend trials, 683–684

CABLE POLICY ACT OF 1984
See Cable Television

CABLE TELEVISION
Ban on telephone company control, 751
Cable Policy Act of 1984, pp. 427–428
Compulsory copyright license, 407, 426
FCC regulation, 93–94, 402–408
First Amendment issues, 428–429
History of, 402–408
Limitations on FCC authority, 93, 406
Mandatory carriage rules, 424–425
Microwave importation restrictions, 407
Municipal authority over, 405, 427–428
"Must carry" requirement, 424–425
New media competition, 414–423
Satellite delivered services, 411–412, 414–415
Syndicated exclusivity rules, 426
Telephone carrier competition, 755–756
Vertical integration issues, 735
Urban tactics in 1980s, pp. 412–413

CAMERAS
See, also, Photography
In courtrooms, 644–651
Invasion of privacy, 261–262, 268, 285–286, 291–292, 299–300, 302

CAVEAT EMPTOR
"Let the buyer beware", 432

CENSORSHIP
Alien and Sedition Acts, 27–30
Antitrust prosecution not censorship, 642–644
British origins, 11, 15, 53
Broadcast regulation and, 89, 373–374
Cable TV regulation and, 431
"Free speech" guarantees in U.S.S.R., 8
High school press, 49–52
Jehovah's Witness cases, 53–55
Licensing schemes, 52–55
Motion picture, 344
Nazi marches in Skokie, 53
Near v. Minnesota, 39–43
Obscenity not protected from, 356
Pentagon Papers, 41–44
Prior restraint, 37
Progressive Magazine case, 46–47
Restrictive orders by courts, 501–510
Secrecy contracts of CIA, 47–49

CHAFEE, ZECHARIAH
Antitrust law, 697

CHAFEE, ZECHARIAH—Cont'd
Gitlow case nationalized First Amendment, 12
On clear and present danger test, 18

CIVIL LAW
Defined, 4

CLEAR AND PRESENT DANGER
Test discussed, 17–18

COMMON LAW
Copyright, 492–494
Defined, 3
Denied as basis for federal crimes, 29
Privacy law growth, 253
Reporter's privilege and, 564–565

COMMUNICATION COMMON CARRIERS
Effects on the growth of cable TV, 744
Importance to modern newspapers, 743–744
Significance for network broadcasting, 744

CONSTITUTION OF THE UNITED STATES
See, also, Fifth Amendment; First Amendment; Fourteenth Amendment
Antifederalist opposition, 10
Drafted in secret, 9
First Amendment, historical position, 10
Intent of Framers, 19–21

CONSTITUTIONAL LAW
Defined, 2
"Free speech" guarantee in U.S.S.R., 8

CONSTITUTIONS, STATE
Pennsylvania constitution of 1790, p. 11
Qualify press freedom, 9, 11

CONTEMPT
Blackstone on, 545–546
Branzburg case, 552
Colonial, early national legislatures, 544, 546
Confidentiality and reporters, 560–564
Confidentiality pledges as contracts, 577–580
"Constructive" contempt, 76
Direct or in-court, 544
Freedom to criticize courts, 78
Janet Cooke incident, 575–576
Legislative power of, 547–548
Newsroom searches, 583
Out-of-court publications, 546–547
Relation to reporter's privilege, 550
Shield laws and libel, 571

CONTEMPT—Cont'd
State shield laws, 566
Summary powers of judges, 76, 545–546
U.S. statute of 1831, p. 77

CONVERGENCE OF MEDIA
Decreasing differences among media, 96–99
Merging of media systems, 749–753
Newspapers and electronic publishing, 754

COOLEY, THOMAS
"Right to be let alone" and privacy, 248

COOLIDGE, CALVIN
Urges regulation of broadcasting, 87

COPYRIGHT
Act of 1909, p. 489
Act of 1976, pp. 489, 493, 498, 500–501
Berne copyright convention, 499
Cable TV compulsory license, 409–410
Common law, 492–494
Comparative advertising, 527–528
Conflict with state law, 493
Copyright Royalty Tribunal, 409–410
Criminal penalties for infringement, 513
Damages for infringement, 506
Defined, 490
Duration of, 498–499
"Fair use" defenses, 520–527
"Fair use" and parody, 536–538
"Fair use" and public interest, 522–527
"Fair use" and technology, 533–536
"First sale" doctrine and the VCR, 533–536
History of, 490–494
Infringement, 503–512
Mark Twain on, 489
Musical licensing, 538–542
Nature of, 494–495
Originality, 501–503
Registration and deposit, 499–500
Securing a copyright, 496–500
Statute of 8 Anne, 492
Unfair competition and news, 513–520
Zapruder case, 525–527

COURT OF STAR CHAMBER
Symbol of repressive secret courts, 13

CRIMINAL LAW
Defined, 4

CRIMINAL LIBEL
Beauharnais case, 65–66
Breach of peace in, 66–67
Croswell defended by Alexander Hamilton, 63
Garrison case, 67–68

CRIMINAL LIBEL—Cont'd
Hate-crime legislation, 66
Libel of a group, 65–67
Theodore Roosevelt charges, 64

DEFAMATION
See, also, Libel
Altered quotations, 179
Broadcasting as libel or slander, 133–137
Defined, 100–105
Libel and slander distinguished, 103
Political candidate and broadcaster, 138–139

DIRECT BROADCAST SATELLITE (DBS)
See Federal Communications Commission

EMOTIONAL DISTRESS
Falwell case, 129–131
In libel cases, 128–131

EQUAL ACCESS REQUIREMENTS
See Federal Communications Commission

EQUITY
Defined, 3

ESPIONAGE ACT OF 1917
Discussed, 30–32
Sedition amendment to Act of 1917, p. 30

FAIR TRIAL
See Free Press–Fair Trial

FAIRNESS DOCTRINE
See Federal Communications Commission

FALSE LIGHT
Invasion of privacy, 290–298

FEDERAL COMMUNICATIONS COMMISSION
Barred from censorship, 89
"Citizen group" license challenges, 376–378
Creation of, 90
Deregulatory policies, 95–96, 382, 394–396, 752–753
Direct broadcast satellites (DBS), 414–418
Equal access requirements, 388–392
Fairness doctrine requirements, 392–399
Fairness doctrine rescission, 394–397
Financial interest rules, 731–734
Format changes, 381–383

FEDERAL COMMUNICATIONS COM-MISSION—Cont'd
Indecent programming, 383–387
Investigation of network practices, 90–91
Licensing review and renewal process, 376–379
Lottery licensing, 420–421
LPTV policies, 421–422
Marketplace policies, 423–431
Minority ownership policies, 726–730
MMDS policies, 419–421
Network regulation, 380–381
New media policies, 414–423
"Open Skies" satellite policy, 745
Ownership policies, 701–706, 730–731,
Personal attack rules, 397–399
Political Editorials, 398
"Prime Time access" rule, 735–736
Review of programming practices, 379–387
Satellite policies, 414–418
SMARTV policies, 418–419

FEDERAL RADIO COMMISSION
Creation of, 87
Licensing policies, 88–90
Programming practice policies, 379

FEDERAL TRADE COMMISSION
Authority of, 434–436
Corrective advertising orders, 449–451
FTC Improvement Act of 1975, pp. 442–443
FTC Improvement Act of 1980, pp. 444–445
Sandpaper shave case, 447–448
Structure of, 434–436

FESSENDEN, REGINALD
Added voice and music to radio, 81

FICTIONALIZATION
Invasion of privacy, 293–298

FIFTH AMENDMENT
Right against self incrimination, 13–14

FIRST AMENDMENT
See, also, Free Speech and Press
Absolute protection not provided, 14–15
Access to government not included, 592–593
Basic guarantee of free expression, 2, 10
Broadcast free speech, 79, 88–93, 373–374
Cable television and, 428–429
Difference in application among media, 52
Discriminatory taxation of media forbidden, 69–76
Fairness doctrine and, 392–397

FIRST AMENDMENT—Cont'd
Intention of Framers, 19–21
Left undefined by Framers, 19–21
Limited source confidentiality, 550–571
Obscenity not protected, 336–338
Relationship to Fourteenth Amendment, 12–14
Restricts control by states, 11–13
Richmond Newspapers v. Virginia, 681
Right to gather information under Richmond Newspapers case, 681–686
Rights of telephone carriers, 757

FOURTEENTH AMENDMENT
Curbs state control of expression, 12–14

FREE PRESS–FAIR TRIAL
Camera in courtrooms, 647–651
CNN and the Noriega tapes, 672–673
Contempt sanctions suggested in Reardon Report, 660
"Gannett cards", 686
Gannett v. DePasquale, 675
In general, 636–640
Judge's role, 656–659
Lindbergh case, 644
Pre-trial proceeding openings, 688–691
Pre-trial publicity, 640–642, 645
Publicity during trial, 644, 647
Remedies, in general, 657–658
　Change of venue, 657
　Contempt, 658
　Continuance or postponement, 657
　Sequestration of jury, 658
　Voir Dire, 657–658
Restrictive "gag" orders, 663–670
Sheppard case, 651–656
Televising trials, 644–651
Trial reporting guidelines, 659–663
Trials, open, 681
Warren Commission on Kennedy assassination, 637

FREE SPEECH AND PRESS
　See, also, Constitutions, State; First Amendment
"Absolute" freedom to Black, Meiklejohn, 14–15
Bill of Rights, 19–21
Blackstone definition, 11
Communist party cases, 32–37
Limited under Smith Act, 32

GENERAL ELECTRIC
Early radio activities, 82–83
Ownership of NBC, 703

GITLOW v. NEW YORK
Curbs on state power over expression, 11–13

HAMILTON, ANDREW
Defends John Peter Zenger, 24–26

HOLMES, OLIVER WENDELL, JR.
Clear and present danger test, 31

HOOVER, HERBERT
Commerce Secretary, radio administrator, 84–87

HURST, JAMES WILLARD
On right of privacy, 250

INCITEMENT
Soldier of Fortune case, 326

INDECENT PROGRAMMING
See Federal Communications Commission

INTRUSION
An invasion of privacy, 255–268

JEFFERSON, THOMAS
Opposed Alien and Sedition Acts, 28

JEHOVAH'S WITNESS CASES
Licensing and prior restraint issues, 54–56

KOVNER, VICTOR A.
Definitional problems of privacy, 305

LEVY, LEONARD W.
Origins of Bill of Rights, 20
Power of colonial assemblies over press, 26

LEWIS, ANTHONY
Right to gather information, 517–518

LIBEL
　See, also, Actual Malice, Defined in New York Times v. Sullivan; Seditious Libel
Actual injury, 111–112
Actual malice, 171–184
Advertisements, 131
Awards skyrocket, 141–144
Broadcast ad lib, 135
Broadcast defamation, 133–139
Broadcasts of candidates for public office, 138
Compensatory damages, 141–144
Criminal libel, 61–69
　Actual malice, 67
　Application to groups, 64
　Breach of peace, 64–65, 67
　Defense of truth must not be limited, 68
　Effect of Sullivan rule, 67
　Public officials, 66–69

LIBEL—Cont'd
Damage through ridicule, 117–120
Damage to corporation's credit or integrity, 122–125
Damage to esteem or social standing, 112–117
Damage to trade or profession, 121–122
Damages, 141–144
　Compensatory, 141
　Emotional distress, 128–131
　Punitive, 141–142
　Special, 141
Defense costs, 142
Defenses, 145–184
　Constitutional, 146–147
　Fair comment, 227–232
　　Relation to First Amendment, 232
　　Separating fact, opinion, 232–241
　First Amendment, 146
　Qualified privilege, 207
　　Destroyed by extraneous matter, 211
　　Destroyed by malice, 209
　　Destroyed by opinion, 209
　　Fair and accurate reports, 210
　　Executive bodies, 215
　　Judicial proceedings, 213–215
　　Legislative reporting, 217
　　Official proceedings, 213
　　Public proceedings, 217
　　Retraction, 241
　　Truth, 222
Defined, 99
Discovery problems, 192–194
Disease or mental illness, imputation of, 120
Distinguishing public from private persons, 159–171
Electronic news gathering (ENG) problems, 137
Elements of libel, 105
"Extreme departure" test, 158
Extrinsic facts, 139
Fault, 110
Headlines, 128
Identification of defamed, 106
Injury to reputation, 111
Inventing quotations, 179
Investigative reporting, 174
Jury problems in, 184–186
Knowing falsehood, 152, 179
Mental illiness, imputation of, 120
Minor inaccuracy, 225
Necessary allegations in suing, 105
Negligence standard, 199
Neutral reporting, 189
Opinion, 123
Per quod, 139
Per se, 139
Pictures, 131
Private persons, 195–198

LIBEL—Cont'd
Public figures, 151
Public officials, 146
Public principle, 146
Publication necessary to action, 105
Qualified privilege, 207–221
Reckless disregard for truth, 176
Reform proposals, 144
Retraction, 241
Rhetorical hyperbole, 125
Strict liability ended, 198
Summary judgment, 186
Truth, burden of proving, 223–227

LOCKE, JOHN
On natural rights, 6

LOW POWER TELEVISION (LPTV)
See Federal Communications Commission

MADISON, JAMES
Draft of Bill of Rights, 10

MAGNA CHARTA
British charter of rights of 121, p. 9

MALICE
See Actual Malice; Libel

MARCONI, GUGLIELMO
"Father" of radio, 79

MARKETPLACE OF IDEAS
Concept discussed, 17

MEIKLEJOHN, ALEXANDER
Absolute freedom of political expression, 15

MICROPHONES
Invasion of privacy, 249, 258–260, 262–265

MOSS–MAGNUSON ACT
Increased Federal Trade Commission powers, 442–443

MULTI–CHANNEL, MULTI–POINT DISTRIBUTION SYSTEMS (MMDS)
See Federal Communications Commission

NATIONAL ASSOCIATION OF BROADCASTERS (NAB)
Opposition to complete deregulation, 424–425, 430–431
Private programming standards overturned, 736

NATIONAL CABLE TELEVISION ASSOCIATION (NCTA)
Cable Policy Act, 427
Negotiations with NAB, 406, 425

NEWS
Definitions attempted in privacy cases, 307–312

NEWSPAPER PRESERVATION ACT
Exception to antitrust law, 715

NEWSWORTHINESS
Defense in privacy suits, 311

NIEMOELLER, MARTIN
On the Holocaust, 5

NIXON, RICHARD M.
Executive privilege denied, 446–447

OBSCENITY
See, also, Federal Communications Commission
Balancing societal interests, 354–372
Broadcast obscenity, 383
Comstock Law of 1873, p. 330
Conduct of seller, 340–341
Contemporary community standards, 333, 346, 347–352, 367
Customs censorship, 332
Definition elusive, 329, 332–335, 337–339, 343–346
Hicklin rule, 331
Indianapolis ordinance, 365
Kidporn, 361–365
Local standards (Miller case), 347–350
Mapplethorpe case, 352–353
Meese report, 368
Miller v. California, 347–350
"Pandering" test, 340–341
"Partly obscene" test, 331
Prior censorship, allowable for movies, 357
Privacy concerns, 344–346
Protection for minors, 361–365
Rap music, 353–354
Roth landmark case, 336–338
"SLAPS test", 349, 351–352
Ulysses case, 332
Variable obscenity concept, 342
Women's rights and, 360–361, 365–367

OPEN MEETINGS AND RECORDS
See Access to Government Information

OSWALD, LEE HARVEY
Assassination of, and free press-fair trial dispute, 637–638

OWNERSHIP OF MEDIA
See Antitrust

PATENT POOL
US Navy administration of, 82

PENTAGON PAPERS CASE
New York Times v. US; prior restraint, 43–46

PHOTOGRAPHY
Copyright, 496, 525–527
Courtrooms, 644–647
Invasion of privacy, 255–259, 261–262, 266–267, 291–295, 299–301, 302–304

POSADAS CASE
Weakens constitutional protection for advertising, 482–485

POSTAL POWERS
Advertising regulation, 455

PRE–TRIAL CLOSURES
Overturned, 690
Upheld, 674–680

PRE–TRIAL PUBLICITY
In general, 640–644

PRIOR RESTRAINT
Broadcasting licensing, 52, 84–93
CIA secrecy agreements, 49–51
Forcing communication to occur, 58
H-bomb secrecy, 45–47
High school press, 49–52
Jehovah's Witness cases, 53–55
Licensing, 52–57
Nazi's Skokie March, 53
Near v. Minnesota limits, 41
Presumption against constitutionality, 39–40
Use of, historically, 37–39

PRIVACY
Appropriation concept, 298–307
As constitutional right, 250
Cable television implications for, 248–249
Consent as defense, 317–320
Consent exceeded, 320–322
Constitutional defense, 312–317
Development of tort, 245–255
Dietemann v. Time, 258
False light, 290–293
False publications invading privacy, 290–292
Fictionalization, 293–298
Incitement, 326
Intrusion, 255
Intrusion and trespass, 266–268
Miller, Arthur, "Assault on Privacy", 248
Newsworthiness as defense, 307–312
Prosser, William L., four categories, 253

PRIVACY—Cont'd
Publication of private matters, 269
Rape cases, 272–274, 285
Right of publicity, 303–307
"Social value" test, California, 278
Tape recorders' use, 262
"Time lapse" as element in suits, 282
Truthful publications may invade, 286
Warren & Brandeis 1890 article, 251–252

PROSSER, WILLIAM L.
Categorized four privacy torts, 253
Privacy torts as threats to press freedom, 324

PUBLIC ACCESS TO MEDIA
Denied in Tornillo case, 60
Fairness doctrine provided; repealed in 1987, pp. 394–397
Right of, proposed by Jerome Barron, 60

PUBLIC BROADCASTING
Ban on editorializing overturned, 401
Carnegie Commission and, 400
Not a "public forum", 401

PUBLICATION OF PRIVATE MATTERS
Privacy invasions, 269–289

QUALIFIED PRIVILEGE
Major defense in libel, 207

RADIO ACT OF 1912
Description of, 87–88

RADIO ACT OF 1927
Adoption of, 90
Makes broadcasting a "privilege", 90, 373–374

RADIO CONFERENCES
Activities, 1921–1925, p. 87

RADIO CORPORATION OF AMERICA (RCA)
Early radio activities, 82–83

RADIOTELEGRAPHY
"Wireless" radio, 81–82

REPORTING COURTS
See Legal Problems in Reporting Courts, pp. 635–693

RIGHT OF PUBLICITY
Privacy law concept, 303–307

RIGHT TO REFUSE SERVICE
Broadcast advertising, 469–471
Newspaper advertising, 462–464

RIGHT TO TRAVEL
Limited, 433

SATELLITE MASTER ANTENNA TV (SMARTV)
See Federal Communications Commission

SCHORR, DANIEL
Rationale for refusing to testify, 549–550

SECRECY IN GOVERNMENT
See Access to Government Information

SECTION 315, COMMUNICATIONS ACT
Equal opportunities requirements for broadcasters, 388–392

SEDITIOUS LIBEL
Alien and Sedition Acts, 27
Defined, 22
Discredited by Jeffersonians, 29
Espionage Act (1917), p. 30
Growth and decline in 20th century, 32–37
Smith Act (1940), p. 32
World War I, 30
Zenger trial, 24

SHIELD LAW
See Contempt

SIEBERT, FREDRICK S.
Licensing, censorship in England, 22

SINCLAIR, UPTON
The Jungle, novel which aided passage of Pure Food and Drug Act, 433

SMITH ACT
See Alien Registration Act of 1940

STATE BAR TRIAL COVERAGE GUIDELINES
Dangers seen by journalists if made mandatory, 662–663
Free press-fair trial, 659–661

STATIONERS COMPANY
Controller of English printers, 491

STATUTE OF 8 ANNE
First copyright statute of England, 492

STATUTORY LAW
Defined, 2–3

STEWART, POTTER
Knew obscenity when he saw it, 329
Supports reporter's privilege, 393

STORY, JOSEPH
"Originality" in Copyright Law, 502

TAPE RECORDERS
Privacy invasion problems, 262

TAXATION
Grosjean case, 70–73
Media not exempt from non-discriminatory taxes, 73–74
Minneapolis Star & Tribune case, 75–76
Stamp taxes, 70
"Taxes on knowledge", 69

TELCO
See Bell Operating Companies (BOC)

"TOPLESS" RADIO
See Broadcasting

TREASON
Defined, 23

TRUTH
Defense in libel, 222

WARREN COMMISSION
News coverage of Oswald slaying, 637–638

WARREN, EARL
Exploitation of obscene literature opposed, 337
Opposed to televising criminal trials, 646–647

WARREN, SAMUEL D.
Co-author of seminal privacy article, 251

WESTINGHOUSE
Early radio activities, 82–83

WHEELER–LEA AMENDMENT
Increased Federal Trade Commission power over advertising, 438–439

WIRELESS SHIP ACT OF 1910
First radio law of US, 80

WOOLSEY, JOHN
Ulysses decision and obscenity law, 332–33

ZENGER, JOHN PETER
Free press champion, 24

ZENITH RADIO CORPORATION
Challenges Radio Act of 1912, pp. 86–87

†